SIXTEENTH EDITION

THE NAVAL INSTITUTE GUIDE TO THE Ships and Aircraft of the U.S. Fleet

Norman Polmar

Naval Institute Press
Annapolis, Maryland

ISBN: 1-55750-686-8

This edition is authorized for sale only in the United States, its territories and possessions, and Canada.

Printed in the United States of America on acid-free paper ♾

04 03 02 01 00 99 98 97   9 8 7 6 5 4 3 2

First printing

To the Memory of
Susan Thompson and
Peter Gookin
Friends and Colleagues

Contents

The SEAWOLF (SSN 21) on initial sea trials during July 1996. The SEAWOLF and the other submarines of her class were the most controversial Navy ships of the 1980s and into the 1990s. (U.S. Navy, courtesy General Dynamics/Electric Boat)

Preface

This edition of *Ships and Aircraft* appears at a pivotal time for the U.S. Navy. The end of the Cold War brought the need to reassess defense spending and the roles and missions of the military services. Before these issues could be adequately addressed, the Navy found itself embroiled in a maelstrom: a turret explosion on a battleship with an unfortunate rush to judgment; controversies related to sexual transgressions; a variety of problems at the Naval Academy; a series of aviation accidents; a failed submarine program; and the tragic suicide of the Chief of Naval Operations, Admiral J. M. (Mike) Boorda—an officer who rose from the enlisted ranks to the head of the service.

In this problem-strewn environment, the Navy continues to maintain, under way or forward deployed, more than half of its surface ships and almost half of its submarines. Similarly, several battalions of Marines are embarked in amphibious ready groups that are forward deployed, and a division-wing team is forward based on Okinawa and in Japan.

The record of Navy–Marine Corps participation in crises and confrontations during the past few years is indeed impressive; these services have operated off Korea and Bosnia, in the Taiwan Straits and the Persian Gulf, and near trouble spots in Africa. These operations were conducted in addition to several major humanitarian actions.

This edition of *Ships and Aircraft* discusses the Navy's structure, force levels, ships, aircraft, weapons, electronics, and—most important—personnel during this tumultuous period.

Many individuals and organizations have provided assistance in producing this book. First and foremost I am in debt to the photographers who have provided a veritable stream of photographs of U.S. ships and aircraft. As always, Dr. Giorgio Arra—the dean of ship photographers—has taken the majority of the ship photos in this edition. Leo Van Ginderen was unsparing in providing his photos and those of his colleagues, while several provided by Stephan Terzibaschitsch, Dr. Wilhelm Donko, and others were extremely valuable. Aviation writer-photographer Peter Mersky has provided a number of his own photos for this edition. Many of the photos submitted to the author and not used in the book were invaluable in helping to identify changes to ships.

Those photos credited to the U.S. Navy came from many sources, most from the Navy's Office of Information, whose still photo section under Russ Egnor has provided outstanding service. His staff—JOC Richard Toppings, USN, Diane Mason, Lt. Christopher Madden, USN, and Henrietta Wright—have demonstrated both knowledge and patience in their continued assistance.

Help with illustrations has also been provided by Kenneth Carter and Patricia Toombs of the public affairs directorate of the Department of Defense.

Samuel L. Morison has been most cooperative in researching and keeping track of the status of U.S. Navy ships; he is unequaled in this regard. The indefatigable Ted Minter also checked on the status of Navy ships.

Others who have provided assistance are: Lt. John W. Albright, USN, executive officer, Sustain (AFDM 7); Barbara Anderson, public relations, McDonnell Douglas; Dr. William Armstrong, historian, Naval Air Systems Command; Lt.(jg) Ralph Benhart, USCG, assigned to Marinette Marine; Greg Beaudoin, United Communications Group; Lisa Brihagen, public relations, Alliant Techsystems; Operations Specialist First Class D. K. Buchanan, USN, Assault Craft Unit 4; Lt. Comdr. Rick Burgess, USN, formerly editor of *Naval Aviation News;* Marilyn Carlson, public affairs officer, Special Projects Program Office; M. P. (Blade) Chapman, naval analyst; Comdr. Steve Clawson, USN, public affairs officer, Bureau of Naval Personnel; Chris Cocco, public relations, National Steel & Shipbuilding Company; Tony Cochran, marketing, Alliant Techsystems; Adrienne M. Combs, public affairs, U.S. Army Transportation Center; Cary J. Dell, management staff, Loral Defense Systems-Akron; Lt. Chuck Diorio, USCG, and CPO Wayne Paugh, USCG, public affairs, Headquarters, U.S. Coast Guard; JOC David T. Farmer, USN, Naval Submarine Base, New London, Connecticut; Susan Fili, public affairs, Naval Sea Systems Command; Patricia A. Frost, senior specialist-communications, McDonnell Douglas; WO Randy George, USMC, public affairs, Headquarters, U.S. Marine Corps; Col. John Greenwood, USMC (Ret.), editor of the *Marine Corps Gazette;* Bob Harper, editor, *SkyPower,* Lockheed Aeronautical Systems Company; Carl L. Harris, Director of Public Affairs/Advertising, Bell Helicopter Textron; Elizabeth K. Healy, public relations, Kaman Corporation; Col. Richard Herrington, USMC, Naval Air Warfare Directorate; Margaret Holtz, public affairs officer, Military Sealift Command, and her most helpful assistants Nancy Breen and Barry Lake; Comdr. Glenn King, USN, public affairs officer, Naval Special Warfare Command; Marc P. Lasky, office of ship construction, Maritime Administration; Steven Llanso, United Communications Group; Denny Lombard, photographer of the Lockheed Martin Skunk Works; Paul Martineau, Washington representative, Litton/Ingalls Shipbuilding; Donna McKinney, public affairs, Naval Research Laboratory; Ed Offley, military reporter, *Seattle Post-Intelligencer;* Lt. Rob Newell and Lt. Maureen Olson, public affairs office, Bureau of Medicine and Surgery; Penny Norman, historian's office, Joint Chiefs of Staff; Lt. Flex Plexico, USN, public affairs officer, Navy Strategic Communications Wing 1; Dr. Scott Price, historian, U.S. Coast Guard; Capt. Rosario Rausa, USNR (Ret.), editor, *Wings of Gold;* Capt. Carter B. Refo, USN, commanding officer, USS Independence (CV 62); John Romer, public affairs, Naval Air Warfare Center (Patuxent River, Maryland); Troy (Jim) Roop, director, program development, unmanned aerial vehicles, TRW; JOC David A. Rourk, USN, public affairs, Enterprise (CVN 65); Ronald O'Rourke, Congressional Research Service; Sandy Russell, managing editor, *Naval Aviation News;* Lt. Comdr. Nicholas Sabalos Jr., USN, editor in chief, *Surface Warfare* magazine; Lt. Chris Sims, USN, public affairs, Naval Air Training Command; Hal Sisson, marketing, Textron Marine Systems; Maj. D. L. Spasojevich, USMC, administrative officer, squadron HMX-1; Daryl Stephenson, public relations, McDonnell Douglas; James P. Stevenson, aviation historian; Julia D. Stone, manager, marketing communications, Gulfstream Aircraft; William S. Tuttle, manager, public relations, United Technologies/Sikorsky Aircraft; Barbara J. Tweedt, manager, marketing/communications, Schweizer Aircraft; Judy Van Benthuysen, Navy Office of Information; Comdr. Kevin M. Wensing, public affairs officer, Naval Air Force, Atlantic Fleet; and Tommy L. Wilson, corporate communications, Loral Vought Systems.

Dr. Scott C. Truver of the TECHMATICS Corporation and members of his staff have been most helpful in my research efforts, especially Robert Anderson, Edward Feege, John Kellar, John Patrick, and Maren Smith.

Several members of the U.S. Naval Institute staff contributed greatly to making this edition a reality, most especially my editor, Linda O'Doughda; my most perceptive proofreader, Jack Brostrom; designer Karen White; Susan Artigiani and Tom Harnish of marketing; Mary Beth Straight Kiss, Susan Brook, and Chuck Mussi who provided photo research; and Eve Secunda, administrative assistant par excellence.

As with many of my editorial projects, I appreciate the guidance and support of Fred Rainbow, editor in chief of the Naval Institute *Proceedings,* and his staff, especially Julie Olver, who edits my regular column in the *Proceedings.*

The compilation of the next edition of *Ships and Aircraft* begins almost immediately, to be published three years after this volume went to press. Comments and photographs should be submitted directly to the author in care of the U.S. Naval Institute.

NORMAN POLMAR

THE NAVAL INSTITUTE GUIDE TO THE

Ships and Aircraft of the U.S. Fleet

CHAPTER 1

State of the Fleet

An E-2C Hawkeye takes off from the carrier THEODORE ROOSEVELT (CVN 71), operating in the Adriatic Sea. Despite the end of the Cold War, naval forces—and especially aircraft carriers—have proven to be invaluable in support of U.S. overseas interests. The F/A-18 Hornets and S-3B Viking in the foreground are from Carrier Air Wing (CVW) 8. (Jon R. Anderson/Army Times Publishing)

The U.S. Navy is approaching the 21st century in confusion and frustration. The confusion arises primarily because of an ongoing debate among the military services over roles and missions as U.S. military forces are being "downsized." Not since the infamous roles-and-missions debate of the late 1940s has there been such an acrimonious debate among the services.[1] The Navy and Air Force are in direct competition for long-range strike capability, i.e., manned land-based bombers versus carrier aircraft and Tomahawk cruise missiles. The Navy and the Army are competing over Theater Ballistic Missile Defense (TBMD). Together, the Navy and Marine Corps are competing with the Army (and at times the Air Force) over the rapid projection of ground forces into crisis areas.

These and several other areas of interservice rivalry are increasing. Despite the Republican leadership in both houses of Congress (which supports a relatively high level of defense spending) and continued crises and conflicts that demand U.S. military readiness, if not participation, the real spending levels available to the services are decreasing. Furthermore, within the Navy the warfare communities, or "unions"—aviation, surface, and submarine—continue to compete for the available funds with little regard for overall roles and missions. Indeed, Navy infighting has accelerated since the reduction in 1992 of the "platform sponsors," or "barons," within the Office of the Chief of Naval Operations from three-star to two-star rank. That move, however, was intended to *reduce* bureaucratic infighting (see chapter 5). Although the aviation and surface warfare communities now have two-star directors, in reality the submarine community is still run by a four-star admiral in the position of Director Naval Nuclear Propulsion (see chapter 9). Officially, he is not a platform sponsor—he is responsible for training and safety within the Navy's nuclear propulsion program—but nevertheless the close-knit and dogmatic nuclear submarine community answers to him, not to the two-star Director Submarine Warfare Division in OPNAV nor to the three-star Commander Submarine Force Atlantic Fleet, nominally the Navy's senior submarine commander.[2]

Significantly, neither President Bill Clinton's 1994 promise of $25 *billion* to improve defense readiness and modernization over the next six years nor the Commission on Roles and Missions of the Armed Forces—established by Congress—that met in 1994–1995 is having much impact on the defense establishment or the core problems between the services. For example, just days after Mr. Clinton's 1 December 1994 statement that he was adding money to the next six defense budgets (that may well extend beyond his time in the White House), the Defense Department revealed $7.7 *billion* in cutbacks in weapons procurement, including Navy-Marine programs for ships, aircraft, submarines, and assault vehicles.

The roles and missions commission, chaired by Dr. John P. White, Director of the Center for Business and Government at Harvard's Kennedy School of Government and a former Assistant Secretary of Defense, did not take on the "tough issues," nor did the committee make recommendations that would help the services resolve their current controversies.

Rather, Secretary of Defense William J. Perry's hard-line, no-nonsense approach to managing the defense establishment appears to be the best possibility of bringing some order to the controversies surrounding the armed services. He has support from President Clinton and respect from Congress. (The Defense Department was undoubtedly hurt, however, by the departure of his deputy, John M. Deutch, in 1995 to become the Director of Central Intelligence.)

This issue of roles and missions is especially frustrating for the Navy's leadership because, on a day-to-day basis, the forward-deployed Navy and Marine Corps personnel provide the most ready and available U.S. military forces. Still, the public perceptions of the post–Cold War crises and conflicts that have involved U.S. forces—Panama, Desert Storm, Somalia, and Bosnia—are that Army and Air Force components had the major or only significant roles. The Navy and (to a lesser degree) the Marine Corps have failed to effectively articulate their participation, especially in Somalia (starting with the remarkable evacuation of the U.S. Embassy in January 1991); the Persian Gulf conflict, including the buildup and the continuing blockade of Iraq; international disaster assistance efforts; Tomahawk strikes against Iraqi targets after the 1991 war in the gulf, and later against targets in Bosnia; and, most recently, in support of U.S.-NATO-United Nations operations in Bosnia.

These perceptions affect congressional actions and hence the funding for and controversies among the military services.

The Navy–Marine Corps leadership attempted to define future roles in the strategy paper . . . *From the Sea,* published in 1992.[3] Navy leaders hailed that paper as reflecting a "landmark shift" in its operational focus and a reordering of priorities. The thrust of that shift was to develop naval forces that could carry out regional missions "from the sea" rather than forces that would fight on the sea and strike the Soviet empire in the face of a global maritime threat. But there was relatively little change from forces that had been advocated for the Cold War era, in part because the flexibility of naval forces had been amply demonstrated during the Cold War.

Indeed, the areas in which . . . *From the Sea* could be seen to offer a change became almost irrelevant. Submarines were hardly mentioned in the paper, which came as the Bush administration canceled the SEAWOLF (SSN 21) program after a single submarine. However, spurred on by the Director Naval Nuclear Propulsion, Admiral Bruce DeMars, and the SEAWOLF's builder, General Dynamics/Electric Boat, Congress did approve a second, then a third, submarine of the class.

A new strategy statement, *Forward . . . From the Sea,* was published in 1995. It was an attempt to refine Navy-Marine strategy for the contemporary world—one inundated with conflicts and crises—stating, most fundamentally, that, short of war, the role of Navy-Marine forces is to be continually engaged in forward areas with the objectives of preventing conflict and controlling crises. Being engaged in forward areas—generally referred to as forward presence—is thus critical to the Navy. The 1994 National Security Strategy put forward by the White House states, "[forward] presence demonstrates our commitment to allies and friends, underwrites regional stability, gains U.S. familiarity with overseas operating environments, promotes combined training among the forces of friendly countries, and provides timely initial response capabilities."

Currently, Navy and Marine Corps personnel constitute less than 20 percent of all U.S. military personnel deployed overseas. By the end of the decade that proportion will be about 50 percent, and possibly more, under current planning. The naval forces normally forward-deployed have considerably more mobility than, for example, an Army division in Korea or an Air Force tactical wing in the United States, unless secure ports and bases are available and politically usable in the crisis area. While a Navy carrier or amphibious group may require some number of days to reach a crisis area, its movement can be initiated at the earliest indication of a problem, with minimal attention being called to itself. Once on scene, the naval group can remain on station almost indefinitely, without the need for land bases in the area.

In addition, if advantageous, this presence can be visible. The ships can entertain visitors—a CNN camera team or local political leaders—to publicize their presence. Or, the ships can remain beyond the horizon, largely out of sight, but with targets several hundred miles inland still within range of their F/A-18 Hornet strike aircraft or Tomahawk land-attack missiles.

Naval forces are also well suited for coalition operations, a hallmark of future U.S. military operations. Navies easily carry out joint exercises, practicing "interoperability" with minimal political impact. The longstanding series of naval exercises in the Atlantic and

1. The late 1940s debate centered on the role of the newly established Air Force vis-à-vis naval aviation, both carrier- and land-based, including Marine aviation. A recent analysis of this debate is Jeffrey G. Barlow, *Revolt of the Admirals: The Fight for Naval Aviation, 1945–1950* (Washington, D.C.: Naval Historical Center, 1994).
2. The Commander Submarine Force Pacific Fleet is a two-star officer.
3. In effect . . . *From the Sea* was a successor to the highly successful *Maritime Strategy* put forward by the Navy's leadership in the early 1980s, which was well articulated by Secretary of the Navy John Lehman as a "tool" for building his 600-ship fleet.

The submarine SEAWOLF (SSN 21) fitting out. She is probably the most capable undersea craft built in the West, but she is too large and too expensive for series production. Some observers consider the SEAWOLF a relic of the Cold War. (General Dynamics/Electric Boat)

Mediterranean with NATO navies (including the French), and with South American fleets, as well as those of Australia, New Zealand, and some Asian nations, ensure compatibility during crisis or combat operations. The ease of naval interoperability was fully demonstrated during the Persian Gulf conflict, when 50 ships from 17 nations joined with the 100 U.S. Navy ships that took part in gulf-area operations. Tactical assignments, communications, logistics, and other aspects of the multinational naval participation were carried out without any difficulties.

These and other factors make it evident why naval forces have been extensively engaged in support of current U.S. policies in many areas of the world. But the internal Navy "union" conflicts, the failure of the Navy to develop a unified position on restructuring and force requirements, and the pressure of force reductions and Army and Air Force competition for roles and missions, coupled with the Navy's failure to effectively articulate its Cold War and post-1991 accomplishments, make one apprehensive about the Navy's future.

The frustrations affecting Navy effectiveness tend to center on the massive and continuing failure of the Navy to conform to the "new world *social* order." It is difficult to discern the precise causes or the precise starting point for this situation, but the manifestations are very clear. The beginning has been traced by some observers to the turret explosion in the battleship IOWA (BB 61) on 19 April 1989. In a rush to declare judgment, the Navy's leadership sought an individual to blame, and a dead sailor was identified as the culprit, a suicide intent on taking his comrades with him. But the evidence was questionable at best, and more objective and capable analyses subsequently determined that it was undoubtedly a problem with the powder bags that caused the detonation that killed 47 men aboard the dreadnought.

The IOWA incident and a series of other accidents led to a "stand down" of essentially all naval operations for a day of briefings, lectures, and discussions. While the numbers of accidents declined, the Navy's problems continued, as did the manner in which they were handled by the Navy's leaders. The Tailhook Association's convention of 1991 in Las Vegas, Nevada, featured a variety of sexual activities; senior Navy officials were in the vicinity of some of those events. More important than the actual occurrences at Tailhook was the Navy's initial handling of complaints by a young female helicopter pilot who told her commanding officer about the events. Her complaints were initially disregarded; when an investigation was begun by the Naval Investigative Service, it was thoroughly botched. Then the Navy's leadership again mishandled the situation, which eventually led to the resignation of the Chief of Naval Operations—just two months before his normal retirement. In the meantime, numerous junior and mid-grade officers were censured, some of whom were brought up on charges and finally court-martialed.

But there was no "closure" to Tailhook. Naval aviators (Navy and Marine) who were not even in the continental United States at the time had promotions delayed and came under scrutiny. Then, in January 1996, the promotion of Commander Robert E. Stumpf to captain was withdrawn by Secretary of the Navy John H. Dalton because Stumpf had watched a stripper at Tailhook—a perfectly legal activity.[4] Stumpf had been selected for promotion by a board of flag officers, Secretary Dalton had personally interviewed and approved Stumpf, and his promotion had been approved by the Senate. At that stage only Dalton or President Clinton could legally have halted his promotion. Stumpf, former leader of the prestigious Blue Angels flight demonstration team and an outstanding leader, was "left out to dry" by the Navy's leadership although he had been fully investigated and cleared of any wrongdoing at Tailhook.

A long list of personnel problems—including major episodes of sexual harassment—continues. The Naval Academy was rocked by charges of sexual harassment against female midshipmen, the worst incidence involving one being manacled to a urinal in December 1989. The academy was further rocked by a major cheating scandal in December 1992 and a drug scandal in 1995. In recent years a series of charges have been pressed against relatively senior naval officers for sexual harassment, with some captains not being promoted and a full admiral being denied assignment to the post of Commander in Chief Pacific Command. (The admiral who did get the position was summarily discharged for an ill-advised comment related to the rape of a young Okinawan girl by a couple of Marines and a sailor.)

Officers have not been the only culprits. In December 1995 a hospital corpsman third class was sentenced to five years in the brig for touching women and getting them to expose themselves when he took X-rays of them. A few days before his sentencing, a first class petty officer was arrested for groping a woman on a commercial aircraft while several of his colleagues looked on, among them a Navy chaplain.

The situation with respect to sexual problems was exacerbated in 1994 with the first assignment of women to a combatant ship (see chapter 9). Beyond the social disorder caused within the close living conditions of warships—coupled with prolonged deployments measured in terms of months—officers and chief petty officers found that their male sailors objected to having to do more of the "heavy work" during underway replenishments because the women, it was felt (rightly or wrongly), could not handle the numerous "muscle jobs" aboard a warship.

Furthermore, seniors were apprehensive of rewarding or chastising enlisted women for fear of being accused of sexual harassment (or rewarding the more attractive females). While the Navy has attempted to integrate women at several levels aboard ship so that female chiefs would be the ones to chastise enlisted women, this interferes with the basic chain of command in a ship populated mainly by men. The author has been told of at least one woman who was not made the master chief of a command because of the executive officer's concern (supported by the commanding officer) that the traditional close

4. Stumpf, at the time of Tailhook, was commanding officer of Navy Strike Fighter Squadron 83; he was asked by his superiors to attend the Tailhook convention to receive an award for his squadron, which had been voted the Navy's best unit of that type for the year. He retired from the Navy effective 1 October 1996.

relationship between an executive officer (male) and leading chief (female) could lead to problems.

The Navy was forced to take women into carrier air wings, aircraft carriers, cruisers, and destroyers under conditions that were far different than integrating them into Army and Air Force tactical units.[5] Under the 1994 dictum, women cannot serve in ground combat units nor in submarines, the latter because of constrained living conditions. However, on 14 February, 1996, Secretary Dalton said that a study was under way to determine how to put women aboard submarines. (Up to the time this edition went to press the Navy's Office of Information was unable to identify that study.)

As various aspects of integration were discussed in the early years of the Clinton administration—which was determined that homosexuals as well as women would have totally equal opportunities within the armed forces—the Navy failed to make a convincing case to the White House and Congress of the extent of the problems caused by the new social order. Moreover, once the decision was made, the Navy again failed to properly make the changes in an effective and professional manner.[6]

The Navy's failure to cope with the changing social environment came after the outspoken and controversial, but highly effective, John Lehman stepped down as Secretary of the Navy (1981 to 1987). In that position Lehman had assumed several of the duties traditionally undertaken by the Chief of Naval Operations (CNO). Since Lehman's departure, a succession of CNOs have attempted to "restore" the Navy. This began under Admiral James Watkins (1982 to 1986), followed as CNO by Admiral Carlisle A. H. Trost (1986 to 1990) and Frank B. Kelso (1990 to 1994). These men were somewhat limited by their relatively narrow experience as nuclear submariners.[7] Two had not served in or commanded surface warships. (Watkins, the first nuclear submariner to serve as CNO, had been executive officer of the nuclear-propelled cruiser LONG BEACH/CGN 9.)

Their commands had been strategic missile submarines and attack submarines. These undersea craft, with crews numbering about 130, were manned by volunteers within a volunteer service, men who were carefully selected and had specialized training and received extra pay in comparison to the sailors on surface ships. Submariners make up less than 8 percent of the Navy's personnel; they are not a cross section of the people and the problems that officers in the surface and air communities have to face every day.

The selection of Admiral J. M. (Mike) Boorda as CNO in 1994 brought a new perspective to the Navy's leadership. He is a surface officer who has literally gone from seaman to four-star admiral; he held several important shore assignments, including Chief of Naval Personnel and Commander in Chief of NATO's Allied Forces Southern Europe. He held the NATO billet when his forces became involved in the Bosnian conflict and peacekeeping efforts.

While concerned about the role of the Navy in the post–Cold War era, developing a "littoral" operating strategy, preparing and "selling" Navy shipbuilding and aircraft procurement programs, and a multitude of other activities, Boorda needed to manage the complex social changes of the Navy. These social changes are determined outside of the Departments of Defense and the Navy, but they have a bearing on the military services nonetheless. Although they may or may not be valid social changes, they are generally imposed by people who have no direct knowledge of the naval operating environment. Popular writer Erica Jong has addressed this situation in a broader social context: "But being zealots, they never care very much about truth. They are idealists, and theirs is only to theorize. The implementation of their theories is left to others. . . ."[8]

But Boorda served just a little more than half of his expected four-year term as Chief of Naval Operations. The Navy's budget and social problems, and questions about the "V" insignia that he had previously worn on two of his commendation awards, probably led Mike Boorda—the first person ever to rise from an enlisted man to Chief of Naval Operations—to commit suicide on 16 May 1996.

His death was an unexpected and grievous loss to the Navy and to the nation. The Navy's morale and image had improved during his two-year tenure, but his demise severely hurt the service.

THE SHIPS

The U.S. Navy continues to reduce the number of active ships, declining to the goals specified in the Bottom-Up Review conducted by the Department of Defense in 1993.[9] That review established the architecture for the Clinton administration's long-term defense program. Conducted by civilian and military personnel from the Department of Defense, as well as representatives of the military services, unified commands, and other defense agencies, the review determined the forces required to simultaneously carry out two Major Regional Conflicts (MRC). These were defined as Persian Gulf–type conflicts, i.e., the large-scale deployment of U.S. air, naval, and ground forces for a conventional conflict. The two "most probable" areas of MRCs involving U.S. participation were estimated to be the Middle East–Persian Gulf and the Korean peninsula.

The accompanying table indicates the overall Navy force structure proposed under the Bottom-Up Review; the Army and Air Force are included for comparative purposes. As indicated, the strategic missile submarines are being reduced by 60 percent, a reflection of the shift in U.S. relations with the Soviet Union from a superpower nuclear confrontation to an era of U.S.–Russia cooperation. Also, the strategic missile submarines of the OHIO (SSBN 726) class, each with 24 Trident missiles, are far superior to the Poseidon/Trident submarine mix of the late 1980s. The attack submarine force, with a 50 percent reduction, also reflects the end of the Cold War as well as the Navy's problems in developing an acceptable submarine design and procurement program.

U.S. MILITARY FORCE STRUCTURE

	End of Cold War	FY 1995	Bottom-Up Review FY 1999 Plan
Navy			
Strategic Missile Submarines*	35	16	17
Attack Submarines	97	85	45–55
Aircraft Carriers**	15	11/1	11/1
Carrier Air Wings#	13/2	10/1	10/1
Surface Ships	427	373	346
Marine Corps			
Active Divisions	3	3	3
Reserve Divisions	1	1	1
Active Personnel	197,000	174,000	174,000
Reserve Personnel	44,000	42,000	42,000
Army			
Active Divisions	18	12	10
National Guard Divisions	10	8	5+
Air Force			
Active Fighter Wings##	26	13	13
Reserve Fighter Wings##	13	8	7
B-1B Bombers	90	60	60
B-2 Bombers	—	6	20
B-52 Bombers	187	74	56

Notes: *Strategic missile submarines (SSBN) were not addressed by the Bottom-Up Review (see chapter 11).
**Active/Naval Reserve Force (NRF) carriers.
#Active/Reserve Forces.
##Fighter wing equivalents.

5. See "The Law and Women in the Navy," U.S. Naval Institute *Proceedings* (February 1996), p. 29. A recent analysis of the situation and recommendations are found in Capt. John L. Byron, USN (Ret.), "End Sexism," *Proceedings* (February 1996), pp. 27–31.
6. Although there were major differences, an example of how a naval institution can be successfully breached by females was the integration of women into the Naval Academy in 1975.
7. Three earlier CNOs had been qualified in submarines: E. J. King (1942–1945), Chester W. Nimitz (1945–1947), and Louis E. Denfield (1947–1949). All had served in and commanded surface ships.
8. Erica Jong, "Is Sex Sexy Without Power?" *Penthouse* (April 1996), p. 58.
9. Secretary of Defense Les Aspin, *Report of the Bottom-Up Review* (Washington, D.C.: October 1993).

FY 1996 THROUGH 2001 SHIPBUILDING PROGRAM

Type/Class		FY 1996 Actual	FY 1997 Planned	FY 1998 Planned	FY 1999 Planned	FY 2000 Planned	FY 2001 Planned
SSN 21	SEAWOLF	1*	—	—	—	—	—
NSSN		—	—	1	1	1	1
DDG 51	ARLEIGH BURKE	2	4	2	3	3	3
LHD 1	WASP	1	—	—	—	—	—
LPD 17		1	—	1	1	2	2
PC 1	CYCLONE	—	1**	—	—	—	—
ADC(X)	support ship	—	—	—	—	1	—
T-AGS	research ship	1	—	—	1	—	—
T-AGOS	surveillance ship	—	—	1	1	—	—
LMSR	large medium-speed roll-on/roll-off ship	2	2	2	2	—	—
Total		*9*	*7*	*7*	*8*	*7*	*5*

Notes: *Originally authorized in FY 1992; final funding in FY 1996.
**Not in DOD plan; see text.

The carrier reduction of 20 percent causes the unusual status of the JOHN F. KENNEDY (CV 67), with a composite active–Naval Reserve Force (NRF) crew. The ship will be deployable should it be necessary, unlike previous U.S. training carriers (CVT/AVT types). Similarly, other surface ships are suffering a 20 percent reduction, with some 115 surface combatants (cruisers, destroyers, frigates) planned for the end of the century.

"Real-life" experience of the past few years has already demonstrated that the planned reductions in attack submarines, surface combatants, and amphibious ships will not permit the current tempo of Navy operations. For example, during the fall of 1995 the Navy—on a standard day—had almost 50 percent of its attack submarines, as well as 55 percent of its surface ships, under way. Of the latter, more than 30 percent were forward-deployed, including an average of 4 of 12 carrier battle groups and 4 of 12 amphibious groups.

The ongoing Fleet reductions mean that, with the same ratio of ships to forward-deployed ships, the Navy will not be able to meet current deployment requirements. Thus, radical Fleet restructuring or changes in requirements must be forthcoming.

Moreover, the current shipbuilding programs will not support even the fiscal 1999 force-level goals. A nominal ship life of 30 years must be calculated against the number of ships authorized per year to produce the expected force levels. In the late 1980s, for example, after the departure of John Lehman—who was able to garner almost unlimited funds for the Navy—the shipbuilding programs averaged almost 20 ships per year, i.e., enough to support a Fleet of almost 600 ships.[10]

In contrast, the fiscal 1993 through 1995 programs have averaged just over six ships per year, i.e., a potential Fleet of just 180 ships. And the trend has been downward, with the Clinton administration requesting just three ships in the fiscal 1996 shipbuilding program. Congress has authorized funds for seven ships in fiscal 1996, however, an action based on both naval requirements and providing work for shipyards, a major political issue. It is dubious if such largess can continue.

Significantly, two new warship concepts were under discussion in the Departments of Defense and the Navy as this edition of *Ships and Aircraft* went to press.

Theater Ballistic Missile Defense. The Iraqi use of Scud-type ballistic missiles against targets in Saudi Arabia and Israel during January 1991 has led to extensive U.S. interest in developing a Theater Ballistic Missile Defense (TBMD) competence. Secretary of Defense William J. Perry stated, "The capability to protect noncombatants will become increasingly vital to the U.S. leadership role in the world as ballistic missiles proliferate and aggressors attempt to deter the formation of defensive coalitions through the threat of missile attacks."[11]

The Department of Defense is sponsoring a multi-tier TBMD. The first phase consists of near-term improvement to existing systems, using low-cost, low-risk, quick-reaction solutions. The second phase expands the current capacity. Two core efforts are under way: the Army's Patriot Advanced Capability Level-3 (PAC-3) and the Navy's Theater High-Altitude Area Defense (THAAD) program.

The PAC-2 missile was used against Iraqi missiles during the Gulf War with very limited effectiveness. The Patriot, an air-transporable mobile system, is being upgraded to the PAC-3 configuration. (A follow-on to the PAC-3 is also being considered.)

The THAAD program is based on using Aegis-fitted cruisers and destroyers, using upgraded Standard Block IVA missiles, and modifying software in the existing Aegis system. The Navy THAAD offers many advantages over the PAC-3 concept, primarily because of the mobility of the ships, their territorial independence, and the ability to deploy them early in a crisis—the traditional characteristics of warships.

The down side of THAAD is that fitting ballistic-missile intercept weapons in an Aegis ship would detract from the number of vertical launch cells available for "naval" weapons, i.e., standard SAMs (Surface-to-Air Missiles), TLAMs (Tomahawk Land-Attack Missiles), and the vertical-launch ASROC (Anti-Submarine Rocket). The arsenal ship program could provide some relief from the weapon load-out problems of Aegis ships (as could increased numbers of Aegis warships).

Arsenal Ship. The war against Iraq also gave impetus to the arsenal ship concept. The arsenal ship is envisioned as a floating missile battery, carrying perhaps 500 to 750 vertical-launch missiles. Several weapons are envisioned for the ship: Tomahawk TLAMs for striking targets ashore at distances of almost 1,000 miles (1,610 km); the Army's ATACMS missile, with a range of almost 100 miles (160 km); and possibly standard SAMs, including the Block IVA missiles configured for the anti-theater ballistic missile role.[12] These missiles would be controlled by other ships, aircraft, or forces ashore under the Cooperative Engagement Capability (CEC) now being developed.

These weapons would be used to provide commanders with massive amounts of firepower early in a crisis or conflict while reducing the strategic airlift and sealift needed to move weapons from the United States or other areas to the crisis location. This concept would permit the available (and generally limited) strategic lift resources to be used to move combat and support forces rather than ordnance.

Furthermore, political constraints and limitations on airfield and port facilities can reduce the firepower that can rapidly be brought to a crisis area. These were important factors in the 1990 buildup for the Gulf War. Navy planners are quick to point out that during that conflict, on 16 February 1991, an Iraqi Scud-type missile hit close to the pier at Al Jubayl, Saudi Arabia. At that moment, four cargo ships, a U.S. helicopter carrier, two aviation support ships, a Polish training ship, and a U.S. Army barge were alongside the pier, while hundreds of vehicles and tons of munitions were on the pier. A few yards

10. This does not include the small, special warfare ships and craft, including the 13 units of the CYCLONE (PC 1) class.
11. Secretary of Defense William J. Perry, *Annual Report to the President and Congress* (Washington, D.C.: February 1995), p. 241.

12. ATACMS = Army Tactical Missile System.

separated the near miss from a major disaster. Arsenal ships standing offshore would have greatly reduced the need for cargo ships carrying munitions, the amount of ordnance piled on piers, and the need to transport missiles to Army and Marine firing batteries ashore.

Some Marine leaders look at the arsenal ship to partially fulfill the long-time need for naval fire support. Although the Marines have long cited the shortfalls in fire support, the Marine commandants have not used their "blue chits" with Congress to force the issue, either in terms of new fire-support ships, keeping battleships in commission, or rearming existing ships with an improved weapon for shore bombardment. The now-stricken dreadnoughts of the IOWA class were severely limited in this role: their 16-inch (406-mm guns) had a range of less than 30 n.miles (55.6 km). While a major modification could have permitted them to fire small-diameter rounds to three times that distance, the funds for keeping these ships in commission, each manned by some 1,500 men, were simply beyond realistic budget planning. Despite the efforts by battleship buffs and others within the Navy and Marine Corps to retain the battleship, the fiscal 1996 appropriation report states, "None of the funds provided in this Act shall be available either to return any IOWA Class Battleships to the Naval Register, or to retain the logistical support necessary for support of any IOWA Class Battleships in active service."

Finis for the battleship? Well . . . despite legislation that specified no funds could be used to retain the battleships, other congressional legislation directed that the Navy retain some of the ships. Accordingly, the Secretary of the Navy has directed that the NEW JERSEY (BB 62) and WISCONSIN (BB 64) be retained as possible "mobilization assets," but they have not been reinstated on the Naval Vessel Register, and only minimal funds (from the Operations & Maintenance account) are being expended on them. Meanwhile, the IOWA (BB 61) and the MISSOURI (BB 63) have been offered as memorial-museum ships; a considerable number of interested parties are competing for these dreadnoughts (see appendix D).

The Navy has begun development of the arsenal ship, responding to interest expressed by then-Chief of Naval Operations Admiral Boorda. His view was that:

> the arsenal ship is the gun barrel, or the airplane, or the missile tube . . . that takes the information from somebody else that says please put your thing here and the arsenal ship shoots it. Simple operation—not a very sophisticated ship with respect to elaborate fire control systems. It merely gets told where the target is—probably by some data links, like CEC—and it unloads the right weapon on the target. . . . The whole idea is that it isn't a specific-weapon ship. [The weapon] is whatever the Defense Department builds that can be launched vertically, that can be fired off of the ship.[13]

(The modern concept of a warship carrying hundreds of missiles is not new. Vice Admiral Joseph Metcalf III, while Deputy Chief of Naval Operations for Surface Warfare, publicly advanced this idea in 1988, calling for a specialized warship with up to 200 vertical-launch missiles.[14] The idea was elaborated upon a few months later by Dr. Scott C. Truver, an astute naval analyst and defense consultant.[15] But their goal was a warship to stand in battle with other naval forces to strike Soviet targets ashore and afloat. Their ship carried not only vertical-launch systems but also had an anti-submarine capability, being fitted with bow-mounted sonar and SH-60 Seahawk helicopters. Propelled by gas turbines, the ship would sail with other warships in the battle group.)

The arsenal ship is "intended for presence, crisis response, and regional conflicts," according to a Navy official.[16] And the ship would be different from the vertical-launch warship proposed during the Cold War. Merchant construction techniques would be employed, possibly with double-hull configuration with transverse frames and stiffeners. Various protective systems could be fitted within a double hull to help defeat attacking cruise missiles. The ship would have a small Radar Cross Section (RCS) and other passive defense features, as well as innovative damage control systems.

The propulsion concepts currently being examined center on electric propulsion to provide a transit speed of about 25 knots for the ship to reach the crisis area. The ship would have a high degree of automation, making a crew as small as 25 to 30 feasible. (Such a ship would have only passive/stealth defensive features; an active defense would require a larger crew.)

The Navy believes that four to six such arsenal ships could provide a continuous war-fighting presence in two or three areas. To permit the ships to remain on station for long periods, the crews would probably be rotated, as is now done for some maritime prepositioning ships. Under current Navy planning, the fiscal 1998 budget would provide for a prototype arsenal ship—an Advanced Concept Technology Demonstrator (ACTD), in defense gobbledygook. Construction of the lead ship as an ACTD would shorten construction time and reduce technical risks, according to Navy statements. A contract for design of an ACTD prototype could be awarded as early as fiscal 1997. The most significant difference between the ACTD prototype and the envisioned operational units would be the number of launch cells provided. A single 64-cell unit would be installed in the prototype, with the ship capable of being upgraded to a full 500-missile battery. (The actual number of vertical-launch cells installed would be a multiple of 64 launch cells, plus possibly one 32 cell module, i.e., 480 or 512 missiles.)

While most of the discussion of the arsenal ship centers on surface ships, the submarine community has proposed a submarine arsenal ship that would be based on the Trident submarine. The Navy has 17 OHIO-class submarines in commission; one more is under construction. The 1994 review of U.S. strategic forces provides for a force of 14 Trident submarines after the year 2000; thus, four of the older units will be retired.

Rear Admiral Dennis A. Jones, Director Submarine Warfare Division, has touted use of these nonstrategic Trident submarines in the arsenal ship role. He has noted that there is no reason why any weapon in the military inventory "cannot be shot submerged. . . . We are also exploring this option: a sub-surface to air or a sub-surface to surface missile."[17] According to Admiral Jones, the Navy recently completed a feasibility study that showed the ATACMS could be launched from a standard attack submarine VLS with only minor modifications being required.

The Trident submarine in the arsenal ship role has the following advantages: it is readily available; it has a high degree of stealth; and, even rearmed with nonstrategic missiles, it would retain traditional torpedo/mine capabilities. Each Trident could be converted to carry 162 Tomahawk-size missiles in place of 24 Trident weapons. Admiral Jones, who refers to the nonstrategic Trident as the "LSC"—Large Stealth Combatant—contends that the Trident submarines could "do, and do as well, in shallow water, every role that the present [SSN] 688 and the [planned] New Attack Submarine will be able to do."[18]

But an ex-Trident boat in this role would still have a relatively limited missile load, compared to a specialized arsenal ship; it would be expensive to operate; and it could possibly cause some confusion in strategic arms negotiations.

A more realistic approach to a submarine arsenal ship would be to convert some submarines of the LOS ANGELES (SSN 688) class that are being retired long before their predicted 30-year service life. These missile ships would consist of a basic SSN 688 submarine with the following modifications:

- reconfigure the "front end" to provide for 12 VLS tubes (as in Improved SSN 688s)
- insert an amidships hull section of approximately 100 feet (30 m) fitted with approximately 100 to 120 VLS cells
- provide appropriate fire control equipment.

13. Adm. Boorda interview with Eric Schmitt, *The New York Times*, 24 August 1995.
14. Vice Adm. Metcalf, "Revolution at Sea," U.S. Naval Institute *Proceedings* (January 1988), pp. 34–39.
15. Dr. Truver, "Whither the Revolution at Sea?" U.S. Naval Institute *Proceedings* (December 1988), pp. 68–74.
16. Capt. Mark Edwards, USN, Office of the Chief of Naval Operations (N863), interview, 2 October 1995.
17. Rear Adm. Jones, Office of the Chief of Naval Operations (N87), address to the Naval Submarine League, Fort Myer, Va., 8 November 1995.
18. Rear Adm. Jones, op. cit.

An artist's concept of the proposed arsenal ship. Some proposals call for converting a laid-up oiler of the Henry J. Kaiser (T-AO 187) class as a prototype arsenal ship; other proposals call for a highly stealthy surface ship, while the submarine community advocates the conversion of four ex-Trident missile submarines to that role. (Lockheed Martin)

The SSN 688 missile ship would retain four torpedo tubes and full sonar and torpedo fire control capability. The current internal stowage of some 25 torpedoes, however, may be reduced in favor of additional Tomahawk missiles (torpedo-tube launched), or some stowage space may have to be reconfigured for fire control equipment. Such a modified submarine could thus carry more than 100 Tomahawks or other missiles, plus a nominal number of torpedoes.

The hull section insertion would be similar to the U.S. program of the late 1950s in which the Skipjack (SSN 585) design was modified by the insertion of a 130-foot (40-m) section, including 16 missile launch tubes, to provide the Polaris submarine design. There have been several other submarine conversions of this type, undertaken by the U.S. and other navies. In this regard, the SSN 688 is far superior to the SSN 585 for such a conversion, e.g., the SSN 688 has a 30,000-horsepower reactor plant compared to 15,000 horsepower for the SSN 585. Few, if any, additional personnel would be required in the reconfiguration of an SSN 688 to the arsenal ship role.[19]

(The Russians have already reconfigured several former Yankee strategic missile submarines to carry the SS-N-21 Sampson cruise missile, a weapon similar to the U.S. Tomahawk.)

There are many pros and cons to the arsenal ship concept. For example, what is the relative value of increasing the missile capacity of a variant of the Arleigh Burke (DDG 51) class in place of producing arsenal ships? Or could a removable vertical-launch module be dropped into the docking well of LSD-type amphibious ships? And, should the relative cost of defending an arsenal ship with an Aegis destroyer be included in budgeting for the program?

The submarine concept is more difficult to address. The issue of stealth, for example, could become moot if the submarine has to remain in a specific area, or "box," for a sustained period, shooting missiles at the orders of a ground commander and thus becoming relatively vulnerable to detection. Also, if an Army or Marine commander needs an arsenal ship to provide his forces with missile support, there would most likely be amphibious and cargo ships in the area with their defensive escorts, lessening the value of a stealth arsenal ship.

It is obviously too early to make such definitive judgments on the arsenal ship concept. But as the U.S. Navy enters the 21st century, it is obvious that many of the weapons, ships, aircraft, and concepts that were employed in the Cold War will not be effective in the future, especially if that future demands sustained operations in relatively shallow water, close to the shore. New weapons and new operations concepts will be needed. The arsenal ship may be one of the right ones.

Strategic missile submarines: Under the strategic arms agreements with the late Soviet Union, the United States was limited in the number of weapons that could be deployed. The ultimate U.S. strategic force planned at the end of the Cold War was to include 18 Ohio-class submarines armed with 432 Trident C-4 and D-5 missiles. The strategic force will now be based on 14 submarines, all armed with the D-5 missile. (These will be supplemented by 450 to 500 single-warhead, land-based ballistic missiles. There will also be a U.S. "strategic" bomber force, but those aircraft will be assigned to primarily conventional/theater strike missions.)

Attack submarines: The attack submarine (SSN) program continues without guidance. Despite efforts by the Bush and Clinton administrations to halt the Seawolf (SSN 21) program with a single submarine, the second and third units have been funded. The third Seawolf will have a Department of Defense price tag of at least $3 *billion.* This does not take into account the Department of Energy cost for reactor development, procurement, and fueling.

Forced by the White House and Congress to seek a less expensive alternative, the New Attack Submarine (NSSN) was conceived. But intelligence analyses late in 1994 that indicated the improved Akula-class SSNs being produced by Russia were quieter than the improved Los Angeles design caused consternation over U.S. submarine programs to surface.[20]

In frustration, Congress stepped into the picture in September 1995, when Newt Gingrich, Speaker of the House, personally met with outside submarine specialists and analysts. A House hearing on 7 September 1995 led to congressional support for several prototype designs to be produced instead of series production of the basic NSSN design, which, by logical deduction, would be inferior to its Soviet counterparts in quieting as well as other features.

The fiscal 1996 appropriation bill provides funding to complete the third Seawolf as well as long-lead component funding for two advanced nuclear submarines, to be authorized in fiscal 1998 and 1999 or 2000. And, there is continued interest in several quarters for the Navy to objectively evaluate the issue of nonnuclear submarines. Such craft could be especially important as the Navy emphasizes its potential role in littoral operations. The submarine picture remains very murky.

Aircraft carriers: These behemoths continue to serve as the nation's "911" force—when there is a crisis, the first question still asked in the White House situation room seems to be "where are the carriers?"

No less than eight nuclear-propelled carriers (CVN) are in service, with two more under construction. Thus, without any further production of these ships, the Navy will have at least that number well into

19. For a discussion of potential SSN 688 modifications see N. Polmar, "There Are Alternatives to the Third *Seawolf,*" U.S. Naval Institute *Proceedings* (March 1995), pp. 121–22.

20. N. Polmar, "The Quest for the Quiet Submarine," U.S. Naval Institute *Proceedings* (October 1995), pp. 119–21.

the next century. For a number of reasons, however, it seems unlikely that additional ships of the NIMITZ (CVN 68) class will be built, mainly because of their cost and nuclear-related issues.

A large number of designs and concepts are being considered by the Navy for follow-on aviation ships, and Congress seems ready to support future aviation ships. The Department of Defense has planned funding beginning in fiscal 2000 for aviation ships to be procured after 2001, although such long-term planning is more political than practical.

In the near-term, several oil-fueled carriers remain operational, with one—the JOHN F. KENNEDY—in the unusual status of being an NRF-training ship that can be deployed.

Surface combatants: Production of the Aegis-configured destroyers of the BURKE class continues, with the improved Flight III ships beginning construction. Looking toward the future, the surface navy is developing an advanced warship under the rubric Surface Combatant (SC) 21. The surface community is examining every possible concept for the SC 21.

Amphibious ships: The decision by Congress to procure a large helicopter carrier (LHD 7) in the fiscal 1996 appropriation bill, when the Department of Defense had planned the ship in fiscal 2001, again demonstrates the effectiveness of Navy-Marine "marketing" and the understanding of the value of amphibious forces—as well as the political factors of building the ship at a specific shipyard. The LHD 7 will give the Navy 12 large helicopter carriers (LHA/LHD), permitting the preservation of 12 amphibious ready groups.

Also worthy of mention is the demise of the tank landing ship (LST), invaluable for amphibious and logistic operations. The Navy had planned to dispose of all 20 ships of the NEWPORT (LST 1179) class, but Congress has forced a few to be retained. (Those that are being discarded have a ready market in other navies.)

Special warfare and patrol craft: The 13 coastal patrol ships of the CYCLONE (PC 1) class have been completed. Despite the limitations of their design, these are useful ships for special operations. Two deployed to European waters in 1995, demonstrating their endurance.

Without a Navy request, Congress funded $20 million for the advance procurement of another ship of the CYCLONE class in the fiscal 1996 budget, with full funding expected in fiscal 1997. The ship is not included in the Department of Defense shipbuilding plan but is likely to be fully funded and built.

Mine countermeasures ships and craft: The rehabilitation of the Navy's mine force is almost complete, with the new construction MCM and MHC classes and the acquisition of the powerful MH-53E Sea Dragon helicopters. A long-needed specialized support ship is now available in the INCHON (MCS 12), a converted LPH helicopter carrier. However, there are no plans for a required second support ship. This, coupled with the basing of most of the surface units at Ingleside, Texas, imposes significant limitations on the force.

Indeed, the limitations of basing the entire mine countermeasures force at Ingleside have already been recognized by the Navy. Two MCMs are being homeported in Japan, two will probably be on the West Coast, and two are forward deployed to the Persian Gulf.

Proposals for a more capable, deployable MHC(V) class have been dropped.

Sealift: The success of the Navy's sealift efforts in Desert Shield/Desert Storm has led to additional support for increasing both the maritime prepositioning force and the sealift ships. Special problems identified in the Persian Gulf included obtaining sufficient merchant seamen to man the ships, U.S. and overseas port facilities, and cargo handling. These problems are being addressed in light of the Army, Marine Corps, Navy, and Air Force all employing forward-deployed matériel ships.

THE AIRCRAFT

The Navy and Marine Corps air arms are being reduced in size and, in several respects, in capability. The phasing out of the A-6E Intruder in 1996 deletes a highly competent aircraft from the Fleet, and the reduction in the F-14 Tomcat forces also reduces the adequacy of carrier aviation.

The flexible F/A-18 Hornet is being produced in prodigious numbers to fill carrier decks and Marine squadrons. After the year 2000 the F/A-18 and the aging AV-8B Harrier will be the only fighter-attack aircraft in the Navy-Marine arsenal. Nevertheless, a long-term Joint Advanced Strike Technology (JAST) program is intended to provide a tactical aircraft for the Air Force as well as the Navy and Marine Corps. But such programs are rarely successful. History is replete with examples of unsuccessful efforts to take a land-based aircraft and adapt it for carrier use. The most publicized example was probably the F-111, developed in the 1960s under the designation TFX for use by the Air Force, Navy, and Marine Corps. In the event, it proved highly unsatisfactory for carrier use and was procured only by the Air Force as a tactical and strategic (FB-111) strike aircraft, the latter variant forced on the Air Force by then-Secretary of Defense Robert S. McNamara.[21] One qualified exception to this tendency has been the adoption of the YF-17 lightweight fighter

21. Forty-four F-111 aircraft were subsequently converted to the EF-111 Raven electronic countermeasures variant; they are now being replaced by the Navy EA-6B Prowler in support of Air Force strike operations.

"A close one": the coastal minehunter OSPREY (MHC 51) undergoes shock trials at the Army's Aberdeen Test Center at Aberdeen, Maryland. The Navy's mine countermeasures force is vital to future naval operations in littoral areas. It is undergoing a belated modernization that began during the Reagan Administration. (U.S. Navy)

Even nuclear-propelled warships require the support of fleet auxiliaries: The carrier THEODORE ROOSEVELT takes on ordnance via VERTREP from the ammunition ship SANTA BARBARA off the Atlantic coast after the carrier completed a yard period in December 1995. The SANTA BARBARA transferred the munitions with her UH-46 Sea Knight helicopters from Helicopter Combat Support Squadron (HC) 6. Two NATO Sea Sparrow missile launchers and two Phalanx CIWS mounts are visible on the after part of the ROOSEVELT. (1995, U.S. Navy, PH2 Michael Turner)

to the F/A-18 Hornet design, although the naval aircraft was highly modified from the original design.

In contrast, several aircraft designed from the outset for carrier use have been highly successful in land-based operations. The most notable examples are probably the F-4 Phantom fighter, and A-7 Corsair, A-3 Skywarrior, and A-4 Skyhawk attack aircraft. The Phantom, Corsair, and Skyhawk have been flown by a large number of air forces, while the large, 35-ton Skywarrior was adopted by the U.S. Air Force as the B-66. (The Air Force was directed by the Defense Department and Congress to produce the Corsair; it did so, but for reserve components.)

However, the abortive AX and A-12 Avenger programs demonstrate the difficulties—political and technical—in developing advanced carrier-based tactical aircraft. In the category of tactical aircraft, there will be a need to replace the AV-8B in the midterm. This is a neglected area of development, although the JAST program is supposed to answer this need.

The other planes that fill a carrier deck, especially the E-2C Hawkeye and EA-6B Prowler, are also becoming dated. Upgrades will keep them flying, but a realistic replacement program is needed. (The Navy's Prowler force is also replacing the Air Force's EF-111A Raven electronic aircraft.)

The S-3B Viking and its derivative ES-3A electronic reconnaissance aircraft are robust aircraft that should serve well into the next century.

With respect to the important land-based P-3 Orion, that aircraft is also expected to fly well into the next century. Its planned successor, the P-7, was stillborn, another example of the Navy's inability to develop advanced aircraft.

The rotary-wing picture is much brighter. After many delays, the V-22 Osprey tilt-rotor aircraft is now in production, primarily for the Marine Corps. The Navy will buy some for search-and-rescue missions, and the Army and Air Force are expected to follow. Assuming that the production aircraft meets its "specs," this could also be an attractive aircraft for foreign sales.

Production of the ubiquitous H-60 for naval roles is winding down, as is production of the H-53E series. Both of these are excellent aircraft and—with the V-22—will provide a strong rotary-wing force for the foreseeable future. (The Navy does plan a vertical-replenishment helicopter for future procurement, to replace the UH-46D Sea Knight.)

The Navy is also participating in the extensive Department of Defense program to deploy Unmanned Aerial Vehicles (UAV). While these vehicles offer promise in many areas of naval warfare, the support for them is not unanimous within the Navy. The arguments heard against UAVs are reminiscent of those used in previous years against putting helicopters and then VSTOL aircraft aboard ships.[22]

The major problem facing naval aviation, however, is the low rate of procurement. The large number of aircraft planned in later years may be too late for the Navy to retain its current number of carrier air wings, while the number of patrol aircraft—which are useful in a variety of crisis as well as combat operations—will decline precipitously. The maritime patrol role could be taken over to a significant degree by satellite surveillance, however, if the funding for such activities is forthcoming.

The Navy that enters the 21st century should be far different from the Navy that fought the Cold War, but institutions are slow to change. If the Navy is unable to sail smartly into the next century, it will find its roles and missions—and funds—greatly diminished.

22. VSTOL = Vertical/Short Take-Off and Landing.

FY 1996 THROUGH 2001 AIRCRAFT PROCUREMENT PROGRAM

Aircraft	FY 1996 Actual	FY 1997 Planned	FY 1998 Planned	FY 1999 Planned	FY 2000 Planned	FY 2001 Planned
F/A-18C/D Hornet	18	—	—	—	—	—
F/A-18E/F Hornet	—	12	24	36	42	48
E-2C Hawkeye	3	2	3	4	4	4
AH-1W SeaCobra	6	—	—	—	—	—
V-22 Osprey	—	4	5	7	9	10
VERTREP helicopter*	—	—	—	4	8	9
T-45TS Goshawk	12	12	12	12	12	12
T-39N Sabre	17	—	—	—	—	—
JPATS training aircraft	—	—	—	—	8	24
Total	*56*	*30*	*44*	*63*	*83*	*107*

Notes: *Vertical Replenishment helicopter.

CHAPTER 2

Glossary

AA	Anti-Aircraft
AAM	Air-to-Air Missile
AAW	Anti-Air Warfare
ABL	Armored Box Launcher
APF	Afloat Prepositioning Force
ASM	Air-to-Surface Missile
ASROC	Anti-Submarine Rocket
ASUW	Anti-Surface Warfare
ASW	Anti-Submarine Warfare
barrel	42 U.S. gallons (159.6 liters)
beam	extreme width of hull
bhp	brake horsepower (for diesel engines)
BPDMS	Basic Point Defense Missile System
cal	caliber: (1) the diameter of a gun's bore; U.S. naval guns with a diameter of less than one inch (25.4 mm) are measured in "calibers"—fractions of an inch, as .50 calibers—or millimeters (mm) (2) the nominal length of the gun's bore expressed in multiples of its bore; thus, a 76-mm/62-cal gun has a bore, or inner barrel length, of 4,712 mm, or approximately 185½ inches (4.7 m).
CBR	Chemical-Biological-Radiological
CINC	Commander in Chief
CIWS	Close-In Weapon System
COD	Carrier On-Board Delivery
comm.	commission
CVBG	Carrier Battle Group
DASH	Drone Anti-Submarine Helicopter
decomm.	decommission
displacement	*light* (ship) is displacement of the ship and all machinery without crew, provisions, fuel munitions, other consumables, or aircraft *standard* is displacement of ship fully manned and equipped, ready for sea, including all provisions, munitions, and aircraft, but without fuels *full load* is displacement of ship complete and ready for service in all respects, including all fuels (aviation as well as ship)
DP	Dual Purpose (for use against air and surface targets)
draft	maximum draft of ship at full load, including fixed projections beneath the keel (e.g., sonar dome)
DWT	Deadweight Tonnage (ship's carrying capacity)

Sailors aboard the carrier AMERICA (CV 66), operating in the Adriatic Sea, share their mess spaces with 1,000-pound (454-kg) laser-guided bombs being readied for transfer to the flight deck. Even in the giant aircraft carriers, space is at a premium. (U.S. Navy, PH3 Brandon A. Teeples)

ECM	Electronic Countermeasures
ESM	Electronic Surveillance Measures
EW	Electronic Warfare
extreme width	maximum width at or about a carrier's flight deck, including fixed projections (e.g., "gun tubs")
FBM	Fleet Ballistic Missile (now referred to as SLBM)
FCS	Fire Control System
FLIR	Forward-Looking Infrared
FLO/FLO	Float-On/Float-Off
FRAM	Fleet Rehabilitation and Modernization
FSS	Fast Sealift Ship
FY	Fiscal Year: from 1 October of the calendar year until 30 September of the following year (since June 1976; previously from 1 July through 30 June); S in front of the year indicates Supplemental authorization
GFCS	Gunfire Control System
GRP	Glass-Reinforced Plastic
GRT	Gross Registered Tons (ship's tonnage measured in total cubic contents expressed in units of 100 cubic feet, or 2.83 m^3)
HTS	High Tensile Steel
HY	High Yield (steel)
ICIR	In Commission, In Reserve
IOC	Initial Operational Capability
IR	Infrared
IVDS	Independent Variable Depth Sonar
LAMPS	Light Airborne Multi-Purpose System (helicopter)
LASH	Lighter Aboard Ship
lbst	pounds static thrust
length	*waterline* indicates length on waterline (this length is generally the same as between perpendiculars [bp]) *overall* indicates length overall
Mach	speed of sound at sea level; from the name of German physicist Ernest Mach
mack	[combined] mast and stack
MAD	Magnetic Anomaly Detection
manning	the number of personnel assigned to the ship or craft; the term *complement* is no longer used by the U.S. Navy
MarAd	Maritime Administration
MCLWG	Major Caliber Lightweight Gun
MCM	Mine Countermeasures
MEB	Marine Expeditionary Brigade
MEF	Marine Expeditionary Force
MEU	Marine Expeditionary Unit
Mk	Mark
Mod	Modification
MPS	Maritime Prepositioning Ship
MSC	Military Sealift Command (changed from Military Sea Transportation Service in 1970)
MSTS	Military Sea Transportation Service (established 1 October 1949; changed to MSC in 1970)
NASA	National Aeronautics and Space Administration
NDRF	National Defense Reserve Fleet
n.mile	nautical mile (1.15 statute miles, or 1.852 km)
NOAA	National Oceanic and Atmospheric Administration
NRF	Naval Reserve Force
NTDS	Navy Tactical Data System
NTU	New Threat Upgrade
NVR	Naval Vessel Register[1]
OSP	Offshore Procurement
PAIR	Performance and Integration Retrofit (sonar)
psi	pounds per square inch (kg/cm^2) (boiler pressure)
RAST	Recovery Assistance, Securing, and Traversing System[2]
RCOH	Refueling/Complex Overhaul
reactors	the first letter of the reactor designation indicates the platform (A = Aircraft carrier, C = Cruiser, D = frigate [DL/DLG], S = Submarine); numeral indicates the sequence of the reactor design by specific manufacturer (G = General Electric, W = Westinghouse)
RFA	Royal Fleet Auxiliary (British)
RO/RO	Roll-On/Roll-Off
ROS	Reduced Operating Status
RPV	Remotely Piloted Aircraft
RRF	Ready Reserve Force
RWR	Radar Warning Receiver
SABAR	Service Craft and Boat Accounting Report
SAG	Surface Action Group
SAM	Surface-to-Air Missile
SAR	Search and Rescue
SATCOMM	Satellite Communications
SCB	Ships Characteristics Board's sequential number of Navy ship designs reaching the advanced planning stage; numbered in a single sequential series from 1947 (SCB No. 1 was the Norfolk/CLK 1, later DL 1) through 1964 (SCB No. 252 was the Flagstaff/PGH 1); from 1964 on numbered blocks: 001–009 cruisers, 100 carriers, 200 destroyers/frigates, 300 submarines, 400 amphibious, 500 mine warfare, 600 patrol, 700 auxiliary, 800 service craft, 900 special purpose. The latter numbers have suffix of fiscal year of prototype with, for example, 400.65 being the LCC of fiscal 1965 design
SEABEE	Sea Barge
SEAL	Sea-Air-Land (team)
shp	shaft horsepower
SLBM	Submarine-Launched Ballistic Missile
SLEP	Service Life Extension Program
SOSUS	Sound Surveillance System
SSM	Surface-to-Surface Missile
Status	**AA** Atlantic Active
	AR Atlantic Reserve
	GL Great Lakes (Coast Guard)
	PA Pacific Active
	PR Pacific Reserve
	R&D Research and Development
	TRA Training
STOL	Short Take-Off and Landing
STOVL	Short Take-Off/Vertical Landing
str.	stricken
SUBROC	Submarine Rocket
SURTASS	Surveillance Towed Array Sensor System
SWATH	Small Waterplane-Area Twin Hull (ship)
TACAN	Tactical Air Navigation
TACTAS	Tactical Towed Array Sonar
TALD	Tactical Air-Launched Device
TAR	Training and Administration of Reserves
TAS	Target Acquisition System
TASM	Tomahawk Anti-Ship Missile
TASS	Towed Array Sonar SystemTactical Air-Launched Decoy
TLAM	Tomahawk Land-Attack Missile
UNREP	Underway Replenishment
UAV	Unmanned Aerial Vehicle
USCGC	U.S. Coast Guard Cutter
USNS	U.S. Naval Ship
USS	U.S. Ship
URG	Underway Replenishment Group
UUV	Unmanned Underwater Vehicle
VDS	Variable Depth Sonar
VERTREP	Vertical Replenishment
VLA	Vertical Launch ASROC
VLS	Vertical Launch System
VOD	Vertical Onboard Delivery
VSTOL	Vertical/Short Take-Off and Landing

1. The official U.S. Navy listing of ships owned by the Navy.
2. The RAST system was developed for the Canadian Navy; it has been used in U.S. Navy ships since the late 1980s.

Note: Aviation abbreviations are found in chapter 28.

CHAPTER 3

Ship Classifications

U.S. Navy ships and small craft, with a few specific exceptions, are classified by type and by sequence within that type. The list of classifications is issued periodically, updating a system that was begun in 1920.

The following classifications appear on the current list, which was last revised in 1988. The letter prefixes to the basic symbols indicate:

F	being constructed for foreign government
T-	assigned to Military Sealift Command (formerly Military Sea Transportation Service)
W	Coast Guard cutter

The suffix N is used to denote nuclear-propelled ships. For service craft the suffix N indicates a non–self-propelled version of a similar self-propelled craft. While the prefix letter W in the list indicates that Coast Guard classifications are included in the Navy list of classifications, in fact they are not.

There are many inconsistencies in the current classification list. The suffix letter X—which does not appear in the classification list—is used unofficially to indicate new designs or classes, as DDX, LHDX, AKX, and ARX. More formal designations often exist for several years in official documents and usage before they appear in the ship classification instruction, as MSH (added to the list in 1982) and LHD (added in 1983).

Parentheses are not used in designations.

In the following list the ships are arranged in the order of the current Navy instruction on classifications; some levels of subcategorization are deleted here for purposes of readability. Note that combat logistics ships are listed—as combat ships—ahead of mine warfare ships and are separated from other auxiliary ships.

WARSHIP CLASSIFICATION

Aircraft Carrier Type

CV	Multi-purpose aircraft carrier
CVN	Multi-purpose aircraft carrier (nuclear propulsion)

Surface Combatant Type

BB	Battleship
CG	Guided missile cruiser
CGN	Guided missile cruiser (nuclear propulsion)
DD	Destroyer
DDG	Guided missile destroyer
FF	Frigate
FFG	Guided missile frigate
FFT	Frigate (Reserve Training)

Submarine Type

SSN	Submarine (nuclear propulsion)
SSBN	Ballistic missile submarine (nuclear propulsion)

OTHER COMBATANT CLASSIFICATION

Patrol Ships

PHM	Patrol combatant missile (hydrofoil)

Amphibious Warfare Type Ships

LCC	Amphibious command ship
LHA	Amphibious assault ship (general purpose)
LHD	Amphibious assault ship (multi-purpose)
LKA	Amphibious cargo ship
LPD	Amphibious transport dock
LPH	Amphibious assault ship (helicopter)
LSD	Dock landing ship
LST	Tank landing ship

Combat Logistics Type Ships

AE	Ammunition ship
AF	Store ship
AFS	Combat store ship
AO	Oiler
AOE	Fast combat support ship
AOR	Replenishment oiler

Mine Warfare Type Ships

MCM	Mine countermeasures ship
MCS	Mine countermeasures support ship
MHC	Minehunter, coastal
MSO	Minesweeper—ocean

Coastal Defense Ships

PC	Patrol, coastal

AUXILIARY CLASSIFICATION

Mobile Logistic Type Ships

AD	Destroyer tender
AR	Repair ship
AS	Submarine tender

Support Type Ships

ACS	Auxiliary crane ship
AG	Auxiliary general
AGDS	Deep submergence support ship
AGF	Miscellaneous command ship
AGFF	Auxiliary general frigate
AGM	Missile range instrumentation ship
AGOR	Oceanographic research ship
AGOS	Ocean surveillance ship
AGS	Surveying ship
AGSS	Auxiliary research submarine
AH	Hospital ship
AK	Cargo ship
AKB	Auxiliary cargo barge/lighter ship
AKF	Auxiliary cargo float-on/float-off ship
AKR	Vehicle cargo ship
AOG	Gasoline tanker
AOT	Transport oiler
AP	Transport
ARC	Cable repairing ship
ARS	Salvage ship
ASR	Submarine rescue ship
ATF	Fleet ocean tug
ATS	Salvage and rescue ship
AVB	Aviation logistic support ship
AVT	Auxiliary aircraft landing training ship

COMBATANT CRAFT CLASSIFICATION

Patrol Type Craft

ATC	Mini-armored troop carrier
PB	Patrol boat
PBR	River patrol craft
PCF	Patrol craft (fast)
PTF	Fast patrol craft

Amphibious Warfare Type Craft

LCAC	Landing craft, air cushion
LCM	Landing craft, mechanized
LCPL	Landing craft, personnel, large
LCU	Landing craft, utility
LCVP	Landing craft, vehicle, personnel
LSSC	Light SEAL support craft
LWT	Amphibious warping tug
MSSC	Medium SEAL support craft
SDV	Swimmer delivery vehicle[1]
SLWT	Side loadable warping tug
SWCL	Special warfare craft, light
SWCM	Special warfare craft, medium

SUPPORT CRAFT CLASSIFICATION

Dry Docks (non–self-propelled)

AFDB	Large auxiliary floating dry dock
AFDL	Small auxiliary floating dry dock
AFDM	Medium auxiliary floating dry dock
ARD	Auxiliary repair dry dock
ARDM	Medium auxiliary repair dry dock
YFD	Yard floating dry dock

Tugs (self-propelled)

YTB	Large harbor tug
YTL	Small harbor tug
YTM	Medium harbor tug

Tankers (self-propelled)

YO	Fuel oil barge
YOG	Gasoline barge
YW	Water barge

Lighters and Barges (self-propelled)

CSP	Causeway section, powered
YF	Covered lighter
YFR	Refrigerated covered lighter
YFU	Harbor utility craft
YG	Garbage lighter

Lighters and Barges (non–self-propelled)

CSNP	Causeway section, non-powered
YC	Open lighter
YCF	Car float
YCSS	Cargo semi-submersible barge
YCV	Aircraft transportation lighter
YFN	Covered lighter
YFNB	Large covered lighter
YFNX	Lighter (special purpose)
YFRN	Refrigerated covered lighter
YFRT	Range tender
YGN	Garbage lighter
YOGN	Gasoline barge
YON	Fuel oil barge
YOS	Oil storage barge
YSR	Sludge removal barge
YWN	Water barge

Other Craft (self-propelled)

DSRV	Deep submergence rescue vehicle
DSV	Deep submergence vehicle
NR	Submersible research vehicle (nuclear propulsion)
YAG	Miscellaneous auxiliary service craft
YFB	Ferryboat or launch
YM	Dredge
YP	Patrol craft, training
YSD	Seaplane wrecking derrick
YTT	Torpedo trials craft

Other Craft (non–self-propelled)

APL	Barracks craft
YD	Floating crane
YDT	Diving tender
YFND	Dry dock companion craft
YFP	Floating power barge
YHLC	Salvage lift craft, heavy
YLC	Salvage lift craft, light
YMN	Dredge
YNG	Gate craft
YPD	Floating pile driver
YR	Floating workshop
YRB	Repair and berthing barge
YRBM	Repair, berthing and messing barge
YRDH	Floating dry dock workshop (hull)
YRDM	Floating dry dock workshop (machine)
YRR	Radiological repair barge
YRST	Salvage craft tender

Unclassified Miscellaneous

IX	Unclassified miscellaneous unit

COAST GUARD CUTTERS AND BOATS

The cutter designations currently in use for Coast Guard cutters and boats:

WAGB	Icebreaker
WAGO	Oceanographic cutter
WHEC	High endurance cutter (multi-mission; 30 to 45 days at sea without support)
WIX	Training cutter
WLB	Offshore buoy tender (full sea-keeping capability; medium endurance)
WLI	Inshore buoy tender (short endurance)
WLIC	Inland construction tender (short endurance)
WLM	Coastal buoy tender (medium endurance)
WLR	River buoy tender (short endurance)
WLV	Light vessel
WMEC	Medium endurance cutter (multi-mission; 10 to 30 days at sea without support)
WPB	Patrol boat (multi-mission; 1 to 7 days at sea without support)
WSES	Surface effect ship

The Coast Guard uses the term icebreaker for a variety of vessels with the following categories:

Type A	late GLACIER (WAGB 4)
Type B	MACKINAW (WAGB 83) and late Wind class (WAGB 281)
Type C	Bay class (WTGB 140)
Type D	medium harbor tugs (WYTM)
Type E	small harbor tugs (WYTL)
Type P	Polar class (WAGB 10)

MARITIME ADMINISTRATION

The following are Maritime Administration design classifications that were developed in the late 1930s by the Maritime Commission. They are currently assigned only to auxiliary/sealift ships; during World War II the escort aircraft carriers, frigates, and tank landing ships designed by the Maritime Commission also had these design classifications.

The first letter-number series indicates ship type (e.g., C4), with an adjacent letter indicating size.

C	Cargo
P	Passenger
R	Refrigerator (reefer)
S	Special type
T	Tanker
VC	Victory-Cargo

The second letter-number series indicates propulsion.

M	Motor (diesel)
ME2	Motor; 2 shafts (diesel)
MET	Diesel-electric; 2 shafts
S	Steam
S2	Steam; 2 shafts
SE	Turbo-electric
SE2	Turbo-electric; 2 shafts
ST	Steam; 2 shafts

The third letter-number series indicates specific ship design, usually beginning with A1 or 1; later designs have lower-case letters, as 1b.

1. SDV is usually referred to as SEAL delivery vehicle.

CHAPTER 4

Defense Organization

Soldiers of the Army's 75th Special Forces Group climb aboard an MH-53J Pave Low helicopter on the aircraft carrier GEORGE WASHINGTON (CVN 73) during Fleet Exercise 2-94 in the Western Atlantic. Such joint exercises—and operations—are becoming more routine as the military services are becoming more operationally integrated. (U.S. Navy, JOC Gregg Snaza)

The United States has a unified defense establishment that is responsible for the conduct of military operations—in peace and in war—in support of the national security strategy. That strategy has changed dramatically in the past few years, with the end of the Cold War—as manifested in the demise of the Soviet Union and the termination of Soviet control over Eastern Europe and the Baltic states.

The unexpected rapidity of the demise of the Soviet regime, the breakup of the Warsaw Pact, and the ensuing massive reductions in U.S. military forces and direct U.S. military involvement in crises and conflicts around the world have led to new assessments of U.S. defense requirements. However, the structure of the late 1990s remains essentially the same as at the beginning of the decade.

This structure developed during the Cold War and was reinforced by the Goldwater-Nichols Department of Defense Reorganization Act of 1986, which emphasizes both the role of the Chairman of the Joint Chiefs of Staff, as the principal military adviser to the Secretary of Defense and the President, and the role of the unified commanders in chief.

The President, under the provisions of the Constitution, is the Commander in Chief of the U.S. armed forces. The Secretary of Defense, the President's immediate subordinate, serves as the day-to-day decision maker in defense matters. Together, the President and Secretary of Defense—and, in an emergency, their designated alternates—make up the National Command Authority (NCA), empowered to command all U.S. combat forces and to release nuclear weapons for operational use.

From the President the operational chain-of-command goes through the Secretary of Defense, with orders transmitted to operational commanders through the Chairman of the Joint Chiefs of Staff.

The Secretary of Defense and the Chairman of the Joint Chiefs of Staff are the principal military advisers to the President. In addition, by statute the President is assisted by an advisory body, called the National Security Council (NSC), that provides advice on a broad range of national security and intelligence matters. Chaired by the President, the permanent members of the NSC are the Vice President, the Secretaries of Defense, State, and Treasury, the Chairman of the Joint Chiefs of Staff, and the Director of Central Intelligence. The official who coordinates NSC activities and directs its staff activities is known as the President's National Security Adviser.

The principal components of the defense establishment are: (1) the Department of Defense, (2) the Joint Chiefs of Staff, (3) military departments and their subordinate services, and (4) unified commands. Four of the U.S. military services are within the Department of Defense; the fifth military service, the Coast Guard, is part of the Department of Transportation. That service has responsibilities to both departments (see chapter 32).

DEPARTMENT OF DEFENSE

The Department of Defense is headed by the Secretary of Defense, a member of the President's cabinet, and a member of the National Security Council. By custom, the Secretary of Defense is a civilian, not a professional military officer.[1]

The principal deputies to the Secretary of Defense are the Deputy Secretary, Under Secretary for Policy, Under Secretary for Personnel and Readiness, Under Secretary for Acquisition and Technology, and Comptroller and Chief Financial Officer. The under secretaries, in turn, are supported by eight persons at the Deputy Under Secretary (DUS) level:

- DUS for Policy
- DUS Personnel and Readiness
- DUS Acquisition and Technology
- DUS Advanced Technology
- DUS Readiness
- DUS Acquisition Reform
- DUS Environmental Security
- Deputy Comptroller

There are 17 Assistant Secretaries of Defense (ASD) and others at that level:

- ASD International Security Affairs
- ASD Strategy and Requirements
- ASD International Security Policy
- ASD Special Operations and Low-Intensity Conflict
- ASD Reserve Affairs
- ASD Health Affairs
- ASD Legislative Affairs
- ASD Command, Control, Communications, and Intelligence
- ASD Atomic Energy
- ASD Economic Security
- ASD Force Management
- Director Program Analysis and Evaluation
- Director Defense Research and Engineering
- Director Net Assessment
- Director Small and Disadvantaged Business Utilization
- Deputy Comptroller for Financial Systems
- Defense Advisor, U.S. Mission to NATO

The large staff that supports these officials is the Office of the Secretary of Defense (OSD). There are approximately 500 military personnel and 1,635 civilians assigned to OSD.[2]

There are 16 separate agencies under the Secretary of Defense that support the Department of Defense and the military services. These agencies generally perform functions that affect all U.S. military activities. Of these agencies, ten are headed by military officers (indicated by asterisks) and six by civilians:

- Ballistic Missile Defense Organization*
- Defense Advanced Research Projects Agency
- Central Imagery Office
- Defense Commissary Agency*
- Defense Contract Audit Agency
- Defense Finance and Accounting Service
- Defense Information Systems Agency*
- Defense Intelligence Agency*
- Defense Investigative Service
- Defense Legal Services Agency
- Defense Logistics Agency*
- Defense Mapping Agency*
- Defense Nuclear Agency*
- Defense Security Assistance Agency*
- National Security Agency/Central Security Service*
- On-Site Inspection Agency*

The Defense Intelligence Agency (DIA), in addition to performing intelligence analysis for OSD, serves as the intelligence staff for the Joint Chiefs of Staff (the equivalent of a J-2 staff). The National Security Agency (NSA) performs electronic intercept and cryptological activities to support the entire U.S. intelligence community as well as the defense establishment. That agency also supervises the cryptologic activities of the Army, Navy, and Air Force.

Historical: Congress established the War Department in 1789 and the Navy Department in 1798 (see below). These two departments administered their respective services (with the Navy Department administering the Navy and Marine Corps). The secretaries of these two departments reported directly to the President and were members of the President's cabinet.

This arrangement continued until the National Security Act of 1947, which became effective on 18 September 1947 and created the National Military Establishment as well as the National Security Council and Joint Chiefs of Staff. The Departments of the Army, Navy, and Air Force were established as cabinet-level departments,

---

1. The exception was General of the Army George C. Marshall, who was Chief of Staff of the U.S. Army during World War II. He subsequently served as both Secretary of State (1947–1949) and Secretary of Defense (1950–1951).

2. During the past few years there has been a decline of military personnel and an increase in civilians assigned to OSD.

Secretary of Defense William J. Perry and the Minister of Defense of Ukraine, Colonel-General Vitaliy Radetsky, discuss the destruction of strategic missiles at Pervomaysk in Ukraine. A U.S. Assistant SecDef, Ashton Carter, is behind them. (Department of Defense, R.D. Ward)

with the newly created Secretary of Defense functioning primarily as a coordinator of these military departments.

In 1949, amendments to the National Security Act established the Secretary of Defense as the principal assistant to the President on defense matters and changed the National Military Establishment to the Department of Defense. These amendments also made the three military departments subordinate to the Department of Defense and removed their secretaries from the cabinet. Subsequent actions by various Secretaries of Defense have taken away many of the decision-making prerogatives of the military departments and assigned them to OSD and the various defense agencies.

The Defense Reorganization Act of 1958 established a new chain of command from the President and Secretary of Defense to the unified and specified commanders, who were given "full operational command" over the forces assigned to them. However, the Secretary of Defense could delegate the Joint Chiefs of Staff to exercise operational control over forces when he deemed it appropriate. Previously, the military departments acted as executive agencies for the control of forces.

DEPARTMENT OF DEFENSE MANPOWER*

Service	Active Duty	Reserve & National Guard	Civilians
Army	495,000	603,000	265,800
Navy	424,500	98,900	246,200**
Marine Corps	174,000	42,300	—
Air Force	388,200	186,700	186,400
Other agencies	—	—	142,800
Total DOD	1,481,700	930,900	841,200

Notes: *Data for 30 September 1995; totals are rounded.
**Department of the Navy employees (i.e., Navy and Marine Corps).

JOINT CHIEFS OF STAFF

The Joint Chiefs of Staff (JCS) consists of a Chairman, Vice Chairman, and the military chiefs of the Army, Navy, Air Force, and Marine Corps. The Chairman and the Vice Chairman are four-star officers (i.e., full generals or admirals), as are the military service chiefs.[3]

The JCS collectively serves as the principal military advisers to the President, Secretary of Defense, and the National Security Council. In addition, under the Goldwater-Nichols Act of 1986, the Chairman of the JCS is in the chain-of-command between the National Command Authority and the unified commanders with orders and other communications transmitted to unified commanders through the Chairman of the JCS. Commenting on the Goldwater-Nichols Act and its influence on the Persian Gulf conflict of 1991, journalist Michael R. Gordon and Marine Lieutenant General Bernard (Mick) Trainor, also a distinguished journalist, wrote in *The General's War:*

> [the act] also strengthened the role of the chairman of the JCS and of field commanders. As a result, [JCS Chairman Colin L.] Powell wielded power and influence beyond that exercised by previous chairmen. His fellow members provided the forces. As for [General Norman] Schwarzkopf [Commander in Chief Central Command], he was king of his domain. During the war, no serious attempt was made by any of the services to go around Schwarzkopf. A service chief not could even visit the Gulf without his permission.[4]

The JCS has a Joint Staff composed of seven directorates that perform military staff functions for the Joint Chiefs and, to some extent, for the unified commands. The staff directorates are:

- J-1 Manpower and Personnel
- J-3 Operations
- J-4 Logistics
- J-5 Strategic Plans and Policy
- J-6 Command, Control, and Communications
- J-7 Operational Plans and Interoperability
- J-8 Force Structure, Resource, and Assessment

The directors of these staff directorates are three-star officers (i.e., lieutenant generals or vice admirals). Their staffs consist mostly of military officers from all services. There are approximately 1,260 military personnel and 260 civilians assigned to the Joint Staff. Unlike the former Soviet General Staff and the senior military staffs of some other nations, the officers assigned to the Joint Staff are not professional staff officers; rather, they are assigned from the separate services, often without any prior staff experience or education.

Historical: President Franklin D. Roosevelt and Prime Minister Winston Churchill decided at their wartime meeting in Washington during December 1941–January 1942 to create the Anglo-American Combined Chiefs of Staff. The British component already existed as the Chiefs of Staff Committee; there was no comparable U.S. body of senior military officers.

Without specific executive action or congressional legislation, the senior U.S. military officers met as a body for the first time with their British colleagues to form the Combined Chiefs of Staff on 23 January 1942. At the time, the term Joint Chiefs of Staff (JCS) was used for the Americans, although several members were not the chiefs of their services. The JCS initially consisted of the Chief of Naval Operations, Commander in Chief U.S. Fleet, Army Chief of Staff, and Chief of the Army Air Forces.[5] In July 1942 retired Admiral William D. Leahy was appointed Chief of Staff to the Commander in Chief (Roosevelt) and became *de facto* Chairman of the JCS. The JCS membership stabilized at four for the remainder of the war: Leahy, Chief of Staff of the Army (George C. Marshall), CINC U.S. Fleet (Ernest J. King), and Chief of the Army Air Forces (H. H. Arnold.) The JCS membership served as both the U.S. component of the Combined Chiefs of Staff and as the executive body for the direction of U.S. military forces during the war.

The JCS was formally established by the National Security Act of 1947, but not until the 1949 amendments was the position of chairman

---

3. Of the 14 Chairmen of the Joint Chiefs of Staff since 1942, four have been naval officers:

Fleet Adm. William D. Leahy	July 1942–Mar 1949
Adm. Arthur W. Radford	Aug 1953–Aug 1957
Adm. Thomas H. Moorer	July 1970–June 1974
Adm. William J. Crowe Jr.	Oct 1985–Sep 1989

Adm. Leahy's official position was Chief of Staff to the President; he served as the *de facto* Chairman of the JCS.

4. Michael R. Gordon and Lt. Gen. Bernard E. Trainor, USMC (Ret.), *The General's War: The Inside Story of the Conflict in the Gulf* (Boston: Little, Brown and Co., 1995), p. 471.
5. The Chief of the Army Air Forces was changed to Commanding General in March 1942; the position of Chief of Naval Operations was combined with that of CINC U.S. Fleet in March 1942, giving the JCS three members—the heads of the Army, Army Air Forces, and Navy—in addition to the chairman.

authorized. The chairman thereafter rotated, although in no particular order, among the Army, Navy, and Air Force. Some, but certainly not all, of the chairmen were former chiefs of their services.

In 1952 the Commandant of the Marine Corps was authorized to sit with the JCS and to vote on issues of direct interest to the Marine Corps. In 1979 the Commandant was made a full member of the JCS.

The position of Vice Chairman of the JCS was established in 1987. Previously, when the Chairman was absent, the other members served in his place by rotation. In addition to being a "stand-in" for the Chairman, the Vice Chairman chairs the most powerful Joint Requirements Oversight Council (JROC), which controls the acquisition of weapon systems for the military services.

MILITARY DEPARTMENTS

There are three military departments within the Department of Defense: Army, Navy, and Air Force. Each department is headed by a civilian Secretary, Under Secretary, and several Assistant Secretaries. These are civilian positions although, on occasion, a military officer has been appointed to one of the Assistant Secretary positions.

Reporting directly to the civilian secretary is the chief of the service assigned to the department, who is the senior military officer of that department (except for officers assigned as Chairman or Vice Chairman of the JCS, who rank above service chiefs). The Navy and the Marine Corps are two military services within the Navy Department.

The military departments are responsible for the training, provision of equipment, and administration of their military services. They do not direct military operations; that function was taken away by the Defense Reorganization Act of 1958. The influence and prerogatives of the military departments have varied considerably in recent years on the basis of the personality, influence, and attitudes of the service secretaries and, to a lesser degree, on the service chiefs.

Historical: The Second Continental Congress authorized the first increment of national troops on 14 June 1775, with their officers responsible to Congress. The U.S. Constitution of 1789 provided that the President should be Commander in Chief of the Army and Navy, his powers over them exclusive, limited only "by their nature and by the principles of our institutions." On 7 August 1789, Congress created the War Department.

The U.S. Navy originated with the decision by General George Washington in 1775 to dispatch vessels to prey on British shipping. In October of that year the Continental Congress established a Naval Committee to acquire and fit out vessels for naval operations. (The following month the Continental Congress established the Marine Corps.)

At the end of the American Revolution, in 1783, the weak and almost bankrupt Congress ordered the Navy to disband. Although the Constitution, adopted in 1789, directed Congress "to provide and maintain a navy," a separate Navy Department was not considered necessary, and naval affairs—such as they were—were included under the jurisdiction of the War Department. Not until the Navy Act of 1794, which authorized the procurement of six frigates, was the Navy reestablished.[6] Not until 30 April 1798 did Congress create the Navy Department.

The 1949 amendments to the National Security Act removed the secretaries of the three military departments from the cabinet and placed them under the supervision of the Secretary of Defense.

6. These six frigates included the CONSTITUTION and CONSTELLATION (see chapter 25).

The role of naval forces—especially submarines—in future joint operations must be better clarified than has been done to date. Submarines tend to lack the flexibility of surface ships for carrying out the missions of political presence and projection of military force ashore that tend to characterize the post–Cold War era. Here the ALEXANDRIA (SSN 757) steams off Andros Island in the Bahamas. (U.S. Navy, F. E. Zimmerman)

NATIONAL DEFENSE COMMAND STRUCTURE

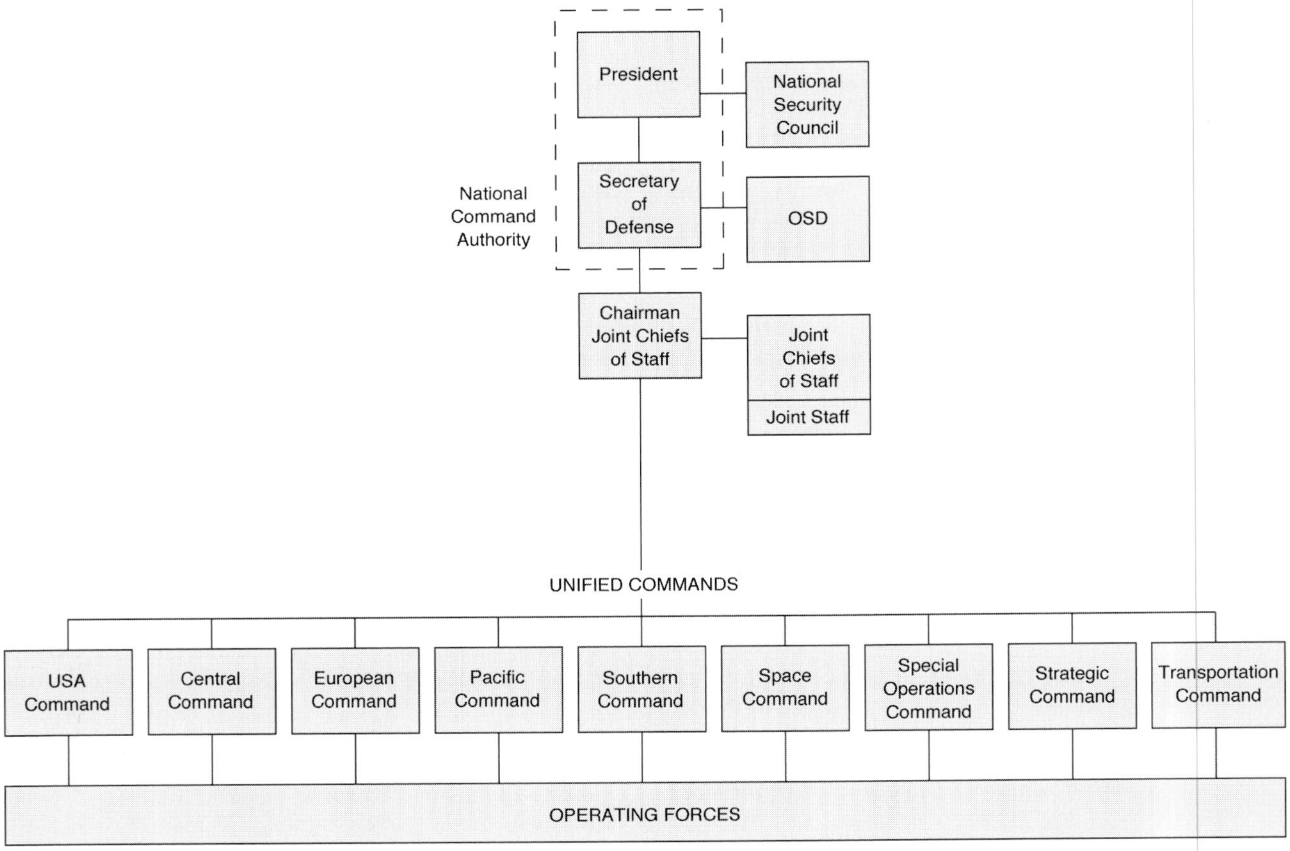

UNIFIED COMMANDS

Essentially all U.S. operating forces are assigned to *unified* commands, which plan for military operations, direct exercises, and control combat operations, in addition to having operational control of specifically assigned U.S. forces. The 1958 reorganization of the Department of Defense established the chain of command of the operating forces from the National Command Authority (President and Secretary of Defense) directly to the Commanders in Chief of the unified commands.

Unified commands contain forces from two or more services; most are responsible for specific geographic areas. Whereas the Atlantic and Pacific commands continually have large forces assigned to them, other unified commands are mainly planning staffs until specific forces are placed under them during an exercise, a crisis, or in wartime. To illustrate, prior to the Iraqi invasion of Kuwait in August 1991, the Central Command (CENTCOM) was a planning staff of several hundred men and women in the United States. Except for exercises, no major military units were assigned to CENTCOM. When Operation Desert Shield was initiated in early August, CENTCOM took command of the buildup, with more than 500,000 U.S. military personnel—and large numbers of ships, aircraft, and ground units—being assigned to CENTCOM. Subsequently, in coordination with the commander of Saudi forces, CENTCOM directed Operation Desert Storm, the assault on occupied Kuwait and Iraq.

The newest unified command is the U.S. Atlantic Command (USACOM), whose concept is generally credited to the then-Chairman of the Joint Chiefs of Staff, General Colin L. Powell. In 1993, in a report to the Secretary of Defense on the roles, missions, and functions of the armed forces, General Powell lamented:

> The unified command structure works well overseas, where CINCs [Commanders in Chief] with a geographic area of responsibility effectively direct the forces assigned to them from the Services in accomplishing a wide range of missions. . . .
>
> But unification has never been achieved in the United States to the same degree as overseas. While forces based in the United States are assigned, by law, to one CINC, many are assigned to overseas CINCs and have limited opportunities to train jointly with the overseas-based forces they would join for military operations in crisis or war.[7]

Twice before, the Joint Chiefs of Staff had attempted to establish a single command to oversee military forces in the United States. In 1961 the U.S. Strike Command (STRICOM) was activated to provide unified control over Army and Air Force units based in the United States, being given responsibility to train forces, develop joint doctrine, and plan for and execute contingency operations as ordered. Later, STRICOM was additionally given geographic responsibility for contingency planning for the Middle East, South Asia, and Africa south of the Sahara. General Powell has noted that, "In attempting to fulfill its functional responsibilities as trainer and provider of forces, STRICOM frequently collided with the Services' authority under Title X [U.S. code] to organize, train, and equip forces."[8]

In 1971 Strike Command was replaced by the Readiness Command (REDCOM), which had the same training and readiness functions as STRICOM, but with no geographic areas of responsibility. REDCOM, according to Powell, experienced some of the same resistance by the military services as did its predecessor. Still, over time REDCOM was given additional responsibilities, including a requirement to plan for and provide Joint Task Force (JTF) headquarters for operations in areas that were not assigned to existing unified commands.

What began as REDCOM's Rapid Development Joint Task Force (RDJTF) eventually grew into a new unified combat command, the Central Command, established in 1983. With headquarters at MacDill Air Force Base in Tampa, Florida, CENTCOM was given responsibility for Southwest Asia and related areas. REDCOM was abolished in 1987. (Significantly, USACOM does not control Pacific Fleet forces based on the U.S. West Coast; those forces—including Fleet Marine Force Pacific—continue to come under the Pacific Command. Al-

7. Chairman, Joint Chiefs of Staff, "1993 Report on the Roles, Missions and Functions of the Armed Forces," 10 February 1993, p. III-3.
8. Ibid.

though there has been increased emphasis on "universal" doctrine and structure for U.S. forces, many factors, such as geography, personality, and allies, do make operations in the Pacific very different from the European-Atlantic and other regions. This could lead to problems if USACOM forces are assigned to Pacific Command for operations in time of crisis and war. This appears to be one of the most significant potential problems of the USACOM concept.)

Subsequently, with the end of the Cold War and the withdrawal of large numbers of U.S. military forces from overseas areas, the need was perceived for a better structure for training and organizing forces in the United States. As General Powell expressed it, "not just for occasional exercises, but as a way of life."[9]

There are currently nine unified commands, some of which date to World War II. The Commanders in Chief of the unified forces are four-star officers; some CINC positions rotate among the services, while some are assigned to officers of only one or two services. In 1996 there were four unified commands under Army generals, three commands under Air Force generals, one command under a Navy admiral, and one command under a Marine general.

The unified commands are:

Atlantic Command (USACOM): U.S. forces in the Atlantic area, including the Caribbean. The CINC U.S. Atlantic Command is also the NATO Supreme Allied Commander Atlantic and, until 1985, additionally served as CINC Atlantic Fleet.

The U.S. Atlantic Command (USACOM)—which replaced the previous U.S. Atlantic Command (LANTCOM)—is the largest U.S. unified command, being responsible for the readiness of virtually all military forces within the continental United States. Established on 1 October 1993, USACOM's principal mission is to develop joint force "packages" of Army, Navy, Air Force, and Marine Corps components that can be rapidly deployed to overseas areas and operate effectively upon arrival in forward areas. Under this concept, the major service commands in the United States report to USACOM for training and deployment. In addition, USACOM remains the unified or operational commander for the Atlantic Fleet as well as for its readiness and training.

The service component commands under USACOM are, in addition to the Atlantic Fleet, Air Combat Command (Air Force), Marine Force Atlantic (Marine Corps), and Forces Command (Army).

The Commander in Chief (CINC) of USACOM continues to serve as the NATO Supreme Allied Commander (SACLANT), one of the two major NATO military commands, with responsibility for NATO operations in the North Atlantic area.

Headquarters: Norfolk, Virginia

Established: December 1947 as Atlantic Command; October 1993 as U.S. Atlantic Command

CINC: From its establishment until 1994, CINCLANT/USACOM/LANTCOM has been a Navy officer. On 31 October 1994, General John J. Sheehan became the first Marine to serve in this position. (Previously, the Central Command was the only unified command to have had a Marine as CINC.)

Central Command (CENTCOM): U.S. forces operating in the Middle East area. The Central Command directed U.S. military operations in the buildup and war in the Persian Gulf area in 1990–1991; it is the successor to the Rapid Deployment Force (see 13th Edition/pages 22–25).

Headquarters: MacDill Air Force Base, Tampa, Florida

Established: January 1983

CINC: Central Command is headed by an Army or Marine officer; the current CINCCENT is General James H. B. Peay III, USA.

European Command (EURCOM): U.S. forces in Europe, including U.S. naval forces in the Mediterranean. The CINC European Command is also the NATO Supreme Allied Commander Europe.

Headquarters: Stuttgart-Vaihingen, Germany

Established: March 1947[10]

CINC: The European Command is headed by an Army or Air Force officer; the current CINCEUR is General George A. Joulwan, USA.

Pacific Command (PACCOM): U.S. forces in the Pacific and Indian Ocean areas as well as on the Asian mainland. The CINC Pacific Command additionally served as CINC Pacific Fleet until 1958.

Headquarters: Camp H. M. Smith, Oahu, Hawaii

Established: January 1947

CINC: From its establishment in 1947 PACCOM has been headed by a Navy officer. The current CINCPAC is Admiral Joseph W. Prueher, USN.

Southern Command (SOUTHCOM): U.S. forces in Central America and South America. The command was known as the Caribbean Command (CINCCARIB) until June 1963.

Headquarters: Quarry Heights, Panama

(In 1995 it was announced that the Southern Command Headquarters will move to the Coast Guard facility at Richmond Heights in Dade County, Florida, near Miami. As part of the Panama Canal Treaty, all U.S. military forces must leave Panama by 31 December 1999; the approximately 700 uniformed and civilian personnel at SOUTHCOM Headquarters are expected to move to the new location in the summer of 1998.)

Established: November 1947

CINC: Southern Command is commanded by an Army officer; the current CINCSOUTH is Lieutenant General Wes Clark, USA.

Space Command (SPACECOM): U.S. activities and forces in space, including the monitoring of foreign space activities.

Headquarters: Peterson Air Force Base, Colorado Springs, Colorado

Established: September 1985

CINC: SPACECOM has always been commanded by an Air Force officer; the current CINC is General Joseph W. Ashy, USAF.

Special Operations Command (SOCOM): Directs U.S. special forces activities (primarily Air Force Special Operations Command, Army Green Berets and Delta Force, and Navy SEALs).

SOCOM differs from most other unified commands because it (1) does not have any geographic responsibilities, and (2) does have major budget planning and manpower management responsibilities that are similar to those of the military services. For example, the Navy's CYCLONE (PC 1)-class patrol ships are sponsored by the Special Operations Command, as are fixed-wing aircraft and helicopters from all of the services configured for special operations.

Headquarters: MacDill Air Force Base, Tampa, Florida

Established: April 1987

CINC: CINCSOCOM has always been an Army officer; the current CINC is General Wayne A. Downing, USA.

Strategic Command (STRATCOM): All U.S. land-based and sea-based strategic forces. The Strategic Air Command (SAC), a specified command with only Air Force components, was abolished in 1992, at which time most of its resources were assigned to the newly formed Strategic Command. Also incorporated into the Strategic Command was the Joint Strategic Target Planning Staff (JSTPS), a multiservice agency that planned the targets for U.S. strategic weapons and various Navy activities related to strategic missile submarine operations.

(Despite some writers stating that the new U.S. Strategic Command combined the separate Air Force and Navy strategic commands, in fact the Navy never had a strategic command. Previously, the naval strategic forces—carrier-based aircraft and ballistic missile submarines—were assigned to the Atlantic, Pacific, and European unified commands.)

9. Ibid., p. III-4.

10. From March 1947 until July 1952 this position was Commander in Chief Europe (CINCEUR), largely a U.S. Army command and only nominally a unified command.

U.S. Special Operations Forces (SOF)—including Navy SEALs—have gained unprecedented prominence in U.S. military planning. The creation of the Special Operations Command (SOCOM) in 1987 as a unified command with subordinate SOF commanders assigned within other unified commands has, in some respects, established a fifth military service within the Department of Defense. SOCOM is the sponsor of numerous special operations programs within the armed services, it keeps track of personnel, and it has budget responsibilities beyond that of other unified commands.

Among the Navy's special operations programs are:

Top: The new Advanced SEAL Delivery System (ASDS), a manned "combatant submersible" that is, according to Navy statements, capable of operating in a "high-threat" environment. This will be a "dry" submersible, propelled by battery-powered electric motors and carried into its operational area on the after deck of an attack submarine. (U.S. Navy)

Center: The attack submarine Archerfish (SSN 678) at Port Everglades, Florida, shows a Dry Deck Shelter (DDS) with the main hatch open. Either a small SEAL Delivery Vehicle (SDV) or swimmers can be locked out of the DDS at shallow depths. The DDS is connected through its pressure chamber (forward) to the submarine's amidships hatch. (Giorgio Arra)

Bottom: The stern of the coastal patrol ship Tempest (PC 2) shows the platform transom of this design, which is intended to facilitate SEAL operations. Above the transom is a 20-foot (6.1-m) Rigid Inflatable Boat (RIB) and its quick-launching crane. (U.S. Navy, Don S. Montgomery)

Headquarters: Offutt Air Force Base, Nebraska
Established: June 1992
CINC: STRATCOM has been headed by both Air Force and Navy officers; the current CINC is General Eugene E. Habiger.

Transportation Command (TRANSCOM): All air and sea transport resources, including the sea transportation assets of the Navy's Military Sealift Command.
Headquarters: Scott Air Force Base, Illinois
Established: July 1987
CINC: TRANSCOM has always been commanded by an Air Force officer; the current CINC is General Robert L. Rutherford, USAF.

There are currently no U.S. specified commands. That term was applied to commands that had forces assigned from only one military service and were headed by a CINC from that service.

Previously, there were three specified commands. The Strategic Air Command (SAC) and the Military Airlift Command (MAC) were both staffed by Air Force personnel. The Forces Command (FORCECOM) was composed of Army personnel. SAC and MAC (previously Military Air Transport Service) were disestablished in 1992, and most of their components were transferred either to the new Strategic Command or the Transportation Command, respectively.

FORCECOM, which was responsible for all U.S. Army forces (active and inactive) in the United States, became the Army's component command within the U.S. Atlantic Command. Established in July 1987, FORCECOM was disestablished as a specified command in 1993.

The number of unified and specified commands is not fixed by law or regulation, and it may be changed from time to time at the discretion of the President and the Secretary of Defense.

Within most unified commands there are air, ground, and naval component commanders who direct the operations of their respective services.

Historical: The official history of the U.S. Joint Chiefs of Staff states: "The surprise attack [on Pearl Harbor] indicated dramatically the difficulties inherent in coordinating responsibility for defense of the whole Hawaiian area. It likewise made President Roosevelt and his advisors determine that there be no uncertainty as to responsibility for protection of the Panama Canal."[11] Consequently, on 12 December 1941, in a meeting with the President, U.S. military leaders established the first unified commands. All U.S. military forces in the Hawaii area were placed under the Commander in Chief Pacific Fleet and those in the Panama area under the CINC Panama (an Army Air Forces officer).

11. Grace Person Hayes, *The History of the Joint Chiefs of Staff in World War II: The War Against Japan* (Annapolis, Md.: Naval Institute Press, 1982), p. 29.

Subsequent U.S. unified commanders were also Allied commanders with responsibility for directing U.S. and British forces in a specific area (with some other Allied forces being present in some commands). The complexity of strategic bombing operations against Germany (including coordination with the British bombers), and later Japan, led to the JCS establishing the U.S. Strategic Air Forces in Europe and U.S. Strategic Air Forces in the Pacific. These were all-Army Air Forces commands that were operationally outside the control of the respective theater commanders and, in reality, the first U.S. specified commands.

Unified and specified commanders were in a sort of limbo after World War II, as the military departments tended to direct operations of their forces within specific geographic areas. The 1958 defense reorganization gave the unified commands responsibility for all military forces and operations within a specific area and established specified commands when the component forces were all from one service.

JOINT TASK FORCES

Periodically, unified Joint Task Forces (JTF) are organized within unified commands for specific operations. In 1989 several JTFs were established to help combat the influx of illegal drugs into the United States. In 1995 there were three such JTFs engaged in counternarcotics operations:

Unified/Specified Command	*Task Force*	*Area*
U.S. Atlantic Command	JTF-4	U.S. East Coast–Caribbean
U.S. Pacific Command	JTF-5	U.S. West Coast
U.S. Forces Command	JTF-6	U.S.–Mexican border

These task forces serve as their respective command's counternarcotics coordinators, with forces from all military services, including the Coast Guard, being assigned to the task forces. The JTFs also coordinate activities with other unified and service commands and with other government agencies. Coast Guard flag officers currently serve as Commander JTF-4, with headquarters in Key West, Florida, and Commander JTF-5, with headquarters in Alameda, California. The Commander JTF-6, an Army officer, has his headquarters at Fort Bliss in El Paso, Texas.

Historical: The first joint task force of the post–World War II era was JTF-1, established in 1946 to conduct the multiservice atomic bomb tests at the Bikini atoll in the Pacific in July of 1946. Task forces are nonpermanent organizations, being formed and disestablished as required.

CHAPTER 5

Navy Organization

The cruiser Antietam (CG 54), shown here launching a Standard Surface-to-Air Missile (SAM), like all Navy ships and aircraft, belongs to both operational and administrative organizations. The distinction is important, and the bilinear organization has been successful. (U.S. Navy, PH3 Jeffrey S. Viano)

The Navy is responsible for organizing, training, and equipping the Navy and Marine Corps to conduct prompt and sustained combat operations at sea. Specifically, the Navy and Marine Corps are to seek out and destroy enemy naval forces and to suppress enemy sea commerce; to gain and maintain general naval supremacy; to control vital sea areas; to protect vital sea lines of communication; to establish and maintain local superiority (including air) in an area of naval operations; to seize and defend advance naval bases; and to conduct such land and air operations as may be essential to the prosecution of a naval campaign.[1]

To carry out these functions, the Navy is part of a dual command structure: (1) an administrative structure that originates with the Secretary of the Navy and the Chief of Naval Operations, and (2) an operational structure that originates with the unified commanders in chief. The administrative structure fulfills the institutional need for civilian control and the balancing of service interests by enabling the Navy to support deployed forces without intervening in combat operations directed by the unified command system. The operational structure relieves the fleet and task force commanders from the administrative and procurement workload that would otherwise distract them from their primary task—the command of combat forces.

The Navy has long had a bilinear organizational structure, with squadron and later fleet commanders and, after 1942, the Chief of Naval Operations exercising military command over the operating forces, while the Secretary of the Navy, through civilian assistants and chiefs of the various bureaus and agencies, directs its business, research and development, procurement, and support activities. The responsibility for military command of operating forces has subsequently been transferred to the unified commands (see chapter 4).

John H. Dalton, Secretary of the Navy since July 1993. (U.S. Navy, Art Gibson)

Admiral Jay L. Johnson, USN, Chief of Naval Operations since June 1996. (U.S. Navy)

Admiral J. M. (Mike) Boorda, USN, Chief of Naval Operations from April 1994 to 16 May 1996. (U.S. Navy, PH2 John Sokolowski)

1. See "Functions of the Department of Defense and Its Major Components," Department of Defense Directive No. 5100.1, with changes.

OPERATIONAL ORGANIZATION

The operating forces of the Navy and Marine Corps—like those of the Army and Air Force—are subordinate to unified commands. Most naval forces are assigned to the naval component commanders of three unified commands; their basic command structure is shown below.

Unified Command	*Naval Component*	*Operating Fleet*
U.S. Atlantic Command	Atlantic Fleet	Second Fleet
U.S. Central Command	Naval Forces Central Command	Fifth Fleet
U.S. European Command	Naval Forces Europe	Sixth Fleet
U.S. Pacific Command	Pacific Fleet	Third Fleet
		Seventh Fleet

Three naval component commanders are full admirals, while Commander Naval Forces Central Command is a vice admiral; all have shore-based staffs.[2]

Atlantic Fleet: The CINC Atlantic Fleet functions in both the administrative and operational chains of command. Until 1986 the position of CINC Atlantic Fleet was an additional duty of the CINC Atlantic Command (who is additionally NATO Supreme Allied Commander Atlantic). The Second Fleet is the major operational component of the Atlantic Fleet.

Headquarters: Norfolk, Virginia

Naval Forces Central Command: The Commander Naval Forces Central Command is the component commander of CENTCOM, responsible for naval activities in the Arabian Sea, Persian Gulf, Red Sea, and portions of the Indian Ocean. Previously, the Commander Middle East Force, a rear admiral, commanded naval forces in the area under the aegis of CENTCOM. During the 1990–1991 naval buildup and conflict in the gulf, the Commander Seventh Fleet exercised command of naval forces in the region as the CINCENT naval component commander.

The naval component commander was upgraded to vice admiral in 1992 and additionally designated as the Fifth Fleet in 1995 (see below). The Deputy Commander Naval Forces Central Command, a rear admiral, is at CENTCOM headquarters at MacDill Air Force Base, near Tampa, Florida.

Headquarters: Bahrain

Naval Forces Europe: The CINC Naval Forces Europe is responsible for U.S. naval operations in the European area, including the Sixth Fleet in the Mediterranean. The CINC simultaneously holds the NATO position of CINC Allied Forces Southern Europe, responsible to the NATO Supreme Allied Commander Europe.

The CINC Naval Forces Europe does not have administrative responsibilities for support of U.S. naval forces in Europe; they come under the cognizance of the CINC Atlantic Fleet.

Headquarters: Naples, Italy

Pacific Fleet: Like CINC Atlantic Fleet, the CINC Pacific Fleet functions in both the administrative and operational chains of command. In the latter role (as a naval component commander), he is responsible for naval operations in the Pacific–Indian Ocean area. The principal operating commands are the Third Fleet and Seventh Fleet.

Headquarters: Pearl Harbor, Hawaii

The numbered fleet commanders are vice admirals. Their staffs are normally "split" between the fleet flagship and a component ashore.

Second Fleet: Operating in the Atlantic area, the Second Fleet serves as the NATO strike force, is responsible for anti-submarine operations in the Atlantic, and, increasingly, has operational requirements in the Caribbean area and off Central America. Most ships of

2. All active-duty U.S. Navy admirals and Marine Corps generals are listed, with their current positions, in the May issue of the U.S. Naval Institute *Proceedings* (Naval Review issue).

the Second Fleet rotate at regular intervals to the Sixth Fleet in the Mediterranean and to the Fifth Fleet.
Fleet headquarters: Norfolk, Virginia
Flagship: MOUNT WHITNEY (LCC 20)

Third Fleet: The Third Fleet operates in the Eastern Pacific and rotates ships to the Seventh Fleet in the Western Pacific–Indian Ocean area and the Fifth Fleet. The Third Fleet originally had an anti-submarine orientation, derived from its origins as ASW Force Pacific. The growth of Soviet naval capabilities in the Pacific during the 1980s led to an increase in carrier battle force operations in the Third Fleet, with regular North Pacific operations, some within air-strike range of Russian bases in Siberia.

Fleet headquarters: Naval Air Station North Island (San Diego), California. Fleet headquarters were shifted from Ford Island in Pearl Harbor to San Diego in August 1991.
Flagship: CORONADO (AGF 11)

Fifth Fleet: The Commander Naval Forces CENTCOM is additionally the Commander Fifth Fleet, that position having been established on 1 July 1995. The fleet has no ships permanently assigned. Rather, ships from other fleets that deploy into the area are assigned to the Fifth Fleet. There are an average of more than ten active Navy ships in the area at any given time, plus about 25 Maritime Prepositioning Ships (MPS) and Afloat Prepositioning Ships (APF). Most of the latter ships are anchored at Diego Garcia.

Various task forces (TF) are activated within the Fifth Fleet depending upon the ships in the area. For example, TF 50 (Naval Expeditionary Force) is activated when a carrier battle group and amphibious ready group (ARG) are in the area; TF 51 (Amphibious Force) is activated when an ARG but no carrier is in the area. The normal commanders of these forces retain command, but they are additionally assigned to the Fifth Fleet.

Commander Task Force 53 (Logistics Force) has a permanent staff at Bahrain. He also serves as Commander Service Force for NAVCENT and has control of all underway replenishment ships, tenders, tugs, and the MPS/APF ships in the area.

(The LA SALLE/AGF 3 was previously flagship of Commander Middle East Force, based at Mina' Sulman, Bahrain.)
Headquarters: Bahrain

Sixth Fleet: The Sixth Fleet operates in the Mediterranean Sea and has both U.S. and NATO responsibilities, the latter as the NATO Striking and Support Forces, Southern Europe. Several NATO allies provide direct support to the Sixth Fleet in terms of shore bases and ASW and reconnaissance forces.

A few Sixth Fleet support ships and the fleet flagship are homeported in the Mediterranean. Most Sixth Fleet ships and aircraft squadrons are on rotation from the Atlantic Fleet; those units normally spend 6 months in transit and operating in the Mediterranean, and 12 months in their home port and in Atlantic operations.
Fleet headquarters: Gaeta, Italy
Fleet flagship: LA SALLE (AGF 3)

Seventh Fleet: The Seventh Fleet has broad responsibilities for naval operations in the Western Pacific and Indian Ocean areas—from the Kamchatka Peninsula of Russian Siberia to the western Indian Ocean. Thus, the Seventh Fleet has complex and wide-ranging mission requirements with only limited allied support available. The aircraft carrier INDEPENDENCE (CV 62), a cruiser-destroyer group, and an amphibious group are homeported in Japan.

During the Persian Gulf operations of 1990–1991 (Desert Shield/Desert Storm), the Commander Seventh Fleet became the naval component commander for Central Command.
Fleet headquarters: Yokosuka, Japan
Flagship: BLUE RIDGE (LCC 19)

Historical: The U.S. Navy's numbered fleets were established from 1942 onward within the U.S. Atlantic and Pacific Fleets. Those in the Atlantic-Mediterranean area were given even numbers; those in the Pacific area received odd numbers. The U.S. numbered fleets were:

First Fleet: Established in the Eastern Pacific as the First Task Fleet from 1947 to 1950, when changed to the First Fleet; disestablished in 1973.

Second Fleet: Established for operations in the North Atlantic as the Second Task Fleet from 1947 to 1950, when changed to Second Fleet.

Third Fleet: Established for operations in the Western Pacific from 1943 to 1946. The Third Fleet generally shared the same naval forces with the Fifth Fleet; while one fleet commander and his staff were at sea operating against the Japanese, the other commander and staff would be ashore at Pearl Harbor planning the next operation. It was reestablished in 1973 for operations in the Eastern Pacific.

Fourth Fleet: The U.S. South Atlantic Force as renamed in 1943; disestablished in 1946.

Fifth Fleet: Established for operations in the Western Pacific from 1944 to 1946, it was reestablished in 1995 for operations in the Persian Gulf–Indian Ocean area.

Sixth Fleet: Established as the Sixth Task Fleet in 1948 for operations in the Mediterranean; that designation was changed to Sixth Fleet in 1950.

Seventh Fleet: Called "MacArthur's Navy," the Seventh Fleet was formed in 1943 to provide naval support to operations by General Douglas MacArthur. From 1949 to 1950 it was designated the Seventh Task Fleet.

Eighth Fleet: Established in 1943 to conduct operations in the Mediterranean; disestablished in 1946.

Ninth Fleet: Designation not used.

Tenth Fleet: "Paper" fleet established in the Navy Department to coordinate anti-submarine warfare. The Tenth Fleet was belatedly established on 20 May 1943 under the direct command of the Chief of Naval Operations and CINC U.S. Fleet, Admiral Ernest J. King.[3]

Eleventh Fleet: Designation not used.

Twelfth Fleet: This fleet was established in 1943 and set up its headquarters in London, as the U.S. Navy's planning staff for European operations. It was disestablished in 1946.

ADMINISTRATIVE ORGANIZATION

The administrative organization of the Navy begins with the Secretary of Defense and then goes through the Secretary of the Navy and the Chief of Naval Operations (CNO), as shown in simplified form in the accompanying figure. The CNO is "double hatted" as both the uniformed head of the Navy and as a member of the Joint Chiefs of Staff.

The Secretary of the Navy and the CNO—as the uniformed head of the Navy—are essentially managers charged with supporting unified commanders. They are responsible for logistics, maintenance, personnel management, procurement of naval systems and supplies, and research and development.

To accomplish these tasks, the Secretary and the CNO each have staff organizations; the Secretary's staff are mostly civilians and the CNO's mostly naval personnel. The Secretary of the Navy has the following principal assistants, most of whom are civilians:[4]

- Under Secretary
- Assistant Secretary (Financial Management)
- Assistant Secretary (Manpower and Reserve Affairs)
- Assistant Secretary (Research, Development, and Acquisition)
- Assistant Secretary (Shipbuilding and Logistics)
- General Counsel
- Inspector General (★★★)
- Judge Advocate General (★★)
- Chief of Legislative Affairs (★)
- Chief of Naval Research (★)
- Chief of Information (★)

3. The Battle of the Atlantic was essentially won in May 1943, almost simultaneous with setting up the Tenth Fleet. The delay was caused largely by Admiral King, who wished to keep direct control of the anti-submarine campaign, and the bitter controversy between the Army Air Forces and the Navy over the control of land-based anti-submarine aircraft.

4. The rank of military incumbents is shown in parentheses; ★ = rear admiral (lower half); ★★ = rear admiral; ★★★ = vice admiral.

These officials handle Marine Corps as well as Navy matters within their areas of responsibility. With the CNO and his staff, these officials are jointly responsible for the administration of numerous commands of the shore establishment. The principal commands, all headed by naval officers, are:

- Bureau of Medicine and Surgery* (★★★)
- Bureau of Naval Personnel* (★★★)
- Naval Air Systems Command (★★★)
- Naval Data Automation Command (captain)
- Naval Doctrine Command (★★)
- Naval Education and Training Command* (★★★)
- Naval Facilities Engineering Command (★★)
- Naval Intelligence Command (★)
- Naval Investigative Service Command (★)
- Naval Legal Service Command (★★)
- Naval Meteorology Oceanography Command (★)
- Naval Safety Center (★)
- Naval Sea Systems Command (★★★)
- Naval Security Group Command (★)
- Naval Space Command (★)
- Naval Supply Systems Command (★★)
- Naval Telecommunications Command (captain)
- Navy Recruiting Command (★)
- Space and Naval Warfare Systems Command (★★)

The commanders of three of these commands—indicated by asterisks—are "double hatted" on the staff of the Chief of Naval Operations as N093, N01, and N07, respectively (see below). The Naval Space Command also serves as the naval component of the U.S. Space Command and is thus an operational as well as administrative organization.

The Chief of Naval Operations has several deputies and assistants and a large staff historically known as the Office of the Chief of Naval Operations (OPNAV). The most far reaching reorganization of the U.S. Navy headquarters in almost 50 years has changed the OPNAV staff to the Chief of Naval Operations staff and destroyed the so-called platform barons, the vice admirals who directed the submarine, surface, and air "communities." The reorganization, announced on 22 July 1992, also eliminated several flag billets, including four vice admirals, and cut the size of the headquarters staff by about 150 positions.

Administrative Chain of Command

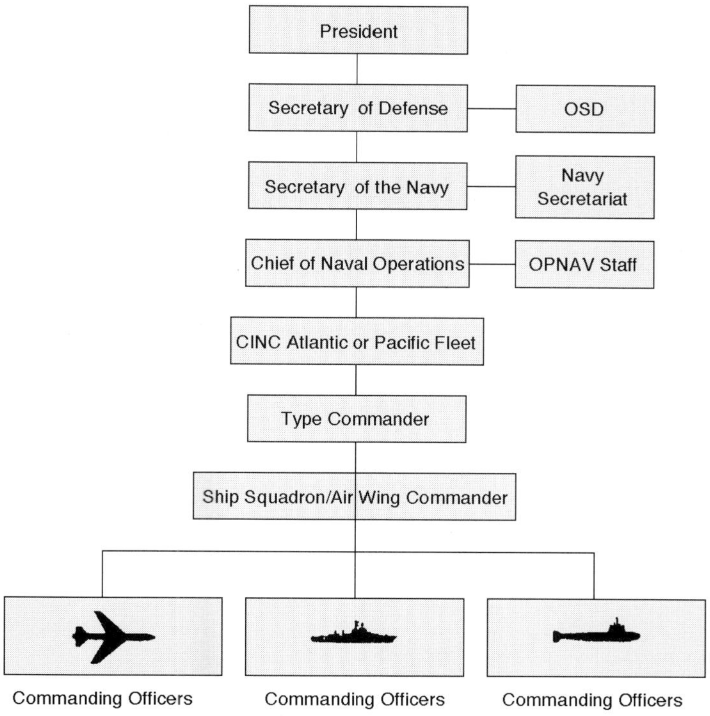

Fleet Command Structure

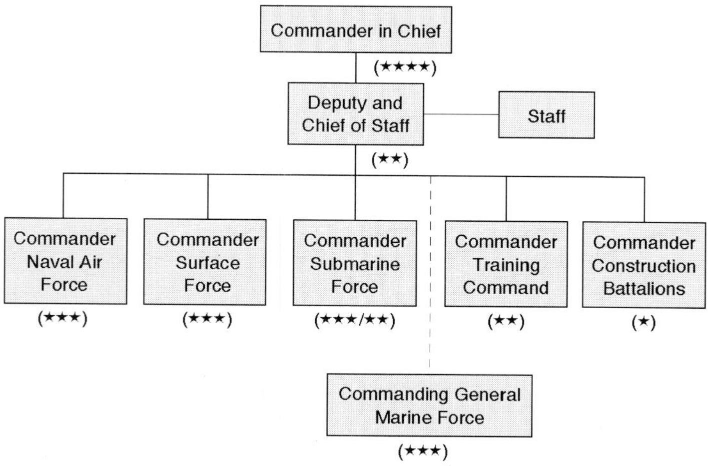

These changes were made, according to the Navy's statement to Congress, because: "The dramatic changes that have taken place and are continuing to take place in the world situation have dictated a reduction in the force structure of the U.S. Navy. This reduction also requires that the Navy review how its command and administrative structure is organized. Navy leadership has recognized for some time the need to have a tighter, leaner headquarters organization, better tailored and coordinated to deal with [Department of Defense] and [Joint Chiefs of Staff] as well as operational staffs."[5]

However, the reorganization reflected a long-standing desire by Department of Defense officials as well as senior Army and Air Force officers to bring the Navy's executive staff "into line" with the other services. The new organization brings the Navy into closer alignment to the staff of the Joint Chiefs of Staff as well as the other services. The principal subordinates to the Chief of Naval Operations and their N-series OPNAV codes are:

- N09 Vice CNO (★★★★)
- N091 Director Test and Evaluation and Technology Requirements (★★★)
- N093 Director Naval Medicine (★★★)
- N095 Director of Naval Reserve (★★)
- N096 Oceanographer of the Navy (★★)
- N097 Chief of Chaplains (★)
- N1 Deputy CNO Manpower and Training (★★★)
- N2 Director Naval Intelligence (★★)
- N3/5 Deputy CNO Plans, Policy and Operations (★★★)
- N4 Deputy CNO Logistics (★★★)
- N6 Director Space and Electronic Warfare (★★★)
- N7 Director Naval Training (★★★)
- N8 Deputy CNO Resources, Warfare Requirements, and Assessments (★★★)

The principal 1992 organizational change was the elimination of the "barons," or "platform" sponsors, at the three-star level—the Assistant CNOs for undersea warfare (OP-02), surface warfare (OP-03), and air warfare (OP-05). The concept of these offices, which sought to control their respective communities as fiefdoms, dates to August 1943, when the Deputy CNO for air was established with responsibility for "the preparation, readiness and logistic support" of naval aviation. Accordingly, as a result of the reorganization, N85 was established as the Director Expeditionary Warfare (a Marine major general), N86 as Director Surface Warfare, N87 as Director Submarine Warfare, and N88 as Director Air Warfare.

5. Memorandum from Capt. J. R. McCleary, USN, subject: "Reorganization of the Naval Headquarters Staff," 22 July 1992.

An F-14A Tomcat from Fighter Squadron 101 taxies after landing aboard the aircraft carrier GEORGE WASHINGTON (CVN 73) during the squadron's carrier qualifications. Naval forces are flexible, with ships and aircraft squadrons being able to readily shift from one fleet command to another, as political considerations, crises, and conflicts dictate. (Peter B. Mersky)

Surface and submarine warfare matters were directed by a single Deputy CNO until 1971, who also had general sponsorship responsibilities for aviation ships. Pleading for "equality" by Admiral H. G. Rickover, then head of naval nuclear propulsion, and the submarine community led then-CNO Admiral E. R. Zumwalt to establish a separate Deputy CNO for submarine warfare (OP-02) in 1971. Zumwalt believed that, "Setting up the DCNO for Submarines made it easier to deal with the submarine community and with Rickover."[7]

This move, in turn, led to OP-03 becoming the Deputy CNO for surface warfare, and it initiated two decades of intra-Navy, or "union," competition as the "platform barons" competed for resources, political position, and even flag billets. For example, prior to the establishment of OP-02, submarine-qualified officers could serve as OP-03, while the air and surface communities worked much more closely together. Beyond the competitive aspects of the new arrangement, it was easy for non-platform specific programs (especially mine warfare programs) to "fall through the cracks"—to become lost or underfunded.

Then-Secretary of the Navy Sean O'Keefe, in announcing the changes, stressed that: "[O]ne of my primary concerns is ending rivalries and jealousies between the various key warfare fighting communities in the Navy. . . . We believe there can be no jealousy among the fingers of a strong fist. This Navy reorganization will begin the process of bringing our warfare fighters together into a tighter, stronger fist."[8]

Unfortunately, the 1992 reorganization missed opportunities to return anti-submarine warfare programs and mine warfare programs to a realistic staff level, especially when one considers their increasing importance for potential operations in littoral areas. They should have been placed at the same level within N8 as the air, surface, and subsurface offices.

At the time of his death in May 1996, Admiral Boorda, the CNO, was reported to be preparing to approve an OPNAV reorganization. While details of the reorganization had not been made public when this edition went to press, it was primarily intended to rectify several shortcomings in the 1992 restructuring.

Historical: The Navy Department was formally established by an act of Congress on 30 April 1798, and the first Secretary of the Navy was Benjamin Stoddart, installed on 18 June 1798. As originally established, the Secretary of the Navy's role was to exercise direct control over the Navy's shore establishment as well as the operating forces.

From 1842 onward, Congress established a series of bureaus to provide effective procurement of ships and supplies, to manage personnel, and to operate shore activities. These bureaus, commanded by naval officers, also reported directly to the Secretary of the Navy. This organizational concept continues today, with the original bureaus having evolved into the modern systems commands and bureaus.

The position of Aide for Operation was established from 1990 to 1915 to provide a flag officer (rear admiral) on the staff of the Secretary of the Navy to be responsible for ship operations as well as training, planning, intelligence, and logistics, and to recommend officer appointments. In 1915, as a result of the war in Europe, the position was changed to Chief of Naval Operations (with the rank of full admiral, the first appointee being Admiral William S. Benson).

Operational Chain of Command

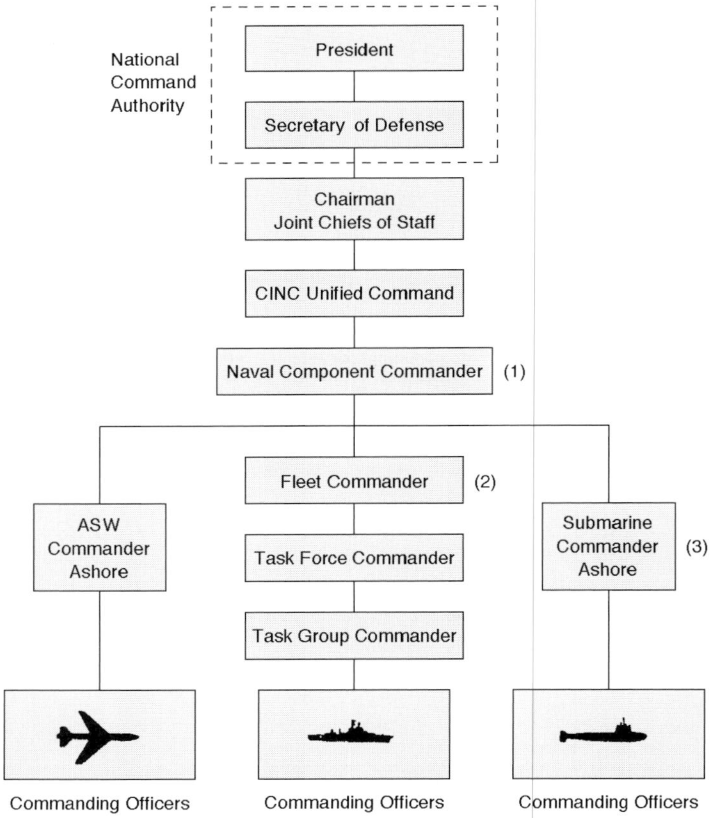

(1) Nominally CINC U.S. Atlantic Fleet, Pacific Fleet, or Naval Forces Europe
(2) Nominally numbered fleet commander.
(3) Nominally Commander Submarine Force Atlantic Fleet or Submarine Force Pacific Fleet.

7. Adm. H. G. Rickover, head of naval nuclear propulsion from 1948 until 1992.
8. Secretary of the Navy Sean O'Keefe, press conference, the Pentagon, 22 July 1992.

However, the CNO did not direct naval forces afloat. Rather, various squadron and, from 1906, fleet commanders exercised command of ships, with their commands based on geographic areas. In 1919 the position of Commander in Chief U.S. Fleet (CINCUS) was established as the overall commander of U.S. naval forces afloat. The CINCUS reported to the Secretary of the Navy, independent of the Chief of Naval Operations.

The positions of CNO and CINCUS remained separate until Admiral Ernest J. King, who had become Commander in Chief U.S. Fleet in December 1941, was additionally named Chief of Naval Operations in March 1942. From that time on the CNO had *de facto* operational command of forces afloat. At the same time, the CNO was also the Navy member of the Joint Chiefs of Staff. The position of Commander in Chief U.S. Fleet (which King had changed to COMINCH—pronounced com-*INCH*) was abolished in October 1945, immediately after World War II.

There have been continuous organizational changes within the Navy. Among the more significant, in 1963 the separate technical bureaus were incorporated under a central Naval Material Command headed by the Chief of Naval Material (a full admiral). This had the effect of increasing the influence of the CNO over the bureaus. In 1966 the Secretary of the Navy placed the Naval Material Command (and hence the system commands) directly under the CNO, giving him full responsibility for material, personnel, and medical support of the operating forces. Also in this period, the technical bureaus were redesignated as systems commands—air, ship, ordnance, electronic, supply, etc.

The intermediate administrative organization of the Naval Material Command was abolished in 1985 by Secretary of the Navy John Lehman. Under his revisions, the Secretary and the CNO would jointly exercise direction of the five systems commands then in existence: the Naval Air Systems Command, Naval Sea Systems Command, Space and Naval Warfare Systems Command, Naval Facilities Engineering Command, and Naval Supply Systems Command.

The Bureau of Naval Personnel and Bureau of Medicine and Surgery had remained outside of the Naval Material Command. Those bureaus survived with those titles until 1978 and 1982, when they were renamed the Naval Military Personnel Command and the Naval Medical Command, respectively. Those awkward and bureaucratic titles survived only until 1989, when the traditional bureau names were restored.[9]

9. The Bureau of Personnel was created in October 1942, evolving from the Bureau of Navigation (1862) and the predecessor Bureau of Ordnance and Hydrography (1842); the Bureau of Medicine and Surgery was one of the five bureaus originally established by Congress in August 1842.

Frigates—at times during the Cold War the most numerous U.S. surface combatants—will survive into the 21st century in relatively small numbers, if at all. Here the Samuel B. Roberts (FFG 58) cuts through the Adriatic Sea after taking on fuel during a multi-ship replenishment operation with the aircraft carrier George Washington. Both ships were participating in Operation Joint Endeavor during 1996, supporting NATO efforts to keep peace in Bosnia. (U.S. Navy, PH2 Jim Vidrine)

CHAPTER 6

Fleet Organization

The destroyers COMTE DE GRASSE (DD 974) and SCOTT (DDG 995) and the attack submarine SAN JUAN (SSN 751) lie moored together at Port Everglades, Florida. Increasingly, the Navy is deploying warships in fixed battle groups and other task groups, with all ships training and working up for deployments together. (John Bouvia)

The Navy has made major changes in its fleet organization and the assignment of ships, aircraft, and submarines in the wake of the end of the Cold War. Significant revisions were made in 1995, developed from the earlier efforts to establish "permanent" carrier battle groups.

As noted in chapter 5, all naval forces are assigned to both administrative and operational commands. Within the new fleet structures, however, the distinction is becoming blurred. For example, the carrier battle group commander is responsible for both the "workup" and training of his force as well as its forward (overseas) deployment. Similarly, an attempt is made to keep destroyer squadrons together for both workup and deployment. Note that the organizational concept of destroyer squadron is ambiguous, with such units being combinations of destroyers and frigates and, occasionally, cruisers. Carrier-based squadrons are assigned to air wings when deployed aboard ship, but to "type" commanders when ashore.

Each battle group normally consists of an aircraft carrier and two missile cruisers; they are collocated at the same U.S. home port. During pre-deployment workup and training, a destroyer squadron—normally four ships—will join up with the core battle-group elements. From that point on, this seven-ship battle group, along with submarines, if assigned, will train and deploy together. Some carrier battle groups are commanded by the surface warfare admiral in command of a cruiser-destroyer group.

The operational organizations are based primarily on task forces/groups. The Task Force (TF) and Task Group (TG) organizations listed in this chapter under the commanders in chief of Atlantic and Pacific Fleets are mainly for contingency operations; exceptions include the respective submarine force commanders, who have both operational and administrative roles. TF organizations are employed for exercises, forward-deployment operations, and in war.

Naval administrative organizations are asymmetrical; the hierarchy, organization, and composition of units vary within the fleets and from fleet to fleet. Major organizational changes are taking place in the mid-1990s as the size of the active fleet is reduced and organizations are realigned. Ship squadrons that do not have ships assigned are usually operational command staffs that control forward-deployed task forces or groups or training workups.

The Western Hemisphere Group of the Atlantic Fleet, established in 1995, deploys ships for four- and five-month operations, such as Caribbean ops and the South American training cruise UNITAS.

The following tables show a breakdown of naval organizations and nominal ship assignments as of 1996. Ships assigned to type commanders are indicated under the administrative organizations. Such assignments change regularly as new ships are commissioned, older ships are stricken, and ships are reassigned for overhaul or modernization. Specific aircraft carriers and fleet flagships are identified. The fleet flagships (⚑) are listed under their administrative commands (see chapter 18 for operational details).

The ships listed are active unless indicated as Naval Reserve Force (NRF) ships. Headquarters locations or flagship home ports are indicated, although all ships of a command may not be at the same port. Although some ships listed here are under construction, they are close enough to completion to warrant their fleet assignment. Note that major Atlantic Fleet units generally have even numbers and Pacific Fleet units use odd numbers.

In the summer of 1992, "permanent" organizations were instituted for the battle groups of the Atlantic and Pacific Fleets. These were to be "transparent" battle groups in the contemporary vernacular, all with essentially the same composition and capabilities, intended to be easily shifted from one unified command to another. Each of the battle groups nominally consisted of one carrier with an embarked carrier air wing; cruiser, destroyer, and frigate units; and two attack submarines. The initial compositions of these battle groups as they were established may be found in the 15th Edition/page 36 of *Ships and Aircraft*. Those assigned quickly changed as older ships were retired earlier than expected. The current battle group assignments are listed below.

The Marine Force organizations are described in chapter 7 and operational naval aviation units (air wings and squadrons) are listed in chapter 28.

Notes are listed at the end of this chapter.

PACIFIC FLEET

TF 10	Temporary Operations Force
TF 11	Training Force
TF 12	Anti-Submarine Force
TF 14	Submarine Force
TF 15	Surface Force
TF 16	Maritime Defense Zone[1]
TF 17	Naval Air Force
TF 18	Sealift Forces
TF 19	Marine Force[2]
TF 91	Naval Forces Alaska
TF 199	Naval Support Force Antarctica
THIRD FLEET	
TF 30	Battle Force
TF 31	Command and Coordination Force
TF 32	Ready Force
TF 33	Combat Logistics Support Force
TF 34	Submarine Force
TF 35	Surface Combatant Force
TF 36	Amphibious Force
TF 37	Carrier Strike Force
TF 39	Landing Force[2]
SEVENTH FLEET	
TF 70	Battle Force
TF 71	Command and Coordination Force
TF 72	Patrol and Reconnaissance Force
TF 73	Logistic Support Force
TF 74	Submarine Force
TF 75	Surface Combatant Force
TF 76	Amphibious Force
TF 77	Carrier Strike Force
TF 79	Landing Force[2]

CARRIER BATTLE GROUPS	
Carrier Group 1	North Island, Calif.
Carrier Group 3	Alameda, Calif.
CVN ABRAHAM LINCOLN	Everett, Wash.
1 CGN	
2 CG	
Carrier Group 5	Yokosuka, Japan
CV INDEPENDENCE	Yokosuka, Japan
2 CG	
Carrier Group 7	North Island, Calif.
CVN NIMITZ	Bremerton, Wash.
1 CGN	
2 CG	
Cruiser-Destroyer Group 1	Pearl Harbor, Hawaii
CV CONSTELLATION	San Diego, Calif.
2 CG	
Cruiser-Destroyer Group 3	San Diego, Calif.
CVN VINSON	Alameda, Calif.
1 CGN	
3 CG	
Cruiser-Destroyer Group 5	San Diego, Calif.
CVN KITTY HAWK	San Diego, Calif.
2 CG	
NAVAL AIR FORCE PACIFIC	North Island, Calif.
Carrier Air Wing 2	Miramar, Calif.
Carrier Air Wing 5	Yokosuka, Japan
Carrier Air Wing 9	Lemoore, Calif.
Carrier Air Wing 11	Miramar, Calif.
Carrier Air Wing 14	Miramar, Calif.
Carrier Air Wing 15	Miramar, Calif.
Helicopter Tactical Wing Pacific	North Island, Calif.
HC-3, HC-11	
HM-15	
VXE-6	
Sea Control Wing Pacific	North Island, Calif.
VS-41	
VQ-5	
Helicopter Anti-Submarine Wing Pacific	North Island, Calif.
HS-10	
Helicopter Anti-Submarine Light Wing Pacific	North Island, Calif.
HSL-37, HSL-41, HSL-43, HSL-45, HSL-47, HSL-49, HSL-51	
Fighter Wing Pacific	Miramar, Calif.
Airborne Early Warning Wing Pacific	Miramar, Calif.
VRC-30	
Strike Fighter Wing Pacific	Lemoore, Calif.
VFA-125, VFA-127	
Patrol Wings Pacific	Barbers Point, Hawaii
VP-1, VP-4, VP-9, VP-17, VP-40, VP-46, VP-47	
VPU-2	
VQ-1	
Attack Wing Pacific	Whidbey Island, Wash.
VA-128	
Electronic Combat Wing Pacific	Whidbey Island, Wash.
VAQ-129, VAQ-130, VAQ-132, VAQ-140, VAQ-141	
Strategic Communications Wing 1	Tinker AFB, Okla.
VQ-3, VQ-4	
Fleet Air Western Pacific	Atsugi, Japan
HC-5	
NAVAL SURFACE FORCE PACIFIC	Coronado, Calif.
Amphibious Group 1	White Beach, Okinawa
LCC BLUE RIDGE (⚑ Seventh Fleet)	Sasebo, Japan
Amphibious Squadron 11	Sasebo, Japan
1 LHA	
1 LPD	
1 LSD	

PACIFIC FLEET (continued)

Amphibious Group 3	San Diego, Calif.
Amphibious Squadron 1	San Diego, Calif.
Amphibious Squadron 3	San Diego, Calif.
Amphibious Squadron 5	San Diego, Calif.
Amphibious Squadron 7	San Diego, Calif.
Amphibious Squadron 9	San Diego, Calif.
AGF Coronado (⚑ Third Fleet)	San Diego, Calif.
2 LHA	
2 LHD	
2 LPH	
5 LPD	
7 LSD	
Naval Beach Group 1	Coronado (San Diego), Calif.
Amphibious Construction Battalion 1	
Assault Craft Units 1, 5	
Beachmaster Unit 1	
Destroyer Squadron 1	San Diego, Calif.
7 FFG (NRF)	
1 LST (NRF)	
Destroyer Squadron 5	Pearl Harbor, Hawaii
2 DDG	
1 DD	
1 FFG	
Destroyer Squadron 7	San Diego, Calif.
2 DDG	
3 DD	
Destroyer Squadron 9	Everett, Wash.
2 DD	
2 FFG	
Destroyer Squadron 13 Disestablished 1996	
Destroyer Squadron 15	Yokosuka, Japan
3 DD	
4 FFG	
Destroyer Squadron 17	San Diego, Calif.
Destroyer Squadron 21	San Diego, Calif.
1 DDG	
3 DD	
1 FFG	
Destroyer Squadron 23	San Diego, Calif.
3 DD	
2 FFG	
Destroyer Squadron 31	Pearl Harbor, Hawaii
3 DD	
2 FFG	
Destroyer Squadron 33 Disestablished 1996	
Readiness Support Group	San Diego, Calif.
1 AFDM	
Combat Logistics Group 1	Everett, Wash.
5 AE	
3 AOE	
2 AOR	
Logistics Group Western Pacific	Singapore
1 AFS	
2 ATS	
Naval Surface Group Mid-Pacific	Pearl Harbor, Hawaii
3 DDG	
4 DD	
2 FFG	
2 AO	
2 ARS	
Explosive Ordnance Disposal Group 1	San Diego, Calif.
SUBMARINE FORCE PACIFIC	Pearl Harbor, Hawaii
Submarine Development Group 1	San Diego, Calif.
1 SSN	
1 AGSS	
2 DSRV (submersibles)	
2 DSV (submersibles)	
Submarine Group 5	San Diego, Calif.
1 SSN	
Submarine Group 7	Yokosuka, Japan
1 AS	
Submarine Group 9	Bangor, Wash.
Submarine Squadron 1	Pearl Harbor, Hawaii
9 SSN[3]	
Submarine Squadron 3	San Diego, Calif.
7 SSN	
1 AS	
1 ARD	
Submarine Squadron 7	Pearl Harbor, Hawaii
7 SSN[3]	
Submarine Squadron 11	San Diego, Calif.
7 SSN	
1 AS	
1 ARDM	
Submarine Squadron 17	Bangor, Wash.
8 SSBN	
TRAINING COMMAND PACIFIC	San Diego, Calif.
3RD NAVAL CONSTRUCTION BRIGADE	Pearl Harbor, Hawaii
Mobile Construction Battalions 3, 4, 5, 40	
Underwater Construction Team 2	

ATLANTIC FLEET

TF-40 Naval Surface Force
TF-41 Naval Air Force
TF-42 Submarine Force
TF-43 Training Command
TF-44 Coast Guard Forces[1]
TF-45 Marine Force[2]
TF-46 Mine Warfare Force
TF-47 Naval Construction Battalions
TF-49 Poseidon Operational Test Force
TF-80 Naval Patrol and Protection of Shipping
TF-81 Sea Control and Surveillance Force
TF-82 Amphibious Task Force
TF-83 Landing Force[2]
TF-84 ASW Task Force
TF-85 Mobile Logistic Support Force
TF-86 Patrol Air Task Force
TF-87 Tactical Development and Evaluation and Transit Force
TF-88 Training Force
TF-89 Maritime Defense Zone[1]
TF-134 Naval Forces Caribbean
TF-137 Eastern Atlantic
TF-138 South Atlantic Force
TF-139 Multilateral Special Operations Force
TF-142 Operational Test and Evaluation Force

SECOND FLEET
TF-20 Battle Force
TF-21 Sea Control and Surveillance Force
TF-22 Amphibious Force
TF-23 Landing Force[2]
TF-24 ASW Task Force
TF-25 Mobile Logistics Support Force
TF-26 Patrol Air Task Force
TF-28 Caribbean Contingency Force

CARRIER BATTLE GROUPS	
Carrier Group 2	Norfolk, Va.
CV John F. Kennedy	Mayport, Fla.
Cruiser Group 6	
3 CG	
Carrier Group 4[4]	Norfolk, Va.
Carrier Group 6[5]	Mayport, Fla.
CV America	Norfolk, Va.
Cruiser-Destroyer Group 2	Norfolk, Va.
2 CG	
Carrier Group 8	Norfolk, Va.
CVN Theodore Roosevelt	Norfolk, Va.
Cruiser Group 8	
1 CGN	
2 CG	
Cruiser-Destroyer Group 2	Norfolk, Va.
CVN George Washington	Norfolk, Va.
1 CGN	
1 CG	
Cruiser-Destroyer Group 8	Norfolk, Va.
CVN Dwight D. Eisenhower	Norfolk, Va.
2 CG	
Cruiser-Destroyer Group 12	Mayport, Fla.
CVN Enterprise	Norfolk, Va.
2 CG	
NAVAL AIR FORCE ATLANTIC	Norfolk, Va.
VX-1	
Carrier Air Wing 1	Oceana, Va.
Carrier Air Wing 3	Oceana, Va.
Carrier Air Wing 7	Oceana, Va.
Carrier Air Wing 8	Oceana, Va.
Carrier Air Wing 17	Cecil Field, Fla.
Helicopter ASW Wing Atlantic	Jacksonville, Fla.
HS-1, HS-3, HS-5, HS-7, HS-11, HS-15	
Helicopter ASW Light Wing Atlantic	Mayport, Fla.
HSL-40, HSL-42, HSL-44, HSL-46, HSL-48	
Helicopter Tactical Wing Atlantic	Norfolk, Va.
HC-2, HC-6, HC-8	
HM-14	
VC-6	
Fighter Wing Atlantic	Oceana, Va.
VF-14, VF-32, VF-41, VF-84, VF-101, VF-102, VF-103, VF-142, VF-143	
VC-8	
Attack Wing Atlantic	Oceana, Va.
VA-34, VA-35, VA-75	
Airborne Early Warning Wing Atlantic	Norfolk, Va.
VAW-120, VAW-121, VAW-122, VAW-123, VAW-125, VAW-126	
VRC-40	
Strike Fighter Wing Atlantic	Cecil Field, Fla.
VFA-15, VFA-37, VFA-81, VFA-82, VFA-83, VFA-86, VFA-87, VRA-106, VFA-131, VFA-136	
VF-45	
Sea Control Wing Atlantic	Cecil Field, Fla.
VS-22, VS-24, VS-30, VS-31, VS-32	
Patrol Wings Atlantic	Norfolk, Va.
Patrol Wing 5	Brunswick, Maine
VP-8, VP-10, VP-11, VP-23, VP-26	
VPU-1	
Patrol Wing 11	Jacksonville, Fla.
VP-5, VP-16, VP-24, VP-45, VP-30	
Fleet Air Mediterranean	Naples, Italy
HC-4	
VQ-2	
NAVAL SURFACE FORCE ATLANTIC	Norfolk, Va.
Destroyer Squadron 2	Norfolk, Va.
1 DDG	
2 DD	
1 FFG	
Destroyer Squadron 6	Pascagoula, Miss.
8 FFG (NRF)	
Destroyer Squadron 14	Mayport, Fla.
1 DDG	
2 DD	
1 FFG	
Destroyer Squadron 18	Norfolk, Va.
1 DDG	
2 DD	
1 FFG	
Destroyer Squadron 20	Norfolk, Va.
2 DDG	
1 DD	
2 FFG	

ATLANTIC FLEET (continued)

Destroyer Squadron 22	Norfolk, Va.
2 DDG	
1 DD	
1 FFG	
Destroyer Squadron 24	Mayport, Fla.
1 DDG	
2 DD	
1 FFG	
Destroyer Squadron 26	Norfolk, Va.
1 DDG	
2 DD	
1 FFG	
Destroyer Squadron 28	Norfolk, Va.
1 DDG	
1 DD	
2 FFG	
Destroyer Squadron 32	Norfolk, Va.
1 DDG	
1 DD	
2 FFG	
Western Hemisphere Group 6[6]	
2 CG	
2 DDG	
2 DD	
10 FFG	
Naval Surface Group Norfolk/Combat Logistics Group 2	Norfolk, Va.
1 AFDL	
1 AFDM	
3 AD	
3 AOE	
2 AOR	
Amphibious Group 2[7]	Norfolk, Va.
LCC Mt. Whitney (⚑Second Fleet))	Norfolk, Va.
AGF La Salle (⚑Sixth Fleet)	Norfolk, Va.
2 LHA	
2 LHD	
5 LPD	
6 LSD	
Amphibious Group 4	Mayport, Fla.
Amphibious Squadron 2	Norfolk, Va.
Amphibious Squadron 4	Norfolk, Va.
Amphibious Squadron 6	Norfolk, Va.
Amphibious Squadron 8	Little Creek, Va.
Naval Beach Group 2	
Beach Master Unit 2	
Amphibious Construction Battalion 2	
Assault Craft Unit 2	
Assault Craft Unit 4	
Combat Logistic Squadron 2	Earle, N.J.
4 AE	
3 AO	
Support Squadron 8	Little Creek, Va.
2 ARS	
1 ATS	
MINE WARFARE COMMAND[8]	Corpus Christi, Texas
2 MCM	
12 MCM (NRF)	
2 MHC	
2 MHC (NRF)	
COOP Mine Squadron 1	Charleston, S.C.
Mine Division 121 (NRF)	Newport, R.I.
Mine Division 123	Little Creek, Va.
Mine Division 126 (NRF)	Mayport, Fla.
SUBMARINE FORCE ATLANTIC	Norfolk, Va.
Submarine Group 2	Groton, Conn.
2 SSBN	
4 SSN	
Submarine Group 8	Naples, Italy
Submarine Group 10	Kings Bay, Ga.
Submarine Squadron 2	Groton, Conn.
14 SSN	
2 ARDM	
NR-1 (submersible)	
Submarine Squadron 4	Charleston, S.C.
4 SSN	
1 AS	
1 ARDM	
Submarine Squadron 6	Norfolk, Va.
1 SSBN	
11 SSN	
1 AS	
Submarine Squadron 8	Norfolk, Va.
16 SSN	
1 AS	
1 AFDM	
Submarine Development Squadron 12	Groton, Conn.
7 SSN	
Submarine Squadron 20	Kings Bay, Ga.
7 SSBN	
1 ARDM	
Submarine Squadron 22	——
1 AS	
TRAINING COMMAND ATLANTIC	Norfolk, Va.
2ND NAVAL CONSTRUCTION BRIGADE	Little Creek, Va.
Mobile Construction Battalions 1, 7, 13, 14, 20, 21, 23, 24, 26, 27, 74, 133	
Underwater Construction Team 1	

FIFTH FLEET

Bahrain

TF 50 Naval Expeditionary Force
TF 51 Amphibious Force
TF 53 Logistics Force
Destroyer Squadron 50/Middle East Force Surface Action Group

SIXTH FLEET

Gaeta, Italy

TF 60 Battle Force
TG 60.1 Battle Group 1
TG 60.2 Battle Group 2
TF 61 Amphibious Force
TF 62 Landing Force 2
TF 63 Service Force
TF 66 ASW Force
TF 67 Maritime Surveillance and Reconnaissance Force
TF 68 Special Operations Force
TF 69 Attack Submarine Force

1. Commanded by a Coast Guard officer.
2. Commanded by a Marine Corps officer.
3. In 1996 several submarines are being transferred from San Diego to Pearl Harbor.
4. Training group for battle groups prior to deployment.
5. When the carrier America is decommissioned on 30 September 1996, the John C. Stennis was to be assigned to Carrier Group 6.
6. This group controls all cruisers, destroyers, and frigates not assigned to the nine Atlantic Fleet destroyer squadrons. The group is under the operational control of Task Force 125 at Mayport, Fla.
7. Combined with Amphibious Squadron 10 in 1994.
8. See chapter 22 for details of the Mine Warfare Command.

CHAPTER 7

Marine Forces

Marines from the 24th Marine Expeditionary Unit are shown during a training exercise. Men from this unit went into hostile territory in western Bosnia-Herzegovina to rescue a downed Air Force pilot. Their CH-53E Super Stallion helicopter is one of several ways—by air, surface, and submarine—in which Marines can enter hostile territory. (U.S. Marine Corps)

The Marine Corps is a separate service—along with the U.S. Navy—within the Department of the Navy. The primary mission of the Marine Corps is to provide the Atlantic and Pacific Fleets with combat-ready air-ground task forces to conduct amphibious operations.

In addition to maintaining the Marine Forces assigned to the Atlantic and Pacific Fleets, the Marine Corps provides:

- Afloat detachments in aircraft carriers.[1]
- Security detachments for selected Navy shore installations in the United States.
- Security detachments for U.S. embassies and diplomatic missions abroad.

The U.S. Marine Corps is the world's largest "naval infantry force," with its early 1996 strength of approximately 17,800 officers and 156,800 enlisted men and women.[2] This strength is down from a post–Vietnam War peak of approximately 200,000 in the late 1980s. The current Marine Corps has the smallest percentage of women of all five U.S. military services: 3.6 percent of the officers and 4.4 percent of the enlisted personnel are female. (The number of female officers has increased very slightly over the past few years, while the number of enlisted women has declined.)

The two Marine Forces—the "muscle of the Corps"—currently number some 76,000 troops in the Pacific Fleet and 40,000 troops in the Atlantic Fleet. From 1933 to 1994 the Marines assigned to fleets were designated the Fleet Marine Force (FMF); they provided the tactical and support organizations for amphibious operations. In July 1994 the term FMF was dropped in favor of Marine Forces.

The change from FMF to Marine Forces (MARFOR) came about after Operations Desert Shield/Desert Storm in the Persian Gulf in 1990–1991. During that campaign the Marines ashore in Saudi Arabia became the Marine component of Central Command (CENTCOM), on an equal basis with the Army, Air Force, and Navy components. (The Marine units afloat in the gulf were under the Navy component commander.)

The Marine Corps is a "combined arms" force possessing armor and heavy artillery and a large tactical air arm that includes fixed-wing aircraft and helicopters. The Marine Corps is the only such service with its own air arm, except for a small number of helicopters and light fixed-wing aircraft flown by the British and Russian marines. (The U.S. Marine Corps aviation structure is described in chapter 28, and Marine aircraft are listed in chapter 29).

The Marine Corps is nominally organized into three ground divisions and three aircraft wings, with a large combat support force formed into three service support groups. The basic structure of the Marine Forces is shown in the accompanying table. The Marine Corps Reserve consists of an additional ground division, aircraft wing, and support group. However, these divisions and wings can be considered primarily an administrative structure for Marine units deployed in Marine Air-Ground Task Force (MAGTF, pronounced "*mag*-taf") formations.

The Marine Corps has followed a basic triangular organization since the start of World War II, with each division having three infantry regiments (plus an artillery regiment), each infantry regiment having three rifle battalions, and each battalion having three rifle companies (plus a weapons company).[3] In light of post–Cold War reductions, however, the divisions have been reorganized: each has only two infantry regiments, each regiment having three infantry battalions and a reconnaissance company. A combined arms regiment has been added, which has a light armored reconnaissance company, two light armored infantry battalions, and—in two active divisions—a tank battalion.

Marine divisions are among the world's largest, with a total strength of 14,000 Marines and 932 Navy personnel. The figures at the end of this chapter show the nominal Marine division organization. The division totals vary in actual units because of differing organizations of artillery regiments, tank battalions, and assault amphibian battalions.

Marine divisions are generally considered to be "light" or

1. Previously, Marine detachments were provided to battleships as well as heavy cruisers and submarine tenders, the latter to provide security for nuclear warheads.
2. At the time of the demise of the Soviet Union, in December 1991, the Soviet Naval Infantry, or marines, consisted of some 18,000 troops. However, in the late 1980s four motorized rifle divisions of the Soviet Ground Forces had been transferred to the Navy and, with the Naval Infantry and Navy-controlled Coastal Missile-Artillery Force (some 14,000 troops), formed the Coastal Defense Force within the naval establishment.
   The next largest Marine forces are those of China, with an estimated 50,000+ troops; Taiwan, with 39,000; Vietnam, with 27,000; South Korea, with 25,000; and Thailand, with 20,000. Britain's Royal Marines has a strength of some 7,700.
3. In 1988–1989 eight Marine battalions, designated as MEU (Special Operations Capable) were provided with a fourth rifle company. However, the drawdown of Marine strength forced a reduction to three rifle companies in those battalions during 1991.

MAGTF ORGANIZATIONS

	Marine Expeditionary Unit (MEU)	Marine Expeditionary Brigade (MEB)	Marine Expeditionary Force (MEF)	Special Purpose Force (SPF)
Total personnel	1,000–4,000	4,000–18,000	30,000–60,000	100–1,000
Commander	colonel	brigadier general	lieutenant general	varies
Ground combat element	infantry battalion	infantry regiment	one or more divisions	rifle company
Aviation combat element	composite squadron (helicopters + STOVL)	aircraft group	aircraft wing	aviation detachment
Combat service support element	MEU service support group	brigade service support group	force service support group	combat service support detachment
Self-sustainment capability*	15 days	30 days	60 days	as required
Amphibious lift	4–6 ships	21–26 ships	approx. 50 ships	varies
Major equipment	5 tanks 8 155-mm howitzers 8 81-mm mortars 9 60-mm mortars 32 Dragon anti-tank launchers 8 TOW anti-tank launchers** 12 assault amphibian vehicles 5 Stinger SAM teams 6 fixed-wing aircraft (STOVL) ~20 helicopters	17 tanks 24 155-mm howitzers 6 8-inch (203-mm) howitzers 24 81-mm mortars 27 60-mm mortars 96 Dragon anti-tank launchers 48 TOW anti-tank launchers 47 assault amphibian vehicles 36 light armored vehicles 6 Hawk SAM launchers 15 Stinger SAM teams ~75 fixed-wing aircraft ~100 helicopters	70 tanks 108 155-mm howitzers 12 8-inch (203-mm) howitzers 72 81-mm mortars 81 60-mm mortars 288 Dragon anti-tank launchers 144 TOW anti-tank launchers 208 assault amphibian vehicles 147 light armored vehicles 24 Hawk SAM launchers 75 Stinger SAM teams ~150 fixed-wing aircraft ~150 helicopters	varies

*Varies with tactical situation, level of combat, etc.
**Additional TOW launchers are mounted on AH-1 SeaCobra helicopters.

"mechanized" combat units. There are currently only two active tank battalions (44 tanks each) and two reserve battalions (8 tanks each); each of the three divisions has a light armored vehicle battalion.[4] This limited number of armored vehicles and the lack of armored personnel carriers reduces the effectiveness of Marine units against heavily armored forces. The Marines do use AAV-series tracked amphibious vehicles for battlefield transport; however, those vehicles are limited in that role (see chapter 20).

After the Gulf War the Marine Corps reorganized the division structure to consist of some 14,000 Marines (plus Navy personnel), a reduction of almost 4,000 troops per division. The new divisions have enhanced reconnaissance capabilities, an increased number of Light Armored Vehicles (LAV), and the Multiple-Launch Rocket System (MLRS).

The three Marine artillery regiments (10th, 11th, and 12th Marines) were reorganized in late 1992, with each regiment being assigned three or four direct support battalions and each battalion having three firing batteries with six M198 155-mm howitzers. In addition to the M198 heavy towed howitzers, each MEF has available 48 M101A1 105-mm towed howitzers for use in special contingencies where the 16,000-pound (7,258-kg) M198s are not suitable. The present plan is to retain the M198s in artillery battalions until the Marine Corps receives the lightweight 155-mm howitzer, which weighs less than 9,000 pounds (4,082 kg).[5]

The Marine Corps does not have medical, dental, or chaplain personnel, but relies upon the Navy to provide these services. These Navy personnel are fully integrated into Marine units and, when in the field, dress in Marine uniforms. In turn, Marine representatives are assigned to all appropriate Navy staffs, including those of the Secretary of the Navy and the Office of the Chief of Naval Operations (OPNAV). A Marine major general serves as the Director Expeditionary Warfare (code N85) in OPNAV, and the lieutenant general who serves as Deputy Chief of Staff for Aviation at Marine Headquarters is additionally assigned as the Principal Advisor, Marine Aviation (code N88M) to the Director of the Air Warfare Division in OPNAV.

General Charles C. Krulak, USMC, Commandant of the Marine Corps since July 1995. (Department of Defense, R. D. Ward)

MARINE FORCE ORGANIZATION

The Marine Forces are the amphibious assault component of what are now called Naval Expeditionary Forces: Marine assault units, amphibious ships, supporting carrier task forces, and other forces required to project American military power by sea.

The combined arms Marine Air-Ground Task Forces (MAGTF) can be tailored to the size and composition required to meet a broad range of operational requirements, and for transport by various methods. There are four generic types of MAGTFs:

Marine Expeditionary Unit (MEU)
Marine Expeditionary Brigade (MEB)
Marine Expeditionary Force (MEF)
Special Purpose Force (SPF)

During the 1980s some MEUs underwent special training and qualifications to be designated as Special Operations Capable (SOC); that qualification was dropped in late 1991. Each MAGTF has four fundamental elements that are drawn from the ground divisions, aircraft wings, and support groups as needed; those elements are shown in the figure below.

The buildup of MAGTFs from the component "building blocks" is not linear. For example, while a Marine regiment and aircraft group are the ground and air elements of a Marine Expeditionary Brigade, a division-wing team cannot form three MEBs because of the shortfall of command and support units. Thus, the Marine Forces, with three divisions and three wings, can effectively deploy two MEFs or perhaps four MEBs, plus some smaller units.

NOTIONAL MARINE AIR-GROUND TASK FORCE STRUCTURE

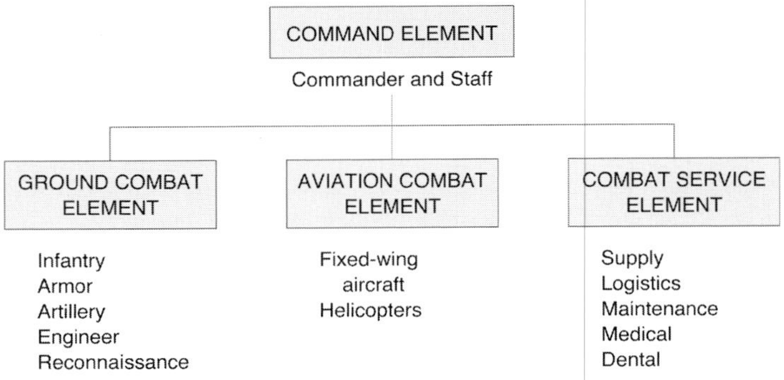

MARINE CORPS DIVISION

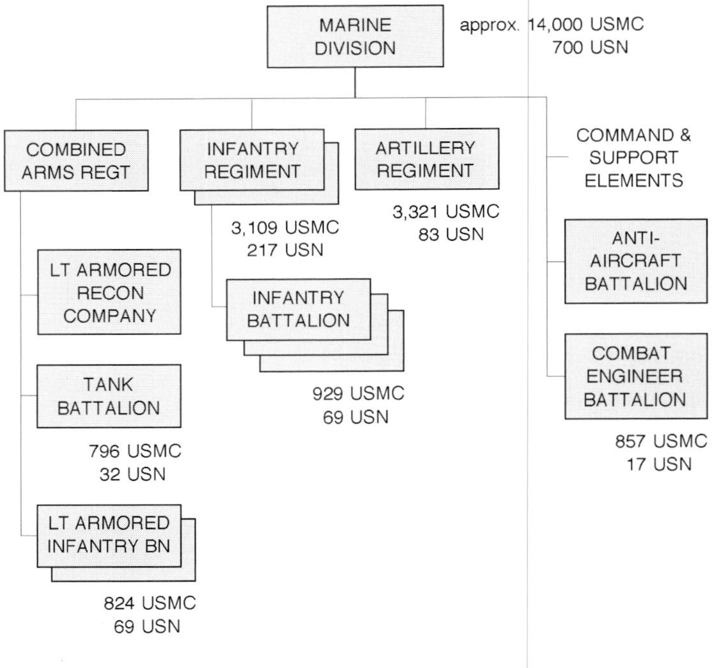

The Special Purpose Force (SPF) units are employed for both conventional and "unconventional" operations; they can be deployed into forward areas by aircraft, surface ships, or the Navy's transport submarines.

Originally the MAGTFs, when established in the late 1970s, were not permanent organizations, but were to be "task organized for a specific mission and, after completion of that mission, dissolved."[6] In

4. The Marines currently have some 271 M1A1 tanks: 30 afloat with each of the three Maritime Prepositioning Squadrons; 116 in active tank battalions; 16 in reserve tank battalions; and 47 for pipeline, training, and war reserves.
5. The M198 can be helicopter lifted only by the CH-53E Super Stallion. The lightweight LW 155 gun can be lifted by the CH-46 Sea Knight and CH-53D Sea Stallion helicopters as well as the CH-53E.

6. Commanding General, Marine Corps Development and Educational Command, *Marine Air-Ground Task Force Doctrine* (FMFM 0–1) (Quantico, Va., June 1978), p. 1–5.

MARINE INFANTRY REGIMENT

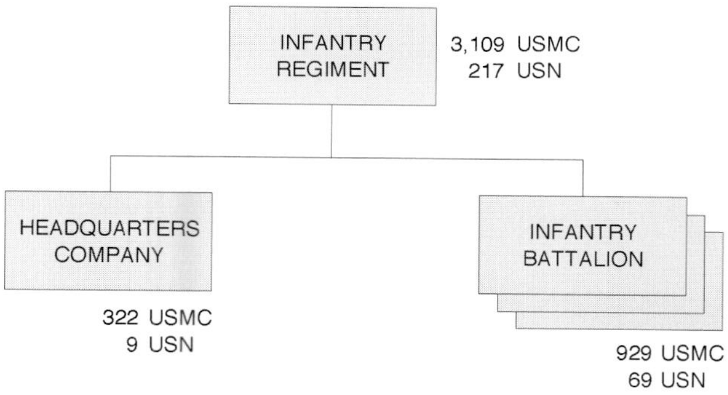

MARINE INFANTRY BATTALION

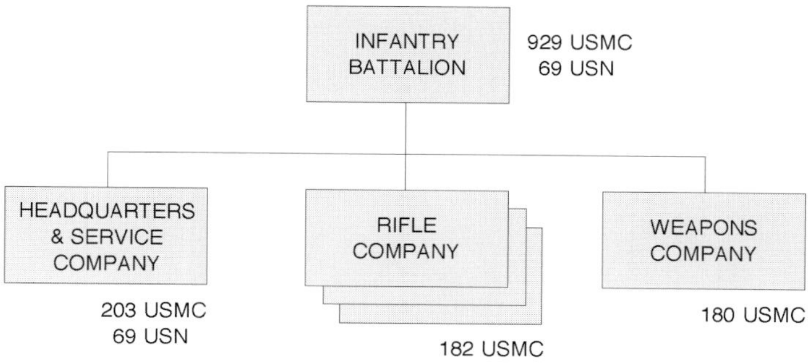

NOMINAL MARINE ARTILLERY REGIMENT

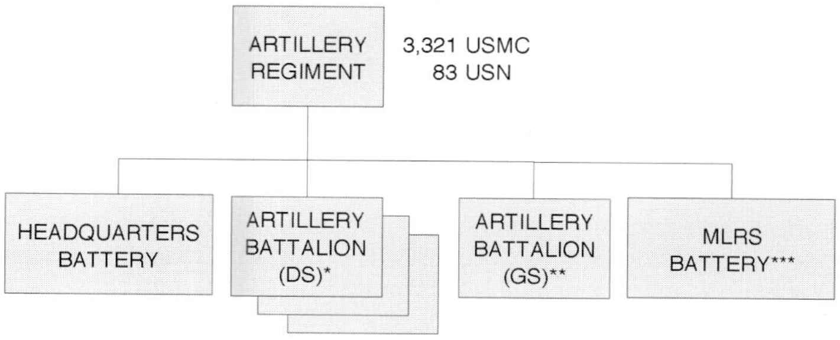

Notes: *DS = Direct Support; 24 M198 155-mm towed howitzers per battalion.
**GS = General Support; 12 M109A3 self-propelled 155-mm howitzers and 12 M110A2 8-inch (203-mm) self-propelled howitzers.
***MLRS = Multiple-Launch Rocket System; 9 self-propelled MLRS launchers attached to some artillery regiments.

the 1980s the MAGTF units took on an increasingly permanent structure. This shift came in large part because of commitments to "marrying" Marine combat units with weapons and material in Maritime Prepositioning Ships (MPS) deployed in various ocean areas and prepositioned ashore in Norway. The permanent assignment of MAGTFs to specific prepositioned equipment and to specific geographic areas has reduced the flexibility of Marine units.

During 1992, as a consequence of force-level reductions and the lessons learned in Desert Shield and Desert Storm, the Marine Corps began to reform their MAGTF structure. Since 1982 a total of 15 permanent MAGTF command elements have been formed: 3 MEFs, 6 MEBs, and 6 MEUs. With the cutback in personnel strength, all six standing brigade-level (MEB) command elements have been deactivated. Instead, when Marine units larger than MEUs deploy they will be commanded by a forward component of the MEF command element. In a related move, the staffs of the I and II MEF headquarters have been expanded; the III MEF has been deactivated, having been replaced by the I MEF (Forward) command element, which retains all of the functions previously found in the III MEF.

The standing MEUs are the 11th, 13th, 15th, and 31st in MARFOR Pacific, and the 22nd, 24th, and 26th in MARFOR Atlantic.

MARINE SECURITY FORCES

The Marine Corps Security Force (MCSF) provides security force detachments on board all active aircraft carriers, at various ammunition storage sites, at major bases in the United States and overseas, at the Naval Academy in Annapolis, Maryland, and at U.S. embassies and consulates abroad. Approximately 200 officers and 5,000 enlisted men and women are assigned to the MCSF.

On board aircraft carriers the Marines primarily serve as the cadre for a landing force, and they perform ceremonial functions. The standard detachment on aircraft carriers is 1 officer and 25 enlisted. (Prior to the early 1990s force reductions, Marine carrier detachments numbered 2 officers and 64 enlisted; beyond their current duties, the detachment was also responsible for the security of on-board nuclear weapons.)

The security companies, detachments, and "barracks" at more than 100 locations vary considerably in size. The largest such units are the Marine barracks at the Guantánamo Bay (Cuba) naval base and Washington, D.C. The "Gitmo" barracks, commanded by a colonel, has 21 officers and 323 enlisted personnel. In addition to base security, that barracks has the responsibility for safeguarding refugees who are incarcerated at the base.[7]

The barracks at Washington, D.C., also commanded by a colonel, has 54 officers and 1,000 enlisted personnel. The Marines at the historic 8th and I Street barracks have several assignments in addition to security at the nearby Washington Navy Yard and White House duties. The other MCSF units that survive as barracks are at the Naval Academy in Annapolis, Maryland, and in Yokosuka, Japan.

The current MCSF structure was established in late 1987 in response to a directive by the Secretary of the Navy for the reorganization of naval security forces to meet the growing threat of terrorism and to strengthen the Navy Department's ability to detect and defeat attacks targeted at military personnel and their families. The Marine Corps responded by creating two MCSF battalions—Atlantic and Pacific—to supervise the operations of companies and detachments at shore bases around the world. Only the Atlantic battalion survives; its headquarters are in Norfolk, Virginia. (The Pacific battalion had its headquarters at Mare Island, California.)

In addition to the companies and detachments that safeguard various shore facilities, the MCSF battalion also has a Fleet Antiterrorism Security Team (FAST) company of 8 officers and 313 enlisted men. The FAST unit is specially trained and equipped to rescue hostages and contain terrorists. The battalion has a special school to instruct personnel in counter-terrorist operations.

MARINE FORCE MOBILITY

Mobility is a principle of naval operations and is a key characteristic of the Fleet Marine Forces. There are several aspects to FMF mobility:

Forward afloat forces. Marine units are normally afloat in amphibious ships in forward areas. Normally, one MEU is afloat in the Mediterranean area and one in the Pacific–Indian Ocean area; at times, additional MEUs or larger formations are at sea, in transit to relieve forward-deployed MEUs, or involved in exercises. As a crisis begins to evolve, the afloat MEUs, like other naval forces, can be dispatched to the problem area without creating an intrusion in foreign territory or air space.

Amphibious assault. The Marines have a significant amphibious assault capability when they employ helicopters, landing craft, and vehicles from the Navy's amphibious ships (see chapter 19). The existing amphibious force has a theoretical lift capacity equivalent to the assault echelon of approximately one MEF, i.e., a reinforced division and the helicopter and STOVL portions of an aircraft wing.[8] (The "assault echelon" is the portion of the force that makes the actual

---

7. The Guantánamo barracks was the subject of the movie *A Few Good Men,* starring Jack Nicholson and Tom Cruise.

8. The term VSTOL for Vertical/Short Take-Off and Landing was used by the Marine Corps until early 1995, when the less accurate term STOVL was adopted by Headquarters, Marine Corps.

Marines come ashore during an exercise featuring the traditional over-the-beach assault technique. An LCAC and LCM are behind them. Such amphibious techniques are outmoded in the era of widely proliferated guided weapons and naval and ground mines. (U.S. Navy, PHC Jeff Elliott)

landing; that is, about two-thirds of the troops, one-half the vehicles, and one-quarter of the cargo of the unit.)

Recent reductions in the Fleet have seen a decline in the lift capacity to only 2½ MEBs, i.e., reinforced regiments. More budget reductions could further reduce this lift capacity.

Maritime prepositioning. Three squadrons of Maritime Prepositioning Ships (MPS) are forward deployed: one in the Atlantic, one off Diego Garcia in the Indian Ocean, and one off the Mariana Islands in the Western Pacific. Each MPS squadron carries weapons, vehicles, equipment, munitions, and provisions for a MEB (see chapter 8). These ships can be sent into a port to be "married" with Marines flown into the area by transport aircraft. While this force does not have the ability to make a forcible entry—it requires a friendly port or sheltered unloading area and nearby airfield—the viability of the MPS concept was nevertheless demonstrated in Operation Desert Shield in August 1991.

Airlift. Marines, as with other light combat forces, can be airlifted into an area by transport aircraft. The Marine Corps has a small force of C-130 Hercules transport-tanker aircraft, but a sizable troop commitment would require the use of U.S. Air Force transport aircraft.

Aircraft carriers. In 1992 the U.S. Atlantic Command began examining the feasibility of putting Marine *ground* combat troops aboard large-deck carriers. The rationale for such a move was reported as:

- To better justify large-deck carriers by giving them an assault capability.
- To provide more fleet flexibility by being able to rapidly embark a Marine assault force in a carrier.
- To provide an assault capability in an area without deploying an amphibious ready group, i.e., three to five amphibious ships with a MEU of some 2,000 Marines embarked.

Accordingly, in mid-January 1993, 538 Marines embarked in the carrier THEODORE ROOSEVELT (CVN 71) for a month of at-sea training and workup. Designated as a Special-Purpose Marine Air-Ground Task Force (SPMAGTF), the Marines consisted of a rifle company (190 men) from the 3rd Battalion, 6th Marines; a command staff and various detachments, including an 18-man reconnaissance platoon; and a heavy helicopter squadron (HMH-362) with a component from a utility and attack helicopter squadron (HMLA-167) with six CH-53 Sea Stallion and four UH-1N Huey helicopters.[9]

Following the month-long workup, the ROOSEVELT battle group departed Norfolk on 11 March 1993, steaming for the Mediterranean and a six-month forward deployment as a component of the Sixth Fleet. Aboard the ROOSEVELT—in addition to the 638 Marines—was Carrier Air Wing (CVW) 8. To make space for the Marines and their helicopters, CVW 8 left on the beach Air Anti-Submarine Squadron 24, the wing's S-3B Vikings. Also, Marine squadron VMFA-312, with F/A-18C Hornets, was embarked in the ship in place of the second F-14 Tomcat squadron of CVW 8.

The loss of the Vikings was of particular concern to some Navy planners because of their anti-submarine prowess, but also their effectiveness for general surveillance and their value as tankers for extending the range of the Hornets. The two latter roles were of particular importance as the ROOSEVELT operated in the Adriatic Sea area, supporting the efforts to stop the racial fighting in former Yugoslavia.

Although the Atlantic Command had at one point envisioned the Marines aboard the ROOSEVELT as a substitution for an Amphibious Ready Group (ARG), in fact an ARG with a MEU embarked was also deployed in the Med. But the focus was on the ROOSEVELT and the 600-man SPMAGTF.

The ROOSEVELT deployment identified a number of problems with Marines aboard large-deck carriers. These included:

Tactical: Under the new doctrine articulated in the Navy's 1992 policy statement . . . *From the Sea,* the Navy and Marine Corps will "respond to crises and can provide the initial, 'enabling' capability for joint operations in conflict—as well as continued participation in any

9. The aviation personnel totaled about 230 men.

sustained effort." In this context, the forward-deployed Marines are referred to as the "tip of the spear" of the enabling forces. The concerns about the ROOSEVELT operation centered on that "tip" being 190 Marine riflemen, too small a force to be effective at essentially any level of crisis or conflict. Their largest organic weapons were three 60-mm mortars, six 7.62-mm machine guns, and a few anti-tank weapons—far too few to counter any significant Third World opposition.

The argument had been made that support for the SPMAGTF rifle company is an entire carrier air wing. However, this response assumed that the carrier would remain within tactical range of the Marines ashore (see below) and that weather and visibility would permit the carrier aircraft to fly close air support missions.

ACTIVE MARINE CORPS BASING
Camp H.M. Smith, Hawaii
Headquarters Marine Force Pacific
Kaneohe, Hawaii
 3rd Marine Regiment (infantry)
 1st MAW Aviation Support Element (formerly Marine Aircraft Group 24)
Camp Pendleton, Calif.
Headquarters I Marine Expeditionary Force
1st Marine Division
 1st, 5th Marine Regiments (infantry)
 11th Marine Regiment (artillery)
 Marine Aircraft Group 39
 1st Combat Engineer Battalion
 3rd Assault Amphibian Battalion
1st Force Service Support Group
Twenty-nine Palms, Calif.
 7th Marine Regiment (infantry)
 3rd Tank Battalion
 3rd AA Battalion
El Toro, Calif.
3rd Marine Aircraft Wing
 Marine Aircraft Group 11
Tustin, Calif.
 Marine Aircraft Group 16
Yuma, Ariz.
 Marine Aircraft Group 13
Okinawa
Headquarters III Marine Expeditionary Force (Camp Courtney)
3rd Marine Division
 4th Regiment (infantry)
1st Marine Aircraft Wing
 Marine Aircraft Group 36 (Futenma)
3rd Force Service Support Group
Iwakuni, Japan
 Marine Aircraft Group 12
Norfolk, Va.
Headquarters 4th Marine Expeditionary Brigade (Little Creek)
Camp Lejeune, N.C.
Headquarters Marine Force Atlantic
Headquarters II Marine Expeditionary Force
2nd Marine Division
 2nd, 6th, 8th Marine Regiments (infantry)
 10th Marine Regiment (artillery)
 2nd Tank Battalion
 2nd Assault Amphibian Battalion
 2nd Combat Engineer Battalion
2nd Force Service Support Group
Cherry Point, N.C.
2nd Marine Aircraft Wing
 Marine Aircraft Group 14
New River, N.C.
 Marine Aircraft Groups 26, 29
Beaufort, S.C.
 Marine Aircraft Group 31

RESERVE MARINE CORPS BASING
New Orleans, La.
Headquarters Marine Forces Reserve
4th Marine Division
4th Marine Aircraft Wing
4th Force Service Support Group
Willow Grove, Pa.
 Marine Aircraft Group 49
Marietta, Ga.
 Marine Aircraft Group 42
Dallas, Texas
 14th Marine Regiment (artillery)
 Marine Aircraft Group 41
Overland Park, Kan.
 Reserve Support Command
San Rafael, Calif.
 23rd Marine Regiment
Miramar, Calif.
 Marine Aircraft Group 46
Kansas City, Mo.
 24th Marine Regiment
Worcester, Mass.
 25th Marine Regiment
Glenview, Ill.
 Marine Air Control Group 48
Selfridge, Mich.
 Marine Wing Service Group 47

Such a force had little real combat capability, and there was fear that Navy and national planners would commit the small force to a situation far beyond its capabilities. As a senior Marine officer remarked to the author, "this concept could get 600 lightly armed people in trouble in a heartbeat."

Support: With their limited cargo helicopter capability (six CH-53Ds), even in suitable flying weather the Marines on the ROOSEVELT could not bring ashore heavy trucks and other equipment. While ARGs have helicopters for landing troops, including the heavy lift CH-53E Super Stallion, they also have air cushion landing craft (LCAC), conventional landing craft (LCM/LCU), and tracked amphibian vehicles (AAV) that could provide seaborne logistics to the troops ashore, regardless of weather conditions.

Operational: The aircraft carrier with its air wing is one of the most flexible and mobile weapon systems in existence. Should the SPMAGTF be lifted ashore, would the battle group commander be required to remain in the area to provide air support—and possibly air evacuation—for the Marines?

The carrier's flight deck situation also became a problem. Carrier flight decks operate on the basis of launch and recovery cycles that are quite different from the helicopter carriers in which Marines embarked. This caused major difficulties for the flight deck crewmen when the Marine aviators wanted to spread rotors and fly between the normal aircraft cycles.

Political: Possibly most significant in the long term, it was unlikely that embarking the Marines in large-deck carriers would have little or no positive impact on justifying carrier force levels. *If* successful, the concept could have led politicians to reconsider the construction of additional amphibious ships, believing that carriers with Marines on board could substitute for new "amphibs."

Certainly there were benefits to be gained and lessons to be learned from experiments such as placing the SPMAGTF aboard the ROOSEVELT. However, the costs and disadvantages far outweighed the benefits and the concept was discontinued.

MARINE OPERATIONS

The Marines had a major role in the U.S. buildup in the Middle East from August 1990 (Operation Desert Shield) and the subsequent war with Iraq in early 1991 (Operation Desert Storm). With fears that Iraq would launch an assault on Saudi Arabia immediately after consolidating its position in Kuwait, in early August 1990 the President ordered the deployment of U.S. combat forces into Saudi Arabia.

The first squadron of prepositioning ships arrived at the port of Al Jubayl, Saudi Arabia, on 15 August 1991 and were met by troops of the 7th MEB (based on the 7th Marines), who had been airlifted from Twenty-nine Palms, California.[10] Additional Marines followed, by air and sea, with all three MPS squadrons unloading their material in Saudi Arabia. When the Gulf War began on 17 January 1991, there were 76,000 Marines "in country" in the 1st and 2nd Marine Divisions, with a massive Marine air force consolidated under the 3rd Marine Aircraft Wing and a large support establishment designated as the 1st Force Service Support Group. The Marine air component in Desert Storm—both on amphibious ships and ashore—totaled 20 fixed-wing and 24 helicopter squadrons, plus detachments of other aviation units.

The entire Marine force within Saudi Arabia was under the command of the I Marine Expeditionary Force, with the commanding general, Lieutenant General Walter E. Boomer, also serving as Commander, U.S. Marine Force Central Command (MARCENT). Separate from this command were the 17,000 Marines on board 31 amphibious ships in the Persian Gulf. This afloat force consisted of two separate Marine brigades (4th and 5th MEBs), plus a separate MEU. For political reasons there was no overall Marine commander assigned for the afloat force, which represented the largest amphibious task force assembled since World War II. (Another 5,000 Marines were embarked in amphibious ships in the Eastern Mediterranean.)

10. These were the ships of Maritime Prepositioning Squadron 2. They had been anchored at Diego Garcia in the Indian Ocean and were ordered on 8 August to get under way for the Persian Gulf.

Marines share the THEODORE ROOSEVELT's flight deck with a part of the carrier's air wing. Whereas the experiment demonstrated that these "soldiers of the sea" are not really at home on large-deck carriers, the flexibility of aircraft carriers was shown once again. (U.S. Navy)

During the ground assault against occupied Kuwait and Iraq, the I MEF was to the right wing of the allied line and saw considerable combat. The Marines' shortfall in armored vehicles was a major consideration to allied planners, however, and an Army tank brigade was attached to the I MEF and, in the field, some Marine units also exchanged their M60A1 tanks for the new M1A1 Abrams tank.[11]

Although the 17,000 afloat Marines were not employed in an amphibious assault, the threat of such a landing did force the Iraqi high command to deploy several frontline divisions along the coast of Kuwait and away from the main line of defense along the Kuwaiti border. During January 1991, the 5th MEB was landed some 20 miles (32 km) south of the Kuwait-Saudi border, behind the advancing I MEF. Eight air cushion landing craft (LCAC) brought ashore 7,300 Marines along with almost 2,400 tons of vehicles and weapons in less than 24 hours; the ship-to-shore transfer required 55 trips by the LCACs, made in heavy seas with 40-knot winds. Portions of the 4th MEB were subsequently brought ashore.

During Operations Desert Shield/Desert Storm some 85 percent of the Fleet Marine Force was deployed to Southwest Asia; 25,710 men and women of the Marine Corps Reserve—61 percent of that force—were mobilized in that period, with many of them sent into the desert with their active-duty counterparts. Then-Commandant A. M. (Al) Gray declared: "There are four kinds of Marines: those in Saudi Arabia, those going to Saudi Arabia, those who want to go to Saudi Arabia, and those who don't want to go to Saudi Arabia but are going anyway!"

Simultaneous with Desert Shield, a Navy-Marine amphibious force remained off the coast of strife-torn Liberia for seven months, providing security for the U.S. embassy in Sierra Leone. During that operation—code named Sharp Edge—the Marines helped evacuate 2,400 American diplomats and citizens. A small Navy amphibious force, with an escorting destroyer, remained off Liberia from the end of May 1990 until early December.

During the buildup in the Persian Gulf, the political crisis in Somalia boiled over. At the urgent request of the U.S. ambassador in Mogadishu, in the pre-dawn darkness of 4 January 1991, two Marine CH-53E Super Stallion helicopters took off from an amphibious ship and carried 70 Marines on a 460-n.mile (852-km) flight to Mogadishu. The CH-53E flight was made with in-flight refuelings from Marine KC-130 tankers. The Marines helped secure the embassy, and then the helicopters shuttled out 260 American diplomats and foreign nationals to the amphibious ships GUAM (LPH 9) and TRENTON (LPD 14) to conclude the successful operation, given the code name Eastern Exit.

Following Operation Desert Shield, Navy-Marine amphibious forces were engaged in humanitarian assistance to Kurds in northern Iraq, and in assisting survivors of the flooding in Bangladesh.

Subsequently, the frustrating U.S. attempts to help alleviate the starvation and gang-rule in Ethiopia saw Marines at the forefront of American activities in that ravaged country. While no combat was involved in that humanitarian action, Marines were involved in conflicts with local gangs. After an Army patrol suffered heavy casualties—and with the hunger situation partially alleviated—U.S. forces were hurriedly withdrawn. (The 1992–1994 Somalia operation was an international effort in which large contingents of French and Italian military forces participated.)

With the decision to have U.S. forces support United Nations/North Atlantic Treaty Organization activities in the Bosnian civil war, Marine F/A-18 Hornet strike fighters have been based on a continuous basis at Aviano, Italy, since April 1994. Periodically, Marine EA-6B Prowlers, as well as Navy Prowlers, have flown from the NATO base. In addition, Marine aircraft have flown from carriers operating in the Adriatic Sea, with a Marine MEU embarked in an amphibious ready group in the Mediterranean-Adriatic area.

When the Air Force F-16 fighter pilot Captain Scott O'Grady was shot down by a surface-to-air missile over western Bosnia-Herzegovina on 2 June 1995, the intrepid aviator was able to evade

11. The Marine Corps completed transition from the M60 to the M1A1 tank in mid-1992.

capture for six days until he was rescued—by Marines. A TRAP (Tactical Recovery of Aircraft and Personnel) mission was mounted by Marines flying from the helicopter carrier KEARSARGE (LHD 3), operating in the Adriatic. Early on the morning of 8 June, CH-53Es lifted off the KEARSARGE's deck, escorted by helicopter gunships and fixed-wing aircraft. They flew the 87 miles (140 km) to the downed pilot's location, pinpointed by his survival-radio transmissions. Although the Western press played up O'Grady as a hero, the real heroes were the 57 Marines and 4 Navy hospital corpsmen who flew in to successfully evacuate him. The operation was completed without casualties.

MARINE FORCES RESERVE

The Marine Forces Reserve (formerly Marine Corps Reserve) consists of the 4th Marine Division, 4th Marine Aircraft Wing, and 4th Force Service Support Group. These units generally parallel active units in organization, but in some categories they have older equipment and lack several service support components. Based on command problems during the reserve call-up in Desert Shield and Desert Storm, the Marine Corps reorganized its reserves in 1992 under one command structure. The Marine Forces Reserve oversees the training, equipping, and leadership of the Marine reserve components.

The principal Marine Forces Reserve units and their basing are shown in the accompanying box.

Marine reservists have training sessions on a weekly or monthly basis, and for two weeks during the summer. The latter periods include participation in exercises with active units in the United States and overseas.

In 1996 the Marine Forces Reserve had 9,400 officers and 99,200 enlisted personnel in a ready-reserve status; of these, 3,850 officers and 36,860 enlisted are assigned to reserve units, i.e., Selected Marine Forces Reserve.

Historical: The Marine Corps was established on 10 November 1775 by the Continental Congress, which called for two battalions of troops to be raised who were "good seamen, or so acquainted with maritime affairs as to be able to serve to advantage by sea, when required." Subsequently, Marines have fought at sea and ashore in almost all American conflicts. The Corps reached a peak strength of 485,000 men and women during World War II, with six divisions and five aircraft wings (plus numerous separate squadrons).

During the 1950s the United States began the practice of maintaining battalion landing teams (and later MEUs) afloat, embarked in amphibious ships that tranversed the Mediterranean, the Western Pacific, and, at times, the Caribbean and Persian Gulf areas.

From its beginning, the Marine Corps has been a separate service within the Navy Department. The senior Marine officer is the Commandant, holding the rank of full general. He is a member of the Joint Chiefs of Staff (JCS), and, although responsible for the readiness and training of the Marine Corps, he does not have operational command of Marine combat forces except as specifically assigned by the JCS or the Secretary of Defense. Rather, the senior organizational commands of the Marine Corps—Marine Forces in the Atlantic and Pacific Fleets—are essentially "type" commands within those two fleets.

Marines on the stern of the transport submarine KAMEHAMEHA (SSBN 642) recover a Combat Rubber Raiding Craft (CRRC) after an exercise. The KAMEHAMEHA is one of two ex-Polaris submarines engaged in this role (see chapter 12). In addition, several submarines of the STURGEON (SSN 637) class regularly operate with Marines as well as SEALs and other special forces. (U.S. Marine Corps, Cpl. Robert A. Berry)

CHAPTER 8

Military Sealift Command

The surveying ship PATHFINDER (T-AGS 60) represents one of the Military Sealift Command's newest special mission support ships. Although this force is being reduced in size, a limited modernization program is under way. These ships support all of the armed services as well as some civilian agencies. (Leo Van Ginderen collection)

Sealift is the term used for the movement of weapons and matériel to forward areas by sea. This aspect of strategic mobility is of increasing importance for future U.S. participation in world affairs as U.S. overseas bases are closed down and the number of troops abroad is reduced. The United States in the late 1990s will have fewer bases and troops abroad than at any time since mid-1950, the eve of the Korean War. While troops can be flown into forward areas, it is prohibitive to consider airlift for overseas buildups in terms of tanks, munitions, fuel, and other war matériel. For example, a C-5 Galaxy cargo aircraft, flying from the United States to the Middle East, can carry but a single M1-series main battle tank.

The Military Sealift Command (MSC) operates a variety of ships for the Department of Defense and for the Navy. Under this dual-command concept, the Military Sealift Command is responsible for the operation of several categories of ships: (1) strategic sealift, (2) naval fleet auxiliary force, and (3) special mission support force. These are three diverse, relatively large, and important maritime activities.

STRATEGIC SEALIFT

The Military Sealift Command is responsible for the ocean transport for all Department of Defense materials and supplies. This mission is the command's predominant task in terms of numbers of ships and people, and dollars expended. Further, the strategic sealift is currently undergoing a large-scale expansion with the procurement of 19 Large Medium-Speed Roll-On/Roll-Off (LMSR) cargo ships as well as additional ships for the Afloat Prepositioning Force (APF). These programs are intended primarily to support Army troops, improving their rapid-response capabilities.

Strategic sealift ships are described in chapter 24 of this edition of *Ships and Aircraft*.

There are three basic categories of strategic sealift ships:

Active. These are operational ships, generally at sea, under long-term charter by the MSC as well as the Maritime Prepositioning Ships (MPS) that carry weapons, equipment, and vehicles for the Marine Corps and the APF ships that carry matériel for the Army, Navy, and Air Force.

The three Marine MPS squadrons embark the equipment and supplies for a Marine Expeditionary Brigade (MEB), sufficient for sustaining up to 17,000 Marines for up to 30 days, depending upon the level of combat. A 14th ship is being procured with fiscal 1995 funds for this force. MPS Squadron 1, with four ships, is normally based in the Atlantic area, off the Azores; MPS Squadron 2, with five ships, at Diego Garcia in the Indian Ocean; and MPS Squadron 3, with four ships, in the Pacific, at Guam. In 1994 some ships of MPS Squadron 1 were moved into the Mediterranean in conjunction with U.S. contingency plans for participating in the Bosnian conflict.

The MPS concept has now been adopted by the Army, with the MSC deploying eight prepositioning ships at Guam to support an Army armored brigade for 15 days of combat operations. These are seven Roll-On/Roll-Off (RO/RO) ships and one crane ship, the GOPHER STATE (T-ACS 4).[1] This force is referred to as the Army War Reserve (AWR) 3 program. These are interim ships, to be replaced by the specially constructed LMSR ships. When the LMSRs become available, the interim-AWR ships will be returned to Ready Reserve Force (RRF) status.

The APF ships are located at Diego Garcia and in the Mediterranean. These consist of eight cargo ships—loaded with munitions, a 500-bed field hospital, and military equipment—and two fully laden tankers.

The MPS-APF ships steam toward ports available in the crisis area at the first indication of trouble. Simultaneously, troops are airlifted to bases near the ports to "marry up" with the matériel as it is unloaded. Thus, unlike amphibious assaults, MPS-APF operations require an available port (or at least sheltered anchorage), and adjacent airfield, in a permissive environment.[2] The RRF ships include several crane

1. Along with munitions, supplies, spare parts, lubricants, and other equipment, these ships carry:

   123 M1A1 Abrams main battle tanks
   154 Bradley armored fighting vehicles
   100 armored personnel carriers
   24 self-propelled 155-mm howitzers
   9 Multiple-Launch Rocket Systems (MLRS)

2. The forward-deployment concept was first introduced by Secretary of Defense Robert S. McNamara in the mid-1960s, when he proposed that a force of 30 Fast Deployment Logistic (FDL) ships be constructed in addition to a force of long-range transport aircraft. Congress refused to fund the FDL ships, but the aircraft were developed, i.e., the C-5 Galaxy program. However, the Department of Defense did modify several existing cargo ships and tank landing ships (LST) to be forward deployed, carrying munitions and supplies.

MSC COMMAND RELATIONSHIPS

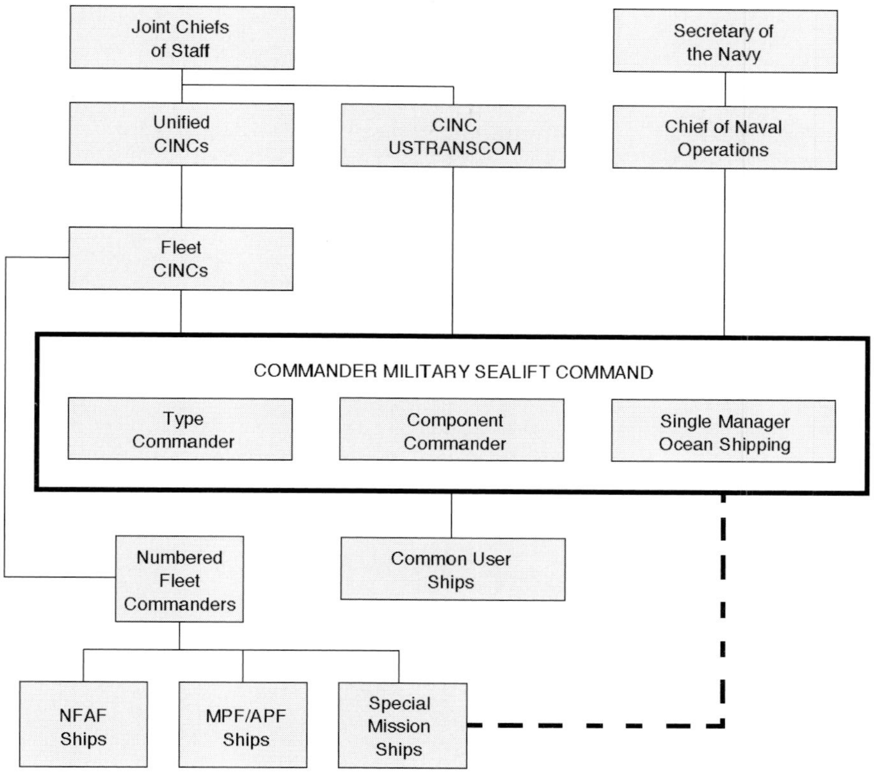

ships (T-ACS) that have heavy cranes for unloading main battle tanks; those ships can also carry break-bulk and containerized cargo.

Inactive. These are the eight Fast Sealift Ships (FSS) and a large number of merchant-type ships in the RRF. The FSS-type ships—converted SL-7 merchant ships—have partial crews on board and are designed to begin loading troops at U.S. East Coast and Gulf ports within 96 hours of an alert (see *Operational* notes). There are 75 cargo ships and two troop ships in RRF status (in addition to ten RRF ships that are currently assigned to the APF and AWR programs). The RRF ships consist of 22 RO/RO vehicle cargo ships, with small crews aboard, on a four-day standby; some 25 other ships in a 10- to 20-day readiness status; and almost 30 more ships maintained in a 30-day readiness condition.

There are also four highly specialized ships in this category: two hospital ships (T-AH) and two aviation support ships (T-AVB).

National Defense Reserve Fleet. These are older merchant ships laid up in the Maritime Administration's National Defense Reserve Fleet (NDRF). These NDRF ships receive far less maintenance than the RRF ships, and they require between 30 and 120 days of work to reactivate them. In a 1985 test two ships, the American Victory and Hattiesburg Victory, were reactivated in 60 days and 108 days, respectively; those were among the NDRF's World War II–built Victory ships in best condition. Few of these ships remain, and their usefulness is doubtful because of their limited cargo capacity, slow speed, and generally poor condition.

Operational: During the U.S. buildup in the Middle East from August 1990 to January 1991 (Operation Desert Shield), MSC-operated or chartered ships carried 95 percent (by weight) of the war matériel moved into the Middle East from the United States and Europe. Undertaken in five months and without hostile interference, it was the largest U.S. military buildup for a single campaign since World War II.

"Sail orders" were issued on 7 August 1990 to the MPS squadrons at Diego Garcia and at Guam, directing them to steam for the Persian Gulf to support Desert Shield. The ships of MPS Squadron 2 began unloading on 15 August, and the ships from MPS Squadron 1 reached Saudi Arabia on 26 August. Although the Marines were relatively "light" units, the ships did carry M60 tanks and 155-mm howitzers as well as light armored vehicles and amphibian tractors that could serve as armored personnel carriers in the desert. The 11 APF ships that were at Diego Garcia began arriving in the gulf on 17 August to unload their Army and Air Force cargoes. At the same time, MPS Squadron 3 in the Atlantic set course for the Persian Gulf. (After unloading their prepositioned cargoes, the MPS ships departed the gulf for U.S. ports and employment in resupply operations.)

In the United States the eight Fast Sealift Ships (FSS) that had been procured specifically to move heavy Army equipment to a crisis—the RO/RO ships of the SL-7 class—began loading the Army's 24th Mechanized Infantry Division at Savannah, Georgia. The SL-7s, with a maximum speed of 33 knots, were intended to be ready to receive cargo within 96 hours; the first of these RO/RO ships was ready in just 48 hours, and all seven met the 96-hour goal. The eighth fast RO/RO ship was in a shipyard for overhaul; she was hastily "put back together" and sailed ten days after the call.

On 27 August—12 days after the first MPS ships had arrived—the first fast sealift ships began to unload in Saudi Arabia the M1A1 Abrams tanks of the Army's 24th Mechanized Infantry Division. There followed a continuous flow of ships carrying U.S. military equipment. The major bottleneck in the sealift effort was the lack of shore facilities. For example, only two loading berths at Savannah were available to embark the 24th Division, while the massive shipping effort from several U.S. and overseas ports had to be unloaded through only five berths at the Saudi port of Ad Dammam and two at the port of Jubail.

More merchant ships followed. On 28 September 1991 the Desert Shield sealift reached a peak, with 90 ships at sea; 69 were en route to the Middle East from the United States and Europe, and 21 "empties" were returning for more cargo. Had the ships been evenly spaced on the route from the U.S. East Coast to the Persian Gulf, there would have been one ship every 100 n.miles (185 km). When "phase II" of Desert Shield was undertaken in November 1990 to build up a U.S. offensive force in the Persian Gulf, a peak of 172 sealift ships at sea was reached on 2 January 1991.

In addition to the "common user ocean transport" ships that were already operational under the aegis of the MSC, all of the maritime prepositioning ships and afloat prepositioning ships, the eight fast RO/RO ships (one of which broke down), several ships from the RRF,

MILITARY SEALIFT COMMAND SHIPS

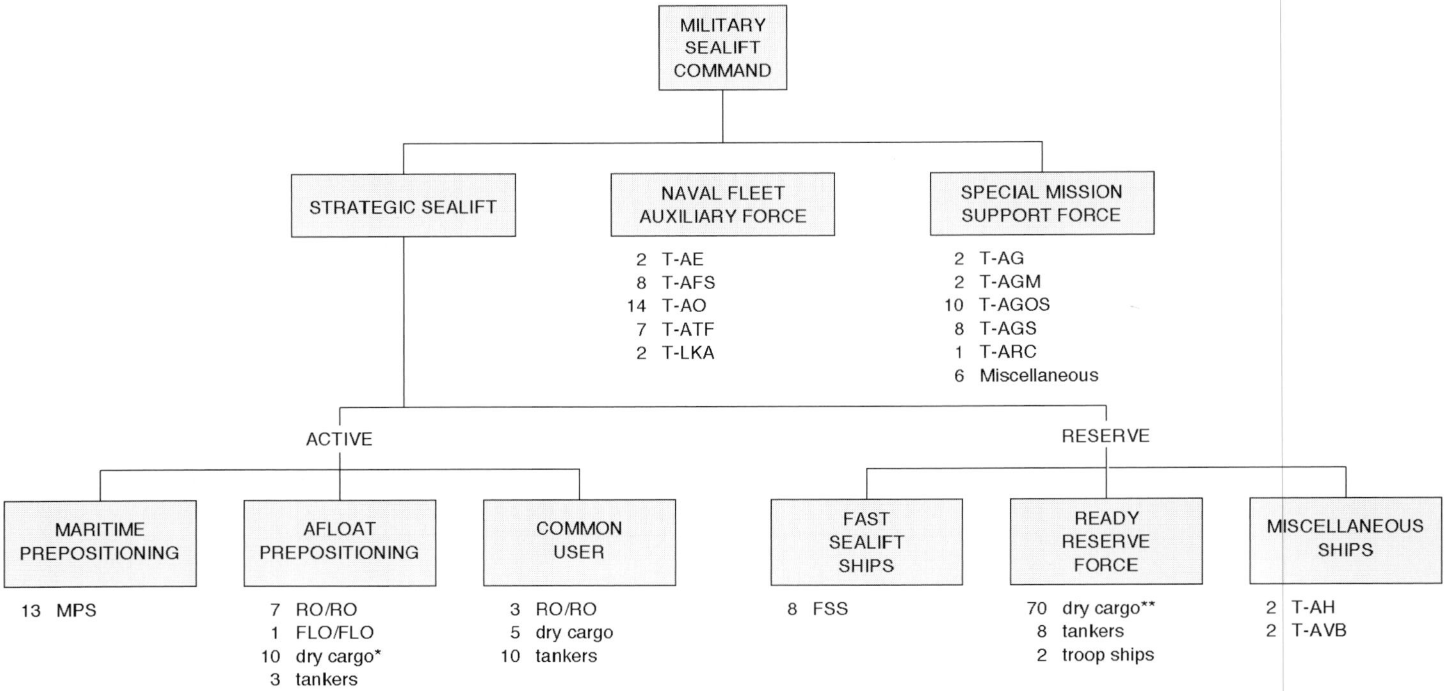

Notes: * Includes one crane ship.
** Includes seven crane ships.

The MSC-operated ocean surveillance ship ABLE (T-AGOS 20) is one of the few sonar surveillance ships that will be in service in the post–Cold War era. Her SWATH hull improves stability for operations in northern seas. (Leo Van Ginderen collection)

and 206 operating commercial merchant ships (29 U.S. flag and 177 foreign flag) were chartered by the MSC between 10 August 1990 and 18 January 1991 to support operations Desert Shield and Desert Storm. Also activated by the MSC and sent to the gulf were the two hospital ships and two aviation support ships maintained in standby reserve.

Subsequent to the Gulf War, the MSC carried out a massive sealift operation to *remove* thousands of tons of vehicles, munitions, and supplies from Saudi Arabia. Sealift ships have also been employed in small military buildup operations around the world since the Gulf War. Twice, in late 1994 and again in September 1995, prepositioning ships were dispatched to the Persian Gulf during confrontations with Iraq. Also in 1995, 14 RRF ships were activated in support of Operation Uphold Democracy, the U.S. operations in Haiti.

Several RRF ships have been activated to support U.S.–North Atlantic Treaty Organization operations in war-torn Bosnia. Two, the CAPE DIAMOND (T-AKR 5055) and CAPE RACE (T-AKR 9960), were activated in June 1995 to carry military supplies to British troops engaged in peacekeeping operations.

NAVAL FLEET AUXILIARY FORCE

The Military Sealift Command currently operates 31 naval auxiliary ships that provide direct support to the fleet. These include underway replenishment ships (AE/AFS/AO types) and all seven of the Navy's fleet tugs (ATF). These ships are operated by civil service mariners, with some ships having a small Navy detachment on board to provide communications and to support ordnance handling and helicopter operations.

The NFAF also includes two amphibious cargo ships, the MOBILE (T-LKA 115) and EL PASO (T-LKA 117). They are laid up in Reduced Operating Status (ROS), manned with 50-person nucleus crews and capable of being reactivated within five days. They were assigned to the MSC in 1996 and changed from LKA to T-LKA on 1 February 1996. (The three other LKAs of the CHARLESTON/LKA 113 class are retained in the Navy's Category B reserve, suitable for activation within 180 days.)

Note that the two hospital ships and two avaiation support ships are considered by the MSC to be sealift vice auxiliary ships. Because of their specialized nature, however, they are listed with other fleet auxiliary ships in chapter 23 of this edition of *Ships and Aircraft.*

SPECIAL MISSION SUPPORT FORCE

The MSC provides and operates ships to support specialized military activities, especially oceanographic and hydrographic surveys, undersea surveillance, acoustic research, missile range instrumentation, and the collection of telemetry intelligence against foreign missile tests. A total of 25 ships in this category are currently operated by the MSC (AG/AGM/AGOS/AGS/ARC types). This is a major reduction from the end of the Cold War era, when there were 20 T-AGOS/SURTASS ocean surveillance ships in MSC service.

These ships support a number of Department of Defense agencies as well as the Navy and Air Force.

ORGANIZATION

Military Sealift Command Headquarters is located in Washington, D.C., with MSC area commands in London, England; Bayonne, New Jersey; Oakland, California; and Yokohama, Japan. Smaller, sub-area commands are located in other ports.

The Commander MSC is a Navy vice admiral with an executive staff consisting of both Navy and civilian personnel. The MSC has more than 5,000 civilian employees and almost 1,000 uniformed personnel ashore and afloat. In addition, more than 2,000 contract mariners are employed on MSC ships.

In wartime, the MSC's command structure would be augmented by some 2,000 reserve personnel who would serve at MSC Headquarters and various area and sub-area offices. During Operation Desert Shield, 274 naval reservists were called to active duty to assist in chartering and scheduling activities. Another 130 reservists performed their annual active training duty in support of the MSC.

The Commander MSC is "double hatted" as the Assistant for Naval Control of Shipping on the staff of the Chief of Naval Operations. As such, he is the program sponsor for some 3,000 naval reservists in the Naval Control of Shipping Organization, which is responsible for the control of merchant shipping during a national emergency or war. In wartime, this organization would organize convoys and embark in merchant ships as staffs for convoy commodores. These personnel regularly participate in exercises.

Vice Admiral Philip M. Quast, USN, Commander Military Sealift Command since August 1994. (U.S. Navy)

Historical: The Military Sealift Command was established in response to a directive issued by the Secretary of Defense in August 1949, making the Secretary of the Navy the single manager for ocean transportation for the defense establishment. Accordingly, the Military Sea Transportation Service was established within the Navy on 1 October 1949. The basis for the new service was the ships of the Naval Ocean Transport Service (NOTS). The following year, oceangoing cargo ships and transports of the Army Transportation Corps were transferred to MSTS. Through 1950, additional Army ships were transferred to the Navy agency.

Under the aegis of MSTS some of these ships were manned by Navy crews (designated USS) and others by civilians (USNS). Initially, only the civilian-manned and then all of the ships had the prefix *T-* added to their designations. Some of the Navy-manned ships were armed. The last Navy crew went ashore in the 1960s, after which all ships were manned by civil service civilian or contract civilian crews.

On 1 August 1970 MSTS was renamed the Military Sealift Command to bring the name in line with the Air Force's Military Airlift Command (MAC). The latter was a specified command within the defense establishment, however, while the MSC remained a Navy command, reporting to the Chief of Naval Operations.

On 1 July 1987 the unified U.S. Transportation Command (USTRANSCOM) was established; the Military Sealift Command as well as the Military Airlift Command were its principal components. The Commander MSC is "double hatted" as a component commander of USTRANSCOM while also reporting to the Chief of Naval Operations because of the MSC's specialized ship operations.

(The Air Force's Military Air Transport Service [MATS] was renamed Military Airlift Command on 1 January 1966; it was inactivated on 1 June 1992, and its components were allocated to other Air Force commands.)

Two of the Military Sealift Command "fleets" are represented here: at left, the Maritime Prepositioning Ship 1st Lt Jack Lummus (T-AK 3011) refuels from the MSC-operated fleet oiler Passumpsic (T-AO 107), now discarded. MSC-operated fleet auxiliaries have demonstrated high standards of effectiveness in supporting the fleet. (U.S. Navy)

Ships of the Military Sealift Command come in all shapes and sizes. The force inventory changes continually as the ships' statuses change, especially between the active and reserve (RRF) categories in response to varying shipping requirements of the Department of Defense.

Top: The STRONG TEXAN is an unusual ship. Short and broad, the Dutch-built ship was rebuilt at a U.S. shipyard into a heavy lift ship by fitting her with two 160-ton-capacity cranes that can work in tandem. The ship can ballast down to float cargoes on and off. Here the STRONG TEXAN is carrying 34 house trailers that belong to the U.S. Army's 1302nd Medium Port Command. (U.S. Navy, courtesy *Sealift*)

Center: The long-serving gasoline tankers ALATNA (T-AOG 81), left, and CHATTAHOOCHEE (T-AOG 82) are now in inactive reserve, laid up in Tsuneishi, Japan, under MSC jurisdiction. They were built for Arctic operations. These ships and the World War II-built NODAWAY (T-AOG 78), also laid up at Tsuneishi, are the only AOG-type gasoline tankers retained by the Navy. They are maintained in a ten-day callup status. (U.S. Navy, courtesy *Sealift*)

Bottom: The massive lines of the BELLATRIX (T-AKR 288) belie the ship's high speed (33 knots). One of the world's fastest merchant ships, she and seven sister ships have been extensively converted to carry main battle tanks and other heavy equipment for the Army. These fast sealift ships and other modern RO/RO ships are vital for the rapid movement of heavy ground forces which cannot be airlifted to crisis or conflict areas. (Leo Van Ginderen collection)

CHAPTER 9

Naval Personnel

Clad in foul-weather gear (some are also wearing safety harnesses), crewmen wait atop the sail structure as their attack submarine approaches the submarine base at New London–Groton, Connecticut. These men and their colleagues are well trained and professional, representing some of the best and the brightest of the nation. (U.S. Navy, courtesy *The Dolphin*)

U.S. Navy personnel strength continues to decline as the size of the active fleet is reduced. At the same time, the closure of a large number of shore installations and the realignment of others will result in additional personnel reductions, although the major cutbacks in personnel are based on the reduction in operating ships and aircraft wings and squadrons. Navy personnel strength is being reduced by about 30 percent from 1991—the end of the Cold War—to the year 2000. This is, however, the smallest percentage reduction of the four military services in the Department of Defense in this period.

The Navy is scheduled to have an active personnel strength of 395,000 officers and enlisted men and women by the fall of the year 2000. This will be a net reduction of some 33,000 from the current (1996) Navy strength and of almost 200,000 men and women from the peak Navy strength of the Reagan naval buildup of nearly 593,000 personnel in the late 1980s (see table).[1]

The reductions in personnel strength are being achieved by cutting back on new accessions and by the forced retirement of large numbers of officers and enlisted personnel, some under special programs prior to their reaching 20 years of service, the historic retirement point for military personnel.

ACTIVE-DUTY NAVAL PERSONNEL (End of fiscal year)*

	FY 1995 Actual	FY 1996 Planned	FY 1997 Planned	FY 1998 Planned	FY 1999 Planned	FY 2000 Planned
Officers	58,788	58,327	56,108	54,648	54,550	54,550
Enlisted	371,670	361,852	346,876	339,159	336,350	336,350
Midshipmen	4,159	4,000	4,000	4,000	4,000	4,000
Total	434,617	424,179	406,984	397,807	394,900	394,900

*Totals are rounded.

NAVAL OFFICERS

Related to the general personnel reductions, the number of flag officers on active duty is also being reduced, but at a much smaller ratio than the overall fleet/personnel reductions. This is due, in part, to the large number of flag officers assigned to joint and unified staffs, including the Joint Staff of the Joint Chiefs of Staff. Still, the reductions are at a very different ratio than the reductions in other personnel. There were some 330 admirals on active duty during the 1980s; by June 1996 there were 308 flag officers on active duty, a reduction of only 9 percent.[2] Included in these tabulations are captains selected for flag rank, some of whom are authorized to assume the title and wear the uniform of a rear admiral (lower half), although they are still paid at the captain level.

While the number of flag officers has declined since the end of the Cold War, the number of rear admirals (upper half) has increased significantly. The Navy has eight full, four-star admirals on active duty. The full admirals include the Director Naval Nuclear Propulsion and the Superintendent U.S. Naval Academy.

The nuclear propulsion assignment is currently held by Admiral Frank Bowman. The assignment evolved from the position of Admiral H. G. Rickover, head of Navy nuclear propulsion from 1948 until he was fired in January 1982. Subsequently, the position remained a four-star billet, although today it primarily manages nuclear propulsion training and safety. Those functions could certainly be managed by a rear admiral.

The Naval Academy position has historically been a rear admiral's billet, with several incumbents being promoted to three-star rank while at the academy. The incumbent, Admiral Charles R. (Chuck) Larson, took the academy post in July 1994, following the worst cheating scandal in the school's history. Larson, who had been superintendent from 1983 to 1986, came back to the academy from the position of Commander in Chief of the Pacific Command. He retained four-star rank (although all active-duty admirals have a permanent rank of only rear admiral [upper half]). Although that scandal, coupled with incidents of sexual harassment at the Naval Academy, demanded new leadership, it could certainly have been provided by an astute, aggressive rear admiral. Unfortunately, the Naval Academy still suffers from scandals and lesser problems. Thus, two of the eight four-star admirals are filling billets that should, by logic, be two-star positions.

The Navy continues to suffer from significant shortfalls in certain officer areas:

Aviation. The Navy still has a pilot shortfall, although the situation has improved during the past few years because of the phasing out of aircraft and aviation units. However, the Navy's personnel managers are concerned about forecasts of increases in civilian airline hiring over the next few years. This could have a significant impact on the Navy's pilot retention program.

Nuclear. The Navy continues to suffer a severe shortfall in submarine officers, a situation exacerbated by the lowest junior officer retention over the last two years that the Navy has experienced in more than a decade. This is reflected in more first-tour officers resigning after completing their minimum service obligation rather than taking assignments ashore. This is occurring despite a submarine duty incentive pay of some $17,000 per year.

Despite the reality of this situation, officials at the Bureau of Naval Personnel contend that the nuclear personnel program "got well" at the end of the Cold War.[3] This, they contend, came about because of the rapid phasing out of strategic missile submarines (SSBN) as well as attack submarines (SSN). In addition, increasing numbers of nuclear officers are ashore: (1) serving in joint billets (i.e., a multiservice command); (2) attending postgraduate and war-college-level schools; and (3) assigned as instructors/company officers at the Naval Academy and in the Naval Reserve Officer Training Corps (NROTC). In the Cold War era very few nuclear submariners could hope for such assignments.

The joint billets are especially important because of the legal requirement that a U.S. military officer have service in a joint or unified assignment to be eligible for promotion to flag rank. The hard-core submarine community, however, has fought for a permanent deferral of this provision of the 1986 Goldwater-Nichols defense reorganization act, which will apply to submarine officers beginning on 1 January 1997.[4] The community wants the deferral of joint duty to stand until an officer is ready for a rear-admiral (upper half) assignment.

Meanwhile, the viewpoint of the nuclear officer situation in the fleet is not positive. Rear Admiral Jon M. Barr, Commander Submarine Force Pacific Fleet, declared in 1995 that "retention is not good" in his command, with "bleak career prospects for junior officers."[5] He attributed the situation to the submarine force "not having a focused mission to justify [why] we do long time at sea." Barr also foresees problems in the area of enlisted retention, especially for sonar technicians, because of the high operational tempo: "more demands for submarines in the Pacific than we can possibly fill."

In response to the deteriorating situation, Barr viewed the only alternative to be a cutback in operations after the year 2000, especially in non–forward-deployment activities.

The Navy's nuclear manpower situation at the end of the Cold War, the plan for fiscal 1995, and the plan for fiscal 2000 are:

1. The planned 600-ship fleet of the Reagan administration would have required some 622,000 personnel for full manning.
2. The names and assignments of Navy and Coast Guard flag officers, as well as Marine Corps general officers, are listed annually in the May (Naval Review) issue of the U.S. Naval Institute *Proceedings.*
3. Interview with Rear Adm. Albert H. Konetzni Jr., Bureau of Naval Personnel, Arlington, Va., 2 June 1995.
4. See, for example, Capt. C. H. Griffiths Jr., USN, "How About A Permanent Waiver?" U.S. Naval Institute *Proceedings,* December 1993, pp. 68–71.
5. Rear Adm. Jon M. Barr, USN, presentation to Naval Submarine League, Arlington, Va., 6 June 1995.

	Actual 1990	*Plan FY 1995*	*Plan FY 2000*
Nuclear surface officers	1,070	1,020	954
Nuclear submarine officers	5,119	4,316	3,712
Nuclear surface enlisted	5,597	5,586	5,099
Nuclear submarine enlisted	10,301	7,883	5,841

Significantly, the nuclear-trained personnel retention problems have existed for three decades, since the massive Polaris SSBN program of the early 1960s, when 41 missile submarines were completed in a seven-year period, each with two highly trained crews of some 135 men. In addition, 13 SSNs were completed in the same period, each with crews of almost 100 men. The selection and training of these crews, personally managed by Admiral Rickover, never caught up with the force manning requirements. The policies of that period—exacerbated by the "firing" of several hundred non–nuclear-trained officers from the submarine forces in 1988—have created a perpetual submarine manpower crisis. Finally, like the civilian market for Navy pilots, nuclear-trained officers are highly sought after in the civilian nuclear community.

Medical. The retention of medical personnel—physicians and nurses—continues to be a problem for the Navy, in large part because of higher pay and family stability in the civilian sector. There have been modest improvements in this field in the past few years, in large part through incentive pay/bonus programs and the recent awarding of four-year scholarships.

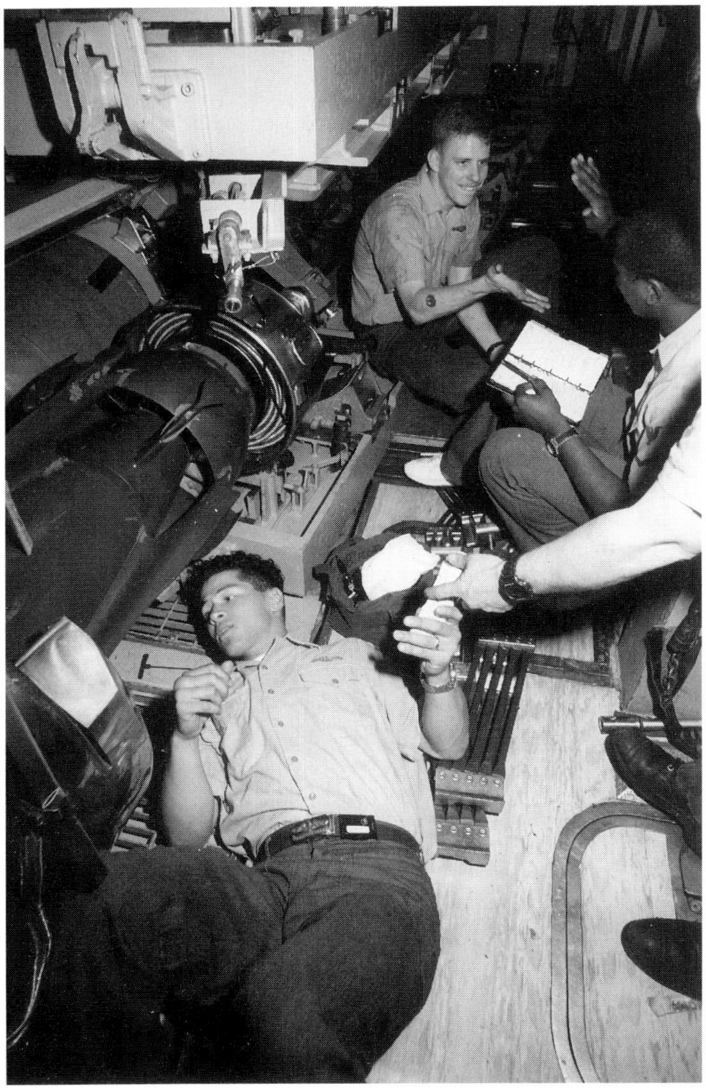

The modern Navy is a high-tech force, although muscle power is still needed for many jobs. Here a technician in the attack submarine NORFOLK (SSN 714) attaches a control cable to a practice Mk 48 ADCAP torpedo. The submarine's close quarters and long patrols prohibit women from serving in them. (U.S. Navy, PH2 Todd Cichonowicz)

NAVY FLAG OFFICERS

Rank	Category	1988	June 1996
Admirals	Line	10	8
Vice Admirals	Line	30	26
	Engineering	1	—
	Aerospace Engineering	—	1
	Intelligence	—	—
	Medical Corps	1	1
	Supply Corps	—	1
Rear Admirals *Upper Half*	Line	55	86
	Engineering	7	7
	Aerospace Engineering	3	3
	Cryptology	1	2
	Intelligence	2	2
	Public Affairs	—	1
	Fleet Support	—	1
	Medical Corps	7	3
	Health Care Executive	—	8
	Dental Corps	1	1
	Supply Corps	8	12
	Chaplain Corps	1	1
	Civil Engineer Corps	3	2
	Judge Advocate General's Corps	2	3
Rear Admirals *Lower Half*	Line	144	80
	Engineering	8	5
	Aerospace Engineering	5	4
	Cryptology	2	1
	Intelligence	2	3
	Public Affairs	1	1
	Fleet Support	—	3
	Oceanography	3	1
	Medical Corps	9	4
	Dental Corps	4	1
	Medical Service Corps	2	2
	Health Care Executive	—	8
	Supply Corps	11	11
	Chaplain Corps	2	3
	Civil Engineer Corps	4	6
	Judge Advocate General's Corps	1	—
	Nurse Corps	1	1

ENLISTED PERSONNEL

The Navy is an all-volunteer force. The current personnel cutbacks permit the Navy to accept enlisted men and women who have a high aptitude for technical training. Of the 53,982 men and women enlisted in fiscal 1994 (the last year for which complete data are available), 95.1 percent had high school diplomas.[6] The enlistment of the 5 percent who were not high school graduates was a conscious Navy decision to permit certain high achievers with low academic grades to have an opportunity for naval service. Indeed, a "seaman-to-admiral" program selects about 50 sailors for specialized career paths to take advantage of the diversity and talent of the Navy's junior enlisted personnel.

Quality is also being improved through a continued reduction in first-term attrition, i.e., the loss of sailors who leave after their first enlistment, who desert, or who have unauthorized absences. Improvement in these areas has led to an overall improvement in the quality of personnel. The Navy also saves resources each time a sailor reenlists or each time the desertion rate or unauthorized absence rate falls since personnel and other resources are not spent to find and train a replacement sailor.

The Navy—like the remainder of the armed forces—has developed a minorities accession plan. The "goals" of the plan are to have a Navy of 12 percent Blacks (African-Americans), 12 percent Hispan-

6. By comparison, of the Navy's enlisted intake in 1990, 92 percent were high school graduates.

ics, and 5 percent Asian-American/Pacific islanders across all enlisted rates and officer designators by the year 2000. In terms of actual numbers, the Navy's enlisted ranks are very close to this composition: 16 percent Black, 6½ percent Hispanic, and 5½ percent other. The challenge in the enlisted community is to correct an uneven representation across the various enlisted ratings.

Navy officials stress that the so-called 12/12/5 goal "is not something that can be achieved in a short time, and it is not the only answer to enhancing an environment of equal opportunity in our Navy."[7] However, the Navy—like other parts of the American society—must exercise considerable caution that the establishment of such "goals" does not prevent qualified nonminority officers and enlisted personnel from being promoted and receiving appropriate assignments.

WOMEN IN THE NAVY

Just over 12 percent of the Navy's officers and almost 11 percent of the Navy's enlisted personnel are women. These are smaller percentages than in the respective categories of the Army and Air Force, but they are significantly higher than in the Marine Corps (see chapter 7).

The Navy has six active-duty rear admirals who are women. Of the six, one is a line officer, assigned as the Superintendent Naval Postgraduate School, one is in the Nurse Corps, one is a senior health care specialist, and three are Fleet Support specialists. The latter hold major staff and major shore command assignments—Commander Naval Space Command, Commander Great Lakes Naval Training Center, and Director of Manpower and Personnel (J-1) on the Joint Staff.

On 13 May 1996, Rear Admiral Patricia A. Tracey, the Great Lakes commander, was nominated to serve as Chief of Naval Education and Training and Director of Naval Training (the latter on the OPNAV staff) in the grade of vice admiral. She is the second female to be nominated for three-star rank in the U.S. armed forces.[8]

Women have long served at sea in U.S. Navy hospital ships and transports. Since 1979 women have also been assigned to noncombatant ships and craft, mostly tenders, repair ships, and fleet oilers. The aircraft carrier Dwight D. Eisenhower (CVN 69) was the first U.S. warship to deploy with women, departing Norfolk, Virginia, on 20 October 1994, with 367 female officers and enlisteds on board. The ship deployed for six months, operating in the Mediterranean-Adriatic areas. By the beginning of 1996, more than 9,000 women were at sea: 500 officers and 8,535 enlisted. By 1997, 28 combatant ships are to have been modified to embark women. They are also fully integrated into all of the Navy's mobile construction battalions—the Seabees.

The first woman to head a Navy aircraft squadron took command of Electronic Warfare Squadron (VAQ) 34 in July 1990, and in December 1990 the first woman took command of a U.S. Navy ship, the salvage ship Opportune (ARS 41).[9] Subsequently, female commanding officers have been named to other ships.

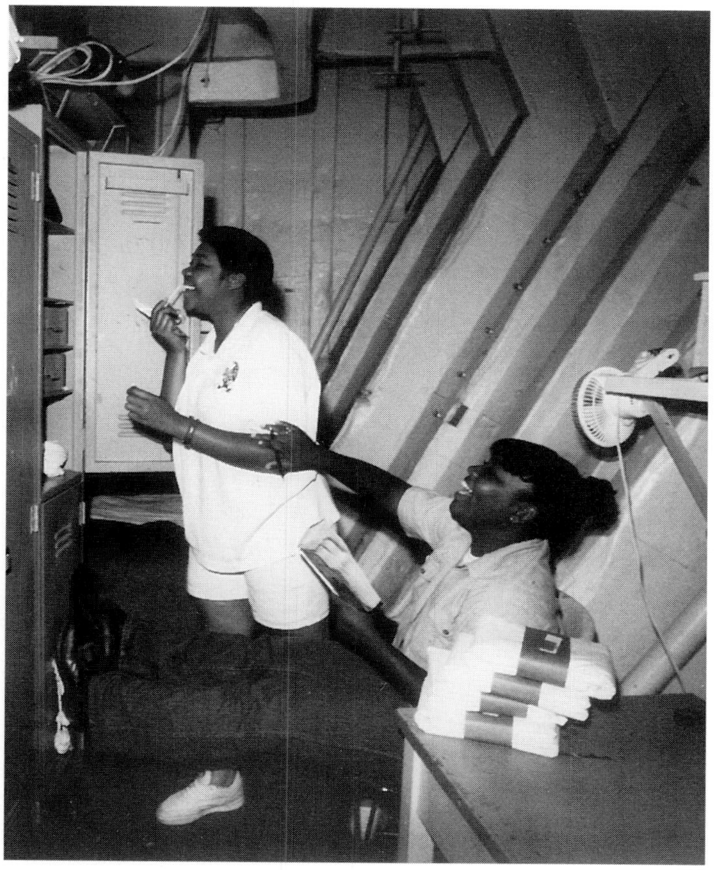

A seaman on the large harbor tug Neodesha (YTB 815) gets ready for liberty while a shipmate jokes with her. The Navy's all-volunteer force is drawing almost all high school graduates or higher for the enlisted ranks. Indeed, the Navy today probably has a higher educational level than ever before. (U.S. Navy, PH1 Don Bray)

Of concern to the Navy's personnel managers is the impact of large increases of women in the Navy. This could cause major problems with respect to the impact of pregnancy on crew stability and the Navy's currently stringent policy of assigning service husbands and wives to the same base or station. A high pregnancy rate among Navy women, especially those in ships' crews, can disrupt operations and increase medical-care requirements.

Also, a significant number of Navy personnel are married: as of January 1996, 2,774 officers and 18,332 enlisted personnel. Most of these are women, and most are married to Navy men (with both spouses included in these numbers). The Navy attempts to assign married service personnel to the same base and to transfer them at the same time. Obviously, this situation complicates personnel rotation and assignments, while those married personnel with children have the added complication of child care during deployments, especially emergency operations. Here again, the social standards of the nation are imposed upon military personnel with relatively little concern for military readiness.

7. Vice Adm. Frank L. Bowman, Chief of Naval Personnel, statement before the House National Security Committee, 14 March 1995.
8. In March 1996 the Marine Corps, with one woman general officer, selected the first woman in the U.S. armed forces to be promoted to three-star rank, Carol A. Mutter. As a lieutenant general she became Deputy Chief of Staff for Manpower and Reserve Affairs for the Marine Corps. The Coast Guard has no female flag officers.
9. Lt. Comdr. Darlene M. Iskra took command after the ship's commanding officer was taken off in a medical emergency; the Opportune had an all-male crew at the time.

CHAPTER 10

Naval Reserve

A naval aviator from Tactical Electronic Countermeasures Squadron (VAQ) 209 hugs his daughter upon returning to his home base of Naval Air Facility Washington after flying combat missions over Bosnia. Reservists —both the surface and the air reserve—regularly "pull" deployments, thus supplementing the regular Navy on a regular basis. (U. S. Navy)

In the post–Cold War period of military reductions, the Naval Reserve is being reduced while, at the same time, its importance is increasing because of the drawdown in active naval forces.

The Naval Reserve currently consists of approximately 16,000 TAR (Training and Administration of Reserve) personnel and 79,500 selected reservists—a total of more than 95,500 men and women. Another 167,500 men and women are in the individual ready reserve.

The selected reserve operates 23 ships and numerous aviation units, provides staff augmentation, and mans construction battalions and other specialized units. These personnel normally train 48 days per year, plus serving two weeks on active duty; most receive pay for their services. The TAR personnel, along with some other reserve personnel, are on full-time active duty, most in conjunction with training reserves.

During their drill periods, some ready reserve personnel participate in Navy day-to-day operational activities. For example, reserve patrol squadrons routinely conduct ASW patrols from bases in the United States and overseas during their training periods. These and other reserve air units have regularly flown drug-interdiction missions in the Caribbean and off the U.S. East and West Coasts, while reserve transport aircraft regularly carry personnel and cargo between the United States and overseas points. Also, in 1995, reserve Tactical Electronic Countermeasures Squadron (VAQ) 209 deployed personnel and EA-6B Prowler aircraft to the Aviano airfield in Italy to carry out flights over Bosnia in collaboration with an active VAQ squadron.

NAVAL RESERVE PERSONNEL*

	FY 1995 Actual	FY 1996 Planned	FY 1997 Planned	FY 1998 Planned	FY 1999 Planned	FY 2000 Planned
TAR officers	1,843	1,880	1,818	1,815	1,838	1,838
TAR enlisted	15,312	15,209	14,393	14,253	14,261	14,261
Total	17,155	17,089	16,211	16,068	16,099	16,099
Selected Reserve						
officers	19,235	18,776	18,286	18,248	18,328	18,324
enlisted	63,965	62,342	61,149	61,330	61,219	61,223
Total	83,200	81,118	79,435	79,578	79,547	79,547

*End of fiscal year

ORGANIZATION

The Director of Naval Reserve (in the Office of the Chief of Naval Operations/OPNAV Code N095), a rear admiral, manages the Naval Reserve programs. The surface ships of the Naval Reserve Force (NRF) report directly to the respective Atlantic and Pacific fleet commanders and, administratively, to the Commander Naval Surface Reserve Force; the aviation units of the Naval Air Reserve Force report through the Commander Naval Air Reserve Force to the Chief of Naval Operations.

The headquarters of the Commander Naval Surface Reserve and the Commander Naval Air Reserve, both rear admirals, are located in New Orleans, Louisiana.

Those Naval Reserve activities that report directly to the Director of Naval Reserve are:

Naval Air Reserve Centers
Naval Reserve ASW Training Center
Naval Reserve Construction Force/1st Naval Construction Battalion Brigade
Naval Reserve Intelligence Program
Naval Reserve Readiness Regions

There are five Naval Air Reserve Centers, located at Columbus, Ohio; Minneapolis, Minnesota; Olathe, Kansas; Lemoore, California; and Denver, Colorado. The 1st Naval Construction Battalion Brigade consists of 17 mobile construction battalions—the famed Seabees. These provide two-thirds of the Navy's total construction battalion force.

The Naval Reserve Mobile Inshore Warfare units provide all of the Navy's capability in this area, while reserve Naval Control of Shipping and Cargo Handling units provide more than 90 percent of the Navy's capabilities.

NAVAL SURFACE RESERVE

The surface Naval Reserve operates 22 ships in addition to making a significant contribution to manning a large-deck aircraft carrier, the John F. Kennedy (CV 67). The "JFK" is designated as an "operational reserve/training" ship, providing carrier landing training for pilots while having the capability of deploying as an operational carrier on short notice. This is the first time an aircraft carrier has ever been "assigned" to the NRF. The ship replaces the specialized training carriers (AVT) that were not capable of deploying with an air wing.

The "JFK" has a crew of some 2,600. The ship embarked some 300 TAR personnel in mid-1995, i.e., 11 percent of the crew. About 300 selected (part-time) reservists will join the ship in late 1997, when the Kennedy returns from a post-overhaul overseas deployment. This will bring the reserve component to about 22 percent.

Another reserve first has been the assignment of the mine countermeasures support ship Inchon (MCS 12) to the NRF. A converted helicopter carrier (LPH 12), the Inchon ranks as the second largest ship to have an NRF component. With a total manning of just over 700 personnel, the ship has a reserve component of some 170, i.e., 24 percent.

As of late 1996, 20 additional ships were assigned to the NRF with composite active duty–reserve crews: 12 frigates of the Oliver Hazard Perry (FFG 7) class, 2 tank landing ships of the Newport (LST 1179) class, 2 mine countermeasures ships of the Avenger (MCM 1) class, and 4 coastal minehunters of the Osprey (MHC 51) class. For several years the Navy had planned to assign most if not all MCM/MHC–type ships to the NRF. After the Persian Gulf conflict in 1991, however, the decision was made to retain 10 of the 14 Avenger-class ships and one of the Ospreys in active status. The minuscule COOP (Craft-of-Opportunity) minehunting program is also a reserve component.

In addition, four reserve Small Boat Units (SBU) operate a number of small craft.

The surface reserve program has undergone a massive revision since the end of the Cold War. Prior to the assignment of the "JFK" and the Inchon, the largest ships operated by the NRF were the Newport-class LSTs. With respect to warships, the NRF previously operated destroyers, the last being the Edson (DD 946); the ship was assigned to the NRF on 1 April 1977 and was stricken on 15 December 1988.

With the end of the Cold War, the Navy had initiated an unprecedented program based on the decommissioning of all 40 frigates of the Knox (FF 1052) class. In December 1991 eight ships were reclassified as training frigates (FFT), and the remaining 32 ships were laid up in specialized reserve. The latter would be reactivated in a crisis or war, employing reserve personnel trained aboard the FFTs. This program had been dubbed the Innovative Naval Reserve Concept (see 15th Edition/pages 147–50 for details). However, the decision was soon made to phase out all Knox-class ships, with additional Perry-class frigates being assigned to the NRF.

Previous plans to transfer other auxiliary ships to the Naval Reserve have been discarded.

The NRF frigate FLATLEY (FFG 21) manned by a composite active-reserve crew. Reservists are now assigned to a large carrier and a helicopter carrier/mine countermeasures support ship, the largest ships to be assigned to NRF status. (Leo Van Ginderen collection)

NAVAL AIR RESERVE

The Naval Air Reserve consists of one carrier air wing (CVWR) plus a large number of land-based squadrons that largely mirror the active fleet in organization and aircraft. The carrier-based components consist of a single carrier air wing, CVWR-20, with:

Squadron		*Aircraft*
1 VF	fighter squadron	F-14A Tomcat
2 VFA	strike-fighter squadrons	F/A-18A Hornet
2 VFC	fighter composite squadrons	F/A-18A Hornet
1 VA	attack squadron	A-6E Intruder
1 VAQ	tactical ECM squadron	EA-6B Prowler
1 VAW	airborne early warning squadron	E-2C Hawkeye

In addition, one Marine reserve F/A-18 squadron—VMFA-142—is assigned to the wing.

The land-based naval air reserve components are:

Squadron		*Aircraft*
1 VAW	airborne early warning squadron	E-2C Hawkeye
9 VP	patrol squadrons	P-3C Orion
12 VR	fleet logistic support squadrons	C-9 Skytrain DC-9 C-20 Gulfstream C-39 Sabreliner C-130 Hercules
1 HC	helicopter combat support squadron	H-3 Sea King series
2 HCS	helicopter combat SAR/ special warfare support squadrons	HH-60H Seahawk
1 HS	helicopter ASW squadron	SH-3H Sea King
2 HSL	helicopter light ASW squadrons	SH-2G LAMPS I

The two reserve mine countermeasures squadrons, HM-18 and HM-19, have been merged with the active squadrons HM-14 and HM-15, respectively. These constitute the Navy's first combined active-reserve aircraft squadrons.

Most reserve air squadrons fly the same type of aircraft as their active-duty counterparts. The principal exceptions are the lack of S-3 Viking fixed-wing ASW aircraft in a VS squadron for the reserve carrier air wing, and the lack of SH-60 ASW helicopters in the HS/HSL squadrons.

OPERATIONAL

The Naval Reserve had major roles in World War II, the Korean War, and the Vietnam War, as well as periodic operations in the NRF and active Navy ships during normal "peacetime" naval operations. The Navy activated 21,109 reservists or almost 16 percent of the ready reserve force, during Operations Desert Storm/Desert Shield. (Reportedly, 134,000 reservists requested active duty in conjunction with the gulf buildup.)

These reservists were called up mainly for their individual skills, with medical personnel (physicians, nurses, medical service, corpsmen) accounting for almost one-half of those activated. Many of those medical personnel were used to "backfill" positions at U.S. medical facilities while the active-duty personnel were sent to the Persian Gulf, and to serve in two reserve field hospitals and two hospital ships deployed in the gulf area. Cargo handling, construction (Seabee), and Mobile Inshore Undersea Warfare (MIUW) units were sent to the gulf. The Naval Reserve strength at the time was 123,593 men and women; the personnel activated were:

Specialty	*Reserve Total*	*Activated*
Medical	19,986	10,452
Ship augmentees	18,687	1,838
Construction	14,731	2,475
Aviation	16,736	1,111
Cargo handling	1,924	961
Military sealift	1,885	469
Other	49,644	3,803

Some of the Navy reservists listed above were activated after the cease-fire in Iraq to provide logistics support in the redeployment of personnel and equipment to the United States. No NRF ships were deployed to the gulf area; portions of nine reserve aircraft squadrons, however, were deployed to Europe and the Middle East. Of those, four were fleet logistic support squadrons, activated to assist the Air Force's Military Airlift Command in the European theater. This marked the first joint service military aircraft operation since the Berlin airlift of 1948.

HISTORICAL

The naval reserve concept can be traced to the American Revolution, when several of the colonies employed armed merchant ships to resist British military activities within their state's waters. By the time of the signing of the Declaration of Independence in July 1776, 11 colonies had some form of navy, most composed of men who served the state governments on essentially a part-time basis—a defacto naval reserve.

During the next century, various schemes of state volunteers were introduced, with a volunteer force participating in the Union Navy during the Civil War. Then, beginning in 1888, several states established naval components as part of their state militias. These naval militias were intended for harbor and coastal defense; they had no federal standing, and rules for applicants and levels of competence varied considerably.

Beginning in 1891 the Navy offered to allow state militias to participate in some fleet exercises, and soon there was federal cooperation in a number of training areas. Two years later the training ship New Hampshire (launched in 1864, although laid down 45 years earlier!) was transferred from the Navy to the New York State Naval Militia.

By the eve of the Spanish-American War of 1898 more than 4,000 men were enrolled in state naval militias. When the conflict erupted, the militias were used to patrol the coasts (there was a perceived threat of a Spanish assault), while thousands more militiamen were taken into the Navy. Their outstanding service in the war led to Navy Department recommendations for the creation of a national Naval Reserve. This was opposed—mostly by state interests—until 1914, when Congress passed legislation that largely placed the naval militias under supervision of the Navy Department. In time of war they would become part of the Navy (as the state National Guard units would become part of the Army). A year later, in 1915, the U.S. Naval Reserve was established, a reserve force to consist of men honorably discharged from the active Navy.

With the entry of the United States into World War I in April 1917, the militias were mobilized as the National Naval Volunteers. Almost the total strength of just over 10,000 men came onto active duty in the Navy. By September 1917 their ranks had grown to almost 17,000 men. These volunteers were consolidated with the Naval Reserve in July 1918, creating the current U.S. Naval Reserve organization. (The states of California, Illinois, and New York continue to maintain state naval forces, whose members are additionally in the Naval Reserve.)

An F/A-18 Hornet from Strike-Fighter Squadron (VFA) 303 taxis toward a catapult on the carrier Kitty Hawk (CV 63) shortly before the squadron was dis-established in December 1994. Naval Reserve squadrons fly first-line aircraft, providing a backup carrier air wing as well as patrol, logistics, and specialized squadrons that are important to the active fleet, especially in this era of "downsizing" the active forces. (U.S. Navy, PHCM Dave Fraker)

CHAPTER 11

Strategic Missile Submarines

The Trident submarine NEBRASKA. Her fine, harmonious lines belie the striking power of the 24 Trident D-5 submarine-launched ballistic missiles fitted amidships. The NEBRASKA and 13 sister ships will provide the major portion of U.S. nuclear striking power in the early 21st century. (1994, Giorgio Arra)

The U.S. strategic missile submarine (SSBN) force provides about half of the U.S. strategic nuclear warheads and is the most flexible and survivable component of the U.S. strategic force. According to Secretary of Defense William J. Perry, the SSBN force, "which is virtually undetectable when on patrol, is the most survivable and enduring element of the strategic nuclear triad. A significant portion of the SSBN force is at sea at any given time, and all submarines that are not in the shipyard for long-term maintenance can be generated during a crisis."[1]

In the fall of 1996 the SSBN force consisted of 17 operational nuclear-propelled undersea craft of the OHIO class, with one additional submarine under construction. When the Cold War ended in late 1991, it was anticipated that these 18 submarines, carrying a total of 432 multi-warhead Trident missiles, would constitute the principal component of the nation's strategic offensive capability in the post–Cold War era, at least through the year 2011. This was assuming a 30-year service life for these submarines. With each Trident missile armed with eight warheads, these 18 submarines, then, would have carried an aggregate of 3,456 warheads.

However, the Clinton administration's comprehensive Nuclear Posture Review (NPR), completed in September 1994, provides for reducing the strategic submarine force to 14 submarines with 336 missiles. This review of U.S. strategic arms programs calls for retiring four of the Trident C-4 submarines, completed from 1981–1986, and rearming four other C-4 submarines with the Trident D-5 missile. Thus, the surviving 14 Trident submarines will all carry the D-5 missile.

These reductions in strategic nuclear weapons will be compatible with the START II agreement with Russia. By the year 2003 (the end of the time period considered by the NPR), it is expected that START II limitations would be in effect, allowing a total of only 3,000 to 3,500 strategic weapons each for the United States and Russia. Of those, the U.S. strategic missile submarine force would carry some 1,680 warheads (i.e., about five warheads per Trident missile) on 14 submarines, plus 450 to 500 warheads on single-warhead Minuteman III Intercontinental Ballistic Missiles (ICBM) and the remainder on manned bombers—66 B-52H Stratofortress and 20 B-2 "stealth" aircraft. (Presumably, more than half of the Russian strategic nuclear warheads would similarly be in submarines.)

The four older Trident C-4 submarines probably will be retired, but they could be converted to other roles.

The Trident D-5 is a longer-range and more accurate weapon compared to the C-4. Also, the D-5 can deliver 75 percent more payload than the C-4, carrying eight of the Mark 5 reentry bodies, each fitted with a W88 nuclear warhead having an explosive force of about 300 to 475 kilotons. However, of the approximately 1,680 Trident warheads, only about 400 will have W88s; the others will be armed with a W76, having a yield of about 100 kilotons (see chapter 30). To meet START II requirements, the D-5 missiles will be downloaded to only four or five warheads. The backfitting of four submarines to carry the D-5 missile, and the providing of those missiles, will also preserve an industrial base for strategic missiles following the cancellation of further production of the MX Peacekeeper ICBM and the mobile, small-ICBM program called "Midgetman."

Beyond the cutback to 14 submarines, the operating tempo of the Trident submarines has been reduced. But no action has been taken on some proposals that the Trident force shift from the historic two-crew operating concept to a single crew. While this action could result in considerable financial savings, it would severely reduce Trident submarine time at sea and flexibility in scheduling.

The Navy has also considered a Trident D-5 missile in a configuration for carrying a conventional, high-explosive warhead. This concept has been suggested by the Navy's Strategic Systems Project Office as a means of striking time-sensitive, heavily defended, high-value targets. Such a weapon could enable the Navy to retain the four nonstrategic submarines for a conventional role. However, there could be significant problems in the concept, such as a nation's early warning system indicating that ballistic missiles were being fired with no way of knowing the intended target or whether they were nuclear or conventional weapons. Further, the modification of existing treaties and their missiles count would be required. Thus, employing Trident SSBNs in a conventional strike role is highly unlikely.

While the Nuclear Posture Review has been called the "first such review of U.S. nuclear policy in 15 years, and the first study ever to include policy, doctrine, force structure, command and control, operations, supporting infrastructure, safety and security and arms control in a single review," it actually follows several reviews of strategic forces during the Reagan and Bush administrations.[2] President George Bush announced major changes in the U.S. nuclear forces—strategic as well as tactical—on 27 September 1991. The "Fiscal Year 1992 Base Force" for strategic forces, announced in 1990, and the "New Base Force," revealed in 1992, both made significant changes in U.S. strategic forces.

No U.S. nuclear weapons or launching platforms are now under development.

The last of the 41 earlier Polaris-Poseidon ballistic missile submarines, completed from 1959 to 1967, have been removed from service. They were armed with a succession of Polaris missiles (41 submarines), Poseidon missiles (31), and Trident C-4 missiles (12). Of those submarines, 37 are being partially dismantled and stored at Bremerton, Washington; two others, the KAMEHAMEHA and the JAMES K. POLK, are in active service as special operations submarines (now designated SSN 642 and 645, respectively). Two retired LAFAYETTE-class SSBNs have been modified for use as Moored Training Ships (MTS) for nuclear propulsion operators. They are moored at Charleston, South Carolina.

The dismantling of nuclear-propelled submarines requires more than a year. Because U.S. Navy nuclear-propelled ships, by law, must have personnel on board until the reactor is permanently closed down and the fuel removed, nuclear ships and submarines are placed In Commission, In Reserve (ICIR) upon deactivation. After the reactor shutdown requirements have been met, the ships are formally decommissioned and, in recent years, stricken on the same date. Once a ship has been placed in ICIR status, she cannot be returned to service. In particular, SSBNs have their missile compartments cut out and the forward and after sections welded back together.

Builders: The Electric Boat Division of General Dynamics in Groton, Connecticut, is the only U.S. shipyard currently constructing strategic missile submarines. That yard built all 18 of the Trident submarines (as well as 17 of the 41 U.S. Polaris-Poseidon submarines).

The Polaris submarine program reflected a spectacular U.S. submarine construction effort, with the 41 submarines being completed in a 7½-year period following a highly compressed development period. (In addition to the Polaris submarines, the Navy completed 17 other nuclear-propelled submarines in that period, an average of almost 8 nuclear submarines per year.)

Classification: See chapter 12 for a complete list of post–World War II SS-series hull numbers, including SSBNs.

Manning: All operational U.S. SSBNs are assigned two complete crews (designated Blue and Gold). The crews alternate on deterrent patrols. While one crew is at sea, the other is engaged in training (mostly with system simulators), leave, medical treatment, and other shore activities. The normal deployment patrol (with one crew) is up to 70 days.

Studies are under way on the means of accommodating female crew members on board Trident submarines.

Missiles: All Polaris and Poseidon missiles have been retired from the U.S. submarine fleet (see table and chapter 30).

The Polaris A-3 missile, fitted with a British-developed nuclear warhead, remains in Royal Navy SSBNs of the RESOLUTION class (Chevaline A3TK version). Those submarines have not been upgraded to fire the Poseidon or Trident C-4 missile and will be replaced by new-construction submarines of the VANGUARD class armed with the Trident D-5 missile, also carrying British warheads.

1. William J. Perry, "Annual Report to the President and the Congress" (Washington, D.C.: Department of Defense, February 1995), p. 88.

2. "DOD Review Recommends Reduction in Nuclear Force," (Department of Defense News Release, 22 September 1994), p. 1.

Names: The 41 Polaris strategic missile submarines completed from 1960 to 1967 were named for "famous Americans," although several were in fact named for persons never in the American colonies or United States.

The subsequent Trident submarines completed from 1981 are named for "States of the Union," beginning with the OHIO. Previously, state names were assigned to battleships and, later, to guided missile cruisers (CGN 36–41). The exception to the state name source for SSBNs was made on 27 September 1983, when the RHODE ISLAND was renamed for the late Senator Henry M. (Scoop) Jackson.

Operational: Approximately two-thirds of the force is normally at sea on deterrent patrol. The Trident SSBN force is based at Bangor, Washington, for patrols in the North Pacific, and at Kings Bay, Georgia, for patrols in the North Atlantic.

As of 1 July 1996, U.S. ballistic missile submarines had completed 3,227 deterrent patrols. The total number does not take into account the 41 patrols conducted by five Regulus-armed *guided* missile submarines in the North Pacific from mid-1960 to mid-1964.[3]

The TENNESSEE completed the 3,000th U.S. fleet ballistic missile submarine deterrent patrol in April 1992—31 years after the pioneer GEORGE WASHINGTON conducted the first such patrol. These included 1,245 Polaris patrols and 1,182 Poseidon patrols.

3. The operational Regulus submarines were the TUNNY (SSG 282), BARBERO (SSG 317), GRAYBACK (SSG 574), GROWLER (SSG 577), and HALIBUT (SSGN 586). They deployed with the Regulus I surface-launched cruise missile in the Northwest Pacific area.

STRATEGIC MISSILE SUBMARINE PATROLS

Missile	First patrol begun	Last patrol completed
Polaris A-1	15 Nov 1960 GEORGE WASHINGTON	14 Oct 1965 ABRAHAM LINCOLN
Polaris A-2	26 June 1962 ETHAN ALLEN	9 June 1974 JOHN MARSHALL
Polaris A-3	28 Sep 1964 DANIEL WEBSTER	1 Oct 1981 ROBERT E. LEE*
Poseidon C-3	31 Mar 1971 JAMES MADISON	1 Oct 1991 KAMEHAMEHA and ULYSSES S. GRANT**
Trident C-4	20 Oct 1979 FRANCIS SCOTT KEY	(in service)
Trident D-5	29 Mar 1990 TENNESSEE	(in service)

*This is the date that the ROBERT E. LEE was taken off alert. She was still at sea at the time, but Polaris patrols officially ended on 1 October 1981.

**The KAMEHAMEHA and ULYSSES S. GRANT were taken off alert on this date. The submarines were still at sea, returning to port on 15 and 16 October 1981, respectively; their deterrent patrols officially ended on 1 October 1991.

17 + 1 STRATEGIC MISSILE SUBMARINES: "OHIO" CLASS

Number	Name	FY	Builder	Start	Laid down	Launched	Commissioned	Status
SSBN 726	OHIO	74	General Dynamics/Electric Boat	19 July 1974	10 Apr 1976	7 Apr 1976	11 Nov 1981	**PA**
SSBN 727	MICHIGAN	75	General Dynamics/Electric Boat	15 Aug 1975	4 Apr 1977	26 Apr 1980	11 Sep 1982	**PA**
SSBN 728	FLORIDA	75	General Dynamics/Electric Boat	27 Feb 1976	9 June 1977	14 Nov 1981	18 June 1983	**PA**
SSBN 729	GEORGIA	76	General Dynamics/Electric Boat	17 Jan 1977	7 Apr 1979	6 Nov 1982	11 Feb 1984	**PA**
SSBN 730	HENRY M. JACKSON	77	General Dynamics/Electric Boat	28 Feb 1978	19 Jan 1981	15 Oct 1983	6 Oct 1984	**PA**
SSBN 731	ALABAMA	78	General Dynamics/Electric Boat	6 Apr 1979	27 Aug 1981	19 May 1984	25 May 1985	**PA**
SSBN 732	ALASKA	78	General Dynamics/Electric Boat	12 Oct 1979	9 Mar 1983	12 Jan 1985	25 Jan 1986	**PA**
SSBN 733	NEVADA	80	General Dynamics/Electric Boat	17 Feb 1981	8 Aug 1983	14 Sep 1985	16 Aug 1986	**PA**
SSBN 734	TENNESSEE	81	General Dynamics/Electric Boat	15 Jan 1982	9 June 1986	13 Dec 1986	17 Dec 1988	**AA**
SSBN 735	PENNSYLVANIA	83	General Dynamics/Electric Boat	29 Nov 1982	2 Mar 1987	23 Apr 1988	9 Sep 1989	**AA**
SSBN 736	WEST VIRGINIA	83	General Dynamics/Electric Boat	21 Nov 1983	18 Dec 1987	14 Oct 1989	20 Oct 1990	**AA**
SSBN 737	KENTUCKY	84	General Dynamics/Electric Boat	13 Aug 1985	18 Dec 1987	11 Aug 1990	13 July 1991	**AA**
SSBN 738	MARYLAND	85	General Dynamics/Electric Boat	22 Mar 1986	18 Dec 1987	10 Aug 1991	13 June 1992	**AA**
SSBN 739	NEBRASKA	86	General Dynamics/Electric Boat	6 June 1987	18 Dec 1987	15 Aug 1992	10 July 1993	**AA**
SSBN 740	RHODE ISLAND	87	General Dynamics/Electric Boat	23 Apr 1988	—	17 July 1993	9 July 1994	**AA**
SSBN 741	MAINE	88	General Dynamics/Electric Boat	4 Apr 1989	—	16 July 1994	29 July 1995	**AA**
SSBN 742	WYOMING	89	General Dynamics/Electric Boat	27 Jan 1990	—	22 July 1995	13 July 1996	**AA**
SSBN 743	LOUISIANA	90	General Dynamics/Electric Boat	15 May 1991	—	27 July 1996	1997	Building

Displacement:	16,764 tons standard 18,750 tons submerged
Length:	560 feet (170.7 m) overall
Beam:	42 feet (12.8 m)
Draft:	36¼ feet (11.05 m)
Propulsion:	2 steam turbines (General Electric); approx. 35,000 shp; 1 shaft
Reactors:	1 pressurized-reactor S8G (General Electric)
Speed:	28 knots surface approx. 30 knots submerged
Manning:	163 (15 officers + 148 enlisted)
Missiles:	SSBN 726–733 24 tubes for Trident C-4 SLBM SSBN 734–743 24 tubes for Trident D-5 SLBM
Torpedo tubes:	4 21-inch (533-mm) tubes Mk 68 (amidships)
ASW weapons:	Mk 48 torpedoes
Radars:	BPS-15A surface search on SSBN 726–740 BPS-16 surface search on SSBN 741–743
Sonars:	BQQ-6 bow mounted passive BQR-15 towed array; to be replaced by TB-29 BQR-19 active navigation BQS-13 active BQS-15 under ice
Fire control:	1 CCS Mk 2 Mod 3 1 Mk 98 missile FCS 1 Mk 118 torpedo FCS
EW systems:	WLR-8(V)5 WLR-10

These are the largest submarines to be built in the United States and second in size only to the six Soviet Typhoon-class (Project 941) SSBNs, which are almost twice as large. The OHIO was laid down nine years after completion of the previous U.S. strategic missile submarine, the WILL ROGERS. The original contract delivery date for the OHIO was April 1979.

Incorporation of the D-5 missile in SSBNs 734–736 resulted in a one-year delay in their construction; the SSBN 737 and later submarines were ordered as D-5 ships (see *Missiles* notes).

Builders: Note that four submarines of this class were laid down at the General Dynamics/Electric Boat yard on the same date. The last four submarines did not have formal keel layings.

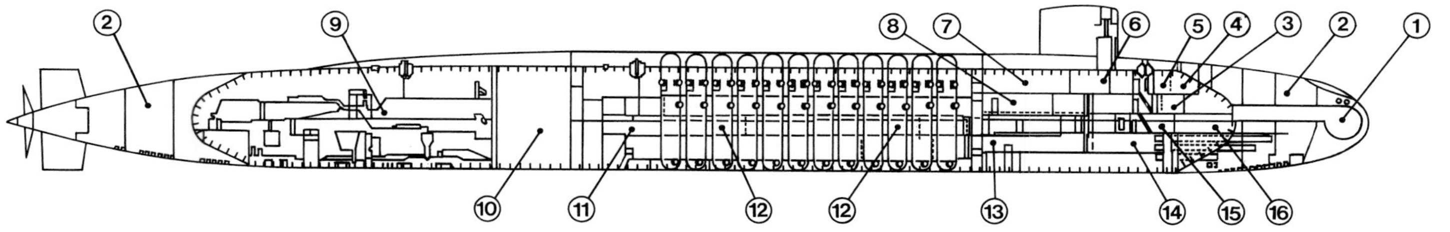

Ohio class
1. Sonar sphere. 2. Ballast tanks. 3. Computer room. 4. Radio room. 5. Sonar room. 6. Command and control center. 7. Navigation center. 8. Missile control center. 9. Engine room. 10. Reactor compartment. 11. Auxiliary machinery. 12. Crew's berthing. 13. Crew's mess. 14. Torpedo room. 15. Wardroom. 16. Chief petty officer quarters. (William Clipson)

Class: The basis for the Trident program was the Department of Defense–sponsored STRAT-X study of 1967–1968 to determine future strategic weapon requirements. The study recommended two land-based and two sea-based strategic systems, with one of the latter being the Underwater Long-range Missile System (ULMS). This evolved into the Trident system; the name was changed from ULMS to Trident on 16 May 1972.

The Trident program lagged considerably behind the schedule established in May 1972 when the weapon system was approved for development. The lead submarine was funded in fiscal 1974; a schedule was put forward at that time for constructing an initial series of ten Trident SSBNs at an annual rate of 1-3-3-3. These ten submarines were to have been completed by 1982.

The first Trident submarine was ordered on 25 July 1974, with a planned delivery date of 30 April 1979. However, the shipyard agreed to attempt to make delivery in December 1977 because of the high priority of the program. Subsequent delays caused by the Navy management of the project, design changes, and problems at the shipyard resulted in the late deliveries of the early submarines, with authorizations for the first ten submarines covering a ten-year period vice four years. Navy planning in the early 1980s called for a class of at least 20 Ohio-class SSBNs.

The SALT I strategic arms agreement with the Soviet Union in 1972 required the decommissioning of the Polaris A-3 submarines Theodore Roosevelt and Abraham Lincoln to compensate for the Ohio entering service. Those were the first U.S. SSBNs to be decommissioned (see below).

Design: SCB No. 304.74. These are the largest submarines to be built in the West, the size of the craft having been determined primarily by their reactor plant. The Ohio-class submarines have a conservative design, with the bow sonar dome and amidships torpedo tubes similar to later attack submarine designs. These are the only 24-tube strategic missile submarines built by any nation (the Soviet Typhoon-class SSBNs have 20 missile tubes).

The Trident submarines have comfortable accommodations for their crews. Three logistic hatches—in the forward (control-accommodation section), center (missile), and after (engineering) compartments—have escape trunks that can be removed when in port to provide large, six-foot (1.8-m)-diameter resupply and repair openings. These provide for the rapid transfer of supply pallets, equipment replacement modules, and even machinery components, permitting a significant reduction in the time required for replenishment and maintenance. (The standard U.S. submarine hatches are 26 inches/0.66 m in diameter.)

These submarines are reported to have a 985-foot (300-m) operating depth.

Engineering: The S8G reactor plant was originally intended to provide up to 60,000 shp, having been based on an earlier design for a large, high-speed cruise missile submarine. Its actual horsepower is publicly reported as being in excess of 30,000 shp, but that is significantly less than the original 60,000 goal.

The S8G reactor plant, a land-based prototype of the Ohio plant, is installed at West Milton, New York.

Reportedly, the Ohio is quieter than the ship's design goals for self-quieting, and at low speeds (i.e., when using natural convection rather than pumps for the circulation of pressurized water in the primary loop) the Ohio may be the quietest nuclear submarine yet constructed.

Missiles: The first eight Trident submarines were originally armed with the C-4 missile, referred to as Trident I. Beginning with the ninth submarine, the D-5 missile capability was provided, referred to as Trident II.

Four of the C-4 submarines will be backfitted with the D-5 capability during subsequent overhauls.

The Ohio fired the first Trident C-4 to be launched from this class on 17 January 1982. The Tennessee launched the first D-5 missile from a submarine on 21 March 1989; the missile failed. The first successful Trident D-5 launch from the Tennessee occurred on 2 August 1989.

The Nebraska. Note the large sail-mounted diving planes and the deck structure over the 24 missile tubes. (1994, Giorgio Arra)

Stern aspect of the Nebraska. The lack of limber or flood holes reveals the single-hull design of U.S. nuclear submarines. (1994, Giorgio Arra)

The TENNESSEE at Port Everglades, Fla. The low-lying appearance of the Trident submarines disguises their size; they are the largest submarines to be built in the West. But they are dwarfed by the six Russian Typhoon-class submarines (Project 941), which have about twice their displacement. (1993, Giorgio Arra)

Names: The SSBN 730 was originally named the RHODE ISLAND, which was changed later to honor Senator "Scoop" Jackson, longtime supporter of nuclear and defense programs.

Operational: The OHIO made the first operational patrol of this class from 1 October 1982 to 10 December 1982.

The first squadron of eight submarines operates in the Pacific, based at Bangor, Washington (Submarine Squadron 17), established on 5 January 1981. The second Trident submarine squadron (SubRon 20) operates in the Atlantic, based at Kings Bay, Georgia.

These submarines are designed to conduct 70-day patrols interrupted by 25-day overhaul/replenishment periods, during which time the Blue/Gold crews change over. Under this schedule the submarines undergo a lengthy overhaul and reactor refueling every 20 years.

The sail of the NEBRASKA with two periscopes raised. There is a short-range sonar "window" at the front of the sail, just below the diminutive bridge area. (1994, Giorgio Arra)

STRATEGIC MISSILE SUBMARINES: "LAFAYETTE" CLASS

Number	Name	Comm.	Notes
SSBN 616	LAFAYETTE	1963	decomm. 12 Aug 1991; stricken 25 Feb 1992
SSBN 617	ALEXANDER HAMILTON	1963	decomm./stricken 23 Feb 1993
SSBN 619	ANDREW JACKSON	1963	decomm./stricken 31 Aug 1989
SSBN 620	JOHN ADAMS	1964	decomm./stricken 30 Sep 1989
SSBN 622	JAMES MONROE	1963	decomm./stricken 25 Sep 1990
SSBN 623	NATHAN HALE	1963	decomm./stricken 31 Dec 1986
SSBN 624	WOODROW WILSON	1963	decomm./stricken 1 Sep 1994
SSBN 625	HENRY CLAY	1964	decomm./stricken 6 Nov 1990
SSBN 626	DANIEL WEBSTER	1964	decomm. 27 Apr 1990/to MTS
SSBN 627	JAMES MADISON	1964	decomm./stricken 20 Nov 1992
SSBN 628	TECUMSEH	1964	decomm./stricken 23 July 1993
SSBN 629	DANIEL BOONE	1964	decomm./stricken
SSBN 630	JOHN C. CALHOUN	1964	decomm./stricken 1 Oct 1994
SSBN 631	ULYSSES S. GRANT	1964	decomm./stricken 12 June 1992
SSBN 632	VON STEUBEN	1964	decomm./stricken
SSBN 633	CASIMIR PULASKI	1964	decomm./stricken
SSBN 634	STONEWALL JACKSON	1964	decomm./stricken 9 Feb 1995
SSBN 635	SAM RAYBURN	1964	decomm. 31 Aug 1989; to MTS
SSBN 636	NATHANAEL GREENE	1964	decomm./stricken 31 Jan 1987
SSBN 640	BENJAMIN FRANKLIN	1965	decomm./stricken 23 Nov 1993
SSBN 641	SIMON BOLIVAR	1965	decomm./stricken
SSBN 642	KAMEHAMEHA	1965	to transport submarine
SSBN 643	GEORGE BANCROFT	1966	decomm./stricken 21 Sep 1993
SSBN 644	LEWIS AND CLARK	1965	decomm./stricken 1 Aug 1992
SSBN 645	JAMES K. POLK	1966	to transport submarine
SSBN 654	GEORGE C. MARSHALL	1966	decomm./stricken 24 Sep 1992
SSBN 655	HENRY L. STIMSON	1966	decomm./stricken 5 May 1993
SSBN 656	GEORGE WASHINGTON CARVER	1966	decomm./stricken 18 Mar 1993
SSBN 657	FRANCIS SCOTT KEY	1966	decomm./stricken 2 Sep 1993
SSBN 658	MARIANO G. VALLEJO	1966	decomm./stricken
SSBN 659	WILL ROGERS	1967	decomm./stricken 12 Apr 1993

These strategic missile submarines were enlarged and improved versions of the previous ETHAN ALLEN class. The last 12 submarines of the class had quieter machinery installations and other minor differences which led to their being referred to as the BENJAMIN FRANKLIN sub-class.

All LAFAYETTE submarines have been removed from the strategic missile role; all but four have now been partially dismantled. The SAM RAYBURN and DANIEL WEBSTER have been modified (and immobilized) to serve as Moored Training Ships (MTS) in which to train nuclear propulsion plant operators. Their propellers were removed and missile tubes filled with concrete. They are officially listed as "floating equipment" by the Navy and are moored at Charleston, South Carolina.

KAMEHAMEHA and JAMES K. POLK have been converted to special operations/transport submarines (see chapter 12).

Missiles: The first eight LAFAYETE-class submarines were completed with the Polaris A-2 missile and the subsequent 23 with the A-3 variant; all were refitted between 1970 and 1978, inclusive, to launch the Poseidon C-3 missile. Subsequently, 12 units were refitted in 1978–1982 to fire the Trident C-4 missile (SSBN 627, 629, 630, 632–634, 640, 641, 643, 655, 657, 678).

See 15th Edition/pages 59–61 for characteristics.

STRATEGIC MISSILE SUBMARINES: "ETHAN ALLEN" CLASS

Number	Name	Comm.	to SSN	Decomm.	Stricken
SSBN 608	ETHAN ALLEN	1961	1 Sep 1980	31 Mar 1986	(same)
SSBN 609	SAM HOUSTON	1962	10 Nov 1980	12 Aug 1991	6 Dec 1991
SSBN 610	THOMAS A. EDISON	1962	6 Oct 1980	1 Dec 1983	30 Apr 1986
SSBN 611	JOHN MARSHALL	1962	20 June 1981	22 July 1992	(same)
SSBN 618	THOMAS JEFFERSON	1963	3 Mar 1981	1 Feb 1985	30 Apr 1986

These were the first U.S. submarines designed from the outset as SSBNs, the previous GEORGE WASHINGTON class having been converted during design/construction.

All five units were reclassified as attack submarines (SSN) after discarding their Polaris missiles. They had limited effectiveness in the SSN role because of their sonar, noise levels, and number of torpedoes. In 1984–1986 two, the JOHN MARSHALL and SAM HOUSTON, were extensively converted to transport submarines to carry SEALs or other special forces. (They retained SSN designations in the transport role.) The HOUSTON was employed in the mid-1980s as a test platform for the UQQ-2 Surveillance Towed Array Sonar System (SURTASS); the SURTASS is carried by T-AGOS surveillance ships (see chapter 23).

The five submarines of the ETHAN ALLEN class have been partially dismantled and are laid up pending ultimate disposal.

Missiles: These submarines originally deployed with the Polaris A-2 missiles, being upgraded to the A-3 variant in 1974–1976.

See 12th Edition/page 22 for characteristics as SSBNs.

STRATEGIC MISSILE SUBMARINES: "GEORGE WASHINGTON" CLASS

Number	Name	Comm.	to SSN	Decomm.	Stricken
SSN 598	GEORGE WASHINGTON	1959	20 Nov 1981	24 Jan 1985	30 Apr 1986
SSN 599	PATRICK HENRY	1960	24 Oct 1982	25 May 1984	25 May 1985
SSBN 600	THEODORE ROOSEVELT	1961	—	28 Feb 1981	30 Apr 1986
SSN 601	ROBERT E. LEE	1960	1 Mar 1982	1 Dec 1983	30 Apr 1986
SSBN 602	ABRAHAM LINCOLN	1961	—	28 Feb 1981	(same)

These were the U.S. Navy's first ballistic missile submarines. They were based on the SKIPJACK (SSN 585) design, being lengthened 130 feet (39.6 m) to provide space for 16 Polaris missile tubes and related navigation and fire-control equipment. These submarines were completed after a remarkably rapid design-and-construction period.

All five submarines originally carried the Polaris A-1 missile, being modified in 1966–1967 to carry the A-3 version. Three submarines served briefly in the attack submarine role, but they were of limited effectiveness as SSNs.

The five submarines of the WASHINGTON class have been partially dismantled and are laid up pending ultimate disposal.

See 12th Edition/page 23 for characteristics as SSBNs.

Partners under the sea: The Trident submarine ALABAMA and the smaller attack submarine SAN FRANCISCO (SSN 711) are representative of the current U.S. submarine force. The ALABAMA's large snorkel induction mast is raised. In the background is the Aegis missile cruiser CHOSIN (CG 65), a destroyer, and a frigate moored at Pearl Harbor. (1991, John Bouvia)

CHAPTER 12

Submarines

The SEAWOLF at "rollout"—the largest, most expensive, most controversial, and costliest attack submarine ever built by any navy. The massive sonar dome and bow section are encased in Glass Reinforced Plastic (GRP); the torpedo tube openings are just visible behind the scaffolding. (1995, General Dynamics/Electric Boat)

In the post–Cold War era the Navy's submarine community is seeking to redefine the roles of attack submarines (SSN) because the quantity of potentially opposing submarine and surface naval threats has diminished greatly.

The attack submarine force in the fall of 1996 consisted of just over 75 nuclear-propelled submarines, including one SSN configured for special ocean search-and-recovery missions (PARCHE), one employed in the research and development role (MEMPHIS), and two fitted as transports for special operations forces (KAMEHAMEHA and JAMES K. POLK).

The attack submarine force—like strategic missile submarines (SSBN)—is being reduced precipitously, from a force-level goal of 100 SSNs at the end of the Cold War (which was never achieved) to only 45 to 55 SSNs by about the year 2000, as proposed under the Department of Defense's Bottom-Up Review of 1993. The Navy has proposed both new missions and a shift of mission emphasis away from the attack submarine's primary Cold War role of ASW against Soviet nuclear-propelled submarines.

The SSN roles most stressed by their supporters are:[1]

Support of the battlefield: The use of submarines in forward areas to provide Indications and Warning (I&W) of enemy activity; mine warfare surveillance and destruction using Unmanned Underwater Vehicles (UUV); general reconnaissance through links to Unmanned Air Vehicles (UAV); and fire support of ground forces using the Army-developed Advanced Tactical Missile System (ATACMS) launched from submerged submarines.

Stealth strike: The use of attack submarines to launch Tomahawk Land-Attack Missiles (TLAM) to strike targets that cannot easily be attacked by aircraft. This could be a major consideration as detection methods against "stealth" aircraft improve, especially advanced infrared and low-frequency search-rate radars.

Special forces: Landing, supporting, and recovering special operations forces (Navy SEALs, Army Green Berets, etc.).

Another SSN role is, of course, operations in littoral (coastal) areas against diesel-electric submarines. This role differs substantially from ASW against Soviet-type submarines in the deep-ocean environment for which the U.S. submarine force was developed, armed, and trained during the Cold War. Consequently, this new role is the most difficult one for relatively large nuclear-propelled attack submarines to perform. The potential "arsenal ship" role for submarines is discussed in chapter 1.

The Navy is examining possible modifications for the third SEAWOLF-class submarine and the NSSN design to enable them to better perform post–Cold War SSN roles. These include the ability to remove torpedo skids and handling gear from the SSN torpedo room to provide additional accommodations for special operations forces.

The Navy had planned to construct SEAWOLF-class submarines as replacements for pre–LOS ANGELES SSNs as those older units were retired after about 30 years of service. However, with the end of the Cold War, the SEAWOLF program was quickly reduced by the Bush administration from a planned 30 units to only the lead ship. Congressional pressure—supported by the Navy's nuclear submarine community—had already funded a second SEAWOLF in fiscal 1991 and partially funded a third in fiscal 1992. Procurement of the third unit was again halted as other attack submarine options were considered (see below) and the SSN controversy continued. The third unit (SSN 23) was then authorized in the fiscal 1996 shipbuilding program in an effort to keep the Electric Boat Division of the General Dynamics Corp. and several component supplies in the submarine-construction business. The interval between the second SEAWOLF (1991 authorization) and the third (1996)—if built—is probably the longest interval between submarines in the history of the U.S. Navy.

As the high cost of SEAWOLF construction and congressional opposition became evident, the Chief of Naval Operations, Admiral Frank B. Kelso II, proposed in 1990 a lower-cost SSN, given the project name Centurion. This submarine was intended as an alternative to the SEAWOLF, with the lead ship to be authorized in fiscal 1998. In 1993 the craft was redesignated the New Attack Submarine (NAS and then NSSN). The fate of this submarine is also questionable because of the high costs of development and design, although follow-on submarine unit costs are estimated to be significantly lower than follow-on SEAWOLFS (about $1.5 *billion* compared to estimates of almost $3 *billion* for the third SEAWOLF).

In some respects the future construction rate is more significant than the number of SSNs because of the impact on the submarine industrial base. With the end of the Cold War, the Navy has decided to maintain only the General Dynamics/Electric Boat shipyard in Groton, Connecticut, to build submarines. This compares to seven yards that were building nuclear-propelled submarines in the 1960s and 1970s.

The Bottom-Up Review accepted the Navy nuclear-propulsion community's recommendation to concentrate future SSN construction at the Electric Boat shipyard. This action would maintain the Newport News shipyard (which will complete construction of the improved LOS ANGELES class in 1996) as a nuclear-capable yard through the construction and refueling of nuclear carriers.

However, the Newport News yard, which had designed the LOS ANGELES class as well as the "front end" of the SEAWOLF, had sought to build some units of the SEAWOLF class, taking the issue to court in 1991 (see below). Subsequently, in 1995, Newport News proposed that it could build the NSSN without the Navy having to build the third SEAWOLF (SSN 23) to "bridge" the construction gap between the second SEAWOLF (SSN 22) and the NSSN, as is required at Electric Boat. This is possible because Newport News has a broader business base than Electric Boat, including the Navy's carrier program, deactivating nuclear cruisers, commercial ship construction and overhaul, and possibly frigate construction for other navies.

Several proposals have been made for the U.S. Navy to procure nonnuclear submarines, particularly designs fitted with Air Independent Propulsion (AIP) to supplement the diesel-electric propulsion plant. Such submarines could carry out some missions as well as nuclear units could, among them anti-submarine training (against nonnuclear submarine targets), special operations in low-threat areas, and research and development. However, nonnuclear submarine construction has been strongly opposed by the nuclear submarine leadership, as has the construction of conventional submarines in U.S. shipyards for foreign navies.

The last U.S. Navy diesel-electric attack submarine was the BLUEBACK, stricken in 1990 after more than 30 years of service. In 1994 the Litton/Ingalls yard obtained U.S. State Department permission to explore the construction and/or fitting out of submarines in the United States for the Egyptian Navy. (Previously, the yard was involved in the procurement—albeit not construction—of German-built submarines for the Israeli Navy.)

All PERMIT and earlier submarines have been stricken, while submarines of the STURGEON and early LOS ANGELES classes are now being decommissioned at a rapid rate. Nuclear-propelled submarines cannot be laid up in reserve for possible future reactivation because of the measures necessary for shutting down their reactor plants and removing possibly radioactive components.

All diesel-electric combat attack submarines (SS) have been discarded from the U.S. Navy, although one diesel-electric research submarine, the DOLPHIN, remains in service.

Several submarines of the ETHAN ALLEN and GEORGE WASHINGTON classes served briefly in the SSN role during the 1980s; they were not successful as SSNs because of their relatively high self-noise levels, limited sonar capability, and few torpedo reloads. These submarines are listed in chapter 11 under the GEORGE WASHINGTON (SSBN 598) and ETHAN ALLEN (SSBN 608) entries.

Several submersibles, including the nuclear-propelled NR-1, are also in service (see chapter 26).

---

1. See, for example, Vice Adm. William A. Owens, USN, "The View from OPNAV," *The Submarine Review* (July 1993), pp. 18–26, and Adm. William A. Owens, USN, *High Seas: The Naval Passage to an Unchartered World* (Annapolis, Md.: Naval Institute Press, 1995). In 1993 Owens was Deputy Chief of Naval Operations (Resources, Warfare Requirements, and Assessments [N8]); in 1995 he was the Vice Chairman of the Joint Chiefs of Staff.

SUBMARINE FORCE LEVELS (FALL 1996)

Type	Class/Ship	Comm.	Active*	Building**	Notes
SSN 21	Seawolf	1996–	—	3	in production.
SSN 751	Improved Los Angeles	1988–	23	—	in production.
SSN 688	Los Angeles	1976–1989	35	—	1 serves in research role.
SSN 671	Narwhal	1969	1	—	to be deactivated late 1990s.
SSN 683	Parche	1974	1	—	special mission submarine.
SSN 637	Sturgeon	1967–1975	18	—	class being deactivated.
SSN 616	Lafayette	1965–1966	2	—	ex-SSBNs; transport submarines.
AGSS 555	Dolphin	1968	1	—	deep-diving research submarine.

*Some submarines are in the process of "standing down" in preparation for being decommissioned and stricken.
**Submarines authorized through fiscal 1996.

Classification: Historically, all U.S. submarines were numbered in a single series—with the exception of six specialized craft—until the advent of the Seawolf, which is designated SSN 21.[2] Originally, SSN 21 indicated a design concept, i.e., a submarine for the 21st century. Subsequently, the SSN 21 was adopted as a hull number, although it violates the 1920 Secretary of the Navy instruction that establishes the Navy hull-numbering system that prohibits hull numbers being reused. (The first SS 21 was named Barracuda, later changed to F-2; she was commissioned in 1912 and stricken in 1922.)

Names: Attack submarines have had several name sources. The Navy's first submarine, the Holland (SS 1), was named for its designer, Irish immigrant and schoolteacher John P. Holland, who was living when the craft was accepted by the Navy and named in 1900. Subsequent U.S. submarines were given "fish" names until 1911, when class letters and numerals were assigned (as A-2). This scheme continued until 1931, at which time fish names were again used (in addition to a scheme of class letter designations and hull numbers).

After World War II the class letter-number names were again used for the small T (training) and K (hunter-killer) submarines, but they were soon given fish names. Postwar submarines continued the use of fish or other marine-life names until 1971, when Vice Admiral H. G. Rickover, then head of the Navy's nuclear propulsion program, instituted the practice of naming attack submarines for deceased members of Congress who had supported nuclear programs. Four SSNs were so named: Glenard P. Lipscomb, L. Mendel Rivers, Richard B. Russell, and William H. Bates.

The naming source for attack submarines was changed to city names in 1974, with the first being the Los Angeles. In 1983, however, Secretary of the Navy John Lehman directed that the SSN 705 (then under construction) be named Hyman G. Rickover for Admiral Rickover, whom Lehman had helped force to leave the Navy in January 1982. (This was only the second recent U.S. Navy ship to be named for a living person, the first being the carrier Carl Vinson/CVN 70). Lehman's action was intended to prevent Congress from naming an aircraft carrier for Admiral Rickover.

The SSN 21 reverted to a fish name for submarines with the Seawolf, but the SSN 22 carries a state name, Connecticut. (Other U.S. Navy ships named for states are battleships, strategic missile submarines, and cruisers.)

Operational: Peacetime SSN missions include intelligence collection and anti-submarine training for air, surface, and submarine forces. In wartime the primary mission of U.S. attack submarines would be operations against enemy "attack" and strategic missile submarines as well as carrying out anti-surface ship, land-attack (with Tomahawk), and mining operations.

Two Los Angeles-class SSNs participated in the Gulf War by firing Tomahawk missiles against targets in Iraq. Those submarines fired 4 percent, or 12 of the 288, Tomahawk missiles launched in that conflict. Those launches were made primarily for "public relations" purposes, although the launchings were a valuable test of the concept.

Weapons: All U.S. combat submarines (SSBN/SSN) have 21-inch (533-mm) torpedo tubes. This diameter has been the standard in U.S. submarines since the submarine AA-2 (SS 60) was completed in 1922. The Seawolf class will introduce 26½-inch (673-mm) diameter torpedo tubes to U.S. submarines. The plan for these submarines is for them to carry only variants of the 21-inch Mk 48 torpedo, but the larger-diameter tubes, fitted with skids, will permit quiet "swim-out" launch of torpedoes. The research submarine Memphis has also been fitted with a single 30-inch torpedo tube.

All operational U.S. attack submarines can carry Harpoon anti-ship missiles and Tomahawk Anti-Ship (TASM) and Land-Attack Missiles (TLAM). These missiles are launched from standard 21-inch torpedo tubes with the later Los Angeles-class units additionally having 12 vertical-launch cells for Tomahawk missiles.

The Sea Lance ASW Stand-Off Weapon (SOW) has been canceled. Ostensibly, it was to replace the outdated SUBROC (Submarine Rocket), an ASW weapon carrying a nuclear depth bomb that was discarded in the late 1980s. With the subsequent cancellation of the Sea Lance, no ASW stand-off weapon is available to U.S. submarines. (The Sea Lance was to have carried both a nuclear depth bomb and the Mk 50 conventional, lightweight torpedo as a warhead, with the latter having development priority.)

The Sturgeon and later Los Angeles submarines can carry Submarine-Launched Mobile Mines (SLMM) in place of torpedoes.

The development of a lower-cost SSN was initiated in 1988–1990 in response to the increasing costs of the Seawolf class as well as questions about that submarine's tasks and missions. The current goal

2. The six exceptions were three hunter-killer submarines (SSK 1–3, one of which was later redesignated SST 3); two target and training submarines (SST 1, 2); and the midget submarine X-1.

40+ NUCLEAR-PROPELLED NEW ATTACK SUBMARINES: FORMERLY CENTURION PROJECT

Number	FY	Commission	Status
NSSN No. 1	1998	2004	Planned
NSSN No. 2	1999		Planned
NSSN No. 3	2000		Planned
NSSN No. 4–30	2001		Planned
NSSN No. 31–45	2002–2020		Proposed

Builders:	NSSN No. 1, 3 General Dynamics/Electric Boat, Groton, Conn. NSSN No. 2, 4 Newport News Shipbuilding, Va.
Displacement:	______ 7,700 tons
Length:	377 feet (114.93 m) overall
Beam:	34 feet (10.37 m)
Draft:	
Propulsion:	2 steam turbines; approx. 25,000 shp; 1 shaft
Reactors:	1 pressurized-water S9G reactor (General Electric)
Speed:	25+ knots
Manning:	134 (14 officers + 120 enlisted)
Missiles:	Harpoon SSM and Tomahawk TLAM launched from torpedo tubes and VLS 12 vertical launch cells for Tomahawk TLAM
Torpedo tubes:	4 21-inch (533-mm) amidships (24 weapons)
ASW weapons:	Mk 48 torpedoes
Radars:	BPS-16 surface search
Sonars:	bow-mounted spherical array lightweight Wide-Aperture-Array (WAA) mine hunting TB-16 fat-line towed array TB-29 thin-line towed array
EW systems:	

for this program is to develop a multi-mission attack submarine that is: (1) substantially less expensive than the SEAWOLF design; (2) capable of maintaining U.S. undersea superiority against a reduced but continuing Russian submarine effort; (3) more capable than the SEAWOLF or improved LOS ANGELES classes for operations in littoral areas; and (4) better able than the SEAWOLF or improved LOS ANGELES designs to incorporate major new submarine technologies as they become available.

This program was initially known as "Centurion," reflecting a submarine for the year 2000.[3] The designation was changed to New Attack Submarine in 1993 (originally NAS and, subsequently, NSSN).

The Navy originally announced plans to construct two or three Centurion SSNs per year to maintain a force level of some 80 attack submarines. On 19 March 1991 Secretary of the Navy H. Lawrence Garrett III testified before Congress that:

> the Navy face[s] a long-term problem of maintaining an adequate force of first-line ships when the [SSN] 688 class begins to be retired. As part of an overall effort to seek economies in all our ships and aircraft, I have recently directed the Chief of Naval Operations . . . to begin studies for a new submarine that would incorporate the technologies developed for SSN 21 and new technologies, in a smaller, less expensive platform as an option when the LOS ANGELES-class submarines reach the end of their service lives after the year 2000. . . . The proposed new submarine will complement the SEAWOLF in the multi-mission environment of the twenty-first century. While the SEAWOLF design strongly emphasizes ASW capability against the very best projected Soviet submarines, this new submarine design will emphasize capability in other kinds of contingencies. Both of these ships will allow us to maintain an adequate force level as we move past the year 2010.

Through mid-1991 the Navy had maintained that the Centurion SSN would be a complement rather than a successor to the SEAWOLF. In late June 1991, however, there were reports that the SEAWOLF procurement would cease about the year 2000 to permit acceleration of the new, lower-cost attack submarine.

On 28 August 1992 the Under Secretary of Defense for Acquisition approved concept definition studies for the new attack submarine with the Defense Acquisition Board (DAB), directing the Navy to keep the cost of the Centurion SSN program at $1 *billion* or less per submarine and to examine a variety of SSN alternatives for the Centurion. The *minimum* alternatives listed in the directive were:

> *SSN 21:* Assume continued production of the SEAWOLF at the rate of one per year at one shipyard. Assume two different start (authorization) dates: Fiscal Year (FY) 1996 and FY 1998. This alternative will serve as the cost and analysis baseline.
>
> *SSN 21 (V):* Assume at least two lower-cost variants of the SSN 21 with displacements in the range of 10,000 tons.
>
> *SSN 688 [Improved]:* Assume variations of the SSN 688I class that incorporate all available technology. Examine two different start dates: FY 1996 and FY 1998.
>
> *New nuclear-powered attack submarines:* Examine a range of alternative new nuclear attack submarines. Include alternatives with reduced capabilities relative to those of the SSN 21, and designs smaller than that of the SSN 688I. Examine designs smaller than 5,000 tons and options with reduced or deleted mission capabilities, e.g., power projection. These designs should be more affordable ($1 *billion*), less than or equal to the cost of the SSN 688I. Examine three different start dates: FY 1998, FY 2002, and FY 2008.
>
> *Trident [Variant]:* Assume selected variations including differences in tube volume of the Trident design, including a conversion of existing units, with emphasis on power projection mission.
>
> *Conventional submarines:* Examine a range of conventionally powered submarines, including as a minimum the following technologies: Diesel, closed-cycle diesel, air independent propulsion,[4] fuel cell, Stirling engine, a hybrid submarine using a small nuclear reactor to recharge batteries (SSn), and advanced batteries. Display the effect of overseas basing on this alternative.

As a result of the DAB review on 12 January 1994, the Navy was directed to study several nuclear-propelled attack submarine concepts and their impact on the industrial base. On 1 August 1994 the DAB approved Phase I design efforts focused on the authorization of a lead ship in fiscal 1998.

The General Accounting Office (GAO) has released a report proposing that the Navy save $9 *billion* by cutting the number of attack submarines planned for procurement over the next 20 years by six units, or one-fifth of the SSN building program. The SEAWOLF and 30 of the new attack submarines (NSSN) procured from fiscal 1998 and 2014 would cost an estimated $48 *billion.*[5]

The GAO calculated that a purchase of only 25 SSNs would save the $9 *billion* while permitting a force of 55 attack submarines through 2013, thereafter declining to 45 units. The 45-to-55 SSN range was recommended by the Bottom-Up Review of conventional forces carried out in 1995 by the Clinton administration. The GAO plan calls for retaining some LOS ANGELES submarines longer than now planned, i.e., up to their full 30-year service life expectancy. Various Navy and unified commander in chief studies call for more SSNs—up to 67—but the likelihood of such a force is highly improbable.

In 1995 the Navy had planned the lead ship for construction in fiscal 1998, with an identical follow-on submarine in fiscal 2001 and series production of two or three submarines per year to begin in fiscal 2002. Congress has now dictated that the NSSN program will provide one submarine per year in fiscal years 1998 through 2001, with Electric Boat and Newport News alternating construction of these four submarines.

Further, the submarine leadership wanted all NSSNs to be of the same design, with incremental improvements being made as production continues. But Rep. Duncan Hunter (R-Calif.), chairman of the powerful procurement subcommittee of the House National Security Affairs Committee, with the full backing of House speaker Newt Gingrich (R-Ga.), has directed that the fiscal 1998–2001 submarines be competitive prototypes, evaluating new designs, machinery, different quieting concepts (acoustic and non-acoustic), and other advanced features. Only after the four designs are evaluated would series production begin of the design judged most effective.

Cost: In 1994 the Navy estimated that the lead submarine would cost about $3.4 *billion* (including about $1.1 *billion* in nonrecurring detailed design costs) and the fifth and follow-on submarines would cost $1.54 *billion* (in fiscal 1998 dollars). The 1994 study that was prepared for the Navy estimated the following costs for the first three units:[6]

FY 1998	NSSN No. 1	$2.237 *billion*
FY 2000	NSSN No. 2	$1.843 *billion*
FY 2001	NSSN No. 3	$1.746 *billion*
Nonrecurring costs		$4.681 *billion*

(The nonrecurring costs are for design, research and development, etc.)

Design: The NSSN is expected to have an acoustic signature (self-radiated noise) at the same level as the SEAWOLF design. The submarine will be configured to operate unmanned underwater vehicles.

The torpedo room will be configured for rapid removal of weapon stowage and handling equipment to facilitate the use of the submarine as a special operations transport or possibly for other specialized roles. In addition, the design would provide for follow-on units to be built with different hull sections, i.e., modular reconfigurability.

The sail will house an Electronic Support Measures (ESM) mast, multi-function communication masts, and two photonics masts for improved imaging functions. The latter will be "non-penetrating" of the pressure hull. A modular sail concept will permit rapid replacement of specialized masts and antennas.

The pressure hull is to be fabricated of HY-100 steel, but the NSSN will have the operating depth of the LOS ANGELES class (HY 80), not the deeper operating SEAWOLF.

Torpedoes: The NSSN will stow fewer weapons in the torpedo room/tubes than can the SEAWOLF class (probably some 25 weapons).

3. There has never been a U.S. Navy ship with the name Centurion. Since 1650, the Royal Navy has had nine ships, including two battleships, named CENTURION.
4. Closed-cycle diesel is a form of Air Independent Propulsion (AIP), as are the Stirling engine, fuel cells, SSn, and advanced batteries concepts.
5. "Navy Shipbuilding Programs: Nuclear Attack Submarine Issues" (Washington, D.C.: General Accounting Office, 16 May 1995).
6. "New Attack Submarine (NSSN) Independent Characteristics Review," prepared for the Assistant Secretary of the Navy for Research, Development, and Acquisition (May 1994).

(3) NUCLEAR-PROPELLED ATTACK SUBMARINES: "SEAWOLF" CLASS

Number	Name	FY	Builder	Start*	Launch	Commission	Status
SSN 21	Seawolf	89	General Dynamics/Electric Boat	25 Oct 1989	24 June 1995	late 1996	Building
SSN 22	Connecticut	91	General Dynamics/Electric Boat	14 Sep 1992		1998	Building
SSN 23	———	92/96	General Dynamics/Electric Boat			2002	Planned

*These ships do not have a formal keel laying; dates are for start of construction.

Displacement:	7,460 tons surface 9,137 tons submerged (see *Design* notes)
Length:	353 feet (107.6 m) overall
Beam:	40 feet (12.2 m)
Draft:	35 feet (10.9 m)
Propulsion:	2 steam turbines (General Electric); approx. 40,000 shp; 1 shaft/propulsor
Reactors:	1 Westinghouse S6W reactor
Speed:	——— 35 knots submerged (see Propulsion notes)
Manning:	134 (14 officers + 120 enlisted)
Missiles:	Harpoon SSM and Tomahawk TLAM launched from torpedo tubes
Torpedo tubes:	8 26½-inch (673-mm) amidships (50 weapons)
ASW weapons:	Mk 48 torpedoes
Radars:	BPS-16 surface search
Sonars/Fire Control:	BSY-2 with bow-mounted transducers BQG-5D hull-mounted Wide Aperture Arrays (WAA) BQS-24 navigation/ice-avoidance TB-16D fat-line towed array TB-29 thin-line towed array
EW systems:	BLD-1D/F WLQ-4(V)1

The Seawolf was developed as a follow-on to the Los Angeles class with the primary mission of anti-submarine operations against advanced Soviet submarines.

The Navy originally planned to construct about 30 submarines of this class, to be authorized in fiscal years 1989 to 2000: one was to be authorized in fiscal 1989, two each in fiscal 1991 and 1992, and an average of 3⅓ ships in the following years. However, controversy over the design, the issue of concurrent BSY-2 system development and submarine construction, and high costs led to reductions in the program. On 13 August 1990, as a result of a four-month Department

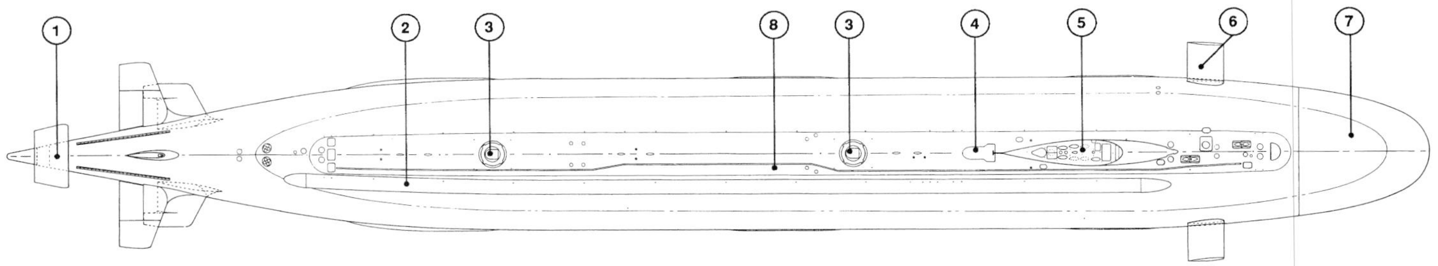

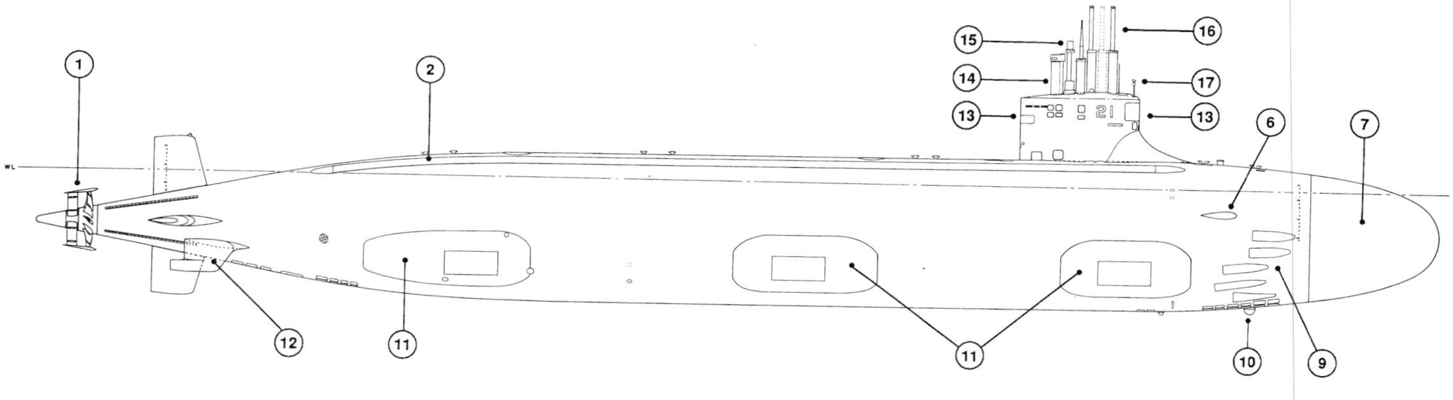

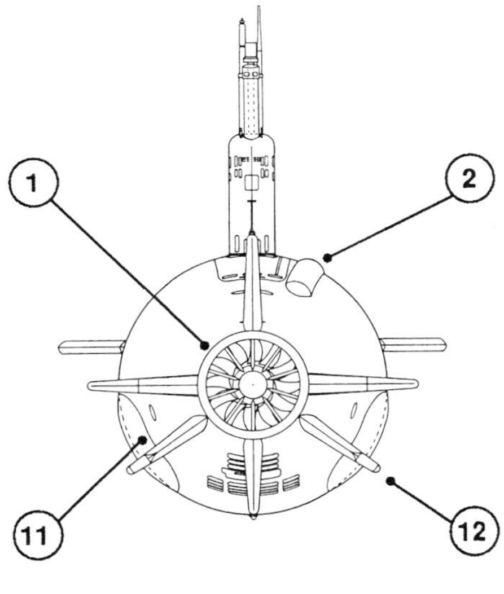

Seawolf class
1. Pump jet propulsor. 2. Towed array fairing. 3. Escape trunk and DSRV mating hatch. 4. Weapons shipping hatch. 5. Sail structure. 6. Retractable bow plane. 7. Sonar dome. 8. Safety track. 9. Torpedo tube shutters (8). 10. Low-frequency hydrophone. 11. Wide Aperture Array (WAA) sonar fairings. 12. Anhedral stabilizer with towed array lead. 13. High-frequency array. 14. Snorkel intake. 15. ESM mast. 16. Periscopes and antennas. 17. BPS-16 radar. (Deep Sea Designs/Greg Sharpe)

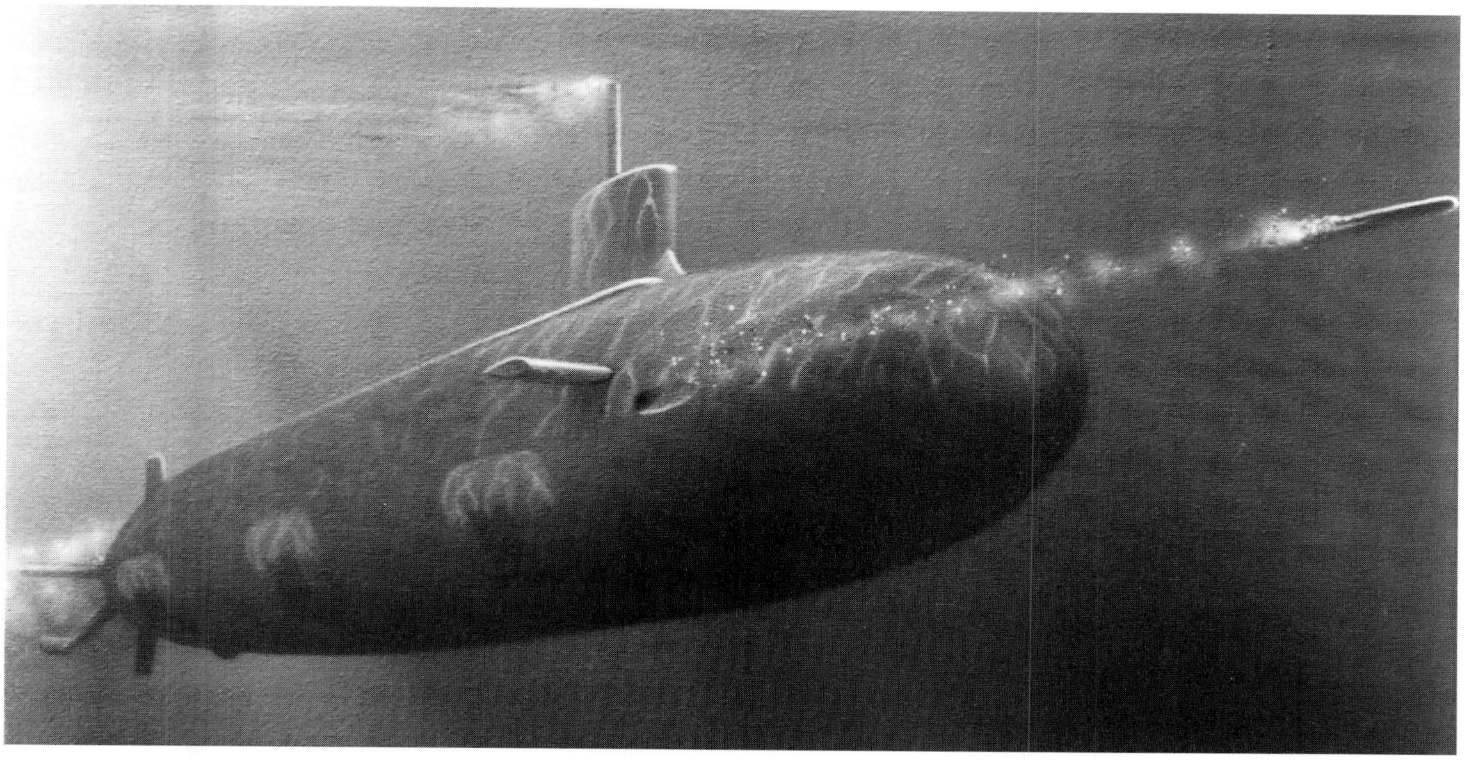

A Navy artist's concept of the SEAWOLF launching a torpedo. Note the position of the retractable bow diving planes, the "fillet" at the forward base of the sail, and the Wide Aperture Array (WAA) sonar fairings amidships. Details of the propeller-in-shroud propulsor have not been revealed. (U.S. Navy)

of Defense major warship and threat review, the SEAWOLF procurement was reduced to 12 submarines and the production rate was reduced to three submarines every two years (i.e., 1½ per year). The six-year defense plan submitted to Congress in February 1991 reduced the planned procurement rate to one SSN per year through fiscal 1995; after that there would be a 2-1-2-1 pattern, starting in fiscal 1996.

In September 1991 the Chief of Naval Operations, Admiral Frank B. Kelso II, said that he expected only one SEAWOLF per year to be constructed until the lead Centurion SSN was authorized; this statement indicated that he did not anticipate a total program of more than seven or eight SEAWOLFS. In January 1992 the Department of Defense announced that the entire SEAWOLF program would be canceled; only the first unit would be completed. The funds previously voted by Congress for the SSN 22 and SSN 23 were to be rescinded.

(The SEAWOLF became a political issue when, during the presidential primary campaign of 1992, then-Arkansas Governor Bill Clinton told Connecticut voters that he would continue production of the SEAWOLF class beyond the first unit; primary candidate Paul Tsongas observed that Clinton, a Democrat, was supporting a defense program that even the Republican president did not wish to continue.)

The SSN 21 delivery was originally scheduled for November 1994; the delivery of the lead ship was delayed by at least six months (to May 1995) because of changes in the BSY-2 system configuration.[7] On 1 August 1991 the Navy announced that massive weld failures had been discovered in the hull that would delay the lead submarine at least into 1996. The cracks in the welding, which were first discovered in June 1991, required the replacement of all welds completed up to that time. The SEAWOLF contract was increased by $58,825,590 to cover the costs of the corrections.

Subsequently, the funding for the second SEAWOLF (SSN 22), authorized in fiscal 1991, was retained by Congress, with an additional $540,200,000 to be used for either the third SEAWOLF or some other project to preserve the submarine construction base.

The third SEAWOLF (SSN 23) was originally authorized in 1992 but the administration withheld the funds pending various studies of alternative submarine programs. The fiscal 1996 defense budget requested additional funding for the third SEAWOLF to keep the submarine production line at Electric Boat "hot" until the planned new NSSN is authorized in fiscal 1998.

Builders: On 9 January 1989 a fixed-price, incentive-plus-fee contract to build the lead submarine of the class was awarded to Electric Boat. Construction began on 25 October 1989, with a scheduled delivery date of May 1995.

The Navy awarded a contract for the second submarine of the class to Electric Boat on 3 May 1991. Four days later Newport News Shipbuilding filed a lawsuit protesting the decision, basing its case on a congressional mandate to preserve a two-yard submarine construction capability.[8]

On 31 August 1991 a federal judge voided the contract award with Electric Boat and directed the Navy to open the contract for the second SEAWOLF to competitors.

Class: The decision to construct a new SSN class was taken in July 1982. This followed a Navy decision one year earlier not to construct a new SSN (see the 13th Edition/page 54). When the SEAWOLF was conceived in 1982 the SSN force level goal was increased from 90 to 100 submarines.[9] But from the outset of the SEAWOLF effort even a cursory look at the program made it apparent that it would be impossible to procure a 100-submarine force because of the development and unit costs of the SEAWOLF class.

Classification: The Navy has designated this class as SSN 21, indicating an attack submarine for the 21st century. That hull number was previously carried by the submarine F-2 (initially named BARRACUDA), completed in 1912.

Cost: The construction of 29 submarines at an eventual production rate of three or four submarines per year was estimated in 1988 at $36 *billion.* The Secretary of the Navy's cost ceiling for the program (in fiscal 1985 dollars) was $1.6 *billion* for the lead ship and $1 *billion* for

7. The first *Naval Sea Systems Command Monthly Progress Report* issued after the construction contract was awarded listed the SSN 21 projected launch date as 28 January 1994 and completion on 26 May 1995.

8. On 7 May 1991 the Navy terminated a contract with Newport News Shipbuilding to participate in the design of the Centurion. This was one day after Newport News filed its suit challenging the selection of Electric Boat to build the second SEAWOLF. Navy officials denied that the two events were linked.

9. Ninety attack submarines was the Navy's force goal from 1973 to 1981; that goal was never achieved. Before that a force of 120 attack submarines, both diesel and nuclear, was authorized.

The SEAWOLF high and dry while under construction. The propulsor is just visible as is her unusual six-"surface" tail configuration. The SEAWOLF has a significantly larger displacement than did the Polaris strategic missile submarines. (1995, General Dynamics/Electric Boat)

the fifth and later ships; the latter unit cost excludes the cost of constructing the ninth and later ships with HY-130 steel. (These cost estimates do not take into account the welding problems and resulting delays.) In addition, the development cost of the BSY-2 was estimated at $1 *billion.*

In 1987 the Navy awarded Newport News Shipbuilding a $303 million (fiscal 1987 dollars) contract for the overall SEAWOLF design and detailed design of the submarine's forward half; Newport News awarded a $48,800,000 subcontract to Electric Boat for the detailed design of the submarine's rear half. By the end of 1992 Newport News estimated that the total cost of the SEAWOLF-class design would be $683 million (then-year dollars), a 125 percent increase over the original design cost estimate.

The SSN 21 total cost was estimated at $718 million (fiscal 1987 dollars) at the time the contract was awarded; in mid-1994 the estimated cost of the submarine was in excess of $1.1 *billion.*

The SSN 22 cost was estimated at $689 million (fiscal 1991) at the time the contract was awarded.

The fiscal 1991 defense appropriation provided $2.4 *billion* to build the SSN 23 and to cover advanced procurement items for follow-on SEAWOLFS. On 18 January 1994 then-Chief of Naval Operations, Admiral Frank B. Kelso II, stated in his briefing "Restructuring Naval Forces" that $900 million had already been spent on the SSN-23 and that $1.5 *billion* was required to complete the submarine—an estimated total of $2.4 *billion.* (A year later the Congressional Research Service identified a formal obligation of only $578,700,000 as of January 1995.[10] Of that amount, only $382,500,000 actually had been expended.)

By 1996 the SSN 23 cost was estimated at $3 *billion.* (All costs are exclusive of Department of Energy costs for reactor and fuel development and procurement.)

Design: The basic SEAWOLF design was established in 1982–1983. It emphasized improved machinery, quieting, and improved combat systems, both sensors and additional weapons.

The SEAWOLF is considered the first "top-to-bottom" U.S. attack submarine design since the SKIPJACK design of the late 1950s. These submarines will be slightly faster than the LOS ANGELES class and will have more torpedo tubes and more internally stowed weapons; there will be no Tomahawk launch tubes external to the pressure hull, as in the later units of the LOS ANGELES class. The design provides for a smaller length-to-beam ratio than in previous U.S. attack submarine classes. A six-surface tail configuration is used with the single propeller shaft common to U.S. SSNs since the late 1950s, but the propeller has a circular shroud or duct similar to the installation in some British TRAFALGAR-class SSNs and (on a smaller scale) the Mk 48 torpedo. The submarines have bow-mounted diving planes (vice sail-mounted), which retract into the bow for under-ice operations.

According to Electric Boat statements, "The SEAWOLF will be less detectable at high speed than a LOS ANGELES class SSN sitting at the pier," and the SEAWOLF is the "world's quietest submarine." Both statements were made before the SEAWOLF was launched.[11]

The submerged displacement (9,150 tons) listed above is the limit imposed by the Secretary of the Navy circa 1986. The actual submerged displacement is approximately 9,300 tons; about 150 tons is the water trapped in the bow sonar dome, which is normally flooded and closed when the submarine is at sea. However, in this class, to keep within the Secretary of the Navy's ceiling, the sonar dome is "open" to the sea when flooded.

Innovative modular construction techniques are employed in the construction of these submarines.

The ninth and subsequent units were to have had HY-130 steel vice the HY-100 steel used in the earlier SEAWOLF-class submarines. All U.S. submarines from the THRESHER through the LOS ANGELES class were constructed of HY-80 steel.[12] (HY-100 steel was originally proposed for the LOS ANGELES class.)

A one-quarter scale model of the SEAWOLF is being used to evaluate SEAWOLF design concepts (see end of this chapter).

Electronics: These submarines have the BSY-2 combat system, previously known as SUBACS for Submarine Advanced Combat System (see chapter 31 for characteristics). The BQG-5D WAA system has three rectangular arrays fitted to each side of the submarine's hull.

Changes in the design of the BSY-2 caused redesign of portions of the SEAWOLF. In addition to the large bow spherical array, there are three WAA panels along each side of the submarine.

Engineering: The maximum submerged speed has been officially stated to be 35 knots, apparently making the SEAWOLF class faster than any previous U.S. submarine design. The SEAWOLF is expected to have a maximum "acoustic speed" in excess of 20 knots (i.e., the speed at which the submarine can transit while maintaining a sufficiently low noise level to still employ passive sonar with a narrow-band capability; a comparative Soviet speed was reported at 6 to 8 knots for submarines built in the 1980s).

Names: The name SEAWOLF was chosen for the lead submarine of this class in 1986 with the assumption that the existing SEAWOLF (SSN

10. Ronald O'Rourke, "Navy Attack Submarine Programs: Issue for Congress," CRS Issue Brief (Washington, D.C.: Congressional Research Service, 17 January 1995), p. 3.

11. "Seawolf," on the reverse of an artist's concept prepared by General Dynamics/Electric Boat Division [n.d.].

12. HY-80 was used in the SKIPJACK class, but the THRESHER was the first to have a complete HY-80 pressure hull, permitting a deeper operating depth.

575) would be stricken by the time the new craft was launched; the SSN 575 was stricken on 10 July 1987.

The previous SEAWOLF was the Navy's second nuclear-propelled submarine. That submarine was built with a liquid-sodium reactor plant (vice pressurized-water); it was not considered successful and was removed. An earlier submarine named SEAWOLF (SS 197) was one of two U.S. submarines to be sunk by American forces in World War II.

Torpedoes: The Navy originally planned to place the torpedo tubes in the bow of these craft, where they would be less vulnerable to water-flow problems during weapon launches at high speed. Following tests, the launch tubes were retained in the amidships position used in all designs since the TULLIBEE and THRESHER classes. Firing tests, however, demonstrated the feasibility of high-speed torpedo firing from amidship tubes, and the SEAWOLF design was modified.

23 NUCLEAR-PROPELLED ATTACK SUBMARINES: IMPROVED "LOS ANGELES" CLASS

Number	Name	FY	Builder	Laid down	Launched	Commissioned	Status
SSN 751	SAN JUAN	83	General Dynamics/Electric Boat	16 Aug 1985	6 Dec 1986	6 Aug 1988	AA
SSN 752	PASADENA	83	General Dynamics/Electric Boat	20 Dec 1985	12 Sep 1987	11 Feb 1989	PA
SSN 753	ALBANY	84	Newport News Shipbuilding	22 Apr 1985	13 June 1987	7 Apr 1990	AA
SSN 754	TOPEKA	84	General Dynamics/Electric Boat	13 May 1986	23 Jan 1988	21 Oct 1989	PA
SSN 755	MIAMI	84	General Dynamics/Electric Boat	24 Oct 1986	12 Nov 1988	30 June 1990	AA
SSN 756	SCRANTON	85	Newport News Shipbuilding	29 Aug 1986	3 July 1989	26 Jan 1991	AA
SSN 757	ALEXANDRIA	85	Newport News Shipbuilding	19 June 1987	23 June 1990	29 June 1991	AA
SSN 758	ASHEVILLE	85	Newport News Shipbuilding	9 Jan 1987	24 Feb 1990	28 Sep 1991	AA
SSN 759	JEFFERSON CITY	85	Newport News Shipbuilding	21 Sep 1987	17 Aug 1990	29 Feb 1992	AA
SSN 760	ANNAPOLIS	86	General Dynamics/Electric Boat	15 June 1988	18 May 1991	11 Apr 1992	AA
SSN 761	SPRINGFIELD	86	General Dynamics/Electric Boat	29 Jan 1990	4 Jan 1992	9 Jan 1993	AA
SSN 762	COLUMBUS	86	General Dynamics/Electric Boat	7 Jan 1991	1 Aug 1992	24 July 1993	PA
SSN 763	SANTA FE	86	General Dynamics/Electric Boat	9 Sep 1991	12 Dec 1992	8 Jan 1994	AA
SSN 764	BOISE	87	Newport News Shipbuilding	25 Aug 1988	23 Mar 1991	7 Nov 1992	AA
SSN 765	MONTPELIER	87	Newport News Shipbuilding	19 May 1989	23 Aug 1991	13 Mar 1993	AA
SSN 766	CHARLOTTE	87	Newport News Shipbuilding	17 Aug 1990	3 Oct 1992	16 Sep 1994	AA
SSN 767	HAMPTON	87	Newport News Shipbuilding	2 Mar 1990	28 Sep 1991	6 Nov 1993	AA
SSN 768	HARTFORD	88	General Dynamics/Electric Boat	27 Apr 1992	4 Dec 1993	10 Dec 1994	AA
SSN 769	TOLEDO	88	Newport News Shipbuilding	6 May 1991	28 Aug 1993	24 Feb 1995	AA
SSN 770	TUCSON	88	Newport News Shipbuilding	15 Aug 1991	20 Mar 1994	18 Aug 1995	AA
SSN 771	COLUMBIA	89	General Dynamics/Electric Boat	21 Apr 1993	24 Sep 1994	9 Oct 1995	AA
SSN 772	GREENEVILLE	89	Newport News Shipbuilding	28 Feb 1992	17 Sep 1994	16 Feb 1996	AA
SSN 773	CHEYENNE	90	Newport News Shipbuilding	6 July 1992	16 Apr 1995	13 Sep 1996	AA

Displacement:	6,300 tons standard except SSN 771–773 6,330 tons 7,147 tons submerged except SSN 771–773 7,177 tons
Length:	360 feet (109.7 m) overall
Beam:	33 feet (10.1 m)
Draft:	32 feet (9.75 m)
Propulsion:	2 steam turbines; approx. 30,000 shp; 1 shaft
Reactors:	1 pressurized-water S6G (General Electric)
Speed:	22 knots surface approx. 33 knots submerged
Manning:	141 (14 officers + 127 enlisted)
Missiles:	Harpoon and Tomahawk SSMs launched from torpedo tubes 12 vertical launch cells for Tomahawk SSM
Torpedo tubes:	4 21-inch (533-mm) amidships Mk 67 (25 weapons)
ASW weapons:	Mk 48 torpedoes
Radars:	BPS-15A surface search
Sonars:	BQQ-5C/D multi-function bow mounted (being upgraded to BQQ-5E) BQR-15 towed array BQR-26 in some units BQS-13 active BQS-15 under ice/mine detection BSY-1 combat system TB-23 and/or TB-29 towed array
Fire control:	1 CCS Mk 2 Mod 2 1 Mk 117 torpedo FCS
EW systems:	BRD-7 direction finder WLR-8(V) WLR-9 WLR-12

These are improved LOS ANGELES-class submarines having Tomahawk vertical-launch missile cells, minelaying and under-ice capabilities, and improved machinery quieting. See the LOS ANGELES-class entry for additional information and notes on these submarines.

Class: The LOS ANGELES class is the world's largest series of nuclear-propelled submarines, with 62 submarines built and under construction. The "final" program was for 65 units, but the Navy did not request funds for the last four units, supporting instead the SEAWOLF program. Congress authorized one of those LOS ANGELES-class submarines (SSN 773). This is the largest class of submarines built since World War II by any nation except for the Soviet diesel-electric Whiskey class (215 units completed 1949–1957) and Foxtrot class (62 built for Soviet service, plus 17 for foreign navies, 1958–1973).

Electronics: These submarines are fitted with the BSY-1 sonar/fire-control "combat system." Major problems were encountered in late 1986 in installing the initial system in the SSN 751, which resulted in a completion delay of the submarine.

Engineering: These submarines will be refueled at 16- to 20-year intervals. The SSN 768 and later units have improved quieting features and two additional stern fins (as in the SEAWOLF).

Missiles: The Harpoon and Tomahawk missiles can be launched from the torpedo tubes in this class. All have 12 vertical launch tubes for Tomahawk missiles fitted forward—between the pressure hull and sonar sphere—in space previously used for ballast tanks.

The SANTA FE at Port Canaveral, Florida, shows all of the hatches open for the 12 vertical launch cells. These weapons greatly enhance SSN capabilities. (1994, John Bouvia)

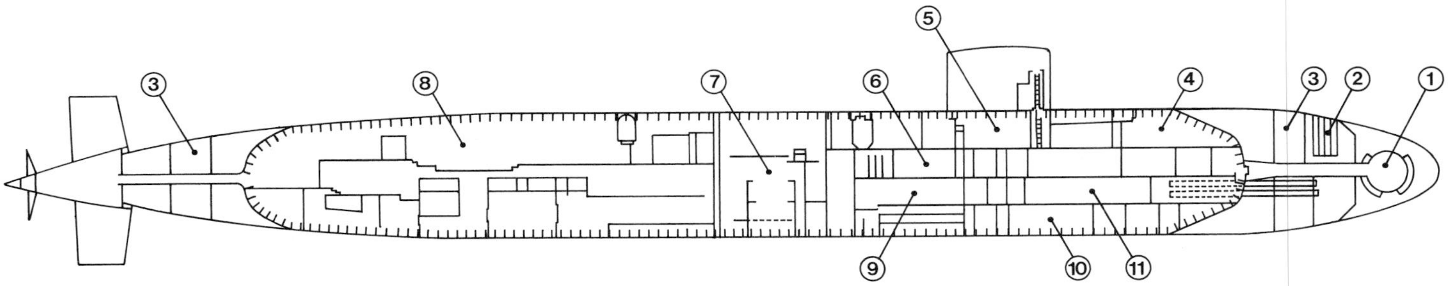

Improved Los Angeles class
1. Sonar sphere. 2. Vertical-launch cells. 3. Ballast tanks. 4. Sonar room. 5. Control room/attack center. 6. Crew's mess. 7. Reactor compartment. 8. Engine room. 9. Auxiliary machinery. 10. Battery compartment. 11. Torpedo room. (William Clipson)

The Boise at Port Everglades, Florida. The retractable, bow-mounted diving planes of the Improved Los Angeles-class submarines permit them to navigate under ice, which was an important aspect of Cold War submarine operations. (1994, Giorgio Arra)

Moored at Hong Kong, the Jefferson City shows the rounded hull of the Los Angeles design. A commercial navigation radar is rigged atop her bridge. (1994, Giorgio Arra)

34 NUCLEAR-PROPELLED ATTACK SUBMARINES / 1 NUCLEAR-PROPELLED RESEARCH SUBMARINE — "LOS ANGELES" CLASS

Number	Name	FY	Builder	Laid down	Launched	Commissioned	Status
SSN 688	Los Angeles	70	Newport News Shipbuilding	8 Jan 1972	6 Apr 1974	13 Nov 1976	**PA**
SSN 689	Baton Rouge	70	Newport News Shipbuilding	18 Nov 1972	26 Apr 1975	25 June 1977	decomm./str. 13 Jan 1995
SSN 690	Philadelphia	70	General Dynamics/Electric Boat	12 Aug 1972	19 Oct 1974	25 June 1977	**AA**
SSN 691	Memphis	71	Newport News Shipbuilding	23 June 1973	3 Apr 1976	17 Dec 1977	**AA-R&D**
SSN 692	Omaha	71	General Dynamics/Electric Boat	27 Jan 1973	21 Feb 1976	11 Mar 1978	decomm./str. 5 Oct 1995
SSN 693	Cincinnati	71	Newport News Shipbuilding	6 Apr 1974	19 Feb 1977	10 June 1978	decomm./str. 31 July 1995
SSN 694	Groton	71	General Dynamics/Electric Boat	3 Aug 1973	9 Oct 1976	8 July 1978	**AA**
SSN 695	Birmingham	72	Newport News Shipbuilding	26 Apr 1975	29 Oct 1977	16 Dec 1978	**PA**
SSN 696	New York City	72	General Dynamics/Electric Boat	15 Dec 1973	18 June 1977	3 Mar 1978	decomm./str. early 1997
SSN 697	Indianapolis	72	General Dynamics/Electric Boat	19 Oct 1974	30 July 1977	5 Jan 1980	**PA**
SSN 698	Bremerton	72	General Dynamics/Electric Boat	6 May 1976	22 July 1978	28 Mar 1981	**PA**
SSN 699	Jacksonville	72	General Dynamics/Electric Boat	21 Feb 1976	18 Nov 1978	16 May 1981	**AA**
SSN 700	Dallas	73	General Dynamics/Electric Boat	9 Oct 1976	28 Apr 1979	18 July 1981	**AA**
SSN 701	La Jolla	73	General Dynamics/Electric Boat	16 Oct 1976	11 Aug 1979	24 Oct 1981	**PA**
SSN 702	Phoenix	73	General Dynamics/Electric Boat	30 July 1977	8 Dec 1979	19 Dec 1981	**AA**
SSN 703	Boston	73	General Dynamics/Electric Boat	11 Aug 1978	19 Apr 1980	30 Jan 1982	**AA**
SSN 704	Baltimore	73	General Dynamics/Electric Boat	21 May 1979	13 Dec 1980	24 July 1982	**AA**
SSN 705	City of Corpus Christi	73	General Dynamics/Electric Boat	4 Sep 1979	25 Apr 1981	8 Jan 1983	**AA**
SSN 706	Albuquerque	74	General Dynamics/Electric Boat	27 Dec 1979	13 Mar 1982	21 May 1983	**AA**
SSN 707	Portsmouth	74	General Dynamics/Electric Boat	8 May 1980	18 Sep 1982	1 Oct 1983	**PA**
SSN 708	Minneapolis-Saint Paul	74	General Dynamics/Electric Boat	20 Jan 1981	19 Mar 1983	17 Mar 1984	**AA**
SSN 709	Hyman G. Rickover	74	General Dynamics/Electric Boat	24 July 1981	17 Aug 1983	8 Sep 1984	**AA**
SSN 710	Augusta	74	General Dynamics/Electric Boat	1 Apr 1982	21 Jan 1984	19 Jan 1985	**AA**
SSN 711	San Francisco	75	Newport News Shipbuilding	26 May 1977	27 Oct 1979	24 Apr 1981	**PA**
SSN 712	Atlanta	75	Newport News Shipbuilding	17 Aug 1978	16 Aug 1980	6 Mar 1982	**AA**
SSN 713	Houston	75	Newport News Shipbuilding	29 Jan 1979	21 Mar 1981	25 Sep 1982	**PA**
SSN 714	Norfolk	76	Newport News Shipbuilding	1 Aug 1979	31 Oct 1981	21 May 1983	**AA**
SSN 715	Buffalo	76	Newport News Shipbuilding	25 Jan 1980	8 May 1982	5 Nov 1983	**PA**
SSN 716	Salt Lake City	77	Newport News Shipbuilding	26 Aug 1980	16 Oct 1982	12 May 1984	**PA**
SSN 717	Olympia	77	Newport News Shipbuilding	31 Mar 1981	30 Apr 1983	17 Nov 1984	**PA**
SSN 718	Honolulu	77	Newport News Shipbuilding	10 Nov 1981	24 Sep 1983	6 July 1985	**PA**
SSN 719	Providence	78	General Dynamics/Electric Boat	14 Oct 1982	4 Aug 1984	27 July 1985	**AA**
SSN 720	Pittsburgh	79	General Dynamics/Electric Boat	15 Apr 1983	8 Dec 1984	23 Nov 1985	**AA**
SSN 721	Chicago	80	Newport News Shipbuilding	5 Jan 1983	13 Oct 1984	27 Sep 1986	**PA**
SSN 722	Key West	80	Newport News Shipbuilding	6 July 1983	20 July 1985	12 Sep 1887	**AA**
SSN 723	Oklahoma City	81	Newport News Shipbuilding	4 Jan 1984	2 Nov 1985	9 July 1988	**AA**
SSN 724	Louisville	81	General Dynamics/Electric Boat	16 Sep 1984	14 Dec 1985	8 Nov 1986	**PA**
SSN 725	Helena	82	General Dynamics/Electric Boat	28 Mar 1985	28 June 1986	11 July 1987	**PA**
SSN 750	Newport News	82	Newport News Shipbuilding	3 Mar 1984	15 Mar 1986	3 June 1989	**AA**

Displacement:	SSN 688–699	6,080 tons standard
		6,927 tons submerged
	SSN 700–715	6,130 tons standard
		6,977 tons submerged
	SSN 716–718	6,165 tons standard
		7,012 tons submerged
	SSN 719–750	6,255 tons standard
		7,102 tons submerged
Length:	360 feet (109.7 m) overall	
Beam:	33 feet (10.1 m)	
Draft:	32 feet (9.75 m)	
Propulsion:	2 steam turbines; approx. 30,000 shp; 1 shaft	
Reactors:	1 pressurized-water S6G (General Electric)	
Speed:		
	approx. 33 knots submerged	
Manning:	141 (14 officers + 127 enlisted) except SSN 691	
	165 (14 officers + 151 enlisted)	
Missiles:	Harpoon and Tomahawk SSMs launched from torpedo tubes	
	SSN 719–725, 750 12 vertical launch cells for Tomahawk TLAM	
Torpedo tubes:	4 21-inch (533-mm) amidships Mk 67 (25 weapons)	
ASW weapons:	Mk 48 torpedoes	
Radars:	BPS-15A or BPS-16 surface search	
Sonars:	BQQ-5 multi-function bow mounted (BQQ-5E in later and updated units)	
	BQR-15 towed array	
	BQR-26 in some submarines	
	BQS-13 active	
	BQS-15 under ice/mine detection	
	TB-16 (BQQ-5A) or TB-23 (BQQ-5D) towed array in later and updated units	
Fire control:	SSN 688–719 1 CCS Mk 2 Mod 0	
	SSN 719–725, 750 1 CCS Mk 2 Mod 1	
	1 Mk 117 torpedo FCS	
EW systems:	BRD-7 direction finder	
	WLR-8(V)	
	WLR-9	
	WLR-12	

These are large attack submarines, originally developed to counter the Soviet Victor fast-attack submarines that were first completed in 1967–1968. The Memphis is employed as a Research and Development (R&D) platform; but she retains her combat capabilities.

The Los Angeles submarines are about five knots faster than the previous U.S. Sturgeon class, the higher speed being the principal advantage over the earlier class (see Propulsion notes). However, the Los Angeles class is about one-half again as large in terms of displacement and considerably more expensive (see *Cost* notes). Also, the original Los Angeles design lacked under-ice and minelaying capabilities, both vital for modern submarine warfare. The SSN 756 and later units have a minelaying capability.

The San Juan and later units are considered an "improved" design (see previous listing).

Class: The Memphis, formerly a "straight" SSN, began operating a full-time "interim" R&D platform in August 1989. She provides an at-sea testing environment for the Advanced Research Projects Agency (ARPA), Navy, and industry programs. One of the first projects to be evaluated in the Memphis is a non-penetrating periscope (i.e., mounted on a flexible cable employing fiber optics). In 1993–1994 she underwent extensive modifications to serve in the research role, including provision of a 30-inch torpedo tube, advanced towed sonar arrays, an oversize logistics hatch to facilitate equipment installation and removal, and fitting of a "turtleback" structure for carrying Unmanned Underwater Vehicles (UUV).

The Memphis project was the result of congressional criticism of the Navy's failure to pursue advance submarine technology. There is no plan to reclassify the submarine; properly, she should be designated SSAGN.

A pilot boat comes alongside the KEY WEST off Port Everglades, Florida. The LOS ANGELES-class submarines can be readily identified by the rise in the hull forward of the sail. The sail-mounted diving planes were discarded in the improved submarines of this design; they had been introduced in U.S. nuclear submarines in the late 1950s. (1994, Giorgio Arra)

Classification: Submarine hull numbers 726 through 749 were reserved for Trident SSBNs.

Design: SCB No. 303. These are large SSNs; the increase in size over the STURGEON class is due primarily to the installation of the larger, more capable S6G reactor plant in an effort to regain the speed loss in the PERMIT and STURGEON classes. These submarines were designed to be constructed of HY-100 steel; however, they were built with HY-80. The ALBANY and TOPEKA have some hull sections of HY-100 to serve as a materials test bed for the SEAWOLF class; those submarines have not encountered the welding problems sustained by the later submarine.

The LOS ANGELES also has improved sonar and fire-control systems (these were being retrofitted to the STURGEON class) compared to previous classes. These submarines are not fitted to carry mines nor are they configured for under-ice operations; such shortcomings are corrected in the Improved LOS ANGELES class.

These submarines originally had berthing for only 95 enlisted men; the remainder either used sleeping bags in available space or "hot bunked." Additional berthing has been added, but the ships are considered to be quite crowded in comparison with earlier SSNs.

Electronics: The large towed array passive sonar is carried in a sheathlike housing fitted to the upper starboard side of the hull.

The early submarines were fitted with the Mk 113 (analog) fire-control system and could carry the Tomahawk missile, while those with the Mk 117 (digital) cannot carry the SUBROC. All have been refitted with the Mk 117.

Engineering: The S6G reactor is estimated to have an initial fuel core operating life of 10 to 13 years. According to official Navy statements, with the LOS ANGELES "the speed threshold which had been established by SKIPJACK 18 years earlier was finally surpassed."

Missiles: The Harpoon and Tomahawk missiles can be launched from the torpedo tubes in this class. The ATLANTA was the first SSN to deploy with the Tomahawk, in November 1983.

The ALBUQUERQUE is representative of the largest class of nuclear attack submarines built by any nation. Temporary bridge guards are rigged and her sail is crowded with the officer of the deck, the captain, and lookouts. (1994, Giorgio Arra)

The SALT LAKE CITY alongside the fleet tug CATAWBA (T-ATF 168) in Hong Kong. Note the huge fenders rigged by the CATAWBA to protect both ships. The SALT LAKE CITY has most of her periscopes and antennas raised despite the large number of foreign intelligence officers stationed in Hong Kong. (1994, Giorgio Arra)

Names: Most of the earlier submarines of this class carry names previously borne by cruisers; many later names were carried by lesser warships (e.g., frigates [PF]).

The SSN 705 was originally to be CORPUS CHRISTI for the Texas port city of that name. That name was previously borne by the frigate PF 44 (launched in 1943); the seaplane tender ALBEMARLE (AV 5) was converted to a helicopter repair ship (ARVH 1) during the Vietnam War and renamed CORPUS CHRISTI BAY (she was operated by the Military Sealift Command for the Army). After protests from Catholic groups the SSN 705 name was changed on 10 May 1982 to CITY OF CORPUS CHRISTI. (This corrects data in the previous edition.)

The SSN 708 honors the "twin cities" in Minnesota that are actually named Minneapolis–St. Paul (vice *Saint* Paul).

The SSN 709 was named on 4 March 1983 for Admiral H. G. Rickover, longtime head of the U.S. Navy's nuclear propulsion program. The move to honor Rickover while he was still alive was, in part, an effort to preempt congressional pressure to name an aircraft carrier for the controversial admiral.

The SSN 719 was named PROVIDENCE in September 1983 to honor the state of Rhode Island after the SSBN 730 (having previously been named for that state) was renamed HENRY M. JACKSON.

The SSN 757 was originally named ASHEVILLE; the name was changed to ALEXANDRIA on 27 February 1987. The SSN 764 was originally named HARTFORD and the SSN 768 the BOISE; they swapped names on 3 March 1989.

Operational: The LOUISVILLE and PITTSBURGH launched TLAM missiles against targets in Iraq during the 1991 Gulf War. The latter submarine fired the first "war shot" against an enemy by a U.S. submarine since World War II. The LOUISVILLE fired eight missiles and the PITTSBURGH fired four; this represented 4 percent of the 288 missiles fired in the Gulf War.

The AUGUSTA struck a Soviet nuclear-propelled strategic missile submarine underwater in the North Atlantic in October 1986 (at least one other Soviet submarine was in the area at the time). Repairs to the AUGUSTA cost $2.7 million.

The BATON ROUGE collided with a Russian nuclear-propelled submarine in the Barents Sea on 11 February 1992. U.S. officials said that the incident occurred in international waters, beyond the 12-n.mile (22.2-km) territorial zone recognized by the United States. Russian officials declared that the collision was off Murmansk, within their territorial waters. Neither submarine was reported to have suffered serious damage, and there were no injuries. However, the Navy placed the BATON ROUGE In Commission, In Reserve (ICIR) on 11 January 1993 for later disposal.

1 NUCLEAR-PROPELLED SPECIAL MISSION SUBMARINE: MODIFIED "STURGEON" CLASS

Number	Name	FY	Builder	Laid down	Launched	Commissioned	Status
SSN 683	PARCHE	68	Litton/Ingalls Shipbuilding	10 Dec 1970	13 Jan 1973	17 Aug 1974	PA

Displacement:	
	7,800 tons submerged
Length:	401 5/12 feet (122.4 m) overall
Beam:	31 2/3 feet (9.65 m)
Draft:	35 feet (10.67 m)
Propulsion:	2 steam turbines (De Laval or General Electric); 15,000 shp; 1 shaft
Reactors:	1 pressurized-water S5W (Westinghouse)
Speed:	approx. 15 knots surface
	approx. 28 knots submerged
Manning:	179 (22 officers + 157 enlisted)
Missiles:	Harpoon and Tomahawk SSMs launched from torpedo tubes
Torpedo tubes:	4 21-inch (533-mm) amidships Mk 63 (25 weapons)
ASW weapons:	Mk 48 torpedoes
Radars:	BPS-15 surface search
Sonars:	BQQ-5 multi-function bow mounted
	BQS-13 active
	towed array
Fire control:	Mk 117 torpedo FCS
EW systems:	WLR-9

Built as a unit of the STURGEON class, the PARCHE has been extensively modified to perform ocean-engineering and other "special" missions. The PARCHE replaced the HALIBUT in this role in 1976; the SEAWOLF (SSN 575) was also employed in special missions.

The PARCHE was transferred from the Atlantic to the Pacific in October 1976 and underwent modifications at the Marie Island Naval Shipyard for the ocean-engineering role. She was refueled and extensively modified at the Mare Island Naval Shipyard from January

The PARCHE, showing her lengthened forward section with the small superstructure added ahead of the sail structure. The submarine has been extensively modified for ocean-engineering activities, including deep-ocean search and recovery. The yard tug MANHATTAN (YTB 779) maneuvers alongside off the submarine base at Bangor, Washington. (1994, Ed Offley)

The PARCHE under way at high speed near her home port of Bangor, Washington. Note the raised forward structure and the sonar dome aft. (U.S. Navy)

1987 to May 1991; these later modifications included the addition of a 100-foot (30.5-m) section forward of the sail to accommodate special search-and-recovery equipment. The latter is reported to include a clawlike device that can be lowered by cable to recover satellites and other equipment from the ocean floor.

Design: SCB No. 300. See STURGEON class for design details.

Electronics: The original BQQ-2 system has been upgraded to the BQQ-5 configuration. Built with the Mk 113 analog fire-control system, but that was replaced by the Mk 117 digital system during overhaul.

Operational: The PARCHE relieved the HALIBUT in the special missions role in 1976. The later submarine participated in Operation Ivy Bells beginning shortly after her completion. In this super-secret U.S. Navy project, nuclear-propelled submarines planted "taps" on seafloor communication cables in the Sea of Okhotsk between the major submarine base at Petropavlovsk on Kamchatka peninsula (and its surrounding air, naval, and military bases) and the mainland of Soviet Siberia.

(Ivy Bells was revealed to the Soviets by Ronald W. Pelton, a 14-year employee of the U.S. National Security Agency, who provided the Soviets with intelligence information from January 1980 until his arrest in November 1985. He was subsequently sentenced to life imprisonment. The Soviets paid him an estimated $35,000 during his five years of spying.)

The PARCHE's special operations have earned the submarine five Presidential Unit Citations and three Navy Unit Citations.

NUCLEAR-PROPELLED ATTACK SUBMARINE: "GLENARD P. LIPSCOMB"

The GLENARD P. LIPSCOMB (SSN 685), commissioned in 1974, was constructed to evaluate a Turbine Electric Drive (TED) propulsion plant that sacrificed speed to reduce machinery noises. The TULLIBEE, constructed more than a decade earlier, was, in part, a similar effort to replace reduction gear with electric drive. No additional submarines of the LIPSCOMB type were built because of a decision to make the faster LOS ANGELES class the Navy's standard SSN design.

The LIPSCOMB was decommissioned and stricken on 18 June 1988. See 14th Edition/page 56 for characteristics.

Details of the PARCHE's sail and the forward superstructure. The submarine is covered with anechoic tiles. (1994, Ed Offley)

18 NUCLEAR-PROPELLED ATTACK SUBMARINES: "STURGEON" CLASS

Number	Name	FY	Builder	Laid down	Launched	Commissioned	Status
SSN 637	Sturgeon	62	General Dynamics/Electric Boat	10 Aug 1963	26 Feb 1966	3 Mar 1967	decomm./stricken 1 Aug 1994
SSN 638	Whale	62	General Dynamics/Electric Boat	27 May 1964	14 Oct 1966	12 Oct 1968	decomm./stricken 20 June 1996
SSN 639	Tautog	62	Litton/Ingalls Shipbuilding	27 Jan 1964	15 Apr 1967	17 Aug 1968	**PA**
SSN 646	Grayling	63	Portsmouth Naval Shipyard	12 May 1964	22 June 1967	11 Oct 1969	**AA**
SSN 647	Pogy	63	Litton/Ingalls Shipbuilding	4 May 1964	3 June 1967	15 May 1971	**PA**
SSN 648	Aspro	63	Litton/Ingalls Shipbuilding	23 Nov 1964	29 Nov 1967	20 Feb 1969	decomm./stricken 3 Mar 1995
SSN 649	Sunfish	63	General Dynamics, Quincy, Mass.	15 Jan 1965	14 Oct 1966	15 Mar 1969	**AA**
SSN 650	Pargo	63	General Dynamics/Electric Boat	3 June 1964	17 Sep 1966	5 Jan 1968	decomm./stricken 14 Apr 1995
SSN 651	Queenfish	63	Newport News Shipbuilding	11 May 1965	25 Feb 1966	6 Dec 1966	decomm./stricken 8 Nov 1991
SSN 652	Puffer	63	Litton/Ingalls Shipbuilding	8 Feb 1965	30 Mar 1968	9 Aug 1969	decomm./stricken 20 June 1996
SSN 653	Ray	63	Newport News Shipbuilding	1 Apr 1965	21 June 1966	12 Apr 1967	decomm./stricken 16 Mar 1993
SSN 660	Sand Lance	64	Portsmouth Naval Shipyard	15 Jan 1965	11 Nov 1969	25 Sep 1971	**AA**
SSN 661	Lapon	64	Newport News Shipbuilding	26 July 1965	16 Dec 1966	14 Dec 1967	decomm./stricken 8 Aug 1992
SSN 662	Gurnard	64	Mare Island Naval Shipyard	22 Dec 1964	20 May 1967	6 Dec 1968	decomm./stricken 28 Apr 1995
SSN 663	Hammerhead	64	Newport News Shipbuilding	29 Nov 1965	14 Apr 1967	28 June 1968	decomm./stricken 3 Mar 1995
SSN 664	Sea Devil	64	Newport News Shipbuilding	12 Apr 1966	5 Oct 1967	30 Jan 1969	decomm./stricken 16 Oct 1991
SSN 665	Guitarro	65	Mare Island Naval Shipyard	9 Dec 1965	27 July 1968	9 Sep 1972	decomm./stricken 29 May 1992
SSN 666	Hawkbill	65	Mare Island Naval Shipyard	12 Dec 1966	12 Apr 1969	4 Feb 1971	**PA**
SSN 667	Bergall	65	General Dynamics/Electric Boat	16 Apr 1966	17 Feb 1968	13 June 1969	decomm./stricken 11 June 1996
SSN 668	Spadefish	65	Newport News Shipbuilding	21 Dec 1966	15 May 1968	14 Aug 1969	**AA**
SSN 669	Seahorse	65	General Dynamics/Electric Boat	13 Aug 1966	15 June 1968	19 Sep 1969	decomm./stricken 17 Aug 1995
SSN 670	Finback	65	Newport News Shipbuilding	26 June 1967	7 Dec 1968	4 Feb 1970	**AA**
SSN 672	Pintado	66	Mare Island Naval Shipyard	27 Oct 1967	16 Aug 1969	11 Sep 1971	**PA**
SSN 673	Flying Fish	66	General Dynamics/Electric Boat	30 June 1967	17 May 1969	29 Aug 1970	decomm./stricken 16 May 1996
SSN 674	Trepang	66	General Dynamics/Electric Boat	28 Oct 1967	27 Sep 1969	14 Aug 1970	**AA**
SSN 675	Bluefish	66	General Dynamics/Electric Boat	13 Mar 1968	10 Jan 1970	8 Jan 1971	**PA**
SSN 676	Billfish	66	General Dynamics/Electric Boat	20 Sep 1968	1 May 1970	12 Mar 1971	**AA**
SSN 677	Drum	66	Mare Island Naval Shipyard	20 Aug 1968	23 May 1970	15 Apr 1972	decomm./stricken 30 Oct 1995
SSN 678	Archerfish	67	General Dynamics/Electric Boat	19 June 1969	16 Jan 1971	17 Dec 1971	**AA**
SSN 679	Silversides	67	General Dynamics/Electric Boat	13 Oct 1969	4 June 1971	5 May 1972	decomm./stricken 2 Aug 1994
SSN 680	William H. Bates	67	Litton/Ingalls Shipbuilding	4 Aug 1969	11 Dec 1971	5 May 1973	**PA**
SSN 681	Batfish	67	General Dynamics/Electric Boat	9 Feb 1970	9 Oct 1971	1 Sep 1972	**AA**
SSN 682	Tunny	67	Litton/Ingalls Shipbuilding	22 May 1970	10 June 1972	26 Jan 1974	**PA**
SSN 684	Cavalla	68	General Dynamics/Electric Boat	4 June 1970	19 Feb 1972	9 Feb 1973	**PA**
SSN 686	L. Mendel Rivers	69	Newport News Shipbuilding	26 June 1971	2 June 1973	1 Feb 1975	**AA**
SSN 687	Richard B. Russell	69	Newport News Shipbuilding	19 Oct 1971	12 Jan 1974	16 Aug 1975	decomm./stricken 24 June 1994

Displacement:	4,250 tons standard except SSN 678–687 4,460 tons
	4,780 tons submerged except SSN 678–687 4,960 tons
Length:	292 feet (89.0 m) overall except SSN 678–687 302 feet (92.1 m)
Beam:	31⅔ feet (9.65 m)
Draft:	28⅚ feet (8.8 m)
Propulsion:	2 steam turbines (De Laval or General Electric); 15,000 shp; 1 shaft
Reactors:	1 pressurized-water S5W (Westinghouse)
Speed:	approx. 15 knots surface
	approx. 28 knots submerged
Manning:	136 (14 officers + 122 enlisted)
Missiles:	Harpoon and Tomahawk SSMs launched from torpedo tubes
Torpedo tubes:	4 21-inch (533-mm) amidships Mk 63 (25 weapons)
ASW weapons:	Mk 48 torpedoes
Radars:	BPS-14 or BPS-15 surface search
Sonars:	BQQ-5 multi-function bow mounted
	BQR-15 or TB-23 towed array
	BQR-26 in SSN 666
	BQS-11 passive
	BQS-14A active
Fire control:	Mk 117 torpedo FCS
EW systems:	BRD-7D/F
	WLQ-4E Sea Nymph
	WLR-9

The Grayling shows the high sail structure of the Sturgeon class, a major improvement over the previous Permit class. The higher sail permits sail-mounted sail planes to provide better depth control, and the additional space within the sail can be employed for surveillance antennas. (1993, Giorgio Arra)

These submarines are improved versions of the PERMIT class, the principal visible difference being the taller sail structure and under-ice operational capability (see *Design* notes). After the LOS ANGELES class, this is the largest U.S. series of nuclear-propelled submarines.

The class originally consisted of 37 units. The extensively modified PARCHE is listed separately. Other units have been decommissioned and stricken; the remaining submarines should be decommissioned by 2000.

The GUITARRO sank on 15 May 1969, while still under construction, alongside a pier at the San Francisco Naval Shipyard. The cause: faulty ballasting and workman errors. There were no casualties. She was subsequently raised and rebuilt.

Builders: The POGY was begun by the New York Shipbuilding Corporation, Camden, New Jersey. The contract for her construction was terminated on 5 June 1967, and the unfinished submarine was towed to the Litton/Ingalls yard for completion under a contract awarded on 7 December 1967.

Design: SCB No. 188A (through SSN 664) and subsequently SCB No. 300 in the new series. These submarines are similar to the previous PERMIT class, but the several deficiencies of the earlier design have been corrected. An improved electronics suite was provided as well as a larger sail structure, which provides more space for masts and under-ice operational features and allows the submarine to maintain specific depth when near the surface. These modifications resulted in a larger submarine which, with the S5W reactor plant, suffered a further loss of speed over the PERMIT and SKIPJACK classes.

The under-ice features include upward- and forward-looking navigational sonars, strengthened sail and rudder caps, and provision for the sail-mounted diving planes to rotate 90° for breaking through ice.

The SSN 678 and later units were lengthened during construction to permit installation of the BQQ-5 sonar (vice BQQ-2).

Electronics: The original BQQ-2 system has been upgraded to the BQQ-5 configuration during overhauls. The HAWKBILL has a protruding BQR-26 sonar fitted in the forward part of her sail structure. A few ships have been fitted with the TB-23 thin-line array.

Many, if not all, of these submarines have an acoustic device known as GNAT fitted just forward of the upper rudder fin.

This class was built with the Mk 113 analog fire-control system; it was replaced by the Mk 117 digital system during overhauls.

Missiles: The GUITARRO was the trials ship for the submarine-launched Tomahawk.

Modifications: The CAVALLA was modified in August–December 1982 with fittings to carry a removable Dry Deck Shelter (DDS)

The BLUEFISH with crewmen on deck standing by to enter port. There is a non-skid material on deck, laid over the anechoic tiles. (1993, Giorgio Arra)

The SUNFISH with line handlers on deck. Above the American flag atop her sail is the BPS-14/15 radar antenna and the slightly raised snorkel intake mast. (1994, Giorgio Arra)

The WHALE at high speed on the surface. Now retired, she carried out numerous missions under the Arctic ice pack. The sail-mounted diving planes rotate to a vertical position to reduce damage while surfacing through the ice. (1994, Giorgio Arra)

hangar that can accommodate a SEAL Delivery Vehicle (SDV) or lock out a group of 16 commandos/swimmers while the submarine is fully or partially submerged. There is no reduction of submarine combat capability except for a slightly reduced speed and higher (flow) noise level when the hangar is installed. Five other "long-hull" submarines were similarly modified in fiscal 1988–1991 (SSN 678–680, 682, 686).

The Navy has six DDSs, with three assigned to each fleet. These are also carried by the two modified LAFAYETTE-class transport submarines (two each).

Names: The SSN 680 was originally to be named REDFIN; she was renamed for a deceased member of Congress on 25 June 1971.

Operational: The QUEENFISH was the first of several submarines of this class to conduct extensive operations under the Arctic ice pack and was the first single-screw submarine of any nation to surface through the ice, in February 1967.[13] The WHALE and PARGO were the first submarines of this class to surface at the North Pole, in April 1969. (The QUEENFISH surfaced at the North Pole during her July–August 1970 under-ice operations.)

13. See N. Polmar, "Sailing Under the Ice," U.S. Naval Institute *Proceedings* (June 1984), pp. 121–23.

1 NUCLEAR-PROPELLED ATTACK SUBMARINE: "NARWHAL"

Number	Name	FY	Builder	Laid down	Launched	Commissioned	Status
SSN 671	NARWHAL	64	General Dynamics/Electric Boat	17 Jan 1966	9 Sep 1966	12 July 1969	AA

Displacement:	5,284 tons standard
	5,830 tons submerged
Length:	314 11/12 feet (96.0 m) overall
Beam:	37 3/4 feet (11.5 m)
Draft:	25 11/12 feet (7.9 m)
Propulsion:	2 steam turbines (General Electric); 17,000 shp; 1 shaft
Reactors:	1 pressurized-water S5G (General Electric)
Speed:	approx. 20 knots surface
	approx. 25 knots submerged
Manning:	136 (14 officers + 122 enlisted)
Missiles:	Harpoon and Tomahawk SSMs launched from torpedo tubes
Torpedo tubes:	4 21-inch (533-mm) amidships Mk 63 (25 weapons)
ASW weapons:	Mk 48 torpedoes
Radars:	BPS-14 surface search
Sonars:	BQQ-5 multi-function bow mounted
	BQS-8 under ice/mine detection
	towed array
Fire control:	Mk 117 torpedo FCS
EW systems:	BRD-7 direction finder

This one-of-a-kind submarine was constructed to evaluate the natural-circulation S5G reactor plant. Weapons, sensors, and other features of the NARWHAL are similar to the STURGEON-class SSNs.

The NARWHAL is scheduled to "stand down" on 30 September 1998 and to be decommissioned/stricken in 1999.

Design: SCB No. 245.

Electronics: The BQQ-2 has been upgraded to a BQQ-5 configuration. The Mk 117 torpedo fire-control system has been installed in place of the original Mk 113.

Reactor: The S5G reactor plant uses natural convection rather than pumps for heat transfer/coolant transfer at slow speeds, thus reducing self-generated machinery noises. This concept is used in the subsequent LOS ANGELES and OHIO (SSBN 726) classes. A land-based prototype of the S5G plant was built at Arco, Idaho.

The one-of-a-kind submarine NARWHAL. (1993, Giorgio Arra)

The NARWHAL has been modified for special operations. Those modifications included this structure being fitted aft, apparently for carrying a remote-control underwater vehicle. (Giorgio Arra)

2 NUCLEAR-PROPELLED TRANSPORT SUBMARINES: "LAFAYETTE" CLASS

Number	Name	FY	Builder	Laid down	Launched	Commissioned	Status
SSN 642	Kamehameha	63	Mare Island Naval Shipyard	2 May 1963	16 Jan 1965	10 Dec 1965	**PA**
SSN 645	James K. Polk	63	General Dynamics/Electric Boat	23 Nov 1963	22 May 1965	16 Apr 1966	**AA**

Displacement:	7,350 tons standard 8,250 tons submerged
Length:	425 feet (129.6 m) overall
Beam:	33 feet (10.06 m)
Draft:	31½ feet (9.6 m)
Propulsion:	2 steam turbines; 15,000 shp; 1 shaft
Reactors:	1 pressurized-water S5W (Westinghouse)
Speed:	approx. 20 knots surface approx. 25 knots submerged
Manning:	130
Troops:	65
Missiles:	removed
Torpedo tubes:	4 21-inch (533-mm) Mk 65 (bow)
Torpedoes:	Mk 48
Radars:	BPS-15 surface search
Sonars:	BQR-7E passive detection BQR-15 towed array BQR-19 navigation BQR-21 passive array BQS-4 active/passive detection
Fire control:	Mk 113 torpedo/missile FCS
EW systems:	WLR-8 WLR-10

The James K. Polk as a transport submarine for special forces. A single Dry Deck Shelter (DDS) is fitted on the port side, aft of the sail. Several Sturgeon-class SSNs are fitted to carry a single DDS for transporting SEALs and other special forces, plus SEAL Delivery Vehicles (SDV). (1994, Giorgio Arra)

A deck shelter is lifted from a transport ship, the Sam Houston, which has since been replaced in the transport role. The current submarines fitted to carry the DDS, both the Lafayette and Sturgeon units, will be retired by the year 2000; it is not clear how they will be replaced. (U.S. Navy)

The KAMEHAMEHA at Pearl Harbor with two deck shelters fitted amidships. The door of the starboard DDS is partially open. (U.S. Navy)

These submarines were built to carry the Polaris A-3 SLBM, and they were subsequently converted in 1972 to carry the Poseidon C-3 missile. (They were not among the 12 LAFAYETTE-class submarines later upgraded to fire the Trident C-4 missile; see *Missiles* notes.)

The KAMEHAMEHA and POLK were subsequently converted to serve as transport submarines for special operations forces such as Navy SEALs. They were converted at Mare Island in 1992–1993. They replaced the ex-Polaris submarines SAM HOUSTON (SSBN/SSN 609) and JOHN MARSHALL (SSBN/SSN 611) in this role.

Marines crowd the deck of the KAMEHAMEHA during a (rather unusual) daylight exercise in the Hawaiian Islands. At left is an open missile tube hatch, now giving access to the Marines' gear. (1994, U.S. Marine Corps, Cpl. Robert A. Berry)

Class: Thirty-one submarines of the LAFAYETTE class were built (see chapter 11 for class data).

Classification: Changed from SSBN to SSN on 31 August 1992 and 1 October 1993, respectively.

Design: SCB No. 216. As transport submarines they can each carry two Dry Deck Shelters (DDS) aft of the sail structure. Each DDS can accommodate a SEAL Delivery Vehicle (SDV) or be used as a lock-out chamber for swimmers. (See STURGEON-class entry for details.)

Internally, all missile support and launch equipment as removed; air, electrical, internal communications, and drain systems were installed for the DDS. Berthing and sanitary facilities are provided for 65 troops. Some of the former missile tubes are used for SEAL equipment stowage.

NUCLEAR-PROPELLED ATTACK SUBMARINES: "THRESHER/PERMIT" CLASS

Number	Name	Comm.	Notes
SSN 593	THRESHER	1961	sunk 10 Apr. 1963
SSN 594	PERMIT	1962	decomm./stricken 12 June 1991
SSN 595	PLUNGER	1962	decomm. 3 Jan 1990; stricken 2 Feb 1990
SSN 596	BARB	1963	decomm./stricken 20 Dec 1989
SSN 603	POLLACK	1964	decomm./stricken 1 Mar 1989
SSN 604	HADDO	1964	decomm. 12 June 1991; stricken 30 Aug 1991
SSN 605	JACK	1967	decomm./stricken 11 July 1990
SSN 606	TINOSA	1964	decomm./stricken 15 Jan 1992
SSN 607	DACE	1964	decomm. 2 Dec 1988; stricken 1 Mar 1989
SSN 612	GUARDFISH	1966	decomm./stricken 4 Feb 1992
SSN 613	FLASHER	1966	decomm./stricken 14 Sep 1992
SSN 614	GREENLING	1967	decomm./stricken 18 Apr 1994
SSN 615	GATO	1968	decomm./stricken 24 April1996
SSN 621	HADDOCK	1967	decomm./stricken 7 Apr 1993

These submarines established the basic design for subsequent U.S. Navy SSNs and SSBNs, having a deep-diving capability (approx. 1,300 feet/396 m), quiet machinery, and large bow-mounted sonar; their torpedo tubes are angled out from amidships. Fourteen submarines were completed from 1961 through 1967; the later units were delayed following the 1963 loss of the THRESHER for modification under the so-called "subsafe" program.

Class: After the loss of the THRESHER the class was officially called the PERMIT class.

Operational: The THRESHER was lost on post-overhaul sea trials off New England on 10 April 1963; all 112 naval personnel and 17 civilians on board were lost. This was the world's first nuclear submarine loss and the worst submarine disaster on record.

See 14th Edition/pages 62–64 for characteristics.

NUCLEAR-PROPELLED ATTACK SUBMARINE: "TULLIBEE"

The TULLIBEE (SSN 597) was commissioned on 9 November 1960 as a small, hunter-killer submarine intended to operate off enemy ports and in narrow waterways (as were the earlier diesel-electric submarines of the SSK 1 class). The construction of additional submarines of this design was halted in favor of the larger and more versatile PERMIT class. The TULLIBEE was decommissioned and stricken on 18 June 1988.

Design: This was the first U.S. submarine to have bow-mounted sonar; the torpedo tubes were fitted amidships and angled out to port and starboard. This sonar arrangement, followed in later SSNs and the OHIO (SSBN 726) class, places the acoustic detection equipment in the best position with respect to ship movement and machinery noises. The TULLIBEE was not fitted to fire SUBROC, as were later SSNs.

Engineering: The TULLIBEE's nuclear power plant was smaller and less powerful than in other U.S. submarines, with turbo-electric drive used in place of steam turbines and reduction gear to reduce self-generated noise.

See 14th Edition/page 67 for characteristics.

NUCLEAR-PROPELLED RESEARCH SUBMARINE: "HALIBUT"

The HALIBUT (SSGN 587) was commissioned on 4 January 1960 as the U.S. Navy's only nuclear-propelled guided missile submarine (SSGN), having been designed and constructed to launch the Regulus II strategic cruise missile. After that weapon was canceled in December 1958, the ship was armed with the Regulus I missile, carrying that weapon on deployments to the Western Pacific from 1960 to 1964.

After deletion of her missile equipment the HALIBUT was reclassified as an attack submarine (SSN) on 15 August 1965 and subsequently served as a research/ocean-engineering submarine until being decommissioned on 30 June 1976. In the latter role the HALIBUT's forward missile hangar was modified for research equipment, a ducted bow-thruster was provided for precise control and maneuvering, and provisions were made for carrying submersibles on the after deck (mated to the after escape hatch).

She was decommissioned on 30 June 1976 and stricken on 30 April 1986.

Class: The HALIBUT was originally ordered as a diesel-electric submarine, but on 27 February 1956 the Navy announced that she would be provided with nuclear propulsion. No additional submarines of this design were built. An improved Regulus II–armed SSGN class was planned, but those submarines were reordered as PERMIT-class SSNs.

See 14th Edition/page 68 for characteristics.

NUCLEAR-PROPELLED ATTACK SUBMARINE: "TRITON"

The TRITON (SSRN 586), commissioned on 10 November 1959, was designed to serve as a radar picket submarine (SSRN) to provide early warning of air attack against a carrier task force. The real reason for her construction, however, was Admiral Rickover's desire to test a two-reactor nuclear plant in a submarine, in part as a precursor to multi-reactor surface warships.

The Navy phased out the radar picket submarine program in the late 1950s because of the greater effectiveness of Airborne Early Warning (AEW) aircraft. The TRITON was reclassified as an SSN on 1 March 1961 and employed in general submarine operations until being decommissioned on 29 March 1969. She was stricken on 30 April 1986.

Design: The TRITON was the only Western submarine built with two reactors.

The TRITON's hull configuration was designed for high-speed surface operations to operate with aircraft carriers. A large, retractable SPS-26 air search radar was fitted in the sail structure. A large Combat Information Center (CIC) was provided as well as extensive communications equipment.

See 14th Edition/page 69 for characteristics.

NUCLEAR-PROPELLED ATTACK SUBMARINES: "SKIPJACK" CLASS

Number	Name	Comm.	Notes
SSN 585	SKIPJACK	1959	decomm. 19 Apr 1990; stricken 19 Apr 1990
SSN 588	SCAMP	1961	decomm./stricken 26 Apr 1988
SSN 589	SCORPION	1960	sunk 27 May 1968
SSN 590	SCULPIN	1961	decomm./stricken 3 Aug 1990
SSN 591	SHARK	1961	decomm./stricken 15 Sep 1990
SSN 592	SNOOK	1961	decomm./stricken 14 Nov 1986

The SKIPJACK-class submarines were the first to combine nuclear propulsion with the high-speed, "tear-drop" hull design of the experimental submarine ALBACORE. These were the fastest nuclear submarines in the U.S. Navy when built (up to 33 knots); their speed was not equaled until the LOS ANGELES class. The ALBACORE attained a submerged speed of 37 knots in one of her several configurations.

The SCORPION (SSN 589) was lost with all 99 men on board in May 1968 while some 400 n.miles (741 km) southwest of the Azores.

Design: The first U.S. fleet ballistic missile submarine, the GEORGE WASHINGTON (SSBN 598), was based on this design, which then formed the basis for U.S. fleet ballistic missile submarines constructed during the late 1950s and 1960s.

See 14th Edition/pages 70–71 for characteristics.

NUCLEAR-PROPELLED ATTACK SUBMARINES: "SKATE" CLASS

Number	Name	Comm.	Notes
SSN 578	SKATE	1957	decomm. 3 Aug 1986; stricken 30 Oct 1986
SSN 579	SWORDFISH	1958	decomm./stricken 30 June 1989
SSN 583	SARGO	1958	decomm./stricken 21 Apr 1988
SSN 584	SEADRAGON	1959	decomm. 12 June 1984; stricken 30 Apr 1986

This class was the first U.S. effort to develop a nuclear-propelled submarine for series production. Additional units were deferred in favor of the high-speed SKIPJACK class. All of the SKATE-class submarines except the SWORDFISH were employed extensively in Arctic operations.

See 14th Edition/pages 71–72 for characteristics.

ATTACK SUBMARINES: "BARBEL" CLASS

Number	Name	Comm.	Decomm.	Stricken
SS 580	BARBEL	1959	4 Dec 1989	17 Jan 1990
SS 581	BLUEBACK	1959	1 Oct 1990	30 Oct 1990
SS 582	BONEFISH	1959	28 Sep 1988	28 Feb 1989

These were the last diesel-electric combat submarines built in the United States and the last in U.S. Navy service. They were the first combat submarines to incorporate the ALBACORE—or high-speed, tear-drop hull—design. The BARBEL was decommissioned following a diving accident on 1 May 1989. The BONEFISH was severely damaged by fire off the coast of Florida on 24 April 1988; 1 officer and 2 sailors were killed in the blaze, and 89 others survived.

See 14th Edition/page 75 for characteristics.

ATTACK SUBMARINE: "DARTER"

The DARTER (SS 576) was built to an improved TANG-class design; the construction of further submarines of this class differed in favor of the more capable BARBEL class. Commissioned in 1956, the DARTER's service life was extended several times until she was decommissioned on 1 December 1989 and stricken on 17 January 1990. (The GRAYBACK and GROWLER were to have been of this class, but they were completed instead as Regulus guided-missile submarines, the SSG 574 and SSG 577, respectively.)

See 14th Edition/page 76 for characteristics.

NUCLEAR-PROPELLED ATTACK SUBMARINE: "SEAWOLF"

The SEAWOLF (SSN 575), commissioned on 30 March 1957, was the U.S. Navy's second nuclear-propelled submarine. She was designed to evaluate a nuclear plant competitive to that of the NAUTILUS. She was engaged in research/ocean-engineering activities from 1969 until her decommissioning on 30 March 1987. The SEAWOLF was stricken on 10 July 1987.

Design: For her research/ocean-engineering role the SEAWOLF was fitted with four side thrusters, two forward and two aft. She was configured to carry a submersible on her after deck.

Engineering: The SEAWOLF was built with a liquid-sodium reactor plant (S2G) in lieu of the pressurized-water plant in the NAUTILUS and all other U.S. nuclear submarines. After almost two years of limited operations, the original plant was shut down in December 1958 and a modified NAUTILUS-type plant was installed. The submarine was recommissioned on 30 September 1960. SEAWOLF's original reactor was towed to sea by barge and scuttled off the U.S. Atlantic coast on 8 April 1959.

See 14th Edition/page 73 for characteristics.

NUCLEAR-PROPELLED ATTACK SUBMARINE: "NAUTILUS"

The NAUTILUS (SSN 571) was the world's first nuclear-propelled submarine, having been commissioned on 30 September 1954, although she did not get under way until 3 January 1955. On 3 August 1958, while sailing under the Arctic ice pack, she became the first ship to reach the North Pole. The NAUTILUS was decommissioned on 3 March 1980; after being defueled and modified at the Mare Island Naval Shipyard, Vallejo, California, in 1985, she was towed to Groton, Connecticut, and formally transferred to private control on 6 July 1985 for use as a museum.[14]

See 13th Edition/page 74 for characteristics.

ATTACK SUBMARINES: "TANG" CLASS

Number	Name	Comm.	Notes
SS/AGSS 563	TANG	1951	to Turkey 18 Feb. 1980; stricken 6 Aug 1987
SS 564	TRIGGER	1952	stricken/to Italy 10 July 1973
SS 565	WAHOO	1952	stricken 15 July 1983
SS 566	TROUT	1952	stricken/to Iran 19 Dec 1978 (not transferred)
SS/SSAG 567	GUDGEON	1952	to Turkey 30 Sep 1983; stricken 6 Aug 1987
SS 568	HARDER	1952	stricken/to Italy 20 Feb 1974

This was the first U.S. post–World War II submarine design, incorporating many features of the German high-performance Type XXI U-boat design. All TANG-class submarines have been transferred or stricken. Three submarines of this class—the TANG, WAHOO, and TROUT—were to have been transferred to Iran, but their transfer was canceled in 1979 after the fall of the Shah.

See 12th Edition/page 45 for characteristics.

14. The Navy had decided to moor the ship at the Washington Navy Yard in the nation's capital. However, President Jimmy Carter directed that the ship be moored at New London, Conn.

1 RESEARCH SUBMARINE: "DOLPHIN"

Number	Name	FY	Builder	Laid down	Launched	Commissioned	Status
AGSS 555	DOLPHIN	61	Portsmouth Naval Shipyard	9 Nov 1962	8 June 1968	17 Aug 1968	PA

Displacement:	860 tons standard 950 tons submerged
Length:	165 feet (50.3 m) overall
Beam:	19 5/12 feet (5.9 m)
Draft:	16 feet (4.9 m)
Propulsion:	2 diesel engines (General Motors 12V71) 1 electric motor (Elliott); 1,650 shp; 1 shaft
Speed:	7.5 knots surface 15 knots submerged
Manning:	48 (4 officers + 44 enlisted)
Missiles:	none
Torpedo tubes:	removed
Radars:	SPS-53 navigation (portable)
Sonars:	BQR-2 passive (bow mounted) BQS-15 active
Fire control:	none

The DOLPHIN is an experimental, deep-diving submarine. Reportedly, she has operated at greater depths than any other operational U.S. submarine. The DOLPHIN is assigned to Submarine Development Group 1, providing support to the Naval Ocean Systems Center and several other Navy research activities. The DOLPHIN has been modified to test HY-130 steel components.

Design: SCB No. 207. The DOLPHIN has a constant-diameter pressure hull with an outside diameter of approximately 15 feet (4.57 m) and hemisphere heads at both ends.

An improved rudder design and other features permit maneuvering without conventional submarine diving planes. There are minimal penetrations of the pressure hull (e.g., only one access hatch) and built-in safety systems that automatically surface the submarine in an emergency.

The experimental torpedo tube that was originally fitted was removed in 1970.

Electronics: Various experimental sonars have been fitted in the DOLPHIN. Her original bow sonar, which had four arrays that could be extended at 90° angles to the submarine's bow-stern axis, has been removed.

Engineering: Submerged endurance is approximately 24 hours; her sea endurance is about 14 days.

The deep-diving research submarine DOLPHIN is the only nonnuclear submarine in U.S. naval service. The submarine's SPS-53 navigation radar is mounted at the after end of her sail, behind the periscope. (1985, Giorgio Arra)

Operational: The DOLPHIN's activities have supported research in air-submarine laser communications, deep submergence, sonar, oceanography, and ASW.

POST–WORLD WAR II SUBMARINES

Number	Name/Class	Comm.	Notes
SS 551	BASS (ex-K-2/SSK 2)	1951	stricken 1965
SS 552	BONITA (ex-K-3/SSK 3)	1952	stricken 1965
SS 553	(KINN) Norway OSP	completed 1964	
SS 554	(SPRINGEREN) Denmark OSP	completed 1964	
AGSS 555	DOLPHIN	1968	
SS 556–562	not used		
SS 563–568	TANG class		
AGSS 569	ALBACORE	1953	stricken 1980
AGSS 570	completed as SST 1		
SSN 571	NAUTILUS	1954	memorial
SSR 572	SAILFISH (later SS)	1956	stricken 1978
SSR 573	SALMON (later SS)	1956	stricken 1977
SSG 574	GRAYBACK (later LPSS/SS)	1958	stricken 1984
SSN 575	SEAWOLF	1957	stricken 1987
SS 576	DARTER	1956	stricken 1990
SSG 577	GROWLER	1958	stricken 1980
SSN 578, 579	SKATE class		
SS 580–582	BARBEL class		
SSN 583, 584	SKATE class		
SSN 585	SKIPJACK class		
SSRN 586	TRITON (later SSN)		
SSGN 587	HALIBUT (later SSN)		
SSN 588–592	SKIPJACK class		
SSN 593	THRESHER		
SSN 594–596	PERMIT class		
SSN 597	TULLIBEE		
SSBN 598–602	GEORGE WASHINGTON class		
SSN 603–607	PERMIT class		
SSBN 608–611	ETHAN ALLEN class		
SSN 612–615	PERMIT class		
SSBN 616–617	LAFAYETTE class		
SSBN 618	ETHAN ALLEN class		
SSBN 619, 620	LAFAYETTE class		
SSN 621	PERMIT class		
SSBN 622–636	LAFAYETTE class		
SSN 637–639	STURGEON class		
SSBN 640–645	LAFAYETTE class		
SSN 646–653	STURGEON class		
SSBN 654–659	LAFAYETTE class		
SSN 660–670	STURGEON class		
SSN 671	NARWHAL		
SSN 672–684	STURGEON class		
SSN 685	GLENARD P. LIPSCOMB		
SSN 686, 687	STURGEON class		
SSN 688–725	LOS ANGELES class		
SSBN 726–743	OHIO class		
SSBN 744–749	reserved for SSBNs		
SSN 750–773	LOS ANGELES class		

U.S. submarine programs reached hull number SS 562 during World War II; hulls 526–562 were canceled late in the war. Subsequently, five of these numbers were assigned to postwar submarines: three U.S. submarines and two American-financed, foreign-built submarines (Offshore Procurement).

The last war-built submarine on the Naval Vessel Register was the transport submarine SEALION (LPSS 315), decommissioned and laid up in 1970 and stricken on 15 March 1977. The last active submarine of World War II construction was the TIGRONE (AGSS 419), which was decommissioned on 30 June 1975 and stricken on 27 June 1975 (i.e., three days before being formally decommissioned).

Note the large number of submarine designs developed and built from the late 1940s into the early 1960s. This was a period of highly innovative thinking in the submarine community, in part while searching for new roles for submarines and exploring the potential impact of emerging technologies on submarine warfare. In particular, the research submarine ALBACORE introduced many of the features found in subsequent undersea craft; in many respects she was the beginning of the modern submarine era.

All postwar U.S. submarines—including ballistic missile craft—have been numbered in the same series except for three small, hunter-killer submarines (SSK) and three training submarines (SST), which were in separate series.

The U.S. Navy's lone midget submarine, the X-1 completed in 1955, was stricken in 1973. She is on display at the Naval Academy in Annapolis, Maryland.

HUNTER-KILLER SUBMARINES

Number	Name	Comm.	Notes
SSK 1	BARRACUDA (ex-K-1)	1951	to SST 3
SSK 2	BASS (ex-K-2)	1951	to SS 551
SSK 3	BONITA (ex-K-3)	1952	to SS 552

These purpose-built SSKs were small (1,000-ton, 196-foot/59.75-m), hunter-killer submarines, intended to lie in wait to intercept Soviet submarines off their home ports and in narrow waterways. Several hundred SSKs were to have been produced in time of war. They were originally assigned K-number "names" that were changed to fish names in 1955. The BASS and BONITA were reclassified SS in 1959 for use in the training role; the BARRACUDA was changed to SST in 1959 for the training role.

In addition to these built-for-the-purpose SSKs, the nuclear-propelled TULLIBEE was built as an SSKN (although designated SSN 597). Seven GATO (SS 212)-class diesel submarines were converted to hunter-killer submarines in the 1950s and redesignated SSK (214, 240–244, 246).

TRAINING SUBMARINES

Number	Name	Comm.	Notes
SST 1	MACKEREL (ex-T-1)	1953	stricken 1973
SST 2	MARLIN (ex-T-2)	1953	stricken 1973
SST 3	BARRACUDA (ex-K-1/SSK 1)	1951	stricken 1973

The SST 1 and 2 were small (310-ton, 133-foot/40.5-m) submarines developed for training and target use. The MACKEREL was ordered as AGSS 570 and completed as the SST 1. Originally assigned T-number "names," they were given fish names in 1956.

ADVANCED SEAL DELIVERY SYSTEMS

The Navy is developing an Advanced SEAL Delivery System (ASDS) centered on a submersible with a length of about 50 feet (16 m) and a capacity for carrying eight SEALs in a "dry" environment. The SEALs would be able to "lock out" of the submersible in forward areas. This craft will be carried on the deck of a submarine, aft of the sail. The SEALs and operating crew would board the craft directly from the submarine through a coupling between the submarine's amidships escape hatch and a bottom hatch in the submersible.

This craft will not be a replacement for the SEAL delivery vehicles listed below; rather, it will provide a different, longer-range capability for special operations.

Reportedly, the Navy has a requirement for 11 of the new vehicles. A design contract was awarded in September 1994; delivery of the first vehicles is expected about the year 2001.

SEAL DELIVERY VEHICLES

The Navy has about 15 SEAL Delivery Vehicles (SDV) that can be carried into forward areas in Dry Deck Shelter (DDS) hangars fitted onto attack or special operations submarines. These are Mk VIII Mod 1 fiberglass "wet" vehicles which can carry eight SEALs, each wearing a self-contained underwater breathing apparatus (SCUBA).

The vehicles are all upgrades of earlier SDVs, with improved propulsion and electronics equipment. The use of more efficient "packaging" has increased their capacity from six to eight SEALs.

A follow-on SDV program was canceled in 1992 because of cost overruns and schedule slippage. That craft was being built by the UNISYS Corp.

A Mk VIII Mod 1 SDV, which shows the pilots' compartment open and passenger compartment covers closed. A swimmer is at the port quarter. These craft can be carried in deck shelters on SSNs; the planned advanced SEAL delivery system vehicle will be a dry, mini-submarine carried on the after deck of an SSN. (U.S. Navy)

The Lockheed-developed UUV configured for the mine field surveillance role during in-situ testing. (1994, Lockheed)

A Mk VIII Mod 0 SDV, which shows both the pilot and passenger compartments open. The acoustic "window" in the bow has been deleted in the conversion to the Mod 1 configuration. The craft has a six-blade propeller powered by battery-supplied electric motors. (U.S. Navy)

UNMANNED UNDERWATER VEHICLES

The U.S. Navy is developing a series of Unmanned Underwater Vehicles (UUV). In the underwater environment, unmanned craft—either tethered or Autonomous Underwater Vehicles (AUV)—would undertake a number of missions, some considered too dangerous to risk a manned submarine. The missions being considered for UUVs include:

Submarine warfare: A variety of UUV configurations could support friendly submarine operations, among them serving as a decoy to draw out hostile submarines, a sustained remote communication relay (as a link for radio or, in the future, lasers), an offboard platform for acoustic or wake sensors, area search and reconnaissance to expand a submarine's "search horizon," laying mines, and specific intelligence collection (as off an enemy port or in a transit area).

Offboard acoustic sensors (i.e., AUV-carried active and passive systems) would permit submarines to use bi-static and multi-static, low-frequency detection techniques. These are already in use with surface ships that tow active low-frequency sonars.

Anti-submarine warfare: In addition to the above operations, an ASW-configured AUV would perform barrier surveillance, towing an array through an area and automatically transmitting detections to another platform (ship, submarine, or satellite). Future technology might enable an AUV to pick up and trail an enemy submarine as it leaves port or transits through a barrier line.

Ocean surveillance: As an extension of the ASW mission, AUVs could be programmed in their ocean-surveillance role to patrol wide ocean areas with passive sensors. Or, they could be employed as an active sound source wherein reflections of their acoustic pulses would be monitored by fixed underwater Sound Surveillance Systems (SOSUS) or Surface Towed Array Surveillance Systems (SURTASS).

Mine warfare: A Mine Countermeasures (MCM) vehicle could transit enemy mine fields, map them for future reference, or guide a friendly submarine or surface ship through them. Active sonar would be used to detect the mines, while a bottom-matching sonar—coupled with an inertial navigation system—would provide precise information on the UUV's position.

A mine field picture would be maintained that could be transmitted back to friendly units via an acoustic data link or a fiber-optic cable, or the picture could be retained for the physical return of the vehicle to a recovery ship, submarine, or even aircraft. The MCM vehicle could also provide "route maintenance," periodically transmitting a friendly mine field to ensure that an enemy submarine had not penetrated the field to plant mines on the safe routes used by friendly submarines.

Special warfare: In this warfare area the AUV could perform friendly harbor patrol/defense, beach reconnaissance prior to a clandestine operation, and intelligence collection.

Noncombat operations: These AUV activities are primarily search and recovery of foreign or friendly objects dropped on the ocean floor. These could include satellites and weapons.

A number of UUVs are already in foreign and U.S. naval use. Since the 1960s the U.S. Navy has employed cable-controlled torpedo recovery devices,[15] the Mk 30 submarine target, the Mk 71 MOSS decoy used by ballistic missile submarines, and tethered mine countermeasures vehicles. Classified deep-ocean search-and-recovery devices have also been used to exploit Soviet objects lost on the ocean floor. (Numerous commercial UUV-type vehicles are likewise in service, often referred to as ROV, for remote operating vehicles. These are used mostly for exploration and support of offshore oil fields. As an indication of the state of the art, some of the commercial vehicles can operate to almost 10,000 feet/3,050 m and have a 350-hour mission duration at five or six knots.)

The new family of UUVs will expand the "operational envelope" of underwater drones. The Navy and the Advanced Research Projects Agency (ARPA) have initiated a joint advanced-technology UUV program in 1986. Through this effort, ARPA has developed two prototypes for test bed/mission hardware demonstrations. One vehicle took the first mission "package"—a tactical acoustic decoy system developed by Martin Marietta—to sea in 1990 and has since been transferred to the Navy for testing. According to a Navy spokesman, the initial payoff for this UUV would be increased submarine survivability, but it would pave the way for UUV applications to a number of classified submarine scenarios.[16] The second ARPA vehicle, also completed in 1990, has a Lockheed-developed mine search system package. A third mission package for ocean surveillance is also being developed under ARPA contract.

Several Navy laboratories are also working in the UUV field. While most will not discuss their efforts, a notional vehicle for long-duration ocean surveillance is being designed by the David Taylor Research Center (DTRC) in Carderock, Maryland. This vehicle would be much larger than the torpedo-like ARPA devices: 68 feet (20.7 m) long, with a tail ring some ten feet in diameter that would stream a multi-line passive acoustic array. Under the DTRC concept, the AUV would operate in the deep ocean powered by a hydrogen liquid-fuel-cell power plant that could provide a mission duration of several weeks. When a contact is made and evaluated as a possible hostile intruder, an expendable communications buoy would be launched, pop up to the surface, and broadcast the data or serve as a data link.

In all of these efforts, the key to success will be component or "enabling" technologies: navigation, composite hull materials, guidance, energy source, propulsion, communication links, and signal processing, as well as the specific mission packages. Advanced AUVs will require an enhanced sensor and decision-making capability; while these are within the scope of near-term technologies, they could be very expensive. (A handful of relatively unsophisticated autonomous vehicles has been used by the U.S. Navy since the early 1960s.)

The operating Navy, however, is cautious about moving toward UUVs. While most vehicles are considered in the context of enhancing submarine operations, a submarine may be the most difficult platform for supporting a UUV. Limited space, the problems of hull openings and maintenance on vehicles, and other factors make it a problem for submarines to support UUVs. Even if they are sized for torpedo tubes—now 21-inch diameter and 30-inch diameter in the SEAWOLF class—keeping UUVs aboard submarines will displace torpedoes and missiles. Whereas a double-hull submarine configuration might accommodate a UUV more easily, that design concept is anathema to leaders of the Navy's nuclear propulsion activities. Further, underwater-to-underwater communications will be more troublesome than underwater-to-surface, air, or satellite platforms.

Surface ships, submarines, and even aircraft (fixed-wing and helicopters) could also deploy and recover UUVs. Surface ships would be the most feasible to support UUV operations; however, even a preliminary review of vehicle potential indicates that some UUVs, such as a DTRC-type area surveillance vehicle, would best be supported by surface ships. Nevertheless, the submarine is the ideal launch/support platform for many UUV missions.

---

15. One of these vehicles—a Cable-controlled Underwater Research Vehicle (CURV)—recovered a hydrogen bomb from a depth of 2,800 feet (854 m) off the coast of Palomares, Spain, in 1966.
16. Rear Adm. D. J. Wolkensdorfer, USN, "Joint DARPA/Navy Technology program," presentation at IEEE Conference, Dulles Airport, Va., 5 June 1990.

1 LARGE SCALE VEHICLE: "KOKANEE"

Number	Name	Completed	Builder
(none)	KOKANEE	1988	Southwest Research Institute, San Antonio, Texas

Weight:	155 tons
Length:	88⅚ feet (27.1 m) overall
Beam:	10⅙ feet (3.1 m)
Draft:	9½ feet (2.9 m)
Propulsion:	direct-drive electric motor; 3,000 shp; 1 shaft
Speed:	
Range:	see *Engineering* notes
Manning:	unmanned

The KOKANEE is a submarine-design test vehicle operated in Lake Pend Oreille, Bayview, Idaho, by the David Taylor Research Center's acoustic research detachment. Known as the Large Scale Vehicle (LSV), the craft has been employed to test variations of submarine propulsors for the submarine SEAWOLF.

The LSV concept was proposed in 1972 by Dr. M. M. Sevik of the DTRC as an extension of the center's model-testing program. The construction contract was awarded in February 1984. The completed vehicle was delivered to Bayview in October 1987 and dedicated at ceremonies there on 7 March 1988. She was transported from San Antonio to Bayview by train.

The KOKANEE is the world's largest autonomous, free-swimming submersible.

Cost: Construction cost of the KOKANEE was $65 million.

Design: The KOKANEE has a conventional submarine configuration with a modified sail or fairwater structure that can be removed. The forward portion of the submarine contains electric storage batteries; the after portion has the DC electric motor and auxiliary machinery as well as data recorders and guidance and navigation equipment.

The operationing depth of the craft is not known; the lake has a maximum depth of 1,150 feet (350 m).

Engineering: The craft is controlled by on-board computers that are programmed before each test run. Lead-acid batteries are employed. Endurance is approximately six hours for medium-power runs and two or three hours for full-power runs.

Names: The Kokanee is a salmon found in Lake Pend Oreille.

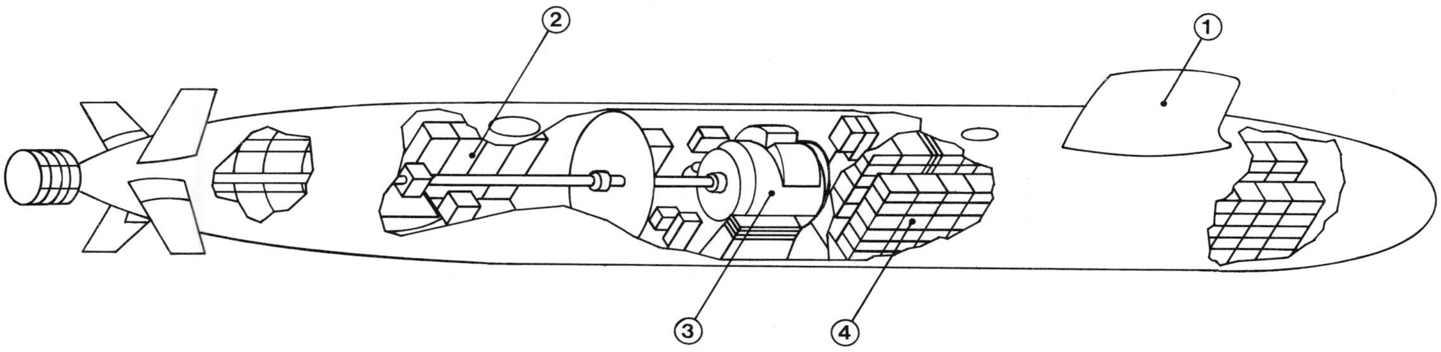

KOKANEE
1. Removable fairwater. 2. Data recorders and navigation equipment. 3. DC electric motor. 4. Batteries. (William Clipson)

The KOKANEE immediately after surfacing in Lake Pend Oreille, Bayview, Idaho. Note the similarity of the sail structure to that of the new SEAWOLF. The craft's hull is gray and the sail structure is red. (U.S. Navy)

CHAPTER 13

Aircraft Carriers

The DWIGHT D. EISENHOWER demonstrated the flexibility of aircraft carriers when the ship embarked 1,800 soldiers and 64 Army helicopters of the 10th Mountain Division for the U.S. military occupation of Haiti. A Navy SH-3 Sea King helicopter is in front of the island; Army UH-60 Black Hawks are visible on the flight deck; Army AH-1T Cobra gunships and Navy MH-53E Sea Dragon helicopters are forward, with more helicopters on the hangar deck. (1994, U.S. Navy, PH2 Steve Enfield)

Aircraft carriers remain the backbone of U.S. conventional naval forces. The U.S. carrier force in the fall of 1996 consisted of 11 fully operational carriers: seven nuclear-propelled ships (CVN) and four conventional, oil-burning ships (CV). In addition, the conventional carrier JOHN F. KENNEDY has a composite active-reserve crew and is employed as an "operational reserve/training" ship, capable of deploying with a relatively short work-up period.

An additional new-construction aircraft carrier is working up and two more are under construction; these ships are to replace conventional ones to maintain a force level of 11 fully operational carriers plus the KENNEDY. The Department of Defense's Bottom-Up Review of 1993 provides for this 11-plus-1 force to be maintained indefinitely, with four carriers being tentatively scheduled for construction after the turn of the century to replace older ships being retired.

A 15-carrier force is required to provide a virtually full-time presence in three key regions where the Department of Defense considers a naval presence to be important: the Mediterranean, the Western Pacific, and the Indian Ocean/Persian Gulf. A 12-carrier force could provide a full-time presence in one region, with a minimum of two-month "gaps" in carrier presence in the other two. With only 11 fully operational carriers, the gap in coverage increases, with amphibious groups centering on a large helicopter carrier (LHA/LHD) substituting for carrier battle groups in some, but not all, "presence" missions.

When the ninth NIMITZ-class carrier (CVN 76) is completed in 2003, it will have been 28 years after the completion of the lead ship—the preliminary design of the NIMITZ began in 1964—a remarkable and probably unique life span for a warship design. (Many minor changes have been made to the design in the 27-year period [see below].) The NIMITZ class also represents the largest number of carriers built to the same basic design since World War II by any nation except for the U.S. helicopter carriers of the TARAWA (LHA 1) and WASP (LHD 1) classes (see chapter 19).

The ninth NIMITZ was authorized in fiscal 1995, seven years after the previous ships of the class. The earlier ships were the second pair of CVNs funded under the Reagan-Lehman naval buildup of the 1980s. The CVN 76 was funded after the Cold War ended, having been put forward by the Clinton administration and approved by Congress with relatively little debate and only minor opposition—a true testimony to the aircraft carrier's utility.

The Department of Defense envisions an additional carrier being authorized about fiscal 2002 (with $30 million for long-lead components being funded in fiscal years 2000 and 2001). It is probable that the ship will *not* have nuclear propulsion.

A comprehensive analysis by the Greenpeace organization has concluded that:

> The cost of nuclear power is not justified in peacetime or in wartime, in terms of useful military capability. Nuclear ships are more expensive, less available, and only comparable in generating and sustaining air operations. They operate as part of integrated and increasingly joint military missions close to land, and nuclear-powered carriers are not used any differently than their conventional counterparts.[1]

The Greenpeace report bases its findings largely on an analysis of three U.S. Navy claims for nuclear-propelled carriers:[2]

- virtually unlimited range at maximum speed
- ability to remain on-station indefinitely without refueling
- greater storage capacity for combat consumables, such as bombs and jet fuel.

Using Navy data, the report concludes that during the Vietnam and Persian Gulf Wars, the period between the two conflicts, and the operation of carriers in crisis response (as well as deployments in general), operations have not matched either the promises or expectations of nuclear propulsion.

> Nuclear-powered carriers do not transit faster to a region, remain longer on-station, or drop significantly more ordnance or launch more aircraft sorties than do conventionally powered carriers. In fact the Navy itself does not appear to distinguish between nuclear and conventional carriers in its operational planning or crisis preparation.[3]

The Greenpeace paper also makes points against nuclear-propelled carriers in this context: One, they require more shipyard time, with a related reduction in at-sea time. Two, the costs associated with their uranium fuel cores—from design through disposal—are significant but barely factored in, in program costs. Three, political liabilities such as foreign port calls and overseas basing and transit through certain straits and canals are associated with nuclear carriers. And four, the current plan is to discard the nine nuclear-propelled cruisers, which will further reduce the potential effectiveness of nuclear carriers.

(Not mentioned in the Greenpeace report, but another important factor nonetheless, is the increased cost of nuclear-trained engineering personnel for nuclear carriers compared to oil-burning ships. Also, with the demise of the nuclear cruiser force the promotion/command opportunities for those men and women are reduced significantly, which will have an impact on their recruitment, retention, and cost.)

A variety of technologies and designs are being looked at by the Navy in anticipation of the CV/CVN 77 program (see below).

Future budgetary constraints may force a further decline in carrier force levels; according to some budget projections, possibly to only ten operational ships.

The Navy no longer operates a dedicated pilot training ship (AVT). The FORRESTAL was to have replaced the venerable LEXINGTON, an ESSEX/HANCOCK-class carrier completed in 1943 that served in the pilot training role from 1963 to 1990. The FORRESTAL was instead decommissioned as part of the post–Cold War cutback of naval forces (the ship had been reclassified as AVT 59). The "Lex" had succeeded the ANTIETAM, the first large-deck dedicated training carrier, which served in that role from 1957 to 1962. Basic pilot training in carrier landings is now carried out on board the KENNEDY.

All World War II–built carriers of the MIDWAY and ESSEX/HANCOCK classes have been retired, the last being the MIDWAY, decommissioned in 1992 after 46 years of service.

In addition to the ships described in this chapter, the Navy operates several large helicopter carriers (amphibious assault ships) of the LPH/LHA/LHD type; these ships are described in chapter 19.

Aircraft: The composition of carrier air wings is described in chapter 28. Air wings vary in aircraft composition and personnel strength; nominal wing strengths are provided in this chapter based on a composition of one fighter squadron (VF), two strike-fighter squadrons (VFA), and one attack squadron (VA), plus electronic countermeasures (VAQ), early warning (VAW), fixed-wing ASW (VS), and helicopter ASW (HS) aircraft.

Builders: Newport News Shipbuilding in Newport News, Virginia, is the only U.S. shipyard now constructing aircraft carriers. The Litton/Ingalls Shipyard in Pascagoula, Mississippi, constructs carrier-type amphibious ships of some 50,000 tons.

The New York Naval Shipyard in Brooklyn, New York, and the New York Shipbuilding Company, in Camden, New Jersey, had also built carriers of the FORRESTAL class. All nuclear-propelled carriers were built at Newport News.

Design: Displacements of carriers have been continuously increased with the addition of new equipment during overhauls and modernization. The data below have been updated for this edition.

Marines: Aircraft carriers are the only U.S. ships that now carry permanent Marine security detachments. Previously, they were also carried on board battleships and larger cruisers (CA, CB, CL types).

The carrier detachments consisted of 2 officers and 64 enlisted until 1993. The Chief of Naval Operations approved a Marine Corps proposal on 28 May 1993 to reduce the detachment, and by June 1993 all carrier detachments numbered 1 officer and 25 enlisted.

Marine aircraft squadrons periodically serve on board aircraft carriers (as well as helicopter carriers). All Marine tactical aircraft are carrier capable, and Marine aviators are trained in carrier operations.

---

1. Hans M. Kristensen, William M. Arkin, and Joshua Handler, *Aircraft Carriers: The Limits Of Nuclear Power* (Washington, D.C.: Greenpeace, June 1994), p. 2.
2. "Navy kicks off campaign to sell CVN-76 carrier to Congress," *Inside the Navy* (12 March 1994), pp. 7–8.
3. Kristensen, et al., p. 3.

The Navy's newest carrier, the JOHN C. STENNIS, on trials. The radar mast immediately behind the island is a pylon structure that supports the SPS-49 long-range search radar, not clearly seen from this angle. The ship's 4½-acre flight deck is empty except for a few tractors near the island and on the portside elevator. (1995, U.S. Navy, Bob Sitar)

CARRIER FORCE LEVELS (FALL 1996)

Number	Class/Ship	Comm.	Active	Building*	Reserve	Notes
CVN 68	NIMITZ	1975–	7	2	—	nuclear-propelled
CV 63	KITTY HAWK	1961–1968	3	—	1	includes 1 operational reserve/training carrier
CVN 65	ENTERPRISE	1961	1	—	—	nuclear-propelled.
CV 59	FORRESTAL	1959	1	—	—	to be retired in 1998
CV 41	MIDWAY	1945	—	—	1	in reserve

*Carriers authorized through fiscal 1996.

Names: U.S. aircraft carriers were traditionally named for older American warships and battles except for the first carrier, LANGLEY (CV 1), named for aviation pioneer Samuel P. Langley.[4] In 1945 the CVB 42 was named for President Franklin D. Roosevelt, who had died in office; CVA 59 was named for the first Secretary of Defense, James V. Forrestal, who committed suicide soon after leaving office; and CVA 67 was named for President John F. Kennedy, assassinated while in office.

Subsequently, the Navy named the CVN 68 for Fleet Admiral Chester W. Nimitz, who died in 1966, and from that point on, naming carriers became a political issue. The Navy's three other fleet admirals—William D. Leahy, Ernest J. King, and William F. Halsey—were remembered by guided missile frigates (DLG, later designated CG or DDG). (Two other ships were named for five-star officers: the Polaris submarine SSBN 654, named the GEORGE C. MARSHALL for the Army Chief of Staff in World War II who subsequently became the Secretary of State and Secretary of Defense; and the large troop transport GEN. R.E. CALLAN/AP 139, which was converted by the Air Force to a missile range instrumentation ship and renamed the GEN. H.H. ARNOLD/T-AGM 9, honoring the World War II commander of the Army Air Forces. Thus, of nine five-star officers in the U.S. armed forces, seven have been honored with U.S. ships. Only Generals of the Army Omar Bradley and Douglas MacArthur have been slighted.)

As a result of the Navy naming the CVN 68 for Admiral Nimitz, White House or congressional intervention led to the CVN 69, 75, and 76 being named for former presidents, and the CVN 70 and 74 for influential members of Congress.

The CVN 71–73 have names previously assigned to ballistic missile submarines (SSBN). The CVN 72 and CVN 73 were named prior to their start, in part to preempt potential congressional pressure for naming one of those ships for Admiral H. G. Rickover (the SSN 709 was named for the admiral).

Operational: From the late 1940s into the late 1980s the Navy attempted to forward deploy two carriers in the Mediterranean and three (subsequently, two) in the Western Pacific/Indian Ocean regions. With the remaining carriers either in transit to or from deployment areas, engaged in fleet exercises or other types of training, or in overhaul, there was a 1:3 deployment cycle, which meant a ship was forward deployed for about six months at a time. Higher deployment rates, as during the Vietnam War and various crises, invariably resulted in lower retention rates, a critical factor in an all-volunteer, high-technology service. Also, the 1:3 cycle did not take into account carriers undergoing the long-term Service Life Extension Project (SLEP) modernization.

The crises and conflicts of the early 1980s, especially the Soviet invasion of Afghanistan (1979) and the Iran-Iraq War (1980–1988) led to more flexible carrier deployment patterns—called FLEXOPS—whereby carriers were withdrawn from some areas and spent more time at sea to provide for multi-carrier exercises or to support special operations, as in the continuing crisis in Lebanon, the invasion of Grenada in October 1983, operations against Libya in 1986, and Operations Desert Shield/Desert Storm (1990–1991). Carrier deployments have thus significantly exceeded the nominal ratio of 6 months' deployment to 12 months in transit/overhaul/in port/local operations.

The situation has become exacerbated in the 1990s because of the general concern for the Indian Ocean area in the wake of the Gulf War. The steaming distances from U.S. ports to the Indian Ocean require on the order of five carriers to maintain one ship on a six-month deployment.

Torpedo countermeasures: U.S. warships have long been fitted with torpedo countermeasures to decoy anti-ship torpedoes. The T-Mk 6 Fanfare, a towed noisemaker, has been phased out of the fleet, succeeded in surface ships by the SLQ-25 Nixie, an advanced towed noisemaker.

4. The most notable exception to the traditional naming scheme was the SHANGRI-LA (CV 38), so named by the Navy when journalists asked where the Doolittle bombers that struck Tokyo and other Japanese cities in April 1942 had flown from. President Franklin D. Roosevelt replied "Shangri-La," referring to the mythical Asian kingdom in James Hilton's novel *Lost Horizon*. The Doolittle bombers had flown from the carrier HORNET (CV 8).

However, the revelation in the mid-1980s of several unexpected Soviet submarine and torpedo developments led to a new emphasis in torpedo countermeasures. The Surface Ship Torpedo Decoy System (SSTDS) was initiated (see chapter 31) and has been fitted to most active aircraft carriers. Some carriers have been fitted with 12.75-inch (324-mm) Mk 32 torpedo tubes (in triple mounts) for launching modified Mk 46 torpedoes to counter the Russian Type 65-80 wake-homing torpedo.

FUTURE CARRIER PROJECTS

The Bottom-Up Review calls for the construction of four additional *nuclear* carriers to be authorized during the period fiscal year 2000 to 2008 to maintain the 11-plus-1 carrier force. The lead ship—generally referred to as CVX—would be completed about 2007. These ships would replace older oil-burning carriers to maintain a force of 11 or 12 large-deck carriers.

About $630 million is currently programmed by the Department of Defense for fiscal years 2000 and 2001 for advanced procurement and design of the CVX.

The Navy is examining a variety of configurations for the CVX. Several of the concepts being examined have conventional, not nuclear, propulsion (although the designation CVN 77 is also used in some Navy planning documents). A joint study report of the Center for Naval Analyses (CNA) and Naval Sea Systems Command (NAVSEA) in early 1995 proposed six design concepts for the CVX; their basic characteristics are listed in the accompanying table.[5]

5. "Future Carrier Project—NAVSEA Status Report" (Brief to the Commander Naval Sea Systems Command), 1 Feb. 1995.

FUTURE CARRIER PROJECTS

Concept	Displacement	Length*	Beam*	Aircraft	Catapults	Elevators	Missiles
Ultra-Large	214,000 tons	1,550 ft	176 ft	120+	2	5	—
SWATH	84,000 tons	784 ft**	164 ft	~30	2	2	—
Monohull	47,000 tons	770 ft#	121 ft	~30	2	2	—
CGV-CTOL (Version 1)	35,800 tons	770 ft	109 ft	14	0	2	192
CGV-CTOL (Version 3)	43,200 tons	770 ft	102 ft	12##	0	0	192
CGV-STOVL	26,500 tons	700 ft	96 ft	14–22	0	0	64–192

*Waterline dimensions.
**Length of submerged hulls approximately 960 feet overall.
#Flight deck overhang provides overall length of 814 feet.
##Aircraft hangared on flight deck.

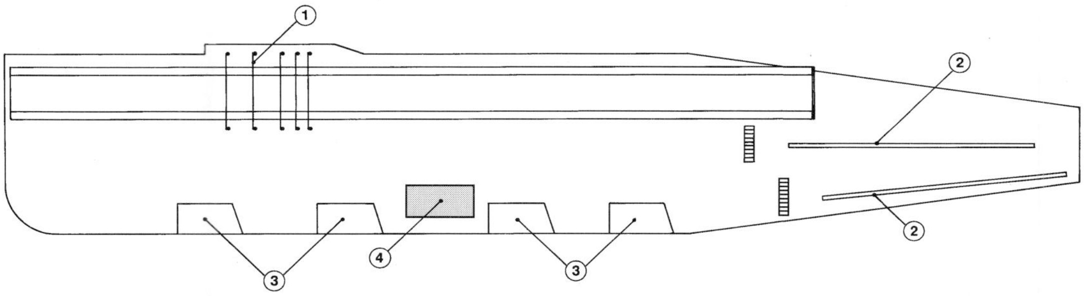

ULTRA-LARGE STOAL CONCEPT
1. Arresting wires (4). 2. Catapults (2). 3. Elevators (4). 4. Island structure.

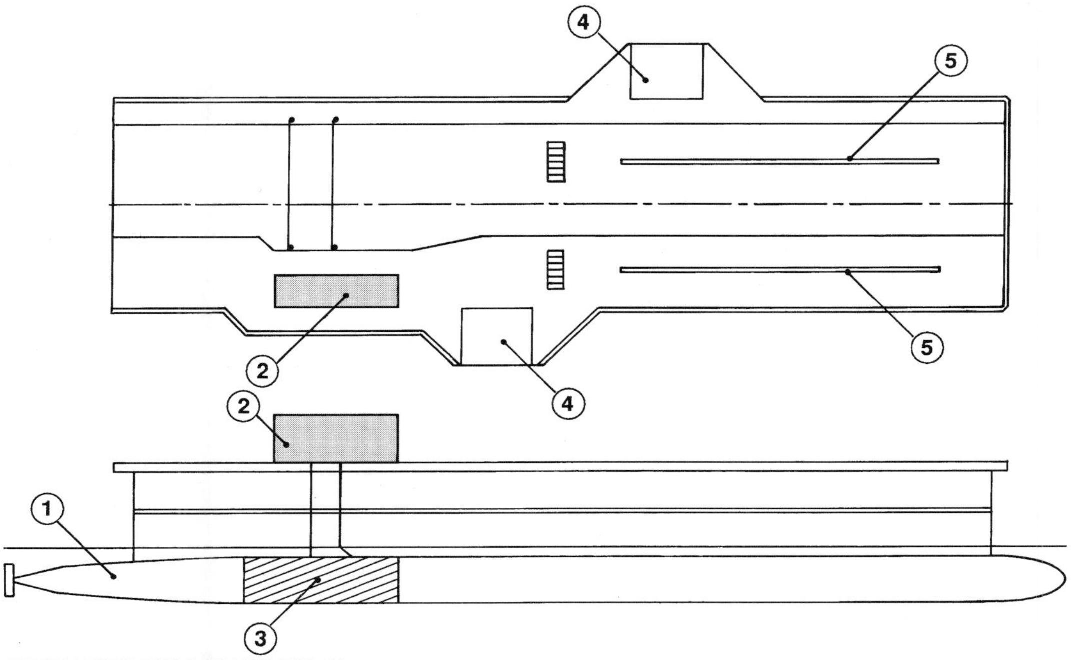

SWATH MINIMUM CAPABILITY CV
1. Submerged twin hulls. 2. Island structure. 3. Electric motors. 4. Elevators (2). 5. Catapults (2).

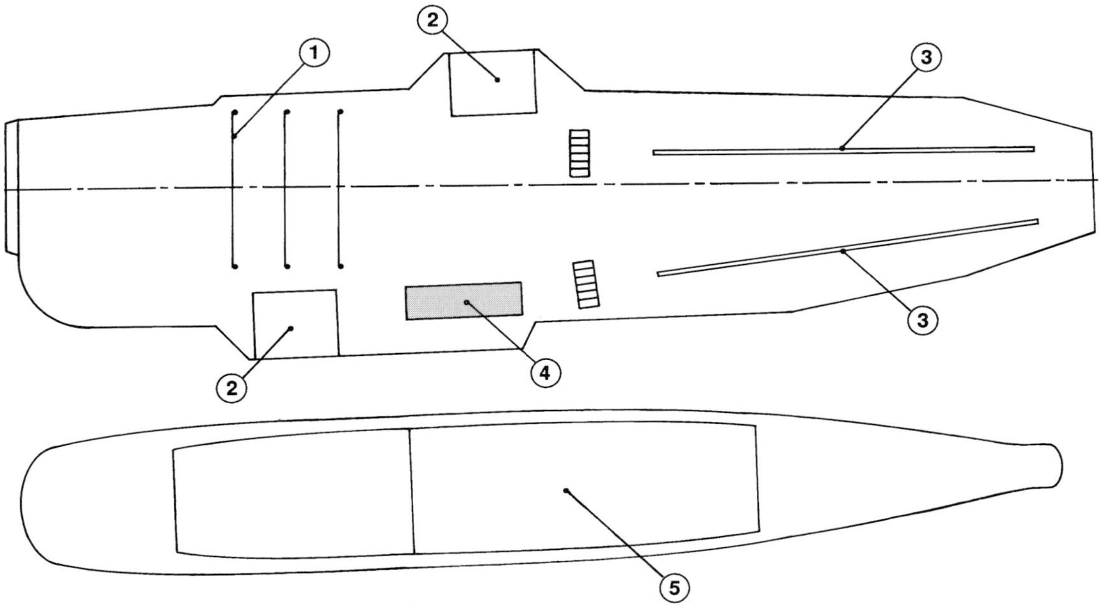

MONOHULL MINIMUM CAPABILITY CV
1. Arresting wires (3). 2. Elevators (2). 3. Catapults (2). 4. Island structure. 5. Hangar deck.

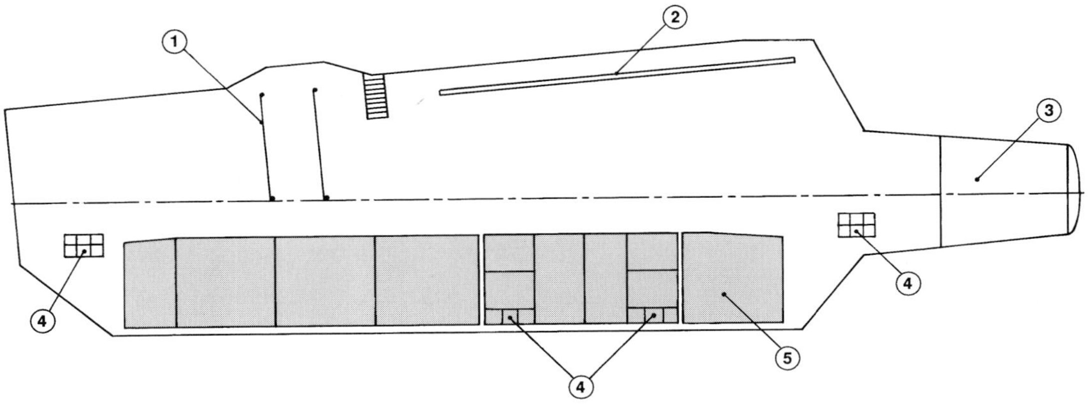

CGV-CTOL VERSION 3
1. Arresting wires (2). 2. Catapult. 3. Ski ramp. 4. Missile launchers (VLS). 5. Island structure with on-deck hangars for 10 fixed-wing aircraft and 2 helicopters.

Ultra-Large STOAL Concept:[6] This is an enlargment of the NIMITZ design, estimated to displace 214,000 tons and to carry an air wing about twice as large as that on board a NIMITZ. The ship would have a small starboard-side island structure, one port and four starboard deck-edge elevators, and two catapults with a "parallel-deck" configuration.

SWATH Minimum Capability CV Concept: This ship would employ the Small Waterplane Area Twin-Hull (SWATH) configuration with a rectangular flight deck; there would be a small island structure aft (starboard side) and two deck-edge elevators and two catapults. This ship would have electric-drive propulsion. About 30 aircraft would be carried.

Monohull Minimum Capability Concept: A relatively small, conventional carrier design, with electric drive.

CGV-CTOL Version 1 Concept:[7] A small angled-deck carrier with a missile capability; it will displace about 35,800 tons. This ship would also have 192 vertical-launch cells for surface-to-air and strike missiles. Only two arresting wires would be fitted with a ski-ramp forward (no catapults). There would be two off-center elevators.

CGV-CTOL Version 3 Concept: A small angled-deck carrier with the aircraft hangared on the flight deck. This is similar to the Mk II strike cruiser proposed in the late 1970s (see page 120). This CGV-CTOL configuration would have a displacement of 34,200 tons and carry 12 aircraft (8 F-14 Tomcats, 2 E-2C Hawkeyes, 2 SH-60 Seahawks). The ship would have 192 vertical-launch missiles.

CGV-STOVL Concept:[8] This ship would be similar to the British INVINCIBLE-class STOVL carriers; it would be larger, however, and carry a large missile battery. The U.S. ship would displace 26,500 tons and operate an air wing of 14 to 22 STOVL aircraft and helicopters. The ship would have a ski-ramp, but no arresting wires or catapults. Between 64 and 192 missiles would be provided in vertical-launch cells.

Note that only the largest of the six conceptual designs would have nuclear propulsion; most of the others would make use of gas turbine/electric propulsion systems, signature control to reduce detection by various kinds of sensors, fiber-optic highway, and dynamic armor.

Not included in the CNA-NAVSEA analysis is an aviation platform concept put forward by Admiral William A. Owens, former Vice Chairman of the Joint Chiefs of Staff. In a recent book, he describes large mobile sea bases made up of components that could be towed to a given crisis area and assembled at sea.[9] These ships—referred to in the Bottom-Up Review as "floating islands"—would be as large as National Airport in Washington, D.C., displacing more than

6. STOAL = Short Take-Off Arrested Landing.
7. CGV = Guided missile cruiser with aviation capability; CTOL = Conventional Take-Off and Landing.
8. STOVL = Short Take-Off Vertical Landing (formerly VSTOL).
9. Adm. William A. Owens, USN, *High Seas: The Naval Passage to an Uncharted World* (Annapolis, Md.: Naval Institute Press, 1995).

500,000 tons and capable of handling from 150 to almost 300 aircraft, including C-130 Hercules transports, depending upon their type. These platforms would be non–self-propelled. One CNA study addressed a Mobile Offshore Base (MOB) concept composed of six modules assembled to form a platform 3,000 feet (914.6 m) long and 300 feet (91.46 m) wide.

This concept, however, would violate the advantages of mobility and ready on arrival that have traditionally characterized warships.

The efficiency of the designs is difficult to compare. For example, the Ultra-Large STOAL ship and the SWATH ship would require enlarging dry docks and port facilities to accommodate the ships; also, their unit costs may be too great for Congress to accept in the post–Cold War era. The Monohull design appears to be the most cost-effective platform from the viewpoint of aircraft-per-ton displacement. However, if one accepts STOVL aircraft as the equivalent of Conventional Take-Off and Landing (CTOL) aircraft, and one assigns value to missile capability, then the CGV-STOVL ship—the smallest of the platforms proposed—ranks as the "best" option.

MULTI-PURPOSE CARRIERS

Separate from the above design concepts, some U.S. naval leaders also see a confluence of the CVN and LHA/LHD designs. Admiral Owens labels such a development—by the 2020 decade—as "presence" carriers.[10] Owens views the development of his presence carriers, which would normally be forward deployed, to parallel the development of the large Mobile Offshore Bases which, when assembled in a forward area and operating up to 300 aircraft, would be "war fighting" platforms (see figure 13-1).

This union of large carriers and large helicopter carriers has also been proposed by Vice Admiral George R. Sterner, Commander NAVSEA, and hence responsible for warship design, development, and construction.[11]

This concept would result in a large carrier that would combine air strike and fighter capabilities with amphibious assault capabilities. While these may not be compatible in an operational sense, the development of advanced STOVL aircraft (i.e., planes that would not require catapults or arresting gear) could ease the interface and support problems. Still, there would be significant operational problems. For example, would the amphibious component demand that the ship remain offshore in a restricted operating area to support Marines ashore, while the strike/fighter component is needed elsewhere? Or, will the strike/fighter aircraft and troop-carrying helicopters be compatible on the flight deck? How will missile launches affect flight operations?

More feasible could be the combining of cruiser-destroyer features (e.g., SPY-1 radar, vertical-launch missiles) with an "attack" carrier—a concept used by the Soviet Navy in its KIEV and TBILISI carrier designs.[12] Such a U.S. ship could be similar to the CGV-series cruiser designs discussed above.

Admiral Owens has also proposed a merger of the surface combatant (DDG 51) and amphibious ship (LX/LPD 17) designs to produce the "littoral supremacy ship." But his ship would be primarily an amphibious ship (LHA/LHD)—operating helicopters and tilt-rotor aircraft—fitted with vertical-launch missiles forward; it would still have the large docking well of an amphibious ship. The ship, according to Owens,

> . . . could provide air and ballistic-missile defense across the littoral, joint-task-force C³I, strike and close air support, and direct and indirect fire support [with missiles]. With five to six hundred marines, twenty helicopters, and three or four air-cushioned landing craft . . . it would, as its name suggests, be a very strong asset, allowing the United States to dominate the littoral battle space from a single platform.[13]

But the ship would suffer from the interference of differing missions, support requirements, etc. The current operation of a handful of AV-8B Harrier STOVL from helicopter-carrying LHA/LHD ships is not a reasonable model for such an aviation ship. And, as Owens notes, "Such a ship would not be cheap, however, and as an expensive investment that creates something very valuable, the littoral-supremacy ship would pose two perennial problems:

- Would it be too valuable to risk in dangerous areas?
- What would we do with such a specialized ship if the Navy's mission shifted back to sea control?"[14]

For these and other reasons, more likely approaches to multi-purpose carriers in the coming years would be the Monohull or CGV-series ships, with conventional propulsion, as well as enhanced LHA/LHD designs as follow-on ships to the NIMITZ class.

Modern aircraft carriers are floating repair shops: Here, mechanics from Fighter Squadron (VF) 143 work on an F-14B Tomcat on the flight deck of the GEORGE WASHINGTON as the ship steams in the Persian Gulf. (U.S. Navy, AN Joe Hendricks)

10. Ibid., p. 163.
11. Admiral Sterner at Navy League Sea-Air-Space symposium, Washington, D.C., 12 April 1995.
12. The latter ship was originally named RIGA, then LEONID BREZHNEV, then TBILISI, and, after the breakup of the Soviet Union, the ADMIRAL FLOTA SOVETSKOGO SOYUZA KUZNETSOV.
13. Owens, p. 167.
14. Ibid.

7 + 2 NUCLEAR-PROPELLED AIRCRAFT CARRIERS: "NIMITZ" CLASS

Number	Name	FY	Builder	Laid down	Launched	Commissioned	Status
CVN 68	NIMITZ	67	Newport News Shipbuilding	22 June 1968	13 May 1972	3 May 1975	**PA**
CVN 69	DWIGHT D. EISENHOWER	70	Newport News Shipbuilding	15 Aug 1970	11 Oct 1975	18 Oct 1977	**AA**
CVN 70	CARL VINSON	74	Newport News Shipbuilding	11 Oct 1975	15 Mar 1980	13 Mar 1982	**PA**
CVN 71	THEODORE ROOSEVELT	80	Newport News Shipbuilding	31 Oct 1981	27 Oct 1984	25 Oct 1986	**AA**
CVN 72	ABRAHAM LINCOLN	83	Newport News Shipbuilding	3 Nov 1984	13 Feb 1988	11 Nov 1989	**PA**
CVN 73	GEORGE WASHINGTON	83	Newport News Shipbuilding	25 Aug 1986	21 July 1990	4 July 1992	**AA**
CVN 74	JOHN C. STENNIS	88	Newport News Shipbuilding	13 Mar 1991	13 Nov 1993	9 Dec 1995	**AA**
CVN 75	HARRY S. TRUMAN	88	Newport News Shipbuilding	29 Nov 1993	7 Sep 1996	1998	Building
CVN 76	RONALD REAGAN	95	Newport News Shipbuilding	1998	2000	2002	Building

Displacement:		*Light*	*Full load*
	CVN 68–70	74,042 tons	95,413 tons
	CVN 71–73	77,606 tons	97,574 tons
	CVN 74–76	78,127 tons	99,050 tons
	CVN 72–76	102,000 tons combat load (see *Design* notes)	

Length: 1,040 feet (317.2 m) waterline
1,092 feet (332.9 m) overall
Beam: 134 feet (40.85 m)
Flight deck: 250⅚ feet (76.5 m)
Draft: CVN 68–70 37 feet (11.3 m)
CVN 71–76 38 5/12 feet (11.7 m)
CVN 72–76 39 feet (11.9 m) combat load
Propulsion: 4 steam turbines (General Electric); 280,000 shp; 4 shafts
Reactors: 2 pressurized-water A4W (Westinghouse)
Speed: 30+ knots

Manning:		*Total*	*Officers*	*Enlisted*
	CVN 68	3,062	158	2,904
	CVN 69	3,008	159	2,849
	CVN 70	3,068	158	2,910
	CVN 71	3,059	159	2,900
	CVN 72	3,058	158	2,900
	CVN 73	3,054	160	2,894
	CVN 74	3,060	160	2,900
Marines:		26	1	25

Flag: approx. 70 (25 officers + 45 enlisted) when embarked
Air wing: approx. 2,000
Aircraft: approx. 80
Catapults: 4 steam Mk 13-1 in CVN 68–71
4 steam Mk 13-2 in CVN 72 and later ships
Elevators: 4 deck edge (85 × 52 feet/25.9 × 15.85 m); 130, 000-lb (58,500 kg) capacity
Missiles: 3 8-tube NATO Sea Sparrow launchers Mk 29
Guns: 3 20-mm Phalanx CIWS Mk 16 (3 multi-barrel) in CVN 68, 69; 4 guns in later ships
Radars: SPS-48E 3-D air search
SPS-49(V)5 air search
SPS-64(V)9 navigation
SPS-67(V)1 surface search
Mk 23 Target Acquisition System (TAS)
Sonars: none
Fire control: 3 Mk 91 missile FCS
EW systems: SLQ-25A Nixie torpedo countermeasures
CVN 68, 69 SLQ-29 (SLQ-17A + WLR-8)
CVN 70–76 SLQ-32(V)4
WLR-1H

These are the largest warships ever built. Seven ships are in commission; two more are under construction. Details vary as improvements have been made with succeeding ships (see *Design* notes). The class is expected to total nine ships.

The STENNIS is being assigned to the Pacific Fleet; the TRUMAN is scheduled to be assigned to the Atlantic Fleet, the REAGAN to the Pacific Fleet.

Class: A program to construct the first three CVNs of this class was approved by Secretary of Defense Robert S. McNamara during the Vietnam War as replacements for the three MIDWAY-class carriers to provide a force of 12 large carriers (i.e., CV 59–64, 66, 67, and CVN 65, 68–70). The first three ships were delayed during construction by labor strikes and schedule problems at the Newport News yard. The NIMITZ was seven years from keel laying to commissioning, compared to less than four years for the more complex (eight-reactor) ENTERPRISE.

The CVN 71 was forced on the Carter administration by Congress in 1980; the CVN 72 and CVN 73 were approved through the efforts of Secretary of the Navy John Lehman early in the Reagan administration. The CVN 74 was originally included in the last year of the five-year (FY 1984–1988) shipbuilding program put forward by the Reagan administration in January 1983. That ship was included for "planning" purposes only, however, and appeared to be a backup in the event that Congress declined to authorize one of the two NIMITZ-class ships in the fiscal 1983 program. In mid-1986 several members of Congress urged the construction of CVN 74, but budget limitations and the overall budget deficit prevented serious consideration of the ship. In December 1986 it was learned that the Reagan

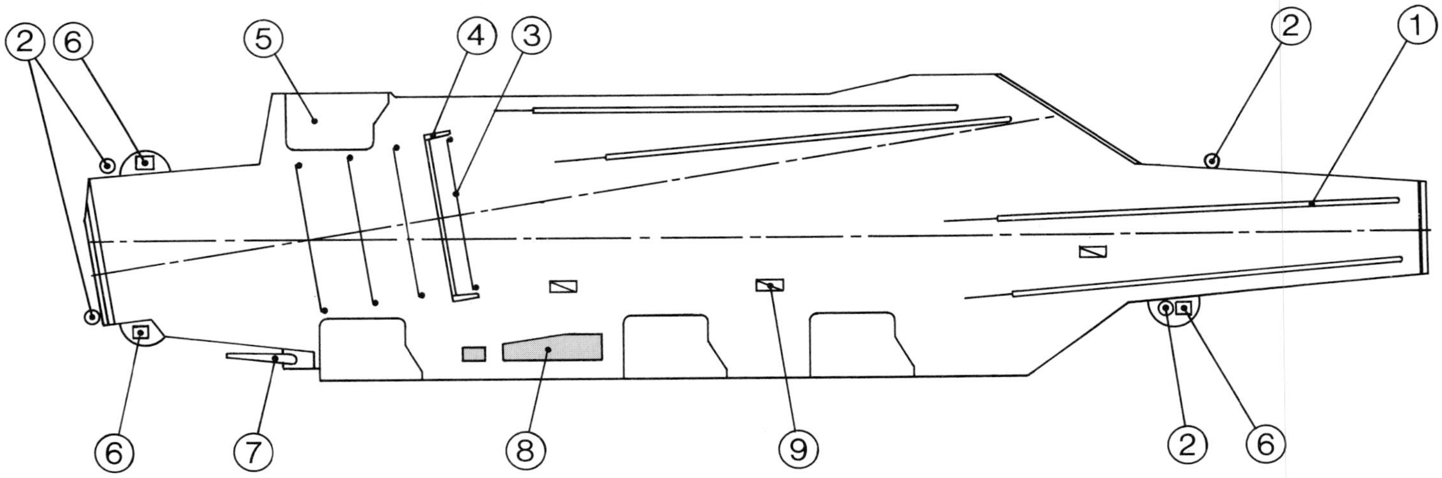

GEORGE WASHINGTON
1. Catapults (4). 2. Phalanx CIWS (4). 3. Arresting wires (4). 4. Barricade. 5. Elevators (4). 6. NATO Sea Sparrow missile launchers (3). 7. Crane. 8. Island structure. 9. Bomb elevators (3). (William Clipson)

The GEORGE WASHINGTON at sea off the Virginia Capes shows the long, angled lines of U.S. supercarriers, which originated with the canceled UNITED STATES (CVA 58) of 1949. Note that aircraft are parked on the port quarter, still allowing use of the angled landing deck. (1994, U.S. Navy, JOC Gregg L. Snaza)

administration would request two additional CVNs, with Lehman becoming the principal advocate; in January 1987 the fiscal 1988 defense budget proposed the construction of the CVN 74 and CVN 75.

Classification: The NIMITZ and EISENHOWER were ordered as attack aircraft carriers (CVAN); they were changed to multi-mission aircraft carriers (CVN) on 30 June 1975. The VINSON and later ships were ordered as CVN.

Design: SCB No. 102. The general arrangement of these ships is similar to the previous KITTY HAWK class with respect to flight deck, hangar, elevators, and island structure (e.g., the island structure is aft of the No. 1 and No. 2 elevators; the No. 4 elevator is on the port side, aft of the angled deck and opposite the No. 3 elevator on the starboard side). The angled deck is canted to port at 9° 3′ and is 796 ⅔ feet (242.9 m) long.

The hangar deck is 684 feet (208.5 m) long, 108 feet (32.9 m) wide, and 26½ feet (8.1 m) high.

This class has been in production longer than any other carrier design in history. The uncertainty of future CVN construction and the general excellence of the NIMITZ design precluded major changes in the later ships. The CVN 71 and subsequent ships incorporate improved magazine protection; the CVN 73 and later ships have improved topside ballistic protection; and the CVN 74 and units were constructed with HSLA-100 steel. There have also been incremental improvements in the ships' electrical and electronics systems.

"Combat load" is maximum displacement after underway replenishment at sea of full ordnance and aviation fuel capacity. Payload includes approximately 2,900 tons of aviation ordnance and up to 3.5 million gallons (13.2 million liters) of jet fuel (JP-5).

Electronics: Several carrier-landing systems are provided—SPN-42A Carrier Controlled Approach (CCA) in CVN 68–71; SPN-43C marshaling in all ships; SPN-44 landing aid in CVN 71 and later ships; two SPN-46 air traffic control in CVN 72 and subsequent ships.

Engineering: These carriers have only two reactors compared to eight in the first nuclear carrier, the ENTERPRISE. The fuel cores in the early ships were estimated to have a service life of at least 13 years (800,000 to one million n.miles/1,481,000 to 1,850,350 km); however, the later cores have been pushed out to 23 years. This means that the later ships would be refueled only once during a service life of 45 to 50 years.

The Refueling/Comprehensive Overhaul (RCOH) schedule for the

The NIMITZ maneuvering in the Northern Persian Gulf. Following the Gulf War of January 1991 the United States has maintained a carrier battle group in the area on an almost continuous basis. The ship is not ready to launch aircraft, as a number of planes are parked on all four of her catapults. (1993, John Bouvia)

The EISENHOWER shows the port-side sponsons of the NIMITZ design, a small one forward for a Phalanx CIWS, and the large sponsons aft supporting the angled flight deck. The enclosed bow dates to the immediate post–World War II period, intended to reduce damage from heavy seas. (1994, Giorgio Arra)

NIMITZ-class ships when this edition went to press was:

NIMITZ	fiscal 1998–2000
EISENHOWER	fiscal 2001–2003
VINSON	fiscal 2005–2007
ROOSEVELT	fiscal 2010–2012

Manning: Aircraft carriers were the first U.S. combatant ships to have women assigned as permanent crew members; the EISENHOWER was the first to deploy with women, departing Norfolk, Virginia, on 20 October 1994 with 367 female officers and enlisted on board. The ship deployed for six months, operating in the Mediterranean and Adriatic areas.

Missiles: The CVN 68 and CVN 69 were built with the Sea Sparrow Mk 25 missile launchers (with Mk 115 fire-control system); they have been rearmed with the NATO Sea Sparrow system.

Names: The CVN 68 is named for one of three fleet admirals appointed during World War II; the CVN 69 is named for the 34th president, a former general of the army; the CVN 70 is named for the longtime chairman of the House Armed Services Committee, a major supporter of the U.S. naval buildup on the eve of World War II; the CVN 71 is named for the 26th president; the Polaris submarine SSBN 600 previously honored Roosevelt; the CVN 72 honors the 16th president; the Polaris submarine SSBN 602 previously carried that name; the CVN 73 honors the first president and commander of American forces in the Revolutionary War (the SSBN 598 was also named GEORGE WASHINGTON); and the CVN 74 recalls a Navy supporter who served in the House of Representatives from 1947 to 1988.

The CVN 75 was originally named UNITED STATES for one of the six sailing frigates authorized by Congress in 1794, and she was the first to be launched; the other ships in the series included the frigates CONSTITUTION and CONSTELLATION. The second UNITED STATES was a battle cruiser (CC 6), laid down in 1920, but cancelled; sister ships were completed as the carriers LEXINGTON (CV 2) and SARATOGA (CV 3). The next UNITED STATES was the first "super carrier" (CVA 58), laid down in April 1949 and promptly cancelled, which led to the carrier-versus-B-36 controversy. On 2 February 1995 the CVN 75 was renamed for the 33rd president.

The CVN 76 is named for the 40th president, who rebuilt U.S. military forces in the 1980s.

Operational: The VINSON shifted to the Pacific Fleet in 1983, the NIMITZ in 1987, and the LINCOLN in 1990.

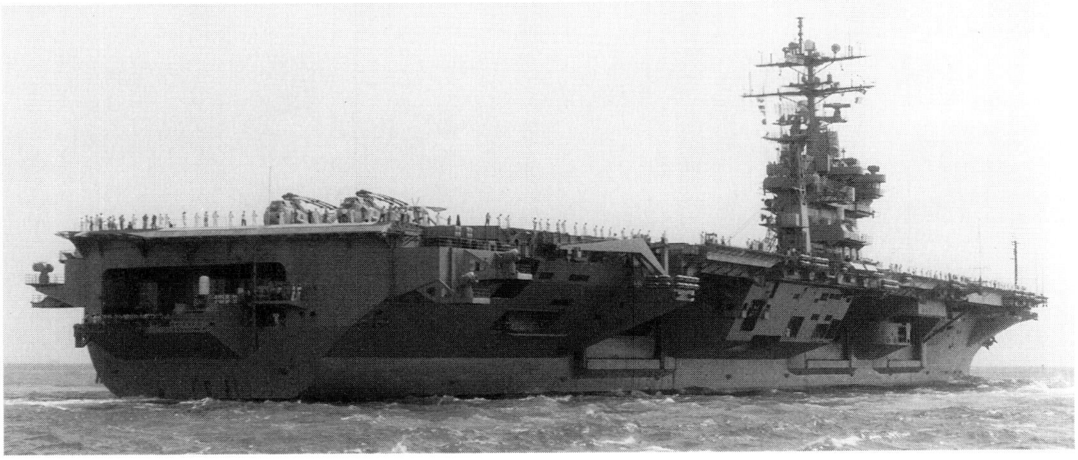

The stern aspect of the EISENHOWER shows the Phalanx CIWs mounted on the fantail and a Mk 91 Sea Sparrow fire-control antenna silhouetted on the port quarter. On the starboard quarter is the aircraft crane, which is used for handling the ship's boats as well as aircraft when alongside a pier. (1994, Giorgio Arra)

The island structure of the EISENHOWER. The SPS-48 is mounted forward of the mast with an SPS-67 fitted immediately above it, on the mast. Two Mk 91 Sea Sparrow fire-control antennas are in "tubes" on the starboard side of the island. An SPS-49 air search radar tops the lattice mast aft the island. (1994, Giorgio Arra)

GEORGE WASHINGTON has a pylon mast aft of the island structure in place of the lattice radar mast in other NIMITZ-class ships. An SPS-49(V)5 radar is fitted on the mast. There are twin OE-82 satellite communication "dishes" topping the array of antennas on the main mast. (1992, Giorgio Arra)

3 MULTI-PURPOSE AIRCRAFT CARRIERS: "KITTY HAWK" CLASS
1 OPERATIONAL RESERVE/TRAINING CARRIER: "JOHN F. KENNEDY"

Number	Name	FY	Builder	Laid down	Launched	Commissioned	Status
CV 63	Kitty Hawk	56	New York Shipbuilding, Camden, N.J.	27 Dec 1956	21 May 1960	29 Apr 1961	**PA**
CV 64	Constellation	57	New York Naval Shipyard, Brooklyn, N.Y.	14 Sep 1957	8 Oct 1960	27 Oct 1961	**PA**
CV 66	America	61	Newport News Shipbuilding	9 Jan 1961	1 Feb 1964	23 Jan 1965	**AR**
CV 67	John F. Kennedy	63	Newport News Shipbuilding	22 Oct 1964	27 May 1967	7 Sep 1968	**NRF-TRA**

Displacement: *Light* / *Full load*
- CV 63, 64: 61,057 tons / 81,985 tons
- CV 66: 61,174 tons / 85,490 tons
- CV 67: 60,660 tons / 80,940 tons

Length: 990 feet (301.9 m) waterline
- CV 63, 64: 1,045$\frac{2}{3}$ feet (318.8 m) overall
- CV 66: 1,047$\frac{1}{2}$ feet (319.25 m) overall
- CV 67: 1,052 feet (320.3 m) overall

Beam: 129$\frac{11}{12}$ feet (39.6 m) except CV 67 128$\frac{1}{2}$ feet (39.2 m)
Flight deck: 265$\frac{1}{2}$ feet (80.9 m) except CV 67 267$\frac{1}{2}$ feet (81.5 m)
Draft: 37 feet (11.3 m) except CV 67 36$\frac{1}{2}$ feet (11.1 m)
Propulsion: 4 steam turbines (General Electric); 280,000 shp; 4 shafts
Boilers: 8 1,200 psi (83.4 kg/cm^2) (Foster Wheeler)
Speed: 33 knots
Range: 12,000 n.miles (22,225 km) at 20 knots

Manning:

	Total	*Officers*	*Enlisted*
CV 63	2,914	148	2,766
CV 64	2,900	148	2,752
CV 66	2,890	147	2,743
CV 67	2,578	135	2,443
Marines:	26	1	25

Flag: approx. 70 (25 officers + 45 enlisted) when embarked
Air wing: approx. 2,000
Aircraft: approx. 80
Catapults: 4 steam C13 in CV 63, 64
3 steam C13 + 1 steam C13-1 in CV 66, 67
Elevators: 4 deck edge (85 × 52 feet/25.9 × 15.9 m) 130,000-lb (58,500 kg) capacity
Missiles: 2 8-tube NATO Sea Sparrow launchers Mk 29 in CV 64; 3 launchers in other ships
Guns: 4 20-mm Phalanx CIWS Mk 16 (3 multi-barrel) in CV 64; 3 guns in other ships
Radars: SPS-48E 3-D air search except SPS-48C in CV 66
SPS-49(V)5 air search
SPS-64(V)9 surface search
SPS-67(V)1 surface search
Mk 23 Target Acquisition System (TAS)
Sonars: (removed from CV 66)
Fire control: 3 Mk 91 missile FCS
EW systems: SLQ-29 (SLQ-17 + WLR-8)
WLR-1H
WLR-11

These ships have a modified FORRESTAL configuration with improved elevator and flight deck arrangements. The KITTY HAWK was delayed because of shipyard problems; the CONSTELLATION was delayed because of a fire on board while under construction; and the KENNEDY was delayed because of length debates over whether the ship should have nuclear or conventional propulsion. (All subsequent U.S. large carriers have been nuclear propelled.) The AMERICA was decommissioned at ceremonies on 9 August 1996; her official date is 30 September. She will be retained in reserve.

The CONSTELLATION is scheduled to replace the INDEPENDENCE as

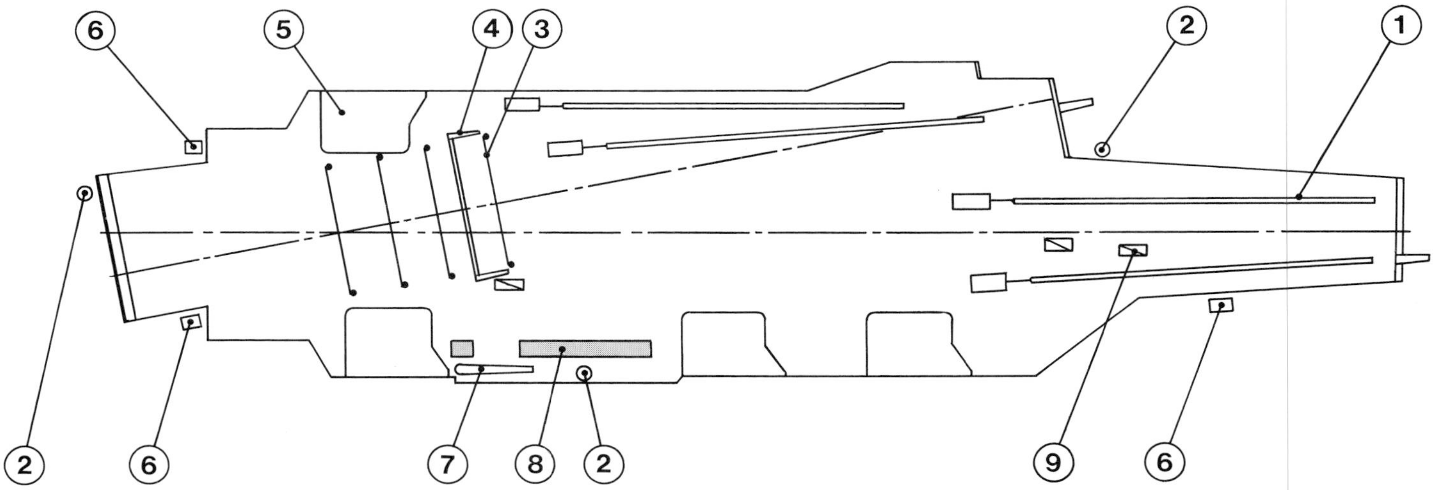

AMERICA
1. Catapults (4). 2. Phalanx CIWS (3). 3. Arresting wires (4). 4. Barricade. 5. Elevators (4). 6. NATO Sea Sparrow launchers (3). 7. Crane. 8. Island structure. 9. Bomb elevators (3). (William Clipson)

the Navy's forward-based carrier at Yokosuka, Japan, in fiscal 1998. The KENNEDY was changed from active status to the Naval Reserve Force (NRF) on 1 October 1994; she serves as an "operational reserve/training carrier," providing carrier landing training for pilots while being capable on short notice of deploying as an operational carrier. This is the first time an aircraft carrier has ever been assigned to the NRF. She is homeported in Mayport, Florida (AVT training carriers were based at Pensacola, Florida).

The KITTY HAWK is to be retired in fiscal 2003, the CONSTELLATION in fiscal 2008, and the KENNEDY in fiscal 2012.

Builders: This class includes the last U.S. aircraft carriers to be built by shipyards other than Newport News.

Class: The KENNEDY is officially a separate, one-ship class. All four ships are often grouped with the FORRESTAL class in force-level discussions.

Classification: All four ships were originally attack aircraft carriers (CVA). Two ships were changed to multi-mission carriers (CV) when modified to operate ASW aircraft: the KITTY HAWK, on 29 April 1973, and the KENNEDY, on 1 December 1974. The CONSTELLATION and AMERICA were changed to CV on 30 June 1975, prior to being modified.

Design: SCB No. 127, 127A, 127B, and 127C, respectively. These ships are larger than the FORRESTAL class and have an improved flight deck arrangement, with two elevators forward of the island structure and the port-side elevator on the stern quarter rather than at the forward end of the angled flight deck.

The hangar deck in the first three ships is 740 feet (225.6 m) long, 101 feet (30.8 m) wide, and 25 feet (7.6 m) high; in the KENNEDY the hangar deck is 688 feet (209.75 m) long, 106 feet (32.3 m) wide, and 25 (7.6 m) feet high. The angled deck is canted to port at 11° 20′; the KENNEDY is canted at 11°; the KITTY HAWK and CONSTELLATION angled decks are 722 7/12 feet (220.3 m) long, the AMERICA's is 741 feet (225.9 m) long, and that of the KENNEDY 754 feet (229.9 m) long. The KENNEDY has her stack angled out to starboard to help carry exhaust gases away from the approach path to the flight deck.

Electronics: Several carrier-landing systems are provided in these

The KITTY HAWK under way off Hong Kong with most of Air Wing 2 on her flight deck. Satellite and other "white" antenna domes abound on her bridge and mast; a white-domed Phalanx CIWS is on a sponson on the starboard bow. (1964, Giorgio Arra)

Stern aspect of the CONSTELLATION at Hong Kong, with her starboard anchor visible. The large after sponson on the starboard side was built for a Terrier Mk 10 missile launcher, long since removed. (1994, Giorgio Arra)

ships: SPN-35 blind-landing approach radar, SPN-41 landing aid, SPN-42 CCA, SPN-43C marshaling, and two SPN-46 air traffic control.

The AMERICA and KENNEDY have bow sonar domes, but only the AMERICA had sonar installed. She was the only postwar U.S. carrier so fitted at the time; the set, an SQS-23, was removed in late 1981.

Manning: As an NRF ship, the KENNEDY embarked some 300 Navy Training and Administration of Reserves (TAR) personnel in mid-1995. TARs are full-time reserve personnel. Selected (part-time) reservists will not join the ship until late 1997, when the KENNEDY returns from a post-overhaul overseas deployment. About 300 selected reservists will then be assigned to the crew.

Missiles: The first three ships were built with two Terrier missile launchers (Mk 10 Mod 3 on starboard quarter and Mk 10 Mod 4 on port quarter) with SPQ-55B missile control "searchlight" radars. The KENNEDY originally had three Sea Sparrow Mk 25 launchers and Mk 115 FCS.

Modernization: The KITTY HAWK and CONSTELLATION have been modernized under the SLEP upgrade. The AMERICA will not be upgraded and is scheduled to be decommissioned in 1996–1997. She will be the first of the class to be retired (in 1996–1997) because of higher maintenance and overhaul costs. This was caused by thinner hull plating and other cost-reduction methods employed in her construction.

The Secretary of Defense in early 1991 canceled the planned SLEP for the KENNEDY; however, Congress placed language in the fiscal 1991 supplemental appropriation to force the SLEP to be undertaken at the Philadelphia Naval Shipyard.[15] Congress voted only $405 million for the KENNEDY work, though, about one-half the estimated cost of a SLEP. Instead, the Navy undertook a two-year Comprehensive Overhaul (COH) modernization in 1993–1994 (vice about three years for a SLEP); cost of the COH is $491 million.

	Arrival at yard	Modernization start	Modernization complete
CV 63	7 Apr 1987	28 Jan 1988	31 Aug 1991
CV 64	11 Apr 1990	2 July 1990	10 Mar 1993
CV 67	13 Sep 1993	13 Sep 1993	15 Sep 1995

The upgrades add an estimated 15 years to the ships' nominal 30-year service life.

See FORRESTAL class for SLEP details.

15. The Philadelphia yard was closed in 1996.

The KITTY HAWK at sea in the Western Pacific. The dark areas on the starboard side indicate the open hangar bays, with the three starboard-side elevators at the flight deck level in this view. (1994, Giorgio Arra)

The CONSTELLATION's island shows an SPS-49 antenna atop the bridge, with a host of other antennas mounted on the island structure. A Phalanx CIWS is mounted beneath the bridge (starboard side); an SPS-48E radar is fitted atop the mast aft of the island. (1994, Giorgio Arra)

The KENNEDY is the only carrier with an angled funnel, which helps keep exhaust gases away from the aircraft approach path. When this photo was taken the "JFK" had an SPS-49 antenna atop the bridge with an SPS-67 antenna mounted above it; an SPS-48C antenna is fitted onto the lattice mast. (1989, Giorgio Arra)

1 NUCLEAR-PROPELLED AIRCRAFT CARRIER: "ENTERPRISE"

Number	Name	FY	Builder	Laid down	Launched	Commissioned	Status
CVN 65	ENTERPRISE	58	Newport News Shipbuilding	4 Feb 1958	24 Sep 1960	25 Nov 1961	**AA**

Displacement:	73,570 tons light 93,970 tons full load
Length:	1,040 feet (317.2 m) waterline 1,101½ feet (335.8 m) overall
Beam:	133 feet (40.5 m)
Flight deck:	248⅓ feet (75.7 m)
Draft:	39 feet (11.9 m)
Propulsion:	4 steam turbines (Westinghouse); approx. 280,000 shp; 4 shafts
Reactors:	8 pressurized-water A2W (Westinghouse)
Speed:	33 knots
Manning:	3,276 (168 officers + 3,108 enlisted)
Marines:	26 (1 officer + 25 enlisted)
Flag:	approx. 70 (25 officers + 45 enlisted) when embarked
Air wing:	approx. 2,000
Aircraft:	approx. 80
Catapults:	4 steam C13-1
Elevators:	4 deck edge (85 × 52 feet/25.9 × 15.9 m); 130,000-lb (58,500 kg) capacity
Missiles:	3 8-tube NATO Sea Sparrow launchers Mk 29
Guns:	3 20-mm Phalanx CIWS Mk 16 (3 multi-barrel)
Radars:	SPS-48E 3-D air search SPS-49(V)5 air search SPS-64(V)9 navigation SPS-67(V)1 surface search Mk 23 Target Acquisition System (TAS)
Sonars:	none
Fire control:	3 Mk 91 missile FCS
EW systems:	SLQ-32(V)4 WLR-1H

The ENTERPRISE was the world's second nuclear-propelled surface warship, and at the time of construction she was the world's largest and most expensive warship. Estimated construction cost was $444 million (contemporary conventional carrier construction cost in same-year dollars was estimated at $265 million).

The ship operated in the Pacific from 1965 until early 1990. She arrived at Norfolk, Virginia, on 16 March 1990, in preparation for a three-year refueling/modernization at Newport News Shipbuilding (see *Modernization* notes). She resumed operations with the Atlantic Fleet in 1995.

The "Big E" is scheduled to be retired in fiscal 2015.

Class: Congress provided $35 million in the fiscal 1960 budget for long-lead-time nuclear components for a second aircraft carrier of this type. The Eisenhower administration (1953–1961), however, deferred the project. The next nuclear carrier, the NIMITZ, was not ordered until almost ten years after the ENTERPRISE; two oil-burning carriers were constructed in the interim period.

Classification: Originally classified as an attack aircraft carrier (CVAN), the ENTERPRISE was changed to a multi-mission carrier (CVN) on 30 June 1975.

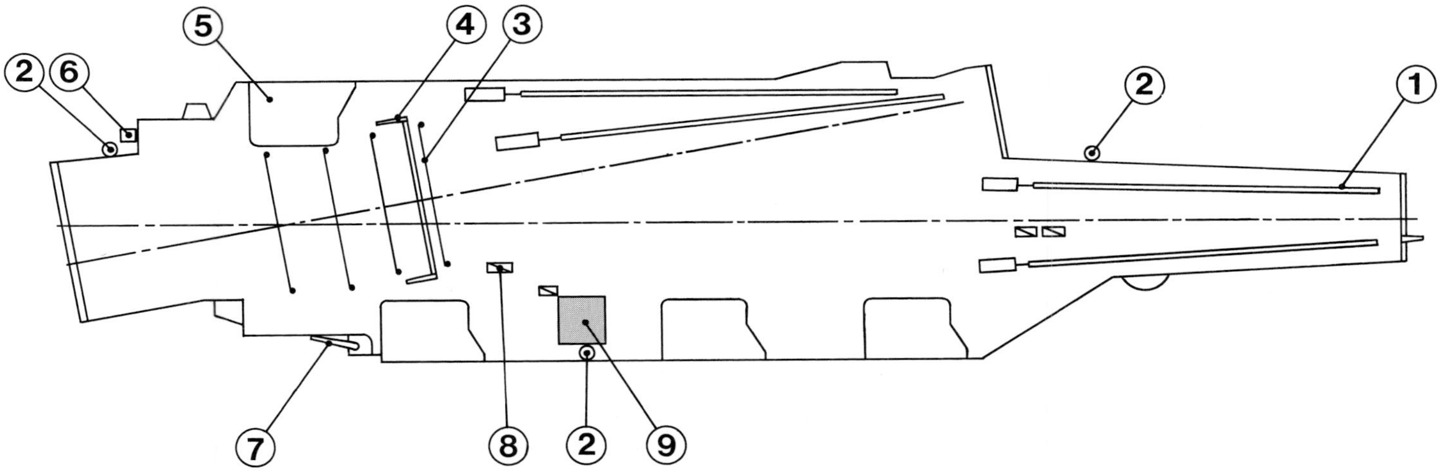

Enterprise
1. Catapults (4). 2. Phalanx CIWS (3). 3. Arresting wires (4). 4. Barricade. 5. Elevators (4). 6. NATO Sea Sparrow launchers (3 now mounted). 7. Crane. 8. Bomb elevators (4). 9. Island structure. (William Clipson)

Design: SCB design No. 160. The Enterprise was built to a modified Kitty Hawk design, but in her original configuration she had a distinctive island structure because of the arrangement of "billboard" radar antennas (see *Radars* notes).

Her hangar deck is 860 feet (262.2 m) long, 107 feet (32.6 m) wide, and 25 feet (7.6 m) high. The angled deck is canted to port at 10° 8′ 44″; the angled deck is 755⅚ feet (230.4 m) long.

Electronics: The Enterprise and cruiser Long Beach (CGN 9) were the only ships fitted with the Hughes SPS-32 and SPS-33 fixed-array radars. The radars were difficult to maintain and were replaced during the 1979–1981 modernization with conventional SPS-48 and SPS-49 radars.

Carrier-landing systems provided in the Enterprise are the SPN-41 landing aid, SPN-43C marshaling, and two SPN-46 air traffic control.

Engineering: At the time of her construction the Enterprise was estimated to have a cruising range of more than 200,000 n.miles (370,400 km) without refueling. On her initial set of fuel cores the ship traveled 207,000 n.miles (383,365 km).

The two-reactor A1W prototype of the Enterprise propulsion plant was constructed at Arco, Idaho.

Missiles: As built, the Enterprise had neither defensive missiles nor guns, the planned Terrier system having been deleted from the design because of cost. Late in 1967 she was fitted with two Sea Sparrow Mk 25 launchers. During her 1979–1982 overhaul the NATO Sea Sparrow launchers were installed, as were the Phalanx CIWS.

Modernization: The Enterprise underwent a Refueling/Complex Overhaul (R/COH) modernization and nuclear refueling at Newport News Shipbuilding; she arrived at the yard on 12 October 1990 and the modernization began on 8 January 1991. She carried out initial post-overhaul sea trials on 27–30 September 1994. After additional at-sea operations, the carrier returned to Newport News and completed fitting out on 6 December 1994. She then entered the Norfolk Naval Shipyard for several months to undertake work that was not done during the modernization. The work at Norfolk and additional work at Newport News was completed on 21 July 1995.

Congress authorized $79.5 million in fiscal 1989 and $1.4 billion in fiscal 1990 to refuel and upgrade the ship. The actual costs are expected to be approximately $2.5 billion. However, the amount of modernization has been reduced because of cost constraints. The refueling was expected to provide cores with a service life of about 20 years, i.e., until about 2115.

The Enterprise modernization and refueling was called an R/COH, not a SLEP, for arbitrary reasons at the direction of the Navy's nuclear propulsion directorate.

Operational: During August–October 1964 the Enterprise, in company with the cruiser Long Beach and frigate Bainbridge (DLGN 25, now CGN 25), formed all-nuclear Task Force 1. The ships

The Enterprise at sea after her lengthy rehabilitation. Note the island structure, long without the distinctive SPS-32/33 "billboard" antennas that were originally mounted. Here an A-6E Intruder lands aboard while an SH-60 Seahawk hovers off her starboard side. (1995, U.S. Navy)

The "Big E" heels to starboard as she makes a high-speed turn after her extensive rehabilitation. A lone SH-3G Sea King helicopter sits on her broad flight deck. (1995, U.S. Navy)

The starboard side of the extensively modified island structure of the "Big E." Her SPS-49(V)5 radar antenna is visible behind her heavy mast; the SPS-40E antenna is forward of the mast (above the bridge). A Phalanx CIWS is mounted below the "65"; the twin white domes to the right house extremely high-frequency antennas. (1995, U.S. Navy)

steamed around the world without refueling or replenishing, traveling 32,600 n.miles (60,375 km) in 64 days, including time for port visits in several countries. They took on no fuel or provisions during the cruise, except for special food for a kangaroo that was picked up in Australia.

The ENTERPRISE shifted to the Pacific Fleet in 1965 and in November of that year began flying air strikes against North Vietnam, becoming the first nuclear ship to enter combat. She remained in the Pacific until 1990, when she returned to the Atlantic in preparation for overhaul at Newport News Shipbuilding.

The ENTERPRISE completed her last operational cruise prior to the R/COH on 16 March 1990; she conducted local flight operations through 18 July 1990, followed by a one-day dependents' cruise on 20 July 1990. From 7 to 14 August 1990 she went to sea with a team of engineers to observe the operation of her nuclear plant; the plant was shut down at the Norfolk Naval Base on 15 August 1990. She was towed to the Newport News yard on 12 October 1990 for modernization.

Her overhaul/refueling and sea trials were completed on 6 December 1994. From January to mid-July 1995 the ENTERPRISE was back at Newport News for installation of components of her combat system. She then began work-up operations with the Fleet.

1 AIRCRAFT CARRIER: "FORRESTAL" CLASS

Number	Name	FY	Builder	Laid down	Launched	Commissioned	Status
CV 62	INDEPENDENCE	55	New York Naval Shipyard	1 July 1955	6 June 1958	10 Jan 1959	**PA**

Displacement;	61,000 tons light 81,500 tons full load
Length:	990 feet (301.8 m) waterline 1,052 feet (320.7 m) overall
Beam:	130 feet (39.6 m)
Flight deck:	250 feet (76.2 m)
Draft:	37 feet (11.3 m)
Propulsion:	4 steam turbines (General Electric); 280,000 shp; 4 shafts
Boilers:	8 1,200 psi (83.4 kg/cm²) (Babcock & Wilcox)
Speed:	33 knots
Range:	12,000 n.miles (22,225 km) at 20 knots
Manning:	3,126 (147 officers + 2,979 enlisted)
Marines:	26 (1 officer + 25 enlisted)
Flag:	approx. 70 (25 officers + 45 enlisted) when embarked
Air wing:	approx. 2,000
Aircraft:	approx. 80
Catapults:	4 steam C7
Elevators:	4 deck edge (63 × 52 feet/19.2 × 15.9 m); 110,000-lb (49,500 kg) capacity
Missiles:	2 8-tube NATO Sea Sparrow Launchers Mk 29
Guns:	3 20-mm Phalanx CIWS Mk 16 (3 multi-barrel)
Radars:	SPS-10 surface search SPS-49 air search
Sonars:	none
Fire control:	2 Mk 91 missile FCS
EW systems:	SLQ-29 (SLQ-17 + WLR-8) WLR-1 WLR-3 WLR-11

The sole survivor of the FORRESTAL class, the INDEPENDENCE is homeported in Yokosuka, Japan, having replaced the MIDWAY as the only U.S. aircraft carrier based overseas. The INDEPENDENCE arrived at Yokosuka on 11 September 1991. She is scheduled to be decommissioned in fiscal 1998, to be replaced by the CONSTELLATION. At that time the "Indy" would be retained in the reserve (replacing the mothballed carrier MIDWAY).

Class: The FORRESTAL class was the world's first aircraft carrier design to be constructed from the keel up after World War II. The ships were intended specifically to operate heavy and high-performance turbojet attack aircraft. Originally, four ships were in this class, completed from 1955 to 1959. The FORRESTAL (CV 59) made her last operational deployment in mid-1991, after which she was to become the Navy's pilot landing training ship (AVT 59) in 1992. She was decommissioned and stricken on 10 September 1993, however, prior to undertaking that role; the FORRESTAL was changed from CV to AVT on 4 February 1991.

The SARATOGA (CV 60) was decommissioned and stricken on 30 September 1994. The RANGER (CV 61) was decommissioned on 10 July 1993 but not immediately stricken; it was expected that she would be by the time this edition went to press.

Classification: The INDEPENDENCE was built as an attack aircraft carrier (CVA), changed to multi-mission aircraft carrier (CV) when modified to operate S-3A Viking ASW aircraft and SH-3 Sea King ASW helicopters and reclassified on 28 February 1973.

Design: SCB No. 80. This class incorporated many design features of the aborted carrier UNITED STATES (CVA 58). The original design provided for an axial (straight) flight deck. The FORRESTAL was modified during construction to incorporate the British-developed angled flight deck. Details of these ships differed considerably.

The hangar deck is 740 feet (225.6 m) long, 101 feet (30.8 m) wide, and 25 feet (7.6 m) high.

Electronics: The INDEPENDENCE is fitted with the SPN-41 landing aid, SPN-43A marshaling, SPN-44 landing aid, and two SPN-42 CCA systems.

Guns: These were the last U.S. aircraft carriers built with a major gun armament. As built, all ships had eight 5-inch/54-cal DP Mk 42 single guns, mounted in pairs on sponsons, both sides, forward and aft. The forward sponsons were removed (except for the RANGER) early in their service because of damage in heavy seas. The after guns were removed as Sea Sparrow launchers became available for these ships.

Modernization: The INDEPENDENCE underwent SLEP modernization intended to add 15 years to her nominal 30-year service live. The SLEP update was undertaken at the Philadelphia Naval Shipyard. The INDEPENDENCE arrived at the yard on 14 April 1985, and conversion began the following day. The SLEP was completed on 30 April 1988.

The SLEP update included rehabilitation of the ship's hull, propulsion, auxiliary machinery, and piping systems, with improved radars, communications equipment, and aircraft launch-and-recovery systems provided.

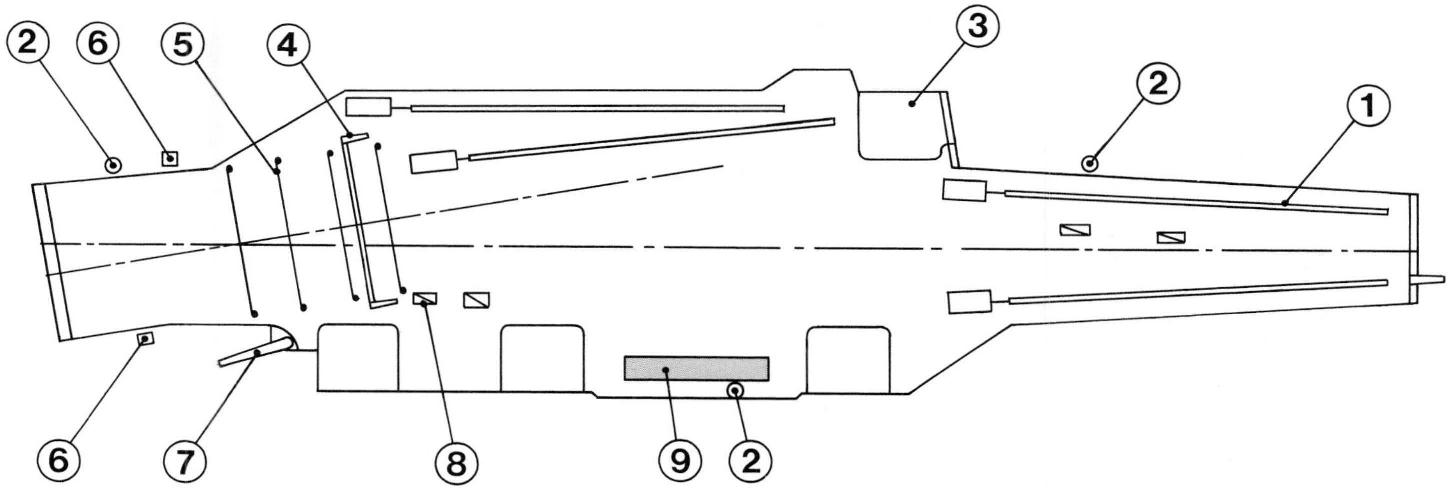

INDEPENDENCE
1. Catapults (4). 2. Phalanx CIWS (3). 3. Elevators (4). 4. Barricade. 5. Arresting wires (4). 6. NATO Sea Sparrow launchers (2). 7. Crane. 8. Bomb elevators (3). 9. Island structure. (William Clipson)

The INDEPENDENCE arrives in Tokyo Bay en route to her home port of the Yokosuka naval station. The guided missile cruiser BUNKER HILL (CG 52), also based at Yokosuka, is at left. Basing the "Indy" in Japan provides an important saving in "ship days" that would be needed for a carrier based in the United States to transit to and from the Western Pacific. (1991, U.S. Navy, PH3 Shawn James)

The island structure of the INDEPENDENCE shows a variety of radar and aircraft control antennas. A small pole mast at the after end of the island is used to carry radio antenna wires from the main mast. (1991, U.S. Navy, PH1 R.J. Oriez)

The INDEPENDENCE—the only survivor of the original FORRESTAL class—is shown bow on. Note the SPS-48 radar antenna above the bridge and the SPS-49 offset to starboard. The later large carriers have a radar mast aft of the island. (1990, John Bouvia)

1 AIRCRAFT CARRIER: "MIDWAY" CLASS

Number	Name	FY	Builder	Laid down	Launched	Commissioned	Status
CV 41	Midway	42	Newport News Shipbuilding	27 Oct 1943	20 Mar 1945	10 Sep 1945	PR

Displacement:	52,972 tons light
	69,873 tons full load
Length:	900 feet (274.3 m) waterline
	976 feet (297.5 m) overall
Beam:	141 feet (43.0 m)
Flight deck:	263½ feet (80.3 m)
Draft:	35 feet (10.7 m)
Propulsion:	4 steam turbines (Westinghouse); 212,000 shp; 4 shafts
Boilers:	12 600 psi (41.7 kg/cm²) (Babcock & Wilcox)
Speed:	32 knots
Range:	15,000 n.miles (27,780 km) at 15 knots
Manning:	2,534 (123 officers + 2,411 enlisted)
Marines:	64 (2 officers + 62 enlisted)
Air wing:	approx. 1,715 (245 officers + 1,470 enlisted)
Aircraft:	approx. 75
Catapults:	2 steam C13
Elevators:	3 deck edge (63 × 52 feet/19.2 × 15.9 m); 130,000-lb (58,500 kg) capacity
Missiles:	2 8-tube Sea Sparrow Mk 25 launchers
Guns:	3 20-mm Phalanx CIWS Mk 16 (3 multi-barrel)
Radars:	SPS-48C 3-D air search
	SPS-49(V)5 air search
	SPS-64(V)9 surface search
	SPS-67(V)1 surface search
Sonars:	none
Fire control:	2 Mk 115 missile FCS
EW systems:	SLQ-29 (SLQ-17 + WLR-8)
	WLR-1H
	WLR-11

The Midway was the last World War II–era warship in commission in the U.S. Navy. She was decommissioned on 11 April 1992 and is laid up in reserve.

The ship was scheduled to remain as a first-line carrier until the late 1990s, when she was to be replaced by the CVN 74 to maintain a 15-carrier force. The early 1990s fleet reductions led to the Midway's being mothballed immediately after returning from Operation Desert Storm.

The above manning numbers reflect her last year in commission. The Navy plans to retain the ship in reserve (mothball) status until about fiscal 1998, when the Independence is to be decommissioned.

Aircraft: The Midway did not operate F-14 Tomcat fighters or S-3 Viking ASW aircraft because of limited hangar space and support facilities. Prior to being mothballed the Midway carried Carrier Air Wing (CVW) 5—which operated three F/A-18 Hornet squadrons, two A-6E Intruder squadrons, and an SH-3H Sea King squadron—plus combat support aircraft.

Class: Six ships of this class were authorized in 1942–1945: CVB 41–44, 56, and 57. The CVB 44 was canceled on 1 November 1943; the CVB 56 and CV 57 were canceled on 28 March 1945. None had been laid down.

The Franklin D. Roosevelt (CVB 42, later CVA/CV) was commissioned in 1945. Active for virtually her entire career, the "FDR" was stricken on 1 October 1972 and scrapped. The Coral Sea (CVB 43, later CVA/CV), commissioned in 1947 and in almost continuous active service thereafter, was decommissioned and stricken on 30 April 1990. She is being scrapped.

Classification: These ships were built as large carriers (CVB), sometimes being referred to as "battle" carriers. They were reclassified as attack aircraft carriers (CVA) on 1 October 1952 and as aircraft carriers (CV) on 30 June 1975.

Design: The Midways were the largest warships designed by the U.S. Navy during World War II, being significantly larger than the previous Essex class.[16] The Midways had a larger aircraft capacity and heavier gun battery than their predecessors, and they were the first U.S. aircraft carriers with an armored flight deck. As built, each ship had two hydraulic catapults and three elevators (two centerline and one port deck edge). Aircraft capacity was rated at 137 at the time completed. They were the first U.S. warships constructed with a beam too great to permit passage through the 110-foot (33.5-m)-wide locks of the Panama Canal. (Several U.S. battleships damaged at Pearl Harbor on 7 December 1941 were rebuilt with beam blisters that prevented them from passing through the canal.)

The Midway hangar deck is 692 feet (211 m) long, 85 feet (25.9 m) wide, and 17½ feet (5.3 m) high. Her flight deck is canted 13° to port and is 682 feet (207.9 m) long.

16. The original displacements of the major war-built classes are shown below (source: Department of the Navy, *Ships' Data U.S. Naval Vessels*, Vol. I, 15 April 1945 [Confidential]):

		Standard	*Full load*
CVB 41	Midway	45,000 tons	60,100 tons
BB 61	Iowa	45,000 tons	57,540 tons
CV 9	Essex	27,100 tons	33,000 tons

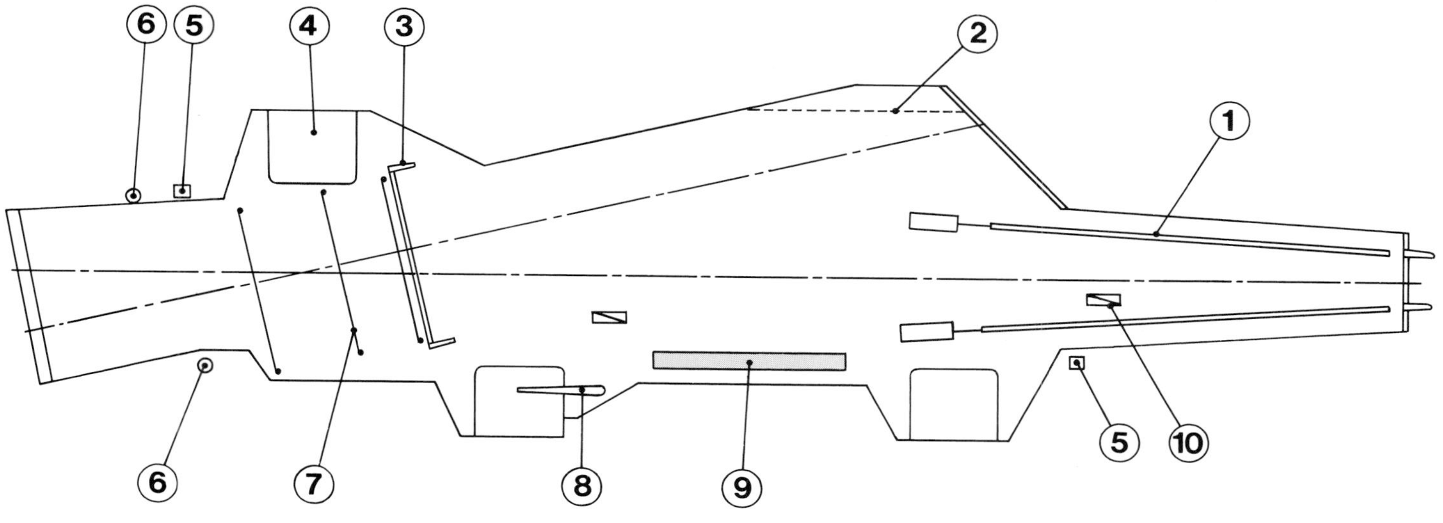

Midway
1. Catapults (2). 2. Removable deck extension. 3. Barricade. 4. Elevators (3). 5. BPDMS Sea Sparrow launchers (2). 6. Phalanx CIWS (2). 7. Arresting wires (3). 8. Crane. 9. Island structure. 10. Bomb elevators (2). (William Clipson)

Sailors form a message of farewell on the deck of the carrier MIDWAY as she departs Yokosuka, her home port from 1973 to 1991. The MIDWAY is the only aircraft carrier currently being retained in "mothballs." (1991, U.S. Navy, PH1 Glen Walker)

Electronics: When decommissioned, the MIDWAY was fitted with the SPN-41 landing aid, two SPN-42 CCA, SPN-44A marshaling, and SPN-44 landing aid systems.

Guns: As built, the MIDWAY mounted 18 single 5-inch/54-cal DP Mk 39 guns; these were arranged on both sides at the main deck level. Her secondary gun armament consisted of 84 40-mm AA guns and 28 20-mm AA guns at completion. The 40-mm and 20-mm guns were replaced by twin 3-inch/50-cal AA gun mounts. The gun armament was reduced until, by the 1970s, she mounted only three 5-inch guns. Subsequently, all conventional guns were removed.

Modernization: The MIDWAY has been extensively rebuilt. A major modernization, which provided an enclosed ("hurricane") bow, angled flight deck, strengthened flight deck and elevators, and steam catapults, was accomplished at the Puget Sound Naval Shipyard from September 1955 to September 1957 (SCB 110 under the old SCB scheme) and at the San Francisco Naval Shipyard from February 1966 to January 1970 (SCB 101 under the new SCB scheme). The MIDWAY's 1966–1970 modernization was delayed because of the workload for West Coast shipyards during the Vietnam conflict.

Her 1966–1970 refit gave the MIDWAY her definitive deck layout: she has two bow-mounted C13 catapults (none on the angled deck), two starboard, deck-edge elevators (one forward and one aft of the island), and one elevator on the port quarter. She has an ordnance storage capacity of 1,210 tons and can carry 1,186,000 gallons (4,489,010 liters) of jet fuel.

During a 1986 overhaul in Japan the MIDWAY was fitted with blisters to improve buoyancy and stability, but those changes caused a reduction in roll time, i.e., the ship tried to right herself more quickly from a roll with a negative effect on flight operations. During sea trials in December 1986 the ship rolled up to ten degrees at nine knots in four- to six-foot (1.2- to 1.8-m) seas, and she took water over the flight deck. (The above beam and draft are as refitted with bulges; see 14th Edition/page 96 for pre-bulge dimensions.)

The bulge caused a Senate appropriations subcommittee to vote in late 1987 to retire the MIDWAY as a cost-saving measure, concluding that the mistake would be too costly to repair. (The Navy had sought $138 million for repairs.) That decision was reversed by a congressional appropriations conference committee after lobbying by the Navy. In April 1988, the MIDWAY underwent modifications to solve her stability problems, but very little of the $113 million finally appropriated for those repairs was spent.

Operational: The MIDWAY initially operated in the Atlantic and Mediterranean areas; she transferred to the Pacific Fleet in 1955.

The MIDWAY was based at Yokosuka, Japan, from 1973 until 1991, the first U.S. carrier ever to be based in a foreign country. (Another U.S. carrier was planned for homeporting in Pireaus, Greece, in the early 1970s; that proposal was dropped because of problems within the Greek government.)

The MIDWAY and her battle group arrived in the Persian Gulf region in early November 1990 as part of Operation Desert Shield, the international response to Iraq's August 1990 invasion and annexation of Kuwait. When the Desert Storm air campaign began in January 1991, the MIDWAY's air wing (CVW-5) delivered 1,500 tons of ordnance on Iraqi targets. During her time in the region, CAW-5 flew more than 4,000 sorties. She left the Desert Storm theater of operations on 14 March and arrived in her home port of Yokosuka on 16 April.

In June 1991 the MIDWAY and the ABRAHAM LINCOLN—the oldest and newest carriers in the U.S. Navy, respectively—evacuated thousands of U.S. dependents and service personnel from Subic Bay in the Philippines following the eruption of Mount Pinatubo. It was the LINCOLN's first deployment and the MIDWAY's last.

VSTOL SUPPORT SHIPS

During the mid-1970s there was increased U.S. Navy interest in VSTOL aircraft; a major analysis (known as the Sea-Based Air Master Study) developed a long-term program for several categories of VSTOL aircraft. In 1975 the Chief of Naval Operations, Admiral James L. Holloway III, proposed a VSTOL aircraft carrier of approximately twice the size of the aborted SCS that would be able to operate a number of improved AV-8 Harrier combat aircraft in addition to ASW aircraft. About 50 design alternatives were considered, with some having a small number of catapults and arresting wires to permit the use of E-2 Hawkeye AEW aircraft and S-2 Viking ASW aircraft. The primary aircraft to have been embarked in this ship would be VSTOL fighter and attack variants.

No ships of this type were constructed because Holloway lacked the ability to push through such an innovative program.

MEDIUM AIRCRAFT CARRIER

The Ford administration (1974–1977) and Carter administration (1977–1981) both proposed the construction of large-deck conventional aircraft carriers of 50,000 to 60,000 tons—designated CVV—to be constructed in lieu of additional NIMITZ-class ships at a ratio of about 2:1. A variety of designs was considered under this concept, ranging from about 40,000 tons full-load displacement (i.e., about the size of a HANCOCK-class ship) up to a repeat of the KENNEDY design.

A CVV program was put forth to Congress in the fiscal 1979 budget of the Carter administration, but the ship was strongly opposed by proponents of the nuclear-powered NIMITZ, especially Admiral Rickover, and none was authorized.

SEA CONTROL SHIPS

Several proposals were put forward in the 1960s for providing ASW helicopters as the primary armament of convoy escorts (with the ship designations DH, DDH, and DHK being used). Subsequently, in 1970, the Chief of Naval Operations, Admiral Elmo R. Zumwalt, proposed a class of at least eight Sea Control Ships (SCS) that would carry several SH-3 Sea King ASW helicopters, plus a small number of AV-8 Harriers for self-defense. The SCS concept was evaluated at sea from October 1971 to January 1972, with the helicopter carrier GUAM (LPH 9) operating AV-8A Harriers and SH-3 Sea King helicopters.

Although the lead SCS was planned for the fiscal 1975 shipbuilding program, Congress (strongly supported by the advocates of large carriers) refused to authorize such ships because of their limited capability. A modified version of the SCS design was built for the Spanish Navy: the 16,700-ton PRINCIPE DE ASTURIAS was launched in 1982. The Spanish Bazan shipyard in Ferrol, which built the Spanish SCS, is building the similar, but smaller, 11,367-ton aviation ship CHAKKRINAREUBET for the Thai Navy.

HEAVY AIRCRAFT CARRIERS

Four ships of this class of large carriers, intended primarily to operate nuclear strike aircraft, were planned; the lead ship, the UNITED STATES (CVA 58), was authorized in fiscal 1948. That ship was laid down at Newport News Shipbuilding on 18 April 1949, but she was canceled on 23 April 1949.

Although never completed, she served as the procreator of the FORRESTAL and subsequent large U.S. aircraft carriers. The UNITED STATES design provided for a flush-deck configuration that could simultaneously launch two heavy attack aircraft and two fighters from a pair of forward catapults and a pair of waist catapults. Three deck-edge elevators and one stern elevator would lift aircraft to the flight deck. The ship was to have had a standard displacement of 65,000 tons and 80,000 tons full load.

"ESSEX" AND "HANCOCK" CLASSES

All 24 ships of the World War II–built ESSEX and HANCOCK classes have been stricken. These aircraft carriers formed the backbone of U.S. carrier strength from 1943 through the Korean War. They operated alongside the larger MIDWAY- and FORRESTAL-class ships through the Cold War and the Vietnam War. The LEXINGTON was the last active ship, serving as a training carrier until decommissioned on 8 November 1991 (date of ceremony; official decommission date is 26 November 1991). The last fully operational carrier was the ORISKANY, which was decommissioned on 30 September 1976.

Most were modernized to various degrees after World War II, with the most extensive mods being designated as the HANCOCK class (see previous editions). Construction of the ORISKANY was suspended in 1946; resumed in 1947, she was completed to a modified design, the prototype for later modernization. The ANTIETAM was the first U.S. carrier modified to an angled-deck configuration (1952).

Twenty-four ships were completed of the 32 that were ordered from 1940 to 1942. Originally designated CV, all were changed to CVA in 1952. Subsequently, several became ASW carriers (CVS), three amphibious assault ships (LPH), one a training carrier (CVT/AVT), and several (while in mothballs) aviation transports (AVT). All except the amphibious assault ships (LPH) and transports (AVT) retained their original CV hull number.

In March 1991 the Navy ordered a halt to LEXINGTON (AVT 16) training operations because of maintenance problems. Her last arrested aircraft landing took place in February 1991: landing No. 493,248, undoubtedly more than any other aircraft carrier of any nation. The BUNKER HILL was retained as a moored electronics test ship in San Diego harbor until November 1972 (after being stricken).

The following table lists U.S. aircraft carriers from the ESSEX class onward.

See 14th Edition/pages 98–101 for ESSEX/HANCOCK characteristics.

POST–WORLD WAR II AIRCRAFT CARRIERS

World War II aircraft carrier programs reached hull number CVB 57 (a canceled MIDWAY-class ship). After the war there were several proposals to construct new-design aircraft carriers, but the large number of fleet (CV), light (CVL), and escort (CVE) carriers available precluded any serious consideration of new construction except for "heavy" carriers (CVA) to carry heavy, long-range nuclear-strike aircraft.

Number	Name	Comm.	Classifications	Stricken
CV 9	ESSEX	1942	CVA/CVS	1 June 1973
CV 10	YORKTOWN#	1943	CVA/CVS	1 June 1973
CV 11	INTREPID#	1943	CVA/CVS	30 Sep 1980
CV 12	HORNET	1943	CVA/CVS	25 July 1989
CV 13	FRANKLIN	1944	CVA/CVS/AVT 8	1 Oct 1964
CV 14	TICONDEROGA	1944	CVA	16 Nov 1973
CV 15	RANDOLPH	1944	CVA/CVS	1 June 1973
CV 16	LEXINGTON	1943	CVA/CVS/CVT/AVT*	30 Nov 1991
CV 17	BUNKER HILL	1943	CVA/CVS/AVT 9	1 Nov 1966
CV 18	WASP	1943	CVA/CVS	1 July 1972
CV 19	HANCOCK	1944	CVA/CV	31 Dec 1975
CV 20	BENNINGTON	1944	CVA/CVS	20 Sep 1989
CV 21	BOXER	1945	CVA/CVS/LPH 4	1 Dec 1969
CVL 22–30	INDEPENDENCE-class light carriers#			
CV 31	BON HOMME RICHARD	1944	CVA	20 Sep 1989
CV 32	LEYTE	1946	CVA/CVS/AVT 10	1 June 1969
CV 33	KEARSARGE	1946	CVA/CVS	1 May 1973
CV 34	ORISKANY	1950	CVA/CV	25 July 1989
CV 35	REPRISAL	canceled 1945		
CV 36	ANTIETAM	1945	CVA/CVS	1 May 1973
CV 37	PRINCETON	1945	CVA/CVS/LPH 5	30 Jan 1970
CV 38	SHANGRI-LA	1944	CVA/CVS	15 July 1982
CV 39	LAKE CHAMPLAIN	1945	CVA/CVS	1 Dec 1969
CV 40	TARAWA	1945	CVA/CVS/AVT 12**	1 June 1967
CVB 41–44	MIDWAY-class large carriers			
CV 45	VALLEY FORGE	1946	CVA/CVS/LPH 8	15 Jan 1970
CV 46	IWO JIMA	canceled 1945		
CV 47	PHILIPPINE SEA	1946	CVA/CVS/AVT 11	1 Dec 1969
CVL 48, 49	SAIPAN-class light carriers			
CV 50–55	ESSEX class	canceled 1945		
CVB 56, 57	MIDWAY-class large carriers			
CVA 58	UNITED STATES heavy carrier			
CV 59–64	FORRESTAL and modified FORRESTAL classes			
CVAN 65	ENTERPRISE			
CV 66, 67	modified FORRESTAL classes			
CVN 68–76	NIMITZ class			

*Training carrier; the other AVTs are aviation transports.

**The TARAWA operated as an LPH in the late 1950s while retaining a CVS classification.

#The YORKTOWN and INTREPID are memorials, as is the light carrier CABOT (CVL 28); see appendix D.

CHAPTER 14

Battleships

The NEW JERSEY, mothballed at the Bremerton Naval Shipyard (Washington). She will probably go to the breakers. Alongside is a mothballed HANCOCK (CV-19)-class aircraft carrier, also due to become scrap metal. It is expected that the MISSOURI and possibly one other IOWA-class battleship will be retained as memorial-museum ships. They were too expensive and too manpower intensive for their limited combat capabilities. (1991, Robert Kaplan)

The battleship era officially ended for the U.S. Navy on 12 January 1995 when the four dreadnoughts of the IOWA class were stricken from the Naval Vessel Register. These were the world's last operational battleships. Steel battleships had been in the U.S. Navy continuously since the second class battleship TEXAS was placed in commission in August 1895.

Shortly after the deletion of the ships, however, members of Congress—urged on primarily by battleship veterans and buffs—began efforts to force the Navy to retain some or all of the IOWAS. The strongest language was in a Senate amendment to the fiscal 1996 defense authorization act that directed, "The Secretary of the Navy shall list on the Naval Vessel Register, and maintain on such register, at least two of the IOWA class battleships that were stricken from the register in February [*sic*] 1995." Further, the amendment proposed that the Secretary maintain the two IOWAS until the Navy has an "operational surface fire support capability that equals or exceeds the fire support capability that the IOWA class battleships . . . would, if in active service, be able to provide for Marine Corps amphibious assaults and operations ashore."

Significantly, the leadership of the Marine Corps did not protest strongly after the battleships were stricken. Congressional legislation to force the Navy to retain some of the IOWAS was passed by the House-Senate conference in September 1995, but the reality of the retention was not clear when this edition went to press. The most likely candidates for retention appeared to be the NEW JERSEY and WISCONSIN, although there is also legislation stating that no funds may be spent on maintaining battleships.

Battleships had been in active service from 1895 until 8 March 1958, when the WISCONSIN was decommissioned following service in the Korean War. Subsequently, the NEW JERSEY was reactivated in 1968–1969 for service in the Vietnam War, and all four IOWA-class ships were recommissioned during the Reagan-Lehman naval buildup of the 1980s. Two of the latter ships, the MISSOURI and WISCONSIN, saw action in the Persian Gulf conflict of 1991. All four ships were again mothballed in 1990–1992, the MISSOURI having been held in service with a reduced crew to participate in ceremonies at Pearl Harbor on 7 December 1991 that commemorated the 50th anniversary of the Japanese sneak attack on U.S. naval and air bases in Hawaii.

The MISSOURI steamed into the Long Beach Naval Shipyard (California) on 21 December 1991 for deactivation and was decommissioned there on 31 March 1992; she was then towed to the Bremerton Naval Shipyard (Washington) for storage. (Correction to previous edition.)

The four IOWAS were stricken in 1995 "due to the expenditure necessary to ensure continued, reliable service; the costs of which would be disproportionate to the ships' value."[1]

Although there has been considerable pressure from outside of the Navy to retain some or all of the IOWAS in active service (even during the Cold War–era), their operation was untenable because:

First, battleships are expensive to operate. The 1980s' reactivation of the battleships cost only some $300 to $500 million per ship (i.e., enough for the four battleships to buy two or three FFG 7-class frigates); the dreadnoughts each require a crew of 1,600 and cost about $65 million per year to operate. Each battleship's crew is enough to man more than four Aegis missile cruisers or almost eight anti-submarine frigates (albeit these are smaller ships requiring higher skill levels). The expense is considerable for a single-mission warship.

Second, battleships are too limited in capability. The battleships have no anti-submarine and no effective anti-air capability; they must be escorted in most operational scenarios. An IOWA's main batteries are nine 16-inch (406-mm) guns and 32 Tomahawk cruise missiles. The guns are useful for amphibious gunfire support, but they are outdistanced by modern assault methods (helicopters and air cushion landing craft), and there are too many Third World nations with modern aircraft, mines, submarines, and missiles for the United States to *politically* risk those ships in assault areas. (A few hits with napalm or an under-the-keel torpedo explosion could severely injure them.)

Their Tomahawks are a potent weapon, but most of the SPRUANCE (DD 963)-class anti-submarine destroyers, for example, are fitted with 61 vertical launch cells for Tomahawk missiles with no loss of their other capabilities. A SPRUANCE has a crew of about 340, making them far more efficient Tomahawk launch platforms.

Third, battleships are too few in number. With only four battleships—one of which is normally in overhaul at any given time, and the others widely scattered—the probability of a battleship being available at short notice in a crisis area was small. This is partially compensated for by their sustained high speed, although in the face of air or submarine threats, they would require escort ships with a lesser high-speed endurance.

While useful in "showing the flag" in peacetime, in the Korean and Vietnam Wars the IOWAS were employed exclusively in the shore bombardment role. The Reagan-Lehman reactivation of all four IOWAS included providing each ship with 32 Tomahawk and 16 Harpoon cruise missiles. This expanded their capabilities (in addition to the shore-bombardment role) to strike and anti-ship beyond the range of their guns, i.e., 41,622 yards (38,069 m) against shore targets. Thus modified, the MISSOURI launched 28 Tomahawk missiles and the WISCONSIN launched 24 in the Persian Gulf conflict. Totaled, these were equivalent to 18 percent of the 288 Tomahawks launched in the conflict. In addition, the MISSOURI fired 759 16-inch rounds and the WISCONSIN fired 324 16-inch rounds against shore targets during Operation Desert Storm (January–February 1991).

The 1980s' reactivation plan for the IOWAS included a future Phase II modernization that was to have added more Tomahawks—to be fired from vertical launchers, removing the after 16-inch gun turret—plus making other upgrades. This proposal was dropped in 1983. Proposals to fit these ships as numbered fleet flagships and to provide facilities for operating AV-8 Harrier STOVL aircraft were made, but these were not carried out, primarily because of funding limitations.

The accompanying table shows the active service of the IOWA-class ships. Characteristics of the IOWA class are provided in the 15th Edition/pages 98–101.

Classification: The U.S. Navy's first two steel battleships, the TEXAS and MAINE (both completed in 1895), were not assigned hull numbers. The U.S. Navy classification scheme of 1920 established the designation BB for battleships in existence at that time; the INDIANA (1895) became BB 1.

The IOWA class reached hull number BB 66 (the canceled KENTUCKY), with the subsequent, never-started MONTANA class being assigned hull numbers BB 67–71.

Status: When this edition of *Ships and Aircraft* went to press, efforts were under way to preserve some of the IOWA-class ships as memorials. The high cost of such undertakings, and the number of dreadnoughts already preserved in the United States, make it unlikely that more than one or two will be preserved. The MISSOURI, site of the Japanese surrender at the end of World War II, will most likely be preserved, either at Bremerton, Washington, where she is now moored, or at Pearl Harbor.[2]

1. Vice Adm. W. A. Earner, USN, Deputy Chief of Naval Operations (Logistics), letter to Secretary of the Navy, subject: "Striking of Iowa Class Battleships," 5 January 1995. The Secretary of the Navy approved the recommendation to dispose of the ships on 12 January 1995.

2. The instruments of surrender were signed by Allied and Japanese officials on board the MISSOURI on 2 September 1945 while the battleship was anchored in Tokyo Bay.

"IOWA" CLASS ACTIVE SERVICE

Number	Name	World War II	Korean War	Vietnam War	600-ship Fleet
BB 61	IOWA	22 Feb 1943–24 Mar 1949	25 Aug 1951–24 Feb 1958	—	28 Apr 1984–26 Oct 1990
BB 62	NEW JERSEY	23 May 1943–30 June 1948	21 Nov 1950–21 Aug 1957	6 Apr 1968–17 Dec 1969	28 Dec 1982–8 Sep 1991
BB 63	MISSOURI	11 June 1944–	–26 Feb 1955	—	10 May 1986–31 Mar 1992
BB 64	WISCONSIN	16 Apr 1944–1 July 1948	3 Mar 1951–8 Mar 1958	—	22 Oct 1988–30 Sep 1991

CHAPTER 15

Cruisers

A TICONDEROGA-class Aegis cruiser fires a salvo of two Standard SM-2 surface-to-air missiles. The ships of this class—the most capable surface combatants of any nation—will soon be the only cruisers in service with the U.S. Navy. (U.S. Navy)

Guided missile cruisers are employed primarily to screen carrier battle groups; the Improved TICONDEROGA-class ships, fitted with vertical-launch missile systems, have a potent land-attack/strike capability. The Navy is retiring all cruisers except for the 27 ships of the TICONDEROGA class. These Aegis cruisers are highly capable, multi-purpose warships. Thus, by the year 2000 only these 27 ships will be in service in the cruiser category; further, budget constraints may dictate that the first five ships, without a Tomahawk strike capability, be retired before the end of the decade.

The U.S. cruiser force in the fall of 1996 consisted of 27 TICONDEROGA-class ships (CG) and 4 nuclear-propelled missile cruisers (CGN). The latter, all of which will be decommissioned by the year 2000, are inferior to the Aegis ships in all combat capabilities despite their virtually unlimited steaming range and relatively high acquisition costs. No additional cruisers are under construction or planned. The next-generation Surface Combatant—currently designated SC 21—is a follow-on to the ARLEIGH BURKE (DDG 51) destroyers and is discussed in chapter 16. (The Reagan administration had included a nuclear cruiser in the last year of the fiscal 1983–1987 shipbuilding plan, but that ship has "slipped" into oblivion. According to Navy officials, the ship was placed in the long-range program for "planning purposes" and will not be pursued in the near future. The rapid decommissioning of the nuclear cruiser force means that the Navy's nuclear-propelled aircraft carriers will operate with only oil-burning screening ships.)

In most respects the TICONDEROGA-class ships are the most capable surface combatants afloat. Their Aegis AAW system is undoubtedly the best anti-air missile system in service with any navy, while the ships also have the most capable ASW suite available in the U.S. Navy, the same as in the SPRUANCE (DD 963)-class destroyers. The 22 ships with Vertical Launch Systems (VLS)—able to carry 122 Standard and Tomahawk missiles—additionally possess an unequaled missile strike capability against land targets.

The lines between the cruiser and destroyer categories blur when examining the TICONDEROGAS, which have the same hull and propulsion plant and some of the same combat systems as the destroyers of the SPRUANCE (DD 963) and KIDD (DDG 993) classes, and essentially the same anti-air system as the ARLEIGH BURKE class. The term "cruiser" tends to indicate a ship that is commanded by a captain (rather than a commander in destroyers) and costs more than a contemporary destroyer (although this is not true with respect to the ARLEIGH BURKE and TICONDEROGA classes, with the cruiser being less expensive).[1]

The Navy's nine nuclear-propelled cruisers are being retired, six before the end of their postulated 30-year service life. These six ships had significantly less combat capability than oil-burning, conventional U.S. cruisers. In particular, the nuclear ships lacked an effective ASW helicopter capability, a key factor in anti-submarine operations. There were proposals in the 1970s to provide the large cruiser LONG BEACH with the Aegis AAW system during her "mid-life" modernization and even to complete the ARKANSAS (then under construction) with an Aegis system. But those efforts were halted, in large part through the efforts of Admiral H. G. Rickover, then-head of the naval nuclear propulsion program, who feared that making those ships more capable would reduce the chances of additional cruiser construction. In the event, the Navy lost both ways: Neither the LONG BEACH nor ARKANSAS were fitted with Aegis, and no more nuclear cruisers have been built.

The 18 conventional cruisers of the LEAHY and BELKNAP classes have been discarded. Those ships, graceful in appearance and capable warships for their time, were decommissioned with the end of the Cold War, the RICHMOND K. TURNER having been retained longer than the other ships for the Navy's Lightweight Exoatmospheric Projectile (LEAP) tests for a sea-based Theater Ballistic Missile Defense (TBMD) system.

No "gun ships" remain in commission. The largest guns in active U.S. cruisers are 5-inch (127-mm) weapons. The last two heavy cruisers (CA), which were armed with 8-inch (203-mm) guns, were laid up in reserve and finally stricken in 1991. At the start of the battleship recommissioning program in the early 1980s proposals were made to reactivate those two surviving heavy cruisers, the DES MOINES (CA 134) and SALEM (CA 139), instead of or in addition to the battleships. The Navy rejected those proposals, preferring the larger guns of the more impressive IOWA (BB 61)-class dreadnoughts.

Builders: The TICONDEROGA-class ships were being built by the Bath Iron Works in Maine and the Litton/Ingalls Shipbuilding yard (the lead yard) at Pascagoula, Mississippi. The keel-laying date for the Ingalls-built ships is the date of the start of erection of the first module on the horizontal building position at the yard; the ships are lowered into the water on a floating dock (launching) and are formally christened at a later date.

Classification: The Aegis program office within the Naval Sea Systems Command has established its own classification of Aegis ships with variations known as "baselines." The following are the principal baseline characteristics; note that there are some system overlaps in the TICONDEROGA-class cruisers.

Baseline 0: cruisers CG 47, 48	SPY-1A radar Mk 26 launchers UYK-7 computers SH-2F LAMPS I helicopter
Baseline 1: cruisers CG 49–51	SPY-1A radar Mk 26 launchers UYK-7 computers SH-60B LAMPS III helicopter
Baseline 2: cruisers CG 52–58	VLS/Tomahawk SQQ-89 ASW system
Baseline 3: cruisers CG 59–64	SPY-1B radar improved communications
Baseline 4: cruisers CG 65–73	SPY-1B(V) radar SQS-53C sonar UYK-43/44 computers

Guns: During the 1980s and 1990s, cruisers have been fitted with .50-cal/7.62-mm machine guns, 20-mm cannon, and 25-mm Mk 38 Bushmaster "chain" guns for close-in defense against small craft. This armament is especially important for ships deploying into the Persian Gulf area. The weapons are shifted from ship to ship as they forward deploy; accordingly, they are not listed under the specific class entries.

Names: U.S. cruisers traditionally had been named for major cities in the United States, with the CANBERRA (CA 70, later CAG 2) being named for an Australian cruiser sunk in 1942 while operating with U.S. forces. From 1971 to 1978 six cruisers were assigned state names (DLGN/CGN 36–41).

From 1981 on, cruisers have been named for famous American battles, although even this scheme was corrupted when the CG 51 was named for a deceased Secretary of the Navy and Secretary of Defense, Thomas Gates.

CRUISER FORCE LEVELS (FALL 1996)

Number	Class/Ship	Comm.	Active	Reserve
CG 47	TICONDEROGA	1983–1994	27	—
CGN 38	VIRGINIA	1978	2	1*
CGN 36	CALIFORNIA	1974–1975	2	—
CGN 25	BAINBRIDGE	1962	—	1*

*In Commission, In Reserve in preparation for being stricken.

1. Only four nations now have warships rated as cruisers in their navies: Italy (1), Peru (1), Russia (approximately 12), and the United States (31). The ambiguous category cruiser should include some French ships that were previously rated as "frigates" (DLG). No nation is currently building "cruisers."

22 GUIDED MISSILE CRUISERS: IMPROVED "TICONDEROGA" CLASS

Number	Name	FY	Builder	Laid down	Launched	Christened	Commissioned	Status
CG 52	Bunker Hill	82	Litton/Ingalls Shipbuilding	11 Jan 1984	11 Mar 1985	19 Apr 1985	20 Sep 1986	**PA**
CG 53	Mobile Bay	82	Litton/Ingalls Shipbuilding	6 June 1984	22 Aug 1985	12 Oct 1985	21 Feb 1987	**PA**
CG 54	Antietam	83	Litton/Ingalls Shipbuilding	15 Nov 1984	14 Feb 1986	19 Apr 1986	6 June 1987	**PA**
CG 55	Leyte Gulf	83	Litton/Ingalls Shipbuilding	18 Mar 1985	20 June 1986	11 Oct 1986	26 Sep 1987	**AA**
CG 56	San Jacinto	83	Litton/Ingalls Shipbuilding	24 July 1985	14 Nov 1986	24 Jan 1987	23 Jan 1988	**AA**
CG 57	Lake Champlain	84	Litton/Ingalls Shipbuilding	3 Mar 1986	3 Apr 1987	25 Apr 1987	12 Aug 1988	**PA**
CG 58	Philippine Sea	84	Bath Iron Works, Maine	8 May 1986	12 July 1987	—	18 Mar 1989	**AA**
CG 59	Princeton	84	Litton/Ingalls Shipbuilding	15 Oct 1986	25 Sep 1987	17 Oct 1987	11 Feb 1989	**PA**
CG 60	Normandy	85	Bath Iron Works, Maine	7 Apr 1987	19 Mar 1988	—	9 Dec 1989	**AA**
CG 61	Monterey	85	Bath Iron Works, Maine	19 Aug 1987	23 Oct 1988	—	16 June 1990	**AA**
CG 62	Chancellorsville	85	Litton/Ingalls Shipbuilding	24 June 1987	15 July 1988	23 July 1988	4 Nov 1989	**PA**
CG 63	Cowpens	86	Bath Iron Works, Maine	23 Dec 1987	11 Mar 1989	—	9 Mar 1991	**PA**
CG 64	Gettysburg	86	Bath Iron Works, Maine	17 Aug 1988	22 July 1989	—	22 June 1991	**AA**
CG 65	Chosin	86	Litton/Ingalls Shipbuilding	22 July 1988	1 Sep 1989	14 Oct 1989	12 Jan 1991	**PA**
CG 66	Hue City	87	Litton/Ingalls Shipbuilding	20 Feb 1988	1 June 1990	21 July 1990	14 Sep 1991	**AA**
CG 67	Shiloh	87	Bath Iron Works, Maine	1 Aug 1989	8 Sep 1990	—	18 July 1992	**PA**
CG 68	Anzio	87	Litton/Ingalls Shipbuilding	21 Aug 1989	2 Nov 1990	10 Nov 1990	2 May 1992	**AA**
CG 69	Vicksburg	88	Litton/Ingalls Shipbuilding	30 May 1990	2 Aug 1991	12 Oct 1991	14 Nov 1992	**AA**
CG 70	Lake Erie	88	Bath Iron Works, Maine	6 Mar 1990	13 July 1991	—	24 July 1993	**PA**
CG 71	Cape St. George	88	Litton/Ingalls Shipbuilding	19 Nov 1990	10 Jan 1992	13 June 1992	12 June 1993	**AA**
CG 72	Vella Gulf	88	Litton/Ingalls Shipbuilding	22 Apr 1991	30 May 1992	25 July 1992	18 Sep 1993	**AA**
CG 73	Port Royal	88	Litton/Ingalls Shipbuilding	20 Nov 1991	20 Nov 1992	5 Dec 1992	9 July 1994	**PA**

Displacement:	8,910 tons standard 9,466 tons full load
Length:	532⅔ feet (162.4 m) waterline 567 feet (172.9 m) overall
Beam:	55 feet (16.75 m)
Draft:	31½ feet (9.6 m)
Propulsion:	4 gas turbines (General Electric LM 2500); 80,000 shp; 2 shafts
Speed:	30+ knots
Range:	6,000 n. miles (11,110 km) at 20 knots
Manning:	387 (28 officers + 359 enlisted) + LAMPS detachment
Helicopters:	2 SH-60B Seahawk LAMPS III
Missiles:	2 61-cell VLS for Standard-MR SM-2/Tomahawk (122 weapons) Mk 41 Mod 0 8 Harpoon SSM Mk 141 (2 quad canisters)
Guns:	2 5-inch (127-mm) 54-cal DP Mk 45 (2 single) 2 20-mm Phalanx CIWS Mk 16 (2 multi-barrel) several light machine guns or cannon
ASW weapons:	6 12.75-inch (324-mm) torpedo tubes Mk 32 (2 triple)
Radars:	SPS-49(V)6/7/8 air search SPS-55 surface search SPS-64(V)9 navigation CG 52–58 (4) SPY-1A multi-function CG 59–73 (4) SPY-1B multi-function
Sonars:	CG 52–55 SQS-53A bow mounted CG 56–67 SQS-53B bow mounted CG 68–73 SQS-53C bow mounted SQR-19 TACTAS
Fire control:	1 Mk 7 Aegis weapon system 1 Mk 86 GFCS with SPQ-9A radar 4 Mk 99 missile directors with SPG-62 radar 1 Mk 116 ASW FCS 1 SQQ-89(V)3 ASW system in CG 54–73 1 SWG-3 weapon control system (Tomahawk)
EW systems:	SLQ-25 Nixie SLQ-32(V)3

These later Ticonderoga-class cruisers differ from the first five ships in having the VLS for missiles. The VLS permits them to carry Tomahawk missiles, providing a land-attack capability as well as more missiles (122 compared to 88) than in the earlier ships. (See Ticonderoga class, below.)

Like the earlier Ticonderogas, these are the world's most capable AAW ships, developed to provide carrier battle group defense against aircraft and anti-ship missiles. In addition, the ships have major ASW capabilities.

The Ingalls-built ships are launched from a floating dock; their christening—public relations—ceremony is held at a later date. Some of these ships received administrative commissioning ceremonies at their building yard; their formal commissioning dates are listed above (e.g., the Bunker Hill was formally commissioned in Boston).

The Cowpens under way in the Far East. The massive forward and amidships superstructures dominate these ships. Note the placement of the SPY-1B radar antennas' "faces" on the forward superstructure looking forward and on the amidships structure looking to port. (1994, Giorgio Arra)

The COWPENS with an SH-60B LAMPS III helicopter on her flight deck (with hangar door open). Eight Harpoon canisters are mounted on the stern, supplementing the 122 vertical-launch missiles and thus providing the largest missile battery of any warship afloat. (1994, Giorgio Arra)

The BUNKER HILL and MOBILE BAY are homeported in Yokosuka, Japan, the only U.S. cruisers based in another country. They are part of the INDEPENDENCE (CV 62) carrier battle group.

Class: This is the largest cruiser class built by any Navy in the post–World War II period. The only other cruiser class of this size built by any nation was the 27-ship CLEVELAND (CL 55) class of light cruisers, built for the U.S. Navy and completed in 1942–1945.[2]

When conceived, the TICONDEROGA class was intended to complement the nuclear-propelled strike cruiser (CSGN), which also was to be fitted with the Aegis AAW system. However, Congress refused to fund the strike cruiser, and only the conventionally propelled Aegis ships were built. The Aegis system was subsequently fitted in the ARLEIGH BURKE-class destroyers.

Classification: These ships were changed from guided missile destroyers (DDG with the small hull numbers) to guided missile cruisers on 1 January 1980 to better reflect their capabilities and cost.

Design: SCB No. 226. These ships are based on the SRUANCE design, employing the same hull and propulsion plant. The superstructure has been enlarged to accommodate the Aegis/SPY-1 equipment, with two fixed-array radar antennas on the forward deckhouse facing forward and to starboard, and two on the after deckhouse facing aft and to port. Internal changes include limited armor plating for the magazine and critical electronic spaces, increases in the ship's service generators from three 2,000 kw to three 2,500 kw, additional accommodations, and additional fuel tanks.

During construction the design was changed to provide higher exhaust stacks and a bow bulwark; the latter was required to reduce water over the bow due to the greater draft compared to the SPRUANCE class.

The VINCENNES and later ships have tripod (vice quadrapod) lattice masts that provide a reduction of some nine tons in topside weight.

Electronics: All ships have the SQR-17 sonar data processor.

Helicopters: These ships have the RAST helicopter-hauldown system (see OLIVER HAZARD PERRY/FFG 7 class). The sizes of the twin helicopter hangars in these ships vary; they are approximately 39 feet (11.9 m) long, 26½ to 29 feet (8.1 to 8.8 m) wide, and 14⅓ to 15½ feet (4.35 to 4.7 m) high.

Missiles: The VLS provides these ships with a Tomahawk launch capability. The BUNKER HILL was the first U.S. naval ship other than the missile test ship NORTON SOUND (AVM 1) and experimental surface effect ship SES-100B to launch a missile at sea from a VLS installation, on 20 May 1986.

These ships are candidates for carrying the Navy's proposed sea-based Theater Ballistic Missile Defense (TBMD) system, which would employ the Standard SM-2/Block IVA missile as a forward, high-altitude interceptor against theater ballistic missile attacks. Modifications will also be made to the Aegis radar/fire-control system for the TBMD role.

Modernization: A proposed update for this class includes the provision of five-foot (1.5-m) blisters on either side along about three-fifths of the ship length; this would provide additional side protection from anti-ship missiles. The shear line of the weather deck would be raised. The blisters would increase displacement and reduce maximum speed by less than one knot.

Names: All ships of this class are named for battles except for the CG 51, named for a deceased Secretary of the Navy and Secretary of Defense. Most of these ship names also remember World War II–era aircraft carriers of the ESSEX (CV 9) and INDEPENDENCE (CVL 22) classes (see also WASP/LHD 1 class amphibious ships). The CG 66 is the second U.S. warship to be named for a battle of the Vietnam War; the PELELIU (LHA 5) was originally named DA NANG, but that ship was renamed on 15 February 1978, after the fall of the Republic of (South) Vietnam to Communist forces.

The CG 69, originally PORT ROYAL, changed names while under construction. (The CG 65 and 66 did not trade names, as reported in a previous edition.)

Operational: The VINCENNES shot down an Iranian commercial airliner on 3 July 1988 over the southern Persian Gulf. All 290 passengers and crew were killed. The VINCENNES's combat information center had identified the target as probably an Iranian F-14 Tomcat making a dive on the ship. Two Standard missiles were fired.

Seven ships of this class fired 105 Tomahawk missiles during Operation Desert Storm (1991):

BUNKER HILL	28 missiles
MOBILE BAY	22 missiles
LEYTE GULF	2 missiles
SAN JACINTO	14 missiles
PHILIPPINE SEA	10 missiles
PRINCETON	3 missiles
NORMANDY	26 missiles

These missiles represented 36 percent of the Tomahawks fired during the conflict.

2. In addition to the 27 ships that were completed, one CLEVELAND was canceled and nine were converted to light carriers (CVL); nine modified CLEVELANDS were planned, but only two were completed in 1945–1946: the FARGO class (CL 106 and 107).

On 18 February 1991, during the Gulf War, the PRINCETON struck a bottom-laid influence mine that damaged the ship (a second mine was detonated by the explosion of the first). The damage to the PRINCETON required her being towed to port, although at no time was the ship in danger of sinking, and most of her combat systems remained operational. (The ship could have proceeded under her own power, but the commanding officer decided on the tow to avoid strain on the ship's hull until an examination could be made in a dockyard.) Repairs were made during a seven-week "availability" at Dubai in the United Arab Emirates followed by a two-month yard period in the United States.

On 26 June 1993 another 23 Tomahawk missiles were launched against targets in Iraq: 9 by the cruiser CHANCELLORSVILLE and 14 by the destroyer PETERSON (DD 969).

The ANZIO showing the general arrangement of the TICONDEROGA class. The innocuous vertical-launch missile batteries between the forward 5-inch gun and superstructure, and between the helicopter deck and after 5-inch gun, belie the ship's striking power. (1991, Litton/Ingalls Shipbuilding)

The VINCENNES at speed in the Far East. The forward 5-inch gun and Mk 26 missile launcher are barely visible over the forward gunnels. The stem anchor is characteristic of ships with SQS-26/53 sonar domes. In addition to the large missile battery, these ships have an ASW capability. (1994, Giorgio Arra)

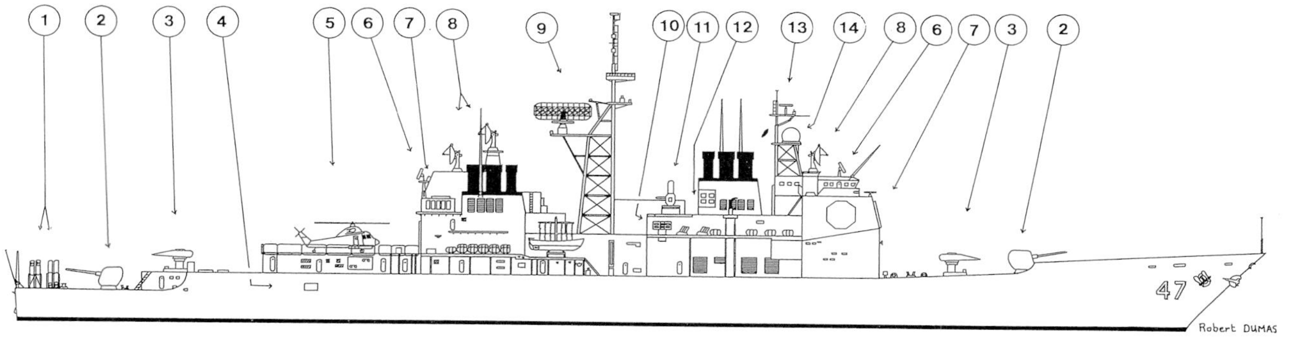

TICONDEROGA

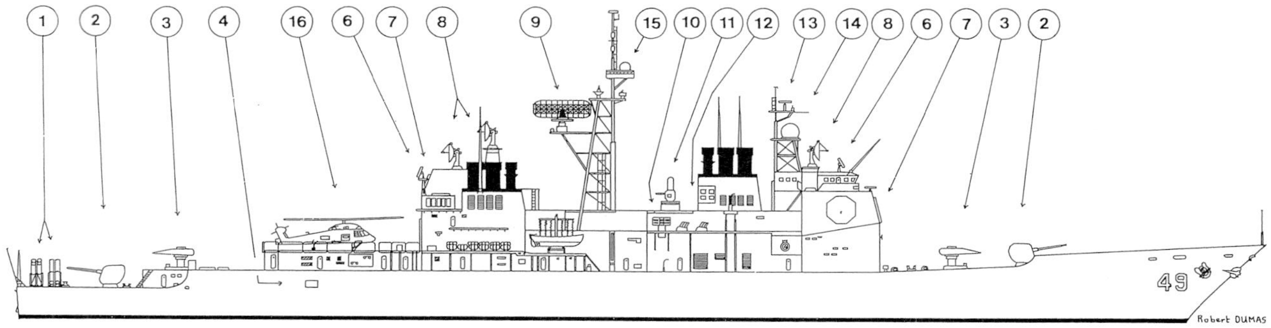

VINCENNES

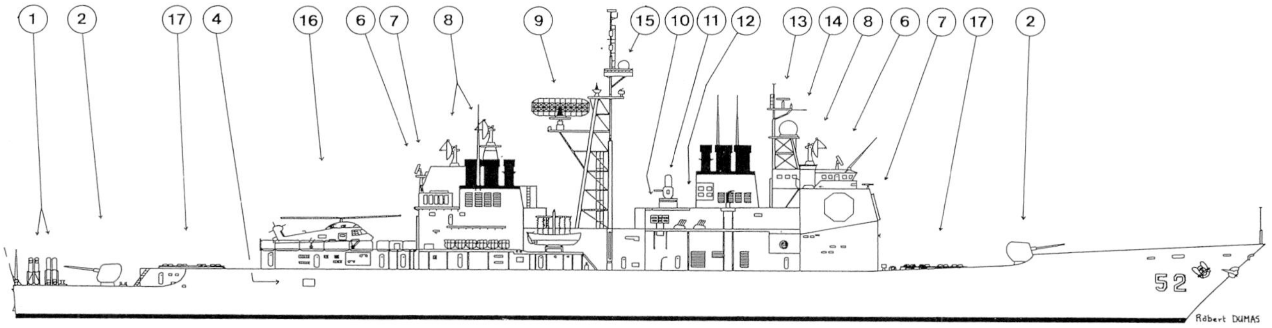

BUNKER HILL

1. Harpoon missile canisters (8 missiles). 2. 5-inch DP guns Mk 45 (2). 3. Surface-to-air missile launchers Mk 26 (2). 4. 12.75-inch triple torpedo tubes Mk 32 (2). 5. SH-2F LAMPS I helicopter. 6. OE-82 satellite antennas (2). 7. SPY-1 fixed radars (4). 8. SPG-62 radar illuminators (4). 9. SPS-49(V)6 air search radar. 10. SLQ-32(V)3 EW antennas (2). 11. Phalanx CIWS (2). 12. SUBROC decoy launcher Mk 36. 13. SPS-55 surface search radar. 14. SPQ-9A surface/gunfire control radar. 15. SPS-64(V)9 navigation radar. 16. SH-60B LAMPS III helicopter. 17. Vertical-launch system Mk 41. (Robert Dumas)

5 GUIDED MISSILE CRUISERS: "TICONDEROGA" CLASS

Number	Name	FY	Builder	Laid down	Launched	Christened	Commissioned	Status
CG 47	Ticonderoga	78	Litton/Ingalls Shipbuilding	21 Jan 1980	25 Apr 1981	16 May 1981	22 Jan 1983	**AA**
CG 48	Yorktown	80	Litton/Ingalls Shipbuilding	19 Oct 1981	17 Jan 1983	16 Apr 1983	4 July 1984	**AA**
CG 49	Vincennes	81	Litton/Ingalls Shipbuilding	20 Oct 1982	14 Jan 1984	18 Apr 1984	6 July 1985	**PA**
CG 50	Valley Forge	81	Litton/Ingalls Shipbuilding	14 Apr 1983	23 June 1984	29 Sep 1984	11 Jan 1986	**PA**
CG 51	Thomas S. Gates	82	Bath Iron Works, Maine	31 Aug 1984	14 Dec 1985	—	22 Aug 1987	**AA**

Displacement:	CG 47, 48 7,019 tons light
	CG 49–51 7,014 tons light
	CG 47, 48 9,589 tons full load
	CG 49–51 9,407 tons full load
Length:	532⅔ feet (162.4 m) waterline
	567 feet (172.9 m) overall
Beam:	55 feet (16.75 m)
Draft:	31½ feet (9.6 m)
Propulsion:	4 gas turbines (General Electric LM 2500); 80,000 shp; 2 shafts
Speed:	30+ knots
Range:	6,000 n. miles (11,110 km) at 20 knots
Manning:	380 (27 officers + 353 enlisted)
	+ LAMPS detachment in CG 49–51
Helicopters:	2 SH-60B Seahawk LAMPS III in CG 49–51
Missiles:	2 twin Mk 26 Mod 1 launchers for Standard-MR SM-2/ASROC (88 weapons)
	8 Harpoon SSM Mk 141 (2 quad canisters)
Guns:	2 5-inch (127-mm) 54-cal DP Mk 45 (2 single)
	2 20-mm Phalanx CIWS Mk 16 (2 multi-barrel)
	several light machine guns or cannon
ASW weapons:	ASROC fired from Mk 26 launcher in CG 47–51
	6 12.75-inch (324-mm) torpedo tubes Mk 32 (2 triple)
Radars:	SPS-49(V)6/7/8 air search
	SPS-53 surface search
	SPS-55 surface search
	SPS-64(V)9 navigation
	(4) SPY-1A multi-function
Sonars:	SQS-53A bow mounted
	SQR-19 towed array
Fire control:	1 Mk 7 Aegis weapon system
	1 Mk 86 GFCS with SPQ-9A radar
	4 Mk 99 missile directors with SPG-62 radar
	1 Mk 116 ASW FCS
EW systems:	SLQ-25 Nixie
	SLQ-32(V)3

These first five ships of the Ticonderoga class have Mk 26 twin-arm missile launchers in lieu of the more capable VLS in the later 22 ships.

The Ingalls-built ships are launched from a floating dock; their christening—public relations—ceremony is held at a later date. Some of these ships received administrative commissioning ceremonies at their building yard; their formal commissioning dates are listed here.

The Yorktown will be modified in an automation/crew-reduction program in the late 1990s to permit a major cut in the size of the crew—possibly as large as one-quarter to one-third.

See Improved Ticonderoga class entry for *Class, Classification,* and *Design* notes.

Electronics: All ships have the SQR-17 sonar data processor. The SQQ-89(V)3 suite consists of the SQS-53 series plus SQR-19 sonars.

Helicopters: The first two ships of this class carried the SH-2F LAMPS I helicopter, now discarded; the CG 49–51 were fitted to carry the SH-60B Seahawk LAMPS III.

Names: The CG 51 is named for a deceased Secretary of the Navy and Secretary of Defense. (Other Secretaries of the Navy are remembered by destroyers and cruisers, the former having been named for secretaries when they were built as DLG "frigates" in the destroyer family; the only other Secretaries of Defense to have had Navy ships named in their honor were James V. Forrestal, also a former Secretary of the Navy, and George C. Marshall.)

Operational: The Vincennes shot down an Iranian commercial airliner on 3 July 1988 over the southern Persian Gulf. All 290 passengers and crew were killed. The Vincennes's combat information center had identified the target as probably an Iranian F-14 Tomcat making a dive on the ship. Two Standard missiles were fired.

The Thomas S. Gates is the only ship of the Ticonderoga class not named for a battle. Most surface combatants have their SLQ-32 antenna system mounted on the bridge structure; in the "Ticos" the SLQ-32 is amidships, below the Phalanx CIWS mount. (1995, John Bouvia)

2 NUCLEAR-PROPELLED GUIDED MISSILE CRUISERS: "VIRGINIA" CLASS

Number	Name	FY	Builder	Laid down	Launched	Commissioned	Status
CGN 40	Mississippi	72	Newport News Shipbuilding	22 Feb 1975	31 July 1976	5 Aug 1978	**AA**
CGN 41	Arkansas	75	Newport News Shipbuilding	17 Jan 1977	21 Oct 1978	18 Oct 1980	**PA**

Displacement:	10,500 tons light 11,400 tons full load
Length:	585 feet (178.4 m) overall
Beam:	63 feet (19.2 m)
Draft:	31½ feet (9.6 m)
Propulsion:	2 steam turbines; approx. 70,000 shp; 2 shafts
Reactors:	2 pressurized-water D2G (General Electric)
Speed:	30+ knots
Manning:	554 (38 officers + 516 enlisted)
Helicopters:	VERTREP area only (see notes)
Missiles:	2 twin Mk 26 Mod 0/1 launchers for Standard-MR SM-2 SAM (68 weapons) 8 Harpoon SSM Mk 141 (2 quad canisters) 16 Tomahawk SSM Mk 143 (2 quad ABL)
Guns:	2 5-inch (127-mm) 54-cal DP Mk 45 (2 single) 2 20-mm Phalanx CIWS Mk 16 (2 multi-barrel)
ASW weapons:	ASROC fired from forward Mk 26 launcher 6 12.75-inch (324-mm) torpedo tubes Mk 32 (2 triple)
Radars:	SPS-48E 3-D air search SPS-49(V)5 air search SPS-55 surface search SPS-64(V)9 navigation
Sonars:	SQS-53A bow mounted
Fire control:	1 Mk 14 weapon direction system 1 Mk 86 GFCS with SPG-60D and SPQ-9A radars 1 Mk 74 missile FCS 1 Mk 116 ASW FCS 2 SPG-51D radar 1 SWG-2 weapon control system (Tomahawk)
EW systems:	SLQ-25 Nixie SLQ-32(V)3

These were the last nuclear-propelled surface combatants to be built for the U.S. Navy.[3]

The number of nuclear-propelled fleet escorts (DLGN/CGN) proposed for the fleet has varied considerably, apparently reaching a peak of 28 ships in Navy program proposals of 1970—the cruiser Long Beach, the four then-DLGN ships already built and under construction, plus 23 of the DXGN design, which evolved into the Virginia class. This ambitious program was soon reduced to more fiscally possible numbers, and in May 1971 the Department of Defense decided to hold this class at three ships (then DLGN 38–40), i.e., a total of eight CGN/DLGNs to provide escorts for two all-nuclear carrier groups. Subsequent Navy efforts to garner support for nuclear ships led to congressional funding of a fourth ship (DLGN 41) and for long-lead components of a fifth ship (DLGN 42) that was to be authorized in fiscal 1975. However, Congress then declined to fund the latter ship when the Navy proposed the more capable strike cruiser (CSGN) for later construction, and the DLGN/CGN 42 was never built.

Hence, the number of nuclear-propelled escorts reached a peak of nine ships in 1980, at which time the Navy had three nuclear-propelled carriers.

3. From 1980 to 1988 the Soviet Navy completed three nuclear-propelled "battle" cruisers of the 28,300-ton Kirov class; a fourth ship, the Petr Velikiy (ex-Yuri Andropov) was completed in 1996. See N. Polmar, *Guide to the SovietNavy* (Annapolis, Md.: Naval Institute Press, 1991), pp. 148–52.

Class: Originally a class of four ships; the Texas (CGN 39), commissioned in 1977, was decommissioned and stricken on 16 July 1993; the Virginia (CGN 38) was decommissioned and stricken on 29 Nov 1994.

The Texas was the first U.S. nuclear-propelled surface ship to be decommissioned; the event occurred without prior notice, fanfare, or major ceremonies at the Puget Sound Naval Shipyard in Bremerton, Washington. The ship had entered the Puget Sound yard in September 1992 for a major overhaul and refueling; prior to loading new fuel cores, the decision was made to decommission the ship, and all work was halted.

The Mississippi is scheduled to be placed In Commission, In Reserve on 30 September 1996 in preparation of being decommissioned and stricken, and the Arkansas will be placed ICIR on 30 September 1997.

Classification: CGN 38–40 were originally classified as frigates (DLGN 38–40); they were changed to cruisers on 30 June 1975. The Arkansas was ordered as CGN 41.

Design: These ships are of an improved design that is superior to the previous California class, with Mk 26 missile launchers and provision for a helicopter hangar and elevator in their stern. These were the first U.S. ships built since World War II to have the latter feature.

Helicopters: As built, the ships had a stern hangar with a folding hatch cover and elevator arrangement to accommodate a single SH-2F LAMPS. The hangar was 42 feet (12.8 m) long, 14 feet (4.3 m) wide, and 14¼ feet (4.3 m) high. The ships encountered problems with the

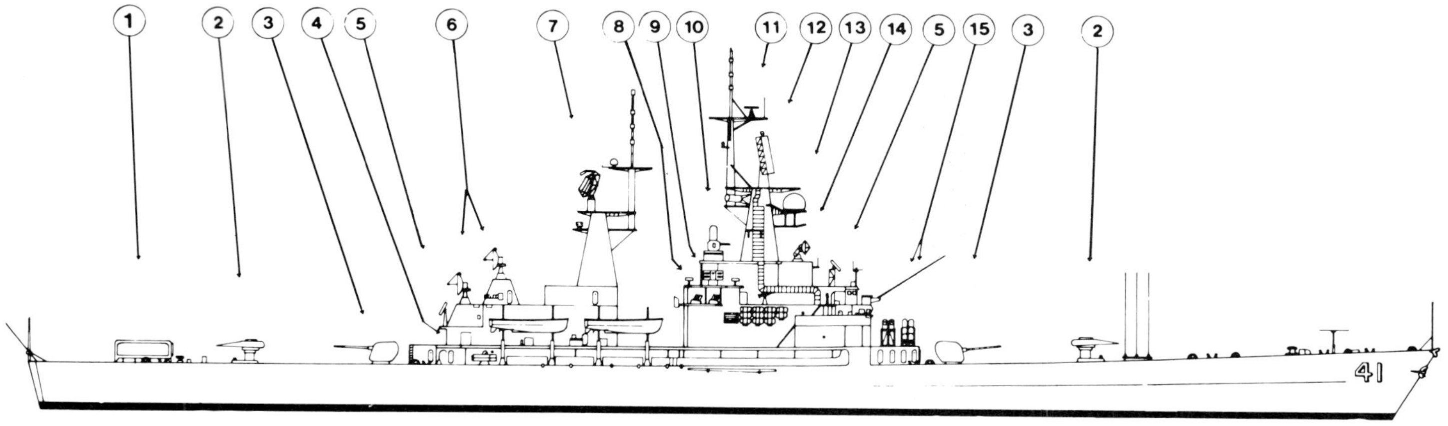

Arkansas
1. Tomahawk ABL (8 missiles). 2. Surface-to-air missile launchers Mk 26 (2). 3. 5-inch DP guns Mk 45 (2). 4. 12.75-inch triple torpedo tubes Mk 32. 5. OE-82 satellite antennas (2). 6. SPG-51D radar illuminators (2). 7. SPS-40B radar (replaced by SPS-49(V)5). 8. SUBROC decoy launcher Mk 36. 9. SLQ-32(V)3 EW antennas (2). 10. Phalanx CIWS (2). 11. SPS-55 surface search radar. 12. SPS-48E air search radar. 13. SPQ-9A surface/gunfire control radar. 14. SPG-50D gun/missile control radar. 15. Harpoon missile canisters (8 missiles). (Robert Dumas)

elevators and in keeping the hangars watertight. Accordingly, in the early 1980s the decision was made to delete the helicopters in favor of the Tomahawk box launchers. The ships have small VERTREP areas forward and on the fantail.

Missiles: These ships were fitted with Tomahawk cruise missiles in armored box launchers on the fantail, aft of the second Mk 26 launcher. Earlier proposals to provide a VLS for Tomahawk missiles in place of the hangar were dropped. The Harpoon canisters were installed forward of the bridge, on the 01 level.

Modernization: From the late 1980s on, these ships had a weapons upgrade, although they did not receive a full New Threat Upgrade (NTU) modernization. Their Mk 13 weapons direction system was replaced by the Mk 14; the SPS-40B radar was replaced by the SPS-49(V); and the SPS-48B was upgraded to the SPS-48C variant.

Operational: The Virginia fired two Tomahawk missiles and the Mississippi launched five during Operation Desert Storm in 1991; these amounted to 2 percent of the TLAM missiles fired in the war. (The only other cruisers to launch Tomahawks in the conflict were Ticonderoga-class ships.)

The Mississippi, the penultimate nuclear-propelled surface combatant built for the U.S. Navy. The same year as the Arkansas was completed (1980), the Soviet Navy completed the first of four nuclear cruisers of the Kirov class of almost twice the tonnage of the U.S. ships. (1991, Giorgio Arra)

The Mississippi at Port Everglades, Fla. Her port Tomahawk armored box launcher is in the raised position, while the after twin Mk 26 launcher has missiles on both rails. The twin openings in the stern counter are for the SLQ-25 Nixie torpedo countermeasures. (1994, John Bouvia)

2 NUCLEAR-PROPELLED GUIDED MISSILE CRUISERS: "CALIFORNIA" CLASS

Number	Name	FY	Builder	Laid down	Launched	Commissioned	Status
CGN 36	CALIFORNIA	67	Newport News Shipbuilding	23 Jan 1970	22 Sep 1971	16 Feb 1974	**PA**
CGN 37	SOUTH CAROLINA	68	Newport News Shipbuilding	1 Dec 1970	1 July 1972	25 Jan 1975	**AA**

Displacement:	9,676 tons light 10,530 tons full load
Length:	596 feet (181.8 m) overall
Beam:	61 feet (18.6 m)
Draft:	31½ feet (9.6 m)
Propulsion:	2 steam turbines; 70,000 shp; 2 shafts
Reactors:	2 pressurized-water D2G (General Electric)
Speed:	30+ knots
Manning:	CGN 36 528 (38 officers + 490 enlisted) CGN 37 547 (38 officers + 509 enlisted)
Helicopters:	VERTREP area only
Missiles:	2 single Mk 13 Mod 3 launchers for Standard-MR SM-1 SAM (80 weapons) 8 Harpoon SSM Mk 141 (2 quad canisters)
Guns:	2 5-inch (127-mm) 54-cal DP Mk 45 (2 single) 2 20-mm Phalanx CIWS Mk 16 (2 multi-barrel)
ASW weapons:	ASROC launcher Mk 16 (removed) 4 12.75-inch (324-mm) torpedo tubes Mk 32 (4 fixed single)
Radars:	SPS-48E 3-D air search SPS-49(V)5 air search SPS-64(V)9 navigation SPS-67(V)1 surface search
Sonars:	SQS-26CX bow mounted
Fire control:	1 Mk 11 Mod 3 weapon direction system 2 Mk 74 missile FCS 1 Mk 86 GFCS with SPG-60 and SPQ-9A radars 1 Mk 114 ASW FCS 4 SPG-51D radar
EW systems:	SLQ-25 Nixie SLQ-32(V)3 SLQ-34 combat D/F

These "double-end" ships are essentially nuclear-propelled versions of guided missile designs proposed in the early 1960s, with the so-called Tartar-D missile system vice the more capable missile systems of other U.S. cruisers and some destroyer classes. Their construction was delayed because of Secretary of Defense Robert McNamara's opposition to nuclear ship construction and the fiscal demands of the Vietnam War. Funds for their construction were released only after strong congressional efforts.

This was the first class of nuclear-propelled surface warships intended for series production.

These ships were overhauled and refueled in 1992–1994, hence they will remain in service longer than other U.S. nuclear-propelled surface combatants, i.e., until about the year 1999.

Class: A third ship of this design was authorized in fiscal year 1968 but was not built because of rising costs and the development of the more capable VIRGINIA design.

Classification: Both ships originally were classified as guided missile frigates (DLGN); they were changed to cruisers on 30 June 1975.

Design: SCB No. 241; this SCB number was part of the new SCB series (241.65). These ships have a large helicopter landing area aft, but no hangar or maintenance facilities. They have a separate ASROC box launcher because their Mk 13 missile launchers cannot accommodate the anti-submarine rockets.

Guns: Unlike earlier CG/CGN-type ships built with 5-inch guns, these ships were not built with a secondary gun battery of 3-inch/50-cal weapons.

Missiles: These are the Navy's only cruisers armed with the SM-1 series Standard missiles (*né* Tartar-D system).

No Tomahawk missiles are provided. The starboard-firing Harpoon canister is fitted amidships, between the "mack" structures, and the port-firing canister is at the after end of the superstructure, at the 01 level.

The ASROC launcher was removed in 1993.

NUCLEAR-PROPELLED GUIDED MISSILE CRUISER: "TRUXTUN"

The guided missile cruiser TRUXTUN (CGN 35), commissioned in 1967, was built as a nuclear-propelled version of the BELKNAP class. The Navy had requested seven oil-burning frigates (DLG) in the fiscal 1962 program; however, Congress directed that one of the ships have nuclear propulsion, which led to the one-of-a-kind TRUXTUN. The ship was decommissioned and stricken on 30 August 1995.

Classification: Originally classified as a guided missile frigate (DLGN 35); changed to cruiser (CGN) on 30 June 1975.

Design: A "single-end" Terrier/Standard missile ship, the TRUXTUN was built to a modified BELKNAP-class design with the gun and missile-launcher positions reversed. The ship had a distinctive appearance, what with four-legged lattice masts having replaced the macks of the oil-burning ships.

See 15th Edition/pages 112–13 for characteristics.

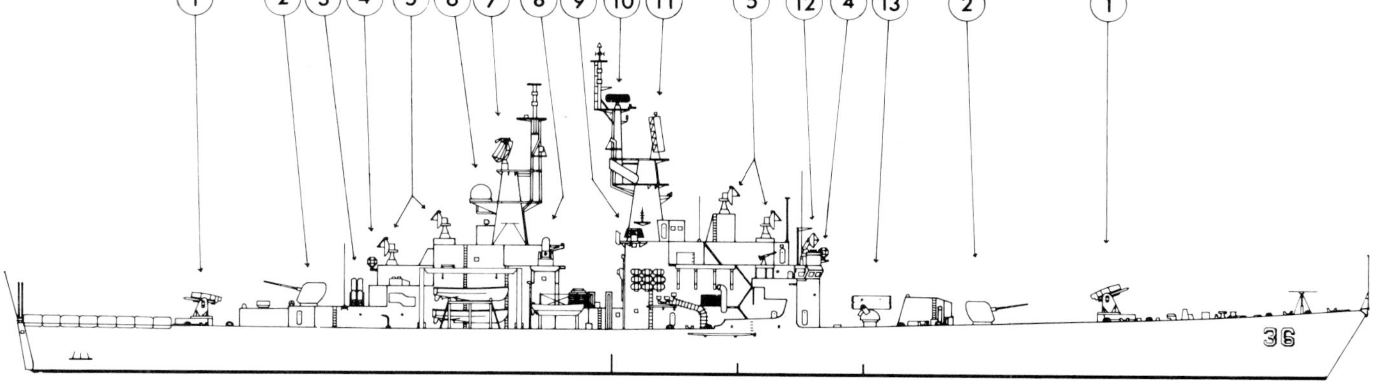

CALIFORNIA
1. Surface-to-air missile launchers Mk 13 (2). 2. 5-inch DP guns Mk 45 (2). 3. Harpoon missile canisters (8). 4. OE-82 satellite antennas (2). 5. SPG-51D radar illuminators (2). 6. SPQ-9A surface/gunfire control radar. 7. SPS-40B radar (replaced by SPS-49(V)5). 8. Phalanx CIWS (2). 9. SLQ-32(V)3 EW antennas. 10. SPS-67(V)1 surface search radar. 11. SPS-48C air search radar. 12. SPG-60 gun/missile radar illuminator. 13. ASROC launcher. (Robert Dumas)

This stern view of the CALIFORNIA reveals her lack of a helicopter hangar and flight deck. The after 5-inch gun mount is on the 01 level vice the main deck of other nuclear cruisers. (1994, Giorgio Arra)

The large, graceful CALIFORNIA at Hong Kong. These ships had a limited missile capability, outfitted with only the single-arm Mk 13 surface-to-air launchers. Her Harpoon canisters are amidships. The ASROC launcher, fitted behind the forward 5-inch gun, has been inactivated. (1994, Giorgio Arra)

GUIDED MISSILE CRUISERS: "BELKNAP" CLASS

Name	Number	Comm.	Notes
CG 26	BELKNAP	1964	decomm./stricken 15 Feb 1995
CG 27	JOSEPHUS DANIELS	1965	decomm./stricken 22 Jan 1994
CG 28	WAINWRIGHT	1966	decomm./stricken 10 Nov 1993
CG 29	JOUETT	1966	decomm./stricken 28 Jan 1994
CG 30	HORNE	1967	decomm./stricken 4 Feb 1994
CG 31	STERETT	1967	decomm./stricken 24 Mar 1994
CG 32	WILLIAM H. STANDLEY	1966	decomm./stricken 11 Feb 1994
CG 33	FOX	1966	decomm./stricken 15 Apr 1994
CG 34	BIDDLE	1967	decomm./stricken 30 Nov 1993

These were single-end Terrier/Standard-ER guided missile cruisers built to screen aircraft carriers. After suffering major damage in a collision with the carrier JOHN F. KENNEDY (CV 67), the BELKNAP was rebuilt in 1978–1980 and configured as the Sixth Fleet flagship. She served in that role until 1995.

Classification: These ships were originally classified as guided missile frigates (DLG 27–34); they were changed to CG on 30 June 1975.

Design: These ships were built to an improved LEAHY-class design, with a 5-inch gun being substituted for the after missile launcher. They carried 60 surface-to-air missiles in place of the 80 in the "double-end" LEAHYS.

See 15th Edition/pages 113–16 for characteristics.

NUCLEAR-PROPELLED GUIDED MISSILE CRUISER (CGN): "LONG BEACH"

The LONG BEACH (CGN 9), commissioned in 1961, was the world's first nuclear-propelled surface warship.[4] The LONG BEACH was the first U.S. cruiser to be constructed since World War II and the world's first warship to be built with guided missiles as the main battery, carrying two Terrier/Standard surface-to-air launchers (forward) and a Talos surface-to-air launcher (aft).

The ship was placed In Commission, In Reserve on 2 July 1994 to begin the retirement process. She was decommissioned and stricken on 1 May 1995.

4. The Soviet nuclear-propelled icebreaker LENIN was completed in September 1959.

Classification: The LONG BEACH was ordered as a guided missile light cruiser (CLGN 160) on 15 October 1956, reclassified as a guided missile cruiser (CGN 160) on 6 December 1956, and renumbered CGN 9 on 1 July 1957.

Design: The LONG BEACH was initially proposed as a large destroyer or "frigate" (DLGN) of some 7,800 tons (standard displacement); her design subsequently was enlarged to accommodate additional missile systems to take maximum advantage of the benefits of nuclear propulsion.

This was the first U.S. warship built without guns; she was subsequently fitted with two 5-inch/38-cal DP guns to provide minimal defense against attacks by subsonic aircraft or small craft. (Two Phalanx CIWS were later installed.)

See 15th Edition/pages 119–21 for characteristics.

The LONG BEACH shortly before being taken out of service in preparation for her disposal. Once hailed as the prototype of future surface combatants, the LONG BEACH was the world's first nuclear-propelled surface warship and the first ship built with an all-missile armament. She retained her square superstructure although her SPS-32/33 "billboard" fixed-array antennas were long gone. (1994, Giorgio Arra)

The LONG BEACH with her stepped Phalanx CIWS mounts and Tomahawk box launchers aft. Her two 5-inch/38 single gun mounts, their directors, and her ASROC box launcher are between the forward superstructure and the lattice mast. (1994, Giorgio Arra)

NUCLEAR-PROPELLED GUIDED MISSILE CRUISER: "BAINBRIDGE"

The BAINBRIDGE (CGN 25) was the world's first nuclear-propelled "destroyer" type ship, being built as the guided missile frigate DLGN 25 and commissioned in 1962. She was a double-end Terrier/Standard-ER missile ship. The ship was placed In Commission, In Reserve on 31 October 1995, and was scheduled to be decommissioned and stricken on 1 December 1996.

Classification: Originally classified as a guided missile frigate (DLGN 25); changed to cruiser on 30 June 1975.

See 15th Edition/page 117 for characteristics.

GUIDED MISSILE CRUISERS: "LEAHY" CLASS

Number	Name	Comm.	Notes
CG 16	LEAHY	1962	decomm./stricken 1 Oct 1993
CG 17	HARRY E. YARNELL	1963	decomm./stricken 29 Oct 1993
CG 18	WORDEN	1963	decomm./stricken 10 Oct 1993
CG 19	DALE	1962	decomm./stricken 23 Sep 1994
CG 20	RICHMOND K. TURNER	1964	decomm./stricken 30 June 1995
CG 21	GRIDLEY	1963	decomm./stricken 21 Jan 1994
CG 22	ENGLAND	1962	decomm./stricken 21 Jan 1994
CG 23	HALSEY	1963	decomm./stricken 28 Jan 1994
CG 24	REEVES	1964	decomm./stricken 12 Nov 1993

These were double-end Terrier/Standard-ER missile cruisers with surface-to-air missile launchers forward and aft. They were the smallest U.S. Navy ships to be classified as cruisers in the post–World War II era, having been classified as frigates (DLG 16–24) from their completion until 1975.

Design: They were also the only U.S. cruisers to be built with only 3-inch/50-cal guns; the gun mounts were later replaced by Harpoon missile canisters.

See 15th Edition/pages 118–19 for characteristics.

STRIKE CRUISERS

The strike cruiser (CSGN) was an outgrowth of the DLGN concept, developed in 1973–1974 as an enlarged DLGN intended specifically to carry the Aegis weapon system. As more weapons were added—especially the Harpoon and Tomahawk cruise missiles—the ship was enlarged and the twin-reactor D2G propulsion plant was upgraded.

The ship was proposed as a carrier escort, with up to four CSGNs being considered to screen each carrier. The cost of the lead strike cruiser in fiscal 1976 was estimated at $1.371 *billion,* and the ship was to have been completed in December 1983. After the ship was ignored by Congress, the Naval Sea Systems Command hurriedly developed a strike cruiser Mk II design that retained the same armament but added a flight deck, presenting a superficial similarity to the Soviet KIEV-class VTOL carriers.[5] However, the U.S. ship, with two vertical launch systems in place of the two Mk 26 launchers, would have had an enlarged island structure with hangars for several Harrier VSTOL aircraft and LAMPS III helicopters (far fewer than the KIEV operates).

A further modification of the Mk II design considered a hangar above the main deck, resulting in a design somewhat similar to the Navy's small or light carriers of World War II (CVL 22–30). That ship would have carried about 18 Harriers on a displacement of some 18,000 tons. The concept of combining a missile cruiser with a limited aircraft capability is again being considered by the Navy (see page 00).

See 13th Edition/pages 136–37 for additional strike cruiser details.

5. See N. Polmar, *Guide to the Soviet Navy* (Annapolis, Md.: Naval Institute Press, 1991), pp. 138–44.

GUIDED MISSILE CRUISERS

Number	Name	Notes
CAG 1	BOSTON (ex-CA 69)	reverted to CA 69; stricken 1973
CAG 2	CANBERRA (ex-CA 70)	reverted to CA 70; stricken 1978
CLG 3	GALVESTON (ex-CL 93)	stricken 1973
CLG 4	LITTLE ROCK (ex-CL 92)	changed to CG 4; stricken 1977
CLG 5	OKLAHOMA CITY (ex-CL 91)	changed to CG 5; stricken 1982
CLG 6	PROVIDENCE (ex-CL 82)	changed to CG 6; stricken 1978
CLG 7	SPRINGFIELD (ex-CL 66)	changed to CG 7; stricken 1978
CLG 8	TOPEKA (ex-CL 67)	stricken 1973
CGN 9	LONG BEACH (ex-CLGN/CGN 160)	
CG 10	ALBANY (ex-CA 123)	stricken 1985
CG 11	CHICAGO (ex-CA 136)	stricken 1984
CG 12	COLUMBUS (ex-CA 74)	stricken 1976
CG 13	BALTIMORE/OREGON CITY class	conversion canceled
CG 14	BREMERTON (CA 130)	conversion canceled
CG 15	BALTIMORE/OREGON CITY class	conversion canceled
CG 16	ROCHESTER (CA 124)	conversion canceled
CG 16–24	LEAHY class (ex-DLG 16–24)	
CGN 25	BAINBRIDGE (ex-DLGN 25)	
CG 26–34	BELKNAP (ex-DLG 26–34)	
CGN 35	TRUXTUN (ex-DLGN 35)	
CGN 36, 37	CALIFORNIA class (ex-DLGN 36, 37)	
CGN 38–41	VIRGINIA class (ex-DLGN 38–41)	
CGN 42	VIRGINIA class	canceled
CG 43–46	not used	
CG 47–73	TICONDEROGA (ex-DDG 47) class	

Cruisers planned, authorized, and/or built during World War II reached hull number CL 159 (hulls 154–159 were canceled in 1945). All heavy (CA), light (CL), and anti-aircraft (CLAA) cruisers were numbered in the same series. Only one ship—the LONG BEACH—was added to this series in the postwar period. She was ordered as CLGN 160, changed to CGN 160, and completed as CGN 9. Further "cruiser" construction was halted in favor of the smaller and comparatively less expensive "frigates" that could carry most of a cruiser's missile armament.

The guided missile cruiser classifications were established in 1952 to reflect the specialized weapons and AAW roles of these ships. Eleven war-built cruisers were converted to a missile configuration (CAG 1, 2, CLG 3–8, CG 10–12). Two BALTIMORE (CA 69)-class cruisers with 8-inch (203-mm) guns and six CLEVELAND-class cruisers with 6-inch (152-mm) guns were converted to a gun-missile configuration (CAG and CLG, respectively). These 19 ships have all been stricken, the last being the OKLAHOMA CITY, which was decommissioned in 1979 and stricken in 1982. The CAGs had two Terrier launchers aft; the CLGs were fitted with either a single Talos or Terrier launcher aft; four of the CLGs were especially modified to serve as numbered fleet flagships. The two CAGs lost their missile systems and reverted to CA designations during the Vietnam War; four of the CLGs were changed to CG in 1975 even though they retained 6-inch and 5-inch (127-mm) guns forward. Three other heavy cruisers were converted to all-missile configurations (CG 10–12). Known as the ALBANY class, these too have been stricken, the last being the ALBANY in 1985. (The above table, revised from the 15th Edition, shows the candidate cruisers for conversion to CG 14 and 16 among four canceled Talos CG ships. Note that the hull number 16 was "reused.")

One cruiser hull, the NORTHAMPTON, was completed as a command ship after the war. Begun as a heavy cruiser (CA 125), she was canceled in 1945 when partially complete, reordered in 1948, completed as a tactical command ship in 1953 (CLC 1), and later changed to a national command ship (CC 1). She was stricken in 1977. (See 11th Edition/page 121 for characteristics.)

In 1975, 25 guided missile frigates (DLG/DLGN) were changed to cruisers, and in 1980 the Aegis-equipped destroyers were reclassified as cruisers. The latter ships began with CG 47, their former DDG number.

HUNTER-KILLER CRUISERS

Number	Name	Notes
CLK 1	Norfolk	completed as DL 1
CLK 2	New Haven	deferred 1949; canceled 1951

After World War II the U.S. Navy established the classification of hunter-killer cruiser (CLK) for a planned series of small cruisers intended for ASW operations against high-speed submarines. Only the lead ship, the Norfolk, was completed; she was reclassified as a frigate (DL) while under construction. She was employed mainly in ASW test and evaluation, being decommissioned in 1970 and stricken in 1973.

See 8th Edition/pages 11–12 for characteristics.

FRIGATES

The frigate classification (DL) was established in 1951 for large *destroyer*-type ships that were designed to operate with fast carrier forces. While initially intended as highly capable ASW ships, the deployment of missile systems in these ships (DLG/DLGN) puts the emphasis on AAW systems, although some ships additionally had the most capable ASW systems available (i.e., large sonar, drone helicopter, ASROC).

The frigate classification was abolished on 30 June 1975, and frigate (FF/FFG) was established to indicate smaller escort ships (formerly DE/DEG). One class of DLGs was reclassified as destroyers (DDG); the other DLG/DLGN ships became cruisers (CG/CGN).

Number	Name	Comm.	Notes
DL 1	Norfolk (ex-CLK 1)	1953	stricken 1973
DL 2	Mitscher (ex-DD 927)	1953	converted to DDG 35
DL 3	John S. McCain (DD 928)	1953	converted to DDG 36
DL 4	Willis A. Lee (ex-DD 930)	1954	stricken 1972
DL 5	Wilkinson (ex-DD 930)	1954	stricken 1974
DLG 6–15	Farragut class		changed to DDG 37–46
DLG 16–24	Leahy class		changed to CG 16–24
DLGN 25	Bainbridge		changed to CGN 25
DLG 26–34	Belknap class		changed to CG 26–34
DLGN 35	Truxtun		changed to CGN 35
DLGN 36–37	California class		changed to CGN 36–37
DLGN 38–40	Virginia class		changed to CGN 38–40

The hunter-killer cruiser Norfolk was completed as the DL 1, while four Mitscher-class ships ordered as destroyers were completed as DL 2–5. These ships were built with an all-gun armament plus the Weapon Afla ASW rocket launcher and other ASW weapons. (See 11th Edition/pages 11 and 12 for characteristics as DLs.) The DLG 6–8 were ordered as DL 6–8 and changed to DLG in 1956 (see page 131).

Note that the all-gun and missile-armed frigates were numbered in the same series; in the cruiser, destroyer, and frigate/destroyer escort categories the missile and non-missile ships were assigned hull numbers in separate series.

The Aegis cruiser Anzio of the Ticonderoga class and the destroyer Hayler (DD 997) of the Spruance (DD 963) class. The two classes have similar hulls and machinery; visible here are the cruiser's Harpoon canisters on the fantail and SPY-1 radar antennas atop the after deckhouse. (1994, Leo Van Ginderen collection)

CHAPTER 16

Destroyers

The hunted and the hunter: The nuclear-propelled attack submarine BOISE (SSN 764) and the guided missile destroyer BARRY. Anti-submarine warfare was the principal mission of U.S. destroyers in World War I and one of two primary missions in World War II, the other being anti-air warfare. The BARRY—fitted with Aegis and vertical-launch missiles—is oriented primarily toward AAW; the destroyer lacks the helicopter support facilities vital for modern ASW operations. (1993, Giorgio Arra)

Destroyers—like guided missile cruisers—serve primarily as screening ships for carrier battle groups and other naval forces (e.g., amphibious and logistic groups). However, the ARLEIGH BURKE-class destroyers and most SPRUANCE-class ships additionally have a land-attack/strike capability with Tomahawk missiles. The provision of the Vertical Launch System (VLS) and the Aegis radar/weapons control system in the BURKE-class ships has further blurred the distinction between the cruiser and destroyer categories.

In the fall of 1996 the Navy had 20 guided missile destroyers (DDG) and 31 ASW destroyers (DD) in commission. This is a considerable reduction from the destroyer force at the end of the Cold War, although destroyer force levels had already been declining in the late 1980s because of the availability of the Aegis cruisers of the TICONDEROGA (CG 47) class. In 1980, for example, the Navy had 80 destroyers in commission; that number declined to 68 in 1988 and to only 57 in 1990 (see appendix A). The six SPRUANCE-class ships without a VLS capability may be retired during the next few years.

The BURKE class is in series production, the only major surface combatant now under construction for the U.S. Navy. The so-called Surface Combatant (SC 21) is now being developed to succeed the BURKE class on the building ways. Although the BURKE class was intended to replace several classes of older cruisers (CG/CGN) and destroyers, the retirement of older ships was accelerated with the end of the Cold War, and the current production rate of just under three ships per year is too low to sustain the force goal of 110 to 116 surface combatants proposed by the Department of Defense in 1995. Rather, the current rate will sustain merely a force of some 90 ships on a long-term basis (i.e., three ships per year with a 30-year service life).

Builders: The BURKE-class ships are being built by the Bath Iron Works in Maine (lead yard) and the Litton/Ingalls Shipbuilding yard at Pascagoula, Mississippi. The keel-laying date for the Ingalls-built ships is defined as the day on which workers start to erect the first module on the horizontal building position at the yard; the ships are lowered into the water on a floating dock (i.e., their launching) and are formally christened at a later date.

Classification: The Aegis program office in the Naval Sea Systems Command has developed its own "baseline" designation scheme for Aegis ships. The following are the principal baseline characteristics for destroyers:

Baseline 4: destroyers DDG 51–67	SPY-1D radar SQS-53C sonar UYK-43/44 computers
Baseline 5: destroyers DDG 68–78	SLQ-32(V)3 EW suite Standard SM-2 Block IV missile JTID[1]
Baseline 6: destroyers DDG 79–	helicopter hangar

Guns: All destroyers have 5-inch (127-mm) guns, the largest weapons now carried in active U.S. Navy warships. The 8-inch (203-mm) Major Caliber Lightweight Gun (MCLWG), at one time proposed for the entire SPRUANCE class, was terminated. The gun was successfully evaluated at sea in the destroyer HULL in 1975–1979. The loss of 16-inch (406-mm) guns with the retirement of the four IOWA (BB 61)-class battleships raised the issue of providing an MCLWG or similar shore-bombardment weapon in the SPRUANCE class. The proposal died rapidly, however, because of the lack of funding.

Names: Destroyers have traditionally been named for naval heroes and leaders, including deceased Secretaries of the Navy, admirals, and inventors.

DESTROYER FORCE LEVELS (FALL 1996)

Number	Class/Ship	Comm.	Active	Building*
DDG 51	ARLEIGH BURKE	1991–	16	18
DDG 993	KIDD	1980–1981	4	—
DD 963	SPRUANCE	1975–1983	31	—

*Includes ships authorized through fiscal 1996.

ADVANCED SURFACE COMBATANT: SC 21 PROGRAM

An advanced surface combatant is being developed to succeed the destroyers of the BURKE class in series production. Designated SC 21 in the development stage, the new ship may be a further modification of the DDG 51 design, possibly the Flight III variant. The Navy plans to request authorization in fiscal 2003 for the lead ship, which is to be completed in 2010. Follow-on ships would be procured at a rate of at least three per year (i.e., the DDG 51 acquisition rate).

The SC 21 is intended to replace the SPRUANCE-class destroyers and TICONDEROGA-class cruisers.

A variety of ship configurations are being considered, with (standard) displacements ranging from 2,000 to 40,000 tons, accord-

1. JTIDS = Joint Tactical Information Distribution System.

This configuration, envisioned by Newport News Shipbuilding, is one of the proposals for the Navy's surface combatant for the 21st century. Forward is a 5-inch gun, a Phalanx CIWS, and a VLS; amidships are Harpoon missiles, RAM launchers, and ASW torpedo tubes (in hull); and af are another Phalanx CIWS, two other CIWS mounts, and facilities for a large multi-purpose helicopter. Note that the ship carries an "F" (frigate) identification letter. (Newport News Shipbuilding)

ing to the SC 21 program officer. Most likely, however, the ship will be at least as large as the Improved BURKE class.

Alternative designs being considered include the LPD 17 (formerly designated LX), a docking-well amphibious ship of some 23,000 tons full load. In place of the docking well the ship would have a large VLS battery and advanced electronics, including an advanced version of the SPY-1 multi-purpose radar.

The SC 21 program replaces the earlier surface combatant program, designated DD(V), that sought to determine the characteristics for a new guided missile destroyer intended for construction beginning with the fiscal 1998 shipbuilding program. In the event, it was decided to continue construction of the BURKE class (Flight IIA) into the 21st century.

IMPROVED "ARLEIGH BURKE" CLASS (FLIGHT III)

The so-called Flight III was a proposed enhancement of the ARLEIGH BURKE design, the principal changes being the provision of a two-helicopter hangar and reduced radar and infrared signatures. This variant would have displaced 10,722 tons full load; weapons and sensors would have been similar to the basic BURKE class except that an improved SPY-1 radar (designated SPY-1E in some publications) was to have been provided.

(21) GUIDED MISSILE DESTROYERS: IMPROVED "ARLEIGH BURKE" CLASS (FLIGHT IIA)

Number	Name	FY	Builder	Laid down	Launch	Christen	Commission	Status
DDG 79	OSCAR AUSTIN	94	Bath Iron Works, Maine	1997	1998	—	2000	Building
DDG 80		95	Litton/Ingalls Shipbuilding	1997	1999	—	2000	Building
DDG 81	WINSTON CHURCHILL	95	Bath Iron Works, Maine	1998	1999	—	2000	Building
DDG 82		95	Litton/Ingalls Shipbuilding	1998	1999	—	2001	Building
DDG 83		96					2002	Building
DDG 84		96					2002	Building
DDG 85		97					2003	Authorized
DDG 86		97					2003	Authorized
DDG 87		97					2003	Authorized
DDG 88		97					2003	Authorized
DDG 89, 90 (2 ships)		98					2004	Planned
DDG 91–93 (3 ships)		99					2005	Planned
DDG 94–96 (3 ships)		2000					2006	Planned
DDG 97–99 (3 ships)		2001					2007	Planned

Displacement:	9,217 tons full load
Length:	509 feet (155.18 m) overall
Beam:	66 11/12 feet (20.4 m)[2]
Draft:	30 7/12 feet (9.3 m)
Propulsion:	4 gas turbines (General Electric LM 2500-30); 100,000 shp; 2 shafts
Speed:	31 knots
Range:	4,400 n.miles (8,150 km) at 20 knots
Manning:	359 (26 officers + 333 enlisted) + LAMPS detachment 21 (6 officers + 15 enlisted)
Helicopters:	2 SH-60R LAMPS III
Missiles:	96-cell VLS for Standard-MR SM-2/Tomahawk/VLA (ASROC) Mk 41 Mod 0
Guns:	1 5-inch (127-mm) 54-cal DP Mk 45 2 20-mm Phalanx CIWS Mk 16 (2 multi-barrel)
ASW weapons:	VLA (ASROC) 6 12.75-inch (324-mm) torpedo tubes Mk 32 (2 triple)
Radars:	SPS-64 navigation SPS-67(V)3 surface search (4) SPY-1D(V) multi-function
Sonars:	SQS-53C bow mounted
Fire control:	3 Mk 99 illuminators with SPG-62 radar 1 Mk 116 ASW control system 1 Mk 160 GFCS SQQ-89(V) ASW system SWG-3 weapon control system (Tomahawk)
EW systems:	SLQ-25A Nixie SLQ-32(V)3

These are improved ARLEIGH BURKE-class ships, the most significant differences being six additional vertical launch missile cells and full facilities for supporting two SH-60B Seahawk helicopters. The Flight IIA ships are larger, however, and do not have Harpoon canisters (as do all other active cruisers and destroyers).

The ships are being constructed at the rate of just under three ships per year; that rate was determined in January 1995 when Secretary of Defense William Perry announced that the fiscal 1996–2001 shipbuilding plan would provide 16 ships instead of the 18 previously proposed, resulting in an expected saving of $2.1 *billion.*

Assuming that construction of the SC 21 design is initiated in 2003, the Navy would probably acquire 23 Improved BURKE-class ships through fiscal 2002, plus possibly another couple of ships in fiscal 2003–2004 as the SC 21 program gets under way.

These ships may be configured for the Theater Ballistic Missile Defense (TBMD) role.

Design: In addition to the supplementary VLS cells and helicopter facility, the Flight IIA ships have the two after SPY-1 radar "faces" mounted one deck (8 feet/2.4 m) higher than in the earlier ships to improve line-of-sight performance over the after end of the ship. The after superstructure will be extended to accommodate the dual hangar, and the transom will also be extended—accounting for the greater length—to accommodate the stern helicopter deck.

Electronics: Beginning with the DDG 79, the SPY-1D radar will be a modified variant to enhance performance in littoral areas (i.e., against background land clutter).

The SQS-53C sonar will be fitted with the Kingfisher modification for mine detection.

The SQR-19 TACTAS towed array found in earlier ships will not be fitted in these ships, although it could be "reconstituted" if necessary.

Helicopters: The Recovery Assist, Secure, and Traverse (RAST) system will be fitted in these ships. The helicopter hangar doors will be of an accordion type, folding upward.

Missiles: The self-loading feature of the two VLS batteries will be deleted in these ships, permitting 32 VLS cells forward and 64 cells aft for a total of 96 weapons (or more if multiple rounds are fitted in a single cell; see chapter 30).

The eight-canister Harpoon missile battery found in all other U.S. cruisers and destroyers are expected to be deleted from these ships as a weight-saving measure. However, they could be mounted at a future date, between the funnels.

2. The beam at waterline is 59 feet (18.0 m).

An artist's concept of the Flight IIA of the Arleigh Burke design. This ship has six additional VLS missile cells and—most significant—facilities to support two SH-60 LAMPS III helicopters. (Gibbs and Cox)

16 + 12 GUIDED MISSILE DESTROYERS: "ARLEIGH BURKE" CLASS (FLIGHTS I/II)

Number	Name	FY	Builder	Laid down	Launched	Christened	Commissioned	Status
DDG 51	Arleigh Burke	85	Bath Iron Works, Maine	31 July 1986	16 Sep 1989	—	4 July 1991	**AA**
DDG 52	Barry	87	Litton/Ingalls Shipbuilding	26 Feb 1990	10 May 1991	8 June 1991	12 Dec 1992	**AA**
DDG 53	John Paul Jones	87	Bath Iron Works, Maine	8 Aug 1990	26 Oct 1991	—	18 Dec 1993	**PA**
DDG 54	Curtis Wilbur	89	Bath Iron Works, Maine	12 Mar 1991	16 May 1992	—	19 Mar 1994	**PA**
DDG 55	Stout	89	Litton/Ingalls Shipbuilding	12 Aug 1991	16 Oct 1992	24 Oct 1992	13 Aug 1994	**AA**
DDG 56	John S. McCain	89	Bath Iron Works, Maine	3 Sep 1991	26 Sep 1992	—	2 July 1994	**PA**
DDG 57	Mitscher	89	Litton/Ingalls Shipbuilding	12 Feb 1992	7 May 1993	15 May 1993	10 Dec 1994	**AA**
DDG 58	Laboon	89	Bath Iron Works, Maine	24 Mar 1992	20 Feb 1993	—	18 Mar 1995	**AA**
DDG 59	Russell	90	Litton/Ingalls Shipbuilding	24 July 1992	20 Oct 1993	23 Oct 1993	20 May 1995	**PA**
DDG 60	Paul Hamilton	90	Bath Iron Works, Maine	24 Aug 1992	24 July 1993	—	27 May 1995	**PA**
DDG 61	Ramage	90	Litton/Ingalls Shipbuilding	4 Jan 1993	11 Feb 1994	23 Apr 1994	22 July 1995	**AA**
DDG 62	Fitzgerald	90	Bath Iron Works, Maine	9 Feb 1993	29 Jan 1994	—	14 Oct 1995	**PA**
DDG 63	Stethem	90	Litton/Ingalls Shipbuilding	10 May 1993	17 June 1994	16 July 1994	21 Oct 1995	**PA**
DDG 64	Carney	91	Bath Iron Works, Maine	3 Aug 1993	23 July 1994	—	13 Apr 1996	**AA**
DDG 65	Benfold	91	Litton/Ingalls Shipbuilding	27 Sep 1993	19 Nov 1994	12 Nov 1994	30 Mar 1996	**PA**
DDG 66	Gonzalez	91	Bath Iron Works, Maine	3 Feb 1994	18 Feb 1995	—	1996	Building
DDG 67	Cole	91	Litton/Ingalls Shipbuilding	28 Feb 1994	10 Feb 1995	8 Apr 1995	June 1996	**AA**
DDG 68	The Sullivans	92	Bath Iron Works, Maine	27 July 1994	12 Aug 1995	—	1997	Building
DDG 69	Milius	92	Litton/Ingalls Shipbuilding	8 Aug 1994	1 Aug 1995	1 Aug 1995	1996	Building
DDG 70	Hopper	92	Bath Iron Works, Maine	23 Feb 1995	6 Jan 1996	—	1997	Building
DDG 71	Ross	92	Litton/Ingalls Shipbuilding	10 Apr 1995	23 Mar 1996	23 Mar 1996	1997	Building
DDG 72	Mahan	92	Bath Iron Works, Maine	17 Aug 1995	1996	—	1997	Building
DDG 73	Decatur	93	Bath Iron Works, Maine	1996	1996	—	1998	Building
DDG 74	McFaul	93	Litton/Ingalls Shipbuilding	12 Feb 1996	1997		1998	Building
DDG 75	Donald Cook	93	Bath Iron Works, Maine	1996	1997	—	1998	Building
DDG 76	Higgins	93	Bath Iron Works, Maine	1996	1997	—	1999	Building
DDG 77	O'Kane	94	Bath Iron Works, Maine	1997	1998	—	1999	Building
DDG 78	Porter	94	Litton/Ingalls Shipbuilding	1997	1998		1999	Building

Displacement:	DDG 51 6,624 tons light
	later units 6,682 tons light
	DDG 51 8,315 tons full load
	later units 8,373 tons full load
Length:	465 5/6 feet (142.0 m) waterline
	504 1/3 feet (153.8 m) overall
Beam:	66 11/12 feet (20.4 m)[3]
Draft:	30 7/12 feet (9.3 m)
Propulsion:	4 gas turbines (General Electric LM 2500-30); 100,000 shp; 2 shafts
Speed:	31 knots
Range:	4,400 n.miles (8,150 km) at 20 knots
Manning:	DDG 51–53 316 (21 officers + 295 enlisted)
	later units 337 (22 officers + 315 enlisted)
	+ LAMPS detachment 21 (6 officers + 15 enlisted)
Helicopters:	landing deck only

Missiles:	90-cell VLS for Standard-MR SM-2/Tomahawk/VLA (ASROC) Mk 41 Mod 0
	8 Harpoon SSM Mk 141 (2 quad canisters)
Guns:	1 5-inch (127-mm) 54-cal DP Mk 45
	2 20-mm Phalanx CIWS Mk 16 (2 multi-barrel)
ASW weapons:	VLA (ASROC)
	6 12.75-inch (324-mm) torpedo tubes Mk 32 (2 triple)
Radars:	1 SPS-64(V)9 navigation
	1 SPS-67(V)3 surface search
	(4) SPY-1D multi-function
Sonars:	SQS-53C bow mounted
	SQR-19 TACTAS towed array
Fire control:	3 Mk 99 illuminators with SPG-62 radar
	1 Mk 116 ASW control system
	1 Mk 160 GFCS
	SQQ-89(V)4 ASW system
	SWG-3 weapon control system (Tomahawk)
EW systems:	SLQ-25A Nixie
	SLQ-32(V)2 in DDG 51–67
	SLQ-32(V)3 in DDG 68–78

3. The beam at waterline is 59 feet (18.0 m).

These destroyers emphasize AAW capabilities and are intended to complement Aegis cruisers of the TICONDEROGA class in the air/missile defense of carrier battle groups. Initial plans for a more advanced radar and propulsion plant for these ships were dropped in favor of the propulsion plant in the CG 47/DDG 993/DD 963 classes and a derivative of the CG 47 Aegis radar.

The production DDG 51 units were planned to cost approximately 75 percent of a CG 47-class cruiser. The significant differences in the weapon and sensor for the DDG 51 from the CG 47 are:

- three vice four missile illuminators
- 90 vice 122 VLS missiles
- no helicopter hangar
- no AAW commander/coordination facilities

The lead ship of the class was completed 21 months behind schedule, the original contract with Bath Iron Works requiring delivery in October 1989. The Navy states that the delays were caused by: (1) a 90-day labor strike at Bath Iron Works; (2) corrections to government-furnished information for the main reduction gear; (3) Navy changes to engine room piping; (4) extension of the combat system testing program; and (5) limitations of Bath's design and production capacity.

Builders: In the late 1980s Congress attempted to open construction of the BURKE class to a third shipyard, the most probable candidates being Todd Pacific Shipyards at Long Beach, California, and Avondale Shipyards, New Orleans, Louisiana. Because of the low production rate that was envisioned at that time, the Navy limited construction to two yards.

Class: Original Navy planning provided for 50 to 60 advanced missile destroyers to be authorized in fiscal 1985–1994 to replace about the same number of older cruisers and destroyers. The Carter administration proposed the construction of 49 ships of this class, while the Reagan administration initially (1981) envisioned a program of 63 ships. It now appears that the basic Flight I/II ships will total 28 units, followed by the Flight IIA ships.

The DDG 51–67 are known as Flight I ships, and the DDG 68–78 are designated Flight II. The later ships have a number of combat capability improvements such as the Joint Tactical Information Distribution System (JTIDS), Tactical Data Information Exchange (TADIX) subsystem, the upgraded SLQ-32(V)3, and the Standard-MR Block IV missile. The later ships will also have the ability to refuel and rearm helicopters (see below).

The Japanese KONGO-class destroyers, being fitted with the Aegis/VLS system, have a similar configuration, but they are smaller.

The ninth ARLEIGH BURKE-class destroyer, the RUSSELL, at sea. Note the broad beam and the angled superstructure and funnels, the latter feature intended to reduce the ship's radar cross section. Unfortunately, the mast, the Phalanx CIWS, and other projections enhance radar returns. (1995, Litton/Ingalls Shipbuilding)

Four ships have been funded (the first completed in 1993) and four additional ships have been proposed.

Classification: The initial Navy study conducted in 1979, which led to the preliminary design of this ship, used the designation DDX and subsequently DDGX. Of the various design/capability options developed in the study, sub-type 3A was selected for development as the DDG 51.

Cost: Early cost estimates stipulated $550 million per ship (FY 1982 dollars) for the 6,000-ton ship in series production. In February 1983 the Secretary of the Navy established a cost ceiling of $1.1 *billion* for the lead ship and $700 million each for ships no. 6 through 10. In early 1987 the Navy estimated that in FY 1983 dollars, the lead ship would cost $1.048 *billion* and the later ships $677 million.

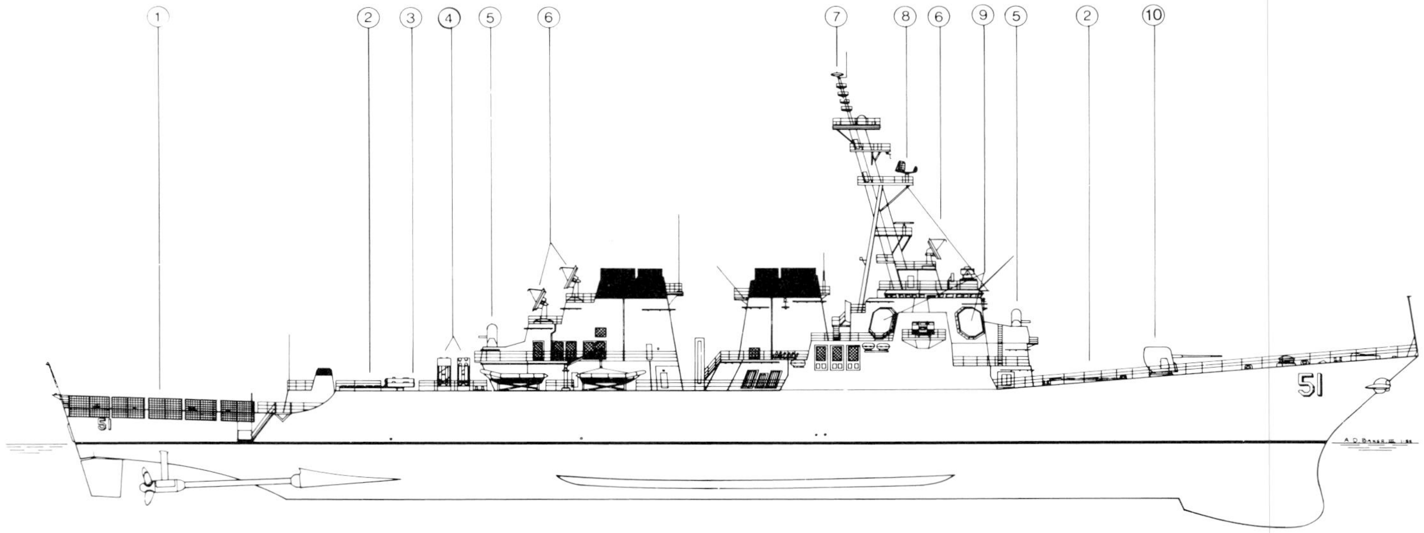

ARLEIGH BURKE
1. Helicopter deck. 2. Vertical-launch system Mk 41. 3. 12.75-inch triple torpedo tubes Mk 32 (2). 4. Harpoon missile canisters (8 missiles). 5. Phalanx CIWS (2). 6. SPG-62 radar illuminators (3). 7. URN-20 TACAN. 8. SPS-67(V)3 search radar (above SPS-64(V)9 navigation radar). 9. SPY-1D fixed radar (4). 10. 5-inch DP gun Mk 45. (A. D. Baker III)

The costs for current ships are (in millions):

	Ship cost	*Outfitting*	*Post delivery*
FY 1996 ships	$1,084.6 M	$30.7 M	$44.6 M
FY 1997 ships	$ 952.4 M	$20.1 M	$20.3 M

Design: From the outset these ships were directed by the Chief of Naval Operations to be smaller and less expensive than the DDG/CG 47 design. Early design concepts envisioned a ship with a full-load displacement as small as 6,000 tons.

These are the first U.S. destroyers of post–World War II construction to have steel superstructures. That decision was made as a result of the cruiser BELKNAP (CG 26) colliding with an aircraft carrier in 1975 (*not* after the loss of a British destroyer to an Argentine-launched Exocet air-to-surface missile in the 1982 conflict in the Falklands). The steel construction provides increased resistance to blast overpressure and fragment and fire damage, plus Electromagnetic Pulse (EMP) protection. The ships have 130 tons of Kevlar armor plating to protect vital spaces.

This is the first class of U.S. Navy ships to be built with the so-called Level III collective protection features against Chemical-Biological-Radiological (CBR) attack. This provides the maximum protection possible within a ship, including berthing, medical, and control spaces. (The second class to be so fitted is the SUPPLY/AOE 6 class.)

The ships have been designed with a significantly reduced radar cross section over previous destroyer-type ships.

Early designs provided for a 61-foot (18.6-m) beam; it was subsequently reduced to 59 feet (18 m).

Electronics: A derivative of the CG 47 Aegis system is provided, with all four SPY-1D radar "faces" mounted on a single, forward deckhouse.

Engineering: Essentially the same propulsion plant as in the CG 47/DD 963/DDG 997 classes is fitted in this class. At congressional urging, the Navy looked into the possibility of the Rankin regenerative system to enhance the efficiency of the gas turbines, but that system was found to require too much internal volume to be practical for the class.

The BURKE reportedly attained 32 knots on sea trials, with 103,000 shp. The sustained horsepower for these ships is approximately 90,000 shp.

Guns: The original DDGX proposal called for a gun armament of only two Phalanx CIWS. Subsequently, a single 76-mm OTO Malera Mk 75 gun was provided in the design and later the single 5-inch/54-cal Mk 45 was dictated, in addition to the two CIWS.

Helicopters: These ships have a large helicopter landing area on their fantail and a VERTREP position forward; however, no hangar is provided, and helicopters will not normally be deployed in these ships. The DDG 52 and later ships have the RAST haul-down system plus helicopter refueling and rearming capabilities (adding 58 tons to full-load displacement).

Manning: The BENFOLD is the first U.S. Navy ship being built with certain living spaces specifically designed to accommodate female crew members. An estimated 46 of the ship's crew will be female.

Names: In 1983 the not-yet-started DDG 51 was named for Admiral Arleigh Burke, Chief of Naval Operations from 1955 to 1961. This was the second U.S. ship to be named in recent years for a living person, the first being the CARL VINSON (CVN 70).

The DDG 52 was originally named JOHN BARRY. The name was changed to BARRY on 1 February 1988, back to JOHN BARRY on 9 May 1988, and again back to BARRY on 8 December 1989—further testimony to the confusion in the U.S. Navy ship-naming process. (Correction to previous edition.)

The DDG 68 is named for the five Sullivan Brothers who were killed on 12–13 November 1942 when the light cruiser JUNEAU (CLAA 52) was sunk by Japanese forces. Only 10 men from a crew of 700 survived. The destroyer DD 537 previously carried the name.

Detail of the BARRY's bridge structure and forward funnel. Note the insignificant appearance of the forward VLS; the placement of the visible SPY-1D radar antenna; and the location of the port-side SLQ-32(V)2 EW antenna array (i.e., below the bridge). (1993, Giorgio Arra)

Stern aspect of the BARRY showing the openings for the SLQ-25 Nixie towed torpedo countermeasures (right) and the SQR-19 TACTAS towed array (center). The port-side, aft-facing SPY-1D radar can also be seen. (1993, Giorgio Arra)

The BARRY at high speeds shows the attractive, almost rakish, lines of the ARLEIGH BURKE class. These were the first U.S. destroyers (DD/DDG) to have been built with a single 5-inch gun mount. (1993, Giorgio Arra)

4 GUIDED MISSILE DESTROYERS: "KIDD" CLASS (FORMER IRANIAN SHIPS)

Number	Name	FY	Builder	Laid down	Launched	Christened	Commissioned	Status
DDG 993	KIDD	79S	Litton/Ingalls Shipbuilding	26 June 1978	11 Aug 1979	13 Oct 1979	27 July 1981	**AA**
DDG 994	CALLAGHAN	79S	Litton/Ingalls Shipbuilding	23 Oct 1978	1 Dec 1979	19 Jan 1980	29 Aug 1981	**PA**
DDG 995	SCOTT	79S	Litton/Ingalls Shipbuilding	12 Feb 1979	1 Mar 1980	29 Mar 1980	24 Oct 1981	**AA**
DDG 996	CHANDLER	79S	Litton/Ingalls Shipbuilding	7 May 1979	24 May 1980	24 May 1980	13 Mar 1982	**PA**

Displacement: 6,950 tons light
9,574 tons full load
Length: $528\frac{5}{6}$ feet (161.2 m) waterline
$563\frac{1}{3}$ feet (171.8 m) overall
Beam: 55 feet (16.8)
Draft: 33 feet (10.1 m)
Propulsion: 4 gas turbines (General Electric LM 2500); 86,000 shp; 2 shafts
Speed: 30+ knots
Range: 6,000 n.miles (11,112 km) at 20 knots
3,300 n.miles (6,112 km) at 30 knots
Manning: 331 (21 officers + 310 enlisted)
Helicopters: removed
Missiles: 2 twin Mk 26 Mod 0/1 launchers for Standard-ER SM-2 SAM/ASROC (68 weapons)
8 Harpoon SSM Mk 141 (2 quad canisters)
Guns: 2 5-inch (127-mm) 54-cal DP Mk 45 (2 single)
2 20-mm Phalanx CIWS Mk 16 (2 multi-barrel)
ASW weapons: ASROC fired from forward Mk 26 launcher
6 12.75-inch (324-mm) torpedo tubes Mk 32 (2 triple)
Radars: SPS-48E 3-D air search
SPS-49(V)5 air search
SPS-55 surface search
SPS-64(V)9 navigation
Sonars: SQS-53A bow mounted
Fire control: 1 Mk 14 weapon direction system
2 Mk 74 missile FCS with SPG-51D radars
1 Mk 86 GFCS with SPG-60 and SPQ-9A radars
1 Mk 116 ASW FCS
1 SYS-2 weapon control system
EW systems: SLQ-25 Nixie
SLQ-32(V)5 with Sidekick jammer

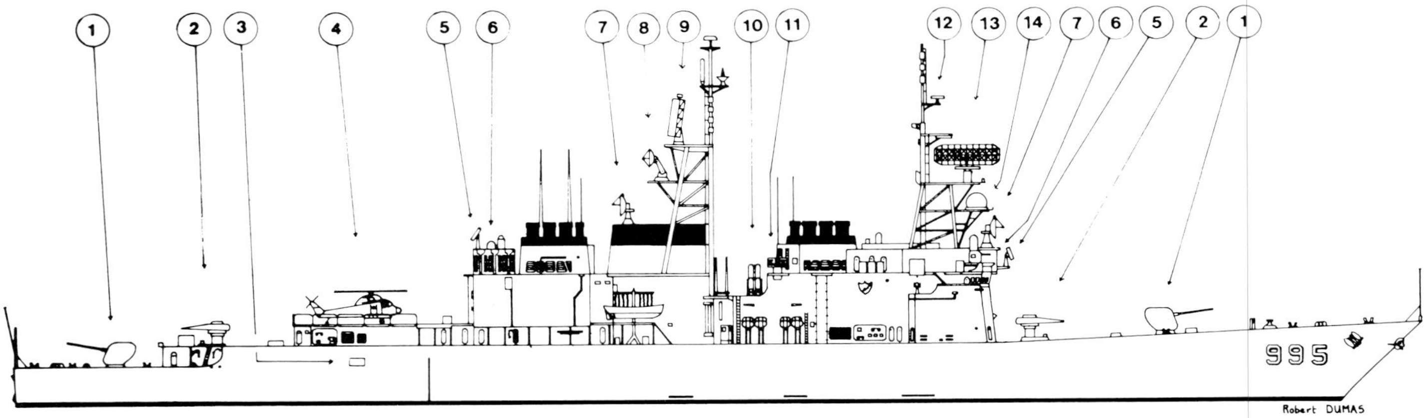

SCOTT (KIDD class)
1. 5-inch DP gun Mk 45. 2. Surface-to-air missile launchers Mk 26 (2). 3. 12.75-inch triple torpedo tubes Mk 32 (2). 4. SH-2F LAMPS I helicopter. 5. OE-82 Satellite antennas (2). 6. Phalanx CIWS (2; after mount to port side of gas turbine intake structure). 7. SPG-51D radar illuminator (2). 8. SPG-60 gun/missile fire-control radar. 9. SPS-48E air search radar. 10. Harpoon missile canisters (8 missiles). 11. SLQ-32(V)5 EW antenna (2). 12. SPS-55 surface search radar. 13. SPS-49(V)5 surface search radar. 14. SPQ-9A gun fire-control radar. (Robert Dumas)

These were the most capable destroyers in U.S. service prior to the advent of the BURKE class, being the guided missile variant of the SPRUANCE class. However, the KIDD design provided considerably more ASW capability prior to the removal of the LAMPS helicopters.

The four ships were ordered by the government of the Shah of Iran, which fell in 1979. Subsequently, the U.S. Navy sought to acquire these ships, which were then under construction. The FY 1979 supplemental budget provided $1.353 *billion* for the purchase of these ships, and they were formally acquired on 24 July 1979.

The ships differ from the contemporary CG 47 Aegis cruisers primarily in not having the Aegis/SPY-1A AAW system.

All have been modernized to the equivalent of the New Threat Upgrade (NTU) configuration.

Class: The Iranian government announced plans to order two AAW ships based on the SPRUANCE design on 15 December 1973; they announced their intention to procure four additional ships on 27 August 1974. Two ships were canceled in June 1976. Four ships were ordered on 23 March 1978 under the U.S. foreign military sales program.

Classification: These ships were originally ordered as the DD 993, 994, 996, and 998, respectively, indicating that they were basically SPRUANCE-class ships. (Correction to previous edition.) They were changed to DDG, bearing the same non-missile hull numbers, on 8 August 1979.

Design: The original SPRUANCE-destroyer concept consisted of a missile-armed variant (designated DXG) as well as the basic ASW ship (DX). These are the only ships that were built to the DXG design, none having been ordered for the U.S. Navy.

The Iranian government required that these ships be provided with increased air-conditioning capacity and dust separators for their engine air intakes. See SPRUANCE class for additional notes.

Electronics: The SQR-19A TACTAS towed-array sonar was considered for these ships; it is unlikely that it will be installed, however, because of funding constraints.

Helicopters: The ship's configuration provides for two SH-60B LAMPS III helicopters to be embarked, but only one SH-2F has been assigned to these ships, and that was removed in 1994 when that helicopter was phased out of the fleet. It is unlikely that these ships will be fitted with the SH-60B helicopter, as was once planned.

Missiles: The Mk 26 Mod 0 missile launcher installed forward was provided with a smaller (24-missile) magazine than the after Mk 26 Mod 1 launcher to provide space for possible installation of the 8-inch Mk 71 gun in place of the existing 5-inch gun. The after 44-missile magazine is used for ASROCs in these ships.

Modernization: The SCOTT completed the NTU modernization in March 1988, KIDD in September 1989, CALLAGHAN in July 1990, and CHANDLER in August 1990.

Names: See page 135 for Iranian names assigned to these ships.

Details of the KIDD's superstructure show the large SPS-49 air search radar on the forward mast, a feature absent from the similar SPRUANCE-class destroyers. These ships have an SPS-48E radar on the after mast in lieu of the SPS-40 of the non-missile ships. (1990, Giorgio Arra)

The KIDD head-on shows the stem anchor of ships fitted with the large SQS-26/53 bow-mounted sonar. An OE-82 satellite antenna is adjacent to the forward SPG-51D radar (below the spherical SPQ-9A radar). (1990, Giorgio Arra)

The KIDD at sea with Standard missiles on her forward and after Mk 26 launchers and a now-discarded SH-2F LAMPS I helicopter on the flight deck. The U.S. Navy had planned to build similar ships, but in the event, only the four ships ordered by Iran were constructed and acquired by the U.S. Navy. (1990, Giorgio Arra)

The KIDD is shown here with her two stern openings (starboard side) for the SLQ-25 Nixie closed over to stop seas from entering. The after Phalanx CIWS is on the port side; the forward CIWS is on the starboard side. With the demise of the SH-2F helicopter, these ships lack an effective ASW capability. (1990, Giorgio Arra)

GUIDED MISSILE DESTROYERS: "CHARLES F. ADAMS" CLASS

Number	Name	Comm.	Status
DDG 2	Charles F. Adams	1960	decomm./stricken 20 Nov 1992
DDG 3	John King	1961	decomm. 30 Mar 1990; stricken 12 Jan 1993
DDG 4	Lawrence	1962	decomm. 30 Mar 1990; stricken 16 May 1990
DDG 5	Claude V. Ricketts	1962	decomm. 31 Oct 1989; stricken 1 June 1990
DDG 6	Barney	1962	decomm. 17 Dec 1990; stricken 20 Nov 1992
DDG 7	Henry B. Wilson	1960	decomm. 2 Oct 1989; stricken 26 Jan 1990
DDG 8	Lynde McCormick	1961	decomm. 1 Oct 1991; stricken 20 Nov 1992
DDG 9	Towers	1961	decomm. 1 Oct 1990; stricken 1 Oct 1990
DDG 10	Sampson	1961	decomm. 24 June 1991; stricken 20 Nov 1992
DDG 11	Sellers	1961	decomm. 31 Oct 1989; stricken 20 Nov 1992
DDG 12	Robison	1961	decomm. 1 Oct 1991; stricken 20 Nov 1992
DDG 13	Hoel	1962	decomm. 1 Oct 1990; stricken 20 Nov 1992
DDG 14	Buchanan	1962	decomm. 1 Oct 1991; stricken 20 Nov 1992
DDG 15	Berkeley	1962	decomm. 1 May 1992; to Greece 30 Sep 1992
DDG 16	Joseph Strauss	1963	decomm. 1 Feb 1990; to Greece 1 Oct 1991
DDG 17	Conyngham	1963	decomm. 29 Oct 1990; stricken 30 May 1991
DDG 18	Semmes	1962	decomm. 12 Sep 1991; to Greece 12 Sep 1991
DDG 19	Tattnal	1963	decomm. 18 Jan 1991; stricken 12 June 1993
DDG 20	Goldsborough	1963	decomm./stricken 29 Apr 1993; to Australia 17 Sep 1993
DDG 21	Cochrane	1964	decomm. 1 Oct 1990; stricken 20 Nov 1992
DDG 22	Benjamin Stoddert	1964	decomm. 20 Dec 1991; stricken 20 Nov 1992
DDG 23	Richard E. Byrd	1964	decomm. 27 Apr 1990; to Greece 1 Oct 1991
DDG 24	Waddell	1964	decomm. 1 Oct 1992; to Greece 1 Oct 1992

This large class of Tartar-armed missile destroyers was decommissioned and stricken immediately after the Cold War ended. They were highly capable destroyers for their relatively small size, although they lacked helicopter facilities. Numerically, this was the largest class of missile-armed surface warships to be constructed for the U.S. Navy prior to the Oliver Hazard Perry (FFG 7) class. The Conyngham suffered a major fire off the Virginia Capes on 8 May 1990; the ship was not repaired (one officer was killed).

Class: Three additional ships of this class were built for Australia (assigned U.S. hull numbers DDG 25–27) and three for West Germany (DDG 28–30).

After being decommissioned from U.S. service, four ships were transferred to Greece; three for service and the DDG 23 for spare parts. The last of these guided missile destroyers was stricken from the Naval Vessel Register on 1 October 1992. The DDG 20 was transferred to Australia for spare parts.

Classification: The first eight ships of this class were authorized as all-gun/ASW destroyers (DD 952–959); they were changed to guided missile ships and reclassified DDG 952–959 on 16 August 1956; they were changed again on 26 June 1957 to DDG 2–9.

Design: The Adams design was based on an improved Forrest Sherman arrangement, with a Tartar missile launching system in place of the Sherman's aftermost 5-inch gun. The last five ships have their sonar in the improved, bow position.

See 15th Edition/pages 133–35 for characteristics.

GUIDED MISSILE DESTROYERS: "FARRAGUT" CLASS

Number	Name	Comm.	Notes
DDG 37	Farragut	1960	decomm. 31 Oct 1989; stricken 20 Nov 1992
DDG 38	Luce	1961	decomm. 1 Apr 1991; stricken 20 Nov 1992
DDG 39	MacDonough	1961	decomm. 23 Oct 1992; stricken 30 Nov 1992
DDG 40	Coontz	1960	decomm. 2 Oct 1989; stricken 6 May 1993
DDG 41	King	1960	decomm. 28 Mar 1991; stricken 20 Nov 1992
DDG 42	Mahan	1960	decomm. 15 June 1993; stricken 15 June 1993
DDG 43	Dahlgren	1961	decomm. 31 July 1992; stricken 20 Nov 1992
DDG 44	William V. Pratt	1961	decomm. 30 Sep 1991; stricken 20 Nov 1992
DDG 45	Dewey	1959	decomm. 31 Aug 1990; stricken 20 Nov 1992
DDG 46	Preble	1960	decomm. 15 Nov 1991; stricken 20 Nov 1992

These ships were built as "single-end" guided missile frigates (DLG) armed with the Terrier/Standard-ER missile. All were decommissioned and stricken following the end of the Cold War. Although effective AAW ships, they lacked a helicopter capability.

Class: These ships are also referred to as the Coontz class, that ship being the first ordered with the DLG designation.

Classification: The first three ships of this class were ordered on 27 January 1956 as all-gun frigates (DL 6–8); they were changed to guided missile frigates (DLG 6–8) on 14 November 1956.

All ten ships were classified as DLG (6–15) from the time of their commissioning until 30 June 1975, when they were changed to guided missile destroyers (DDG 37–46).

See 15th Edition/pages 131–32 for characteristics.

The Decatur, having been discarded after service as a fleet destroyer (DD 936) and guided missile destroyer (DDG 31), is making a comeback as a demonstration platform for self-defense systems. A helicopter deck is aft, something not found when the Forrest Sherman-class destroyers were in the fleet. (U.S. Navy)

31 DESTROYERS: "SPRUANCE" CLASS

Number	Name	FY	Builder	Laid down	Launched	Commissioned	Status
DD 963	Spruance	70	Litton/Ingalls, Pascagoula, Miss.	27 Nov 1972	10 Nov 1973	20 Sep 1975	AA
DD 964	Paul F. Foster	70	Litton/Ingalls, Pascagoula, Miss.	6 Feb 1973	23 Feb 1974	21 Feb 1975	PA
DD 965	Kinkaid	70	Litton/Ingalls, Pascagoula, Miss.	19 Apr 1973	25 May 1974	10 July 1976	PA
DD 966	Hewitt	71	Litton/Ingalls, Pascagoula, Miss.	23 July 1973	24 Aug 1974	25 Sep 1976	PA
DD 967	Elliot	71	Litton/Ingalls, Pascagoula, Miss.	15 Oct 1973	19 Dec 1974	22 Jan 1977	PA
DD 968	Arthur W. Radford	71	Litton/Ingalls, Pascagoula, Miss.	14 Jan 1974	1 Mar 1975	16 Apr 1977	AA
DD 969	Peterson	71	Litton/Ingalls, Pascagoula, Miss.	29 Apr 1974	21 June 1975	9 July 1977	AA
DD 970	Caron	71	Litton/Ingalls, Pascagoula, Miss.	1 July 1974	24 June 1975	1 Oct 1977	AA
DD 971	David R. Ray	71	Litton/Ingalls, Pascagoula, Miss.	23 Sep 1974	23 Aug 1975	19 Nov 1977	PA
DD 972	Oldendorf	72	Litton/Ingalls, Pascagoula, Miss.	27 Dec 1974	21 Oct 1975	4 Mar 1978	PA
DD 973	John Young	72	Litton/Ingalls, Pascagoula, Miss.	17 Feb 1975	7 Feb 1976	20 May 1978	PA
DD 974	Comte De Grasse	72	Litton/Ingalls, Pascagoula, Miss.	4 Apr 1975	26 Mar 1976	5 Aug 1978	AA
DD 975	O'Brien	72	Litton/Ingalls, Pascagoula, Miss.	9 May 1975	8 July 1976	3 Dec 1977	PA
DD 976	Merrill	72	Litton/Ingalls, Pascagoula, Miss.	16 June 1975	1 Sep 1976	11 Mar 1978	PA
DD 977	Briscoe	72	Litton/Ingalls, Pascagoula, Miss.	21 July 1975	18 Dec 1976	3 June 1978	AA
DD 978	Stump	72	Litton/Ingalls, Pascagoula, Miss.	22 Aug 1975	21 Mar 1977	19 Aug 1978	AA
DD 979	Conolly	74	Litton/Ingalls, Pascagoula, Miss.	29 Sep 1975	3 June 1977	14 Oct 1978	AA
DD 980	Moosbrugger	74	Litton/Ingalls, Pascagoula, Miss.	3 Nov 1975	23 July 1977	16 Dec 1978	AA
DD 981	John Hancock	74	Litton/Ingalls, Pascagoula, Miss.	16 Jan 1976	28 Sep 1977	10 Mar 1979	AA
DD 982	Nicholson	74	Litton/Ingalls, Pascagoula, Miss.	20 Feb 1976	29 Nov 1977	12 May 1979	AA
DD 983	John Rodgers	74	Litton/Ingalls, Pascagoula, Miss.	12 Aug 1976	25 Feb 1978	14 July 1979	AA
DD 984	Leftwich	74	Litton/Ingalls, Pascagoula, Miss.	12 Nov 1976	8 Apr 1978	25 Aug 1979	PA
DD 985	Cushing	74	Litton/Ingalls, Pascagoula, Miss.	2 Feb 1977	17 June 1978	20 Oct 1979	PA
DD 986	Harry W. Hill	75	Litton/Ingalls, Pascagoula, Miss.	1 Apr 1977	10 Aug 1978	17 Nov 1979	PA
DD 987	O'Bannon	75	Litton/Ingalls, Pascagoula, Miss.	24 June 1977	25 Sep 1978	15 Dec 1979	AA
DD 988	Thorn	75	Litton/Ingalls, Pascagoula, Miss.	29 Aug 1977	14 Nov 1978	16 Feb 1980	AA
DD 989	Deyo	75	Litton/Ingalls, Pascagoula, Miss.	14 Oct 1977	20 Jan 1979	22 Mar 1980	AA
DD 990	Ingersoll	75	Litton/Ingalls, Pascagoula, Miss.	16 Dec 1977	10 Mar 1979	12 Apr 1980	PA
DD 991	Fife	75	Litton/Ingalls, Pascagoula, Miss.	6 Mar 1978	1 May 1979	31 May 1980	PA
DD 992	Fletcher	75	Litton/Ingalls, Pascagoula, Miss.	24 Apr 1978	16 June 1979	12 July 1980	PA
DD 997	Hayler	78	Litton/Ingalls, Pascagoula, Miss.	22 Oct 1980	27 Mar 1982	5 Mar 1983	AA

Displacement: 6,156 tons light
8,280 tons full load
Length: 528 11/12 feet (161.25 m) waterline
563 1/6 feet (171.7 m) overall
Beam: 55 feet (16.8 m)
Draft: 29 feet (8.8 m)
Propulsion: 4 gas turbines (General Electric LM 2500); 86,000 shp; 2 shafts
Speed: 32.5 knots
Range: 6,000 n.miles (11,112 km) at 20 knots
3,300 n.miles (6,112 km) at 30 knots
Manning: approx. 325 (21 officers + 304 enlisted) (see *Manning* notes)
+ LAMPS detachment 21 (6 officers + 15 enlisted)
Helicopters: 2 SH-60B Seahawk LAMPS III
Missiles: 1 8-tube NATO Sea Sparrow launcher Mk 29
8 Harpoon SSM Mk 141 (2 quad canisters)
8 Tomahawk TASM/TLAM Mk 143 (2 quad ABL) in DD 974, 976, 979, 983, 984, 989, 990 (7 ships)
61-cell VLS for Tomahawk/VLA(ASROC) Mk 41 Mod 0 in 24 ships
Guns: 2 5-inch (127-mm) 54-cal DP Mk 45 (2 single)
2 20-mm Phalanx CIWS Mk 16 (2 multi-barrel)

ASW weapons: ASROC launcher Mk 16 (removed)
6 12.75-inch (324-mm) torpedo tubes Mk 32 (2 triple)
Radars: Mk 23 Target Acquisition System (TAS) in most ships
SPS-40B/C/D/E air search except SPS-49(V)2 in DD 997
SPS-53 or SPS-64(V)9 or LN-66 navigation
SPS-55 surface search
Sonars: SQS-53B bow mounted except SQS-53C in DD 978
SQR-19A/B TACTAS towed array in most ships
Fire control: 1 Mk 86 GFCS with SPG-60 and SPQ-9A radars
1 Mk 91 missile FCS
1 Mk 116 ASW FCS
SQQ-89(V)1 ASW system
SWG-2 weapon control system (Tomahawk) in ships with ABL
SWG-3 weapon control system (Tomahawk) in ships with VLS
EW systems: SLQ-25 Nixie
SLQ-32(V)2 except SLQ-32(V)5 with Sidekick jammer in DD 969, 973, 976–979, 983, 997 (8 ships)
SLQ-34 combat DF in 16 ships

The Spruances were originally built as specialized ASW ships. The Harpoon missile gives them an anti-ship capability; the Tomahawk missile gives them a long-range anti-ship/land-attack capability.

The four Kidd-class missile destroyers and Ticonderoga-class missile cruisers have the same hull, propulsion, and auxiliary systems. The Spruance class represents the largest destroyer class built by any Western navy since World War II.

The Hewitt and O'Brien are homeported in Yokosuka, Japan, the only U.S. destroyers based in another country. They are part of the Independence (CV 62) carrier battle group.

Builders: The entire Spruance class was contracted with a single shipyard to facilitate design and mass production. A contract for the development and production of 30 ships was awarded on 23 June 1970 to a new yard established by the Ingalls Shipbuilding Division of Litton Industries at Pascagoula, Mississippi. Labor and technical problems delayed the construction of these ships. The 31st ship was placed under contract in 1979 (see *Class* notes).

Class: The Spruance-class destroyers were developed as replacements for the large number of World War II–built general purpose destroyers of the Allen M. Sumner (DD 692) and Gearing (DD 710) classes that reached the end of their service lives in the mid-1970s. In addition to these 31 ships, four similar ships were ordered with the Mk

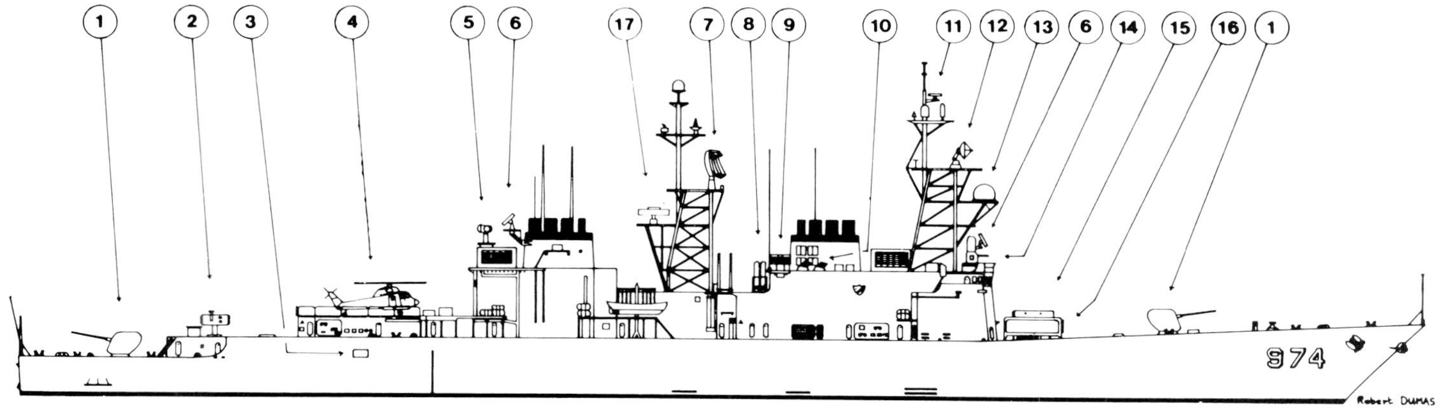

SPRUANCE
1. 5-inch DP gun Mk 45 (2). 2. Sea Sparrow launcher Mk 29. 3. 12.75-inch triple torpedo tubes Mk 32 (2). 4. SH-2F LAMPS I helicopter. 5. Radar director for Sea Sparrow control system Mk 91 Mod 0. 6. OE-82 satellite antenna (2). 7. SPS-40 air search radar. 8. Harpoon missile canisters (8 missiles). 9. SLQ-32(V)2 EW antenna (2). 10. SRBOC decoy launchers. 11. SPS-55 surface search radar. 12. SPG-60 gun/missile control radar. 13. SPQ-9A gun fire control radar. 14. Phalanx CIWS (2). 15. ASROC launcher Mk 16. 16. Tomahawk ABL (2). 17. Mk 23 TAS radar. (Robert Dumas)

26/Standard AAW missile system for the Iranian Navy, but they were completed as the U.S. KIDD class, accounting for hull numbers DD 993–996.

One additional ship of this class was ordered on 29 September 1979 (DD 997). This ship was one of two authorized (one funded) by Congress with the proviso that, in the wording of the Senate Committee on Armed Services, "The committee does not intend for these funds to be used for acquisition of two standard DD 963-class destroyers; rather, it is the committee's intention that these ships be the first element in a new technology approach to the problems of designing surface escorts. The standard [DD] 963 class design should be modified to substantially increase the number of helicopter aircraft carried." This feature could permit the eventual modification of the ships to operate VSTOL aircraft as well. However, the Navy chose to build the ship as a standard SPRUANCE, and no additional ships were funded by Congress. (The ship was initially listed as DDH 997 in Navy working papers.)

Design: SCB No. 224. The original concept for this class provided for an AAW missile version (DXG) as well as the ASW version (DX); these designs became the KIDD and SPRUANCE classes, respectively.

The SPRUANCE design provided for the subsequent installation of additional weapon systems, specifically the Mk 26 missile launcher (later the Mk 41 VLS) forward—with removal of the ASROC launcher—and aft—with removal of the Sea Sparrow launcher (see *Missiles* notes). In addition, the forward 5-inch gun could be replaced by the now-canceled 8-inch Mk 71 Major Caliber Lightweight Gun.

The ASROC was automatically reloaded, with a vertical magazine that provides 16 reloads. ASROC launchers were removed from the non-VLS ships in the early 1990s.

The Sea Sparrow launcher is reloaded "by hand," with a total of 24 Sea Sparrow missiles carried on board.

Electronics: The Mk 23 TAS is not provided in six of the ships, (DD 984–986, 988, 990, and 992).

Original plans provided for these ships to have the SQS-35 Independent Variable Depth Sonar (IVDS) in addition to their bow-mounted SQS-53. The IVDS was deleted because of the effectiveness of the SQS-53. The decision was subsequently made to fit these ships with the SQR-19 TACTAS; the SQR-19 is not fitted in ten ships (DD 969, 972, 976, 982–985, 986, and 988–990).

The STUMP was fitted with the engineering development model of the SQS-53C sonar; the MOOSBRUGGER was refitted with the SQS-53B sonar and was the first Navy ship to have the SQQ-89 system.

Four ships were fitted with the SQR-15 TASS, which was removed by 1992.

Engineering: These are the first U.S. Navy surface combatants to have gas-turbine propulsion. Gas turbines previously were installed in Navy patrol combatants (PGM/PG 84 class) and in the Coast Guard HAMILTON (WHEC 715) class, as well as some RELIANCE (WMEC 615)-class cutters.

The SPRUANCE-class ships have four LM 2500 gas turbines, which are modified TF39 aircraft turbofan engines. Their maximum horsepower is about 86,000; sustained shp is shown above. One engine can

The O'BRIEN at Hong Kong. The backfitting of a 61-missile VLS to these ships was accomplished with no reduction in their primary mission capability of ASW. The SPRUANCE class was the world's first surface combatant design to accommodate two large ASW helicopters. (1994, Giorgio Arra)

The MOOSBRUGGER is shown here with an SH-60B LAMPS III helicopter on her flight deck. The Mk 23 TAS is visible just behind the pole mast (below the SPS-40 air search radar). The Mk 32 torpedo tubes are within the hull, behind shutters (below the nose of the helicopter), which facilitates maintaining and reloading them. (1993, Giorgio Arra)

propel the ships at about 19 knots, two engines at about 27 knots, and three and four engines can provide speeds in excess of 30 knots. The engines have a maximum rating of 86,000 shp; 80,000 shp is the sustained rating.

Helicopters: The sizes of the twin helicopter hangars in these ships vary; they are 49 to 54 feet (14.9 to 16.5 m) long, 21 to 23½ feet (6.4 to 7.2 m) wide, and at least 16 feet (4.9 m) high.

Manning: The crews of these ships vary from 319 to 350 (20–22 officers + 308–28 enlisted).

Missiles: The MERRILL was fitted with armored box launchers for eight Tomahawk cruise missiles in October 1982, the first U.S. surface ship to carry that weapon. The ABLs are mounted forward of the superstructure, alongside the ASROC launcher and aft of the 5-inch gun mount.

The Mk 41 VLS installation replaces the ASROC launcher and magazine. The VLS installation carries vertical-launch ASROCs, thus reducing the number of Tomahawks that can be loaded from a theoretical 61 missiles.

Names: The DD 974 carries the *title* of the admiral who led the French fleet that protected American forces from the British fleet and reinforcements in the Battle of Yorktown (1781), the last major battle in the American Revolution. The admiral's full name was Comte [Count] Francois Joseph Paull, Marquis de Grasse-Tilly.

Operational: Five ships of this class fired Tomahawk missiles during Operation Desert Storm:

CARON	2 missiles
FIFE	60 missiles
LEFTWICH	8 missiles
PAUL F. FOSTER	40 missiles
SPRUANCE	2 missiles

These 112 missiles constituted 39 percent of the Tomahawks fired during the Gulf War. The FOSTER fired the first Tomahawk missile—hence the "opening shot" of the Gulf War—on 17 January 1991. While the FIFE had 61 missile cells, the Navy would not comment on whether a 61st missile was carried or if it failed to launch or if it was simply not required.

In Tomahawk attacks against Iraq on 17 January 1993, 45 missiles were launched by the destroyers CARON, HEWITT, and STUMP; on 26 June 1993, the PETERSON launched 14 missiles (with the cruiser CHANCELLORSVILLE/CG 62 launching nine missiles in the later strike).

The O'BRIEN's massive superstructure mounts a variety of antennas; the structure in the similar TICONDEROGA (CG 47)-class cruisers is larger, with still more antennas. (1994, Giorgio Arra)

These details of the JOHN RODGERS show the armored box launchers—each holding four Tomahawk missiles—that flank the ship's ASROC launcher. ASROC reloads were in a below deck magazine, with pairs of the eight ASROC cells rotating to a vertical position for reloading. The box launcher has since been deleted. (1989, Giorgio Arra)

GUIDED MISSILE DESTROYERS

Number	Name	Comm.	Notes
DDG 1	GYATT (ex-DD 712)	1956	stricken as DD 712
DDG 2–24	CHARLES F. ADAMS class		
DDG 25	(Australian PERTH)	1965	
DDG 26	(Australian HOBART)	1965	
DDG 27	(Australian BRISBANE)	1967	
DDG 28	(German LÜTJENS)	1969	
DDG 29	(German MÖLDERS)	1969	
DDG 30	(German ROMMEL)	1970	
DDG 31	DECATUR (ex-DD 936)	1956	stricken 16 Mar 1988
DDG 32	JOHN PAUL JONES (ex-DD 932)	1956	stricken 31 Apr 1986
DDG 33	PARSONS (ex-DD 949)	1959	stricken 15 May 1984
DDG 34	SOMERS (ex-DD 947)	1959	stricken Apr 1988
DDG 35	MITSCHER (ex-DL 2)	1968	stricken 1 June 1978
DDG 36	JOHN S. MCCAIN (ex-DL 3)	1969	stricken 29 Apr 1978
DDG 37–46	FARRAGUT class (ex-DLG 6–15)		
DDG 47–50	TICONDEROGA class	changed to CG 47–50	
DDG 51–	ARLEIGH BURKE class		

The guided missile destroyer (DDG) classification was established in 1956. The first DDG was the GEARING-class destroyer GYATT (DD 712), fitted with a twin Terrier SAM launcher that replaced the ship's after 5-inch twin gun mount. The GYATT became DDG 712 on 3 December 1956 and DDG 1 on 23 April 1957. Subsequent DDGs were fitted with the smaller Tartar (later Standard-MR) missile system until the FARRAGUT-class frigates were reclassified as destroyers in 1975, those ships being armed with the Terrier/Standard-ER missile. Six ADAMS-class DDGs built for Australia and West Germany in U.S. shipyards were assigned the hull numbers DDG 25–30.

DESTROYERS: "FORREST SHERMAN" CLASS

Number	Name	Comm.	Notes
DD 931	FORREST SHERMAN	1955	stricken 27 July 1990
DD 932	JOHN PAUL JONES	1956	to DDG 32; stricken 30 Nov 1985
DD 933	BARRY	1956	to floating equipment 31 Jan 1983
DD 936	DECATUR	1956	to DDG 31; stricken 16 Mar 1988; retained as test ship
DD 937	DAVIS	1957	stricken 27 July 1990
DD 938	JONAS INGRAM	1957	stricken 15 June 1983
DD 940	MANLEY	1957	stricken 1 June 1990
DD 941	DU PONT	1957	stricken 1 June 1990
DD 942	BIGELOW	1957	stricken 1 June 1990
DD 943	BLANDY	1957	stricken 27 July 1990
DD 944	MULLINNIX	1958	stricken 26 July 1990
DD 945	HULL	1958	stricken 15 Oct 1983
DD 946	EDSON	1958	stricken 31 Jan 1989
DD 947	SOMERS	1959	to DDG 34; stricken Apr 1988
DD 948	MORTON	1959	stricken 7 Feb 1990
DD 949	PARSONS	1959	to DDG 33; stricken 15 May 1984
DD 950	RICHARD S. EDWARDS	1959	stricken 7 Feb 1990
DD 951	TURNER JOY	1959	stricken 13 Feb 1990

These were the first U.S. Navy ships to be built after World War II and completed with the designation "destroyer"; the four large destroyers of the MITSCHER class were built earlier, but they were completed with the classification "frigate" (DL). Further construction of this class was deferred in favor of the missile-armed CHARLES F. ADAMS class, which had the same general arrangement, but was fitted with a Tartar missile launcher in place of the third 5-inch gun.

All but the BARRY have been stricken; she was reclassified as "floating equipment" in 1983 and since 2 February 1984 has been permanently moored at the Washington Navy Yard as a memorial-museum ship. Adjacent to the Navy Museum, the BARRY hosted her one millionth visitor on 17 May 1993. The ship is manned by 34 active-duty Navy personnel.

The last ship to be decommissioned was the EDSON, which served as an Officer Candidate School/NRF training ship at Newport, Rhode Island; she was assigned to NRF on 1 April 1977 and decommissioned on 15 December 1988. Stricken in 1989, she was transferred to the INTREPID (CVS 11) Sea-Air-Space Museum in New York City on 30 June 1989. The INGRAM, stripped of weapons and radars, serves as a test hulk at the Philadelphia Naval Shipyard.

The stricken DECATUR serves as a test hulk for the Ship Self-Defense System (SSDS), operating out of the Puget Sound (Washington) Naval Shipyard. She is fitted with the following systems:

Mk 23 Target Acquisition System (TAS)
Phalanx CIWS Mk 16 Block 1
RAM missile launcher (RIM-116A)
Sea Sparrow missile launcher (RIM-7P)
SLQ-32(V) electronic countermeasures

The stricken SOMERS serves as a target hulk for the Naval Air Weapons Center at Point Mugu, California.

Class: Originally a class of 18 ships, four were converted to a guided missile configuration (DDG 31–34); further conversions were canceled, primarily because of cost. (The 14 others were scheduled for ASW modernization, but only eight were completed.)

See 14th Edition/pages 156–57 for DD characteristics; see 13th Edition/pages 146–47 for DDG characteristics.

POST–WORLD WAR II DESTROYERS

Number	Name	Notes
DD 927–930	MITSCHER class	completed as DL 2–5
DD 931–933	FORREST SHERMAN class	
DD 934	ex-Japanese HANAZUKI	
DD 935	ex-German T-35	
DD 936–938	FORREST SHERMAN class	
DD 939	ex-German Z-39	
DD 940–951	FORREST SHERMAN class	
DD 952–959	CHARLES F. ADAMS class	completed as DDG 2–9
DD 960	(AKIZUKI)	Japan OSP 1960
DD 961	(TERUZUKI)	Japan OSP 1960
DD 962	(ex-British CHARITY)	to Pakistan 1958 (SHAH JAHAN)
DD 963–992	SPRUANCE class	
DD 993	(ex-Iranian KOUROSH)	completed as U.S. DDG 993
DD 994	(ex-Iranian DARYUSH)	completed as U.S. DDG 994
DD 995	(Iranian ARDESHIR)	canceled June 1976
DD 996	(ex-Iranian NADER)	completed as U.S. DDG 995
DD 997	(Iranian SHAPOUR)	canceled June 1976; reassigned to SPRUANCE class
DD 998	(ex-Iranian ANOUSHIRVAN)	completed as U.S. DDG 996

U.S. World War II destroyer programs reached hull number DD 926 (hulls DD 891–926 were canceled in 1945). Two destroyers were built for the Japanese Maritime Self-Defense Force with U.S. funds under the Offshore Procurement (OSP) program. Many ships built during the war were subsequently reclassified as escort destroyers (DDE), hunter-killer destroyers (DDK), radar picket destroyers (DDR), and experimental destroyers (EDD). One GEARING-class ship was converted to a missile configuration (DDG 712) to evaluate the Terrier system in a destroyer-size ship; she was subsequently changed to DDG 1. All except the DDG retained their DD hull numbers in their new roles.

All surviving special-configuration destroyers reverted to "straight" DD classification except for six DDRs during the early 1960s. Most ships were updated under the FRAM (Fleet Rehabilitation and Modernization) program of the early 1960s.

As indicated above, several war prizes and foreign-built ships (Offshore Procurement) had DD-series hull numbers, as did one British destroyer transferred to Pakistan with U.S. funds.[4]

Six missile-armed ships of the SPRUANCE class ordered by Iran were assigned DD hull numbers by the U.S. Navy. The four ships actually built went to the U.S. Navy with DDG designations, but they retained their DD-series hull numbers. The two other ships were canceled; one of their hull numbers was subsequently assigned to the 31st SPRUANCE-class ship.

4. While three Axis destroyers were given DD numbers, the Japanese battleship NAGATO, the German heavy cruiser PRINZ EUGEN, and several German and Japanese submarines acquired after World War II were not given warship designations. The German CA was assigned the designation IX 300 (sunk, along with the NAGATO, in the Bikini atomic bomb tests of 1946). The German supply ship CONECUH became the IX 301 and, subsequently, saw U.S. Navy service as the AO/AOR 110.

CHAPTER 17

Frigates

The frigate KAUFFMAN tows the refugee-carrying Haitian ship *Valerie 1* to the U.S. naval base at Guantánamo Bay, Cuba. Frigates serve as excellent ships for short-of-war operations. However, the attraction of the high capabilities of Aegis/SPY-1 and of large numbers of vertical-launch missiles in cruisers and destroyers is too great at this juncture to risk trading off "high-mix" warships for "low-mix" frigates. (1994, U.S. Navy, Lt. Scott Gureck)

The frigate has become the least important U.S. Navy warship in the post–Cold War era. Procured in large numbers to combat the threat posed by Soviet submarines, the number of frigates has been reduced precipitously since the collapse of the Soviet Union, and by the year 2000 the type could disappear entirely from the U.S. Fleet.

The Navy in the fall of 1996 had 45 frigates in service: 33 active ships and 12 assigned to the Naval Reserve Force (NRF), the latter manned by composite active-reserve crews. All are of the OLIVER HAZARD PERRY class. Several additional frigates will be decommissioned by the end of 1996, with only a small number—probably all NRF ships—expected to remain in service after the year 2000.

This declining force compares to a peak of 115 frigates (94 active and 21 NRF ships) in 1985, when the Navy maintained a large number of ocean escort ships to counter the large Soviet submarine force. Although the PERRY-class ships are considered multi-purpose ships because of their surface-to-air/Harpoon missile capability and major helicopter capability, their predecessors were too highly specialized for the ASW mission against the Soviet undersea fleet to be retained in service in the post–Cold War era.

Frigates are primarily ASW ships, with the PERRY class intended to provide limited AAW defense to convoys and amphibious and replenishment groups. Despite the higher speed and missile capabilities of the PERRY-class frigates, these ships are still not capable of serving as effective escorts for carrier battle groups in wartime. These ships, however, can fire Harpoon anti-ship missiles from their Mk 13 missile launcher, albeit at the expense of anti-air missiles.

As Navy force levels are reduced to some 110 to 116 surface combatants (cruisers, destroyers, frigates), the emphasis will be on the more capable cruisers and destroyers. Thus, the PERRY-class ships will be retired as new-construction ARLEIGH BURKE (DDG 51)-class destroyers enter service.

No frigate-type ships are under construction, the last ship of the PERRY class having been completed in 1989. No future development or acquisition of frigates is planned. In the mid-1980s the Navy began to design an advanced frigate for construction in the 1990s to replace the KNOX and earlier frigate classes. That effort, however, was canceled in 1986 by the Deputy Chief of Naval Operations (Surface Warfare) because of the large size of those designs (see below).

A smaller frigate intended specifically for NRF service was planned by the Carter administration in the late 1970s, but it was not built nor will the long-gestation surface effects ship frigate (FFGS).[1]

Classification: This type of warship was officially classified as "escort vessel" (DE) from its inception in the U.S. Navy in 1941 although the DE type was invariably called "destroyer escort"—often in official publications. Only in the early 1950s—as the Soviet submarine threat emerged and DE production began to accelerate—were these ships generally referred to as escort vessels. (At that time the term "frigate" was applied to large destroyer-type ships—DL/DLG.)

Subsequently, missile-armed escort ships were designated DEG; the escort research ship GLOVER was designated AGDE. All escort ships were changed to "frigate" (FF/FFG/AGFF) on 30 June 1975.

Guns: Beginning during the 1990–1991 crisis and war in the Persian Gulf, several PERRY-class frigates were fitted with .50-cal machine guns and 25-mm Mk 38 Bushmaster "chain" guns for close-in defense against small craft. The weapons are shifted from ship to ship as they forward deploy; accordingly, they are not listed under the specific class entries.

Names: The frigate ship type evolved from the World War II–era destroyer escort (DE) and thus the ships have destroyer-type names. The HAROLD E. HOLT remembers the deceased Australian prime minister who supported U.S. policy in the Vietnam War.

ADVANCED GUIDED MISSILE FRIGATE DESIGN

A low-level Navy design effort to develop a multi-purpose frigate for construction in the 1990s was canceled in April 1986 because of dissatisfaction with the efforts to date. Those efforts had produced preliminary designs of some 7,000 tons for a monohull ship and 9,200 tons for a SWATH (Small Waterplane-Area Twin Hull) design.

The SWATH configuration would have been approximately 300 feet (91.5 m) in length and, in some versions, could accommodate large helicopters (H-46/H-53 series) or the V-22 Osprey tilt-rotor aircraft.

The ships were considered too large and too expensive for the anticipated ship construction budgets of the 1990s.

1. In 1989 the Soviet Navy completed the first Dergach-class (Project 1239) guided missile surface effects ship, a heavily armed corvette-type ship of some 850 tons full load. See N. Polmar, *Guide to the Soviet Navy*/5th Edition (Annapolis, Md.: Naval Institute Press, 1991), p. 192.

The CROMMELIN is shown here with an SH-60B LAMPS III helicopter on her landing deck. Helicopters are the primary means of localization and attack in modern anti-submarine operations. The Mk 32 torpedo tubes (amidships) are of questionable effectiveness against submarines armed with long-range torpedoes or anti-ship guided missiles. (1994, Giorgio Arra)

49 GUIDED MISSILE FRIGATES: "OLIVER HAZARD PERRY" CLASS

Number	Name	FY	Builder	Laid down	Launched	Commissioned	Status
FFG 7	Oliver Hazard Perry	73	Bath Iron Works, Maine	12 June 1976	25 Sep 1976	17 Dec 1977	**NRF-A**
FFG 8	McInerney	75	Bath Iron Works, Maine	16 Jan 1978	4 Nov 1978	15 Dec 1979	**AA**
FFG 9	Wadsworth	75	Todd Shipyards, San Pedro, Calif.	13 July 1977	29 July 1978	28 Feb 1980	**NRF-P**
FFG 10	Duncan	75	Todd Shipyards, Seattle, Wash.	29 Apr 1977	1 Mar 1978	24 May 1980	PR; decomm. 17 Dec 1994
FFG 11	Clark	76	Bath Iron Works, Maine	17 July 1978	24 Mar 1979	9 May 1980	**NRF-A**
FFG 12	George Philip	76	Todd Shipyards, San Pedro, Calif.	14 Dec 1977	16 Dec 1978	15 Nov 1980	**NRF-P**
FFG 13	Samuel Eliot Morison	76	Bath Iron Works, Maine	4 Dec 1978	14 July 1979	11 Oct 1980	**NRF-A**
FFG 14	Sides	76	Todd Shipyards, San Pedro, Calif.	7 Aug 1978	19 May 1979	30 May 1981	**NRF-P**
FFG 15	Estocin	76	Bath Iron Works, Maine	2 Apr 1979	3 Nov 1979	10 Jan 1981	**NRF-A**
FFG 16	Clifton Sprague	76	Bath Iron Works, Maine	30 July 1979	16 Feb 1980	21 Mar 1981	AR; decomm. 2 June 1995
FFG 19	John A. Moore	77	Todd Shipyards, San Pedro, Calif.	19 Dec 1978	20 Oct 1979	14 Nov 1981	**NRF-P**
FFG 20	Antrim	77	Todd Shipyards, Seattle, Wash.	21 June 1978	27 Mar 1979	26 Sep 1981	AR; decomm. May 1996
FFG 21	Flatley	77	Bath Iron Works, Maine	13 Nov 1979	15 May 1980	20 June 1981	AR; decomm. May 1996
FFG 22	Fahrion	77	Todd Shipyards, Seattle, Wash.	1 Dec 1978	24 Aug 1979	16 Jan 1982	**NRF-A**
FFG 23	Lewis B. Puller	77	Todd Shipyards, San Pedro, Calif.	23 May 1979	15 Mar 1980	17 Apr 1982	**NRF-P**
FFG 24	Jack Williams	77	Bath Iron Works, Maine	25 Feb 1980	30 Aug 1980	19 Sep 1981	AR; decomm. 27 Oct 1995
FFG 25	Copeland	77	Todd Shipyards, San Pedro, Calif.	24 Oct 1979	26 July 1980	7 Aug 1982	**NRF-P**; to decomm. 1996
FFG 26	Gallery	77	Bath Iron Works, Maine	17 May 1980	20 Dec 1980	5 Dec 1981	AR; decomm. June 1996
FFG 27	Mahlon S. Tisdale	78	Todd Shipyards, San Pedro, Calif.	19 Mar 1980	7 Feb 1981	13 Nov 1982	**NRF-P**; to decomm. 1996
FFG 28	Boone	78	Todd Shipyards, Seattle, Wash.	27 Mar 1979	16 Jan 1980	15 May 1982	**AA**
FFG 29	Stephen W. Groves	78	Bath Iron Works, Maine	16 Sep 1980	4 Apr 1981	17 Apr 1982	**AA**
FFG 30	Reid	78	Todd Shipyards, San Pedro, Calif.	8 Oct 1980	27 June 1981	19 Feb 1983	**PA**
FFG 31	Stark	78	Todd Shipyards, Seattle, Wash.	24 Aug 1979	30 May 1980	23 Oct 1982	**AA**
FFG 32	John L. Hall	78	Bath Iron Works, Maine	5 Jan 1981	24 July 1981	26 June 1982	**AA**
FFG 33	Jarrett	78	Todd Shipyards, San Pedro, Calif.	11 Feb 1981	17 Oct 1981	2 July 1983	**PA**
FFG 34	Aubrey Fitch	78	Bath Iron Works, Maine	10 Apr 1981	17 Oct 1981	9 Oct 1982	**AA**
FFG 36	Underwood	79	Bath Iron Works, Maine	3 Aug 1981	6 Feb 1982	29 Jan 1983	**AA**
FFG 37	Crommelin	79	Todd Shipyards, Seattle, Wash.	30 May 1980	1 July 1981	18 June 1983	**PA**
FFG 38	Curts	79	Todd Shipyards, San Pedro, Calif.	1 July 1981	6 Mar 1982	8 Oct 1983	**PA**
FFG 39	Doyle	79	Bath Iron Works, Maine	23 Oct 1981	22 May 1982	21 May 1983	**AA**
FFG 40	Halyburton	79	Todd Shipyards, Seattle, Wash.	26 Sep 1980	13 Oct 1981	7 Jan 1984	**AA**
FFG 41	McClusky	79	Todd Shipyards, San Pedro, Calif.	21 Oct 1981	18 Sep 1982	10 Dec 1983	**PA**
FFG 42	Klakring	79	Bath Iron Works, Maine	19 Feb 1982	18 Sep 1982	20 Aug 1983	**AA**
FFG 43	Thach	79	Todd Shipyards, San Pedro, Calif.	6 Mar 1982	18 Dec 1982	17 Mar 1984	**PA**
FFG 45	De Wert	80	Bath Iron Works, Maine	14 June 1982	18 Dec 1982	19 Nov 1983	**AA**
FFG 46	Rentz	80	Todd Shipyards, San Pedro, Calif.	18 Sep 1982	16 July 1983	30 June 1984	**PA**
FFG 47	Nicholas	80	Bath Iron Works, Maine	27 Sep 1982	23 Apr 1983	10 Mar 1984	**AA**
FFG 48	Vandegrift	80	Todd Shipyards, Seattle, Wash.	13 Oct 1981	15 Oct 1982	24 Nov 1984	**PA**
FFG 49	Robert G. Bradley	80	Bath Iron Works, Maine	28 Dec 1982	13 Aug 1983	11 Aug 1984	**AA**
FFG 50	Jesse L. Taylor	81	Bath Iron Works, Maine	5 May 1983	5 Nov 1983	1 Dec 1984	**AA**
FFG 51	Gary	81	Todd Shipyards, San Pedro, Calif.	18 Dec 1982	19 Nov 1983	17 Nov 1984	**PA**
FFG 52	Carr	81	Todd Shipyards, Seattle, Wash.	26 Mar 1982	26 Feb 1983	27 July 1985	**AA**
FFG 53	Hawes	81	Bath Iron Works, Maine	22 Aug 1983	17 Feb 1984	9 Feb 1985	**AA**
FFG 54	Ford	81	Todd Shipyards, San Pedro, Calif.	16 July 1983	23 June 1984	29 June 1985	**PA**
FFG 55	Elrod	81	Bath Iron Works, Maine	21 Nov 1983	12 May 1984	6 July 1985	**AA**
FFG 56	Simpson	82	Bath Iron Works, Maine	27 Feb 1984	31 Aug 1984	9 Nov 1985	**AA**
FFG 57	Reuben James	82	Todd Shipyards, San Pedro, Calif.	19 Nov 1983	8 Feb 1985	22 Mar 1986	**PA**
FFG 58	Samuel B. Roberts	82	Bath Iron Works, Maine	21 May 1984	8 Dec 1984	12 Apr 1986	**AA**
FFG 59	Kauffman	83	Bath Iron Works, Maine	8 Apr 1985	29 Mar 1986	21 Feb 1987	**AA**
FFG 60	Rodney M. Davis	83	Todd Shipyards, San Pedro, Calif.	8 Feb 1985	11 Jan 1986	9 May 1987	**PA**
FFG 61	Ingraham	84	Todd Shipyards, San Pedro, Calif.	30 Mar 1987	25 June 1988	5 Aug 1989	**PA**

Displacement: 2,769 tons light except 3,210 tons for ships with LAMPS III modification
3,658 tons full load except 3,900–4,100 tons for ships with LAMPS III modification

Length: 413 feet (125.9 m) waterline
445 feet (135.6 m) overall except 455¼ feet (138.8 m) for ships with LAMPS III modification

Beam: 45 feet (13.7 m)

Draft: $21\frac{11}{12}$ feet (6.7 m)

Propulsion: 2 gas turbines (General Electric LM 2500); 40,000 shp; 1 shaft

Speed: 29 knots (sustained; see *Engineering* notes)

Range: 5,000 n.miles (9,260 km) at 18 knots
4,200 n.miles (7,778 km) at 20 knots

Manning: active ships approx. 214 (16 officers + 198 enlisted) + LAMPS detachment 21 (6 officers + 15 enlisted)
NRF ships approx. 162 active (14 officers + 148 enlisted) + 76 reserve (4 officers + 72 enlisted)

Helicopters: 1 or 2 SH-60B Seahawk LAMPS III in FFG 8, 36–61
1 SH-2G LAMPS I in FFG 7, 9–35

Missiles: 1 single Mk 13 Mod 4 launcher for Standard-MR SM-1 SAM/Harpoon SSM (40 weapons)

Guns: 1 76-mm/62-cal AA Mk 75
1 20-mm Phalanx CIWS Mk 16 (multi-barrel) in active ships and FFG 13

ASW weapons: 6 12.75-in (324-mm) torpedo tubes Mk 32 (2 triple)

Radars: SPS-49(V)4 air search except SPS-49(V)5 in FFG 50, 51, 53, 55, 56, and 61
SPS-55 surface search

Sonars: SQS-56 keel mounted
SQR-19 TACTAS towed array except none in FFG 10, 24, 27, 31, 34, 51, 52, 54

Fire control: 1 Mk 13 weapon direction system
1 Mk 92 weapons FCS except Mk 92 Mod 6 CORT in FFG 50, 51, 53, 55, 56, 61
1 STIR radar
SQQ-89(V)2 ASW system in active ships and FFG 7
SYS-2(V)2 Integrated Automatic Detection and Tracking (IADT) system in FFG 50 and FFG 61

EW systems: SLQ-25 Nixie
SLQ-32(V)2 except SLQ-32(V)5 with Sidekick in FFG 29, 30, 54, and some other units

This is the second largest class of major surface warships to be built by any nation since World War II; 51 PERRY-class ships were completed for the U.S. Navy between 1977 and 1989; additional ships were built for foreign navies in the United States and in other countries (see *Class* notes). The Soviet SKORYY class of destroyers was larger, with 72 ships completed between 1950 and 1954.

The PERRY class was initiated in the early 1970s—together with the planned Sea Control Ship (SCS)—to provide a viable capability for defending Sea Lines Of Communications (SLOC) against Soviet air and submarine attacks. After the cutbacks in the DX/DXG program (SPRUANCE/DD 963 class), the FFG 7 class was additionally looked upon as a replacement for GEARING (DD 710)-class destroyers.

These frigates lack the large, hull-mounted active/passive sonar and ASROC launcher of previous U.S. frigate classes. However, their towed-array and ability to support two large LAMPS III helicopters make them useful ASW ships. In addition, they have a surface-to-air missile system, a feature lacking in all but six of the previous U.S. post–World War II frigates.[2] And, despite their relatively light construction, according to the reference work *Combat Fleets of the World,* "The soundness of the design has permitted the expansion [of capabilities], and the ships have proven remarkably sturdy."[3]

Two ships have been decommissioned and six additional units will be taken out of service by the end of 1996; these and other units will be made available to foreign navies under lease arrangements.

Note the short interval between the PERRY's keel laying and launching due to modular construction; fabrication of modules began on 17 December 1974.

The CURTS, MCCLUSKY, THACH, and RODNEY M. DAVIS are homeported in Yokosuka, Japan.

Anti-submarine: The only ship-mounted ASW weapons are Mk 32 torpedo tubes, with the SH-60B helicopters being their primary ASW weapon. These are the first U.S. surface combatants that have been built without ASROC since that weapon became available in the early 1960s.

Class: Early U.S. Navy planning provided for approximately 75 ships of this class. Shipbuilding programs of the early 1970s reduced the number of ships to be built in "later" years, in part because of the planned FFX, a smaller frigate intended specifically for NRF operation (see below).

2. The point-defense missile system fitted in a number of previous frigates does have a limited anti-air capability, but its intended purpose is primarily to defeat incoming Styx-type anti-ship cruise missiles.

3. Bernard Prézelin and A. D. Baker III, *Combat Fleets of the World 1995* (Annapolis, Md.: Naval Institute Press, 1995), p. 883.

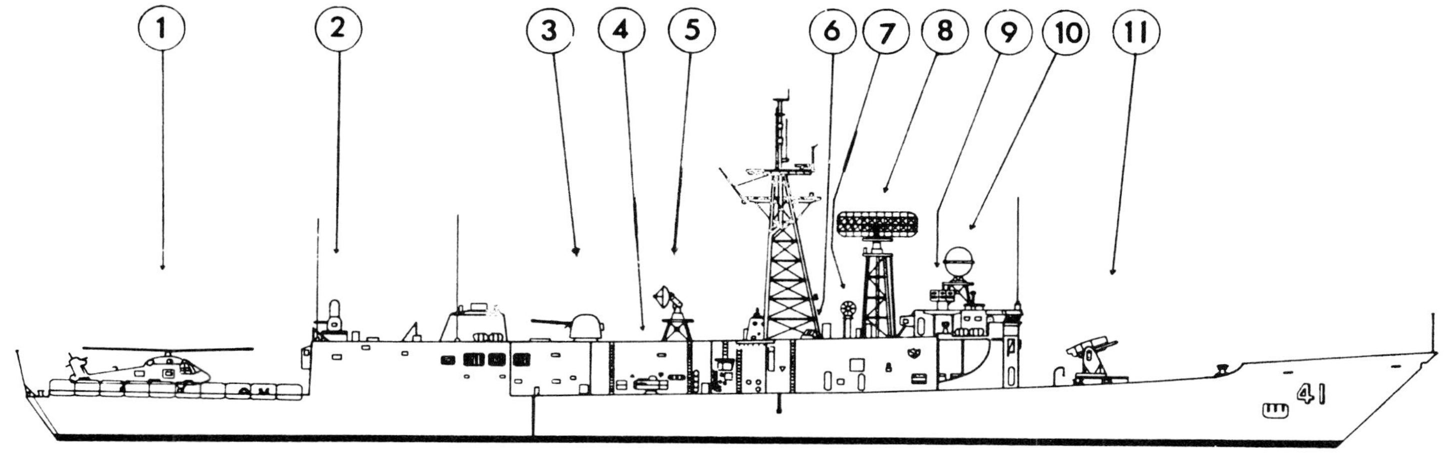

MCCLUSKY
1. SH-60B LAMPS III helicopter. 2. Phalanx CIWS. 3. 76-mm AA gun Mk 75. 4. 12.75-inch triple torpedo tubes Mk 32 (2). 5. STIR fire-control radar. 6. SRBOC decoy launcher. 7. OE-82 satellite antenna (2). 8. SPS-49 air search radar. 9. SLQ-32(V)2 EW antenna. 10. Mk 92 fire-control radar. 11. Surface-to-air missile launcher Mk 13. (Robert Dumas)

The MCCLUSKY at Hong Kong. The ship is still under way: upon anchoring she will fly the "jack" at the bow and the national ensign at the stern. Note the rigid inflatable boat and the Mk 32 torpedo tubes amidships, in the "notch" in the deck structure. (1994, Giorgio Arra)

The last Carter administration five-year plan (fiscal 1982–1986) deleted all FFG 7 construction after one ship in the 1983 program. However, the Reagan administration's shipbuilding program put forward in January 1982 for fiscal 1983–1987 provided for 12 additional FFGs in those years; Congress voted the two ships in the fiscal 1983 budget, but the Reagan administration's subsequent five-year plan (fiscal 1984–1988) deleted all further frigate construction, thus halting the FFG 7 program at 50 ships. In the event, Congress funded one additional ship in the fiscal 1984 budget specifically for construction at the Todd San Pedro yard (FFG 61).

The Todd Seattle yard built four ships of this class for the Australian Navy (given the U.S. designations FFG 17, 18, 35, and 44), which were delivered from 1980 to 1983. Additional ships of this design have been constructed in Australia (two), Spain (six), and Taiwan (seven) for their respective navies. Thus, the total number of ships built to the PERRY design is 70.

Sixteen ships were assigned to the NRF; 12 remained in this role in 1996 (mobilization category A). The locations of NRF ships in 1996 are listed below:

FFG 7	PERRY	to NRF 31 May 1984	New York, N.Y.
FFG 9	WADSWORTH	to NRF 30 June 1985	San Diego, Calif.
FFG 11	CLARK	to NRF 30 Sep 1985	Norfolk, Va.
FFG 12	PHILIP	to NRF 18 Jan 1986	San Diego, Calif.
FFG 13	MORISON	to NRF 30 June 1986	Charleston, S.C.
FFG 14	SIDES	to NRF 9 Aug 1986	San Diego, Calif.
FFG 15	ESTOCIN	to NRF 30 Sep 1986	Norfolk, Va.
FFG 19	MOORE	to NRF 30 Jan 1987	San Diego, Calif.
FFG 20	ANTRIM	to NRF 30 Jan 1987	Pascagoula, Miss.
FFG 21	FLATLEY	to NRF 30 Nov 1987	Pascagoula, Miss.
FFG 22	FAHRION	to NRF 30 Sep 1988	Charleston, S.C.
FFG 23	PULLER	to NRF 1 June 1987	San Diego, Calif.
FFG 25	COPELAND	to NRF 30 Sep 1989	San Diego, Calif.
FFG 27	TISDALE	to NRF 31 Jan 1988	San Diego, Calif.

Foreign transfers scheduled for 1996–1997 are:

FFG 10	DUNCAN to Egypt
FFG 16	CLIFTON SPRAGUE to Turkey
FFG 20	ANTRIM to Turkey
FFG 21	FLATLEY to Turkey
FFG 24	JACK WILLIAMS to Bahrain
FFG 25	COPELAND to Egypt
FFG 27	MAHLON S. TISDALE to Oman

Classification: When conceived, these ships were classified as "patrol frigates" (PF), a designation previously applied to a series of smaller World War II–era ships (PF 1–102) and postwar coastal escorts that were constructed specifically for foreign transfer (PF 103–108). The PERRY was designated PF 109 until changed to "frigate" FFG 7 on 30 June 1975.

Design: SCB design No. 261. During the design phase the Chief of Naval Operations, Admiral Elmo R. Zumwalt, placed the following constraints on the ships' cost, displacement, and crew size:

- $50 million in then-year dollars
- 3,530 tons full load
- 185 crew (17 officers + 168 enlisted)

All three parameters were exceeded, although the design did arrest the upward trend in frigate (DE/FF) cost, size, and manning requirements.

These ships were designed specifically for modular assembly and mass production. All major components were tested at sea or in land facilities before completion of the lead ship. Space and weight were reserved for fin stabilizers, which were installed during construction in FFG 36 and later units. Early designs provided for a single hangar aft with twin funnels ("split" by the hangar). The design was revised to provide separate, side-by-side hangars to accommodate two SH-60B helicopters (see *Helicopters* notes).

The hangars vary in size: they are approximately 41 to 46 feet (12.5 to 14 m) long, each 13⅔ to 16 feet (4.2 to 4.9 m) wide, and 13½ to 15½ feet (4.1 to 4.7 m) in height. In addition to the fantail landing area, the ships have a VERTREP area forward.

Electronics: The STIR (Separate Target Illumination Radar) is a modified SPG-60 radar. The Sperry Corporation had lobbied Congress and the Navy to install a phased-array radar in the later ships of this class, with a backfit to the earlier ships. However, the cost was considered prohibitive by the Navy.

The INGRAHAM was completed with an improved combat system developed by Sperry/Unisys referred to as CORT (Coherent Receiver/Transmitter). It consists of the Mk 92 Mod 6 fire-control system with the SYS-2(V)2 automatic tracking system. The ship's SPS-49(V)5 digital radar has enhanced ECM capabilities. A similar CORT refit followed for five other ships. However, the weight and cost of the modification was deemed unacceptable, and no further modifications followed.

The Sidekick ECM installation provides an active countermeasures capability to the otherwise passive SLQ-32(V)2; suites so modified are redesignated SLQ-32(V)5.

The SQR-18A towed array sonar is fitted in the NRF ships and the SQR-19 TACTAS towed-array sonar is provided in the active units and FFG 7. The first ship to be built with the SQR-19 was the ELROD, with the array to be backfitted in the earlier ships. The limited capabilities of hull-mounted SQS-56 will make these ships rely primarily on the towed array for effective ASW.

The NICHOLAS was provided with the Kingfisher modification to the SQS-26 sonar for mine detection.

Engineering: These ships have two LM 2500 gas turbine main propulsion engines and can attain 25 knots on one engine. On trials some ships reportedly have reached 36 knots. The maximum rated horsepower is 41,000; the sustained shp is shown above.

The ships have two 350-hp electric-drive, retractable auxiliary propulsion pods for precise maneuvering; they also provide a "come-home" capability at six knots in the event of main propulsion failure. They are fitted with four 1,000-kilowatt diesel ship's service generators, thus lacking the elaborate silencing of the SPRUANCE-class destroyers, which have gas turbine generators.

Guns: Early designs addressed a variety of guns for these ships, among them a twin 35-mm rapid-fire gun in place of the later 76-mm

The superstructure of the McCLUSKY. The massive block structure and lattice masts of these ships, as well as other features, give them a large radar cross edition, especially in comparison with newer, European frigates and corvettes. The omniscient SLQ-32 antennas are above the bridge, port and starboard. (1994, Giorgio Arra)

The JARRETT shows the massive deckhouse of the PERRY-class frigates. The 76-mm gun is lost amidst the topside clutter. The Mk 13 missile launcher (forward) is in the vertical position; a circular missile magazine for Standard SM-1 and Harpoon missiles lies beneath the launcher. (1994, Giorgio Arra)

gun and CIWS. These are the first U.S. surface combatants since the early 1960s to be built without a 5-inch gun.

Helicopters: These were the first U.S. ships fitted with a helicopter haul-down system. The MCINERNEY tested the RAST haul-down system and conducted FFG sea trials with the SH-60B in 1981. It permits the recovery of helicopters while the ship is rolling through 28° and pitching up to 5°. RAST was backfitted in those ships completed prior to the TAYLOR (ships that have LAMPS III capability), which was the first ship to be completed with the RAST system.

The NRF-operated ships are intended to take aboard an SH-2G LAMPS I helicopter operated by the Naval Air Reserve (squadrons HSL-84 and HSL-94).

The DOYLE served as trials ship for the Canadair CL-227 Sentinel unmanned aerial reconnaissance vehicle, a peanut-shaped Vertical Take-Off and Landing (VTOL) aircraft.

Manning: The original complement was to be 179 (12 officers + 167 enlisted); that number rose to 185 by the time the design was completed (17 officers + 168 enlisted). The crews of active ships vary considerably, from 13 to 19 officers, and from 184 to 215 enlisted, in addition to LAMPS detachments.

Operational: While operating in the Persian Gulf the STARK was struck by two Exocet missiles launched by an Iraqi Mirage F1 aircraft on the night of 17 May 1987 that mistook the frigate for an Iranian ship. The STARK suffered 37 dead as one of the missile warheads detonated, and unexpended fuel in both missiles set fire and caused heavy damage to the ship. The STARK's crew fought fires for 24 hours; at one point the accumulation of water on board from fire-fighting efforts caused the ship to list 16°. (The STARK was able to return to the United States under her own power and underwent months of repairs at the Litton/Ingalls yard from November 1987 to August 1988. The repairs cost an estimated $90 million.)

The SAMUEL B. ROBERTS struck an Iranian-laid mine in the Persian Gulf on 14 April 1988. The ship suffered a 22-foot (6.7-m) gash in the side, a 9-foot (2.7-m) tear in the bottom, and a cracked superstructure. The ship's gas turbines were knocked from their mountings, and there was heavy flooding. Ten sailors were injured, but there were no fatalities. (After emergency repairs, the crippled ROBERTS departed the gulf on 1 July 1988 on board the Dutch-flag heavy lift ship MIGHTY SERVANT 2; the frigate was brought back to the United States and underwent 18 months of repairs at Bath Iron Works from May 1988 to October 1989. The repairs cost an estimated $37.5 million.)

GUIDED MISSILE FRIGATES: "BROOKE" CLASS

Number	Name	Comm.	Notes
FFG 1	BROOKE	1966	decomm. 16 Sep 1988; to Pakistan 8 Feb 1989
FFG 2	RAMSEY	1967	decomm. 1 Sep 1988; stricken 25 Jan 1992
FFG 3	SCHOFIELD	1968	decomm. 8 Sep 1988; stricken 25 Jan 1992
FFG 4	TALBOT	1967	decomm. 30 Sep 1988; to Pakistan 31 May 1989
FFG 5	RICHARD L. PAGE	1967	decomm. 30 Sep 1988; to Pakistan 31 Mar 1989
FFG 6	JULIUS A. FURER	1967	decomm. 10 Nov 1988; to Pakistan 31 Jan 1989

These were the Navy's first frigates to be armed with surface-to-air missiles, being fitted with a Tartar/Standard launcher in place of the second 5-inch (127-mm) gun of the similar GARCIA class. Additional ships of this configuration were planned but not built because of the significantly higher costs of the missile variants compared to all-gun ASW frigates. The TALBOT conducted at-sea tests of the gun, fire control, and sonar systems for the PERRY class.

These and the GARCIA-class all-gun frigates were the first ships to be taken out of active service after Secretary of the Navy John Lehman stepped down from that office in 1987, ending the effort to build a 600-ship fleet. Four ships have been leased to Pakistan. The RAMSEY and SCHOFIELD were to go to Turkey but were rejected by that Navy; they are stored at Bremerton, Washington, awaiting final disposition. (The BROOKE was returned from Pakistan on 14 November 1993 and stricken on that date; the FURER and TALBOT were returned on 11 December 1993 and stricken on the same date; and the PAGE was returned on 15 January 1994 and stricken on that date.)

See 14th Edition/pages 168–69 for characteristics.

FRIGATES: "KNOX" CLASS

Number	Name	Comm.	Notes
FF 1052	Knox	1969	decomm. 14 Feb 1992
FF 1053	Roark	1969	to NRF 1 June 1987; decomm. 14 Dec 1991
FF 1054	Gray	1970	to NRF 15 July 1982; decomm. 30 Sep 1991
FF 1055	Hepburn	1969	to NRF 1 Oct 1989; decomm. 20 Dec 1991
FF 1056	Connole	1969	decomm./to Greece 30 Aug 1992
FF 1057	Rathburne	1970	decomm. 14 Feb 1992
FF 1058	Meyerkord	1969	to NRF 30 Sep 1989; decomm. 14 Dec 1991
FF 1059	W. S. Sims	1970	to NRF 30 Sep 1990; decomm. 6 Sep 1991
FF 1060	Lang	1970	to NRF 17 Jan 1982; decomm. 12 Dec 1991
FF 1061	Patterson	1970	to NRF 15 June 1983; decomm. 30 Sep 1991
FF 1062	Whipple	1970	decomm. 14 Feb 1992
FF 1063	Reasoner	1971	decomm./to Turkey 28 Aug 1993
FF 1064	Lockwood	1970	decomm. 30 Sep 1993; to NDRF 4 Oct 1993
FF 1065	Stein	1972	decomm. 19 Mar 1992
FF 1066	Marvin Shields	1971	decomm. 2 July 1992
FF 1067	Francis Hammond	1970	decomm. 2 July 1992
FF 1068	Vreeland	1970	decomm. 30 June 1992; to Greece 25 July 1992
FF 1069	Bagley	1972	decomm. 30 Sep 1991
FF 1070	Downes	1971	decomm. 5 June 1992
FF 1071	Badger	1970	decomm. 20 Dec 1991
FF 1072	Blakely	1970	to NRF 11 June 1983; decomm. 15 Nov 1991
FF 1073	Robert E. Peary	1972	decomm. 7 Aug 1992; to Taiwan 7 Aug 1992
FF 1074	Harold E. Holt	1971	decomm. 2 July 1992
FF 1075	Trippe	1970	decomm./to Greece 30 July 1992
FF 1076	Fanning	1971	decomm./to Turkey 31 July 1992
FF 1077	Ouellet	1970	decomm. 6 Aug 1993
FFT 1078	Joseph Hewes	1971	to NRF 30 Sep 1991; decomm./to Taiwan 30 June 1994
FFT 1079	Bowen	1971	to NRF 30 Sep 1991; decomm./to Turkey 3 June 1994
FF 1080	Paul	1971	decomm. 14 Aug 1992
FF 1081	Aylwin	1971	decomm. 15 May 1992
FF 1082	Elmer Montgomery	1971	decomm./stricken 30 June 1993; to Turkey 13 Dec 1993
FF 1083	Cook	1971	to NRF 1 Oct 1989; decomm. 30 Apr 1992; to Taiwan 31 May 1994
FFT 1084	McCandless	1972	to NRF 31 Dec 1991; decomm./to Turkey 6 May 1994
FFT 1085	Donald B. Beary	1972	to NRF 30 Sep 1991; decomm./to Turkey 20 May 1994
FF 1086	Brewton	1972	decomm. 2 July 1992; to Taiwan 23 July 1992
FF 1087	Kirk	1972	decomm./to Taiwan 6 Aug 1993
FF 1088	Barbey	1972	to NRF 15 Jan 1991; decomm. 20 Mar 1992; to Taiwan 21 June 1994
FFT 1089	Jesse L. Brown	1973	to NRF 31 Dec 1991; decomm./to Egypt 27 July 1994
FFT 1090	Ainsworth	1973	to NRF 30 Sep 1990; decomm./to Turkey 27 May 1994
FF 1091	Miller	1973	to NRF 17 Jan 1982; decomm. 15 Oct 1991
FF 1092	Thomas C. Hart	1973	decomm./to Turkey 30 Aug 1993
FF 1093	Capodanno	1973	decomm./to Turkey 30 July 1993
FF 1094	Pharris	1974	decomm. 15 Feb 1992
FFT 1095	Truett	1974	to NRF 31 Dec 1991; decomm./to Thailand 30 July 1994
FF 1096	Valdez	1974	to NRF 14 Aug 1982; decomm. 16 Dec 1991
FFT 1097	Moinester	1974	to NRF 31 Dec 1991; decomm./to Egypt 28 July 1994

This was the largest class of surface combatants prior to the Perry-class frigates to be constructed in the West since World War II, with 46 ships completed. The Knox-class ships were highly criticized for their large size (comparable to World War II–era destroyers), a single propeller shaft, and limited AAW/ASUW capabilities. The latter limitation has been partially corrected with the Harpoon missile fired from the ASROC launcher.

The Truett was the last ship to be decommissioned; the ship had been in service for 22 years.

Class: Ten additional ships were authorized in the fiscal 1968 budget (DE 1098–1107). The construction of the last six ships (DE 1102–1107) was deferred in 1968 in favor of the more capable Spruance-class destroyers, and three other ships (DE 1099–1101) were deferred later that year to help pay for cost overruns of nuclear submarines; one ship (DE 1098) was deferred in 1969. Note that hull number 1098 was reassigned to the *earlier* Glover (formerly AGDE/AGFF 1, later AGFF 1).

Five similar ships were built in Spain with a SAM launcher amidships; they were designated DEG 7–11 for U.S. Navy record purposes.

Thirteen ships had been assigned to the NRF through early 1991 when the decision was made to take the entire class out of service. The Kirk was scheduled to shift to NRF status prior to being decommissioned.

Classification: These ships were built as ocean escorts (DE) and were changed to frigates on 30 June 1975. Eight ships were changed to training frigates (FFT): the FF 1078, 1079, 1085, and 1090 were changed to FFT on 15 December 1991; the FF 1084, 1089, 1095, and 1097 changed to FFT on 31 December 1991.

Design: These ships are considerably larger than the previous Brooke and Garcia classes because of the use of non–pressure-fired boilers. The superstructure is topped by a distinctive cylindrical "mack" that combines mast and stacks; it was to mount an advanced electronic warfare suite, but that was not developed.

The original DASH hangar was enlarged to accommodate the SH-2F LAMPS I helicopter.

As built, the ships took water over their bows in rough seas. Beginning in 1980 they have had raised bulwarks and spray strakesfitted forward. These changes added 9.1 tons and extended their overall length from the original 438⅙ feet (133.6 m).

Engineering: The canceled DE 1101 was to have had gas turbine propulsion to evaluate that plant for future use in surface combatants. The Barbey and Patterson evaluated controllable-pitch propeller configurations for subsequent use with LM 2500 gas turbine propulsion plants.

During the late 1980s it was proposed to refit these ships with LM 2500 gas turbines in place of their steam propulsion plants as part of the upgrade package. In the event, the massive force cutbacks of the early 1990s halted these considerations.

Missiles: Thirty-one ships were fitted, after completion, with Sea Sparrow point-defense systems. Installation of the Sea Chapparal, adopted from an Army SAM system, was planned for 14 other ships but was not undertaken.

The Downes served as evaluation ship for the NATO Sea Sparrow missile, being fitted with a Mk 29 missile launcher aft and a Mk 23 Target Acquisition System (TAS) in place of SPS-40 radar. Both systems were removed in 1983 when the Phalanx CIWS fitted aft.

Modernization: During the late 1980s several proposals were put forward to upgrade these ships and extend their nominal 30-year service life by ten years. Proposals—some termed a Service Life Extension Program (SLEP)—included fitting a vertical launch missile system, adding a second Phalanx CIWS forward, replacing the steam turbine and boilers with LM 2500 gas turbines, and upgrading the electronics, including provision of the Mk 68 fire-control system and SLQ-32(V)3 electronic countermeasures. In the event, funding constraints and then the 1990–1991 retirement decisions ended all consideration of major upgrades to this class.

Operational: In 1991, in conjunction with the massive fleet reductions, the Navy decided to take the entire Knox class out of active service: six ships were to be leased to other navies; 32 ships were preserved in a state of "reduced maintenance" (mobilization category B); and eight ships were designated as training frigates (FFT), operated to train nucleus crews for the other 32 ships. Each of the eight operational NRF ships were to be responsible for nucleus crew training for four laid-up ships. The reservists were to train on board the operational ship one weekend per month and to be on board, under way, for two weeks every year.

The 32 laid-up ships were to be stored in an "as is" condition, with the radar antennas removed and stowed on deck, but with their Phalanx CIWS and SLQ-32 systems removed and stored ashore. It is estimated that the reduced-maintenance ships could be returned to full operational capability—*if* crews and industrial facilities are available—within 180 days. In addition, the ships would require some 60 to 90 days of at-sea training before they could be considered fully operational.

The eight FFTs were to have had active-duty crews of 12 officers and 104 enlisted personnel, with a selected reserve crew of 10 officers and 55 enlisted personnel forming the nucleus for each of the laid-up ships. They were to be based in three ports: Staten Island, New York (FFT 1079, 1085, 1090); Mobile, Alabama (FFT 1089, 1097); and Inglewood, Texas (FFT 1078, 1084, 1095).

This program was dropped in 1991—as it was beginning—because of opposition in Congress and by the General Accounting Office. Accordingly, all KNOX-class ships are being stricken and/or transferred.

See 15th Edition/pages 147–50 for characteristics.

FRIGATES: "GARCIA" CLASS

Number	Name	Comm.	Notes
FF 1040	GARCIA	1964	decomm. 10 Nov 1988; to Pakistan 31 Jan 1989
FF 1041	BRADLEY	1965	decomm. 30 Sep 1988; to Brazil 15 Apr 1989
FF 1043	EDWARD MCDONNELL	1965	decomm. 30 Sep 1988; stricken 15 Dec 1992
FF 1044	BRUMBY	1965	decomm. 31 Mar 1989; to Pakistan 31 Mar 1989
FF 1045	DAVIDSON	1965	decomm. 31 Dec 1988; to Brazil 25 July 1989
FF 1047	VOGE	1966	decomm. 23 Aug 1989; stricken 15 Dec 1992
FF 1048	SAMPLE	1968	decomm. 23 Sep 1988; to Brazil 24 Aug 1989
FF 1049	KOELSCH	1967	decomm. 31 May 1989; to Pakistan 31 May 1989
FF 1050	ALBERT DAVID	1968	decomm. 18 Sep 1989; to Brazil 18 Sep 1989
FF 1051	O'CALLAHAN	1968	decomm. 20 Dec 1988; to Pakistan 8 Feb 1989

These ten ships incorporated the DASH, ASROC, and SQS-26 sonar of the previous BRONSTEIN class in a larger, more seaworthy hull. These ships were similar to the contemporary BROOKE-class frigates but with a second 5-inch gun in place of the FFG's Mk 22 launcher.

(The O'CALLAHAN was returned from Pakistan on 14 November 1993; the GARCIA was returned on 13 November 1994; and the BRUMBY and KOELSCH were returned on 19 August 1994. All were stricken on the same date.)

See 14th Edition/pages 176–77 for characteristics.

FRIGATES: "BRONSTEIN" CLASS

Number	Name	Comm.	Notes
FF 1037	BRONSTEIN	1963	decomm. 13 Dec 1990; stricken 4 Oct 1991
FF 1038	MCCLOY	1963	decomm. 14 Dec 1990; stricken 4 Oct 1991

The two frigates of the BRONSTEIN class were prototypes for a new generation of ASW ocean escorts, featuring large SQS-26 bow-mounted sonar, ASROC, and a DASH capability. These features were provided in the next 63 escort ships built by the U.S. Navy as well as in several foreign ASW ships. However, the BRONSTEIN class was too slow and lacked the seakeeping and range necessary for effective ASW to counter contemporary Soviet submarines. During the 1970s and 1980s they were employed extensively to evaluate the Towed Array Surveillance System (TASS) and to monitor Soviet naval activities.

Both ships were transferred to Mexico on 1 October 1993.

See 14th Edition/page 177–78 for characteristics.

NAVAL RESERVE FORCE FRIGATE

During the late 1970s the Navy proposed the construction of a class of small frigates (design designation FFX) for use by the Naval Reserve Force. These ships were intended to augment the FFG 7 force in the ASW role in low-threat areas. A class of approximately 12 ships was planned; the lead ship was intended for authorization in fiscal 1984. For several reasons the FFX class was not started. Subsequently, the Naval Reserve Force has been provided with frigates of the KNOX and PERRY classes to replace the aging GEARING-class ships previously assigned to the NRF.

The tentative characteristics of the FFX are provided in the 13th Edition/page 176.

POST–WORLD WAR II ESCORT/FRIGATES

U.S. World War II–destroyer escort programs reached hull number DE 1005 (with DE 801–1005 being canceled in 1943). After the war several destroyer escorts were converted to radar picket escorts (DER), seven for the tactical fleet role, and 36 for strategic early warning of a Soviet bomber attack against the continental United States. A few were also modified to an escort control (DEC) configuration to support amphibious landings.

The first postwar DEs were actually envisioned as successors to the war-built, steel-hulled submarine chasers (PC). With the start of the postwar programs in the early 1950s these ships were reclassified as ocean escorts (DE), partly to avoid confusion with escort destroyers (DDE).

U.S. hull numbers were assigned to 17 ships built in Europe with American Offshore Procurement, or OSP, funding. Thirteen U.S. ships of the DEALEY design (DE 1006, 1014, 1015, 1021–1030) were completed between 1954 and 1957, and ships of the CLAUD JONES design (DE 1033–1036) were completed in 1959–1960. All of these designs were intended for mass production in wartime; significantly, while the massive World War II–era DE program included large numbers of diesel-propelled ships, in the postwar era only the four ships of the JONES class were diesel, the remainder being steam powered until the advent of the PERRY class (gas turbine).

The GLOVER was built as an experimental frigate with a modified propeller configuration. The ship was commissioned in 1965 as the AGDE 1, which was subsequently changed to AGFF 1 and then FF 1098. She was again changed to the research role and given the auxiliary designation T-AGFF 1 on 15 June 1990; the GLOVER was assigned on that date to the Military Sealift Command (see chapter 23).

Number	Ship/Class	Comm.	Notes
DE 1006	DEALEY	1954	to Uruguay 1972
DE 1007	(French LE NORMAND)	OSP 1956	
DE 1008	(French LE LORRAIN)	OSP 1956	
DE 1009	(French LE PICARD)	OSP 1956	
DE 1010	(French LE GASCON)	OSP 1957	
DE 1011	(French LE CHAMPENPOIS)	OSP 1957	
DE 1012	(French LE SAVOYARD)	OSP 1957	
DE 1013	(French LE BOURGUIGNON)	OSP 1957	
DE 1014	CROMWELL	1954	stricken 1972
DE 1015	HAMMERBERG	1955	stricken 1973
DE 1016	(French LE CORSE)	OSP 1952	
DE 1017	(French LE BRESTOIS)	OSP 1952	
DE 1018	(French LE BOULONNAIS)	OSP 1953	
DE 1019	(French LE BORDELAIS)	OSP 1953	
DE 1020	(Italian CIGNO)	OSP 1957	
DE 1021	COURTNEY	1956	stricken 1973
DE 1022	LESTER	1957	stricken 1973
DE 1023	EVANS	1957	stricken 1973
DE 1024	BRIDGET	1957	stricken 1973
DE 1025	BAUER	1957	stricken 1973
DE 1026	HOOPER	1958	stricken 1973
DE 1027	JOHN WILLIS	1957	stricken 1972
DE 1028	VAN VOORHIS	1957	stricken 1972
DE 1029	HARTLEY	1957	to Colombia 1972
DE 1030	JOSEPH K. TAUSSIG	1957	stricken 1972
DE 1031	(Italian CASTORE)	OSP 1957	
DE 1032	(Portuguese PERO ESCORBAR)	OSP 1957	
DE 1033	CLAUD JONES	1959	to Indonesia 1974
DE 1034	JOHN R. PERRY	1959	to Indonesia 1973
DE 1035	CHARLES BERRY	1959	to Indonesia 1974
DE 1036	MCMORRIS	1960	to Indonesia 1974
DE 1037, 1038	BRONSTEIN class		
DE 1039	(Portuguese ALMIRANTE PEREIRA DA SILVA)	OSP 1966	
DE 1040, 1041	GARCIA class		
DE 1042	(Portuguese ALMIRANTE GAGO COUTINHO)	OSP 1967	
DE 1043–1045	GARCIA class		
DE 1046	(Portuguese ALMIRANTE MAGALHAES CORREA)	OSP 1967	
DE 1047–1051	GARCIA class		
DE 1052–1007	KNOX class*		

*The hull number FF 1098 subsequently was reassigned to the GLOVER (former AGFF/AGDE 1).

CHAPTER 18

Command Ships

The MOUNT WHITNEY and a MARS (AFS 1)-class replenishment ship rendezvous in the western Atlantic. The Navy's four command ships are invaluable for providing communications, working spaces, and accommodations for the commanders of four of the Navy's numbered fleets. (U.S. Navy)

The U.S. Navy has four fleet-level command ships in service: the La Salle, flagship of the Commander, Sixth Fleet, in the Mediterranean; the Blue Ridge, flagship of Commander, Seventh Fleet, in the Western Pacific; the Mount Whitney, flagship of Commander, Second Fleet, in the Atlantic; and the Coronado, flagship of Commander, Third Fleet, in the Eastern Pacific.

From the end of World War II until the 1970s, the four numbered fleets generally had cruisers for flagships. The cruisers now in service do not have major flag facilities and accommodations. The last true cruiser flagship, the Belknap (CG 26), was partially converted in 1986 to accommodate a portion of the Sixth Fleet staff. The Belknap retained a full missile cruiser capability.

These are large command ships, the only ones to be designed from the outset specifically for the amphibious command ship role. The Navy's earlier command ships could not operate with the 20-knot amphibious ships built from the 1960s onward. Both ships are now employed as fleet flagships.

The Blue Ridge is homeported in Yokosuka, Japan, having relieved the cruiser Oklahoma City (CG 5) in October 1979 as flagship of the Seventh Fleet; the Mount Whitney is based at Norfolk, Virginia, having relieved the cruiser Albany (CG 10) in January 1981 as flagship of the Second Fleet.

The Iowa (BB 61)-class battleships reactivated in the 1980s were not fitted to serve as major flagships.

Classification: The Blue Ridge and Mount Whitney retain their amphibious command ship LCC designation in the fleet command ship role; the miscellaneous flagships (AGF) retain their previous LPD hull numbers with the AGF designation.

Names: Amphibious command ships (AGC/LCC) have traditionally been assigned the names of American mountains and mountain ranges. The AGFs retain their amphibious ship names.

Class: A third ship of this class (AGC 21) was planned; she was to have been configured for service as both an amphibious flagship and a fleet flagship.

Classification: These ships were originally classified as amphibious force flagships (AGC); they were changed to amphibious command ships (LCC) on 1 January 1969.

Design: SCB No. 400. The hull and propulsion machinery are similar to that of the Iwo Jima (LPH 2)-class helicopter carriers. The command ship facilities originally provided in this class were for a Navy amphibious task force commander and a Marine Corps assault force commander and their staffs. Their designed flag/staff accommodations were for 200 officers and 500 enlisted.

The ships have large open deck areas to provide for optimum

2 AMPHIBIOUS COMMAND SHIPS: "BLUE RIDGE" CLASS

Number	Name	FY	Builder	Laid down	Launched	Commissioned	Status
LCC 19	Blue Ridge	65	Philadelphia Naval Shipyard, Penna.	27 Feb 1967	4 Jan 1969	14 Nov 1970	**PA**
LCC 20	Mount Whitney	66	Newport News Shipbuilding, Va.	8 Jan 1969	8 Jan 1970	16 Jan 1971	**AA**

Displacement:	16,790 tons light LCC 19 18,390 tons full load LCC 20 18,646 tons full load
Length:	579 11/12 feet (176.8 m) waterline 636 5/12 feet (194.0 m) overall
Beam:	82 feet (25.0 m)
Extreme width:	108 feet (32.9 m)
Draft:	27 7/12 feet (8.4 m)
Propulsion:	1 steam turbine (General Electric); 22,000 shp; 1 shaft
Boilers:	2 600 psi (41.7 kg/cm^2) (Foster Wheeler)
Speed:	22 knots
Range:	13,500 n.miles (25,000 km) at 16 knots
Manning:	LCC 19 784 (42 officers + 742 enlisted) LCC 20 717 (43 officers + 674 enlisted)
Flag:	LCC 19 196 (47 officers + 149 enlisted) LCC 20 160 (51 officers + 109 enlisted)
Troops:	LCC 19 16 (1 officer + 15 enlisted)
Helicopters:	landing area only
Missiles:	removed
Guns:	2 25-mm Mk 38 Bushmaster guns (2 single) 2 20-mm Phalanx CIWS Mk 16 (2 multi-barrel) 4 12.7-mm machine guns (4 single)
Radars:	SPS-40E air search SPS-48C 3-D search SPS-64(V)9 navigation SPS-67(V)1 surface search
Fire control:	removed
EW systems:	SLQ-25 Nixie SLQ-32(V)3A

The Blue Ridge in the Far East. Note the bridge extensions, the boat stowage, and the antenna array fitted in these ships. Designed as amphibious command ships, the Blue Ridge and Mount Whitney are invaluable as fleet-task force flagships. (1995, Giorgio Arra)

antenna placement. There is a helicopter landing area aft, but no hangar. (A small vehicle hangar is serviced by an elevator.) Davits provide stowage for five LCPL/LCVP–type personnel craft, plus a ship's launch.

Electronics: Fitted with the Naval Tactical Data System.

Engineering: Maximum sustained speed is 20 knots.

Guns: The early designs for this ship provided for six 3-inch/50-cal AA Mk 33 guns in twin mounts: two pair forward of the bridge structure in enclosed gun houses were fitted, but the third pair on the forecastle was not installed. The two 3-inch mounts were removed in 1992.

Phalanx CIWS mounts were long scheduled for installation in these ships. Two were installed in the BLUE RIDGE in 1985, mounted forward on a small deckhouse fitted on the main deck and on a sponson at the stern (increasing the ship's length approximately 16 feet/4.9 m). The MOUNT WHITNEY was fitted in 1987 with two CIWS mounts.

Helicopters: A UH-3H Sea King is usually assigned to each ship.

Missiles: Two 8-tube Sea Sparrow BPDMS launchers were fitted abaft of the bridge structure in 1974. They were removed from both ships in 1992, as were the two Mk 115 missile fire control systems.

Operational: In addition to the Seventh Fleet staff, the BLUE RIDGE carries a Marine communications detachment. For exercises, the BLUE RIDGE normally embarks the staffs of Commander, Amphibious Group 1/Amphibious Force Seventh Fleet (48 officers + 95 enlisted), and the Commander, III Marine Expeditionary Force/Landing Force Seventh Fleet (80 officers + 127 enlisted).

For exercises, the MOUNT WHITNEY carries the staff of Amphibious Group 2 (26 officers + 47 enlisted), in addition to the Second Fleet staff.

AMPHIBIOUS COMMAND SHIPS

Amphibious command ships—originally called amphibious force flagships—reached hull number AGC 18 during World War II. A variety of ships comprised the type: 15 C2 merchant ships completed as AGCs, a converted liner, a converted seaplane tender, and a converted Coast Guard cutter. The last was one of six 327-foot (99.7-m) cutters of the Secretary class (WPG 31–37) that served as amphibious flagships, although only the DUANE (WPG 33) was reclassified (AGC 6).

Five surviving ships were changed from AGC to LCC on 1 January 1969. The last war-era AGC to see active naval service was the ELDORADO (AGC/LCC 11), decommissioned in 1973. She and the others were transferred to the Maritime Administration for disposal.

The yacht WILLIAMSBURG, which served as a gunboat (PG 56) from 1941 to 1945, was assigned as the presidential yacht after World War II, being redesignated AGC 369 on 10 November 1945. She served in that role for Presidents Truman and (for one cruise) Eisenhower. The WILLIAMSBURG was decommissioned in 1953 and stricken in 1962. (The ship was then employed as a civilian oceanographic research ship from 1962 to 1968; she was undergoing rehabilitation to a yacht configuration in an Italian shipyard when this edition went to press.)

The stern aspect of the MOUNT WHITNEY. While fitted with a helicopter deck, these ships unfortunately lack hangar facilities for supporting helicopters. (1994, U.S. Navy, PH2 John Sokolowski)

1 MISCELLANEOUS FLAGSHIP: CONVERTED "AUSTIN" CLASS

Number	Name	FY	Builder	Laid down	Launched	Commissioned	Status
AGF 11 (ex-LPD 11)	CORONADO	64	Lockheed Shipbuilding & Constn., Seattle, Wash.	3 May 1965	30 July 1966	23 May 1970	**PA**

Displacement:	11,050 tons light 16,912 tons full load
Length:	568¾ feet (173.4 m) overall
Beam:	84 feet (25.6 m)
Draft:	23⁷⁄₁₂ feet (7.2 m)
Propulsion:	2 steam turbines (De Laval); 24,000 shp; 2 shafts
Boilers:	2 600 psi (41.7 kg/cm²) (Foster-Wheeler)
Speed:	21 knots
Range:	7,700 n.miles (14,260 km) at 20 knots
Manning:	457 (24 officers + 433 enlisted)
Flag:	approximately 50
Helicopters:	1 SH-3 Sea King
Missiles:	none
Guns:	2 20-mm Phalanx CIWS Mk 16 (2 multi-barrel) 2 12.7-mm machine guns (2 single)
Radars:	SPS-10F surface search SPS-40E air search SPS-64(V)9 navigation
Fire control:	local control only
EW systems:	SLQ-32(V)2 WLR-1H intercept

The CORONADO was built and served as a dock landing ship until 1980 when she was modified to serve as a temporary flagship to permit the Middle East flagship LA SALLE to undergo a lengthy overhaul at the Philadelphia Naval Shipyard. After an overhaul in 1983–1984 she became flagship of the Sixth Fleet in August 1985 and was homeported in Gaeta, Italy. The CORONADO replaced the destroyer tender PUGET SOUND (AD 38) as Sixth Fleet flagship.

In June 1986, with the BELKNAP assigned as Sixth Fleet flagship, the CORONADO departed the Mediterranean, and the following month she was shifted to the Pacific to become flagship for Commander, Third Fleet (then based at Pearl Harbor). Prior to breaking his flag in the CORONADO on 26 November 1986, the Commander, Third Fleet, had flown his flag ashore since the end of World War II. In August 1991 the Commander, Third Fleet, sailing on board the CORONADO, shifted her home port to North Island Naval Air Station at San Diego, California.

Classification: Changed from LPD 11 to AGF 11 on 1 October 1980.

Conversion: The CORONADO's telescoping hangar is 49½ feet (15.1 m) long, 18½ feet (5.6 m) wide, and 17⅔ feet (5.4 m) high; it expands to a length of about 75 feet (22.9 m). The ship retains a docking well.

Design: SCB No. 187C. See AUSTIN (LPD 4) listing for additional details. The ship is similar to, but larger than, the LA SALLE.

Guns: Phalanx CIWS mounts have been installed on an extension of the bridge structure, forward to port, and amidships, on the starboard side.

The two 3-inch/50-cal Mk 33 AA twin gun mounts previously carried in the AGF role were removed in the early 1990s.

The CORONADO moored at San Francisco. The antenna rigs of the command ships are periodically changed. (1988, Giorgio Arra)

The Third Fleet flagship CORONADO. She has a telescoping hangar aft of the superstructure. Small sponsons at the main deck level, port and starboard, provide additional working spaces. (1991, U.S. Navy, OS2 John Bouvia)

1 MISCELLANEOUS FLAGSHIP: CONVERTED "RALEIGH" CLASS

Number	Name	FY	Builder	Laid down	Launched	Commissioned	Status
AGF 3 (ex-LPD 3)	La Salle	61	New York Naval Shipyard, N.Y.	2 Apr 1962	3 Aug 1963	22 Feb 1964	AA

Displacement:	8,040 tons light 13,900 tons full load
Length:	500 feet (152.4 m) waterline 521¾ feet (159.0 m) overall
Beam:	84 feet (25.6 m)
Draft:	21 feet (6.4 m)
Propulsion:	2 steam turbines (De Laval); 24,000 shp; 2 shafts
Boilers:	2 600 psi (41.7 kg/cm²) (Babcock & Wilcox)
Speed:	21.6 knots (20 knots sustained)
Range:	9,600 n.miles (17,780 km) at 16 knots 16,500 n.miles (30,558 km) at 10 knots
Manning:	455 (24 officers + 431 enlisted)
Flag:	138 (48 officers + 90 enlisted)
Helicopters:	landing area
Missiles:	none
Guns:	2 25-mm Mk 38 Bushmaster cannon (2 single) 2 20-mm Phalanx CIWS Mk 16 (2 multi-barrel) 2 12.7-mm machine guns (2 single)
Radars:	SPS-10F surface search SPS-40E air search SPS-64(V)9 navigation
Fire control:	local control only
EW systems:	SLQ-32(V)3 WLR-1H

The La Salle was converted from an amphibious transport dock specifically to serve as flagship for the Commander, U.S. Middle East Force (now Commander, U.S. Naval Forces, Central Command). In November 1994 she replaced the cruiser Belknap as flagship of the Sixth Fleet in the Mediterranean.

The La Salle initially served as an amphibious ship.

Class: The La Salle was one of three Raleigh (LPD 1)-class amphibious transport docks.

Classification: Built as LPD 3, she served as an amphibious ship until 1 July 1972, when the designation changed to AGF 3.

Conversion: The ship was converted to a flagship in 1972, when she was fitted with command and communication facilities, a helicopter hangar, and additional air-conditioning. The amidships hangar is 47⁵⁄₁₂ feet (14.6 m) long, 18¹⁄₁₂ feet (5.5 m) wide, and 19⅓ feet (5.9 m) high. Her docking well has been converted into office space.

Design: SCB No. 187A.

Guns: Phalanx CIWS mounts have been installed amidships, port and starboard.

The two 3-inch (76-mm) 50-cal Mk 33 AA twin gun mounts previously mounted as an AGF have been deleted.

Operational: The La Salle operated in the Persian Gulf–Indian Ocean area from 1972 to 1980, when she was relieved by the Coronado. The La Salle underwent an extensive overhaul at the Philadelphia Naval Shipyard from December 1980 to September 1982. After that overhaul she, in turn, relieved the Coronado as flagship of the Middle East Force on 16 June 1983 at Minā Sulman, Bahrain. She served in that role during the Persian Gulf War, shifting to the Mediterranean in late 1994. She is currently homeported in Gaeta, Italy.

In response to the mining of the Red Sea by a Libyan merchant ship in 1984, the La Salle operated RH-53D Sea Stallion mine countermeasures helicopters.

Prior to the conversion of the La Salle, the flagship of the Commander, Middle East Force, had been a small seaplane tender of the Barnegat (AVP 10) class from the time that command was established in the late 1940s (see below) onward.

FLEET/NATIONAL COMMAND SHIPS

In addition to the two amphibious command ships (AGC/LCC) listed above, the Navy has built one ship and converted another since World War II specifically for use as major command ships. A third such ship was planned for conversion.

The heavy cruiser Northampton (CA 125) was canceled on 11 August 1945 while under construction (she was about 50 percent complete). She was subsequently reordered in 1948 as a tactical light command ship (CLC 1) and completed in that configuration in 1953. After operating as a fleet flagship, the Northampton was reconfigured to serve as a National Emergency Command Post Afloat (NECPA) in 1961 and reclassified as CC 1. She was decommissioned in 1970 and laid up in reserve until stricken in 1977.

The light aircraft carriers Wright (CVL 49) and Saipan (CVL 48), completed in 1946–1947, were similarly designated for conversion to the NECPA role. The Wright, also designated AVT 7 while in reserve, was converted to a national command ship in 1962–1963 and became CC 2. She operated in the NECPA role until being laid up in reserve in 1970. She was stricken in 1977.

The Saipan, designated AVT 6 while in reserve after World War II, began conversion to CC 3 in 1964, but she was completed instead as a

The La Salle, the last ship of the innovative Raleigh class in active service. She has a pole mast, while the Coronado, of the later Austin class, has a tripod mast. The La Salle's two Phalanx CIWS mounts can be seen amidships. (U.S. Navy)

major communications relay ship in 1966 (renamed ARLINGTON and designated AGMR 2).

In the NECPA role these ships were to provide afloat facilities for the President in the event of a national emergency or war. (A more interesting, though never undertaken, proposal was to convert the large, nuclear-propelled submarine TRITON/SSRN 586 to an under-water NECPA.)

In the fiscal 1953 conversion program the unfinished large cruiser HAWAII (CB 3) was authorized for conversion to a fleet command ship (CBC), but no work was undertaken on that project and it was ultimately canceled. The HAWAII would have been an enlarged version of the NORTHAMPTON (as CLC 1).

MISCELLANEOUS FLAGSHIPS

From 1949 until 1965 the Navy rotated three small seaplane tenders (AVP) as flagship for U.S. forces in the Persian Gulf area. They were the DUXBURY BAY (AVP 38), GREENWICH BAY (AVP 41), and VALCOUR (AVP 55). The VALCOUR was reclassified as a miscellaneous flagship (AGF 1) on 15 December 1965 and homeported in Bahrain. She was replaced in that role by the LA SALLE in 1972. Since 1994 various U.S. cruisers and destroyers operating in the gulf area have served as flagship for the Commander, Naval Forces, U.S. Central Command; the first was the FLETCHER (DD 992), in 1994.

The Middle East AVP/AGF flagships were painted white to help counter the intensive heat in the Persian Gulf.

This overhead view shows the LA SALLE during Operation Southern Watch in the Persian Gulf. The amidships hangar and awnings are visible; the large amidships crane handles the admiral's barge and ship's boats. (1993, U.S. Navy, PH2 Tim W. Tow)

CHAPTER 19

Amphibious Ships

The large helicopter carrier ESSEX takes aboard an air cushion landing craft. The Marines and helicopters on her flight deck demonstrate the versatility of amphibious forces. AV-8B Harrier STOVL aircraft and unmanned aerial "vehicles" can easily be accommodated in these large ships, providing a potent capability across a spectrum of conflicts. (Litton/Ingalls Shipbuilding)

The U.S. Navy's amphibious lift in the fall of 1996 consisted of 37 ships in active service and two in the Naval Reserve Force (NRF), the latter manned by composite active-reserve crews. Four more amphibious-type ships (LCC/LPD) are employed as command ships for fleet/force commanders and are not available to provide amphibious lift (see chapter 18).

In addition, several amphibious ships are being maintained in reserve, two of them in Reduced Operating Status (ROS) to offset the retirement of older ships and delays in procurement of the new LPD 17 class (formerly designated LX). The ROS ships can be reactivated in a few days; the other ships—in "mothball" status—will take several months to bring into service.

Currently under construction are large helicopter-dock ships (LHD) and amphibious transport docks (LPD). A replacement for the TARAWA class is also being designed (designated LHX).

One former LPH, the INCHON, is currently undergoing conversion to a mine countermeasures support ship (MCS).

The current active "amphib" force has a theoretical lift capacity of the assault elements of 2½ Marine brigade equivalents. A better measure is that each of 12 Amphibious Ready Groups (ARG) can embark a Marine Expeditionary Unit (MEU) consisting of a reinforced infantry battalion and a composite aircraft squadron—a total of some 2,500 men and women. Thus 12 ARGs provide a total lift of almost 30,000 troops. While the current amphibious force can provide approximately the desired lift in terms of people, helicopters, and landing craft, there is a shortage of vehicle lift that will not be remedied until the LPD 17 class begins to enter service, after the year 2000.

This amphibious capability compares to an amphibious ship force objective at the end of the Cold War of 72 ships to provide lift for the assault elements of one Marine Expeditionary Force (MEF) plus one Marine Expeditionary Brigade (MEB).

The Reagan administration's buildup of amphibious ships in the 1980s was the third major "spurt" of amphibious ship construction since World War II. The first, during the Korean War, produced the LSD 28 and LST 1156 classes (23 ships); the second, in the Kennedy-Johnson administrations of the early 1960s, produced the LCC 19, LHA 1, LKA 112, LPD 12, LSD 36, and LST 1179 classes (49 ships).

The third postwar amphibious ship buildup effort began with the WHIDBEY ISLAND, the first amphibious ship authorized for the U.S. Navy in a decade. That ship was funded by Congress in fiscal 1981 over the objections of the Carter administration. With the Reagan administration entering the White House in January 1981, amphibious ship construction was accelerated. This third amphibious buildup included the WASP, WHIDBEY ISLAND, and HARPERS FERRY classes. Eighteen ships of these three classes were funded in the fiscal 1984–1993 shipbuilding programs.

The accompanying table of Nominal Amphibious Lift Capabilities shows the capacity of current amphibious ships.

Aircraft: A normal LHA/LHD "air wing" consists of a Marine composite squadron of 18 CH-46 Sea Knights, 4 CH-53 Sea Stallions, and 4 AH-1W SeaCobra helicopters, plus a couple of UH-1N Huey command/utility helicopters.

An LPH embarks 12 CH-46s, 4 CH-53Es, 4 AH-1Ws, plus UH-1Ns.

These ships regularly operate AV-8B Harrier STOVL fixed-wing attack aircraft.[1] They also operate Unmanned Aerial Vehicle (UAV)–type aircraft.

No catapults or arresting gear are fitted to the LHD/LHA/LPH–type ships.

Guns: Beginning in the 1980s LSD- and LPD-type amphibious ships were fitted with .50-cal/7.62-mm machine guns, 25-mm Mk 38 Bushmaster "chain" guns, and 20-mm cannon for close-in defense against small craft. This armament suite was especially important for ships deploying into the Persian Gulf.

All 3-inch/50-cal (76-mm) guns have been removed from surviving amphibious ships except for NEWPORT-class LSTs and CHARLESTON-class LKAs, all in reserve. The only "major" guns fitted in active amphibious ships are 5-inch/54-cal (127-mm) guns in the TARAWA-class LHAs.

Names: Amphibious assault ships (LHA/LPH) are named for battles fought by Marines; the LHD series, however, carries the names of World War II–era aircraft carriers, which, in turn, were named for early Navy ships and battles.

Amphibious cargo ships (LKA) and tank landing ships (LST) are named for counties and parishes, the latter term being the equivalent of counties in the state of Louisiana.[2]

Amphibious transport docks (LPD) are named for cities that honor explorers and pioneers.

Dock landing ships (LSD) carry the names of historic sites and cities.

Operational: The current amphibious force is organized into 12 amphibious ready groups, with each ARG based on an Amphibious Squadron (PhibRon). One group is normally deployed to the Mediterranean with a MEU embarked, and a group is similarly deployed to the Western Pacific–Indian Ocean area with a MEU embarked. Periodically, a third amphibious group operates in the Caribbean area and another in the Western Pacific. Including groups that are en route to and from deployments, or on special exercises, a significant fraction of the Navy's amphibious lift capability is at sea in widely separated areas at any given time. (This peacetime deployment pattern could inhibit the rapid assembly of a large number of amphibious ships in times of crisis or war.)

After the end of the Cold War the Department of Defense planned an initial reduction to 11 ARGs; however, the unanticipated deployment of the helicopter carrier INCHON to Haiti in support of operations there in 1994—coupled with the crises-conflicts in Bosnia, Somalia, and North Korea—led to a reevaluation of amphibious force requirements, and the decision was made to maintain 12 amphibious groups. The Navy envisions amphibious groups after the turn of the century to each consist of one LHA/LHD, one LSD, and one LPD 17-class (LX) ship, for a total force of 36 amphibious ships.

AMPHIBIOUS WARFARE SHIPS (FALL 1996)

Type	Class/Ship	Comm.	Active	NRF	Reserve	Building*
LHD 1	WASP	1989–	4	—	—	3
LHA 1	TARAWA	1976–1980	5	—	—	—
LPH 2	IWO JIMA	1961–1970	2	—	—	—
LPD 17	. . . . . .	2002	—	—	—	1
LPD 4	AUSTIN	1965–1971	11	—	—	—
LPD 1	RALEIGH	1962–1964	—	—	1	—
LSD 49	HARPERS FERRY	1995–	3	—	—	1
LSD 41	WHIDBEY ISLAND	1985–1992	8	—	—	—
LSD 36	ANCHORAGE	1969–1972	5	—	—	—
LST 1179	NEWPORT	1969–1972	—	2	7	—
LKA 113	CHARLESTON	1968–1970	—	—	5**	—

*Ships authorized through fiscal 1996.
**Two ships are in Reduced Operating Status (see class entry).

NOMINAL AMPHIBIOUS LIFT CAPABILITIES

Class	Troops	Vehicle space (square feet)	Cargo space (cubic feet)	Helicopter spots*	LCAC spots**
LHD 1	1,685	20,900	185,000	46	3
LHA 1	1,710	25,400	105,900	41	1
LPH 2	1,490	3,400	49,500	26	—
LPD 17	720	25,000	25,000	6	2
LPD 4	#	12,000	40,000	4	1
LSD 49	450	16,200	50,700	2	2
LSD 41	450	13,500	5,100	1	4
LSD 36	300	15,200	1,400	1	3
LST 1179	350	17,300	3,400	1	—
LKA 113	210	32,900	66,100	1	—

*Hangar and flight deck capacity (CH-46E equivalents) for ships that normally embark helicopters.
**Docking well capacity.
#LPD 4–6, 14, 15 can accommodate 930 troops; LPD 7–10, 12, 13 can accommodate 840 troops.

1. The term Vertical/Short Take-Off and Landing (VSTOL) was previously used for the Harrier aircraft. It was changed by the U.S. Marine Corps in February 1995 to Short Take-Off/Vertical Landing (STOVL).

2. When LSTs were first assigned names on 1 July 1955, all names had the suffix county or parish. This naming scheme was continued until the naming of the NEWPORT and several of her sister ships, which do not have prefixes.

AMPHIBIOUS ASSAULT SHIPS: LHX DESIGN

The LHX is planned as a replacement for the LHA-type ships as they reach the end of their projected 35-year service life (although they will probably serve longer with SLEP/modernization work). The principal difference from the LHA/LHD will be the replacement of the docking well with a "dry-well" for three LCACs or other vehicles that would be unloaded via a stern ramp.

The design was previously referred to as LVX.

The first LHX is planned for authorization about 2005 and completion about 2011.

4 + 3 AMPHIBIOUS ASSAULT SHIPS: "WASP" CLASS

Number	Name	FY	Builder	Laid down	Launched	Christened	Commissioned	Status
LHD 1	WASP	84	Litton/Ingalls Shipbuilding, Pascagoula, Miss.	30 May 1985	4 Aug 1987	19 Sep 1987	6 July 1989	**AA**
LHD 2	ESSEX	86	Litton/Ingalls Shipbuilding, Pascagoula, Miss.	20 Mar 1989	7 Jan 1991	16 Mar 1991	17 Oct 1992	**PA**
LHD 3	KEARSARGE	88	Litton/Ingalls Shipbuilding, Pascagoula, Miss.	6 Feb 1990	26 Mar 1992	16 May 1992	16 Oct 1993	**AA**
LHD 4	BOXER	89	Litton/Ingalls Shipbuilding, Pascagoula, Miss.	8 Apr 1991	13 Aug 1993	28 Aug 1993	11 Feb 1995	**PA**
LHD 5	BATAAN	91	Litton/Ingalls Shipbuilding, Pascagoula, Miss.	22 June 1994	15 Mar 1996	18 May1996	1998	Building
LHD 6	BONHOMME RICHARD	93	Litton/Ingalls Shipbuilding, Pascagoula, Miss.	18 Apr 1995	1997	1997	1998	Building
LHD 7	......	96	Litton/Ingalls Shipbuilding, Pascagoula, Miss.				2000	Authorized

Displacement:	28,233 tons light 40,530 tons full load
Length:	777⅚ feet (237.1 m) waterline 844 feet (257.3 m) overall
Beam:	106 feet (32.3 m) waterline
Extreme width:	140 feet (42.7 m)
Draft:	26⅔ feet (8.1 m)
Propulsion:	2 steam turbines; 77,000 shp; 2 shafts
Boilers:	2 720 psi (49.3 kg/cm²) (Combustion Engineering)
Speed:	24 knots (22 knots sustained)
Range:	9,500 n.miles (17,594 km) at 20 knots
Manning:	1,146 (62 officers + 1,084 enlisted)
Troops:	1,685
Aircraft:	amphibious role: approx. 30 CH-46 Sea Knight and CH-53 Sea Stallion helicopters + 6 AV-8B Harrier STOVL carrier role: approx. 20 AV-8B Harrier STOVL + 6 SH-60B/F ASW helicopters
Elevators:	2 deck edge (50 × 45 feet 15.2 × 13.7 m)
Missiles:	2 8-tube NATO Sea Sparrow missile launchers Mk 29
Guns:	3 20-mm Phalanx CIWS Mk 16 (3 multi-barrel) 8 12.7-mm machine guns M2 (8 single)
Radars:	Mk 23 Target Acquisition System (TAS) SPS-48E 3-D air search in LHD 2–6 SPS-49(V)5 or (V)9 air search SPS-52C 3-D air search in LHD 1 SPS-64(V)9 navigation SPS-67(V)3 surface search
Fire control:	2 Mk 91 missiles FCS 1 SYS-2(V)3 weapon control system
EW systems:	SLQ-25 Nixie SLQ-32(V)3 SRS-1 combat D/F

These ships and the similar TARAWA class are the world's largest amphibious ships. The only larger ships that have been employed in this role were the converted ESSEX (CV 9)-class fleet carriers that operated in the LPH role (see below). The WASP class was initially planned as helicopter-carrying amphibious ships that would be smaller and less costly than the TARAWA class. In the event, the basic LHA design was adopted, with the following principal differences: (1) increased Harrier STOVL aircraft support capability; (2) movement of the stern elevator to the starboard side of the flight deck; (3) redesign of the docking well to accommodate three LCAC with an LPD/LSD stern gate vice the sectional, "split" gate of the LHA; and (4) modification of the self-defense armament.

Class: A seventh LHD was planned in the fiscal 2001 shipbuilding program to provide 12 large-deck helicopter ships (LHA/LHD) to maintain 12 amphibious ready groups. However, Congress authorized the LHD 7 in fiscal 1996 to reduce procurement costs and to accelerate modernization of amphibious lift. The ship was ordered on 28 December 1995.

Classification: During the preliminary design stage these ships were designated LHDX. They should correctly have been designated in the LHA series (i.e., LHD 6–12), as the differences in the two types are minor.

Cost: The BONHOMME RICHARD is officially listed as a fiscal 1993 ship, although advanced funds were provided in fiscal 1993 ($303.1 million) and the majority of the funds in fiscal 1994 ($893.8 million). The ship will also require outfitting and post-delivery funding, i.e., a total of about $1.2 *billion.*

Design: Whereas the basic configuration of these ships is similar to the LHA 1 class, they have less vehicle storage space and bulk cargo space. Nevertheless, they carry more aircraft, and the arrangement of the docking well permits more air cushion landing craft (three LCACs) to be embarked. Alternatively, the well can hold 12 LCM(6)s or 6 LCM(8)s or 2 LCU 1610s. The LHDs also have communications and certain command spaces moved into the hull (vice island structure) for better protection.

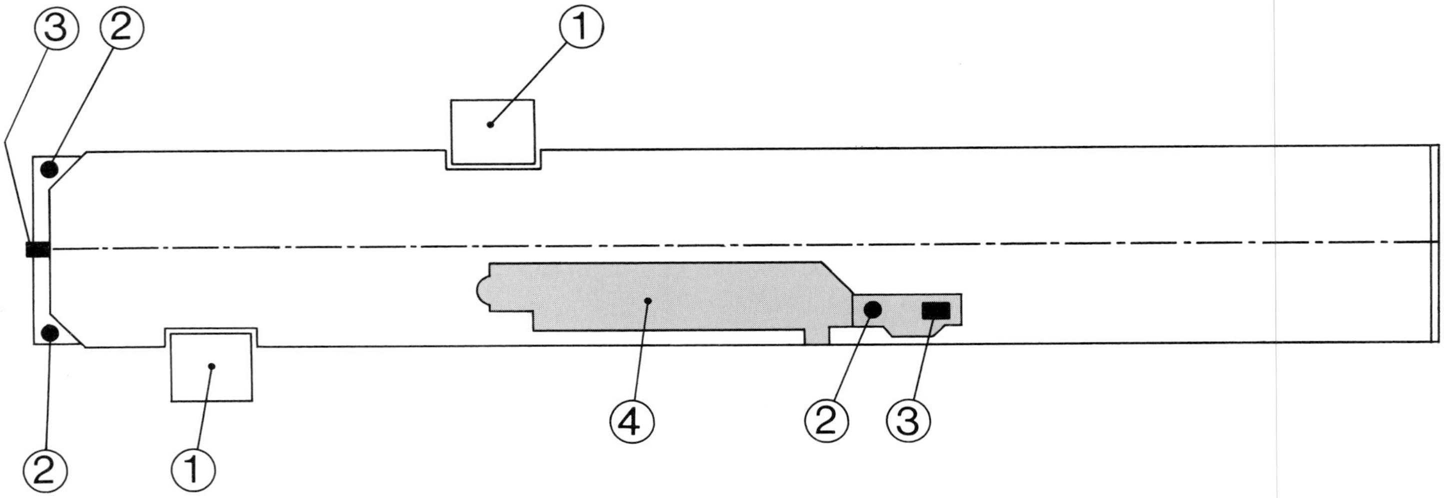

WASP
1. Deck-edge elevator (2). 2. Phalanx CIWS (3). 3. NATO Sea Sparrow missile launcher (2). 4. Island structure.

The stern centerline elevator of the LHA design has been moved to the starboard side, aft.

Although intended from the outset to operate Harriers as well as helicopters, these ships do not have ski-jump ramps to assist STOVL operations because the size of the flight deck is considered sufficiently large to enable rolling takeoffs for heavily laden STOVL aircraft.

Medical facilities include beds for 600 patients, with four main operating rooms and extensive dental facilities.

Electronics: Fitted with SPN-35A marshaling and SPN-43B and SPN-47 aircraft approach/control systems.

Engineering: Maximum horsepower is indicated above; the sustained ship is 70,000. Note that these ships and the TARAWA class have had their boilers upgraded from the original 600 psi (41.7 kg/cm^2).

Names: These ships honor World War II–era fleet carriers (CV/CVL). The WASP remembers both the CV 7, which was sunk in 1942, and her namesake, the CV 18.

The BONHOMME RICHARD is named for the carrier CV 31 (although that ship was named BON HOMME RICHARD) and the original frigate BONHOMME RICHARD, commanded by John Paul Jones in 1779 during her heroic battle with the British frigate SERAPIS.

A "sense-of-Congress" resolution passed in late 1995 proposed naming the LHD 7 the IWO JIMA. Previous ships with that name were the CV 46 (canceled) and the LPH 2.

Troops: Approximately 200 additional troops can be embarked for short transits (i.e., several days).

The WASP under way off the coast of Haiti during Operation Support Democracy. Five large H-53E series helicopters are parked forward, with a variety of other helicopters visible on her flight deck. These ships have the same hull as the earlier TARAWA class. (1994, U.S. Navy, PH2 John Sokolowski)

The ESSEX at Hong Kong. The principal differences between the LHD and LHA designs are the configuration of the docking well and the movement of the after aircraft elevator from the centerline to the starboard side, as shown here on the ESSEX. Note the two Phalanx CIWS mounts and the NATO Sea Sparrow launcher above the well gate. (1994, Giorgio Arra)

The ESSEX island structure has a Phalanx CIWS and NATO Sea Sparrow launcher stepped forward of the bridge. The mast and radar configurations differ in the LHA/LHD designs. The SLQ-32(V)3 ECM antenna is shown just forward of the refueling rig, above the bridge level. (1994, Giorgio Arra)

The docking well of the KEARSARGE with an LCAC at rest. Three LCACs can be accommodated. There are overhead rails for cranes to load equipment from the storage holds of the LHD. (1994, Leo Van Ginderen collection)

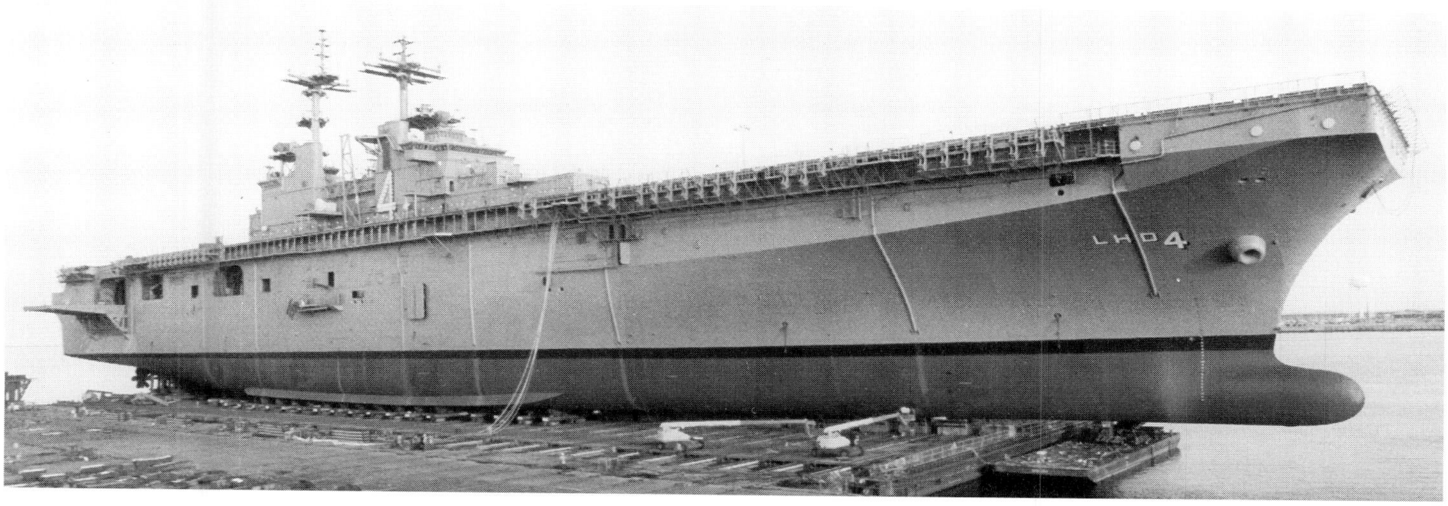

The BOXER is seen high and dry on her launch platform. The massive carrier-like hull has a prominent bow bulb. The starboard deck-edge elevator is far aft; the port deck-edge elevator is opposite the after end of the island structure. These ships are larger than any foreign warships except for Russian aircraft carriers. (1993, Litton/Ingalls Shipbuilding)

5 AMPHIBIOUS ASSAULT SHIPS: "TARAWA" CLASS

Number	Name	FY	Builder	Laid down	Launched	Christened	Commissioned	Status
LHA 1	TARAWA	69	Litton/Ingalls Shipbuilding, Pascagoula, Miss.	15 Nov 1971	1 Dec 1973	1 Dec 1973	29 May 1976	**PA**
LHA 2	SAIPAN	70	Litton/Ingalls Shipbuilding, Pascagoula, Miss.	21 July 1972	18 July 1974	20 July 1974	15 Oct 1977	**AA**
LHA 3	BELLEAU WOOD	70	Litton/Ingalls Shipbuilding, Pascagoula, Miss.	5 Mar 1973	11 Apr 1977	11 June 1977	23 Sep 1978	**PA**
LHA 4	NASSAU	71	Litton/Ingalls Shipbuilding, Pascagoula, Miss.	13 Aug 1973	21 Jan 1978	28 Jan 1978	28 July 1979	**AA**
LHA 5	PELELIU	71	Litton/Ingalls Shipbuilding, Pascagoula, Miss.	12 Nov 1976	25 Nov 1978	6 Jan 1979	3 May 1980	**PA**

Displacement: 33,536 tons light
39,967 tons full load
Length: 777⅔ feet (237.1 m) waterline
833¾ feet (254.2 m) overall
Beam: 106 feet (32.3 m)
Extreme width: 132 feet (40.2 m)
Draft: 26 feet (7.9 m)
Propulsion: 2 steam turbines (Westinghouse); 77,000 shp; 2 shafts
Boilers: 2 720 psi (49.3 kg/cm^2) (Combustion Engineering)
Speed: 24 knots (22 knots sustained)
Range: 10,000 n.miles (18,520 km) at 20 knots
Manning: LHA 1 1,063 (58 officers + 1,005 enlisted)
LHA 2 1,067 (58 officers + 1,009 enlisted)
LHA 3 1,058 (58 officers + 1,000 enlisted)
LHA 4, 5 1,064 (58 officers + 1,006 enlisted)
Troops: 1,710
Aircraft: approx. 30 CH-46 Sea Knight and CH-53 Sea Stallion + 6 AV-8B Harrier STOVL
Elevators: 1 deck edge (50 × 34 feet | 15.2 × 10.3 m)
1 stern (59¾ × 34¾ feet | 18.2 × 10.6 m)

Missiles: 2 8-tube Sea Sparrow BPDMS launchers Mk 25 except 1 launcher in LHA 2
2 21-tube RAM launchers Mk 49
Guns: 2 5-inch (127-mm) 54-cal DP Mk 45 (2 single)
6 20-mm/70-cal cannon Mk 67 (6 single)
2 20-mm Phalanx CIWS Mk 16 (2 multi-barrel)
8 12.7-mm machine guns M2 (8 single)
Radars: Mk 23 Target Acquisition System (TAS) in LHA 5
SPS-40E air search
SPS-52B 3-D air search
SPS-64(V)9 navigation
SPS-67(V)3 surface search
Fire control: 1 Mk 86 GFCS with SPG-60 and SPQ-9A radars
2 Mk 115 missile FCS
1 SWY-2 weapon control system (RAM)
EW systems: SLQ-25 Nixie
SLQ-32(V)3

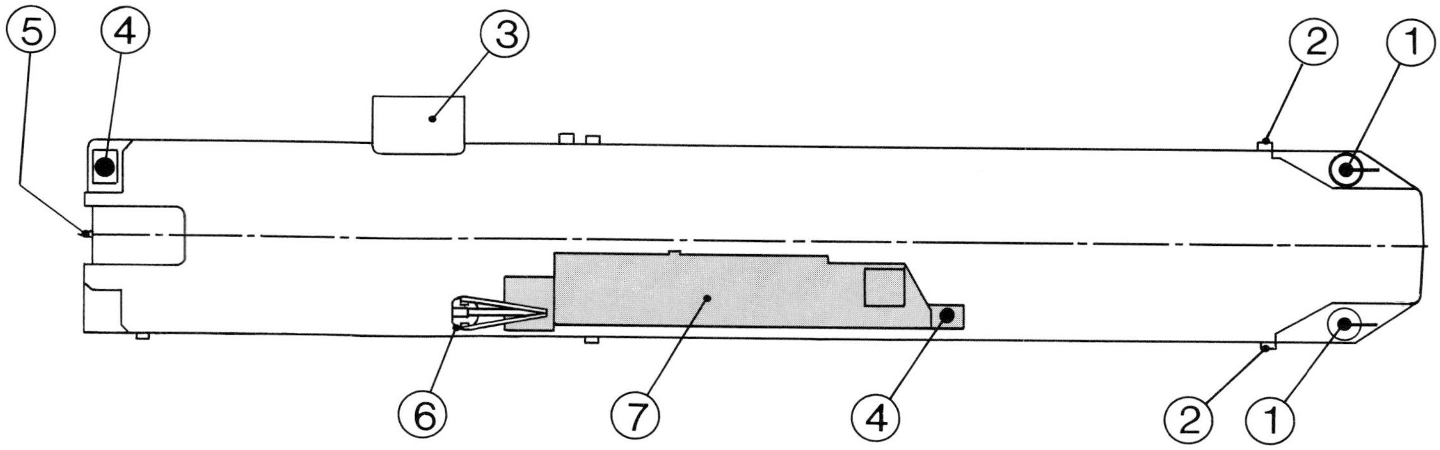

TARAWA
1. 5-inch DP gun Mk 45 (2). 2. 20-mm cannon Mk 67 (6). 3. Deck-edge elevator. 4. Phalanx CIWS (4). 5. Stern elevator. 6. Aircraft/boat crane. 7. Island structure.

The TARAWA-class ships combine the capabilities of several types of amphibious ships in a single hull. In addition, these ships periodically have operated AV-8 Harrier STOVL aircraft and OV-10 Bronco STOL aircraft.[3]

Note that the TARAWA was christened on the same date that she was launched ("floated off" her assembly dock).

The BELLEAU WOOD is homeported at Sasebo, Japan, the flagship for the ships of Amphibious Group 1 based there.

Class: Nine ships of this class were originally planned in the early 1960s. The Navy announced on 20 January 1971 that LHA 6–9 would not be constructed.

Design: SCB No. 410. Special features of this class include an 18-foot (5.5-m) section of the mast that is hinged to permit passage under bridges; a 5,000-square-foot (450-m^2) training and acclimatization room to permit troops to exercise in a controlled environment; the vehicle storage decks connected by ramps to the flight deck and docking well; and five cargo elevators to move equipment between the holds and flight deck. Extensive command and communications facilities are provided for an amphibious force commander.

The hangar deck is 820 feet (250 m) long and 78 feet (27.8 m) wide, with a 20-foot (6.1-m) overhead.

The stern docking well is 268 feet (81.7 m) long and 78 feet (23.8 m) wide and can accommodate 4 LCU 1610 landing craft or 7 LCM(8)s or 17 LCM(6)s or 45 AAV/LVTP-7 amphibian vehicles. Because of the arrangement of the docking well, only one LCAC can be carried. In addition, 35 amphibian vehicles can be carried on the third deck of an LHA.

Extensive medical facilities are provided, including three operating rooms and bed space for 300 patients.

3. STOL = Short Take-Off and Landing.

Electronics: SPN-35 aircraft marshaling and SPN-43B approach/control systems are fitted. The ships' radars have been upgraded.

Engineering: Maximum horsepower is indicated above; the sustained shp is 70,000. A 900-hp through-tunnel thruster is fitted in the forward part of the hull to assist in maneuvering while launching landing craft.

The ships' boilers are the largest ever manufactured in the United States.

Guns: These are the only U.S. amphibious ships currently armed with 5-inch guns. As built, three 5-inch guns were fitted; the 5-inch gun originally mounted aft, starboard side, has been replaced by drone (UAV) aircraft controls.

Missiles: These ships originally had two Sea Sparrow BPDMS Mk 25 launchers (one in LHA 2) controlled by two Mk 71 directors with Mk 115 radars. These have been replaced by two RAM (Rolling Airframe Missile) launchers, beginning with the 1992 refitting of the PELELIU and BELLEAU WOOD.

Names: The PELELIU was originally named DA NANG; the ship was renamed on 15 February 1978 after the fall of the Republic of (South) Vietnam to Communist forces.

Operational: The NASSAU evaluated the "sea control" configuration for these ships during a 1981 deployment when she successfully operated 19 AV-8A Harrier STOVL aircraft. That same year the TARAWA made the first extended deployment of an amphibious ship, with Harriers on board, carrying six AV-8A aircraft during a deployment to the Western Pacific. Subsequent studies showed that an LHA in the sea-control role could effectively operate 20 Harriers, plus 4 to 6 SH-60B LAMPS III helicopters. (See also *Operational* notes for GUAM, page 158.)

These ships were the first ones of any navy to be constructed specifically to operate helicopters. Unlike the Royal Navy's commando carriers of the 1960s and 1970s, and the later TARAWA/WASP classes, the LPHs do not carry landing craft (except that LCVP davits were provided in the INCHON).

The NASSAU with a Phalanx CIWS forward of the island structure, replacing a Sea Sparrow launcher. The starboard SLQ-32(V)3 ECM antenna is mounted between the funnels; beneath it hang refueling hoses. The SPS-40B radar is hidden by the lattice mast. (1989, Giorgio Arra)

The five TARAWA-class LHAs are the only amphibious ships that still mount 5-inch guns, with a pair of the Mk 45 weapons mounted forward. The later WASP-class LHDs have "square cut" flight decks. (1989, Giorgio Arra)

The BELLEAU WOOD with a pair of H-53E helicopters maneuvering nearby. Several helicopters are parked forward, five AV-8B Harrier STOVL aircraft are parked aft. The lattice masts help distinguish these ships from the similar WASP class. (1995, U.S. Navy, PH2 David P. Gallant)

2 AMPHIBIOUS ASSAULT SHIPS: "IWO JIMA" CLASS

Number	Name	FY	Builder	Laid down	Launched	Commissioned	Status
LPH 9	GUAM	62	Philadelphia Naval Shipyard, Penna.	15 Nov 1962	22 Aug 1964	16 Jan 1965	AA
LPH 11	NEW ORLEANS	65	Philadelphia Naval Shipyard, Penna.	1 Mar 1966	3 Feb 1968	16 Nov 1968	PA

Displacement:	11,000 tons light 18,300 tons full load
Length:	556 feet (169.5 m) waterline 602¼ feet (183.6 m) overall
Beam:	83⅔ feet (25.5 m) waterline
Extreme width:	104 feet (31.7 m)
Draft:	26 feet (7.9 m)
Propulsion:	1 steam turbine (Westinghouse); 23,000 shp; 1 shaft
Boilers:	2 600 psi (41.7 kg/cm²) (Combustion Engineering except Babcock and Wilcox in LPH 9)
Speed:	23 knots (21 knots sustained)
Range:	16,600 n.miles (30,743 km) at 11.5 knots 10,000 n.miles (18,520 km) at 20 knots
Manning:	LPH 9 699 (48 officers + 651 enlisted) LPH 11 819 (49 officers + 770 enlisted)
Troops:	1,490
Aircraft:	approx. 24 CH-46 Sea Knight and CH-53 Sea Stallion helicopters
Elevators:	2 deck edge (50 × 34 feet| 15.2 × 10.4 m)
Missiles:	2 8-tube Sea Sparrow BPDMS launchers Mk 25
Guns:	2 25-mm M38 cannon (2 single) 2 20-mm Phalanx CIWS Mk 16 (2 multi-barrel) 4 to 8 12.7-mm machine guns (4 to 8 single)
Radars:	SPS-40 air search SPS-64(V)9 navigation SPS-65(V)1 air/surface search SPS-67(V)1 surface search
Fire control:	2 Mk 115 missile FCS (Sea Sparrow)
EW systems:	SLQ-25 Nixie SLQ-32(V)3

The GUAM is tentatively scheduled to be decommissioned in 1996; however, the Navy is examining the feasibility of extending the service life of the ship beyond the year 2000.

The NEW ORLEANS is scheduled to be decommissioned about 1998.

Class: Originally a class of seven ships.

		Comm.	*Decomm.*	*Stricken*
LPH 2	IWO JIMA	1961	10 July 1993	(same)
LPH 3	OKINAWA	1962	17 Dec 1992	(same)
LPH 7	GUADALCANAL	1963	31 Aug 1994	15 Sep 1994
LPH 10	TRIPOLI	1966	16 Sep 1995	(same)

After being stricken, the OKINAWA was transferred to the NDRF on 16 January 1993.

The INCHON (LPH 12) of this class is being converted to a mine countermeasures support ship (MCS 12); see chapter 22.

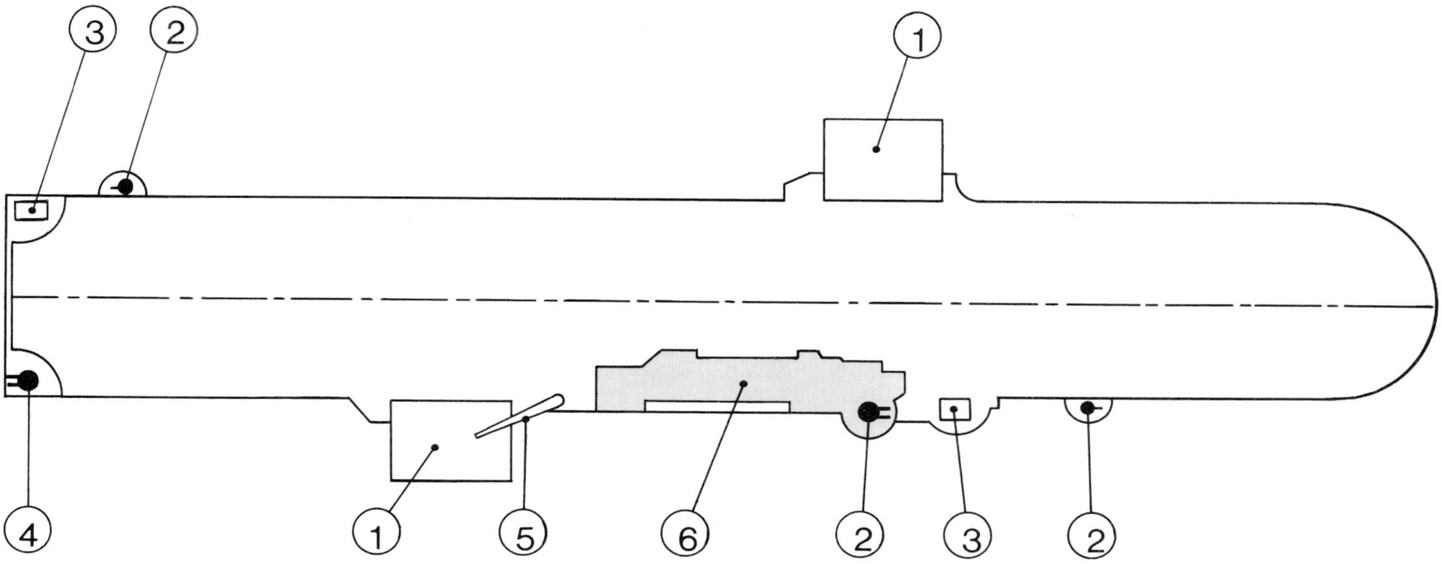

IWO JIMA Class
1. Deck-edge elevator (2). 2. Phalanx CIWS (2). 3. Sea Sparrow missile launcher (2). 4. Twin 3-inch AA gun Mk 33 (2). 5. Aircraft/boat crane. 6. Island structure. (Armament varied in the class; see text.)

Design: SCB No. 157. These ships represent an improved World War II–type escort carrier design with accommodations for a Marine battalion and supporting helicopter squadron.

These ships have extensive medical facilities, including a 155-bed sick bay.

Electronics: The ships' radars have been upgraded. SPN-35A aircraft marshaling and SPN-43B approach/control systems are fitted in these ships.

Guns: As built, these ships had four 3-inch twin gun mounts; two forward of the island structure and two on the after corners of the flight deck. Between 1970 and 1974 all ships had two of their 3-inch gun mounts replaced by Sea Sparrow launchers (one forward of the island and one on the port quarter); the remaining guns were later removed. The ships were subsequently fitted with two Phalanx CIWS mounts.

Helicopters: The ships have the capability of operating up to seven CH-46 Sea Knight or four CH-53 Sea Stallion helicopters on their flight decks. The hangar deck can accommodate 19 Sea Knights or 11 Sea Stallions or various mixes of these and other aircraft.

Operational: The Guam operated as an interim Sea Control Ship (SCS) from 1972 to 1974 to evaluate the concept of flying STOVL aircraft and ASW helicopters from a ship of about this size in the convoy defense role. She operated AV-8A Harriers and SH-3D Sea Kings. The ship reverted to an amphibious assault role.

These ships have also operated H-53 helicopters in the mine countermeasures role off North Vietnam and in the Suez Canal. In December 1990, upon arrival in the Middle East, the Tripoli became flagship of the U.S. mine countermeasures group for operations in the Persian Gulf and took aboard Mine Countermeasures Squadron (HM) 14. On 18 February 1991 the Tripoli struck a moored contact mine in the gulf that blasted a 20 × 30-foot (6.1 × 9.1-m) hole in the ship's starboard side, below the waterline. No crewmen were killed and injuries were slight.

The Tripoli was repaired in a dry dock in Bahrain; after repairs that took one month, she returned to MCM duties in the gulf. Her last helicopter mine mission was flown on 18 June 1991, after which she departed the gulf on 23 June and returned to the United States.

The island structure of the Guam, dominated by the SPS-40 air search radar (forward), pole mast, and antenna dome for an aircraft control radar. The LPHs will soon be retired from the amphibious role, with the Inchon converting to a mine warfare support role. (1990, Giorgio Arra)

The Guam off the coast of Normandy, France, 50 years after the massive Allied D-Day assault. The forward Phalanx CIWS is on a small, starboard-side sponson; the starboard elevator is lowered to the hangar-deck level. Antenna domes can be seen on the flight deck, forward and aft. (1994, Leo Van Ginderen collection)

The GUAM at New Orleans. CH-53E Super Stallion helicopters dominate the after flight deck. Her starboard deck-edge elevator is folded against the hull, a feature that permits passage through narrow canals and passages. The twin 3-inch/50-cal gun mounts are still fitted forward of the island and at the stern in this view. (1990, Giorgio Arra)

AMPHIBIOUS ASSAULT SHIPS

The LPH classification was established in 1955. The World War II–era escort carrier BLOCK ISLAND was to have been LPH 1, but her conversion was canceled. Three ESSEX (CV 9)-class aircraft carriers subsequently were modified to LPHs, as was the escort carrier THETIS BAY. The smaller ship had been designated a helicopter assault carrier (CVHA 1) at the start of her 1955–1956 conversion; she was changed to LPH to avoid confusion and budget competition with the CV-type aircraft carriers.

In addition to the three ESSEX-class ships changed to LPH, the TARAWA (CVS 40) operated extensively with Marine helicopters in the late 1950s (see 8th Edition/page 42).

The designation LPH has *never* signified "Landing Platform Helicopter," as used in some documents.

Number	Name	Notes
LPH 1	BLOCK ISLAND (ex-CVE 106)	conversion canceled
LPH 2–3	IWO JIMA class	
LPH 4	BOXER (ex-CV/CVA/CVS 21)	to LPH 1959; stricken 1969
LPH 5	PRINCETON (ex-CV/CVA/CVS 37)	to LPH 1959; stricken 1970
LPH 6	THETIS BAY (ex-CVE 90)	to CVHA 1/LPH 1956; stricken 1966
LPH 7	IWO JIMA class	
LPH 8	VALLEY FORGE (ex-CV/CVA/CVS 45)	to LPH 1961; stricken 1970
LPH 9–12	IWO JIMA class	

(12) AMPHIBIOUS TRANSPORT DOCKS: LX DESIGN

Number	Name	FY	Status
LPD 17	......	96	Authorized
LPD 18	......	98	Planned
LPD 19	......	99	Planned
LPD 20, 21	(2 ships)	2000	Planned
LPD 22–28	(7 ships)	2001–2004	Planned

Displacement: approx. 23,000 tons full load
Length: 684 feet (208.5 m) overall
Beam: 101 feet (30.8 m)
Draft: 23 feet (7.0 m)
Propulsion: gas turbines; 2 shafts
Speed: 22 knots
Range:
Manning: 463
Troops: 720
Helicopters: 6
Missiles: 2 21-tube RAM launchers Mk 49
Guns: 2 20-mm Phalanx CIWS Mk 16 (2 multi-barrel)
Radars: Mk 23 Target Acquisition System (TAS)
SPS-49(V)5 surface search
SPS-64(V)9 navigation
Fire control: 1 SWY-2 weapon control system (RAM)
EW systems: SLQ-25 Nixie
SLQ-32(V)3

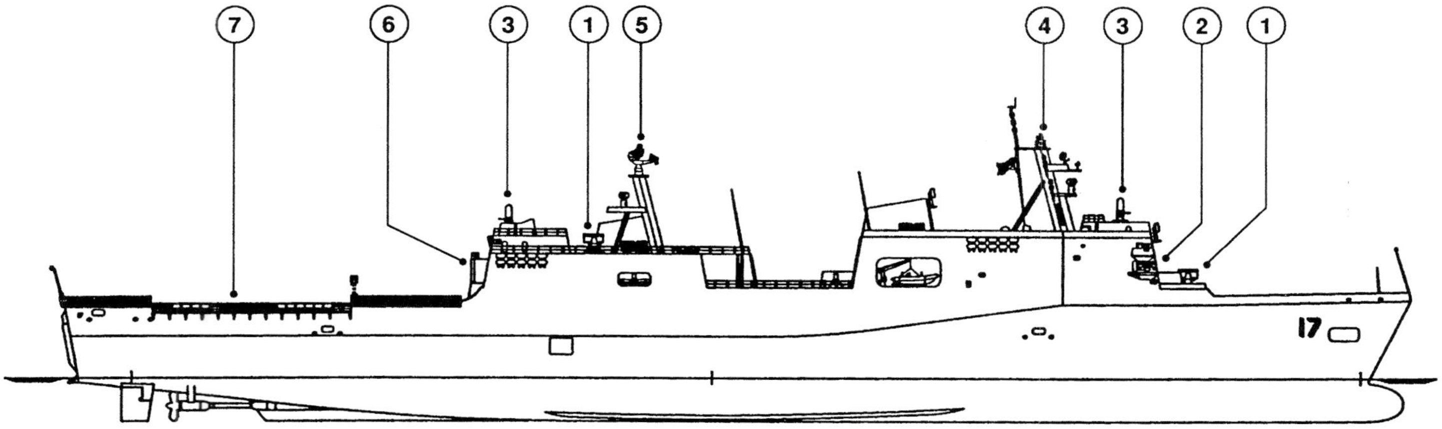

LPD 17 (formerly LX)
1. RAM missile launcher Mk 49 (2). 2. SLQ-32(V)3 EW antenna. 3. Phalanx CIWS (2). 4. SPS-64(V)9 navigation radar. 5. SPS-49(V)5 search radar. 6. Helicopter hangar. 7. Helicopter deck.

The LPD is a development of the dock landing ship (LSD) design, which had its origins in World War II. The LPD has increased troop and vehicle capacity and a relatively small docking well. These ships have fixed helicopter decks above the docking well; the LSDs have removable decks.

The LPD 17 was planned as a functional replacement for 38 ships of the LPD/LSD/LST types. Construction of the lead ship was originally proposed for authorization in fiscal 1995 but was changed by the Clinton administration to fiscal 1998. Congress authorized the ship in fiscal 1996 instead, reflecting support for the rehabilitation of the amphibious force.

Completion will be in about 2002.

Class: The Navy originally proposed a program of 27 LX-type ships to operate with 17 LSD 41 and 15 LHD/LHA ships to provide a MEF + MEB lift capability; the reduced amphibious lift goals, however, have led to plans for a 12-ship LPD 17/LX program.

Cost: In 1993 the Navy estimated acquisition costs at $800 million per ship.

Design: Compared to the previous LPD 4 class, these ships are larger and will have considerably more vehicle storage space at the cost of reduced bulk cargo space. They will also be able to accommodate two LCACs in the docking well, compared to one in the LPD 4 class.

The LPD 17 will have a 130-bed medical facility.

Missiles: The forward RAM launcher is on the port side of the forward superstructure; the amidships RAM launcher is on the starboard side of the after structure.

Space and weight are reserved for possible later installation of the Evolved Sea Sparrow Missile (ESSM) in a vertical-launch system forward, just ahead of the superstructure.

11 AMPHIBIOUS TRANSPORT DOCKS: "AUSTIN" CLASS

Number	Name	FY	Builder	Laid down	Launched	Commissioned	Status
LPD 4	Austin	62	New York Naval Shipyard	4 Feb 1963	27 June 1964	6 Feb 1965	AA
LPD 5	Ogden	62	New York Naval Shipyard	4 Feb 1963	27 June 1964	19 June 1965	PA
LPD 6	Duluth	62	New York Naval Shipyard	18 Dec 1963	14 Aug 1965	18 Dec 1965	PA
LPD 7	Cleveland	63	Ingalls Shipbuilding, Pascagoula, Miss.	30 Nov 1964	7 May 1966	21 Apr 1967	PA
LPD 8	Dubuque	63	Ingalls Shipbuilding, Pascagoula, Miss.	25 Jan 1965	6 Aug 1966	1 Sep 1967	PA
LPD 9	Denver	63	Lockheed SB & Constn., Seattle, Wash.	7 Feb 1964	23 Jan 1965	26 Oct 1968	PA
LPD 10	Juneau	63	Lockheed SB & Constn., Seattle, Wash.	23 Jan 1965	12 Feb 1966	12 July 1969	PA
LPD 12	Shreveport	64	Lockheed SB & Constn., Seattle, Wash.	27 Dec 1965	25 Oct 1966	12 Dec 1970	AA
LPD 13	Nashville	64	Lockheed SB & Constn., Seattle, Wash.	14 Mar 1966	7 Oct 1967	14 Feb 1970	AA
LPD 14	Trenton	65	Lockheed SB & Constn., Seattle, Wash.	8 Aug 1966	3 Aug 1968	6 Mar 1971	AA
LPD 15	Ponce	65	Lockheed SB & Constn., Seattle, Wash.	31 Oct 1966	30 May 1970	10 July 1971	AA

Displacement:	9,128 tons light 16,585 to 17,595 tons full load
Length:	568¾ feet (173.4 m) overall
Beam:	84 feet (25.6 m)
Draft:	23 to 23 7/12 feet (7.0 to 7.2 m)
Propulsion:	2 steam turbines (De Laval); 24,000 shp; 2 shafts
Boilers:	2 600 psi (41.7 kg/cm²) (Foster-Wheeler except Babcock & Wilcox in LPD 5, 12)
Speed:	21 knots
Range:	7,700 n.miles (14,260 km) at 20 knots
Manning:	approx. 402 (28 officers + 374 enlisted)
Troops:	930 in LPD 4–6, 14, 15 840 in LPD 7–10, 12, 13
Flag:	90 in LPD 7–10, 12, 13
Helicopters:	landing area and hangar, except no hangar in LPD 4
Missiles:	none
Guns:	2 25-mm Mk 38 cannon in most ships 2 20-mm Phalanx CIWS Mk 15 (2 multi-barrel) 8 12.7-mm machine guns M2 (8 single)
Radars:	SPS-10F surface search SPS-40B air search except SPS-40E in LPD 13 SPS-64(V)9 navigation
Fire control:	removed
EW systems:	SLQ-25 Nixie SLQ-32(V)1

These ships are enlarged versions of the previous Raleigh-class LPDs. They carry Marines into forward areas and unload them by landing craft and vehicles carried in their docking well and by using helicopters provided mainly from amphibious assault ships. The general configuration of these ships is similar to dock landing ships but with a relatively smaller (covered) docking well and additional space for troop berthing and vehicle parks.

The Dubuque is homeported at Sasebo, Japan.

Aircraft: These ships have deployed with up to six CH-46 Sea Knights embarked for short-term operations. They are rated as being able to deploy with up to four cargo helicopters (CH-46 or CH-53), but this can be done only with a helicopter carrier in company to provide maintenance and other support on a sustained basis.

Builders: The Duluth was completed at the Philadelphia Naval Shipyard after the closing of the New York Naval Shipyard; she was reassigned to Philadelphia on 24 November 1965.

Class: An additional ship of this class (LPD 16) was provided in the fiscal 1966 shipbuilding program, but construction was deferred in favor of the LHA program and officially canceled in February 1969.

The Coronado (LPD 11) of this class was modified for use as a flagship in late 1980 and reclassified AGF 11 (see chapter 18).

Design: LPD 4–10 are SCB No. 187B; LPD 11–13 are No. 187C, changed to No. 402 for LPD 14 and 15 under the new SCB numbering scheme.

The LPD 7–10, 12, and 13 are configured as amphibious squadron flagships and have an additional bridge level, plus flag berthing space and communications equipment. The docking well in these ships is 168 feet long (51.2 m) and 50 feet (15.2 m) wide; it can accommodate 1 LCU and 3 LCM(6)s or 9 LCM(6)s or 4 LCM(8)s or 28 AAV/LVTP-7 amphibian vehicles. In addition, 2 LCM(6)s or 4

The open stern of an Austin-class LPD taking aboard amphibian assault vehicles during operations off the U.S. East Coast during Operation Agile Provider. (1994, U.S. Navy)

LCVP/LCPLs are normally carried on the helicopter deck; up to 16 amphibian vehicles can be parked on the main deck.

One 30-ton-capacity crane and six 4-ton cranes are provided.

Guns: As built, these ships had eight 3-inch (76-mm) 50-cal AA Mk 33 guns in twin mounts. Two mounts were removed in the late 1970s and two in the early 1990s. They had Mk 56 and Mk 63 GFCS.

Helicopters: These ships have a fixed flight deck, with two landing spots, above the docking well. All except the Austin are fitted with a hangar varying from 58 to 64 feet (17.7 to 19.5 m) in length, 18½ to 24 feet (5.6 to 7.3 m) in width, and 17½ to 19 feet (5.3 to 5.8 m) in height; the hangars have an extension that can expand to provide a length of approximately 80 feet (24.4 m).

Modernization: A Service Life Extension Program (SLEP) was developed for these ships to permit them to operate 10 to 15 years beyond a nominal 30-year service life. In addition to general improvements, they were to be fitted with the SPS-67 radar in place of the SPS-10 and modified to carry two LCACs; their aviation capabilities were also to be improved. Budget constraints and congressional opposition to the program, however, resulted in its cancellation.

Operational: During U.S. minesweeping operations in the Persian Gulf in 1988 the Trenton served as tender to minesweepers.

AMPHIBIOUS TRANSPORT DOCKS: "RALEIGH" CLASS

Number	Name	Comm.	Status
LPD 1	Raleigh	1962	decomm. 13 Dec 1991 (see notes)
LPD 2	Vancouver	1963	PR; decomm. 27 Mar 1992
LPD 3	La Salle	1964	converted to AGF 3

These ships were derived from the LSD design, but they have a smaller docking well to provide for larger troop, vehicle, and cargo space. The Raleigh was stricken on 25 January 1992, transferred to NDRF on 23 July 1992 and again stricken on 28 September 1992. On 22 September 1993 she was reinstated in the Naval Vessel Register for use by the Atlantic Fleet as a non-destructive target.

The Vancouver is being temporarily retained in reserve at Pearl Harbor; she is expected to be stricken in the near future.

The La Salle served in the amphibious role until converted to a miscellaneous flagship in 1972 (see chapter 18).

See 15th Edition/pages 174–75 for characteristics.

The Ogden at anchor in Hong Kong. These ships—which will be replaced by the new LSD 17 class—differ from the dock landing ships primarily by having larger troop and vehicle capacities at the cost of a smaller docking well. (1994, Giorgio Arra)

The TRENTON operating in the Caribbean. Long an area for Navy ships to train, the rescue of Cuban and Haitian refugees, and the occupation of Haiti in 1994, gave amphibious ships an important post–Cold War operational mission. (1994, U.S. Navy, PH2 John Sokolowski)

3 + 1 DOCK LANDING SHIPS: "HARPERS FERRY" CLASS

Number	Name	FY	Builder	Laid down	Launched	Commissioned	Status
LSD 49	HARPERS FERRY	88	Avondale Industries, New Orleans, La.	15 Apr 1991	16 Jan 1993	7 Jan 1995	PA
LSD 50	CARTER HALL	90	Avondale Industries, New Orleans, La.	11 Nov 1991	2 Oct 1993	30 Sep 1995	AA
LSD 51	OAK HILL	91	Avondale Industries, New Orleans, La.	21 Sep 1992	11 June 1994	June 1996	AA
LSD 52	PEARL HARBOR	93	Avondale Industries, New Orleans, La.	27 Jan 1995	24 Feb 1996	1998	Building

Displacement:	11,894 tons light 16,695 tons full load
Length:	579 11/12 feet (176.8 m) waterline 609 5/12 feet (185.8 m) overall
Beam:	84 feet (25.6 m)
Draft:	19 3/4 feet (6.0 m)
Propulsion:	4 diesel engines (Colt-Pielstick 16 PC2.5V400); 41,600 bhp; 2 shafts
Speed:	22 knots
Range:	approx. 8,000 n.miles (14,816 km) at 20 knots
Manning:	333 (21 officers + 312 enlisted)
Troops:	approx. 500
Helicopters:	landing area
Missiles:	none
Guns:	2 25-mm Bushmaster cannon Mk 38 (2 single) 2 20-mm Phalanx CIWS Mk 16 (2 multi-barrel) 8 12.7-mm machine guns M2 (8 single)
Radars:	1 SPS-49(V)5 air search 1 SPS-64(V)9 navigation 1 SPS-67(V)1 surface search
Fire control:	none
EW systems:	SLQ-25 Nixie SLQ-32(V)2

These ships are similar to the WHIDBEY ISLAND-class LSDs, but they have a smaller docking well to provide for increased troop, vehicle, cargo, and helicopter capacity. Navy planning documents refer to the class as LSD 41CV for *Cargo Variant.*

Class: The Navy originally planned a class of six ships: the four ships above, plus the LSD 53 and LSD 54; the latter were canceled. The LSD 52 was originally funded in fiscal 1992, but the funds were rescinded by the Bush administration. Congress again funded the ship in fiscal 1993.

Design: The docking well can accommodate two LCACs or one LCU or four LCM(8)s or nine LCM(6) landing craft.

The HARPERS FERRY-class LSDs continue the line of these most useful ships that began with the ASHLAND (LSD 1), completed in 1943. The LSDs can be easily distinguished from the LPD design by the former's removable helicopter platforms, mounted above the sidewalls of the docking well. (1995, Avondale Industries, Ricky Kellum)

Engineering: Maximum horsepower is given above; sustained shp is 33,600.

Missiles: These ships will probably be fitted with the RAM missile system.

Names: LSDs are named for historic sites. Harpers Ferry, West Virginia, was site of a government arsenal that insurrectionist-abolitionist John Brown captured in 1859, a prelude to the American Civil War.

The LSD 52 honors the site of the Japanese surprise attack on the U.S. Fleet on 7 December 1941, not the attack itself.

The HARPERS FERRY takes aboard an LCAC. Designated as the cargo variant of the WHIDBEY ISLAND design, this class has a smaller docking well, which allows the additional internal space to be used for cargo space. (1995, Avondale Industries, Ricky Kellum)

8 DOCK LANDING SHIPS: "WHIDBEY ISLAND" CLASS

Number	Name	FY	Builder	Laid down	Launched	Commissioned	Status
LSD 41	WHIDBEY ISLAND	81	Lockheed Shipbuilding, Seattle, Wash.	4 Aug 1981	10 June 1983	9 Feb 1985	AA
LSD 42	GERMANTOWN	82	Lockheed Shipbuilding, Seattle, Wash.	5 Aug 1982	29 June 1984	8 Feb 1986	PA
LSD 43	FORT MCHENRY	83	Lockheed Shipbuilding, Seattle, Wash.	10 June 1983	1 Feb 1986	8 Aug 1987	PA
LSD 44	GUNSTON HALL	84	Avondale Industries, New Orleans, La.	26 May 1986	27 June 1987	22 Apr 1989	AA
LSD 45	COMSTOCK	85	Avondale Industries, New Orleans, La.	27 Oct 1986	16 Jan 1988	3 Feb 1990	PA
LSD 46	TORTUGA	85	Avondale Industries, New Orleans, La.	23 Mar 1987	15 Sep 1988	17 Nov 1990	AA
LSD 47	RUSHMORE	86	Avondale Industries, New Orleans, La.	9 Nov 1987	6 May 1989	1 June 1991	PA
LSD 48	ASHLAND	86	Avondale Industries, New Orleans, La.	4 Apr 1988	11 Nov 1989	9 May 1992	AA

Displacement:	11,854 tons standard	
	15,165 tons full load	
Length:	580 feet (176.8 m) waterline	
	609 5/12 feet (185.8 m) overall	
Beam:	84 feet (25.6 m)	
Draft:	19 7/12 feet (6.0 m)	
Propulsion:	4 diesel engines (SEMT-Pielstick 16 PC2.5 V400); 41,600 bhp; 2 shafts	
Speed:	22 knots	
Range:	8,000 n.miles (14,816 km) at 20 knots	
Manning:	LSD 41, 44, 46	310 (21 officers + 289 enlisted)
	LSD 42, 43, 47	317 (21 officers + 296 enlisted)
	LSD 45	312 (21 officers + 291 enlisted)
	LSD 48	320 (21 officers + 299 enlisted)

Troops:	560
Helicopters:	landing area
Missiles:	2 21-tube RAM launchers Mk 49 in LSD 41
Guns:	2 25-mm Bushmaster cannon Mk 38 (2 single)
	2 20-mm Phalanx CIWS Mk 16 (2 multi-barrel)
	8 12.7-mm machine guns (8 single)
Radars:	SPS-64(V)9 navigation
	SPS-49(V)1 air search in LSD 41–45; (V)5 in LSD 46–48
	SPS-67(V)1 surface search
Fire control:	1 SWY-2 weapon control system (RAM) in LSD 41
EW systems:	SLQ-25 Nixie
	SLQ-32(V)1

These ships were built to replace the THOMASTON-class LSDs and to provide increased lift for air cushion landing craft.

The GERMANTOWN is based in Sasebo, Japan. (She replaced the ST. LOUIS as Amphibious Group 1's major cargo ship in November 1992.)

Class: Navy planning in the early 1980s called for 9 or 10 ships of this class to replace the LSD 28 class; the number was subsequently increased to 12 ships through the fiscal 1988 shipbuilding program. However, the decision was made in the mid-1980s to produce eight LSD 41s and six LSD 41 cargo variants (HARPERS FERRY class) in place of 12 units of this design.

Design: The docking well is 440 feet (134.1 m) long and 50 feet (15.2 m) wide; it can accommodate 4 LCACs or 3 LCU or 10 LCM(8) or 21 LCM(6) landing craft or 64 AAV/LVTP-7 amphibian vehicles. In addition, several LCVP/LCPL-type landing craft are normally carried on deck.

Fitted with one 60-ton-capacity crane, one 20-ton crane, and one 15-ton crane.

No helicopter hangar or support facilities are provided.

Engineering: These are the first U.S. ships powered by medium speed diesel engines. Of French design, the diesels are produced under license by the Fairbanks Morse Division of Colt Industries.

Maximum horsepower is given above; sustained shp is 33,600.

Missiles: These ships are being fitted with the RAM missile system. The WHIDBEY ISLAND conducted trials with the RAM system (one launcher) in June 1993 using radar inputs from the Phalanx VPS-2 search and track radar.

The WHIDBEY ISLAND shows the massive forward structure of LSDs, with the amidships and after sections devoted to machinery and the docking well. These ships do not normally embark helicopters because of their lack of hangar facilities. Nevertheless, they can carry vehicles on their helicopter deck, lowered into the docking well or onto landing craft alongside by crane. (1993, Hughes Missile Systems)

5 DOCK LANDING SHIPS: "ANCHORAGE" CLASS

Number	Name	FY	Builder	Laid down	Launched	Commissioned	Status
LSD 36	ANCHORAGE	65	Ingalls Shipbuilding, Pascagoula, Miss.	13 Mar 1967	5 May 1968	15 Mar 1969	**PA**
LSD 37	PORTLAND	66	General Dynamics, Quincy, Mass.	21 Sep 1967	20 Dec 1969	3 Oct 1970	**AA**
LSD 38	PENSACOLA	66	General Dynamics, Quincy, Mass.	12 Mar 1969	11 July 1970	27 Mar 1971	**AA**
LSD 39	MOUNT VERNON	66	General Dynamics, Quincy, Mass.	29 Jan 1970	17 Apr 1971	13 May 1972	**PA**
LSD 40	FORT FISHER	67	General Dynamics, Quincy, Mass.	15 July 1970	22 Apr 1972	9 Dec 1972	**PA**

Displacement:	8,200 tons light
	13,680 tons full load
Length:	534 feet (162.8 m) waterline
	553¼ feet (168.66 m) overall
Beam:	85 feet (25.9 m)
Draft:	20 feet (6.1 m)
Propulsion:	2 steam turbines (De Laval); 24,000 shp; 2 shafts
Boilers:	2 600 psi (Foster-Wheeler except Combustion Engineering in LSD 36)
Speed:	22 knots (20 knots sustained)
Range:	14,000 n.miles (25,940 km) at 12 knots
Manning:	322 (18 officers + 304 enlisted)
Troops:	336
Helicopters:	landing area
Missiles:	none
Guns:	2 25-mm Buchmaster cannon Mk 38
	2 20-mm Phalanx CIWS Mk 16 (2 multi-barrel)
	6 12.7-mm machine guns M2 (6 single)
Radars:	SPS-10F surface search
	SPS-40B air search
	SPS-64(V)9 navigation
Fire control:	removed
EW systems:	SLQ-25 Nixie
	SLQ-32(V)1

These LSDs were part of the large amphibious ship construction program of the early 1960s and were to supplement the LPDs and LHAs by carrying additional landing craft to the assault area.

Design: SCB No. 404. The docking well is 430 feet (131.1 m) long and 50 feet (15.2 m) wide; it can accommodate 4 LCACs or 3 LCUs or 9 LCM(8)s or 52 AAV/LVTP-7 amphibian vehicles. Another 15 amphibian vehicles can be stowed on a "mezzanine" deck. A removable helicopter deck is fitted over the docking well. Several additional landing craft are normally stowed on deck.

Two 50-ton-capacity cranes are fitted.

No helicopter hangar or support facilities are provided.

Guns: As built, these ships had eight 3-inch/50-cal Mk 33 guns in twin mounts; one amidships mount and the Mk 56 and Mk 63 GFCS were removed in 1977. An additional 3-inch twin mount was deleted with installation of the two Phalanx CIWS mounts in the 1980s. The remaining 3-inch guns were deleted in the early 1990s.

The FORT FISHER at Hong Kong. Note a Phalanx CIWS atop her bridge and a second Phalanx amidships. The heavy battery of 3-inch/50-caliber guns has been beached from these and all other active amphibious ships. (1994, Giorgio Arra)

The FORT FISHER at anchor. When at rest, U.S. ships fly the Union Jack at the bow and the national ensign at the stern; when under way, the American flag is flown from the masthead. There is a small opening at the bottom of the stern gate for streaming the SLQ-25 Nixie torpedo countermeasures device. (1994, Giorgio Arra)

DOCK LANDING SHIPS: "THOMASTON" CLASS

Number	Name	Comm.	Status
LSD 28	Thomaston	1954	decomm. 5 Sep 1984; stricken 24 Feb 1992
LSD 29	Plymouth Rock	1954	decomm. 30 Sep 1983; stricken 24 Feb 1992
LSD 30	Fort Snelling	1955	decomm. 28 Sep 1984; stricken 24 Feb 1992
LSD 31	Point Defiance	1955	decomm. 30 Sep 1983; stricken 24 Feb 1992
LSD 32	Spiegel Grove	1956	decomm. 2 Oct 1989; stricken 13 Dec 1989
LSD 33	Alamo	1956	decomm. 28 Sep 1990; to Brazil 20 Nov 1990
LSD 34	Hermitage	1956	decomm. 2 Oct 1989; to Brazil 2 Oct 1989
LSD 35	Monticello	1957	decomm. 1 Oct 1985; stricken 24 Feb 1992

This was the first class of docking-well ships to be built for the U.S. Navy after World War II.

See 14th Edition/pages 204–5 for characteristics.

After the tank landing ship (LST), the dock landing ship was in many respects the most innovative amphibious ship developed during World War II. Establishing the basic design for future LSD/LPD classes, the Ashland (LSD 1), commissioned in 1943, had a large superstructure forward and a docking well that took up most of her hull, with machinery fitted in the walls of the dock. The wartime program embraced LSDs 1–27, with LSDs 9–12 being built for Britain.

9 TANK LANDING SHIPS: "NEWPORT" CLASS

Number	Name	FY	Builder	Laid down	Launched	Commissioned	Status
LST 1179	Newport	65	Philadelphia Naval Shipyard	1 Nov 1966	3 Feb 1968	7 June 1969	AR
LST 1182	Fresno	66	National Steel & SB, San Diego, Calif.	16 Dec 1967	20 Sep 1968	22 Nov 1969	PR
LST 1184	Frederick	66	National Steel & SB, San Diego, Calif.	13 Apr 1968	8 Mar 1969	11 Apr 1970	**NRF-P**
LST 1185	Schenectady	66	National Steel & SB, San Diego, Calif.	2 Aug 1968	24 May 1969	13 June 1970	PR
LST 1187	Tuscaloosa	66	National Steel & SB, San Diego, Calif.	23 Nov 1968	6 Sep 1969	24 Oct 1970	PR
LST 1190	Boulder	67	National Steel & SB, San Diego, Calif.	6 Sep 1969	22 May 1970	4 June 1971	AR
LST 1191	Racine	67	National Steel & SB, San Diego, Calif.	13 Dec 1969	15 Aug 1970	9 July 1971	PR
LST 1194	La Moure County	67	National Steel & SB, San Diego, Calif.	22 May 1970	13 Feb 1971	18 Dec 1971	**NRF-A**
LST 1195	Barbour County	67	National Steel & SB, San Diego, Calif.	15 Aug 1970	15 May 1971	12 Feb 1972	PR

Displacement:	4,975 tons light 8,576 tons full load
Length:	522⅙ feet (159.2 m) overall 561⅚ feet (171.3 m) over derrick arms
Beam:	69½ feet (21.2 m)
Draft:	5 11/12 feet (1.8 m) forward 17½ feet (5.3 m) aft
Propulsion:	6 diesel engines (General Motors 16-645-E5 in LST 1179–1181; Arco 16-251 in others); 16,500 bhp; 2 shafts
Speed:	22 knots (20 knots sustained)
Range:	14,250 n.miles (26,400 km) at 14 knots
Manning:	active ships approx. 262 (15 officers + 247 enlisted) NRF ships 191 active (11 officers + 180 enlisted) + approx. 70 reservists
Troops:	350
Helicopters:	landing area
Guns:	4 3-inch (76-mm) 50-cal AA Mk 32 (2 twin) in some ships 1 20-mm Phalanx CIWS Mk 16 (multi-barrel) in LST 1179–1183, 1187, 1189, 1194 4 12.7-mm machine guns M2 (4 single)
Radars:	SPS-10F surface search SPS-64(V)9 navigation
Fire control:	local control only for 3-inch guns
EW systems:	none

These ships represent the ultimate design in landing ships that can be "beached," but they generally unload onto pontoon causeways. They depart from the traditional LST bow-door design to obtain a hull design for a sustained speed of 20 knots.

Seven ships are laid up in reserve in mobilization Category B, i.e., intended for reactivation within 180 days.

Five ships have served in the Naval Reserve Force; two are currently in NRF status. Twelve have been transferred to other navies; more will probably follow.

The decommissionings and shifts of these ships to NRF in 1994–1995 mark the first time since 1942 that there have not been LSTs in the active U.S. amphibious force.

		to NRF	*Decommissioned*	*Notes*
LST 1179	Newport	—	30 Sep 1992	
LST 1180	Manitowoc	—	30 June 1993	to Taiwan 15 July 1995
LST 1181	Sumter	—	30 Sep 1993	to Taiwan 15 July 1995
LST 1182	Fresno	30 Sep 1990	8 Apr 1993	
LST 1183	Peoria	—	28 Jan 1994	to Venezuela 30 Dec 1995
LST 1184	Frederick	31 Jan 1995	—	
LST 1185	Schenectady	—	10 Dec 1993	
LST 1186	Cayuga	—	29 July 1994	to Brazil 26 Aug 1994
LST 1187	Tuscaloosa	—	18 Feb 1994	
LST 1188	Saginaw	—	28 June 1994	to Australia 24 Aug 1994
LST 1189	San Bernardino	—	30 Sep 1995	to Chile 30 Sep 1995
LST 1190	Boulder	1 Dec 1980	28 Feb 1994	
LST 1191	Racine	15 Jan 1981	2 Oct 1993	
LST 1192	Spartanburg C.	—	16 Dec 1994	to Malaysia 16 Dec 1994
LST 1193	Fairfax C.	—	17 Aug 1994	to Australia 27 Sep 1994
LST 1194	La Moure C.	30 Sep 1995	—	
LST 1195	Barbour C.	—	30 Mar 1992	to Venezuela 1996
LST 1196	Harlan C.	—	14 Apr 1995	to Spain 14 Apr 1995
LST 1197	Barnstable C.	—	29 June 1994	to Spain 26 Aug 1994
LST 1198	Bristol C.	—	9 July 1994	stricken 29 July 1994; to Morocco 16 Aug 1994

The LST 1193 departed from Little Creek, Virginia, en route to Australia on 15 August 1994 as a U.S. Navy ship carrying a combined U.S. (150) and Australian (20) crew; she was decommissioned and stricken at sea and formally transferred to Australia upon arrival at Sydney.

(The LST 1188 and LST 1193 in Australian service were converted in 1995–1996 to serve as training and helicopter support ships; they support Army Black Hawk helicopters as well as Navy S70B-2 Seahawk helicopters, the latter flown from Australian frigates of the Oliver Hazard Perry/FFG 7 design.)

Class: Twenty ships of this class were completed from 1969 to 1972. Seven additional ships were planned for the fiscal 1971 shipbuilding program; they were canceled.

Design: SCB No. 405. The design provides bow and stern ramps for unloading tanks and other vehicles. The aluminum bow ramp is 112 feet (34.1 m) long and is handled over the bow by the twin, fixed derrick arms. Vehicles can be driven between the main deck forward and aft through a passage in the superstructure. The stern ramp permits unloading AAV/LVTP–type amphibious vehicles directly into the water while the ships are either under way or "mating" the LST to landing craft or a pier. They can carry 2,000 tons of vehicles or cargo but only 500 tons when beaching. The tank (lower) deck can accommodate 23 AAV/LVTP-7 amphibian vehicles or 41 2½-ton 6 × 6 cargo trucks; another 29 trucks can be carried on the main (upper) deck. Two 10-ton-capacity cranes are fitted amidships.

Four LCVP/LCPL–type landing craft are carried in amidship davits. Four pontoon causeway sections can be carried on the hull, amidships.

There is a large helicopter landing area aft, but no hangar or support facilities.

Electronics: In the 1970s the Navy planned to equip these ships with the SLQ-32(V)1; EW systems will not be installed, however. (A few ships do have chaff launchers, originally planned for the entire class).

Guns: These ships were all built with four 3-inch/50-cal guns in twin mounts atop the superstructure; their Mk 63 GFCS were removed in 1977–1978. The 3-inch guns were removed from most surviving ships. One Phalanx CIWS has been mounted above the bridge; a planned second Phalanx has not been provided.

Missiles: Proposals to mount the Army's Assault Ballistic Rocket System (ABRS) on some or all of these ships for the fire support role have been dropped.

Names: The first 13 ships of the NEWPORT class do not have county or parish name suffixes, as had all previous named LSTs. County and parish names were assigned to 158 existing LSTs on 1 July 1955 (36 Japanese-manned T-LSTs were not named). All subsequent LSTs were assigned names when built.

Operational: Congress had wanted both NRF ships to be based in Hawaii, to be able to transport Marine and Army equipment from Oahu to the island of Hawaii for training. When this edition went to press, however, the LA MOURE COUNTY was homeported at Little Creek, Virginia, and the FREDERICK at San Diego, California.

The HARLAN COUNTY bow on, showing the large derrick arms that lift the unloading ramp over the bow (which partially opens). This ship has since been transferred to the Spanish Navy for service in the LST role. (1993, Giorgio Arra)

The SAN BERNARDINO showing the unusual lines of this ultimate class of LSTs. The ship-type prow was necessary to permit 20-knot speeds; previous LST designs had nearly flat bows and large doors covering the bow ramp. (1994, Giorgio Arra)

TANK LANDING SHIPS: "DE SOTO COUNTY" CLASS

Number	Name	Comm.	Notes
LST 1171	De Soto City	1958	to Italy 1972
LST 1172	. . . . .	canceled 1955	
LST 1173	Suffolk County	1957	stricken 16 Feb 1989
LST 1174	Grant County	1957	to Brazil 1973
LST 1175	York County	1957	to Italy 1972
LST 1176	Graham County	1958	to AGP 1176
LST 1177	Lorain County	1958	stricken 16 Feb 1989
LST 1178	Wood County	1959	stricken 16 Feb 1989

The seven ships of this class were completed, the last U.S. Navy LSTs to be built with the traditional bow doors and ramp and the superstructure aft. The Graham County (LST 1176) was converted to a gunboat support ship to support the Asheville (PG 84)-class ships operating in the Mediterranean. The Wood County was to have been converted to support the Pegasus (PHM 1)-class hydrofoil missile craft; her conversion was canceled in 1977. She was to have been designated AGHS.

See 14th Edition/page 209 for characteristics.

TANK LANDING SHIPS: "TERREBONNE PARISH" CLASS

Number	Name	Comm.	Status
LST 1156	Terrebonne Parish	1952	to Spain 1971
LST 1157	Terrell County	1954	to Greece 1977
LST 1158	Tioga County	1953	stricken 1 Nov 1973
LST 1159	Tom Green County	1953	to Spain 1972
LST 1160	Traverse County	1953	to Peru 1984
LST 1161	Vernon County	1953	to Venezuela 1973
LST 1162	Wahkiakum County	1953	stricken 11 Jan 1973
LST 1163	Waldo County	1953	to Peru 1984
LST 1164	Walworth County	1953	to Peru 1984
LST 1165	Washoe County	1953	to Peru 1984
LST 1166	Washtenaw County	1953	to MSS 2 (stricken 30 Aug 1973)
LST 1167	Westchester County	1954	to Turkey 1974
LST 1168	Wexford County	1954	to Spain 1971
LST 1169	Whitfield County	1954	to Greece 1977
LST 1170	Windham County	1954	to Turkey 1973

These 15 ships were built during the Korean War. They were the Navy's first post–World War II LST design. All but one were in Navy service until their decommissioning in 1970; the Walworth County was decommissioned in 1971. The LST 1158, 1160, and 1162–1165 then served with the Military Sealift Command in 1972–1973 (designated T-LST). Upon being laid up, the ex-T-LSTs were retained in NDRF for possible future use; two remain. Most transferred to other navies (lease or sale); four ships were leased to Peru on 7 August 1984.

The Washtenaw County was reclassified as a "minesweeper special" and used as an experimental mine countermeasures craft.

See 14th Edition/pages 210–11 for characteristics.

POST–WORLD WAR II TANK LANDING SHIPS

From December 1942 to June 1945 a total of 1,052 LSTs were completed for the U.S. Navy (numbered LST 1–1152, with 100 units canceled). All were of the same basic design. Three larger, improved LSTs with steam-turbine propulsion were ordered late in the war. Two were completed: the LST 1153 (in 1947) and the LST 1154 (in 1949). The third ship was canceled. (All other U.S. LSTs have had diesel propulsion.)

Number	Name	Notes
LST 1153	Talbot County	stricken 1973
LST 1154	Tallahatchee County	to AVB 2
LST 1155		canceled 1946
LST 1156–1170	Terrebonne Parish class	
LST 1171	De Soto County class	
LST 1172		canceled 1955
LST 1173–1178	De Soto County class	
LST 1179–1198	Newport class	

The Navy is retaining the five Charleston-class amphibious ships in reserve because of their valuable break-bulk cargo capability. Here the El Paso is seen lowering an LCM-type landing craft, one of several carried by these ships. (1991, Giorgio Arra)

5 AMPHIBIOUS CARGO SHIPS: "CHARLESTON" CLASS

Number	Name	FY	Builder	Laid down	Launched	Commissioned	Status
LKA 113	CHARLESTON	65	Litton/Ingalls Shipbuilding, Pascagoula, Miss.	5 Dec 1966	2 Dec 1967	14 Dec 1968	AR
LKA 114	DURHAM	65	Litton/Ingalls Shipbuilding, Pascagoula, Miss.	10 July 1967	29 Mar 1968	24 May 1969	PR
T-LKA 115	MOBILE	65	Litton/Ingalls Shipbuilding, Pascagoula, Miss.	15 Jan 1968	19 Oct 1968	29 Sep 1969	PR-ROS
LKA 116	SAINT LOUIS	65	Litton/Ingalls Shipbuilding, Pascagoula, Miss.	3 Apr 1968	4 Jan 1969	22 Nov 1969	PA
T-LKA 117	EL PASO	65	Litton/Ingalls Shipbuilding, Pascagoula, Miss.	22 Oct 1968	17 May 1969	17 Jan 1970	AR-ROS

Displacement:	10,000 tons light
	20,700 tons full load
Length:	549¾ feet (167.6 m) waterline
	576 feet (175.6 m) overall
Beam:	62 feet (18.9 m)
Draft:	27 11/12 feet (8.5 m)
Propulsion:	1 steam turbine (Westinghouse); 22,000 shp; 1 shaft
Boilers:	2 600 psi (41.7 kg/cm²) (Combustion Engineering)
Speed:	20 knots
Range:	9,600 n.miles (17,800 km) at 16 knots
Manning:	approx. 363 (25 officers + 338 enlisted)
Troops:	210
Helicopters:	landing area only
Missiles:	none
Guns:	6 3-inch (76-mm) 50-cal AA Mk 33 (3 twin) except 4 guns in LKA 113, 117
	2 20-mm Phalanx CIWS Mk 16 (2 multi-barrel) in LKA 113, 117
Radars:	LN-66 navigation except SPS-64(V)9 in LKA 115
	SPS-10F surface search
Fire control:	local control only for 3-inch guns
EW systems:	SLQ-25 Nixie in LKA 117
	SLQ-32(V)1

These ships carry heavy equipment and supplies for amphibious assaults. They are configured for rapid unloading of equipment into landing craft and helicopters.

During 1979–1981 four of the ships were shifted to the NRF; they were returned to active Navy service in the early 1980s to improve amphibious readiness in response to the crises in the Persian Gulf, Lebanon, and Caribbean areas. All were decommissioned in 1992–1994.

The LKA 113, 114, and 116 are retained in reserve ("mothballs"); the LKA 115 and 117 are in ROS, manned with nucleus crews of 50 and capable of being reactivated within five days. They are assigned to the Military Sealift Command, having been changed to T-LKA 115 and T-LKA 116 on 1 February 1996. The three other LKAs are in Category B reserve, suitable for activation within 180 days.

The LKA 113 was transferred to the NDRF on 29 September 1992, but the ship was returned to the Naval Vessel Register on 31 May 1994.

	To NRF	*Returned to Active Fleet*	*Decomm.*
LKA 113	21 Nov 1979	18 Feb 1983	27 Apr 1992
LKA 114	1 Oct 1979	1 Oct 1982	25 Feb 1994
LKA 115	1 Sep 1980	30 Sep 1983	4 Feb 1994
LKA 116	—	—	2 Nov 1992
LKA 117	1 Mar 1981	1 Oct 1982	21 Apr 1994

Classification: These ships were ordered as attack cargo ships (AKA). The CHARLESTON was changed to LKA on 14 December 1968, and the others were changed to LKA on 1 January 1969.

Design: SCB No. 403. This is the first class of ships designed specifically for this role; all previous ships of the LKA/AKA type were converted from or built to merchant designs.

These ships have a large helicopter landing area aft, but no hangar or maintenance facilities. There are two 78-ton-capacity booms, two 40-ton booms, and eight 15-ton booms.

The ships normally carry as deck cargo 4 LCM(8)s, 5 LCM(6)s, 2 LCVPs, and 2 LCPLs.

Engineering: Maximum horsepower is shown above; sustained shp is 19,250.

Guns: As built, four 3-inch twin gun mounts were installed. One mount was removed from each ship, as was the Mk 56 GFCS in 1977–1978. Subsequently, a second 3-inch twin mount is being removed to accommodate the installation of the CIWS.

Two Phalanx CIWS mounts are fitted in these ships. One CIWS is fitted forward, to the left of the remaining forward 3-inch gun mount, and the other Phalanx is fitted on the superstructure in place of the starboard 3-inch gun mount.

AMPHIBIOUS CARGO SHIP: MARINER TYPE (C4-S-1A)

The Navy's only other post–World War II amphibious cargo ship, the TULARE (AKA/LKA 112), was stricken on 1 August 1981 and placed in the NDRF. She was reinstated on the Naval Vessel Register in May 1984 but stricken again on 31 August 1992.

The LKA 112, LPA 248, and LPA 249 were acquired by the Navy while under construction as Mariner-class merchant ships; two others became support ships for the Polaris program (AG 153, AG 154).[4] One ship of this design remains on the Navy List as a missile range instrumentation ship, the OBSERVATION ISLAND (T-AGM 23); see chapter 23.

See 12th Edition/page 141 for TULARE characteristics.

AMPHIBIOUS TRANSPORTS: MARINER TYPE (C4-S-1A)

The Navy had two postwar-built amphibious transports, the PAUL REVERE (APA/LPA 248) and FRANCIS MARION (APA/LPA 249); both ships were stricken on 1 January 1980 and sold to Spain in January 1980 and July 1980, respectively.

See 11th Edition/page 131 for characteristics.

FIRE SUPPORT SHIPS

In World War II numerous production landing ships were modified during construction or converted to the fire support role for amphibious landings. They were the LCIG, LCIM, LCIR, LSMR, and LCSL (the only one constructed specifically for that role). One inshore fire support ship, the CARRONADE (IFS 1), was constructed after the war. She was an improved LSMR with a single 5-inch gun and rapid-fire rocket launchers. Her designation was changed to LFR on 1 January 1969, along with the surviving war-built LSMRs. The CARRONADE was commissioned in 1955 and stricken in 1973. (The CARRONADE and three LSMRs saw active service in the Vietnam War.)

There have been subsequent proposals to build fire support ships (IFS, LFR, LFS), but none has been authorized. The recommissioning of the four IOWA (BB 61)-class battleships made consideration of such ships superfluous in the 1980s, while funding constraints will probably negate construction efforts in the 1990s.

CHAPTER 20

Landing Craft and Vehicles

An air cushion landing craft comes ashore near Trondheim, Norway, during a multinational exercise. The LCAC provides an excellent means of bringing ashore vehicles and material in the follow-on to an initial amphibious lodgment. However, the craft could be highly vulnerable in an assault environment. (1995, Royal Navy, CPOA [Photo] Ric Burch)

The U.S. Navy operates several hundred landing craft. The larger landing craft air cushion (LCAC) and utility landing craft (LCU) are usually identified by "hull" numbers.

All landing craft are operated by Navy personnel. The smaller landing craft are identified by the ship, unit, or base to which they are assigned. The assault amphibian vehicles (formerly amphibious tractors) operated by the Marine Corps are listed in the latter section of this chapter.

Numerous LCUs have been transferred to other navies, reclassified, or stricken; others serve as test support craft (IX), ferryboats (YFB), and harbor utility craft (YFU). These are all described in chapter 25. The Army operates several LCUs in the same designation series as the Navy craft, as well as LCMs (see chapter 34).

Additional landing craft of the smaller types are laid up in various forms of storage.

The amphibious forces also operate warping tugs (LWT) and side-loading warping tugs (SLWT); both types are used to move pontoon causeways in amphibious areas. They can be transported to forward areas by amphibious ships.

Operational: In the Pacific Fleet, Naval Beach Group 1, based at the Naval Amphibious Base Coronado (San Diego), California, has Assault Craft Unit (ACU) 1 that operates conventional landing craft and ACU-5 that operates LCACs. In the Atlantic Fleet, Naval Beach Group 2 at Little Creek (Norfolk), Virginia, has ACU-2 for conventional landing craft and ACU-4 for LCACs.

LANDING CRAFT

86 + 5 LANDING CRAFT AIR CUSHION: LCAC TYPE

Number	FY	In service	Assignment	Number	FY	In service	Assignment	Number	FY	In service	Assignment
LCAC 1	82	Dec 1984	ACU-5	LCAC 32	86	May 1991	ACU-5	LCAC 63	91	Sep 1993	ACU-5
LCAC 2	82	Feb 1986	ACU-5	LCAC 33	86	June 1991	ACU-5	LCAC 64	91	Oct 1993	ACU-5
LCAC 3	82	June 1986	ACU-5	LCAC 34	89	May 1992	ACU-4	LCAC 65	91	Nov 1993	ACU-5
LCAC 4	83	Aug 1986	ACU-5	LCAC 35	89	May 1992	ACU-4	LCAC 66	91	Dec 1993	NCSL*
LCAC 5	83	Nov 1986	ACU-5	LCAC 36	89	May 1992	ACU-4	LCAC 67	91	Feb 1994	ACU-4
LCAC 6	83	Dec 1986	ACU-5	LCAC 37	89	July 1991	ACU-4	LCAC 68	91	Mar 1994	ACU-4
LCAC 7	84	Mar 1987	ACU-4	LCAC 38	89	Sep 1991	ACU-4	LCAC 69	91	Apr 1994	ACU-4
LCAC 8	84	June 1987	ACU-4	LCAC 39	89	Sep 1991	ACU-4	LCAC 70	91	June 1994	ACU-4
LCAC 9	84	June 1987	ACU-4	LCAC 40	89	Nov 1991	ACU-4	LCAC 71	91	June 1994	ACU-4
LCAC 10	84	Oct 1987	ACU-4	LCAC 41	89	Nov 1991	ACU-4	LCAC 72	91	July 1994	ACU-5
LCAC 11	84	Dec 1987	ACU-4	LCAC 42	89	Dec 1991	ACU-5	LCAC 73	92	Sep 1994	ACU-5
LCAC 12	84	Dec 1987	ACU-4	LCAC 43	89	Feb 1992	ACU-5	LCAC 74	92	Nov 1994	ACU-5
LCAC 13	85	Sep 1988	ACU-5	LCAC 44	89	Feb 1992	ACU-5	LCAC 75	92	Jan 1995	ACU-5
LCAC 14	85	Nov 1988	ACU-5	LCAC 45	89	Mar 1992	ACU-5	LCAC 76	92	Feb 1995	ACU-5
LCAC 15	85	Sep 1989	ACU-4	LCAC 46	89	May 1992	ACU-4	LCAC 77	92	Mar 1995	ACU-4
LCAC 16	85	Jan 1990	ACU-5	LCAC 47	89	June 1992	ACU-5	LCAC 78	92	May 1995	ACU-4
LCAC 17	85	Feb 1990	ACU-5	LCAC 48	89	July 1992	ACU-5	LCAC 79	92	July 1995	ACU-4
LCAC 18	85	Nov 1988	ACU-5	LCAC 49	90	Oct 1992	ACU-4	LCAC 80	92	Aug 1995	ACU-5
LCAC 19	85	June 1990	ACU-4	LCAC 50	90	Feb 1993	ACU-4	LCAC 81	92	Oct 1995	ACU-5
LCAC 20	85	Sep 1990	ACU-4	LCAC 51	90	June 1993	ACU-4	LCAC 82	92	Dec 1995	
LCAC 21	85	Mar 1989	ACU-4	LCAC 52	90	Aug 1992	ACU-5	LCAC 83	92	Feb 1996	
LCAC 22	86	Nov 1990	ACU-5	LCAC 53	90	Oct 1992	ACU-4	LCAC 84	92	1996	
LCAC 23	86	June 1991	ACU-5	LCAC 54	90	Oct 1992	ACU-4	LCAC 85	93	1996	
LCAC 24	86	Mar 1990	ACU-5	LCAC 55	90	Nov 1992	ACU-4	LCAC 86	93	1996	
LCAC 25	86	June 1990	ACU-4	LCAC 56	90	Jan 1993	ACU-5	LCAC 87	93	1996	
LCAC 26	86	June 1990	ACU-4	LCAC 57	90	Feb 1993	ACU-5	LCAC 88	93	1997	
LCAC 27	86	Aug 1990	ACU-4	LCAC 58	90	Mar 1993	ACU-5	LCAC 89	93	1997	
LCAC 28	86	Oct 1990	ACU-4	LCAC 59	90	Apr 1993	ACU-5	LCAC 90	93	1997	
LCAC 29	86	Dec 1990	ACU-5	LCAC 60	90	May 1993	ACU-4	LCAC 91	93	1997	
LCAC 30	86	Dec 1990	ACU-5	LCAC 61	91	July 1993	ACU-5				
LCAC 31	86	Feb 1991	ACU-5	LCAC 62	91	Aug 1993	ACU-5				

*NCSL = Naval Coastal Systems Laboratory, Panama City, Fla.

Builders:	Bell-Aerospace/Textron Marine Systems, New Orleans, La., except LCAC 15–23, 34–36, 49–51 by Avondale Gulfport Marine, La.
Displacement:	102.2 tons light 169 tons full load 184 tons overload
Length:	81 feet (24.7 m) overall (structure) $87\frac{11}{12}$ feet (26.8 m) on cushion
Beam:	$43\frac{2}{3}$ feet (13.3 m) (structure) 47 feet (14.3 m) on cushion
Draft:	3 feet (0.9 m) structure
Propulsion/lift:	4 gas turbines (Avco-Lycoming TF-40B); 15,820 shp; 2 shrouded propellers and 2 bow thrusters/4 centrifugal lift fans
Speed:	50 knots maximum on cushion 40+ knots with payload on cushion in sea state 2 30+ knots with payload on cushion in sea state 3 25 knots maximum on hull
Range:	200 n.miles (370 km) at 40 knots with payload
Manning:	5 (enlisted)
Troops:	24
Guns:	(see notes)
Radars:	navigation

These landing craft are the first advanced-technology surface ships to be produced in series by the U.S. Navy. They carry heavy vehicles and cargo from amphibious ships onto the beach at higher speeds and for longer distances than can conventional landing craft.

Builders: Lockheed Shipyard in Seattle, Washington, was originally the second source for LCAC construction; beginning in June 1988, however, that firm divested itself of shipbuilding activities, and the Gulfport Marine division of Avondale Industries took over the Lockheed contracts.

Class: The original Navy-Marine plan was for 107 LCACs to support an amphibious assault force of one Marine Expeditionary Force (MEF) plus one Marine Expeditionary Brigade (MEB). In early 1984 the Department of Defense announced a plan for "at least 90" units, although the 107 force-level goal was listed in official documents through fiscal 1991. The fiscal 1993 Department of Defense budget request provided for the final 7 LCACs for a total of 91 units.

Design: The Navy began development of air cushion craft in 1960.

The LCAC 50, carrying a test tank and a trailer, enters the water at Panama City, Florida. This view shows the drive-through configuration of these craft, which facilitates loading and unloading while in a ship's docking well. The control compartment is on the starboard side, just ahead of the starboard gas-turbine exhaust. (1993, U.S. Navy)

The LCAC design is based on the JEFF(B), one of two competitive prototypes delivered to the Navy in 1977.

The LCAC has a modular design that facilitates construction, maintenance, and damage repairs. The craft are fully "skirted"; they are amphibious and can clear land obstacles up to four-feet (1.2 m) high. Bow and stern ramps are fitted. The cargo deck area is 81 feet (24.7 m) × 27 feet (8.2 m), for a total of 1,809 square feet (162.8 m^2).

The design payload is 120,000 pounds (54,545 kg), with a maximum overload of 150,000 pounds (68,182 kg). An LCAC can accommodate one M1 Abrams tank or four Light Armored Vehicles (LAV) or three AAV7/LVTP-7 amphibian vehicles (two AAVs if appliqué armor is fitted) or two M198 155-mm towed howitzers.

The control compartment is located on the starboard side; it has an aircraft-type cockpit in which the operator sits on the far right, the engineer in the center, and the navigator on the left.

Design problems occurred in the early craft, with operational tests revealing that the craft shipped water that could cause electrical shorts and interrupt operations. The early craft have been modified, but the Navy did not request additional units in the fiscal 1987–1988 budgets because the five units completed to that time would require additional testing before modifications could be developed.

All units were built with composite (ceramic tile) armor for the control station module. The LCAC 34 and later units have one engine on each side armored; the LCAC 61 and subsequent units have additional engine armor. Armor, modular arrangement, and redundancy provide a relatively high degree of survivability.

Electronics: The modified LN-66 is combined with a Unisys-developed system to provide multiple functions.

Engineering: The gas turbines are fitted in modules, two per side, in the port and starboard sides. The clutch/gearbox system permits a high degree of flexibility. Two engines are normally employed for propulsion and two for lift; under emergency conditions, one engine can provide propulsion and one can provide lift. The craft have a high degree of maneuverability and can turn 180° within their own length.

The propellers are four-blade, 11¾-foot (3.6-m) diameter, reversible, each fitted with two rudders; the lift fans are 5¼ feet (1.6 m) in diameter.

Guns: Although no armament is fitted, three mounting positions are provided: one for a 7.62-mm M60 machine gun and two for either a 7.62-mm M60 or .50-cal M2HB machine gun or a 40-mm Mk 19 grenade launcher.

Mine countermeasures: In December 1993 the decision was made to provide a Mine Countermeasures (MCM) capability to some LCACs. Operational test and evaluation began with the reconfigured LCAC 66 in February 1994 at Panama City, Florida.

A total of eight LCACs are planned to be configured for rapid conversion to the MCM role. These craft are referred to as multipurpose air cushion vehicles (MCAC). They can be modified to employ the Mk 104, Mk 105, and Mk 106 MCM systems as well as the M-58 line charges, the latter to be eventually replaced by the SABER line charge system (see chapter 31). Towing speed for the Mk 104/105/106 systems is 25 knots. The AQS-14 mine-hunting sonar can also be fitted.

(The Royal Navy conducted mine countermeasure trials with the 55-ton BH7 Mk 2 Hovercraft [pennant P 235] in 1983. An enlarged, specialized BH7 Mk 20 Hovercraft configured for the MCM role—using U.S. helicopter equipment—was designed, but not procured.)

Operational: Each LCAC is commanded by a craftmaster, i.e., a chief petty officer who also pilots the craft; the other crew members are the engineer, navigator, loadmaster, and deck seaman.

The LCACs are assigned in approximately equal numbers to Assault Craft Unit 4 at Little Creek (Norfolk), Virginia, and Assault Craft Unit 5 at Camp Pendleton, California. ACU-4 was established in 1987 and ACU-5 in 1983.

ACU-5 rotates three LCACs to Sasebo, Japan, at 18-month intervals.

The LCACs can be carried in the following amphibious ships: LHD (3), LHA (1), LPD 17 (2), LPD 4 (1), LPD 1 (1), LSD 49 (2), LSD 41 (4), and LSD 36 (3).

Seventeen LCACs were deployed on board amphibious ships participating in Operation Desert Storm in January–February 1991. All were "mission-ready" and operated in day-and-night exercises and administrative (noncombat) landings with 100 percent availability. (This was exactly one-half the number of LCACs in service at the time.)

The LCAC 27 comes ashore during NATO exercise Strong Resolve in Norway. Two gun barrels protrude over the bow of the craft, which is loaded with guns and vehicles. The "propeller shaft" of the port gas-turbine engine is just visible above the letters U.S. Navy. (1995, U.S. Navy, PH2 Franklin P. Call)

An LCAC from Assault Craft Unit 4 comes aboard the dock landing ship Ashland (LSD 48) during Exercise Agile Provider off the North Carolina coast. The enlisted men who pilot these craft often have a difficult job launching and recovering in seaways. (1994, U.S. Navy, PH1 Alexander C. Hicks).

The LCAC 37 backs out of the dock landing ship Nashville (LPD 13) during a port visit to Nina Sulman, Bahrain. Note the small stern gate, four-blade aircraft propellers, and trainable gas-turbine exhausts, forward of the shrouded propellers. (1993, John Bouvia)

High and dry: The LCAC 10 ashore at the Naval Amphibious Base Little Creek, Virginia. Note the twin steering vanes fitted to each ducted propeller and the propeller drive shafts. Although LCACs are faster and more efficient than conventional landing craft, helicopters and the new MV-22 Osprey will be the principal amphibious assault vehicle into the 21st century. (U.S. Navy)

40 UTILITY LANDING CRAFT: "LCU 1610" CLASS

Number	Assignment*	Number	Assignment*	Number	Assignment*
LCU 1614	NADC, Key West, Fla.	LCU 1656	ACU-2	LCU 1657	ACU-2
LCU 1616	ACU-1	LCU 1643	ACU-2	LCU 1658	ACU-2
LCU 1617	ACU-1	LCU 1644	ACU-2	LCU 1659	ACU-2
LCU 1619	ACU-1	LCU 1645	ACU-2	LCU 1660	ACU-2
LCU 1624	ACU-1	LCU 1646	ACU-1	LCU 1661	ACU-2
LCU 1627	ACU-1	LCU 1647	NUSWC, Andros Range, Caribbean	LCU 1662	ACU-2
LCU 1629	ACU-1	LCU 1648	ACU-1	LCU 1663	ACU-2
LCU 1630	ACU-1	LCU 1649	ACU-2	LCU 1664	ACU-2
LCU 1631	ACU-1	LCU 1650	ACU-2	LCU 1665	ACU-1
LCU 1632	ACU-1	LCU 1651	ACU-1	LCU 1666	ACU-1
LCU 1633	ACU-1	LCU 1652	ACU-1	135CU8501	reserve training; Buffalo, N.Y. (LCU 1680)
LCU 1634	ACU-1	LCU 1653	ACU-2	135CU8502	reserve training; Tampa, Fla. (LCU 1681)
LCU 1635	ACU-1	LCU 1654	ACU-2		
LCU 1641	EOD Mobile Unit 6	LCU 1655	AUX-2		

*ACU = Assault Craft Unit; EOD = Explosive Ordinance Disposal; NAB = Naval Amphibious Base; NADC = Naval Air Development Center; NUSWC = Naval Undersea Warfare Center.

Builders:	Defoe SB, Bay City, Wisc.: LCU 1646–1666
	General Ship & Engine Works, East Boston, Mass.: LCU 1627, 1628, 1631–1635
	Gunderson Bros., Portland, Ore.: LCU 1616–1619, 1623, 1624
	Marinette Marine, Wisc.: LCU 1643–1645
	Moss Point Marine, Escatawpa, Miss.: LCU 1680, 1681
	Southern SB, Slidell, La.: LCU 1626, 1629, 1630
Displacement:	190 tons light
	390 tons full load except LCU 1680, 1681 404 tons
Length:	134¾ feet (41.1 m) overall
Beam:	29¾ feet (9.1 m)
Draft:	6 11/12 feet (2.1 m)
Propulsion:	4 diesel engines (General Motors Detroit 6-71); 1,200 bhp; 2 Kort-nozzle propellers except LCU 1646 and later units 4 General Motors 12V71N, 1,700 bhp
Speed:	11 knots
Range:	1,200 n.miles (2,222 km) at 8 knots with payload
Manning:	6 (enlisted) except LCU 1680, 1681 14 (2 officers + 12 enlisted)
Troops:	8
Guns:	2 20-mm cannon or 2 .50-cal machine guns M2 (2 single)
Radars:	SPS-69 Pathfinder navigation

These are improved LCUs with 15 units (LCU 1610–1624) completed in 1959–1960 and the remainder from 1967 to 1976, except the LCU 1680 and LCU 1681, in 1987.

Class: This class originally consisted of hull numbers LCU 1610–1624 and 1627–1681.

The LCU 1680 and LCU 1681 were built to a modified design. The LCU 1667–1679 went to the U.S. Army.

The LCU 1621, 1623, and 1628 have been converted to auxiliary swimmer delivery vehicles (ASDV) to support diving operations, and others became service craft (YFU). The latter are described in chapter 25.

Classification: Two LCUs assigned to naval reserve training activities have hull registry numbers.

Design: The LCU 1610–1624 were SCB No. 149; the LCU 1627 and later units were SCB No. 149B (new series SCB No. 406).

These LCUs have a "drive-through" configuration with bow and stern ramps and a small, starboard-side island structure housing controls and accommodations. Previous LCU/LCT–type landing craft had a small deck structure aft. They are of welded-steel construction; the mast folds down for entering well decks of amphibious ships.

A Marine M1A1 Abrams tank plunges into the surf from the LCU 1658 at Camp Lejeune, North Carolina. A radar "pot" is situated on the pole mast above the LCU's bridge; it folds down to permit entry into a docking-well amphibious ship. (1994, U.S. Marine Corps, Cpl. R. D. Clayton)

The LCU 1659 maneuvers off the docking well of the helicopter carrier NASSAU (LHA 4) during Exercise Agile Provider. These craft are valuable for carrying ashore vehicles and materiél in a nonhostile environment. (1994, U.S. Navy, PHC Johnny R. Wilson)

Cargo capacity is one M1 Abrams tank or up to about 190 tons of cargo or, for short distances, 350 to 400 troops.

Engineering: The LCU 1621 had vertical shafts fitted with vertical axis, cycloidal six-bladed propellers. All other units have Kort-nozzle propellers. The LCU 1680 and 1681 have improved engines; LCU 1646 and higher have been backfitted.

Guns: Weapons are not normally fitted in these craft.

Operational: Most LCUs are assigned to Assault Craft Units 1 and 2, as indicated above.

The LCU 1641 is used as a training minelayer, having been fitted with a stern mine rail and a recovery crane.

The LCU 1663 shows the lines of the ultimate LCT/LSU/LCU design. The craft has a drive-through design, with bridge and accommodations on the starboard side. In this view the mast is raised (note yard at top of photo); the radar "pot" is lowered (white circle adjacent to the "3"). (1994, Leo Van Ginderen collection)

3 UTILITY LANDING CRAFT: "LCU 1466" CLASS

Number	Assignment
119WB1561 (ex-LCU 1561, YFU 61)	Naval Station Roosevelt Roads, P.R.
LCU 1580 (ex-Army Vera Cruz)	on loan to Maritime Administration
LCU 1590 (ex-Army Spotsylvania)	Mobile Diving and Salvage Unit 2

Displacement:	180 tons light 360 tons full load
Length:	119 feet (39.0 m) overall
Beam:	34 feet (10.4 m)
Draft:	6 feet (1.8 m)
Propulsion:	3 geared diesel engines (Gray Marine 64 YTL); 675 bhp; 3 shafts
Speed:	8 knots
Range:	700 n.miles (1,300 km) at 7 knots with payload
Manning:	6 (enlisted)
Troops:	8
Guns:	removed
Radars:	navigation

These are the survivors of a large series of LCUs. The LCU 1580 supports the National Defense Reserve Fleet at Suisun Bay (Vallejo), California. These craft were completed in 1954.

Class: This class covered hull numbers LCU 1466–1609: 14 units were constructed in Japan under the offshore procurement program for foreign service (LCU 1594–1607, completed in 1955). Other ships of this design were built for the U.S. Army.

An LCU 1466-class landing craft carrying three Marine M48 Patton tanks (with turrets turned to the rear) during a landing exercise. Several of these craft are operated by the Army (see chapter 34). These craft have only a bow ramp; twin 20-mm cannon are fitted on either side of the bridge. (U.S. Navy)

Numerous U.S. units were transferred to other nations; others became service craft (YFUs and YFBs).

Classification: The LCU 1466–1503 series was ordered as utility landing ships (LSU) on 31 October 1951; they were reclassified as LCUs on 15 April 1952.

Design: SCB-25. These craft have a deckhouse-aft configuration.

Guns: Built with gun "tubs" on either side of the bridge structure for .50-cal machine guns or 20-mm cannon.

POST–WORLD WAR II TANK LANDING CRAFT

The tank landing craft designs LCT(1), (2), (3), and (4) were British. The first U.S. design was the LCT(5); No. 1–500 were completed in 1942; many were transferred to Great Britain. The LCT(6) followed, with No. 501-1465 being completed in 1943–1944; a few went to Britain and six became coastal minehunters, designated AMc(U) 1–6.[1] The LCT(6) had an "island" structure on the port side, introducing the "drive-through" design to landing craft.

The American LCT(7) design, No. 1501–1830, was for oceangoing craft, completed as medium landing ships (LSM/LSMR). The British LCT(8) design was for similar oceangoing craft.

In 1949 the surviving LCT(6)s were reclassified as LSUs with their LCT hull numbers. Landing craft Nos. 1466–1503 were ordered in 1951 as LSUs but changed to LCU in May 1952. Subsequent LCUs follow in sequence, ignoring the numbers initially assigned to the LCT(7) series.

APPROX. 75 MECHANIZED LANDING CRAFT: LCM(8) MK 3, MK 5

Weight:	34 tons light 121 tons full load
Length:	73 7/12 feet (22.4 m) overall
Beam:	21 feet (6.4 m)
Draft:	4 7/12 feet (1.4 m) aft
Propulsion:	4 diesel engines (General Motors Detroit 6-71); 1,300 bhp; 2 shafts (see *Engineering* notes)
Speed:	12 knots
Range:	150 n.miles (278 km) at 12 knots
Manning:	5 (enlisted)
Guns:	none (see notes)

These are standard landing craft intended to carry vehicles and cargo. Capacity is 58 tons of cargo or light vehicles. No accommodations are provided in these or other LCM-type craft.

1. AMc(U) = minesweeper, coastal (underwater locator); see chapter 22.

Most of these craft are assigned to Assault Craft Units 1 and 2.

Guns: A pair of .50-cal machine guns can be fitted.

Engineering: Most have four GM 6-71 diesels; a few have two of the larger GM 12V71 diesels. The last 20 units (delivered 1991–1992) have GM 8V92N engines.

APPROX. 25 MECHANIZED LANDING CRAFT: LCM(8) MK 2, MK 4

Weight:	36.5 tons light 106.75 tons full load
Length:	$74\frac{1}{12}$ feet (22.6 m) overall
Beam:	$21\frac{1}{12}$ feet (6.4 m)
Draft:	$4\frac{1}{2}$ feet (1.4 m)
Propulsion:	4 diesel engines (General Motors); 1,300 bhp; 2 shafts
Speed:	12 knots
Range:	150 n.miles (278 km) at 12 knots
Manning:	5 (enlisted)
Guns:	none

An LCM(8) assigned to the Naval Amphibious Base in Coronado (San Diego), California. Bow ramps vary in these craft. The mast protruding from the conning position mounts a navigation light. (1985, Giorgio Arra)

An LCM(8) from Assault Craft Unit 2 off Norfolk, Virginia. A glass-windowed cover is installed over the conning position. LCMs and smaller landing craft are identified by their parent unit, base, or ship. (1985, Giorgio Arra)

An aluminum LCM(8) is shown being loaded aboard the amphibious cargo ship MOBILE (LKA 115). The LCMs and other landing craft types had their beginnings in World War II. (1988, Leo Van Ginderen collection)

These are aluminum versions of the steel-hulled LCM(8), originally developed for use with the CHARLESTON (LKA 113)-class amphibious cargo ships (Mk 2). Subsequently, additional units were ordered for use aboard maritime prepositioning ships (Mk 4).

Cargo capacity is 65 tons of cargo or light vehicles.

Engineering: Some units have been refitted with Kort nozzles.

APPROX. 60 MECHANIZED LANDING CRAFT: LCM(6) TYPE

Weight:	26.7 tons light 62.35 tons full load
Length:	56 feet (17.1 m) overall
Beam:	$14\frac{1}{3}$ feet (4.4 m)
Draft:	$3\frac{5}{6}$ feet (1.2 m)
Propulsion:	2 diesel engines (Gray Marine 64HN9 or General Motors 8V71); 625 bhp; 2 shafts
Speed:	12 knots
Range:	130 n.miles (240 km) at 9 knots
Manning:	5 (enlisted)
Guns:	none

Additional units of this type serve in various support roles. Numerous LCMs of this type were converted to riverine combat craft during the Vietnam War. Of the above total, about ten are normally carried aboard amphibious ships.

Of welded steel construction, they can carry 34 tons of cargo or, for short distances, 120 troops.

Engineering: Above horsepower and speed for GM engines; those with Gray Marine have 450 bhp and can make 10 knots.

This "short-hull" LCM(6) shows the wear and tear on these craft. LCMs usually display dents from being smashed against docking-well walls in amphibious ships. (1983, Giorgio Arra)

An LCM(6) modified to serve as a tender at the Naval Surface Warfare Center facility in Florida. A life raft canister is fitted alongside the elevated pilothouse. (1990, Giorgio Arra)

2 MECHANIZED LANDING CRAFT: LCM(3) TYPE

Weight:	23.2 tons light 50 tons full load
Length:	50 feet (15.28 m) overall
Beam:	14 feet (4.27 m)
Draft:	4 feet (1.22 m)
Propulsion:	2 diesel engines (Gray Marine 64HN9); 450 bhp; 2 shafts
Speed:	9.5 knots
Range:	130 n.miles (240 km) at 9.5 knots with payload
Manning:	4 or 5 (enlisted)
Guns:	none

These are outdated landing craft, the survivors of a large class. Capacity is 26.5 tons of cargo or light vehicles.

One unit is assigned to Fleet Activities Okinawa and one to the Mare Island Naval Shipyard.

APPROX. 130 LANDING CRAFT PERSONNEL LIGHT (LCPL): Mk 11–13

Weight:	10 tons full load
Length:	36 feet (11.0 m) overall
Beam:	13 feet (4.0 m)
Draft:	$3\frac{1}{2}$ feet (1.1 m)
Propulsion:	1 diesel engine (General Motors 8V71); 350 bhp; 1 shaft (see notes)
Speed:	17 knots
Range:	150 n.miles (278 km) at 15 knots
Manning:	3 (enlisted)
Guns:	none (see notes)

These small landing craft are used for passenger transport and for the control of other landing craft. About 100 are currently carried in amphibious ships; the remainder are assigned to shore activities. Additional Mk 13 units are being built by Peterson Builders, Sturgeon Bay, Wisconsin.

LCPLs are built of fiberglass-reinforced plastic. They carry 17 passengers or two tons of cargo.

Engineering: The newer LCPLs have Cummins lightweight engines fitted.

Guns: During the Vietnam War several LCPLs were armed with one or more .50- and .30-cal machine guns and employed for inshore patrol (some with a navigation radar fitted).

An LCPL of the Mk 12 series. These are now the most numerous landing craft in Navy service. They are used mainly as personnel transports, not in the traditional landing craft role. (1992, George R. Schneider)

APPROX. 10 LANDING CRAFT VEHICLE AND PERSONNEL (LCVP): Mk 7

Weight:	13.5 tons full load
Length:	$35\frac{3}{4}$ feet (10.9 m) overall
Beam:	$10\frac{1}{2}$ feet (3.2 m)
Draft:	$3\frac{1}{2}$ feet (1.1 m)
Propulsion:	1 diesel engine (Gray Marine 64HN9); 225 bhp; 1 shaft
Speed:	10 knots
Range:	110 n.miles (204 km) at 8 knots
Manning:	2 or 3 (enlisted)
Guns:	none

These small landing craft can be carried by amphibious ships. Most of these are currently aboard "amphibs."

LCVPs are built of wood or fiberglass-reinforced plastic. They have a bow ramp and can carry light vehicles or four tons of cargo or 40 troops.

An LCVP from the Blue Ridge (LCC 19); two or, at most, three are the normal crew of these craft. (Giorgio Arra)

2 AUXILIARY SWIMMER DELIVERY VEHICLES: MODIFIED LCU

Number	Built	Assignment
ASDV 2 (ex-LCU 1623)	1960	Special Boat Unit 20
ASDV 3 (ex-LCU 1628)	1967	SEAL Delivery Team 1

These are former utility landing craft modified to support training operations for combat swimmers/SEALs. See page 174 for basic characteristics of these craft.

They are fitted with a recompression chamber and associated air compressors, storage flasks, and an electrical generator. Manning varies from 10 to 14 enlisted crew, depending upon whether or not the mission requires use of the decompression chamber. A crane is fitted for handling swimmer delivery vehicles, small boats, and underwater equipment. Sleeping quarters are provided for embarked personnel.

Class: A third craft of this type, the ASDV 1 (ex-LCU 1610) has been discarded.

Operational: SBU-20 is based at Little Creek (Norfolk), Virginia, and SEAL Delivery Team 1 at Coronado, California.

The ASDV 1 off San Diego. These former utility landing craft have been extensively modified internally, but they retain their original LCU lines. The bow ramp is still operational. (1986, Giorgio Arra)

The stern aspect of the ASDV 3 shows the support facilities installed in these craft. The crane stowed athwartships is for handling rigid inflatable boats. (1986, Giorgio Arra)

AMPHIBIOUS WARPING TUGS

The Navy operates a large number of these craft, which are fabricated from pontoon sections. They are used to ferry materiél from amphibious and Maritime Prepositioning Ships (MPS) to shore, to install amphibious fuel and water transfer systems, and to maneuver and support causeways. One warping tug (SLWT) and three or four powered causeway sections (CSP) are carried by each MPS vessel; with some equipment removed and the A-frame lowered, the tugs can be side loaded on tank landing ships of the Newport (LST 1179) class.

The tugs are operated by Amphibious Construction Battalions (ACB) under the Commanders, Naval Beach Group 1 (Coronado, California) and Naval Beach Group 2 (Norfolk, Virginia).

21 SIDE LOADABLE WARPING TUGS

Builders:	Oregon Iron Works, Klackamas, Ore.
Displacement:	
Length:	80 feet (24.38 m) overall
Beam:	22 feet (6.71 m)
Draft:	
Propulsion:	2 diesel engines (Harbormaster); 860 bhp; aximuth propulsors
Speed:	5 knots
Range:	
Manning:	

These units were delivered in 1994–1995.

3 SIDE LOADABLE WARPING TUGS

Number	Number	Number
SLWT 4013	SLWT 4014	SLWT 4015

Builders:	PACECO, Gulfport, Miss.
Weight:	110 tons loaded
Length:	84 feet (25.6 m) overall
Beam:	21¼ feet
Draft:	2⅔ feet (0.8 m)
Propulsion:	2 turbo-charged diesel engines (Detroit Diesel 8V71TI; 850 bhp; 2 waterjet propulsion units with 360° rotating nozzles with 12,500 lbs (5,625 kg) thrust
Speed:	8.5 knots
Range:	75 n.miles (140 km)
Manning:	8 (enlisted)

These side loadable warping tugs are modular, consisting of 33 replaceable pontoon "cans" that are bolted together plus three engine modules, a small control station, and an A-frame lifting device. They can be connected as "pushers" to one to six unpowered pontoon causeways to form barge ferries; each causeway can carry 100 tons of containerized cargo or vehicles. Without the A-frame and minor modifications, these craft are designated as causeway section, powered (CSP); that designation is now found on the Navy's ship classification list (see chapter 3).

The SLWT has a double-drum, diesel-powered A-frame/winch (turbo-charged Detroit Model 4-53T) with a lifting capacity of 12 tons. The tug is fitted with a 1,120-pound (504-kg) stern anchor. Fuel capacity is 625 gallons (2,375 liters).

Classification: In the fleet these craft are (incorrectly) referred to as side-loading warping tugs (SLWT).

AMPHIBIOUS WARPING TUGS

The LWT 1 and LWT 2 have been stricken. Two units, built by Campbell Machine Works, San Diego, California, were delivered in 1970. Series production of this design was not undertaken. These craft were 85 feet (25.9 m) long and were propelled by two diesel engines.

The SLWT 35 from ACB 1 pushes two pontoon causeways loaded with several Marine trucks. These "tugs" and pontoon causeways are necessary for unloading amphibious ships and, in some situations, Maritime Prepositioning Ships (MPS). (1992, U.S. Navy, Tom Hollinberger)

An SLWT from Amphibious Construction Battalion 1 is seen beaching at San Diego. Note the control station (offset to starboard), removable mast, and A-frame. (1992, U.S. Navy, Tom Hollinberger)

The SLWT 35 from ACB-1 serves as a pusher for pontoon causeways. (1992, U.S. Navy, Tom Hollinberger)

LANDING VEHICLES

Assault amphibian vehicles (AAV) are used by the Marine Corps for assault landings and for subsequent movement ashore. The Marine Corps currently operates 1,323 assault amphibian vehicles of the AAV7 series. Most of these are troop carriers (AAVP7), 106 of which are configured as command vehicles (AAVC7) and 64 as recovery/repair vehicles (AAVR7).

An Advanced Assault Amphibian Vehicle (AAAV) is under development. The definitive Defense Acquisition Board, the Penta-

Marines stand by their AAVP7A1 amphibian assault vehicles inside the docking well of the Harpers Ferry (LSD 49). Another vehicle is coming aboard. These vehicles have limited utility in over-the-horizon landings, now made possible by helicopters and LCACs. (1993, Hughes Missile Systems)

gon's major review agency for new weapon programs, approved the AAAV moving from the initial concept and exploration phase into the demonstration and validation phase on 15 March 1995. A contract for full-scale development of prototype vehicles is expected to be awarded in 1996. Production will probably not begin until 2005 (see below). Total program price—for development and procurement—is estimated between $3 and $5 *billion*.

However, the high cost of the program and the Marine Corps' need for the MV-22 Osprey tilt-rotor aircraft, as well as other high-cost weapons, could place the AAAV program in jeopardy.

The AAV7 series was previously designated landing vehicle tracked, personnel LVTP-7. The term AAV was adopted in the 1970s as a "sexy" designation for the next generation of assault amphibian vehicle. In 1985 the designation LVTP and the terms amphibious tractors, or "amtrac," were discarded from AAV terminology.

Increasingly, the Marines have employed these vehicles on land as well as for ship-to-shore movement. The AAV/LVT is limited as an armored personnel carrier because of: (1) its high noise level, (2) the height of the vehicle, (3) treads that are vulnerable to heavy land use, (4) its slow speed over certain terrain, and (5) its light armor. Also, there is now no effective method of protecting the troops in the AAV7 vehicles from a chemical/biological weapons attack.

The Marine Corps has three battalions that operate amphibian tractors. These battalions are:

- 1st Armored Assault Battalion on Okinawa to support the 3d Marine Division (2 amphibian companies);
- 2d Assault Amphibian Battalion at Camp Lejeune, North Carolina, to support the 2d Marine Division (4 amphibian companies);
- 3d Assault Amphibian Battalion at Camp Pendleton, California (3 amphibian companies);
- Company D, 3d Assault Amphibian Battalion, at Twenty Nine Palms, California;
- Detachment A, 3d Assault Amphibian Battalion (2 platoons), at Kaneohe Bay, Hawaii.

Note that the battalion on Okinawa is an *armored* unit, with two tank companies in addition to the amphibian companies. The standard amphibian battalion has a total of 1,166 personnel and 208 amphibian vehicles—187 AAVP7s, 15 AAVC7s, and 6 AAVR7s.

MARINE ASSAULT AMPHIBIAN BATTALION

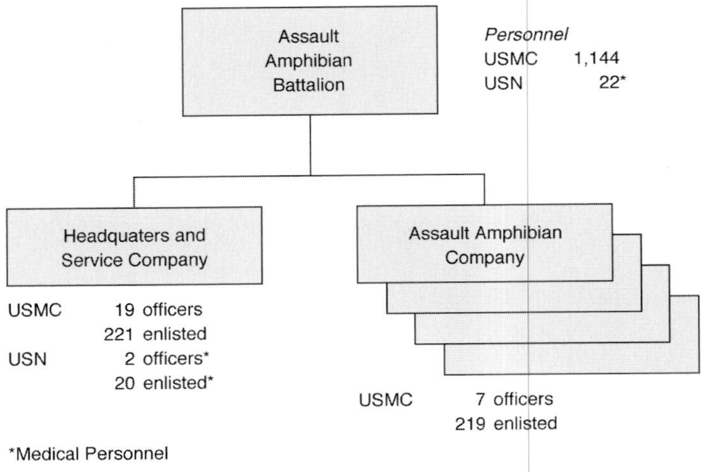

The 2d and 3d Battalions are each capable of simultaneously lifting the assault elements of a Marine Expeditionary Brigade (i.e., reinforced regiment), while the 1st Battalion can provide lift for a Marine Expeditionary Unit (i.e., reinforced battalion).

Another 327 AAVs are forward deployed on board the maritime pre-positioning ships. Additional AAVs are assigned to the Marine Corps Reserve and are in the pipeline for maintenance, training, etc.

The service life of the present AAV7 "family" of vehicles was expected to end in the mid-1980s. However, the failure to gain approval for a follow-on amphibian vehicle led the Marines to embark on an extensive Service Life Extension Program (SLEP) for existing vehicles (with modified vehicles receiving the designation suffix A1).

Two proposed successors to the AAV7/LVTP-7 were the landing assault vehicle (LVA), initiated in 1973 and canceled in 1979, followed by the advanced tracked landing vehicle, designated LVT(X). The abortive LVT(X), which was canceled in 1985, is described in the 13th Edition/page 212.

Modernization: The AAV7 SLEP upgrade program includes the following changes:

- Replacing the existing gun turret mounting a single .50-cal M85 machine gun with an electric-drive turret mounting a 40-mm Mk 19 grenade launcher as well as the older but more-reliable .50-cal M2 machine gun.

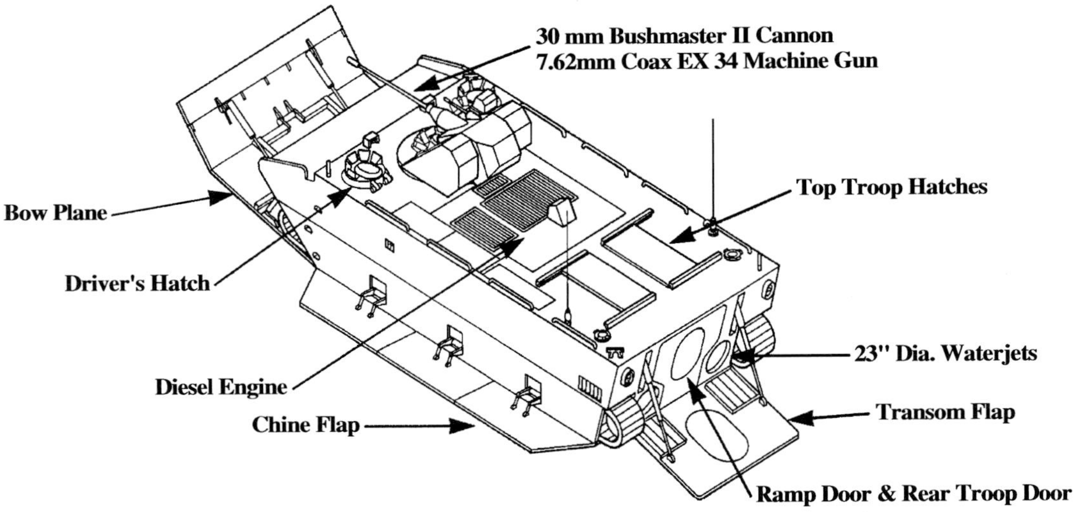

The AAAV has a bow plane and chine flaps that extend to provide a high-speed configuration for water transit. The turret houses the 30-mm version of the Bushmaster chain gun as well as a coaxial machine gun.

- An advanced mine-clearing system that fires explosive "snakes" for detonating ground mines. The system—including a possible later version with fuel-air explosive—can be installed on top of a tractor.
- A limited Chemical-Biological-Radiological (CBR) alarm and protection system.
- Appliqué steel armor that can be bolted on to the vehicle by the crew. This P-900 armor will defeat 14.7-mm gunfire. The armor weighs 3,500 pounds (1,591 kg), which the vehicle can easily handle. In fact, the weight actually improves the water stability of the craft. A lighter, improved armor is being developed.
- A bow plane that extends when the craft is in the water to reduce the tendency to push down into seas.
- An automatic fire sensor and suppression system is being installed to reduce the possibility of fuel fires in the troop compartment.
- Improved transmission and suspension.
- Magnetic heading device.

These improvements add weight to the vehicle, which is not a concern because of the craft's great payload. More critical is space because the changes reduce the troop capacity to perhaps 21 riflemen. If crew-served weapons such as mortars are carried, the troop capacity is even less.

An advanced propulsion system that will provide enhanced mobility is being considered. A rotary engine of about 750 hp with all-electric drive has been evaluated in a prototype AAV7.

ADVANCED AMPHIBIAN ASSAULT VEHICLE

Weight:	62,000 to 72,000 pounds (28,182 to 32,727 kg) full load
Length:	27⅚ feet (8.48 m) on land
	37 feet (11.28 m) in water
Width:	12 feet (3.66 m)
Height:	10 feet (3.05 m)
Propulsion:	1 diesel engine (MTU MT883 Ra-523); 2,600 hp in water mode, 800 hp in land mode; tracked running gear on land
	2 waterjets in water
Speed:	45 mph on land
	23 to 29 mph in water
Range:	300 miles (483 km) on land
Crew:	3
Troops:	17
Guns:	1 30-mm Bushmaster II cannon (200 rounds ready)
	1 7.62-mm machine gun (800 rounds ready)

The development of an Advanced Amphibian Assault Vehicle "remains our primary developmental research effort," according to the Commandant of the Marine Corps.[2] This development program—referred to as AAAV for the advanced amphibious assault—seeks to provide a high-speed tracked vehicle to move assault troops from amphibious ships beyond the horizon to inland objectives.

The Marine AAAV envisions a so-called "high-speed" seacraft with the land mission capabilities of the U.S. Army's Bradley Armored Fighting Vehicle (AFV). The new craft is intended to be able to move at speeds in excess of 20 knots through three-foot (0.9-m) seas.

The Marine Corps plans to procure 1,013 AAAVs to replace the 1,300 AAV7s. Two groups, the United Defense (formerly FMC Corporation's Ground Systems Division, which built all AAV7s) and General Dynamics' Land Systems Division teamed with AAI Corporation, competed in the development of the new vehicle. Following tests with demonstration vehicles, GD was chosen in 1996 to produce 15 prototype vehicles, namely, 13 troop carriers and 2 command and control vehicles. Initial production would begin about 2005.

Design: The FMC design had a hydrofoil-assisted planing hull, a concept that demonstrated 33-knot speeds in a half-scale demonstrator model. The GD-AAI design has a planing hull.

AAI has produced three AAV technology test beds under contract to the Navy, with the last—called a Propulsion System Demonstrator (PSD)—achieving a planing speed of 25 mph (40 km/h) for 33 n.miles (61 km) in trials, with a top speed of 45 mph (72.4 km/h). Vehicle weight was 57,000 pounds (25,855 kg). The craft had a Cummins VTA 903T diesel engine and (for high speed in water) a General Electric LM 120/T700/TC7 gas turbine engine. Such a combat vehicle, with a crew of 3, could carry 15 troops.

Gun: The 25-mm cannon and 7.62-mm machine gun would be coaxially mounted in a turret atop the vehicle.

2. Gen. A. M. Gray, USMC, testimony before the House Armed Services committee, 21 February 1991.

An AAAV prototype achieving a planing speed of 45 mph. Note the massive wake created by the vehicle. The bow plane and chine flaps retract for slow-speed and land operations. (1992, General Dynamics/Land Systems)

A mock-up of the AAAV on land, capable of serving as an armored personnel carrier. The bow plane and chine flaps are retracted, providing additional protection to the vehicle. The 17 combat-equipped troops leave the vehicle through a rear door-ramp arrangement. (General Dynamics/Land Systems)

An "amtrac" shown carrying Marines in the assault on occupied Kuwait during the Persian Gulf conflict. The troops have hung their gear from the vehicle, whose name is "Pressure Point." (1991, U.S. Navy, CWO2 Ed Bailey)

AAVP7A1 assault vehicles—fitted with appliqué armor—drive along the beach at Vladivostok in the Russian Far East during a joint exercise with the Russian Navy called Cooperation from the Sea. A Russian landing ship is at left. (1994, U.S. Navy, PH1 Charles W. Alley)

The turret of an AAVP7A1 showing the .50-cal machine gun and 40-mm grenade launcher. Previous generations of "amtracs" included vehicles armed with heavier guns and howitzers up to 105 mm. (1991, U.S. Navy, CWO2 Ed Bailey)

An AAVP7A1 assault vehicle prepares to come aboard the SHREVEPORT (LPD 12) during Exercise Agile Provider. These vehicles are low in the water when at sea. (1994, U.S. Navy, PH1 Robert N. Scoggin)

An AAVP7A1 employed ashore as an armored personnel carrier; the roof plates are open, and Marines with their M16 rifles are at the ready in the troop compartment. (FMC Corporation)

An AAVP7A1 fitted with a mine-clearance kit; the three-rocket launcher for deploying explosive line charges is in the raised position at the rear of the vehicle. (U.S. Marine Corps)

An AAVR7A1 vehicle with crane raised. There is a towing winch at the rear of the vehicle, above the ramp. (FMC Corporation)

1,153 PERSONNEL VEHICLES: AAVP7A1 SERIES (FORMERLY LVTP-7)

Weight:	38,450 pounds (17,477 kg) empty
	50,350 pounds (22,886 kg) loaded
Length:	26 feet (7.9 m) overall
Width:	10¾ feet (3.3 m)
Height:	10¼ feet (3.1 m)
Draft:	5⅔ feet (1.7 m)
Propulsion:	turbo-supercharged diesel engine (Cummins VT400);
	400 hp; tracked running gear on land
	2 waterjets in water (3,025 lbs each)
Speed:	40 mph maximum, 20–30 mph cruise on land
	8.4 mph maximum, 8 mph cruise in water
Range:	300 miles at 25 mph on land
	approx. 55 miles at 8 mph in water
Crew:	3 (enlisted)
Trrops:	21
Guns:	1 .50-cal machine gun M2
	1 40-mm grenade launcher Mk 19

The AAVP7 is a full-tracked amphibian vehicle that provides an over-the-beach capability for landing troops and equipment through heavy surf. It is the world's only vehicle capable of operating in rough seas and plunging surf (up to ten feet high). Several hundred are being modernized and are designated AAV7A1 (see below).

These vehicles were designed and manufactured by the Ordnance Division of FMC Corporation, San Jose, California. They are also used by the marine forces of Argentina, Brazil, Italy, South Korea, Spain, and Thailand.

Armament: The LVTP-7 was designed to mount a 20-mm cannon coaxially with a machine gun; because of development problems, however, the cannon was deleted. The current .50-cal machine gun is co-mounted with a 40-mm grenade launcher in a 360° powered turret that holds 200 .50-cal rounds and 98 40-mm rounds.

A mine-clearance kit can be fitted for clearing beach obstacles. This consists of a rack launcher that fires three 350-foot-long explosive line charges. Detonation is controlled by wire from within the vehicle.

Class: The prototypes for the LVTP-7 design were the 15 LVTPX-12 vehicles delivered to the Marines in 1967–1968. These were followed by a production run of 965 LVTP-7s delivered from 1970 to 1974, plus the specialized LVTC and LVTR vehicles described below. In addition, one LVTE-7 prototype of an assault engineer/mine-clearance vehicle was delivered in 1970, but none was series produced. Additional vehicles have been produced for use by the maritime pre-positioning forces.

Design: The LVTP-7 was designed to replace the LVTP-5 series amtracs and offered increased land and water speeds and more range, with less vehicle weight. In lieu of troops, the newer vehicle can carry 10,000 pounds (4,545 kg) of cargo. The LVTP-7 has a rear door and ramp for loading/unloading troops and cargo; it can turn 360° within its own length on land or in water.

Modernization: The SLEP upgraded vehicles were designated LVTP-7A1 prior to the change to AAV7A1. The first updated vehicles were delivered to the Marine Corps on 24 October 1983.

106 COMMAND VEHICLES: AAVC7A1 SERIES (FORMERLY LVTC-7)

Weight:	40,187 pounds (18,267 kg) empty
	44,111 pounds (20,050 kg) loaded
Crew:	12 (3 vehicle crew, 5 radiomen, 1 unit commander, and 3 staff)
Troops:	none
Guns:	1 7.62-mm machine gun M60D

Except as indicated above, the AAVC7 command vehicle characteristics are similar to those of the basic AAV7 series. Eighty-five of these vehicles were originally procured for use as command vehicles in amphibious landings. Additional vehicles were procured in the 1980s.

These vehicles are fitted with radios, crypto equipment, and telephones. Seventy-seven of the original vehicles are being modernized to the 7A1 configuration.

64 RECOVERY/REPAIR VEHICLES: AAVR7A1 SERIES (FORMERLY LVTR-7)

Weight:	47,304 pounds (21,502 kg) empty
	49,853 pounds (22,660 kg) loaded
Crew:	5 (3 vehicle crew, 2 mechanics)
Troops:	none
Guns:	1 7.62-mm machine gun M60D

Except as indicated above, the characteristics of the recovery/repair vehicle are similar to the AAV7 series. Sixty of these vehicles were originally procured for the recovery of damaged amtracs during amphibious landings. Additional units were procured during the 1980s.

They are fitted with a 6,000-pound (2,727-kg) capacity telescoping boom-type crane and 30,000-pound (13,636-kg) pull winch, plus maintenance equipment.

POST–WORLD WAR II AMPHIBIOUS TRACTORS

The U.S. Marine Corps procured 18,620 "amtracs" of various LVT/LVTA models during World War II. The first postwar LVT design produced for the Marines was the LVTP-5 troop carrier and the derivative LVTH-6, the latter mounting a 105-mm howitzer, LVTE-1 engineer vehicle, LVTC-1 command vehicle, and LVTR-1 recovery vehicle. A total of 1,332 of these vehicles were manufactured between 1951 and 1957.

This series was followed by the LVT-7 (now AAV7) series.

CHAPTER 21

Special Warfare and Patrol Craft

The FIREBOLT at high speed with her crew at battle stations. These coastal patrol ships, primarily intended to support SEAL operations, will be employed in a variety of roles as the U.S. Navy seeks to improve its capabilities in littoral/coastal areas. The FIREBOLT was the first Navy ship ever to be placed in commission in Alexandria, Virginia. (1994, U.S. Navy)

The role of special warfare craft in the U.S. Navy has increased significantly in the 1990s with the new emphasis on littoral warfare and special operations forces. The CYCLONE-class ships are the first major patrol craft to be built for the U.S. Navy in a decade, replacing smaller, less capable craft.

The CYCLONE class of 14 ships follows a series of failures in U.S. Navy efforts in the 1980s to develop patrol/special warfare craft. Those craft had the design designations PBM, PCM, SWCM (Sea Viking), and PXM, the last being a hydrofoil patrol craft.[1] Small patrol-series craft are also being procured by the Navy, primarily to support special operations.

A number of inshore and special warfare craft are also operated by the Naval Reserve Force.

The U.S. Navy has historically showed little interest in small combatants in peacetime, in part because of the emphasis on long-range, blue-water operations that support the Navy's primary missions, and in part because of the belief that the tactics and craft needed for coastal and inshore operations can be rapidly developed in wartime.

The CYCLONE class is the Navy's third series of post–World War II "large" patrol ships to be built. The Navy's six hydrofoil missile craft have been discarded, most after little more than a decade of operational service. Designed as Cold War attack craft to counter Soviet warships in coastal areas (such as the Aegean Sea), they were never forward-deployed and spent virtually all of their service in the Caribbean area engaged in anti-drug operations. Also discarded have been the ASHEVILLE-class patrol gunboats produced in the 1960s, which participated in offshore patrol operations during the Vietnam War.

The Navy evaluated several advanced technology combat craft in the 1960s and produced several hundred coastal and riverine patrol and support craft. Those too have been discarded. During the Vietnam War the lack of a capability in small combatant craft forced the Navy to procure Norwegian-built fast patrol boats and to adopt commercial designs for naval use. Subsequently, the Navy has sought to keep abreast of small craft design, and during the early 1980s American shipyards delivered a series of Navy-designed missile craft (PCG/PGG types) to Saudi Arabia in addition to selling smaller inshore and riverine combat craft to several other countries.

Armament: No anti-submarine weapons are carried by U.S. patrol craft.

Classification: The smaller unnamed patrol boats and craft are individually designated by their hull length, hull type, calendar year of construction, and consecutive hull of that type built during the year. Thus, 68PB842 indicates the second 68-foot PB-type craft built in 1984. The first two letters in this scheme are generally used in the designation:

AT	armored troop carrier
HS	harbor security
PB	patrol boats
RP	river patrol boat

Operational: Navy special warfare forces are under the operational control of the U.S. Special Operations Command (a unified command) and the administrative control of the U.S. Atlantic and Pacific Fleets.

Most of the Navy's smaller combat craft are assigned to Special Boat Units (SBU) under Special Boat Squadron 1 at the Naval Amphibious Base Coronado (San Diego), California, and Special Boat Squadron 2 at Naval Amphibious Base Little Creek (Norfolk), Virginia.

Squadron 1 has active units SBU-11 and SBU-12, and one Naval Reserve Force (NRF) unit, SBU-13; Squadron 2 has active SBU-20 and reserve SBU-22 and SBU-24. The active SBUs regularly deploy detachments overseas. The SBUs also operate SEAL Delivery Vehicles (SDV) (see page 82).

ADVANCED SPECIAL WARFARE CRAFT

The Navy's Surface Warfare Plan through 1989 had proposed a series of advanced special warfare craft in addition to the PC series, described below.

SWCX: The Navy planned to procure 20 special warfare craft, designated SWCX, to be delivered from 1994 to 1998. These craft, smaller than the PBC/PC design, were intended specifically to "insert" SEAL teams into hostile territory.[2] Thus, they were to have had an enhanced "stealth" capability.

RIB: The rigid inflatable boat, a 30-foot (9.1-m) craft, and an undefined high-speed interceptor craft were intended to replace the Seafox special warfare craft—light. The RIB was to be a lightweight, highly seaworthy craft that could be easily launched from an amphibious ship or a surface combatant.

SWCR: The special warfare craft, riverine, was intended as a shallow-draft boat to replace the existing 32-foot (9.75-m) PBRs.

MATCX: This was to be a replacement for the mini-armored troop carrier (mini-ATC).

1. See 13th Edition/page 221 and 14th Edition/pages 227–28 for characteristics.

2. SEAL = Sea-Air-Land; these are the Navy's special operations forces, akin to the U.S. Army's Green Berets.

A new Mk V special operations craft is unloaded from an Air Force C-5A Galaxy cargo plane at the Naval Air Station Jacksonville, Florida, demonstrating the strategic mobility of Special Operations Forces. The Mk V was flown into "Jax" in 1995 for trials in Tampa Bay. (John Bouvia)

13 + 1 (?) COASTAL PATROL SHIPS: "CYCLONE" CLASS

Number	Name	FY	Laid down	Launched	Commissioned	Status
PC 1	CYCLONE	90	22 June 1991	1 Feb 1992	7 Aug 1993	**AA**
PC 2	TEMPEST	90	30 Sep 1991	4 Apr 1992	21 Aug 1993	**AA**
PC 3	HURRICANE	90	20 Nov 1991	6 June 1992	15 Oct 1993	**PA**
PC 4	MONSOON	90	15 Feb 1992	10 Oct 1992	22 Jan 1994	**PA**
PC 5	TYPHOON	90	15 May 1992	3 Mar 1993	12 Feb 1994	**AA**
PC 6	SIROCCO	90	20 June 1992	29 May 1993	11 June 1994[3]	**AA**
PC 7	SQUALL	90	17 Feb 1993	28 Aug 1993	4 July 1994	**PA**
PC 8	ZEPHYR	90	6 Mar 1993	3 Dec 1993	15 Oct 1994	**PA**
PC 9	CHINOOK	91	16 June 1993	6 Feb 1994	28 Jan 1995	**AA**
PC 10	FIREBOLT	91	17 Sep 1993	10 June 1994	10 June 1995	**AA**
PC 11	WHIRLWIND	91	4 Mar 1994	9 Sep 1994	1 July 1995	**PA**
PC 12	THUNDERBOLT	91	9 June 1994	2 Dec 1994	7 Oct 1995	**PA**
PC 13	SHAMAL	91	22 Sep 1995	3 Mar 1995	27 Jan 1996	**AA**
PC14	......	97 (?)				Proposed

Builders:	Bollinger Machine Shop & Shipyard, Lockport, La.
Displacement:	328.5 tons full load
Length:	170½ feet (52.0 m) overall
Beam:	25 feet (7.6 m)
Draft:	7⅚ feet (2.4 m)
Propulsion:	4 diesel engines (Paxman Valenta 16 RP200); 13,400 bhp; 4 shafts
Speed:	35 knots
Range:	2,000 n.miles (3,700 km) at 12 knots
Manning:	28 (4 officers + 24 enlisted)
Troops:	9 (SEALs or other passengers)
Missiles:	1 Stinger point-defense missile launcher (6 missiles)
Guns:	2 25-mm Bushmaster cannon Mk 38 (2 single)
	2 .50-cal machine guns M2HB (2 single)
	2 7.62-mm machine guns M60 (2 single)
	2 40-mm grenade launchers Mk 19 (2 single)
Radars:	2 Sperry RASCAR 2500 surface search (S and X bands)
Sonars:	Wesmar side-scanning (fish-finder) (HF)
EW systems:	APR-39A(V)1 radar warning receiver

These are small combatants intended for coastal interdiction and the support of special operations forces, primarily Navy SEALs. They were specifically intended as replacements for the Navy's overage PB Mk III craft.

Thirteen PCs were built under the original program, funded in fiscal 1990–1991. In the fiscal 1996 budget, without a Navy request, Congress funded $20 million for advance procurement of another ship of the CYCLONE class; full funding is expected in the fiscal 1997 budget. The ship is not included in the Department of Defense shipbuilding plan, but it is likely to be fully funded and built.

The CYCLONE class was designed to cost, hence a readily available foreign design was adopted. According to the reference work *Combat Fleets of the World,* these ships "have limited endurance for their size, and their combat systems and ammunition allowance do not compare with those of similar ships in most other navies."[4]

Armament: These ships are eventually to be fitted with the Stabilized Weapon Platform System (SWPS), which will be installed on the fantail. The SWPS will launch a variety of missiles, including the Hellfire, Stinger, and Hydra-70, with a co-mounted 25-mm or 30-mm cannon, a television camera, laser range finder and designator, and Forward-Looking Infrared (FLIR) sensor.

The existing Stinger launcher has six ready rounds.

Class: The Navy planned to construct 16 of these ships (PBC) when the program was defined in the late 1980s; by the time the lead ship was ordered, however, the program had been reduced to 13 units.

Bollinger was awarded a contract for the construction of eight ships, with an option for five additional units, on 3 August 1990. The five-ship option was exercised on 19 July 1991.

Classification: These ships were originally designated PBC for patrol boat, coastal. The designation was changed to PC—for patrol, coastal—on 26 July 1991.

The classification PC originated in World War I as the *hull numbers* for a series of 110-foot (33.5-m) wood-hull submarine chasers; they were given *names* in the SC series. Beginning in 1940 a series of steel-hull submarine chasers were built with PC designations, and in October 1942 all wood-hull submarine chasers were given SC hull numbers.

The World War II steel-hull program reached hull number PC 1603 (completed in 1944). Most ships were 173-foot (52.7-m) oceangoing craft designated PC, although the PCE-PCS-SC types shared the same numbering series. Postwar ships with PC-PCE designations that were built in the United States and abroad, all for use by foreign navies, took the series to PC 1646. The PC 1647 and 1648 were canceled; thus, the new-construction American PCs should properly have begun with hull No. 1649—not PC 1.

Design: The PC hull/propulsion design is based on the Vosper Thornycroft–built missile craft of the Province class, constructed for Egypt (six units completed 1981–1982), Oman (four units completed 1982–1989), and Kenya (two units completed 1987).

The U.S. ships have steel hulls with aluminum superstructures; one-inch (25-mm) appliqué armor is fitted to portions of the superstructure for protection against small arms fire. Endurance is ten days.

Two 16-foot (4.9-m) combat rubber raiding craft (CRRC) and one 20-foot (6.1-m) rigid inflatable swimmer delivery craft can be carried by each PC.

Electronics: The ships have two Mk 52 chaff/decoy launchers. An Identification Friend or Foe (IFF) transponder is fitted, but no interrogator.

Engineering: The Paxman Valenta engines are the same as those used in the Coast Guard's "Island"-class patrol boats.

Manning: These ships are commanded by lieutenants. The last such commands in the U.S. Navy were the ASHEVILLE-class patrol gunboats. (The PEGASUS class was commanded by lieutenant commanders.)

Names: The ships are named for weather elements.

Operational: These ships were initially placed "In Commission, Special" at the Bollinger yard to permit a Navy crew to take them to ports where they were then placed "In Commission, Full," the formal commissioning ceremony listed above.

The first four ships of the class participated in the U.S. occupation of Haiti in 1994; the MONSOON ran aground during coastal patrol activities. During the operations off Haiti the boats carried up to 25 SEALs while on multi-day patrols.

The first overseas deployment of this class began on 21 April 1995, when the TYPHOON and SIROCCO departed Norfolk, Virginia, for operations in the Baltic and Mediterranean Seas.

---

3. The SIROCCO was commissioned at the Washington Navy Yard; this was the first U.S. Navy ship to be placed in commission at the yard—the Navy's oldest—since the steam/sail corvette NIPSIC was commissioned on 11 October 1879, the last of 22 ships built at the Washington Navy Yard.
4. Bernard Prézelin and A. D. Baker III, *Combat Fleets of the World 1995* (Annapolis, Md.: Naval Institute Press, 1995), p. 887. The CYCLONE ammunition allowance is:

Stinger SAM	6 ready missiles
25-mm cannon Mk 38	2,000 rounds
.50-cal machine guns	2,000 rounds
7.62-mm machine guns	2,000 rounds
Mk 19 grenade launchers	1,000 rounds

The TYPHOON wears a camouflage paint scheme while on deployment in European waters. She carried this scheme during the first overseas deployment of these ships. The last U.S. Navy ship to wear camouflage markings was the submarine tender PROTEUS (AS 19) during a deployment to Australia in 1992 (see chapter 25). (1995, Leo Van Ginderen collection)

The SIROCCO returns to Little Creek, Virginia, after a four-month deployment to the Mediterranean and Baltic areas in company with the TYPHOON. Machine guns are fitted on the SIROCCO's bridge wings. (1995, U.S. Navy, PH2 Richard Rosser)

The lead ship of the CYCLONE class, showing the unusual deckhouse arrangement, open stern area with crane for handling rigid inflatable boats, and step-on stern counter for swimmers. An armament increase is planned. (1994, Bollinger Machine Shop & Shipyard)

SPECIAL WARFARE CRAFT

The Navy has selected the Trinity-Halter design for production as the Mk V patrol craft. The Navy had sponsored two competitive designs in August 1993: two craft produced by Trinity-Halter and one by Peterson Builders. The production of 14 Mk V craft is envisioned, intended primarily for SEAL insertion in clandestine operations where the CYCLONE-class ships are not suitable or cannot be used because of their detectability. The Mk V craft are to be air transportable in C-5 Galaxy aircraft.

2 + 14 SPECIAL OPERATIONS CRAFT: MK V TYPE

Builders:	Trinity-Halter Marine, Gulfport, Miss.
Displacement:	approx. 75 tons full load
Length:	82 feet (25.0 m) overall
Beam:	18 feet (5.49 m)
Draft:	$4\frac{1}{3}$ feet (1.32 m)
Propulsion:	(1) 3 diesel engines (GM Detroit); 3 shafts
	(2) 2 diesel engines (MTU 16V396 TE94); 2 waterjets
Speed:	50+ knots
Range:	500 n.miles (926 km) at 35 knots
Manning:	
Troops:	16 (SEALS or other passengers)
Guns:	combinations of .50-cal machine guns M2HB
	7.62-mm machine guns M60
	40-mm grenade launchers Mk 19
Radars:	navigation

The first two units were competitive designs for an advanced special operations craft. The first craft was of Kevlar construction and the second of aluminum.

1 SPECIAL OPERATIONS CRAFT: MK V PROTOTYPE (SEA STALKER)

Builders:	Peterson Builders, Sturgeon Bay, Wisc.
Displacement:	39 tons standard
	75 tons full load
Length:	71 feet (21.64 m) overall
Beam:	18 feet (5.49 m)
Draft:	$4\frac{7}{12}$ feet (1.4 m)
Propulsion:	2 diesel engines (MTU 164396 TE94); 7,000 bhp; 2 shafts + 1 diesel engine (Seatek 64V-9L); 570 bhp; 1 waterjet for low-speed/loiter operations
Speed:	50+ knots
Range:	500 n.miles (926 km) at 35 knots
Manning:	5
Troops:	16 (SEALs or other passengers)
Guns:	combinations of .50-cal machine guns M2HB
	7.62-mm machine guns M60
	40-mm grenade launchers Mk 19
Radars:	navigation

Completed in May 1994 as a prototype special operations craft, this craft has an unusual "asymmetric catamaran" hull configuration based on the British Cougar Cat 2100 "Dark Moon" design.

A prototype Mk V special operations craft at high speed. The craft will replace the discarded Seafox type. This craft has a pot-dome radar antenna on a pole mast. (1994, Halter Marine)

A Mk V prototype being procured for SEAL operations. A bar-type radar antenna is fitted above the deckhouse and a rigid inflatable boat is carried amidships. (1995, John Bouvia)

The competitive prototype for Mk V procurement was the Sea Stalker, an asymmetric catamaran design. A pot-dome radar can be seen on the structure above the cockpit. (1994, Peterson Builders)

3 PATROL BOATS: PB MK IV TYPE (SEA SPECTRE)

Number	Launched	Completed	Assignment
68PB841	23 Sep 1985	1 Feb 1986	SBU-26
68PB842	11 Nov 1985	1 Feb 1986	SBU-26
68PB843	31 Dec 1985	15 Feb 1986	SBU-26

Builders:	Atlantic Marine, Ft. George Island, Fla.
Displacement:	42.25 tons full load
Length:	68 5/12 feet (20.85 m) overall
Beam:	18 1/12 feet (5.5 m)
Draft:	3½ feet (1.1 m)
Propulsion:	3 diesel engines (General Motors 12V71 TI); 1,950 bhp; 3 shafts
Speed:	30 knots
Range:	
Manning:	5 (1 officer + 4 enlisted) minimum
Guns:	1 25-mm Bushmaster cannon Mk 38 1 20-mm cannon 1 81-mm mortar Mk 2/1 .50-cal machine gun M2HB 2 40-mm grenade launchers Mk 19 (2 single)
Radars:	navigation

These are slightly enlarged variants of the PB Mk III series. They are referred to by the design name Sea Spectre. Authorized in fiscal 1985, they were intended specifically for patrol operations in the Panama Canal area.

The Mk IVs are constructed of aluminum.

Guns: Originally armed with two 20-mm cannon; one gun was replaced by the rapid-fire Bushmaster cannon in 1987. PB armament can be easily changed. The .50-cal machine gun is mounted above the 81-mm mortar.

The 68PB851 with a lengthened deckhouse; 20-mm cannon are mounted fore and aft in this view, plus machine guns. PB armament can be easily changed. (1986, U.S. Navy)

The 68PB851 at high speed; a life raft canister is fitted amidships. (1986, U.S. Navy)

A heavily armed PB Mk III in the Persian Gulf. The 40-mm cannon mounted forward has been succeeded by the 25-mm Bushmaster "chain gun" in the gunboat configuration. (1987, U.S. Navy)

13 PATROL BOATS: PB MK III TYPE (SEA SPECTRE)

Number	Built	Assignment
65PB731	1974	NSWC Norfolk, Va.
65PB734	1975	NSWC Norfolk, Va.
65PB735	1975	SBU-26
65PB737	1976	SBU-12
65PB751	1976	SBU-12
65PB755	1976	SBU-12
65PB757	1976	SBU-12
65PB758	1977	SBU-12
65PB759	1977	SBU-26
65PB775	1979	SBU-12
65PB776	1979	SBU-12
65PB777	1979	NSWC Norfolk, Va.
65PB778	1979	SBU-20

Builders:	Peterson Builders, Sturgeon Bay, Wisc.
Displacement:	28 tons light
	36.7 tons full load
Length:	64 11/12 feet (19.8 m) overall
Beam:	18½ feet (5.5 m)
Draft:	5⅚ feet (1.8 m)
Propulsion:	3 diesel engines (General Motors 8V71); 1,950 bhp; 3 shafts
Speed:	26 knots (see notes)
Range:	2,000 n.miles (3,700 km) at slow speeds
	450 n.miles (835 km) at 26 knots
Manning:	5 (1 officer + 4 enlisted) minimum
Missiles:	(see notes)
Guns:	1 25-mm Bushmaster cannon Mk 38
	1 or 2 7.62-mm machine guns (1 or 2 single) (see notes)
Radars:	navigation

The PB Mk III was developed as a multi-mission inshore warfare craft for U.S. and foreign naval service. The U.S. craft are operated by Special Boat Units (SBU), except that three are used by the Naval Surface Warfare Center detachment at Norfolk. Although these craft are named Sea Spectre, they are generally referred to simply as PB Mk IIIs.

Class: Twenty-two of these craft were built for the U.S. Navy and four for the Philippines. PB Mk IIIs were procured from Peterson Builders as well as Marinette Marine Corporation, Wisconsin.

No PB Mk II was built; the last of the Mk I units have been discarded (see 15th Edition/page 201 for characteristics).

Classification: These craft were also designated as special warfare craft—medium (SWCM). The Naval Sea Systems Command designates these craft as PB Mk 3; however, they are listed as Mk III in most Navy documentation.

Design: The Mk III is a modified commercial craft used to support offshore drilling platforms in the Gulf of Mexico. These craft are of all-aluminum construction with their pilothouse offset to starboard to provide maximum deck space for weapons and equipment. The craft has a low radar cross section and quiet engines for clandestine operations. Mission duration is up to five days.

Engineering: Note that these craft have three engines; the centerline engine is specially silenced for slow, quiet operations.

Guns: These craft were originally fitted with an automatic 40-mm Bofors cannon or a manually operated 20-mm cannon forward and up to four .50-cal machine guns on pintle mountings. There are hard points on the deck for fitting other guns as well as missiles. The craft can also be rigged to carry mines, torpedoes, or minesweeping gear.

Missiles: Four stowage/launcher containers were fitted on the after portion of the deck of a PB III to evaluate the Norwegian-developed Penguin SSM.

PATROL CRAFT—FAST (PCF): SWIFT BOATS

All of the so-called Swift boats (PCF) have been discarded. A total of 139 units were built from 1965 onward, most of which were used by the U.S. Navy in Vietnam. One hundred four boats were transferred to South Vietnam in 1968–1970. Other Swift boats were built specifically for South Korea, the Philippines, and Thailand. Variations used by the U.S. Navy were a torpedo weapons recovery craft (TWR) and utility/rescue craft.

In 1995 the French firm Aérospatiale test fired an MM15 missile from a PCF on Lake Pontchartrain near New Orleans, Louisiana. The MM15 is a ship-launched version of the AS 15TT helicopter-launched missile.

The PCF 1 arrived at the Washington Navy Yard on 17 June 1995 for display at the Navy Museum. The craft was used for training at San Diego and was not deployed to South Vietnam.

See 15th Edition/page 201 for PCF characteristics.

25+ RIVERINE ASSAULT CRAFT: STINGER TYPE

Builders:	No. 1–7 SeaArk Marine, Monticello, Ark. others Swiftships, Morgan City, La.
Displacement:	7.48 tons full load
Length:	34 11/12 feet (10.64 m) overall
Beam:	9 1/4 feet (2.8 m)
Draft:	2 1/6 feet (0.66 m)
Propulsion:	2 diesel engines (Cummins BTA5.9M2); 600 bhp; 1 waterjet
Speed:	38 knots (34.6 knots sustained)
Range:	
Manning:	4 (enlisted)
Troops:	10
Guns:	2 .50-cal machine guns M2 (2 single) 2 7.62-mm machine guns M60 (2 single)
Radars:	SPS-60 navigation

These are replacements for the PBR-type patrol boats. The first seven units entered service in 1990, the next 18 in 1991–1994.

A variety of light weapons can be mounted, including 40-mm M19 grenade launchers.

These craft can be airlifted by a C-130 Hercules or larger aircraft.

The Stinger riverine assault craft are another manifestation of the U.S. Navy's current interest in regional or littoral combat operations. (SeaArk, 1990)

25 RIVERINE PATROL BOATS: PBR MK 2 TYPE

Number	Built	Assignment
31RP664	1965	SBU-11
31RP66137	1966	SBU-11
31RP673	1967	SBU-22
31RP674	1967	SBU-11
31RP6880	1968	SBU-11
31RP6883	1968	SBU-22
31RP6884	1968	SBU-22
31RP6887	1968	SBU-26
31RP6889	1968	SBU-11
31RP6893	1968	SBU-26
31RP6894	1968	SBU-26
31RP6923	1969	SBU-11
31RP6924	1969	SBU-11
31RP7021	1970	SBU-26
31RP7118	1972	SBU-22
31RP721	1972	SBU-22
31RP7210	1972	SBU-11
31RP723	1972	SBU-11
31RP724	1972	SBU-11
31RP7329	1979	SBU-22
31RP7330	1982	SBU-22
31RP7331	1974	SBU-22
31RP7334	1974	SBU-22
31RP7335	1974	SBU-22
31RP7337	1974	SBU-22

Builders:	Uniflite, Bellingham, Wash.
Displacement:	7.5 tons light 8.9 tons full load
Length:	32 feet (9.75 m) overall
Beam:	11 2/3 feet (3.6 m)
Draft:	2 7/12 feet (0.8 m)
Propulsion:	2 diesel engines (General Motors 6V53 or 6V53T or 4-53N); 430 bhp; 2 waterjets
Speed:	24 knots
Range:	150 n.miles (278 m) at 23 knots
Manning:	4 or 5 (enlisted)
Missiles:	none
Guns:	1 60-mm mortar Mk 4 in some units 1 40-mm grenade launcher Mk 19 3 .50-cal machine guns (1 twin, 1 single)
Radars:	navigation

These heavily armed craft were developed for riverine warfare in Vietnam. All U.S. survivors are operated by the NRF.

Class: More than 500 PBRs were built between 1965 and 1973; most of them were transferred to South Vietnam after being used by the U.S. Navy.

Additional units were built for the U.S. Navy in the early 1980s (with GM 4-53N diesel engines). Subsequently, replacement hulls have been procured commercially for refit/replacement of existing boats in a one-for-one "swap" procedure. The newer boats are being provided with GM 6V53T engines.

A PBR Mk 2 under way in San Francisco Bay. The Coast Guard aids-to-navigation boat 55101 is in the background. Several PBRs were used in the Persian Gulf from the late 1980s. (1988, Giorgio Arra)

The 31RP66108, 31RP7023, and 31RP9999 are at the Naval Historical Center at the Washington Navy Yard.

Design: These craft have fiberglass hulls and ceramic armor.

Engineering: The waterjet propulsion enables the boats to operate in shallow and debris-filled water with a very high degree of maneuverability.

A PBR Mk 2. These craft were also widely used in the Vietnam War. (1988, Giorgio Arra)

SPECIAL WARFARE CRAFT—LIGHT: SEAFOX TYPE

The small, 36-foot (10.8-m), high-speed Seafox craft, intended primarily to support SEAL operations, have been stricken. One prototype (built in 1976–1977) plus 36 operational units were procured for the U.S. Navy; others were built for foreign service.

See 15th Edition/page 203 for characteristics.

21 ARMORED TROOP CARRIERS: MINI-ATC TYPE

Number	Built	Assignment
36AT721	1972	SBU-22
36AT7213	1972	SBU-22
36AT7214	1973	SBU-22
36AT7215	1973	SBU-22
36AT7216	1973	SBU-22
36AT7217	1973	SBU-22
36AT722	1973	SBU-11
36AT723	1973	SBU-11
36AT724	1973	SBU-11
36AT725	1973	SBU-11
36AT726	1973	SBU-11
36AT727	1973	SBU-11
36AT729	1973	SBU-11
36AT7212	1973	SBU-11
36AT763	1977	SBU-22
36AT764	1977	SBU-11
36AT768	1977	SBU-22
36AT783	1979	SBU-11
36AT784	1979	SBU-22
36AT785	1979	SBU-22
36AT786	1979	SBU-22

Builders:	Marinette Marine, Wisc. Tacoma Boatbuilding, Wash.
Displacement:	11 tons light 14.75 tons full load
Length:	36 feet (11.0 m) overall
Beam:	12¾ feet (3.9 m)
Draft:	3½ feet (1.0 m)
Propulsion:	2 diesel engines (General Motors 8V53N); 566 bhp; 2 waterjets
Speed:	28 knots
Range:	
Manning:	2 (enlisted)
Troops:	16
Guns:	2 .50-cal machine guns (2 single)
Radars:	LN-66 navigation

These craft were developed from lessons learned in the Vietnam War and are intended for clandestine operations during riverine campaigns. They have low radar signatures and quiet engines.

Design: The mini-ATCs have aluminum hulls and ceramic armor. At high speed they have a one-foot (0.3-m) draft. They can carry two tons of cargo.

Additional weapons can be mounted.

A mini-ATC under way in San Francisco Bay. (1988, Giorgio Arra)

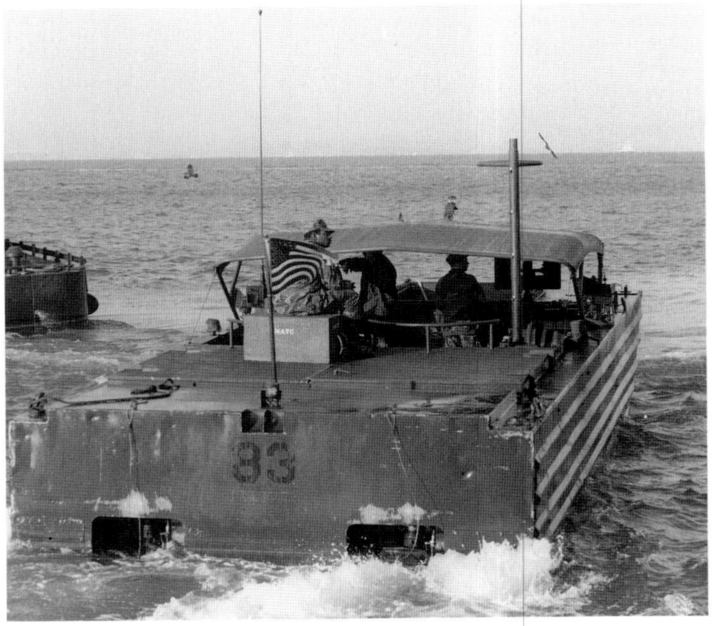

A mini-ATC without the radar "pot" fitted. (1986, Giorgio Arra)

SMALLER SPECIAL WARFARE CRAFT

The Navy's SBUs operate several other types of craft, most for use by SEALs in clandestine operations. Small craft operated by SBUs and other Navy special warfare organizations include the following (see list below). Some LCUs are also assigned to boat units and SEAL delivery teams (see chapter 20).

Type	Hull designation	Length
landing craft mechanized	CM	56 ft (17.1 m)
landing craft, personnel light	PL	36 ft (11.0 m)
rigid inflatable boat	MRB	32⅔ ft (10 m)
rigid inflatable boat	RB	30 ft (9.1 m)
utility boat	UB	25 ft (7.62 m)
patrol boat	PB	25 ft (7.62 m)
rigid inflatable boat	RB	24 ft (7.3 m)
rigid inflatable boat (nonstandard)	RX	24 ft (7.3 m)
utility boat	UB	22 ft (6.7 m)
combat rubber raiding craft	—	16 ft (4.9-m)

SEALs ride their rigid inflatable boat en route to check out a Danish cargo ship during the embargo of Iraq by the United Nations. These craft are widely used by the world's special operations forces as well as by the U.S. Navy, Marine Corps, and Coast Guard. (1994, U.S. Navy, PH1 Richard Piening)

73 HARBOR SECURITY BOATS

Number	Built
24HS8701	1988–1989
24HS8703–24HS8709	
24HS8711–24HS8728	
24HS8733–24HS8735	
24HS8738–24HS8745	
24HS8748–24HS8750	
24HS8801–24HS8810	
24HS8813–24HS8825	
24HS8901–24HS8910	

Builder:	Peterson Builders, Sturgeon Bay, Wisc.
Displacement:	2.5 tons light 3.8 tons full load
Length:	24 feet (7.3 m) overall
Beam:	7 7/12 feet (2.3 m)
Draft:	5 1/6 feet (1.6 m)
Propulsion:	2 diesel engines (Volvo Penta AGAD 41A); 2 outboard drives
Speed:	22.5 knots
Range:	
Manning:	4 (enlisted)
Guns:	see notes
Radars:	none

These craft are employed for harbor patrol at various bases, shipyards, and forward operating areas. They are aluminum construction craft. No armament is provided, but light machine guns can be mounted.

Class: Originally 75 craft numbered 24HS8701–24HS8750 and 24HS8801–24HS8825.

A harbor security boat approaches the Middle East flagship LA SALLE (AGF 3) during operations in the Persian Gulf. (1991, U.S. Navy)

A harbor security boat in the Persian Gulf, patrolling against Iraqi or Iranian swimmers or floating mines. (1991, U.S. Navy)

RIVERINE AND INSHORE COMBAT CRAFT

During the Vietnam War (1963–1972) the U.S. Navy operated several hundred riverine and inshore combat craft built for the purpose or converted from landing craft. These were used mainly for Operation Market Time (coastal surveillance), Game Warden (river patrol), and operations with U.S. Army troops in the Rung Sat special zone. About 650 river and coastal craft were turned over to South Vietnamese forces in 1970–1971 as the United States withdrew from the conflict.

In addition to the PCF and PBR types listed above, the principal Vietnam-era small craft were:

ASPB	assault support patrol boat
ATC	armored troop carrier
CCB	command and control boat (converted LCM)
MON	monitor (converted LCM)
PACV	patrol air cushion vehicles

All of the above craft were produced in large numbers except for the air cushion craft. Several other craft were also developed and evaluated during the war.

PATROL SHIPS AND VESSELS

The ex-Soviet Tarantul I missile craft—previously employed in a research role by the U.S. Navy—is listed below, as are the major patrol ships and vessels constructed by the U.S. Navy since World War II.

The "destroyer escorts" of the post–World War II era were previously designated as patrol vessels; they are listed as frigates in this edition (chapter 17).

1 GUIDED MISSILE CRAFT: EX-SOVIET TARANTUL I CLASS

Number	Name	Commissioned	Status
185NS9201	(ex-HIDDENSEE)	2 Apr 1985	discarded Apr 1996

Builders:	Volodarskiy Shipyard (No. 341), Rybinsk (USSR)
Displacement:	480 tons standard 540 tons full load
Length:	172⅙ feet (52.5 m) waterline 185⅓ feet (56.5 m) overall
Beam:	34 5/12 feet (10.5 m)
Draft:	8¼ feet (2.5 m)
Propulsion:	COGAG: 2 gas turbines (NK-12M); 24,000 shp + 2 gas turbines; 8,000 shp = 32,000 shp; 2 shafts
Speed:	46 knots
Range:	400 n.miles (740 km) at 36 knots
Complement:	39
Missiles:	4 SS-N-2c Styx anti-ship (2 twin) 4 SA-N-5 anti-air launcher (1 quad)
Guns:	1 76.2-mm/59-cal DP 2 30-mm/65-cal close-in (2 multi-barrel)
Radars:	1 Bass Tilt (fire control) 1 Plank Shave (targeting) 1 TSR-333 (navigation)
Sonars:	none
EW systems:	4 . . . . (passive) 1 Square Head IFF 1 High Pole-B IFF

This Soviet-built missile craft was transferred upon completion to the East German Navy, one of five such craft to enter that navy. Following the reunification of Germany in 1990, this was the only ship of the five to be placed in German service.

She was transferred to the U.S. Navy in November 1991 for trials and evaluation; the craft was transported to the United States on a heavy-lift ship in early 1992. She was placed on the Navy's service craft list with the above number on 14 February 1992. She was operated by the Naval Air Warfare Center at Patuxent River, Maryland, until 18 April 1996. She was in storage when this edition went to press, awaiting transfer to the Sea-Air-Space Museum in New York City.

Class: Two Tarantul I-class units are believed to be in Russian service; additional units were built in the Soviet Union for East Germany, India, and Poland, with still other units being constructed in India.

The improved Tarantul II continued in production for Russian naval service at least into 1991; the Tarantul I/II variants in Soviet service carry the Styx missile (as above); the Tarantul III variant has four SS-N-22 anti-ship missiles in place of the Styx.[5]

Design: The Tarantul hull is similar to the Pauk-class ASW corvette, but it has a different propulsion system. The craft has seven watertight hull compartments.

The Tarantul I and II/III designs differ primarily in electronics, and the Tarantul III has a more capable anti-ship missile. All three designs are fitted with a Chemical-Biological-Radiological (CBR) protective system.

Names: In East German service the craft was named RUDOLF EGELHOFER (pennant 572); she was renamed HIDDENSEE (pennant P6166) by the unified German Navy (Hiddensee is an island in the Baltic Sea).

PATROL COMBATANTS—MISSILE (HYDROFOIL): "PEGASUS" CLASS

Number	Name	Comm.	Notes
PHM 1	PEGASUS	1977	Decommissioned and stricken 30 July 1993
PHM 2	HERCULES	1983	
PHM 3	TAURUS	1981	
PHM 4	AQUILA	1982	
PHM 5	ARIES	1983	
PHM 6	GEMINI	1983	

These were high speed, heavily armed missile craft, originally intended to conduct sea control operations in restricted seas. Upon their completion, however, they were employed primarily in anti-drug operations in the Caribbean area.

Class: This design was one of the new warship types initiated by Admiral Elmo R. Zumwalt when he was Chief of Naval Operations (1970–1974). A class of at least 30 missile craft of this type were planned. When Zumwalt left office the Navy reduced the program to only the prototype, but congressional pressure led to completing the first "flight" of six ships, which were already funded.

5. See N. Polmar, *Guide to the Soviet Navy*/5th Edition (Annapolis, Md.: Naval Institute Press, 1991), pp. 192–93.

A former East German Tarantul I-class missile corvette during U.S. Navy trials in the Chesapeake Bay. She is one of five ships of this class built in the Soviet Union for East Germany. Ships of this class were built for the Soviet and foreign navies. (1992, U.S. Navy)

Engineering: These craft had Combination Diesel or Gas (CODOG) turbine propulsion that could drive them up to 55 knots when foilborne, with a remarkably smooth operation.

Operational: The six PEGASUS-class PHMs were assigned to Patrol Combat Missile Hydrofoil Squadron 2, based at Key West, Florida. Earlier plans to deploy the PHMs to the Mediterranean, supported by a specially configured LST, were discarded. The support ship was to have been the WOOD COUNTY (LST 1178).

PATROL GUNBOAT (HYDROFOIL): "TUCUMCARI"

The TUCUMCARI (PGH 2) was the Boeing-built competitive prototype for the PHM 1 class. Completed in 1968, the craft was wrecked on a reef on 16 November 1972 and taken out of service on 7 November 1973 (her hulk was used for tests). Both the TUCUMCARI and FLAGSTAFF were used off South Vietnam in the late 1960s.

See 9th Edition/pages 94–95.

PATROL GUNBOAT (HYDROFOIL): "FLAGSTAFF"

The FLAGSTAFF (PGH 1) was a competitive prototype for the PHM 1 class built by Grumman. Completed in 1968, she conducted Navy trials and was then evaluated by the Coast Guard in 1974 (designated WPBH 1). She was subsequently stricken.

See 10th Edition/page 73 for characteristics.

SUBMARINE CHASER (HYDROFOIL): "HIGH POINT"

The hydrofoil submarine chaser HIGH POINT (PCH 1) was the U.S. Navy's first operational hydrofoil. She was built to evaluate structural and hydrodynamic features of hydrofoils, as well as to develop ASW concepts for hydrofoils. The HIGH POINT was placed in service in 1963. After extensive Navy evaluation, she was transferred to the Coast Guard in 1975 for evaluation by that service (designated WMEH 1). She was subsequently returned to the Navy for continued test-and-evaluation work.

The HIGH POINT was taken out of service in October 1978. She was employed at Boeing's hydrofoil facility for several years, then sold on 29 March 1990 to a private firm.

See 15th Edition/pages 197–98 for characteristics.

PATROL GUNBOATS: "ASHEVILLE" CLASS

Number	Name	Comm.	Notes
PG 84	ASHEVILLE	1966	stricken 31 Jan 1977; to Massachusetts Maritime Academy 11 Apr 1977
PG 85	GALLUP	1966	stricken 31 Jan 1977*
PG 86	ANTELOPE	1967	to Enviromental Protection Agency 17 Jan 1978
PG 87	READY	1968	stricken 6 Jan 1977; to Massachusetts Maritime Academy 1 Mar 1978
PG 88	CROCKETT	1967	to Environmental Protection Agency 18 Apr 1977**
PG 89	MARATHON	1968	stricken 31 Jan 1977; to Massachusetts Maritime Academy 18 Apr 1977
PG 90	CANON	1968	stricken 31 Jan 1977*
PG 92	TACOMA	1969	to Colombia 16 May 1983
PG 93	WELCH	1969	to Colombia 16 May 1983
PG 94	CHEHALIS	1969	became Navy research ship ATHENA I
PG 95	DEFIANCE	1969	to Turkey 11 June 1973
PG 96	BENICA	1970	to South Korea 15 Oct 1971
PG 97	SURPRISE	1969	to Turkey 28 Feb 1973
PG 98	GRAND RAPIDS	1970	became Navy research ship ATHENA II
PG 99	BEACON	1969	stricken 1 Apr 1977; to Greece 22 Nov 1989†
PG 100	DOUGLAS	1971	stricken 1 Oct 1977; became Navy research ship LAUREN
PG 101	GREEN BAY	1969	stricken 1 Apr 1977; to Greece 22 Nov 1989†

*Both units were reinstated on the Naval Vessel Register on 17 July 1981 and placed in reserve at Bremerton, Wash. They were again stricken on 9 October 1984.

**Declared excess in 1982 and transferred to Great Lakes Navy Association for use as a museum.

†Retained in storage at Little Creek, Va., until transferred to Greece.

The Navy built 17 ASHEVILLE-class patrol gunboats, originally intended for operations in the Caribbean in reaction to the Communist regime on the island. Fourteen have been stricken, loaned to other U.S. government or state agencies, or transferred to other nations. The three other ships—the CHEHALIS, GRAND RAPIDS, and DOUGLAS—have been stripped of armament and are employed by the U.S. Navy as research craft (see chapters 25 and 34).

The last two U.S. Navy units in service as combat craft—the TACOMA and WELCH—were used in the late 1970s to train Saudi Arabian naval personnel at Norfolk, Virginia.

Classification: These ships were originally classified as motor gunboats (PGM) and were changed to patrol combatants (PG) on 1 April 1967; they retained their PGM hull numbers, which repeated World War II–era gunboat (PG) numbers. (The PGM 33–83, 91, and 102–124 were gunboats built in the United States or overseas from 1955 onwards specifically for transfer to foreign navies; none served in the U.S. Navy.)

(Some of those PG hull numbers duplicate the designations assigned to corvettes built in Britain and Canada for U.S. service during World War II; those ships encompassed hull numbers PG 62–100.)

Engineering: These were the first U.S. Navy combat ships with gas turbine propulsion.

Missiles: Several ships were armed with Standard anti-ship missiles.

See 12th Edition/page 165 for characteristics. Note corrected/additional dates in the above table.

COASTAL PATROL AND INTERDICTION CRAFT

A single coastal patrol and interdiction craft (CPIC) was built for the U.S. Navy as the prototype for a craft to succeed the PT/PTF–type small combatants in U.S. service and for foreign sales. The prototype CPIC was launched in 1974 and, after exhaustive trials, was transferred to South Korea on 1 August 1975. (Additional craft of this type were built in South Korea.)

The CPIC was returned to U.S. custody in the Philippines in 1981 and brought back to San Diego in 1982. After being surveyed, the craft was rated unsuitable for further evaluation or service and consequently was discarded.

See 13th Edition/page 226 for characteristics.

FAST PATROL BOATS

The classification fast patrol boat (PTF) was established in 1963 for fast seagoing craft to conduct clandestine operations off the coast of Vietnam. The PTF 3–16 were Nasty-class boats built in Norway and taken over by the U.S. Navy upon completion in 1962–1965. The first four units had been assigned Norwegian names in preparation for service in that navy. The subsequent PTF 17–22 were built by John Trumpy yacht builders (Annapolis, Maryland) to the Nasty design; the PTF 23–26, built by Sewart Seacraft, were of a different design.

Most saw combat service in Vietnam; all have been stricken; some were expended as targets.

See the 13th Edition/pages 224–25 for details and characteristics.

POST–WORLD WAR II MOTOR TORPEDO BOATS

U.S. motor torpedo boat construction began in 1939. World War II programs reached hull number PT 808, with 774 units being completed through 1945 (another 34 were canceled before completion). Many survivors served with allied fleets after the war. The similar PTC series—armed with depth charges in place of torpedoes—reached PTC 60, but most of those were transferred to other navies or completed as torpedo boats.

Four competitive prototype PT-boats of advanced designs were completed in 1950–1951: the PT 809 by Electric Boat (Groton, Connecticut), PT 810 by Bath Iron Works (Maine), PT 811 by Trumpy (Annapolis, Maryland), and PT 812 by the Philadelphia Naval Shipyard. They were reclassified (as PTs) from patrol vessels to service craft on 13 April 1951. All were stricken, but the PT 810 and 811 were reinstated on the Naval Vessel Register in service (vice in commission) as the PTF 1 and PTF 2 on 21 December 1962 for Vietnam service.

The PT 809, renamed the GUARDIAN, was reinstated in service for use by the Secret Service as an escort for craft carrying the president. Subsequently, the craft was employed by the Navy as the drone recovery craft RECOVERY (DR-1).

CHAPTER 22

Mine Countermeasures Ships and Craft

The mine countermeasures ship WARRIOR at Fort Lauderdale, Florida, represents the new mine warfare ships of the U.S. fleet. These new ships, supplemented by the capable MH-53E Sea Dragon helicopters, provide a considerable capability against hostile mines. These MCM capabilities are limited, however, in view of the potential mine threat to U.S. interests. (1994, Giorgio Arra)

The Navy's Mine Countermeasures (MCM) force is completing a long-delayed modernization, with new ships and helicopters (MH-53E) entering the fleet. In the fall of 1996 the surface mine countermeasures force consisted of 14 mine countermeasures ships and 7 coastal minehunters (MHC). Five additional coastal minehunters were under construction. The Navy also has 11 diminutive COOP mine countermeasures craft in service. (All of the U.S. minesweepers of the MSO and MSC types built during the Korean War era have been stricken, although many continue to serve in other navies.)

In addition, eight air-cushion landing craft (LCAC) have been modified to undertake mine countermeasures operations in shallow water. These craft are described in chapter 20.

The helicopter carrier INCHON has undergone conversion to an MCM support ship (designated MCS). There has long been a need for such a ship to enhance the effectiveness and on-station time of deployed MCM forces, both surface ships and helicopters. Unfortunately, only one such support ship is now envisioned for at least the next decade.

These forces have the primary mission of clearing U.S. waters, strategic choke points, and a path for amphibious assaults. It should be noted that the helicopters have a limited night-flying capability and cannot effectively counter bottom-laid mines.

The current MCM buildup was initiated under the Reagan-Lehman naval program of the early 1980s. After an almost 30-year hiatus in the series production of minesweepers, the two new ship classes were initiated; the AVENGER-class MCM ships and the CARDINAL-class air-cushion minehunters (MSH). Both the MCM and MSH encountered major construction problems. The CARDINAL class was canceled and the OSPREY class (MHC), adopted from an Italian design, was built in its place.

The new mine warfare ships are modern, outfitted with advanced MCM equipment. However, their numbers are relatively small in view of the worldwide political-military interests of the United States and the proliferation of naval mines, the ease with which they can be planted, and the recent precedents of their use by Third World nations (e.g., by Libya in the Red Sea in 1984 and by Iraq in the Persian Gulf in the 1980s and early 1990s).

In May 1991 the Navy announced plans to move the headquarters for the newly established Mine Warfare Command to Ingleside, Texas (near Corpus Christi), and to homeport all mine countermeasures ships there beginning in early 1992. In a report to the Secretary of the Navy issued on 27 December 1991, the General Accounting Office attacked the Navy's plan, criticizing the Navy for not spending enough time analyzing the issue and indicating that the cost of the relocation could be prohibitive. (The Mine Warfare Command and several mine warfare ships were previously based at Charleston, South Carolina.)

The move to Ingleside, hailed by the Navy in 1992 as improving efficiency, in reality will detract from the force effectiveness by: (1) removing mine warfare ships and people from the major fleet operating bases, thus inhibiting the exchange of ideas; (2) making exercises with the fleet more difficult and costly; and (3) increasing deployment transits to forward areas for the relatively low-speed MCM forces.

Subsequently, the Navy has decided that two MCMs will be based in Astoria, Oregon, and two MCMs in Sasebo, Japan, and two will be continuously forward deployed in the Persian Gulf.

The problems in the belated MCM and MSH programs, the mining of the supertanker BRIDGETON in the first convoy escorted by U.S. forces in the Persian Gulf in 1987, the mining of the U.S. frigate SAMUEL B. ROBERTS (FFG 58) in the Persian Gulf in 1988, and the damage inflicted by mines on the helicopter carrier TRIPOLI (LPH 10) and the Aegis cruiser PRINCETON (CG 59) in the gulf in 1991 have all raised questions about the fundamental ability of the U.S. Navy to cope with modern mine warfare problems. According to then-Deputy Chief of Naval Operations (Surface Warfare), Vice Admiral Robert L. Walters, speaking in 1983, "No segment of Naval Warfare has been underfunded for so many years as has the Mine Warfare community. Despite the large stockpiles of sophisticated modern mines possessed by the Soviets, we have only recently begun to respond to the threat."[1]

1. Vice Adm. Robert L. Walters, USN, Deputy CNO (Surface Warfare), statement before the House Appropriations Committee, 20 April 1983.

MINE COUNTERMEASURES FORCES

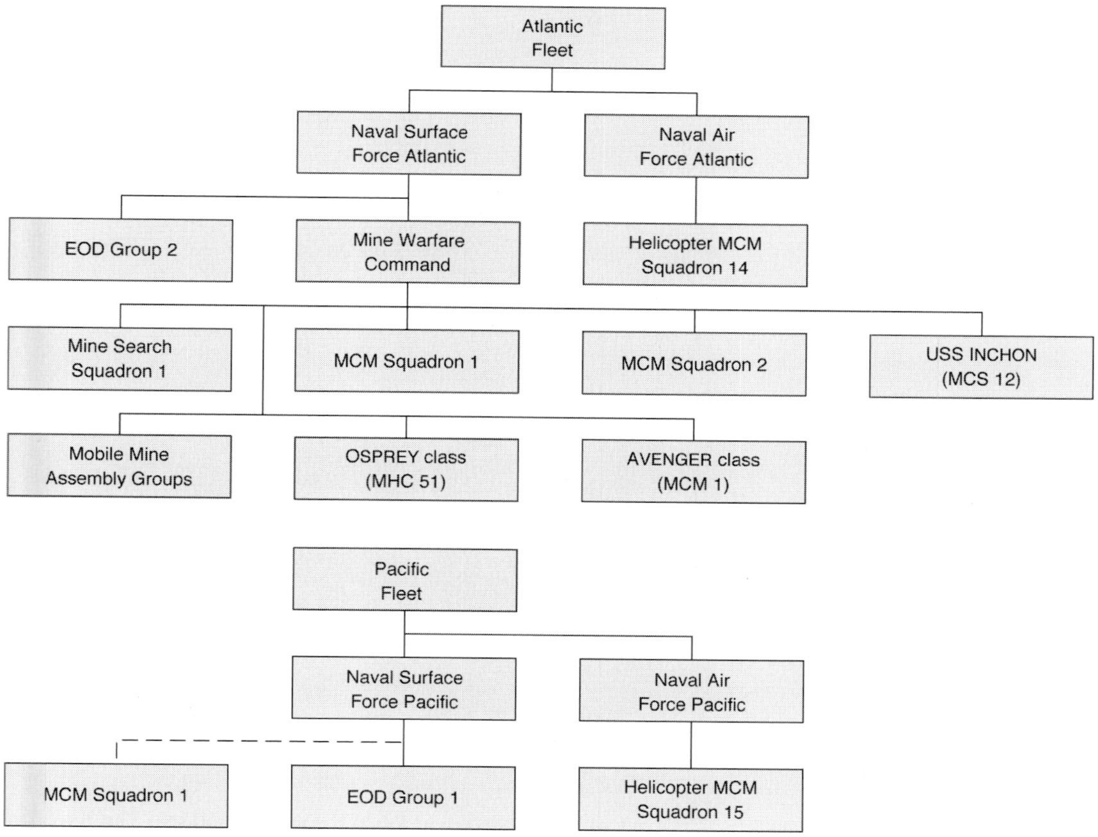

NOTES: Only MCM forces are shown.
EOD = Explosive Ordnance Disposal
MCM = Mine Countermeasures

The Persian Gulf minings—like the experiences faced by the United States in the Korean War (1950–1953)—demonstrate that even Third World nations can effectively employ sea mines. But a lack of understanding of that truth came to the fore in 1987 when a U.S. Navy captain observed at a press briefing that the Iranians "have some potential capability to moor mines . . . but nothing that we would think of as minelaying capability in military terms and no modern mines. . . . So we would say that their mine warfare capability is limited."[2] A month later an Iranian-laid mine damaged the supertanker BRIDGETON, embarrassing the United States and questioning U.S. ability to escort reflagged Kuwaiti tankers.[3]

Even with the demise of the Soviet Union as a military threat to the United States in the near term, sea mines remain a major threat to the maritime operations of the United States and other nations. The Department of Defense report on the Persian Gulf conflict states:

> Operation Desert Shield and Desert Storm highlighted the dangers that sea mines pose to naval forces. Mines will continue to pose a difficult problem. Refocusing our national defense strategy away from the European theater and toward regional contingencies has exposed a gap in U.S. mine warfare capability that our European allies were previously expected to fill.[4]

No additional mine countermeasures ships are planned by the U.S. Navy. Thus, by the year 2000 the surface MCM Force is expected to consist of the 14 AVENGER-class ships and 12 smaller coastal minehunters of the OSPREY class. These 26 ships will fall short of providing the Navy's minimum goal for mine countermeasures capabilities. That goal, as stated in 1991, was 45 new MCM/MHC ships, plus helicopters. (Studies of wartime requirements indicate a need for at least 60 mine countermeasures ships, with the high end of estimates in the hundreds—much too large a force for American peacetime budgets *or* interest.)

Mine countermeasures: The MCM and MHC classes both use hull-mounted Variable Depth Sonar (VDS) as their primary means of mine detection and cable-controlled SLQ-48 Mine Neutralization System (MNS) to examine and clear the mines (see a description at the end of this chapter).[5]

Names: The larger minesweepers have adjective names and smaller units have bird names (except for the MHC 58, which is named for an American Indian tribe). The bird names date to World War I, having been the name source for most U.S. minesweepers until the 1950s, except for the larger, destroyer-minesweepers (DMS series), which retained their destroyer names.

Operational: U.S. minesweepers in the Persian Gulf in the late 1980s escorted Kuwaiti tankers and other merchant ships during the Iran-Iraq conflict and again in 1990–1991 during Operations Desert Shield/Desert Storm. The Navy sent four MSOs as well as MSBs to the Persian Gulf in 1988; the AVENGER, GUARDIAN, and three MSOs were deployed there in 1990–1991.

In July 1994 the mine countermeasures ships GUARDIAN and PATRIOT were deployed from Ingleside, Texas, in company with the JUNEAU (LPD 10) to the Far East to support U.S. interests in South Korea. The JUNEAU carried four MH-53E Sea Dragon MCM helicopters.

The operation demonstrated the need to deploy mine countermeasures forces in forward areas and raised the issue of forward-basing MCM units in the Far East and, possibly, the Mediterranean–Middle East areas.

The entire U.S. Navy surface ship/craft mine countermeasures force was originally scheduled to be operated by the Naval Reserve Force (NRF). However, following the mine countermeasures effort in Operation Desert Storm, the decision was made to retain ten AVENGER-class ships in the active fleet. All but one of the smaller OSPREY-class ships will be operated by the NRF with composite active-reserve crews.

MINE WARFARE SHIPS AND CRAFT (FALL 1996)

Type	Ship/Class	Commissioned	Active	NRF	Building*
MCS 12	INCHON	1970	1	—	—
MHC 51	OSPREY	1992–	1	6	5
MCM 1	AVENGER	1987–1994	12	2	—
CT	COOP	—	—	11	—

*Ships authorized through Fiscal 1996.

2. Press conference, Pentagon, Washington, D.C., 18 June 1987.
3. The BRIDGETON, 401,400 deadweight tons, was damaged about 20 n.miles (37 km) south of Farsi Island by a 1908-vintage, Russian-design M08/39 moored contact mine. A similar mine devastated the SAMUEL B. ROBERTS in 1988. The PRINCETON was damaged by an Italian Manta magnetic-acoustic influence mine; the TRIPOLI struck an Iraqi-produced LUGM-145 "cheeseburger" contactmine.
4. Department of Defense, *Conduct of the Persian Gulf Conflict* (Washington, D.C.: July 1992), p. 6–9.
5. The MNS was previously referred to as MNV for Mine Neutralization Vehicle.

The INCHON is shown at sea off the coast of Haiti as an LPH shortly before she began conversion to an MCM support ship. The Navy has long needed a specialized support ship that could support MCM ships and helicopters in forward areas, a serious shortfall in U.S. mine warfare capabilities. A second support ship is needed. (1994, U.S. Navy, PH2 John Sokolowski)

1 MCM SUPPORT SHIP: CONVERTED "IWO JIMA" CLASS

Number	Name	FY	Builder	Laid down	Launched	Commissioned	Status
MCS 12 (ex-LPH 12)	Inchon	66	Ingalls Shipbuilding, Pascagoula, Miss.	8 Apr 1968	24 May 1969	20 June 1970	AA

Displacement:	11,000 tons light 18,798 tons full load
Length:	556 feet (169.5 m) waterline 602¼ feet (183.6 m) overall
Beam:	83⅔ feet (25.5 m) waterline)
Extreme width:	104 feet (31.7 m)
Draft:	26 feet (7.9 m)
Propulsion:	1 steam turbine (Westinghouse); 23,000 shp; 1 shaft
Boilers:	2 600 psi (41.7 kg/cm^2) (Combustion Engineering)
Speed:	23 knots (21 knots sustained)
Range:	16,600 n.miles (30,743 km) at 11.5 knots 10,000 n.miles (18,520 km) at 20 knots
Manning:	1,420 (113 officers + 1,307 enlisted)
Troops:	see notes
Aircraft:	8 MH-53E Sea Dragon MCM helicopters
Elevators:	2 deck edge (50 × 34 feet/15.2 × 10.4 m)
Missiles:	removed
Guns:	2 25-mm Bushmaster cannon Mk 38 (2 single) 2 20-mm Phalanx CIWS Mk 16 (2 multi-barrel) 8 .50-cal machine guns M2HB (8 single)
Radars:	SPS-40E air search SPS-64(V)9 navigation SPS-67(V)1 surface search
Fire control:	removed
EW systems:	SLQ-25 Nixie SLQ-32(V)3

The Inchon was converted from an Iwo Jima-class helicopter carrier (amphibious assault ship) to a mine countermeasures support ship to operate MH-53E helicopters and to provide services to surface mine countermeasures ships. She was the last of the seven Iwo Jima-class ships to be completed (see chapter 19).

The supporters of this program have sought a ship that could (1) support and provide underway replenishment for mine countermeasures ships, (2) provide command and control facilities for MCM operations, and (3) carry and operate MH-53E helicopters.

Earlier, the Navy had considered the conversion of two Cleveland (LPD 4)-class dock landing ships for this role. The LPD conversions would have provided a limited transport capability for MHC-type ships, but their command and control and helicopter support facilities were too limited for the MCS role.

The Inchon will be manned by a composite active-reserve crew; she will be homeported at Ingleside, Texas, and assigned to the NRF.

A second LPH conversion is tentatively planned for the period 2005–2010.

Conversion: The ship was converted to the MCM support role at the Ingalls Shipyard in Pascagoula. The conversion began on 6 March 1995 and was completed the end of May 1996, with fitting out to be completed by July 1996. The planned cost of the conversion was $28.7 million.

Design: LPH project number was SCB No. 157. The Inchon is the only Iwo Jima (LPH 2)-class ship with boat davits for four LCVP-type landing craft. The hangar can accommodate 11 MH-53E helicopters, although only eight will normally be assigned to the ship.

The ship's medical facilities include 155 beds.

In the MCS role the ship can provide over-the-stern refueling of mine ships while under way and alongside refueling while stationary.

Classification: This ship should properly be designated MCS 8; however, the Navy is initially listing her as MCS 12, using her LPH number.

Electronics: The ship has SPN-35A marshaling and SPN-43B approach systems.

Guns: As built, the ship had four 3-inch Mk 33 twin gun mounts, two forward of the island structure and two on the after corners of the flight deck. Two gun mounts were replaced in the 1970s by Sea Sparrow launchers; the remaining pair of twin gun mounts was removed during MCS conversion.

Missiles: The two 8-tube Sea Sparrow BPDMS launchers Mk 25 were removed during MCS conversion. Two Mk 115 missile fire-control systems were provided for the Sea Sparrow battery.

Operational: Several ships of this class had previously operated helicopters in the countermeasures role off North Vietnam (1973), in the Suez Canal (1974–1975), and in the Persian Gulf (1991).

MINE WARFARE COMMAND AND SUPPORT SHIPS

The designation MCS was established in 1956 for mine countermeasures ships; it was subsequently changed to mine warfare command and support ships. The Catskill and Ozark were converted in 1963–1967; their near sister ships LSV 3–5 were not converted and remained laid up in "mothballs" while carrying the MCS designation. The Orleans Parish supported minesweepers for several years with an LST designation before being changed to MCS.

Number	Name	Comm.	MCM Comm.	Notes*
MCS 1	Catskill	1944	1967	ex-LSV 1, CM 6, AP 106
MCS 2	Ozark	1944	1967	ex-LSV 2, CM 7, AP 107
MCS 3	Osage	1944	—	ex-LSV 3, AN 3, AP 108
MCS 4	Saugus	1945	—	ex-LSV 4, AN 4, AP 109
MCS 5	Monitor	1944	—	ex-LSV 5
MCS 6	Orleans Parish	1945		ex-LST 1069
MCS 7	Epping Forest	1943	1962	ex-LSD 4
MCH 8	Inchon	1970	1996	ex-LPH 12

*AP = transport; CM = minelayer; LPH = amphibious assault ship; LSD = dock landing ship; LST = tank landing ship; LSV = vehicle landing ship

ADVANCED COASTAL MINEHUNTERS

In early 1991 the Navy put forth proposals to build an enlarged coastal minehunter, with the first unit planned for the fiscal year 1995 shipbuilding program. These ships—given the planning designation MHC(V) and MHC 51(V)—were to be larger than the Osprey Lerici class and would be capable of long-range deployments.

By the fall of 1991, however, the proposal was dropped in favor of having a planned mine countermeasures mother ship that could transport the Osprey class. Still, the six-year (FY 1992–1997) shipbuilding plan presented to Congress in late January 1992 by the Department of Defense provided for the construction of the lead ship of the new MHC class in the fiscal 1995 budget; two follow-on ships in fiscal 1997 and approximately eight later ships were also planned for construction. In the event, the entire MHC(V) program was dropped.

This class, probably fabricated of glass-reinforced plastic, was to have had the SQQ-32 minehunting sonar and the SLQ-48 mine neutralization system.

AIR-CUSHION MINE HUNTERS: "CARDINAL" CLASS

The planned minesweeper hunter (MSH) program was a fiasco. It was halted by the Navy on 25 August 1986 and formally canceled on 24 November 1986. That program had envisioned the construction of 17 air-cushion minehunters of some 470 tons displacement to be authorized from fiscal 1984 through 1989 (see 13th Edition/page 230).

The lead ship Cardinal (MSH 1) was authorized in fiscal 1984, and a contract was awarded to Bell-Halter of New Orleans for construction of the ship. The MSH 2–5 were authorized in fiscal 1986 and MSH 6–9 were requested in fiscal 1987. However, explosive shock testing of a 103-ton fiberglass MSH hull section caused the fiberglass to delaminate. These and other problems, including major difficulties with the Isotta-Fraschini diesel engines (also being used in the MCM class), led then-Assistant Secretary of the Navy for Shipbuilding, Everett Pyatt, to admit: "The Navy wasn't very good. The naval architect was terrible. And the shipbuilders weren't very good."

The lead ship, laid down on 13 February 1986, was never completed.

5 + 7 COASTAL MINEHUNTERS: "OSPREY" CLASS

Number	Name	FY	Builder	Start*	Launched	Commissioned	Status
MHC 51	Osprey	86	Intermarine USA, Savannah, Ga.	16 May 1988	23 Mar 1991	20 Nov 1993	**AA**
MHC 52	Heron	89	Intermarine USA, Savannah, Ga.	7 Apr 1989	21 Mar 1992	6 Aug 1994	**NRF-A**
MHC 53	Pelican	89	Avondale Industries, New Orleans, La.	6 May 1991	27 Feb 1993	18 Nov 1995	**NRF-A**
MHC 54	Robin	90	Avondale Industries, New Orleans, La.	28 Jan 1992	11 Sep 1993	11 May 1996	**NRF-A**
MHC 55	Oriole	90	Avondale Industries, New Orleans, La.	8 May 1991	22 May 1993	16 Sep 1995	**NRF-A**
MHC 56	Kingfisher	91	Avondale Industries, New Orleans, La.	24 Mar 1992	18 June 1994	1996	**NRF-A**
MHC 57	Cormorant	91	Avondale Industries, New Orleans, La.	8 Apr 1992	21 Oct 1995	1997	Building
MHC 58	Blackhawk	92	Intermarine USA, Savannah, Ga.	12 May 1992	27 Aug 1994	11 May 1996	**NRF-A**
MHC 59	Falcon	92	Intermarine USA, Savannah, Ga.	3 Apr 1993	3 June 1995	1997	Building
MHC 60	Cardinal	92	Intermarine USA, Savannah, Ga.	1 Feb 1994	9 Mar 1996	1997	Building
MHC 61	Raven	93	Intermarine USA, Savannah, Ga.	15 Nov 1994	1996	1998	Building
MHC 62	Shrike	93	Intermarine USA, Savannah, Ga.	1 Aug 1995	1997	1999	Building

*These ships do not have a formal keel laying.

Displacement:	803 tons light
	918 tons full load
Length:	$174\frac{1}{6}$ feet (53.1 m) waterline
	$187\frac{3}{4}$ feet (57.25 m) overall
Beam:	$35\frac{11}{12}$ feet (10.95 m)
Draft:	$9\frac{1}{2}$ feet (2.9 m)
Propulsion:	2 diesel engines (Isotta-Fraschini ID 36 SS 6V-AM) 1,160 bhp; 2 cycloidal propellers
	2 180-ship hydraulic motors for quiet operation
Speed:	12 knots
Range:	2,500 n.miles (1,350 km) at 12 knots
Manning:	MHC 51, 52 (5 officers + 47 enlisted)
	others: active 51 (5 officers + 46 enlisted) + reservists
Guns:	2 .50-cal machine guns M2HB (2 single)
Radar:	SPS-64(V)9 navigation
Sonar:	SQQ-32 mine detection

These ships are intended for harbor clearance, port breakout, and deep-water coastal mine countermeasures. This class was developed in place of the canceled Cardinal class of air-cushion minehunters.

The Heron was transferred to NRF status on 11 July 1995. Subsequent ships will be initially commissioned into active service and, after a one-year trials and shakedown period, will be transferred to NRF service.

Some ships were initially placed "In Commission, Special" at the building yard to permit a Navy crew to take them to a port where they were placed "In Commission, Full," the formal commissioning ceremony listed above.

Class: Congress added one ship to the Bush administration's request for two MHCs each in the fiscal 1992 and 1993 programs, reflecting an increase in concern over the U.S. Navy's mine countermeasures capabilities. Still, only 12 MHCs will be procured, although the initial program was planned at 17 units. The follow-on, enlarged MHC(V) program was canceled in 1991.

The Italian Navy procured four similar ships of the Lerici class, completed in 1985; additional ships were built in Italy for Malaysia and Nigeria. The U.S. design is slightly larger to accommodate U.S. sonars, MNS, and navigation gear; also, a different propulsion system is provided. (Indonesia did not procure ships of this design, as previously reported.)

Classification: The MHC designation originated in the early 1950s as AMc(U)—mine vessel underwater locator. Those ships were intended to locate and plot mines for subsequent destruction by minesweepers. The Bittern (MHC 43), completed in 1957, was built for the purpose on a 144-foot (43.9-m) MSC hull with a full-load displacement of 350 tons; the planned series production of similar MHCs was canceled, and the hull numbers MHC 44 and 45 were allocated to conversions (see below).

The AMc(U) 1–10 were converted LCT(6)s; the AMc(U) 7–11, 15–42 were converted LSI(L)s; the AMc(U) 12 and 13 were converted coastal survey ships (AGSc/AGS), which, in turn, had been converted from YMS motor minesweepers; the AMc(U) 14 was a converted AMC, originally built as a PCS/PC; and the MHC 44, 45, and AMc(U) 46–50 were converted YMS minesweepers. Some of the LSI(L) conversions were not completed.

The designation AMc(U) was changed to coastal minehunter (MHC) on 7 February 1955.

Design: These are the first U.S. Navy ships to be constructed of Glass-Reinforced Plastic (GRP), a material long used in foreign mine countermeasures craft. The hull has a monocoque design, with no longitudinal or transverse framing.

The ships are fitted with the SYQ-13 tactical navigation/command system. One Mine Neutralization System (MNS) vehicle is carried.

At-sea endurance is 12 to 15 days.

Engineering: Each ship is fitted with a 180-shp bow thruster.

Names: All named for birds except the MHC 58, which bears the name of an American Indian tribe.

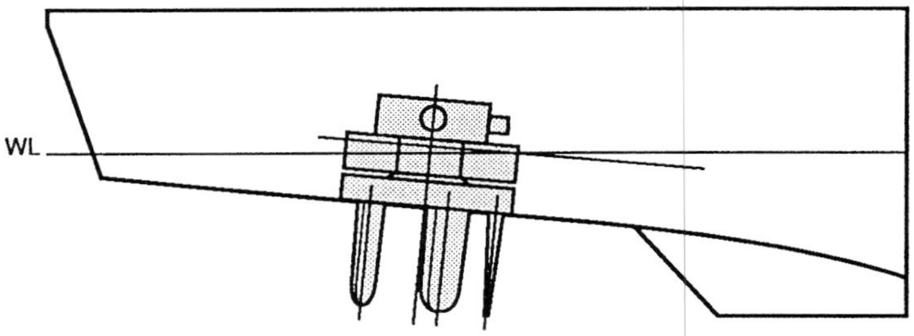

A diagram of the Voith-Schneider propeller arrangement in the Osprey-class ships. This arrangement provides a very high degree of maneuverability, as shown in an accompanying photo.

The OSPREY under way. These coastal minehunters are built to a modified Italian design. The winch for the SQQ-32 sonar, which is lowered from the hull, is fitted forward of the bridge. (1994, Giorgio Arra)

Another aspect of the lead ship of the OSPREY class, showing the open working area aft with a crane for handling minesweeping gear, including the Mine Neutralization System (MNS) vehicle. Note the position of the mast, forward of the short, squat funnel. (1994, Giorgio Arra)

A trio of OSPREY-class mine countermeasures ships being completed at Avondale Industries in New Orleans. The U.S. Navy will have only 26 MCM/MHC mine countermeasures ships well into the 21st century. (1995, Leo Van Ginderen collection)

14 MINE COUNTERMEASURES SHIPS: "AVENGER" CLASS

Number	Name	FY	Builder	Laid down	Launched	Commissioned	Status
MCM 1	Avenger	82	Peterson Builders, Sturgeon Bay, Wisc.	3 June 1983	15 June 1985	12 Sep 1987	NRF-A
MCM 2	Defender	83	Marinette Marine, Marinette, Wisc.	1 Dec 1983	4 Apr 1987	30 Sep 1989	NRF-A
MCM 3	Sentry	84	Peterson Builders, Sturgeon Bay, Wisc.	8 Oct 1983	20 Sep 1986	6 Oct 1990	PA
MCM 4	Champion	84	Marinette Marine, Marinette, Wisc.	28 June 1984	15 Apr 1989	8 Feb 1991	AA
MCM 5	Guardian	84	Peterson Builders, Sturgeon Bay, Wisc.	8 May 1985	20 June 1987	16 Dec 1989	PA
MCM 6	Devastator	85	Peterson Builders, Sturgeon Bay, Wisc.	9 Feb 1987	11 June 1988	6 Oct 1990	AA
MCM 7	Patriot	85	Marinette Marine, Marinette, Wisc.	31 Mar 1987	15 May 1990	13 Dec 1991	PA
MCM 8	Scout	85	Peterson Builders, Sturgeon Bay, Wisc.	8 June 1987	20 May 1989	15 Dec 1990	AA
MCM 9	Pioneer	85	Peterson Builders, Sturgeon Bay, Wisc.	5 June 1989	25 Aug 1990	7 Dec 1992	AA
MCM 10	Warrior	86	Peterson Builders, Sturgeon Bay, Wisc.	25 Sep 1989	8 Dec 1990	30 Dec 1992	AA
MCM 11	Gladiator	86	Peterson Builders, Sturgeon Bay, Wisc.	7 May 1990	29 June 1991	4 June 1993	AA
MCM 12	Ardent	90	Peterson Builders, Sturgeon Bay, Wisc.	22 Oct 1990	16 Nov 1991	18 Sep 1993	AA
MCM 13	Dextrous	90	Peterson Builders, Sturgeon Bay, Wisc.	11 Mar 1991	20 June 1992	9 July 1994	AA
MCM 14	Chief	90	Peterson Builders, Sturgeon Bay, Wisc.	19 Aug 1991	12 June 1993	5 Nov 1994	AA

Displacement: 1,195 tons light
1,312 tons full load
Length: 212¾ feet (64.85 m) waterline
224¼ feet (68.4 m) overall)
Beam: 38 11/12 feet (11.9 m)
Draft: 11¼ feet (3.4 m)
Propulsion: MCM 1, 2 4 diesel engines (Waukesha L-1616); 2,280 bhp; 2 shafts
MCM 3–14 4 diesel engines (Isotta-Fraschini ID36 SS 6V-AM); 2,600 bhp; 2 shafts (see notes)
2 low-speed motors (Hansome); 400 shp (geared to propellers)

Speed: 13.5 knots
Range:
Manning: 81 (6 officers + 75 enlisted) except early ships 70 (6 officers + 64 enlisted)
Guns: 2 .50-cal machine guns M2HB (2 single)
Radars: SPS-55 surface search
SPS-64(V)9 navigation
Sonars: MCM 2–9 SQQ-30 mine detection
MCM 1, 10–14 SQQ-32 mine detection

These are relatively large mine countermeasures ships intended to locate and destroy mines that cannot be countered by conventional minesweeping techniques.

The Avenger class has suffered a number of design and construction problems. The first two ships were fitted with American engines from existing stocks; they were installed improperly and tests later revealed a potential fire hazard from lubricating oil leakage through the turbocharger into the exhaust stack. (This engine design had been blamed for a series of fires in previous minesweepers.) The Italian engines planned for the later MCMs failed in their endurance tests.

The MCMs are also overweight: one of two planned DC generators for sweep gear and mine-hunting had to be deleted because of space/weight problems. The ships have also had electronic interference problems. During Operation Desert Storm in 1991 the Avenger suffered both main engine and generator problems as she hunted mines in the Persian Gulf, but evidence did show that her acoustic signature was greater than expected.

The Avenger was ordered on 29 June 1982, becoming the first large minesweeper under construction for the U.S. Navy since the Assurance was completed 25 years earlier. The Avenger was almost two years behind her original contract schedule and the Defender more than 15 months behind.

Some ships were initially placed "In Commission, Special" at the building yard to permit a Navy crew to take them to a port where they were placed "In Commission, Full," the formal commissioning ceremony listed above.

The Avenger and Defender were transferred from active status to the NRF on 30 September 1995. Ten ships are homeported in Ingleside, Texas. The Guardian and Patriot are based in Sasebo, Japan, and two other ships are expected to be based at Pearl Harbor.

Class: The Navy originally planned a two-year "program gap" between the fiscal 1982 lead ship and four ships in fiscal 1984. The Navy later sought to accelerate the program with four ships in fiscal 1983. Congress, citing problems with the MCM design, instead funded only one ship in fiscal 1983 and directed the Navy to develop a second source shipyard (i.e., Marinette).

Design: The current MCM design is similar to previous MSO classes. Their hulls are constructed of fiberglass-sheathed wood (laminated oak framing, Douglas fir planking, and deck sheathing with reinforced fiberglass covering). One or two MNS vehicles can be carried in addition to conventional sweep gear.

The MCM concept has undergone several changes in the past few years, originally being proposed in the late 1970s as an oceangoing ship to protect U.S. strategic missile submarines against Soviet

The Warrior head on. The winch for lowering and raising the SQQ-32 sonar is forward of the bridge. These ships have a "heavy" tripod mast atop the bridge. (1994 Giorgio Arra)

deep-ocean mines. A Small Waterplane-Area Twin Hull (SWATH) design was considered for that concept to provide improved seakeeping in northern waters. Under that concept the MCMs would have operated in pairs, towing a sweep gear between them. Nineteen of these ships were proposed; they were to have displaced 1,640 tons and to have been 265 feet (80.8 m) long.

Electronics: Fitted with SSN-2(V) precise navigation system and SYQ-13 navigation/command system; the improved SYQ-15 is to replace the latter system.

Early ships were fitted with the SQQ-30 variable-depth mine-hunting sonar. This equipment, an upgraded SQQ-14, has severe limitations and is replaced in later ships by the SQQ-32. It was planned to backfit the SQQ-32 into the earlier ships; in 1990 the Avenger was hurriedly refitted with the engineering development model of the SQQ-32 for operations in the Persian Gulf. Deployed to the gulf (with several MSOs), the Avenger detected the first Manta bottom mine to be discovered, but the ship then suffered mechanical and power-generation problems and was forced to withdraw from the mined area.

Engineering: All ships have four very-low-magnetic diesel engines for propulsion; electrical power for minesweeping gear is provided by gas turbines. The low-speed motors are geared to the propellers. A 350-hp bow thruster is fitted for precise maneuvering. Maximum mine-hunting speed is five knots.

Congress directed that the MCM 10–14 would have American-made diesel engines; however, foreign engines were procured for them.

Names: Navy publicity at the time of the commissioning of the Chief stated that the ship "was named Chief in honor of the chief petty officers" of the Navy. In reality, the ship was named (on 3 July 1990) along with several other MCMs to "commemorate the service of World War II minecraft that saw significant service. . . . Chief (MCM-14) commemorates Chief (AM-315), that earned five battle stars in World War II." The AM-315 was named for "the head or leader of a group," according to the U.S. Naval Historical Center.

Operational: The Avenger was deployed to the Persian Gulf for Operations Desert Shield/Desert Storm, having been transported to the area by a heavy-lift ship, along with three MSOs.[6] The Avenger returned to the United States in June 1991 under her own power. She was relieved in the gulf by the Guardian.

6. The four mine warfare ships were carried by the Dutch heavy-lift ship Super Servant 3, which departed Norfolk on 29 August 1990 and arrived at Bahrain on 3 October 1991. The use of a heavy-lift ship saved debilitating wear-and-tear on the ships and crews during the long transit.

The Guardian at rest in Hong Kong. These ships suffered several design and construction problems. (1994, Giorgio Arra)

The Guardian, showing the mine gear towing reel and a variety of mine countermeasures devices on her stern. These ships are intended to detect and destroy floating, moored, and bottom mines. (1994, Giorgio Arra)

OCEAN MINESWEEPERS: "ACME" CLASS

Number	Name	Comm.	Notes
MSO 508	ACME	1956	decomm. 6 Nov 1970; stricken 15 May 1976
MSO 509	ADROIT (NRF)	1957	decomm. 12 Dec 1991; stricken 8 May 1992
MSO 510	ADVANCE	1958	decomm. Dec 1970; stricken 15 May 1976
MSO 511	AFFRAY (NRF)	1958	decomm./stricken 31 Dec 1992

This was an improved ocean minesweeper design based on the earlier AGILE and AGGRESSIVE classes. The four ships built for the U.S. Navy have been stricken; two were assigned to the Naval Reserve Force in their later years. Seven additional ships were built for allied navies (MSO 512–518).

The ADROIT participated in Operation Desert Storm (1991).

See 15th Edition/pages 213–14 for characteristics.

OCEAN MINESWEEPERS: "AGILE" AND "AGGRESSIVE" CLASSES

Number	Name	Comm.	Notes
MSO 427	CONSTANT	(NRF) 1954	decomm. 30 Sep 1992; stricken 9 Mar 1994
MSO 433	ENGAGE	(NRF) 1954	decomm. 30 Dec 1991; stricken 20 Apr 1992
MSO 437	ENHANCE	(NRF) 1954	decomm. 13 Dec 1991; stricken 21 Feb 1992
MSO 438	ESTEEM	(NRF) 1954	decomm./stricken 20 Sep 1991
MSO 439	EXCEL	(NRF) 1955	decomm. 30 Sep 1992; stricken 28 Mar 1994
MSO 440	EXPLOIT	(NRF) 1954	decomm. 16 Dec 1993; stricken 28 Mar 1994
MSO 441	EXULTANT	1954	decomm. 30 June 1993; stricken 9 Mar 1994
MSO 442	FEARLESS	(NRF) 1955	decomm. 23 Oct 1990; stricken 28 Oct 1990
MSO 446	FORTIFY	(NRF) 1954	decomm. 31 Aug 1992; stricken 9 Mar 1994
MSO 448	ILLUSIVE	(NRF) 1955	decomm. 30 Mar 1990; stricken 1 June 1990
MSO 449	IMPERVIOUS	(NRF) 1955	decomm. 12 Dec 1991; stricken 18 Mar 1992
MSO 455	IMPLICIT	(NRF) 1954	decomm./to Taiwan 30 Sep 1994 (stricken 29 Nov 1994)
MSO 456	INFLICT	(NRF) 1954	decomm. 30 Mar 1990; stricken 23 May 1990
MSO 464	PLUCK	(NRF) 1954	decomm. 29 Nov 1990; stricken 16 Jan 1991
MSO 488	CONQUEST	(NRF) 1955	decomm./stricken 29 June 1994; to Taiwan 3 Aug 1994
MSO 489	GALLANT	(NRF) 1955	decomm./stricken 29 Apr 1994; to Taiwan 3 Aug 1994
MSO 490	LEADER	1955	decomm. 12 Dec 1991; stricken 18 Mar 1992
MSO 492	PLEDGE	(NRF) 1956	decomm./stricken 31 Jan 1994; to Taiwan 3 Aug 1994

All ocean minesweepers of the massive Korean War–era program have been discarded. Fifty-eight ships of this design were built for the U.S. Navy (MSO 421–449, 455–474, 488–496); another 27 ships were built for allied navies (MSO 450–454, 475–487, 498–507), with the MSO 497 being canceled.

The above list contains ships stricken since 1990 (note revisions to previous edition). Most were assigned to the Naval Reserve Force prior to their disposal (indicated by NRF).

All three ships of the similar ABILITY class (MSO 519–521) built for the U.S. Navy have been discarded. The MSO 522 of that design was built for foreign use.

Operational: The ENHANCE, EXCEL, and FEARLESS were deployed to the Persian Gulf in 1987 (along with several MSBs). The IMPERVIOUS, INFLICT, and LEADER were deployed to the Persian Gulf in 1990–1991, participating in Desert Shield/Desert Storm.

COASTAL MINESWEEPERS

The 24 coastal minesweepers of the similar BLUEBIRD (MSC 121, 122), FALCON (MSC 190–209), and ALBATROSS (MSC 289, 290) classes have been discarded, the last in 1976. Most of the 145-foot (44.2-m) craft, completed from 1953 to 1955 (except MSC 289, 290 in 1961), were assigned to the NRF during their last years of U.S. service. Another 154 American-built MSCs and 41 near sisters built overseas with U.S. funds went to allied navies upon completion; some U.S. units were also transferred overseas after active Navy service. The MSC 155–166 were canceled.

See 8th Edition/page 22 for characteristics.

INSHORE MINESWEEPERS

Two inshore minesweepers—the COVE (MSI 1) and CAPE (MSI 2)—were built for the U.S. Navy, completed in 1958 and 1959, respectively. After several years of operation in the mine warfare role, they were employed as research craft. Additional MSIs were built for foreign navies.

See 13th Edition/page 334 for characteristics.

MINESWEEPING BOATS

The Navy's long-serving minesweeping boats (MSB) have all been discarded from the MCM role, the last in 1993. These craft, which saw extensive service in the Vietnam War and also in the Persian Gulf in the late 1980s, were assigned to Mine Division 125 at Charleston, South Carolina. That formation was disestablished on 1 April 1992, and the last of the MSBs were stripped of their sweep gear and assigned to utility duties. The MSB 15 and 51 were discarded in 1992; MSB 25, 28, 29, and 41 were transferred to Panama on 3 March 1993. The ex-MSB 17 remains in service in a utility role for U.S. naval forces in the Panama Canal Zone (redesignated 57UB753).

See 14th Edition/pages 241–42 for characteristics.

RIVERINE MINESWEEPING CRAFT

A variety of minesweeping craft were employed during the Vietnam War for clearing rivers of mines and booby traps. These were the patrol minesweepers (MSR), river minesweepers (MSM), and drone (radio-controlled) minesweepers (MSD).

CRAFT OF OPPORTUNITY PROGRAM

The Navy developed the Craft of Opportunity Program (COOP) plan in the 1980s to provide a mine countermeasures capability for U.S. ports. The COOP craft have towed side-looking sonar; they locate enemy bottom mines and then direct larger minecraft or swimmers to the target mines to place charges next to them.

The Navy initially planned a force of 22 COOP sweepers, each to have had four reserve (NRF) crews, for a total of 88 crews. In wartime up to 66 previously identified civilian, trawler-type craft would be taken over by the Navy and employed in the harbor sweep role with the additional COOP crews.

The COOP effort was essentially canceled by the Navy in 1990 (zero funded), but funds were again requested in 1991 (fiscal 1992 budget). With the end of the Cold War and the apparent end of the danger of Soviet submarines mining U.S. ports, the Navy sought to discard the COOP program. The effort has generally been supported by Congress, however. The House Armed Services Committee report on fiscal 1993 Navy programs (May 1992) states:

> The committee continues to believe that the COOP program provides a significant deterrent to, and capability in response to, terrorism in United States Harbors. The COOP program also provides a cost effective and useful means of mine countermeasures training for both active and reserve forces.
>
> Accordingly, the committee directs the Secretary of the Navy to continue the COOP program in the Naval Reserve and to maintain 15 units geographically dispersed on the Atlantic, Pacific and Gulf coasts.

Although many Navy leaders opposed the COOP effort, it appears to have been successful. For example, a former Commander, Mine Warfare Command, stated in 1989 that in a then-recent test the Navy had laid 30 bottom mines and COOP craft had found 29 of them on the first pass, "just dragging [a trawler net]. . . ." He concluded his description of the COOP effort with the evaluation "[I]t works well."[7]

Classification: Note that CT (for COOP trainer) is not an "official" designation; a hyphen is used in the designation. Several CT numbers have been used twice.

Manning: Each COOP craft is operated by nine enlisted personnel, with four reserve crews assigned. These crews (designated Blue, Gold, Red, and Green) were to alternate operating the craft on weekends. In addition, each craft has two active enlisted personnel assigned, plus an administrative staff of two officers and two enlistees.

7. Rear Adm. Charles F. Horne III, USN, U.S. Naval Institute symposium "Mine Warfare: Which Platform?" Charleston, S.C., 26 February 1987.

Operational: Mine Group 11 (Seattle, Washington) and Mine Squadron 22 (Charleston, South Carolina) previously operated the COOP craft. The surviving units are now under the command of Inshore Boat Squadron 1 at Ingleside, Texas.

COOP MINESWEEPERS: "FRIGATEBIRD" CLASS

The FRIGATEBIRD (CT-21) and ALBATROSS (CT-22), prototypes for new construction COOP craft, were completed in 1988 and transferred in 1993–1994 from Navy explosive ordnance disposal units to the National Oceanic and Atmospheric Administration.

11 COOP MINESWEEPERS: CONVERTED YP TRAINING CRAFT

Number	Built
CT-1 (ex-YP 675)	1979
CT-2 (ex-YP 668)	1968
CT-4 (ex-YP 669)	1971
CT-5 (ex-YP 654)	1960
CT-6 (ex-YP 664)	1958
CT-8 (ex-YP 661)	1958
CT-9 (ex-YP 660)	1958
CT-10 (ex-YP 659)	1966
CT-11 (ex-YP 666)	1966
CT-15 (ex-YP 662)	1959
CT-19 (ex-YP 673)	

Builders:	YP 654–662 Stephen Brothers, Stockton, Calif. YP 664 Elizabeth City Shipbuilders, N.C. YP 666–675 Peterson Brothers, Sturgeon Bay, Wisc.
Displacement:	60 tons light 71 tons full load
Length:	80⅓ feet (24.5 m) overall
Beam:	18⅓ feet (5.6 m)
Draft:	5⅓ feet (1.7 m)
Propulsion:	2 diesel engines (General Motors Detroit Diesel 6-71); 660 bhp; 2 shafts
Speed:	13.5 knots
Range:	
Manning:	9 to 11 (enlisted)
Guns:	none
Radars:	Raytheon 1220 navigation
Sonar:	C Mk 2 side-scan towed sonar

Seventeen former Naval Academy seamanship training craft (YP) were to be adopted for the COOP effort, but only 12 were modified in 1989; the five others were subsequently assigned to the Naval Postgraduate School at Monterey, California, as training craft.

Class: This YP class originally consisted of YP 654–675 (originally SCB No. 139; changed to No. 800 in the new SCB series). They were completed between 1965 and 1979.

The following have been discarded:

CT-12 (ex-YP 665)
CT-13 (ex-YP 663)
CT-16 (ex-YP 670)
CT-17 (ex-YP 671)
CT-18 (ex-YP 672)
CT-19 (ex-YP 673)
CT-20 (ex-YP 674)

The status of other COOP craft is as follows:

CT-1 (ex-IDA GREEN)—returned to owner in October 1986.
CT-2 (ex-65WB601, ex-TIKI)—still held by the U.S. Navy.
CT-12 (ex-58NS850)—still held by the U.S. Navy.
CT-19 FALCON—in storage at San Diego since 1992.
CT-20 SISKIN (ex-SIROD)—in storage at San Diego since 1993.

MINESWEEPING SHRIMP BOAT

The prototype for the COOP effort was the so-called minesweeping shrimp boat ROBIN GAIL II (designated MSSB 1 and later CT-3 by the Navy). She was acquired in 1980 under rental contract to evaluate the feasibility of configuring such small fishing craft for MCM activities. Placed in service in 1985, the 101-foot (30.8-m) craft had been seized by the U.S. Customs Service in February 1980 while carrying marijuana. An additional electric generator, minesweeping gear, a small sonar (WQS-1), and other special equipment was installed before the craft could be evaluated.

The craft was subsequently given the Navy small boat designation 103WB831; she was discarded in 1986 and transferred to Panama on 22 July 1992.

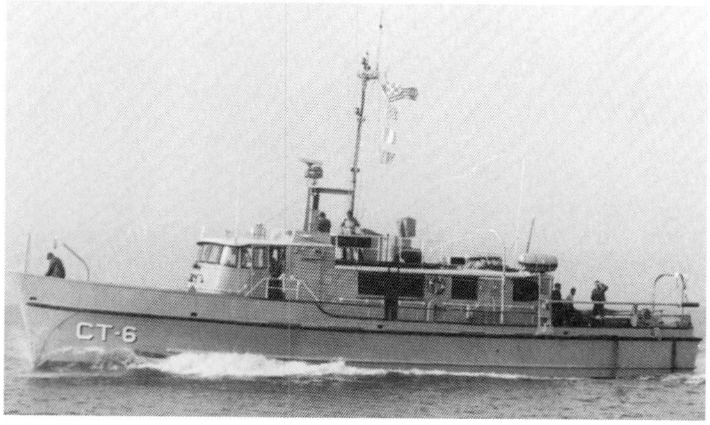

The CT-6 is typical of the Naval Academy training craft (YP) converted to a minesweeping role. Originally praised and then criticized by the Navy, the program has been retained on a small scale but can be expected to end soon. (1991, Giorgio Arra)

UNMANNED MINESWEEPERS

The U.S. Navy is developing several unmanned mine countermeasures devices. One is a joint U.S.–Swedish project, referred to as SAM II, and another is the RMOP project. Also see page 83.

The RMOP vehicle. The structure that protrudes above the water has a location light and transceiver antenna for remotely controlling the vehicle. (1994, U.S. Navy, courtesy of *Surface Warfare* magazine)

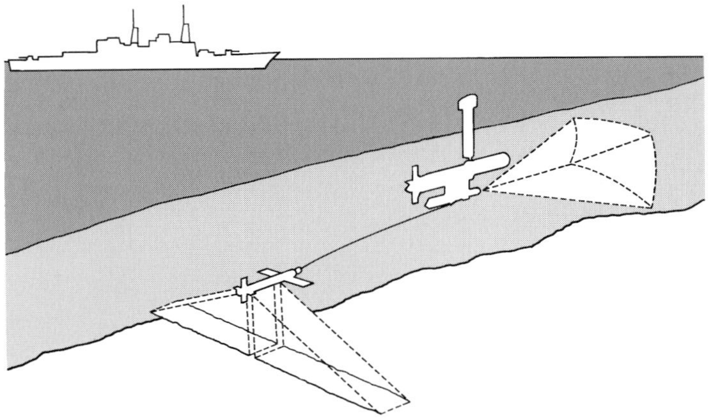

A diagram of the Remote Minehunting Operational Prototype (RMOP) being developed by the Navy. The RMOP—with sensors fitted underneath—tows an AQS-14 airborne mine-detecting sonar. The RMOP is shown here controlled by a destroyer operating several miles away.

REMOTE MINEHUNTING OPERATIONAL PROTOTYPE

The Navy's Remote Minehunting Operational Prototype (RMOP) is an unmanned undersea vehicle configured to hunt mines. It is controlled from a surface ship although, in the future, it could be additionally controlled by a fixed-wing aircraft or helicopter.

As shown in the accompanying diagram and photos, the RMOP has a torpedo-like body with a fixed "sail" that contains a navigation light, antenna for its controls/sensors, and a snorkel for its diesel engine. The RMOP has a Reason SeaBat 6012 forward-looking sonar for mine detection in its "keel" and tows an AQS-14 helicopter minehunting sonar.

The system employs Global Positioning System (GPS) navigation and, after launching from a mother ship, conducts its mission in a semiautonomous manner, running preprogrammed tracks. Sonar and mission data are displayed to the operator aboard the mother ship in real time. Aboard ship, the sonar operator identifies and classifies contacts that are detected by RMOP sonar.

The RMOP can operate for 24 hours at a speed of five knots before it requires refueling and servicing aboard its mother ship. (Of course, helicopter recovery should also be possible). Upon completion of a mission the RMOP winches the AQS-14 sonar body into a stowed position. The RMOP can be refueled, checked, and begin another mission in less than one hour.

Development of the RMOP began in September 1993.

MARINE MAMMAL SYSTEMS

The U.S. Navy also has a fully operational minehunting capability that employs trained dolphins. Designated as the Marine Mammal Systems (MMS) Mk 4 and Mk 7, the dolphins are assigned to Explosive Ordnance Disposal (EOD) Mobile Unit 3 at San Diego.

The dolphins are employed to locate mines in poor minehunting environments, especially shallow water, where mine-detecting sonars do not function effectively. The dolphins are housed in open-water enclosures and work untethered in the open ocean. They are particularly effective in finding bottom mines, including those buried by silt, and close-tethered mines.

The dolphins can be transported and supported aboard ship. For example, in the multinational RIMPAC '94 exercise, dolphins and their supporting personnel and equipment were based on the amphibious ship JUNEAU (LPD 10). They lived in specially designed saltwater pools kept in the ship's docking well. Operating one at a time, the dolphins then swam to the operating area, accompanied by their handlers riding in small boats.

Once in their operating area, the dolphins are directed by acoustic or hand signal to search for mines. After searching an area, the dolphins report the presence or absence of mines by pushing a paddle on the side of the boat. When a dolphin reports a mine, the handler gives it a marker that the mammal places next to the mine, which will be avoided or subsequently detonated. The handlers use the Global Positioning System (GPS) to ensure their exact location.

The Navy has employed dolphins in minehunting and other ocean-engineering activities since the early 1970s. Employing dolphins to deter enemy swimmers from entering an area has also been considered by the Navy.

The U.S. Navy used two unmanned, Swedish-developed catamaran minesweepers in the Persian Gulf campaign. There is an ongoing U.S.–Swedish development program in this area. Here the PEGGY (foreground) and GERRY are maneuvered by U.S. sailors; the discs above their fantail are on marker buoys. (1991, U.S. Navy, Capt. Joseph Davis)

UNMANNED CATAMARAN MINESWEEPERS

Names	Completed	Acquired
GERRY (ex-SAM 03)	1983	5 Feb 1991
PEGGY (ex-SAM 05)	1983	5 Feb 1991

Builders:	Karlskronavarvet, Karlskrona (Sweden)
Displacement:	15 tons light 20 tons full load
Length:	59 feet (18.0 m)
Beam:	20 feet (6.1 m)
Draft:	5¼ feet (1.6 m) over propellers 2⅓ feet (0.7 m) hulls
Propulsion:	1 diesel engine (Volvo-Penta TAMD 70D); 210 bhp; 1 shrouded propeller
Speed:	8 knots
Range:	330 n.miles (611 km) at 7 knots
Manning:	unmanned

The Navy purchased two unmanned, remote-controlled catamaran minesweepers from the Swedish Navy just after the outbreak of the Gulf War in early 1991. They were employed in gulf operations.

The craft—known as SAM from their Swedish acronym—perform several functions. According to their manufacturer, a SAM can execute "magnetic minesweeping by hull-integrated coils; acoustic minesweeping by a towed acoustic transmitter; clearing the way to get a higher security for minesweepers and minehunters; and marking out of 'free passages' with buoys on board."

Eight swept-channel marker buoys are carried on each SAM.

Several of these craft are in Swedish service. The former Swedish designations are indicated above.

Names: The craft were named for relatives of the U.S. Navy project manager.

Operational: The U.S. Navy previously employed drone minesweepers in riverine operations during the Vietnam War.

POST–WORLD WAR II MINESWEEPERS

A large number of minesweepers of various types were acquired by the U.S. Navy during the past 35 years, beginning with the massive ocean minesweeper (AM/MSO) and coastal minesweeper (AMS/MSC) series built in the early 1950s. During the 1960s a large number of smaller, riverine sweep craft were developed for use in the Vietnam War (all of which have been discarded, as have all previous craft except for the MSO type listed in this edition).

The various types of post–World War II minesweepers are discussed in the 13th Edition/pages 236–37 and previous editions of *Ships and Aircraft*.

MINE NEUTRALIZATION SYSTEM

One Mine Neutralization System (MNS) vehicle is carried on board ships of the AVENGER and OSPREY classes. Formerly called Mine Neutralization Vehicle (MNV), the device is controlled and powered through a 5,000-foot (1,524-m) cable. A closed-circuit television and close-range sonar provide viewing of objects detected by shipboard sonar; the vehicle can then cut cables for moored mines or plant a small explosive charge to detonate bottom mines.

The Navy took delivery of 67 systems from 1987 to 1995.

Builders:	Honeywell (subsequently Alliant Techsystems)
Weight:	2,750 lbs (1,247 kg)
Length:	12½ feet (3.8 m)
Width:	3 feet (0.9 m)
Height:	3 feet (0.9 m)
Propulsion:	2 electric motors; 30 hp
Speed:	6 knots
Manning:	unmanned

An SLQ-48 MNS vehicle is carried on each U.S. MCM and MHC. Once the vehicle is in the water, the lifting cables (right and left) are released and the vehicle is tethered by a single cable carrying electrical power and control, sonar, and video signals. (Alliant Techsystems)

CHAPTER 23

Auxiliary Ships

The aircraft carrier GEORGE WASHINGTON (CVN 73), with ordnance on flight deck, during a Vertical Replenishment (VERTREP) operation with the fast combat support ship SUPPLY (AOE 6). A UH-46D Sea Knight helicopter is off the WASHINGTON's port side, and an SH-2G LAMPS I from a reserve squadron is between the ships. No transfer lines are rigged between GEORGE WASHINGTON and the SUPPLY. (1995, U.S. Navy, PH3 Shane Hebert)

Auxiliary ships provide support to the "fighting fleet." A large number of different types of specialized auxiliary ships are in U.S. naval service. Sealift ships, although nominally considered to be auxiliary ships, are described in chapter 24 of this edition.

The Reagan-Lehman naval programs of the 1980s emphasized the construction of underway replenishment ships to support battle groups. This effort, and the procurement of large numbers of sealift ships, was undertaken while several planned (and needed) destroyer tenders and repair ships were deleted from shipbuilding programs of the 1980s. Since the start of the post–Cold War era there has been a major cutback in auxiliary ships—especially tenders and repair ships—as well as a proportional cutback in replenishment ships as the number of battle groups has been reduced.

Further, the "tender" force, which consists of destroyer and submarine tenders and repair ships, will be reduced to four ships at the following home ports by the end of this decade: Norfolk, Virginia; Apra Harbor, Guam; La Maddalena, Italy; and Bahrain.

Six auxiliary ships were under construction in the fall of 1996: one oceanographic research ship (AGOR), one ocean surveillance ship (AGOS), three surveying ships (AGS), and one fast combat support ship (AOE). No additional auxiliary ships are scheduled for construction until the AGOR and the AGOS planned for fiscal 1998–1999. The next major auxiliary class planned for construction is a replenishment/dry cargo ship in the fiscal 2000 building program. That ship, tentatively designated ADC(X), will be series produced to replace the existing underway replenishment (UNREP) ships (see page 212).

All of the large numbers of auxiliary ships built in the 1940s and 1950s have been discarded from active naval service. The Military Sealift Command (MSC) still operates specialized research/range support ships built in the 1940s.

Classification: Auxiliary ships are listed in this chapter in alphabetical order according to classification. The U.S. Navy arranges auxiliary ships according to their function, using the following categories:

(1) Combat Logistic Type Ships[1]

Ships that have the capability to provide underway replenishment to fleet units.

(a) Underway Replenishment: AE, AF, AFS, AO, AOE, AOR

(2) Mobile Logistic Type Ships

Ships that have the capability to provide underway replenishment to fleet units and/or to provide direct material support to other deployed units operating far from home base.

(a) Material Support: AD, AR, AS

(3) Support Type Ships

Ships designed to operate in the open ocean in a variety of sea states to provide general support to either combatant forces or shore-based establishments. (Includes smaller auxiliaries which, by the nature of their duties, rarely leave inshore waters.)

(a) Fleet Support: ARS, ASR, ATF, ATS

(b) Other Auxiliaries: ACS, AG, AGDS, AGF, AGFF, AGM, AGOR, AGOS, AGS, AGSS, AH, AK, AKB, AKF, AKR, AOG, AOT, AP, ARC, AVB, AVT.

While overly simplistic, this scheme does attempt to indicate the types of support the various auxiliaries provide to the fleet. This Navy scheme was initiated in 1978.

Several ships officially classified as auxiliaries are listed elsewhere in this volume and are not included in the following table:

AGF	miscellaneous command ship	chapter 18
AGSS	auxiliary submarine	chapter 12
ASDV	swimmer delivery vessel	chapter 20

Sealift ships are listed in chapter 24.

Guns: None of the ships operated by the MSC is armed. Most Navy-manned auxiliaries have a minimal armament of 20-mm or .50-cal guns and 40-mm grenade launchers for close-in self-defense. The major underway replenishment ships, which in wartime would provide direct support to battle groups, have 20-mm Phalanx CIWS and/or Sea Sparrow point-defense missiles as well as SLQ-32 electronic countermeasures gear.

No active auxiliary ships retain the 5-inch guns that populated such ships from the late 1930s onward, nor the 3-inch guns that were common in auxiliary ships from the early 1950s. The KILAUEA (AE 26)-class ammunition ships were the last to carry 3-inch weapons.

Missiles: The AOE/AOR–type replenishment ships are the only U.S. Navy auxiliary ships that are armed with guided missiles.

Names: The historic naming scheme for auxiliary ships, like those for combatants, has undergone a considerable degree of corruption during the past few years, mainly for political purposes.

Destroyer tenders (AD) are named for geographic areas, except for the SAMUEL GOMPERS (AD 37), which honors a labor leader.

Ammunition ships (AE) carry the names of explosives and volcanoes.

Combat stores ships (AFS), fast combat support ships (AOE), and replenishment oilers (AOR) have city names except that the MARS (AFS 1) honors the Roman god of war while the SUPPLY (AOE 6)-class ships carry the names of earlier supply ships (AE/AF/IX types).

Missile range instrumentation ships (AGM) have carried a variety of names, including cities (WHEELING/T-AGM 8), "range" names (RANGE SENTINEL/T-AGM 22), and missile project names (REDSTONE/T-AGM 20), while the ships formerly "owned" by the Air Force honored generals (GEN. H.H. ARNOLD/T-AGM 9).

Oceanographic research ships (AGOR) and surveying ships (AGS) are generally named for oceanographers and Navy oceanographic officers. The PATHFINDER (T-AGS 60) commemorates the Coast and Geodetic Survey ship by that name that was operated by the Navy (AGS 1) during World War II.

Surveillance ships (AGOS) have names that convey traits of capability or accomplishment.

Hospital ships (AH) are assigned "mercy" names.

Oilers (AO) historically have been named for rivers with Indian names. The lead ship of the latest class, the HENRY J. KAISER (T-AO 187), however, is named for an American industrialist and World War II master shipbuilder. The succeeding eight ships of the class are named for industrialists, engineers, and naval architects; Indian names are assigned to the final nine ships of the class.

Repair ships (AR) and cable ships (ARC) are assigned mythological names.

Salvage ships (ARS) are named for terms related to salvage activity.

Submarine tenders (AS) have a variety of name sources, mostly mythological (PROTEUS/AS 19) and submarine pioneers (SIMON LAKE/AS 33).

Submarine rescue ships (ASR) have historically had bird names, because the first ASRs were converted World War I–era minesweepers with bird names.

Tugs (ATF) have Indian names. British-built salvage and rescue ships (ATS), quite understandably, carry the names of English cities with American namesakes.

Aviation logistic ships (AVB) are named for aviation pioneers.[2]

Operational: Auxiliary ships are operated by the active Navy and the MSC, the latter with civil service or contractor civilian crews. Auxiliary ships are no longer assigned to the Naval Reserve Force (NRF), which previously manned several salvage ships (ARS) with composite active-reserve crews.

Several Navy ships are on loan to academic institutions that are conducting naval research projects.

The MSC ships have the prefix USNS for U.S. Naval Ship and the prefix T- is appended to their hull numbers.

1. These are considered warship/combatant ships.

2. The first two AVBs were converted LSTs and continued to carry their landing ship names after conversion to aviation base ships.

AUXILIARY SHIPS (FALL 1996)

Type		Active Total	Active Navy	Active MSC	Active Academic	Building*	Reserve
AD	Destroyer Tenders	2	2	—	—	—	4
AE	Ammunition Ships	8	4	4	—	—	2
AFS	Combat Store Ships	8	—	8	—	—	—
AG	Miscellaneous Auxiliaries	2	—	2	—	—	1
AGM	Missile Range Instrumentation Ships	2	—	2	—	—	—
AGOR	Oceanographic Research Ships	5	—	—	5	1	—
AGOS	Ocean Surveillance Ships	9	—	9	—	1	1
AGS	Surveying Ships	9	—	9	—	2	1
AH	Hospital Ships	—	—	—	—	—	2
AO	Oilers	18	5	13	—	—	2
AOE	Fast Combat Support Ships	7	7	—	—	1	—
AOR	Replenishment Oilers	—	—	—	—	—	6
ARC	Cable Ships	1	—	1	—	—	—
ARS	Salvage Ships	4	4	—	—	—	—
AS	Submarine Tenders	5	5	—	—	—	1
ATF	Fleet Tugs	7	—	7	—	—	—
ATS	Salvage and Rescue Ships	3	3	—	—	—	—
AVB	Aviation Logistic Ships	—	—	—	—	—	2

*Ships authorized through fiscal 1996.

AUXILIARY CRANE SHIPS

The auxiliary crane ships (ACS) are listed with sealift ships (see chapter 24). The Navy's one previous ship in this general category was the ex-battleship KEARSARGE (BB 5, redesignated IX 16 and then AB 1). Completed in 1900, the KEARSARGE was converted in 1920, having been fitted with a 250-ton-capacity crane and hull blisters to provide more stability; she was non–self-propelled. In 1941 she was renamed CRANE SHIP NO. 1 when the name KEARSARGE was assigned to the carrier CV 12 (renamed HORNET) and then CV 33. The crane ship was stricken in 1955 and sold for scrap.

DESTROYER TENDERS

6 DESTROYER TENDERS: "SAMUEL GOMPERS" CLASS

Number	Name	FY	Launched	Commissioned	Status
AD 37	SAMUEL GOMPERS	64	14 May 1966	1 July 1967	PR
AD 38	PUGET SOUND	65	16 Sep 1966	27 Apr 1968	AR
AD 41	YELLOWSTONE	75	27 Jan 1979	28 June 1980	AR
AD 42	ACADIA	76	28 July 1979	6 June 1981	PR
AD 43	CAPE COD	77	2 Aug 1980	17 Apr 1982	PR
AD 44	SHENANDOAH	79	6 Feb 1982	15 Aug 1983	**AA**

Builders:	AD 37, 38	Puget Sound Naval Shipyard
	AD 41–44	National Steel & Shipbuilding, San Diego, Calif.
Displacement:	AD 37, 38	13,600 tons light
	AD 41–44	13,318 tons light
	AD 37, 38	20,500 tons full load
	AD 41–44	20,224 tons full load
Length:	643⅚ feet (196.3 m) overall	
Beam:	85 feet (25.9 m)	
Draft:	22½ feet (6.9 m)	
Propulsion:	2 steam turbines (De Laval); 20,000 shp; 1 shaft	
Boilers:	2 600 psi (41.7 kg/cm²) (Combustion Engineering)	
Speed:	20 knots (18 knots sustained)	
Range:		
Manning:	AD 37	625 (43 officers + 582 enlisted)
	AD 38	625 (42 officers + 583 enlisted)
	AD 41, 43	626 (43 officers + 583 enlisted)
	AD 42	631 (47 officers + 584 enlisted)
	AD 44	621 (43 officers + 578 enlisted)
Helicopters:	landing area (see *Design* notes)	
Guns:	2 40-mm grenade launchers Mk 19 (2 single)	
	2 20-mm cannon Mk 67 (2 single), except 4 guns (4 single) in AD 37, 38	
Radars:	LN-66 navigation	
	SPS-10 surface search	

The Navy's first post–World War II destroyer tenders, these ships are designed to support modern surface combatants, including ships with nuclear and gas turbine propulsion.

The PUGET SOUND served as flagship of the U.S. Sixth Fleet from May 1980 to August 1985, when she was relieved by the command ship CORONADO (AGF 11). When serving as the Sixth Fleet flagship the PUGET SOUND was homeported at Gaeta, Italy; she has since shifted her home port to Norfolk, Virginia. As fleet flagship the PUGET SOUND carried some 225 flag personnel.

All ships of this class are being decommissioned and laid up in reserve:

SAMUEL GOMPERS	decomm. 27 Oct 1995
PUGET SOUND	decomm. 31 Jan 1996
YELLOWSTONE	decomm. 31 Jan 1996
ACADIA	decomm. 16 Dec 1994
CAPE COD	decomm. 30 Sep 1995

The SHENANDOAH is scheduled to be decommissioned and laid up late in 1996.

Class: The AD 39 was authorized in the fiscal 1969 shipbuilding program but was canceled prior to the start of construction because of cost overruns in other new-ship programs. The AD 40 was authorized in fiscal 1973 but was not built. An AD 45 was planned for the fiscal 1980 program but was not funded. Two additional tenders planned for fiscal 1987 and 1988 were deleted from the five-year program of January 1984.

The AD 41 and later ships are officially considered the YELLOWSTONE class. The SHENANDOAH was placed in commission special at San Diego and in full commission at Norfolk on the date shown above.

Design: The SAMUEL GOMPERS was SCB No. 244; subsequent ships were No. 700 in the new SCB series. These ships are similar to the L.Y. SPEAR (AS 36)-class submarine tenders.

A landing platform and hangar for DASH helicopters were provided in the AD 37 and 38. The hangar on the SAMUEL GOMPERS has been converted to a repair shop; the PUGET SOUND's hangar is 54⅓ feet (16.55 m) long, 22⅓ feet (6.8 m) wide, and 16 feet (4.9 m) high; she also has TACAN.

The ships have two 30-ton-capacity cranes and two 6½-ton cranes.

Guns: As built, the AD 37 and 38 had a single 5-inch/38-cal DP gun forward with a Mk 56 GFCS; this armament was removed. Plans to install NATO Sea Sparrow missile launchers in these ships were dropped.

The lead ship of the SAMUEL GOMPERS class shows the massive bulk of a tender's hull, filled with workshops, storerooms, compartments for weapons stowage, and accommodations for a large crew. (1994, Giorgio Arra)

The CAPE COD at anchor in Hong Kong. Tenders have large cranes amidships to lift weapons and parts for ships being serviced and to handle the tender's workboats. Note the stern anchor. (1994, Giorgio Arra)

DESTROYER TENDERS: "DIXIE" CLASS

Number	Name	Comm.	Notes
AD 14	Dixie	1940	stricken 15 June 1982
AD 15	Prairie	1940	decomm./stricken 26 Mar 1993
AD 17	Piedmont	1944	stricken 30 Sep 1982; to Turkey on 18 Oct 1982
AD 18	Sierra	1944	decomm./stricken 29 Oct 1993
AD 19	Yosemite	1944	decomm./stricken 27 Jan 1994; to NDRF 12 Apr 1994

This five-ship class was one of three series of large tender-type ships begun in the late 1930s, the others being the Vulcan (AR 5) and Fulton (AS 11) classes. During their very long careers the above ships were modernized to support surface warships fitted with ASROC, improved electronics, etc.

See 15th Edition/pages 221–22 for Dixie class characteristics.

POST–WORLD WAR II DESTROYER TENDERS

World War II destroyer tenders reached hull number AD 36, with many of these ships serving well into the Cold War era.

Three destroyer tenders were reclassified as repair ships: Klondike (AD 22) to AR 22 in 1960, Markab (AD 21) to AR 23 in 1959, and Grand Canyon (AD 28) to AR 28 in 1971.

Number	Name	Notes
AD 22–25	Klondike class	modified C3 design
AD 26–29	Shenandoah class	modified C3 design
AD 30	Shenandoah class	canceled 1945
AD 31	Tidewater	Shenandoah class
AD 32	New England (ex-AS 28)	canceled 1945
AD 33	Shenandoah class	canceled 1945
AD 34	Alcor (ex-AR 10, AG 34)	
AD 35	Shenandoah class	canceled 1945
AD 36	Bryce Canyon	Shenandoah class

REPLENISHMENT SHIPS

AUXILIARY DRY CARGO SHIPS: NEW CONSTRUCTION

A major class of UNREP ships is being planned with the designation ADC(X) for replenishment/dry cargo ship. This class is intended to eventually replace the AE/AFS type ships.

During the early stages of design and development, the ADC(X) is being based on a commercial cargo ship design. The lead ship is planned for authorization in fiscal 2000; series production is to begin with one ship in fiscal 2002.

AMMUNITION SHIPS

AMMUNITION SHIPS: MODIFIED "KILAUEA" CLASS

The planned ammunition ships of the modified Kilauea class (AE 36–40) were deferred in favor of the construction of additional AOE-type replenishment ships. With the lead ship initially planned for the fiscal 1986 shipbuilding program, the ships were continually delayed until, when the program was halted, one ship was planned for fiscal 1991, one for fiscal 1992, two for fiscal 1993, and one for fiscal 1994.

These ships were to have been slightly larger than the Kilauea class, with gas turbine propulsion (two LM 2500s). See 14th Edition/pages 250–51 for characteristics.

8 AMMUNITION SHIPS: "KILAUEA" CLASS

Number	Name	FY	Launched	Commissioned	Status
T-AE 26	Kilauea	65	9 Aug 1967	10 Aug 1968	**MSC-PA**
T-AE 27	Butte	65	9 Aug 1967	29 Nov 1968	**MSC-AA**
AE 28	Santa Barbara	66	23 Jan 1968	11 July 1970	**AA**
AE 29	Mount Hood	66	17 July 1968	1 May 1971	**PA**
T-AE 32	Flint	67	9 Nov 1970	20 Nov 1971	**MSC-PA**
AE 33	Shasta	67	3 Apr 1971	26 Feb 1972	**PA**
AE 34	Mount Baker	68	23 Oct 1971	22 July 1972	**AA**
T-AE 35	Kiska	68	11 Mar 1972	16 Dec 1972	**MSC-PA**

Builders:	AE 26, 27	General Dynamics, Quincy, Mass.
	AE 28, 29	Bethlehem Steel, Sparrows Point, Md.
	AE 32–35	Ingalls Shipbuilding, Pascagoula, Miss.
Displacement:	9,238 tons light	
	19,937 tons full load	
Length:	563⅝ feet (171.9 m) overall	
Beam:	81 feet (24.7 m)	
Draft:	27¹¹⁄₁₂ feet (8.5 m)	
Propulsion:	3 steam turbines (General Electric); 22,000 shp; 1 shaft	
Boilers:	3 600 psi (41.7 kg/cm²) (Foster Wheeler)	
Speed:	22 knots (20 sustained)	
Range:	18,000 n.miles (33,336 km) at 11 knots	
	10,000 n.miles (18,520 km) at 20 knots	
Manning:	T-AE 26	123 civilian + 40 Navy (2 officers + 38 enlisted)
	AE 28, 34	407 (21 officers + 386 enlisted)
	AE 29	400 (21 officers + 379 enlisted)
	AE 33	405 (21 officers + 384 enlisted)
Helicopters:	2 UH-46 Sea Knight	
Guns:	2 20-mm Phalanx CIWS Mk 16 (2 multi-barrel) in Navy-manned ships	
	4 .50-cal machine guns (4 single) in Navy-manned ships	
Radars:	SPS-10F surface search	
	SPS-64(V)9 navigation	
EW systems:	SLQ-25 Nixie in Navy-manned ships	
	SLQ-32(V)1 in Navy-manned ships	

These are high-capability underway replenishment ships, fitted with the FAST system for the rapid transfer of missiles and other munitions.

All of these ships are being taken out of Navy commission and transferred to the Military Sealift Command for operation by civilian crews with Navy communications and helicopter detachments. (Navy manning data for the most recently transferred ships are indicated above.)

Kilauea	transferred to MSC	1 Oct 1980
Butte	transferred to MSC	June 1996
Flint	transferred to MSC	4 Aug 1995
Kiska	transferred to MSC	Aug 1996

The four other ships will be transferred at a later date.

Design: SCB No. 703. The Kilauea design provides for the ship's main cargo spaces forward of the superstructure and a helicopter landing area aft. A hangar approximately 50 feet (15.2 m) long, 15½ to 17½ feet (4.7 to 5.3 m) wide, and 16⅔ to 17¾ feet (5.1 to 5.4 m) high is built into the superstructure. Cargo capacity is approximately 6,500 tons.

Guns: As built, the ships had eight 3-inch/76-cal Mk 33 guns in twin mounts with two Mk 56 GFCS. Their armament was reduced during the late 1970s; the Navy-manned ships lost their last two 3-inch gun mounts in the late 1980s. Those ships assigned to the MSC are disarmed.

The KISKA at anchor, showing the four replenishment masts forward. These ships can transfer a limited amount of fuel as well as munitions to ships during alongside Underway Replenishment (UNREP) operations. A Phalanx CIWS is mounted forward, port side, and on the after superstructure, starboard side. (1994, Giorgio Arra)

The FLINT when still manned by Navy personnel, prior to transfer to the Military Sealift Command. A UH-46D Sea Knight VERTREP helicopter is parked aft; the ship can hangar two of these aircraft. The Phalanx CIWS mounts were on the starboard side (forward) and port side (amidships). (1994, Giorgio Arra)

AMMUNITION SHIPS: "SURIBACHI" CLASS

Number	Name	Comm.	Notes
AE 21	SURIBACHI	1956	decomm./stricken 2 Dec 1994
AE 22	MAUNA KEA	1957	decomm. 11 July 1995; in reserve (PR)
AE 23	NITRO	1959	decomm. 28 Apr 1995; in reserve (AR).
AE 24	PYRO	1959	decomm. 31 May 1994
AE 25	HALEAKALA	1959	decomm./stricken 10 Dec 1993

These ships were designed specifically for underway replenishment of munitions. The MAUNA KEA was transferred to the Naval Reserve Force on 1 October 1979 and the PYRO on 1 September 1980; however, the heavy operating tempo in the Indian Ocean–Persian Gulf area in the early 1980s led to their being returned to the active fleet on 1 January 1982 and 1 June 1982, respectively.

The HALEAKALA was transferred to the National Defense Reserve Fleet on her strike date. The MAUNA KEA is being temporarily retained in reserve as a "mobilization asset" and may be returned to service as an MSC-operated ship. The NITRO is scheduled to be retained for spare parts until fiscal 1998, and then she will be scrapped.

Class: The three later ships were also referred to as the NITRO class. (The AE 21 and AE 22 are SCB No. 114; AE 23–25 are No. 114A.)

World War II–era ammunition ships reached hull AE 20.

See 15th Edition/pages 224–25 for SURIBACHI class characteristics.

STORE SHIPS

These ships carried refrigerated stores and general cargo for the underway replenishment of ships at sea.

STORE SHIP: "RIGEL" CLASS

The RIGEL (T-AF 58), the Navy's last refrigerated store ship, was placed out of service on 9 September 1992, stricken on 16 May 1994, and transferred to the NDRF. She had been commissioned in 1955. (The RIGEL was not returned to naval service as reported earlier.)

Class: Two ships of this class were constructed, the RIGEL and VEGA (AF 59). They were built specifically for naval service as "reefers."

World War II–era store ships reached hull number AF 47. The AF 48–60 were merchant hulls configured as store ships; their role in the fleet was taken over by the more versatile AFS/AOE/AOR types.

See 15th Edition/page 226 for RIGEL class characteristics.

COMBAT STORE SHIPS

These ships combined the capabilities of early store ships (AF), stores-issue ships (AKS), and aviation store ships (AVS), carrying refrigerated and dry stores as well as parts and other cargo for underway replenishment of ships at sea. They do not carry bulk petroleum products as do the AOE-AOR replenishment ships.

3 COMBAT STORE SHIPS: EX-BRITISH STORE SUPPORT SHIPS

Number	Name	Launched	Completed	U.S. In Service	Status
T-AFS 8	Sirius	7 Apr 1966	22 Dec 1966	17 Jan 1981	**MSC-AA**
T-AFS 9	Spica	22 Feb 1967	21 Mar 1967	4 Nov 1981	**MSC-PA**
T-AFS 10	Saturn	16 Sep 1966	10 Aug 1967	30 Sep 1984	**MSC-AA**

Builders:	Swan Hunter & Wighman Richardson, Wallsend-on-Tyne (England)
Displacement:	9,010 tons light 16,792 tons full load
Length:	489⅚ feet (149.35 m) waterline 523¼ feet (159.5 m) overall
Beam:	72 feet (22.0 m)
Draft:	25½ feet (7.8 m)
Propulsion:	1 turbo-charged diesel engine (Wallsend-Sulzer 8RD76); 12,700 bhp; 1 shaft
Speed:	19 knots
Range:	27,500 n.miles (50,930 km) at 12 knots 11,000 n.miles (20,372 km) at 19 knots
Manning:	110–125 civilian + 49 Navy (5 officers + 44 enlisted)
Helicopters:	2 UH-46 Sea Knight
Radars:	2 . . . . navigation

These ships are former Royal Navy replenishment ships acquired by the U.S. Navy because of the increased logistics demands of maintaining two carrier battle groups in the Persian Gulf–Indian Ocean area following the crises and conflicts in that region that began with the Iranian Revolution of 1979. The ships were all previously operated as Royal Fleet Auxiliaries (RFA) with civilian crews.

With the purchase of the third British ship, the Navy dropped plans to construct an additional AFS under the fiscal 1987 shipbuilding program.

Class: This was a three-ship class, their British names being Lyness, Tarbatness, and Stromness, respectively. The Lyness was originally acquired on 17 January 1981 by the U.S. government on a bare-boat charter for one year. At that time she was placed in U.S. service (renamed Sirius). She was permanently acquired by the Navy on 1 March 1982.

The Tarbatness was acquired on time charter on 30 September 1981; that status changed to bare-boat charter on 4 November 1981, at which time she was placed in U.S. service (and renamed Spica). The Navy permanently acquired her on 30 September 1982.

The Stromness was acquired on 1 October 1983 (renamed Saturn).

The Sirius and Spica were purchased under the fiscal 1982 program at a total cost of $37 million. The Saturn was purchased in fiscal 1984 for $13 million (plus $3.1 million in spare parts for the entire class).

Modernization: In U.S. service the ships have been modernized with the provision of improved communication and UNREP facilities, plus automated data processing. All have been fitted with twin helicopter hangars.

The Saturn is one of eight British-built auxiliary ships acquired by the U.S. Navy since the early 1970s: three store ships, two ocean survey ships (AGS), and three salvage and rescue ships (ATS). In U.S. service the store ships have been fitted with helicopter facilities, greatly enhancing their UNREP capability. (1992, Leo Van Ginderen collection)

The SIRIUS showing the three replenishment stations on the starboard side; three are also to port. U.S. UNREP ships can replenish to both sides simultaneously. Carriers are always replenished to port of the UNREP ship because of the starboard location of the carriers' island structure. (1995, Leo Van Ginderen collection)

5 COMBAT STORE SHIPS: "MARS" CLASS

Number	Name	FY	Launched	Commissioned	to MSC	Status
T-AFS 1	MARS	61	15 June 1963	21 Dec 1963	1 Feb 1993	**MSC-PA**
T-AFS 3	NIAGARA FALLS	64	26 Mar 1966	29 Apr 1967	23 Sep 1994	**MSC-PA**
T-AFS 5	CONCORD	65	17 Dec 1966	27 Nov 1968	15 Oct 1992	**MSC-AA**
T-AFS 6	SAN DIEGO	66	13 Apr 1968	24 May 1969	11 Aug 1993	**MSC-AA**
T-AFS 7	SAN JOSE	67	12 Dec 1969	23 Oct 1970	2 Nov 1993	**MSC-PA**

Builders:	National Steel & Shipbuilding, San Diego, Calif.
Displacement:	9,200–9,400 tons light 16,070 tons full load
Length:	529⅚ feet (161.5 m) waterline 580⅚ feet (177.1 m) overall
Beam:	79 feet (24.1 m)
Draft:	24 feet (7.3 m)
Propulsion:	2 steam turbines (De Laval except Westinghouse in AFS 6); 22,000 shp; 1 shaft
Boilers:	3 600 psi (41.7 kg/cm²) (Babcock & Wilcox)
Speed:	21 knots
Range:	18,000 n.miles (33,336 km) at 11 knots 10,000 n.miles (18,520 km) at 20 knots
Manning:	124–134 civilian + 49 Navy (5 officers + 44 enlisted)
Helicopters:	2 UH-46 Sea Knight
Guns:	removed
Radars:	LN-66 navigation SPS-10 surface search

These are large, built-for-the-purpose underway replenishment ships that combine the capabilities of store ships (AF) and stores-issue ships (AKS). Seven ships of this class were originally in active Navy service; six have been transferred to MSC operation with civilian crews. During modification for MSC operation their cargo-handling capability was enhanced (e.g., the addition of more cargo elevators).

Class: Originally, this class consisted of seven ships. The SYLVANIA (AFS 2) was decommissioned from the active fleet on 26 May 1994 and stricken on 5 January 1995; the WHITE PLAINS (AFS 4) was decommissioned and stricken on 17 April 1995 (to be retained for spare parts until fiscal 1998).

Three additional ships of this class were originally planned in the fiscal 1977–1978 shipbuilding programs; they were not requested by the administration in those years.

Design: The AFS 1–3 were SCB No. 208; the later ships were No. 705 in the later SCB series. These ships have five cargo holds (one refrigerated) for a 7,000-ton total cargo capacity. A large helicopter deck is fitted with a hangar 46¾ to 51 feet (14.25 to 15.55 m) in length and 16 to 23 feet (4.9 to 7.0 m) wide.

Electronics: When manned by a Navy crew, these ships had the SLQ-32(V)1 ECM system and SLQ-25 Nixie towed acoustic torpedo decoy.

Engineering: Two boilers are normally used for full-power steaming, with the third shut down for maintenance.

Guns: These ships were completed with four 3-inch twin gun mounts: one pair of mounts was installed forward and a second pair aft of the funnel. Two mounts were deleted from all ships but the WHITE PLAINS during the late 1970s; all ships lost their Mk 56 GFCS as well as their SPS-40 air-search radar.

The WHITE PLAINS carried eight 3-inch guns into the mid-1980s, when she beached two twin mounts in favor of two Phalanx CIWS. The other ships were to be similarly rearmed, but only the SYLVANIA was so armed prior to transfer to MSC operation. All guns have now been removed for MSC service.

The WHITE PLAINS, with twin 3-inch/50-cal AA mounts forward and low-visibility markings on her bow. Five of the MARS-class combat store ships have been transferred to the Military Sealift Command for operation with civilian crews; the SYLVANIA and WHITE PLAINS have been stricken. These ships have five replenishment stations to starboard and five to port. (1994, Giorgio Arra)

The SAN DIEGO showing her large helicopter landing area and twin hangars for UH-46D Sea Knights. Helicopters speed the transfer of munitions and provisions, and VERTREP often begins long before the UNREP ship comes alongside the ship being replenished. (1992, Giorgio Arra)

MISCELLANEOUS AUXILIARIES

1 SOUND TRIALS SHIP: "HAYES"

Number	Name	FY	Launched	Commissioned	Status
T-AG 195 (ex-T-AGOR 16)	HAYES	67	2 July 1970	21 July 1971	**MSC-AA**

Builders:	Todd Shipyards, Seattle, Wash.
Displacement:	3,543 tons light 4,037 tons full load
Length:	220 feet (67.1 m) waterline 246 5/12 feet (75.1 m) overall
Beam:	75 feet (22.9 m)
Draft:	22 5/6 feet (6.97 m)
Propulsion:	diesel-electric (3 Caterpillar 3516 geared diesels); 5,400 shp; 2 shafts
Speed:	12 knots
Range:	2,000 n.miles (3,700 km) at 10 knots
Manning:	19 civilian + 30 technicians
Helicopters:	no facilities
Radars:	Raytheon TM 1650/6X navigation Raytheon TM 1660/12S navigation

The HAYES is a catamaran built specifically for use as an oceanographic research ship. She has been converted to an acoustic research ship to replace the sound barge MONOB ONE (YAG 61) in support of noise measuring nuclear-propelled submarines. In her new role the HAYES can transport, deploy, and retrieve acoustic arrays, as well as conduct acoustic research. She is operated by an MSC civilian crew.

Following service as an oceanographic research ship (T-AGOR 16), the HAYES was laid up from 1983 until 1989, when her conversion to a sound trials ship began. That work was completed and the ship returned to service on 19 June 1992.

The HAYES operates in the Exuma Sound and Tongue of the Ocean in the Bahama Islands under sponsorship of the David Taylor Research Center. She is homeported at Port Canaveral, Florida.

Classification: Changed from T-AGOR 16 to T-AGS 195 on 20 March 1989.

Conversion: The HAYES was to have been converted to a sound trials ship under a contract awarded on 20 February 1987 to the Tacoma Boatbuilding Company, in Tacoma, Washington. Conversion began on 27 August 1989, but the contract with Tacoma was terminated and the ship towed to the Puget Sound Naval Shipyard on 1 December 1990 for completion at that yard. She was placed in MSC service in 1992.

Design: SCB No. 726. The HAYES has two hulls, each with a 24-foot (7.3-m) beam, spaced 27 feet (8.2 m) apart for an overall ship beam of 75 feet (22.9 m). Berthing and messing spaces are located in the forward superstructure "block," while the laboratory is located aft.

The catamaran design provides a stable work platform with a large open-deck area; also, a centerline well makes it possible to lower research equipment into sheltered water between the two hulls. Some sea-keeping problems were encountered in the design, however, and consequently, it has not been repeated. In particular, the HAYES suffered excessive pitching in her AGOR role and was not considered particularly successful as a seagoing research ship.

The HAYES was built simultaneously with the catamaran submarine rescue ships of the PIGEON (ASR 21) class. This design differs considerably from the SWATH design employed for ocean surveillance (AGOS) ships (see below).

Electronics: The ship conducts noise measurements with a towed array at a towing speed of 3 to 10 knots.

Engineering: The AG conversion included providing a high degree of automation in the engineering spaces; the original four high-speed diesel engines driving controllable-pitch propellers were replaced. The three diesel-electric propulsion engines, as well as two laboratory ship service generators, are located in large enclosures above the main deck and between the two deckhouses, totally isolated from the ship's "skin."

An auxiliary 165-hp diesel engine is provided in each hull to permit a "creeping" speed of 2 to 4 knots when the main propulsion is shut down.

The HAYES, which supports research and development of advanced acoustic sensors in addition to work on submarine noise reduction efforts. (1992, Courtesy Capt. David W. Muir/USNS HAYES)

The HAYES, following an extensive conversion to a sound trials ship. The ship now meets the very stringent self-generated noise levels required to measure other ships' ship-generated noises specified in the Navy's submarine noise reduction program. (1994, Courtesy Capt. David W. Muir/USNS HAYES)

1 NAVIGATION RESEARCH SHIP: CONVERTED OILER (T2-SE-A2)

Number	Name	Launched	Acquired	T-AGM in service	Status
T-AG 194 (ex-T-AGM 19, AO 122)	VANGUARD	25 Nov 1943	21 Oct 1947	28 Feb 1966	**MSC-AA**

Builders:	Marine Ship, Sausalito, Calif.
Displacement:	16,800 tons light 21,478 tons full load
Length:	595 feet (181.4 m) overall
Beam:	75 feet (22.9 m)
Draft:	25 feet (7.6 m)
Propulsion:	1 steam turbine with turbo-electric drive (General Electric); 8,700 shp; 1 shaft
Boilers:	2 600 psi (41.7 kg/cm^2) (Babcock & Wilcox)
Speed:	16 knots
Range:	27,000 n.miles (50,000 km) at 16 knots
Manning:	200 civilian
Helicopters:	no facilities
Radars:	Raytheon 1650/9X navigation Raytheon 1660/12S navigation

The VANGUARD is a former Mission-class tanker that was extensively converted for the missile range instrumentation role; she was subsequently modified for use as a navigation test ship for Trident strategic missile submarines.

The ship initially served as a merchant tanker (MISSION SAN FERNANDO) and was then acquired by the Navy (date above) and placed in service as an oiler (AO 122) with the Naval Transportation Service (NTS); she was transferred to MSTS service and changed to T-AO 122 when that service was created on 1 October 1949. She has been in and out of service as the oiler/tanker requirements have changed: to the NDRF on 10 May 1946; reacquired by the Navy on 21 October 1947 and placed in NTS/MSTS operation; to the NDRF on 24 May 1955; stricken on 22 June 1955; reacquired by the Navy on 21 June 1956; stricken and returned to the NDRF on 4 September 1957; reacquired by the Navy on 28 September 1964 for conversion to T-AGM 19; and converted and employed as AGM (see *Conversions* notes).

The ship was assigned to the Navy's Strategic Systems Programs on 1 October 1978 for conversion to a navigation research ship to replace the COMPASS ISLAND (AG 153). She initially served as T-AGM 19 but was changed to T-AG 194 on 30 September 1980.

Class: The three AGMs of this type were the largest of the 23 range instrumentation ships operated by the United States.

The similar tanker MISSION DE PALA was acquired as the AO 114 and converted to the missile range instrumentation ship REDSTONE (T-AGM 20). She was taken out of MSC service and assigned to the NDRF on 6 August 1993 and stricken on 7 December 1993.

A third ship of this type, the tanker MISSION SAN JUAN, was acquired by the Navy as the AO 126. She was converted to the MERCURY (T-AGM 21), stricken on 28 April 1970, and sold for commercial service.

Conversions: The VANGUARD was extensively converted in 1964–1966 to the AGM configuration at the General Dynamics yard in Quincy, Massachusetts. A 72-foot (21.95-m) section was installed amidships, increasing the ship's original length and beam from 523½ feet (159.6 m) and 68 feet (20.7 m), respectively. The ship was fitted with missile/space tracking systems, extensive communications equipment, and accommodations for a large technical staff.

The VANGUARD was converted in 1980 to a navigation research ship at the Todd Corporation's San Francisco yard.

Names: The VANGUARD was built as the MISSION SAN FERNANDO; she was renamed MUSCLE SHOALS on 8 April 1965 and then VANGUARD on 1 September 1965.

Operational: The ex-tankers were converted specifically to support the Apollo lunar flight program, with the VANGUARD operating in the Atlantic during manned flights to the moon.

The VANGUARD entering the harbor at Port Canaveral, Florida. As a navigation research ship she lost the impressive array of antennas that she carried as a missile range instrumentation ship. The VANGUARD has a tall, slender funnel aft of the after superstructure. (1995, John Bouvia)

1 HEAVY LIFT SHIP: "GLOMAR EXPLORER"

Number	Name	Launched	Completed	Status
AG 193	GLOMAR EXPLORER	14 Nov 1972	July 1973	NDRF

Builders:	Sun Shipbuilding and Dry Dock, Chester, Pa.
Displacement:	63,300 tons full load
Tonnage:	39,705 DWT
	27,445 GRT
	18,511 tons net
Length:	556 11/12 feet (169.8 m) waterline
	618 3/4 feet (188.7 m) overall
Beam:	115 2/3 feet (35.3 m)
Draft:	46 11/12 feet (14.3 m)
Propulsion:	diesel-electric (5 Nordberg diesel engines; 6 General Electric motors); 13,200 shp; 2 shafts
Speed:	10.8 knots
Range:	
Manning:	approx. 180 civilian
Helicopters:	landing area
Radars:	2 . . . . navigation

The GLOMAR EXPLORER was built and operated by the Central Intelligence Agency specifically to lift the remains of a Soviet Golf-class (Project 629) ballistic missile submarine (SSB) that sank in the mid-Pacific in 1968. The ship lifted the forward portion of the submarine from a depth of three miles (4.8 km) in 1974 in a clandestine operation given the code name Jennifer. (The ship's cover story was a seafloor mining operation under the aegis of millionaire Howard Hughes through the Summa Corporation for his Global Marine Development firm.)

The ship was acquired by the Navy on 30 September 1976; she was transferred to the Maritime Administration on 17 January 1977 and laid up in the National Defense Reserve Fleet in Suisun Bay, California.

Subsequent Navy efforts to sell the ship failed, and in 1978 she was leased to Global Marine Development for a commercial seafloor mining venture. She was to be operated by the Lockheed Missiles and Space Company in that role, but that lease was terminated and the ship was returned to Navy control on 25 April 1980 and again assigned to the Maritime Administration on the same date.

In late 1979 it was planned to provide the ship to the National Science Foundation as a deep-sea drilling ship. After modification she was to have the capability of drilling into the earth at an operating depth of approximately 15,000 feet (4,573 m). That project was not funded.

The ship remains on the Naval Vessel Register and is laid up in Suisun Bay.

Classification: When acquired by the Navy in 1976 the GLOMAR EXPLORER was assigned hull number AG 193.

Cost: The cost of the ship at the time of construction was estimated at approximately $350 million. Certain related equipment and the cost of the HMB-1 submersible barge, plus personnel, brought the total project cost to an estimated $550 million.

Design: The ship was designed specifically to lift the sunken Golf-class submarine from a depth of 16,500 feet (5,030 m), employing a heavy-lift system that included attaching a grappling claw to the ship clandestinely via a submersible barge (designated HMB-1). Reportedly, the barge would also be used to hide the Soviet submarine had the entire 330-foot (100.6-m) submarine been salvaged. In the event, the portion salvaged could be accommodated in a large underwater hangar, or Moon Pool, within the GLOMAR EXPLORER.

Engineering: Three bow and two stern thrusters are fitted with an automatic position-keeping system to permit precise maneuvering or holding directly over an object on the ocean floor.

Name: As built, the ship was named HUGHES GLOMAR EXPLORER. Although no Navy name notice was ever promulgated, she is listed in the Naval Vessel Register and other official documents as the GLOMAR EXPLORER.

Operational: The GLOMAR EXPLORER arrived at the submarine lift site on 4 July 1974 and, during the month-long operation, lifted the forward portion of the submarine. The amidships section containing three SS-N-5 ballistic missiles with nuclear warheads was not salvaged. Torpedoes were recovered, however, including two reported to have nuclear warheads. The remains of the submarine were studied within the GLOMAR EXPLORER, then either cut apart and packaged for further analyses or jettisoned.

The deep-sea salvage ship GLOMAR EXPLORER at sea. Efforts to employ her as a seafloor exploration/drilling ship have failed, and there is little likelihood that she will ever again be employed in a recovery role. However, the associated HMB-1 submersible barge is being used with the SEA SHADOW project (see chapter 25). A photo of the GLOMAR EXPLORER as laid up in the NDRF appears in the 13th Edition/page 249.

SURVEYING SHIP: "S.P. LEE"

The small surveying ship S.P. LEE (AG 192, formerly AGS 31) was loaned to the U.S. Geological Survey in February 1974; the ship was carried in the Naval Vessel Register in a lease status until formally being transferred on 1 August 1992.

The LEE was taken out of service on 1 August 1992, stricken on 1 October 1992, and transferred to Mexico on 7 December 1992.

HYDROGRAPHIC RESEARCH SHIP: CONVERTED VICTORY TYPE

The hydrographic research ship KINGSPORT (T-AG 164, formerly T-AK 239) was stricken on 31 January 1984 and laid up in the James River (Virginia) group of the NDRF. Stricken *again* on 20 August 1990 due to a Navy records error, she has since been sold for scrap.

See 14th Edition/pages 259–60 for characteristics.

SONAR TRIALS SHIP: "GLOVER"

The MSC-operated sonar trials ship GLOVER (T-AGFF 1) was placed out of service on 28 September 1992 and transferred to the NDRF on that date. She was stricken on 18 August 1994.

The GLOVER was built as an experimental frigate with a modified propeller configuration. The ship was used primarily for research into the 1970s, after which she served as an operational frigate. In 1990 she was reconfigured as a trials ship for the wide-aperture array sonar and placed in MSC service on 15 June 1991. (The forward 5-inch gun mount was retained while she was in MSC service. The GLOVER was the only MSC-operated warship.)

Classification: The GLOVER was authorized as a miscellaneous auxiliary (AG 163), completed as an escort research ship (AGDE 1), and changed to a frigate research ship (AGFF 1) on 30 June 1975. The ship was redesignated as a frigate (FF 1098) on 1 October 1979, being assigned the hull number of a canceled KNOX-class frigate.

She was again changed to AGFF and designated T-AGFF 1 on 15 June 1990.

Design: The ship was similar to the BROOKE (FFG 1) and GARCIA (FF 1040) frigate classes, but with a modified hull and propulsor. The ship had no after weapon (i.e., 5-inch gun or Mk 22 missile launcher).

See 15th Edition/pages 231–32 for characteristics.

INTELLIGENCE COLLECTION SHIPS

The U.S. Navy converted eight cargo hulls to intelligence collection ships in the 1960s; a large force of these platforms was intended to supplement aircraft, submarines, and surface warships employed in this role. The force of converted ships was to be the equivalent of the large force of Soviet intelligence collection ships (AGI).

Converted for the collection of Signals Intelligence (SIGINT), the ships were manned by Navy personnel, but they operated under the aegis of the National Security Agency, with some civilian specialists on board. The ships' cover story was that they were collecting oceanographic and other environmental information, although their real role was readily apparent from their operations and electronic antennas. The ships were designated AGER for Environmental Research and AGTR for Technical Research. They carried a minimal armament of machine guns and small arms.

Three FS/AKL-type cargo ships were converted to this role (AGER 1–3), as were five larger, Liberty- and Victory-type ships (AGTR 1–5). Two smaller cargo-type ships—the PRIVATE JOSEPH E. VALDEZ (AG 169) and SERGEANT JOSEPH E. MULLER (AG 171)—were also employed in the intelligence role in the 1960s.

The U.S. program was abandoned after the Israeli attack on the LIBERTY (AGTR 5) in 1967 and the capture of the PUEBLO (AGER 2) by North Korea in 1968. The PUEBLO remains listed as "Active, In Commission," although the ship has been interned since being captured on 23 January 1968 while some 12 miles off the coast of Wonsan in international waters. The ship remains at Wonsan, having been opened in 1995 for selective tourist visits.

INTELLIGENCE COLLECTION SHIP: EX-REPAIR SHIP

The SPHINX (ARL 24, ex-LST 963) was the last of several scores of LSTs converted to various types of repair and support ships to be operated by the U.S. Navy. Originally completed in 1944, she was in service from 1944 to 1947, 1950 to 1956, and 1967 to 1971; she was recommissioned on 26 July 1985, reportedly to operate off Central America to intercept radio and radar emissions from Marxist Nicaragua.

For her intelligence collection role, the SPHINX was fitted with electronic intercept and direction-finding gear; a helicopter platform was also installed. The SPHINX was decommissioned and stricken on 19 June 1989. She was transferred to the NDRF on 15 June 1990 and allocated in 1994 to the Rio Grande Military Museum, Rio Hondo, Texas.

The SPHINX originally served as a small craft repair ship, one of 39 tank landing ships converted to the ARL configuration to repair and support landing craft in advanced areas: ARL 1–24, 26–33, and 35–41, with the ARL 25 and 34 canceled. Several of these ships survive in foreign navies. The INDRA (ARL 37, ex-LST 1147), which was stricken on 31 December 1977, remained at the Norfolk Naval Shipyard as an accommodations hulk until being transferred to the NDRF on 12 April 1990.

See 14th Edition/pages 316–17 for SPHINX characteristics.

DEEP SUBMERGENCE SUPPORT SHIPS

The hybrid missile test support ship POINT LOMA (T-AGDS 2) was taken out of MSC service and stricken on 1 October 1993; she was transferred to the NDRF on 4 October 1993.

The POINT LOMA was built as a "wet well" dock cargo ship (originally the POINT BARROW, T-AKD 1) to carry vehicles, supplies, and landing craft to support U.S. radar installations in the Arctic. She was assigned to the MSTS upon completion in 1958 and operated in the cargo role until 1965. (The ship was modified that year to carry Saturn missile boosters and other space program equipment from California to Cape Kennedy and served in that role until 1970; she also made some trips to Vietnam during that period to carry landing craft.)

The ship was laid up in 1971–1972 and then returned to general cargo work under the MSC. The ship was shifted to Navy operational control in 1974 and was converted in 1974–1976 to transport and support the research submersible TRIESTE and, subsequently, to support other submersibles. During her 1980–1982 overhaul the POINT LOMA was modified to serve as the support ship for operational test firings of Trident submarine missiles, having been fitted with extensive tracking gear. (The submersible support capability was retained.)

The POINT LOMA was transferred back to MSC operation in 1986 and subsequently supported Trident missile tests in the Pacific. The POINT LOMA was operated by Navy personnel as the AGDS 2 in the submersible support role until 1 October 1986, when she was assigned to the MSC, with a civilian crew, and changed to T-AGDS 2.

Classification: The classification AGDS was established on 3 January 1974. The previous TRIESTE II support ship, the modified floating dry dock WHITE SANDS (ARD 20), was briefly assigned the hull number AGDS 1.

See 15th Edition/pages 233–34 for POINT LOMA characteristics.

MISSILE RANGE INSTRUMENTATION SHIPS

1 MISSILE RANGE INSTRUMENTATION SHIP: MARINER TYPE (C4-S-1A)

Number	Name	Launched	Commissioned	Status
T-AGM 23 (ex-AG 154)	OBSERVATION ISLAND	15 Aug 1953	5 Dec 1958	**MSC-AA**

Builders:	New York Shipbuilding, Camden, N.J.
Displacement:	13,060 tons light
	16,076 tons full load
Length:	563 feet (171.6 m) overall
Beam:	76 feet (23.2 m)
Draft:	29⅚ feet (9.1 m)
Propulsion:	2 steam turbines (General Electric); 22,000 shp; 1 shaft
Boilers:	2 600 psi (41.7 kg/cm²) (Combustion Engineering)
Speed:	20 knots
Range:	17,000 n.miles (31,500 km) at 13 knots
Manning:	80 civilian + 60 technicians
Helicopters:	no facilities
Radars:	Raytheon 1650/9X navigation
	Raytheon 1660/12S navigation
	SPQ-11 missile tracking
	. . . . missile tracking

The OBSERVATION ISLAND is a former missile test ship now employed as a range instrumentation ship, primarily to monitor Russian missile flights in the Pacific.

The ship, completed in February 1954, was built for commercial cargo service. After operating for a brief period she was laid up in the National Defense Reserve Fleet in November 1954. She was transferred to the Navy on 10 September 1956 for conversion to a missile test ship for the Polaris SLBM and commissioned in 1958. She was subsequently modified to launch the Poseidon missile. After completion of the Poseidon development program, the ship was decommissioned on 25 September 1972 and again laid up in the NDRF.

The OBSERVATION ISLAND was reacquired for conversion to a missile range instrumentation ship on 18 August 1977. Converted in 1979–1981, she is now operated by the MSC with a civilian crew in support of the Air Force and the National Aeronautics and Space Administration in the Pacific.

Class: Five Mariner-class merchant ships were acquired by the Navy, three of which were converted to amphibious assault ships

The OBSERVATION ISLAND is the last of five Mariner-class ships acquired by the Navy for conversion to amphibious and research ships. The OBSERVATION ISLAND now serves as a missile range instrumentation ship, tracking U.S. and Soviet-Russian missile and space launches in the Pacific area. (1987, Leo Van Ginderen collection)

The OBSERVATION ISLAND, with the massive Cobra Judy phased array radar antenna facing to port. This photo was taken before the addition of a conventional tracking antenna at the after end of the deckhouse and installation of a king-post type mast forward. Like most research and missile range ships, she is rarely photographed. (1981, U.S. Navy)

(AKA 112, APA 248, APA 249) and two, the COMPASS ISLAND (AG 153) and OBSERVATION ISLAND, to support ships for the Polaris program. A third Mariner was planned to support the Polaris effort (AG 155), but she was not acquired. The COMPASS ISLAND was configured to test strategic missile submarine navigation systems; she was decommissioned on 1 May 1980 and stricken on 1 October 1981.

Classification: The OBSERVATION ISLAND was originally classified YAG 57 for naval service; that was changed to AG 154 on 19 June 1956 when the ship was listed as EAG 154. On 1 April 1968 the ship was "reclassified" as AG 154 to avoid confusion. The ship was changed again to T-AGM 23 on 1 May 1979.

Conversion: The ship was converted to AGM configuration at the Maryland Shipbuilding & Dry Dock Company in Baltimore from July 1977 to April 1981. She was fitted with the Cobra Judy phased-array radar (SPQ-11) aft, and two radar spheres were installed atop her superstructure.

Design: As an AG she was fitted with two SLBM launch tubes.

Engineering: Two bow thrusters are fitted for precise position keeping.

Names: Her merchant name was EMPIRE STATE MARINER.

1 MISSILE RANGE INSTRUMENTATION SHIP: VICTORY TYPE (VC2-S-AP5)

Number	Name	Launched	APA Comm.	T-AGM in service	Status
T-AGM 22 (ex-APA 205)	RANGE SENTINEL	10 July 1944	20 Sep 1944	14 Oct 1971	**MSC-AA**

Builders:	Permanente Metals, Richmond, Calif.
Displacement:	11,860 tons full load
Tonnage:	8,306 GRT 5,301 DWT
Length:	436½ feet (133.1 m) waterline 455 feet (138.8 m) overall
Beam:	62 feet (18.9 m)
Draft:	28⅚ feet (8.8 m)
Propulsion:	2 steam turbines (Westinghouse); 8,500 shp; 1 shaft
Boilers:	2 465 psi (32.3 kg/cm^2) (Combustion Engineering)
Speed:	17.7 knots
Range:	10,000 n.miles (18,520 km) at 15.5 knots
Manning:	68 civilian + 27 technicians
Helicopters:	no facilities
Radars:	Raytheon TM 1650/9X navigation Raytheon TM 1660/12S navigation SPQ-7 missile tracking 3 . . . . missile tracking

The RANGE SENTINEL is a former Navy attack transport that was converted to a missile range instrumentation ship. She served in the amphibious role during World War II, then was laid up and stricken on 1 October 1958. She was reacquired from the Maritime Administration on 22 October 1969 for conversion to an AGM.

The ship operates in support of Trident missile firings in the Atlantic under the sponsorship of the Navy's Strategic Systems Programs.[3]

Class: A total of eight Victory-type merchant ships served in various AGM configurations (T-AGM 1, 3–8, 22).

Classification: Changed from APA 205 to AGM 22 on 16 April 1971.

Converted: Converted between October 1969 and October 1971 to a support ship for Poseidon and later Trident test firings.

Names: The ship's name as APA 205 was SHERBURNE; she was renamed on 26 April 1971.

3. Formerly Strategic Systems Projects Office and, before that, Special Projects Office.

The RANGE SENTINEL is the last Victory-type merchant ship in U.S. government service. A total of 531 Victory ships were built during World War II: 414 as Navy, Army, and merchant cargo ships, and 117 as Navy attack transports (designated APA). The RANGE SENTINEL has four OE-82 satellite communication "dishes" at the after end of the superstructure. (1994, John Bouvia)

The large converted troop transport GEN H.H. ARNOLD (T-AGM 9, ex-AP 139) was transferred to the NDRF on 23 February 1982 and stricken on 1 March 1982. The GEN HOYT S. VANDENBERG (T-AGM 10, ex-AP 145) was transferred to MarAd on 8 February 1983 and remained in the NDRF until stricken on 29 April 1993. These World War II–built ships had been converted to support Air Force ICBM tests, with the VANDENBERG later supporting Navy SLBM test firings.

See 13th Edition/pages 254–55 for characteristics.

MISSILE RANGE INSTRUMENTATION SHIPS: EX-TRANSPORTS

Number	Name	In service*	Notes
T-AGM 1	RANGE TRACKER	1961	ex-AG 160; VC2-S-AP3 design
T-AGM 2	RANGE RECOVERER	1962	ex-AG 161, FS 278
T-AGM 3	LONGVIEW	1960	ex-AK 238; VC2-S-AP3 design
T-AGM 4	RICHFIELD	1959	ex-AK 253; VC2-S-AP2 design
T-AGM 5	SUNNYVALE	1960	ex-AK 256; VC2-S-AP3 design
T-AGM 6	WATERTOWN	1961	VC2-S-AP3 design
T-AGM 7	HUNTSVILLE	1961	VC2-S-AP3 design
T-AGM 8	WHEELING	1964	VC2-S-AP3 design
T-AGM 9	GEN H.H. ARNOLD	1963	ex-AP 139; C4-S-A1 design
T-AGM 10	GEN HOYT S. VANDENBERG	1963	ex-AP 145; C4-S-A1 design
T-AGM 11	TWIN FALLS VICTORY	1964	VC2-S-AP3 design
T-AGM 12	AMERICAN MARINER		EC2 design
T-AGM 13	SWORD KNOT		C1-M-AV1 design
T-AGM 14	ROSE KNOT		C1-M-AV1 design
T-AGM 15	COASTAL SENTRY	1964	ex-AK 212; C1-M-AV1 design
T-AGM 16	COASTAL CRUSADER		C1-M-AV1 design; to AGS 36
T-AGM 17	TIMBER HITCH		C1-M-AV1 design
T-AGM 18	SAMPAN HITCH		C1-M-AV1 design
T-AGM 19	VANGUARD	1966	ex-AO 122; T2-SE-A2 design
T-AGM 20	REDSTONE	1966	ex-AO 114; T2-SE-A2 design
T-AGM 21	MERCURY	1966	ex-AO 126; T2-SE-A2 design
T-AGM 22	RANGE SENTINEL	1971	ex-APA 205; VC2-S-AP5 design
T-AGM 23	OBSERVATION ISLAND	1981	ex-AG 154; C4-S-1a design

*In service as Navy/USAF missile range instrumentation ship.

MISSILE RANGE INSTRUMENTATION SHIPS

Thirteen merchant and naval ships have been acquired by the Navy and ten by the U.S. Air Force (AGM 9–18) to support military and NASA missile/space operations, providing a worldwide telemetry and communications network. All of the ships were eventually operated by the MSC for the Navy, Air Force, and NASA. The ten USAF ships were initially operated on the Atlantic Missile Range by personnel under contract to that service and transferred to the MSC on 28 April 1964. Some were immediately taken out of service.

The submersible support ship POINT LOMA (AGDS 2) also served as a range instrumentation ship (see page 221).

Only three of the 23 ships remain on the Naval Vessel Register.

OCEANOGRAPHIC RESEARCH SHIPS

Oceanographic research ships perform a broad spectrum of basic ocean research. A major U.S. oceanographic research/surveying ship construction program is under way to replace the large number of such ships procured in the 1960s. The older ships have reached the end of their effective service life and are technologically inadequate for modern oceanographic operations. Their replacement ships will be multi-mission designs.

The former oceanographic research ship HAYES (T-AGOR 16) has been reclassified as the T-AG 195 (see page 217).

Operational: All of these ships are operated by civilian crews under the aegis of the MSC (T-AGOR) or by academic institutions under the Navy's University National Oceanographic Laboratory System (UNOLS).

2 + 1 OCEANOGRAPHIC RESEARCH SHIPS: "THOMPSON" CLASS

Number	Name	FY	Launched	In service	Status
AGOR 23	THOMAS G. THOMPSON	87	27 July 1990	9 May 1991	**Academic**
AGOR 24	ROGER REVELLE	93	20 Apr 1995	11 May 1996	**Academic**
AGOR 25	ATLANTIS	94	1 Feb 1996	1997	Building

Builders:	Trinity/Halter Marine, Moss Point, Miss.
Displacement:	2,100 tons light 3,250 tons full load
Length:	274 feet (83.5 m) overall
Beam:	52 feet (15.85 m)
Draft:	17 feet (5.2 m)
Propulsion:	diesel-electric (3 diesel generators/Caterpillar 3516TA, 2 electric motors/General Motors CD6999); 6,000 shp; 2 azimuth propellers
Speed:	15 knots
Range:	11,300 n.miles (20,940 km) at 12 knots
Manning:	20 civilian + 35–40 scientists and technicians
Helicopters:	no facilities
Radars:	. . . . navigation
Sonar:	Krupp-Atlas seafloor mapping

This is a new class of oceanographic research ships especially suited to support Navy research laboratories, academic institutions, and commercial contractors involved in Navy projects (replacing the CONRAD-class ships). The program was designated AGX during the design phase.

A fourth ship of this class is being built for NOAA.

The lead ship, the THOMPSON, was laid down on 29 March 1989.

Design: The ships are being built to commercial standards. They are especially designed for extended at-sea operations. One or more ships may be configured for supporting deep submergence vehicles. They are fitted with a dynamic positioning system to maintain station during research activities. Four laboratory/accommodation vans can be carried on deck in addition to more than 4,000 square feet (372 m^2) of laboratory space.

Endurance is 60 to 70 days.

The AGOR 23 is configured for oceanographic research and coastal survey.

Engineering: In addition to three diesel generators for propulsion, the ship has three ships service power generators (3508TA), plus one emergency generator (3406TA).

The ships are fitted with all-azimuth (or Z-drives) having 360° rotating propellers; there is also a rotating 360°, 1,180-shp bow thruster to provide precise station keeping.

Names: The AGOR 23 was initially to be named EWING. The AGOR 25 honors two previous oceanographic research ships operated by Woods Hole Oceanographic Institution (WHOI), the ATLANTIS I and ATLANTIS II.

Operational: The THOMPSON is operated by the University of Washington (state), replacing her namesake, the former AGOR 9 (subsequently IX 517); the REVELLE will be operated by the Scripps Institution of Oceanography in La Jolla, California; the ATLANTIS by WHOI (in Massachusetts); and the AGOR 26 will be operated by NOAA.

The THOMAS G. THOMPSON is the first of a new series of oceanographic research ships intended for operation by academic institutions in support of naval activities. (1991, Trinity/Halter Marine)

The ROGER REVELLE being side-launched at the Trinity/Halter shipyard. The yard is producing a large number of research ships for the Navy. (1995, Trinity/Halter Marine)

1 OCEANOGRAPHIC RESEARCH SHIP: "GYRE" CLASS

Number	Name	FY	Launched	Delivered	Status
AGOR 22	MOANA WAVE	71	18 June 1973	16 Jan 1974	**Academic**

Builders:	Trinity/Halter Marine, New Orleans, La.
Displacement:	946 tons light
	1,190 tons full load
Length:	204⅙ feet (62.25 m) overall
Beam:	36 feet (11.0 m)
Draft:	14½ feet (4.4 m)
Propulsion:	2 geared diesel engines (Caterpillar); 1,700 bhp; 2 shafts
Speed:	12.5 knots (sustained 11.5 knots)
Range:	8,000 n.miles (14,816 km) at 10 knots
Manning:	13 civilian + 19 scientists
Helicopters:	no facilities
Radars:	. . . . navigation

The MOANA WAVE was one of two small "utility" research ships built specifically for use by academic research institutions. She is operated for the Oceanographer of the Navy by the Hawaii Institute of Geophysics, having been assigned to that institution upon completion. During the early 1980s the MOANA WAVE was employed for at-sea testing of the T-AGOS/SURTASS towed sonar array.

She was laid down on 9 October 1972.

Class: The GYRE (AGOR 21), completed in 1973, was immediately assigned to Texas A&M University for operation. She was stricken on 17 August 1992 and transferred on that same date to the school.

Design: SCB No. 734. This design is based on that of a commercial offshore oil-rig resupply ship. The open deck aft provides space for special-purpose vans and research equipment. Endurance is 40 to 50 days.

Engineering: A 175-hp bow thruster is fitted.

Modifications: The MOANA WAVE conducted trials in 1979–1984 with satellite communications equipment and with the towed SURTASS array for the T-AGOS program. In 1984–1985 the ship was lengthened, adding a deckhouse aft.

The MOANA WAVE as a research ship. She was previously employed as a test ship for the T-AGOS/SURTASS program (see 14th Edition/page 266). In addition to cranes and other lifting gear, she now has a large housing amidships for lowering equipment into the sea. (1991, Leo Van Ginderen collection)

2 OCEANOGRAPHIC RESEARCH SHIPS: "MELVILLE" CLASS

Number	Name	FY	Launched	Commissioned	Status
AGOR 14	MELVILLE	66	10 July 1968	27 Aug 1969	**Academic**
AGOR 15	KNORR	66	21 Aug 1968	14 Jan 1970	**Academic**

Builders:	Defoe Shipbuilding, Bay City, Mich.
Displacement:	1,915 tons standard 2,670 tons full load
Tonnage:	2,100 GRT
Length:	279 feet (85.1 m) overall
Beam:	46⅓ feet (14.1 m)
Draft:	15 feet (4.6 m)
Propulsion:	diesel-electric (4 diesel generators); 3,000 shp; 3 azimuth propellers (1 forward retractable, 2 aft)
Speed:	14 knots
Range:	12,000 n.miles (22,224 km) at 12 knots
Manning:	24 civilian + 34 scientists
Helicopters:	no facilities
Radars:	. . . . navigation

These ships are large research ships. They were extensively modified from 1988 to 1991 (see *Engineering* notes).

The MELVILLE is operated by the Scripps Institution of Oceanography and the KNORR by the Woods Hole Oceanographic Institution, both for the Office of Naval Research under the technical control of the Oceanographer of the Navy. They were assigned to those institutions upon completion.

The MELVILLE was laid down on 12 July 1967 and the KNORR on 9 August 1967.

Class: The AGOR 19 and AGOR 20 were authorized in the fiscal 1968 program, but their construction was canceled.

Design: SCB No. 710. Although these ships have the same SCB number as the CONRAD class, they are quite different. A bow observation dome is fitted. Endurance is 35 to 40 days.

Engineering: These ships were built with a single diesel engine driving two cycloidal (vertical) propellers through long, internal shafts; the forward propeller is located just behind the bow observation dome, and the after propeller is just in front of the rudder. The ships could hold a fixed position in heavy seas with winds up to 35 knots. Cycloidal propulsion—controlled by a "joystick"—allowed the ships to be propelled in any direction and to turn up to 360° in their own length. This type of propulsion also allowed precise station keeping and slow speeds without the use of auxiliary propulsion units.

The ships experienced transmission system difficulties with their original propulsion plant. They were reengined in 1988–1991 to the configuration described above. They have all-azimuth (or Z-drives) with 360° rotating propellers.

Modernization: Both ships were extensively modernized when reengined. See 14th Edition/page 267 for original characteristics.

Operational: The KNORR located the wreck of the British liner TITANIC in the North Atlantic on 1 September 1985 using a remote-controlled search submersible.

The MELVILLE (above) and the similar KNORR have an unusual configuration. Their "mack"—combined mast and stack—structure is amidships, with an enclosed lookout position. These ships are well equipped for their academic role. (1989, Giorgio Arra)

Stern aspect of the research ship KNORR. (1991, Woods Hole Oceanographic Institution)

OCEANOGRAPHIC RESEARCH SHIPS: "CONRAD" CLASS

Number	Name	Completed	Notes
AGOR 3	ROBERT D. CONRAD	1962	to NDRF 26 July 1989
AGOR 4	JAMES M. GILLIS	1962	to Mexico 15 June 1983
AGOR 5	CHARLES H. DAVIS	1963	to New Zealand 10 Aug 1970
AGOR 6	SANDS	1965	to Brazil 1 July 1974
T-AGOR 7	LYNCH	1965	decomm. 21 Oct 1991; stricken 6 Nov 1991
AGOR 9	THOMAS G. THOMPSON	1965	to IX 517 in 1989
AGOR 10	THOMAS WASHINGTON	1965	decomm. 1 Aug 1992; to Chile 28 Sep 1992
T-AGOR 12	DE STEIGUER	1969	decomm. 2 Nov 1992; to Tunisia (same date)
T-AGOR 13	BARTLETT	1969	decomm. 26 July 1993; to Morocco (same date)

Nine ships of this class were built for the U.S. Navy for operation by the MSC and oceanographic institutions. They were small but capable oceanographic research ships. Three ships were operated by the MSC and six by academic institutions.

Those ships marked "decommissioned" were actually taken out of MSC service on the date indicated (MSC ships are not commissioned ships).

The THOMAS G. THOMPSON (AGOR 9) was reclassified as IX 517 on 11 December 1989 (see chapter 25).

See 15th Edition/pages 241–42 for characteristics.

OCEANOGRAPHIC RESEARCH SHIPS

The AGOR 2 was built for the Norwegian government with U.S. offshore procurement funds. The highly capable ELTANIN and MIZAR were extensively converted from Arctic cargo ships (see 14th Edition/pages 269–70 for characteristics).

Number	Name	Completed*	Notes
AGOR 1	JOSIAH WILLIARD GIBBS	1958	ex-AVP 51
AGOR 2	(H.U. SVERDUP)	1960	built in Norway
AGOR 3–7	CONRAD class		
T-AGOR 8	ELTANIN	1961	ex-T-AK 270; C1-ME2-13a design
AGOR 9, 10	CONRAD class		
AGOR 11	MIZAR	1962	ex-T-AK 272; C1-ME2-13a design
AGOR 12, 13	CONRAD class		
AGOR 14, 15	MELVILLE class		
AGOR 16	HAYES	1971	to T-AG 195
AGOR 17	CHAIN	1958	ex-ARS 20
AGOR 18	ARGO	1960	ex-ARS 27
AGOR 19	canceled 1969		
AGOR 20	canceled 1969		
AGOR 21, 22	GYRE class		
AGOR 23–25	THOMAS G. THOMPSON class		

*In service as oceanographic research ships.

OCEAN SURVEILLANCE SHIPS

These ships are configured for operating the Surveillance Towed Array Sensor System (SURTASS), a submarine detection system intended to supplement the seafloor Sound Surveillance System (SOSUS). These ships were designed to operate where SOSUS coverage is inadequate or where the seafloor arrays are damaged or destroyed. The SURTASS data are sent via satellite link to shore facilities for processing and further transmission to ASW forces; however, the ships can provide "raw" acoustic data to ASW ships in the area. (The SURTASS concept differs from the tactical TACTAS system in that the latter is tactical hydrophone arrays towed by warships to supplement hull-mounted sonars.)

The SURTASS carried by the later ocean surveillance ships is being supplemented by a Low-Frequency Active (LFA) system considered suitable for effective submarine detection in shallow/littoral areas as well as deep-ocean areas.

The initial Navy planning for the T-AGOS/SURTASS program called for 18 ships. This was later reduced to 12 ships because of fiscal constraints; however, because of the success of the early ships and the increasing Soviet submarine threat, in the late-1980s the Navy sought a force of at least 27 surveillance ships: the 18 monohull ships of the STALWART class, four SWATH-P ships, and five SWATH-A ships.

In January 1992 the Navy announced its intention to dispose of the monohull ships by the year 1997 because of budget constraints, although the decline of the Soviet submarine threat is usually cited as the reason for this action.[4] Accordingly, the planned force level was reduced to nine SWATH-type ships. Subsequently, contractual problems with the first of the larger SWATH-P ships led to delays in procuring the five ships of this design.

These ships are not armed.

Costs: In 1992, as the Navy revised its T-AGOS force planning, it listed the cost of the SWATH acquisition program as $487 million for the first five SWATH ships (T-AGOS 19–23) and $674 million for the last four ships, for a total of $1.2 *billion.* At that time, annual operating costs were postulated as:

$6.3 million for monohull ships
$7.0 million for SWATH-P ships
$7.7 million for SWATH-A ships

Electronics: The UQQ-2 SURTASS array is a flexible, tubelike structure some 2,600 feet (800 m) long that contains numerous hydrophones. The whole structure is towed by a 6,000-foot (1,830-m) cable. It is neutrally buoyant, with the depth being varied to compensate for environmental conditions. Typical array operating depths are 500 to 1,500 feet (152 to 457 m).

Data from the hydrophone array are generated at a very high rate that is "pre-processed" on board the T-AGOS and sent at a much lower rate, reduced by a factor of ten, via satellite to shore stations. The data rate from ship to shore is about 32,000 bits (32 kilobits) per second.

Operational: The massive decommissioning of T-AGOS ships is taking place despite the Navy's inability to meet certain surveillance operational requirements. For example, early in 1994 Rear Admiral James Prout, the Deputy Chief of Staff for Resources, Requirements,

4. *Undersea Surveillance: Navy Continues to Build Ships Designed for Soviet Threat* (Washington, D.C.: General Accounting Office, December 1992).

and Assessment of the U.S. Pacific Fleet, told the Senate Armed Services Committee, "We were recently unable to support a U.S. Central Command request for full-time deployment of a T-AGOS ship to the Persian Gulf for surveillance purposes."[5]

(5) OCEAN SURVEILLANCE SHIPS: SWATH-A DESIGN

Number	Name	FY	Launched	In service	Status
T-AGOS 23	IMPECCABLE	90	(see notes)	1999	Building
T-AGOS 24	. . . .	99			Planned
T-AGOS 25	. . . .				Planned
T-AGOS 26	. . . .				Planned
T-AGOS 27	. . . .				Planned

Builders:	T-AGOS 23 American Shipbuilding, Tampa, Fla. (see notes)
Displacement:	5,368 tons full load
Length:	281½ feet (85.8 m) overall
Beam:	95¾ feet (29.2 m)
Draft:	26 feet (7.9 m)
Propulsion:	diesel-electric (3 diesel generators; 2 electric motors); 5,000 shp; 2 shafts
Speed:	12 knots sustained
Range:	8,000 n.miles (14,816 km) at 15 knots
Manning:	26 civilian + 19 Navy technicians
Helicopters:	no facilities
Radars:	. . . . navigation
Sonars:	Low-Frequency Active (LFA) UQQ-2 SURTASS

These enlarged SWATH ships will support SURTASS missions in higher sea states, specifically for operations in high-latitude areas. They are intended to operate through sea state 6 on all headings and sea state 7 on the best heading.

The planned production rate of these ships has been slowed. The lead ship was ordered from the Tampa shipyard on 28 March 1991, but work has been halted due to contractual problems with the American Shipbuilding Corporation.[6] The IMPECCABLE was originally to have been laid down in December 1993, launched in March 1994, and completed in January 1995.

The ship was floated in 1995 and transferred to the Halter Marine yard at Gulfport, Mississippi, for completion.

Design: The Small Waterplane Area Twin-Hull (SWATH) form was evaluated in the research craft KAIMALINO (see chapter 25). The SWATH concept differs from that of a catamaran, which has two

5. Barbara Starr, "SOSUS suffers as USN stretches its funding," *Jane's Defence Weekly* (26 March 1994), p. 3.

6. The American Shipbuilding Corporation also defaulted on the construction of two Navy oilers (T-AO 191, 192); see page 237.

An artist's concept of the IMPECCABLE, the "ultimate" U.S. Navy T-AGOS design. The delays in construction of the lead ship may jeopardize the entire planned class of five ships. Note the projection from the stern to keep the towed array clear of the propellers. (U.S. Navy)

The stern of the VICTORIOUS showing the twin, five-blade propellers. The torpedo-like submerged hulls have a streamlined appearance, but a SWATH is built for stability, not for speed. (1990, McDermott)

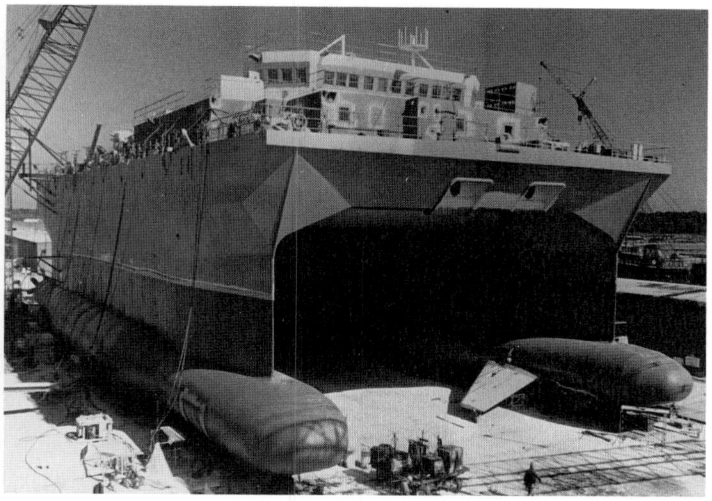

The twin, submerged hulls of the VICTORIOUS have stabilizing fins facing inward, both forward and aft. Twin anchors are set into the bow of the ship. (1990, McDermott)

conventional ship hulls joined together; the SWATH design provides two fully submerged underwater hulls with structures rising through the water to support the ship's superstructure.

The SWATH design provides a large deck space and a high degree of ship stability in rough waters. It was adopted because the monohull T-AGOS ships experienced sea-keeping difficulties in northern latitudes during winter.

Endurance will be 50 to 60 days. Normal SURTASS towing speed will be three knots.

Engineering: To be fitted with two 360° thrusters for station keeping.

Beam:	93½ feet (28.5 m)
Beam of "box":	80½ feet (24.5 m)
Draft:	25 feet (7.6 m)
Propulsion:	diesel-electric (4 Caterpillar-Kato 3512-TA diesel generators; 2 General Electric motors); 3,200 bhp; 2 shafts
Speed:	16 knots; 9.6 knots array towing speed
Range:	3,000 n.miles (5,556 km) at 10 knots
Manning:	22 civilian + 12 Navy technicians
Helicopters:	no facilities
Radars:	. . . . navigation
Sonars:	Low-Frequency Active (LFA) UQQ-2 SURTASS

4 OCEAN SURVEILLANCE SHIPS: "VICTORIOUS" CLASS (SWATH-P)

Number	Name	FY	Launched	In service	Status
T-AGOS 19	Victorious	87	2 May 1990	13 Aug 1991	**MSC-P**
T-AGOS 20	Able	89	14 Feb 1991	24 Mar 1992	**MSC-A**
T-AGOS 21	Effective	89	26 Sep 1991	27 Jan 1993	**MSC-P**
T-AGOS 22	Loyal	89	19 Sep 1992	1 July 1993	**MSC-A**

Builders:	McDermott, Morgan City, La.
Displacement:	2,676 tons light 3,438 tons full load
Length:	190⅔ feet (58.1 m) waterline 234½ feet (71.5 m) overall

These are improved, SWATH-configured SURTASS ships.

A contract was awarded to the McDermott firm in October 1986 for the detailed design and construction of the lead ship of this class, the Victorious , which was laid down on 12 April 1988.

Design: These are the world's first operational military ships with the Small Waterplane Area Twin-Hull design. The design is based on the Navy's research/range support ship Kaimalino (see chapter 25).

Mission endurance is 90 days.

Engineering: The ship's steering system uses a pair of angled rudders aft and a pair of angled canards forward; two azimuth thrusters are fitted forward.

The SWATH design provides the Able with extensive working spaces amidships. No helicopter facilities or combat capabilities are provided in these ships. VERTREP spaces are marked on the deck, amid ships, port and starboard. (U.S. Navy)

The VICTORIOUS was the Navy's first SWATH surveillance ship, the twin, submerged-hull configuration providing enhanced sea-keeping in northern waters. With the planned retirement of the T-AGOS 1–18, the SURTASS force will consist entirely of SWATH ships. (1990, McDermott)

6 OCEAN SURVEILLANCE SHIPS: "STALWART" CLASS

Number	Name	FY	Launched	In service	Status
T-AGOS 1	STALWART	79	11 July 1983	9 Apr 1984	**MSC-A**
T-AGOS 7	INDOMITABLE	81	16 July 1985	1 Dec 1985	**MSC-A**
T-AGOS 8	PREVAIL	81	7 Dec 1985	5 Mar 1986	**MSC-A**
T-AGOS 12	BOLD	82	22 May 1989	20 Oct 1989	**MSC-A**
T-AGOS 16	CAPABLE	86	28 Oct 1988	9 June 1989	**MSC-A**
T-AGOS 17	TENACIOUS	87	17 Feb 1989	29 Sep 1989	PR

Builders:	T-AGOS 1–12 Tacoma Boatbuilding, Wash.
	T-AGOS 13–18 Trinity/Halter Marine, New Orleans, La.
Displacement:	1,600 tons light
	2,285 tons full load
Tonnage:	1,584 GRT
	786 DWT
Length:	203⅔ feet (62.1 m) waterline
	224 feet (68.3 m) overall
Beam:	43 feet (13.1 m)
Draft:	15 feet (4.6 m)
Propulsion:	diesel-electric (4 Caterpillar D-398B diesel generators with General Electric motors); 3,200 bhp; 2 shafts
Speed:	11 knots; 2 to 3 knots array towing speed
Range:	3,000 n.miles (5,556 km) at 11 knots + 90 days on station at 3 knots
Manning:	19 civilian + 9 Navy technicians (enlisted)
Helicopters:	no facilities
Radars:	2 . . . . navigation
	SPS-49 air search in STALWART
Sonars:	UQQ-2 SURTASS

These are monohull SURTASS ships. The program suffered from significant cost increases over original estimates and equipment failures, resulting in at least a several-year delay over the original 1974 schedule.

The TENACIOUS was taken out of T-AGOS service on 14 Feb 1995. The others will be taken out of service and laid up during the next few years.

Class: Originally a class of 18 ships, all are being taken out of service as surveillance ships (see table at end of entry). A plan to provide the Coast Guard with six of the ships withdrawn from the T-AGOS role was rejected by that service because of the ships' slow speed and lack of a helicopter capability. The VINDICATOR and PERSISTENT were the first to have been modified: the berthing and galley areas were changed and Coast Guard electronic equipment as well as minimal armament were added. The Coast Guard service crew was to number 45. The cost of converting the first two ships was $3.7 million.

Three ships have been transferred to NOAA; see chapter 33.

The CONTENDER has been transferred to the Merchant Marine Academy, Kings Point, New York, for service as a training ship (renamed KINGS POINTER). The INVINCIBLE was transferred to the Southern Maine Technical College.

When this edition went to press, three ships were under consideration for transfer to the U.S. Air Force.

Design: The T-AGOS hull is similar to that of the T-ATF 166 class. For MSC operation, a high degree of crew habitability is provided, including single staterooms for all crewmen and three single and four double staterooms for technicians. The T-AGOS 1–12 have four additional berths; the later ships have seven. The T-AGOS 13–18 also have a larger SURTASS operations center and modified machinery layout.

Endurance is rated at 98 days (see *Operational* notes).

Engineering: The four diesel generators drive two main propulsion motors. A bow-thruster powered by a 550-hp electric motor is fitted for station keeping. Special features reduce machinery noise.

Names: T-AGOS 11 was originally named DAUNTLESS, T-AGOS 12, VIGOROUS, and T-AGOS 17, INTREPID; all were renamed during construction.

Operational: Early Navy planning provided for the ships to have 90-day patrol periods, plus 8 days in transit; this would result in more than 300 days at sea per year. This intensity of operations was rejected by the MSC as impractical and unrealistic; they proposed instead a patrol duration of 60 to 74 days, which was undertaken.

Rapidly being discarded, the STALWART class saw little operational service before the end of the Cold War reduced the need for the T-AGOS program. Here the INVINCIBLE reveals the basic appearance of these ships, with their long superstructure, twin funnels, and tripod mast topped with a satellite communications antenna. (1992, Giorgio Arra)

The BOLD, barely under way, shows the large cable reel aft that holds the towed array. (1992, Giorgio Arra)

Another aspect of the BOLD, showing the stern opening for the towed array. These ships are highly specialized; an effort to modify them for Coast Guard use was unsuccessful. (1992, Giorgio Arra)

FORMER OCEAN SURVEILLANCE SHIPS

Number	Name	Comm.	OSIR*	Notes
T-AGOS 2	CONTENDER	1984	1 Oct 1992	stricken 11 Dec 1992; to Merchant Marine Academy, Kings Point, N.Y.
T-AGOS 3	VINDICATOR	1984	30 Mar 1993	stricken 30 Mar 1993
T-AGOS 4	TRIUMPH	1985	20 June 1994	striken 6 Jan 1995; to USAF?
T-AGOS 5	ASSURANCE	1985	28 Mar 1994	stricken 6 Jan 1995; to USAF?
T-AGOS 6	PERSISTENT	1985	11 Oct 1994	stricken 6 Jan 1995
T-AGOS 9	ASSERTIVE	1986	14 Feb 1995	stricken 9 May 1995
T-AGOS 10	INVINCIBLE	1986	6 Feb 1995	stricken 9 May 1995; to Maritime Academy
T-AGOS 11	AUDACIOUS	1989	30 Nov 1995	stricken same date; to USAF?
T-AGOS 13	ADVENTUROUS	1988		to NOAA 1 June 1982
T-AGOS 14	WORTHY	1989		to Geological Survey 17 Mar 1993; stricken 20 May 1993
T-AGOS 15	TITAN	1989	30 Aug 1993	to NOAA 31 Aug 1993
T-AGOS 18	RELENTLESS	1990	17 May 1993	to NOAA 25 Mar 1993; stricken 20 May 1993

*Out of Service, In Reserve.

SURVEYING SHIPS

Surveying ships conduct ocean surveys and collect data in support of fleet operations and systems development. All Navy surveying ships are operated by the Military Sealift Command under the sponsorship of the Naval Oceanographic Command.

The confusion in the numbering of AGS-series ships requires that a list be provided for the convenience of readers of this volume (see table at the end of this section).

None of these ships is armed.

3 + 2 OCEAN SURVEYING SHIPS: "PATHFINDER" CLASS

Number	Name	FY	Launched	In service	Status
T-AGS 60	PATHFINDER	90	4 Oct 1993	5 Dec 1994	**MSC-Active**
T-AGS 61	SUMNER	90	28 Feb 1994	29 May1995	**MSC-Active**
T-AGS 62	BOWDITCH	90	15 Oct 1994	10 June 1996	**MSC-Active**
T-AGS 63	MATTHEW HENSON	94	1997	1998	Building
T-AGS 64	......	96			Authorized

Builders:	Trinity/Halter Marine, Moss Point, Miss.
Displacement:	3,019 tons light 4,762 tons full load
Length:	329 feet (103.3 m) overall
Beam:	58 feet (17.7 m)
Draft:	19 feet (5.8 m)
Propulsion:	diesel-electric (2 General Electric electric motors); 8,000 bhp; 2 azimuth propellers
Speed:	16 knots
Range:	12,000 n.miles (22,236 km) at 12 knots
Manning:	25 civilian + 27 scientists
Helicopters:	no facilities
Radars:	.... navigation

This is a new class of ships for long-range ocean survey and research. Research for a variety of ocean sciences can be conducted. Their design is based on the AGOR 23; the third ship in the series has special features for ice operations.

The PATHFINDER and SUMNER were laid down on 30 January 1991.

Engineering: These ships are propelled and steered through a Z-drive arrangement to azimuth thrusters. A retractable 1,500-hp bow thruster is fitted.

The PATHFINDER shows the graceful, yacht-like lines of this class of ocean surveying ships. The large deck structure houses a variety of laboratories and other working spaces. (U.S. Navy)

The PATHFINDER is fitted with cranes amidships and aft for handling research and surveying gear. (U.S. Navy)

2 COASTAL SURVEYING SHIPS: "JOHN MCDONNELL" CLASS

Number	Name	FY	Launched	In service	Status
T-AGS 51	JOHN MCDONNELL	87	13 Dec 1990	15 Nov 1991	**MSC-AA**
T-AGS 52	LITTLEHALES	87	14 Feb 1991	10 Feb 1992	**MSC-AA**

Builders:	Trinity/Halter Marine, Moss Point, Miss.
Displacement:	2,000 tons full load
Length:	208⅙ feet (63.5 m) overall
Beam:	45 feet (13.7 m)
Draft:	14 feet (4.3 m)
Propulsion:	diesel engines; 1 shaft
Speed:	16 knots sustained
Range:	13,800 n.miles (25,535 km) at 16 knots
Manning:	23 civilian + 10 scientists
Helicopters:	no facilities
Radars:	. . . . navigation

These coastal surveying ships were laid down on 10 November 1988. They are intended to collect bathymetric/hydrographic data in shallow and deep water. They carry small survey launches.

The keel for the MCDONNELL was laid down on 3 August 1989 and that of the LITTLEHALES on 25 October 1989.

The stern of MCDONNELL-class ships has working space and gear, with a crane on the starboard side. (1991, Trinity/Halter Marine)

The LITTLEHALES on builder's trials. She is one of several new research and surveying ships being built for the Navy and Navy-sponsored academic institutions. They replace several old and a few relatively new ships. (1991, Trinity/Halter Marine)

1 OCEAN SURVEYING SHIP: "WATERS"

Number	Name	FY	Launched	In service	Status
T-AGS 45	WATERS	90	1992	26 May 1993	**MSC-PA**

Builders:	Avondale Industries, New Orleans, La.
Displacement:	12,208 tons full load
Length:	442 feet (134.75 m) overall
Beam:	69 feet (21.0 m)
Draft:	21⅙ feet (6.45 m)
Propulsion:	diesel-electric; 7,400 shp; 2 shafts
Speed:	13.2 knots sustained
Range:	
Manning:	62 civilian + 6 Navy (enlisted) + 21 civilian technicians
Helicopters:	no facilities
Radars:	. . . . navigation

This is a large, multifunction surveying ship constructed to replace the MIZAR (T-AGOR 11). The new ship is capable of performing bathymetric, oceanographic, and hydrographic surveys, and she is able to launch and recover a variety of remotely operated vehicles.

The keel for the WATERS was laid down on 21 May 1991.

Design: The ship is fitted with bow and stern thrusters for precise maneuvering.

The WATERS under way in the Gulf of Mexico. Most of her hull volume—except for engineering spaces—is largely void, with 7,339 tons of water ballast being carried. Working spaces and accommodations are in the superstructure. (1993, Avondale Industries)

OCEAN SURVEYING SHIPS: "MAURY" CLASS

Number	Name	In service	Notes
T-AGS 39	Maury	1989	stricken on 28 Oct 1994
T-AGS 40	Tanner	1990	stricken on 14 Jan 1994

These built-for-the-purpose ocean survey ships replaced the outdated Bowditch and Dutton. They were the largest purpose-built U.S. Navy research ships, having been designed, primarily, to conduct hydrographic, magnetic, and gravity surveys.

Note that they were discarded after unprecedentedly short service lives; they were taken out of service and stricken on the same dates. The Tanner suffered major engineering problems and was taken out of service after having steamed only 166,000 n.miles (307,600 km). She is laid up in the James River (Virginia) NDRF as a "spare parts bin" for the Maury.

The Maury was transferred to the California Maritime Academy on 16 September 1994 and renamed Golden Bear (in place of the H.H. Hess; see below).

See 15th Edition/pages 248–49 for characteristics.

OCEAN SURVEYING SHIP: "H.H. HESS"

The large surveying ship H.H. Hess (T-AGS 38) was taken out of service on 5 February 1992, transferred to the NDRF on 21 February 1992, and stricken on 28 July 1992. Although she was to have been transferred to the California State Maritime Academy as a training ship, she was rejected because of a burned-out boiler.

The H.H. Hess was built as a merchant ship, launched in 1964, and acquired by the Navy in 1976 for conversion to an ocean surveying ship.

See 15th Edition/page 249 for characteristics.

4 SURVEYING SHIPS: "SILAS BENT" CLASS

Number	Name	FY	Launched	In service	Status
T-AGS 26	Silas Bent	63	16 May 1964	23 July 1965	**MSC-PA**
T-AGS 27	Kane	64	20 Nov 1965	19 May 1967	**MSC-AA**
T-AGS 33	Wilkes	67	31 July 1969	28 June 1971	PR
T-AGS 34	Wyman	67	30 Oct 1969	3 Nov 1971	**MSC-AA**

Builders:	T-AGS 26 American Shipbuilding, Lorain, Ohio T-AGS 27 Christy Corp., Sturgeon Bay, Wisc. T-AGS 33, 34 Defoe Shipbuilding, Bay City, Mich.
Displacement:	1,790 to 1,935 tons light T-AGS 26, 27 2,558 tons full load T-AGS 33 2,540 tons full load T-AGS 34 2,420 tons full load
Length:	265 feet (80.8 m) waterline 285⅓ feet (87.0 m) overall
Beam:	48 feet (14.6 m)
Draft:	15 feet (4.6 m)
Propulsion:	diesel-electric (2 Alco diesel engines; Westinghouse or General Electric motors); 3,600 bhp; 1 shaft
Speed:	14 knots
Range:	5,800–6,300 n.miles (10,742–11,668 km) at 14 knots 8,000 n.miles (14,816 km) at 13 knots
Manning:	50 civilian + 26 scientists except 41 civilian + 20 scientists in T-AGS 34
Helicopters:	no facilities
Radars:	Raytheon TM 1650/9X navigation Raytheon TM 1660/12S
Sonars:	BQN-17 BOTOSS in T-AGS 34

These ships were designed specifically for surveying operations. They differ in detail. All four ships were operated by the MSC, with some supporting the Navy's SOSUS program.

The Wilkes was taken out of MSC service in 1995.

Design: The first two ships are SCB No. 226; the Wilkes is No. 725 in the new series and the Wyman No. 728.

Electronics: The Wyman is fitted with a BQN-17 bottom survey system.

Engineering: These ships have 350-hp bow propulsion units for precise maneuvering and station keeping.

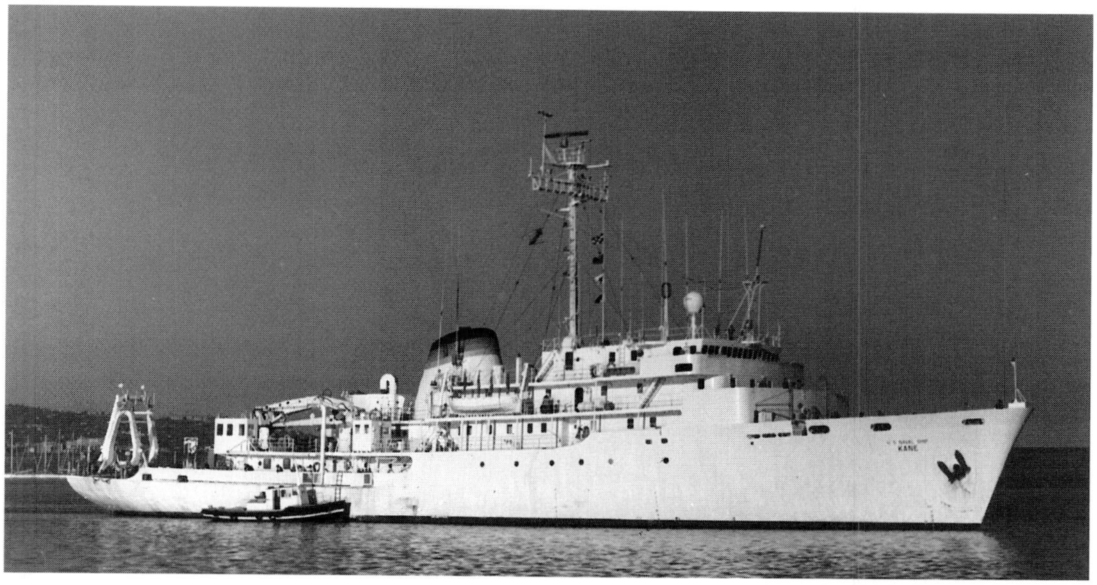

The Kane is typical of a useful class of small surveying ships that are, nevertheless, reaching the end of their effective service life. The Kane has a lifting device aft for handling surveying gear. (1994, Leo Van Ginderen collection)

The WYMAN, which has a clear fantail (i.e., no crane or derrick). (1991, Giorgio Arra)

OCEAN SURVEYING SHIPS: "CHAUVENET" CLASS

Number	Name	In service	Notes
T-AGS 29	CHAUVENET	1970	decomm. 7 Nov 1992; stricken 30 Nov 1992
T-AGS 32	HARKNESS	1971	decomm./stricken 15 Mar 1993

These surveying ships were built in Britain specifically for the U.S. Navy's research role. The "decommission" dates were actually the dates they were taken out of MSC service (MSC ships are not commissioned ships). The CHAUVENET was transferred to the Texas State Maritime Academy and the HARKNESS to the Maine State Maritime Academy as training ships.

See 15th Edition/page 251 for characteristics.

OCEAN SURVEYING SHIPS: VICTORY TYPE

Three former Victory-type merchant ships, acquired by the Navy in 1957 and converted for seafloor charting and magnetic surveys to support the Navy's SSBN programs, have been stricken.

The BOWDITCH (T-AGS 21) was stricken on 26 May 1987 and transferred to the NDRF; she had been heavily damaged during a hurricane while anchored in Rio de Janeiro, Brazil, in January 1987, being rammed by two ships that broke loose from their moorings during the storm.

The DUTTON (T-AGS 22) was taken out of service and transferred to MarAd on 25 October 1989 pending disposal. She was stricken on 14 February 1990.

The MICHELSON (T-AGS 23) was stricken on 15 April 1975.

See 14th Edition/page 277 for characteristics.

The SILAS BENT, lead ship of a long-serving class of surveying ships. (1991, Giorgio Arra)

POST–WORLD WAR II SURVEYING SHIPS

World War II–era surveying ships reached hull number AGS 14. The designations AGSc 12–15 were used for coastal surveying ships (assigned in the same numerical series as AGS). The SAN PABLO and REHOBOTH retained their AVP numbers as surveying ships, throwing the AGS numbering scheme out of sequence, which led to confusion.

Number	Name	In service*	Notes
AGS 15	TANNER	1946	ex-AKA 34; S4-SE2-BE1 design
AGS 16	MAURY	1946	ex-AKA 36; S4-SE2-BE1 design
AGS 17	PURSUIT	1950	ex-MSF 108
AGS 18	REQUISITE	1950	ex-MSF 109
AGS 19	SHELDRAKE	1952	ex-AM 62
AGS 20	PREVAIL	1952	ex-MSF 107
AGS 21	BOWDITCH	1958	VC2-S-AP3 design
AGS 22	DUTTON	1958	VC2-S-AP3 design
AGS 23	MICHELSON	1958	VC2-S-AP3 design
AGS 24	SERRANO	1960	ex-ATF 112
AGS 25	KELLAR	1968	to Portugal 1972
AGS 26, 27	SILAS BENT class		
AGS 28	TOWHEE	1964	ex-MSF 388
AGS 29	CHAUVENET	1970	
AGS 30	SAN PABLO	1948	ex-AVP 30
AGS 31	S.P. LEE	1968	to AG 192 (see above)
AGS 32	HARKNESS	1971	
AGS 33, 34	SILAS BENT class		
AGS 35	SGT GEORGE D. KEATHLEY	1967	ex-APc 117; C1-M-AV1 design
AGS 36	COASTAL CRUSADER	(1969**)	ex-AGM 16
AGS 37	TWIN FALLS	†	ex-AGM 11; VC2-S-AP3 design
AGS 38	H.H. HESS	1976	C4-S-1a design
AGS 39	MAURY	1989	
AGS 40	TANNER	1990	
AGS 41–44	not used		
AGS 45	WATERS	1993	
AGS 46–49	not used		
AGS 50	REHOBOTH	1948	ex-AVP 50
AGS 51	JOHN MCDONNELL	1992	
AGS 52	LITTLEHALES	1992	
AGS 53–59	not used		
AGS 60–64	PATHFINDER class		

*In service as oceanographic surveying ships.
**Never operational as AGS.
†Not converted.

HOSPITAL SHIPS

During the early 1980s the Department of Defense decided to provide two hospital ships to support the deployment of U.S. forces overseas in conventional combat operations. Several alternatives were considered, both merchant ship conversions and new construction.

The candidates for conversion included the superliner UNITED STATES, laid up since her final transatlantic voyage in November 1969. The 990-foot (301.8-m) liner, completed in 1952, carried up to 2,000 passengers and was designed from the outset for conversion to a transport for 14,000 troops. In the AH role she would have had 2,000 to 2,500 beds.

(The UNITED STATES averaged 35.59 knots on her maiden transatlantic voyage and reached 38.32 knots on her sea trials—the fastest merchant ship ever built.)

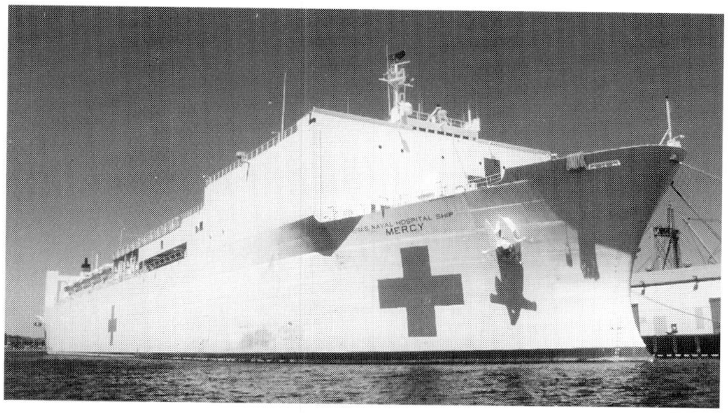

The MERCY displays the high sides of these converted tankers. The principal means of bringing casualties aboard these ships is by helicopter. (1995, Leo Van Ginderen collection)

2 HOSPITAL SHIPS: CONVERTED TANKERS (T8-S-100B)

Number	Name	Launched	In service	Status
T-AH 19	MERCY	19 July 1975	15 Dec 1986	MSC-RRF-P
T-AH 20	COMFORT	12 Feb 1976	1 Dec 1987	MSC-RRF-A

Builders:	National Steel and Shipbuilding, San Diego, Calif.
Displacement:	24,752 tons light 69,360 tons full load
Length:	$854\frac{5}{6}$ feet (260.6 m) waterline 894 feet (272.6 m) overall
Beam:	$105\frac{3}{4}$ feet (32.25 m)
Draft:	$32\frac{5}{6}$ feet (10.0 m)
Propulsion:	1 steam turbine (General Electric); 24,500 shp; 1 shaft
Boilers:	2
Speed:	17.5 knots
Range:	13,400 n.miles (24,817 km) at 17.5 knots
Manning:	73 civilian + 43 Navy communications and support + 1,204 medical/dental (see *Manning* notes)
Patients:	900+ beds (see *Conversion* notes)
Helicopters:	landing area
Radars:	. . . . navigation SPS-67 surface search

These ships are former commercial tankers that have been fully converted to support U.S. forward-deployed troops. They were delivered as tankers to commercial customers on 19 February 1976 and 23 July 1976, respectively.

These are the first ships of the type in U.S. service since the SANCTUARY was decommissioned in March 1974; at that time the SANCTUARY was serving as a naval dependents support ship. They are intended to be based at U.S. ports; in times of crisis or war they would be assigned medical staffs from military hospitals and go to sea with five days' notice as part of the MSC Ready Reserve Force (RRF). The MERCY is based at Oakland, California, and the COMFORT at Baltimore, Maryland.

Conversion: Both ships were converted at the National Steel and Shipbuilding yard in San Diego; the T-AH 19 conversion was authorized in fiscal 1983 (begun July 1984) and the T-AH 20 in fiscal 1984 (begun April 1985).

As hospital ships they have 12 operating rooms, four X-ray rooms, a pharmacy, a blood bank, an 80-bed intensive care facility, and 920 other beds; up to 1,000 additional patients can be accommodated for limited care. The ships are designed to handle a peak admission rate of 300 patients in 24 hours, with surgery required by 60 percent of the admissions and an average patient stay of five days.

The ships are designed to take aboard casualties primarily by helicopter; there is a limited capability for taking on casualties from boats on the port side.

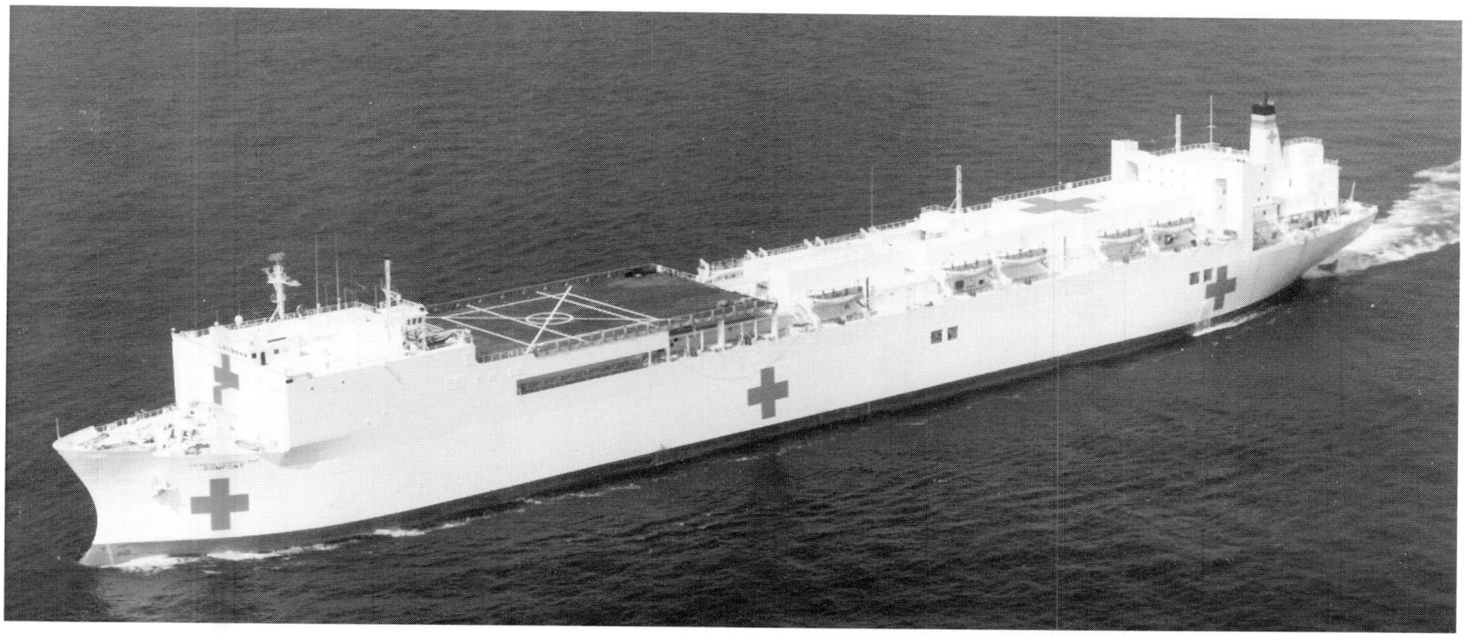

The MERCY displays the high sides of these converted tankers. The principal means of bringing casualties aboard these ships is by helicopter. (1995, Leo Van Ginderen collection)

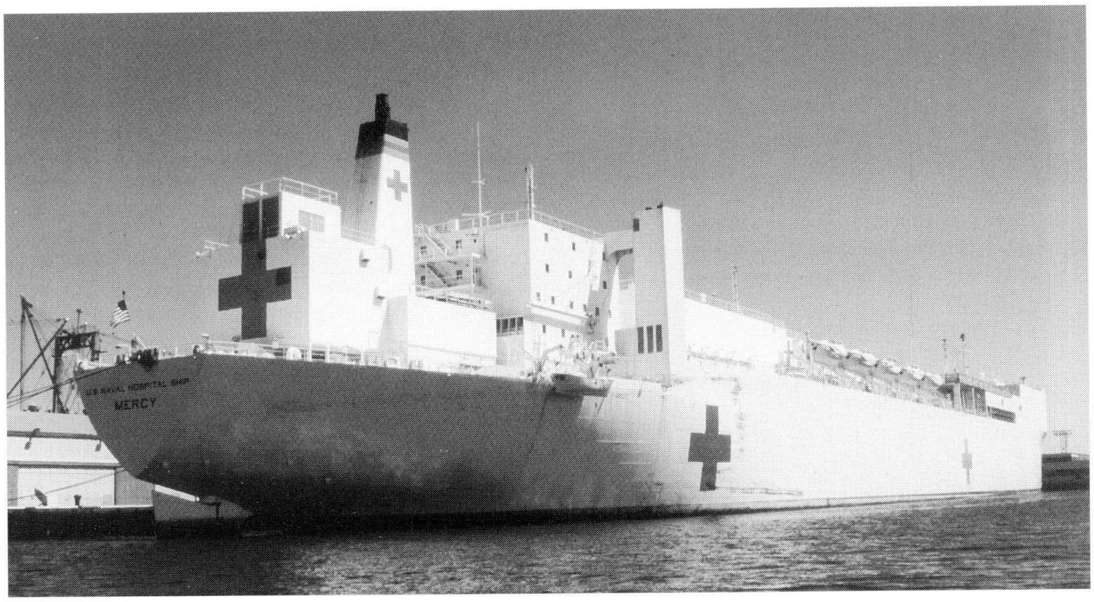

The machinery-aft configuration of the Navy's two hospital ships reveals their tanker origins. Note the row of lifeboats, port and starboard, and the markings—red crosses on white hull and superstructure, with the MSC's black-gold-blue funnel stripes. (1995, Leo Van Ginderen collection)

There are facilities for preparing 7,500 meals and distilling 75,000 gallons (285,000 liters) of fresh water daily.

Manning: The ships operate as medical treatment facilities in the RRS status; upon full mobilization, each ship would be manned by 1,204 Navy personnel. The following table lists the planned Navy manning for the ships in each category. The Navy's breakdown of mobilization personnel does not total 1,204 (the composition was being revised when this edition went to press).

The nonmedical personnel assigned to the medical activity are supply corps, maintenance, etc.

	Treatment Facility	*Full Mobilization*
Medical Corps officers	—	55
Dental Corps officers	—	6
Nurse Corps officers	2	172
Medical Service Corps officers	3	20
Nonmedical officers	1	16
Hospital enlisted	21	674
Dental enlisted	1	16
Non-hospital/dental enlisted	16	205
Total	44	1,164

Names: The merchant names of the ships were WORTH and ROSE CITY, respectively.

Operational: The MERCY operated in the Philippines as a hospital facility from March to June 1987. She was staffed with 375 medical personnel from all of the U.S. military services as well as the Public Health Service. The ship treated almost 63,000 patients during the three-month period.

Both ships were activated in August 1990 in response to the Kuwaiti crisis. They departed their respective home ports on 13 August; the COMFORT arrived in the Persian Gulf on 8 September and the MERCY on 14 September. They were manned by some 450 medical personnel who were assigned from the naval hospitals at Oakland, California, and Bethesda, Maryland; they were subsequently augmented by about 700 additional personnel from those hospitals who were flown to the Middle East to rendezvous with the ships. Both ships were in the Persian Gulf during Operations Desert Shield/Desert Storm.

The COMFORT was sent to Jamaica in June 1994 to support Haitian refugee processing; she subsequently sailed to the U.S. naval base at Guantánamo Bay, Cuba, to support Haitian and Cuban refugees interned there. She returned to her home port of Baltimore in July 1994.

Both ships undertake periodic sea trials.

HOSPITAL SHIPS: "HAVEN" CLASS

The last surviving hospital ship of the World War II–built HAVEN class, the SANCTUARY (AH 17) was stricken on 16 February 1989. She was transferred to Life International on 18 September 1989 for use as a civilian hospital facility in Africa. Sufficient funds were not made available for that goal, however, and she remains at Baltimore.

In 1980 the SANCTUARY was considered for reactivation to support the prepositioning of U.S. military equipment in the Indian Ocean. Instead, the decision was made to acquire and convert two merchant ships.

The HAVEN class originally consisted of five ships (AH 12–16). See 14th Edition/page 278 for characteristics.

FBM SUPPLY SHIPS

These ships transported missiles, spare parts, provisions, and other equipment to forward-deployed FBM tenders at Holy Loch, Scotland; Rota, Spain; and Apra Harbor, Guam, when those bases were active.

All other AK-series ships in naval service are listed in chapter 24.

FBM SUPPLY SHIP: CONVERTED MORMAC CARGO SHIP

The VEGA (T-AK 286) was the last of seven merchant ships configured to support U.S. Fleet Ballistic Missile (FBM) submarine tenders deployed to Holy Loch, Scotland; Rota, Spain; and Apra Harbor, Guam. Launched in 1960 as a commercial cargo ship, she was acquired by the Navy in 1981 for conversion to an FBM supply ship.

The FBM supply ships carried ballistic missiles, stores, packaged fuels, and spare parts. They were manned by civilian crews with Navy security detachments. A total of seven merchant ships were converted to this role.

The VEGA was taken out of MSC service on 28 April 1994 and assigned to the NDRF. She was stricken on 7 November 1994. With the concentration of U.S. Trident missile submarines at Kings Bay, Georgia, and Bremerton, Washington, there was no further need for these supply ships.

See 15th Edition/pages 254–55 for characteristics.

FBM SUPPLY SHIPS: VICTORY TYPE

Number	Name	In service	Notes
T-AK 259	Alcor	1960	stricken 1968
T-AK 260	Betelgeuse		stricken 1974
T-AK 279	Norwalk	1964	stricken 1 Aug 1979
T-AK 280	Furman	1963	stricken 13 Apr 1992
T-AK 281	Victoria	1965	stricken 31 Mar 1986
T-AK 282	Marshfield	1970	stricken 30 Nov 1992

These are former merchant ships extensively converted to support deployed FBM submarine tenders. The Marshfield was the last Victory-type ship to be taken out of service, on 1 October 1992.

The Furman was further modified in 1982–1983 to transport undersea cable. The ship was operated by the MSC under the sponsorship of the Naval Space and Warfare Systems Command.

See 15th Edition/pages 255–56 for characteristics.

ARCTIC CARGO SHIP: "ELTANIN" CLASS

The specialized Arctic cargo ship Mirfak (T-AK 271), completed in 1957, was laid up in the NDRF on 11 December 1979. She was stricken on 21 February 1992. The ship had a strengthened hull, icebreaking prow, enclosed crow's nest and control spaces, and other features for Arctic operation.

Class: Sister ships Eltanin (AK 270) and Mizar (AK 272) were converted to oceanographic research ships, redesignated AGOR 8 and AGOR 11, respectively.

See 14th Edition/page 290 for characteristics.

OILERS

Oilers—also referred to as fleet oilers—provide underway replenishment of naval forces. These ships differ from tankers, which provide point-to-point transfer of fuels, at times replenishing oilers at sea (see chapter 24).

16 FLEET OILERS: "HENRY J. KAISER" CLASS

Number	Name	FY	Launched	In service	Status
T-AO 187	Henry J. Kaiser	82	5 Oct 1985	19 Dec 1986	MSC-ROS
T-AO 188	Joshua Humphreys	83	22 Feb 1986	3 Apr 1987	AR
T-AO 189	John Lenthall, Jr.	84	9 Aug 1986	25 June 1987	**MSC-A**
T-AO 190	Andrew J. Higgins	84	17 Jan 1987	22 Oct 1987	To scrap
T-AO 191	Benjamin Isherwood	85	15 Aug 1988	canceled 1993	
T-AO 192	Henry Eckford	85	14 Aug 1989	canceled 1993	
T-AO 193	Walter S. Diehl	85	10 Oct 1987	13 Sep 1988	**MSC-P**
T-AO 194	John Ericsson	86	21 Apr 1990	19 Mar 1991	**MSC-P**
T-AO 195	Leroy Grumman	86	3 Dec 1988	2 Aug 1989	**MSC-A**
T-AO 196	Kanawha	87	22 Sep 1990	10 Dec 1991	**MSC-A**
T-AO 197	Pecos	87	23 Sep 1989	13 July 1990	**MSC-P**
T-AO 198	Big Horn	88	2 Feb 1991	21 May 1992	**MSC-A**
T-AO 199	Tippecanoe	88	16 May 1992	8 Feb 1993	**MSC-P**
T-AO 200	Guadalupe	89	5 Oct 1991	25 Sep 1992	**MSC-P**
T-AO 201	Patuxent	89	23 July 1994	21 June 1995	**MSC-A**
T-AO 202	Yukon	89	6 Feb 1992	25 Mar 1994	**MSC-P**
T-AO 203	Laramie	89	6 May 1995	5 Apr 1996	**MSC**
T-AO 204	Rappahannock	89	14 Jan 1995	7 Nov 1995	**MSC-P**

Builders:	Avondale Shipyards, New Orleans, La., except T-AO 191 and 192 by Pennsylvania Shipbuilding (Chester, Pa.) and American Shipbuilding (Tampa, Fla.)
Displacement:	9,500 tons light 40,700 tons full load
Tonnage:	26,500 deadweight
Length:	649¾ feet (198.1 m) waterline 677½ feet (206.6 m) overall
Beam:	97½ feet (29.7 m)
Draft:	36 feet (11.0 m)
Propulsion:	2 diesel engines (Colt-Pielstick 10PC4.2V); 32,540 bhp; 2 shafts
Speed:	20 knots
Range:	6,000 n.miles (11,112 km) at 20 knots
Manning:	95 civilian + 23 Navy (1 officer + 22 enlisted)
Helicopters:	landing area
Guns:	none (see notes)
Radars:	2 . . . . navigation
EW systems:	(see notes)

These fleet oilers were built to civilian specifications. Although civilian manned, they operate regularly with forward-deployed battle groups. These ships provide the majority of the Navy's fleet oiler strength.

The lead ship was laid down on 22 August 1984. The Kaiser was assigned to the Afloat Prepositioning Force (APF) in 1995; she carries JP-4 fuel for the U.S. Air Force and is normally moored at Diego Garcia. She is manned by a civilian crew of 23.

The Kaiser and Higgins initially operated as MSC-manned oilers supporting the fleet.

The Kaiser was placed in five-day ROS status on 31 January 1995; the Humphreys was taken out of service and placed in reserve in June 1996; and the Higgins was taken out of service on 1 April 1996 (to be stricken/scrapped).

Builders: Contracts for the construction of T-AO 191, 192, 194, and 196 were awarded to Pennsylvania Shipbuilding in 1985–1986; those contracts were canceled on 31 August 1989 because of default on construction. The first two ships were towed to the Philadelphia Naval Shipyard in October 1989 and subsequently were transferred to American Shipbuilding (Tampa) for completion; they were reordered on 16 November 1989. The T-AO 194 and 196, for which assembly had not yet begun, were awarded to Avondale for construction.

The two ships towed to the Tampa yard were, according to shipyard officials, "a mess." The Tampa yard sued the Navy, which argued that they were forced to send the ship to Tampa because of political pressure, even though the yard did not have the trained work force to complete the ships. Despite additional congressional funding to the Tampa yard, the ships were not completed and the Navy terminated the contract on 15 August 1993. The ships were then towed to the James River (Virginia) NDRF anchorage. The Isherwood was 95.3 percent complete and the Eckford was 84 percent.

The government had paid Pennsylvania Shipbuilding $331 million and American Shipbuilding $102 million for the two ships. They are not completed and there is no plan to finish them.

Design: These are mid-size petroleum carriers with a 180,000-barrel cargo capacity; in addition, they can carry 25,000 gallons (95,000 liters) of lubrication oil as bulk cargo, plus 105,000 gallons (399,000 liters) of potable water and 88,000 gallons (334,400 liters) of boiler feed water. The ships have seven UNREP stations.

The Patuxent and later ships are the first "double hulled" oilers built for MSC operation.

The ships have a limited UNREP capacity for dry stores as well as fuels. A tunnel for forklift trucks runs through the superstructure to permit moving cargo aft to the helicopter deck. Crew requirements have been increased by about ten from the early designs, with space also provided for another ten transient personnel.

Electronics: Space and weight are reserved for the SLQ-25 Nixie torpedo countermeasures, but no SLQ-32 installation is planned.

Guns: There are provisions for 20-mm Phalanx CIWS mounts on the bow and after superstructure in wartime.

5 FLEET OILERS: "CIMARRON" CLASS

Number	Name	FY	Launched	Commissioned	Status
AO 177	Cimarron	76	28 Apr 1979	10 Jan 1981	**PA**
AO 178	Monongahela	76	4 Aug 1979	5 Sep 1981	**AA**
AO 179	Merrimack	77	17 May 1980	14 Nov 1981	**AA**
AO 180	Willamette	78	18 July 1982	18 Dec 1982	**PA**
AO 186	Platte	78	30 Jan 1982	16 Apr 1983	**AA**

Builders:	Avondale Shipyards, New Orleans, La.
Displacement:	37,866 tons full load
Length:	708⅓ feet (215.95 m) overall
Beam:	83 feet (25.3 m)
Draft:	33⅓ feet (10.2 m)
Propulsion:	1 steam turbine; 24,000 shp; 1 shaft
Boilers:	2 600 psi (41.7 kg/cm²) (Combustion Engineering)
Speed:	19.4 knots
Range:	
Manning:	approx. 268 (15 officers + 253 enlisted)
Helicopters:	landing area
Guns:	2 20-mm Phalanx CIWS Mk 15 (2 multi-barrel)
Radars:	LN-66 navigation SPS-55 surface search except SPS-10E in AO 180, 186
EW systems:	SLQ-25 Nixie SLQ-32(V)1

The PECOS is representative of the largest class of oilers built for U.S. naval service since World War II. These ships have three fueling stations to port, two to starboard, and one solid stores transfer station on each side. They can be armed with point-defense systems. (U.S. Navy)

These fleet oilers are designed to provide two complete refuelings to a conventional aircraft carrier and six to eight accompanying escort ships. All five ships have been lengthened or "jumboized" (see below).

These are the only fleet oilers that are manned by the Navy.

Classification: The AO hull numbers 182–185 were assigned to the Falcon-class transport tankers (T-AOT) and the USNS POTOMAC is T-AOT 181 (see chapter 24).

Conversion: All five ships have undergone a "jumbo" conversion to increase their cargo capacity to 183,000 barrels of petroleum products (from 72,000) and to fit self-defense CIWS guns and EW systems. The ships were lengthened by 117 feet (35.7 m), with a reduction in speed of 0.6 knots. The ships have four UNREP stations to port and three to starboard.

The conversions, carried out at Avondale Shipyards, were:

AO 177 June 1990 to Mar 1992
AO 178 Jan 1990 to Oct 1991
AO 179 Mar 1989 to Dec 1990
AO 180 Oct 1989 to May 1991
AO 181 Nov 1990 to Sep 1992

See 14th Edition/pages 295–96 for previous characteristics.

Design: SCB No. 739. The ships have an elliptical underwater bow for improved sea-keeping. A Vertical Replenishment (VERTREP) platform is provided aft, but no helicopter hangar or support facilities are installed.

Manning: Originally to be manned by approximately 135 personnel, that number was increased to provide improved maintenance self-sufficiency for prolonged deployments.

FLEET OILERS: "NEOSHO" CLASS

Number	Name	Comm.	Notes
T-AO 143	NEOSHO	1954	decomm. 10 Aug 1992; stricken 16 Feb 1994
T-AO 144	MISSISSINEWA	1955	decomm. 30 July 1991; stricken 16 Feb 1994
T-AO 145	HASSAYAMPA	1955	decomm. 2 Oct 1991; stricken 16 Feb 1994
T-AO 146	KAWISHIWI	1955	decomm. 31 July 1992; stricken 7 Nov 1994
T-AO 147	TRUCKEE	1955	decomm. 21 Oct 1991; stricken 18 July 1994
T-AO 148	PONCHATOULA	1956	decomm. 1 Apr 1992; stricken 31 Aug 1992

These were the first fleet oilers built for the U.S. Navy after World War II. They were large, graceful, heavily armed ships. All were originally active Navy-manned ships; the AO 144 was transferred to the MSC in 1976–1980 for civilian manning. All were laid up in 1991–1992 and assigned to the NDRF. (The "decommission" dates were actually the dates they were taken out of MSC service; MSC ships are not commissioned ships.) All were subsequently stricken.

See 15th Edition/page 260 for characteristics.

The stern of the KANAWHA showing the massive superstructure, helicopter deck, and opening in the stern for the SLQ-25 Nixie towed torpedo countermeasures. (U.S. Navy)

The PLATTE under way. The five Navy-manned fleet oilers are armed with Phalanx CIWS mounts forward and aft, and both the SLQ-25 Nixie torpedo countermeasures and SLQ-32(V)1 ECM suite are installed. SRBOC launchers are also installed. (1989, Giorgio Arra)

FLEET OILERS: "MISPILLION" CLASS

Number	Name	Comm.	Notes
T-AO 105	MISPILLION	1945	decomm. 8 Feb 1990; stricken 15 Feb 1995
T-AO 106	NAVASOTA	1946	decomm. 2 Oct 1991; stricken 2 Jan 1992
T-AO 107	PASSUMPSIC	1946	decomm./stricken 17 Dec 1991
T-AO 108	PAWCATUCK	1946	decomm./stricken 21 Sep 1991
T-AO 109	WACCAMAW	1946	decomm./stricken 11 Oct 1989

These were the last of a large class of twin-screw naval oilers built during World War II (T3-S2-A3 design) as Navy fleet oilers. They were jumboized (enlarged) in the mid-1960s to increase their cargo capacity, forming a new five-ship class. The ships were transferred from the active Navy to the MSC, with civilian manning in 1973–1975. They were later taken out of service and transferred to the NDRF. (The "decommission" dates were actually the dates they were taken out of MSC service; MSC ships are not commissioned ships.) All were subsequently stricken.

Designation: The WACCAMAW was intended for conversion to a replenishment oiler (AOR 109), but that conversion was not undertaken.

See 15th Edition/pages 260–61 for characteristics.

FLEET OILERS: "CIMARRON" CLASS

Number	Name	Comm.	Notes
AO 51	ASHTABULA	1943	decomm. 30 Sep 1982; stricken 6 Sep 1991
T-AO 57	MARIAS	1944	decomm. 15 Aug 1982; stricken 11 Dec 1992
T-AO 62	TALUGA	1944	decomm. 29 Aug 1983; stricken 21 Feb 1992
AO 98	CALOOSAHATCHEE	1945	decomm. 2 Oct 1989; stricken 18 July 1994
AO 99	CANISTEO	1945	decomm. 2 Oct 1989; stricken 31 Aug 1992

These were the last of a large class of twin-screw fleet oilers (T3-S2-A1) that formed the backbone of Navy UNREP capabilities in World War II. Three ships (with Navy crews) were jumboized (enlarged) in the mid-1960s to increase their carrying capacity. Two ships were transferred to MSC operation in 1972–1973. All were assigned to the NDRF after being taken out of service, but they remained in the naval reserve.

Class: A total of 39 ships of this design were delivered from 1938; nine were initially assigned to commercial operators before being transferred to the Navy. Four ships of this class were converted to escort aircraft carriers (CVE 26–29); this design served as the basis for later war-built oilers and for the COMMENCEMENT BAY (CVE 105) class of carriers.

See 15th Edition/page 262 for characteristics.

POST–WORLD WAR II OILERS

War-built fleet oilers reached hull AO 109. The ex-German submarine tender DITHMARSCHEN (built in 1938) became the USS CONECUH (IX 301) after the war. The ship's designation was later changed to AO 110 and, because of ordnance and stores, to AOR 110. (The AOR classification was established in 1952 as a fleet replenishment tanker to provide "one stop" fuel and munitions replenishment. The classification AOR was reestablished as replenishment oiler in 1964.)

AO 111–142 were "Mission" class T2 merchant tankers operated by the MSC. The MISSION CAPISTRANO (AO 112) was converted to a sonar trials ship (AG 162).

AO 143–148 were the NEOSHO class, built specifically as naval fleet oilers (see above).

AO 149–152 were large tankers of the MAUMEE class built specifically for MSTS/MSC service; they were subsequently designated AOT (see chapter 24). The similar AMERICAN EXPLORER (AO 165) was built for merchant use but upon completion was acquired by the Navy.

AO 153–164 were commercial T2 tankers acquired during the 1956 Suez crisis for MSTS operations, then stricken in 1957–1958.

AO 166, 167 were reserved for planned "Mission" class "jumbo" conversions.

AO 168–176 were the "Sealift" class of tankers built for MSC operation (see chapter 24).

AO 177–180, 186 are the CIMARRON class built specifically for naval service (see above).

AO 181 was assigned to the POTOMAC, having been constructed from portions of an earlier POTOMAC (AO 150) (see chapter 24).

AO 182–185 were merchant tankers taken over for naval use (see chapter 24).

AO 187–204 are the HENRY J. KAISER class (see above).

The MONONGAHELA, one of the five Navy-manned fleet oilers now in service. These ships have four replenishment stations to port, three to starboard. Replenishment ships have more UNREP stations to port to resupply aircraft carriers on that side. (1990, Leo Van Ginderen collection)

FAST COMBAT SUPPORT SHIPS

These ships are intended to operate as part of fast carrier battle groups, providing petroleum products, munitions, and other supplies to aircraft carriers and their screening surface combatants. In practice, they combine the functions of fleet oilers (AO) and ammunition ships (AE) and, to a limited extent, the combat stores ships (AFS).

3 + 1 FAST COMBAT SUPPORT SHIPS: "SUPPLY" CLASS

Number	Name	FY	Launched	In service	Status
AOE 6	SUPPLY	87	6 Oct 1990	26 Feb 1994	**AA**
AOE 7	RAINIER	89	28 Sep 1991	1 Dec 1994	**PA**
AOE 8	ARCTIC	90	30 Oct 1993	16 Sep 1995	**AA**
AOE 10	BRIDGE	93	1996	1998	Building

Builders:	National Steel, San Diego, Calif.
Displacement:	19,700 tons light
	48,800 tons full load
Length:	754¾ feet (230.1 m) overall
Beam:	107 feet (32.6 m)
Draft:	39 feet (11.9 m)
Propulsion:	4 gas turbines (General Electric LM 2500); 100,000 shp; 2 shafts
Speed:	26 knots
Range:	
Manning:	AOE 6 579 (28 officers + 551 enlisted)
	AOE 7 565 (27 officers + 538 enlisted)
	AOE 8 561 (27 officers + 534 enlisted)
Helicopters:	3 UH-46 Sea Knight
Missiles:	1 8-tube NATO Sea Sparrow launcher Mk 29
Guns:	2 25-mm Bushmaster cannon Mk 38 (2 single)
	2 20-mm Phalanx CIWS Mk 16 (2 multi-barrel)
	4 .50-cal machine guns (4 single)
Radars:	SPS-64(V)9 navigation
	SPS-67(V) surface search
Fire control:	1 Mk 25 Target Acquisition System (TAS)
	2 Mk 91 missile FCS
EW systems:	SLQ-25 Nixie
	SLQ-32(V)3

23QQ

These are large, multi-product replenishment ships. They are based on the SACRAMENTO design, the principal difference in the two classes being in their propulsion plants.

The lead ship, the SUPPLY, was laid down on 24 February 1989.

The first three ships suffered major delays, caused mainly by late delivery of reduction gears, a major propulsion system component. The original estimated ship delivery dates were:

	Original
AOE 6	Apr 1991
AOE 7	July 1992
AOE 8	Aug 1993

Related to these delays has been a major increase in cost. In August 1991 the Navy stated that the ships will cost 30 percent more than the original estimates. When this edition went to press the Navy had not exercised its option for AOE 9, and it is unlikely that the ship will be procured in view of the cutback in carrier battle groups.

Class: The AOE 9 was authorized in fiscal 1992; tentatively named CONECUH, her construction was deferred; building funds were employed to pay for shipbuilding cost overruns. The ship was reauthorized in fiscal 1993 as the AOE 10.

Design: Cargo capacity is 156,000 barrels of petroleum products, plus 1,800 tons of munitions, 400 tons of refrigerated provisions, and 250 tons of dry stores.

This is the second class of U.S. Navy ships to be built with the so-called Level III collective protection features against CBR attack, the first having been the ARLEIGH BURKE (DDG 51)-class destroyers. Level III provides the maximum protection possible within a ship, including berthing, medical, and control spaces.

Names: The AOE 10 is named for the first U.S. Navy ship built from the keel up as a stores ship, the BRIDGE (AF 1); she, in turn, was named for Commodore Horatio Bridge, USN, the first Chief of the Bureau of Provisions and Clothing before the Civil War and a pioneer in fleet supply.

The AOE 7 was originally named PAUL HAMILTON, but that changed while the ship was under construction. The former name was assigned to the destroyer DDG 60.

The ARCTIC, the latest of the large AOE replenishment ships, at high speed. These ships can be easily distinguished from the previous SACRAMENTO class by their tripod masts abaft the bridge and the Phalanx CIWS fitted forward of the bridge. (1995, National Steel & Shipbuilding, Kim Lee)

The RAINIER is a high-capability, heavily armed UNREP ship. Note the NATO Sea Sparrow missile launcher and Phalanx CIWS mounted forward; there is another Phalanx CIWS aft. A pair of 25-mm Bushmaster cannon are fitted for defense against small surface craft. (1994, National Steel and Shipbuilding, Kim Lee)

4 FAST COMBAT SUPPORT SHIPS: "SACRAMENTO" CLASS

Number	Name	FY	Launched	Commissioned	Status
AOE 1	SACRAMENTO	61	14 Sep 1963	14 Mar 1964	PA
AOE 2	CAMDEN	63	29 May 1965	1 Apr 1967	PA
AOE 3	SEATTLE	65	2 Mar 1968	5 Apr 1969	AA
AOE 4	DETROIT	66	21 June 1969	28 Mar 1970	AA

Builders:	AOE 1, 3, 4 Puget Sound Naval Shipyard, Bremerton, Wash.
	AOE 2 New York Shipbuilding, Camden, N.J.
Displacement:	18,700 tons light
	53,600 tons full load
Length:	707⅚ feet (215.8 m) waterline
	794¾ feet (242.4 m) overall
Beam:	107 feet (32.6 m)
Draft:	38 feet (11.6 m)
Propulsion:	2 steam turbines (General Electric); 100,000 shp; 2 shafts
Boilers:	4 600 psi (41.7 kg/cm^2) (Combustion Engineering)
Speed:	27.5 knots (26 knots sustained)
Range:	10,000 n.miles (18,520 km) at 17 knots
	6,000 n.miles (11,112 km) at 26 knots
Manning:	612 (27 officers + 585 enlisted)
Helicopters:	2 UH-46 Sea Knight
Missiles:	1 8-tube NATO Sea Sparrow launcher Mk 29
Guns:	2 20-mm Phalanx CIWS Mk 16 (2 multi-barrel)
	4 .50-cal machine guns (4 single)
Radars:	SPS-10F surface search
	SPS-40E air search in AOE 1, 2
	SPS-64(V)9
Fire control:	2 Mk 91 missile FCS
	1 Mk 23 TAS in AOE 3
EW systems:	SLQ-25 Nixie
	SLQ-32(V)3

These are the world's largest underway replenishment ships, designed to provide a carrier battle group with full fuels, munitions, dry and frozen provisions, and other supplies. (The largest foreign UNREP ship is the one-of-a-kind Soviet BEREZINA, completed in 1977, which displaces some 40,000 tons full load.)

Class: The AOE 5 of this class was planned for the fiscal 1968 program but canceled on 4 November 1968.

Design: SCB No. 196. These ships can carry 156,000 barrels of fuels, 2,100 tons of munitions, 250 tons of dry stores, and 250 tons of refrigerated stores. The ships have highly automated cargo-handling equipment.

A large helicopter deck is fitted aft with a three-bay hangar for VERTREP helicopters. Each bay is 47 to 52 feet (14.3 to 15.85 m) long, 17 to 19 feet (5.2 to 5.8 m) wide, and 18 to 18½ feet (5.5 to 5.6 m) high.

Electronics: The hull has provision for SQS-26 sonar, but it has not been installed. The earlier WLR-1 ECM systems have been replaced by the SLQ-32 system.

Details of the SACRAMENTO's bridge structure, showing sailors manning the rail adjacent to the NATO Sea Sparrow launcher. Above the bridge are the SLQ-32(V)3 antennas, port and starboard, and two Mk 91 FCS antennas for the Sea Sparrow. The SUPPLY class has a lattice mast abaft the bridge. (1995, Giorgio Arra)-

Engineering: The first two ships were provided with the machinery produced for the canceled battleship KENTUCKY (BB 66).

Guns: As built, these ships were armed with eight 3-inch guns in twin mounts and associated Mk 56 GFCS. They were removed in the mid-1970s, and a NATO Sea Sparrow launcher was installed forward. The remaining 3-inch guns have been removed; two Phalanx CIWS mounts have been fitted to each ship.

The SACRAMENTO, the first of the massive AOE "one-stop" replenishment ships. These are larger and considerably more capable UNREP ships than the AFS type, which are being retired. Two Mk 95 FCS antennas are mounted atop the bridge; the SACRAMENTO and CAMDEN have an SPS-40E air search radar fitted on their forward mast. (1995, Giorgio Arra)

The SACRAMENTO in the Western Pacific, under way at slow speed. The superstructures of the newer SUPPLY class are considerably different from the first four AOEs. (1995, Giorgio Arra)

REPLENISHMENT OILERS

These ships combine the capability of a fleet oiler (AO) with a limited capability for the services of an ammunition ship (AE) and combat stores ship (AFS).

6 REPLENISHMENT OILERS: "WICHITA" CLASS

Number	Name	FY	Launched	Commissioned	Status
AOR 1	WICHITA	65	18 Mar 1968	7 June 1969	NDRF
AOR 2	MILWAUKEE	65	17 Jan 1969	1 Nov 1969	AR
AOR 3	KANSAS CITY	66	28 June 1969	6 June 1970	PR
AOR 4	SAVANNAH	66	25 Apr 1970	5 Dec 1970	AR
AOR 5	WABASH	67	6 Feb 1971	20 Nov 1971	PR
AOR 6	KALAMAZOO	67	11 Nov 1972	11 Aug 1973	AR

Builders:	AOR 1–6 General Dynamics, Quincy, Mass.
	AOR 7 National Steel and Shipbuilding, San Diego, Calif.
Displacement:	12,500 tons light except AOR 7, 13,000 tons
	41,350 tons full load
Length:	659 feet (200.9 m) overall
Beam:	96 feet (29.3 m)
Draft:	33⅙ feet (10.1 m)
Propulsion:	2 steam turbines (General Electric); 32,000 shp; 2 shafts
Boilers:	3 600 psi (41.7 kg/cm²) (Foster Wheeler)
Speed:	20 knots
Range:	10,000 n.miles (18,520 km) at 17 knots
	6,500 n.miles (12,038 km) at 20 knots
Manning:	AOR 4 466 (23 officers + 443 enlisted)
	AOR 5, 6 467 (23 officers + 444 enlisted)
	AOR 7 461 (23 officers + 438 enlisted)
Helicopters:	2 UH-46 Sea Knight
Missiles:	1 NATO Sea Sparrow launcher Mk 29 in AOR 2–7
Guns:	2 20-mm Phalanx CIWS Mk 15 (2 multi-barrel) in AOR 2–7
	2 20-mm cannon Mk 67 (2 single) in AOR 2
Radars:	SPS-10F surface search
	SPS-64(V) navigation
Fire control:	1 Mk 25 TAS in AOR 6
	2 Mk 91 missile FCS in AOR 2–7
EW systems:	SLQ-25 Nixie
	SLQ-32(V)3

These are smaller variations of the AOE-type ships. In 1993 they began to be decommissioned and laid up in reserve.

WICHITA	decomm. 12 Mar 1993; to the NDRF 7 Apr 1994
MILWAUKEE	decomm. 27 Jan 1994
KANSAS CITY	decomm. 7 Oct 1994
SAVANNAH	decomm. 28 July 1995
WABASH	decomm. 30 Sep 1994
KALAMAZOO	decomm. Sep 1996

The ROANOKE's high stern typifies these ships. The directors for the two Mk 91 missile fire-control systems are atop small lattice masts just forward of the funnels. A UH-46D Sea Knight, with rotors folded, is on the ROANOKE's helicopter deck. (1994, Giorgio Arra)

The ROANOKE, with refueling hoses visible at her port-side refueling stations. This class has four fuel transfer stations to port and three to starboard, in addition to two stations on each side for the transfer of solid stores. The forward Phalanx CIWS is on the port side, the after one to starboard, atop the superstructure. (1994, Giorgio Arra)

The KALAMAZOO will be decommissioned in late 1996; she and the SAVANNAH are under consideration for foreign transfer.

The seventh ship of this class, the ROANOKE (AOR 7), was decommissioned and stricken on 6 October 1995.

Design: SCB No. 707. These ships can carry 175,000 barrels of petroleum, 600 tons of munitions, 200 tons of dry stores, and 100 tons of refrigerated stores. All ships except the ROANOKE were built with helicopter decks but without hangars (see below).

Engineering: The ships can steam at 18 knots on two boilers while the third is being maintained.

Guns: The AOR 1–6 were built with an armament of two 3-inch/50-cal twin AA gun mounts aft and the Mk 56 GFCS. The 3-inch guns were removed from all ships when the helicopter hangars were installed. A minimal 20-mm gun armament was installed in some ships prior to installation of the Phalanx CIWS (which was planned for all units). The WICHITA remained unarmed when decommissioned.

Note that all apparently were fitted with the SLQ-25 and SLQ-32(V)3 systems.

Helicopters: The ROANOKE was built with a twin-bay helicopter hangar aft. The other ships have been similarly fitted; the hangar bays are 61½ to 63 feet (18.75 to 19.2 m) long, 18 to 21 feet (5.5 to 6.4 m) wide, and 17¾ to 18⅓ feet (5.4 to 5.6 m) high.

Missiles: NATO Sea Sparrow launchers and the associated Mk 91 missile FCS are fitted to five ships of the class (atop the hangar structure, aft of the funnel).

The WICHITA refuels the destroyer PAUL F. FOSTER (DD 964) during operations off the California coast. Two hoses are rigged between the two ships. UNREP operations—at speeds of up to 15 knots or more—are a hallmark of U.S. Navy operations. (1993, U.S. Navy, PHC Bill Wallace)

REPAIR SHIPS

These ships provided major repairs to ship hulls, machinery, and equipment. They did not carry the weapons and specialized stores and parts stocked on destroyer, submarine, and seaplane tenders.

The Navy planned a new class of repair ships to replace the VULCAN-class ships, with the lead ship included in the fiscal 1994 shipbuilding program and then slipped to fiscal 1998. This class was to eventually replace older destroyer tenders (AD) as well as the VULCAN-class repair ships.

In the event, the plan was canceled in the early 1990s when the decision was made to dispose of all repair ships (as well as most of the tenders).

REPAIR SHIPS: "VULCAN" CLASS

Number	Name	Comm.	Notes
AR 5	VULCAN	1941	decomm. 30 Sep 1991; stricken 28 July 1992
AR 6	AJAX	1943	decomm. 31 Dec 1986; stricken 16 May 1989
AR 7	HECTOR	1944	decomm. 31 Mar 1987; to Pakistan 20 Apr 1989
AR 8	JASON	1944	decomm./stricken 24 June 1995

These were large, highly capable repair ships, although they lacked the ability to support more sophisticated weapon and electronic systems. The VULCAN class was one of three series of large tender-type ships begun in the late 1930s, the others being the DIXIE (AD 14) and FULTON (AS 11) classes.

Consideration was given in the mid-1990s to assigning some or all of these ships to NRF operation; none was transferred.

Classification: The JASON was completed as a heavy hull repair ship (ARH 1); she was reclassified as AR 8 on 9 September 1957.

See 15th Edition/pages 267–68 for characteristics.

POST–WORLD WAR II REPAIR SHIPS

World War II repair ships reached hull number AR 21. Three destroyer tenders were later reclassified as repair ships, indicating their employment in general repair and support work. The hull numbers AR 24–27 were not used.

Number	Name	Comm.	Notes
AR 22	KLONDIKE	1945	ex-AD 22 (reclassified 1960)
AR 23	MARKAB	1941	ex-AD 21, AK 31 (reclassified 1959)
AR 28	GRAND CANYON	1946	ex-AD 28 (reclassified 1971)

CABLE REPAIR SHIPS

The Navy's cable ships supported SOSUS and other underwater cable activities. In addition to supporting these undersea projects, cable ships conduct special oceanographic and acoustic surveys in support of the Naval Electronic Systems Command under the Oceanographer of the Navy. (Commercial ships are also used under contract to support U.S. seafloor cable installations.)

1 CABLE REPAIR SHIP: "ZEUS"

Number	Name	FY	Launched	In service	Status
T-ARC 7	ZEUS	79	30 Oct 1982	19 Mar 1984	**MSC-PA**

Builders:	National Steel and Shipbuilding, San Diego, Calif.
Displacement:	8,297 tons light 14,225 tons full load
Length:	454 feet (138.4 m) waterline 502½ feet (153.2 m) overall
Beam:	73⅙ feet (22.3 m)
Draft:	23⅚ feet (7.3 m)
Propulsion:	diesel-electric (5 General Motors EMD diesel engines); 12,500 shp; 2 shafts
Speed:	15.8 knots
Range:	10,000 n.miles (18,520 km) at 15 knots
Manning:	88 civilian + 6 Navy (enlisted) + 32 civilian technicians
Helicopters:	no facilities
Radars:	2 . . . . navigation

The ZEUS is the first cable ship built specifically for the U.S. Navy. Two ships of this type were planned, originally to replace the now-stricken THOR (ARC 4) and AEOLUS (ARC 3). The second ship, planned for the fiscal 1986 budget, was not requested.

The ZEUS was delayed because of design and construction problems; her keel was laid down 1 June 1981. She is operated by the MSC under sponsorship of the Naval Space and Warfare Systems Command.

The Navy personnel are communications specialists.

Design: The ship can lay up to 1,000 miles (1,610 km) of cable in depths down to ten miles (16 km).

Electronics: The ZEUS is fitted with the SSN-2 precise seafloor navigation system.

Engineering: Two 1,200-hp bow and two 1,200-hp stern thrusters are fitted for station keeping while handling cables.

The ZEUS is the only cable ship to have been constructed specifically for U.S. naval use. Commercial cable ships also support the Navy's SOSUS seafloor acoustic detection and Air Force missile impact arrays. (1991, Giorgio Arra)

The bow cable sheaves of the Zeus. (1990, Giorgio Arra)

The stern cable sheaves of the Zeus. The ship does not have a helicopter deck. (1990, Giorgio Arra)

CABLE REPAIR SHIPS: "NEPTUNE" CLASS

Number	Name	Comm.	Notes
T-ARC 2	Neptune	1953	decomm. 24 Sep 1991; stricken 20 Aug 1992
T-ARC 6	Albert J. Myer	1963	decomm. 13 Feb 1944; stricken 7 Nov 1944

These were built-for-the-purpose cable ships initially intended for Army use. Both ships were completed in 1946 and laid up in Maritime Administration reserve. The Myer was acquired by the Navy in 1952 and the Neptune in 1953 to support the SOSUS program; they were subsequently placed in Navy commission (ARC) and operated as commissioned ships (USS). The Myer was transferred outright to the Navy and the Neptune was on loan until permanently acquired in 1966. Both ships were transferred to MSC operation in 1973 (T-ARC).

After being taken out of service they were assigned to the NDRF. (The "decommission" dates were actually the dates the ships were taken out of MSC service; MSC ships are not commissioned ships.)

See 15th Edition/pages 269–70 for characteristics.

CABLE REPAIR SHIPS

Number	Name	Comm.*	Notes
ARC 1	Protunus	1952	ex-LSM 275
T-ARC 2	Neptune	1953	
T-ARC 3	Aeolus	1955	ex-AKA 47; stricken 28 Mar 1945
T-ARC 4	Thor	1956	ex-AKA 49; stricken 1 Mar 1978
ARC 5	Yamacraw	1948**	ex-USCG WARC 333, ex-USN ACM 9
T-ARC 6	Albert J. Myer	1963	

*Commission or in service as cable ships.
**Transferred to Coast Guard in 1948; returned to Navy in 1959 and commissioned as ARC 5.

The Navy's first designated cable ship, the Protunus, originally completed in 1944 as the LSM 275, was transferred to Portugal in 1959 and connected to a diving tender.

SALVAGE SHIPS

In addition to naval salvage activities, the Navy has a national responsibility for salvaging all U.S. ships, both government and private (Public Law 80-513).

The ATS-type oceangoing tugs are listed in this subsection because they are employed primarily as salvage and (submarine) rescue ships. In the latter role they would employ the McCann submarine rescue chamber, previously carried by ASR-type rescue ships.

SALVAGE SHIPS: NEW CONSTRUCTION

A new class of ARS-type ships was planned to replace the older ARS/ASR–type ships in their salvage, heavy towing, and diving roles. The lead ship was scheduled for authorization in the fiscal 1994 shipbuilding program. However, the program was canceled in the early 1990s.

4 SALVAGE SHIPS: "SAFEGUARD" CLASS

Number	Name	FY	Launched	Commission	Status
ARS 50	Safeguard	81	12 Nov 1983	17 Aug 1985	**PA**
ARS 51	Grasp	82	21 Apr 1984	14 Dec 1985	**AA**
ARS 52	Salvor	82	28 July 1984	14 June 1986	**PA**
ARS 53	Grapple	83	8 Dec 1984	15 Nov 1986	**AA**

Builders:	Peterson Builders, Sturgeon Bay, Wisc.
Displacement:	2,725 tons light 3,193 tons full load
Length:	240 feet (73.15 m) waterline $254\frac{11}{12}$ feet (77.7 m) overall
Beam:	51 feet (15.5 m)
Draft:	$15\frac{5}{12}$ feet (4.7 m)
Propulsion:	4 geared diesel engines (Caterpillar D399 BTA); 4,200 bhp; 2 shafts (Kort nozzle propellers)
Speed:	13.5 knots
Range:	8,000 n.miles (14,816 km) at 12 knots
Manning:	110 (6 officers + 104 enlisted) except ARS 53, 105 (6 officers + 99 enlisted)
Helicopters:	VERTREP area
Guns:	2 .50-cal machine guns (2 single)
Radars:	Raytheon 1900 navigation SPS-64(V)9 navigation

These ships replaced several of the long-serving salvage ships of the Escape class in the salvage and towing role. The three large ATS-type tugs plus these four ships will permit the continuous peacetime deployment of one salvage-capable ship in the Western Pacific and one in the Mediterranean.

Design: The ship is fitted for towing and heavy lift, with a limited diving support capability. A 40-ton-capacity boom is fitted aft, and a 7.5-ton boom is located forward.

Engineering: A 500-hp bow thruster is provided.

Operational: In July 1990 the Grasp salvaged an S-3B Viking anti-submarine aircraft off the coast of Virginia from a depth of more than 10,000 feet (3,049 m). The aircraft had crashed at sea during a takeoff from the carrier John F. Kennedy (CV 67) on 7 October 1989.

The Grapple shows the unusual Safeguard-class design. The ship's bow and stern facilitate deep-sea, four-point mooring to keep the ship over a salvage target. There are booms forward and aft, with a pair of workboats stowed amidships. (1991, Giorgio Arra)

The Grasp's stern aspect shows the all-around bridge visibility of these ships, an important feature for mooring and for salvage operations. Her fantail work area is relatively small, reflecting the compact design of these highly capable ships. (1989, Giorgio Arra)

SALVAGE SHIPS: "DIVER" AND "BOLSTER" CLASSES

Number	Name	Comm.	Notes
ARS 8	Preserver*	1944	decomm. 7 Aug 1992; stricken 16 Mar 1994
ARS 38	Bolster*	1945	decomm./stricken 24 Sep 1994
ARS 39	Conserver	1945	decomm./stricken 1 Apr 1994
ARS 40	Hoist*	1945	decomm./stricken 30 Sep 1994
ARS 41	Opportune	1945	decomm. 30 Apr 1993/stricken 5 Aug 1993
ARS 42	Reclaimer*	1945	decomm./stricken 16 Sep 1994
ARS 43	Recovery	1946	decomm./stricken 30 Sep 1994

*Ships transferred to NRF in 1979–1986.

These ships were fitted for deep-sea salvage and towing operations. Originally, these two classes included 22 ships: ARS 5–9, 19–28, and 38–43 (plus the canceled ARS 44–49). The lead ship of this design was the Diver (ARS 5); after she was sold in 1949 the Navy listed Escape as the class name. The Bolster (ARS 38) and later ships are considered a separate class; the differences are minimal (e.g., beam, fuel capacity).

Four ships were transferred to the Naval Reserve Force (NRF) in 1979–1986 and manned by composite active-reserve crews. The Preserver and Conserver were decommissioned on 30 September 1986; both ships were recommissioned on 26 September 1987 for salvage and anti-drug patrol duties in the Caribbean. The Preserver then shifted on 30 April 1989 to the NRF in exchange for the Hoist, which returned to active service. The Preserver was decommissioned again in 1992.

When this edition went to press, the Conserver was on "hold" for transfer to Mexico, the Hoist for Eriteria, and the Recovery for Bulgaria.

The Escape (ARS 6) was reactivated from the NDRF and transferred to the Coast Guard on 4 December 1980. (Now stricken, the Escape is on "hold" for transfer to Mexico.)

Class: Two ships of this class were converted to oceanographic ships: the AGOR 17 (ex-ARS 20) and AGOR 18 (ex-ARS 27). Three others served with the Coast Guard: WMEC 167 (ex-ARS 9), WMEC 168 (ex-ARS 26), and WMEC 6 (ex-ARS 6).

Historical: In December 1990 the Opportune became the first U.S. naval ship to be commanded by a woman.

See 15th Edition/pages 271–72 for characteristics.

3 SALVAGE AND RESCUE SHIPS: "EDENTON" CLASS

Number	Name	FY	Launched	Commissioned	Status
ATS 1	Edenton	66	15 May 1968	23 Jan 1971	**AA**
ATS 2	Beaufort	67	20 Dec 1968	22 Jan 1972	**PA**
ATS 3	Brunswick	67	14 Oct 1969	10 Dec 1972	**PA**

Builders:	Brooke Marine, Lowestoft (England)
Displacement:	2,650 tons standard
	3,200 tons full load
Length:	264 feet (80.5 m) waterline
	288⅔ feet (88.0 m) overall
Beam:	50 feet (15.25 m)
Draft:	15⅙ feet (4.6 m)
Propulsion:	4 diesel engines (Paxman 12 YLCM); 6,000 bhp; 2 shafts
Speed:	16 knots
Range:	10,000 n.miles (18,520 km) at 13 knots
Manning:	117 (7 officers + 110 enlisted)
Helicopters:	VERTREP area
Guns:	2 20-mm cannon Mk 67 (2 single)
Radars:	SPS-53 surface search
	SPS-64(V)9 navigation

These are tug-type ships with extensive salvage and diving capabilities. They are one of two classes of auxiliary ships to be constructed in British shipyards for the U.S. Navy, the other being the two Chauvenet (T-AGS 29)-class ships. The more recently acquired British-built stores ships (T-AFS) were constructed for RFA service.

All three ships will be stricken in 1996–1997.

Class: The ATS 4 was authorized in fiscal 1972 and the ATS 5 in fiscal 1973. Their construction was deferred in 1973, and plans for additional ships of the class were canceled because of their high cost. Instead, the less able ATF 166 class was procured.

The Brunswick showing the bow arrangement for deep-sea mooring gear; a 10-ton-capacity crane is fitted forward. The supports for the crane flank the bridge face. (1995, Giorgio Arra)

The Beaufort, barely under way. These ships will be stricken in late 1996 and probably transferred to other navies. (1995, Giorgio Arra)

Classification: ATS, which originally indicated salvage tug, was changed to salvage and rescue ship on 16 February 1971.

Design: SCB No. 719. These ships have large open work spaces forward and aft. Four mooring buoys are carried (as in submarine rescue ships) to assist in four-point moors for diving and salvage activities. A 10-ton-capacity crane is fitted forward and a 20-ton crane aft. The ships have compressed air (not helium-oxygen) diving equipment.

Engineering: The ships have a through-bow thruster for precise maneuvering and station keeping.

SUBMARINE TENDERS

Submarine tenders have extensive maintenance shops for various submarine systems and equipment, as well as major weapon and provision storage. Tenders also provide ample hospital facilities in addition to extra berths for submarine relief personnel.

Tenders are no longer required to support the U.S. Navy's Trident fleet ballistic missile submarines; those craft are supported by their two extensive built-for-the-purpose submarine/missile facilities at Kings Bay, Georgia, and Bangor, Washington.

3 SUBMARINE TENDERS: "EMORY S. LAND" CLASS

Number	Name	FY	Launched	Commissioned	Status
AS 39	Emory S. Land	72	4 May 1977	7 July 1979	**AA**
AS 40	Frank Cable	73	14 Jan 1978	5 Feb 1980	**PA**
AS 41	McKee	77	16 Feb 1980	15 Aug 1981	**PA**

Builders:	Lockheed Shipbuilding and Construction, Seattle, Wash.
Displacement:	13,842 tons light
	22,650 tons full load
Length:	645⅔ feet (196.9 m) overall
Beam:	85 feet (25.9 m)
Draft:	25½ feet (7.8 m)
Propulsion:	1 steam turbine (De Laval); 20,000 shp; 1 shaft
Boilers:	2 650 psi (43.6 kg/cm²) (Combustion Engineering)
Speed:	20 knots (18 knots sustained)
Range:	7,600 n.miles (14,075 km) at 18 knots
Manning:	AS 39, 41 620 (65 officers + 555 enlisted)
	AS 40 619 (64 officers + 555 enlisted)
Flag:	69 (25 officers + 44 enlisted)
Helicopters:	VERTREP area
Guns:	4 20-mm cannon Mk 67 (4 single)
	2 40-mm grenade launchers Mk 19 (2 single)
Radars:	SPS-10 surface search
	1 . . . . navigation

These are improved versions of the L.Y. Spear-class tenders; the later ships have been fitted specifically to support the Los Angeles (SSN 688)-class attack submarines. Up to four SSNs can be supported alongside simultaneously.

The Frank Cable replaced the Holland at Guam in 1996.

Design: SCB No. 737. The ships are fitted with a 30-ton-capacity crane and two 5-ton traveling cranes. Medical facilities include an operating room, dental clinic, and 23-bed ward.

1 SUBMARINE TENDER: "L.Y. SPEAR" CLASS

Number	Name	FY	Launched	Commissioned	Status
AS 36	L.Y. Spear	65	7 Sep 1967	28 Feb 1970	**AA**

Builders:	General Dynamics, Quincy, Mass.
Displacement:	12,770 tons light
	23,493 tons full load
Length:	645⅔ feet (196.9 m) overall
Beam:	85 feet (25.9 m)
Draft:	24⅔ feet (7.5 m)
Propulsion:	1 steam turbine (General Electric); 20,000 shp; 1 shaft
Boilers:	2 650 psi (43.6 kg/cm²) (Foster Wheeler)
Speed:	20 knots (18 knots sustained)
Range:	7,600 n.miles (14,075 km) at 18 knots
Manning:	593 (59 officers + 534 enlisted)
Flag:	69 (25 officers + 44 enlisted)
Helicopters:	VERTREP area
Guns:	4 20-mm cannon Mk 67 (4 single)
Radars:	SPS-10 surface search
	1 . . . . navigation

The Frank Cable entering port. The tenders of the Emory S. Land class resemble the Samuel Gompers–class destroyer tenders, although their internal arrangements and shops are very different. (1993, Giorgio Arra)

The Frank Cable showing the small helicopter deck—which cannot accommodate modern helicopters—and stern anchor. The red "E" and chevron on the funnel indicate two awards for engineering excellence. (1993, Giorgio Arra)

The L.Y. SPEAR was one of the first submarine tenders constructed for the U.S. Navy specifically to support nuclear-propelled attack submarines. Her heavy cranes handle spare parts and submarine propellers and loading torpedoes and cruise missiles into SSNs. (1990, Giorgio Arra)

The L.Y. SPEAR showing the stern anchor and mooring cleats notched into her stern. Tenders have several side ports for laying gangplanks and conveyors onto ships moored alongside. (1990, Giorgio Arra)

The two ships of this class were the U.S. Navy's first submarine tenders designed specifically to support nuclear-propelled attack submarines; they could support four submarines alongside at one time.

The DIXON (AS 37) was placed out of commission "special" on 4 August 1995; she was decommissioned and stricken on 15 December 1995.

Class: The AS 38 of this design was authorized in the fiscal 1969 budget but was not built because of funding shortages in other ship programs. The ship was canceled on 27 March 1969.

Design: SCB No. 702.

Guns: As built, these ships each had two 5-inch/38-cal DP guns. They were deleted in favor of the minimal 20-mm gun armament.

1 FBM SUBMARINE TENDER: "SIMON LAKE" CLASS

Number	Name	FY	Launched	Commissioned	Status
AS 33	SIMON LAKE	63	8 Feb 1964	7 Nov 1964	**AA**

Builders:	Puget Sound Naval Shipyard, Bremerton, Wash.
Displacement:	12,000 tons light
	19,934 tons full load
Length:	643¾ feet (196.3 m) overall
Beam:	85 feet (25.9 m)
Draft:	28½ feet (8.7 m)
Propulsion:	1 steam turbine (De Laval); 20,000 shp; 1 shaft
Boilers:	2 650 psi (43.6 kg/cm²) (Combustion Engineering)
Speed:	18 knots
Range:	7,600 n.miles (14,075 km) at 18 knots
Manning:	612 (62 officers + 550 enlisted)
Helicopters:	VERTREP area
Guns:	4 20-mm cannon Mk 67 (4 single)
Radars:	LN-66 navigation
	SPS-10 surface search

The SIMON LAKE was one of four new construction tenders designed to service fleet ballistic missile submarines.

The CANOPUS (AS 34), a sister ship of the SIMON LAKE, was decommissioned and stricken on 3 May 1995.

Class: The AS 35 of this design was authorized in fiscal 1965, but construction was deferred and the ship was not built. The ship would have provided one tender for each of five Polaris SSBN squadrons, with a sixth ship in overhaul or transit. However, the Polaris SSBN program was reduced from the proposed 45 to 41 submarines, and only four squadrons were formed, with four tenders built (AS 31–34), plus one conversion (AS 19).

Design: SCB No. 238. Two 30-ton-capacity cranes and four 5-ton traveling cranes are fitted.

These ships were originally built to support the Polaris missile. In 1970–1971 the SIMON LAKE was modified to support the Poseidon missile and has since been modified further to handle the Trident C-4 missile. With her missile support capabilities removed, she now supports only nuclear-propelled attack submarines.

Guns: As built, the ships had 3-inch/50-cal Mk 33 guns in two twin mounts, which were removed in the late 1980s.

Operational: The SIMON LAKE was the last submarine tender to be based at Holy Loch, Scotland, where the U.S. Navy had maintained an SSBN base from 1961 until 1992. The ship is now homeported at La Maddalena, Italy, where she serves as tender for U.S. submarines operating in the Mediterranean.

The SIMON LAKE still mounting twin 3-inch/50-cal AA guns alongside the funnel. These ships were among the last to carry these weapons that were once abundant on U.S. warships and fleet auxiliaries. (1985, Giorgio Arra)

The SIMON LAKE off Charleston, South Carolina, with the aircraft carrier YORKTOWN (CV 10) and nuclear-propelled merchant ship SAVANNAH moored at Patriot's Point in the background. Note the funnel-aft design used for later submarine tenders. (1985, Giorgio Arra)

The HOLLAND with an SSN moored alongside. The HOLLAND and HUNLEY were designed specifically to support Polaris SSBNs at forward bases. With the reduction in SSBN force levels they were reassigned to support attack submarines. (1994, Leo Van Ginderen collection)

1 FBM SUBMARINE TENDER: "HUNLEY" CLASS

Number	Name	FY	Launched	Commissioned	Status
AS 32	HOLLAND	62	19 Jan 1963	7 Sep 1963	**PA**

Builders:	Ingalls Shipbuilding, Pascagoula, Miss.
Displacement:	11,000 tons light 19,819 tons full load
Length:	599 feet (182.7 m) overall
Beam:	83 feet (25.3 m)
Draft:	24¼ feet (7.4 m)
Propulsion:	diesel-electric (10 Fairbanks-Morse 38D⅛ diesel engines); 15,000 shp; 1 shaft
Speed:	19 knots
Range:	10,000 n.miles (18,520 km) at 12 knots
Manning:	612 (58 officers + 554 enlisted)
Helicopters:	VERTREP area
Guns:	4 20-mm cannon Mk 67 (4 single)
Radars:	LN-66 navigation SPS-10 surface search

The HUNLEY (AS 31) and her sister ship HOLLAND were the first tenders designed specifically to service fleet ballistic missile submarines. The HUNLEY was decommissioned and stricken on 30 September 1994; the HOLLAND is scheduled to be decommissioned late in 1996.

Design: SCB No. 194. As built, these ships could support the Polaris missile. The HUNLEY was modified in 1973–1974 and the HOLLAND in 1974–1975 to support Poseidon-armed submarines.

As built, the ships had a 32-ton-capacity hammerhead crane fitted aft. It has been replaced in both ships with two amidships cranes, as in the later SIMON LAKE class; these are 30-ton-capacity devices.

Guns: The original armament for these ships was four 3-inch/50-cal AA guns in twin mounts.

SUBMARINE TENDERS: "FULTON" CLASS

Number	Name	Comm.	Notes
AS 11	FULTON	1941	decomm. 17 May 1991; stricken 20 Dec 1991
AS 12	SPERRY	1942	decomm./stricken 30 Sep 1982
AS 15	BUSHNELL	1943	stricken 15 Nov 1980
AS 16	HOWARD W. GILMORE	1944	stricken 1 Dec 1980
AS 17	NEREUS	1960	stricken 27 Oct 1971
AS 18	ORION	1943	decomm./stricken 30 Sep 1993
AS 19	PROTEUS	1944	to IX 518 (see notes)

These large tenders were similar to the contemporary DIXIE (AD 14)-class destroyer tenders and VULCAN (AR 5)-class repair ships. The ships had been modernized but had a limited capability to support nuclear-propelled attack submarines.

The stricken FULTON was assigned to the NDRF in 1994, the NEREUS in 1993, and the GILMORE in 1995.

The PROTEUS was rebuilt in 1959–1960 to service Polaris missile submarines, and she subsequently served in that role at Holy Loch, Scotland; Rota, Spain; and Apra Harbor, Guam. She later served as a general repair ship at Diego Garcia. She was decommissioned and stricken on 30 September 1992 but was reinstated in the Naval Vessel Register on 1 February 1994 as the IX 518 (see chapter 25).

Names: The GILMORE was the first submarine tender to be named for an individual, honoring a submarine commander who went down with his boat in World War II.

See 15th Edition/pages 278–79 for characteristics.

SUBMARINE RESCUE SHIPS

All submarine rescue ships have been stricken. These ships carried out general salvage and diving duties but were configured to carry the McCann submarine rescue chamber. The large PIGEON and ORTOLAN could also carry two of the Deep Submergence Rescue Vehicles (DSRV) (see chapter 26) and were fitted with the fleet's most advanced deep-diving system (Mk II).

SUBMARINE RESCUE SHIPS: "PIGEON" CLASS

Number	Name	Comm.	Notes
ASR 21	PIGEON	1973	decomm./stricken 31 Aug 1992
ASR 22	ORTOLAN	1973	decomm./stricken 31 Mar 1995

These ships were constructed specifically to carry DSRV submarine rescue vehicles and to support deep-ocean diving operations. They were large, catamaran ships. Their completion was delayed by problems in design, construction, and fitting out.

The PIGEON class was developed after the loss of the submarine THRESHER (SSN 593) in 1963 to provide an ASR/DSRV force for submarine rescue down to the collapse depth of contemporary submarines. Up to ten ASRs were planned, but delays and funding constraints reduced the program to two ships. (The DSRVs can also be carried by SSNs.)

See 15th Edition/pages 279–80 for characteristics.

SUBMARINE RESCUE SHIPS: "CHANTICLEER" CLASS

Number	Name	Comm.	Notes
ASR 9	FLORIKAN	1943	decomm. 3 Sep 1991; stricken
ASR 13	KITTIWAKE	1946	decomm./stricken 30 Sep 1994
ASR 14	PETREL	1946	decomm. 30 Aug 1991; stricken 9 Oct 1991
ASR 15	SUNBIRD	1950	decomm./stricken 30 Sep 1993

These were the last of a series of large tug-type ships fitted for salvage and helium-oxygen diving operations. They had a limited submarine rescue capability employing the McCann chamber. Originally, eight ships were in this class: ASR 7–11 and 13–15 (plus the canceled ASR 16–18).

The SUNBIRD was accepted by the Navy on 15 January 1947 and towed (inactivated) to the Charleston Naval Shipyard. She was not commissioned for 3½ years.

The PETREL and SUNBIRD were transferred to the NDRF after being stricken.

The last of a type: The ORTOLAN was the last Navy submarine rescue ship to be placed in commission and the last to be stricken. The ASR series began in 1923 when the minesweeper WIDGEON (AM 22) was converted for submarine salvage and, subsequently, rescue duties. She was not changed to ASR 1 until 1936. Five other AM conversions followed, after which tug-type ships were built for the ASR role until the advent of the PIGEON class. (1990, Giorgio Arra)

OCEANGOING TUGS

The ATS-series salvage and rescue ships (formerly salvage tugs) are listed as salvage ships in this edition of *Ships and Aircraft* (see page 246).

The attack submarine JEFFERSON CITY (SSN 759) alongside the CATAWBA at Hong Kong. These ships, with diesel-electric power plants, can easily provide electric power to submarines. (1994, Giorgio Arra)

7 FLEET TUGS: "POWHATAN" CLASS

Number	Name	FY	Launched	In service	Status
T-ATF 166	POWHATAN	75	24 June 1978	15 June 1979	**MSC-A**
T-ATF 167	NARRAGANSETT	75	28 Nov 1978	9 Jan 1979	**MSC-P**
T-ATF 168	CATAWBA	75	22 Sep 1979	28 May 1980	**MSC-P**
T-ATF 169	NAVAJO	75	20 Dec 1979	13 June 1980	**MSC-P**
T-ATF 170	MOHAWK	78	5 Apr 1980	16 Oct 1980	**MSC-A**
T-ATF 171	SIOUX	78	30 Oct 1980	12 May 1981	**MSC-P**
T-ATF 172	APACHE	78	20 Dec 1980	30 July 1981	**MSC-A**

Builders:	Marinette Marine, Wisc.
Displacement:	2,000 tons standard 2,260 tons full load
Length:	225 11/12 feet (68.9 m) waterline 240 1/12 feet (73.2 m) overall
Beam:	42 feet (12.8 m)
Draft:	15 feet (4.6 m)
Propulsion:	diesel-electric (2 General Motors EMD 20 645×7 diesel engines); 4,500 shp; 2 shafts (Kort nozzle propellers)
Speed:	15 knots
Range:	10,000 n.miles (18,520 km) at 13 knots
Manning:	20 civilian + 4 Navy (enlisted) + 20 transients
Helicopters:	VERTREP area
Radars:	SPS-53 surface search Raytheon TM 1660/12S navigation

These are oceangoing tugs based on a commercial design. They have replaced the war-built ATFs in the active fleet. The new ATF differs from the ASR and ATS types because it lacks the salvage and diving equipment of the earlier ships and has a limited towing capability. A portable Mk 1 Mod 1 diving/decompression module can be loaded on the stern of these ships.

Design: SCB No. 744. These craft are easily distinguished by their side-by-side funnels and low, open sterns. The Navy personnel are communications specialists and the transients are salvage and diving specialists. There is a 10-ton-capacity crane.

In wartime, two 20-mm guns and two .50-cal machine guns can be fitted.

Engineering: The ships have a 300-hp bow thruster.

The CATAWBA, with containers on her fantail. The POWHATAN design differs greatly from previous U.S. Navy oceangoing tugs. (1995, Giorgio Arra)

FLEET TUGS: "CHEROKEE" CLASS

Number	Name	Comm.	Notes
ATF 91	SENECA	1943	trials ship (immobilized)
ATF 105	MOCTOBI	1944	decomm. 30 Sep 1985; stricken 7 Feb 1995
ATF 110	QUAPAW	1944	decomm. 30 Aug 1985; stricken 26 Jan 1995
ATF 113	TAKELMA	1944	decomm. 20 Feb 1992; stricken 30 June 1992
ATF 149	ATAKAPA	1944	decomm. 1 Oct 1981; stricken 21 Feb 1992
ATF 158	MOSOPELEA	1945	decomm. 1 Oct 1981; stricken 21 Feb 1992
ATF 159	PAIUTE	1945	decomm. 7 Aug 1992; stricken 14 Feb 1995
ATF 160	PAPAGO	1945	decomm. 28 July 1992; stricken 14 Feb 1995

These were the last of a class of 48 large oceangoing tugs, many of which saw extensive combat service in World War II. All of the above ships were laid up in the NDRF after being decommissioned except for the SENECA, which was reacquired from the NDRF on 21 November 1985 for use as an immobilized trials craft at the David Taylor Research Center, Annapolis, Maryland.

The PAIUTE was decommissioned on 23 August 1985, and the PAPAGO on 28 June 1985. They were recommissioned into active naval service for anti-drug patrols in the Caribbean on 26 September 1987; they were decommissioned again in 1992.

Class: The AT 64–76 and 81–118 were built to the same basic design. The class was officially known as the CHEROKEE (ATF 66) after the loss of the NAVAJO (AT 64) in 1943 and the SEMINOLE (AT 65) in 1942. Later ships are unofficially referred to as the ABNAKI (ATF 96) class. (Ships numbered below ATF 96 have four diesel engines, four generators, and four electric motors driving through a gear to a single propeller shaft. The later ships have only one, very large electric motor.)

Ships of this class served in the U.S. Coast Guard as well as several foreign navies.

Classification: All of these ships were ordered with the AT designation. The AT 66 and later ships were changed to ATF on 15 May 1944.

See 15th Edition/page 282 for characteristics.

AUXILIARY TUGS: "SOTOYOMO" CLASS

All tugs of this series (ATA 121–125, 146, 170–213, and 219–238) have been stricken; none is retained in the NDRF.

See 14th Edition/page 330 for characteristics.

AVIATION LOGISTIC SHIPS

2 AVIATION LOGISTIC SUPPORT SHIPS: CONVERTED "SEABRIDGE" CLASS

Number	Name	Built	In service	Status
T-AVB 3	WRIGHT	1970	14 May 1986	MSC-RRF-A
T-AVB 4	CURTISS	1969	18 Aug 1987	MSC-RRF-P

Builders:	Litton/Ingalls Shipbuilding, Pascagoula, Miss.
Displacement:	12,409 tons light
	27,580 tons full load
Length:	$559\frac{5}{6}$ feet (170.7 m) waterline
	$600\frac{11}{12}$ feet (183.2 m) overall
Beam:	90 feet (27.4 m)
Draft:	34 feet (10.4 m)
Propulsion:	2 steam turbines (General Electric); 30,000 shp; 1 shaft
Boilers:	2 (Combustion Engineering)
Speed:	23.6 knots
Range:	9,000 n.miles (16,668 km) at 23.6 knots
Manning:	33 civilian
Troops:	300+
Helicopters:	landing area (forward)
Radars:	2 . . . . navigation

These ships were converted from RO/RO-container ships to provide maintenance and logistic support for Marine Corps aircraft in forward areas. Providing peacetime support for Marine aviation, the ships are normally in the United States and partially loaded with a Marine intermediate maintenance unit. The WRIGHT is normally based at Philadelphia, Pennsylvania, and the CURTISS at Port Hueneme, California. During war or crisis periods, the remainder of that Marine unit and other personnel are loaded on board and the ships deployed to forward areas to support Marine tactical aircraft.

The majority of the maintenance unit's facilities used ashore are packaged mainly in standard freight containers. Access ladders, scaffolding, and shipboard electrical power and other services will permit the unit to function while embarked in the ship.

The CURTISS (above) and her sister ship WRIGHT provide extensive maintenance and parts stowage facilities for Marine fixed-wing aircraft and helicopters. The amidships cargo covers can be stacked with aviation support containers. (U.S. Navy)

The WRIGHT with a Marine CH-53 helicopter on her flight deck. The T-AVBs are generally considered in the category of sealift ships, being intended primarily to support forward-deployed Marine aviation units. (U.S. Navy)

Most of the embarked troops are associated with the maintenance unit; the remainder are communications and other support personnel.

Class: The previous AVB 1 and AVB 2 were tank landing ships converted to support land-based patrol aircraft from unimproved airfields and seaplanes in the Mediterranean area. They were Navy manned in the AVB role. The ALAMEDA COUNTY (LST 32) became the AVB 1 and, after she was stricken in 1962, the TALLAHATCHIE COUNTY (LST 1154) became the AVB 2.

Conversion: Both ships were converted at Todd Shipyards in Galveston, Texas. The WRIGHT was converted from December 1984 to May 1986, the CURTISS from December 1985 to August 1987.

Design: The ships are combination RO/RO and self-sustaining container ships. The conversion included fitting a helicopter deck above the two forward holds; the deck can be removed to permit full access to the holds with the use of off-board cranes.

There are seven cargo holds, with the No. 7 hold, aft, having troop berthing and mess facilities installed above it. As a maintenance ship the AVB can embark 300 standard containers, plus 52 access modules; in the resupply role, 684 containers can be carried. Some 35,000 square feet (3,150 m^2) of vehicle storage space are provided.

The ships have been fitted with ten 30-ton-capacity booms (which can be joined to form 60-ton lifts); a single 70-ton Stuelcken boom is also installed.

Their merchant design was C5-S-78A.

Names: Original merchant names were YOUNG AMERICA and GREAT REPUBLIC, respectively; these were changed when the ships were acquired by the Navy for conversion to AVB.

GUIDED MISSILE SHIPS

GUIDED MISSILE SHIP: "NORTON SOUND"

The long-serving test and evaluation ship NORTON SOUND (AVM 1, ex-AV 11) was stricken on 26 January 1987. Built as a seaplane tender and commissioned in 1945, she served as a gun/missile/electronics test ship from 1948 until her decommissioning on 11 December 1986.

See 14th Edition/pages 334–35 for characteristics.

UNCLASSIFIED MISCELLANEOUS SHIPS

These ships (designated IX) are officially considered to be service craft (see chapter 25).

Almost one-half of the Navy's active fleet auxiliaries are UNREP ships, providing the Fleet with a high degree of mobility, a vital factor in sustained forward presence operations. Here, UH-46 Sea Knight helicopters from the ammunition ship SANTA BARBARA transfer ordnance to the carrier THEODORE ROOSEVELT (CVN 71) off the Atlantic coast in December 1995 after the carrier completed a yard period. (U.S. Navy, PH2 Michael Turner)

CHAPTER 24

Sealift Ships

The fast sealift ship ALGOL and some of her load of combat vehicles, the latter in desert camouflage colors for use in the Middle East–Persian Gulf region. The massive U.S. investment in strategic sealift in the 1980s created the sealift that carried virtually all of the matériel and fuels used by U.S. forces in the Gulf War and in other crises of the 1990s. (U.S. Navy)

Sealift ships provide point-to-point transportation of cargo—including dry and liquid cargoes, and troops—for all of the U.S. military services. Also included in this category are the forward-deployed or prepositioned merchant ships that carry guns, vehicles, munitions, provisions, fuels, field hospitals, and other supplies for U.S. troops that will be flown into forward areas to "marry up" with the material.

All sealift ships are operated by civilian crews under contract to the Military Sealift Command (MSC). The official categories of sealift ships are described in chapter 8. In the entries listed below, the following status abbreviations have been used:

APF	Afloat Prepositioning Force
FSS	Fast Sealift Ship
MPS	Maritime Prepositioning Ship
NDRF	National Defense Reserve Fleet
ROS	Reduced Operating Status
RRF	Ready Reserve Force

Ships marked **MSC-Active** are employed by the Military Sealift Command on worldwide transportation assignments for the Department of Defense. Ships marked **Academic** are assigned to state maritime academies for the training of students.

The MPS ships are forward-deployed, carrying matériel for the Marine Corps only; the APF ships carry matériel for all of the services. The 13 MPS ships and eight FSS ships were procured in the 1980s as part of the Reagan-Lehman naval buildup. Also procured at that time were 12 Near-Term Prepositioning Ships (NTPS) and 96 RRF ships to provide sealift for the rapid deployment of U.S. military forces to forward areas.

The forward prepositioning concept dates to the early 1960s when then-Secretary of Defense Robert S. McNamara proposed the acquisition of Fast Deployment Logistic (FDL) ships to carry weapons and supplies to marry up with troops and vehicles flown into forward areas in large C-5 Galaxy transports. Congress refused to fund the FDL program, although the aircraft were procured. Nevertheless, several U.S. merchant ships and LSTs were deployed in the Far East with military equipment, although on a much smaller scale than McNamara envisioned.

The second major buildup of sealift ships occurred in the mid-1990s in the aftermath of the Gulf War. The Department of Defense–developed strategy of being able to fight two Major Regional Conflicts (MRC) simultaneously has led to the establishment of a 16-ship component of the Afloat Prepositioning Force (APF) to support the Army. This is in addition to MPS sealift that supports the Marine Corps and APF that supports Navy and Air Force operations.

On an interim basis the Army force will consist of seven Roll-On/Roll-Off (RO/RO) ships drawn from the RRF, plus one crane ship (ACS). These ships will carry the weapons, vehicles, and equipment for an Army heavy brigade with 30 days of matériel.[1]

For the permanent Army APF the MSC is supervising the procurement of 19 Large Medium-Speed RO/RO (LMSR) ships—14 new construction and five conversions—to be available by the year 2001.

This force is based upon the comprehensive "Mobility Requirements Study" conducted by the Joint Chiefs of Staff after the Gulf War of January 1991 and released on 23 January 1992. The study recommended the construction of 20 large RO/RO ships and the leasing of two container ships (2,000-container-capacity each) for the maritime prepositioning role. This will provide a total of 5 million square feet (450,000 m^2) of vehicle space. Under the JCS plan, 9 ships were to be assigned to carry Army prepositioned equipment, and 11 ships would be used for the rapid deployment of heavy Army divisions from the United States (to be added to eight FSS ships currently employed in this role). In addition to these new acquisitions, under the JCS study the Ready Reserve Force was to be increased from the then-current 96 ships to 142 ships by fiscal 1999, of which 104 would be dry cargo ships and the remainder tankers and several specialized ships.

1. The Army program is officially designated AWR-3 for Army War Reserve Afloat.

In the event, a large number of ships will be procured under the LMSR category, in addition to existing APF ships and the MPS ships that support the Marine Corps.

In this chapter, ships are arranged in the following order:

Container Ships
Crane Ships
Fast Sealift Ships
Float-On/Float-Off (FLO/FLO) Ships
General Cargo Ships
Lighter-Aboard-Ship (LASH) Ships
Prepositioning Ships
Range Support Ships
Sea Barge (SEABEE) Ships
Tankers
Gasoline Tankers
Troop Ships
Vehicle Cargo Ships

Within these categories the ships are grouped on the basis of naval hull number (T-ACS ships) or launch date.

In addition to the ships listed below, the two hospital ships (AH) and two aviation support ships (AVB) listed in chapter 23 are generally included in this category because they primarily support forward-deployed forces.

Designations: Two types of hull numbers are used in this chapter: the four-digit Navy Ships and Aircraft Supplementary Data Tables (SASDT) numbers, which are assigned for accounting purposes but are not actual hull numbers in the normal context, and the one- to three-digit numbers that are traditional Navy hull numbers, which are assigned when the ship is ordered and are derived from the ship designation scheme that began in 1920.

The Maritime Administration's code scheme for American-built merchant ship designs is explained in chapter 3. A few ships constructed in the United States to private designs do not have MarAd designations.

Guns/Missiles: These ships are not armed.

Helicopters: The 13 MPS ships and the eight converted SL-7 fast sealift ships, as well as some of the ships under construction/conversion, have explicit helicopter landing decks. Some other sealift ships have open areas that could be used in an emergency.

Operational: Maritime prepositioned matériel was used by all of the U.S. military services in the Persian Gulf buildup and conflict of 1990–1991. The first U.S. ground combat units brought into Saudi Arabia with tanks, heavy artillery, etc., were two Marine Expeditionary Brigades (MEB) that married up with MPS squadrons.

The third MPS squadron followed. In addition, several APF ships were at Diego Garcia, loaded with field hospitals, Air Force and Army equipment, and potable water.

During the early 1990s, 14 RRF ships were reactivated to support U.S. military and humanitarian operations in Haiti and Somalia.

The vehicle cargo ships CAPE RACE and CAPE DIAMOND were activated in July 1995 to carry equipment for the British troops engaged in peacekeeping operations in Bosnia. The ships were fully crewed and operational within four days of being called into service by the MSC.

Status: Sixteen RRF ships were downgraded to NDRF status on 7 October 1994 because of a lack of funds to maintain them in a high state of readiness.

Ships that are not active are mostly assigned to the RRF, where they are maintained and kept ready for rapid reactivation or for the Maritime Administration's NDRF. The RRF maintains 22 RO/RO ships in a four-day readiness status to load Army and Marine vehicles; 29 other ships are maintained in a 10- to 20-day readiness status; the remaining ships are kept in a 30-day readiness status.

The NDRF ships would take considerably longer to reactivate. On a periodic basis they are "broken out" of RRF and "exercised" by employing them in cargo carrying for the Department of Defense.

U.S. Naval Ships (USNS) are indicated under *Status* notes; all others have the prefix SS (steamship) or MV (motor vessel, i.e., diesel propulsion); the few exceptions are noted. State maritime academy training ships are designated TS.

CONTAINER SHIPS

Container capacity is measured in TEU containers, which are 8 × 8 × 20 feet/2.4 × 2.4 × 6.1 m.[2]

1 CONTAINER SHIP: GERMAN BUILT

Number	Name	Launched	Status
T-AK 9205	Strong Virginian (ex-St. Magnus, Jolly Indaco)	1984	**MSC-APF**

Builders:	Bremer Vulkan A.G., Bremen-Vegesack (Germany)
Displacement:	approx. 29,000 tons full load
Tonnage:	16,169 GRT 21,541 DWT
Length:	475⅔ feet (145 m) waterline 511⅚ feet (156.06 m) overall
Beam:	105 feet (32 m)
Draft:	29½ feet (9 m)
Propulsion:	2 diesel engines (MaK 6M601AK); 16,320 bhp; 2 shafts
Speed:	16.5 knots
Range:	
Manning:	
Radars:	. . . . navigation

This is a combination RO/RO-container ship that has been fitted to carry a 500-bed portable military hospital.

She was chartered by the MSC in July 1992 and assigned to MSC Pacific on 30 September 1993.

The ship has a stern ramp and angled side ramps for loading/unloading vehicles. She can transport 1,413 containers as well as vehicles. Two 50-ton-capacity cranes and one 800-ton heavy-lift derrick have been fitted.

Engineering: The ship has a bow thruster.

2 CONTAINER SHIPS: GERMAN BUILT

Number	Name	Launched	In service	Status
T-AKR 9718	Lt Col Calvin P. Titus (ex-Albert Maersk)	1975	31 Mar 1994	**MSC-APF**
T-AKR 9966	SP5 Eric G. Gibson (ex-Adrian Maersk)	1975	31 Mar 1994	**MSC-APF**

Builders:	Blohm + Voss, Hamburg (Germany)
Displacement:	approx. 50,000 tons full load
Tonnage:	40,600 GRT 30,461 DWT
Length:	725⁵⁄₁₂ feet (221.16 m) waterline 784⅚ feet (239.28) overall
Beam:	100¼ feet (30.56 m)
Draft:	37¾ feet (11.52 m)
Propulsion:	1 diesel engine (Burmeister & Wain-Hitachi 8L90GBE); 31,800 bhp; 1 shaft
Speed:	21 knots
Range:	
Manning:	22 civilians
Radars:	2 . . . . navigation

These ships were chartered on 31 March 1994 from the Danish firm Maersk. They can accommodate 1,600 containers on the forward third of the ship or, alternatively, provide a total of 45,000 square feet (4,050 m^2) of vehicle space. They carry Army matériel. Both are normally moored at Guam.

Each ship has two 40-ton-capacity cranes, and each is fitted with a bow thruster.

Names: Both ships honor Army Medal of Honor recipients.

2. TEU = Twenty-foot (6.1-m) Equivalent Unit.

CRANE SHIPS

These ships are intended to provide an unloading capability for other sealift ships when port facilities are not available. Moored alongside a loaded merchant ship, the T-ACS can lift cargo onto a pier or into landing craft or barges alongside.

Each crane ship has two or three pairs of 30-ton cargo cranes; the cranes can be paired to lift 30 tons. Thus, one crane can lift a fully loaded container, two cranes an M1-series main battle tank. Four cranes, working together, can lift a 105-ton floating causeway.

The C6-S-1 container ship American Banker was to become the T-ACS 11 and another, undesignated ship was to have become the T-ACS 12.

Names: These ships have state nicknames.

2 AUXILIARY CRANE SHIPS: C6-S-MA60D TYPE

Number	Name	Launched	To RRF	Status
T-ACS 9	Green Mountain State (ex-American Altair, Mormacaltair)	20 Aug 1964	24 Sep 1990	MSC-RRF
T-ACS 10	Beaver State (ex-American Draco, Mormacdraco)	14 Jan 1965	1995	MSC-RRF

Builders:	Litton/Ingalls Shipbuilding, Pascagoula, Miss.
Displacement:	16,600 tons light 22,900 tons full load
Tonnage:	14,000 GRT (as built) 12,763 DWT (as built)
Length:	634⅚ feet (193.55 m) waterline 665¾ feet (203.0 m) overall
Beam:	75¹⁄₁₂ feet (22.9 m)
Draft:	31½ feet (9.6 m)
Propulsion:	2 steam turbines (General Electric); 19,000 shp; 1 shaft
Boilers:	2 (Combustion Engineering)
Speed:	21 knots
Range:	17,000 n.miles (31,485 km) at 20 knots
Manning:	64 civilian
Radars:	. . . . navigation

As crane ships these converted container ships can accommodate 650 containers.

Conversion: The Green Mountain was converted at Norfolk Shipbuilding Company in February–March 1989. The Beaver State began conversion to a crane ship on 28 February 1989 at the Norfolk Shipbuilding Company (Virginia). Slowed by lack of funding, the conversion was canceled on 12 January 1990, and she was transferred to MarAd for lay-up on 9 April 1990. The conversion was resumed in 1992 at the Charleston Naval Shipyard but not completed for lack of funds.

Both ships are fitted with three sets of twin 30-ton-capacity cranes.

Engineering: Fitted with highly automated engineering plants. Several ships of this design exceeded 24 knots when new.

The Green Mountain State, like most of the crane ships, is a converted C6-series cargo ship. The sub-types of these ships and the three C5-type crane ships differ in details and dimensions. (1990, Leo Van Ginderen collection)

2 AUXILIARY CRANE SHIPS: C6-S-MA1XB TYPE

Number	Name	Launched	To RRF	Status
T-ACS 7	DIAMOND STATE (ex-PRESIDENT TRUMAN, JAPAN MAIL)	8 Aug 1961	Feb 1989	MSC-RRF
T-ACS 8	EQUALITY STATE (ex-AMERICAN BUILDER, PHILIPPINE MAIL, SANTA ROSA, PRESIDENT ROOSEVELT, WASHINGTON MAIL)	6 Jan 1962	May 1989	MSC-RRF

Builders:	Todd Shipyards, San Pedro, Calif.
Displacement:	15,138 tons light
Tonnage:	16,518 GRT (as built)
	19,871 DWT (as built)
Length:	632$^{11}/_{12}$ feet (192.95 m) waterline
	667$^{5}/_{6}$ feet (203.6 m) overall
Beam:	76 feet (23.2 m)
Draft:	33$^{1}/_{4}$ feet (10.1 m)
Propulsion:	2 steam turbines (General Electric); 22,000 shp; 1 shaft
Boilers:	2 (Combustion Engineering)
Speed:	20 knots
Range:	14,000 n.miles (25,930 km) at 20 knots
Manning:	
Radars:	. . . . navigation

T-ACS 7 and 8 are former container ships that could accommodate 625 containers.

Conversion: The T-ACS 7 was converted November 1987–December 1988 and T-ACS 8 January 1988–February 1989 at the Tampa (Florida) Shipbuilding Company. Each is fitted with three sets of twin 30-ton-capacity cranes.

The crane ship EQUALITY STATE moored outboard of her sister ship DIAMOND STATE. The paired cranes of these ships provide both heavy lift and flexibility. (1994, Leo Van Ginderen collection)

3 AUXILIARY CRANE SHIPS: C5-S-MA73C TYPE

Number	Name	Launched	To RRF	Status
T-ACS 4	GOPHER STATE (ex-EXPORT LEADER)	1973	Oct 1987	**MSC-APF**
T-ACS 5	FLICKERTAIL STATE (ex-LIGHTNING)	1969	Feb 1988	MSC-RRF
T-ACS 6	CORNHUSKER STATE (ex-STAGHOUND)	1969	Apr 1988	MSC-RRF

Builders:	Bath Iron Works, Maine
Displacement:	15,060 tons light
	25,000 tons full load
Tonnage:	16,445 DWT
Length:	581$^{2}/_{3}$ feet (177.35 m) waterline
	609$^{5}/_{6}$ feet (185.9 m) overall
Beam:	91$^{1}/_{6}$ feet (27.8 m)
Draft:	30 feet (9.1 m)
Propulsion:	2 steam turbines; 17,500 shp; 1 shaft
Boilers:	2 (Babcock & Wilcox)
Speed:	20 knots
Range:	9,340 n.miles (17,300 km) at 20 knots
Manning:	52 civilian
Radars:	. . . . navigation

Former container ships.

Conversion: All three ships were converted at Norfolk Shipbuilding Company (Virginia): the T-ACS 4 from October 1986 to October 1987; the T-ACS 5 from December 1986 to February 1988; and the T-ACS 6 from March 1987 to April 1988. They were fitted with two sets of twin 30-ton-capacity cranes.

Operational: The T-ACS 4, as the mercantile EXPORT LEADER, served as test ship for the Arapaho Project of operating and supporting military helicopters from a merchant ship. The 1982 evaluation was totally successful, albeit conducted on a limited scale. (During a 40-hour at-sea period, 178 day and 45 night landings were logged by several helicopter types.)

In early 1990 the FLICKERTAIL STATE and GOPHER STATE were activated and fitted with collective protection spaces for defense against CBR effects. They then carried more than 100,000 artillery projectiles filled with nerve agents from Nordenham, Germany, to Johnston Island in the Pacific. The voyage, from 22 September to 6 November 1990 (via Cape Horn), was conducted under the escort of two guided missile cruisers and was made without incident. The ships were subsequently employed in Desert Shield.

The GOPHER STATE was assigned to the Army's prepositioning force on 30 September 1994.

The GOPHER STATE at Antwerp. In this view the forward pair of cranes is "split," with one crane fore-and-aft and the second handling a container over the port side. (1994, Leo Van Ginderen collection)

The GOPHER STATE, shown here with a deck cargo of containers, represents the largest class of the Navy's auxiliary crane ships. (1994, Leo Van Ginderen collection)

3 AUXILIARY CRANE SHIPS: C6-S-MA1QD TYPE

Number	Name	Launched	To RRF	Status
T-ACS 1	KEYSTONE STATE (ex-PRESIDENT HARRISON)	2 Oct 1965	May 1984	MSC-RRF
T-ACS 2	GEM STATE (ex-PRESIDENT MONROE)	22 May 1965	Oct 1985	MSC-RRF
T-ACS 3	GRAND CANYON STATE (ex-PRESIDENT POLK)	23 Jan 1965	Oct 1986	MSC-RRF

Builders:	National Steel and Shipbuilding, San Diego, Calif.
Displacement:	28,660 tons full load
Tonnage:	17,128 GRT
	13,600 DWT
Length:	$632\frac{11}{12}$ feet (192.95 m) waterline
	$668\frac{1}{2}$ feet (203.8 m) overall
Beam:	$76\frac{1}{6}$ feet (23.2 m)
Draft:	33 feet (10.1 m)
Propulsion:	2 steam turbines (General Electric); 19,250 shp; 1 shaft
Boilers:	2 (Foster Wheeler)
Speed:	20 knots
Range:	13,000 n.miles (24,075 km) at 20 knots
Manning:	64 civilian
Radars:	2 . . . . navigation

These ships can each accommodate 303 containers.

Conversion: The T-ACS 1 was converted by Bay Shipbuilding, Sturgeon Bay, Wisconsin, from March 1983 to May 1984; the T-ACS 2 by Continental Marine, San Francisco, California, from October 1984 to October 1985; and the T-ACS 3 from October 1985 to October 1987 by Dillingham Corporation, San Francisco.

All have been fitted with three sets of twin 30-to-capacity cranes.

The GRAND CANYON STATE with her six paired cranes elevated. They can operate individually or in pairs. (1995, Leo Van Ginderen collection)

The first MSC crane ship, the KEYSTONE STATE, has three sets of paired cranes; one set is aft of the superstructure. (1995, Leo Van Ginderen collection)

The ANTARES with her starboard vehicle port open. The bottom-hinged door forms the ramp that can lead to a pier or, as shown here, to an interim ramp leading to a pontoon barge or landing craft. (1989, U.S. Navy)

FAST SEALIFT SHIPS

These highly capable ships are maintained in U.S. Atlantic and Gulf Coast ports, ready for the rapid loading of Army or Marine Corps equipment and sailing to crisis/war-torn areas. They were employed in the Gulf War in 1991.

8 FAST SEALIFT SHIPS: CONVERTED SL-7 TYPE

Number	Name	Launched	In service	Status
T-AKR 287	ALGOL	22 Sep 1972	19 June 1984	MSC-FSS
T-AKR 288	BELLATRIX	30 Sep 1972	10 Sep 1984	MSC-FSS
T-AKR 289	DENEBOLA	10 May 1973	7 Oct 1985	MSC-FSS
T-AKR 290	POLLUX	18 May 1973	31 Mar 1986	MSC-FSS
T-AKR 291	ALTAIR	28 Apr 1973	13 Nov 1985	MSC-FSS
T-AKR 292	REGULUS	18 Dec 1972	28 Aug 1985	MSC-FSS
T-AKR 293	CAPELLA	9 Sep 1971	1 July 1984	MSC-FSS
T-AKR 294	ANTARES	13 May 1972	12 July 1984	MSC-FSS

Builders: T-AKR 287, 289, 293 Rotterdamsche Dry Dock Maats, Rotterdam (Netherlands)
T-AKR 288, 291 Rheinstahl Nordseewerke, Emden (Germany)
T-AKR 290, 292, 294 A. G. Weser, Bremen (Germany)

Displacement: 31,017 tons light
55,425 tons full load

Tonnage: T-AKR 287, 288 25,915 DWT
T-AKR 289 25,169 DWT
T-AKR 290 24,212 DWT
T-AKR 291, 292 25,595 DWT
T-AKR 293 25,407 DWT
T-AKR 294 24,270 DWT

Length: $946\frac{1}{6}$ ft (288.5 m) overall
Beam: $105\frac{1}{2}$ feet (32.2 m)
Draft: $36\frac{2}{3}$ feet (11.2 m)
Propulsion: 2 steam turbines (General Electric); 120,000 shp; 2 shafts
Boilers: 2 (Foster Wheeler)
Speed: 33 knots
Range: 12,200 n.miles (22,594 km) at 27 knots
Manning: 49 civilian + 56 or 57 troops
Helicopters: landing area
Radars: 2 . . . . navigation

The BELLATRIX showing the unusual stern of the fast sealift ships. They are easily identified by their angular lines, paired cranes forward and aft, large helicopter deck forward of the superstructure, and paired funnels. (1994, Leo Van Ginderen collection)

These are former high-speed merchant ships of the SL-7 class built for the SeaLand Corporation in European shipyards. They have been converted to Fast Sealift Ships (FSS) with an extensive Roll-On/Roll-Off (RO/RO) capability to carry U.S. military cargoes. They are operated by civilian charter crews.

Classification: During the planning stage these ships were designated T-AKRX. Upon acquisition they were designated T-AK and assigned hull numbers in the cargo ship (AK) series. However, upon conversion to RO/RO configuration, they were changed to T-AKR but retained the *AK-series* hull numbers.

T-AK 287 changed to T-AKR on 19 June 1984; T-AK 288 to T-AKR on 10 September 1984; T-AK 289–292 to T-AKR on 1 November 1983; and T-AK 293 and 294 to T-AKR on 30 June 1984.

Conversion: Four ships were converted with fiscal 1982 funds and four with fiscal 1984 funds: the T-AKR 287, 288, and 292 at National Steel and Shipbuilding, San Diego, California; the T-AKR 289 and 293 at Pennsylvania Shipbuilding in Chester; and the T-AKR 290, 291, and 294 at Avondale Shipyards, New Orleans, Louisiana.

These ships have approximately 185,000 square feet (16,650 m^2) of vehicle space. A major container capability remains aft, with provisions for special racks for loading heavy material, including trucks and tanks (being lifted on and off vice RO/RO). Side ports and heavy ramps are provided on both sides of the ship. Twin 35-ton-capacity cranes are fitted forward and twin 50-ton cranes aft. Through limited arcs they can provide a combined lift of 70 and 100 tons, respectively.

A helicopter landing deck is provided amidships that can accommodate the largest U.S. military helicopters (Marine/Navy CH-53E, Army CH-47 Chinook). The four cargo decks beneath the landing deck are connected by ramps and can accommodate helicopters, the first with a height of 19½ feet (5.95 m) and the others with 13½ feet (4.1 m).

In addition to the RO/RO and helicopter space, the ships can each accommodate other vehicles, plus 78 35-foot (10.7-m) flat racks and 46 containers. In the amidships deck structure there is a tunnel for trucks up to a 5-ton capacity to permit passage between the forward and after cargo areas.

Design: As built, the 33-knot SL-7s were the fastest cargo ships ever constructed for the U.S. merchant service.

Names: These ships are assigned traditional Navy cargo ship names (i.e., stars and constellations), reflecting their acquisition on bare-boat charter versus the time charter of MPS ships. Most were previously carried by store ships (AF).

Operational: All eight ships participated in Operations Desert Shield/Desert Storm in 1990–1991, being activated in August 1990. The ANTARES, which had suffered previous machinery problems, had an engine breakdown in the eastern Atlantic during the initial lift of Desert Shield, in August 1990. She was towed into a Spanish port and her cargo was shifted to other sealift ships.

Status: These ships are U.S. Naval Ships.

The REGULUS shows the awkward lines of the fast sealift ships. These are the fastest merchant-type ships flying the American flag. All are held in a ready status, with cadre crews prepared to rapidly proceed to specified ports to load Army and Marine equipment. (1995, Leo Van Ginderen collection)

The REGULUS at slow speed. All eight ships were deployed early in 1990 for Desert Shield, carrying U.S. Army equipment to the Persian Gulf. The ANTARES suffered major engine problems on her first transatlantic trip, however, and was unavailable for the massive U.S. buildup. (1993, Leo Van Ginderen collection)

FLOAT-ON/FLOAT-OFF (FLO/FLO) SHIPS

These ships can be ballasted down to permit small ships and craft to be floated on and off. The STRONG TEXAN listed later in this chapter has a limited FLO/FLO capability.

1 FLO/FLO SHIP: CONVERTED TANKER

Number	Name	Launched	Status
T-AK 2062	AMERICAN CORMORANT (ex-FERNCARRIER, KOLLBRIS)	1975	**MSC-APF**

Builders:	Eriksberg M/V, Göteborg (Sweden)
Tonnage:	10,195 GRT 51,269 DWT
Length:	738⅙ feet (225.1 m) overall
Beam:	135 feet (41.15 m)
Draft:	32⅔ feet (10.0 m); flooded 65¾ feet (20.05 m)
Propulsion:	1 diesel engine (Eriksberg/Burmeister & Wain 10K84EF); 25,000 bhp; 1 shaft
Speed:	16 knots
Range:	23,700 n.miles (43,892 km) at 13 knots
Manning:	19 civilian
Radars:	2 . . . . navigation

The AMERICAN CORMORANT is a semi-submersible, ultra-heavy-lift ship (also referred to as a FLO/FLO ship). The ship has a lifting deck 394 feet (120.1 m) long and 135 feet (41.15 m) wide that can be submerged by ballasting the ship to about 65 feet (19.8 m), at which point the lifting deck is 26 feet (7.9 m) below the surface. Small craft, heavy equipment, and barges up to a total of approximately 45,000 tons can then be positioned over the ship, which is then deballasted. The ship can also carry 25 long (40-foot/12.2-m) containers on her fantail.

This unusual ship was built as a tanker (133,000 deadweight tons). She was laid up almost immediately because of the international shipping glut; she was converted in 1981–1982 at the Gotaverken Cityvarvet yard in Sweden to her current configuration. During the modification process, she was lengthened by 180 feet (54.9 m).

Status: The ship was purchased by the U.S. firm American Automar in 1985 (and renamed). She was chartered by the MSC in October 1985.

The AMERICAN CORMORANT showing her tanker lines, with her cut-out main deck. (1993, Leo Van Ginderen collection)

The AMERICAN CORMORANT loaded with Army barges, landing craft, and a floating crane. This is the only American-flag FLO/FLO ship. Several are in foreign service, having been employed under MSC charter to carry U.S. Navy minesweepers to the Persian Gulf and to bring back a damaged frigate. (1994, Leo Van Ginderen collection)

CARGO SHIPS

These are mostly break-bulk cargo ships. While of limited value in modern commercial shipping operations, these ships have considerable military utility.

1 COMBINATION CARGO SHIP: DANISH BUILT

Number	Name	Launched	Status
....	MAERSK CONSTELLATION (ex-ELIZABETH MAERSK)	1980	**MSC-Active**

Builders:	Odense Stålskibsværft A/S, Lindø (Denmark)
Displacement:	approx. 34,069 tons
Tonnage:	20,529 GRT 21,050 DWT
Length:	551¾ feet (168.2 m) waterline 598 feet (182.3 m) overall
Beam:	90 feet (27.4 m)
Draft:	32 feet (9.75 m)
Propulsion:	2 diesel engines (Sulzer); 15,960 bhp; 1 shaft
Speed:	18.5 knots
Range:	
Manning:	
Radars:	.... navigation

This combination container/vehicle ship was chartered by the MSC on 30 November 1988.

Fitted with a stern ramp, she can carry 566 containers. The ship has two 16-ton and four 30-ton cranes.

2 COMBINATION CARGO SHIPS: GERMAN BUILT

Number	Name	Launched	Status
....	GREEN RIDGE (ex-WOERMAN MERCUR, CAROL MERCUR, SLOMAN MERCUR)	1979	**MSC-Active**
T-AK 2050	GREEN WAVE (ex-WOERMAN MIRA, SLOMAN MIRA)	1980	**MSC-Active**

Builders:	Howaldtswerke (HDW), Kiel (Germany)
Displacement:	18,178 tons full load
Tonnage:	GREEN RIDGE 5,805 GRT 9,549 DWT GREEN WAVE 9,521 GRT 12,487 DWT
Length:	479 1/12 feet (146.1 m) waterline 507 feet (154.6 m) overall
Beam:	69¾ feet (21.25 m)
Draft:	24½ feet (7.45 m)
Propulsion:	2 diesel engines (Krupp-MaK); 10,000 bhp; 1 shaft
Speed:	18 knots
Range:	14,400 n.miles (26,669 km) at 17 knots
Manning:	21 civilian
Radars:	.... navigation

These ships are similar but not identical. Combination break-bulk

The GREEN WAVE in Arctic waters. She has containers stacked four high amidships and rides low in the water from a full load. She has a self-unloading capability with six cranes. Her bulbous bow is partially visible. (1988, U.S. Navy)

and container ships, they were originally chartered by the MSC mainly for Greenland and Antarctic resupply, the GREEN WAVE in August 1984 and the GREEN RIDGE in October 1988.

Both ships have ice-strengthened hulls. Each can carry 543 containers. Each is also fitted with six 25-ton-capacity cranes, four of which can be "ganged" to lift 80 tons from hold No. 4.

1 CARGO SHIP: NORWEGIAN BUILT

Number	Name	Launched	Status
T-AK 5076	NOBLE STAR (ex-CONCORDIA STAR, HOEGH STAR, COSTA ATLANTICA)	1977	**MSC-Active**

Builders:	Kaldnes M/V A/S Tønsberg (Norway)
Displacement:	24,000 tons full load
Tonnage:	10,472 GRT 15,922 DWT
Length:	534⅔ feet (163.0 m) waterline 562¼ feet (171.4 m) overall
Beam:	83 5/12 feet (25.4 m)
Draft:	34 7/12 feet (10.55 m)
Propulsion:	1 diesel engine (Nylands/Burmeister & Wain); 13,100 bhp; 1 shaft
Speed:	17.5 knots
Range:	
Manning:	21 civilian
Radars:	. . . . navigation

Chartered on 31 December 1988, this ship was loaded with a 500-bed deployable field hospital (330 containers) and deployed to Diego Garcia in November 1989 as part of the Afloat Prepositioning Force. She was reassigned to general MSC operation on 30 September 1993.

The NOBLE STAR has a capacity of 570 containers. The ship, with her superstructure aft, has one 5-ton crane, six 10-ton cranes, four 16-ton cranes, and one 150-ton-capacity crane.

Operational: The ship's field hospital was deployed during Operations Desert Storm/Desert Shield.

1 CARGO SHIP: C5 TYPE

Number	Name	Launched	To RRF	Status
T-AK 1014	CAPE NOME (ex-RAPID, AMERICAN RAPID, RED JACKET, MORMACSTAR)	26 Sep 1969	Dec 1987	MSC-RRF

Builders:	Ingalls Shipbuilding, Pascagoula, Miss.
Displacement:	27,980 tons full load
Tonnage:	11,757 GRT 15,694 DWT
Length:	559⅚ feet (170.7 m) waterline 601⅓ feet (183.3 m) overall
Beam:	90 feet (27.4 m)
Draft:	34 feet (10.4 m)
Propulsion:	2 steam turbines (General Electric); 30,000 shp; 1 shaft
Boilers:	2 (Combustion Engineering)
Speed:	23.6 knots
Range:	12,000 n.miles (22,224 km) at 23.6 knots
Manning:	34 civilian
Radars:	. . . . navigation

The capacity of this combination break-bulk/container ship is 70 containers.

The CAPE NOME is an especially attractive, superstructure-aft ship with three king posts that support cargo booms.

Design: Fitted with a stern door for vehicle loading/unloading.

The one-of-a-kind NOBLE STAR. Now employed in general MSC cargo operations, she previously was part of the Afloat Prepositioning Force carrying a largely containerized Navy field hospital. (1994, Leo Van Ginderen collection)

The CAPE NOME with a full load of containers. Her second of three king posts is "split." (1992, Leo Van Ginderen collection)

3 CARGO SHIPS: C5-S-75A TYPE

Number	Name	Launched	To RRF	Status
T-AK 2039	CAPE GIRARDEAU (ex-PRESIDENT ADAMS, ALASKAN MAIL)	1968	Apr 1988	MSC-RRF
T-AK 5051	CAPE GIBSON (ex-PRESIDENT JACKSON, INDIAN MAIL)	1968	Apr 1988	MSC-RRF
. . . .	CLEVELAND (ex-PRESIDENT CLEVELAND)	1969		**MSC-Active**

Builders:	Newport News Shipbuilding, Va.
Displacement:	31,995 tons full load
Tonnage:	15,949 GRT
	CAPE GIRARDEAU 22,273 DWT
	CAPE GIBSON 22,216 DWT
	CLEVELAND 22,180 DWT
Length:	582⅓ feet (177.55 m) waterline
	604⅚ feet (184.4 m) overall
Beam:	82⅙ feet (25.05 m)
Draft:	35 feet (10.7 m)
Propulsion:	2 steam turbines (General Electric); 24,000 shp; 1 shaft
Boilers:	2 (Babcock & Wilcox)
Speed:	21 knots
Range:	14,000 n.miles (25,928 km) at 20.8 knots
Manning:	47 civilian
Radars:	. . . . navigation

These break-bulk cargo ships can carry 409 containers, as well as dry and refrigerated cargo, and 17,000 barrels of liquid cargo. They can accommodate 22 passengers.

One 70-ton-capacity boom and 4 15-ton and 20 20-ton cranes are fitted.

The CAPE GIRARDEAU showing a different C5 configuration than the CAPE NOME. The large, 70-ton-capacity boom is visible behind the superstructure. (1993, Leo Van Ginderen collection)

5 CARGO SHIPS: C4-S-66A TYPE

Number	Name	Launched	To RRF	Status
T-AK 5056	Cape Breton	4 June 1966	May 1985	MSC-RRF
T-AK 5057	Cape Bover	12 Feb 1966	Apr 1985	MSC-RRF
T-AK 5058	Cape Borda	16 Apr 1966	Apr 1985	MSC-RRF
T-AK 5059	Cape Bon	16 July 1965	July 1985	MSC-RRF
T-AK 5060	Cape Blanco	10 July 1965	July 1985	MSC-RRF

Builders:	Avondale Shipyards, New Orleans, La.
Displacement:	21,840 tons full load
Tonnage:	10,723 GRT
	14,662 DWT
Length:	514¾ feet (156.9 m) waterline
	539⅚ feet (164.6 m) overall
Beam:	76 feet (23.2 m)
Draft:	32⅔ feet (9.95 m)
Propulsion:	2 steam turbines (De Laval or Westinghouse); 15,500 shp; 1 shaft
Boilers:	2 (Foster Wheeler)
Speed:	21 knots
Range:	13,660 n.miles (25,300 km) at 20 knots
Manning:	38 civilian
Radars:	1 . . . . navigation

These break-bulk cargo ships can carry 4,000 barrels of liquid cargo in addition to dry cargo.

Design: Fitted with one 80-ton-capacity boom and 20 small booms.

Status: The Letitia Lykes (T-AK 2043) and Tampa Bay of this type were returned to commercial merchant service.

The Cape Breton, fitted with numerous booms for handling break-bulk cargo. Her 80-ton-capacity boom is visible forward of the island structure. (1995, Leo Van Ginderen collection)

The Cape Bover shows the unusual king-post arrangement and twin funnels of this merchant ship design. These are break-bulk ships, very useful for carrying military cargoes that are not wheeled and cannot be easily containerized. (1995, Leo Van Ginderen collection)

5 CARGO SHIPS: C3-S-37D TYPE

Number	Name	Launched	To RRF	Status
T-AK 2035	Gulf Shipper	15 Feb 1964	Aug 1984	MSC-RRF
T-AK 2036	Gulf Trader	28 Dec 1963	Nov 1984	MSC-RRF
T-AK 5044	Gulf Banker	5 Oct 1963	Nov 1984	MSC-RRF
T-AK 5045	Gulf Farmer	3 Aug 1963	Nov 1984	MSC-RRF
T-AK 5046	Gulf Merchant	16 May 1964	Nov 1984	MSC-RRF

Builders: Avondale Shipyards, New Orleans, La.
Displacement: 17,210 tons full load
Tonnage: 8,988 GRT (except T-AK 5044, 5055—8,970 GRT)
11,368 DWT (except T-AK 5044, 5055—11,367 DWT)
Length: 494⅔ feet (150.8 m) overall
Beam: 69⅙ feet (21.1 m)
Draft: 30 1/12 feet (9.2 m)
Propulsion: 2 steam turbines (Westinghouse [except T-AK 5044, 5055 have General Electric]); 10,000 shp; 1 shaft
Boilers: 2 (Combustion Engineering)
Speed: 18.75 knots
Range: 12,000 n.miles (22,224 km) at 17.75 knots
Manning: 45 civilian
Radars: . . . . navigation

These five break-bulk cargo ships were built for the Gulf and South American Steam Ship Company.

Design: The ships have twin exhaust risers (stacks) that resemble king posts. Their machinery spaces are well aft. They have been fitted with one 66-ton-capacity boom, as well as ten 5-ton, two 10-ton, and two 15-ton derricks.

Engineering: Normal horsepower is indicated above; maximum is 11,000 shp.

3 CARGO SHIPS: C4-S-57A TYPE

Number	Name	Launched	To RRF	Status
T-AK 2016	Pioneer Commander (ex-American Commander)	20 Dec 1962	June 1982	MSC-RRF
T-AK 2018	Pioneer Contractor (ex-American Contractor)	22 Mar 1963	Sep 1981	MSC-RRF
T-AK 2019	Pioneer Crusader (ex-American Crusader)	30 July 1963	Sep 1981	MSC-RRF

Builders: Bethlehem Steel, Quincy, Mass.
Displacement: 21,053 tons full load
Tonnage: 11,164 GRT, except Pioneer Commander, 11,105 GRT
13,535 DWT
Length: 560 11/12 feet (171.0 m) overall
Beam: 75 1/12 feet (22.9 m)
Draft: 32⅙ feet (9.8 m)
Propulsion: 2 steam turbines (Bethlehem); 16,500 shp; 1 shaft
Boilers: 2 (Foster Wheeler)
Speed: 21 knots
Range: 12,000 n.miles (22,224 km) at 21 knots
Manning: 43 civilian
Radars: . . . . navigation

Details of these ships differ. Built for the United States Lines, they carry a mixed load of dry cargo, refrigerated provisions, and 8,000 barrels of liquid cargo.

Design: They have one 70-ton boom and several smaller cranes.

Engineering: Normal horsepower is indicated above; maximum is 18,150 shp. The merchant American Charger of this design set a 1963 speed record of 24.9 knots across the Atlantic (3,718 n.miles/ 6,890 km).

4 CARGO SHIPS: C3-S-37C TYPE

Number	Name	Launched	To RRF	Status
T-AK 5036	Cape Chalmers	6 Dec 1962	Nov 1984	MSC-RRF
T-AK 5039	Cape Clear	14 Aug 1963	Nov 1984	MSC-RRF
T-AK 5041	Cape Cod	11 July 1962	Nov 1984	MSC-RRF
T-AK 5042	Cape Carthage	9 Mar 1963	Sep 1984	MSC-RRF

Builders: Bethlehem Steel, Sparrows Point, Baltimore, Md., except Cape Carthage—Avondale Shipyards, New Orleans, La.
Displacement: 18,560 tons full load
Tonnage: 9,296 GRT
12,684 DWT
Length: 494¾ (150.8 m) overall
Beam: 69⅙ feet (21.1 m)
Draft: 32 feet (9.75 m)
Propulsion: 2 steam turbines (General Electric); 11,000 shp; 1 shaft
Boilers: 2 (Combustion Engineering or Foster Wheeler)
Speed: 18.75 knots
Range: 18,300 n.miles (33,892 km) at 17.75 knots
Manning: 34 to 40 civilian
Radars: . . . . navigation

Built for the Lykes Brothers Steamship Company, these break-bulk cargo ships can carry 8,000 barrels of liquid cargo. This was the first series of U.S. oceangoing cargo ships to be built after World War II by a private shipping company.

Design: Twin risers resembling king posts serve as stacks. The ships are fitted with one 60-ton-capacity boom and 20 smaller booms.

Status: Four other ships of this class were transferred from the RRF to be laid up in the NDRF. They are:

Ship		*to NDRF*
T-AK 5037	Cape Canso	1 Apr 1994
T-AK 5038	Cape Charles	8 Dec 1992
T-AK 5040	Cape Canaveral	7 Oct 1994
T-AK 5043	Cape Catoche	7 Oct 1994

The Gulf Trader shows another unusual arrangement of king posts and cargo booms. Twin risers are abaft the bridge structure; additional cargo booms lie aft. (1990, Giorgio Arra)

The CAPE CARTHAGE, fitted with king posts forward and a variety of booms for handling break-bulk cargo. (1993, Leo Van Ginderen collection)

5 CARGO SHIPS: C4-S-58A TYPE

Number	Name	Launched	To RRF	Status
T-AK 5009	CAPE ANN	12 May 1962	Mar 1980	MSC-RRF
T-AK 5010	CAPE ALEXANDER	7 July 1962	Apr 1980	MSC-RRF
T-AK 5011	CAPE ARCHWAY	15 Sep 1962	Apr 1980	MSC-RRF
T-AK 5012	CAPE ALAVA	24 Mar 1962	Apr 1980	MSC-RRF
T-AK 5013	CAPE AVINOF	8 Dec 1962	Apr 1980	MSC-RRF

Builders:	Ingalls Shipbuilding, Pascagoula, Miss.
Displacement:	18,560 tons full load
Tonnage:	11,309 GRT 12,932 DWT
Length:	540$\frac{11}{12}$ feet (164.9 m) waterline 571$\frac{5}{6}$ feet (174.35 m) overall
Beam:	75$\frac{1}{6}$ feet (22.9 m)
Draft:	30$\frac{5}{6}$ feet (9.4 m)
Propulsion:	2 steam turbines (General Electric or Westinghouse); 16,500 shp; 1 shaft
Boilers:	2
Speed:	21.5 knots
Range:	13,300 n.miles (24,632 km) at 20 knots
Manning:	39 civilian
Helicopters:	landing deck in CAPE ANN and CAPE AVINOF
Radars:	. . . . navigation

These large break-bulk cargo ships were built for Farrell Lines specifically for their East African trade. The ships contain special dehumidifying equipment to prevent cargo sweating and odor permeation.

Each ship is fitted with one 60-ton-capacity boom and 14 5-ton and six 10-ton cranes. Two ships were fitted with a helicopter deck aft and other enhancements upon being taken over by the MSC.

Class: Originally, six ships were in this class.

Engineering: Normal horsepower is indicated above; maximum is 19,250 shp. Several ships exceeded their designed speed (above); the AFRICAN NEPTUNE (now T-AK 5011) averaged 22.48 knots on the 6,786 n.mile trip from New York to Cape Town, South Africa.

4 CARGO SHIPS: C4-S-1 TYPE

Number	Name	Launched	To RRF	Status
T-AK 5022	CAPE JOHN (ex-SANTA ANA)	18 Aug 1962	May 1980	MSC-RRF
T-AK 5029	CAPE JACOB (ex-CALIFORNIA)	28 July 1961	Dec 1980	MSC-RRF
T-AK 5075	CAPE JOHNSON (ex-MORMACSAGA, M.M. DANT)	5 May 1962	June 1988	MSC-RRF
T-AK 5077	CAPE JUBY (ex-MORMACSEA, HAWAII)	9 Feb 1962	July 1988	MSC-RRF

Builders: T-AK 5022, 5077 National Steel and Shipbuilding, San Diego, Calif.
T-AK 5029, 5075 Newport News Shipbuilding, Va.

The CAPE ALEXANDER emitting smoke while under way. Some of these ships have landing decks for light helicopters. (1991, Leo Van Ginderen collection)

The CAPE JUBY at Norfolk, Virginia, shortly after having been chartered by the MSC. These ships have a standard king-post/crane arrangement, with a 60-ton-capacity boom on the third king post. (1988, U.S. Navy)

Displacement:	22,629 tons
Tonnage:	CAPE JOHN 12,724 GRT 14,376 DWT CAPE JOHNSON 12,724 GRT 14,467 DWT others 12,691 GRT 14,321 DWT
Length:	528 5/12 feet (161.1 m) waterline 565 feet (172.25 m) overall
Beam:	76 feet (23.2 m)
Draft:	32 feet (9.75 m)
Propulsion:	2 steam turbines (General Electric); 17,500 shp; 1 shaft
Boilers:	2 (Foster Wheeler)
Speed:	20.75 knots
Range:	12,600 n.miles (23,335 km) at 20 knots
Manning:	CAPE JOHN 41 civilian CAPE JACOB 43 civilian others 44 civilian
Radars:	. . . . navigation

These break-bulk cargo ships were built for States Steamship Company or (*Mormac* prefix ships) Moore-McCormack Lines.

Design: One 60-ton-capacity boom, ten 5-ton cranes, two 10-ton cranes, and ten 20-ton cranes.

Engineering: Normal horsepower is indicated above; maximum is 19,200 shp.

2 CARGO SHIPS: C3-S-46A TYPE

Number	Name	Launched	To RRF	Status
T-AK 5008	BANNER	1961	Jan 1983	MSC-RRF
T-AK 5019	COURIER	1962	Aug 1983	MSC-RRF

Builders:	BANNER National Steel and Shipbuilding, San Diego, Calif. COURIER Sun Shipbuilding and Dry Dock, Chester, Pa.
Displacement:	19,400 tons full load
Tonnage:	BANNER 10,659 GRT 12,629 DWT COURIER 11,000 GRT 12,705 DWT
Length:	469 11/12 feet (143.3 m) waterline 493 feet (150.3 m) overall
Beam:	73 feet (22.25 m)
Draft:	30½ feet (9.3 m)
Propulsion:	2 steam turbines (General Electric); 13,750 shp; 1 shaft
Boilers:	2 (Babcock & Wilcox)
Speed:	20 knots
Range:	18,000 n.miles (33,336 km) at 18.5 knots
Manning:	39 civilian
Radars:	. . . . navigation

The BANNER moored in the Elizabeth River, Virginia, awaiting crisis or war. These ships have an amidships bridge structure, with machinery aft. (1987, U.S. Navy)

These are break-bulk cargo ships built for American Export/Isbrandtsen Lines. The COURIER has been modified to carry containers in addition to break-bulk cargo.

Design: Machinery and large superstructure-aft ships with amidships bridge structure. They are fitted with one 60-ton-capacity boom and 20 smaller booms and cranes.

Engineering: Normal horsepower is indicated above; maximum is 13,750 shp.

Names: Note that there is also a tanker named COURIER in MSC service.

Status: The BUYER (T-AK 2033) of this type was downgraded from the RRF to the NDRF on 7 October 1994.

4 CARGO SHIPS: C3-S-33A TYPE

Number	Name	Launched	To RRF	Status
T-AK 284	NORTHERN LIGHT	Apr 1961	Oct 1984	MSC-RRF
T-AK 5016	LAKE	5 Jan 1961	Mar 1977	MSC-RRF
T-AK 5018	SCAN	21 Mar 1961	Feb 1977	MSC-RRF
T-AK 5074	CAPE CATAWBA	1960	Feb 1987	MSC-RRF

Builders:	Sun Shipbuilding and Dry Dock, Chester, Pa., except T-AK 5074—Todd Shipyards, San Pedro, Calif.
Displacement:	18,365 tons full load
Tonnage:	T-AK 284 9,361 GRT 12,537 DWT
Length:	457⅝ feet (139.6 m) waterline 485 11/12 feet (148.15 m) overall
Beam:	68 feet (20.7 m)
Draft:	28½ feet (8.7 m)
Propulsion:	1 steam turbine (General Electric); 11,000 shp; 1 shaft
Boilers:	2 (Combustion Engineering)
Speed:	19 knots
Range:	14,000 n.miles (25,928 km) at 18 knots
Manning:	41 civilian
Radars:	1 . . . . navigation

These were commercial cargo ships built for Moore-McCormack Lines. After merchant service they were laid up in the NDRF. The NORTHERN LIGHT and SOUTHERN CROSS (T-AK 285) were acquired by the Navy in April 1980 for use as prepositioning ships in the Indian Ocean; they were placed in service on 22 April 1980 and 1 May 1980, respectively. Their sister ship VEGA was acquired in April 1981 for conversion to an SSBN supply ship (T-AK 286); see chapter 23.

Two other ships were acquired for conversion to surveying ships but Congress directed new-construction ships instead.

The NORTHERN LIGHT was laid up by the MSC on 26 April 1984 and the SOUTHERN CROSS on 13 September 1984 (correction to previous edition).

Design: The T-AK 284 has a modified bow that makes her slightly longer than other ships of this design. Both ex-T-AK ships are ice strengthened for Arctic operations.

Engineering: Normal horsepower is shown above; maximum is 12,100 shp.

Status: The PRIDE (T-AK 5017) and SOUTHERN CROSS (T-AK 285) were downgraded from the RRF to the NDRF in 1994. The NORTHERN LIGHT and SOUTHERN CROSS were U.S. Naval Ships when active.

VEHICLE/RAILROAD CARGO SHIPS: CONVERTED T2-SE-A2 TYPE

The WASHINGTON (T-AK 5020) and MAINE (T-AK 5021) remain laid up in the NDRF. They are former Mission-type tankers, having been extensively converted to carry railway cars, containers, vehicles, and aircraft. They are invariably referred to as "seatrains."

Formerly assigned to the RRF, both ships are deteriorating because of age and are expected to be stricken in the near future. Both ships shifted from RRF to NDRF status on 12 June 1991.

Class: The WASHINGTON was built as the merchant tanker MISSION SAN DIEGO. She was acquired by the Navy on 17 October 1947 and designated AO 121 (name retained). She was stricken on 22 June 1955; reacquired on 3 July 1956, she served in the MSC until 16 October 1957, when she was stricken again.

The MAINE was built as the Navy tanker TOMAHAWK, designated AO 88. Commissioned on 16 April 1944, she served in the Pacific during 1944–1945 (earning six battle stars). She was decommissioned on 5 January 1946 and stricken on 21 January 1946; she was then acquired for MSTS operation until transferred to the Maritime Administration in September 1961 and laid up.

See 15th Edition/page 197 for characteristics.

CARGO SHIPS: C3-S-76A TYPE

The three cargo ships of this type have been taken out of the RRF and assigned to the NDRF: DEL VIENTO (T-AK 5026), DEL MONTE (T-AK 5049), and DEL VALLE (T-AK 5050). They were break-bulk cargo ships built for the Delta Line.

See 15th Edition/page 309 for characteristics.

CARGO SHIPS: C3-S-38A TYPE

The four cargo ships of this type have been transferred from the RRF to the NDRF: ADVENTURER (T-AK 5005), AIDE (T-AK 5006), AMBASSADOR (T-AK 5007), and AGENT (T-AK 5008). They were break-bulk cargo ships originally built for the American Export/Isbrandtsen Lines.

See 15th Edition/page 310 for characteristics.

The NORTHERN LIGHT with containers on deck, showing the flexibility of break-bulk cargo ships. These ships have a large, squat funnel. Sister ships served in the FBM resupply role. (U.S. Navy)

CARGO SHIP: JAPANESE BUILT

The ADVANTAGE (T-AK 9652) has been taken out of MSC service. She was employed as a prepositioned ammunition ship, carrying Air Force munitions.

See 15th Edition/page 313 for characteristics.

LIGHTER-ABOARD-SHIP (LASH) SHIPS

These merchant ships carry large, fully loaded barges or lighters that can be floated or lifted on and off the ship. This scheme speeds up loading and unloading and allows cargo to be handled at ports where piers or wharves are unavailable. The two principal barge-carrying designs are known as LASH (Lighter Aboard Ship) and SEABEE (Sea Barge); the former ships use cranes to lift barges to the cargo decks and the latter ships have large stern elevators.

SEABEE ships maintained by the MSC are listed on page 278.

1 LASH CARGO SHIP: C9-S-81D TYPE

Number	Name	Launched	Status
T-AK 2049	GREEN VALLEY (ex-BUTTON GWINETT)	1974	**MSC-APF**

Builders:	Avondale Shipyards, New Orleans, La.
Displacement:	62,314 tons full load
Tonnage:	T-AK type 32,278 GRT
Length:	797⅙ feet (243.0 m) waterline
	893⅓ feet (272.35 m) overall
Beam:	100 feet (30.5 m)
Draft:	40⅚ feet (12.4 m)
Propulsion:	2 steam turbines (De Laval); 32,000 shp; 1 shaft
Boilers:	2 (Combustion Engineering)
Speed:	22.75 knots
Range:	15,000 n.miles (27,780 km) at 22 knots
Manning:	27 civilian
Radars:	2 . . . . navigation

LASH ships of this type can carry 89 preloaded barges. A small tug is also embarked to help maneuver barges alongside. Each ship is fitted with a 510-ton traveling crane.

Class: The CAPE FEAR was procured by the MSC in January 1988. She suffered major machinery damage during an MSC-sponsored overhaul, thus delaying her completion.

2 LASH SHIPS: C8-S-81B TYPE

Number	Name	Launched	Status
T-AK 1005	AUSTRAL RAINBOW (ex-CHINA BEAR)	1972	**MSC-APF**
T-AK 2064	GREEN HARBOUR (ex-WILLIAM HOOPER)	1972	**MSC-APF**

Builders:	Avondale Shipyards, New Orleans, La.
Displacement:	44,606 tons full load
Tonnage:	26,456 GRT
	29,820 DWT
Length:	723⅚ feet (220.7 m) waterline
	819⅚ feet (249.9 m) overall
Beam:	100 feet (30.5 m)
Draft:	40¾ feet (12.4 m)
Propulsion:	2 steam turbines (De Laval); 32,000 shp; 1 shaft
Boilers:	2 (Babcock & Wilcox or Combustion Engineering)
Speed:	22.5 knots
Range:	13,000 n.miles (24,076 km) at 22.5 knots
Manning:	33 civilian
Radars:	. . . . navigation

These are former LASH barge carriers that were modified (prior to the MSC charter) to combination barge/container ships. The AUSTRAL RAINBOW can carry 71 standard cargo barges or some 840 containers; the GREEN HARBOUR can carry 1,000 containers.

Each ship is fitted with a 30-ton-capacity traveling crane for handling containers and a 446-ton-capacity traveling barge crane. Two 5-ton cranes are also installed.

LASH ships of this type are similar to the larger C9-S-81d barge carriers.

Class: These were highly innovative ships, 11 having been built to this design. Several ships previously operated by the MSC have been laid up in the NDRF or returned to commercial service.

1 LASH SHIP: JAPANESE BUILT

Number	Name	Launched	Status
T-AK 9204	JEB STUART (ex-ATLANTIC FOREST)	1970	**MSC-APF**

Builders:	Sumitomo Heavy Industries, Uraga, Japan
Displacement:	approx. 65,000 tons
Tonnage:	33,221 GRT
	49,858 DWT
Length:	771½ feet (235.2 m) waterline
	857⅓ feet (261.4 m) overall
Beam:	106⅚ feet (32.6 m)
Draft:	39¾ feet (12.13 m)
Propulsion:	1 diesel engine (Sumitomo-Sulzer 9RND90); 26,000 bhp; 1 shaft
Speed:	18 knots
Range:	29,920 n.miles (55,440 km) at 18 knots
Manning:	
Radars:	. . . . navigation

The AUSTRAL RAINBOW is similar to the C9-type LASH ships, but smaller. These ships have two massive traveling cranes to move full-laden lighters. There are two small lighter-handling tugs near the stern, carried as "deck cargo." (U.S. Navy)

Chartered in July 1992, the ship was assigned to MSC operations on 30 September 1993.

The ship can carry 80 LASH barges, handled by a 510-ton traveling crane.

PREPOSITIONING SHIPS

Nineteen Large Medium-Speed RO/RO (LMSR) ships are to be procured by conversion and new construction for the forward prepositioning of Army vehicles, artillery, munitions, and provisions. The Marine Corps currently has similar matériel afloat in 13 Maritime Prepositioning Ships (MPS) procured during the 1980s.

Names: All ships listed below are named for Medal of Honor recipients of the Army and Marine Corps except for the Bob Hope, which honors a great American comedian who has long entertained U.S. troops throughout the world.

(3+) AFLOAT PREPOSITIONING SHIPS: MODIFIED "BOB HOPE" CLASS

Number	Name	FY	Launch	In service	Status
T-AKR 310	....	93	1997	1998	Building
T-AKR 311	....	95	1998	1998	Building
T-AKR 312	....	95	1998	1999	Building
T-AKR 313–315					Options

Builders:	National Steel and Shipbuilding, San Diego, Calif.
Displacement:	62,968 tons full load
Tonnage:	
Length:	950 feet (289.63 m) overall
Beam:	105¾ feet (32.24 m)
Draft:	34 feet (10.37 m)
Propulsion:	2 gas turbines; 64,000 shp; 1 shaft
Speed:	24 knots
Range:	12,700+ n.miles (23,530+ km) at 24 knots
Manning:	95 civilian (crew + maintenance)
Helicopters:	landing area
Radars:	.... navigation

These ships are similar to the Bob Hope design, but they have gas turbine propulsion. These ships are being constructed following the results of studies conducted after the Gulf War of 1991. Six ships have been funded (T-AKR 300–302, 310–312), and there's a contract option for six additional ships (T-AKR 303–305, 313–315). Together with the five conversions listed below, they would provide 17 of the proposed 19 LMSRs.

All three ships of this class are planned for deployment in the Pacific–Indian Ocean area.

(3+) AFLOAT PREPOSITIONING SHIPS: "BOB HOPE" CLASS

Number	Name	FY	Launch	In service	Status
T-AKR 300	Bob Hope	93	1996	1998	Building
T-AKR 301	....	94	1997	1998	Building
T-AKR 302	....	94	1997	1999	Building
T-AKR 303–305					Options

Builders:	Avondale Industries, New Orleans, La.
Displacement:	62,069 tons full load
Tonnage:	
Length:	950 feet (289.63 m) overall
Beam:	105⅚ feet (32.27 m)
Draft:	34⅔ feet (10.57 m)
Propulsion:	4 medium-speed diesel engines; 65,160 bhp; 1 shaft
Speed:	24 knots
Range:	12,000+ n.miles (22,235+ km) at 24 knots
Manning:	95 civilian (crew + maintenance)
Helicopters:	landing area
Radars:	.... navigation

Similar to the T-AKR 310 class, these ships have diesel propulsion. The Bob Hope was laid down on 29 May 1995.

All three ships of this class and the following three conversions are planned for deployment in the Pacific–Indian Ocean area carrying Army equipment.

2 + 1 AFLOAT PREPOSITIONING SHIPS: CONVERSIONS

Number	Name	In service	Status
T-AKR 295	Sgt 1st Class Randall D. Shughart (ex-Laura Maersk)	1996	**MSC-APF**
T-AKR 297	Sgt 1st Class Rodney J.T. Yano (ex-Leise Maersk)	1996	**MSC-APF**
T-AKR 299	Pfc William A. Soderman (ex-Lica Maersk)	1997	Yard

Builders:	
Displacement:	54,298 tons full load
Tonnage:	
Length:	907 feet (276.52 m) overall
Beam:	105 7/12 feet (32.2 m)
Draft:	34⅚ feet (10.62 m)
Propulsion:	1 slow-speed diesel engine; 47,916 bhp; 1 shaft
Speed:	24 knots
Range:	12,000 n.miles (22,235 km) at 24 knots
Manning:	95 (crew + maintenance)
Radars:	.... navigation

The conversion of these ships was funded under the fiscal 1993 conversion program. The conversion yards and start dates were:

Shughart	National Steel, San Diego	24 June 1994
Yano	National Steel, San Diego	17 May 1995
Soderman	National Steel, San Diego	12 Oct 1995

An artist's concept of the Bob Hope shows a large, superstructure-aft ship designed to carry large numbers of military vehicles as well as containers and other deck cargo. A helicopter landing area is shown just forward of the bridge. Nineteen of these Large Medium-Speed RO/RO (LMSR) ships are planned. (U.S. Navy)

The SGT 1ST CLASS RANDALL D. SHUGHART at San Diego while on post-conversion trials. Note the ship's forward side ramps and paired heavy cranes. (1996, National Steel & Shipbuilding Co., Kim Lee)

Stern aspect of the SHUGHART showing the massive stern structure required to support the vehicle ramp. (1996, National Steel & Shipbuilding Co., Kim Lee)

(2) AFLOAT PREPOSITIONING SHIPS: CONVERSIONS

Number	Name	In service	Status
T-AKR 296	MSGT GARY I. GORDON (ex-JUTLANDIA)	1996	Yard
T-AKR 298	CPL CHARLES L. GILLILAND (ex-SELANDIA)	1996	Yard

Builders:
Displacement: 57,487 tons full load
Tonnage:
Length: 954 feet (290.85 m) overall
Beam: 105⅚ feet (32.25 m)
Draft: 35¾ feet (10.9 m)
Propulsion: 3 slow-speed diesel engines; 65,000 bhp; 1 shaft
Speed: 24 knots
Range: 12,000 n.miles (22,235 km) at 24 knots
Manning: 95 (crew + maintenance)
Radars: . . . . navigation

These conversions, authorized in fiscal 1993, were assigned to the following yards (start dates are indicated):

GORDON	Newport News Shipbuilding, Va.	15 Oct 1993
GILLILAND	Newport News Shipbuilding, Va.	21 Oct 1993

The MSGT GARY I. GORDON in dry dock undergoing conversion to an afloat prepositioning ships at the Newport News Shipbuilding yard. The Army is joining the Marine Corps in the prepositioning of matérial afloat in forward areas. (1995, U.S. Navy)

5 MARITIME PREPOSITIONING SHIPS: "BOBO" CLASS (C8-M-MA134J)

Number	Name	Launched	In service	Status
T-AK 3008	2nd LT JOHN P. BOBO	19 Jan 1985	14 Feb 1985	**MSC-MPS**
T-AK 3009	PFC DEWAYNE T. WILLIAMS	18 May 1985	6 June 1985	**MSC-MPS**
T-AK 3010	1st LT BALDOMERO LOPEZ	26 Oct 1985	21 Nov 1985	**MSC-MPS**
T-AK 3011	1st LT JACK LUMMUS	22 Feb 1986	6 Mar 1986	**MSC-MPS**
T-AK 3012	SGT WILLIAM R. BUTTON	17 May 1986	18 May 1986	**MSC-MPS**

Builders:	General Dynamics, Quincy, Mass.
Displacement:	22,700 tons light 40,846 tons full load
Tonnage:	44,543 GRT 26,523 DWT
Length:	673 feet (205.2 m) overall
Beam:	105½ feet (32.2 m)
Draft:	29½ feet (9.0 m)
Propulsion:	2 diesel engines (Stork Werkspoor 18TM410V); 26,400 bhp; 1 shaft
Speed:	17.7 knots
Range:	11,100 n.miles (20,557 km) at 17.7 knots
Manning:	30 civilian + 25 maintenance personnel (civilian)
Flag:	7 (Navy-civilian) + 8 Navy communications in 1 ship
Helicopters:	landing area
Radars:	2 . . . . navigation

These new-construction ships were classified T-AKX during planning stages. Each of them carries equipment and supplies for about a quarter of a MAB for 30 days. Although built specifically for the MPS role, they are under 25-year charter.

The first two ships were laid down in 1983, others in 1984.

Design: These ships have 162,500 square feet (14,625 m^2) of vehicle deck space and can carry 1,605,000 gallons (6 million liters) of break-bulk petroleum products, plus 81,770 gallons (310,726 liters) of potable water. Up to 522 containers can be carried. A stern ramp is fitted for unloading vehicles into landing craft and onto piers. Five 39-ton-capacity cranes have also been fitted.

Engineering: These ships achieved 18.8 knots on trials; above is sustained speed. A 1,000-hp bow thruster is fitted to permit maneuvering alongside a pier without the aid of tugs.

Manning: All MPS ships will have berthing for a Marine "surge team" that can be embarked to assist in preparing vehicles and unloading. These teams consist of about 100 troops in these and the Waterman ships, and up to 77 in the Maersk ships.

The SGT WILLIAM R. BUTTON, with a deck load of military containers and holds stuffed with munitions, vehicles, and equipment for Marine expeditionary forces. The heavy cranes and stern ramp provide a self-unloading capability. (1995, Giorgio Arra)

The SGT WILLIAM R. BUTTON is typical of the 13 maritime prepositioning ships that carry Marine vehicles, weapons, and equipment. These ships have a raised helicopter deck above their stern, above the main vehicle unloading ramp. (1995, Giorgio Arra)

3 MARITIME PREPOSITIONING SHIPS: WATERMAN CLASS (C7-S-133A)

Number	Name	Launched	Start Conv.	In service	Status
T-AK 3005	SGT MATEJ KOCAK (ex-JOHN B. WATERMAN)	1981	Mar 1983	5 Oct 1984	**MSC-MPS**
T-AK 3006	PFC EUGENE A. OBREGON (ex-THOMAS HEYWOOD)	1982	Nov 1982	15 Jan 1985	**MSC-MPS**
T-AK 3007	MAJ STEPHEN W. PLESS (ex-CHARLES CARROLL)	1983	Mar 1983	1 May 1985	**MSC-MPS**

Builders:	Sun Shipbuilding and Dry Dock, Chester, Pa., except PLESS—General Dynamics, Quincy, Mass.
Displacement:	15,000 tons light 48,754 tons full load
Length:	821 feet (250.3 m) overall
Beam:	105½ feet (32.2 m)
Draft:	32⅙ feet (9.8 m)
Propulsion:	2 steam turbines; 30,000 shp; 1 shaft
Boilers:	2
Speed:	20 knots
Range:	13,000 n.miles (24,076 km) at 20 knots
Manning:	39 civilian + 25 maintenance personnel (civilian)
Flag:	7 (Navy-civilian) + 8 Navy communications in 1 ship
Helicopters:	landing area
Radars:	2 . . . . navigation

Previously commercial container ships operated by the Waterman Corporation, these ships were acquired specifically for conversion to the MPS role, designated T-AKX during the planning stage, and under 25-year charter.

Conversion: As built, these ships were 695 feet (211.9 m) overall, with a full-load displacement of 38,975 tons. A 126-foot (38.4-m) mid-body section was inserted, and the ships were reconfigured for 152,524 square feet (13,727 m^2) of vehicle cargo space and 540 standard cargo containers. They can carry 1,544,000 gallons (5.8 million liters) of bulk fuels and 94,780 gallons (360,164 liters) of potable water. The ships are fitted with vehicle ramps and cranes to provide a self-unloading capability.

All three ships were converted to the MPS role by the National Steel yard in San Diego, California.

The SGT MATEJ KOCAK anchored off Norfolk. The ship has two pairs of heavy cranes forward, as well as a traveling crane for handling containers. (1988, Giorgio Arra)

The PFC EUGENE A. OBREGON with empty main deck. Two helicopter spots are marked on the raised helicopter deck. Unlike UNREP ships, these ships cannot easily move cargo from holds to helicopters. (1989, Giorgio Arra)

5 MARITIME PREPOSITIONING SHIPS: DANISH BUILT

Number	Name	Launched	Start Conv.	In service	Status
T-AK 3000	CPL LOUIS J. HAUGE JR. (ex-ESTELLE MAERSK)	3 Aug 1979	Jan 1984	7 Sep 1984	**MSC-MPS**
T-AK 3001	PFC WILLIAM B. BAUGH JR. (ex-ELEO MAERSK)	1979	Jan 1983	30 Oct 1984	**MSC-MPS**
T-AK 3002	PFC JAMES ANDERSON JR. (ex-EMMA MAERSK)	23 Mar 1979	Oct 1983	26 Mar 1985	**MSC-MPS**
T-AK 3003	1ST LT ALEX BONNYMAN JR. (ex-EMILIE MAERSK)	3 Aug 1979	Jan 1984	26 Sep 1985	**MSC-MPS**
T-AK 3004	PVT HARRY FISHER (ex-EVELYN MAERSK)	12 Oct 1979	Apr 1984	12 Sep 1985	**MSC-MPS**

Builders:	Odense Stålskibsværft, Lindø (Denmark)
Displacement:	28,249 tons light
	46,484 tons full load
Length:	755½ feet (230.3 m) overall
Beam:	90¹⁄₁₂ feet (27.5 m)
Draft:	32¹⁄₁₂ feet (9.8 m)
Propulsion:	1 diesel engine (Sulzer 7RND 76M); 16,800 bhp; 1 shaft
Speed:	17.5 knots
Range:	10,800 n.miles (20,000 km) at 17.5 knots
Manning:	30 civilian + 20 maintenance personnel (civilian)
Flag:	7 (Navy-civilian) + 8 Navy communications in BONNYMAN
Helicopters:	landing area
Radars:	2 . . . . navigation

The CPL LOUIS J. HAUGE JR. showing how the heavy-lift cranes are paired. Military containers are on the forward deck. (1991, Leo Van Ginderen collection)

These former Maersk Line combination container and RO/RO vehicle cargo ships were acquired by the U.S. government specifically for conversion to the MPS role. The ships were designated T-AKX during the design stage.

Conversion: During conversion a new 157½-foot (48-m) midsection was added to each ship (original length 598¹⁄₁₂ feet/182.3 m, with a deadweight tonnage of 29,182 tons). In the MPS role they have 120,080 square feet (10,807 m^2) of vehicle storage space and can carry up to 332 standard freight containers, 1,283,000 gallons (4.8 million liters) of bulk fuels, and 65,000 gallons (247,000 liters) of potable water. Ramps and cranes provide a limited self-unloading capability.

The HAUGE, ANDERSON, and FISHER were converted by the Bethlehem Steel yard at Sparrows Point, Baltimore, Maryland; the BAUGH and BONNYMAN underwent conversion at the Bethlehem Steel yard in Beaumont, Texas.

Names: The ALEXANDER BONNYMAN JR. was changed to ALEX BONNYMAN JR. on 4 March 1986. The PVT HARRY FISHER was to have been changed to PVT FRANKLIN S. PHILLIPS, the former being the pseudonym used by Phillips when he was awarded the Medal of Honor, but the original name has been retained.

The PFC WILLIAM B. BAUGH JR. at Portsmouth, Virginia. The ship is riding high in the water even though a large deck cargo is being carried. (1990, Leo Van Ginderen collection)

RANGE SUPPORT SHIPS

MSC ships of this category support the various tracking stations on the Atlantic Missile Range.

1 RANGE SUPPORT SHIP

Number	Name	Launched	Status
....	SEACOR CLIPPER (ex-NICOR CLIPPER)	20 Apr 1982	**MSC-Active**

Builders:	Moss Point Marine, Escatawpa, Miss.
Displacement:	
Tonnage:	428 GRT 1,200 DWT
Length:	$253\frac{11}{12}$ feet (77.4 m) overall
Beam:	44 feet (13.4 m)
Draft:	13 feet (4.0 m)
Propulsion:	2 diesel engines (General Motors EMD 12-567C); 2,700 bhp; 2 shafts
Speed:	10 knots
Range:	
Manning:	
Radars:	.... navigation

This is a small, open-deck cargo ship employed to support U.S. space tracking and research facilities on various Caribbean islands. The ship was chartered by the MSC on 6 May 1987.

Design: Built as an offshore oil rig supply vessel, a stern ramp has been fitted for carrying small vehicles. A bow thruster has also been fitted.

SEA BARGE (SEABEE) SHIPS

3 SEABEE SHIPS: C8-S-82A TYPE

Number	Name	Launched	To RRF	Status
T-AKR 5063	CAPE MAY (ex-ALMERIA LYKES)	1972	July 1986	MSC-RRF
T-AKR 5064	CAPE MENDOCINO (ex-DOCTOR LYKES)	1972	Oct 1986	MSC-RRF
T-AKR 5065	CAPE MOHICAN (ex-TILLIE LYKES)	1973	Sep 1986	MSC-RRF

Builders:	General Dynamics, Quincy, Mass.
Displacement:	18,880 tons light 57,290 tons full load
Tonnage:	21,667 GRT 38,410 DWT
Length:	$721\frac{1}{3}$ feet (219.9 m) waterline $873\frac{3}{4}$ feet (266.39 m) overall
Beam:	$105\frac{5}{6}$ feet (32.3 m)
Draft:	$39\frac{1}{12}$ feet (11.9 m)
Propulsion:	2 steam turbines (General Electric); 36,000 shp; 1 shaft
Boilers:	2 (Babcock & Wilcox)
Speed:	20.5 knots
Range:	14,300 n.miles (26,484 km) at 19.25 knots
Manning:	39
Radars:	.... navigation

Each ship can carry 38 cargo barges.

Design: Fitted with a 2,000-ton-capacity elevator at the stern for loading and unloading fully laden barges. In addition, these ships can carry 4,000 barrels (CAPE MOHICAN, 11,000 barrels) of liquid cargo.

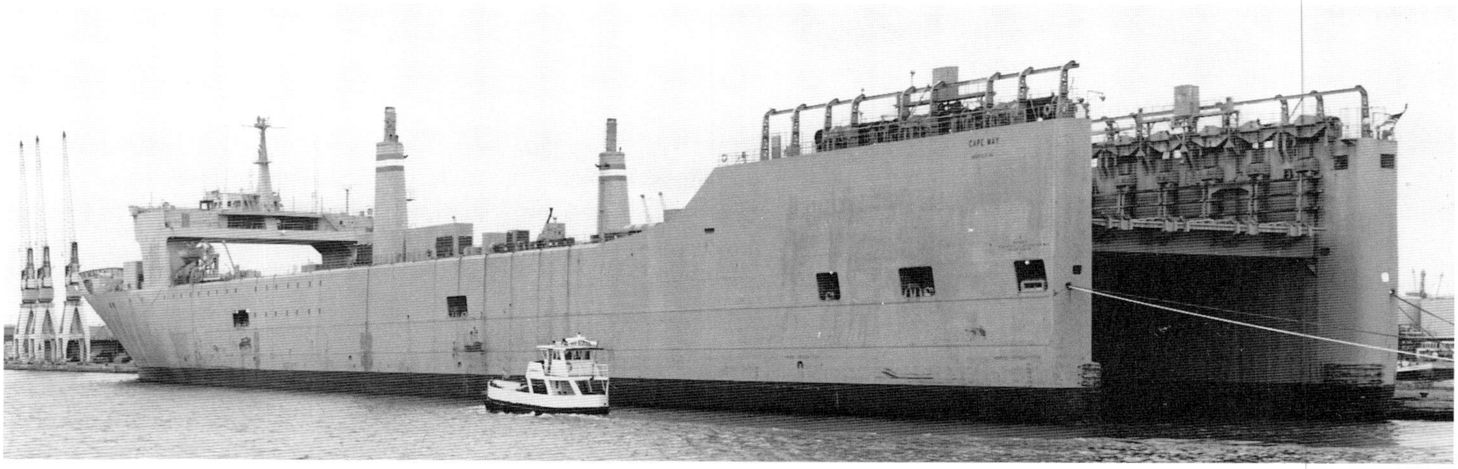

The open stern of the CAPE MAY shows the barge-carrying well of the ship. The stern elevator lifts barges to the storage-deck level. The twin funnels are mounted atop the sidewalls. (1991, Leo Van Ginderen collection)

The CAPE MOHICAN shows the long, straight lines of this barge-carrying design. The bridge straddles the barge well. The machinery is fitted into the side-walls. (1991, Leo Van Ginderen collection)

TANKERS

In addition to the tankers listed below, the Navy-built fleet oilers of the HENRY J. KAISER (T-AO 187) class are being assigned to the sealift role (see page 237).

Several ships are fitted with the OPDS (Offshore Petroleum Discharge System) to transfer fuel ashore without pier facilities, together with a four-mile (6.5-km) flexible floating pipeline.

5 TANKERS: MODIFIED T5 TYPE

Number	Name	Launched	In service	Status
T-AOT 1121	GUS W. DARNELL (ex-OCEAN FREEDOM)	10 Aug 1985	11 Sep 1985	**MSC-Active**
T-AOT 1122	PAUL BUCK (ex-OCEAN CHAMPION)	1 June 1985	11 Sep 1985	**MSC-Active**
T-AOT 1123	SAMUEL L. COBB (ex-OCEAN TRIUMPH)	2 Nov 1985	15 Nov 1985	**MSC-Active**
T-AOT 1124	RICHARD G. MATTHIESEN (ex-OCEAN SPIRIT)	15 Feb 1986	18 Feb 1986	**MSC-Active**
T-AOT 1125	LAWRENCE H. GIANELLA (ex-OCEAN STAR)	19 Apr 1986	22 Apr 1986	**MSC-Active**

Builders:	American Shipbuilding, Tampa, Fla.
Displacement:	9,000 tons light 39,624 tons full load
Tonnage:	19,037 GRT 30,150 DWT
Length:	587⅓ feet (179.1 m) waterline 614⅚ feet (187.45 m) overall
Beam:	90 feet (27.4 m)
Draft:	34 feet (10.4 m)
Propulsion:	1 diesel engine (Mitsubishi or Ishikawajima-Sulzer 5RTA-76); 15,300 bhp; 1 shaft
Speed:	16 knots
Range:	12,000 n.miles (22,224 km) at 16 knots
Manning:	24 civilian
Radars:	1 . . . . navigation

These are build-and-charter oilers constructed specifically for naval service, although they were initially contracted for commercial service. The lead ship was laid down on 26 December 1983.

Builders: Major components for these ships were built by the American Shipbuilding Company at Lorain, Ohio, and Nashville, Tennessee.

Design: Modified T-5 design with ice-strengthened hulls. Cargo capacity is 238,400 barrels in the first three ships, 239,500 barrels in the last two units.

Engineering: Mitsubishi diesels in the first two ships and Ishikawajima in all others.

The SAMUEL L. COBB, a modified T5 type tanker not fitted, however, for alongside UNREP. All of these ships can conduct an astern refueling of a ship (note reel on the fantail of the COBB and GIANELLA). (1988, Giorgio Arra)

The Lawrence H. Gianella refuels the carrier Independence (CV 62), demonstrating the versatility of the MSC point-to-point tankers. The Gianella and Matthiesen of this class have been fitted with Modular Fuel Delivery Systems (MFDS), with two refueling stations on the port side. They can also refuel ships by the astern method. (U.S. Navy)

The Lawrence H. Gianella, one of two tankers of this type provided with an UNREP capability. The port-side location of the refueling stations facilitates fueling carriers, which have starboard-side island structures. This enables the carrier's commanding officer to closely monitor the evolution. (1993, Leo Van Ginderen collection)

TRANSPORT OILER: T5-S-RM2A TYPE

The AMERICAN EXPLORER (T-AOT 165) was transferred from the RRF to the NDRF on 7 October 1994. She was built for merchant use, but upon completion she was acquired by the Navy. The ship is similar to the MAUMEE-class ships.

Class: This design was intended to serve as a prototype for wartime production of large tankers. In the event, only this one ship was built to this design.

See 15th Edition/page 317 for characteristics.

1 COASTAL TANKER: NORWEGIAN BUILT

Number	Name	Launched	Status
....	VALIANT (ex-SETA, CHIMBORAZO, THOMONA)	1973	**MSC-Active**

Builders:	Kleven M/V A/S, Ulsteinvik (Norway)
Displacement:	approx. 10,600 tons full load
Tonnage:	4,375 GRT 7,634 DWT
Length:	396 feet (120.76 m) overall
Beam:	52 7/12 feet (16.03 m)
Draft:	22 2/3 feet (6.9 m)
Propulsion:	2 diesel engines (MaK 6M453AK); 4,200 bhp; 1 shaft
Speed:	13.5 knots
Range:	10,000 n.miles (18,530 km) at 13.5 knots
Manning:	
Radars:	.... navigation

The VALIANT is a small tanker, successor to the Navy-built gasoline tankers (AOG) operated by the MSC.

She has an ice-strengthened hull.

1 TANKER: "DUCHESS"

Number	Name	Launched	Status
....	DUCHESS	1971	**MSC-Active**

Builders:	
Displacement:	
Tonnage:	20,751 GRT 37,276 DWT
Length:	672 feet (208.88 m) overall
Beam:	89 feet (27.13 m)
Draft:	36 feet (10.98 m)
Propulsion:	
Speed:	16.5 knots
Range:	
Manning:	
Helicopters:	
Radars:	

Cargo capacity is 303,000 barrels.

1 TANKER: "FALCON" CLASS

Number	Name	Launched	To RRF	Status
T-AOT 5005	MISSION CAPISTRANO (ex-COLUMBIA, FALCON LADY)	12 Sep 1970	Mar 1988	MSC-RRF

Builders:	Litton/Ingalls Shipbuilding, Pascagoula, Miss.
Displacement:	45,877 tons full load
Tonnage:	20,751 GRT 37,874 DWT
Length:	637 5/6 feet (194.5 m) waterline 672 1/6 feet (204.9 m) overall
Beam:	89 1/6 feet (27.2 m)
Draft:	36 1/4 feet (11.0 m)
Propulsion:	2 diesel engines (Crossley-Pielstick 16 PC-2V400); 16,000 bhp; 1 shaft
Speed:	16.5 knots
Range:	16,000 n.miles (29,632 km) at 16.5 knots
Manning:	23 civilian
Radars:	.... navigation

This ship served on MSC charter from 1974 to 1983 under the name COLUMBIA (designated T-AOT 182); see class notes and 13th Edition/page 288 for additional data. Cargo capacity is 303,000 barrels.

Class: Three other tankers of this class were returned to their owners in 1983–1984 after MSC service: NECHES (T-AOT 183), HUDSON (T-AOT 184), and SUSQUEHANNA (T-AOT 185).

This ship should not be confused with the earlier MISSION CAPISTRANO (AO 112, later AG 162), a World War II–built T2-SE-A2 fleet oiler.

Classification: The ship was designated T-AO 182 upon being chartered by the MSC but was changed to T-AOT in 1979.

1 TANKER: "MISSION BUENAVENTURA"

Number	Name	Launched	To RRF	Status
T-AOT 1012	MISSION BUENAVENTURA (ex-SPIRIT OF LIBERTY)	1968	Oct 1987	MSC-RRF

Builders:	Bethlehem Steel, Sparrows Point, Baltimore, Md.
Displacement:	46,243 tons full load
Tonnage:	20,947 GRT 38,851 DWT
Length:	629 11/12 feet (192.0 m) waterline 660 feet (201.2 m) overall
Beam:	90 1/6 feet (27.5 m)
Draft:	38 1/4 feet (11.7 m)
Propulsion:	2 steam turbines (Bethlehem); 15,000 shp; 1 shaft
Boilers:	2 (Foster Wheeler)
Speed:	16.5 knots
Range:	12,000 n.miles (22,224 km) at 16.5 knots
Manning:	26 civilian
Radars:	.... navigation

Cargo capacity is 326,000 barrels.

The COLUMBIA, later renamed MISSION CAPISTRANO. The tanker is shown here at Ghent while on MSC charter; she is high in the water, her cargo tanks empty. (1981, Leo Van Ginderen collection)

1 TANKER: "POTOMAC"

Number	Name	Launched	In service	Status
T-AOT 181	POTOMAC	(see notes)	12 Jan 1976	**MSC-APF**

Builders: Sun Shipbuilding and Dry Dock, Chester, Pa.
Displacement: 7,333 tons light
34,800 tons full load
Tonnage: 15,739 GRT
27,908 DWT
Length: 591⅙ feet (180.2 m) waterline
619⅚ feet (189.0 m) overall
Beam: 83½ feet (25.5 m)
Draft: 33 7/12 feet (10.2 m)
Propulsion: 1 steam turbine (Westinghouse); 20,460 shp; 1 shaft
Boilers: 2 (Combustion Engineering)
Speed: 18.5 knots
Range: 18,000 n.miles (33,336 km) at 18 knots
Manning: 30 civilian
Radars: 2 . . . . navigation

The POTOMAC was constructed with the mid-body and bow sections built to mate with the stern section of an earlier tanker named POTOMAC (T-AO 150). The "new" tanker was named SHENANDOAH and operated under commercial charter to the MSC for several years until she was purchased on 12 January 1976. At that time the ship was renamed POTOMAC and designated T-AO 181, which was changed to T-AOT 181 on 30 September 1978.

The ship was contractor-operated by the MSC with a civilian crew. She was taken out of service on 26 September 1983 and placed in the RRF on 5 March 1984. Subsequently, the POTOMAC was assigned to the Afloat Prepositioning Force.

(The original POTOMAC was launched on 8 October 1956; she was partially destroyed by fire on 3 October 1961, but the stern section and machinery were relatively intact. She was originally the T5-S-12a type.)

Cargo capacity is 200,000 barrels. The ship has been fitted with OPDS.

Class: Three other tankers that were sister ships of the original POTOMAC have been discarded. They are:

Ship		*Notes*
T-AOT 149	MAUMEE	from NDRF to stricken 13 Apr 1992
T-AOT 151	SHOSHONE	to NDRF 7 Oct 1994
T-AOT 152	ex-YUKON	from NDRF to stricken 13 Apr 1992

Classification: The POTOMAC was built as T-AO, but that was changed to T-AOT on 30 September 1978.

Design: The MAUMEE has an ice-strengthened bow. The T-AO(T) 149 and 150 were the T5-S-12a type.

Names: The T-AOT 152 dropped the name YUKON on 9 May 1989 to make the name available for the T-AO 202.

Status: The POTOMAC was a U.S. Naval Ship prior to transfer to the RRF.

2 TANKERS: "CHESAPEAKE" CLASS

Number	Name	Launched	to RRF	Status
T-AOT 5084	CHESAPEAKE (ex-HESS VOYAGER)	1964	20 July 1991	MSC-RRF
T-AOT 9101	PETERSBURG (ex-SINCLAIR TEXAS, CHARLES KURZ, KEYSTONE)	1963	1 Aug 1991	MSC-RRF

Builders: Bethlehem Steel, Sparrows Point, Baltimore, Md.
Displacement: approx. 65,000 tons full load
Tonnage: CHESAPEAKE 27,015 GRT
50,826 DWT
PETERSBURG 27,469 GRT
50,072 DWT
Length: 704⅚ feet (214.9 m) waterline
736⅙ feet (224.4 m) overall
Beam: 102⅚ feet (31.2 m)
Draft: 39¾ feet (12.1 m)
Propulsion: 2 steam turbines (Bethlehem); 15,000 shp; 1 shaft
Boilers: 2
Speed: 15 knots
Range:
Manning:
Radars: . . . . navigation

Together with the similar MOUNT WASHINGTON, these large merchant tankers are the largest ships in the MSC in terms of displacement. The PETERSBURG was assigned to the RRF on 30 September 1994.

The PETERSBURG is fitted with OPDS.

1 TANKER: "MOUNT WASHINGTON"

Number	Name	Launched	To RRF	Status
T-AOT 5076	MOUNT WASHINGTON	1963	30 Oct 1989	MSC-RRF

Builders: Bethlehem Steel, Sparrows Point, Baltimore, Md.
Displacement: approx. 65,800 tons full load
Tonnage: 27,412 GRT
47,751 DWT
Length: 706⅚ feet (215.5 m) waterline
736⅙ feet (224.4 m) overall
Beam: 102⅚ feet (31.2 m)
Draft: 40¼ feet (12.3 m)
Propulsion: 2 steam turbines (Bethlehem); 21,500 shp; 1 shaft
Boilers: 2
Speed: 17.5 knots
Range:
Manning:
Radars: . . . . navigation

This large commercial tanker is similar to the CHESAPEAKE and PETERSBURG (see above), but with more powerful turbines.

Class: The MOUNT VERNON (T-AOT 3009) of this design was transferred to the NDRF on 7 October 1994.

1 TANKER: "AMERICAN OSPREY"

Number	Name	Launched	To RRF	Status
T-AOT 5075	AMERICAN OSPREY (ex-GULF PRINCE)	1958	June 1987	**MSC-APF**

Builders: Bethlehem Steel, Sparrows Point, Baltimore, Md.
Displacement: 44,840 tons full load
Tonnage: 20,143 GRT
34,723 DWT
Length: 660 11/12 feet (201.5 m) overall
Beam: 89 11/12 feet (27.4 m)
Draft: 36 1/12 feet (11.0 m)
Propulsion: 2 steam turbines (Bethlehem); 15,000 shp; 1 shaft
Boilers: 2 (Foster Wheeler)
Speed: 17 knots
Range: 14,000 n.miles (25,928 km) at 17 knots
Manning: 37 civilian
Radars: . . . . navigation

This is a former merchant tanker, modified at Alabama Dry Dock Company in 1987–1988 to carry a barge-launching device and four-point mooring system to be used when transferring fuel to shore without pier facilities. She has been fitted with OPDS.

TANKERS: SEALIFT CLASS

Number	Name	In service
T-AOT 168	SEALIFT PACIFIC	1974
T-AOT 169	SEALIFT ARABIAN SEA	1975
T-AOT 170	SEALIFT CHINA SEA	1975
T-AOT 171	SEALIFT INDIAN OCEAN	1975
T-AOT 172	SEALIFT ATLANTIC	1974
T-AOT 173	SEALIFT MEDITERRANEAN	1974
T-AOT 174	SEALIFT CARIBBEAN	1975
T-AOT 175	SEALIFT ARCTIC	1975
T-AOT 176	SEALIFT ANTARCTIC	1975

These ships were built specifically for the MSC to replace 16 World War II–era tankers of the T2 type. The ships were contractor-operated under "bareboat" charter for the MSC with civilian crews for a

The AMERICAN OSPREY at Norfolk. Visible on her deck is the fuel transfer system that enables the OSPREY and other tankers moored alongside to transfer fuel ashore through a flexible pipeline. (1988, Giorgio Arra)

20-year period. All were returned to their civilian owners in 1995. By that time the condition of the ships was marginal for safe and efficient service.

Classification: Assigned T-AOT designations on 30 September 1978.

See 15th Edition/pages 320–21 for characteristics.

TANKERS: T6-M-98A TYPE

The four large tankers of this class were returned to their civilian owners: PATRIOT (T-AOT 1001), RANGER (T-AOT 1002), ROVER (T-AOT 1006), and COURIER (T-AOT 1007).

See 15th Edition/pages 315–16 for characteristics.

TRANSPORT TANKERS: OVERSEAS CLASS

These four tankers have been returned to their civilian owners: OMI CHAMPION (no number), OVERSEAS ALICE (T-AOT 1203), OVERSEAS VALDEZ (T-AOT 1204), and OVERSEAS VIVIAN (T-AOT 1205). All were in active MSC service or served in the Afloat Prepositioning Force.

See 15th Edition/pages 318–19 for characteristics.

TANKERS: "SUAMICO" CLASS (T2-SE-A1)

The last of the Navy-operated, World War II–built T2 tankers, the SAUGATUCK (T-AOT 75) was stricken on 15 February 1995. Ships of this class were begun as merchant tankers but were acquired by the Navy in 1942–1943, completed as fleet oilers (AO), and Navy manned. After World War II they were employed in the tanker role by the MSTS (later MSC).

Class: The TALLULAH (T-AOT 50), CACHE (T-AOT 67), MILLICOMA (T-AOT 73), and SCHUYLKILL (T-AOT 76) were stricken on 4 March 1988.

Classification: The SAUGATUCK was changed from T-AO to T-AOT on 30 September 1978 (while laid up).

Status: The SAUGATUCK was laid up in the NDRF on 5 November 1974.

See 15th Edition/page 323 for characteristics.

TANKERS: MISSION TYPE (T2-SE-A2)

The MISSION SANTA YNEZ (T-AOT 134) was the last survivor retained in reserve of the Mission series of merchant tankers built late in World War II and acquired by the Navy after the war. Delivered as a merchant tanker on 13 March 1944 and acquired by the Navy for use as a tanker on 22 October 1947, she was laid up in the NDRF on 6 March 1975. Changed to T-AOT on 30 September 1978, she was stricken on 1 November 1990.

Class: The Mission class encompassed AO 111–137; other fleet oilers and tankers (transport oilers) of this design were in naval service during and after World War II.

See 14th Edition/page 310 for characteristics.

GASOLINE TANKERS

These are small tankers originally intended to carry gasoline and aviation fuels for aircraft, motor torpedo boats, and other special craft.

GASOLINE TANKERS: "ALATNA" CLASS (T1-MET-24A)

The long-serving gasoline tankers ALATNA (T-AOG 81) and CHATTAHOOCHEE (T-AOG 82) were transferred from the RRF to the NDRF on 7 October 1994. This two-ship class was built specifically for operation in support of U.S. military activities in the Arctic. Both ships were operated by the MSTS (later MSC) until being taken out of service on 8 August 1972 and laid up in the NDRF. The ships were reacquired by the Navy on 10 May 1979 and 24 May 1979, respectively, and reactivated for MSC service to replace older AOGs. The ALATNA was placed in MSC service on 3 February 1983 and the CHATTAHOOCHEE on 11 January 1982. Both were taken out of service on 25 January 1985 and placed in the MSC Ready Reserve Force in April 1985 and January 1985, respectively (berthed in Japan).

See page 47. See 15th Edition/page 324 for characteristics.

GASOLINE TANKER: "TONTI" CLASS (T1-M-BT2)

The NODAWAY (T-AOG 78) was transferred from the RRF to the NDRF on 7 October 1994. She was the lone survivor in U.S. service of a once numerous type of small gasoline tanker. Five ships of this specific design were built as merchant tankers, all of which were acquired by the Navy in 1950 and assigned to the MSTS, later Military Sealift Command. The NODAWAY was taken out of service on 22 July 1984 and assigned to the MSC-RRF on 30 September 1985.

Class: This class originally consisted of the T-AOG 76–80; the AOG 64–75 were similar (BT1 design).

See 15th Edition/page 325 for characteristics.

TROOP SHIPS

Although the two troop ships listed here are employed as state maritime academy training ships, they do remain available for immediate use as transports under the jurisdiction of the MSC.

1 TROOP SHIP: S5-S-MA49C TYPE

Number	Name	Launched	Status
T-AP 1000	Patriot State (ex-Santa Mercedes)	30 July 1963	**Academic**

Builders:	Bethlehem Steel, Sparrows Point, Baltimore, Md.
Displacement:	approx. 20,500 tons full load
Tonnage:	11,188 GRT 9,376 DWT
Length:	$508\frac{5}{12}$ feet (155.0 m) waterline $544\frac{11}{12}$ feet (166.1 m) overall
Beam:	$79\frac{1}{6}$ feet (24.1 m)
Draft:	29 feet (8.9 m)
Propulsion:	2 steam turbines (General Electric); 19,800 shp; 2 shafts
Boilers:	2 (Babcock & Wilcox)
Speed:	20 knots
Range:	7,000 n.miles (12,964 km) at 20 knots
Manning:	33 civilian
Passengers:	600
Radars:	. . . . navigation

The Patriot State is a former passenger-cargo liner modified for use as a school ship by the Massachusetts Maritime Academy. She can carry 175 containers, and about 120 cadets are normally embarked for training cruises.

The ship was laid down on 29 October 1962.

Class: One of four similar ships completed in 1963 for the Grace Lines for the Central-South American trade.

Design: As built, the ship was a combination passenger-cargo ship that could accommodate 119 passengers.

Engineering: The shaft horsepower shown above is maximum; normal is 18,000 shp.

The Massachusetts state training ship Patriot State. In an emergency the state training ships could be employed as troop transports, although such employment is unrealistic in most potential conflicts or crises. (1993, Giorgio Arra)

The New York state training ship Empire State at Portsmouth, England. The state training ships carry their state's nickname. (1993, Leo Van Ginderen collection)

1 TROOP SHIP: C5-S-MA1UA TYPE

Number	Name	Launched	In service	Status
T-AP 1001	Empire State (ex-Cape Junction, Mormactide, Oregon)	16 Sep 1961	3 Jan 1990	**Academic**

Builders:	Newport News Shipbuilding and Dry Dock, Va.
Displacement:	22,629 tons full load
Tonnage:	9,298 GRT (before conversion) 12,691 DWT (before conversion)
Length:	528⅓ feet (161.1 m) waterline 564 11/12 feet (172.2 m) overall
Beam:	76⅙ feet (23.2 m)
Draft:	31 7/12 feet (9.6 m)
Propulsion:	2 steam turbines (General Electric); 17,500 shp; 1 shaft
Boilers:	2 (Foster Wheeler)
Speed:	20 knots
Range:	
Manning:	
Radars:	. . . . navigation

This cargo ship was acquired on 14 October 1988 from the National Defense Reserve Fleet for conversion to a training ship for the New York State Maritime Academy, replacing the former USNS Barrett (T-AP 196). She was converted by Bay Shipbuilding, Bay City, Wisconsin. Refitted with classrooms and berthing for students, her troop capacity is consequently small.

The ship was first assigned to the MSC-RRF, then assigned as a school ship in 1990.

TROOP TRANSPORTS: "BARRETT" CLASS (P2-S1-DN3 TYPE)

Number	Name	In service	Status
T-AP 196	Empire State V (ex-USNS Barrett)	1951	to NDRF 4 Apr 1990
T-AP 197	Bay State (ex-USNS Geiger)	1952	hulk
T-AP 198	State of Maine (ex-USNS Upshur)	1952	to NDRF

These veteran troop transports have been discarded. Three ships of this design were begun as combination passenger-cargo liners for the American President Lines; they were taken over by the Navy during construction and completed as troop transports. All were placed in service in 1951–1952 with the MSTS (later MSC) and operated by civilian crews.

All three ships were laid up in the NDRF in 1973, having been the last large transports operated by the Military Sealift Command. They were subsequently transferred on loan to state maritime schools: the Barrett to the New York Maritime Academy, Geiger to the Massachusetts Maritime Academy, and Upshur to the Maine Maritime Academy.

The ex-Geiger (renamed Bay State) was severely damaged by an engine room fire in 1981 and was not returned to service.

See 15th Edition/pages 325–26 for characteristics.

TROOP TRANSPORTS: ADMIRAL TYPE[3] (P2-SE2-R1)

All transports of this design have been stricken. Ten ships were completed in 1944–1945 (AP 120–129). They could carry up to 5,000 troops. Several units served as barracks ships (designated IX); see chapter 23.

The last units to be stricken had been laid up in the NDRF—the Gen Alexander M. Patch (T-AP 122), Gen Simon B. Buckner (T-AP 123), and Gen Maurice Rose (T-AP 126). All were stricken on 20 August 1990. The Gen Nelson M. Walker (T-AP 125) was stricken on 25 January 1981; the ship was donated to Life International for conversion to a civilian hospital ship. When this edition went to press she remained laid up in the James River NDRF.

See 14th Edition/page 313 for characteristics.

TROOP TRANSPORTS: GENERAL TYPE (P2-S2-R2)

All transports of this design have been stricken. Eleven ships were completed from 1943 to 1945 (AP 110–119 and 176). They could accommodate up to 5,300 troops.

The last unit to be stricken had been laid up in the NDRF; this was the Gen John Pope (T-AP 110), stricken on 26 October 1990.

See 14th Edition/page 313–14 for characteristics.

VEHICLE CARGO SHIPS

These are Roll-On/Roll-Off (RO/RO) ships with strengthened cargo decks for carrying heavy vehicles and side and/or stern ramps for loading and unloading vehicles. These ships are extremely important for the sealift of modern ground combat forces.

2 VEHICLE CARGO SHIPS: ITALIAN BUILT

Number	Name	Launched	To RRF	Status
T-AKR 9666	Cape Vincent (ex-Taabo Italia, Merzario Italia)	1984	19 Aug 1994	MSC-RRF
T-AKR 9701	Cape Victory (ex-Merzario Britannia)	1984	2 Sep 1994	MSC-RRF

Builders:	Fincantieri, Genoa (Italy)
Displacement:	approx. 27,000 tons
Tonnage:	22,423 GRT 21,439 DWT
Length:	566¾ feet (172.8 m) waterline 631¾ feet (192.6 m) overall
Beam:	87 feet (26.55 m)
Draft:	27¾ feet (8.47 m)
Propulsion:	1 diesel engine (GMT-Sulzer 6RNB 66/140); 11,850 bhp; 1 shaft

3. As built, these ships had "admiral" names; they were transferred to the Army in 1946 and renamed for generals. On 1 March 1950 they were transferred again to the Navy under the newly established Military Sea Transportation Service. They retained their Army-assigned names.

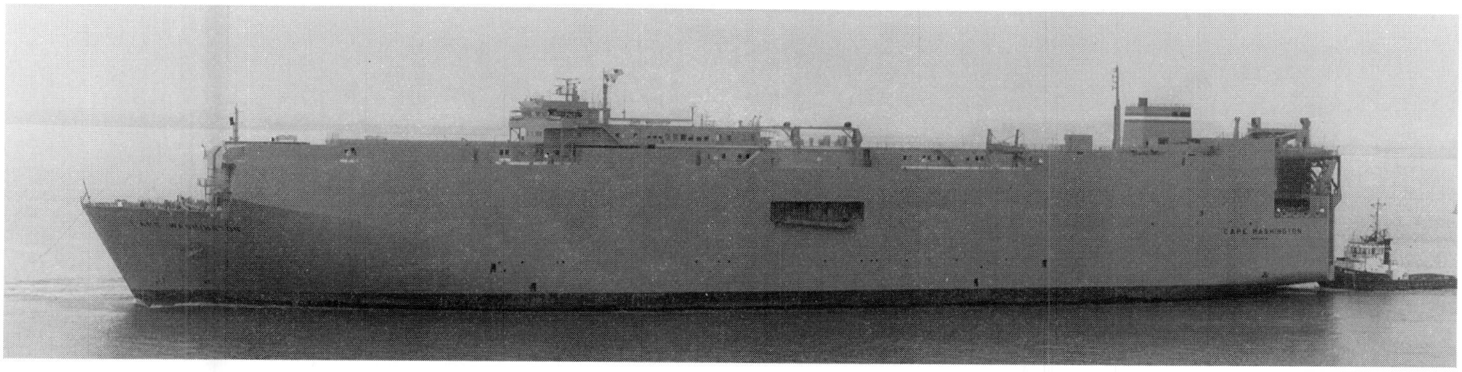

The Cape Washington (above) and her sister ship Cape Wrath are among the most ungainly looking ships afloat. They have a high freeboard, low amidships bridge, and square funnel aft, with a large stern vehicle ramp. (1994, Leo Van Ginderen collection)

Speed:	16 knots
Range:	21,000 n.miles (38,900 km) at 16 knots
Manning:	
Radars:	. . . . navigation

The CAPE VINCENT was acquired for the RRF on 13 May 1993, the CAPE VICTORY on 2 April 1993. The ships can carry 1,306 containers or vehicles, loaded/unloaded via a stern ramp.

The ships each have a bow thruster.

The lowered stern vehicle ramp of the CAPE WRATH, seen while the ship was at Antwerp. The single funnel is offset to starboard; it has red-white-blue stripes, not the black-blue-gold stripes common to most gray-painted MSC ships. (1994, Leo Van Ginderen collection)

2 VEHICLE CARGO SHIPS: POLISH BUILT

Number	Name	Launched	To RRF	Status
T-AKR 9961	CAPE WASHINGTON (ex-HAUL TRANSPORTER)	1981	5 Apr 1994	**MSC-APF**
T-AKR 9962	CAPE WRATH (ex-HAUL TRADER, HOEGH TRADER)	1982	30 Sep 1994	**MSC-APF**

Builders:	Stocznia imeni Komuny Paryskiej, Gdynia (Poland)	
Displacement:	approx. 55,000 tons	
Tonnage:	CAPE WASHINGTON	23,597 GRT
		32,695 DWT
	CAPE WRATH	20,563 GRT
		32,722 DWT
Length:	642 feet (195.76 m) waterline	
	697⅓ feet (212.61 m) overall	
Beam:	105 11/12 feet (32.28 m)	
Draft:	38⅙ feet (11.63 m)	
Propulsion:	1 diesel engine (Cegielski-Sulzer 6RND 90/155); 17,400 bhp; 1 shaft	
Speed:	17 knots	
Range:		
Manning:		
Radars:	. . . . navigation	

The CAPE WASHINGTON was acquired for the RRF on 7 April 1993, the CAPE WRATH on 14 May 1993. Both were assigned to the Army's Afloat Prepositioning Force on 30 September 1994. Both were to return to Navy control in 1997; to RRF.

As former automobile carriers (their capacity was 6,000 cars) these ships can carry as many as 1,203 containers or vehicles, loaded/unloaded through side doors and quarter doors/ramps. Fitted with a bow thruster, each ship also has an ice-strengthened hull.

3 VEHICLE CARGO SHIPS: SWEDISH BUILT

Number	Name	Launched	to RRF	Status
T-AK 2044	CAPE ORLANDO (ex-AMERICAN EAGLE, ZENIT EAGLE, FINNEAGLE)	1981	12 Sep 1994	**MSC-Active**
. . . .	AMERICAN FALCON (ex-ZENIT CLIPPER, FINNCLIPPER)	1981		**MSC-Active**
. . . .	AMERICAN CONDOR (ex-ZENIT EXPRESS, KUWAIT EXPRESS)	1981		**MSC-Active**

Builders:	Kockums AB, Malmö (Sweden)	
Displacement:	approx. 30,000 tons full load	
Tonnage:	CAPE ORLANDO	15,632 GRT
	others	15,636 GRT
	AMERICAN FALCON	20,394 DWT
	others	20,404 DWT
Length:	593 feet (180.8 m) waterline	
	635¼ feet (199.2 m) overall	
Beam:	91⅚ feet (28.0 m)	
Draft:	29½ feet (9.0 m)	
Propulsion:	2 diesel engines (Cegielski-Sulzer 6RND68M); 21,500 bhp; 1 shaft	
Speed:	22 knots	
Range:	16,800 n.miles (31,130 km) at 19 knots	
Manning:	20 civilian	
Radars:	. . . . navigation	

The CAPE ORLANDO was acquired for the RRF as the AMERICAN EAGLE; she had been on charter since 22 August 1983 and was purchased in December 1992. The ship has since been renamed and assigned to MSC operation.

These are large ships with a bridge forward and twin funnels aft. The CAPE ORLANDO can carry 1,040 containers or vehicles, with 116,669 square feet (10,500 m²) of vehicle parking area; the other ships are similar. Vehicles are loaded/unloaded via stern ramps.

There are two bow thrusters.

Names: The CAPE ORLANDO was chartered as the AMERICAN EAGLE and renamed in 1993.

The CAPE ORLANDO as earlier chartered by the MSC and by the British Ministry of Defence (when she was named AMERICAN EAGLE). These ships have an unusual split superstructure, with a large deckhouse, topped by the bridge forward, and a superstructure aft, topped by twin funnels. Note the twin stern vehicle ramps. (1986, Leo Van Ginderen collection)

3 VEHICLE CARGO SHIPS: JAPANESE-NORWEGIAN BUILT

Number	Name	Launched	To RRF	Status
T-AKR 5066	CAPE HUDSON (ex-BARBER TIAF)	1979	Nov 1986	**MSC-APF**
T-AKR 5067	CAPE HENRY (ex-BARBER PRIAM)	1979	Sep 1986	**MSC-APF**
T-AKR 5068	CAPE HORN (ex-BARBER TØNSBERG)	1979	Dec 1986	**MSC-APF**

Builders: T-AKR 5066 Mitsubishi, Nagasaki (Japan)
T-AKR 5067 Kaldnes M/V, A/S Tønsberg (Norway)
T-AKR 5068 Tangen Værft, Kragerø (Norway)
Displacement: approx. 47,200 tons full load
Tonnage: HUDSON 21,976 GRT
HENRY 21,747 GRT
HORN 22,090 GRT
Length: 693¾ feet (211.5 m) waterline
749½ feet (228.5 m) overall
Beam: 105⅚ feet (32.3 m)
Draft: 35 5/12 feet (10.8 m)
Propulsion: 1 diesel engine (Mitsubishi-Sulzer in CAPE HENRY; Burmeister & Wain in others); 30,150 bhp (30,700 bhp in Norwegian-built ships); 1 shaft
Speed: 21 knots
Range: 24,300 n.miles (45,000 km) at 17 knots
Manning: 27 civilian
Radars: . . . . navigation

All three of these large combination RO/RO-container ships were purchased on 1 June 1986. Details vary; they can carry vehicles or 1,607 to 1,626 containers.

They all have one 40-ton-capacity crane forward (the superstructure is aft).

Status: All three ships were assigned to the Army's Afloat Prepositioning Force on 30 September 1994.

The CAPE HENRY at Antwerp shows the unusual design of this series of RO/RO ships. They feature a large superstructure aft and twin, angled funnels attached to the support for the large stern ramp. (1994, Leo Van Ginderen collection)

This stern aspect of the CAPE HENRY reveals the unusual, angled stern ramp. It has an extending feature, indicated by the twin arms projecting above the ramp in this photo that shows it stowed flat against the stern of the ship. (1993, Leo Van Ginderen collection)

3 VEHICLE CARGO SHIPS: JAPANESE BUILT

Number	Name	Launched	To RRF	Status
T-AKR 9678	Cape Rise (ex-Saudi Riyadh, Seaspeed Arabia)	1977	15 Nov 1994	MSC-RRF
T-AKR 9679	Cape Ray (ex-Saudi Makkah, Seaspeed Asia)	1977	17 Dec 1994	MSC-RRF
T-AKR 9960	Cape Race (ex-G and C Admiral, Seaspeed America)	1977	11 Sep 1994	MSC-RRF

Builders: Kawasaki Heavy Industries, Sakaide (Japan)
Displacement:
Tonnage: 14,825 GRT
22,735 DWT
Length: 591 feet (180.22 m) waterline
647⅚ feet (197.52 m) overall
Beam: 105⅚ feet (32.26 m)
Draft: 32⅚ feet (10.0 m)
Propulsion: 2 diesel engines (Kawasaki-MAN 14V 52/55A); 28,000 bhp; 1 shaft
Speed: 19.75 knots
Range:
Manning:
Radars: . . . . navigation

These ships—combination vehicle and container carriers—were acquired on 9 August 1993 (Rise), 20 April 1993 (Ray), and 28 April 1993 (Race), respectively. They can carry 1,315 containers.

Each has been fitted with a bow and a stern thruster.

3 VEHICLE CARGO SHIPS: GERMAN-JAPANESE BUILT

Number	Name	Launched	To RRF	Status
T-AKR 112	Cape Texas (ex-Lyra, Reichenfels)	1977	19 Aug 1994	MSC-RRF
T-AKR 113	Cape Taylor (ex-Thekwini, Cygnus, Rabenfels)		27 July 1994	MSC-RRF
T-AKR 9711	Cape Trinity (ex-Santos, Canadian Forest, Radbod, Norefjord, Rheinfels)		21 Nov 1994	MSC-RRF

Builders: T-AKR 112, 9711 Howaldtswerke, Kiel (Germany)
T-AKR 113 Sasebo Heavy Industries (Japan)
Displacement: Cape Texas 9,870 tons light
Cape Texas 24,555 tons full load
others 26,455 tons full load
Tonnage: 14,174 GRT
15,075 DWT
Length: 583⅚ feet (178.0 m) waterline
627⅚ feet (191.29 m) overall, except Texas 634⅙ feet/193.33 m)
Beam: 89¼ feet (27.2 m)
Draft: 28⅙ feet (8.6 m)
Propulsion: 2 diesel engines (MAN 9L 52/55A heavy-oil); 18,980 bhp; 1 shaft
Speed: 20.5 knots
Range: 22,600 n.miles (41,880 km) at 16.5 knots
Manning: 49 civilian
Radars: . . . . navigation

The Cape Rise at Antwerp, showing the graceful lines of this superstructure-forward, twin-funnels-amidships design. Note the simple stern-ramp arrangement. (1995, Leo Van Ginderen collection)

The Cape Texas has a conventional RO/RO appearance, with superstructure aft, side ports, and a stern ramp. Like other ships of this type, the Cape Texas has (twin) square funnels aft. (1994, Giorgio Arra)

These large RO/RO ships were purchased in December 1992 and acquired in 1993. The CAPE TEXAS initially operated in MSC service as the USNS LYRA.

These ships can accommodate 340 containers, plus vehicles. Hulls are ice strengthened.

4 VEHICLE CARGO SHIPS: C7-S-95A TYPE

Number	Name	Launched	To RRF	Status
T-AKR 10	CAPE ISLAND (ex-MERCURY, ILLINOIS)	21 Dec 1976	Nov 1993	**MSC-Active**
T-AKR 11	CAPE INTREPID (ex-JUPITER, LIPSCOMB LYKES, ARIZONA)	1 Nov 1975	Apr 1986	MSC-RRF
T-AKR 5062	CAPE ISABEL (ex-CHARLES LYKES, NEVADA)	15 May 1976	June 1986	MSC-RRF
T-AKR 5076	CAPE INSCRIPTION (ex-TYSON LYKES, MAINE)	24 May 1975	Sep 1987	MSC-RRF

Builders:	Bath Iron Works, Maine
Displacement:	14,222 tons light
	33,765 tons full load
Tonnage:	13,156 GRT
	19,172 DWT
Length:	639⅚ feet (195.1 m) waterline
	684¾ feet (208.8 m) overall
Beam:	102 feet (31.1 m)
Draft:	$32\frac{1}{12}$ feet (9.8 m)
Propulsion:	2 steam turbines (General Electric); 37,000 shp; 2 shafts
Boilers:	2 (Babcock & Wilcox)
Speed:	24 knots
Range:	12,600 n.miles (23,335 km) at 23 knots
Manning:	36 civilian except 41 in MERCURY
Radars:	1 Raytheon TM 1650/6X navigation
	1 Raytheon TM 1660/12S navigation

The CAPE ISLAND—long the USNS MERCURY—has a small crane forward. The large crane shown here is on the adjacent pier. RO/RO ships have become one of the most important ships of the sealift fleet because of the large numbers of vehicles needed by modern military forces. (1990, Leo Van Ginderen collection)

The CAPE INTREPID—shown here as the USNS JUPITER—has a deck load of military containers. (U.S. Navy)

These ships were built for commercial service by the Lykes Brothers Steamship Company. These ships are RO/RO vehicle carriers, with side ports and a stern ramp for rapidly loading and unloading vehicles. They can also carry containers and 728 tons of liquid cargo.

The MERCURY and JUPITER were acquired by the Navy on long-term charter in 1980 for use as prepositioning ships in the Indian Ocean. Note that they were assigned standard Navy hull designations; they were placed in service on 3 June 1980 and 7 May 1980, respectively.

The MERCURY was taken out of service and transferred to the NDRF on 30 April 1993; she was renamed CAPE ISLAND and assigned to the RRF on 22 November 1993 and subsequently placed in MSC service. The JUPITER was transferred to MarAd (Suisun Bay) on 23 April 1986, assigned to the RRF on 2 May 1986 and renamed in 1993.

Status: The MERCURY and JUPITER were U.S. Naval Ships.

1 HEAVY LIFT CARGO SHIP: DUTCH BUILT

Number	Name	Launched	Status
....	STRONG TEXAN (ex-DOCK EXPRESS TEXAS, HAPPY RUNNER)	1976	**MSC-Active**

Builders:	Arnhemsche Schipswerf Maats, Arnhem (Netherlands)
Displacement:	approx. 4,200 tons full load
Tonnage:	1,382 GRT 2,776 DWT
Length:	244 feet (74.4 m) waterline 268⅓ feet (81.82 m) overall
Beam:	51½ feet (15.7 m)
Draft:	18¼ feet (5.55 m)
Propulsion:	2 diesel engines (Stork-Kromhout 9F-CHD240); 2,500 bhp; 2 shafts
Speed:	12 knots
Range:	
Manning:	
Radars:	.... navigation

This is a small heavy lift/cargo/vehicle ship. She has a 160-ton-capacity crane and ramps for loading/unloading vehicles. This ship has a limited FLO/FLO capability. See page 47.

2 VEHICLE CARGO SHIPS: FRENCH BUILT

Number	Name	Launched	Status
T-AK 9301	AMERICAN MERLIN (ex-UTRILLO)	1975	**MSC-APF**
T-AK 9302	BUFFALO SOLDIER (ex-MONET)	1975	**MSC-APF**

Builders:	Chantiers Navals de la Ciotat (France)
Displacement:	approx. 36,000 tons full load
Tonnage:	26,409 GRT 19,669 DWT
Length:	639 11/12 feet (195.1 m) waterline 669 7/12 feet (204.15 m) overall
Beam:	87 1/12 feet (26.55 m)
Draft:	35¼ feet (10.74 m)
Propulsion:	2 diesel engines (SEMT-Pielstick 18PC2 5V 4000); 1 shaft
Speed:	19 knots
Range:	
Manning:	
Radars:	.... navigation

Chartered in 1992 from a French firm, these ships were assigned to the MSC Atlantic on 30 September 1993.

Primarily vehicle carrying ships, they each can accommodate 637 containers in fixed guides.

Conversion: Both ships were lengthened from their original 538⅙ feet (164.07 m) overall.

2 VEHICLE CARGO SHIPS: CANADIAN BUILT

Number	Name	Launched	To RRF	Status
T-AKR 5077	CAPE LAMBERT (ex-FEDERAL LAKES, AVON FOREST)	1973	Nov 1987	MSC-RRF
T-AKR 5078	CAPE LOBOS (ex-FEDERAL SEAWAY, LAURENTIAN FOREST, GRAND ENCOUNTER)	1972	Mar 1988	MSC-RRF

Builders:	Port Weller Dry Dock, St. Catherines, Ontario (Canada)
Displacement:	30,375 tons full load
Tonnage:	15,005 GRT 20,545 DWT
Length:	621⅓ feet (189.4 m) waterline 681⅚ feet (207.9 m) overall
Beam:	75⅙ feet (22.9 m)
Draft:	30½ feet (9.3 m)
Propulsion:	2 diesel engines (Crossley-Pielstick); 18,000 bhp; 2 shafts
Speed:	19 knots
Range:	6,000 n.miles (11,112 km) at 17.5 knots
Manning:	27 civilian
Radars:	.... navigation

Built as newsprint and vehicle carriers, these ships are ice strengthened for operations on the Great Lakes. They were purchased on 5 June 1987.

The ships have side doors with two vehicle ramps. They have 189,937 square feet (17,094 m^2) of vehicle space. Each has a bow thruster.

The CAPE LOBOS as laid up in the James River reserve group of the NDRF. The king posts are on the ship moored alongside. This design has the bulbous bow common to many modern merchant ships, improving seakeeping in rough seas. (1989, Leo Van Ginderen collection)

5 VEHICLE CARGO SHIPS: FRENCH-SWEDISH BUILT

Number	Name	Launched	To RRF	Status
T-AKR 5051	Cape Ducato (ex-Barranduna)	1972	Dec 1985	MSC-RRF
T-AKR 5052	Cape Douglas (ex-Lalandia)	1973	Nov 1985	**MSC-APF**
T-AKR 5053	Cape Domingo (ex-Tarago)	1973	Oct 1985	MSC-RRF
T-AKR 5054	Cape Decision (ex-Tombarra)	1973	Oct 1985	**MSC-APF**
T-AKR 5055	Cape Diamond (ex-Tricolor)	1972	Oct 1985	MSC-RRF

Builders:	T-AKR 5051, 5052, 5054 Eriksberg M/V, Lindholmen (Sweden) T-AKR 5053, 5055 Chantiers Navals de France, Dunkerque (France)
Displacement:	35,173 tons full load
Tonnage:	23,972 to 24,437 GRT 21,299 to 21,398 DWT
Length:	633⅚ feet (193.24 m) waterline 680¼ feet (207.4 m) overall
Beam:	97 feet (29.57 m)
Draft:	31½ feet (9.59 m)
Propulsion:	*French built:* 3 diesel engines (Ch. d'Atlantic-Pielstick); 28,890 bhp; 1 shaft *Swedish built:* 3 diesel engines (Lindholmen-Pielstick); 27,000 bhp; 1 shaft
Speed:	22 knots
Range:	26,000 n.miles (48,180 km) at 20.6 knots
Manning:	27 civilian
Radars:	2 . . . . navigation

These are combination cargo ships, able to carry heavy vehicles as well as 1,327 containers. They are fitted with a bow and a stern thruster.

Status: The Cape Decision and Cape Douglas were assigned to the Army's Afloat Prepositioning Force on 30 September 1994. (Beyond Army combat equipment, the Cape Douglas carries a 300-bed field hospital.)

The Cape Douglas at Antwerp with her stern ramp lowered to the pier. These ramps can handle the heaviest tanks and trucks in the U.S. military arsenal. (1993, Leo Van Ginderen collection)

The Cape Decision at Antwerp. Large numbers of ventilators are on her deck to clear exhaust fumes from the ship's garage decks. She has no side ports for unloading vehicles. (1993, Leo Van Ginderen collection)

1 VEHICLE CARGO SHIP: SWEDISH BUILT

Number	Name	Launched	To RRF	Status
T-AKR 5069	Cape Edmont (ex-Parralla)	1971	Apr 1987	MSC-RRF

Builders:	Eriksberg M/V, Lindholmen (Sweden)
Displacement:	approx. 32,000 tons full load
Tonnage:	13,355 GRT 20,224 DWT
Length:	602½ feet (183.7 m) waterline 652$^{11}/_{12}$ feet (199.02 m) overall
Beam:	94⅙ feet (28.7 m)
Draft:	31½ feet (9.6 m)
Propulsion:	3 diesel engines (Eriksberg-Pielstick 18PC2V 400); 25,920 bhp; 1 shaft
Speed:	19 knots
Range:	17,000 n.miles (31,500 km) at 19 knots
Manning:	32 civilian
Radars:	. . . . navigation

This combination vehicle and container ship can carry up to 1,212 containers. She was assigned to the RRF on 10 April 1987.

The ship has 118,325 square feet (10,649 m^2) of vehicle space; she has been fitted with a bow thruster.

1 VEHICLE CARGO SHIP: "CALLAGHAN"

Number	Name	Launched	In service	Status
T-AKR 1001	Adm Wm. M. Callaghan	17 Oct 1967	19 Dec 1967	MSC-RRF

Builders:	Sun Shipbuilding and Dry Dock, Chester, Pa.
Displacement:	26,573 tons full load
Tonnage:	13,500 GRT 24,471 DWT
Length:	633$\frac{5}{12}$ feet (193.12 m) waterline 694$\frac{1}{4}$ feet (211.66 m) overall
Beam:	92 feet (28.1 m)
Draft:	29 feet (8.8 m)
Propulsion:	2 gas turbines (General Electric LM2500); 40,000 shp; 2 shafts
Speed:	26 knots
Range:	12,000 n.miles (22,224 km) at 20 knots
Manning:	28 civilian
Radars:	1 . . . . navigation

The Callaghan was an early RO/RO ship and the first one built for the U.S. Navy but operated under charter, rather than outright ownership, to the MSC. The ship was operated by the MSTS/MSC in that status for almost two decades until being purchased outright in 1986.

The ship was assigned to the RRF in May 1987.

The Callaghan has 167,537 square feet (15,078 m^2) of vehicle storage space, with four side ports and a stern ramp for rapid loading and unloading. She can off-load some 750 vehicles in 27 hours, having been fitted with two 120-ton-capacity booms and 12 booms with a capacity of 5 to 10 tons.

Engineering: This was the first all-gas-turbine ship constructed for the U.S. Navy. The engines were originally two Pratt & Whitney FT-4s (rated at 25,000 shp each); these were replaced in 1977 by the widely used LM 2500.

Name: The ship is named for Admiral William M. Callaghan, first commander of the Military Sea Transportation Service (predecessor to the MSC), from 1949 to 1952. He was retired and employed by American Export lines, which built the ship, when she was named in his honor by the firm.

Status: The Callaghan was taken out of service and transferred to the RRF on 31 May 1987 after almost 20 years of continuous MSC service. On 25 June 1987 she was transferred to MarAd for layup and subsequently returned to RRF status. The ship has the prefix GTS for Gas Turbine Ship.

The venerable Adm Wm. M. Callaghan—the first RO/RO ship acquired by the U.S. Navy—was purchased specifically to move Army vehicles between the United States and Europe. There are cargo holds forward; vehicles are loaded/unloaded through side ports as well as a stern ramp. (1985, Leo Van Ginderen collection)

1 VEHICLE CARGO SHIP: C4-ST-67A TYPE

Number	Name	Launched	Commissioned	Status
T-AKR 9	Meteor (ex-Sea Lift)	18 Apr 1965	19 May 1967	MSC-RRF

Builders:	Lockheed Shipbuilding and Construction, Seattle, Wash.
Displacement:	9,154 tons light 21,480 tons full load
Tonnage:	16,467 GRT 12,326 DWT
Length:	540 feet (164.7 m) overall
Beam:	83$\frac{2}{3}$ feet (25.5 m)
Draft:	29 feet (8.8 m)
Propulsion:	2 steam turbines (De Laval); 19,400 shp; 2 shafts
Boilers:	2
Speed:	22 knots
Range:	10,000 n.miles (18,520 km) at 20 knots
Manning:	56 civilian
Radars:	1 Raytheon TM 1650/6X navigation 1 Raytheon TM 1660/12S navigation

The Meteor, originally named Sea Lift, was built specifically as a RO/RO ship for naval service. The ship has four side ramps and a stern ramp. She has 87,735 square feet (7,896 m^2) of vehicle space.

Assigned to the Rapid Deployment Force (RDF) in 1980–1981, she was placed in the RRF on 30 October 1985.

The ship was authorized in the fiscal 1963 naval shipbuilding program and laid down on 19 May 1964.

Classification: Authorized as T-AK 278 but changed to T-LSV 9 while under construction. The designation was changed again to vehicle cargo ship T-AKR 9 on 14 August 1969.

The LSV 1 through 6 were World War II–built vehicle landing ships, all of which served under other designations. The Taurus (LSV 8) was the former AK 273; she had been begun as the Fort Snelling (LSD 23). Note that the later SL-7 conversions to rapid response ships have AK-series hull numbers with the prefix AKR type designation.

Design: The Meteor was one of the few ships to have both an SCB (No. 236) and a MarAd design designation.

Names: Changed from Sea Lift to Meteor on 12 September 1975 to avoid confusion with the Sealift-class tankers.

Status: The Meteor was a U.S. Naval Ship until being transferred to the RRF in 1985.

The long-serving METEOR, a combination cargo–RO/RO ship. (1984, Leo Van Ginderen collection)

1 VEHICLE CARGO SHIP: C3-ST-14A TYPE

Number	Name	Launched	In service	Status
T-AKR 7	COMET	31 July 1957	27 Jan 1958	MSC-RRF

Builders:	Sun Shipbuilding and Dry Dock, Chester, Pa.
Displacement:	8,175 tons light 18,286 tons full load
Tonnage:	13,792 GRT 10,111 DWT
Length:	499 feet (152.2 m) overall
Beam:	78 feet (23.8 m)
Draft:	29⅙ feet (8.9 m)
Propulsion:	2 steam turbines (General Electric); 13,200 shp; 2 shafts
Boilers:	2 (Babcock & Wilcox)
Speed:	18 knots
Range:	12,000 n.miles (22,235 km) at 18 knots
Manning:	44 civilian
Radars:	1 Raytheon TM 1650/6X navigation 1 Raytheon TM 1660/12S navigation

The COMET was built specifically for naval service. The ship can accommodate some 700 vehicles in her two after holds; the two forward holds are intended for general cargo. Vehicle space totals 83,613 square feet (7,525 m^2).

The COMET was assigned to the RRF in March 1985.

She was laid down on 15 May 1956.

Classification: The COMET originally was classified T-AK 269; she was changed to vehicle cargo ship T-LSV 7 on 1 June 1963 and again to T-AKR 7 on 1 January 1969.

Status: The COMET was a U.S. Naval Ship prior to her transfer to MarAd on 15 March 1985.

The COMET, another early cargo–RO/RO ship. Her two port-side ports are clearly visible in this photo. (1982, Leo Van Ginderen collection)

CHAPTER 25

Service Craft

Service craft support virtually all U.S. naval operations. The aircraft carrier DWIGHT D. EISENHOWER (CVN 69) carrying troops and helicopters of the Army's 10th Mountain Division got under way for Haiti with the help of the harbor tugs ANOKA (YTB 810) and PIQUA (YTB 793) when the "Ike" departed Norfolk, Virginia. (1994, U.S. Navy, PHAN Gregory L. Cambell)

The U.S. Navy operates several hundred service craft, both self-propelled and non–self-propelled. Most service craft are at naval bases in the United States; a few are based overseas. These craft perform a variety of fleet and base support services.

In addition, several special ships and craft are listed at the beginning of this chapter. Also listed are the Navy's miscellaneous unclassified ships with the IX designation, which are officially classified as service craft. Although the relic CONSTITUTION has dropped her IX designation, she is included below in her sequential position for historical reasons; she is no longer self-propelled. (The sailing corvette CONSTELLATION, formerly IX 20, is not listed in this volume; she is not owned by the U.S. government nor is she the original frigate built in 1797; see below.)

Only the self-propelled service craft are described below. However, several IX-designated ships that are employed as accommodation/barracks ships but are no longer self-propelled are listed, as well as a few non–self-propelled barges with IX designations. This provides continuity for that "ship" designation series. The non–self-propelled units are indicated by an arrow (↓).

The former East German guided missile craft HIDDENSEE of the Soviet Tarantul I class is designated 185NS9201 in U.S. service; she is listed in chapter 21.

The Navy's manned submersibles and floating dry docks, officially classified as service craft, are listed in chapters 26 and 27.

Classification: Most service craft have Y-series designations, that letter having been established when these were considered yard craft. They were also known as district craft, from being assigned to the now defunct naval districts. Other service craft have hull registry numbers (length + type designation + serial). A few have both; for example, the TWR 821 has the hull registry number 120TR821.

The SEA SHADOW with her upper hatch open and a commercial radar and radio antennas raised. (1993, U.S. Navy)

Only Y-series service craft are listed in the Naval Vessel Register (NVR). All service craft are found in the Service Craft and Boat Accounting Report (SABAR).

Guns: Although service craft are not armed, the seamanship training craft (YP) can be armed with light weapons for use as harbor patrol craft. Some of the utility cargo carriers (YFU) and barracks ships (APB) were armed for service in the Vietnam War. The IX 515/SES-200 has carried out trials with a number of weapons.

Helicopters: The "mini-carrier" IX 514 is the only service craft with a helicopter capability.

Operational: Most service craft are manned by Navy personnel. Those assigned to the Naval Command, Control and Ocean Surveillance Center at San Diego, California, together with a few other service craft, are operated by civilian personnel. That center, established in early 1992, incorporates the former Naval Ocean Systems Center (NOSC).

Builders: The craft was designed and built by the Lockheed "Skunk Works," which developed the U-2, SR-71 Blackhawk, and F-117A stealth fighter, among other projects. Construction began in 1983 inside of the floating dock HMB-1.[1]

Design: The SEA SHADOW has a Small Waterplane Area Twin-Hull (SWATH) configured with twin submerged hulls. The diesel engines are fitted in the "fuselage" and the electric motors in the twin submerged hulls.

1 STEALTH RESEARCH SHIP: "SEA SHADOW"

Number	Name	In service
(none)	SEA SHADOW	1985

Builders:	Lockheed Missiles and Space Co., Sunnyvale, Calif.
Displacement:	560 tons full load
Length:	164 feet (50.0 m) overall
Beam:	68 feet (20.73 m)
Draft:	14 feet (4.27 m)
Propulsion:	diesel-electric; 2 shafts
Speed:	13 knots
Manning:	10 Navy-civilian engineers and technicians

The SEA SHADOW was built as a test platform for several surface-ship technologies, among them ship control, automation, structures, seakeeping, and—especially—signature reduction. The program was sponsored by the Navy, the Advanced Research Projects Agency (ARPA), and Lockheed. Results of the signature reduction research have been used in the ARLEIGH BURKE (DDG 51) class and the SWATH-configured ocean surveillance ships (T-AGOS 19–23).

The Navy announced that the cost of the SEA SHADOW program was $195 million, including ship construction costs of $50 million.

The angled fuselage and supports for the twin submerged hulls help reflect radar signals. Anechoic coatings have been used on the craft to further deter radar detection.

A small, retractable radar is fitted atop the control station. There are no fixed projections from the hull.

Operational: The SEA SHADOW ran sea trials in 1985–1986, after which the craft was stored in the covered floating dock HMB-1 at Redwood City in the San Francisco Bay area. At-sea testing was resumed in April 1993 off Santa Cruz Island and, subsequently, in the San Francisco Bay.

The craft conducted exclusively nighttime test runs off the coast of southern California in 1985–1986, making the first—highly publicized—daylight test run on 11 April 1993.

1. HMB-1 = Hughes Mining Barge. This dock was developed for use with the deep-ocean salvage ship GLOMAR EXPLORER (AG 193); see page 219.

The shape of stealth: head-on, the SEA SHADOW resembles a stealth aircraft as much as she does a naval ship. She has twin submerged hulls of the SWATH configuration. The craft tested several new technologies for future ship designs. The test program has been completed. (1993, U.S. Navy)

The SEA SHADOW at rest in the floating dock HMB-1, her clandestine home. Lockheed's imaginative engineers have produced advanced stealth aircraft as well as the SEA SHADOW. (1993, U.S. Navy)

The SEA SHADOW during her first daylight test run off the coast of southern California on 11 April 1993. Note the lack of masts and other projections from the flat sides and top of the craft. Some of her technologies are incorporated in the VICTORIOUS (T-AGOS 19)-class surveillance ships. (1993, U.S. Navy)

UNCLASSIFIED AUXILIARY SHIPS

Unclassified ship designations reached hull number IX 235 at the end of World War II. The series was continued after the war, with the German heavy cruiser PRINZ EUGEN designated IX 300 (i.e., creating a gap of hull numbers 236–299). The postwar IX series reached hull number 310.

In 1967 the extensively converted ELK RIVER (LSMR 501) was placed in this category and classified IX, using her previous hull number. Subsequent craft were given 500-series designations (i.e., creating a second major sequential gap because hull numbers 311–500 were not used). Thus, there has been an official disregard for the IX numerical series, which dated back to December 1941. (The IX symbol for unclassified vessels was used by the Navy from 1920 onward without hull numbers being assigned.)

1 BARRACKS SHIP: EX-SUBMARINE TENDER ↓

Number	Name	Launched	Commissioned
IX 518 (ex-AS 19)	PROTEUS	12 Nov 1942	31 Jan 1944

Originally a submarine tender of the FULTON (AS 11) class, the PROTEUS has been taken out of service and is employed as a barracks ship at the Puget Sound Naval Shipyard, Bremerton, Washington, replacing the GEN HUGH J. GAFFEY.

The ship was in active service as a tender from 1944 to 26 September 1947, when she was decommissioned and placed "in service." The ship provided support to submarines at New London, Connecticut, until January 1955 when she was taken in hand for extensive conversion to support Polaris fleet ballistic missile submarines. She was recommissioned on 8 July 1960. She served in that role until the 1980s and was subsequently employed in general repair and support activities for surface ships as well as submarines.

The PROTEUS was decommissioned and stricken on 30 September 1992. Her status was changed from "strike" to "In Service, In Reserve" on 1 February 1994 for use as a barracks ship.

Classification: Changed from AS 19 to IX 518 on 1 February 1994.

See 15th Edition/page 278 for characteristics as submarine tender.

The PROTEUS shortly before being decommissioned. Here she wears World War II–era camouflage for a two-month deployment to Australia in the spring of 1992 to commemorate the 50th anniversary of the Battle of the Coral Sea. In that battle the U.S. Navy stopped the Japanese Fleet from assaulting Port Moresby, New Guinea. Northern Australia was that fleet's next invasion target. (1992, U.S. Navy)

1 ESCORT SHIP: EX-OCEANOGRAPHIC RESEARCH SHIP

Number	Name	FY	Launched	In service
IX 517 (ex-AGOR 9)	PACIFIC ESCORT (ex-THOMAS G. THOMPSON)	63	18 July 1964	4 Sep 1965

Builders:	Marinette Marine, Wisc.
Displacement:	1,088 tons light 1,400 tons full load
Length:	195⅚ feet (59.7 m) waterline 208⅚ feet (63.7 m) overall
Beam:	37 feet (11.3 m)
Draft:	16 feet (4.9 m)
Propulsion:	diesel-electric (2 Cummins); 10,000 shp; 1 shaft
Speed:	13.5 knots
Range:	12,000 n.miles (22,235 km) at 9 knots
Manning:	civilian
Radars:	. . . navigation

This is a former CONRAD (AGOR 3)-class oceanographic research ship; she was employed in support of submarines undergoing trials after overhaul at the Mare Island Naval Shipyard (California) from 1990 until early 1995. Her future status had not been determined when this edition went to press.

She replaced a former Army tug of the same name, the 143WB8401 (ex-LT 535); see 15th Edition/page 346.

As an AGOR the ship was operated by the University of Washington (state). All research equipment has been removed.

Class: Nine ships of this class—AGOR 3–7, 9, 10, 12, and 13—were built for Navy (MSC) and academic use. See page 226 for status.

Classification: Redesignated IX 517 on 11 December 1989.

Design: SCB No. 185.

Engineering: The large stack contains a small diesel exhaust funnel and provides space for a small, 620-hp gas turbine engine used to provide "quiet" power when noise generated by the main propulsion machinery could interfere with research activities. The gas turbine can be linked to the propeller shaft for speeds up to 6.5 knots. A retractable bow propeller pod allows precise maneuvering and can propel the ship at speeds up to 4.5 knots.

The THOMAS G. THOMPSON in service as an oceanographic research ship. She is now employed—temporarily—in escort and utility duties. (1986, Giorgio Arra)

1 CLASSROOM BARGE ↓

Number	Name	Built	In service
IX 516	(none)	1976	1988

Displacement:	
Length:	302¾ feet (92.28 m) overall
Beam:	90 feet (27.43 m)
Draft:	22 feet (6.7 m)
Propulsion:	non–self-propelled
Manning:	

The IX 516 is a classroom barge employed at the Naval Nuclear Power Training Unit, Goose Creek, South Carolina. A three-story deckhouse on the barge contains classrooms; the structure is 241 feet (73.5 m) long, 72 feet (21.95 m) wide, and 35 feet (10.7 m) high.

The IX 516 is a floating classroom for nuclear technicians. The craft has emergency power generators but normally uses shore electrical power. (1990, U.S. Navy)

The U.S. Navy's experimental surface effects ship SES-200 after her latest modification. The U.S. Navy has not proceeded with SES development, as has the Russian Navy, which has developed a corvette-size SES, the Dergach class. (Textron Marine Systems)

1 SURFACE EFFECTS SHIP: "SES-200"

Number	Launched	In service
IX 515 (ex-SES-200, WSES-1)	Dec 1978	Feb 1979

Builders:	Bell-Halter, New Orleans, La.
Displacement:	187 tons light
	243 tons full load
Length:	$159\frac{1}{12}$ feet (48.5 m) overall
Beam:	$42\frac{7}{12}$ (13.0 m)
Draft:	6 feet (1.8 m) on hull
	5 feet (1.5 m) on cushion
Propulsion:	2 diesel engines (MTU 16V396 TB94); 5,720 bhp; 2 waterjets
Lift:	2 diesel engines (MTU 6V396 TB83); 1,400 bhp; 4 centrifugal fans
Speed:	16 knots on hull in sea state 0
	14 knots on hull in sea state 3
	40+ knots on cushion in sea state 0
	27 knots on cushion in sea state 3
Range:	2,950 n.miles (5,463 km) at 30 knots in sea state 0
	2,400 n.miles (4,445 km) at 25 knots in sea state 3
Manning:	22 (2 officers + 20 enlisted)
Guns:	(see notes)
Radars:	2 Decca navigation

The SES-200 was built as a prototype for U.S. Navy and Coast Guard evaluation. The craft was designed by Bell Aerospace and built by Halter Marine. After completion, she was leased to the U.S. Coast Guard for trials (beginning January 1980) and then transferred back to the U.S. Navy (from 1982) for continued trials. Following her conversion (see below), the craft was again evaluated by the Coast Guard in late 1984.

In Coast Guard service the craft was named DORADO and designated WSES-1. (Subsequently, the Coast Guard purchased three similar craft; see chapter 32.)

The craft was again placed in U.S. Navy service on 24 September 1982. She is assigned to the David Taylor Research Center and based at the Naval Air Station, Patuxent River, Maryland.[2]

Classification: The hull number IX 515 was assigned on 11 May 1987; previously, the craft was listed as "floating equipment."

Conversion: In January 1982 the craft was returned to Bell-Halter where she was cut in half to accommodate the installation of a 50-foot (15.2-m) midships section. The modified craft was accepted by the Navy on 24 September 1982.

Two additional lift fans were installed in 1984. Her propulsion plant was upgraded from September 1987 through 1988; the older propulsion system was replaced by the current diesel engines and waterjet propulsion in 1990.

Engineering: The original characteristics and propulsion plant are described in the 14th Edition/pages 355–56. The waterjet propulsion is the Swedish KaMeWa system.

Guns: The ship was fitted in 1986–1987 with an Ex-25 25-mm Sea Vulcan rotary-barrel (Gatling) gun to evaluate the effectiveness of such weapons on high-speed craft, especially against slow-moving targets.

Missiles: In 1989 the craft evaluated the LTV-developed Crossbow weapons pedestal, which can be used to launch a variety of short-range missiles.

Operational: In 1985–1986 the craft carried out trials and demonstrations in several European countries and Canada. The craft conducted visits to several South American ports in 1987.

The SES-200 at rest. (1989, Giorgio Arra)

The SES-200 showing the craft's broad stern. (1989, Giorgio Arra)

2. Formerly Naval Ship Research and Development Center, with headquarters at Carderock, Maryland.

The helicopter landing training craft IX 514 at Pensacola, Florida. The TH-57 SeaRanger is flown by student pilots to practice shipboard landings on the IX 514, the world's smallest "aviation ship." (1994, Leo Van Ginderen collection)

1 HELICOPTER TRAINING CRAFT: EX-YFU TYPE

Number	Name	Completed	IX in service
IX 514 (ex-YFU 79)	(none)	1968	Mar 1986

Builders:	Pacific Coast Engineering, Alameda, Calif.
Displacement:	220 tons light
	380 tons full load
Length:	125 feet (38.1 m) overall
Beam:	36 feet (11.0 m)
Draft:	7½ feet (2.3 m)
Propulsion:	2 diesel engines (General Motors 6-71); 1,000 bhp; 2 shafts
Speed:	8 knots
Manning:	
Radars:	1 Decca navigation

Converted in 1985–1986, she is used as a helicopter landing ship to train helicopter pilots. Placed in service on 31 March 1986, she operates in the Gulf of Mexico, based at the Naval Air Station, Pensacola, Florida.

Classification: Changed from YFU to IX on 31 March 1986.

Helicopters: The flight deck landing area is 57⅚ (17.6 m) feet long and 28 feet (8.5 m) wide. There is no helicopter parking area or hangar on the craft; no refueling capability is provided. Lighting is provided for night landings.

The Empress II radiation test barge IX 513. Tests to determine electromagnetic effects on ships have become controversial because of the efforts of environmental groups. (1990, Leo Van Ginderen collection)

1 RADIATION TEST BARGE ↓

Number	In service
IX 513	June 1988

Builders:	Eastern Marine, Panama City, Fla.
Displacement:	approx. 2,200 tons full load
Length:	120 feet (36.57 m) overall
Beam:	90 feet (27.43 m)
Draft:	15 feet (4.57 m)
Propulsion:	non–self-propelled

The IX 513 is an unmanned barge used to produce an electric pulse to evaluate ships' Electro-Magnetic Pulse (EMP) protection under a program termed Empress II. The craft has a 150-foot (45.7-m), four-leg support structure for a 188½-foot (57.5-m) diameter pulse transmission antenna ring. A pulse of 7-million volts can be generated by the craft's two diesel generators.

Delayed by builder problems and environmental impact concerns, the barge began pulse tests against warships in 1990 off the coast of North Carolina; she was subsequently moved to the Gulf of Mexico.

Names: Empress is an acronym for Electromagnetic Pulse Radiation Environment Simulator for Ships.

1 MISSILE TEST BARGE ↓

The unnamed missile test barge IX 512 (ex-BD 6651), built in 1954, was stricken on 15 December 1995. This was a former U.S. Army floating crane converted for simulation of Trident D-5 missile launches. Known as the Simulated Underwater Partial Launch System (SUPLS II), the craft was fitted with a single Trident missile tube. She operated off San Clemente, California.

See 15th Edition/pages 332–33.

RANGE SUPPORT SHIP: EX-TANK LANDING SHIP

The IX 511 (formerly LST 399), constructed during World War II, was deactivated and stricken on 1 November 1973. She was laid up in the NDRF until being reacquired by the Navy on 25 November 1980 for use as a range support ship on the Pacific Missile Range, Point Mugu, California. She was classified as IX and placed in service on 30 September 1982, then stricken on 15 June 1985.

The former troop transport GEN HUGH J. GAFFEY. (1986, Leo Van Ginderen collection)

BARRACKS SHIPS: EX-TROOP TRANSPORTS (P2-SE2-R1) ↓

Number	Name	AP Comm.	Notes
IX 507 (ex-AP 121)	GEN HUGH J. GAFFEY	18 Sep 1944	stricken 26 Oct 1993
IX 510 (ex-AP 127)	GEN WILLIAM O. DARBY	27 Sep 1945	stricken 26 Oct 1993

These former Admiral-type transports were employed as immobilized barracks ships during the 1980s. Built as naval transports, they were transferred to the Army in 1946, then assigned to the Navy's newly established Military Sea Transportation Service (MSTS) on 1 March 1950. As troop transports the AP 121 could carry 4,680 troops and the AP 127 could carry 4,985.

The GAFFEY was stricken from the Naval Vessel Register on 9 January 1969; the ship was reacquired by the Navy on 1 November 1978 for conversion to a barracks ship and reclassified IX 507. She was assigned to the Bremerton Naval Shipyard (Washington) to house the crews of aircraft carriers undergoing conversion and modernization. After being stricken in 1993, the GAFFEY was sold for scrap in 1995.

The DARBY was operational as a transport from her completion until being laid up in NDRF ready reserve status on 1 July 1967. She was reacquired from the NDRF on 27 October 1981 (reclassified IX 510 on that date) for use as a barracks ship. After being modified, she was towed to Norfolk Navy Yard (Virginia) to house crews of ships undergoing conversion and modernization. Her status was "out of service, in reserve." She was laid up again in the NDRF on 23 April 1991; after being stricken, the ship remains in the James River (Virginia) reserve group.

Only the ships' accommodations and messing spaces were rehabilitated. The ships were not capable of steaming in their final condition.

See 15th Edition/page 333 for characteristics.

EXPLOSIVES DAMAGE-CONTROL BARGE

The unnamed IX 509, a non–self-propelled barge configured to support explosives testing, was stricken on 18 December 1992. The craft had been placed in service in 1979.

See 15th Edition/page 333 for characteristics.

1 TEST OPERATIONS SUPPORT SHIP: EX-LCU TYPE

Number	Name	Completed
IX 508 (ex-LCU 1618)	ORCA	1959

Builders:	Gunderson Bros., Portland, Ore.
Displacement:	190 tons light 390 tons full load
Length:	134¾ feet (41.1 m) overall
Beam:	29¾ feet (9.1 m)
Draft:	6⅚ feet (2.1 m)
Propulsion:	4 diesel engines (General Motors 6-71); 1,200 bhp; 2 shafts (Kort nozzles)
Speed:	11 knots
Range:	1,200 n.miles (2,222 km) at 11 knots
Manning:	

This craft is configured to support test operations at the Naval Command, Control and Ocean Surveillance Center at San Diego. Formerly an LCU 1610-class landing craft, she served for severalyears in the test support role before being changed to IX 508 on 1 December 1979.

Electronics: Modified in 1978 to conduct trials with the NAVSTAR satellite global positioning system.

IX 508. (1990, U.S. Navy)

IX 508. (1986, Giorgio Arra)

1 RESEARCH SUPPORT SHIP: EX-YFU TYPE

Number	Name	Completed
IX 506 (ex-YFU 82)	Sea Lion	Oct 1968

Builders:	Pacific Coast Engineering, Alameda, Calif.
Displacement:	220 tons light 380 tons full load
Length:	136 feet (41.5 m) overall
Beam:	36 feet (11.0 m)
Draft:	5½ feet (1.7 m)
Propulsion:	4 diesel engines (General Motors 6-71); 1,000 bhp; 2 shafts
Speed:	8 knots
Torpedo Tubes:	3 12.75-inch (324-mm) tubes Mk 32 (triple)
Manning:	12 (2 officers + 10 enlisted)

IX 506. (1985, Giorgio Arra)

IX 506. (1985, Giorgio Arra)

This former harbor utility craft was converted for use as a research platform by the Naval Command, Control and Ocean Surveillance Center at San Diego (replacing the YTM 759). Her bow was rebuilt, and a forecastle was added. A center well permits lowering test gear to depths of 900 feet (274 m). She was converted in 1978–1982.

Classification: Changed from YFU 82 to IX 506 on 1 April 1978.

2 SELF-PROPELLED BARRACKS SHIPS: MODIFIED LST DESIGN ↓

Number	Name	Launched	Commissioned
IX 502 (ex-APB 39)	Mercer	17 Nov 1944	19 Sep 1945
IX 503 (ex-APB 40)	Nueces	6 May 1945	30 Nov 1945

Builders:	Boston Navy Yard
Displacement:	2,190 tons light 3,640 tons full load
Length:	328 feet (100.0 m) overall
Beam:	50 feet (15.25 m)
Draft:	11 feet (3.4 m)
Propulsion:	2 diesel engines (General Motors 12-267); 1,600 bhp; 2 shafts (see notes)
Speed:	10 knots
Manning:	198 (12 officers + 186 enlisted) as APB
Troops:	approx. 900
Guns:	removed

These ships were built to provide accommodations and support for small craft. Both were completed as barracks ships (APL, later APB). They were modified in 1975–1976 to serve at shipyards for crews of ships being built or in overhaul. They were changed from APB to IX at that time.

Two ships were placed in commission upon original completion; the Echols was placed in service. All three ships were laid up in reserve after World War II. The Mercer and Nueces were recommissioned in 1968 for service in the Vietnam War. They were rearmed at that time with two 3-inch/50-cal AA guns (single), eight 40-mm AA guns (quad), and several machine guns. As modified to support riverine forces in South Vietnam they had crews of 12 officers and 186 enlisted men and could accommodate 900 troops and small-craft crewmen. Both ships were again laid up from 1969–1971 until being reactivated in 1975 as barracks ships on the West Coast; they are now at San Diego.

The Echols was reactivated and placed in service on 1 February 1976 as a barracks ship for the crews of new-construction SSBNs at the General Dynamics/Electric Boat yard in Groton, Connecticut.

Class: There were originally 14 ships of this class, APB 35–48.

The Echols (IX 504, ex-APB 37) was stricken on 22 December 1995.

Classification: APL/APB 39 changed to IX 502 and APL/APB 40 to IX 503 on 1 November 1975; APL/APB 37 changed to IX 504 on 1 February 1976.

Engineering: Their propulsion plants are not operational.

Guns: As built, these ships had eight 40-mm AA guns (quad mounts).

The barracks ship Mercer at San Francisco. Barracks ships provide mess and berthing facilities for crews of ships under construction or in overhaul or conversion. (1986, Giorgio Arra)

1 BARRACKS SHIP: EX-MEDIUM ROCKET LANDING SHIP ↓

Number	Name	Launched	Commissioned
IX 501 (ex-LSMR 501)	ELK RIVER	21 Apr 1945	27 May 1945

Builders: Brown Shipbuilding, Houston, Texas
Displacement: 1,280 tons full load
Length: 230 feet (70.1 m) overall
Beam: 50 feet (15.25 m)
Draft: 9⅚ feet (3.0 m)
Propulsion: 2 diesel engines (General Motors 16-278A); 1,400 bhp; 2 shafts
Speed: 11 knots
Manning:

The ELK RIVER was converted from a rocket landing ship to a test and training ship for deep-sea diving and salvage. She was operated in that role by the NOSC at San Diego from 1969 until 1986. The large gantry crane (see below) and other pieces of equipment were removed in October 1986, and the ship was relegated to service as a barracks hulk at San Diego.

The ship was laid down on 24 March 1945.

Class: The ELK RIVER was one of 48 medium landing ships (LSM) completed as or converted to rocket-fire support ships (LSMR 401–412 and 501–536). All other ships of this type have been stricken, the last three LSMRs having been used in the Vietnam War (redesignated IFS for inshore fire-support ships but retaining their LSMR hull numbers).

A total of 558 LSM-type ships were completed 1944–1946; originally designated LCT(7), these ships had open tank decks to carry five M4 Sherman medium tanks or six LVT amphibious tractors. The LSMRs had 5-inch (127-mm) spin-stabilized rocket launchers and 5-inch/38-cal DP guns, plus lighter weapons.

Classification: Changed from LSMR to IX on 1 April 1967.

Conversion: The ship was converted to a test-range support ship in 1967–1968 at Avondale Shipyards and the San Francisco Naval Shipyard. The basic 203½-foot (62.0-m) LSMR hull was lengthened, and eight-foot (2.4-m) sponsons were added to both sides to improve the ship's stability and to increase working space. A superstructure was added forward, and an open center well was provided for lowering and raising equipment. The 65-ton gantry crane runs on tracks above the opening to handle small submersibles and diver-transfer chambers. An active precision positioning system has been installed for position holding without mooring.

The prototype Mk II Deep Diving System (DDS) was installed in the ship to support eight divers operating at depths of at least 1,000 feet (305 m) in helium-oxygen saturation conditions. This is the most advanced shipboard system in use today; it has also been installed in the two PIGEON (ASR 21)-class ships.

Names: The 48 LSMRs were given river names on 1 October 1955.

1 SONAR TEST BARGE ↓

Number	Name	IX in service
IX 310	(none)	1 Apr 1971

The IX 310 consists of two non–self-propelled barges, moored in Lake Seneca, New York, for sonar research by the Naval Undersea Warfare Center at Newport, Rhode Island (formerly Naval Underwater Sound Laboratory). She was built in 1970.

SOUND TRIALS SHIP: "MONOB ONE"

The MONOB ONE (ex-IX 309, YW 87) has been reclassified as the YAG 61 (pages 304–5).

1 TORPEDO TRIALS SHIP: EX-CARGO SHIP

Number	Name	Completed
IX 308 (ex-AKL 17)	NEW BEDFORD	Mar 1945

Builders: Wheeler Shipbuilding, Long Island, N.Y.
Displacement: 526 tons light
940 tons full load
Length: 176½ feet (53.8 m) overall
Beam: 32¾ feet (10.0 m)
Draft: 10 feet (3.0 m)
Propulsion: 2 diesel engines (General Motors 6-278A); 1,000 bhp; 2 shafts
Speed: 13 knots
Range: 3,200 n.miles (5,926 km) at 11 knots
Torpedo Tubes: 1 21-inch (533-mm) tube
3 12.75-inch (324-mm) tubes Mk 32 (triple)
Manning: approx. 25

The NEW BEDFORD was built as an Army freight and supply ship (FS 289) and was operated by the Coast Guard for the Army. She was

The torpedo trials ship NEW BEDFORD, which has been replaced by the new YTT series but remained in service when this edition went to press. (1978, U.S. Navy)

The ELK RIVER, once an impressive rocket ship and then host ship for the country's most advanced deep-dive system, now reduced to a barracks hulk. (1992, Stefan Terzibaschitsch)

acquired by the Navy on 1 March 1950 for use as a cargo ship and operated by the MSTS as the T-AKL 17. The ship was later converted for torpedo testing in 1963 and since then has been operated by the Naval Undersea Warfare Center, Keyport, Washington (formerly the Naval Torpedo Station).

The NEW BEDFORD is fitted with the CURV torpedo recovery device.[3]

Classification: Originally U.S. Army FS 289, the ship was operated by the MSTS as T-AKL 17. That designation was changed to IX 308 in October 1971.

1 SAILING FRIGATE: "CONSTITUTION" ↓

Number	Name	Launched	Commissioned
(ex-IX 21)	CONSTITUTION	21 Oct 1797	July 1978

Builders:	Harrt's Shipyard, Boston, Mass.
Displacement:	2,200 tons standard
Length:	175 feet (53.35 m) waterline 204 feet (62.2 m) billet head to taffrail
Beam:	43½ feet (13.3 m)
Draft:	22½ feet (6.85 m)
Masts:	fore 198 feet (60.4 m) main 220 feet (67.0 m) mizzen 172½ feet (52.6 m)
Speed:	13+ knots (under sail)
Manning:	54 (2 officers + 52 enlisted) as relic; up to 500 as frigate (including 55 Marines)
Guns:	several smooth-bore cannon (see notes)

The CONSTITUTION is the oldest U.S. ship in Navy commission and the oldest known warship still afloat. Her original commissioning date is not known; she first put to sea on 23 July 1798. She is now moored as a relic at the Boston Naval Shipyard. (She is afloat, unlike the older VICTORY, Admiral Lord Nelson's flagship at the battle of Trafalgar, which is preserved in concrete at the naval dockyard in Portsmouth, England.)

The CONSTITUTION hosts more than one million visitors per year.

As a sail frigate the CONSTITUTION fought in the Quasi-War with France, against the Barbary pirates, and in the War of 1812 against Great Britain. She has been rebuilt several times and is now restored as much as possible to her original configuration.

No sails are fitted; her designed sail area was 42,710 feet^2 (3,844 m^2). Once a year, usually on the Fourth of July, she is taken out into Boston Harbor under tow and "turned around" so that her masts do not bend from the effects of sun and wind. At noon on the Fourth the CONSTITUTION traditionally fires a 21-gun salute from her forward 24-pounder long guns.

Class: The CONSTITUTION was one of six sail frigates built under an act of Congress of 1794. The CONSTELLATION (38 guns), built under the same act and launched on 7 September 1797, was broken up at the Gosport shipyard, Norfolk, Virginia, in 1852–1853. Almost simultaneously, a sailing corvette of that name was built in the same yard. That ship served in the Navy (designated IX 20 in 1941) until her transfer in 1954 to a private group in Baltimore, Maryland, where she is maintained.[4]

Classification: The CONSTITUTION was classified as an "unclassified" ship in 1920 (designated IX, without a hull number). She became IX 21 on 8 December 1941 and carried that classification until 1 September 1975 when it was withdrawn because, according to Navy officials, the designation "tended to demean and degrade the CONSTITUTION through association with a group of insignificant craft of varied missions and configurations."

Design: Three-masted sail frigate designed by Joshua Humphreys. The ship was built at Edmond Harrt's shipyard in Boston; although she has been rebuilt several times, her basic lines and configuration have been retained.

Guns: The CONSTITUTION was authorized as a 44-gun frigate but in fact was completed with a larger gun battery. The ship was usually overgunned: her original armament consisted of 30 24-pounder long guns, 16 18-pounder long guns, and 14 12-pounder long guns—a total of 60 guns. This heavy armament overloaded and strained the ship.

The number and types of guns varied considerably during her service as a frigate. She carries several cannon and two 40-mm saluting guns (installed in 1976).

Names: From 1 December 1917 until 4 July 1925 the ship was named OLD CONSTITUTION while the name CONSTITUTION was assigned to a battle cruiser (CC 5). The cruiser was never completed, and the name reverted to this ship.

Operational: The ship has been at Boston since 7 May 1934, following a sailing tour of 90 ports on the U.S. Atlantic, Pacific, and Gulf Coasts from 1931 to 1934.

The CONSTITUTION, the world's oldest naval ship in commission and afloat. (1986, Robert Selly)

Y-SERIES SERVICE CRAFT

SOUND TRIALS SHIP: "DEER ISLAND"

The sound trials ship DEER ISLAND (YAG 62), a former oil field supply ship built in 1966, was stricken on 6 February 1995. She was acquired by the Navy on 15 March 1982 but retained her commercial name. The craft was used for sound testing by the Naval Surface Warfare Center (formerly David Taylor Research Center), operating from Port Everglades, Florida.

See 15th Edition/page 338 for characteristics.

SOUND TRIALS SHIP: "MONOB ONE"

The sound trials ship MONOB ONE (YAG 61, ex-IX 309, YW 87), built in 1943, was stricken on 4 April 1955. The MONOB ONE—for *Mobile*

3. CURV = Cable-controlled Underwater Research Vehicle.
4. Until 1991 the private organization preserving the ship contended that the Baltimore CONSTELLATION was the frigate of 1797, despite extensive evidence to the contrary. The issue was decisively addressed and the Baltimore ship proven to be the 1853 vessel in an analysis by Dana M. Wegner, et al., *Fouled Anchors: The* Constellation *Questions Answered* (Carderock, Md.: David Taylor Research Center, Sep. 1991); also see Howard I. Chapelle and Leon D. Polland, *The* Constellation *Question* (Washington, D.C.: Smithsonian Institution Press, 1970).

Noise Barge—was converted to a sound trials configuration in 1969 and placed in service in June 1970 for the David Taylor Research Center. She was assigned to the Naval Surface Warfare Center, operating from Port Canaveral, Florida.

See 15th Edition/page 338 for characteristics.

TORPEDO TRIALS CRAFT: "YF 852" CLASS

All torpedo trials craft modified from YF 852-class self-propelled covered lighters have been discarded. The YF 862 (unnamed) was stricken on 15 February 1985, the KODIAK (YF 866) was stricken in 1989, and the KEYPORT (YF 885) was stricken in July 1990.

See 14th Edition/page 343 for characteristics.

FERRYBOATS: "LCU 1610" CLASS

These are former LCU 1610-class utility landing craft modified in 1969 for use as ferryboats. The YFB 88 (ex-LCU 1636) was stricken on 30 June 1993; YFB 89 (ex-LCU 1638), YFB 90 (ex-LCU 1639), and YFB 91 (ex-LCU 1640) were stricken on 9 October 1992.

See 15th Edition/page 339 for characteristics.

1 FERRYBOAT: YFB TYPE

Number	Name	Completed
YFB 87	MOKU HOLO HELE	May 1970

Builders:	Western Boat
Displacement:	773 tons full load
Length:	162 feet (49.4 m) overall
Beam:	59 feet (18.0 m)
Draft:	12 feet (3.7 m)
Propulsion:	2 diesel engines (General Motors); 860 bhp; 2 shafts
Speed:	
Manning:	

This built-for-the-purpose ferryboat is active at Pearl Harbor, Hawaii. She's been in Navy service since completion.

Names: The craft's name in Hawaiian means "Ship that goes back and forth."

The MOKU HOLO HELE, heavily laden with trucks and cars, at Pearl Harbor. (1985, U.S. Navy)

1 FERRYBOAT: YFB TYPE

Number	Name	Completed
YFB 83	WA'A HELE HONUA	Apr 1949

Builders:	John H. Mathis Co., Camden, N.J.
Displacement:	500 tons full load
Length:	180 feet (54.9 m) overall
Beam:	46 feet (14.0 m)
Draft:	
Propulsion:	2 diesel engines; 400 bhp; 1 shaft
Speed:	8.5 knots
Manning:	

This built-for-the-purpose ferryboat is also in operation at Pearl Harbor, Hawaii. She has been in Navy service since March 1965.

Names: The craft's name in Hawaiian means "A canoe that travels on land."

The WA'A HELE HONUA at Pearl Harbor. (1985, U.S. Navy)

10 SPECIAL-PURPOSE LIGHTERS: YFNX TYPE

Number	Completed	YFNX in service
YFNX 24 (ex-YFN 1215)	1965	1966
YFNX 25 (ex-YFN 1224)	1965	May 1965
YFNX 31 (ex-YFN 1249)	1970	1970
YFNX 35 (ex-YFN 1283)		1 Nov 1992
YFNX 36 (ex-YFN 1263)		1 Nov 1992
YFNX 37 (ex-YFN 1198)		1 Nov 1992
YFNX 38 (ex-YFN 1206)		1 Nov 1992
YFNX 39 (ex-YFN 1276)		1 Nov 1992
YFNX 40 (ex-YC 1519)		1 Feb 1994
YFNX 41 (ex-YFN 274)		1 Feb 1994

Builders:	
Displacement:	
Length:	126 feet (38.4 m) overall
Beam:	32⅚ feet (10.0 m)
Draft:	
Propulsion:	diesel
Speed:	
Manning:	

These are self-propelled special-purpose craft that have been converted from non–self-propelled lighters. Six units are active; the YFNX 35 is laid up at Little Creek, Virginia; YFNX 37 and YFNX 38 are laid up at Norfolk, Virginia; and YFNX 38 and YFNX 39 are at Charleston, South Carolina.

Class: The YFNX 23 was stricken on 2 September 1993; YFNX 26 was stricken on 29 July 1994.

The YFNX 32 (ex-YRBM 7) was reclassified as YRBM 7 on 1 May 1992; YFNX 33 (ex-YFN 1192) was reclassified as YLC 1 in August 1986.

1 SPECIAL-PURPOSE LIGHTER: YFNX TYPE

Number	Name	Completed	YFNX in service
YFNX 30 (ex-YFN 1186)	SEA TURTLE	1952	1973

Builders:	
Displacement:	200 tons light
Length:	111½ feet (34.0 m) overall
Beam:	32⅚ feet (10.0 m)
Draft:	5 7/12 feet (1.7 m)
Propulsion:	diesel
Speed:	
Manning:	

The SEA TURTLE with a canvas covering over a triple Mk 32 torpedo tube mounting on her 01 level. (1990, U.S. Navy)

The Sea Turtle is the only named YFNX-type craft. She is assigned to the Naval Command, Control and Ocean Surveillance Center, San Diego, and supports the CURV II recovery vehicle.

The YFNX 30, unofficially named Sea Turtle, is a unique research support craft operated by the Naval Command, Control and Ocean Surveillance Center at San Diego. (1986, Giorgio Arra)

4 SPECIAL-PURPOSE LIGHTERS: YFNX TYPE

Number	Completed	YFNX in service
YFNX 4	1942	1965
YFNX 15 (ex-YNg 22)	1942	1965
YFNX 20	1952	1965
YFNX 22	1941	1965

Builders:	YFNX 15 Dravo Corp., Wilmington, Del.
Displacement:	
Length:	109 11/12 feet (33.5 m) overall
Beam:	32 5/6 feet (10.0 m)
Draft:	5 7/12 feet (1.7 m)
Propulsion:	diesel
Speed:	
Manning:	

These are self-propelled special-purpose craft, having been converted from non–self-propelled lighters. The YFNX 7, previously in reserve, is assigned to the Coast Guard.

The YFNX 15 was built as a non–self-propelled gate craft (originally YNg 22).

Class: The YFNX 7 is on loan to the Coast Guard; she is based at Governors Island, New York. The YFNX 23 (ex-YFN 289) was stricken on 2 September 1993.

2 TORPEDO TRIALS CRAFT: CONVERTED LIGHTERS

Number	Name	Completed	YFRT in service
YFRT 287 (ex-YF 287)		July 1941	1965
YFRT 520 (ex-YF 520)	Potential	Aug 1943	1965

Builders:	YFRT 287 Norfolk Navy Yard, Va.
	YFRT 520 Erie Concrete & Steel, Pa.
Displacement:	300 tons light
	650 tons full load
Length:	133 feet (40.5 m) overall
Beam:	30 feet (9.1 m)
Draft:	9 feet (2.7 m)
Propulsion:	2 diesel engines (Caterpillar D379); 600–800 bhp; 2 shafts
Speed:	9.5 knots
Torpedo Tubes:	3 12.75-inch (324-mm) tubes Mk 32 (triple)
Manning:	

These former YF-type lighters were converted to a torpedo trials configuration. Both craft are active.

Class: The YFRT 523 was stricken on 3 April 1986; YFRT 451 (ex-YF 451) was stricken on 15 November 1993.

One of the few survivors of a series of lighters converted to torpedo trials craft. These craft and the new YTTs launch a variety of operational torpedoes, prototype-research "fish," and underwater "shapes." (1994, Leo Van Ginderen collection)

The now-discarded YFRT 451 at Keyport, Washington, shows the lines of these lighter-type craft that were long employed as torpedo trials craft. (1990, U.S. Navy)

1 HARBOR UTILITY CRAFT: "LCU 1610" CLASS

Number	Completed
YFU 83	1971

Builders:	Defoe Shipbuilding, Bay City, Mich.
Displacement:	190 tons light
	390 tons full load
Length:	134 3/4 feet (41.0 m) overall
Beam:	29 3/4 feet (9.0 m)
Draft:	6 feet (1.8 m)
Propulsion:	4 diesel engines (General Motors 6-71); 2,000 bhp; 2 shafts (Kort nozzles)
Speed:	11 knots
Manning:	6 (enlisted)

The YFU 83 was built as a harbor utility craft. All other YFUs of this design were converted landing craft of the LCU 1610 class.

Class: The class originally consisted of the YFU 83 and 97–102. The YFU 101 was stricken on 3 March 1986 and YFU 98 on 10 March 1986. The YFU 97 was reclassified as LCU 1611 on 15 June 1990. The YFU 100 and YFU 102 were both stricken on 18 June 1991.

One of the YFU/LCU-type craft of the 1610 class, featuring a starboard-side bridge structure and drive-through tank deck. Only the YFU 83 of this type remains in service as a harbor utility craft. Here the YFU 97, assigned to the Atlantic Undersea Test and Evaluation Center (AUTEC), had a container on her after deck. (1988, Giorgio Arra)

1 HARBOR UTILITY CRAFT: LCU 1608 CLASS

Number	Completed
YFU 91 (ex-LCU 1608)	1957

Builders: Defoe Shipbuilding, Bay City, Mich.
Displacement: 351 tons full load
Length: 115⅙ feet (35.1 m) overall
Beam: 34 feet (10.4 m)
Draft: 5 feet (1.5 m)
Propulsion: 3 diesel engines (Gray Marine 64 HN12); 675 bhp; 3 shafts (Kort nozzles)
Speed: 8 knots
Manning:

This is a coastal cargo craft with a cargo capacity of 183 tons. In service at the Naval Undersea Warfare Center detachment at Andros Island, Bahamas, she supports the Anglo-American Atlantic Undersea Test and Evaluation Center (AUTEC) range.

A conventional superstructure-aft LCU-type ship, the YFU 91 is also assigned to AUTEC, supporting U.S. and British undersea weapons and sensor development. (1991, Giorgio Arra)

1 HARBOR UTILITY CRAFT: "YFU 71" CLASS

Number	Completed
YFU 81	1968

Builders: Pacific Coast Engineering Co., Alameda, Calif.
Displacement: 220 tons light
380 tons full load
Length: 125 feet (38.1 m) overall
Beam: 38 feet (11.0 m)
Draft: 7½ feet (2.4 m)
Propulsion: 2 diesel engines (General Motors 6-71); 1,000 bhp; 2 shafts (Kort nozzles)
Speed: 8 knots
Manning:

This craft was constructed specifically for use as a coastal cargo craft in the Vietnam War. Twelve units were built to a modified commercial design (YFU 71–82); they were completed in 1967–1968. The cargo capacity of the craft is 300 tons. Previously laid up, the craft is assigned to Atlantic Fleet Weapons Training Facility, Roosevelt Roads, Puerto Rico.

Class: The YFU 71–77 and 80–82 were transferred to the U.S. Army in 1970 for use in South Vietnam; they were returned to the Navy in 1973. The YFU 74 and YFU 75 were stricken on 30 September 1986. The YFU 71, 72, 76, and 77 were transferred to the Department of the Interior on 1 December 1984; YFU 76 and 77 were subsequently transferred to the government of the Marshall Islands in 1987.

The YFU 82 became the IX 506 and the YFU 79 became the IX 512.

Guns: During their service in Vietnam waters these craft were each fitted with two or more .50-cal machine guns.

The YFU 75 of the YFU 71 class. (U.S. Navy)

3 SELF-PROPELLED DREDGES: YM TYPE

Number	Completed
YM 17	1934
YM 33	1970
YM 35	1970

These are small dredges whose characteristics vary. The YM 17 and 35 are active; YM 33 is laid up.

Class: The YM 38 was stricken on 31 January 1987, the YM 32 on 17 January 1990.

3 FUEL OIL BARGES: "YO 65" CLASS

Number	Completed
YO 220	Aug 1945
YO 223	Sep 1945
YO 230	Dec 1945

Builders:	Jeffersonville Boat and Machinery, Ind.
Displacement:	440 tons light
	1,390 tons full load
Length:	174 feet (53.1 m) overall
Beam:	33 feet (10.0 m)
Draft:	13 feet (4.0 m)
Propulsion:	1 diesel engine (General Motors); 560 bhp; 1 shaft
Speed:	10.5 knots
Manning:	11 (enlisted)

These are coastal tankers with a cargo capacity of 6,570 barrels. All are active.

Class: The YO 130 was immobilized and changed to YON 130 on 5 September 1990; YO 203 was immobilized and changed to YON 320 on 1 February 1994; YO 129 was stricken on 25 March 1994; and YO 224 and YO 225 were stricken on 10 October 1995.

The YO 153 (of a separate class) was stricken on 27 March 1992.

The now-discarded YO 203 of the YO 65 class, seen off San Diego, California. The gun tub aft of the superstructure reflects the craft's World War II vintage. (1992, Stefan Terzibaschitsch)

1 FUEL OIL BARGE: "YO 46" CLASS

Number	Name	Launched	Completed
YO 47	Casing Head	25 Apr 1942	12 Nov 1942

Builders:	Lake Superior Shipbuilding, Superior, Wisc.
Displacement:	950 tons light
	2,660 tons full load
Length:	235 feet (71.6 m) overall
Beam:	37 feet (11.3 m)
Draft:	16½ feet (5.0 m)
Propulsion:	2 diesel engines (Enterprise); 820 bhp; 2 shafts
Speed:	9 knots
Manning:	34

This is the only named YO. Her cargo capacity is 10,000 barrels (1,350 tons). The Casing Head has been laid up in reserve since 1971.

3 GASOLINE BARGES: "YOG 5" CLASS

Number	Completed
YOG 78	1945
YOG 88	1945
YOG 93	1946

Builders:	YOG 88, 93 R.T.C. Shipbuilding, Camden, N.J.
	YOG 78 Puget Sound Navy Yard, Bremerton, Wash.
Displacement:	440 tons light
	1,390 tons full load
Length:	174 feet (53.0 m) overall
Beam:	33 feet (10.1 m)
Draft:	13 feet (4.0 m)
Propulsion:	1 diesel engine (General Motors); 640 bhp; 1 shaft
Speed:	11 knots
Manning:	

These are self-propelled gasoline barges with a cargo capacity of 6,570 barrels. They are virtually identical to the 174-foot fuel oil barges. The YOG 78 and YOG 88 are in service; the YOG 93 is in reserve.

Class: The YOG 58 was stricken on 18 April 1994 and YOG 196 on 26 July 1994.

The YOG 88 at San Diego. (1985, Giorgio Arra)

27 SEAMANSHIP TRAINING CRAFT: "YP 676" CLASS

Number	Launched	In service
YP 676	9 Apr 1984	1 Nov 1984
YP 677	23 June 1984	1 Dec 1984
YP 678	3 Nov 1984	13 May 1985
YP 679	11 Dec 1984	3 June 1985
YP 680	23 Mar 1985	30 July 1985
YP 681	1 June 1985	11 Oct 1985
YP 682	3 Aug 1985	19 Nov 1985
YP 683	19 June 1986	21 Oct 1986
YP 684	14 Aug 1986	21 Oct 1986
YP 685	25 Sep 1986	25 Nov 1986
YP 686	25 Oct 1986	8 Dec 1986
YP 687	17 Mar 1987	22 May 1987
YP 688	13 Mar 1987	22 May 1987
YP 689	20 Mar 1987	10 June 1987
YP 690	17 Apr 1987	10 June 1987
YP 691	19 May 1987	2 July 1987
YP 692	18 June 1987	27 July 1987
YP 693	14 Aug 1987	22 Sep 1987
YP 694	21 Sep 1987	27 Oct 1987
YP 695	26 Oct 1987	1 Dec 1987
YP 696	31 Mar 1988	1 May 1988
YP 697	1 Feb 1988	26 May 1988
YP 698	29 Mar 1988	16 June 1988
YP 699	11 Apr 1988	30 June 1988
YP 700	12 May 1988	21 July 1988
YP 701	14 June 1988	9 Aug 1988
YP 702	19 July 1988	2 Sep 1988

Builders:	YP 676–682 Peterson Builders, Sturgeon Bay, Wisc.
	YP 683–702 Marinette Shipbuilding, Marinette, Wisc.
Displacement:	172 tons full load
Length:	101⅔ feet (31.0 m) waterline
	108 feet (32.9 m) overall
Beam:	24 feet (7.3 m)
Draft:	5¾ feet (1.75 m)
Propulsion:	2 diesel engines (General Motors 12V71N); 875 bhp; 2 shafts
Speed:	12 knots
Range:	1,500 n.miles (2,778 km) at 12 knots
Manning:	6 (2 officers + 4 enlisted) + 24 students

These are seamanship training craft. They have wood hulls; the deckhouse and pilothouse are aluminum. The YP 686 is fitted for oceanographic research studies.

Electronics: Fitted with NAVSAT and Loran C receivers, as well as navigation radar and a fathometer.

Operational: The YP 676–695 are employed for seamanship training at the Naval Academy, Annapolis, Maryland. The YP 697 and YP 701 are assigned to the Marine Corps Air Station, Cherry Point, North Carolina. The YP 696, 698–700, and 702 are at the Naval Education and Training Center, Newport, Rhode Island.[5]

The YP 679 in the Severn River, near Annapolis, Maryland. The YPs and sail-training craft provide Naval Academy midshipmen with basic knowledge of small craft and, to a limited extent, ship handling. (U.S. Navy)

The YP 679 at "high speed." (1990, Giorgio Arra)

1 SEAMANSHIP TRAINING CRAFT: "YP 654" CLASS

Number	Launched	Completed
YP 667	Apr 1966	Jan 1967

Builders:	Peterson Brothers, Sturgeon Bay, Wisc.
Displacement:	approx. 60 tons light
	approx. 71 tons full load
Length:	80$\frac{5}{12}$ feet (24.5 m) overall
Beam:	18$\frac{3}{4}$ feet (5.7 m)
Draft:	5$\frac{1}{4}$ feet (1.6 m)
Propulsion:	2 diesel engines (General Motors 6-71); 590 bhp; 2 shafts
Speed:	13 knots
Range:	400 n.miles (740 km) at 12 knots
Manning:	10 (2 officers + 8 enlisted) + 20 students
Radars:	. . . navigation

This is the last seamanship training craft of this design in naval service.

Class: Seventeen units of this class were reclassified as mine countermeasures craft under the COOP program (YP 654, 659–666, 668–675), see chapter 22.

The YP 655–658 were stricken on 12 February 1993.

Electronics: This craft is fitted with navigation radar and a fathometer.

Operational: The YP 667 is assigned to the Marine Corps Air Station, Cherry Point, North Carolina.

The YP 667—seen here at San Diego—is the last craft of this class to be employed as a training craft. She has a bar-type radar, open navigation bridge (aft of the mast), and the life-raft canister. (1986, Giorgio Arra)

1 SEAPLANE WRECKING DERRICK: "YSD 11" CLASS

Number	Completed
YSD 74	1944

Builders:	Pearl Harbor Navy Yard
Displacement:	240 tons light
	270 tons full load
Length:	104 feet (31.7 m) overall
Beam:	31$\frac{1}{6}$ feet (9.5 m)
Draft:	4 feet (1.2 m)
Propulsion:	2 diesel engines (Superior); 640 bhp; 2 shafts
Speed:	6 knots
Manning:	13–15 (enlisted)

This is a small, self-propelled floating derrick that is fitted with a 10-ton-capacity crane. The YSD 74 is active. YSDs are called "Mary Anns."

Class: The YSD 53 was stricken in May 1991; YSD 63 was stricken on 16 July 1993.

The "Mary Ann" YSD 63 chugging along. Only the YSD 74 of this class survives. "Mary Anns" of this class have been in the fleet since about 1930. (1977, Giorgio Arra)

5. Newport is no longer an Officer Candidate School (OCS); that activity has merged with the OCS at Pensacola, Florida.

69 LARGE HARBOR TUGS: "YTB 760" CLASS

Number	Name	Completed	Number	Name	Completed	Number	Name	Completed
YTB 760	Natick	1961	YTB 787	Kittanning	1966	YTB 813	Poughkeepsie	1971
YTB 761	Ottumwa	1961	YTB 788	Wapato	1966	YTB 814	Waxahachie	1971
YTB 762	Tuscumbia	1961	YTB 789	Tomahawk	1966	YTB 815	Neodesha	1971
YTB 763	Muskegon	1963	YTB 790	Menominee	1967	YTB 816	Campti	1972
YTB 764	Mishawaka	1963	YTB 791	Marinette	1967	YTB 817	Hyannis	1973
YTB 765	Okmulgee	1963	YTB 792	Antigo	1967	YTB 818	Mecosta	1973
YTB 766	Wapakoneta	1963	YTB 793	Piqua	1967	YTB 820	Wanamassa	1973
YTB 767	Apalachicola	1964	YTB 794	Mandan	1968	YTB 821	Tontocany	1973
YTB 768	Arcata	1964	YTB 795	Ketchikan	1968	YTB 822	Pawhuska	1973
YTB 769	Chesaning	1964	YTB 796	Saco	1968	YTB 823	Canonchet	1973
YTB 770	Dahlonega	1964	YTB 797	Tamaqua	1968	YTB 824	Santaquin	1972
YTB 771	Keokuk	1964	YTB 798	Opelika	1968	YTB 825	Wathena	1973
YTB 774	Nashua	1965	YTB 801	Palatka	1969	YTB 826	Washtuena	1973
YTB 775	Wauwatosa	1965	YTB 802	Cheraw	1969	YTB 827	Chetek	1973
YTB 776	Weehawken	1965	YTB 803	Nanticoke	1970	YTB 828	Catahecassa	1974
YTB 777	Nogalesen	1965	YTB 805	Ocala	1970	YTB 829	Metacom	1974
YTB 778	Apopka	1965	YTB 806	Tuskegee	1970	YTB 831	Dekanawida	1974
YTB 779	Manhattan	1965	YTB 807	Massapequa	1970	YTB 832	Petalesharo	1974
YTB 780	Saugus	1965	YTB 808	Wenatchee	1970	YTB 833	Shabonee	1974
YTB 781	Niantic	1965	YTB 809	Agawam	1971	YTB 834	Negwagon	1974
YTB 782	Manistee	1966	YTB 810	Anoka	1971	YTB 835	Skenandoa	1974
YTB 783	Redwing	1965	YTB 811	Houma	1971	YTB 836	Pokagon	1974
YTB 784	Kalispell	1966	YTB 812	Accomac	1971			

Builders:	YTB 760, 761 Jakobson Shipyard, Oyster Bay, N.Y.
	YTB 762 Commercial Iron Works, Portland, Ore.
	YTB 763–766, 799–802 Southern Shipbuilding, Sidell, La.
	YTB 767–771 Mobile Ship Repair, Ala.
	YTB 774–798, 816–836 Marinette Marine, Wisc.
	YTB 803–815 Peterson Builders, Sturgeon Bay, Wisc.
Displacement:	283 tons light
	356 tons full load
Length:	109 feet (33.2 m) overall
Beam:	30½ feet (9.3 m)
Draft:	13½ feet (4.1 m)
Propulsion:	1 diesel engine (Fairbanks-Morse 38D8 1/8); 2,000 bhp; 1 shaft
Speed:	12.5 knots
Range:	2,000 n.miles (3,704 km) at 12 knots
Manning:	10–14 (enlisted)

These tugs are all in active service. Each is fitted with a small commercial navigation radar.

Class: The similar YTB 837 and 838 were transferred to Saudi Arabia in 1975.

The Eufaula (YTB 800) was transferred to the NDRF on 9 November 1992 and the Tonkawa (YTB 786) on 18 November 1992. The Pushmataha (YTB 830) was stricken on 2 October 1995; the Ahoskie (YTB 804) on 10 October 1995; the Natchitoches (YTB 799) on 13 October 1995; the Ikua (YTB 819) on 19 October 1995; and the Winnemucca (YTB 785) on 20 December 1995.

The Pushmataha was transferred to MarAd for service on the date she was stricken.

Design: SCB No. 147A. These and other Navy harbor tugs are used for towing and maneuvering ships in harbors. Their masts fold down to facilitate working alongside large ships.

Tugs are also equipped for fire fighting.

Names: Named tugs honor American towns and small cities.

The Chesaning shows off her fire-fighting water cannon as she steams past the carrier Saratoga (CV 60). She has protective bumpers on her bow and protective rollers on her superstructure; her mast is lowered. (1991, U.S. Navy)

The Accomac showing the stern aspect of the invaluable craft. Her mast is lowered; a radar antenna and a searchlight sit atop her bridge. Like many YTBs, the Accomac had a mixed male-female crew when this photo was taken. (1991, Giorgio Arra)

4 LARGE HARBOR TUGS: "YTB 756" CLASS

Number	Name	Completed
YTB 757	Oshkosh	1959
YTB 758	Paducah	1961
YTB 759	Bogalusa	1961

Builders:	Southern Shipbuilding, Sidell, La.
Displacement:	311 tons light
	409 tons full load
Length:	109 feet (33.2 m) overall
Beam:	30 feet (9.1 m)
Draft:	14 feet (4.3 m)
Propulsion:	1 diesel engine (Fairbanks-Morse); 1,800 bhp; 1 shaft
Speed:	12 knots
Manning:	10–12 enlisted

All of these craft are active.

Class: The Pontiac (YTB 756) was sticken on 18 November 1992.

Design: SCB No. 147 (less streamlined superstructure than similar SCB No. 147A design).

The Oshkosh with her mast raised. She has a "pot" type navigation radar. (1991, Giorgio Arra)

1 LARGE HARBOR TUG: "YTB 752" CLASS

Number	Name	Completed
YTB 752	Edenshaw	1959

Builders:	Christy Corp., Sturgeon Bay, Wisc.
Displacement:	275 tons light
	375 tons full load
Length:	101 feet (30.8 m) overall
Beam:	29 feet (8.8 m)
Draft:	16 feet (4.9 m)
Propulsion:	1 diesel engine (Alco); 1,800 bhp; 1 shaft
Speed:	12 knots
Manning:	11 or 12 (enlisted)

These are large harbor tugs generally similar to the YTB 760 design.

Class: The Marin (YTB 753) was stricken on 21 May 1991.

The Edenshaw, the last of her design in U.S. naval service, helping a frigate of the Perry (FFG 7) class. The tug has a squared-off funnel compared to angled tops in later YTBs. (1983, Giorgio Arra)

1 SMALL HARBOR TUG: "YTL 422" CLASS

Number	Name	Completed
YTL 602	(none)	1945

Builders:	Robert Jacob, City Island, N.Y.
Displacement:	70 tons light
	80 tons full load
Length:	66⅙ feet (20.2 m) overall
Beam:	17 feet (5.2 m)
Draft:	5 feet (1.5 m)
Propulsion:	1 diesel engine (Hoover); 375 bhp; 1 shaft
Speed:	10 knots
Manning:	5 (enlisted)

The YTL 602 is the sole survivor in U.S. Navy service of several hundred small tugs built during World War II. Many others serve in foreign navies. The YTL 602 is active at the Portsmouth Naval Shipyard, New Hampshire.

Classification: These craft were originally classified YT, with the same hull numbers. YTL initially meant harbor tug, *little.*

MEDIUM HARBOR TUGS

All surviving YTM-type tugs have been stricken except for the ex-YTM 404, which is now designated 100WB8501 and serves at the Naval Station Roosevelt Roads, Puerto Rico, and the YTM 394, laid up at Pearl Harbor.

Plans to construct additional YTMs (initially YTM 800–802, authorized in fiscal 1973) were deferred in favor of additional YTB construction. Recent disposal is listed in the 15th Edition/page 347.

See 14th Edition/pages 350–51 for YTM characteristics.

4 TORPEDO TRIALS CRAFT: "YTT 9" CLASS

Number	Name	Launched	In service
YTT 9	Cape Flattery	5 May 1989	30 May 1991
YTT 10	Battle Point	17 Aug 1989	30 Nov 1991
YTT 11	Discovery Bay	22 Feb 1990	30 May 1992
YTT 12	Agate Pass	6 Sep 1990	30 Oct 1992

Builders:	McDermott Shipyard, Morgan City, La.
Displacement:	1,000 tons light
	1,200 tons full load
Length:	186½ feet (56.85 m) overall
Beam:	40 feet (12.2 m)
Draft:	10½ feet (3.2 m)
Propulsion:	diesel-electric (1 Cummins VTA-28 diesel engine); 1,250 shp; 2 azimuth drives
Speed:	11 knots
Torpedo Tubes:	2 21-inch (533-mm) tubes Mk 59 (fixed single; submerged)
	3 12.75-inch (324-mm) tubes Mk 32 (triple)
Manning:	31 + 9 technicians

These are specialized torpedo trials craft that will replace the IX and YFRT craft currently employed in this role. Each craft is fitted with a 350-hp bow thruster. Electric drive on batteries permits quiet operation for launching acoustic-homing torpedoes.

These craft are assigned to the Naval Undersea Warfare Center, Keyport, Washington. The AGATE PASS was never put in service; she was laid up in reserve at the Bremerton Naval Shipyard upon completion.

Class: The classification YTT originally indicated torpedo testing barge. The YTT 1–4 were built in 1912–1916; the YTT 5–7 were of World War II construction. All were non–self-propelled barges. The designation YTT 8 was not assigned.

Classification: Originally planned as YFRT type, they were built as YTT instead.

The BATTLE POINT, with the CAPE FLATTERY astern, at Keyport, Washington, the Navy's principal torpedo testing facility. They have cranes forward and aft for recovering torpedoes and handling specialized torpedo recovery devices. (1990, U.S. Navy)

The CAPE FLATTERY. The broad working area aft is flanked by the craft's twin engine exhausts. Two radar antennas sit atop the large deckhouse. (1990, U.S. Navy)

WATER BARGES: "YW 83" CLASS

These craft were similar to the YO/YOG types, being employed to carry fresh water for ships. The YW 98 was stricken in 1991 and the YW 127 on 18 April 1994.

The similar YW 87 survives as the MONOB ONE (YAG 61, ex-IX 309).

TORPEDO RETRIEVERS

These craft support torpedo testing and submarine practice torpedo launches. The designations TR, TWR (torpedo weapon retriever), and TRB (torpedo recovery boat) are used for these craft. The names listed below are unofficial.

These craft have stern ramps and—in some units—hydraulic cranes for recovering torpedoes.

The torpedo recovery craft TRB 4 ALBATROSS (65TR674) and TRB 10 (72TR653) were taken out of service and transferred to the Sea Scout organization in June 1995 and July 1995, respectively.

8 TORPEDO RETRIEVERS: 120-FOOT TYPE

Number	Name	Launched	In service
TWR 821	SWAMP FOX	17 Oct 1984	4 Nov 1985
TWR 822		18 Oct 1984	20 Nov 1985
TWR 823	PORPOISE	4 May 1985	6 Dec 1985
TWR 825		8 Aug 1985	6 Dec 1985
TWR 832		22 Mar 1986	3 July 1986
TWR 833		4 Apr 1986	3 July 1986
TWR 841		15 Aug 1986	18 Oct 1986
TWR 842	NARWHAL	22 Sep 1986	24 Dec 1986

Builders:	Marinette Marine, Wisc.
Displacement:	174 tons standard
	213 tons full load
Length:	120 feet (36.6 m) overall
Beam:	25 feet (7.6 m)
Draft:	12 feet (3.65 m)
Propulsion:	2 diesel engines (Caterpillar D 3512); 2,350 bhp; 2 shafts
Speed:	16 knots
Range:	1,700 n.miles (3,150 km) at 16 knots
Manning:	15 (1 officer + 14 enlisted)
Radar:	Canadian Marconi LN-66 navigation

These are improved torpedo retrievers capable of recovering and carrying up to 14 Mk 48 torpedoes.

Class: Originally, this was a class of ten units: TR 821–825, 831–833, 841, and 842. The TWR 824 and TWR 831 were sunk by Hurricane Hugo at Roosevelt Roads, Puerto Rico.

The SWAMP FOX is typical of the latest U.S. Navy series of torpedo recovery craft. She has a slew of awards painted on her deckhouse, indicating outstanding performance. (1992, Giorgio Arra)

Classification: These craft have Service Craft and Boat Accounting Report (SABAR) designations that consist of the prefix 120 + TR + the above numbers; thus, TWR 821 has the SABAR designation 120TR821.

Design: A stern ramp and crane are provided for torpedo recovery. Endurance is seven days.

The SWAMP FOX with a couple of "fish" on her roller-covered after deck; she has an angled torpedo recovery chute on the starboard side, with a cutout in her stern counter (below the rail). A rubber raft is under cover beneath her crane. (1992, Giorgio Arra)

4 TORPEDO WEAPON RETRIEVERS: 100-FOOT TYPE

Number	(SABAR)	Name	Completed
TWR 3	(100C13729)	CONDOR	Sep 1963
TWR 6	(100C14251)	FERRET	Mar 1966
TWR 681	(100TR681)	LABRADOR	
TWR 771	(100TR771)	PHOENIX	Dec 1978

Builders:	Peterson Builders, Sturgeon Bay, Wisc.
Displacement:	110 tons light 165 tons full load
Length:	102 feet (31.1 m) overall
Beam:	21 feet (6.4 m)
Draft:	$7\frac{3}{4}$ feet (2.4 m)
Propulsion:	4 diesel engines (General Motors 12V-149); 1,600 bhp; 2 shafts
Speed:	17 knots
Range:	1,920 n.miles (3,556 km) at 10 knots
Manning:	15 (enlisted)

The TWR 3—also known as the 100C13729 and CONDOR—showing the open stern for retrieving torpedoes. Several Mk 48 torpedoes are on her deck. (1984, Giorgio Arra)

These torpedo retrievers are based on the PGM 59-class motor gunboat design.

Class: Stricken units of this type are the DIAMOND (TWR 1/100C13728), CRAYFISH (TWR 682), and the unnamed TWR 711.

Design: Steel construction. Each ship has been fitted with a stern recovery ramp and can carry 17 tons of torpedoes.

2 TORPEDO RETRIEVERS: 85-FOOT TYPE

Number	SABAR	Name	Completed
TWR 7	(85TR762)	CHAPARRAL	1975
TWR 8	(85TR761)	ILIWAI	1975

Builders:	Tacoma Boatbuilding, Wash.
Displacement:	
Length:	85 feet (25.9 m) overall
Beam:	$18\frac{2}{3}$ feet (5.7 m)
Draft:	$5\frac{2}{3}$ feet (1.7 m)
Propulsion:	4 diesel engines; 2 shafts
Speed:	18 knots
Manning:	

Each craft, constructed of aluminum, can carry eight torpedoes (22,000 pounds/9,979 kg). The TWR 7 is laid up at San Diego.

The CHAPARRAL at high speed. Note the engine exhaust arrangement (port and starboard). (1985, Giorgio Arra)

4 TORPEDO RETRIEVERS: 85-FOOT TYPE

Number	SABAR	Completed
TR 651	(85TR651)	July 1965
TR 653	(85TR653)	Dec 1966
TR 654	(85TR654)	Jan 1967
TR 761	(85TR761)	Dec 1977

Builders:	Tacoma Boatbuilding, Wash.
Displacement:	61 tons full load
Length:	85 feet (25.9 m) overall
Beam:	$18\frac{2}{3}$ feet (5.69 m)
Draft:	$5\frac{2}{3}$ feet (1.73 m)
Propulsion:	2 diesel engines (General Motors 16V-71); 1,160 bhp; 2 shafts
Speed:	21 knots
Manning:	8 (enlisted)

Constructed of aluminum, each craft can carry eight torpedoes (22,000 pounds/9,979 kg).

Two similar patrol craft, built without stern ramps, have the SABAR designations 85C14252 and 85C14253.

5 TORPEDO RETRIEVERS: 72-FOOT MK 2 TYPE

Number	(SABAR)	Completed
TRB 31	(72C3211)	Oct 1958
TRB 32	(72TR645)	Mar 1966
TRB 33	(72TR652)	Aug 1966
TRB 36	(72C4560)	Feb 1961
TRB 37	(72C9426)	Oct 1961

Builders:	
Displacement:	53 tons full load
Length:	72⅙ feet (22.0 m) overall
Beam:	17 feet (5.2 m)
Draft:	4⅓ feet (1.3 m)
Propulsion:	8 diesel engines; 1,300 bhp; 2 shafts
Speed:	18 knots
Range:	180 n.miles (333 km) at 18 knots
Manning:	7 (enlisted)
Radar:	SPS-69 navigation

This series of torpedo recovery craft was to be replaced by the new, 120-foot craft but was retained because of the shortfall in TRs. Each craft can carry 24,000 pounds (10,886 kg) of torpedoes. The series was built with SPS-53 radars that were subsequently replaced by SPS-69.

The craft are constructed of wood.

A 72-foot-type torpedo retriever at San Diego. (1986, Giorgio Arra)

4 TORPEDO RETRIEVERS: 65-FOOT TYPE

Number	(SABAR)	Name	Completed
TR 671			Oct 1967
TR 673		Sea Hawk	1968
TRB 5	(65TR675)	Harrier	July 1968
TR 6	(65TR676)	Peregrine	July 1968

Builders:	
Displacement:	34.8 tons full load
Length:	65 feet (19.8 m) overall
Beam:	17¼ feet (5.25 m)
Draft:	3⅚ feet (1.2 m)
Propulsion:	2 diesel engines (General Motors 12V71); 1,800 bhp; 2 shafts
Speed:	18.7 knots
Range:	280 n.miles (518 km) at 18.7 knots
Manning:	6 (enlisted)

This basic 65-foot design was also used for Navy utility and air-sea rescue boats. Constructed of aluminum, the craft can carry four heavy torpedoes (11,000 pounds).

A 65-foot torpedo recovery craft at San Diego. There is a single life-raft canister above the pilothouse. (1986, Giorgio Arra)

A 65-foot torpedo recovery craft bringing aboard a Mk 48 torpedo. (1986, Giorgio Arra)

MISCELLANEOUS CRAFT

These craft do not have Y-series designations; some have hull registry numbers (length + type designation + serial). The following craft are arranged according to length.

Classification: The type designations used below are:

NS	Non-standard (commercial design)
UB	Utility boat
WB	Work boat

The definition of the designation "C" does not appear in the SABAR directory.

1 ACOUSTIC RESEARCH CRAFT: "CORY CHOUEST"

Number	Name	Completed	In service
(none)	CORY CHOUEST	1974	14 Nov 1991

Builders:	Ulstein Hatlo A/S, Ulsteinvik (Norway)
Displacement:	approx. 3,900 tons full load
Tonnage:	1,597 GRT
	1,800 DWT
Length:	265 11/12 feet (81.08 m) overall
Beam:	59 1/6 feet (18.04 m)
Draft:	14 1/6 feet (4.32 m)
Propulsion:	2 diesel engines (Atlas-MaK 6M453AK); 4,000 bhp; 2 shafts
Speed:	13.75 knots
Manning:	approx. 16 + 30 passengers

This is one of several submersible support tenders provided to the Navy under a contract with the Military Sealift Command by the Edison Chouest Offshore Company of Galliano, Louisiana. The ships were built as oil field support ships.

The CORY CHOUEST is employed in research for Low-Frequency Active (LFA) sonar systems. The in-service date above is the date the craft was chartered to the MSC.

Names: Her commercial names were FAR COMET and TENDER COMET.

1 SUBMERSIBLE SUPPORT CRAFT: "AMY CHOUEST" TYPE

Number	Name	Completed	In service
(none)	AMY CHOUEST	1974	14 Nov 1991

Builders:	Ulstein Hatlo A/S, Ulsteinvik (Norway)
Displacement:	approx. 3,900 tons full load
Tonnage:	1,597 GRT
	1,800 DWT
Length:	264 11/12 feet (80.78 m) overall
Beam:	59 1/6 feet (18.04 m)
Draft:	14 1/6 feet (4.32 m)
Propulsion:	2 diesel engines (Atlas-MaK 6M453AK); 4,000 bhp; 2 shafts
Speed:	13.75 knots
Manning:	approx. 16 + 30 passengers

The AMY CHOUEST is similar to the CORY CHOUEST. The in-service date above is the charter date.

Names: Her commercial names were FAR CLIPPER and TENDER CLIPPER.

1 CONSTRUCTION PLATFORM

Number	Name	Launched	Completed
(none) (ex-YFNB 330)	SEACON	22 Mar 1945	25 Oct 1945

Builders:	Missouri Valley Bridge and Iron, Ind.
Displacement:	2,780 tons full load
Length:	260 feet (79.25 m) overall
Beam:	48 feet (14.6 m)
Draft:	9½ feet (2.9 m)
Propulsion:	3 diesel engines (3 General Motors 6-71); 3 shafts (Voith-Schneider vertical cylindrical propellers)
Speed:	7 knots
Manning:	50

This craft was converted from a barge in order to transport rockets for NASA. She was converted in 1974–1976 by the Norfolk Shipbuilding and Dry Dock Company to serve as a seagoing work ship. The craft is towed to work positions and can use her own engines for propulsion and maneuvering in the work area.

The SEACON is used to lay cable and do other deep-sea work. She is fitted with a 25-ton-capacity A-frame gantry crane and a 22-ton traveling crane.

The SEACON under way in harbor. She has a large traveling crane aft of the superstructure and a large open work area aft. (1992, Giorgio Arra)

1 SUBMERSIBLE TENDER

Number	Name	Completed
(none)	LANEY CHOUEST	1985

Builders:	North American Shipbuilding, Larose, La.
Displacement:	approx. 2,600 tons full load
Tonnage:	497 GRT
	1,200 DWT
Length:	234 feet (71.33 m) overall
Beam:	50 feet (15.2 m)
Draft:	14 1/6 feet (4.33 m)
Propulsion:	3 diesel engines (General Motors); 3 shafts
Speed:	16 knots
Manning:	

This former oil field support craft was chartered by the Navy to support the submersibles DSV 3 and DSV 4 in Submarine Development Group 1 at San Diego.

Design: The craft has a large lifting device aft and an ice-strengthened hull. Three thrusters are fitted for station keeping.

2 TRIALS SUPPORT CRAFT

Number	Name	Completed
192UB8701	RANGER	1981
192UB8702	NAWC 38	1981

Builders:	McDermott Shipyard, New Iberia, La.
Displacement:	approx. 1,800 tons full load
Length:	191 11/12 feet (58.52 m) overall
Beam:	40 feet (12.19 m)
Draft:	14 feet (4.27 m)
Propulsion:	2 diesel engines (General Motors 12-645-E6); 3,000 bhp; 2 shafts
Speed:	12 knots
Range:	
Manning:	civilian

Both ships were acquired in 1986 to support ship trials. The NAWC 38 (ex-SEA LEVEL No. 7) operates from Fort Lauderdale, Florida.

The RANGER (ex-SEACOR RANGER and SEA LEVEL No. 27) is employed on the Anglo-American AUTEC range, Andros Island, Bahamas.

The NAWC 38, which previously had a crane fitted on her fantail. (1991, Giorgio Arra)

1 SPACE BOOSTER RECOVERY SHIP: "INDEPENDENCE"

Number	Name	Launched
(none)	INDEPENDENCE	27 Feb 1985

Builders:	Halter Marine, Moss Point, Miss.
Displacement:	1,798 tons full load
Length:	199 11/12 feet (60.96 m) overall
Beam:	40 feet (12.2 m)
Draft:	13½ feet (4.1 m)
Propulsion:	diesel engines (2 Cummins KTA 3067-M); 2,500 bhp; 2 shafts + 2 Azimuth thrusters (1,000 shp each)
Speed:	13 knots
Range:	
Manning:	13 civilian + 14 scientists/technicians

Built for the U.S. Air Force, the INDEPENDENCE recovers solid-propellant missile boosters launched from Vandenberg Air Force Base, California. Transferred to the Navy in 1988, she has been operated by the Naval Facilities Engineering Center at Port Hueneme, California.

The craft can carry 338 tons of deck cargo aft, including laboratory vans, and she is fitted with a 22-ton-capacity crane.

2 TORPEDO RECOVERY CRAFT / 1 SONOBUOY-TORPEDO TRIALS SHIP } EX-OIL-FIELD SUPPORT CRAFT

Number	Name	Completed	In service
180NS8201	HUGO	Jan 1982	20 Mar 1991
180NS8202	HUNTER	Jan 1981	20 Mar 1991
180NS9202	RANGE ROVER	1982	1992

Builders:	McDermott Shipyard, New Iberia, La., except HUNTER—Quality Shipbuilders, Moss Point, Miss.
Displacement:	approx. 1,500 tons full load
Length:	180 feet (54.86 m) overall, except HUNTER
Beam:	40 feet (12.2 m)
Draft:	12¼ feet (3.73 m)
Propulsion:	2 diesel engines (Caterpillar D399 SCAC); 2,250 bhp; 2 shafts
Speed:	12 knots
Range:	
Manning:	

These are former oil field support vessels. Two ships were acquired for the torpedo recovery role; both are assigned to the Atlantic Fleet Weapons Training activity at Roosevelt Roads, Puerto Rico. The RANGE ROVER serves as a trials ship at the Anglo-American AUTEC range, Andros Island, Bahamas. Details of the ships differ.

Names: Commercial names were HUGO, ex-CRYSTAL PELHAM; HUNTER, ex-NOLA PELHAM; and RANGE ROVER, ex-LOUISE PELHAM.

1 SONOBUOY TRIALS CRAFT: "ACOUSTIC PIONEER"

Number	Name	Completed
180WB8701	ACOUSTIC PIONEER	1981

Builders:	Halter Marine, Moss Point, La.
Displacement:	approx. 1,500 tons full load
Length:	179 11/12 feet (54.86 m) overall
Beam:	40 feet (12.2 m)
Draft:	14 feet (4.3 m)
Propulsion:	2 diesel engines (General Motors 12-645-E6); 3,000 bhp; 2 shafts
Speed:	
Manning:	

Formerly the oil-field supply boat SEPTEMBER MORN, the ACOUSTIC PIONEER was acquired by the Navy in 1987 and employed by the Naval Avionics Development Center at St. Croix in the Virgin Islands for sonobuoy testing. The craft was subsequently transferred to Alaskan waters for sonobuoy research.

1 SUBMERSIBLE SUPPORT CRAFT: "DELORES CHOUEST"

Number	Name	Completed
(none)	DELORES CHOUEST	1978

Builders:	North American Shipbuilding, Larose, La.
Displacement:	approx. 1,600 tons full load
Length:	179 11/12 feet (54.86 m) overall
Beam:	40 feet (12.2 m)
Draft:	11⅚ feet (3.64 m)
Propulsion:	2 diesel engines (Caterpillar D399-SCAC); 2,250 bhp; 2 shafts
Speed:	13 knots
Manning:	

The ship is configured to support DSRV rescue submersibles.

3 RESEARCH CRAFT: "ASHEVILLE" CLASS

Number	Name	Launched	PG Commission	To DTRC
165NS761 (ex-PG 94)	ATHENA I	8 June 1968	8 Nov 1969	21 Aug 1975
165NS762 (ex-PG 98)	ATHENA II	4 Apr 1970	5 Sep 1970	3 Oct 1977
165NS763 (ex-PG 100)	LAUREN	19 June 1970	6 Feb 1971	1990

Builders:	Tacoma Boatbuilding, Wash.
Displacement:	approx. 265 tons full load
Length:	164½ feet (50.2 m) overall
Beam:	23¾ feet (7.2 m)
Draft:	9½ feet (2.9 m)
Propulsion:	CODOG: 2 diesel engines (Cummins VT12-875M), 1,400 bhp; 1 gas turbine (General Electric LM 1500), 12,500 shp; 2 shafts
Speed:	16 knots on diesel engines; 40+ knots on gas turbines
Range:	2,400 n.miles (4,445 km) at 14 knots on diesel engines 325 n.miles (602 km) at 37 knots on gas turbines
Manning:	civilian

These are former ASHEVILLE-class patrol combatants/gunboats employed in the research role. They are the last of a class of 17 in U.S. naval service (see chapter 21). These three ships were transferred on the dates indicated to the David Taylor Research Center for use in various offshore research projects; they are based at Panama City, Florida.

The DOUGLAS was stricken on 1 October 1977 for transfer for the DTRC, to be placed in service as the ATHENA III. She was instead discarded in 1984 but retained in storage at Little Creek, Virginia, for possible foreign transfer. She was reacquired and converted in 1991–1992 for use as a test ship in the Athena program under the name LAUREN.

All weapons have been removed.

Classification: When assigned to the David Taylor Research Center, these ships were reclassified as service craft without specific hull designations. They are technically considered "floating equipment."

Design: Aluminum hulls with fiberglass superstructures.

The ATHENA I showing the extension forward of her bridge. The ATHENA I and II have orange hulls with white superstructures. The ATHENA I does not have an "I" after her name. (1991, Giorgio Arra)

The ATHENA II pulling away from the pier. There is a laboratory van amidships, along with winches and lift equipment. (1989, Giorgio Arra)

The ATHENA II with a rounded bridge face. All three craft are employed for research and development work for the David Taylor Research Center. (1991, Giorgio Arra)

The ex-PG 100 undergoing conversion to a research craft, renamed LAUREN. In this view, the 3-inch/50-cal enclosed gun mount is still installed forward. (1981, Giorgio Arra)

Names: Their former names were PG 94 CHEHALIS, PG 98 GRAND RAPIDS, and PG 100 DOUGLAS.

Operational: These ships have participated in a variety of research projects. Possibly the most unusual was one in which the ATHENA II, at maximum speed, towed an in-flight MH-53E helicopter backwards to help assess the helicopter's flight envelope characteristics. Other trials have included sonars and mine countermeasures gear.

SPACE BOOSTER RECOVERY CRAFT: "RSB-1"

The research support boat RSB-1 (ex-A.B. WOOD II), in U.S. Navy service since 1966, was discarded in 1993 (sunk off the coast of Fort Pompano Beach, Florida, in 1984 for use as an artificial fishing reef). The craft was operated by the Naval Surface Weapons Center at Fort Lauderdale, Florida, to recover space-launch booster rockets. She was assigned service craft hull number 157NS762.

See 15th Edition/pages 348–49 for characteristics.

4 SALVAGE TRAINING HULKS: EX-AUXILIARY TUGS ↓

Number	Name	Launched	Commissioned
(none) (ex-ATA 178)	TUNICA	15 June 1944	15 Sep 1944
(none) (ex-ATA 181)	ACCOKEEK	27 July 1944	7 Oct 1944
(none) (ex-ATA 203)	NAVIGATOR	26 Oct 1944	1 Jan 1945
142NS9201 (ex-ATA 213)	KEYWADIN	9 Apr 1945	1 June 1945

These 143-foot (43.6-m) craft are the only auxiliary tugs (ATA) remaining in U.S. naval service. The KEYWADIN is used for fire and salvage training by Mobile Diving and Salvage Unit 2 at Little Creek, Virginia; the others are used as salvage training hulks by other Navy diving and salvage activities. Only the KEYWADIN has a hull number, having been reacquired for service in 1992.

The TUNICA was decommissioned and transferred to the National Defense Reserve Fleet in 1962, the ACCOKEEK in 1972, and the NAVIGATOR in 1960. The KEYWADIN was decommissioned in 1970 and transferred in 1971.

Class: Originally, the SOTOYOMO class consisted of 70 ships: ATA 121–125, 146, 170–213, and 219–238.

See 14th Edition/page 330 for additional data.

1 SONOBUOY TRIALS CRAFT

Number	Name	Completed
111NS8801	ACOUSTIC EXPLORER	Dec 1981

The former oil field supply boat STRONG BRIO was acquired by the Navy in 1988 and employed by the Naval Avionics Development Center at St. Croix in the Virgin Islands for sonobuoy testing.

1 OCEANOGRAPHIC SUPPORT CRAFT

Number	Name	Completed
105UB821	ERLINE	1965

Builders:	Equitable Equipment Co., New Orleans, La.
Displacement:	96 tons light
	120 tons full load
Length:	105 feet (32.0 m) overall
Beam:	20⅔ feet (6.3 m)
Draft:	5$^{11}/_{12}$ feet (1.8 m)
Propulsion:	2 diesel engines; 2 shafts
Speed:	10 knots
Manning:	

The ERLINE, formerly the commercial ORRIN, is a former oil-field crew boat employed by the Underwater Systems Center and based at Tudor Hill, Bermuda.

1 WORKBOAT: EX-HARBOR TUG

Number	Name	Launched	Commissioned
100WB8501 (ex-YTM 404)	COSHECTON	28 Oct 1944	14 Nov 1944

Builders:	Ira S. Bushey, Brooklyn, N.Y.
Displacement:	260 tons standard 310 tons full load
Length:	101 feet (30.8 m) overall
Beam:	27⅚ feet (8.5 m)
Draft:	11⅙ feet (3.4 m)
Propulsion:	2 diesel engines (Fairbanks-Morse); 820 bhp; 1 shaft
Speed:	10.5 knots
Manning:	14 (enlisted)

This is a former harbor tug, stricken from the Naval Vessel Register on 30 September 1985 but retained as a workboat and redesignated. She is at Roosevelt Roads, Puerto Rico.

Classification: Originally YTB 404, that designation was changed on 24 November 1961 to YTM 404.

1 PATROL-ESCORT CRAFT: EX-COAST GUARD CUTTER

Number	Name	Commissioned
95NS8801 (ex-WPB 95310)	VENTURE	15 Dec 1953

Builders:	Coast Guard Yard, Curtis Bay, Md.
Displacement:	87 tons standard 105 tons full load
Length:	95 feet (29.0 m) overall
Beam:	19 feet (5.8 m)
Draft:	6 feet (1.8 m)
Propulsion:	4 diesel engines (Cummins VT-12-M-700); 2,300 bhp; 2 shafts
Speed:	20 knots
Range:	2,600 n.miles (4,820 km) at 9 knots 460 n.miles (850 km) at 20 knots
Manning:	8 (enlisted)
Radar:	SPS-64(V)1 navigation

Formerly the Coast Guard cutter CAPE WASH, this is the last of the 95-foot Cape-class units in U.S. service. She was stricken from the Coast Guard on 1 June 1987 and transferred to the Navy for use at the submarine base in Bangor, Washington, as a patrol-escort craft.

Class: Four ships of this class were transferred to the Navy; of the others, VANGUARD (ex-CAPE HEDGE/WPB 95311) was returned to the Coast Guard for transfer to Mexico in January 1990; unnamed 95NS8902 (ex-CAPE JELLISON/WPB 95317) was transferred from the Navy to the Sea Scouts at San Diego in 1993; and unnamed 95NS8901 (ex-CAPE ROMAINE/WPB 95319) was discarded in 1993.

PROPULSION TRIALS CRAFT: "JUPITER II"

The gas turbine/superconducting propulsion test craft JUPITER II has been discarded. Originally an offshore oil-industry workboat named PRYER, she was acquired by the Navy in 1976 and operated by the David Taylor Research Center in Annapolis, Maryland, for trials of superconducting electric motor technology.

See 15th Edition/page 352 for characteristics.

DRONE RECOVERY BOAT: EX-MOTOR TORPEDO BOAT

The RETRIEVER (DR-1, ex-PT 809), the Navy's last PT-boat, was stricken in 1986. Completed in 1950, the craft was one of four post–World War II motor torpedo boats built as competitive prototypes. After extensive trials and limited service, the PT 809 was laid up in reserve.

She was later reactivated and employed to carry Secret Service agents screening the presidential yacht on the Potomac River (based at the Washington Navy Yard), being named GUARDIAN in that role. In December 1974 the craft was transferred to Fleet Composite Squadron (VC) 6, based at Little Creek, Virginia, for operation as a recovery boat for aerial target drones and a control boat for surface target drones. She was designated DR-1 (for Drone Recovery) and named RETRIEVER.

See 14th Edition/page 356 for characteristics.

RESEARCH SHIPS: EX-MINESWEEPERS

The only two inshore minesweepers operated by the U.S. Navy, the COVE (MSI 1) and CAPE (MSI 2), have been discarded. Completed in 1958–1959, the two craft served for several years in the MSI role, after which they were assigned to research tasks. The COVE was operated by the Naval Ocean Systems Center (NOSC) at San Diego and the CAPE by the Applied Physics Laboratory of the Johns Hopkins University. The COVE was sold in August 1986.

Similar units were built for the Iranian and Turkish navies.

See 13th Edition/page 334 for characteristics.

1 RANGE SUPPORT SHIP (SWATH): "KAIMALINO"

Number	Name	Launched	In service
90WB8701	KAIMALINO	7 March 1973	1973

Builders:	Coast Guard Yard, Curtis Bay, Md.
Displacement:	228 tons full load
Length:	88⅓ feet (26.9 m) overall
Beam:	46½ feet (14.2 m)
Draft:	15¼ feet (4.65 m)
Propulsion:	CODOG: 2 diesel engines (General Motors 6-71), 160 bhp; 2 gas turbines (General Electric T64-6B), 5,000 shp; 2 shafts
Speed:	22 knots
Range:	1,500 n.miles (2,778 km) at 5 knots on diesel engines 450 n.miles (833 km) at 17 knots on gas turbines
Manning:	10 civilian + 6 scientists
Radars:	Raytheon 3610 Raytheon R40

The Stable Semi-submerged Platform (SSP) KAIMALINO is an experimental SWATH craft long employed in the range support role by NOSC on the center's underwater test range in Hawaii. After several years of successful trials and work activities, during 1980–1981 the KAIMALINO was modified (see Conversion notes). She was again placed in service on 24 September 1982.

In 1995 the KAIMALINO was transferred to the Naval Undersea Warfare Center at Newport, Rhode Island.

Classification: The craft is also known as SSP 1 for semi-submerged platform.

Conversion: The KAIMALINO was modified at the Dillingham Shipyard in Hawaii in 1980–1981. The craft was enlarged from 190 to 228 tons through the addition of fiberglass buoyancy modules. Plans to further enlarge the ship to some 600 tons were not carried out.

Design: The SSP is a Small Waterplane Area Twin-Hull (SWATH) craft developed to test this hull concept. The SSP/SWATH concept differs from that of a catamaran, which has two conventional ship hulls joined together. The SWATH design provides a comparatively large deck area with a minimum of heave, pitch, and roll.

The craft has two full submerged, torpedo-shaped hulls, each 6½ feet (2.0 m) in diameter, with vertical struts penetrating the water to support the superstructure and flight deck. The flight deck area is 3,400 feet^2 (306 m^2).

The KAIMALINO has a hull-stabilizing fin connecting the two submerged hulls and two small canard fins forward, one inboard on each hull. There is an opening in the craft's main deck for lowering research and recovery devices. (The opening is covered over for helicopter operations.) The beam listed above is the maximum over both hulls.

Up to 16 tons of mission equipment can be carried.

Engineering: Two T64-GE-6B aircraft-type gas-turbine engines provide propulsion power. Two Detroit diesel engines (8V-71T) are installed for auxiliary propulsion.

Helicopters: The KAIMALINO conducted tests in 1976 on the feasibility of landing helicopters on SSP/SWATH-type ships in high-sea states at speeds up to 25 knots. The operations with an SH-2F LAMPS were completely successful.

Torpedo Tubes: In 1982 the KAIMALINO was fitted with triple Mk 32 torpedo tubes for tests of lightweight torpedoes.

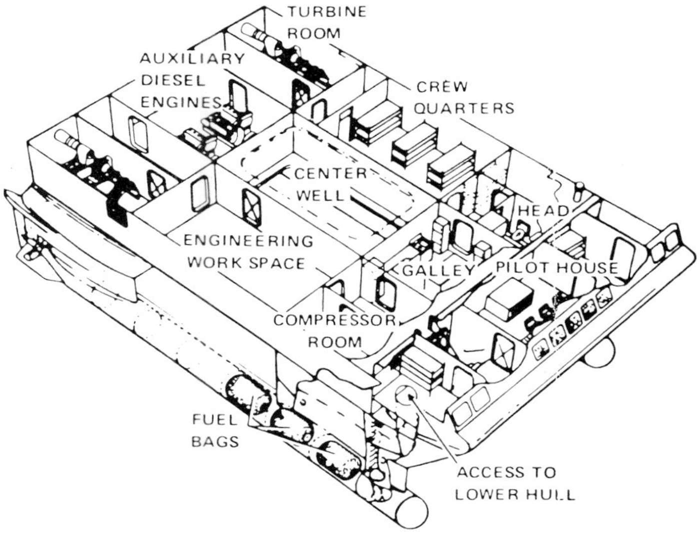

KAIMALINO interior arrangement.

KAIMALINO with the SH-2F. (1976, U.S. Navy)

The KAIMALINO in dry dock showing her twin, torpedo-like submerged hulls. Compare this configuration with the SWATH T-AGOS surveillance ships (chapter 23). (1973, U.S. Navy)

NON–SELF-PROPELLED SERVICE CRAFT

The following are the approximate numbers of various types of non–self-propelled service craft listed on the Naval Vessel Register; almost all are in service. The YCF type transport railroad cars; some of the YD floating cranes have maneuvering propulsion.

Only four of these craft have names: PHOEBUS (YDT 14), SUITLAND (YDT 15), TOM O'MALLEY (YDT 16), and THE BIG W (YSR 6).

APL	Barracks craft	14
YC	Open lighter	249
YCF	Car float	1
YCV	Aircraft transportation lighter	9
YD	Floating crane	68
YDT	Diving tenders	3
YFN	Covered lighter	156
YFNB	Large covered lighter	12
YFND	Dry dock companion craft	4
YFP	Floating power barge	4
YGN	Garbage lighter	3
YLC	Salvage lift craft	1
YMN	Dredge	1
YNG	Gate craft	2
YOGN	Gasoline barge	12
YON	Fuel oil barge	55
YOS	Oil storage barge	13
YPD	Floating pile drive	3
YPK	Pontoon storage barge	2
YR	Floating workshop	25
YRB	Repair and berthing barge	5
YRBM	Repair, berthing and messing barge	38
YRDH	Floating dry dock workshop (hull)	4
YRR	Radiological repair barge	11
YRST	Salvage craft tender	3
YSR	Sludge removal barge	15
YWN	Water barge	7

One of the less seen non–self-propelled service craft, the YSR 39, a sludge removal barge, is moored at Little Creek, Virginia. (1992, Stefan Terzibaschitsch)

The YRBM 31, a multipurpose barge used to support ships undergoing yard work or under construction. The uppermost deck can be used as a recreation area. (1991, Giorgio Arra)

CHAPTER 26

Submersibles

The nuclear-propelled NR-1, the most advanced deep-ocean engineering vehicle in the West, returns to her home port of New London, Connecticut, assisted by the harbor tug NEGWAGON (YTB 834). The proximity of the sailors reveals the small size of the NR-1. (1995, U.S. Navy, courtesy *The Dolphin*)

Six manned submersibles are operated by the U.S. Navy to support deep-ocean search, rescue, research, and recovery activities. These craft have also been employed to maintain seafloor test range and acoustic surveillance equipment.

Submarine Development Group 1 at Point Loma (San Diego), California, operates the rescue submersibles AVALON and MYSTIC, as well as the research submersibles SEA CLIFF and TURTLE. SubDevGru-1 also controls the operations of the special-mission submarine PARCHE (SSN 683) and the deep-diving research submarine DOLPHIN (AGSS 555).

Submarine Group 2 at the Naval Submarine Base New London (Groton), Connecticut, operates the nuclear submersible NR-1, as well as a number of attack submarines. (The NR-1 is based at the Portsmouth Naval Shipyard, New Hampshire.)

The Navy-owned research submersible ALVIN is operated by the Woods Hole Oceanographic Institution in Massachusetts.

In addition to the manned submersibles listed here, the Navy also has several unmanned, tethered research and work submersibles. Some of these are surface controlled/supported, while others can be operated from submerged submarines (see chapter 12).

Classification: The deep-diving bathyscaphe TRIESTE II was designated X-2 and, subsequently, DSV-1 (see 13th Edition/pages 350–51 for characteristics).[1]

The DSV-5 was the unmanned, tethered vehicle NEMO.[2]

Manning: The manning data provided below are the number of Navy personnel assigned to and operating on board each craft, including maintenance and relief operators:

	Total	*Officers*	*Enlisted*
AVALON	20	3	17
MYSTIC	20	3	17
NR-1	26	4	22
SEA CLIFF	16	3	13
TURTLE	16	3	13

Operational: The submersible SEA CLIFF can dive to 20,000 feet (6,100 m), which provides access to 98 percent of the ocean floor. The only other vehicle in the West that has that depth capability is the French submersible NAUTILE, also a three-man craft. The two Finnish-built submersibles of the MIR type operated by Russia are capable of diving to more than 20,000 feet.

1 NUCLEAR-PROPELLED RESEARCH SUBMERSIBLE: "NR-1"

Number	Name	Launched	In service
NR-1	(none)	25 Jan 1969	27 Oct 1969

Builders:	General Dynamics/Electric Boat, Groton, Conn.
Weight:	
	372 tons submerged
Length:	$136\frac{5}{16}$ feet (41.6 m) overall
Beam:	$12\frac{5}{12}$ feet (3.8 m)
Draft:	$15\frac{1}{12}$ feet (4.6 m)
Propulsion:	turbo-electric drive with electric motors; 2 external propeller pods
Reactors:	1 pressurized-water
Speed:	4.6 knots surfaced
	3.6 knots submerged
Operating depth:	2,375 feet (725 m)
Manning:	5 (2 officers + 3 enlisted) + 2 scientists

The NR-1 was originally built as a test platform for a small submarine nuclear power plant. The craft has subsequently been employed as a deep-ocean research and recovery vehicle.

The craft was funded as a nuclear-propulsion effort and was laid down on 10 June 1967. She is commanded by an officer-in-charge rather than a commanding officer.

Classification: NR-1 indicates Nuclear Research vehicle, although the craft is listed as a "submersible research vehicle" in the Naval Vessel Register.

Costs: The estimated cost of the NR-1 in 1965 was $30 million, using state-of-the-art equipment. Subsequently, specialized equipment had to be developed, and a hull larger than the one originally intended was designed. Congress approved allotting $58 million to the project in 1967. The estimated cost of the NR-1 when launched in 1969 was $67.5 million, plus $19.9 million for oceanographic equipment and sensors and $11.8 million for research and development. The total estimated cost was therefore $99.2 million. No final cost data have been released by the Navy.[3]

Design: The hull is constructed of HY-80 steel. The NR-1 does not have periscopes; instead she has a fixed mast with a top-mounted television camera. The craft is fitted with external lights, a remote-control manipulator, and recovery devices. The craft carries 22,000

1. The TRIESTE I is at the Navy Museum at the Washington (D.C.) Navy Yard; the TRIESTE II is at the Naval Undersea Museum at Keyport, Washington.
2. The NEMO is on display at San Diego.
3. Capt. William M. Nicholson, USN, the director of the Navy's Deep Submergence Systems Project (DSSP) at the time of the NR-1's construction, has given the "final" bill as $96 million; see "Truth Is in the Eye of the Beholder," U.S. Naval Institute *Proceedings* (June 1995), p. 10.

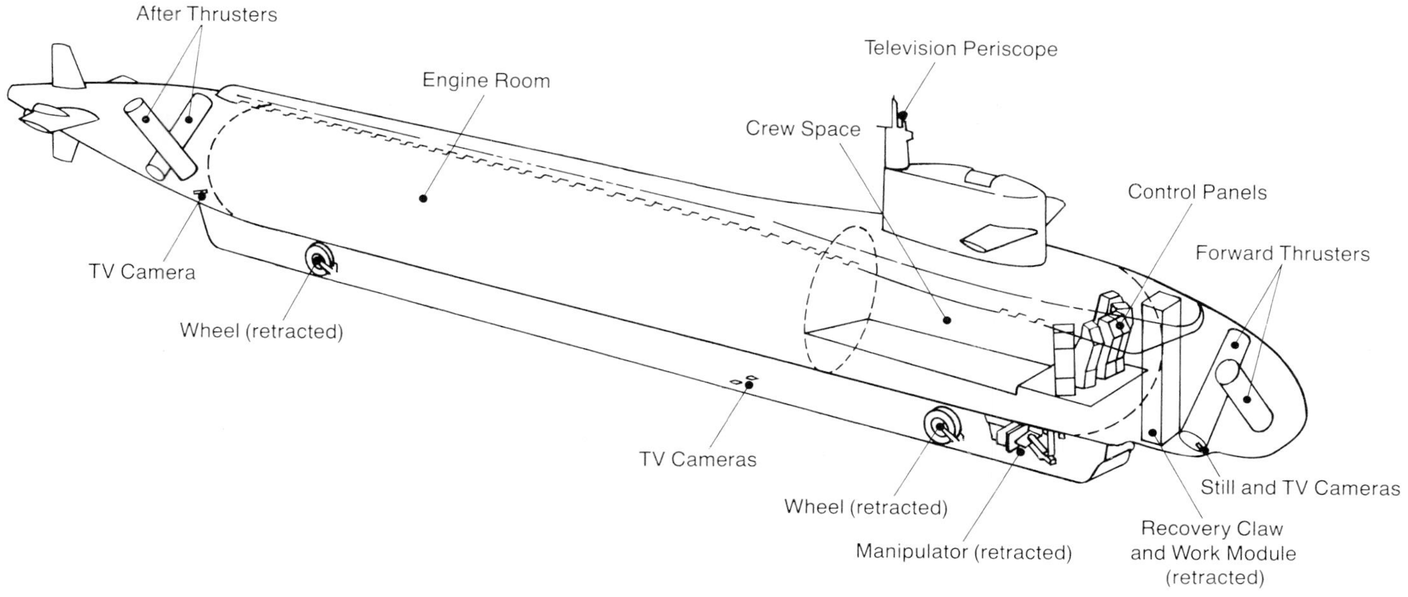

NUCLEAR-PROPELLED RESEARCH SUBMERSIBLE NR-1

pounds (9,980 kg) of expendable lead shot to provide emergency buoyancy.

Three bunks are provided; crew endurance is limited to a maximum of 30-day missions. There is a warming oven for frozen foods and a hot-drink dispenser.

The above operating depth is official Navy unclassified data. Unofficial estimates are approximately 3,000 feet (915 m).

Electronics: Fitted with forward and side-looking sonars; a doppler sonar is provided to measure over-bottom speed. The submersible is also equipped with a BQN-13 rescue pinger beacon.

Engineering: The NR-1 is propelled by twin propellers driven by electric motors outside of the pressure hull. Four ducted thrusters—two horizontal and two vertical—give the NR-1 a capability for precise maneuvering. Bottom wheels are installed.

Operational: Published reports credit the NR-1 with having been used to maintain seafloor equipment and to recover items sunk at great depths.

In 1976 the NR-1 helped recover an F-14 Tomcat fighter armed with a Phoenix missile that rolled off the deck of the carrier JOHN F. KENNEDY (CV 67) and came to rest at a depth of 1,960 feet (600 m) off the coast of Scotland.

In 1986 the NR-1 was employed in the search for wreckage from the crashed space shuttle *Challenger* off Cape Kennedy, Florida.

NUCLEAR-PROPELLED RESEARCH VEHICLE: HTV/NR-2 DESIGN

The so-called Hull Test Vehicle (HTV) was originally proposed as the NR-2 in 1976 by Admiral H. G. Rickover, then head of the Navy's nuclear propulsion program, to provide a deep-ocean (i.e., 3,000+ feet/915+m) test platform for a nuclear reactor and a work submersible. Subsequently, the craft was redesignated HTV to emphasize the use of HY-130 steel. But in the event, neither the Navy nor Congress would support the NR-2 at that time.

Circa 1978 the Navy's leadership decided to proceed with the craft as a vehicle to test the suitability of HY-130 steel for submarines. (HY-140 steel was used for the small pressure capsules of the Deep Submergence Rescue Vehicle [DSRV]; see below.) However, in 1983 the Navy's leadership decided that instead of constructing the nuclear-powered HTV, sections of HY-130 would be added to the conventional deep-diving research submarine DOLPHIN. In addition, the Navy has fabricated several portions of a submarine hull of HY-130 steel in preparation for construction of the SEAWOLF (SSN 21) class.

The NR-1 at Port Lauderdale, Florida, with the now-discarded submarine rescue ship SUNBIRD (ASR 15) in the background. The NR-1 underwent a two-year refueling and overhaul in 1991–1992, which will enable her to operate into the 21st century. (1993, Giorgio Arra)

The NR-1 looks unusual, with a sonar dome protruding from the top of her sail and her fixed mast fitted with a television periscope. The gear on her bow is for towing by a surface ship or a submarine. (1993, Giorgio Arra)

2 DEEP SUBMERGENCE RESCUE VEHICLES: "MYSTIC" CLASS

Number	Name	Launched	Completed
DSRV 1	Mystic	24 Jan 1970	6 Aug 1971
DSRV 2	Avalon	1 May 1971	28 July 1972

Builders:	Lockheed Missiles and Space Co., Sunnyvale, Calif.
Weight:	37 tons
Length:	49⅔ feet (15 m) overall
Diameter:	8 feet (2.4 m)
Propulsion:	1 electric motor; 1 propeller, mounted in control shroud (see *Engineering* notes)
Speed:	4 knots
Operating depth:	5,000 feet (1,524 m)
Manning:	3 + 24 rescuees

These submersibles were developed after the loss of the submarine Thresher (SSN 593) in 1963 to provide a capability for rescuing survivors from submarines disabled on the ocean floor above their hull collapse depth.

After lengthy tests and evaluation, both DSRVs were declared fully operational in late 1977.

With the demise of the Navy's submarine rescue ships carrying the McCann rescue chamber, the DSRVs provide the Navy's only realistic submarine rescue capability.

Class: Initially 12 rescue vehicles were planned, each capable of carrying 12 survivors. Subsequently, the vehicle capability was increased to 24 survivors, and the proposed number of DSRVs was reduced to six. In the event, only two units were built.

The DSRVs were developed by the Navy's Deep Submergence Systems Project, which also had responsibility for the non-propulsion aspects of the NR-1 and had planned for a set of deep submergence search vehicles (DSSV) that were to have had a 20,000-foot (6,100-m) operating capability. The DSSV was designed, but it was neither funded nor built.

Costs: The estimated construction cost of the DSRV 1 was $41 million, the DSRV 2 $23 million. The total development, construction, test, and initial support for these craft have cost in excess of $220 million.

Design: The DSRV consists of three interconnected personnel spheres, each 7½ feet (2.3 m) in diameter, constructed of HY-140 steel encased in a fiberglass-reinforced plastic shell. The forward sphere contains the vehicle's controls and is manned by the pilot and copilot; the center and after spheres can accommodate 24 survivors and a third crew member.

The DSRVs can mate with all U.S. submarines except the Dolphin and NR-1.

The DSRV was configured to be launched and recovered by a submerged attack submarine or by a Pigeon (ASR 21)-class subma-

Crewmen check the mating "skirt" of the Avalon. The skirt mates with the hatch of a submarine and is then pumped dry, permitting passage between the DSRV and the submarine, either the carrying or "mother" submarine or the disabled submarine. (1992, U.S. Navy, PH3 Douglas L. Badders)

The rescue submersible Avalon is carried by the attack submarine Billfish (SSN 676) departing Rota, Spain, for a NATO deep-sea rescue exercise. Location markings are painted on the deck of the Billfish, her sail, and the tops of her diving planes. (1992, U.S. Navy, PH3 Douglas L. Badders)

rine rescue ship. After launching, the DSRV can descend to the disabled submarine, mate with one of the submarine's escape hatches, take on board up to 24 survivors, and return to the "mother" submarine. The submersible can be air-transported in C-141 or C-5 cargo aircraft or ground-transported by a special trailer. It is fitted with a remote-control manipulator.

The two ASRs that could carry and support the DSRVs were stricken in 1992 and 1995.

Electronics: The DSRVs are fitted with elaborate search and navigation sonars, closed-circuit television, and optical viewing devices for locating a disabled submarine and mating with the stricken craft's escape hatches.

Engineering: The DSRVs have a single propeller driven by a 15-hp electric motor for forward propulsion. The propeller is in a rotating control shroud, which alleviates the need for rudders and diving planes (both of which could interfere with a rescue mission). Four ducted thrusters—two vertical and two horizontal—each powered by a 7½-hp electric motor, provide precise maneuvering. The craft has an endurance of five hours at a speed of four knots.

Names: Names were assigned in 1977.

Operational: The DSRV rapid-deployment concept has been tested periodically from U.S. nuclear attack submarines. In 1979 the AVALON was flown by C-5 cargo aircraft from San Diego to Glasgow, Scotland, for deployment on board the British SSBN REPULSE.

The DSRVs are based at the North Island Naval Air Station in San Diego.

Stern aspect of the AVALON on board the submarine BILLFISH. The racks holding the DSRV are easily removed or installed. Note the circular shroud around the craft's propeller. The shroud tilts to steer the craft; just forward of the shroud are openings for the after pair of ducted thrusters. (1992, U.S. Navy, PH3 Douglas L. Badders)

The BILLFISH carrying the AVALON, with mooring parties on deck forward and amidships. The sail markings on the BILLFISH are to aid the AVALON in locating the forward escape hatch. (1992, U.S. Navy, PH3 Douglas L. Badders)

2 RESEARCH SUBMERSIBLES: MODIFIED "ALVIN" CLASS

Number	Name	Launched	Completed
DSV 3	TURTLE	11 Dec 1968	1969
DSV 4	SEA CLIFF	11 Dec 1968	1969

Builders:	General Dynamics/Electric Boat, Groton, Conn.	
Weight:	TURTLE	21 tons
	SEA CLIFF	29 tons
Length:	TURTLE	26 feet (7.9 m) overall
	SEA CLIFF	$30\frac{5}{6}$ feet (9.4 m)
Beam:	8 feet (2.4 m); 12 feet (3.7 m) over propeller pods	
Propulsion:	electric motor, 1 propeller (see *Engineering* notes)	
Speed:	2.5 knots	
Operating depth:	TURTLE	10,000 feet (3,050 m)
	SEA CLIFF	20,000 feet (6,100 m)
Manning:	2 + 1 scientist	

These are small submersibles used for deep-ocean research. They were constructed using an HY-100 steel test sphere and an HY-100 replacement sphere originally fabricated for the ALVIN. Their operating depth with the HY-100 spheres was 6,500 feet (1,980 m); in 1979 the TURTLE was refitted with a modified sphere providing a 10,000-foot (3,050-m) operating depth, and the SEA CLIFF was fitted with a titanium sphere in 1981–1983 for 20,000-foot (6,100-m) operations.

Classification: These craft were designated DSV 3 and DSV 4 on 1 June 1971.

Design: The original HY-100 steel spheres were seven feet (2.1 m) in diameter. A light, fiberglass outer hull is fitted to the spheres. The craft have closed-circuit television, external lights, sonars, cameras, and hydraulic remote-control manipulators.

These craft can be transported by C-5 cargo aircraft.

Engineering: A single stern propeller is fitted, or ahead-propulsion and two pod-mounted external electric motors rotate for maneuvering. No thrusters are fitted. Endurance is one hour at 2.5 knots and eight hours at 1 knot.

Names: During construction these submersibles were named the AUTEC I and II, respectively, because they were initially to be used to support the Anglo-American Atlantic Undersea Test and Evaluation Center (AUTEC). The names TURTLE and SEA CLIFF were assigned at their joint launching.

Operational: The SEA CLIFF dived to 20,000 feet for the first time on 10 March 1985. That was the deepest depth achieved by a U.S. submersible except for the discarded bathyscaphe TRIESTE. The SEA CLIFF deep dive was made in the Middle America Trench off the Pacific coast of Central America.

In September–October 1990, after eight dives carried out in a 17-day period, the SEA CLIFF recovered both halves of a cargo door that tore away from a Boeing 747 jet aircraft in 1989. The doors were recovered from a depth of 14,000 feet (4,297 m) approximately 87 n.miles (161 km) southwest of Hawaii.

1 RESEARCH SUBMERSIBLE: "ALVIN"

Number	Name	Launched	Completed
DSV 2	ALVIN	5 June 1964	1965

Builders:	General Mills Inc., Minneapolis, Minn.
Weight:	16 tons
Length:	$22\frac{1}{2}$ feet (6.9 m) overall
Beam:	8 feet (2.4 m); 12 feet (3.7 m) over propeller pods
Speed:	2 knots
Operating depth:	13,124 feet (4,000 m)
Manning:	1 + 2 scientists

The ALVIN is operated by the Woods Hole Oceanographic Institution for the Office of Naval Research, which sponsored construction of the craft.

The ALVIN accidentally sank in 5,051 feet (1,540 m) of water on 16 October 1968 when her sphere was flooded (there were no casualties). She was raised in August 1969 and refurbished from May 1971 to October 1972 and became operational in November 1972. (The research ship MIZAR/T-AGOR 11 and the commercial submersible ALUMINAUT salvaged the ALVIN.)

Classification: Classified DSV 2 on 1 June 1971.

Design: As built, the ALVIN had a single, 7-foot (2.1-m) diameter pressure sphere made of HY-100 steel, which gave her a 6,000-foot (1,830-m) operating depth. She was refitted with a titanium sphere in 1971–1972, which increased her capabilities. She is fitted with a remote-control manipulator.

Engineering: See the TURTLE and SEA CLIFF for propulsion and maneuvering arrangement.

Operational: In 1985 the ALVIN aided in locating and photographing the sunken ocean liner TITANIC.

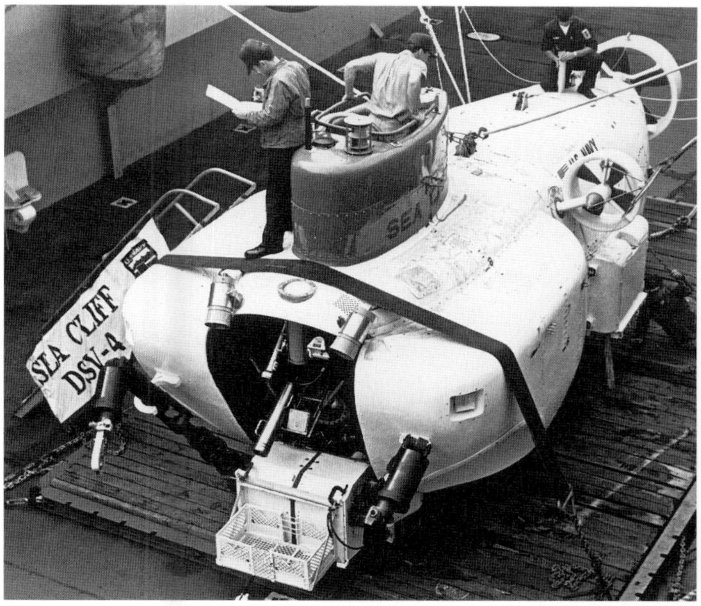

The submersible SEA CLIFF in the docking well of the submersible support ship POINT LOMA (AGDS 2). The craft's work/recovery arms and sample basket in front of the vehicle are visible. Access to the pressure sphere is through a hatch beneath the craft's "sail" structure. (1985, U.S. Navy)

The ALVIN being lifted aboard the FORT SNELLING (LSD 30). (U.S. Navy)

CHAPTER 27

Floating Dry Docks

The floating dry dock SHIPPINGPORT at New London, Connecticut, with a nuclear-propelled attack submarine lifted high and dry. A shroud shields the submarine's propeller. (1994, Leo Van Ginderen collection)

The Navy operates floating dry docks at several bases in the continental United States and in forward areas for the repair and maintenance of surface ships and submarines. Although these are non-self-propelled docks, they do have electrical generators to provide power for their lighting, tools, and equipment. Normally, they operate with a flotilla of non-self-propelled barges that provide specialized services such as messing and berthing for the crews of ships being dry-docked.

All U.S. Navy floating dry docks are open-ended, through-type docks except for the ARD-series docks, which are closed at one end by a distinctive ship-shaped bow.[1]

The larger docks are sectional to facilitate their disassembly and towing. Mounted on their hull sections—which are called "pontoons"—the large AFDB docks have side, or "wing," walls that fold down for storage or towing. These wing walls can be easily shifted between pontoons in the event of damage.

The floating docks are arranged in this chapter alphabetically according to their classification. Floating dry docks are officially considered to be service craft.

The docks in active Navy service have their locations indicated; several others are operated by foreign navies and commercial firms on lease from the Navy. The Coast Guard previously operated one former Navy floating dry dock, the YFD 83.

Class totals represent docks that are in U.S. Navy service or are laid up in reserve. Floating dry docks are listed in both the Naval Vessel Register and Service Craft and Boat Accounting Report (SABAR).

Design: Except where indicated, lift capacity for sectional docks is for all sections when assembled.

Guns: No floating dry docks are armed, although some were originally fitted to mount light anti-aircraft guns.

Names: Dry docks that service nuclear-propelled submarines have been given the names of towns and cities associated with nuclear power; other names signify positive human traits.

Operational: Operational Navy docks are manned by Navy personnel.

1. The ARD-type docks are also referred to as Camel docks because a ship of that name was gutted and fitted with a stern gate to serve as a dock in 1700 at the Russian harbor of Kronshtadt (off St. Petersburg, named Leningrad during most of the Soviet era). The project was undertaken by a captain in the Royal Navy because of the lack of docking facilities at Kronshtadt (which is now a major Russian naval base).

1 LARGE AUXILIARY FLOATING DRY DOCK: CIVILIAN BUILT

Number	Name	Completed
AFDB 9	(unnamed)	1974

Builders: Sunship, Chester, Pa.
Lift capacity:
Length: 700 feet (213.36 m) overall
Width: 220 feet (67.1 m)
Width clear inside:
Draft: 17 feet (5.18 m)
Manning:

The two-section AFDB 9 was taken over by the Navy and placed on the Naval Vessel Register effective 12 July 1990. The dock had been operated by the Pennsylvania Shipbuilding Company, but she was acquired when that firm defaulted on Navy contracts.

The dock is at the Philadelphia Naval Shipyard.

1 LARGE AUXILIARY FLOATING DRY DOCK: GERMAN BUILT

Number	Name	Completed	In USN service
AFDB 8	MACHINIST	1980	5 Aug 1985

Builders: Seebeckwerft, Bremerhaven (West Germany)
Lift capacity: 39,300 tons
Length: 824¾ feet (251.5 m) overall
Width: 175 7/12 feet (53.5 m)
Width clear inside: 140¼ feet (42.8 m)
Draft:
Manning:

The AFDB 8 is a large, one-piece floating dry dock purchased by the Navy from the builder on 5 August 1985 and towed to Subic Bay in the Philippines for operation beginning in March 1986. With the withdrawal of U.S. forces from the Philippines in 1992, she was towed to Pearl Harbor.

Design: The dry dock is fitted with two 7.5-ton capacity traveling cranes on the side walls.

The MACHINIST servicing the frigate KNOX (FF 1052) at Subic Bay. (1987, U.S. Navy)

The MACHINIST while at Subic Bay in the Philippines. The traveling cranes ride along the bridge walls of the dry dock. (1986, U.S. Navy)

1 LARGE AUXILIARY FLOATING DRY DOCK: "AFDB 4" CLASS

Number	Name	In service
AFDB 7	LOS ALAMOS	Mar 1945

Builders:	Mare Island Navy Yard, Vallejo, Calif.[2]
Sections:	6 (A-B-C-D-E-G) in reserve
Lift capacity:	31,000 tons with 4 sections
Length:	413 feet (125.9 m) overall with 4 sections
Width:	240 feet (73.2 m)
Width clear inside:	119½ feet (36.4 m)
Draft:	8⅔ feet (2.6 m) light
	67⅓ feet (20.5) max submerged
Manning:	197 (5 officers + 192 enlisted) with 4 sections

Originally, this was a seven-section dock (A through G). Section F was transferred to the U.S. Army in 1966 for use, initially, as a floating power plant at the Kwajalein atoll in conjunction with anti-ballistic missile tests.[3]

Of the remaining sections, four were operational at Holy Loch, Scotland, to support U.S. Navy SSBNs; they were to be retired with the withdrawal of Submarine Squadron 14 from Holy Loch in 1992; all have been laid up in reserve in the NDRF at James River, Virginia. Four sections were normally at Holy Loch, with two sections in reserve, although only four sets of dock walls are available. The sections were periodically rotated, two at a time, to permit overhaul of the pontoons.

Ownership of these sections has shifted between the Navy and Maritime Administration while they have been in reserve.

Class: The Navy constructed seven advanced base sectional docks (ABSD) in World War II.

	Sections	*Lift capacity*
ABSD 1, 2	10	90,000 tons
ABSD 3	9	81,000 tons
ABSD 4–7	7	55,000 tons

The ABSD 1 was completed in 1943, the ABSD 2–6 in 1944, and the ABSD 7 in 1945. An eighth planned ABSD was canceled.

ABSD 1–3 had the capacity to lift any World War II–era U.S. warship, including the MIDWAY (CVB 41)-class large aircraft carriers. The ABSD 4–7 could lift IOWA (BB 61)-class battleships and ESSEX (CV 9)-class aircraft carriers.

ARTISAN (AFDB 1) sections B-C-D-E were stricken on 27 October 1986; they remain laid up at Pearl Harbor in Navy custody.

AFDB 3 (unnamed) was transferred to the State of Maine in 1982 for use by the Bath Iron Works at Portland.

AFDB 5 (unnamed) was transferred to the city of Port Arthur, Texas, in 1984 for use by Todd Shipyards Corporation.

AFDB 4 (unnamed) sections A through G were stricken on 15 April 1989.

AFDB 6 (unnamed) was stricken in December 1975.

Classification: Originally designated ABSD, with the same hull numbers, these docks were reclassified AFDB in August 1946.

Design: These docks are constructed of steel. The large wing walls can support cranes and, as built, anti-aircraft guns. (The authorized armament when the docks were built was a twin 40-mm Bofors AA mount on each section).

Names: Names were not assigned to these ships until the 1960s.

Operational: Sections A-B-C-D were reactivated from the reserve fleet in 1961 and towed across the Atlantic in February–March 1961 for use at the Holy Loch SSBN refit base. Thus, the AFDB 7 sections were in use at Holy Loch for 30 years.

2. The ABSD sections were erected and assembled at Mare Island; they were fabricated by commercial firms.
3. The dock was fitted with gas turbine generators to serve as a floating power plant that could produce 22 megawatts. The barge was named ANDREW J. WEBER and was used at Subic Bay in the Philippines from 1968 to 1992, when she was towed to Guam for storage.

The now-retired Artisan, with six sections assembled, at Subic Bay. Another AFDB section—with sidewalls raised—is being overhauled within the dock. All AFDBs were similar except for their length when fully assembled. (U.S. Navy)

Two sections of an AFDB (at top) and the Adept at Subic Bay. The wing walls of the AFDB sections fold down for towing and storage. The AFDL 23 still has the gun tubs that held anti-aircraft guns during World War II. (U.S. Navy)

1 LARGE AUXILIARY FLOATING DRY DOCK: "AFDB 1" CLASS

Number	Name	In service
AFDB 2	(unnamed)	Apr 1944

Builders:	Mare Island Navy Yard, Vallejo, Calif.
Sections:	1 (D) in service
Sections:	4 (E-F-H-I) laid up
Lift capacity:	40,000 tons
Length:	approx. 472 feet (143.9 m) overall
Width:	240 feet (73.2 m)
Width clear inside:	119½ feet (36.4 m)
Draft:	9 feet (2.7 m) light
	78 feet (23.8 m) max submerged
Manning:	

Originally, this was a ten-section dock of which only one section remains operational, at Pearl Harbor. Previously, four sections were operational at Subic Bay; the laid-up sections are at Pearl Harbor.

Sections D-E-F-H-I were stricken on 27 October 1986 but reacquired in March 1987; sections A-B-G-J were stricken on 15 April 1989 and put up for sale. The C section was stricken earlier.

2 SMALL AUXILIARY FLOATING DOCKS: "AFDL 1" CLASS

Number	Name	In service
AFDL 6	Dynamic	Mar 1944
AFDL 25	Undaunted	May 1944

Builders:	AFDL 6 Chicago Bridge and Iron, Calif.
	AFDL 25 Doullet, Ewin
Sections:	1
Lift capacity:	1,000 tons
Length:	200 feet (61.0 m) overall
Width:	64 feet (19.5 m)
Width clear inside:	45 feet (13.7 m)
Draft:	3⁵⁄₁₂ feet (1.0 m) light
	28½ feet (8.7 m) max submerged
Manning:	AFDL 6 24 (1 officer + 23 enlisted)

These are steel docks. The AFDL 6 is operational at Little Creek, Virginia, and the AFDL 25 is operational at Guantánamo Bay, Cuba. The Undaunted, which had been stricken earlier, was reacquired in June 1984 for service at Guantánamo Bay, replacing the Endeavor.

Class: AFD/AFDL 1–33 were completed during World War II. The Endeavor (AFDL 1) has been on lease to the Dominican Republic since 8 March 1986; Reliance (AFDL 47) has been on commercial lease since 15 May 1991. Both docks remain on the Naval Vessel Register. Several docks previously on lease to commercial yards were sold on 1 October 1981 (see previous editions). More recent disposals are:

AFDL 10, on lease to the Philippines, was stricken 13 July 1987.

AFDL 21, on commercial lease, was stricken on 31 March 1989 for transfer to another government agency.

AFDL 22, on loan to South Vietnam since 1971, was stricken on 30 July 1985.

AFDL 40, on commercial lease, was stricken on 30 June 1987 and transferred to the Philippines on 30 June 1990.

AFDL 41 was sold in 1983.

Diligence (AFDL 48), on commercial lease, was stricken on 28 August 1986 and sold.

Classification: Originally, an AFD designation was assigned to units No. 1–6, 8–21, and 24–31.

Design: All AFDLs were of one-piece, steel construction except for the Diligence (built after World War II), which is fabricated of concrete. The AFDL 1 type was intended to service minesweeper-size ships (AM/MSF/MSO).

1 SMALL AUXILIARY FLOATING DOCK: MODIFIED "AFDL 1" CLASS

Number	Name	In service
AFDL 23	Adept	Dec 1944

Builders:	George D. Auchter
Sections:	1
Lift capacity:	1,900 tons
Length:	288 feet (87.8 m) overall
Width:	64 feet (19.5 m)
Width clear inside:	45 feet (13.7 m)
Draft:	3¼ feet (1.0 m) light
	31⅓ feet (9.6 m) max submerged
Manning:	

A one-piece steel dock, the Adept was originally intended to service destroyer escorts (DE), tugs, and minesweepers. Formerly at Subic Bay in the Philippines, she is now at Ingleside, Texas, supporting mine countermeasures ships.

The Adept at Subic Bay. There was a Philippine Navy corvette in the dock when this photo was taken. (1987, U.S. Navy)

1 MEDIUM AUXILIARY FLOATING DRY DOCK: "AFDM 14"

Number	Name	Completed
AFDM 14 (ex-YFD 71)	Steadfast	July 1945

Builders:	Pollock-Stockton Shipbuilding, Stockton, Calif.
Sections:	3
Lift capacity:	14,000 tons
Length:	598 feet (182.3 m) overall
Width:	118 feet (36.0 m)
Width clear inside:	87 feet (26.5 m)
Draft:	3⁵⁄₁₂ feet (1.1 m) light
	45¾ feet (13.9 m) max submerged
Manning:	70 (3 officers + 67 enlisted)

This three-piece steel dock is operational at the Naval Station San Diego, California, supporting surface ships.

Classification: Reclassified as an AFDM on 1 February 1983 and named the Steadfast on 9 May 1983.

5 MEDIUM AUXILIARY FLOATING DRY DOCKS: "AFDM 3" CLASS

Number	Name	In service
AFDM 5 (ex-YFD 21)	Resourceful	Feb 1943
AFDM 6 (ex-YFD 62)	Competent	June 1944
AFDM 7 (ex-YFD 63)	Sustain	Jan 1945
AFDM 8 (ex-YFD 64)	Richland	Dec 1944
AFDM 10 (ex-YFD 67)	Resolute	1945

Builders:	Everett Pacific Shipbuilding, Wash., except AFDM 8, Chicago Bridge and Iron, Calif.
Sections:	3
Lift capacity:	18,000 tons
Length:	622 feet (189.6 m) overall
Width:	124 feet (37.8 m)
Width clear inside:	93 to 96 feet (28.35 to 29.27 m)
Draft:	6⅙ feet (1.9 m) light
	52¾ feet (16.1 m) max submerged
Manning:	AFDM 6 155 (5 officers + 150 enlisted)
	AFDM 7 143 (4 officers + 139 enlisted)
	AFDM 10 150 (6 officers + 144 enlisted)

All of these three-piece steel docks are operational.

AFDM 5, formerly at Subic Bay in the Philippines, is now at the Naval Ship Repair Facility at Guam, Marianas; AFDM 6 is at the Naval Submarine Base Pearl Harbor; AFDM 7 is at Norfolk; AFDM 8 is at Guam; and AFDM 10 is assigned to Submarine Squadron 8 at Norfolk.

Class: The AFDM 1, formerly on commercial lease, was stricken on 15 December 1986; AFDM 3 is on commercial lease; and AFDM 9, formerly on lease, was stricken on 31 December 1987.

Classification: These docks were initially classified as floating dry docks (YFD).

Design: Originally, these were intended to dock destroyers, light cruisers, and escort carriers.

The Resourceful riding high out of the water at Subic Bay. (1987, U.S. Navy)

The combat stores ship San Jose (AFS 7) in the Richland at Guam. With the abandonment of the U.S. naval base at Subic Bay, the importance of Guam to U.S. operations in the Pacific–Indian Ocean area has increased. (U.S. Navy)

1 MEDIUM AUXILIARY FLOATING DRY DOCK: "AFDM 1" CLASS

The unnamed AFDM 2 (ex-YFD 4), completed in 1942, was leased to Halter Marine, Gulfport, Mississippi, on 1 September 1992. She was returned to Navy custody on 16 May 1995 and promptly placed in storage.

This is a three-section steel dock with a 15,000-ton lift capacity. She had been laid up in the National Defense Reserve Fleet at Portsmouth, Virginia, since 1987.

See 15th Edition/page 369 for characteristics.

AUXILIARY REPAIR DRY DOCKS: "ARD 12" CLASS

All docks of this class have been stricken. The last in active service was the SAN ONOFRE (ARD 30). The one-piece steel dock had been in service at the Naval Submarine Base San Diego (Point Loma), California, supporting Submarine Squadron 3. She was inactivated on 29 September 1995, stricken on 26 October 1995, and transferred to the Maritime Administration. (See 15th Edition/page 369 for characteristics.)

Class: The ARD 23 and ARD 32, long on lease to Argentina and Chile, respectively, were stricken from the Naval Vessel Register on 25 June 1993 for outright sale to those countries.

Design: The dry dock was originally intended to service destroyers and submarines.

1 AUXILIARY REPAIR DRY DOCK: "ARD 2" CLASS

Number	Name	In service
ARD 5	WATERFORD	June 1942

Builders:	Pacific Bridge, Alameda, Calif.
Sections:	1
Lift capacity:	4,100 tons
Length:	485⅔ feet (148.1 m) overall
Width:	71 feet (21.6 m)
Width clear inside:	49 feet (14.9 m)
Draft:	5¼ feet (1.6 m) light
	32 7/12 feet (9.9 m) max submerged
Manning:	131 (6 officers + 125 enlisted)

This is a one-piece steel dry dock. The WATERFORD is operational at the Naval Submarine Base New London, Connecticut.

Class: The ARD 6 is on loan to Pakistan, ARD 12 to Turkey.

The WEST MILTON (ARD 7) was transferred to the Maritime Administration on 16 July 1981 and laid up. Stricken on 23 August 1990, she was sold for scrap in 1992.

The WATERFORD under tow at New London, Connecticut. The dock has a ship-type bow, three bow anchors, and a navigation bridge. (U.S. Navy, Jean Russell)

The docking well of an ARD 2-class dry dock. Note the keel blocks, which are moved to match specific ship hulls. The stern gate is open in this view. (U.S. Navy)

2 MEDIUM AUXILIARY REPAIR DOCKS: "ARDM 4" CLASS

Number	Name	In service
ARDM 4	SHIPPINGPORT	27 Jan 1979
ARDM 5	ARCO	27 Feb 1986

Builders:	ARDM 4 Bethlehem Steel, Sparrows Point, Baltimore, Md.
	ARDM 5 Todd Shipyards, Seattle, Wash.
Sections:	1
Lift capacity:	7,800 tons
Length:	492 feet (150.0 m) overall
Width:	96 feet (29.3 m)
Width clear inside:	64 feet (19.5 m)
Draft:	54½ feet (16.6 m) max submerged
Manning:	ARDM 4 131 (6 officers + 125 enlisted)
	ARDM 5 130 (5 officers + 125 enlisted)

These were the first floating dry docks built for the U.S. Navy after World War II. They were designed to support nuclear-propelled attack submarines. The SHIPPINGPORT is operational at the Naval Submarine Base New London, and the ARCO is operational at the Naval Submarine Base (Point Loma) San Diego, supporting Submarine Squadron 11.

Class: Two docks were authorized in the fiscal 1975 and 1983 naval shipbuilding programs. A third, similar dock, planned for fiscal year 1984, was not built.

The SHIPPINGPORT under tow by a commercial tug. The dock was designed specifically to support nuclear-propelled submarines. (1992, U.S. Navy, JOSN Connie L. Sanders)

MEDIUM AUXILIARY REPAIR DOCK: "ARDM 1" CLASS

The one-of-a-kind ENDURANCE (ARDM 3, ex-ARD 18) was taken out of service and stricken on 31 July 1995. (See 15th Edition/page 371 for characteristics.)

The ENDURANCE was modified in 1969 to support nuclear-propelled submarines. She had been active at the Charleston Naval Shipyard (South Carolina), supporting Submarine Squadron 20.

This dock differs from the two other units of this type that remain in U.S. service.

The ENDURANCE laid up, without masts, cranes, or other fittings. (U.S. Navy)

1 MEDIUM AUXILIARY REPAIR DOCK: MODIFIED "ARDM 1" CLASS

Number	Name	In service
ARDM 1 (ex-ARD 19)	OAK RIDGE	Mar 1944

Builders:	Pacific Bridge, Alameda, Calif.
Sections:	1
Lift capacity:	8,000 tons
Length:	541 feet (164.9 m) overall
Width:	81 feet (24.7 m)
Width clear inside:	58 feet (17.7 m)
Draft:	7 feet (2.1 m) light
	42$\frac{5}{8}$ feet (13.1 m) max submerged
Manning:	181 (5 officers + 176 enlisted)

The OAK RIDGE is active at the Naval Submarine Base Kings Bay, Georgia, supporting Submarine Squadron 20.

The similar ALAMAGORDO (ARDM 2, ex-ARD 26) was taken out of service on 23 November 1993 in preparation for disposal and was sold for scrap on 21 March 1995. She had been active at Charleston, South Carolina.

YARD FLOATING DRY DOCK: FORMER AFDL

The YFD 83 (ex-AFDL 31), on loan to the Coast Guard since January 1947 for use at the Coast Guard yard at Curtis Bay, Maryland, was stricken and sold in 1994.

Several other YFDs are on commercial lease.

See 15th Edition/page 371 for characteristics.

The OAK RIDGE when at Rota, Spain, servicing an SSBN. Note the two large traveling cranes on the dock wall. (U.S. Navy)

CHAPTER 28

Naval Aviation

Marine AV-8B Harrier STOVL aircraft stand ready on the assault ship Belleau Wood (LHA 3). These highly capable aircraft and the most flexible LHA/LHD amphibious ships form an important component of naval aviation. (U.S. Navy)

The strength and structure of U.S. naval aviation are being reduced at a precipitous rate. U.S. naval aviation—the Navy and Marine Corps air arms—comprises more than 4,200 aircraft, both in active and reserve units. This total includes "pipeline," research, and training aircraft. The current active aircraft inventory is listed in the accompanying table. (U.S. Coast Guard aircraft are listed separately; see chapter 32.)

Naval aviation is undergoing a massive reduction in strength—both in aircraft and units—in the wake of the end of the Cold War. Since the last edition of *Ships and Aircraft,* published in 1993, the Navy and Marine Corps have lost several hundred aircraft and almost 100 squadrons and other aviation units. In 1994 alone, 37 Navy squadrons and one wing (Reserve Carrier Air Wing 30) were disestablished and five Marine squadrons were deactivated. (One Navy and one Marine squadron "stood up" in 1994, VX-9 and HMH-366, respectively.)

The listings for specific squadrons indicate the status of units that have existed since 1990.

NAVAL AIR ORGANIZATION

All naval aviation units belong to an administrative organization; most units also belong to tactical organizations. For example, a strike-fighter squadron is administratively under an administrative "type" wing while at its home base; when deployed on board a carrier, the squadron would come under the air wing commander embarked in that ship. Similarly, a patrol squadron is under the patrol "type" wing commander while in the United States, but if deployed in a forward area, it would be under a fleet commander and his subordinate air commander.

The administrative organization is headed by the Chief of Naval Operations, advised by the Director, Air Warfare Division,[1] and extends through the Commander, Naval Air Force Atlantic Fleet (NavAirLant), and Commander, Naval Air Force Pacific Fleet (NavAirPac), and their respective "type" wing commanders. Details of naval air organization are provided in chapter 6.

Navy wings and squadrons are officially "established" and "disestablished" and are not in commission. However, records and ceremonies continually use the terms "commissioned" and "decommissioned," especially for wings. The Marine Corps uses the terms "activated" and "deactivated" for its aviation units.

In addition to the numbered wings and squadrons described in this chapter, in 1995–1996 the aircraft at various test facilities were organized into two test wings. Naval Test Wing Atlantic comprises four squadrons, all based at NAS Patuxent River, Maryland; they are: Naval Rotary Wing Test Squadron, Naval Strike Aircraft Test Squadron, Naval Force Aircraft Test Squadron, and Naval Test Pilots School. Naval Test Wing Pacific comprises two squadrons: Naval Weapons Test Squadron Point Mugu and Naval Weapons Test Squadron China Lake (both in California).

UNIT DESIGNATIONS

Naval air units are designated in two systems of abbreviations: pronounceable acronyms, and simpler, letter-number combinations. Accordingly, Fighter Squadron 2 is known both as FitRonTwo and VF-2.

All naval aviation units have the prefix V for heavier-than-air or H for helicopter. Previously, Z was employed for lighter-than-air (airship) units.

The V prefix for naval aircraft types and subsequently for aviation units dates from 1922, when V indicated heavier-than-air and Z lighter-than-air airships. VF indicates fighter squadron, VA attack squadron, ZP airship patrol squadron, etc. (The last U.S. Navy airship, a Goodyear ZPG-2W, was taken out of service in 1962.) H was introduced as the helicopter type letter for aircraft (HNS-1) in 1943 and for squadrons in 1947 (the first naval helicopter squadron was Marine Corps HMX-1, followed in 1948 by Navy HU-1 and HU-2). Marine units have the letter M added as the second letter of aviation unit designations.[2]

1. Prior to 1 January 1993 this position was the Assistant Chief of Naval Operations (Air Warfare). The position was originally established in 1944 as the Deputy Chief of Naval Operations (Air); it was a three-star billet from 1944 to 1992.

NAVAL AVIATION UNIT DESIGNATIONS*

CVW	Carrier Air Wing
CVWR	Reserve Carrier Air Wing
HC	Helicopter Combat Support Squadron
HCS	Helicopter Combat Search and Rescue/Special Warfare Support Squadron
HM	Helicopter Mine Countermeasures Squadron
HMAL	(Marine) Attack-Light Helicopter Squadron
HMH	(Marine) Heavy Helicopter Squadron
HMM	(Marine) Medium Helicopter Squadron
HMX	(Marine) Helicopter Squadron
HS	Helicopter Anti-Submarine Squadron
HSL	Light Helicopter Anti-Submarine Squadron
HT	Helicopter Training Squadron
MAG	Marine Aircraft Group
MAW	Marine Aircraft Wing
VA	Attack Squadron
VAQ	Tactical Electronic Warfare Squadron
VAW	Carrier Airborne Early Warning Squadron
VC	Fleet Composite Squadron
VF	Fighter Squadron
VFA	Strike Fighter Squadron
VFC	Fighter Composite Squadron
VMA	(Marine) Attack Squadron
VMA (AW)	(Marine) Attack (All Weather) Squadron
VMAQ	(Marine) Electronic Warfare Squadron
VMFA	(Marine) Fighter-Attack Squadron
VMFA (AW)	(Marine) Fighter-Attack Squadron (All Weather)
VMGR	(Marine) Refueler-Transport Squadron
VMO	(Marine) Observation Squadron
VP	Patrol Squadron
VPU	Patrol Squadron—Special Projects Unit
VQ	Fleet Air Reconnaissance Squadron
VQ	Strategic Communications Squadron
VR	Fleet Logistics Support Squadron
VRC	Fleet Logistics Support (COD) Squadron#
VS	Sea Control Squadron (previously Air Anti-Submarine Squadron)
VT	Training Squadron
VX	Air Test and Evaluation Squadron
VXE	Antarctic Development Squadron
VXN	Oceanographic Development Squadron

Notes: *Marine squadrons add the letter T as a suffix for readiness/transition units.
#COD = Carrier On-board Delivery.

2. The H, V, and Z were also used for ship designations; hence, CV for aircraft carrier, AV for seaplane tender, and AZ for airship tender. Subsequently, H was used in CVHA, CVHE, LPH, LHA, and LHD for helicopter-carrying ships.

An MH-53E Sea Dragon from squadron HC-4 lands aboard the WASP (LHD 1) operating in the Adriatic Sea. HC-4 provides VERTREP services to Navy ships in the Mediterranean area and Persian Gulf. (Lt. Col. P. Croisetiere, USMC)

U.S. NAVAL AIRCRAFT (MID-1996)

Aircraft		Total	Navy Active	Naval Reserve	Marine Active	Marine Reserve	Pipeline
Attack							
A-6E	INTRUDER	92	92	—	—	—	—
AV-8B	HARRIER	179	9	—	145	—	25
Fighter/Strike-Fighter							
F-5E	TIGER II	32	20	—	—	12	—
F-5F	TIGER II	4	3	—	—	1	—
F-14A	TOMCAT	198	140	11	—	—	47
F-14B	TOMCAT	79	56	—	—	—	23
F-14D	TOMCAT	47	45	—	—	—	2
F/A-18A	HORNET	260	92	40	51	31	46
F/A-18B	HORNET	32	21	2	2	—	7
F/A-18C	HORNET	361	256	—	67	—	38
F/A-18D	HORNET	131	32	—	90	—	9
Patrol/Anti-Submarine							
P-3B	ORION	3	2	—	—	—	1
P-3C	ORION	243	146	61	—	—	36
S-3B	VIKING	118	99	—	—	—	19
Electronic/Special Purpose							
E-2C	HAWKEYE	88	56	5	—	—	27
E-6A	MERCURY	16	13	—	—	—	3
EA-6B	PROWLER	118	60	4	22	—	32
EP-3E	ORION	9	8	—	—	—	1
EP-3J	ORION	2	—	1	—	—	1
RP-3A/D	ORION	11	11	—	—	—	—
ES-3A	VIKING	16	12	—	—	—	4
Cargo/Transport							
C-2A	GREYHOUND	38	30	—	—	—	8
C-9B	SKYTRAIN	19	—	17	2	—	—
DC-9	SKYTRAIN	10	—	4	—	—	6
C-20D	GULFSTREAM III	2	—	1	—	—	1
C-20G	GULFSTREAM IV	5	—	4	1	—	—
C-130T	HERCULES	14	—	13	—	—	1
KC-130F	HERCULES	38	—	1	27	—	10
KC-130R	HERCULES	14	—	—	10	—	4
KC-130T	HERCULES	26	—	—	18	—	8
LC-130F	HERCULES	3	3	—	—	—	—
LC-130R	HERCULES	4	3	—	—	—	1
CT-39G	SABRELINER	9	1	5	2	1	—
US-3A	VIKING	2	1	—	—	—	1
VP-3A	ORION	5	5	—	—	—	—
Training							
T-2C	BUCKEYE	110	101	—	—	—	9
TC-18F	—	1	1	—	—	—	1
T-34C	MENTOR	291	285	—	3	—	3
T-38A	TALON	11	7	—	—	—	4
Training (continued)							
T-39D	SABRELINER	1	1	—	—	—	—
T-44A	KING AIR	57	54	—	—	—	3
T-45A	GOSHAWK	55	48	—	—	—	7
TA-4J	SKYHAWK	78	77	—	—	—	1
TAV-8B	HARRIER	18	2	—	15	—	1
TC-130G	HERCULES	1	1	—	—	—	—
TE-2C	HAWKEYE	2	1	—	—	—	1
TP-3A	ORION	5	5	—	—	—	—
Utility/Miscellaneous							
RC-12F	SUPER KING AIR	2	2	—	—	—	—
RC-12M	SUPER KING AIR	2	2	—	—	—	—
UC-12B	HURON	65	42	5	10	3	5
UC-12F	SUPER KING AIR	6	2	—	4	—	—
UC-12M	SUPER KING AIR	10	10	—	—	—	—
UP-3A	ORION	6	6	—	—	—	—
UP-3B	ORION	2	2	—	—	—	—
Rotary Wing							
XV-15A	—	2	2	—	—	—	2
V-22	OSPREY	7	7	—	—	—	—
AH-1W	SEACOBRA	163	3	—	111	28	21
HH-1N	HUEY	33	21	—	5	—	7
UH-1N	HUEY	108	2	—	72	16	18
SH-2G	SEASPRITE	17	1	16	—	—	—
SH-3G	SEA KING	1	1	—	—	—	—
SH-3H	SEA KING	17	10	6	—	—	1
UH-3A	SEA KING	4	4	—	—	—	—
UH-3H	SEA KING	43	34	9	—	—	—
VH-3A	SEA KING	4	4	—	—	—	—
VH-3D	SEA KING	11	—	—	7	—	4
CH-46D	SEA KNIGHT	28	24	—	—	—	4
CH-46E	SEA KNIGHT	240	—	—	185	22	33
HH-46D	SEA KNIGHT	43	29	—	8	—	6
UH-46D	SEA KNIGHT	13	11	—	—	—	2
CH-53D	SEA STALLION	52	13	—	34	—	5
CH-53E	SUPER STALLION	144	5	—	110	—	29
MH-53E	SEA DRAGON	44	22	12	5	—	5
RH-53D	SEA STALLION	16	—	—	—	13	3
TH-57B	SEARANGER	45	45	—	—	—	—
TH-57C	SEARANGER	75	73	—	—	—	2
HH-60H	SEAHAWK	30	12	14	—	—	4
SH-60B/F	SEAHAWK	163	131	—	—	—	32
UH-60A	BLACK HAWK	3	3	—	—	—	—
VH-60N	SEAHAWK	8	—	—	5	—	3
Totals		4,268	2,322	231	1,011	127	577

UNIT CODES

Most naval aviation organizations have two-letter identification codes that are displayed on aircraft tail fins and, in some marking schemes, on wings. Training wings have single-letter designations, while air stations and other special organizations use a number-letter scheme.

Beginning in 1946 the Navy used single-letter codes to identify specific ships to which the planes were attached—as B for BOXER (CV 21) and F for FRANKLIN D. ROOSEVELT (CVB 42)—with land-based units having two-letter codes. The system was revised in 1957 to provide the current fleet "split," with the first letter indicating the fleet assignment: A to M for Atlantic and N to Z for Pacific. To avoid confusion with numerals, the letters I and O are not used. The unit code AF was dropped because of confusing it with Air Force (previously used by Carrier Air Group 6, which then took code letters AE); AF was later reinstated for use by Reserve Carrier Air Wing 20.

The code letters AD and NJ are worn by several fleet readiness-transition squadrons. The letters were formally assigned to Combat Readiness Carrier Air Wing 4 and Combat Readiness Carrier Air Wing 12, respectively. Both of those wings were disestablished on 1 June 1970, but some of their squadrons survive in the Atlantic and Pacific Fleets.

Within carrier air wings the squadrons are identified by blocks of numbers and colors, with the individual aircraft further identified by numbers within the block. The block numbers (e.g., 100, 200) are aircraft flown by the wing commander; the first of each series (e.g., 101, 201) is flown by squadron commanding officers. The color code is rarely used because of the current low-visibility marking scheme.

Side number	*Squadron*	*Color code*	*Aircraft*
100 series	fighter	insignia red	F-14
200 series	fighter or strike-fighter	orange-yellow	F-14 or F/A-18
300 series	strike-fighter	light blue	F/A-18
400 series	strike-fighter	international orange	F/A-18
500 series	medium attack	light green	A-6E
600–609	AEW	black	E-2C
610–619	helicopter ASW	black	HH-60H, SH-60F
620–629	EW	black	EA-6B
700–719	sea control	black	S-3B
720+	ELINT detachment		ES-3A

CARRIER AIR WINGS

The Navy currently has ten active and one reserve carrier air wings (CVW/CVWR). During the 1980s the Navy briefly had 14 active wings as part of the Reagan-Lehman naval buildup; a fifteenth wing was planned but not activated. The reserve carrier air wing flies first-line aircraft and is suitable for deployment on board carriers. In addition, most Marine Corps combat aircraft are carrier capable, with all Marine aviators being carrier trained. Up to three Marine fighter-attack (VMFA) squadrons and one electronic countermeasures squadron (VMAQ) are normally assigned to the carrier force to compensate for Navy shortfalls in carrier squadrons.

The composition of carrier air wings is changing. Into the 1980s the standard wing had two fighter squadrons (24 F-14A), two light attack squadrons (24 A-7E), and one medium attack squadron (10 A-6E + 4 KA-6D tankers), in addition to specialized Anti-Submarine Warfare (ASW), Airborne Early Warning (AEW), and Electronic Warfare (EW) squadrons.

During the 1980s, with the introduction of the F/A-18 Hornet strike-fighter, the Navy evaluated several air wing variations. For example, the so-called "ROOSEVELT air wing" (CVN 71) had double the number of A-6E Intruder aircraft, provided by reducing the numbers of fighters and strike-fighters (the F/A-18 having replaced the A-7E). Under this plan, the A-6Es would be succeeded in service by improved models of the Intruder (A-6F or A-6G) and, subsequently, by the A-12 Avenger. The cancellation of the A-12 in early 1991 and overall budget reductions forced the Navy to drop this plan.

The standard air wing of the mid-1990s is a composite of the 1980s air wing plus the ROOSEVELT wing, although, as discussed below, there will be significant variations based on aircraft availability. Further, the demise of the A-6 Intruder attack aircraft and the reduction in F-14 Tomcat fighters will lead to still more changes. By the late 1990s, carrier air wings are expected to consist of:

Units		*Aircraft*
1 VF	fighter squadron	14 F-14 Tomcat
3 VFA	strike-fighter squadrons	36 F/A-18 Hornet
1 VAQ	tactical electronic warfare squadron	4 EA-6B Prowler
1 VAW	airborne early warning squadron	4 E-2C Hawkeye
1 VS	sea control squadron	8 S-3B Viking
1 HS	helicopter anti-submarine squadron	2 HH-60H Seahawk
		6 SH-60F[3] Seahawk

Carriers with one VF squadron normally have 14 F-14s; ships with two squadrons embark about 10 planes per squadron.

Squadron assignments to carrier air wings change periodically because the shortage of special-mission aircraft (VAQ and VAW) requires some shifts of these squadrons among the air wings to support overseas carrier deployments.

Also, on 13 January 1992 the Secretary of the Navy directed that the Navy and Marine Corps more closely integrate Marine tactical aviation into carrier air wings. The memorandum directed the two services to "undertake innovative measures to enhance the efficiency of naval aviation through . . . closer integration," especially of Marine fighter-attack (VMFA) and electronic warfare (VMAQ) squadrons to reduce Navy aircraft requirements by at least 140 planes in those categories.

(Since November 1931, Marine tactical squadrons have periodically operated from aircraft carriers. At that time Marine scouting squadron VS-15M went aboard the carrier LEXINGTON/CV 2 and VS-14M went aboard the SARATOGA/CV 3 for fleet operations; they remained in those carriers until November 1934.)

In addition to wing aircraft, forward-deployed carriers generally operate an ES-3A Viking aircraft in the ELINT role, these being assigned from fleet air reconnaissance squadrons VQ-5 in the Western Pacific area and VQ-6 in the Mediterranean area.

3. These will be replaced by the SH-60R, a modified SH-60B or an SH-60F modified to a common, multisensor ASW configuration.

Flight deck aircraft handlers and flight deck officers take a break during flight operations aboard the carrier GEORGE WASHINGTON. These personnel use the templates on the two-level flight and hangar deck model in foreground to monitor the position of each aircraft, shifting positions of the 70-odd planes of an air wing. (U.S. Navy, JOC Gregg Snaza)

Historical: The designation carrier air wing (CVW) was established on 20 December 1963 in place of carrier air groups (CVG).[4] Air group designations had reached No. 153 during World War II, albeit with several gaps in the series. The designation ASW carrier air group (CVSG) was established on 1 April 1960 for aircraft assigned to ASW carriers (CVS). Those ships were phased out in the late 1960s and early 1970s, the last CVSG being decommissioned on 30 June 1973. The ASW groups were numbered from CVSG-50 to CVSG-62.

Replacement air groups (RAG) became combat readiness air wings (CRAW) in 1963, but these were phased out over the next few years, the last on 30 June 1973. Some of their squadrons survive, known officially as Fleet Readiness Squadrons (FRS) but also called "replacement," or RAG, squadrons. They provide transition-training to fleet aircraft and are generally assigned to the specialized aircraft wing commands under NavAirLant or NavAirPac.

When the ASW carrier air groups were phased out in the 1960s and early 1970s, the fixed-wing and helicopter ASW aircraft went aboard the larger attack aircraft carriers (which became simply CV/CVN vice CVA/CVAN). The CV/CVN concept was originally intended for the "swing wing" concept, wherein a carrier could be loaded predominately with fighter, attack, or ASW aircraft. In practice, this has not been followed because standard wings have been organized to the extent possible for all carriers. However, in October 1971, in a demonstration of the swing-wing concept, the carrier SARATOGA operated 37 ASW aircraft—21 S-2E Trackers and 16 SH-3D Sea Kings—plus 20 fighters, 9 attack aircraft, and 8 special-mission aircraft.[5]

Specialized reconnaissance aircraft were phased off carrier decks in the late 1970s as both the RA-5C Vigilante and RF-8G Crusader were retired. The active fleet's last "recce" squadrons were RVAH-7, decommissioned on 30 September 1979, and VFP-63, decommissioned on 30 June 1982. (The Naval Air Reserve flew the RF-8G "Photo" Crusader until 1987.) Marine RF-4B Phantoms subsequently provided a limited photographic reconnaissance capability on some carriers pending the availability in the early 1980s of the Tactical Air Reconnaissance Pod System (TARPS) for the F-14A Tomcat on the larger carriers. Flown by non-specialized reconnaissance pilots, however, the TARPS pod does not provide the quality or quantity of tactical reconnaissance that was possible with the RA-5C or RF-8G. This shortfall was keenly felt during Operation Desert Storm (1991). According to the U.S. Director of Naval Intelligence, the TARPS "was totally inadequate" in providing sufficient and timely bomb damage assessment during Operation Desert Storm.[6]

The personnel strength of air wings varies; the nominal carrier squadron strengths are:

VA	medium attack	37 officers + 226 enlisted
VAQ	electronic	27 officers + 167 enlisted
VAW	early warning	32 officers + 127 enlisted
VF	fighter	36 officers + 216 enlisted
VFA	strike-fighter	21 officers + 187 enlisted
VS	sea control	41 officers + 212 enlisted
HS	helicopter ASW	26 officers + 178 enlisted

Carrier air wing staffs number about 10 officers + 17 enlisted, except that Japan-based CVW-5 has 15 officers and 25 enlisted assigned. Most CVW staffs also have one- to three-officer detachments assigned to their home air base.

Air Wing	Code	Ship	Squadrons	
CVW-1	AB	STENNIS	VF-102 VFA-82 VFA-86 VMFA-251	VMAQ-3 VAW-123 VS-32 HS-11

This wing previously operated from the AMERICA, being aboard for that carrier's final deployment in 1996. CVW-1 subsequently transferred to the JOHN C. STENNIS, at the time the Navy's newest aircraft carrier. Note that two Marine squadrons are assigned as part of the scheme to supplement the reduced number of Navy carrier-based squadrons with Marine units.

A Marine EA-6B squadron—the VMAQ-3 Moondogs—stands in for the disestablished VAQ-137. Other carrier air wings have only VMFA squadrons flying the F/A-18 assigned.

The wing is scheduled to go aboard the GEORGE WASHINGTON for a September 1997–March 1998 deployment.

CVW-2	NE	CONSTELLATION	VF-2 VFA-137 VFA-151 VMFA-323	VAQ-131 VAW-116 VS-38 HS-2

CVW-2 previously served aboard the RANGER, shifting to the "Connie" following the decommissioning of the older ship in 1993.

CVW-3	AC	ROOSEVELT	VF-32 VFA-37 VFA-105 VMFA-312	VAQ-130 VAW-126 VS-22 HS-7

The wing went aboard the THEODORE ROOSEVELT after the DWIGHT D. EISENHOWER entered the Newport News Shipbuilding yard in July 1995 for an 18-month refueling/overhaul.

CVW-3 was previously aboard the KENNEDY. The wing was reorganized in 1983 to evaluate an all A-6E attack capability, with the KENNEDY embarking two F-14 squadrons and two A-6E Intruder squadrons (a total of 25 medium attack aircraft) and no light attack squadrons (A-7 or F/A-18). In 1989 CVW-3 was provided with two A-7E squadrons—VA-46 and VA-72—which were the last Corsair squadrons in the fleet. They flew with CVW-3 during Operation Desert Storm, after which they were replaced by VFA-37 and VFA-105, flying the F/A-18 Hornet.

The wing went aboard the "Ike" in April 1993; the KENNEDY entered the Philadelphia Naval Shipyard later in the year for overhaul (and emerged in the fall of 1995 as a reserve/training carrier).

During Operation Uphold Democracy—the U.S. occupation of Haiti in September 1994—the EISENHOWER embarked three Navy helicopter squadrons (HC-2, HCS-4, and HS-7), plus 51 helicopters of the Army's 10th Mountain Division (some 1,800 troops).

CVW-4	Disestablished 1 June 1970			
CVW-5	NF	INDEPENDENCE	VF-154 VFA-27 VFA-192 VA-195	VAQ-136 VAW-115 VS-21 HS-14

CVW-5 previously flew from the carrier MIDWAY, with the entire wing being based at NAF Atsugi, Japan. When assigned to the MIDWAY the wing did not have F-14 Tomcats or S-3 Vikings because of the ship's size and lack of an ASW command center. A detachment of three Marine RF-4B Phantoms from VMFP-3 had provided the ship with a photoreconnaissance capability until 1986, when the MIDWAY wing shifted from F-4 Phantom fighters to F/A-18 Hornets. From 1986 until going aboard the INDEPENDENCE in 1991, the wing had eight squadrons: 3 VFA, 2 VA (flying the A-6E), 1 VAQ, 1 VAW, and 1 HS.

Upon joining the "Indy" in August 1991, CVW-5 lost VFA-151 and VA-185, but it gained two F-14 squadrons and an S-3 squadron, becoming the last wing to receive those aircraft. The F-14s were subsequently combined into a single squadron, and VFA-27 replaced VA-115 in June 1996.

CVW-6	AE	FORRESTAL	Disestablished 1 Apr 1992 VF-11 VF-31 VFA-132 VFA-137 VA-176	 VAQ-133 VAW-122 VS-28 HS-15

4. The term CAG (for Commander Air Group) is still used to refer to an air wing commander.
5. In 1960–1961, in an earlier example of a swing-wing concept in response to Soviet "saber-rattling," U.S. carriers in the Mediterranean and Far East unloaded fighter aircraft to embark more nuclear strike aircraft.
6. Rear Adm. Thomas A. Brooks, USN, comments at a luncheon of the Naval & Maritime Correspondents Circle, Washington, D.C., 15 July 1991.

This wing previously served in the INDEPENDENCE, shifting to the FORRESTAL in 1986 when the "Indy" began her long-term SLEP modernization. After SLEP, the INDEPENDENCE went to the Far East, taking on CVW-5. This wing was decommissioned when the FORRESTAL was shifted to a training role (AVT 59).

See individual squadrons for their status.

CVW-7	AG	WASHINGTON	VF-143 VFA-131 VFA-136 VA-34	VAQ-140 VAW-121 VS-31 HS-5

This wing previously served on board the EISENHOWER. CVW-7 flew from the "Ike" during Operation Desert Shield in 1990, but not Desert Storm (1991). VF-11 will replace VF-143.

CVW-8	AJ	KENNEDY	VF-14 VF-41 VFA-15 VFA-87	VAQ-141 VAW-124 VS-24 HS-3

This wing deployed to the Western Pacific with the NIMITZ when that carrier departed Norfolk on 30 December 1986 for a six-month assignment prior to being homeported at Bremerton, Washington. Upon completion of the deployment, CVW-8 returned to the East Coast for subsequent assignment to the THEODORE ROOSEVELT and now the JOHN F. KENNEDY. Two attack squadrons previously in the wing—VA-36 and VA-65—have been disestablished.

During the ship's March–September 1995 deployment, a Marine F/A-18 squadron, VMFA-312, embarked; it was replaced by VF-14.

CVW-9	NG	NIMITZ	VF-211 VFA-146 VFA-147 VMFA-314	VAQ-138 VAW-112 VS-33 HS-8

Formerly embarked in the KITTY HAWK, the wing was assigned to the NIMITZ in mid-1986 after the nuclear carrier shifted to the Pacific Fleet. The KITTY HAWK, in turn, entered the Philadelphia Naval Shipyard for her SLEP modernization.

CVW-10	Disestablished 1 June 1988

This wing was established on 1 November 1986, having been the Navy's 14th carrier air wing of the Reagan-Lehman naval buildup. The previous CVW-10 was decommissioned on 20 November 1969.

CVW-11	NH	KITTY HAWK	VF-213 VFA-22 VFA-94	VAQ-135 VAW-117 VS-29 HS-6

Previously on board the ENTERPRISE, CVW-11 remained on the West Coast to embark in the LINCOLN when the "Big E" shifted to the East Coast in early 1990 for her extended modernization and refueling at Newport News Shipbuilding. VA-95 from this wing was disestablished in 1995. The wing went aboard the KITTY HAWK in 1996.

CVW-12	Disestablished 1 June 1970
CVW-13	Disestablished 1 Jan 1991

This wing was established on 1 March 1984 at NAS Oceana, Virginia, for assignment to the CORAL SEA, following her transfer to the Atlantic Fleet in 1983. The wing had four F/A-18 squadrons and one A-6E squadron, plus special-mission units.

The previous CVG-13 had been disestablished on 1 October 1962. The new wing made three Mediterranean deployments in the CORAL SEA from 1986 to 1989 before being decommissioned.

CVW-14	NK	VINSON	VF-11 VF-31 VFA-25 VFA-113 VA-196	VAQ-139 VAW-113 VS-35 HS-4

The wing was previously on board the CONSTELLATION, then it shifted to the INDEPENDENCE when the "Connie" entered the Philadelphia Naval Shipyard for SLEP. The wing flew from the "Indy" during Desert Shield (not Desert Storm), after which the INDEPENDENCE took on CVW-5 when she was homeported in Japan in September 1991.

CVW-15	NL	KITTY HAWK	Disestablished 31 March 1995 VF-51 VF-111 VFA-27 VFA-97 VA-52	 VAQ-134 VAW-114 VS-37 HS-4

The wing's last deployment—on board the KITTY HAWK— was in the Western Pacific from June to December 1994. HS-4 from this wing is now assigned to CVW-9.

See individual squadrons for their status.

CVW-16	Disestablished 30 June 1971			
CVW-17	AA	ENTERPRISE	VF-103 VFA-81 VFA-83 VA-75	VAQ-132 VAW-125 VS-30 HS-15

CVW-17 shifted from the FORRESTAL to the SARATOGA when the former ship began SLEP modernization at the Philadelphia Naval Shipyard in 1982, thus ending three decades of the wing's operating from CVA/CV 59. The wing went aboard the "Big E" in 1994 as the "Sara" was decommissioned.

CVW-18	Not used
CVW-19	Disestablished 30 June 1977
CVWR-20	Reserve Air Wing (see below)
CVW-21	Disestablished 12 Dec 1975
CVW-22 to 29	Not used
CVWR-30	Reserve Air Wing; disestablished 31 Dec 1994

PATROL WINGS

Patrol Wings (PatWings) direct the operations of the Navy's patrol squadrons (VP), with East Coast squadrons assigned to Patrol Wings Atlantic (PatWingsLant) at NAS Norfolk, Virginia, and West Coast squadrons assigned to Patrol Wings Pacific (PatWingsPac) at NAS Barbers Point, Hawaii. (PatWingsPac headquarters, previously at NAS Moffett Field, south of San Francisco, California, moved to Barbers Point on 1 July 1993.)

Under PatWingsLant are PatWing-5 at Brunswick, Maine, and PatWing-11 at Jacksonville, Florida. Their P-3 Orion squadrons operate in the Atlantic, Caribbean, and Mediterranean areas. PatWingsLant has administrative control of the Atlantic P-3 readiness squadron (VP-30). PatWing-5 is the administrative command for VPU-1.

PatWingsPac directs Pacific and Indian Ocean VP operations and has direct control over VP squadrons in Hawaii as well as VPU-2. PatWing-1 at Kamiseya, Japan, directs the VP squadrons that rotate to the Western Pacific. PatWing-10, also under PatWingsPac, has administrative control of VP squadrons at NAS Whidbey Island, Washington, and VQ-1. Squadron VP-30 provides P-3 readiness training for both Atlantic and Pacific squadrons flying the Orion. (The Pacific Fleet P-3 readiness squadron, VP-31, has been disestablished.)

Patrol squadron assignments to wings are listed in chapter 6. PatWing-2 in the Pacific was disestablished on 30 September 1993; the wing had been established at NAS Ford Island (Pearl Harbor) on 1 October 1937.

ATTACK SQUADRONS

Squadron	Aircraft	Name/Notes
VA-22	A-7E	to VFA-22 on 4 May 1990
VA-27	A-7E	to VFA-27 on 25 Jan 1991
VA-34	A-6E	to VFA in 1996
VA-35	A-6E	disestablished 31 Jan 1995
VA-36	A-6E	disestablished 31 Mar 1994
VA-37	A-7E	to VFA-37 on 28 Nov 1990
VA-42	A-6E, TC-4C, T-34C	disestablished 30 Sep 1994
VA-46	A-7E	disestablished 30 June 1991
VA-52	A-6E	disestablished 31 Mar 1995
VA-55	A-6E	disestablished 1 Jan 1991
VA-65	A-6E	disestablished 31 Mar 1995
VA-72	A-7E	disestablished 30 June 1991
VA-75	A-6E	to disestablish 1997
VA-85	A-6E	disestablished 30 Sep 1994
VA-94	A-7E	to VFA-94 on 28 June 1990
VA-95	A-6E	disestablished 31 Oct 1995
VA-97	A-7E	to VFA-97 on 25 Jan 1991
VA-105	A-7E	to VFA-105 on 17 Dec 1990
VA-115	A-6E	to VFA in 1996
VA-122	A-7E	disestablished 31 May 1991
VA-128	A-6E, TC-4C	disestablished 30 Sep 1995
VA-145	A-6E	disestablished 1 Oct 1993
VA-155	A-6E	disestablished 30 Apr 1993
VA-165	A-6E	to disestablish 1996
VA-176	A-6E	disestablished 30 Sep 1992
VA-185	A-6E	disestablished 30 Aug 1991
VA-196	A-6E	to disestablish 1996

All attack squadrons are being phased out of service; the last will be VA-34 (Blue Blasters), scheduled to transition to the F/A-18 in 1996. All other VA squadrons have either been transitioned to strike-fighter squadrons (VFA), flying the F/A-18 Hornet, or disestablished. Since 1991 all attack squadrons have flown only the A-6E Intruder, except for two transition-readiness squadrons, VA-42 and VA-128.

All A-7E squadrons were similarly disestablished or converted to VFA units. VA-46 and VA-72 in the Atlantic were the Navy's last A-7E Corsair squadrons; their demise was delayed because of the Persian Gulf War (during which they flew from the KENNEDY). Both squadrons were disestablished on 30 June 1991 (ceremonies were held on 23 May 1991, confusing the records).[7] VA-122, the A-7E readiness-transition squadron, was disestablished in May 1991, the last of three such units (the others being VA-125 and VA-174). This ended the 25-year career of the Corsair as a first-line Navy attack aircraft. (It continued in service briefly in special-purpose roles, but it was not flown by the Marine Corps.)

VA-34 and VA-115 became VFA in 1996, but in "cadre" status; they are to "stand up" as F/A-18E squadrons in 1998.

VA-55, which had been deactivated in 1975, was again established on 7 October 1983 for the new CVW-13; the squadron was again disestablished at the start of 1991. Note that VA-45 has been changed to VF-45 (see below).

Atlantic Fleet A-6E squadrons are based at NAS Oceana, under Attack Wing Atlantic; in the Pacific the A-6E units (as well as most Navy EA-6B Prowlers) are at NAS Whidbey Island, under Attack Wing Pacific. The VA fleet readiness-training squadrons for the A-6E were VA-42 at Oceana and VA-128 at Whidbey Island.

Historical: Attack squadrons (VA) were established on 15 November 1946, replacing the previous carrier-based bombing fighting (VBF), bombing (VB), and torpedo (VT) squadrons.

7. The A-7D variant is no longer flown by the Air Force Reserve; several other countries still fly A-7 variants.

Flight deck personnel scatter as an F/A-18C Hornet from VFA-106 is about to catapult from the carrier GEORGE WASHINGTON. The F/A-18, a flexible and highly effective aircraft, is replacing the long-serving A-6 Intruder as an attack aircraft. But the newer aircraft still cannot match some of the Intruder's attack capabilities. (Peter B. Mersky)

TACTICAL ELECTRONIC WARFARE SQUADRONS

Squadron	Aircraft	Name/Notes
VAQ-33	EA-6A, EP-3J	disestablished 1 Oct 1993
VAQ-34	F/A-18A/B	disestablished 1 Oct 1993
VAQ-35	EA-6B	disestablished 1 Oct 1993
VAQ-128	EA-6B	to establish 1998
VAQ-129	EA-6B	Vikings (NJ)
VAQ-130	EA-6B	Zappers
VAQ-131	EA-6B	Lancers
VAQ-132	EA-6B	Scorpions
VAQ-133	EA-6B	Wizards
VAQ-134	EA-6B	Garudas
VAQ-135	EA-6B	Black Ravens
VAQ-136	EA-6B	Gauntlets
VAQ-137	EA-6B	Rooks
VAQ-138	EA-6B	Yellowjackets
VAQ-139	EA-6B	Cougars
VAQ-140	EA-6B	Patriots
VAQ-141	EA-6B	Shadowhawks
VAQ-142	EA-6B	to establish 1997

There are 12 deploying fleet tactical EW squadrons, with a four-plane squadron normally assigned to a carrier air wing. These squadrons fly the EA-6B Prowler; VAQ-132 was the first to receive the aircraft, in July 1971. All Navy EA-6B units are based at NAS Whidbey Island except for VAQ-136, which is based at NAF Atsugi. VAQ-129 provides EA-6B readiness training for Navy and Marine Prowler crews.

Three squadrons that were previously scheduled to be disestablished or are in the process of being phased out—VAQ-132, VAQ-134, and VAQ-137—are being retained with EA-6B aircraft to provide tactical electronic warfare support for Air Force operations. The Air Force is phasing out its EF-111A Raven aircraft that serve in this role.

A total of five VAQ squadrons are being funded to replace the Ravens; 24 EF-111A aircraft were in service in 1995 when the decision was made to phase them out in favor of the EA-6B. Twelve Ravens will be retained until 1999, at which time the Prowlers will carry out all Navy–Air Force jamming missions. In addition to the three squadrons listed above, VAQ-133 (reestablished on 1 April 1996) and VAQ-142 will provide support for Air Force operations.

All tactical EW squadrons report administratively to Electronic Combat Wing Pacific. VAQ-33, 34, and 35 operated under the Fleet Tactical Readiness Group (FTRG), formerly the Fleet Electronic Warfare Support Group (FEWSG), headquartered at the Naval Amphibious Base Little Creek (Norfolk), Virginia. The FTRG squadrons simulated potential enemy electronic/jamming activities. VAQ-33 was at Key West, Florida; VAQ-34 at the Naval Air Weapons Center Point Mugu, California (formerly Pacific Missile Test Center); and VAQ-35 at NAS Whidbey Island, Washington. Reserve VAQ-209 is assigned the Navy's electronic aggressor role following disestablishment of VAQ-33; however, VAQ-33's EP-3J Orions went to reserve VP-66.

Historical: VAQ-129, 131, and 132 were previously heavy attack squadrons (VAH-10, 4, and 2, respectively); they were changed to VAQ in 1968–1970, when they shifted from EKA-3B Skywarriors to EA-6B aircraft. VAQ-130 is formerly early warning squadron VAW-13, redesignated VAQ in 1968. Most of the other VAQs were built up from EKA-3B detachments that operated from forward-deployed carriers.

In July 1990, VAQ-34 became the first U.S. military aviation squadron to be commanded by a woman.

Operational: Reserve squadron VAQ-209 deployed to the Mediterranean on the carrier THEODORE ROOSEVELT from May to September 1995. This was the first fixed-wing reserve squadron to deploy overseas on a carrier since the Korean War. The squadron's 18 fliers and 29 enlisted maintenance and support personnel teamed with VAQ-141 for the deployment. The VAQ-209 Prowlers flew combat missions over Bosnia during the deployment.

AIRBORNE EARLY WARNING SQUADRONS

Squadron	Aircraft	Name/Notes
VAW-77	E-2C	Night Wolves
VAW-110	E-2C, C-2A	disestablished 30 Sep 1994
VAW-111	E-2C	disestablished 30 Apr 1988
VAW-112	E-2C	Golden Hawks
VAW-113	E-2C	Black Eagles
VAW-114	E-2C	disestablished 31 Mar 1995
VAW-115	E-2C	Liberty Bells (ex-Sentinels)
VAW-116	E-2C	Sun Kings
VAW-117	E-2C	Wall Bangers
VAW-120	E-2C, C-2A	Hummers (AD)
VAW-121	E-2C	Bluetails
VAW-122	E-2C	disestablished 31 Mar 1996
VAW-123	E-2C	Screwtops
VAW-124	E-2C	Bear Aces
VAW-125	E-2C	Tiger Tails
VAW-126	E-2C	Sea Hawks
VAW-127	E-2C	disestablished 30 Sep 1991

The ten deploying AEW squadrons are assigned to carrier air wings, each with four or five E-2C Hawkeye aircraft. VAW-120 at NAS Norfolk now provides all training for E-2C and C-2A Greyhound flight crews. The West Coast readiness squadron was VAW-110.

West Coast squadrons are based at NAS North Island (San Diego), California, under AEW Wing Pacific; East Coast units are at NAS Norfolk, under Carrier AEW Wing Atlantic. VAW-115 is based at NAF Atsugi, Japan, having changed its name upon assignment to the INDEPENDENCE.

In addition to regular carrier deployments, VAW aircraft have operated from Keflavík, Iceland, to provide AEW coverage of the Greenland-Iceland-United Kingdom (GIUK) gap, and in Operation Thunderbolt, the U.S. Customs Service effort to intercept drug smugglers off U.S. coasts. VAW-77 was established on 18 November 1995 for land-based drug surveillance. It is based at NAS Atlanta.

Classification: The two readiness AEW squadrons—VAW-110 and VAW-120—were designated RVAW until 1 May 1983, when they dropped the R prefix; they were the only readiness squadrons with that prefix.

Historical: The first carrier AEW squadrons were VAW-1 and VAW-2, commissioned in 1948 to provide aircraft detachments to Pacific and Atlantic carriers, respectively. (AEW aircraft had earlier flown from carriers, and a land-based squadron, VPW-1, had been established in 1948.)

The current VAW structure dates from 1967, when seven AEW squadrons—numbered in sequence—were established. Previously, VAW-11, 12, 13, and 33 provided AEW detachments to carriers while Barrier Squadron Pacific and AEW Wing Atlantic operated land-based WV/EC-121 Warning Star aircraft as part of the North American air defense efforts until 1965.

This E-2C Hawkeye has its wings "tucked in" ready to be lowered to the hangar deck or parked on the flight deck. Note the rudder configuration; the second tail fin (from left) does not have control surfaces. (U.S. Navy)

FLEET COMPOSITE SQUADRONS

Squadron	Code	Aircraft	Name/Notes
VC-1	UA	TA-4J, CH-53A, VP-3A	disestablished 30 Sep 1992
VC-5	UE	F/A-18, SH-3G	disestablished 31 Aug 1992
VC-6	JG	none assigned	Skeeters
VC-8	GF	TA-4J, SH-3G	Redtails
VC-10	JH	TA-4J	disestablished 15 Aug 1993

Composite squadrons provide utility services for the fleet, including "dissimilar" Air Combat Maneuvering (ACM), noncombat photography, aerial target services, radar calibration, and transport. Two VC squadrons had combat missions: VC-1 and VC-10 had TA-4Js that had the additional role of air defense for the Hawaiian islands and Guantánamo Bay, Cuba, respectively.

VC-6 at NAS Norfolk, Virginia, flies no aircraft, but it operates air and surface target drones. Permanent VC-6 detachments are based at the Fleet Combat Training Center in Dam Neck, Virginia, and at the Naval Amphibious Base, Little Creek, Virginia. Five smaller, mobile detachments operate in the Atlantic-Mediterranean areas and periodically deploy with U.S. ships operating around South America in the UNITAS exercises.

VC-8 is at Roosevelt Roads, Puerto Rico, providing services to Atlantic Fleet training and weapon test activities, including drone launches.

Historical: The current VC squadrons comprise the third series of composite squadrons in the fleet. From 1943 to 1945 the Navy had 83 composite squadrons (VC) that operated from escort carriers.

Beginning in 1949, six VC squadrons were formed with nuclear-strike aircraft (flying P2V-3C Neptunes and AJ Savages); those squadrons became heavy attack squadrons (VAH) in 1955–1956. At the same time, several ASW squadrons were formed but were redesignated VS (see page 345).

On 1 July 1965 the Navy's utility squadrons (VJ and later VU) were changed to VC, with VU-1, 5, 6, 8, and 10 being redesignated as fleet composite squadrons (VC).

VC-2 (Oceana) and VC-7 (Miramar) were disestablished in 1980, and VC-3 (North Island) was disestablished in 1981. The latter squadron flew DC-130A Hercules to launch aerial drones.

FIGHTER SQUADRONS

Squadron	Aircraft	Name/Notes
VF-1	F-14A	disestablished 30 Sep 1993
VF-2	F-14D*	Bounty Hunters
VF-11	F-14D	to disestablish 1996
VF-14	F-14A	to VFA-14 in 1997
VF-21	F-14A	disestablished 31 Jan 1996
VF-24	F-14A	to disestablish 1996
VF-31	F-14D*	Tomcatters
VF-32	F-14A*	Swordsmen
VF-33	F-14A	disestablished 1 Oct 1993
VF-41	F-14A	Black Aces
VF-43	F-5E/F, A-4E/F, F-16N, F-21A, T-2C	disestablished 1 July 1994
VF-45	F/A-18A, F-5E/F	disestablished 31 Mar 1996
VF-51	F-14A	disestablished 31 Mar 1995
VF-74	F-14B	disestablished 30 Apr 1994
VF-84	F-14A*	disestablished 30 Sep 1995
VF-101	F-14A/B/D, T-34C	Grim Reapers (AD)
VF-102	F-14B*	Diamondbacks
VF-103	F-14B*	Sluggers
VF-111	F-14A*	disestablished 31 Mar 1995
VF-114	F-14A	disestablished 30 Apr 1993
VF-124	F-14A/D, T-34C	disestablished 30 Sep 1994
VF-126	TA-4J, F-5E/F, F-16N	disestablished 1 Apr 1994
VF-142	F-14B	disestablished 30 Apr 1995
VF-143	F-14B*	World Famous Dogs
VF-154	F-14A*	Black Knights
VF-191	F-14A	disestablished 30 Apr 1988
VF-194	F-14A	disestablished 30 Apr 1988
VF-211	F-14A*	Fighting Checkmates
VF-213	F-14A*	Black Lions

Note: *TARPS-capable squadrons.

The F-14 Tomcat force has suffered major cutbacks, from a peak of 31 fleet squadrons, plus two readiness-training squadrons, to the current totals of ten fleet squadrons and one readiness squadron. The number will decline further, with one squadron (14 aircraft) assigned to each air wing.

Most F-14 squadrons have 10 to 14 aircraft assigned; in one F-14 squadron on each carrier, three or four of them are wired for the TARPS reconnaissance package, which can be installed or removed in a few hours. VF-211 was the first squadron to deploy with TARPS, in early 1982, on board the CONSTELLATION.

An F-14B Tomcat from VF-142 is stopped abruptly aboard the carrier GEORGE WASHINGTON. The steel arresting cable—one of four stretched across the flight deck—has not yet been released from the Tomcat's arresting tail hook. Steam catapults and this scheme of arresting gear permit high-performance aircraft to operate at sea. (Peter B. Mersky)

West Coast F-14 squadrons are at NAS Miramar under Fighter Wing Pacific; East Coast units are at NAS Oceana under Fighter Wing Atlantic. The West Coast squadrons will consolidate with East Coast units at Oceana. All F-14 fleet-readiness training is provided by VF-101 at Oceana, with a detachment at Miramar. The West Coast F-14 readiness unit, VF-124 (NJ), at Miramar, was disestablished in 1994.

VF-43 (Oceana), VF-45 (Key West), and VF-126 (Miramar) provided adversary training, with the last also providing instrument training. VA-45 was changed to VF-45 on 7 February 1985.

VF-191 and VF-194 were established in 1986 for the Navy's 14th carrier air wing. However, the two squadrons were disestablished in 1988. Plans to establish "new" VF-191 and VF-194 as F-14D squadrons were canceled when VF-11 and VF-31 became available because CVW-6 was decommissioned when the FORRESTAL was named as the training carrier. Those two VF squadrons were then shifted to the West Coast.

The Navy's Fighter Weapons School at NAS Fallon flies F/A-18 and F-14A aircraft. Known as Top Gun, the school was established in September 1969 to develop realistic adversary tactics and training for Navy fliers. It began as a VF-121 detachment and became a separate command on 1 July 1972.[8] (Previously, the school also flew F-16N and TF-16N fighters.) Top Gun moved from NAS Miramar to Fallon in May 1996.

8. Officially, the designation is Topgun (one word); however, it is almost universally known as Top Gun.

These F-14 Tomcats are the only "straight" fighters in Navy service.The F/A-18 Hornet will probably be the only fighter-type aircraft aboard U.S. carriers by about 2015—if not sooner. (U.S. Navy)

The MIDWAY flew the Navy's last two active Phantom squadrons (VF-151 and VF-161), which stood down as Phantom units in 1986. The squadrons then became VFA-151 and VFA-161, flying the F/A-18. The last Phantom fleet-readiness squadron was VF-171, disestablished in 1984. All Navy-Marine readiness training in the Phantom was then being undertaken by VMFAT-101 at MCAS Yuma. (VF-121, the West Coast F-4 readiness squadron, was disestablished in 1980; it had been the Navy's first squadron to fly the F-4.)

Historical: VF-1, which was disestablished in 1993, was the fifth successive squadron to be so designated; the first was established in 1922 (formerly Combat Squadron 4).

Names: VF-143 was the World Famous Pukin' Dogs from 1949 until 1994, when Pukin' was deleted, a casualty of political correctness.

STRIKE-FIGHTER SQUADRONS

Squadron	Aircraft	Name	Notes
VFA-15	F/A-18C	Valions	former VA-15
VFA-22	F/A-18C	Fighting Redcocks	former VA-22
VFA-25	F/A-18C	Fist of the Fleet	former VA-25
VFA-27	F/A-18C	Chargers	former VA-27
VFA-34	F/A-18E	Blue Blasters	former VA-34
VFA-37	F/A-18C	Bulls	former VA-37
VFA-81	F/A-18C	Sunliners	former VA-81
VFA-82	F/A-18C	Marauders	former VA-82
VFA-83	F/A-18C	Rampagers	former VA-83
VFA-86	F/A-18C	Sidewinders	former VA-86
VFA-87	F/A-18C	Golden Warriors	former VA-87
VFA-94	F/A-18C	Mighty Shrikes	former VA-94
VFA-97	F/A-18C	Warhawks	former VA-97
VFA-105	F/A-18C	Gunslingers	former VA-105
VFA-106	F/A-18, T-34C	Gladiators (AD)	former VA-106
VFA-113	F/A-18C	Stingers	former VA-113
VFA-115	F/A-18E	Eagles	former VA-115
VFA-125	F/A-18, T-34C	Rough Riders (NJ)	former VA-125
VFA-127	F/A-18, F-5E/F	disestablished 31 Mar 1996	former VA-127
VFA-131	F/A-18C	Wildcats	
VFA-132	F/A-18A	disestablished 1 June 1992	
VFA-136	F/A-18C	Knighthawks	
VFA-137	F/A-18C	Kestrels	
VFA-146	F/A-18C	Blue Diamonds	former VA-146
VFA-147	F/A-18C	Argonauts	former VA-147
VFA-151	F/A-18C	Fighting Vigilantes	former VF-151
VFA-161	F/A-18A	disestablished 1 Apr 1988	former VF-161
VFA-192	F/A-18C	World Famous Golden Dragons	
VFA-195	F/A-18C	Dambusters	former VA-195

Navy F/A-18s are assigned to strike-fighter squadrons, with all carriers operating two or three such squadrons; the number will be increased to three squadrons per ship, each with 12 aircraft.

The first F/A-18 squadron was Fighter Attack Squadron 125, established on 13 November 1980 as the F/A-18 readiness squadron for training Navy and Marine pilots and ground crews. VFA-125's first aircraft was delivered in February 1981. The squadron is located at NAS Lemoore, California. A second F/A-18 readiness squadron, VFA-106, "stood up" in October 1985 at NAS Cecil Field (Jacksonville), Florida. VFA-27 went to Japan in 1996 to fly from the INDEPENDENCE.

VFA-127 provided adversary training; its functions shifted, however, to VFC-13, a reserve squadron.

VFA-75 and VFA-113 were the Navy's first F/A-18 fleet squadrons, shifting from the A-7E Corsair to F/A-18 in March–June 1983. Most F/A-18 squadrons are former A-7E Corsair units (VA), with two F-14 squadrons (VF-151, VF-161) transitioning to F/A-18s, and more VA and VF squadrons scheduled to shift to F/A-18s. VFA-161 was disestablished in 1988.

VA-34 and VA-115 became VFA in 1996 but are in a cadre status until 1998, when they will be equipped with the F/A-18E variant.

Historical: The Marine Corps has had fighter-attack squadrons (VMFA) since the introduction of the F-4 Phantom into squadron service in 1961. The Navy designation VFA originally indicated fighter attack squadron; this was changed in 1983 to strike-fighter to emphasize the attack role.

An aircraft carrier is more than a base for air operations. It also provides logistic support, munitions, and maintenance for the embarked aircraft. Here, aviation ordnancemen work on the M61 rotary cannon of an F/A-18C Hornet aboard the CARL VINSON while steaming in the Persian Gulf. Five 20-mm gun barrels are lying in the foreground. (U.S. Navy, PH1 Donald E. Bray)

PATROL SQUADRONS

Squadron	Code	Name/Notes
VP-1	YB	Screaming Eagles
VP-4	YD	Skinny Dragons
VP-5	LA	Mad Foxes
VP-6	PC	disestablished 31 May 1993
VP-8	LC	disestablished 31 Mar 1996
VP-9	PD	Golden Eagles
VP-10	LD	Red Lancers
VP-11	LE	disestablished 30 Sep 1996
VP-16	LF	Eagles
VP-17	ZE	disestablished 31 Mar 1995
VP-19	PE	disestablished 31 Aug 1991
VP-22	QA	disestablished 31 Mar 1994
VP-23	LJ	disestablished 28 Feb 1995
VP-24	LR	disestablished 30 Apr 1995
VP-26	LK	Tridents
VP-30	LL	Pro's Nest
VP-31	RP	disestablished 1 Nov 1993
VP-40	QE	Fighting Marlin
VP-44	LM	disestablished 28 June 1991
VP-45	LN	Pelicans
VP-46	RC	Grey Knights
VP-47	RD	Golden Swordsmen
VP-48	SF	disestablished 26 June 1991
VP-49	LP	disestablished 1 Mar 1994
VP-50	SG	disestablished 30 June 1992
VP-56	LQ	disestablished 28 June 1991

The Navy's 11 first-line patrol squadrons each fly eight P-3C Orion aircraft, a reduction from the nine planes per squadron in the 1980s. There were 24 active VP squadrons from the early 1970s until 1991. Budget limitations forced the stand down of four squadrons in 1991, followed by further cutbacks with the end of the Cold War.

All P-3 transition-readiness training is performed by VP-30 at NAS Jacksonville; VP-31 at NAS Moffett Field merged with VP-30 on 9 September 1993 to form the Navy's largest aviation squadron. VP-30 has more than 30 P-3C, VP-3A, UP-3A, and TP-3A aircraft and more than 1,000 personnel.

See discussion of Patrol Wings Atlantic and Pacific on page 339.

Historical: VP indicated patrol squadrons from 1922 to 1944, when patrol and multiengine land-based bombing squadrons were redesignated patrol bombing squadrons (VPB). The squadrons reverted to VP on 15 May 1946.

VP-8 was the first P3V/P-3 Orion squadron, receiving the aircraft in 1962. Previously, VP units flew P2V/P-2 Neptunes and P5M/P-5 Marlin flying boats.

Operational: VP squadrons—active and reserve—regularly deploy in whole or detachments to Roosevelt Roads, Puerto Rico; Keflavík, Iceland; Sigonella, Sicily; Jidda, Saudi Arabia; Masirah, Oman; Diego Garcia; Misawa, Japan; and Kadena, Okinawa. (Previous deployments to Adak, Alaska; Bermuda; Lajes, Azores; Rota, Spain; Cubi Point, Philippines; and Agana, Guam, have ceased.)

PATROL SQUADRONS—SPECIAL PROJECTS UNIT

Squadron	Code	Aircraft	Name
VPU-1	OB	P-3B/C	Order of the Buzzards
VPU-2	SP	P-3/C, UP-3A	Wizards

These two squadrons fly specially modified electronic surveillance variants of the Orion. Normally, they appear to operate with the tail codes of other squadrons. VPU-1 is based at NAS Brunswick, Maine, and VPU-2 at NAS Barbers Point, Hawaii. VPU-1's tail code is unofficial, being derived from "*O*rder of the *B*uzzards"; VPU-2's tail code is derived from *S*pecial *P*rojects.

ELECTRONIC RECONNAISSANCE SQUADRONS

Squadron	Code	Aircraft	Name
VQ-1	PR	UP-3A/B, EP-3E	World Watchers
VQ-2	JQ	P-3C, EP-3E	Batmen
VQ-5	SS	S-3A, ES-3A	Sea Shadows
VQ-6	ET	ES-3A	Black Ravens

These units are officially designated fleet air reconnaissance squadrons; they provide electronic surveillance in direct support of fleet operations and carry out special reconnaissance along the borders of a foreign territory. VQ-1 at Whidbey Island and VQ-2 at Rota, Spain, each fly six ELINT-configured EP-3E Orions. Those squadrons previously flew EA-3B Skywarrior ELINT aircraft as well, with the "Whales" operating from forward-deployed carriers. VQ-2 retired the last EA-3B operated by a VQ squadron in September 1991. (They were flown a while longer by VAQs.)

VQ-5 was established at Agana, Guam, on 15 April 1991, and VQ-6 at Cecil Field on 8 August 1991; VQ-5 is now at NAS North Island, California. The squadrons report to their respective Sea Control Wings. They fly the ES-3A Viking, which replaced the EA-3B as the fleet's carrier-based ELINT aircraft.

Historical: VQ-1 was established as Electronic Countermeasures Squadron 1 at NAS Iwakuni, Japan, on 1 June 1955, initially flying P4M-1Q Mercator aircraft. VQ-2 was established as ECM Squadron 2 on 1 September 1955 at Port Lyautey, Morocco, first flying the P4M-1Q and A3D-1Q (EA-3B) aircraft. VQ was changed to Fleet Air Reconnaissance Squadron on 1 January 1960.

Operational: VQ-2 flew both EP-3s and EA-3Bs in support of Desert Shield/Desert Storm; the latter were the last operational combat-environment flights by the venerable Skywarrior.

STRATEGIC COMMUNICATION SQUADRONS

Squadron	Code	Aircraft	Name
VQ-3	TC	E-6A	TACAMOPAC
VQ-4	HL	E-6A	Shadows

These units—officially designated fleet air reconnaissance squadrons—fly the E-6A Mercury, the navalized version of the Boeing 707-320B airframe. They provide LF/VLF communications relay to strategic missile submarines under a program known as TACAMO (Take Charge and Move Out).

VQ-3 and VQ-4 are under the Navy Strategic Communications Wing 1, which was established on 1 May 1992, the year both squadrons moved to Tinker Air Force Base outside of Oklahoma City, Oklahoma. Operationally, they are under the U.S. Strategic Command and report administratively to Naval Air Force Pacific. (Previously, VQ-3 was at NAS Barbers Point and VQ-4 at NAS Patuxent River, Maryland.)

The two squadrons "forward deploy" aircraft either to March Air Force Base in California or Patuxent River to fly operational patrols.

Two similar 707-320B aircraft, designated TC-18F, are operated by the Naval Training Support Unit at Tinker Air Force Base in Oklahoma to train E-6A pilots.

VQ-3 transitioned from the EC-130Q Hercules to the E-6A Mercury in 1989–1990, and VQ-4 in 1991–1992. Sixteen E-6A aircraft are flown by these squadrons, replacing 22 EC-130Q aircraft. The last EC-130Q TACAMO flight, by a VQ-4 "Herk," was on 7 May 1992.

By the late 1990s the Navy aircraft will also replace 27 Air Force EC-135 aircraft in the "Looking Glass" program, additionally providing airborne control of U.S. strategic weapons. At that time the Navy aircraft will be modified to the E-6B configuration and will carry joint Navy–Air Force operational teams.

FLEET LOGISTIC SUPPORT SQUADRONS

Squadron	Code	Aircraft	Name/Notes
VR-22	JL	C-130F, KC-130F	disestablished 31 Mar 1993
VR-24	JM	C-2A, CT-39G	disestablished 31 Jan 1993
VRC-30	RW	C-2A, UC-12F, CT-39E	Truckin' Traders
VRC-40	CD	C-2A	Rawhides
VRC-50	RG	C-2A, US-3A, C-130F	disestablished 7 Oct 1994

The two surviving fleet logistic support squadrons (VRC) deliver passengers, mail, and high-priority parts to carriers at sea. The Navy's straight "transport" squadrons (VR) have been phased out, their role having been taken over by Naval Reserve VR units and the Air Force's Air Mobility Command (formerly Military Airlift Command).

VRC-30 is at NAS North Island and VRC-40 at NAS Norfolk. The disestablishment of VRC-50 led to setting up VRC-30 Detachment 5 at NAF Atsugi to provide Carrier On-board Delivery (COD) aircraft to support carriers in the Western Pacific. The turboprop C-2A is not normally based aboard carriers because of the aircraft's size.

The KC-130F "Herks" of VR-22 were the Navy's only land-based tanker aircraft. VRC-50 flew the Navy's US-3A Viking COD aircraft. VAW-110 took over readiness training for the C-2 from VRC-30; subsequently, VRC-30 provides transition-readiness training for the UC-12 Huron for the Navy.

Historical: The first Navy transport squadron was VR-1, established on 9 March 1942; it was disestablished in October 1978. The VR squadrons were originally transport squadrons (VR), changed to fleet tactical support squadrons (VR) on 15 July 1957. They became fleet logistic support squadrons on 1 April 1976.

The first COD squadron was VRC-40, established at Norfolk on 1 July 1960.

AIRCRAFT FERRY SQUADRONS

Ferry squadrons provided pilots to transfer Navy and Marine Corps aircraft throughout the world. In 1982 the role of VRF-31, the last such unit, was changed to one of coordination of aircraft movements. Thereafter, fleet units conducted the actual ferry missions.

The Navy's last aircraft ferry squadron was VRF-31, based at NAS Norfolk; it was disestablished on 1 October 1986. The squadron was originally commissioned on 1 December 1943.

SEA CONTROL SQUADRONS

Squadron	Aircraft	Name/Notes
VS-21	S-3B	Fighting Redtails
VS-22	S-3B	Checkmates
VS-24	S-3B	Scouts
VS-27	S-3B	disestablished 30 Sep 1994
VS-28	S-3B	disestablished 1 Oct 1992
VS-29	S-3B	Vikings
VS-30	S-3B	Diamond Cutters
VS-31	S-3B	Topcats
VS-32	S-3B	Maulers
VS-33	S-3B	Screwbirds
VS-35	S-3B	Blue Wolves
VS-37	S-3B	disestablished 31 Mar 1995
VS-38	S-3B	Red Griffins
VS-41	S-3B	Shamrocks (NJ)

The Navy's ten operational sea control squadrons each fly eight S-3B Viking aircraft, a reduction from the ten aircraft assigned to these squadrons in the 1980s, but an increase from the six aircraft assigned in the early 1990s.

VS-41 at NAS North Island provides readiness training for the S-3 community; previously, VS-27 at NAS Cecil Field provided readiness-transition services for the Atlantic Fleet. (VS-30 was an S-2 Tracker readiness-training squadron; it became an operational squadron upon transitioning to the S-3A in 1976.)

On 20 February 1974 the first S-3A Viking was delivered to VS-41; the first fleet squadron, VS-21, shifted to the S-3A in June 1974. The last Viking squadron to be formed was VS-35, on 4 April 1991.

Viking squadrons are assigned to their respective fleet's Sea Control Wings, operating out of North Island and Cecil Field, when they are not working up or deployed with carrier air wings.

Classification: The 13 VS units in service on 16 September 1993 were changed from anti-submarine squadrons (VS) to sea control squadrons, reflecting their more versatile operations.

Historical: Specialized carrier-based ASW squadrons were formed in World War II; most were designated as composite squadrons (VC). In April 1950 eight VC squadrons were changed to air anti-submarine squadrons (VS); each flew 18 TBM-3E Avengers. Four of the squadrons had previously been attack units (VA), which were changed to VC on 1 September 1948.

TRAINING SQUADRONS

Squadron	Aircraft	Name	Training	Location
TRAINING WING 1 (Code A)				
VT-7	TA-4J	Strike Eagles	Advanced jet	Meridian, Miss.
VT-9	T-2C	disestablished 1 Nov 1987		
VT-19	T-2C	Attack Frogs	Intermediate jet	Meridian, Miss.
VT-23	T-2C	Professionals	Intermediate jet	Meridian, Miss.
TRAINING WING 2 (Code B)				
VT-21	T-45A	Redhawks	Intermediate/advanced jet	Kingsville, Texas
VT-22	T-45A	King Eagles	Intermediate/advanced jet	Kingsville, Texas
TRAINING WING 3 (Code C)		disestablished 31 Aug 1992		
VT-24	TA-4J	disestablished 30 Oct 1992		
VT-25	TA-4J	disestablished 30 Oct 1992		
VT-26	T-2C	disestablished 29 May 1992		
TRAINING WING 4 (Code G)				
VT-27	T-34C	Boomers	Primary flight	Corpus Christi, Texas
VT-28	T-34C	Rangers	Primary flight	Corpus Christi, Texas
VT-31	T-44A	Wise Owls	Advanced maritime	Corpus Christi, Texas
TRAINING WING 5 (Code E)				
VT-2	T-34C	Doerbirds	Primary flight	Milton, Fla.
VT-3	T-34C	Red Knights	Primary flight	Milton, Fla.
VT-6	T-34C	Shooters	Primary flight	Milton, Fla.
HT-8	TH-57B/C	Eight Ballers	Advanced helicopter	Milton, Fla.
HT-18	TH-57B/C	Vigilant Eagles	Advanced helicopter	Milton, Fla.
TRAINING WING 6 (Code F)				
VT-4	E-2C, C-2, T-2C	Warbucks	Advanced	Pensacola, Fla.
VT-10	T-34C, T-39N	Wildcats	Primary NFO*	Pensacola, Fla.
VT-86	T-2C, T-39N	Sabrehawks	Advanced NFO*	Pensacola, Fla.

*NFO = Naval Flight Officer (i.e., the "backseater").

These 16 squadrons provide fixed-wing and helicopter training for Navy, Marine Corps, Coast Guard, Air Force, and foreign pilots and navigators under the direction of the Naval Air Training Command. VT-3 provides primary flight training for U.S. Air Force pilots, and VT-31 provides training to Air Force cargo/transport pilots.

Currently, three Air Force Flying Training Squadrons (FTS) train Navy pilots:

Squadron	*Aircraft*	*Training*	*Location*
35th FTS	T-37	Primary	Reese AFB, Texas
52nd FTS	T-1A	E-6A	Reese AFB, Texas
562nd FTS	T-43A	Advanced Navigator/NFO	Randolph AFB, Texas

The T-45A, TA-4J, and T-2C are carrier capable and enable students to practice landings aboard the carrier JOHN F. KENNEDY, operating in the Gulf of Mexico. VT-21 began operating the long-delayed T-45 Goshawk in early 1992; the plane will eventually replace the surviving TA-4J Skyhawks in VT-7.

VT-7, along with VC-1 and VC-10, is the only U.S. Military squadron still flying the A-4 Skyhawk; more than 70 aircraft were on VT-7's roster when this edition went to press. The venerable TA-4J is scheduled to be replaced by the T-45 by 1997 (or later).

VT-31 trains Navy, Marine, and Coast Guard pilots in multi-engine turboprop aircraft. Beginning in fiscal 1998, it will also be the sole training unit for U.S. Air Force C-130 pilots.

VT-86 trains Naval Flight Officers (NFO) as well as U.S. Air Force Weapon System Operators (WSO) for B-1, B-2, F-15, and F-111 bomber/strike aircraft.

The T-39N aircraft of VT-10 and VT-86 are refurbished Sabreliners used to train NFOs. They are flown and maintained by contractor personnel, having replaced T-47A aircraft that were operated under a similar arrangement.

Historical: The letters T and HT (helicopter) have been used for naval aircraft designations since shortly after World War II; however, VT and HT were not used for squadron designations until 1 May 1960, when 17 training units were redesignated as training squadrons (VT). From the 1920s until 15 November 1946 the designation VT indicated torpedo squadron.

AIR TEST AND EVALUATION SQUADRONS

Squadron	Code	Aircraft	Name/Notes
VX-1	JA	P-3C, S-3A/B, ES-3A, SH-60B/F	ASW Pioneers
VX-4	XF	TA-4J, F-14A/D, F/A-18A	disestablished 29 Apr 1994
VX-5	XE	TA-4J, A-6E, EA-6B, AV-8B, F/A-18, AH-1W	disestablished 29 Apr 1994
VX-9	XE	AV-8B, EA-6B, F-14, F/A-18, AH-1W	Evaluators

These squadrons test and evaluate air weapon systems. VX-1 at NAS Patuxent River specializes in operational test and evaluation of airborne ASW under the cognizance of Naval Air Force Atlantic. VX-9, at the Naval Weapons Center China Lake, California, specializes in fighter aircraft, air-to-surface weapons and tactics, and electronic countermeasures programs. It is directly subordinate to Naval Air Force Pacific.

VX-9 was established on 30 April 1994 when VX-4, at Point Mugu, California, and VX-5, at China Lake, were merged. The squadron flies all variants of the F-14 and F/A-18 aircraft.

The VX squadrons fly a variety of aircraft. Two specialized development squadrons—VXE-6 and VXN-8—were numbered in the basic VX series (see below).

Historical: VX-1 had two predecessors. First, the Aircraft Experimental and Development Squadron was established at NAS Anacostia in Washington, D.C., on 13 August 1942. Second, on 1 April 1943, an Air Anti-Submarine Development Detachment was established at Quonset Point, Rhode Island; this unit was recommissioned as

Anti-Submarine Development Squadron 1 in 1946. These units underwent several name changes, and their functions were combined. Air Test and Evaluation Squadron 1 was adopted on 1 January 1969. The squadron was moved to NAS Patuxent River on 15 September 1973.

ANTARCTIC DEVELOPMENT SQUADRON

Squadron	Code	Aircraft	Name
VXE-6	XD	LC-130F/R, TC-130Q	Puckered Penguins

VXE-6, homeported at Point Mugu, California, provides air support of U.S. Antarctic programs sponsored by the National Science Foundation. The squadron flies from McMurdo when operating in Antarctica. It flies two LC-130F and five LC-130R ski-equipped Hercules, plus a "Herk" training aircraft.

The squadron previously operated UH-1N Huey helicopters (fitted with skis). The last VXE-6 UH-1N flight was on 2 February 1996, when the helicopter support role was contracted out to a commercial firm. In 1996 the Navy also began to shift the Antarctic support mission to the 109th Airlift Group, based at Stratton Air National Guard (ANG) Base in Scotia, New York. That ANG group has extensive cold-weather operational experience; it has been flying in the Arctic since 1975 and in the Antarctic since 1988. It will assume all of VXE-6's missions by the year 2000, at which time the Navy squadron will be disestablished.

VXE-6 is the Navy's last active-duty squadron flying the C-130 Hercules except for the Blue Angels.

Historical: The U.S. Navy has had aviation interests in the Antarctic since 1928, when retired Commander Richard E. Byrd took four civilian aircraft on his first expedition to the South Pole.[9] Major Navy support began with Byrd's 1939–1940 expedition, and on his 1947–1948 expedition there were 19 Navy fixed-wing aircraft and four helicopters, including six R4D/C-47 transports that flew from the aircraft carrier PHILIPPINE SEA (CV 47).

Squadron VXE-6 was originally commissioned as Air Development Squadron 6 (VX-6) on 17 January 1955, specifically for Antarctic operations (Operation Deepfreeze). The squadron was redesignated VXE-6 on 1 January 1969.

OCEANOGRAPHIC DEVELOPMENT SQUADRON

Squadron	Code	Aircraft	Notes
VXN-8	JB	RP-3D	disestablished 1 Oct 1993

VXN-8 at NAS Patuxent River operated five RP-3D Orion aircraft in support of worldwide research projects: Project Magnet was a gravity and geomagnetic study; Project Birdseye an ice reconnaissance and physical oceanography study; and Project Seascan an aerial oceanographic effort.

Some of the effort has been taken over by aircraft sponsored by the Naval Research Laboratory (NRL) in Washington, D.C., which operates five research-configured NP-3D aircraft in support of worldwide scientific research projects. Based at NAS Patuxent River, the NRL's NP-3D Orions are extensively modified P-3A/B/C models that support research into gravity and ocean-floor spreading, basic and advanced electronic warfare, space-sensing applications, spaceborne radar, laser projects, and optical systems. These aircraft have the letters NRL and the American flag on their tail fins (no code letters), and they are painted orange and white.

Historical: VXN-8 had its beginnings as Airborne Early Warning Training Unit Atlantic, which, in 1951, was assigned Project Magnet. Projects Birdseye and Outpost Seascan were assigned in 1962 and Project Jenny in July 1965. The last was to provide radio and television broadcasts to South Vietnam pending the completion of ground facilities. Subsequently, the unit became the Oceanographic Airborne Survey Unit and, on 1 July 1967, Air Development Squadron (VX) 8. It was changed to VXN-8 in January 1969.

9. While Byrd was on the expedition, Congress promoted him—on 21 December 1928—to the rank of rear admiral on the retired list.

FLIGHT DEMONSTRATION SQUADRON

Code	Aircraft	Name
BA	F/A-18A/B, TC-130G	Blue Angels

The Blue Angels is the Navy–Marine Corps flight demonstration team that performs throughout the United States to encourage aviation recruiting. The unit currently flies early-model F/A-18 Hornets—eight F/A-18A and one two-seat F/A-18B. The F/A-18s are not carrier capable, have had their guns removed, and are provided with smoke generators, improved flight control systems, and additional navigation equipment.

A Marine-owned TC-130G Hercules is assigned to the team as a support aircraft.

The tail code BA is not shown on Blue Angels aircraft; they have blue-and-gold livery with large numerals indicating the aircraft place in formation.

Historical: Established on 18 April 1946, the unit was designated as the Flight Demonstration Squadron on 1 December 1973. The "Blues" have flown a succession of first-line naval aircraft: F6F Hellcat, F8F Bearcat, F9F-2 and F9F-5 Panther, F9F-6 Cougar, F11F Tiger, F-4J Phantom, A-4F Skyhawk, and, since November 1986, the F/A-18 Hornet.

HELICOPTER COMBAT SUPPORT SQUADRONS

Squadron	Code	Aircraft	Name/Notes
HC-1	UP	SH-3G/D/H, CH-53E	disestablished 29 Apr 1994
HC-2	HU	VH-3A, UH-3H	Circuit Riders
HC-3	SA	HH-46D, CH-46D, UH-46D	Packrats
HC-4	HC	MH-53E	Black Stallions
HC-5	RB	HH-46D	Night Riders
HC-6	HW	CH-46A/D, HH-46D, UH-46A/D	Chargers
HC-8	BR	CH-46A/D, HH-46A, UH-46A/D	Dragon Whales
HC-11	VR	CH-46A/D, HH-46A/D, UH-3H	Gunbearers
HC-16	BF	SH-3D, UH-1N	disestablished 1 Apr 1994

Most of these squadrons provide helicopter detachments for Search and Rescue (SAR) and replenishment (VERTREP/VOD) operations in direct support of the fleet. HC-1 based at NAS North Island had provided SAR helicopters for the command ship BLUE RIDGE (LCC 19) as well as for fleet logistic support and all H-3 helicopter readiness-transition training. The squadron has become HSL-51 Detachment 11. All SH-3 training is now done by HC-2.

HC-2, based at NAS Norfolk, has VH-3A Sea Kings for VIP transport, as well as 12 SH-3H Sea Kings. It gave up two CH-53E Super Stallions used for fleet support. The squadron's Sea Kings provide a VIP ferry service between Norfolk and the Pentagon. The squadron's helicopters serve flagships in the Sixth and Seventh Fleets, as well as the new Fifth Fleet in the Persian Gulf. Since the summer of 1996, HC-2 provides H-3 readiness/transition training.

HC-3 and HC-11 are also at NAS North Island, with HC-3 conducting all Navy readiness-transition training for the H-46 Sea Knight. HC-11 provides a UH-3H for the Commander Third Fleet.

HC-4 at NAS Sigonella, Sicily, provides logistics support for the Sixth Fleet with MH-53Es (having initially flown the CH-53E). In addition, the squadron keeps a pair of helicopters in the Persian Gulf for replenishment operations. (The MH-53Es came from reserve HM-18 and HM-19 when those units combined with active mine countermeasures units.)

HC-5 at Anderson AFB on Guam provides detachments to the Seventh Fleet for VERTREP operations; the squadron, with 12 Sea Knights, also flies a variety of secondary missions on Guam, including SAR, medical evacuation, VIP transport, and support of local police agencies.

HC-6 and HC-8 at NAS Norfolk support Atlantic Fleet ships.

HC-9 was a reserve unit when it was disestablished in 1990.

HC-16 was at NAS Pensacola, having previously been designated HCT-16 from 1974 to 1977. The squadron provided readiness training for Sea Knight crewmen until 1983, when HC-3 took over that role. This, in turn, gave the Pacific Fleet's seagoing VERTREP duties to HC-5 and HC-11. HC-16 then became the readiness squadron for all Navy UH-1N Hueys in addition to providing SAR helicopters for the training carrier in the Gulf of Mexico. With the end of HC-16, all Navy–Marine H-1 training has been assigned to Marine HMT-303.

An SH-3H Sea King hovers above the GEORGE WASHINGTON as an F/A-18C from VFA-106 is taxiing toward a catapult. The venerable Sea King has served in a variety of roles since its fleet introduction in 1961. Few Sea Kings remain in naval service, however, as the ubiquitous H-60 "Hawk" series has taken over most of its roles. (Peter B. Mersky)

Historical: The genesis of these squadrons was VX-3, the Navy's first helicopter squadron, established in 1947.[10] The following year, on 1 April 1948, VX-3 was split into helicopter utility squadrons HU-1 and HU-2, on the East and West Coasts, respectively. All helicopter utility squadrons (HU) were changed to combat support squadrons (HC) on 1 July 1965.

HELICOPTER MINE COUNTERMEASURES SQUADRONS

Squadron	Code	Aircraft	Name/Notes
HM-12	DH	CH/MH-53E	disestablished 30 Sep 1994
HM-14	BJ	MH-53E	Vanguard
HM-15	TB	MH-53E	Blackhawks

HM-14 at NAS Norfolk and HM-15 at NAS Corpus Christi are Airborne Mine Countermeasures (AMCM) squadrons with active and reserve personnel. Originally, HM-14 and HM-16 were established in 1978 for operational deployments, but HM-16 was subsequently disestablished and HM-15 established at Alameda for Pacific operations. (A four-helicopter detachment from HM-15 was previously deployed to Cubi Point in the Philippines until U.S. forces withdrew from there.)

Squadron HM-12 at Norfolk provided AMCM readiness training until it was disestablished in 1994. AMCM flight training is now provided by Marine HMT-302 at MCAS New River, North Carolina.

HM-14 and HM-15 each fly 12 aircraft. HM-15 moved from NAS Alameda to Texas in mid-1996 to support the Mine Warfare Command at Ingleside, Texas.

Reserve HM-18 and HM-19 have been disestablished, and their aircraft and personnel were merged with HM-14 and HM-15 in 1995 and 1994, respectively. This was the first complete merger of active and reserve aviation squadrons in the U.S. Navy.

Historical: The Navy employed helicopters for mine spotting in the Korean War (1950–1953), and beginning in September 1966, squadrons HC-6 and HC-7 provided RH-3A Sea King detachments for mine countermeasures operations. Those helicopters flew from the USS CATSKILL (MCS 1) and OZARK (MCS 2).

HM-12 was established on 1 April 1971 as the world's first helicopter mine countermeasures squadron. Initially flying Navy and Marine CH-53A Sea Stallions and then the specialized RH-53D, HM-12 operated off North Vietnam in 1972 (Operation Endsweep), at the northern end of the Suez Canal in 1974 (Nimbus Star) and again in 1975 (Nimbus Stream), and in the Red Sea in 1984. These squadrons flew MH-53E helicopters in the Persian Gulf area in the late 1980s (escorting Kuwaiti merchant ships) and in Operation Desert Storm and the subsequent mine cleanup.

HELICOPTER ANTI-SUBMARINE SQUADRONS

Squadron	Aircraft	Name
HS-1	SH-60F, HH-60H	Seahorses (AR)
HS-2	SH-60F, HH-60H	Golden Falcons
HS-3	SH-60F, HH-60H	Tridents
HS-4	SH-60F, HH-60H	Black Knights
HS-5	SH-60F, HH-60H	Night Dippers
HS-6	SH-60F, HH-60H	Indians
HS-7	SH-60F, HH-60H	Dusty Dogs (ex-Shamrocks)
HS-8	SH-60F, HH-60H	Eight Ballers
HS-9	SH-3H	disestablished 30 Apr 1992
HS-10	SH-60F, HH-60H	Warhawks (ex-Task Masters) (RA)
HS-11	SH-60F, HH-60H	Dragonslayers
HS-12	SH-3H	disestablished 30 Nov 1994
HS-14	SH-60F, HH-60H	Chargers
HS-15	SH-60F, HH-60H	Red Lions
HS-16	SH-3H	disestablished 1 June 1988
HS-17	SH-3H	disestablished 30 June 1991

Helicopter ASW squadrons are assigned to all carrier air wings; most currently fly four SH-60F Seahawks and two HH-60H combat SAR variants. In addition to ASW, the squadrons provide combat search and rescue, vertical replenishment, passenger transfer, and support to special operations.

HS-10 at NAS North Island handles Navy H-60 readiness-

10. During World War II the Coast Guard undertook helicopter development activities for the Navy.

transition training. HS-1 was the last HS squadron to fly the SH-3 Sea King; it transferred H-3 readiness-transition training to HC-2 in mid-1996. HS-1 will disestablish in early 1997.

Previously, HS units flew the SH-3H Sea King; the first fleet squadron to receive the SH-60F was HS-2, taking delivery in March 1990. Beginning with HS-6 in September 1990, these squadrons were additionally provided with two HH-60H combat SAR helicopters.

Historical: The first helicopter ASW squadron was HS-1, established on 3 October 1951. It flew the Sikorsky HO4S-1 helicopter.

HS-7 made the last SH-3H deployment, aboard the EISENHOWER in early 1995.

LIGHT HELICOPTER ANTI-SUBMARINE SQUADRONS

Squadron	Code	Aircraft	Name/Notes
HSL-30	HT	SH-2F	disestablished 30 Sep 1993
HSL-31	TD	SH-2F	disestablished 31 July 1992
HSL-32	HV	SH-2F	disestablished 31 Jan 1994
HSL-33	TF	SH-2F	disestablished 29 Apr 1994
HSL-34	HX	SH-2F	disestablished 30 Nov 1993
HSL-35	TG	SH-2F	disestablished 4 Dec 1992
HSL-36	HY	SH-2F	disestablished 30 Sep 1992
HSL-37	TH	SH-60B	Easy Riders
HSL-40	HK	SH-60B	Airwolves
HSL-41	TS	SH-60B	Seahawks
HSL-42	HN	SH-60B	Proud Warriors
HSL-43	TT	SH-60B	Battlecats
HSL-44	HP	SH-60B	Swamp Foxes
HSL-45	TE	SH-60B	Wolfpack
HSL-46	HQ	SH-60B	Grand Masters
HSL-47	TY	SH-60B	Saberhawks
HSL-48	HR	SH-60B	Vipers
HSL-49	TX	SH-60B	Scorpions
HSL-51	TA	SH-60B	Warlords

The HSL squadrons provide detachments of ASW helicopters for deployments on board cruisers, destroyers, and frigates. Each operational squadron has 10 to 13 aircraft.

The seven squadrons flying the SH-2F Seasprite have been disbanded; those aircraft flew from active frigates of the KNOX (FF 1052) class and a few cruisers and destroyers. Reserve HSL squadrons now provide SH-2G helicopters for reserve frigates of the OLIVER HAZARD PERRY (FFG 7) class. HSL-30 at NAS Norfolk and HSL-31 at NAS North Island provided SH-2F readiness training for the Atlantic and Pacific squadrons, respectively. HSL-37 at NAS Barbers Point became the only composite SH-2F/SH-60B squadron in early 1992 to support LAMPS operations on Pearl Harbor–based ships. It now flies only the SH-60B.

HSL-51 was established in October 1991 to operate helicopters from Japan-based ships. It is based at Atsugi.

The first Seahawk squadron was HSL-41, established on 21 January 1983 at NAS North Island as the SH-60B readiness-training squadron. The first SH-60B fleet squadrons were established the following year. HSL-40, at Naval Station Mayport, Florida, is the East Coast SH-60B readiness squadron.

Historical: The first SH-2D LAMPS were assigned to helicopter combat support squadrons HC-4 and HC-5, which were redesignated HSL-30 and HSL-31, respectively, on 1 March 1972. The last SH-2F deployment was from HSL-33 in 1994.

HELICOPTER TRAINING SQUADRONS

Squadron	Code	Name	Aircraft	Training
HT-8	E	Eight Ballers	TH-57C	Advanced Helicopter
HT-18	E	Vigilant Eagles	TH-57C	Advanced Helicopter

These squadrons provide helicopter training for Navy, Marine Corps, Coast Guard, and foreign pilots. Students first fly fixed-wing T-34C aircraft before going into helicopters. The squadrons are numbered in the same series as VT squadrons and are part of Training Wing 5.

HT-18 previously operated variants of the H-1 Huey in addition to TH-57A SeaRanger helicopters.

Historical: HT-8 traces its history to HTU-1, established in 1950 and changed to HTG-1 in 1957 and to HT-8 in 1960. HT-18 was established in 1972.

NAVAL AIR STATIONS/NAVAL AVIATION ACTIVITIES

Code	Activity
4L	Naval Air Warfare Center Lakehurst, N.J.
4M	NAS Memphis, Tenn.
7A	NAS Patuxent River, Md.
7B	NAS Atlanta, Ga.
7C	NAS Norfolk, Va.
7D	NAS Fort Worth, Texas
7E	NAS Jacksonville, Fla.
7F	NAS Brunswick, Maine
7G	NAS Whidbey Island, Wash.
7H	NAS Fallon, Nev.
7J	NAS Alameda, Calif.
7L	Naval Air Warfare Center Point Mugu, Calif.
7M	NAS North Island, San Diego, Calif.
7N	NAF Washington, D.C.*
7P	Naval Air Warfare Center China Lake, Calif.
7Q	NAF Key West, Fla.
7R	NAS Oceana, Va.
7S	NAS Lemoore, Calif.
7T	Naval Air Test Center Patuxent River, Md.
7U	NAS Cecil Field, Fla.
7W	NAS Willow Grove, Penna.
7X	NAS New Orleans, La.
7Y	Naval Reserve Selfridge, Mich.
7Z	NAS South Weymouth, Mass.
8A	NAF Atsugi, Japan
8C	NAS Sigonella, Sicily
8D	Naval Station Rota, Spain
8E	Naval Station Roosevelt Roads, P.R.
8F	Naval Station Guantánamo, Cuba
8G	NAF Mildenhall, England
8H	Fleet Activities Okinawa
8J	Naval Station Guam, Marianas
8K	Middle East Force, Bahrain
8M	NAF Misawa, Japan
8N	NAF El Centro, Calif.
8U	Naval Station Mayport, Fla.
SD	Naval Air Test Center Patuxent River, Md.

Note: *NAF Washington is located at Andrews Air Force Base near the Washington suburb of Suitland, Md.

These number-letter codes designate utility and light transport aircraft assigned to the bases and other centers and activities indicated above.

NAVAL AIR RESERVE

The Naval Air Reserve operates approximately 300 aircraft. These are organized primarily into one carrier air wing, nine maritime patrol squadrons, and several helicopter and transport squadrons.

Under the direction of Secretary of the Navy John Lehman, a reserve naval aviator, a major upgrading of reserve aircraft took place in the 1980s, with first-line aircraft being assigned (F-14, F/A-18, A-6E).

All air reserve units are assigned to the Commander, Naval Air Reserve Force, based at New Orleans, Louisiana. The major air reserve subordinate commands are Reserve Patrol Wing Atlantic and Reserve Patrol Wing Pacific that control the VP squadrons; the Reserve Helicopter Wing directs reserve HC, HCS, HSL, and HS squadrons; and the Reserve Tactical Support Wing supervises VR squadrons.

Squadrons within the reserve carrier air wing are designated in sequence based on the wing designation, except for the AEW squadron. Non-carrier air wing squadrons have designations in the standard Navy squadron numerical series. The VF and VFA squadrons are normally assigned 12 aircraft each; the VAQ and VAW squadrons have four aircraft each.

Two reserve carrier air wings (CVWR) were commissioned on 1 April 1970; one has been phased out as part of the post–Cold War reductions. No ASW aircraft (S-3 Viking, SH-3 Sea King, or SH-60 Seahawk) are assigned to the wing (too few S-3 Vikings are available).[11] However, current planning provides for the existing HS (SH-3H) squadrons to be assigned to the carrier wing in wartime. Three reserve helicopter anti-submarine squadrons, which operate from Naval Reserve Force (NRF) frigates, fly the SH-2G LAMPS I helicopter. Three reserve HAL/HC squadrons have been merged to form two combat support squadrons (HCS).

Note that a Marine reserve F/A-18 Hornet squadron and two naval reserve VFC squadrons are now assigned to the reserve air wing.

Bases: The closing of NAS Dallas, Texas, and NAS Glenview, Illinois, and the move of reserve activities to NAS Memphis, Tennessee, is causing a buildup of Navy and Marine aviation units at the newly established NAS Forth Worth, Texas. Fort Worth will be a Joint Reserve Base—hosted by the Navy—with Army, Navy, Marine, Air Force, and Coast Guard reserve units based there.

RESERVE CARRIER AIR WINGS

Wing	Code	Squadron	Aircraft	Location/Notes
CVWR-20	AF	VF-201	F-14A	NAS Fort Worth, Texas
		VF-202	F-14A	disestablished 31 Dec 1994
		VFA-203	F/A-18A	NAS Cecil Field, Fla.*
		VFA-204	F/A-18A	NAS New Orleans, La.
		VMFA-142	F/A-18A	NAS Cecil Field, Fla.*
		VFC-12	F/A-18A/B	NAS Oceana, Va.
		VFC-13	F-5E/F	NAS Fallon, Nev.
		VA-205	A-6E, KA-6D	disestablished 31 Dec 1994
		VAQ-209	EA-6B	NAF Washington, D.C.
		VAW-77	E-2C	NAS Atlanta, Ga.
		VAW-78	E-2C	NAS Norfolk, Va.
CVWR-30	ND	disestablished 31 Dec 1994		
		VF-301	F-14A	disestablished 31 Dec 1994
		VF-302	F-14A	disestablished 31 Dec 1994
		VFA-303	F/A-18	disestablished 31 Dec 1994
		VA-304	A-6E, KA-6D	disestablished 31 Dec 1994
		VFA-305	F/A-18	disestablished 31 Dec 1994
		VAQ-309	EA-6B	disestablished 31 Dec 1994
		VAW-88	E-2C	disestablished 31 Dec 1994

Note: *Scheduled to move to NAS Atlanta, Ga., location of the CVWR-20 wing staff.

ATTACK SQUADRONS

Six reserve VA squadrons—three per wing—flew the A-7E, the last being VA-204, which became VFA-204 on 1 May 1991. Two squadrons traded in their Corsairs for A-6E and KA-6D Intruders—VA-205 and VA-304; the four others shifted to F/A-18 Hornets (see below). Earlier, all six squadrons flew the trouble-plagued A-7B model, and before that, the A-4 Skyhawk.

KA-6D tankers were assigned to these units to replace the KA-3B Skywarrior in the in-flight refueling role.

All reserve VA squadrons are now gone, a harbinger of the active naval air situation.

FIGHTER SQUADRONS

Four reserve fighter squadrons shifted to the F-14A Tomcat in the 1980s, which replaced the F-4 Phantom. VF-301 became the first fully operational reserve F-14A squadron in October 1986. (The last naval squadron to fly the Phantom was VF-202, which transitioned from the F-4S to the F-14A in early 1987.[12]

Three reserve fighter squadrons have been disbanded, with VF-201 (the "Hunters") the only VF survivor of the post–Cold War cutbacks.

STRIKE-FIGHTER SQUADRONS

The F/A-18 Hornet replaced the A-7E Corsairs in four attack squadrons, which became VFA. VA-303 became the first Naval Reserve squadron to fly the F/A-18 Hornet, acquiring its first aircraft in 1985. The two F/A-18 squadrons assigned to CVWR-30 have been disestablished.

FIGHTER COMPOSITE SQUADRONS

The two reserve composite fighter squadrons—VFC-12 and VFC-13—are now assigned to CVWR-20. They provide air combat maneuver training for reserve and active fighter and attack squadrons. Both squadrons previously flew A-4F Skyhawks; they switched to F/A-18s in 1992–1993; VFC-13 now flies only the Tiger II. Prior to being assigned to CVWR-20 the squadrons were assigned tail codes AF and UX, respectively.

Classification: These squadrons were previously designated VC-12 and VC-13, respectively; they were changed to VFC on 22 April 1988 to reflect their emphasis on adversary training.

RECONNAISSANCE SQUADRONS

The last specialized Navy reconnaissance squadron, VFP-206, flying the RF-8G "Photo" Crusader, was disestablished on 1 April 1987. This was a light photoreconnaissance squadron. The unit was based at NAF Washington, D.C. Subsequently, one reserve F-14 squadron in each wing provided a photoreconnaissance capability with TARPS pods (retained in VF-201).

TACTICAL AERIAL REFUELING SQUADRONS

The two reserve tanker squadrons (VAK) have been disestablished: VAK-308 in 1988 and VAK-208 in 1989. These squadrons had been redesignated from tactical EW squadrons (VAQ) to tanker units on 1 October 1979, reflecting the primary role of their Skywarriors. They flew KA-3B and EKA-3B Skywarriors. (The active Navy did not have specialized tanker squadrons.)

TACTICAL ELECTRONIC COUNTERMEASURES SQUADRONS

VAQ-209 and VAQ-309 were established in 1977 and 1979, respectively, to provide the reserve air wings with an organic ECM capability. The reserve VAQ squadrons flew the EA-6A Intruder until 1989, when they began to fly the more capable EA-6B Prowler.

Only VAQ-209 survives. It was additionally assigned the Navy's electronic aggressor role with the disestablishment of active squadron VAQ-33.

Operational: VAQ-209 saw combat over Bosnia in 1995, flying from the carrier THEODORE ROOSEVELT. This was the first fixed-wing reserve squadron to deploy overseas on a carrier since the Korean War.

AIRBORNE EARLY WARNING SQUADRONS

The first E-2C variant of the Hawkeye to be flown by the reserves was assigned to VAW-78 in 1983; VAW-88 began receiving the E-2C in 1986. These squadrons have assisted in U.S. drug enforcement surveillance efforts, as have active AEW squadrons.

A new squadron designated VAW-77 was established on 1 October 1995 at NAS Atlanta. Although assigned to CVWR-20, this is a land-based E-2C squadron intended to support counter-drug operations and to participate in fleet exercises. (It uses the tail letters AF.)

Classification: Note that VAW-78 and VAW-88, both established in 1970, were not numbered in the standard CVWR designation scheme because they were originally assigned to Reserve Carrier Anti-Submarine Air Groups 70 and 80, respectively.

11. When CVWR-20 and CVWR-30 were commissioned, the Navy established two reserve ASW air groups, CVSGR-70 and CVSGR-80, on 1 May 1970.
12. The Phantom flew in the Marine air reserve into 1992.

PATROL SQUADRONS

Squadron	Code	Aircraft	Location/Notes
VP-60	LS	P-3B	disestablished 1 Sep 1994
VP-62	LT	P-3C	NAS Jacksonville, Fla.
VP-64	LU	P-3C	NAS Willow Grove, Penna.
VP-65	PG	P-3C	NAS Point Mugu, Calif.
VP-66	LV	P-3C, EP-3J	NAS Willow Grove, Penna.
VP-67	PL	P-3B	disestablished 30 Sep 1994
VP-68	LW	P-3C	NAF Washington, D.C.
VP-69	PJ	P-3C	NAS Whidbey Island, Wash.
VP-90	LX	P-3B	disestablished 30 Sep 1994
VP-91	PM	P-3C	Moffett Federal Airfield, Mountain View, Calif.
VP-92	LY	P-3C	NAS Brunswick, Maine
VP-93	LH	P-3B	disestablished 30 Sep 1994
VP-94	PZ	P-3C	NAS New Orleans, La.

These squadrons each fly eight Orion patrol aircraft (previously nine). The reserve P-3s regularly supplement active squadrons in U.S. and overseas operational deployments. The reserve VP strength has been reduced from its longstanding strength of 13 squadrons to nine. These squadrons report to Reserve Patrol Wings Atlantic or Pacific (VP-94 has been reporting to ResPatWingPac since 1 April 1994).

VP-94 changed from code LZ to PZ when switched to Pacific Fleet control in 1995. VR-68 is scheduled to disestablish in 1997–1998.

All squadrons fly the P-3C variant; the first to transition to the P-3C from the P-3B was VP-62. The last reserve-flown P-3A was retired by VP-69 in October 1990. VP-67 was the last squadron to fly the SP-2H Neptune, completing transition to the Orion in 1979. In 1993, VP-66 received the two EP-3J aircraft previously flown by VAQ-33.

Two VP Master Augmentation Units (VP-MAU) were based at NAS Brunswick (code LB) and NAS Moffett Field (code PS). These units—using P-3C, UP-3A, and TP-3A Orions—trained crews to augment fleet VP squadrons and often operated detachments overseas. VP-MAU Moffett Field, for example, operated one aircraft and crew in Desert Storm. The two units were disestablished in 1991.

FLEET LOGISTICS SUPPORT SQUADRONS

Squadron	Code	Aircraft	Location/Notes
VR-46	JS	DC-9	NAS Atlanta, Ga.
VR-48	JR	C-20G	NAF Washington, D.C.
VR-51	RV	C-9B	disestablished 30 Sep 1994
VR-52	JT	DC-9	NAS Willow Grove, Penna.
VR-53	WV	C-130T	NAF Washington, D.C.
VR-54	CW	C-130T	NAS New Orleans, La.
VR-55	RU	C-130T	Moffett Federal Airfield, Mountain View, Calif.
VR-56	JU	C-9B	NAS Norfolk, Va.
VR-57	RX	C-9B	NAS North Island, Calif.
VR-58	JV	C-9B	NAS Jacksonville, Fla.
VR-59	RY	C-9B	NAS Fort Worth, Texas
VR-60	RT	DC-9	disestablished 1 Apr 1995
VR-62	JW	C-130T	NAS Brunswick, Maine

These squadrons provide transport support for active and reserve Navy activities within the United States and, on a limited basis, overseas. Five of the squadrons have two or three C-9B aircraft or ex-commercial DC-9 Skytrain aircraft; four squadrons have six C-130T Hercules.

VR-48 in the nation's capital provides C-20G aircraft for VIP flights.

These squadrons have multiple crews for their aircraft.

Historical: VR-48 previously flew the C-131H Samaritan, the last one being retired in mid-1990.

The last C-118 Liftmaster aircraft, long flown by the Naval Reserve, was retired in 1985. (The C-118 was originally designated R6D by the Navy; this was changed in the 1962 redesignation action.[13])

VR originally indicated transport squadrons.

13. This was the military version of the DC-6 transport.

HELICOPTER COMBAT SUPPORT SQUADRONS

Squadron	Code	Aircraft	Location/Notes
HC-9	NW	HH-3A	disestablished 31 July 1990
HC-85	NW	SH-3H, UH-3H	NAS North Island, Calif.

HC-85 operates ASW and utility helicopters capable of flying from carriers with the reserve air wing. Previously designated HS-85, the squadron moved from Alameda to North Island in 1994 to replace squadron HC-1, which provided target/torpedo recovery off San Clemente Island. The squadron received four Sea Kings specially modified for recovery operations and was redesignated HC-85 on 1 October 1994.

HC-9 was the Navy's only active combat SAR unit, flying armed and armored HH-3A Sea Kings. Established in 1975, the squadron was disestablished on 31 July 1990; its mission passed to two reserve squadrons, HCS-4 and HCS-5.

Note that all reserve helicopter squadrons have the code letters NW for the reserve helicopter wing; no helicopter squadrons are assigned to the reserve air wing.

Classification: HC-9 was numbered in the active Navy HC designation series.

HELICOPTER COMBAT SAR/SPECIAL WARFARE SUPPORT SQUADRONS

Squadron	Code	Aircraft	Location
HCS-4	NW	HH-60H	NAS Norfolk, Va.
HCS-5	NW	HH-60H	NAS Point Mugu, Calif.

These squadrons were established in 1989 to provide combat SAR and special warfare support for active and reserve operations. Each squadron flies eight HH-60H Seahawk helicopters. During Operations Desert Shield/Storm in 1990–1991, these two squadrons deployed HH-60H helicopters as a joint unit into Saudi Arabia for combat SAR operations.

The HH-60H is the Navy's only dedicated combat SAR helicopter; it is also being integrated into HS anti-submarine squadrons. (The Coast Guard flies the HH-60J SAR-configured version of the Blackhawk/Seahawk helicopter.)

The HCS squadrons took over the functions of reserve helicopter light attack squadrons HAL-4 and HAL-5, which flew the HH-1K Huey in support of riverine and special operations, and of helicopter composite squadron HC-9, which flew the HH-3A in the combat SAR role. The reserve HALs also had antiterrorist support roles, working with SEAL units.

Historical: HAL-4 and HAL-5 were established in 1976–1977 as helicopter gunship units. The Navy's only active gunship unit was HAL-3, established in 1967 and disestablished in 1972 after extensive service in Vietnam.

HELICOPTER MINE COUNTERMEASURES SQUADRONS

Squadron	Code	Aircraft	Notes
HM-18	NW	RH-53D/MH-53E	disestablished 1 Mar 1995
HM-19	NW	RH-53D/MH-53E	disestablished 5 Nov 1994

Reserve mine countermeasures squadron HM-18 was established in 1986, and HM-19 in 1989. They initially flew the RH-53D Sea Stallion helicopter. They were transitioning to the MH-53E Sea Dragon when the decision was made to merge them with active squadrons HM-14 and HM-15, respectively.

HELICOPTER ANTI-SUBMARINE SQUADRONS

Squadron	Code	Aircraft	Location/Notes
HS-75	NW	SH-3H	NAS Jacksonville, Fla.
HS-85	NW	SH-3H	changed to HC-85

These squadrons operate ASW helicopters capable of flying from carriers with the reserve air wing.

LIGHT HELICOPTER ANTI-SUBMARINE SQUADRONS

Squadron	Code	Aircraft	Location/Notes
HSL-74	NW	SH-2F	disestablished 1 Apr 1994
HSL-84	NW	SH-2G	NAS North Island, Calif.
HSL-94	NW	SH-2G	NAS Willow Grove, Penna.

These are former reserve HS units that previously flew the SH-3G Sea King. They were changed to HSL for the LAMPS role on 1 January 1985, 1 March 1984, and 1 October 1985, respectively. They provide ASW helicopters to NRF frigates.

CHIEF OF NAVAL AIR RESERVE

Several aircraft, mostly C-20s and CT-39s, based at various air stations, have been assigned to the Chief of Naval Air Reserve. These aircraft were formerly assigned to Naval Air Reserve Units (NARU).

Code	Location
6A	NAF Washington, D.C.
6F	NAS Jacksonville, Fla.
6G	NAS Alameda, Calif.
6M	NAS Memphis, Tenn.
6S	NAS Norfolk, Va.

MARINE AVIATION

The U.S. Marine Corps currently operates about 1,000 aircraft in three active aircraft wings, plus about 125 aircraft in a reserve wing. It is the only marine force in the world with a major air arm.[14]

Marine aviation continues to undergo major aircraft changes, with the advanced AV-8B Harrier having replaced the earlier AV-8A/C Short Take-Off/Vertical Landing (STOVL) aircraft, and variants of the F/A-18 Hornet strike-fighter having replaced all A-4 Skyhawk, A-6 Intruder, and RF-4 and F-4 Phantom aircraft.[15] Thus, the F/A-18 has become the most numerous fixed-wing aircraft in the Marine Corps, as it has in the Navy. However, the Marines fly the two-seat F/A-18D variant, a type—so far—eschewed by the Navy.

In the near term the Marine Corps will acquire the long-delayed MV-22 Osprey tilt-rotor STOVL aircraft and, early in the 21st century, the F/A-18E and F variants.

Operational: Marine aviation had a major role in the Gulf War during January–February 1991, with most Marine aircraft flying from shore bases in Saudi Arabia. Harriers flew from the assault ship Nassau in the Persian Gulf, while Marine helicopters flew from more than 30 other U.S. Navy amphibious ships in the Persian Gulf area. (Most Marine air strikes were flown against Iraqi positions in Kuwait, with Marine helicopters and fixed-wing aircraft providing close air support, troop transport, and logistics support to the 1st and 2nd Marine Divisions' drive into Kuwait. There was no amphibious landing in the gulf area, although Marines were flown ashore by helicopter to reinforce those divisions in the drive into Kuwait.)

ORGANIZATION

The Marine Aircraft Wing (MAW) is the major Marine aviation command. There are three active wings and one reserve wing to which all fixed-wing and rotary-wing aircraft are assigned, except for a few utility and cargo aircraft. The wings vary in size and composition; an active wing has a theoretical strength of 325 aircraft of all types. However, only the 2nd and 3rd MAWs actually have full aircraft assignments. The 1st Marine Aircraft Wing is based at Iwakuni, Japan, and Futenma, Okinawa, with most of its aircraft provided on six-month rotation from the other aviation commands, including the newly established 1st MAW Aviation Support Element (Kaneohe), formerly MAG-24 at MCAS Kaneohe Bay, Hawaii.

The 2nd MAW, with headquarters at Cherry Point, North Carolina, has aircraft squadrons based on the East Coast, while the 3rd MAW, with headquarters at MCAS El Toro, California, has its squadrons on the West Coast and at Yuma, Arizona.

In addition to aircraft groups, the Marine aircraft wing contains:

(1) *Marine Wing Headquarters Squadron:* Provides command, administration, and camp facilities for the wing headquarters.

(2) *Marine Air Control Group:* Provides communications, air control, and air support squadrons for the operation of the wing. It also contains a light anti-aircraft missile battalion (with 16 Hawk missile launchers) and a low-altitude air defense battalion (with 90 Stinger missile teams). The air support squadron provides control and coordination for aircraft operating in direct support of Marine ground forces.

(3) *Marine Wing Support Group:* Provides fixed-wing and helicopter maintenance as well as mess, medical, supply, transportation, weather, and airfield services for the wing's components.

An aircraft wing is generally paired with a reinforced division to form a Marine Expeditionary Force (MEF), an aircraft group with a reinforced regiment to form a Marine Expeditionary Brigade (MEB), and a composite squadron with a reinforced battalion to form a Marine Expeditionary Unit (MEU); see chapter 6.

Unlike Navy aircraft wings—in which the principal subordinate command is the squadron—the Marine aircraft wings have several groups. The accompanying chart shows a nominal MAW. The Marine aircraft groups each control specific aircraft squadron types, i.e., fighter and attack, and helicopters.

MAG-70 was established in August 1990 to serve as the aviation vanguard for the deployment of the 7th MEB and 1st MEF in the Persian Gulf area. The advance components of MAG-70 arrived at Shaikh Isa, Bahrain, on 12 August 1990 to supervise the aviation buildup that would reach more than 6,000 personnel. MAG-70 was disbanded on 3 September 1990, when MAG-11 assumed its role for Desert Shield/Desert Storm operations. During Desert Storm all Marine aircraft in Saudi Arabia were assigned to the 3rd MAW, with MAGs 40 and 50 being formed to direct tactical air operations.

A composite squadron generally consists of 4 CH-53, 12 CH-46, 4 AH-1, and 2 UH-1N helicopters deployed on board an LHA/LHD/LPH and accompanying amphibious ships. Additionally, AV-8B Harriers may also be assigned to the squadron, depending upon mission and aircraft and ship availability.

UNIT DESIGNATIONS

The Marine Corps uses the standard naval squadron designation scheme except that the second letter M is used to indicate Marine aviation squadrons; the suffix T indicates Marine readiness-transition squadrons.

Marine CH-46E Sea Knight helicopters are packed tightly on the deck of the Wasp during a dust storm as the helicopter carrier operates off the North African coast. (Lt. Col. P. Croisetiere, USMC)

14. Britain's Royal Marines fly helicopters and light fixed-wing aircraft, while Russian Naval Infantry has some helicopters assigned.
15. The term VSTOL for Vertical/Short Take-Off and Landing was used by the Marine Corps until early 1995, when the less accurate term STOVL was adopted by Headquarters, Marine Corps.

MAG-24 changed to 1st Marine Aircraft Wing Aviation Support Element Kaneohe Bay on 30 September 1994. Its fixed-wing tactical squadrons were reassigned to other MAGs.

The Marine Corps Air Station (MCAS) Kaneohe was changed to Marine Corps Air Facility (MCAF) in 1994.

MCAS Tustin will close down in 1997, at which time MAG-16 and its squadrons, with 118 helicopters and 2,700 Marines, will move to MCAS El Toro, pending completion of permanent facilities for MAG-16 at NAS Miramar, California.

Marine Aircraft Wings	Marine Aircraft Groups	Squadrons	
1st MAW	MAG-12 (Iwakuni)	VMA	(MAW-3)*
		VMAQ	(MAW-2)*
		VMFA	(MAW-2)*
		VMFA	(MAW-3)*
		VMFA (AW)	(MAW-3)*
	MAG-36 (Futenma)	HMH	(MAW-3)*
		HMLA	(MAW-3)*
		VMGR-152	
		HMM-262	
		HMM-265	
	Aviation Support Element (Kaneohe)	HMH-362	
		HMH-363	
		HMH-366	
		HMH-463	
		HMT-301	
2nd MAW	MAG-14 (Cherry Point)	VMAQ-1	
		VMAQ-2	
		VMAQ-3	
		VMAQ-4	
		VMAT-203	
		VMA-223	
		VMA-231	
		VMGR-252	
		VMGRT-253	
		VMA-542	
	MAG-26 (New River)	HMLA-167	
		HMT-204	
		HMM-261	
		HMM-264	
		HMM-266	
		HMH-362	
		HMH-461	
	MAG-29 (New River)	HMM-162	
		HMM-263	
		HMLA-269	
		HMM-365	
		HMH-464	

Note: Asterisks indicate aircraft wing from which these units are rotated.

Marine Aircraft Wings	Marine Aircraft Groups	Squadrons
	MAG-31 (Beaufort)	VMFA-115
2nd MAW (cont.)		VMFA-122
		VMFA(AW)-224
		VMFA-251
		VMFA-312
		VMFA(AW)-332
		VMFA-451
		VMFA(AW)-533
	MAG-32 (Cherry Point); deactivated 30 April 1993	
3rd MAW	MAG-11 (El Toro)	VMFAT-101
		VMFA(AW)-121
		VMFA-212
		VMFA(AW)-225
		VMFA-232
		VMFA-235
		VMFA(AW)-242
		VMFA-314
		VMFA-323
		VMGR-352
		HMM-364
	MAG-13 (Yuma)	VMA-211
		VMA-214
		VMA-311
		VMA-513
	MAG-16 (Tustin)	HMM-161
		HMM-163
		HMM-164
		HMM-166
		HMM-268
		HMT-302
		HMH-361
		HMH-363
		HMH-462
		HMH-465
		HMH-466
	MAG-39 (Camp Pendleton)	HMLA-169
		HMLA-267
		HMT-303
		HMLA-367
		HMLA-369

NOTIONAL MARINE AIRCRAFT WING

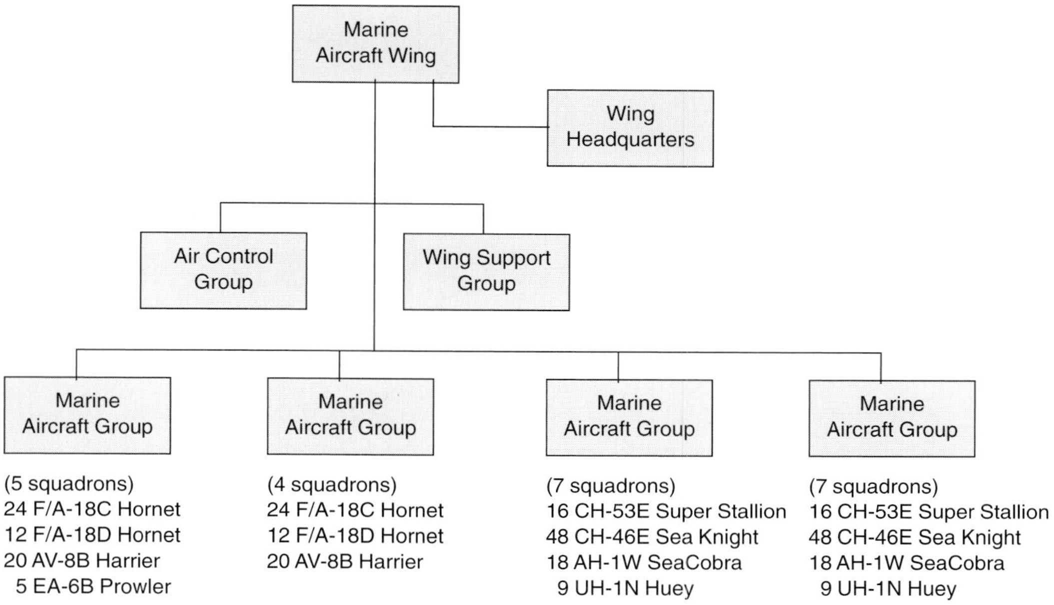

MARINE ATTACK SQUADRONS

Squadron	Code	Aircraft	Notes
VMA(AW)-121	VK	A-6E	changed to VMFA(AW)-121
VMAT-203	KD	AV-8B/TAV-8B	readiness squadron
VMA-211	CF	AV-8B	
VMA-214	WE	AV-8B	
VMA-223	WP	AV-8B	
VMA(AW)-224	WK	A-6E	changed to VMFA(AW)-224
VMA-231	CG	AV-8B	
VMA(AW)-242	DT	A-6E	to VMFA(AW)-242 14 Dec 1990
VMA-311	WL	AV-8B	
VMA-322	QR	A-4M	deactivated 30 June 1992
VMA-331	VL	AV-8B	deactivated 30 Sep 1992
VMA(AW)-332	EA	A-6E	to VMFA(AW)-332 16 June 1993
VMA-513	WF	AV-8B	
VMA(AW)-533	ED	A-6E	to VMFA(AW)-533 1 Oct 1992
VMA-542	CR	AV-8B	

Marine attack squadrons have been reduced to eight units, all flying the AV-8B Harrier. Other squadrons that flew the A-4M Skyhawk or A-6E Intruder have been deactivated or converted to the F/A-18 Hornet. Several A-6E aircraft were transferred to the Navy to make up their shortfall in Intruders.

VMAT-203 at MCAS Cherry Point, North Carolina, provides Harrier readiness-transition training.

Harrier squadrons initially had 15 aircraft; all are receiving 20 aircraft.

History: VMA-513 was the first operational Harrier squadron, with AV-8A deliveries beginning in April 1971. All AV-8A/C models of the Harrier have been retired. VMA-331 was the first AV-8B squadron, established at Cherry Point on 30 January 1985.

The A-6 was flown by the Marines from 1964 until 20 October 1993, when VMA(AW)-332 retired its last A-6E. (Six squadrons plus VMAT-202 had flown the Intruder.)

The A-4 was flown by the Marines from 1957 until 1992.

MARINE ELECTRONIC WARFARE SQUADRONS

Squadron	Code	Aircraft
VMAQ-1	CB	EA-6B
VMAQ-2	CY	EA-6B
VMAQ-3	MD	EA-6B
VMAQ-4	RM	EA-6B

The Marine Corps formed four EW squadrons in 1992, replacing the single active-duty squadron (VMAQ-2 with code CY) and the reserve squadron VMAQ-4 (RM). VMAQ-1 and VMAQ-3 were established on 1 July 1992; VMAQ-4 was deactivated as a reserve unit on 1 October 1992 and reactivated as an active unit the following day. Each of the squadrons has five EA-6B Prowlers assigned.

All four squadrons are at MCAS Cherry Point and provide aircraft or detachments to the 1st and 3rd Wings.

Historical: The Marine Corps originally operated EW and photo-reconnaissance aircraft in three composite reconnaissance squadrons (VMCJ). They were deactivated in 1975 and their aircraft allocated to VMAQ-2 and VMFP-3. VMAQ-2 flew the EA-6A Intruder and then the EA-6B Prowler, providing detachments to the aircraft wings and occasionally to Navy carrier wings.

Operational: VMAQ-3's EA-6B aircraft went ashore at the NATO air base in Aviano, Italy, in November 1994 to begin an almost continuous presence of naval EW aircraft to support Allied air operations over Bosnia. The squadron was succeeded by other Marine and Navy (active and reserve) EA-6B units.

A Marine AH-1 SeaCobra takes off from the deck of the helicopter carrier Kearsarge (LHD 3) as the Marine rescue team prepares to take off in two CH-53E Sea Stallion helicopters to carry out the rescue of Air Force Captain Scott O'Grady, shot down over Bosnia six days earlier, on 2 June 1995. (U.S. Marine Corps, Sgt. Dave A. Garten)

MARINE FIGHTER-ATTACK SQUADRONS

Squadron	Code	Aircraft	Notes
VMFAT-101	SH	F/A-18	readiness squadron
VMFA-115	VE	F/A-18C	
VMFA(AW)-121	VK	F/A-18D	former VMA(AW)-121
VMFA-122	DC	F/A-18C	
VMFA-212	WD	F/A-18C	
VMFA(AW)-224	WK	F/A-18D	former VMA(AW)-224
VMFA(AW)-225	CE	F/A-18D	
VMFA-232	WT	F/A-18C	
VMFA-235	DB	F/A-18C	deactivated 28 June 1996
VMFA(AW)-242	DT	F/A-18D	former VMA(AW)-242
VMFA-251	DW	F/A-18C	
VMFA-312	DR	F/A-18C	
VMFA-314	VW	F/A-18C	
VMFA-323	WS	F/A-18C	
VMFA-332	EA	F/A-18C	former VMA(AW)-332
VMFA-333	DM	F/A-18C	deactivated 31 Mar 1992
VMFA-451	VM	F/A-18C	
VMFA-531	EC	F/A-18C	deactivated 31 Mar 1992
VMFA(AW)-533	ED	F/A-18D	former VMA(AW)-533

The F/A-18 Hornet has succeeded the F-4 Phantom in Marine fighter-attack squadrons. All Marine fighter squadrons have made the transition to the F/A-18A Hornet, the first being VMFA-314, which shifted to the F/A-18 in January 1983. In addition to former VMFA and VMA squadrons that now fly the F/A-18C, five A-6E (VMA[AW]) squadrons have transitioned to the two-place F/A-18D variant. These planes also replaced OA-4M and TA-4F Skyhawks in the tactical air control role.

VMFA squadrons each have 12 aircraft.

VMFAT-101 at MCAS El Toro, California, provides transition-readiness training for Marine *and Navy* F/A-18 pilots.

History: Marine fighter squadrons flew the F-4 from 1961 to 1988. On 1 August 1962 the F-4 squadrons were changed from VMF(AW) to the current VMFA. Proposals to provide the F-14 Tomcat to at least four Marine squadrons were canceled in August 1975 at the request of the Marine Corps (freeing up funds for the procurement of the AV-8A Harrier).

MARINE PHOTORECONNAISSANCE SQUADRONS

The last photoreconnaissance squadron in service with the Navy or Marine Corps, VMFP-3, was deactivated on 10 August 1990. It was the only Navy or Marine squadron to fly the RF-4B Phantom (the U.S. Air Force and German Air Force still fly photoreconnaissance variants of the Phantom).

VMFP-3 flew 21 of the reconnaissance-configured Phantoms. Detachments from the squadron were provided to the other wings (and previously to the carrier MIDWAY).

History: The Marines took delivery of their first RF-4B in 1965.

MARINE REFUELER-TRANSPORT SQUADRONS

Squadron	Code	Aircraft	Notes
VMGR-152	QD	KC-130F	
VMGR-252	BH	KC-130F/R	
VMGR-352	QB	KC-130F/R	
VMGRT-253	GR	KC-130	readiness squadron

These squadrons fly KC-130 Hercules aircraft to provide transport for Marine ground forces and in-flight refueling. One Marine KC-130F "Herk" supports the Navy-Marine Blue Angels flight demonstration team. Each squadron is authorized 12 aircraft.

VMGRT "training" squadron 253 was established at MCAS Cherry Point on 1 October 1986.

VMGR-152 is one of only two aircraft squadrons permanently assigned to the 1st MAW.

MARINE OBSERVATION SQUADRONS

Squadron	Code	Aircraft	Notes
VMO-1	ER	OV-10D	deactivated 31 July 1993
VMO-2	UU	OV-10D	deactivated 20 May 1993

The two Marine observation squadrons flew the STOL-capable OV-10 Bronco. Unlike previous Marine observation aircraft, the Bronco could be heavily armed. Twelve aircraft were assigned to each squadron. (The Navy's lone light attack squadron, VAL-4, flew Broncos during the Vietnam War.)

The VMO mission was taken over by the F/A-18D squadrons.

UNMANNED AERIAL VEHICLE SQUADRONS

Two Marine Unmanned Aerial Vehicle (UAV) squadrons were established on 15 January 1996; VMU-2 at MCAS Cherry Point, North Carolina, and VMU-1 at MCAS Yuma, Arizona. Previously, Marine UAVs were operated by remotely piloted vehicles companies. (Each company consisted of 10 Marine officers, 56 Marine enlisted personnel, and 1 Navy hospital corpsman.) Earlier UAV platoons were the primary drone operating units.

VMU-1 was deployed to Bosnia in June 1996 to support the Army's 1st Armored Division. The squadron had five Pioneer drones and 140 personnel, plus about 50 support personnel from the I Marine Expeditionary Force when it deployed.

MARINE HEAVY HELICOPTER SQUADRONS

Squadron	Code	Aircraft	Notes
HMT-301		CH-53D	readiness squadron; activated 30 Sep 1995
HMT-302	UT	CH/MH-53E	readiness squadron
HMH-361	YN	CH-53E	
HMH-362	YL	CH-53D	
HMH-363	YZ	CH-53D	
HMH-366	HH	CH-53D	activated 30 Sep 1994
HMH-461	CJ	CH-53E	
HMH-462	YF	CH-53E	
HMH-463	YH	CH-53D	
HMH-464	EN	CH-53E	
HMH-465	YJ	CH-53E	
HMH-466	YK	CH-53E	

These 12 squadrons fly the three-engine CH-53E Super Stallion or the twin-engine CH-53D Sea Stallion. Each unit has eight helicopters. The first CH-53E squadron was HMH-464, activated at New River on 27 February 1981. HMT-302, at MCAS Tustin, California, serves as the CH-53E readiness-transition squadron for both Navy and Marine H-53E flight crew training, including Airborne Mine Countermeasures (AMCM) for the Navy. Navy personnel are assigned to the squadron, which took over the Navy training role in 1994. The CH-53D will be replaced by the E variant in all HMH squadrons.

HMT-301 was established on 30 September 1995 at Kaneoohe Bay, Hawaii, to provide CH-53D readiness training. All D variants of the CH-53 will be based there.

MARINE UTILITY AND ATTACK HELICOPTER SQUADRONS

Squadron	Code	Aircraft	Notes
HMLA-167	TV	AH-1W, UH-1N	
HMLA-169	SN	AH-1W, UH-1N	
HMLA-267	UV	AH-1W, UH-1N	
HMLA-269	HF	AH-1W, UH-1N	
HMT-303	QT	AH-1W, UH-1N	readiness squadron
HMLA-367	VT	AH-1W, UH-1N	
HMLA-369	SM	AH-1W, UH-1N	

The Marine light (HML) and attack (HMA) helicopter squadrons were combined, beginning on 1 April 1986, to facilitate the deployment of detachments of combined troop-carrying/command UH-1N Huey helicopters and AH-1W SeaCobra gunships. The last of these squadrons made the transition from the AH-1J/T to the AH-1W model in the early 1990s. Each unit has 18 AH-1W and nine UH-1N helicopters.

HMT-303 provides helicopter readiness training for both helicopter types. With the disestablishment of Navy HC-16 in 1994, all Navy-Marine UH-1N training was assigned to HMT-303.

MARINE MEDIUM HELICOPTER SQUADRONS

Squadron	Code	Aircraft	Notes
HMT-301	US	CH-46E	deactivated 31 Dec 1993
HMM-161	YR	CH-46E	
HMM-162	YS	CH-46E	
HMM-163	YP	CH-46E	
HMM-164	YT	CH-46E	
HMM-165	YW	CH-46E	
HMM-166	YX	CH-46E	
HMT-204	GX	CH-46E	readiness squadron
HMM-261	EM	CH-46E	
HMM-262	ET	CH-46E	
HMM-263	EG	CH-46E	
HMM-264	EH	CH-46E	
HMM-265	EP	CH-46E	
HMM-266	ES	CH-46E	
HMM-268	YQ	CH-46E	
HMM-364	PF	CH-46E	
HMM-365	YM	CH-46E	

Each medium helicopter squadron flies 12 Sea Knight helicopters; this number has been reduced from 18 in some units. The CH-46 is scheduled for eventual replacement by the MV-22 Osprey tilt-rotor aircraft.

HMT-204 provides all CH-46E readiness-transition training. It will be the first Marine squadron to receive the MV-22, with an operating capability to be achieved about the year 2001. The first 12 MV-22s will be assigned to this unit. HMT-301, previously the CH-46 transition squadron, has become a CH-53D squadron; see page 23.

History: Established on 15 January 1951, HMM-161 was the first Marine tactical helicopter squadron. It flew the Sikorsky HRS-1.

Operational: Due to an administrative oversight, HMM-262 and Navy VQ-6 both have the same tail code—ET. VQ-6 was assigned the code after HMM-262 was inadvertently omitted from the official code assignment chart. HMT-301 is assigned the code US according to official documents, but the squadron uses SU on its aircraft.

MARINE HELICOPTER SQUADRONS

Squadron	Code	Aircraft
HMX-1	MX	VH-3D, VH-60N, CH-46E, CH-53D/E

This unique squadron, based at MCAS Quantico, Virginia, fulfills a variety of development and operational functions, including providing helicopter transport for the president with its VH-3D Sea Kings. With the president embarked, a helicopter is designated *Marine One.*

HMX-1 is the only Marine unit to operate the H-60 Black Hawk/Seahawk helicopter.

History: This squadron—sometimes incorrectly called Marine Helicopter *Experimental* Squadron 1 or Marine *Development* Squadron 1—was established on 1 December 1947 to develop helicopter assault tactics for the Marine Corps. HMX-1 began providing helicopter transportation for presidents in September 1957, when a UH-34 from HMX-1 carried President Dwight D. Eisenhower from Newport, Rhode Island, to NAS Quonset Point, Connecticut.[16]

MARINE AIR RESERVE

The Marine Air Reserve consists of the 4th Marine Aircraft Wing, plus a few detachments. The wing, organized similarly to the active MAWs, has about 125 aircraft.

In addition to the aircraft squadrons indicated for the 4th MAW, there are various wing command and support aircraft as well as a detachment of C-12 utility aircraft. (The wing headquarters has the tail code EZ.)

16. President Eisenhower became the first U.S. president to fly in a helicopter, on 12 July 1957.

4TH MARINE AIRCRAFT WING

Group	Squadron	Code	Aircraft	Location
MAG-41	VMFA-112	MA	F/A-18A	NAS Fort Worth, Texas
	VMGR-234	QH	KC-130T	NAS Fort Worth, Texas
MAG-42	VMFA-142	MB	F/A-18A	NAS Cecil Field, Fla.
	HMLA-773	MP	AH-1W, UH-1N	NAS Atlanta, Ga.
	HMM-774	MQ	CH-46E	NAS Norfolk, Va.
MAG-46	VMFA-134	MF	F/A-18A	MCAS El Toro, Calif.
	VMFT-401	WB	F-5E/F	MCAS Yuma, Ariz.
	HMM-764	ML	CH-46E	MCAS El Toro, Calif.
	HMH-769	MS	CH-53E	NAS Alameda, Calif.
	HMLA-775	WR	AH-1W/UH-1N	MCAS Camp Pendleton, Calif.
MAG-49	VMFA-321	MG	F/A-18A	NAF Washington, D.C.
	VMGR-452	NY	KC-130	Stewart AFB, N.Y.
	HMH-772	MT	RH-53D	NAS Willow Grove, Penna.

MARINE ATTACK SQUADRONS

VMA-131 was the last Navy-Marine squadron to fly the single-seat A-4 Skyhawk, retiring its last A-4M "Scooter" in 1992. The squadron—thereafter held in service by congressional edict—was deactivated on 30 September 1996; VMFA-124 was deactivated on the same date.

VMA-133 and VMA-322, flying the A-4M Skyhawk, were deactivated during 1992.

MARINE ELECTRONIC WARFARE SQUADRONS

VMAQ-4 became an active EW squadron in 1992.

MARINE FIGHTER SQUADRONS

VMFA-112 was the last U.S. Navy-Marine squadron to fly the versatile Phantom, the F-4S variant in this instance. The squadron—called the "Cowboys"—converted to F/A-18s in late 1992.

Fighter readiness-training squadron VMFT-401 was established on 21 March 1986 to provide adversary training aircraft for active and reserve Marine squadrons. The squadron—nicknamed "Snipers"—initially flew 13 F-21A Kfir fighters leased from Israel Aircraft Industries from June 1987 until September 1989. They were replaced by 12 F-5E Tiger II and one F-5F aircraft for adversary training.

MARINE OBSERVATION SQUADRONS

The last Marine OV-10 squadron, VMO-4, was deactivated on 30 July 1994.

MARINE HEAVY HELICOPTER SQUADRONS

HMH-769 was activated on 1 April 1993 from Detachment A of HMH-772. Deactivated on the same date were HMH-769 and HMH-772, both flying ex-Navy RH-53D Sea Stallion mine countermeasures helicopters.

MARINE UTILITY AND ATTACK HELICOPTER SQUADRONS

HMA-767 was disestablished on 1 August 1994. HMA-773 changed to HMLA-773 on 1 July 1994, and HMA-775 changed to HMLA-775 on 1 August 1994.

HML-771 at NAS South Weymouth, Massachusetts, flying the UH-1N, was deactivated on 1 August 1994, and HML-776 at NAS Glenview, Illinois, flying the UH-1N, was deactivated on 1 July 1994.

MARINE CORPS AIR STATION AIRCRAFT

Code	Location
5A	NAF Washington, D.C.
5B	MCAS Beaufort, N.C.
5C	MCAS Cherry Point, N.C.
5D	MCAS New River, N.C.
5F	MCAS Futenma, Okinawa
5G	MCAS Iwakuni, Japan
5T	MCAS El Toro, Calif.
5Y	MCAS Yuma, Ariz.

These are mostly administrative and training aircraft, both fixed-wing (UC-12B, CT-39G, C-9B) and helicopter (HH-46A, UH-1N) types.

HH-60H search-and-rescue variants of the Seahawk helicopter are now assigned to helicopter anti-submarine squadrons (HS) aboard aircraft carriers. Beyond their SAR role, these aircraft serve as VERTREP helicopters, like the HH-60H from HS-6 shown here loading cargo on the deck of the Abraham Lincoln while operating in the western Pacific. (U.S. Navy, PH3 Russell S. Cramer)

CHAPTER 29

Naval Aircraft

The first F/A-18E "Super Hornet," with an F/A-18C behind it. The E/F variants are 25 percent larger than their predecessors. The larger size provides increased performance and payload. These planes will be the backbone of U.S. carrier and Marine aviation in the coming years. (McDonnell Douglas, Rich Rau)

This chapter describes the aircraft flown by the U.S. Navy, Marine Corps, and Coast Guard. The Unmanned Aerial Vehicle (UAV), formerly called the Remotely Piloted Vehicle (RPV), or drone, programs are described at the end of this chapter.

The procurement of naval aircraft, both types and numbers, has been severely reduced in the past few years, not only because of the improving world situation but also severe U.S. budget constraints. Further, a combination of technical problems and Navy mismanagement of aircraft programs has caused the cancellation of several aircraft, among them the new attack aircraft projects and the P-7 maritime patrol aircraft. Further F-14 Tomcat fighter production as well as "remanufacture" of the F-14A to the F-14D configuration have also stopped.

The halting of the A-12 effort, following cancellation of the proposed A-6F and A-6G variants of the Intruder, as well as the stillborn AX follow-on to the A-12, have ended the 50-year era of specialized attack aircraft in the U.S. Navy. The last A-6E Intruders will be withdrawn from naval service in 1996. Consequently, the most capable naval strike aircraft flown by the Navy and Marine Corps will be the multipurpose F/A-18 Hornet.

Only three fixed-wing aircraft are now being procured by the Navy and Marine Corps: the E-2C Hawkeye radar aircraft, the F/A-18 Hornet strike-fighter in the C and D models, and the T-45A Goshawk trainer. The production of five helicopters is coming to a close: the AH-1W SeaCobra, the HH-60H and SH-60B Seahawk, and the CH-53E (Super Stallion) and MH-53E (Sea Dragon) helicopters.

With the fiscal 1997 procurement, the F/A-18 production is scheduled to make a transition to the E and F models, the one- and two-seat variants of the advanced Hornet. Also, production of the long-delayed MV-22 Osprey, a tilt-rotor replacement for Marine assault helicopters, is scheduled to begin with the fiscal 1997 aircraft buy.

Navy aircraft "procurement" planning also lists two remanufacture projects: the upgrading of the AV-8B Harrier STOVL aircraft to a "Plus" configuration, and the combining of capabilities of the two ASW variants of the Seahawk—the SH-60B (LAMPS III) and SH-60F (carrier-based)—into a single airframe, designated SH-60R.

Beyond these aircraft, the Navy plans in the 21st century to procure a training aircraft developed under the Joint Primary Aircraft Training System (JPATS) and a strike-fighter aircraft derived from the Joint Advanced Strike Technology (JAST) program. These are both joint Air Force–Navy programs, described below.

Historically, the Marine Corps and Coast Guard have flown Navy aircraft; however, during the 1980s both the Marines and Coast Guard sponsored the procurement of aircraft not acquired by the Navy, principally the AV-8 Harrier series for the Marines and the HU-25 Guardian reconnaissance aircraft and HH-65 Dolphin helicopter for the Coast Guard. All of those programs are completed, although new engines are being installed in the HH-65 helicopters. (The original AV-8A Harrier has been replaced in Marine service by the advanced AV-8B aircraft.)

Planned Navy-Marine aircraft procurement is listed in chapter 1.

AIRCRAFT DESIGNATIONS

The current U.S. military aircraft designation scheme, adopted in 1962, is relatively simple, and the prefix and suffix letters provide considerable detail. But confusion persists as the old and new schemes are mixed or written incorrectly. For example, the McDonnell Douglas F-4B Phantom was often written incorrectly as F4B, which was a Boeing fighter of the 1920s. Similarly, the F4F Wildcat of World War II fame is often written incorrectly as F-4F, the U.S. designation used for F-4 Phantoms configured for West Germany. The phasing out of pre-1962 aircraft, however, will soon alleviate this problem with the current designation scheme.

The military services have also corrupted the system in major ways. The most numerous aircraft in the Navy–Marine Corps inventory—the F/A-18 Hornet—carries an unofficial designation that violates the prescribed designation scheme. In 1975, three years before the first Hornet flew, Vice Admiral William D. Houser, then Deputy Chief of Naval Operations (Air), determined that the designation F-18 would be used for the fighter variant and A-18 for the attack variant.[1] On 5 September 1978, however, shortly before the first Hornet flight, Houser's successor, Vice Admiral Frederick C. Turner, wrote to the Commander, Naval Air Systems Command, stating his preference for the designation F/A-18, which did not follow the official aircraft designation guidance.

> My choice, F/A-18, would be based not so much on conformance with existing directives as with the necessity to designate this aircraft so that it truly reflects its multimission nature. Certainly the designation F-18 is in consonance with the tri-service instruction. . . . I prefer to continue [with F/A-18] even though it may be one that receives its legitimacy through use rather than directive.[2]

The U.S. military services do not follow the 1962 designation system in other respects as well. For example, a new helicopter series was established, beginning with H-1 (formerly the HU-1); that series reached only H-6 before the services began adding to the abandoned Air Force series with H-54 and above. More severe violations have been made by the Air Force, with fighter-series numbers above F-111 being assigned, although a new series had begun with the F-1 and was carried through to the F-23.

Similarly, the 1962 system dictated that the "next" training aircraft would be designated T-41. That was done, with successive training aircraft reaching number T-47. Under the 1962 system, the Navy's T2V-1 Sea Star, a navalized version of the T-33, became the T-1. However, in 1992 the Air Force began receiving a new undergraduate pilot training aircraft, which was designated the T-1A Jayhawk. This was the most flagrant violation of the 1962 Department of Defense directive on designations.

The T-2 was a Navy training aircraft, formerly the T2J Buckeye. The Air Force has subsequently added the designation T-3 to the list, the T-3A Firefly being a flight screening aircraft.

Modifications to aircraft, which in the past have added a new suffix numeral or letter, now have such confusing designations as the P-3C Update III, EA-6B ICAP, and EP-3E Aries II aircraft.

Also, whereas the original 1962 scheme used the prefix M for missile-carrying aircraft, the prefix M now indicates multipurpose aircraft, such as the MH-53E Sea Dragon.

Historical: From 1922 to 1962 the Navy had its own designation scheme that indicated the aircraft mission, the sequence of that aircraft type produced by the manufacturer, the manufacturer's name, (hyphen) the model, and the modification. Thus, the AD-2N indicated the first series of attack aircraft (the "1" omitted) built by Douglas, the second model (2), modified for night operation (N); the second Douglas attack aircraft was A2D, the third A3D, etc.

That scheme became unwieldy as the number of manufacturers of naval aircraft increased. For example, the letter F was used for Grumman (as F9F) because G was already assigned to Gallaudet; Y was used for Consolidated (as PBY), C for Curtiss (and, later, Cessna and Culver); A designated Brewster (as F2A) because B was previously assigned to Boeing (and, later, Beech and Budd Manufacturing). To further complicate the situation, the same aircraft flown by different services had different designations. The famed Boeing B-29 Superfortress had the Navy designation P2B, the North American B-25 was used by the Navy and Marine Corps as the PBJ, and the McDonnell Phantom II entered service as the F4H in the Navy and F-110 in the Air Force.

The U.S. Air Force and Army have used different designation schemes for their respective aircraft since the establishment of the Air Force as a separate service in 1947. (Previously, the Air Force was the U.S. Army Air Forces.)

A unified scheme for U.S. military aircraft went into effect on 1 October 1962 when all existing and new military aircraft were redesignated in a new, simplified series, almost all beginning with the

1. Vice Adm. Houser, "Memorandum for the Chief of Naval Operations," Memo 05/187 (30 October 1975).
2. Vice Adm. Turner, "Memorandum for the Commander, Naval Air Systems Command," ser. 506C5/781084, 5 September 1978. A full discussion of the designation issue may be found in James P. Stevenson, *The Pentagon Paradox: The Development of the F-18 Hornet* (Annapolis, Md: Naval Institute Press, 1993). This excellent book is a program history of the F/A-18.

series number one. The Navy-flown AD Skyraider became the first plane in the new attack series, the A-1; the Navy's TF Trader started the new cargo series as C-1; the FJ Fury became the F-1; the T2V Sea Star the T-1; and the UC-1 Otter the U-1.[3]

There was no P-1 or S-1, as the new system picked up the Navy's P2V Neptune and S2F Tracker as the P-2 and S-2, respectively. The improved P3V Orion was the obvious candidate for P-3 and the P5M Marlin, the Navy's last combat flying boat, for P-5. The designation P-4 was used, albeit briefly, for the drone versions of the Privateer (the P4Y-2K, formerly PB4Y-2). The designations P-4 and P-6 are sometimes cited as having been reserved for the P4M Mercator and the P6M Seamaster. But the last of the combination piston-turbojet Mercators were gone by 1962, and the turbojet Seamaster flying boat had been canceled in 1959. The next patrol aircraft was to be the P-7 (which was the canceled Long-Range Air Anti-submarine warfare Capable Aircraft [LRAACA]).

The 1962 system also introduced the mission designation of special electronic E-series aircraft. The first two planes were Navy: the WF-2 Tracer became the E-1B and the W2F-1 Hawkeye the E-2A.

Variations of the previous Air Force X (for experimental) and V (for VSTOL) designations remained, but official records differ as to which aircraft were part of the old or new series. The Marine AV-8 Harrier is officially in the V series, but apparently the designation A-8 was avoided to reduce confusion. In the V series, however, the Ryan "flying jeep" had already been designated XV-8. The latter program never took off, hence the "8" spot is firmly held by the successful Harrier series.

Planes that were used by both services, such as the Albatross seaplane (Navy UF), generally took on the existing Air Force numerical designation (U-16, formerly SA-16). But the Phantom was recent enough to be given a new designation, the now-familiar F-4, and not the Air Force F-110.

Helicopters proved a more confusing issue because the Army also had its own helicopter designation system before 1962 in addition to those of the Navy–Marine Corps and Air Force. The Sea Knight was the Navy HRB, while the Army called that helicopter the HC-1A (HC for helicopter—cargo). This became the H-46 in the new scheme. The Army's HU-1 Iroquois (HU for helicopter—utility) started the new helicopter series as H-1, with most of the Army and Air Force designations being merged to form the new H series. Navy helicopters were "stuck in" to fill the gaps. The Kaman HU2K became the H-2 and the Sikorsky HSS-2 the H-3, but the Navy-Marine HSS-1/HUS, being similar to the Army–Air Force H-34, took on that designation.

Further, after the new H-series reached H-6, the military reverted to simply adding to the larger numerical series, i.e., H-54 and above.

The accompanying diagram explains the current aircraft designation scheme.

3. The U-2 spy plane was given a utility designation in an effort to hide its real purpose.

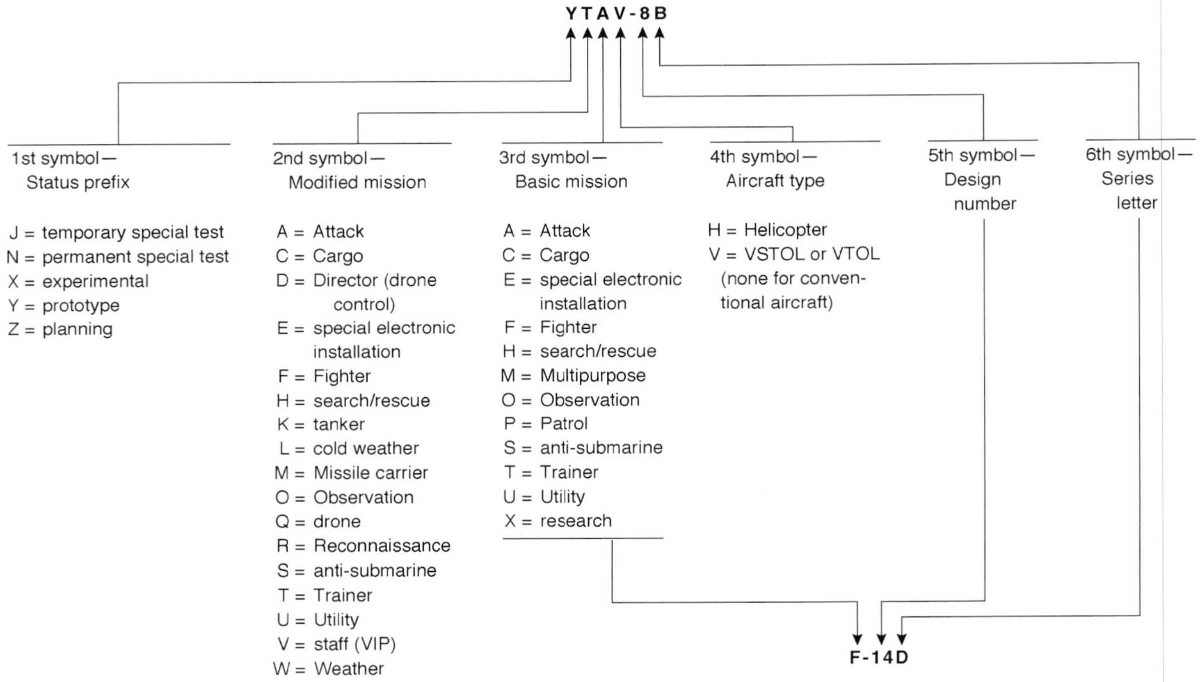

NOTE: Letters I and O are not used as series letters to avoid confusing them with numerals.

AIRCRAFT MARKINGS

Unit markings: These indicate wing, squadron, or base assignment; they consist of letters or letter-number combinations on the tail fin or after body of the aircraft (see chapter 28 for codes).

Side numbers: Generally on the fuselage and upper right and lower left wings, these numbers indicate the aircraft position in a particular squadron or other unit. The side number sequence for carrier air wings is shown on page 336.

Bureau numbers: Assigned to all Navy and Marine Corps aircraft in sequence of their procurement, these numbers are used on the aircraft's after fuselage or tail. On transports, the last three digits are sometimes used as their side numbers. "Bureau" refers to the Bureau of Aeronautics, which directed naval aircraft procurement from 1921 to 1959, when it became the Bureau of Naval Ordnance and, in 1966, the Naval Air Systems Command.

National insignia: The U.S. national insignia consists of a white star within a blue circle, with white rectangles on either side. Those rectangles have a red horizontal stripe and blue border. All naval aircraft have the national insignia on both sides of the fuselage; fixed-wing aircraft also bear it on the upper left and lower right wing surfaces. Most U.S. tactical aircraft now have low-visibility national markings (i.e., no color).

Coast Guard aircraft have the national insignia or an American flag on their tail fin. Some U.S. Navy Carrier On-board Delivery (COD) and other transport aircraft also display the American flag on their fin. Coast Guard aircraft wear that service's wide orange and narrow blue stripe insignia on the forward fuselage with the Coast Guard crest on the orange stripe.

These aircraft have a four-digit side number based on their (Coast Guard) procurement sequence.

ATTACK AIRCRAFT

Specialized attack aircraft are being phased out of naval aviation, except for the AV-8B Harrier, which the Marine Corps will operate well into the 21st century.

Into early 1996 the Navy's few surviving attack squadrons (VA) flew the A-6E Intruder. That plane will be retired in 1996, ending the 50-year history of VA aircraft in the U.S. Navy. (Some TA-4J Skyhawks, training variants of the famed A-4 light attack aircraft, will remain in the service for the next few years.) Subsequently, attack missions will be carried out by the multipurpose F/A-18 Hornet and the small number of F-14 Tomcats that have a limited strike capability.

Several efforts to develop a specialized successor to the A-6 Intruder have either been aborted or were stillborn. The latest was the Navy's A/F-X program, initiated in the early 1990s after the demise of the AX. The A/F-X was a study effort that quickly fell victim to another paper airplane, the so-called Joint Attack Fighter (JAF), an Air Force–sponsored conceptual aircraft. The JAF was to have a range of about 575 miles (926.5 km) carrying a payload goal of four internal air-to-air missiles and up to four external 2,000-pound (907-kg) air-to-surface weapons. The aircraft was to have a low radar cross section and other stealth characteristics. The Air Force examined derivatives of its F-22 fighter aircraft for the JAF requirements.

JOINT ADVANCED STRIKE TECHNOLOGY PROGRAM

The Joint Advanced Strike Technology (JAST) program, a Department of Defense–sponsored effort to develop a tactical strike-fighter, has succeeded the JAF concept. This aircraft, which will employ a variety of advanced technologies, is intended for use by the Air Force, Navy, and Marine Corps, as well as allied air forces.[4] A first prototype flight is planned for the year 2000 and Initial Operational Capability (IOC) in 2010.

The JAST program has been budgeted at $2.3 *billion* through 1999. The total procurement currently envisioned is approximately 3,000 aircraft for the U.S. Air Force, Navy, and Marine Corps, and the Royal Navy.

In 1994 Congress incorporated the related Advanced STOVL (ASTOVL) program into the JAST effort. It is unlikely, however, that the ASTOVL aircraft, being developed primarily for the Marine Corps as a replacement for the AV-8B Harrier, can meet Navy and Air Force strike-fighter requirements (see below).

Under the JAST effort Congress has provided funds to provide an evaluation of a carrier version of the Air Force–Lockheed F-117 stealth strike aircraft.[5] Given the unofficial designation F/A-117X, a carrier variant of the Lockheed aircraft would have to be extensively redesigned from the Air Force F-117A with the following changes:

- provide F414 series afterburning engines in place of the Air Force's F404-GE-F1D2 non-augmented engines
- increase wing span from 43.4 feet (13.23 m) to 61 feet (18.6 m)
- add horizontal stabilizers
- reduce wing sweep angle
- increase length from 66 feet (20.1 m) to 67 feet (20.4 m)
- increase height from 12 5/12 feet (3.79 m) to 17 feet (5.18 m)
- expand lower fuselage to provide larger internal weapons carriage from 4,000 pounds (1,814 kg) to 10,000 pounds (4,536 kg)
- provide fittings for four external payload points for 8,000 pounds (3,629 kg) of stores; although external carriage would destroy the stealth characteristics of the aircraft, the additional payload

4. The U.S. Air Force JAST aircraft is proposed to replace the F-15E Strike Eagle, F-16 Fighting Falcon, and the F-117 stealth attack aircraft.
5. The U.S. Air Force, long eschewing the term "attack aircraft," has insisted on designating strike aircraft in the F (fighter) series. This included such aircraft as the F-105 Thunderchief, F-111, and F-117.

The proposed JAST aircraft would have a very high thrust-to-weight ratio, permitting launch from inclined ski-ramps on carriers and thus reducing dependence on catapults. However, the challenge of developing a single basic aircraft design to meet Navy, Marine Corps, and Air Force requirements is considerable. (Northrop Grumman)

would be useful in later stages of a conflict when stealth requirements are less critical.

(Other weapon-delivery alternatives are to "shape" weapons for external carriage with reduced radar cross sections or to fit them in a "blister" bay on the wings or to coat the weapons with spray-on Radar Absorbing Material [RAM].)

These and other changes to adapt the F-117A to naval use would increase the weight of the aircraft from the F-117A's maximum takeoff weight of 52,500 pounds (23,814 kg) to a maximum launch weight of 68,750 pounds (31,185 kg), i.e., in the range of the A3D/A-3 Skywarrior attack aircraft. While the naval F/A-117X would be larger than the standard F-117A, improvements in stealth technology would provide a *smaller* radar cross section at lower radar frequencies.

Lockheed had earlier proposed a naval version of the F-117 to replace the canceled A-12, the seagoing stealth aircraft then being dubbed Sea Hawk by the firm. The earlier recommendation called for strengthening the F-117's landing gear and fuselage and adding a tail hook and catapult fittings, but otherwise retaining the basic aircraft. That concept was rejected by the Navy as being unsuitable for carrier operation, mainly because of its approach speed of more than 172.5 mph (278 km/h) and its failure to meet naval requirements. (The proposed F/A-117X would have an approach speed of 155.25 mph/250 km/h.)

The new proposal from the firm—now Lockheed Martin—is unlikely to reach fruition because of the high cost of redesign and the questionable effectiveness of a navalized F-117 in comparison to a new-design carrier attack aircraft. And, of course, the Navy has staunchly resisted adopting aircraft that it did not develop for use aboard carriers.[6]

6. The U.S. Air Force and other nations' air forces have successfully adopted several U.S. carrier aircraft—albeit sometimes under protest. The more successful have been the F-4 Phantom, A-3 Skywarrior, A-4 Skyhawk, A-7 Corsair, and E-2 Hawkeye.

The F-117A stealth "fighter" has been proposed for the carrier-based JAST role. The night-only attack aircraft was used without effect in the U.S. occupation of Panama and, with some success, in the Gulf War in 1991. (U.S. Air Force)

ADVANCED STOVL STRIKE-FIGHTER

The Navy has a continuing interest in studies of an Advanced Short Take-Off Vertical Landing (ASTOVL) strike-fighter aircraft, primarily as a replacement for the Marine AV-8B Harrier. The current research effort, announced early in 1992, follows several earlier, unsuccessful efforts to develop a high-performance VSTOL-type aircraft, including the aborted AV-18 Advanced Harrier and XFV-12A

Another view of the proposed JAST aircraft. The Advanced STOVL program has been folded into the JAST program. The latter effort is important as a follow-on to the Marines' AV-8B Harrier. (McDonnell Douglas)

(see 14th Edition/pages 403 and 443). Tentative IOC for the ASTOVL aircraft is 2005.

Studies and development of demonstration aircraft are being undertaken by teams led by the Lockheed Martin and the McDonnell Douglas firms under sponsorship of the Advanced Research Projects Agency (ARPA) and the National Aeronautics and Space Administration (NASA). These efforts include McDonnell Douglas developing and building a full-scale wind tunnel model with an operating gas-coupled lift fan and engine based upon the YF120 Advanced Tactical Fighter (ATF) engine technology. The McDonnell Douglas–led team includes British Aerospace, Northrop Grumman, General Electric Aircraft Engines, and Rolls-Royce. (Northrop Grumman had already been working on the ASTOVL effort at its own expense.)

The Lockheed project is centered on the Pratt & Whitney F119 power plant. However, a combination F100-220 and F100-229 engine will be fitted in the Lockheed demonstration aircraft to save development costs.

The following are the dimensions of the McDonnell Douglas full-scale ASTOVL demonstrator. The aircraft would have the same carrier deck spot factor as the F/A-18C.

Manufacturer:	McDonnell Douglas	
Crew:	(1) pilot	
Engines:	1 General Electric F120	
Weights:		
Dimensions:	length	51 ft 6 in (15.7 m)
	wing span	38 ft 4 in (11.69 m)
	wing area	
	height	12 ft 5 in (3.79 m)

AX ADVANCED ATTACK AIRCRAFT

The Navy's AX effort was initiated after the demise of the A-12 Avenger in another effort to produce a long-range, all-weather attack aircraft for carrier operation to succeed the A-6 Intruder. Near-term proposals for the AX aircraft included variants of the Grumman F-14D, called "Quickstrike," and the McDonnell Douglas–Northrop F/A-18. In addition, the General Dynamics–McDonnell Douglas–Northrop team proposed a design based on the canceled A-12 aircraft, while Lockheed teamed with General Dynamics and Boeing to propose a variant of the Air Force F-22, which was selected in 1991 as the USAF Advanced Tactical Fighter (ATF).

Priorities for the AX design included low-observable (stealth) characteristics and multi-mission potential—attack, electronic warfare, and possibly anti-submarine warfare with the primary missions to be (1) strike and (2) anti-surface warfare. The aircraft was to be capable of carrying all existing and planned Navy air-launched missiles except the Phoenix AAM.

The aerospace firms began design studies in early 1992 with a proposed operational capability in 2005. The effort was canceled, however, because of funding constraints. The following data reflect preliminary AX characteristics.

Manufacturer:	Team #1 Boeing-Grumman-Lockheed
	Team #2 McDonnell Douglas–LTV
	Team #3 General Dynamics–McDonnell Douglas–Northrop
	Team #4 Rockwell-Lockheed
Crew:	(2) pilot, bombardier/navigator
Engines:	2
Weights:	
Dimensions:	
Speed:	
Ceiling:	
Range:	radius 805 miles (1,300 km)
Armament:	up to 12,000 lbs (5,443 kg) of bombs and missiles including 2 AAMs
Radar:	multi-function

A-12 AVENGER

The A-12 Avenger was intended to replace the A-6E Intruder as the "medium" all-weather strike aircraft in carrier air wings. It was also to replace the A-6E in five Marine attack squadrons, but the Marine Corps decided early in the program to forego the A-12 in favor of flying the two-seat F/A-18D in the all-weather attack role.

The Navy and Department of Defense canceled the A-12 program on 7 January 1991, citing "the inability of the contractors to design, develop, fabricate, assemble, and test A-12 aircraft within the contract schedule and to deliver an aircraft that meets contract requirements." Also cited were major cost overruns and misrepresentations by the Naval Air Systems Command; the latter resulted in several officers being censored.[7] Subsequently, General Dynamics and McDonnell Douglas sued the government for improper termination of their contract. On 9 December 1994, the U.S. Court of Federal Claims decided that "Testimony and other evidence at trial showed that the A-12 contract was not terminated because of contractor default. The contract was terminated because the Office of the Secretary of Defense withdrew support and funding from the A-12. Prior to that the Navy did not believe that the contractors' performance justified termination for default."

The design and cost of the A-12 were highly classified until January 1990, when a "slip" in congressional testimony led to revelations that the 620-plane program was to have a unit cost of $96.2 million, making it the most expensive Navy aircraft yet built.[8] Peak A-12 production for the run of 620 aircraft was to be 36 units in fiscal 1994. (When the Marine Corps was also planning to buy the A-12, the procurement goal was 858 aircraft.)

The Air Force had been forced by the Defense Department to join the A-12 program to develop a deep-strike aircraft to succeed the F-111 and F-15E Strike Eagle in that role. Production of the Air Force version—called the Advanced Tactical Aircraft (ATA)—was deferred in 1990 to beyond 1997. The Air Force had planned to buy 400 ATA variants of the aircraft.

Design: The A-12 was to be a low-observable, or stealth, aircraft with a flying-wing configuration sans major tail-fin structures. The official artist's drawings of the A-12—heavily retouched—showed a classic delta flying-wing configuration with the "fuselage" extending slightly rearward from the trailing edge; the wing had a leading-edge sweep of about 48°. There were two large, trapezoidal inlets for the engines just aft and below the leading edges of the wing; no afterburners were fitted. The tandem-seat cockpit was close to the nose of the aircraft, which was sharply pointed and "blended" into the leading edge of the wing. The aircraft was to have been fitted with a digital fly-by-wire control system.

The weapons load—up to 12,000 pounds (5,443 kg)—was to be carried internally (the following table shows armament loadouts for various missions). The A-12 would have had folding wings for carrier stowage. Other features were to include superior range and payload

Mission	Range	Armament	Weight
Strike	900 miles	2 ASMs	4,500 lbs (2,041 kg)
	(1,455 km)	2 AAMs	1,000 lbs (454 kg)
Anti-Surface	940 miles	2 HARM ASMs	1,600 lbs (726 kg)
Warfare	(1,510 km)	2 Harpoon ASMs	2,320 lbs (1,052 kg)
		2 AAMs	1,000 lbs (454 kg)
Close Air	645 miles	16 Mk 82 Snakeye bombs	9,008 lbs (4,086 kg)
Support	(1,040 km)	2 AAMs	1,000 lbs (454 kg)
Tanker*	230 miles	2 AAMs	1,000 lbs (454 kg)
	(370 km)	2 drop tanks (400 gal)	530 lbs (240 kg)

Note: *Performance includes 1½-hour loiter time, with 13,750 pounds (6,237 kg) of fuel for transfer.

7. The Commander, Naval Air Systems Command, was retired and the program's manager and executive officer were transferred; the two latter officers also received administrative letters of censure.
8. See, for example, "A-12 Disclosure," *Aviation Week & Space Technology* (15 January 1990), p. 15.

over the A-6E, a low flight-to-maintenance ratio (expected to be four times better than the A-6E ratio), and dual-function radar/FLIR search and tracking system.

Designation: The designation A-12 was previously assigned by the Central Intelligence Agency to the supersonic aircraft that was the progenitor of the YF-12 fighter aircraft and SR-71 Blackbird reconnaissance aircraft.

Name: The name Avenger was assigned to honor President George Bush, who had flown TBM Avenger torpedo planes in World War II; he was reported to be the Navy's youngest wartime pilot.

Status: Canceled. The A-12 program began in 1984, with the first of six A-12 prototypes originally scheduled to fly in June 1990. At the time that the aircraft was canceled in January 1991, the first flight was scheduled to occur in March 1992. At that point carrier trials were expected in late 1992 or early 1993, with an IOC of 1996.

A-12 CONTRACT SPECIFICATIONS

Manufacturer:	General Dynamics and McDonnell Douglas	
Crew:	(2) pilot, bombardier/navigator	
Engines:	2 General Electric F412-GE-400 turbofans	
Weights:	empty	37,327 lbs (16,952 kg)
	gross T/O	70,146 lbs (31,818 kg)[9]
Dimensions:	length	38 ft (11.6 m)
	wing span	70 ft 3 in (21.42 m)
	wings folded	36 ft 3 in (11.05 m)
	wing area	1,317 ft² (122.48 m²)
	height	11 ft 7 in (3.53 m)
Speed:	maximum	621 mph (999 km/h)
Ceiling:	45,000 ft (13,720 m)	
Range:	see table	
	ferry	2,875 miles (4,630 km)
Armament:	up to 12,000 (5,443 kg) lbs of bombs and missiles	
Radar:	APQ-183 multi-function	

9. This weight is for close air support missions; the gross weight in a tanker configuration would be 74,103 lbs (33,613 kg).

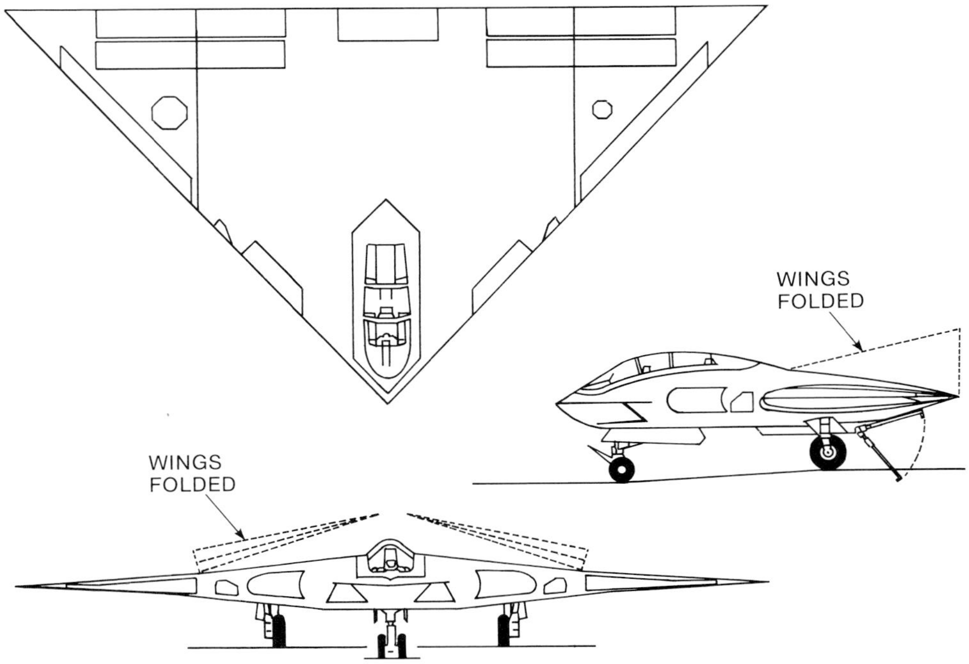

These drawings of the aborted A-12 Avenger are based on official sketches by General Dynamics, courtesy of the American Institute of Astronautics and Aeronautics. (William Clipson)

An artist's concept of the A-12 Avenger. Control surfaces on the A-12 include "elevons" or "flaperons" and pairs of spoilers, plus a single trailing-edge control surface between the elevons. With no vertical tail surfaces, the A-12 would have depended upon differential use of the elevons and/or spoilers for yaw control. (General Dynamics)

Details of the A-12 Avenger show intakes for the two F412-GE-400 turbofan engines fitted flush beneath the leading edge. (Exhausts are below the wing, short of the trailing edge.) Outboard of the intakes are hexagonal dielectronic panels on the wings, believed to be related to the APQ-183 multimode radar. (General Dynamics)

AV-8B HARRIER

The AV-8B is a highly capable STOVL attack aircraft flown by Marine attack squadrons.[10] After 1996 the Harrier will be the only "straight" attack aircraft (VA/VMA) in naval aviation. The aircraft operates from amphibious ships and has flown from large aircraft carriers.

During the Carter administration (1977–1981) the Department of Defense sought to have the Marines procure the F/A-18 Hornet as a replacement for the A-4M, but the Marines—with congressional support—held fast to the AV-8B program.[11] The Marine Corps originally planned to procure 336 operational AV-8B aircraft, plus four full-scale development aircraft, in addition to the two YAV-8B prototypes that were converted from AV-8A aircraft. Procurement was revised downward to the actual production of 256 AV-8B models and 20 of the two-seat TAV-8B trainers, the last procurement being in fiscal 1991.

Design: The AV-8B differs from the earlier AV-8A Harrier flown by the Marines in that it has a supercritical wing shape, larger trailing-edge flaps, drooped ailerons, strakes under the gun pods, redesigned engine intakes, strengthened landing gear, and a more powerful engine. The AV-8B can carry twice the payload of the AV-8A, i.e., up to 9,200 pounds (4,173 kg) of external stores. The aircraft carries one external 25-mm gun pack faired into the under fuselage, with one fuselage and six wing points available for bombs, rockets, missiles, or 300-gallon (1,140-liter) fuel tanks.

Compared to the AV-8A, the new wing has 15 percent greater area, and the aircraft can carry 75 percent more fuel in wing tanks constructed predominately of composites that save weight without losing strength. The AV-8B has six stores stations (compared to four on the AV-8A), plus an updated engine, composite material in some fuselage areas, an elevated cockpit and canopy to improve visibility, redesigned engine intakes, and improved avionics.

The AV-8B has the ASB-19(V)3 angle-rate bombing system. Those aircraft delivered after September 1989 are night-attack capable, having been fitted with nose-mounted FLIR, pilot night-vision goggles, HUD and color head-down displays, and digital moving-map system. Aircraft delivered from 1993 (Harrier II Plus) have the APG-65 multi-mode, synthetic aperture radar and the improved Pegasus 408 engine. The aircraft is also 17 inches (0.43 m) longer in the forward fuselage and weighs some 900 pounds (408 kg) more than the improved (radar-equipped) AV-8B. In addition, 73 earlier AV-8B aircraft are being "remanufactured" to the "Plus" configuration.

Also fitted are the ALR-67 radar warning receiver and the pod-mounted ALQ-164 ECM system.

The two-seat TAV-8B differs from the standard AV-8B in having an enlarged forward fuselage and canopy, plus a vertical fin extension. The two aircraft have a 90 percent component commonality.

Operational: The 86 Marine AV-8B Harriers participating in Operation Desert Storm flew 3,380 combat sorties. (Earlier Harriers flown by Britain's Royal Navy and Royal Air Force from VSTOL carriers achieved remarkable results in the 1982 Falklands conflict.)

Status: Operational; no longer in production, but early AV-8B aircraft are being remanufactured. First flight YAV-8B on 9 November

The AV-8B Harrier can be distinguished from early versions by its massive air intakes for the F402-RR-408 Pegasus turbofan engine that provides both thrust and lift. Note the retracted refueling probe above the port intake. The underwing weapon pylons are evident in this view of a VMA-223 aircraft. (Ted Carlson)

An AV-8B Harrier from VMA-321 taxies after landing on board the amphibious ship NASSAU (LHA 4). The LHA/LHD helicopter carriers regularly deploy with Harrier detachments. During the Gulf War of 1991 the NASSAU operated 19 AV-8B Harriers. (Robert E. Koons)

The two-seat TAV-8B Harrier at rest with both canopies open on the tarmac at MacDill Air Force Base, Florida. Note the raised rear seat position. (John Bouvia)

10. The designation STOVL for the AV-8B Harrier, in place of VSTOL, was made by the Deputy Chief of Staff/Aviation, Headquarters, U.S. Marine Corps, in March 1995.
11. In the event, during the Reagan administration (1981–1989) then-Secretary of the Navy John Lehman procured both the AV-8B and the F/A-18 for the Marine Corps.

1978; first flight AV-8B on 5 November 1981; Harrier II Plus in September 1992. Marine IOC (VMA-331) was in January 1985, Harrier II Plus IOC (VMA-542) in August 1993.

The AV-8B has replaced the A-4M and AV-8A aircraft in Marine VMA squadrons.

(Britain's Royal Air Force procured essentially the same aircraft as the AV-8B–designated GR Mk 5 and the night-attack GR 7 variants; the British T Mk 10 variants are similar to the TAV-8B. AV-8B variants are also flown from VSTOL aircraft carriers by Italy and Spain; earlier Sea Harriers are flown from two Indian aircraft carriers.)

AV-8B "PLUS"

Manufacturer:	McDonnell Douglas and British Aerospace	
Crew:	(1) pilot (2 in TAV-8B)	
Engines:	1 Rolls-Royce F402-RR-408 Pegasus turbofan; 23,800 lbst (10,795 kgst)	
Weights:	empty	12,922 lbs (5,861 kg)
	maximum T/O	VTO 19,550 lbs (8,868 kg)
	maximum T/O	STO 31,000 lbs (14,060 kg) with 1,200-ft (366-m) takeoff run
Dimensions:	length AV-8B	46 ft 4 in (14.12 m)
		TAV-8B 50 ft 3 in (15.32 m)
	wing span	30 ft 4 in (9.25 m)
	wing area	230 ft² (21.37 m²)
	height	11 ft 7¾ in (3.55 m)
Speed:	maximum	668 mph (1,075 km) at sea level
Ceiling:	50,000 ft (15,244 m)	
Range:	radius 173 miles (278 km) with 12 500-lb (227-kg) bombs with 1-hour loiter in STO mode	
	radius 690 miles (1,111 km) with 7 500-lb bombs in STO mode	
	ferry 2,945 miles (4,741 km) with 4 300-gallon (1,140-liter) drop tanks	
Armament:	1 25-mm cannon GAU-12/U (multi-barrel; 300 rounds)	
	11,920 lbs (5,407 kg) bombs, missiles, drop tanks including Sidewinder AAMs	
Radar:	APG-65	

AV-8A HARRIER

The Harrier was the first VSTOL aircraft to enter first-line service with the U.S. armed forces. The British-developed Harrier was procured for three Marine attack squadrons. The Marines deemed it a success despite a high accident rate; several surviving AV-8A aircraft were upgraded to the AV-8C, with two AV-8A Harriers being converted to YAV-8B prototypes for the Harrier II. All AV-8A/C aircraft have been discarded.

The Marine Corps took delivery of 102 single-seat AV-8A (British GR 3 Mk 50) and 8 two-seat TAV-8A (British T 4 Mk 54) aircraft from 1971 to 1976; McDonnell Douglas was the American support contractor.

See 14th Edition/pages 403–4 for characteristics.

A-7 CORSAIR

The Corsair was a carrier-based, light attack aircraft in first-line Navy service from 1966 until 1991. It saw extensive combat in the Vietnam War. The last two A-7E squadrons flew in the Gulf War (VA-46 and VA-72); both units were disbanded in May 1991. The last naval air reserve units to fly the A-7E traded in their Corsairs for the F/A-18 Hornet in April 1991.

The A-7E was replaced in Navy carrier air wings by the F/A-18. (The Marine Corps did not fly the A-7.) Production of the A-7 ended in 1983, with 1,551 Corsairs delivered: 997 for the U.S. Navy, 459 A-7D and 30 two-seat A-7K for the U.S. Air Force, and 65 A-7H and TA-7H models for Greece. (Two A-7D models were upgraded to YA-7F prototypes for an improved close air support aircraft, but no large-scale conversion followed.) Many former U.S. Navy aircraft were modified for foreign use.

Sixty U.S. Navy versions were two-seat TA-7C with dual controls (converted from A-7A and A-7C aircraft); a proposed RA-7E with reconnaissance pods was dropped in favor of the F-14/TARPS, and a proposed twin-engine A-7 variant lost out in the concept stage to the F/A-18 as the new Navy attack aircraft.

Operational: During Operation Desert Storm the 24 A-7E aircraft of VA-46 and VA-72 on the carrier John F. Kennedy flew 737 combat sorties.

See 14th Edition/pages 404–5 for characteristics.

A-6E INTRUDER

A highly versatile attack aircraft, the Intruder is the most capable carrier-based aircraft with respect to weapons payload, and it is able to carry out all-weather, day/night strikes. The aircraft was to be replaced by the A-12 Avenger and its proposed successors. The last Navy A-6E squadrons will be disbanded in 1996; the last Marine A-6E squadrons were disbanded in 1993 (see page 354).

Design: The Intruder is a two-seat, twin-turbojet aircraft. All weapons are carried on five attachment points, each with a 3,600-lb (1,633-kg) capacity with a maximum mission payload of 18,000 lbs (8,165 kg) of ordnance and drop tanks. The A-6E can carry nuclear weapons as well as a variety of laser-guided bombs and guided

An A-6E Intruder from VA-75, at the time aboard the John F. Kennedy, displays the low-visibility markings of U.S. naval aircraft in the post-Vietnam era. The fixed refueling probe projects ahead of the cockpit, which has side-by-side seating for the pilot and bombardier/navigator. (U.S. Navy)

An A-6E Intruder about to touch down on the John F. Kennedy. The aircraft is "dirty": that is, wheels and arresting hook are lowered. The trailing edge of each wingtip splits to form speed brakes, shown open as this A-6E is about to touch down. (U.S. Navy, PH1 Michael D.P. Flynn)

Close-up of an A-6E cockpit as the aircraft prepares for takeoff from the INDEPENDENCE. The pilot, on the left side, sits slightly higher and forward of the bombardier/navigator, on the right. The TRAM pod is visible under the nose, just forward of the aircraft's side number, "504." (John Bouvia)

missiles. The A-6E variant has the Target Recognition Attack Multisensor (TRAM), FLIR, a combination laser designator/range finder, and a laser designation receiver. The ALQ-67 radar warning receiver is also fitted, as are chaff/flare dispensers.

The SWIP (Systems/Weapons Improvement Program) upgrade to 342 A-6Es further increased their attack capability, including the use of Harpoon and Maverick missiles and improved ECM capabilities (ALR-67 and ALQ-126B). More than 100 of the SWIP aircraft were being fitted with composite wings to enable them to serve for a few more years.

An improved A-6F—with new avionics, the APQ-173 radar, GE F404 engines, and composite-material wings—was being developed, with an IOC planned for the late 1980s. That project has been canceled, as has a proposed new A-6G aircraft. As late as 1990, however, the Navy requested cost data from Grumman for 500 A-6G variants—300 new aircraft and 200 remanufactured A-6E aircraft—because of delays in the A-12 program.

The KA-6D tankers (all converted from earlier aircraft) had avionics deleted from the after fuselage to provide space for reel; up to five 300-gallon (1,135-liter) drop tanks could be carried to permit the transfer of more than 21,000 pounds of fuel (9,650 kg)—that is, more than 3,200 gallons (12,110 liters)—immediately after takeoff, or about 15,000 pounds of fuel (6,800 kg)—that is, 2,300 gallons (8,700 liters)—while loitering some 150 n.miles (278 km) from the carrier. Later modifications enabled some aircraft to carry 400-gallon (1,515-liter) tanks. After the phase-out of the KA-6D aircraft, A-6Es were employed as tankers, having been fitted with "buddy store" hose-and-drogue pods. The first A-6A to KA-6D conversion flew on 23 May 1966. The tankers have been discarded.

All Intruder variants have a prominent fixed refueling probe forward of the cockpit; wings fold for carrier stowage.

Designation: The Intruder was originally designated A2F; this was changed to A-6 in 1962.

The EA-6A Intruder and EA-6B Prowler electronic warfare variants are listed separately in this edition (see page 383).

Operational: During Operation Desert Storm the 95 Navy A-6E aircraft flew 4,824 combat sorties, and 20 Marine A-6Es flew 843 sorties.[12]

Status: Operational; no longer in production. First flight A-6A on 19 April 1960. A-6A IOC (VA-42) was in February 1963, KA-6D IOC (VA-176) in September 1970, and A-6E IOC in September 1971.

Grumman built 705 attack variants (including 21 EA-6A models) for the Navy and Marine Corps; the last was delivered in January 1992, an A-6E. Two hundred forty earlier aircraft were upgraded to the A-6E variant (plus 205 built as E models). There were no foreign users.

12. Six U.S. aircraft carriers participated in the Persian Gulf conflict of January 1991: AMERICA, JOHN F. KENNEDY, MIDWAY, RANGER, SARATOGA, and THEODORE ROOSEVELT.

Manufacturer:		Grumman	
Crew:		(2) pilot, bombardier/navigator	
Engines:		2 Pratt & Whitney J52-P-8B turbojets; 9,300 lbst (4,218 kgst) each	
Weights:		empty	26,746 lbs (12,009 kg)
		maximum T/O	60,400 lbs (27,397 kg)
Dimensions:		length	54 ft 9 in (16.69 m)
		wing span	53 ft (16.15 m)
		wing area	528.9 ft^2 (49.1 m^2)
		height	16 ft 2 in (4.93 m)
Speed:		maximum	644 mph (1,036 km/h) at sea level
Ceiling:		42,400 ft (12,927 m)	
Range:		1,010 miles (1,630 km) with combat load	
		ferry 2,730 miles (4,400 km)	
Armament:		30,500 lbs (13,835 kg) bombs and missiles	
	or	10 1,000-lb (454-kg) bombs	
	or	3 2,000-lb (907-kg) bombs + 2 300-gallon (1,140-liter) drop tanks	
	or	HARM, Harpoon, Maverick, Sidewinder, Skipper, SLAM missiles	
Radar:		APQ-148 multi-mode	

A-4 SKYHAWK

See TA-4J Skyhawk under Training Aircraft (page 394).

A-3 SKYWARRIOR

The Douglas A3D (later A-3) was developed as a long-range, carrier-based nuclear strike aircraft. The Skywarrior survived its intended successor, the A3J (later A-5) Vigilante. The A3D was the largest aircraft to operate regularly from an aircraft carrier, the tanker version having a takeoff weight of more than 80,000 pounds (36,288 kg).

The Navy took delivery of 282 Douglas-built Skywarriors of all variants. These included 25 A3D-2Q/EA-3B specialized Electronic Intelligence (ELINT) collection aircraft; many "straight" attack aircraft were subsequently modified to EW/ECM configurations. The ELINT version was the last flown by the Navy, this variant of the "Whale" having been assigned to squadrons VQ-1 and VQ-2 from 1959 until 1991. (From 1987 until 1991 they were restricted to operations from land bases.) The EA-3B was replaced in VQ squadrons by the ES-3 Viking, the last Skywarrior being retired from VQ-2 in September 1991.

(The Air Force flew the similar B-66 Destroyer in the bomber, electronic, reconnaissance, weather, and research roles; B-66 production totaled 206 aircraft.)

Designation: The ELINT aircraft was originally designated A3D-2Q which was changed to EA-3B in 1962.

See 14th Edition/pages 415–16 for characteristics.

FIGHTER AIRCRAFT

The Navy now flies the F-14 Tomcat in the fighter role, and the Navy and Marine Corps fly the multipurpose F/A-18 Hornet. With the halt in both procurement and remanufacture of the F-14, the F/A-18 alone will eventually fill the fighter role for both services.

The proposed Naval Advanced Tactical Fighter (NATF) was essentially stillborn when it was called unaffordable (see below). However, some proposals are still being put forward for a carrier-capable variant of the Air Force's ATF, now the Lockheed-Boeing F-22. This aircraft is scheduled for series production for the Air Force. The Navy's record for adopting non–Navy-developed aircraft for carrier use makes it highly unlikely that there will be a navalized F-22.

NAVAL ADVANCED TACTICAL FIGHTER

The Naval Advanced Tactical Fighter (NATF)—the planned long-term replacement for the F-14 Tomcat—was originally envisioned by the Navy as a navalized version of the F-22 developed by a team comprised of Lockheed, General Dynamics, and Boeing for the U.S. Air Force. A senior official of Lockheed, whose aircraft won the competition, said that the company planned to "give the NATF a swing-wing like the F-14. The swing-wing will let us optimize the plane for the best performance in different [speed and altitude] regions." The official admitted that there would be a penalty for the swing-wing, but performance and stealth would be enhanced in combat environments. Also, Lockheed was to look at a two-seat aircraft for the Navy (the basic F-22 is a single-seat plane) capable of carrying 50 percent more fuel than the Air Force version. Other changes envisioned for the naval aircraft would be additional avionics and engines modified to resist corrosion in a saltwater environment. In short, said the Lockheed official, "The NATF will be designed to a completely different set of requirements."[13]

By early 1991—about the time the Air Force was to select from the YF-22 and YF-23 ATF design competitors—the Navy reached the decision that development and production of a naval ATF was unaffordable.

Two YF-22 prototypes with alternative engines were produced, with one having crashed and the other having completed the aircraft competition and test programs. First flight of nine pre-production F-22 aircraft is scheduled for May 1997,[14] with Air Force production to follow. The estimated IOC is 2004. Naval procurement of the F-22 would follow, with a buy of 546 naval variants of the fighter to replace the F-14.

The existing F-22 can carry two 1,000-pound (455-kg) weapons in its internal weapons bay, as well as two Sidewinder and two AMRAAM missiles on the wings. The aircraft also has two hard points on each wing that can carry up to 5,000 pounds (2,250 kg) of ordnance, although the aircraft suffers a major degrading of radar cross section when carrying external weapons. An M61 rotary-cannon is also fitted.

In 1995 Lockheed announced that it would begin formal studies of precision strike, reconnaissance, and other variants of the F-22.

13. "Lockheed NATF design will be swing-wing," *Navy News* (4 February 1991), pp. 1–2.
14. These are nine Engineering and Manufacturing Development (EMD) aircraft, of which seven are single-seat aircraft and two are two-seat variants.

A prototype YF-22 Advanced Tactical Fighter, showing the semi-stealth configuration of the aircraft. The possibility of a navalized variant of the F-22 is again proposed, but seems unlikely. (Lockheed)

The underside of a prototype YF-22 Advanced Tactical Fighter. Preproduction F-22s are now being built for the Air Force. (Lockheed)

F-21A KFIR

From October 1984 to 1989 the Navy and Marine Corps leased 25 Israeli-built Kfir C1 fighter aircraft to simulate Soviet aircraft in adversary training for pilots.[15] The Kfirs were leased to the United States on a no-cost basis; Israel Aircraft Industries was contracted to maintain the aircraft. All 25 aircraft were returned to Israel when F-16N fighters became available for adversary training. Squadron VF-43 flew 12 of the F-21s and VMFT-401 flew 13 aircraft.

The Kfir was a refinement of the Dassault Mirage 5 design, with a more powerful engine of American origins. IAI had produced 27 Kfir C1 aircraft; one was lost and one was retained in Israel for museum display. After return of the 25 leased aircraft, IAI modified them to extend their service life for further foreign lease or sale.

See 14th Edition/page 395 for F-21A Kfir characteristics.

F/A-18E/F HORNET

This advanced Hornet series is being developed for the Navy and Marine Corps to succeed the F-14 Tomcat fighter, A-6E Intruder attack plane, and, eventually, the earlier F/A-18C/D Hornets in Navy and Marine service. The F/A-18E is a single-seat aircraft and the F/A-18F a two-seat variant.

The requirement for an enhanced F/A-18 was first mentioned in a 15 July 1987 memorandum from then-Secretary of Defense Caspar Weinberger to the Secretaries of the Navy and Air Force. He noted that, because the next-generation Navy attack aircraft and a replacement for the Air Force's F-16 fighter could not be available "for many years," the Navy should study derivatives of the F/A-18 and the Air Force should study F-16 upgrades as interim replacements.

In selecting the F/A-18E as the next-generation carrier-based fighter over several alternatives, including the F-14D, Secretary of Defense Dick Cheney, in a letter to Senator Christopher Bond dated 29 July 1991, said that the F/A-18E "was the clear choice over the F-14" based on reliability, safety, and fewer maintenance personnel and operating costs. "It is three times more reliable, twice as easy to maintain, and has a safety record which is 50 percent better, requires about 25 [percent] fewer maintenance personnel, and costs about 25 percent less to operate per flight hour." Cheney concluded, "When combined, these factors clearly show that the F/A-18E/F is the more cost effective aircraft."

The original Navy–Marine Corps requirement was for 1,000 aircraft; however, by 1994 the E/F procurement goal had been reduced to some 800 aircraft. Procurement will begin with the fiscal 1997 budget, and all 800 aircraft will be acquired by 2015. The latter number is based on a squadron requirement of 630 aircraft (including readiness units), 60 pipeline aircraft, and about 100 aircraft for attrition through the year 2020.

The F/A-18 team—McDonnell Douglas and Northrop Grumman—are also studying the feasibility of an EW/ECM variant of the two-seat F/A-18F to replace the EA-6B Prowler.

15. *Kfir* is Hebrew for lion cub.

The prototype F/A-18E takes to the air for the first time on 29 November 1995. The controversial aircraft will make up the majority of the planes on U.S. large-deck carriers for the foreseeable future. This aircraft has a pitot tube in the nose; the refueling probe is fully retractable. (McDonnell Douglas, D. Martin)

Design: The E/F models are based on a lengthened and upgraded F/A-18C/D design. Compared to the earlier series, the E/F variants will have a center section plug, 25 percent larger wing, and improved engines with 35 percent more thrust. The F414 engine is a derivative of the F404 used in earlier F/A-18s. Two additional wing stores stations boost the total to 11 on the fuselage and wings, plus two wingtip stations for the Sidewinder AAM.

The E/F aircraft will be fitted with the ALE-50 towed countermeasures system, which provides more expendable chaff and flare countermeasures. They will be able to accommodate an in-flight refueling pod to permit the aircraft to serve in a limited tanker role while carrying two 480-gallon (1,817-liter) drop tanks.

The "spotting factor," or footprint, on the carrier deck is 23 percent larger for the F/A-18E than for the F/A-18C.

Status: In development. First flight of an F/A-18E was on 29 November 1995; first flight of an F/A-18F was on 1 April 1996; the planned IOC is for 2000.

Manufacturer:	McDonnell Douglas and Northrop Grumman	
Crew:	(1) pilot in F/A-18E (2) pilot, bombardier/navigator in F/A-18F	
Engines:	2 General Electric F414-GE-400 turbofans; 22,000 lbst (9,979 kgst) each	
Weights:	empty	30,500 lbs (13,835 kg)
	maximum T/O	66,000 lbs (29,937 kg)
Dimensions:	length	60 ft 4 in (18.38 m)
	wing span	44 ft 8½ in (13.63 m) with Sidewinder AAMs fitted
	wing area	500 ft² (45 m²)
	height	15 ft 10 in (4.83 m)
Speed:	maximum	1,185 mph (1,900 km/h) at 37,000 ft (11,280 m); Mach 1.8
Ceiling:	50,000 ft (15,244 m)	
Range:	radius 200 n.miles (370 km) in fighter role with 1.8 hours on station (2 Sidewinders + 4 AMRAAMs) radius 420 n.miles (778 km) in fighter escort role (2 Sidewinders + 2 AMRAAMs) radius 475 n.miles (880 km) in interdiction role (2 Sidewinders + 4 1,000-lb/454-kg bombs)	
Armament:	1 20-mm Vulcan cannon M61A1 (multibarrel; 400 rounds) up to 17,750 lbs (8,051 kg) of bombs, rockets, missiles, and external tanks	
Radar:	APG-73	

The prototype F/A-18E showing pylons loaded with a representative payload of missiles and a laser guidance pod. The "Super Hornet" seeks to overcome the range limitations of the earlier F/A-18 variants, but it does so at a significant increase in size and cost. Nevertheless, the F/A-18 is a highly effective strike-fighter aircraft. (McDonnell Douglas)

F/A-18C/D HORNET

The Hornet is a strike-fighter aircraft flown by the Navy and Marine Corps in significantly larger numbers than any other naval aircraft. In the Navy the F/A-18 replaced the A-7E Corsair light attack aircraft; most carrier air wings have two VFA squadrons flying the F/A-18. In the Marine Corps the F/A-18 replaced the F-4S Phantom fighter, A-6E Intruder, and A-4M Skyhawk attack aircraft, and the RF-4B Phantom and OA-4 Skyhawk special-purpose aircraft.

The development of the F/A-18 came as a result of pressure by Congress for the Navy to obtain a lightweight fighter to complement the F-14 in carrier air wings. Congress originally had directed the Navy to select the winner of the Air Force's lightweight fighter competition of the mid-1970s between the General Dynamics YF-16 and Northrop YF-17 prototypes. The Air Force selected the F-16 for production; the Navy selected the YF-17, but it modified the plane significantly, leading to the F/A-18 model developed jointly by McDonnell Douglas and Northrop. The naval aircraft failed to fully achieve its range/payload goals in the attack role.

The Navy–Marine Corps Blue Angels flight demonstration team began flying the F/A-18 in 1987; these are early, development models of the Hornet that are not carrier capable.[16]

The F/A-18 has been a controversial program for three main reasons: (1) the initial Marine decision to procure the AV-8B Harrier instead of the F/A-18 for the attack role; (2) higher-than-predicted F/A-18 costs; and (3) the F/A-18 has less range than the A-6 and A-7. However, the aircraft's widespread use has had positive cost and support impact, and its performance in Operation Desert Storm equaled that promised by its manufacturers.

Design: A twin-engine, single- or two-seat aircraft, the F/A-18 is characterized by its high maneuverability, the ability to operate in either the fighter or attack role with the push of a button, and comparatively low-maintenance requirements. The initial versions were the F/A-18A strike-fighter and the TF-18 two-seat trainer; the latter is now referred to as the F/A-18B. The F/A-18C is an improved single-seat aircraft, and the F/A-18D is a two-seat aircraft in which a weapons officer sits in the rear seat, with no flight controls. The D variant is also configured for the Marine tactical air control and reconnaissance roles, and it has an austere all-weather capability.

The twin-engine aircraft is distinguished by swept leading wing edges and twin tail fins. The F/A-18 has wingtip Sidewinder AAM positions as well as three fuselage and four wing stations for weapons and sensor/guidance pods. A variety of bombs, missiles, and rockets can be carried, including up to four 2,000-lb (907-kg) bombs.

Initially, the F/A-18 flew with a pod-mounted Forward-Looking Infrared (FLIR) that was developed specifically for the F/A-18 (AAS-38). The F/A-18C/D models delivered since October 1989 have a night-attack capability based on a FLIR sensor called TINS (Thermal Imaging Navigation Set) and designated ARR-50. They also feature an improved HUD. The F/A-18s delivered through mid-1994 have the APG-65 multi-mode, synthetic aperture radar; subsequent aircraft—including the E/F variants—have the APG-73 radar.

Designation: The initial Navy order for 11 development aircraft used the designation YF-18. The designation F/A-18A was used for initial single-seat aircraft and F/A-18B for those with tandem seating. See page 359 for additional discussion of the F/A-18 designation.

Operational: More F/A-18s participated in the Persian Gulf War (January–February 1991) than any other fixed-wing naval aircraft; 13 Navy VFA and 7 Marine VMFA squadrons, plus Canadian Forces, flew the Hornet. The 90 Navy F/A-18s flew 4,449 combat sorties, and the 84 Marine F/A-18s flew 5,239 sorties. These amounted to almost one-third of the 29,363 Navy-Marine combat sorties flown in the Gulf War (including fixed-wing aircraft and helicopters).

On 17 January 1991 two Navy F/A-18C aircraft shot down two Iraqi MiG-21 fighters using both Sparrow and Sidewinder missiles.[17]

Status: Operational; in production. First flight on 18 November 1978. Navy-Marine IOC (VFA-125) was in February 1981, Marine F/A-18A IOC (VMFA-314) in March 1983, and F/A-18D IOC (VMFA[AW]-121) in May 1991. Through 1 January 1996, 1,299 F/A-18s were delivered: 967 to the U.S. Navy and Marine Corps, and 332 to foreign air forces (including 73 coproduced with Aerospace Technologies of Australia). Almost all F/A-18A/B models have been retired from U.S. service.

The original F/A-18 procurement plan was for 11 development aircraft and 1,366 production planes for 24 Navy attack and 6 fighter squadrons, and 12 Marine fighter squadrons, plus 332 aircraft in reserve units and 142 attrition and pipeline aircraft. The current Navy-Marine procurement (including E and F models) is expected to total some 1,200 aircraft; foreign contracts cover another 374 aircraft through 1 January 1996.

Australia, Canada, Kuwait, Finland, Malaysia, Spain, and Switzerland have ordered the F/A-18 for land-based operation; South Korea planned to acquire the F/A-18 in 1989, but in the event it canceled that buy in favor of the F-16 Fighting Falcon. (A proposed Northrop F-18L land-based variant has not been procured.)

16. See page 347 for previous Blue Angel aircraft.

17. On 17 January 1991 the two Navy F/A-18 Hornets from the carrier SARATOGA flew a bombing mission, each carrying four 2,000-pound (907-kg) bombs. They were able to engage two Iraqi MiG-21 fighters. Both of the Iraqi planes were shot down with air-to-air missiles, after which the F/A-18s were able to continue their bombing mission, not having had to jettison their bombs to engage the enemy planes.

F/A-18C

Manufacturer:	McDonnell Douglas and Northrop	
Crew:	(1) pilot in F/A-18A/C	
	(2) pilot, bombardier/navigator in F/A-18D	
Engines:	2 General Electric F404-GE-400 turbofans; 16,000 lbst (7,258 kgst) each; F404-GE-402 engines with 17,700 lbst (8,029 kgst) in fiscal 1992 and later aircraft	
Weights:	empty	23,050 lbs (10,455 kg)
	fighter mission normal	
	takeoff	36,710 lbs (16,651 kg)
	attack mission normal	
	takeoff	49,224 lbs (22,328 kg)
Dimensions:	length	56 ft (17.07 m)
	wing span	37 ft 6 in (11.43 m)
		40 ft 5 in (12.31 m) with Sidewinder AAMs fitted
	wing area	400 ft² (37.16 m²)
	height	15 ft 3½ in (4.66 m)
Speed:	maximum	1,185 mph (1,900 km/h) at 37,000 ft (11,280 m); Mach 1.8
Ceiling:	50,000 ft (15,240 m)	
Range:	radius 200 n.miles (370 km) in fighter role with 1 hour on station (2 Sidewinders + 4 AMRAAMs)	
	radius 303 n.miles (565 km) in fighter escort role (2 Sidewinders + 2 AMRAAMs)	
	radius 277 n.miles (513 km) in interdiction role (2 Sidewinders + 4 1,000-lb/454 kg bombs)	
Armament:	1 20-mm Vulcan cannon M61 (multi-barrel; 570 rounds)	
	2 Sidewinder + 4 Sparrow AAMs in fighter role	
or	2 Sidewinder AAMs + 17,000 lbs (7,711 kg) of bombs, missiles, rockets in attack role	
Radar:	APG-65 or APG-73 multi-mode	

An F/A-18C Hornet from VFA-136, seen from another Hornet, over the Persian Gulf as U.S. naval forces continued to operate in that area following the 1991 conflict. These aircraft have wingtip-mounted Sidewinder AAMs and drop tanks. (U.S. Navy, CWO2 Tony Alleyne)

The rear aspect of an F/A-18C from VMFA-323 about to be catapulted from a carrier. These aircraft have large leading-edge extensions to their wings; the twin tail fins are canted 20° outward and mounted forward of the horizontal tail surfaces. (U.S. Navy)

An F/A-18C Hornet from VMFA-323 sits with wings folded (mounting Sidewinder AAMs) on a carrier flight deck. The small, outer wing panels fold upward through 100° for handling on flight and hangar decks. The AV-8 Harrier and A-4 Skyhawk series are the only fixed-wing carrier aircraft without this feature. (U.S. Navy)

A two-seat F/A-18D Hornet from VMFA(AW)-121 on patrol with drop tanks and wingtip Sidewinder AAMs. The two-seat F/A-18s have replaced several aircraft in Marine aviation; unfortunately, to date no specialized photoreconnaissance variant has been deployed. (McDonnell Douglas)

F-16N FIGHTING FALCON

The Navy flew 26 modified F-16C Fighting Falcon fighters in the adversary training role (replacing the F-21A Kfir). It took delivery of 22 single-seat F-16N and four two-seat TF-16N aircraft in 1987–1988, which were grounded, beginning in 1991, because of structural cracking in the center fuselage. They were subsequently disposed of.

The F-16 is the standard U.S. Air Force lightweight fighter, which is also flown by several allied air forces. The Navy F-16Ns were similar to the F-16C but did not have the M61 20-mm Vulcan cannon; the Navy planes were fitted with the APG-66 radar of the earlier Air Force F-16A/B aircraft and had a more advanced engine.

More than 2,000 F-16s had been delivered to the U.S. Air Force and more than 1,000 aircraft to 16 allied nations through 1995, with additional planes on order.

See 15th Edition/pages 402–3 for characteristics.

F-14 TOMCAT

The F-14 was the principal U.S. Navy carrier-based fighter of the 1970s and 1980s. Two squadrons were assigned to each standard carrier air wing; most wings now have only one F-14 squadron. Designed to intercept Soviet long-range strike aircraft, in several respects the F-14 remains the most capable long-range, all-weather fighter aircraft in service with any air force.

One VF squadron in each carrier can employ the F-14 in the photoreconnaissance role when the standard F-14 is fitted with the removable TARPS (Tactical Air Reconnaissance Pod System). The TARPS package can be fitted to or removed from a standard aircraft in a few hours; it contains a KS-87 frame camera, a KA-99 panoramic camera, and an AAD-5 infrared line scanner.

The F-14 will be succeeded aboard carriers by the F/A-18E and, subsequently, the JAST-developed aircraft.

The F-14 was originally planned for Marine Corps use, but that service turned it down, in part because of the decision to procure the AV-8A Harrier.

Design: A two-seat aircraft, the F-14 has variable-geometry wings that sweep back automatically as the aircraft maneuvers during flight; they extend for long-range flight and landings, sweeping back for high-speed flight (and carrier stowage). Normal sweep range is 20° to 68°, with a 75° "oversweep" position provided for shipboard hangar stowage. Sweep speed is 7.5° per second.

The F-14A has the long-range AWG-9 radar, which can detect hostile aircraft out to more than 100 miles (161 km) and simultaneously track up to 24 targets. The plane carries the Phoenix missile, which can engage targets more than 60 miles (96.5 km) away. The basic F-14 suite includes the ALR-45 and ALR-50 radar warning receiver, ALE-29 and ALE-39 chaff/flare dispensers, and ALQ-100 deception jamming pod. A forward-looking AXX-1 television camera is fitted for long-range visual detection.

Up to 14,500 pounds (6,577 kg) of external stores can be carried by the F-14. The aircraft has a total of four fuselage missile positions (4 Sparrow or 4 Phoenix) and two wing positions (4 Sidewinder or 2 Sparrow or 2 Phoenix); alternatively, fuel tanks or a TARPS can be carried with a reduced missile load. Planned under-fuselage pallets for bombs and air-to-surface missiles were never provided to the basic aircraft, but up to 210 are being fitted with racks for "iron bombs" and laser-guided bombs, called GBUs.[18] The F-14D, however, has pylon adapters for air-to-surface missiles, HARM, and Harpoon missiles, as well as iron bombs and GBUs.

About 80 F-14A variants were originally to have been procured; later aircraft were to have been the F-14B, with F401-PW-400 engines, and an F-14C, also to have an avionics upgrade. In the event, only the F-14A model was produced through the mid-1980s. (The

One of the few F-14B Tomcats—from VF-143—flies with its wings "tucked in" for high-speed flight. The engine intakes are rectangular and sharply angled. The twin tail fins are canted slightly, as are twin ventral fins under the engines. (U.S. Navy)

Still one of the best air-to-air fighters in the world, this F-14A Tomcat from VF-2 shows the aircraft with wings fully extended. They sweep back automatically for high-speed flight. VF-2 has since received the more capable F-14D variant. (U.S. Navy, Lt. Comdr. David Baranek)

Navy had planned an F-14 upgrade with improved engines and air-to-surface weapons in the 1970s, but those programs were halted because of a lack of funds.) Because engine problems plagued the F-14A, the F-14A+ was fitted with F110-GE-400 engines (otherwise, the model was similar to the basic F-14A). The F-14A+ was changed to F-14B in 1991; previously, one F-14A had been reengined and was designated F-14B configuration. The follow-on F-14D has the improved, synthetic-aperture APG-71 radar and other improvements, including a capability for the AMRAAM missile.

The F110-GE-400 engine had a maximum thrust of 28,500 pounds (12,928 kg). This resulted in an increased radius (deck-launched intercept role) from 155 to 240 miles (250 to 390 km) and a maximum catapult weight increase from 59,000 pounds (26,762 kg) to 74,000 pounds (33,566 kg).

The decision to procure 324 F-14D models with the F110-GE-400 engine (formerly F101 DFE) and upgraded avionics was made in early 1984. New procurement was halted by the Department of Defense in April 1989 in favor of the "remanufacture" of 400 earlier F-14 aircraft. In 1991 the Navy decided to remanufacture only 104 F-14As to the F-14D configuration by the year 1997, the cutback having been made in an unsuccessful effort to garner funds for new F-14D production. In the event, only 37 new F-14D aircraft and 18 F-14A upgrades to full F-14D configurations were procured. (Of those, 51 remained flying in 1995.)

The F-14C variant was to have been a development of the original (engine update) F-14B with improved avionics. Several research variants are designated NF-14D.

Operational: The 99 F-14 aircraft that participated in Desert Storm flew 4,124 combat sorties. On 6 February 1991, an F-14A shot down an Iraqi Mi-8 Hip helicopter with a Sidewinder missile. This was one of three Navy air-to-air kills in the conflict. (The two other Navy kills were made by F/A-18s.)

The first use of the Tomcat in the air-to-ground role in combat occurred on 5 September 1995, when an F-14A from the carrier THEODORE ROOSEVELT dropped two 2,000-pound (907-kg) bombs on Serb positions in Bosnia.

Status: Operational; no longer in production. First flight F-14A on 21 December 1970; first flight F-14B (an F-14A with a converted engine) on 29 September 1986; first flight F-14A+ on 24 November 1987. The F-14A IOC (VF-124) was in January 1973, the F-14D IOC in November 1990.

The last F-14 was delivered in May 1992. A total of 632 aircraft were produced for the U.S. Navy: 557 F-14A (including development models), 38 F-14A+ (redesignated F-14B), and 37 new F-14D variants. Subsequently, the following F-14A conversions were undertaken: 1 to F-14B (engine change only in 1973); 32 to F-14A+; 3 to F-14D electronic test bed aircraft; 18 to F-14D.

An additional 80 F-14A aircraft were built for Iran; 79 were delivered in 1976–1979, with 1 retained by Grumman after the Iranian revolution.

18. GBU = Guided Bomb Unit, referring to the guidance package fitted to Mk 82 (500-lb), Mk 83 (1,000-lb), and Mk 84 (2,000-lb) bombs.

F-14A

Manufacturer:	Grumman	
Crew:	(2) pilot, radar-intercept officer	
Engines:	2 Pratt & Whitney TF30-P-414A turbofans; 20,900 lbst (9,480 kgst) each with afterburning	
Weights:	empty	40,104 lbs (18,191 kg)
	takeoff with 4 Sparrow AAMs	59,714 lbs (27,086 kg)
	takeoff with 6 Phoenix AAMs	70,764 lbs (32,098 kg)
	maximum T/O	74,349 lbs (33,724 kg)
Dimensions:	length	62 ft 8 in (19.1 m)
	wing span	64 ft 1½ in (19.54 m) unswept 38 ft 2½ in (11.65 m) swept back
	wing area	565 ft² (52.49 m²)
	height	16 ft (4.88 m)
Speed:	maximum	1,544 mph (2,485 km/h) at altitude 912 mph (1,468 km/h) at low level
	maximum cruise	633 mph (1,019 km/h)
Ceiling:	50,000+ ft (15,240+ m)	
Range:	radius approx. 575 miles (925 km) in strike role; 1,065 miles (1,715 km) in air intercept role ferry 2,000 miles (3,220 km) with 2 267-gallon (1,015-liter) drop tanks	
Armament:	1 20-mm Vulcan cannon M61 (multi-barrel; 676 rounds) 2 Phoenix + 3 Sparrow + 2 Sidewinder AAMs + 2 267-gallon (1,015-liter) drop tanks or 4 Phoenix + 2 Sparrow + 2 Sidewinder AAMs + 2 267-gallon drop tanks or 6 Phoenix + 2 Sidewinder AAMs + 2 267-gallon drop tanks or 6 Sparrow + 2 Sidewinder AAMs + 2 267-gallon drop tanks (*Note:* F-14D can carry AMRAAM in place of Sparrow)	
Radar:	AWG-9 in F-14A APG-71 in F-14D	

An F-14A Tomcat from VF-41, carrying four Sparrow AAMs (under fuselage) and four Sidewinder AAMs (under wings), shows a contemporary missile loadout for these planes. An M61 rotary cannon is fitted in all F-14s. (U.S. Navy, Lt. Gerald B. Parsons)

An F-14A Tomcat from VF-211 with an unlikely loadout of six Phoenix long-range AAMs. Developed for long-range intercept of Soviet bombers, the F-14 has been adopted for more flexible roles, including air-to-ground attack. (U.S. Navy)

An F-14 Tomcat, with canopy open, is being towed on a carrier flight deck. All carrier air wings are being reduced to one squadron of F-14s, a significant loss in night/all-weather air-to-air combat capability. (U.S. Navy)

Photographic specialists prepare a TARPS pod fitted on an F-14 Tomcat of VF-84 aboard the THEODORE ROOSEVELT. Several F-14s on each carrier can carry the TARPS, thus providing a tactical photoreconnaissance capability. (U.S. Navy)

An F-14D Tomcat mounting a 20-mm M61 rotary cannon on the left side. Grouped under the nose are, clockwise, the Television Camera Set (TCS), anti-collision beacon (behind which is the ALQ-165 Airborne Self-Protection Jammer [ASPJ]), and the Infrared Search and Track (IRST) sensor. (U.S. Navy, PHAN Jason Drake)

F-5E/F TIGER II

The F-5E/F variants of the F-5 lightweight fighter are flown by the Navy as an air combat maneuvering/adversary training aircraft. The aircraft was the penultimate design in a long series of trainer/fighter aircraft developed by Northrop, primarily for Third World markets. (The much improved F-5G was redesignated F-20.)

Design: The F-5E Tiger is a single-seat aircraft and the F-5F a two-seat version, both with two turbojet engines. Sidewinder AAMs can be carried on wingtips; there are four wing stations and one fuselage station for ordnance.

The aircraft is not carrier capable.

Status: Operational; no longer in production. First flight F-5A on 30 July 1959; first flight F-5E on 11 August 1972.

More than 3,000 F-5 fighters and similar T-38 Talon trainers have been built for the U.S. Air Force and some 25 foreign nations. The U.S. Navy has mostly F-5E variants and a few F-5F aircraft, plus six T-38s to simulate Russian fighter aircraft in adversary training. The Marines previously flew the F-5E/F in reserve adversary training squadron VMFT-401.

Manufacturer:	Northrop	
Crew:	(1) pilot (2 in F-5F)	
Engines:	2 General Electric J85-GE-21B turbojets; 5,000 lbst (2,268 kgst) each with afterburning	
Weights:	empty F-5E	9,723 lbs (4,410 kg)
	F-5F	10,576 lbs (4,797 kg)
	maximum T/O F-5E	24,722 lbs (11,214 kg)
	F-5F	25,152 lbs (11,409 kg)
Dimensions:	length F-5E	47 ft 4¾ in (14.45 m)
	F-5F	51 ft 4 in (15.65 m)
	wing span	26 ft 8 in (8.13 m)
	wing area	186 ft² (17.3 m²)
	height F-5E	13 ft 4 in (4.06 m)
	F-5F	13 ft 1¾ in (4.01 m)
Speed:	maximum	Mach 1.64 at 36,000 ft (10,975 m)
Ceiling:	51,800 ft (15,790 m)	
Range:	radius	655 miles (1,056 km) with 2 Sidewinder AAMs
		1,775 miles (2,861 km) with external tanks
Armament:	none	
Radar:	APQ-159	

F-4 PHANTOM

Long the principal all-weather, multipurpose fighter of the Navy and Marine Corps, all F-4 Phantoms have been retired from Navy and Marine squadrons. They have been replaced by the F-14 Tomcat in Navy fighter squadrons (VF) and the F/A-18 Hornet in Marine fighter-attack squadrons (VMFA).

McDonnell Douglas produced 5,045 aircraft for U.S. and foreign service, while Japan built 125 F-4EJ variants, including 11 from parts produced by McDonnell Douglas. All production ended in 1979; the last of 1,264 aircraft delivered to the Navy and Marine Corps were completed in December 1971 (including 46 of the RF-4B reconnaissance variant). The principal U.S. naval production versions were the F-4B and F-4J, which were subsequently upgraded to the F-4N and F-4S, respectively. The Phantom remains in service with the U.S. Air Force (F-4G Wild Weasel variant) and in several foreign air forces.[19]

The last Navy squadron to fly the Phantom, reserve VF-202, retired its final F-4S in early 1987; the last Marine unit to fly the Phantom (they also flew the F-4S) was reserve VMFA-112, which phased out its final Phantoms in mid-1992. All RF-4B reconnaissance variants have been retired from Marine service.

Designation: The Phantom was originally designated F4H by the Navy and F-110 by the Air Force; this was changed to F-4 in 1962.

See 14th Edition/pages 401–2 for characteristics.

19. The Royal Navy also flew Phantoms from aircraft carriers; the F-4K was Britain's last non-VSTOL carrier-based fighter-attack aircraft.

The reconnaissance version of the Phantom—RF-4B aircraft in Marine livery—as the last specialized photo aircraft to be assigned to Navy carriers (see page 386). Three cameras were installed in the elongated nose; radar and an infrared sensor also were fitted. (U.S. Navy)

MARITIME PATROL/ANTI-SUBMARINE AIRCRAFT

The U.S. Navy has a requirement for 300 land-based maritime patrol aircraft for active and reserve patrol (VP) squadrons, plus special-purpose aircraft (EP-3, RP-3, etc.). This requirement compares to approximately 400 P-3 aircraft in service in 1990 and just over 300 in service in 1995. All first-line VP aircraft are P-3 variants (with various levels of the Update-series of modernization.)

Following cancellation of the P-7 LRAACA program in 1990, the Navy has been examining options to meet future requirements for maritime patrol aircraft. The most likely options are to resume production of an updated P-3 Orion variant, or remanufacture P-3 aircraft into an improved P-3H configuration. The proposed P-3H variant would have the Update IV avionics, survivability enhancements, extended-range Harpoon capability, and a larger sonobuoy capacity.

(P-3 production ended in the United States in 1995 with eight aircraft for South Korea; P-3 production continues in Japan.)

An F-5E Tiger II flown by the Navy's Fighter Weapons School—better known as Top Gun—flies in formation with an F-4 Phantom from VX-4 shortly before that venerable aircraft was retired from naval aviation. The Tiger II is in camouflage, which is often used by adversary training squadrons. Dummy Sidewinder AAMs are on the Tiger II's wingtips. (U.S. Navy, Lt. Comdr. David Baranek)

The never built P-7A LRAACA was a derivative of the long-serving P-3 Orion. Still, the plane ran afoul of technical problems and delays, which led to cancellation of the program. In this artist's concept a lightweight ASW torpedo has just been released from the weapons bay, and the parachute is opening. A variety of weapons are shown on wing pylons. (Lockheed)

P-7A LONG-RANGE AIR ANTI-SUBMARINE WARFARE CAPABLE AIRCRAFT

The P-7 LRAACA was intended to replace the P-3 Orion in the maritime patrol/ASW roles. Development and procurement of the P-7, however, was canceled on 20 July 1990 by the Navy because the contractor, Lockheed, "failed to make adequate progress toward completion of all contract phases, which were to have resulted in the delivery of two prototype aircraft in April and December 1992." The cancellation also affected 125 production aircraft, in addition to the two prototypes, to have been delivered from 1994 through 2001.

In the mid-1980s the Navy held a competition for the P-3 replacement; the Lockheed design, the Boeing 757, and the McDonnell Douglas MD-90 were proposed. The modified P-3 design submitted by Lockheed Aeronautical Systems of Burbank, California, was selected in October 1988 on the basis of acquisition and life-cycle costs, according to the Navy.[20] The $3.5 *billion* program was badly needed at Lockheed, for the last P-3 Orion then scheduled was to come off the production line in September 1991, and few other aircraft were on order. Lockheed subsequently experienced major cost problems, as well as some technical difficulties, with the P-7 program. In March 1989—shortly before the program was canceled—the total estimated acquisition cost of the 125 P-7A aircraft was about $7.9 *billion,* with an approximate production cost of $56.7 million per aircraft.

The technical problems were particularly perplexing to observers because the Lockheed design was in several respects an enlarged P-3, with less technical innovation than the competitive designs.

The LRAACA bore a strong resemblance to the P-3 Orion; there was to be a large internal weapons bay, plus 12 wing hard points for weapons. Up to 150 A-size and 6 B-size sonobuoys were to be carried; other sensors were to be radar and Magnetic Anomaly Detection (MAD) gear. Up to 150 additional sonobuoys were proposed, to be carried in ten pylon-mounted external packs. The P-7 was to have the equivalent of the P-3 Update IV mission suite (see below). With the UYS-2 Enhanced Modular Signal Processor (EMSP) planned for the P-7, it could then monitor 54 DIFAR sonobuoys at once.

Other avionics included the Texas Instruments APS-137 Inverse Synthetic Aperture Radar (ISAR), AAS-36 infrared detection system, SATCOM receiver, inertial navigation system (INS), Omega Global Positioning Satellite (GPS) navigation, ALR-66(V)5 ESM equipment, and ALE-47 chaff/flare dispensers. (An ALR-77 ESM suite may have been fitted in place of the ALR-66, if available.)

The GE-38 engines were estimated to have a 25 percent lower fuel consumption over the aircraft operating envelope compared with the P-3's T56 engines. The improved performance was due in part to five-blade composite propellers.

Initial Navy planning was for 125 aircraft plus two prototypes, but more aircraft were anticipated to fulfill eventual foreign orders. In April 1988 the German government announced that it planned to select the P-7 to replace its Dassault-Breguet Atlantic ASW aircraft for long-range maritime patrol duties.

20. Boeing proposed a modified version of the 757 twin-engine commercial transport and McDonnell Douglas a modified MD-87 twin-engine transport, the latter with ultra-high-bypass-ratio engines. Gulfstream Aerospace had also proposed a twin-engine, wide-body Gulfstream 4 for the LRAACA program, but it was not accepted as a viable competitor.

APPROXIMATE P-7 CHARACTERISTICS

Manufacturer:	Lockheed	
Crew:	(10)	
Engines:	4 GE-38 turboprops; 5,150 shp each	
Weights:	empty	105,000 lbs (47,628 kg)
	gross	165,000 lbs (74,844 kg)
	maximum T/O	171,350 lbs (77,724 kg)
Dimensions:	length	112 ft 8 in (34.34 m)
	wing span	106 ft 7 in (32.49 m)
	wing area	1,438 ft² (129.42 m²)
	height	32 ft 11 in (10.04 m)
Speed:		
Ceiling:		
Range:	radius	1,840 miles (2,963 km) with 6 hours on station
Armament:	23,661 lbs (10,733 kg) of missiles and ASW torpedoes, including 7,500 lbs (3,402 kg) carried in an internal weapons bay (8 Mk 50 torpedoes or four extended-range Harpoon ASMs or 3 B-57 nuclear depth bombs)	
Radar:	APS-137	

P-3 ORION

The Orion is a long-range maritime reconnaissance and ASW aircraft; its Harpoon anti-ship missile provides a surface attack capability. The P-3C Orion serves in all active and reserve Navy patrol squadrons (VP-VPU), with several specialized electronic surveillance (ELINT), research, and utility variants also in naval service. The current total of some 285 aircraft is down from a peak of about 440 Orions flown by the U.S. Navy in the late 1980s.

The decision not to procure the P-7 will require further upgrades to the P-3 force. P-3s are expected to remain in U.S. Navy patrol squadrons at least through 2015.

Design: The Orion was adopted from the commercial Electra transport that was given a lengthened fuselage and other design modifications. It is powered by four turboprop engines. Up to 15,000 pounds (6,804 kg) of rockets, missiles, mines, ASW torpedoes, or nuclear depth bombs can be carried in the internal weapons bay and on ten wing pylons. The P-3C aircraft are fitted to carry the Harpoon. (In the early 1970s some P-3B

This is one of two EP-3J Orions configured for fleet electronic warfare training. Now flown by reserve VP-66, these aircraft carry internal and pod-fitted deception and jamming equipment. (U.S. Navy, J. Long)

variants were fitted to carry the AGM-12 Bullpup missile.) The plane's ASW equipment includes radar, tail-mounted ASQ-81 MAD, and 48 external (fuselage) sonobuoy chutes, plus 4 in-flight reloadable (internal) chutes. A total of 84 buoys are normally carried.

The P-3C variants have undergone a series of modernizations: Update I of the mid-1970s included a computer upgrade, Omega navigation system, additional tactical displays, and a new tactical program for computer-aided analysis of incoming data. Update II—introduced in 1977—had additional navigation capabilities and provision for the Harpoon anti-ship missile. The latest improvement series is Update III, introduced in 1984; this provides an IBM Proteus signal processor system and new avionics. An Update IV has been developed that will further improve EW, radar, and acoustic systems. Plans to provide an in-flight refueling capability have not been pursued.

An updated P-3C Orion banks while carrying four Harpoon anti-ship missiles and several practice bombs on wing pylons. The weapons bay—fitted forward of the wing—is open. These aircraft also carry various ASW weapons and mines. (U.S. Navy)

The 12 EP-3E Aries II variants (flown by squadrons VQ-1 and VQ-2) have automatic electronic and communication intercept/analysis equipment to provide fleet and task force commanders with real-time intelligence. The aircraft have an ALR-52 multi-band frequency measuring receiver and/or ALR-60 Deepwell communications intercept/analysis system and an ALR-76 combined ESM/radar warning system.

Several NP-3D aircraft are flown in various research configurations by the Navy; these were previously designated RP-3A/D, EP-3A/B, and several UP-3A test bed variants. The Navy also flies a dozen UP-3A/B and five VP-3A "bob-tailed" (sans MAD "stinger") aircraft as executive transports and support aircraft. Two WP-3Ds are operated by the Commerce Department/NOAA and several UP-3A aircraft have been on loan to the Customs Service for anti-drug surveillance since October 1985. A couple of those aircraft have been fitted with an APG-53 radar, as in the Air Force F-15 fighter; one with an APS-125 radar with rotodome antenna, as in the E-2C; and one with an APS-138 radar. NASA flies one P-3B.

A planned P-3G for the U.S. Navy was to have had new engines and updated avionics. (This aircraft was incorrectly identified as a P-3F in some official documents; six P-3F variants were produced for Iran.) The procurement of 125 P-3G models in fiscal 1990–1995 was envisioned; however, the Navy did not pursue the P-3G option because only Lockheed responded to the Navy's request for a proposal, and the P-7 LRAACA was developed in its place. Proposals were also being considered to reengine and upgrade the avionics of the P-3C force, with a possible enlargement of the weapons bay to internally carry extended-range Harpoon missiles. That upgraded version would be labeled P-3H.

Two P-3B aircraft were modified in 1992 to the EP-3J configuration for fleet training (flown by reserve squadron VP-66). The aircraft is fitted with the USQ-113 communications intrusion and deception system and can carry the ALE-43, ALQ-167, ALQ-170, and AST-4/6 pods.

Future upgrades for the P-3C may include: the APS-137 Inverse Synthetic Aperture Radar (ISAR); Cluster Ranger, a long-range, day/night electro-optical imaging system; modernizing the AAS-36 infrared system to improve effectiveness against small targets, both day and night; new tactical displays; UHF satellite communications system; and Maverick air-to-surface missiles.

Designation: The Orion was originally designated P3V, which was changed to P-3 in 1962.

Status: Operational; no longer in production for the U.S. Navy. First flight (aerodynamic airframe) on 19 August 1958; YP-3A on 25 November 1959; P-3A on 15 April 1961; YP-3C on 18 September 1968. P-3A IOC (VP-8) was in August 1962; P-3C IOC in 1969.

Lockheed facilities at Burbank and Palmdale, California, delivered a total of 551 Orions to the U.S. Navy and Naval Air Reserve. The last U.S. Navy Orion to be produced was a P-3C, delivered on 17 April 1990. (The last Palmdale aircraft was a CP-140A, ordered by the Canadian Forces and completed in May 1991. The eight P-3C aircraft for South Korea were delivered by the Lockheed-Martin facility at Marietta, Georgia, in 1995.)

Almost 200 aircraft—new and ex-U.S. Navy—are flown by Australia, Canada, Iran, Japan, South Korea, the Netherlands, New

A P-3C Orion assigned to reserve VP-65 about to land at NAS Point Mugu, California. The wheel doors in the nose and under the inboard engine nacelles are beginning to open. The four-turboprop aircraft has demonstrated considerable effectiveness and reliability. (U.S. Navy, Vance Vasquez)

A P-3C from VP-5 banks away from the camera. The sonobuoy chutes are under the after fuselage, below the star-and-bars insignia. The MAD "stinger" is fixed in the tail—common to VP aircraft—compared to retractable MAD booms in carrier-based ASW aircraft. (U.S. Navy, PH3 Darwin Coligado)

An EP-3E Orion configured for ELINT collection. Flown by VQ-1, the aircraft has a radome under the fuselage and antenna "canoes" mounted in the dorsal and ventral positions; the MAD stinger has been "bobbed." Low-visibility markings are usually worn during ELINT operations. (U.S. Navy, R. Hepp)

Zealand, Norway, Portugal, Spain, and Thailand. Kawasaki in Japan assembled five airframes produced by Lockheed and, under license, built more than 100 P-3C, EP-3, UP-3C, and UP-3D aircraft for the Japanese Maritime Self-Defense Force.[21] Numerous upgrade programs are under way for non–U.S. aircraft.

P-3C

Manufacturer:	Lockheed	
Crew:	(10) command pilot, 2 pilots, flight engineer, navigator/communications officer, tactical coordinator, 3 systems operators; 1 technician; provisions for 2 additional observers	
Engines:	4 Allison T56-A-14 turboprops; 4,910 shp each	
Weights:	empty	61,491 lbs (27,892 kg)
	normal T/O	135,000 lbs (61,236 kg)
	maximum T/O	142,000 lbs (64,411 kg)
Dimensions:	length	116 ft 10 in (35.61 m)
	wing span	99 ft 8 in (30.37 m)
	wing area	1,300 ft^2 (120.77 m^2)
	height	33 ft 8½ in (10.29 m)
Speed:	maximum	473 mph (761 km/h) at 15,000 ft (4,573 m)
	cruise	380 mph (611 km/h) at 25,000 ft (7,622 m)
	loiter	230 mph (370 km/h) with two engines shut down
Ceiling:	28,300 ft (8,628 m)	
Range:	radius	1,550 miles (2,493 km) with 13 hours on station
Armament:	*weapons bay*	*wing points*
	8 Mk 46/50 torpedoes	+ 4 Mk 46/50 torpedoes
or	2 2,000-lb mines	+ 4 Mk 46/50 torpedoes
or	4 1,000-lb mines	+ 4 Mk 46/50 torpedoes
or	8 Mk 46/50 torpedoes	+ 16 5-inch rockets
Radar:	APS-20 in EP-3B/E	
	APS-115 in P-3C	

P-2 NEPTUNE

The P-2 Neptune was a long-range, highly versatile maritime patrol aircraft flown by U.S. Navy patrol squadrons. The last U.S. Neptunes were three EP-2H models in service into the early 1980s, assigned to squadron VC-8 supporting target drones.

Lockheed produced 1,036 Neptunes for U.S. and foreign service, and Kawasaki built another 89 P-2J variants in Japan (with 48 of the Lockheed aircraft assembled in that country). Seven P2V-7U Neptunes were delivered to the U.S. Air Force and flew as RB-69A electronic reconnaissance aircraft. The 12 P2V-3C variants of the late 1940s were configured for carrier launch, but not recovery, to provide the first U.S. ship-based nuclear strike capability.

Japan is the only nation to now fly Neptunes; they will be phased out in the near future, replaced by P-3 Orions.

Designation: Originally designated P2V, the designation was changed to P-2 in 1962.

S-3 VIKING

The S-3 Viking is the Navy's carrier-based ASW aircraft; one eight-plane squadron serves on board each carrier. The Viking replaced the S2F/S-2 Tracker as the Navy's ship-based, fixed-wing ASW aircraft. Existing aircraft are being upgraded to the S-3B configuration.

The S-3 was designed to be within the approximate dimensions of the piston-engine Tracker, but to be faster and to carry more advanced ASW equipment. The internal weapons bay, sized to hold four lightweight ASW torpedoes, can carry 2,400 pounds (1,089 kg) of weapons. There are also two wing pylons, which in the S-3B are upgraded to carry the Harpoon anti-ship missile. ASW systems include the ASQ-81 MAD, FLIR, and 60 sonobuoys in fuselage chutes. The wings and tail fin fold for carrier stowage.

A major avionics upgrade program for 124 S-3B aircraft was begun in 1995.

The S-3B has an improved acoustic processor and the improved APS-137 ISAR radar. Six preproduction S-3A aircraft were modified to a US-3A cargo configuration for operation from carriers in the Western Pacific and Indian Ocean; those planes were taken out of service in the early 1990s (see 15th Edition/pages 414–15). A KS-3 tanker configuration as well as pod tanks and a drogue system have been proposed for the US-3A variant; no development was undertaken.

An S-3B Viking from VS-41 goes belly up for the camera, revealing the closed weapons bay and sonobuoy chutes. Practice weapons are mounted on the wings, outboard of the engine nacelles. (Chris Buhlmann)

21. The single Japanese UP-3C is an in-flight electronic systems test bed aircraft; the UP-3D aircraft support fleet EW training.

Sixteen S-3A aircraft have been converted to the ELINT role and are designated ES-3A (see page 385).

Operational: S-3A/B aircraft served as ground attack aircraft in Operation Desert Storm. The 41 Vikings that participated in Operation Desert Storm flew 1,674 combat sorties.

Status: Operational; no longer in production. First flight on 21 January 1972. S-3A IOC (VS-41) was in February 1974.

The last of 187 S-3A aircraft were completed in 1978. About 160 were upgraded to S-3B by 1994. Proposals for additional S-3 production have not come to fruition.

An S-3B Viking flown by air test and evaluation squadron VX-1 in flight with drop tanks. The MAD stinger is retracted into the tail. S-3B squadrons are assigned to all carriers. (U.S. Navy)

An S-3B Viking from VS-21 serves as a tanker to refuel another carrier-based aircraft. The drogue pod is fitted on the port wing, a drop tank on the starboard wing. The S-3 can also pump fuel from its own tanks. The S-3B has largely replaced the KA-6D Intruder in the tanker role. (U.S. Navy)

This S-3B Viking from VS-22, with two drop tanks under its wings, is about to land on the JOHN F. KENNEDY. In addition to ASW, these aircraft have been employed as tankers, decoy launchers, and bombers. (U.S. Navy, PH1 Michael D.P. Flynn)

Manufacturer:	Lockheed		
Crew:	(4) pilot, copilot, tactical coordinator, systems operator		
Engines:	2 General Electric TF34-GE-400 turbofans; 9,275 lbst (4,207 kgst) each		
Weights:	empty	26,783 lbs (12,149 kg)	
	maximum T/O	52,539 lbs (23,832 kg)	
Dimensions:	length	53 ft 4 in (16.26 m)	
	wing span	68 ft 8 in (20.93 m)	
	wing area	598 ft² (55.56 m²)	
	height	22 ft 9 in (6.94 m)	
Speed:	maximum	506 mph (814 km/h) at sea level	
	cruise	400+ mph (644+ km/h)	
	loiter	240 mph (386 km/h) at 20,000 ft (6,098 m)	
Ceiling:	40,000 ft (12,195 m)		
Range:	patrol	2,645+ miles (4,260+ km)	
	ferry	3,450+ miles (5,556+ km)	
Armament:	*weapons bay*		*wing points*
	4 Mk 46/50 torpedoes		+ 6 500-lb bombs
or	4 500-lb bombs		+ 6 500-lb bombs
Radar:	APS-116 in S-3A		
	APS-137 ISAR in S-3B		

S-2 TRACKER

The S2F was the U.S. Navy's first integrated search/attack ASW aircraft. In U.S. Navy service from 1954 to 1976 in the carrier-based ASW role, it was the progenitor of the E-1 Tracer and C-1 Trader aircraft.

Grumman produced a total of 1,169 Trackers for U.S. and foreign service; another 100 were built in Canada. After service in the U.S. Navy, many aircraft were transferred to other nations, and several remain in foreign air forces. The last U.S. Navy Tracker—called "Stoof" from its S2F designation—was an ES-2D configured as a range support aircraft that was retired in 1986. The last ASW variant was an S-2G, retired from VS-37 in August 1976.

Designation: The Tracker was changed from S2F to S-2 in 1962.

An S-3B Viking showing the sonobuoy chutes mounted aft of the (closed) weapons bay. Two Harpoon air-to-surface missiles are mounted outboard of the twin turbofan engine nacelles. (Lockheed-California)

ELECTRONIC AIRCRAFT

U.S. naval electronic aircraft have two distinct types of designations: those with E-series designations that were designed specifically for an electronic mission (e.g., E-2C, E-6A), and those that have been adopted from other aircraft types and have an E-prefix to their designation (e.g., EA-6B, EC-130Q, EP-3E). In this subsection, all electronic aircraft are listed in alphabetical sequence by designation, which is not their chronological order.

In addition to the electronic aircraft discussed here, the Customs Service flies AEW-configured P-3 Orions, and the Coast Guard evaluated an AEW-configured C-130 Hercules (see pages 377 and 384, respectively).

Studies are under way to determine the feasibility of employing a variant of the F/A-18F Hornet as an EW/ECM aircraft to replace the EA-6B Prowler.

E-6A MERCURY

This aircraft has replaced the EC-130 Hercules in the TACAMO (Take Charge and Move Out) role of providing VLF radio relay to strategic missile submarines at sea. The E-6A is a modified Boeing 707-320B airframe, which also serves as the airframe for the E-3A AWACS (Airborne Warning and Control System). The KC-135/C-135/VC-137/EC-18/E-8A aircraft are similar.

By the late 1990s the Navy E-6A aircraft will also replace 27 Air Force EC-135 aircraft in the "Looking Glass" program, additionally providing airborne control of U.S. strategic weapons. At that time the Navy aircraft will be modified to the E-6B configuration and carry joint Navy–Air Force operational teams.

Design: The Navy had proposed a competition of available airframes; only the Boeing Company responded, however, proposing their modified 707-320B airframe. The E-6A has the familiar lines of the Boeing 707-series commercial transports, but it is fitted with four large GE/SNECMA turbofan engines. (The engine oil tanks have been enlarged to provide for increased flight endurance.)

In the TACAMO role the E-6A has essentially the same communications equipment as the EC-130Q, with two trailing-wire antennas, one almost 5,000 feet (1,524 m) and the other some 30,000 feet (9,146 m) in length; only the shorter wire is electrically charged, with energy re-radiating off of the longer wire. Wingtip pods on the E-6A contain satellite communication antennas. The aircraft are hardened against Electromagnetic Pulse (EMP) effects. They retain the in-flight refueling receptacle for the Air Force flying-boom refueling system. Normal mission duration is 16 hours; with in-flight refueling that can be extended to 72 hours.

Status: Operational; no longer in production. First flight in February 1987. IOC (VQ-3) was in August 1989 and first operational mission completed on 31 October of that year.

The E-6A program consists of one prototype aircraft that has been upgraded to full operational capability and 15 production aircraft. The prototype was delivered in 1987; that aircraft was reconfigured as a standard E-6A and "redelivered" in 1992. The last aircraft was delivered on 7 May 1992.

Manufacturer:	Boeing	
Crew:	(18) 4 flight crew + 6 mission crew + 8 relief crew	
Engines:	4 General Electric/SNECMA F108-CF-100 turbofans; 24,000 lbst (10,886 kgst) each	
Weights:	empty	172,795 lbs (78,380 kg)
	maximum T/O	342,000 lbs (155,131 kg)
Dimensions:	length	152 ft 11 in (46.62 m)
	wing span	148 ft 2 in (45.17 m)
	wing area	3,050 ft^2 (283.4 m^2)
	height	42 ft 5 in (12.93 m)
Speed:	cruise	508 mph (817 km/h)
	maximum	607 mph (977 km/h)
Ceiling:	42,000 ft (12,805 m)	
Range:	7,590 miles (12,223 km)	
	radius 1,150 miles (1,852 km) with 10½-hour loiter on station	
Radar:	APS-133 weather	

A banking E-6A Mercury aircraft reveals its lineage from the Boeing 707/C-135/E-3 series. The wingtip antennas are for satellite communications. (U.S. Navy)

An E-6A Mercury TACAMO aircraft streams a trailing wire antenna. The aircraft will take over the Air Force's Looking Glass responsibilities with an upgrade to the E-6B configuration. The aircraft's name was changed from Hermes (Greek mythology) to Mercury (Roman mythology) to avoid confusion with the disease herpes. (Department of Defense)

E-2C HAWKEYE

The Hawkeye is an Airborne Early Warning (AEW) aircraft developed specifically for carrier operation. The E-2C variant is considered by many authorities as the most capable radar warning and aircraft control plane now in service. A four-plane squadron is provided to each carrier, having replaced the piston-engine WF/E-1 Tracer in AEW squadrons.

Procurement continues through the five-year defense plan at the rate of four aircraft per year. Previously planned rebuilding of the aircraft has been canceled in favor of new E-2C aircraft; a "hot" production line will facilitate continued foreign sales.

Design: The Hawkeye's most distinctive feature is the 24-foot (7.3-m) diameter, saucer-like radome for the APS-120 or APS-125 UHF radar. The radome revolves freely in the airstream at the rate of six revolutions per minute. It provides sufficient lift to offset its own weight in flight, and on board ship it can be lowered to facilitate aircraft handling. The E-2C represents primarily an avionics upgrade over the previous E-2A/B variants (which had the APS-96 radar). Beginning with the fiscal 1986 procurement, the E-2C had the upgraded T56-A-427 engines, providing improved flight safety and an increase in aircraft weight.

The APS-120 radar with over-water surveillance capability was initially installed in E-2C aircraft. Electronic upgrades have included the APS-125 radar, with its effective aircraft detection range of some 275 miles (444.5 km) and over-land/water capability. The aircraft can simultaneously track more than 250 air targets and control up to 30 interceptors. The ALR-73 passive detection system is also installed. The more capable APS-145 radar is being developed as an update for all E-2C aircraft.

Designation: Originally designated W2F, the Hawkeye was changed to E-2 in 1962.

Operational: During Operation Desert Storm the 27 E-2C aircraft on U.S. carriers flew 1,183 combat sorties.

Status: Operational; in production. First flight E-2A on 21 October 1960; first flight E-2C on 20 January 1971. The IOC of E-2A (VAW-11) was in January 1964, IOC E-2C (VAW-123) in November 1973.

Fifty-nine E-2A aircraft were delivered from 1960 to 1967; all have been retired. The E-2B was a designation assigned but not popularly used for E-2A aircraft containing upgraded computers. Two E-2A development aircraft were modified to a YE-2C configuration; these and two early production E-2C aircraft were later employed as trainers (TE-2C).

An E-2C Hawkeye from VAW-120 on a local training flight. The second tail fin does not have control surfaces; it is provided for aerodynamic stability. (Peter B. Mersky)

An E-2C Hawkeye from VAW-125 is about to land aboard a carrier. AEW/AWACS aircraft have become an indispensable part of U.S. air activities in combat and surveillance operations. The Hawkeye has been used extensively in anti-drug operations. (U.S. Navy)

An E-2C Hawkeye taxies on a Middle East runway during a multinational exercise. Hawkeyes have been upgraded to provide an over-land as well as over-water detection capability against low-flying aircraft. (Department of Defense)

An E-2C Hawkeye flown by VAW-120, the transition-readiness training squadron for Navy E-2C airborne early warning and C-2A COD flight crews. The Hawkeye force will require major upgrades or replacement early in the 21st century. (Peter B. Mersky)

A small number of E-2C aircraft were transferred to the Coast Guard in 1987 and to the Customs Service in 1989 for anti-drug operations. The aircraft is also flown by Egypt, Israel, Japan, Singapore, and Taiwan. (Taiwan is receiving E-2B aircraft, designated E-2T, which will subsequently be upgraded to E-2C capability with APS-145 radar.)

Manufacturer:	Grumman	
Crew:	(5) pilot, copilot, combat information center officer, air controller, radar operator or technician	
Engines:	2 Allison T56-A-422 turboprops; 4,591 shp each	
Weights:	empty	37,678 lbs (17,090 kg)
	maximum T/O	51,569 lbs (23,392 kg)
Dimensions:	length	57 ft 7 in (17.56 m)
	wing span	80 ft 7 in (24.58 m)
	wing area	700 ft² (65.03 m²)
	height	18 ft 4 in (5.59 m)
Speed:	maximum	375 mph (603 km/h)
	cruise	310 mph (499 km/h)
Ceiling:	30,800 ft (9,390 m)	
Range:	radius	230 miles (370 km) with 6 hours on station
	ferry	1,755 miles (2,820 km)
Armament:	none	
Radar:	APS-125 (APS-120 in early E-2C aircraft); being replaced by APS-145	

E-1 TRACER

The E-1 Tracer AEW aircraft has been discarded from Navy service. Based on the S-2 Tracker and C-1 Trader cargo aircraft, the E-1 introduced the fixed, aerodynamically shaped radome (for the APS-82 radar) to carrier aircraft. A C-1A flew as the aerodynamic prototype for the AEW configuration, followed by the production of 88 WF-2/E-1B aircraft, with deliveries from 1958 to 1961.

Designation: The Tracer was originally designated WF-2; this was changed to E-1 in 1962.[22]

EA-6B PROWLER

The EA-6B is an extensively modified Intruder that features significantly more EW/ECM capabilities than previous carrier-based electronic aircraft. Four-plane VAQ squadrons flying the Prowler are normally assigned to each carrier.

22. The XWF-1 was Grumman Design No. 95 for an earlier AEW aircraft that was to carry the APS-20A radar based on the S2F initiated in 1951. Two prototypes were ordered, but the project was terminated early in 1953 before either aircraft was completed. The WF-2 was initiated in early 1955.

The Prowler ICAP II variant is the world's most capable, combat-proven tactical jamming aircraft.

The EA-6B is scheduled to take over the Air Force tactical EW mission now flown by EF-111A Raven aircraft.

Design: The Prowler has the basic Intruder configuration with an enlarged cockpit for two additional crew members. A distinctive electronics pod is mounted atop the tail fin, and up to five jamming pods and two fuel tanks can be carried on the fuselage and wing pylons. The total weight of internal avionics/EW equipment is 8,000 pounds (3,636 kg); in addition, 950 pounds (431 kg) can be carried on each of five pylons. Normally, five ALQ-99 pods are carried, each with two jamming transmitters, although a 300-gallon (1,140-liter) drop tank can be substituted for each pod. Beginning in 1986, EA-6B aircraft have been configured to carry the HARM anti-radar missile, their first "hard kill" armament.

A KA-6H tanker based on the enlarged EA-6B airframe was proposed as a successor to the KA-6D, but none was procured.

The EA-6B has undergone a number of EW system upgrades since the original configuration. These modifications have been given the following designations: EXCAP (Expanded Capability), in service from 1973 to 1985; ICAP (Improved Capability), first delivered in 1976; ICAP II, first delivered in 1984; and ADVCAP (Advanced Capability), entering service in 1994. The ADVCAP was terminated in 1994, however, after the ICAP II aircraft were examined in view of predicted post–Cold War threats. These upgrades were made in response to changing foreign radar/SAM threats and have been incorporated into new-production EA-6B aircraft.

The ADVCAP upgrades included adding the low-band ALQ-149 communications ECM, providing two additional ALE-39 chaff/flare dispensers (bringing the total to four), and fitting the J52-P-409 engine to increase allowable landing weight by about 2,000 pounds (907 kg) and to decrease stall speed. The number of wing pylons has been increased to seven, and the Global Positioning System (GPS) is provided. In addition, the jammer pods have been successively upgraded from the basic ALQ-99 to the A/B/C configurations, primarily to increase reliability.

Names: The EA-6B name was changed from Intruder to Prowler in February 1972.

Operational: During Operation Desert Storm the 27 Navy EA-6B aircraft flew 1,126 combat sorties from carriers; the 12 Marine EA-6B aircraft in the area flew 511 sorties from shore bases.

Status: Operational; no longer in production. First flight (converted A-6A) on 25 May 1968; first flight (production EA-6B) November 1970. The IOC (VAQ-129) was in January 1971.

An EA-6B Prowler carrying a jamming pod and drop tank under each wing. This aircraft can be readily distinguished from the A-6E Intruder attack aircraft by the larger, four-place cockpit and the jamming pod atop the tail fin. (U.S. Navy, Comdr. John Leenhouts)

Three A-6A Intruder airframes were modified to serve as development aircraft for the EA-6B program. Grumman Aircraft delivered the last of 170 new production Prowlers to the Navy and Marine Corps in November 1991.

Manufacturer:	Grumman	
Crew:	(4) pilot, 3 electronic countermeasures operators[23]	
Engines:	2 Pratt & Whitney J52-P-408 turbojets; 11,200 lbst (5,080 kgst) each	
Weights:[24]	empty	32,162 lbs (14,589 kg)
	normal T/O	54,461 lbs (24,704 kg)
	maximum T/O	65,000 lbs (29,480 kg)
Dimensions:	length	59 ft 10 in (18.24 m)
	wing span	53 ft (16.15 m)
	wing area	528.9 ft² (49.1 m²)
	height	16 ft 3 in (4.95 m)
Speed:	maximum	613 mph (986 km/h) at sea level
	cruise	483 mph (777 km/h)
Ceiling:	41,000 ft (12,500 m)	
Range:	805 miles (1,296 km)	
Armament:	2 HARM ASM	
Radar:	APQ-129	

23. The ECMO in the right forward seat (next to the pilot) also serves as navigator.
24. Normal takeoff weight, speed, ceiling, and range while carrying five jammer pods.

An EA-6B Prowler from VAQ-140 with two HARM anti-radar missiles on wing pylons; a jamming pod is under the fuselage and the port wing. These aircraft will long survive their progenitor, the A-6 Intruder. (U.S. Navy)

The four-man crew arrangement of the EA-6B Prowler is apparent in this view of an aircraft being readied for takeoff. The previous EA-6A Intruder had but one ECM operator in addition to the pilot. The A-6 Intruder's fixed refueling probe is retained in the EA-6B. (John Bouvia)

EA-6A INTRUDER

This variant of the carrier-based Intruder had a built-in ECM suite to detect and jam hostile radars, primarily for suppressing anti-aircraft missile systems. The aircraft was developed specifically for Marine Corps use; beginning in 1977, it was succeeded in Marine service by the more capable EA-6B Prowler. It was flown by the Navy only in the fleet training role.

The EA-6A differed from the later and larger EA-6B Prowler in having only one ECM operator (vice three in the EA-6B) and significantly less electronics equipment.

Seven A-6A Intruder attack aircraft were converted to the EA-6A configuration, followed by the production of 21 EA-6A aircraft that were delivered by Grumman from 1965. The EA-6A began service in December 1965 with squadron VMCJ-2. The last EA-6A in service was a Navy aircraft (in VAQ-33), which was retired in 1993.

Designation: Originally designated A2F-1H, which was changed to EA-6A in 1962.

See 15th Edition/pages 419–20 for characteristics.

EC-24A

The single EC-24A, flown by the Navy in the electronic warfare simulation/jamming role in support of weapons development and fleet exercises, was discarded in 1992. The aircraft, a converted commercial DC-8 series 54F, was placed in service in November 1987 and operated and supported by a contractor.

This four-turbofan transport was the only U.S. military aircraft given a C-24 series designation. It became operational in 1987.

See 15th Edition/page 421 for characteristics.

EC-130V HERCULES

The EC-130V was an Airborne Early Warning (AEW) conversion of an HC-130H Hercules aircraft developed for U.S. Coast Guard evaluation. It had a large rotating radome (rotodome) for the APS-125 radar of the type fitted in the E-2C Hawkeye.[25]

Flight testing for the aircraft began in July 1991; it was handed over to the Coast Guard on 16 October 1991 for a one-year evaluation. The Coast Guard referred to the project as a High-Endurance Surveillance (HES) aircraft and gave it the nickname "Delphi." The initial funding for the project was based on the aircraft's potential value in anti-drug surveillance operations. The single EC-130V has been transferred to the Air Force.

See 15th Edition/pages 421–22 for characteristics.

EC-130Q HERCULES

The EC-130Q aircraft were C-130 transports extensively modified for the TACAMO role of communications relay with strategic missile submarines (SSBN). These aircraft had the USC-13 airborne VLF communications suite with trailing wire antennas. The E-6A Mercury replaced the 22 TACAMO "Herks" in squadrons VQ-3 and VQ-4.

EP-3E ORION

These are P-3 Orions extensively modified for Electronic Intelligence (ELINT) collection. Twelve P-3C variants are being converted to the EP-3E Aries II configuration, replacing earlier EP-3E Aries I aircraft.

The Japanese Maritime Self-Defense Force is acquiring six Kawasaki-produced EP-3 variants for ELINT missions.

See page 376 for basic characteristics.

25. The aircraft should properly have been redesignated EC-130H; however, that designation is already used for the U.S. Air Force "Compass Call" electronic jamming aircraft.

ES-3A VIKING

The Navy converted 16 S-3A Viking carrier-based ASW aircraft to an ES-3A configuration to serve as electronic surveillance aircraft. The aircraft are generally called *Shadow.*

These aircraft replace the long-serving EA-3B Skywarrior. Sometimes labeled TASES for Tactical Airborne Signal Exploitation System, the aircraft's missions are: (1) electronic warfare reconnaissance (i.e., surveillance); (2) over-the-horizon targeting; and (3) airborne tactical command, control, communications, and intelligence.

The Navy began seeking an EA-3B replacement in the mid-1970s with a planned IOC of 1981. There was little movement toward that goal, however, and the EA-3B "Whales" continued flying in this role until 1987, when they were involved in an increasing number of operational accidents and were assigned exclusively to land-based operations. (They participated in the 1991 war in the Persian Gulf.)

Design: The ES-3A is believed to be fitted with the same systems as the EA-3B; it is also fitted with the APS-137 ISAR radar.

Status: Operational. First flight prototype ES-3A conversion (NS-3A aerodynamic prototype) on 7 September 1989 (the second conversion was the first with a full electronics suite; first flight 21 January 1992.) The IOC (VQ-5) was on 9 May 1992. All aircraft were delivered in 1992–1993 to squadrons VQ-5 and VQ-6; one or two ES-3A aircraft normally operate aboard each forward-deployed carrier.

The ES-3A Viking is the long-awaited replacement for the carrier-based EA-3B Skywarrior in the ELINT role. Sixteen of these aircraft—unofficially referred to as Shadows—are now flown by squadrons VQ-5 and VQ-6. (U.S. Navy)

An ES-3A Viking assigned to test and evaluation squadron VX-1 is about to launch from a carrier steaming in the Mediterranean. The ES-3A has wing-tip antennas and a dorsal antenna "canoe" with a "top hat" antenna. (U.S. Navy, PH3 Bruce Moore)

NKC-135A STRATOTANKER

The Navy's two NKC-135A aircraft employed in the electronic warfare simulation/jamming role in support of weapons development and fleet exercises were discarded in 1992. They replaced a pair of modified EB-47E Stratojet bombers previously flown in this role. The two NKC-135A aircraft entered Navy service in 1977–1978 and were contractor operated.

The aircraft were modified Boeing 707/Air Force KC-135A tankers originally fitted with in-flight refueling equipment. They were modified by the Air Force for research work, their refueling equipment having been removed. Further modifications by the Navy included removal of some of the body fuel cells to provide equipment bays, replacement of the weather track radar with a sea search unit, provision of wing pylons for electronic pods, and an electronic warfare officer/navigator station in the cargo cabin area. Each carried about 12,500 pounds (5,670 kg) of electronic equipment on board and had two wing pylons, thus providing a greater jamming capability than any other aircraft then flying.

Operational: The two NKC-135A and the single EC-24 aircraft were operated by contractor personnel for the Fleet Electronic Warfare Support Group (FEWSG) to provide ECM training for naval forces. These planes had Navy markings but did not carry FEWSG's GD tail code. Squadrons VAQ-33, VAQ-34, and VAQ-35 also operated under FEWSG.

See 14th Edition/page 416 for NKC-135A characteristics.

ADVANCED TACTICAL SUPPORT AIRCRAFT

This plane was viewed by the Navy as a "totally new start": that is, an aircraft to replace the E-2C Hawkeye, EA-6B Prowler, and eventually the S-3B and ES-3A Viking while possibly providing new capabilities to support carrier battle groups. The Advanced Tactical Support (ATS) aircraft was conceived in the late 1980s. Funding for advanced development was provided by Congress until fiscal 1991, when all ATS funding was deleted and the project terminated.

The V-22 Osprey VSTOL aircraft was at one point considered a viable candidate for the ATS role until Secretary of Defense Cheney canceled the V-22 program in 1989. In the ATS role the V-22 was to have had the valuable attributes of being independent of flight deck cycles on large carriers and capable of operating from large surface combatant and amphibious ships. (Meanwhile, British Aerospace and the Bell-Boeing team have revealed proposals for a long-range, anti-submarine version of the V-22, while potential British carrier-based airborne early warning and other variants are being evaluated.)

The Navy had also identified two other potential roles for the ATS: (1) airborne battle management, having the computer power and other facilities to enable a force commander or tactical action officer to direct operations from above the force; and (2) the "missileer" concept. First advanced in the 1960s with the never-built Douglas F6D aircraft, the missileer provides for a relatively low-performance aircraft to remain on station for long periods with advanced air-to-air missiles to intercept incoming attackers.

When this edition went to press it appeared that efforts would be made to extend the service life of the E-2C, EA-6B, and ES-3A, with an ATS not becoming available for service use before 2005–2010.

OBSERVATION/RECONNAISSANCE AIRCRAFT

RU-38A

The Coast Guard operates three Schweizer-built RU-38A lightweight surveillance aircraft for drug surveillance off the coast of Florida. These aircraft, acquired in late 1995, replace two Schweizer RG-8A motorized gliders that were flown at night, in an ultra-quiet mode.

Design: The aircraft has a twin-boom configuration; the main fuselage contains the cockpit, with side-by-side seating, and the engines, with both a tractor and a pusher propeller. They have low-noise signatures. Flight endurance is ten hours, maximum, with no fuel reserves.

RU-38A sensors include FLIR, Low-Light-Level Television (LLLTV), laser range finder, and APN-215 navigation radar. Fitted with GPS.

Status: Operational. First flight in May 1995; the IOC was in 1995. The aircraft are based at Miami, Florida.

Manufacturer:	Schweizer	
Crew:	(2) pilot, observer	
Engines:	2 Continental GIO-550 geared piston; 250 hp each	
Weights:	empty	3,360 lbs (1,524 kg)
	gross T/O	5,300 (2,404 kg)
Dimensions:	length	30 ft 2 in (9.19 m)
	wing span	64 ft (19.51 m)
	wing area	225.86 ft² (20.98 m²)
	height	
Speed:	cruise	103.5 mph (166.5 km/h)
Ceiling:	24,000 ft (7,317 m)	
Range:	890 miles (1,435 km)	
Armament:	none	
Radar:	APN-215 navigation	

An RU-38A motorized glider seen just prior to delivery to the Coast Guard by the Schweizer Aircraft Corporation. The earlier RG-8 motorized gliders were very successful in anti-drug surveillance missions over the Caribbean area. (Schweizer Aircraft)

Another view of a Coast Guard RU-38A before delivery. The aircraft has two piston engines in the center fuselage with pusher/puller propellers. These aircraft are very quiet and have small radar returns. (Schweizer Aircraft)

RG-8A MOTORIZED GLIDERS

Two Schweizer motorized gliders were procured by the Coast Guard in the 1980s for drug-interdiction surveillance. They were obtained from the Department of Defense, which apparently employed the craft in clandestine operations. They have been replaced by the RU-38 gliders.

See 15th Edition/page 452 for characteristics.

OV-10D BRONCO

The last Marine observation squadrons to fly the OV-10D Bronco were disestablished in 1993; the last OV-10D was transferred from the Marine Corps to the Bureau of Alcohol, Tobacco, and Firearms on 24 July 1994. The STOL operating characteristics permitted limited flight operations from LHA/LPH-type ships without the use of catapults or arresting gear.

The turboprop Bronco was developed during the Vietnam War as a multipurpose Counterinsurgency (COIN) aircraft. The Navy also flew the Bronco during the Vietnam War. The Navy and Marine Corps took delivery of 114 aircraft from 1967 to 1969, with additional OV-10s going to the U.S. Air Force and foreign services. Former Marine OV-10D aircraft—stripped of their weapons—were transferred to the ATF Bureau. Other ex-Marine Broncos have been transferred to the Bureau of Land Management and California Forestry Department.

See 15th Edition/page 424 for characteristics.

O-2A SKYMASTER

The Navy flew six former Air Force O-2A Skymaster spotter aircraft during the 1980s as spotting aircraft out of NAS Cecil Field, Florida. The planes, since replaced in that role by T-34C Mentors, were operated by VA-122 and, subsequently, by VFA-125.

The O-2 was a high-wing monoplane with twin tail booms; it was powered by two piston engines, set between the tail booms, a puller forward and a pusher aft. Rocket pods, 7.62-mm Minigun packs, or other light ordnance could be fitted. The aircraft was designed for the forward air control mission, carrying a pilot and observer and having space for two passengers.

All six naval aircraft have been discarded (two each to the National Aviation Museum in Pensacola, Florida, and the Marine Corps Air-Ground Museum in Quantico, Virginia, and two to the U.S. Army). The O-2 series is no longer flown by the Air Force.

RF-8G CRUSADER

The last Navy unit flying the Crusader aircraft, Naval Air Reserve squadron VFP-206, was decommissioned on 1 April 1986. The squadron flew the RF-8G photo version of the Crusader. All U.S. F-8 fighter aircraft have been discarded, although the French Navy still flies the carrier-based F-8E(FN), and the Philippine Air Force has the land-based F-8H.

The Crusader was the first U.S. combat aircraft to achieve more than 1,000 mph (1,609 km/h) in level flight to enter series production. Then-Major John Glenn, later astronaut and U.S. senator, flew an F8U-1P in a speed-record flight across the United States in 1957.

A total of 1,222 F8U/F-8 Crusaders were built for the U.S. Navy and another 42 for the French Navy.

Designation: Originally designated F8U-1P, the "Photo" Crusaders were redesignated RF-8 in 1962.

RF-4B PHANTOM

The Marine Corps operated one squadron of RF-4B photoreconnaissance aircraft. These aircraft were similar to the now-discarded F-4B version of the Phantom; 46 of them were produced.

The U.S. Navy never flew the reconnaissance version of the Phantom, although Marine RF-4s flew from the carrier MIDWAY until 1986, when the ship's fighter and attack squadrons made the transition to the F/A-18 Hornet. Reconnaissance variants of the F-4 were also flown by the U.S. Air Force and several foreign air forces.

Designation: Marine photo variants of the Phantom were originally designated F4H-1P; this was changed in 1962 to RF-4B.

UTILITY AIRCRAFT

UC-27

The Navy acquired one Fokker F-27F light transport in the 1980s for evaluation. Designated UC-27, it was used in support of the Atlantic Underwater Test and Evaluation Center (AUTEC) in the Bahamas. It was discarded in April 1988.

In commercial and military/coast guard use in several nations, more than 200 F27s have been produced in the United States by a joint Fairchild-Fokker venture, in addition to the Dutch production. The Maritime Enforcer version is fitted for electronic surveillance and can carry two Exocet AM-39 or Harpoon anti-ship missiles.

The official Navy designation UC-27 was nonstandard.

See 14th Edition/page 419 for characteristics.

The HU-25A is a multi-mission aircraft developed originally for surveillance and rescue missions. It has been upgraded in the B/C variants for pollution surveillance and anti-drug operations. (U.S. Coast Guard)

HU-25 GUARDIAN

The Guardian is an all-weather, medium-range search-and-surveillance aircraft flown by the Coast Guard. It replaced the HU-16 Albatross and HC-131 Samaritan aircraft.

Design: This aircraft is a modification of the French-developed commercial Falcon 20G. It has two turbofan engines mounted in nacelles outboard of the after fuselage, an arrangement similar to the T-39 Sabreliner. In addition to crew and passengers, 3,200 pounds (1,452 kg) of rescue supplies are carried. A galley and toilet are provided.

The ATF3-6 engines have been difficult and expensive to support.

Seven aircraft were modified with the Aireye sensor system. Infrared/ultraviolet line scanners have been fitted in an underwing pod and an APS-131 Side-Looking Airborne Radar (SLAR) in a fuselage pod. A television camera and other equipment for pollution reconnaissance have also been installed. These seven planes were redesignated HU-25B in 1989.

Nine other aircraft were fitted with FLIR and the APG-66 multi-mode radar to provide for the detection of aircraft out to 80 n.miles (148 km). They were redesignated HU-25C in 1989.

Status: Operational. Coast Guard IOC was in February 1982; the last of 41 aircraft were delivered in 1984. The Guardian Jet Corporation was a jointly owned subsidiary of Dassault Breguet and Pan American.

As part of the downsizing of Coast Guard fixed-wing aircraft, 15 of these aircraft were placed in storage in 1994–1995. Three more will be laid up in 1996. At that time 17 aircraft will be fully operational, with the remaining six in the aircraft pipeline.

(Similar French-built Mystére-Falcon aircraft are flown in a variety of roles by several air forces.)

HU-25A

Manufacturer:	Dassault-Breguet and Guardian Jet	
Crew:	(5) pilot, copilot, drop master, avionics man, air crewman + 3 passengers + 4 litters	
Engines:	2 Garrett AiResearch ATF3-6-2C turbofans; 5,538 lbst (2,512 kgst) each	
Weights:	empty	19,000 lbs (8,618 kg)
	maximum T/O	33,510 lbs (15,200 kg)
Dimensions:	length	56 ft 3 in (17.15 m)
	wing span	53 ft 6 in (16.30 m)
	wing area	450 ft² (41.80 m²)
	height	17 ft 5 in (5.32 m)
Speed:	maximum	531 mph (854 km/h) at 40,000 ft (12,195 m)
Ceiling:	42,000 ft (12,805 m)	
Range:	2,590 miles (4,167 km) with 30 minutes on station	
Radar:	APS-127 search/weather radar except APG-66 in eight HU-25C aircraft	
plus	APS-131 SLAR in eight HU-25B aircraft	

An HU-25B Guardian as upgraded with the Aireye sensor system to detect oil pollution. Russian aircraft as well as satellites have been similarly equipped for this role, which has implications for ASW operations. (U.S. Coast Guard)

U-11A AZTEC

All Navy and Marine U-11A utility aircraft have been discarded. Twenty were acquired in 1960 for use by naval air stations. The aircraft was modified from the commercial Piper Aztec, which was also used by the U.S. Army and other countries.

See 14th Edition/page 420 for characteristics.

CARGO/TRANSPORT AIRCRAFT

C-20 GULFSTREAM

Gulfstream transport aircraft are flown by all three maritime services: the Navy operates four and the Marine Corps one C-20G Gulfstream IV variants; the Marine Corps has two C-20D Gulfstream III variants; and the Coast Guard flies a single C-20B. The last replaces the long-serving VC-11A Gulfstream II.

Design: Designed for the commercial market, the Gulfstreams are swept-wing, T-tail aircraft that feature twin engine pods mounted on the after fuselage. Winglets are fitted (5 ft 4¼ in high).

The C-20G seats can be removed to provide space for up to 4,500 pounds (2,041 kg) of cargo, handled through a large cargo door on the right side, forward.

Navy plans to acquire three additional G variants configured for EW/ECM training (to have been designated EC-20F) were dropped.

Gulfstream Aerospace has proposed a maritime patrol/ASW variant of the improved Gulfstream IV; the Royal Danish Navy now flies the Gulfstream III in a maritime/fisheries patrol variant.

Status: Operational. First flight Gulfstream III on 24 December 1979, Gulfstream IV on 19 September 1985. The Coast Guard's C-20B became operational in 1995. Variants of the C-20 are also flown by the Air Force and Army.

C-20D

Manufacturer:	Gulfstream Aerospace	
Crew:	(2) pilot, copilot + 19 passengers	
Engines:	2 Rolls-Royce Spey Mk 511-8 turbofans; 11,400 lbst (5,171 kgst) each	
Weights:	empty	32,000 lbs (14,515 kg)
	maximum T/O	69,700 lbs (31,616 kg)
Dimensions:	length	83 ft 1 in (25.32 m)
	wing span	77 ft 10 in (23.72 m)
	wing area	934.6 ft² (86.83 m²)
	height	24 ft 4½ in (7.43 m)
Speed:	maximum cruise	576 mph (927 km/h)
	cruise	508 mph (817 km/h)
Ceiling:	45,000 ft (13,720 m)	
Range:		
Radar:	weather radar	

A Marine C-20D Gulfstream, one of three C-20s flown by that service. These aircraft have upturned wingtips called "winglets." (U.S. Marine Corps)

C-20G

Manufacturer:	Gulfstream Aerospace	
Crew:	(4) pilot, copilot, 2 flight crewmen + 26 passengers	
Engines:	2 Rolls-Royce Tay Mk 611-8 turbofans; 13,850 lbst (6,282 kgst) each	
Weights:		
Dimensions:	length	88 ft 4 in (26.92 m)
	wing span	77 ft 10 in (23.73 m)
	wing area	950½ ft² (88.29 m²)
	height	24 ft 5 in (7.44 m)
Speed:	maximum	563.5 mph (907 km/h) at 35,000 ft (10,670 m)
Ceiling:	45,000 feet (13,720 m)	
Range:	4,220 miles (6,790 km)	
Radar:	weather radar	

Navy C-20G Gulfstream from VR-48 with its starboard-side cargo door open. (Gulfstream Aerospace)

This Navy C-20G Gulfstream assigned to reserve squadron VR-48 is retracting its landing gear. The C-20 is one of the few fixed-wing aircraft flown by all five U.S. military services. The lone Coast Guard C-20B is a VIP transport used by that service and officials of the Department of Transportation. (Gulfstream Aerospace)

UC-12B HURON

The Navy and Marine Corps use large numbers of this military version of the Super King Air 200 for transport and utility purposes.

The aircraft's twin turboprop engines are mounted far forward on the low wing; the aircraft has a T-tail compared with the conventional tail configuration of the smaller T-44A King Air trainer. Payload is 2,000 lbs (907 kg) of cargo or eight passengers.

More than 2,800 aircraft of this basic design have been produced, most for civilian use. This is the only fixed-wing aircraft flown by the U.S. Army, Navy, Marine Corps, and Air Force (plus the Army National Guard and Marine Corps Reserve). The Navy flies 49 of these aircraft and the Marine Corps 17 in the UC-12B configuration; another 12 are on order.

Manufacturer:	Beech	
Crew:	(2) pilot, copilot + 8 passengers	
Engines:	2 Pratt & Whitney PT6A-41 turboprops; 850 shp each	
Weights:	empty	7,869 lbs (3,569 kg)
	loaded	12,500 lbs (5,670 kg)
Dimensions:	length	43 ft 9 in (13.34 m)
	wing span	54 ft 6 in (16.61 m)
	wing area	
	height	14 ft 6 in (4.42 m)
Speed:	maximum cruise	
		310 mph (500 km)
	cruise	261 mph (420 km)
Ceiling:	31,000 ft (9,451 m)	
Range:	2,025 miles (3,260 km)	
Radar:	none	

A UC-12B Huron from NAS Jacksonville being refueled at NAS Norfolk. The Army-assigned name, Huron, is not generally used by the Navy; the commercial Super King Air or "Super King" is more often heard. (Peter B. Mersky)

VC-11A GULFSTREAM II

The Coast Guard's single VC-11A, the only such aircraft in U.S. government service, was retired in 1995. It was flown in the executive transport role and based at Washington, D.C.

The Grumman-built aircraft had entered Coast Guard service in July 1968. It suffered from structural integrity problems, communications limitations, and an insufficient range and passenger capacity for current requirements. Accordingly, it has been replaced by a C-20B Gulfstream.

See 15th Edition/page 427 for characteristics.

C-9B SKYTRAIN II

The C-9B is the naval version of the commercial DC-9, series 30, medium-range passenger/cargo aircraft and is convertible to the cargo or passenger transport roles. Both military and commercial versions are flown by the Navy and Marine Corps.

Design: This sleek-looking, swept-wing transport has a T-tail; the turbofan engines in nacelles are mounted on the after fuselage. The cargo compartment can accommodate eight standard 88 × 108-inch (2.2 × 2.7 m) cargo pallets. Payload is 32,444 lbs (14,717 kg) or 90 passengers.

All Skytrains are flown by Navy and Marine Reserve units, replacing the long-serving C-118 Liftmaster (formerly R6D). The U.S. Air Force flies the C-9A Nightingale in the medical evacuation role and the VC-9C as an executive transport. McDonnell Douglas has proposed a maritime patrol/ASW variant of the aircraft (company designation P-9D); it would have General Electric Unducted Fan (UDF) turboprop-type engines.

Status: Operational. First flight DC-9 series 30 on 1 August 1966. IOC Naval Air Reserve in 1976.

Manufacturer:	McDonnell Douglas	
Crew:	(5) pilot, copilot, crew chief, 2 attendants + 90 passengers	
Engines:	2 Pratt & Whitney JT8D-9 turbofans; 14,500 lbst (6,577 kgst) each	
Weights:	empty	59,706 lbs (27,083 kg) in cargo configuration
		65,283 lbs (29,612 kg) in transport configuration
	maximum T/O	110,000 lbs (49,896 kg)
Dimensions:	length	119 ft 4 in (36.37 m)
	wing span	93 ft 5 in (28.47 m)
	wing area	1,000.7 ft² (92.97 m²)
	height	27 ft 6 in (8.38 m)
Speed:	maximum	576 mph (927 km)
	cruise	504 mph (811 km)
Ceiling:	37,000 ft (11,280 m)	
Range:	2,920 miles (4,700 km) with 10,000 lbs (4,536 kg)	
Radar:	weather radar	

A Marine C-9B Skytrain II, flown by the 4th Marine Aircraft Wing. The only transport-cargo aircraft flown by active Marine aviation units is the KC-130 Hercules. (McDonnell Douglas, Harry Gann)

A C-9B Skytrain II from reserve VR-56 showing the aircraft's large cargo door. Only Navy and Marine reserve squadrons fly C-9B/DC-9 aircraft. (Peter B. Mersky)

A C-2A Greyhound from VRC-50 shows the bulky fuselage of these carrier-capable cargo aircraft. They deliver high-priority passengers and cargo as well as mail to the fleet. (U.S. Navy, PH2 John Gay)

C-2A GREYHOUND

The Greyhound is a second-generation built-for-the-purpose COD aircraft, having been derived from the E-2 Hawkeye AEW aircraft.

Nineteen C-2A models were originally procured. In the late 1970s the Navy developed a plan to produce 24 new COD aircraft beginning in fiscal 1983 to replace the existing C-1A and, eventually, C-2A aircraft. The principal candidate for the new COD—designated VCX for planning purposes—was a variant of the S-3A Viking, with several early aircraft having been modified to a US-3A COD configuration. The decision, however, was to procure 39 additional C-2A aircraft (with the first of these "reprocured" aircraft making its first flight on 4 February 1985). The principal difference in the later aircraft was uprated engines.

Design: The cargo aircraft has the E-2's wings, power plant, and tail configuration, but a larger fuselage and rear-loading ramp. This last feature permits the carrying of high-cube cargo, including some aircraft engines. Cargo capacity is 675 cubic feet (20.25 m^3); payload is 10,000 lbs (4,536 kg) of cargo or 26 passengers. The wings fold for carrier stowage, although these planes are not assigned to carrier wings.

Status: Operational. First flight on 18 November 1964. IOC (VRC-50) was in December 1966. Total production was 58 aircraft; 45 C-2A aircraft remain in Navy service.

Manufacturer:	Grumman	
Crew:	(3) pilot, copilot, flight engineer + 26 passengers or 20 litters	
Engines:	2 Allison T56-A-425 turboprops; 4,910 shp each	
Weights:	empty	31,250 lbs (14,175 kg)
	loaded	54,382 lbs (24,668 kg)
Dimensions:	length	56 ft 8 in (17.27 m)
	wing span	80 ft 7 in (24.57 m)
	wing area	700 ft^2 (65.03 m^2)
	height	15 ft 11 in (4.85 m)
Speed:	maximum	352 mph (566 km/h) at 30,000 ft (9,146 m)
	cruise	296 mph (476 km/h) at 30,000 ft
Ceiling:	33,500 ft (10,210 m)	
Range:	normal	1,200 miles (1,930 km)
	maximum	1,800 miles (2,890 km)
Radar:	navigation radar	

A C-2A Greyhound from VRC-40 taxies across the flight deck of the John F. Kennedy, its wings folded. The concept of Carrier On-board Delivery (COD) began in the 1950s to fly atomic bomb components to aircraft carriers. (U.S. Navy, PH1 Michael D.P. Flynn)

A C-2A Greyhound from VRC-40 with its tail ramp lowered and engines turning up at NAS Norfolk. Like the E-2C, one pair of the tail fins has no control surfaces. The ramp permits loading bulky items, including aircraft engines. (Peter B. Mersky)

C-1A TRADER

The Navy's first specialized COD aircraft, the C-1A Trader has been retired from naval service. The plane, which had twin reciprocating engines, was derived from the S2F/S-2 Tracker ASW aircraft.

Grumman produced a total of 87 Traders for the U.S. Navy: four were configured as electronic training aircraft (designated TF-1Q and, after 1962, EC-1A); one was modified as the E-1B aerodynamic prototype (XTF-1W) and then reverted to a COD aircraft. The aircraft were in VR-VRC squadron service from 1955 to 1986; a C-1A was the last piston aircraft to "trap" on a U.S. carrier, coming aboard the USS Lexington (AVT 16) on 27 September 1988.

Designation: Originally designated TF-1; the designation was changed to C-1A in 1962.

See 14th Edition/pages 423–24 for characteristics.

C-131H SAMARITAN

The last Navy-flown C-131 was retired in mid-1990. The C-131 was flown by the Navy and Naval Air Reserve as a transport and by the Coast Guard (HC-131), the latter also having been discarded.

The Convair-built, twin-engine aircraft was also flown by the Air Force as a transport and specialized trainer (T-29).

Designation: The Samaritan was originally designated R4Y by the Navy; the Air Force C-series designation was adopted in 1962.

See 14th Edition/page 424 for characteristics.

C-130 HERCULES

The Hercules, or "Herk," is the most widely flown military transport in the West. The active Navy now flies only the ski-equipped LC-130F/R in support of Antarctic research programs; the Naval Air Reserve flies the C-130T as a logistics aircraft; the Marine Corps uses the KC-130F/R/T as a tactical transport and aerial tanker; and the Coast Guard employs the HC-130H as a long-range search-and-surveillance aircraft.

The Navy's EC-130Q TACAMO aircraft have been retired from the strategic communications role, replaced by the E-6A Mercury.

Design: The basic C-130 is a four-engine cargo aircraft with a high wing. The main landing gear retracts into pods to provide a clear fuselage cargo space; a rear ramp provides access to the cargo compartment and can be opened in flight for parachuting troops or equipment.

The Navy has two ski-fitted LC-130F and five LC-130R aircraft flown by VXE-6.[26] The DC-130 drone carriers are no longer in Navy service.

The Marine KC-130F/R/T are employed as cargo aircraft and tankers, flown by four VMGR squadrons. They can accommodate removable aluminum tanks for 3,600 gallons (13,680 liters) of fuel in the cargo area; two refueling drogues can be streamed simultaneously.

26. LC-130F Bureau No. 148321 was recovered in 1990 after having been buried in Antarctic snow for 16 years. The aircraft began a two-year overhaul in 1991 before being returned to active service.

A Marine KC-130F Hercules from VMGR-152 refuels an A-4E Skyhawk from Navy squadron VC-5 employing the drogue-and-probe technique. Air Force tankers use the rigid-boom technique, but they can also operate a drogue system. (U.S. Navy, PH1 Michael D.P. Flynn)

A KC-130T-30 Hercules flown by Marine reserve squadron VMGR-452 shows the shape of one of the latest variants off the prolific Hercules production lines. (Lockheed)

Two KC-130T-30 stretched aircraft delivered in 1991 to reserve squadron VMGR-452 have two fuselage plugs, adding a total of 14¾ feet (4.5 m) to the fuselage length. The KC-130R has a payload of 26,913 lbs (12,208 kg) of cargo or 92 troops.

One Marine TC-130G is equipped as a maintenance center to support the Navy-Marine Blue Angels flight demonstration team, carrying a crew of 7, plus 30 maintenance personnel. It is called "Fat Albert" in honor of a character created by comedian Bill Cosby. The TC-130G is a converted Navy EC-130G delivered in 1991; previously, "Fat Albert" was a KC-130F.

The Coast Guard HC-130H aircraft carry air-droppable rescue and salvage gear. The HC-130H has increased range, flare launchers, and other improvements over the C-130B aircraft they replaced. (Characteristics are similar to the KC-130R described below.) The HC-130H aircraft have been refitted with the APS-137 ISAR radar; they also have APN-215 weather radar. An external SAMSON sensor pod that contains a FLIR can also be fitted to these aircraft.

A single Coast Guard Hercules has been converted to an AEW configuration for Coast Guard evaluation; it was redesignated EC-130V (see page 384).

Designation: The Navy-Marine variants of the Hercules were originally designated GV-1; this was changed to C-130 in 1962.

Operational: A KC-130F conducted carrier landings and takeoffs from the FORRESTAL in 1963 without the use of arresting gear or catapults. C-130s have also been employed to evaluate minelaying.

Status: Operational; in production. First flight YC-130 on 23 August 1954. Production of the HC-130H continues for the Coast Guard and the KC-130T for the Marine Corps, as does production of other models for other users.

The Hercules is widely used by the U.S. Air Force, and more than 50 other nations also employ military versions. Through the end of 1995 Lockheed had produced some 2,000 military and commercial models of the Hercules, including more than 1,200 for the U.S. military services.

A Coast Guard HC-130H Hercules fitted with auxiliary fuel tanks mounted between the engines. The "Herk" is the largest aircraft flown by the Coast Guard and one of the few four-engine planes to be flown by that service. (Lockheed)

A ski-equipped LC-130R Hercules of VXE-6 takes off from the Antarctic ice cap with the help of JATO rockets. The squadron provides logistic and SAR support for U.S. scientific activities in the Antarctic. (U.S. Navy)

The view from the cockpit of a TA-4J Skyhawk as it approaches a KC-130F Hercules tanker from VMGR-152. Refueling drogues are being streamed from pods mounted on both wings of the tanker. (U.S. Navy)

KC-130R

Manufacturer:	Lockheed (Georgia)	
Crew:	(5) pilot, copilot, navigator, flight engineer, radio operator/loadmaster + 92 troops	
Engines:	4 Allison T56-A-15 turboprops; 4,591 shp each	
Weights:	empty	75,368 lbs (34,187 kg)
	loaded	109,744 lbs (49,780 kg)
	maximum T/O	155,000 lbs (70,308 kg)
Dimensions:	length	99 ft 5 in (30.32 m)
	wing span	132 ft 7 in (40.42 m)
	wing area	1,745 ft^2 (162.12 m^2)
	height	38 ft 3 in (11.66 m)
Speed:	maximum	348 mph (560 km/h) at 19,000 ft (5,790 m)
	cruise	331 mph (533 km/h)
Ceiling:	25,000 ft (7,622 m)	
Range:	radius 2,950 miles (4,749 km) with maximum payload	
	radius 1,150 miles (1,852 km) in tanker role, with 32,140 lbs (14,579 kg) of fuel for transfer	
Radar:	APN-59B	

CT-39 SABRELINER

A few CT-39E/G aircraft are employed to transport high-priority cargo and passengers. The T-39D has been phased out of the training role, having been employed to train bombardier/navigators and radar intercept officers. The aircraft was fitted with the APS-94 radar for that role. The T-39N is flown in the training role (see page 397).

Design: The low, swept-wing configuration of the T-39 has two turbojet engine nacelles mounted on the after fuselage. The aircraft is not carrier capable. The CT-39 aircraft carry a crew of three and seven passengers. These were modified commercial Sabreliner series 40 (E) and 60 (G) aircraft, acquired specifically for the transport role and never used as trainers. One T-39D was fitted as the test bed for the F/A-18 Hornet's APG-65 radar. The aircraft was also used by the Air Force.

Designation: The aircraft was originally flown by the Navy as the T3J; that was changed to CT-39 in 1962.

Status: Operational. First flight modified commercial Sabreliner in September 1958; first flight T-39A in June 1960; first flight T-39D in December 1962.

Manufacturer:	North American Rockwell	
Crew:	(3) pilot, copilot, crewman + 7 passengers	
Engines:	2 Pratt & Whitney J60-P-3A turbojets; 3,000 lbst (1,361 kgst) each	
Weights:	loaded	17,760 lbs (8,056 kg)
Dimensions:	length	43 ft 9 in (13.33 m)
	wing span	44 ft 5 in (13.53 m)
	wing area	342.6 ft^2 (31.83 m^2)
	height	16 ft (4.88 m)
Speed:	432 mph (695 km/h)	
Ceiling:	45,000 ft (13,715 m)	
Range:	2,875 miles (4,630 km)	
Radar:	navigation	

A Marine CT-39G Sabreliner, one of several employed by the Navy and Marine Corps—active and reserve—to carry high-priority cargo and passengers. (McDonnell Douglas, Harry Gann)

CASA 212

The Coast Guard operates a single CASA 212 as a utility transport, flying from Miami, Florida. This type of utility transport is employed in large numbers around the world by commercial, government, and military organizations.

Design: This is a high-wing, STOL aircraft with the turboprop engines mounted on the wings. A rear loading ramp is provided. In the medical evacuation role, 12 litters and four attendants can be carried. When the seats are removed, 5,952 pounds (2,700 kg) of cargo can be carried.

Operational: Operational with the U.S. Coast Guard, as well as several foreign military services.

Manufacturer:	Construcciones Aeronauticas SA (Spain)	
Crew:	(2) pilot, copilot + 25 passengers	
Engines:	2 Garrett TPE331-10R-513C turboprops; 900 shp each	
Weights:	empty	9,700 lbs (4,400 kg)
	maximum T/O	17,637 lbs (8,000 kg)
Dimensions:	length	52 ft $11\frac{3}{4}$ in (16.15 m)
	wing span	66 ft $6\frac{1}{2}$ in (20.28 m)
	wing area	
	height	21 ft $7\frac{3}{4}$ in (6.6 m)
Speed:	maximum	230 mph (370 km/h)
	cruise	186 mph (300 km/h) at 10,000 ft (3,050 m)
Ceiling:	26,000 ft (7,925 m)	
Range:	890 miles (1,433 km)	
Radar:	Bendix weather	

This Coast Guard aircraft is the lone CASA 212 utility transport flown by U.S. military services. This STOL aircraft is used to support Coast Guard activities in the Caribbean area. (U.S. Coast Guard)

TRAINING AIRCRAFT

The following table shows the Navy's "training pipeline" for pilots.

NAVY PILOT TRAINING PIPELINE

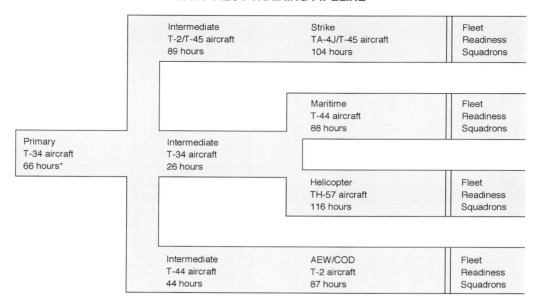

Primary T-34 aircraft 66 hours*	Intermediate T-2/T-45 aircraft 89 hours	Strike TA-4J/T-45 aircraft 104 hours	Fleet Readiness Squadrons
	Intermediate T-34 aircraft 26 hours	Maritime T-44 aircraft 88 hours	Fleet Readiness Squadrons
		Helicopter TH-57 aircraft 116 hours	Fleet Readiness Squadrons
	Intermediate T-44 aircraft 44 hours	AEW/COD T-2 aircraft 87 hours	Fleet Readiness Squadrons

Note: *Flight time in syllabus.

A Beech Mk II aircraft, winner of the Navy–Air Force competition for a Joint Primary Aircraft Training System (JPATS). It will be procured in large numbers by both services. (Raytheon Aircraft/Beech)

JOINT PRIMARY AIRCRAFT TRAINING SYSTEM

The Joint Primary Aircraft Training System (JPATS) is a joint Air Force–Navy program to develop a new training aircraft for production after the year 2000. The Air Force is the lead service for JPATS development.

The Raytheon Aircraft Company's Beech Mk II was selected as the JPATS aircraft in June 1995. Six other aircraft competed for the JPATS role. The JPATS will replace the Navy's T-34 and the Air Force's T-37 trainers, with service requirements for 339 and 372 aircraft, respectively; a total program of 711 aircraft plus three prototypes.

Design: The Beech Mk II is a single-engine, turboprop aircraft with tandem seating. It is derived from the Pilatus PC-9 aircraft. This is a straight-wing aircraft with a pressurized cockpit.

Status: In development for U.S. Navy and Air Force. First flight engineering prototype JPATS in September 1992.

Manufacturer:	Raytheon Aircraft/Beech	
Crew:	(1) pilot + 1 student	
Engines:	1 Pratt & Whitney PT6A-68 turboprop; 1,700 shp	
Weights:	empty	approx. 3,715 lbs (1,685 kg)
	maximum T/O	approx. 7,055 lbs (3,200 kg)
Dimensions:	length	33 ft 4¾ in (10.175 m)
	wing span	33 ft 2½ in (10.12 m)
	wing area	16.9 ft^2 (1.57 m^2)
	height	10 ft 8⅓ in (3.26 m)
Speed:	310.5 mph (500 km/h) at sea level	
Ceiling:	25,000 ft (7,620 m)	
Range:	approx. 1,020 miles (1,642 km)	
Armament:	none	
Radar:	none	

Beech Mk II trainer. (Raytheon Aircraft/Beech)

The Beech Mk II trainer, showing the excellent visibility of this nimble aircraft. (Raytheon Aircraft/Beech)

T-47A CITATION

The Navy's T-47 trainers, a modified commercial Cessna Citation II Model 500 design, have been discarded. The Navy employed 15 T-47A aircraft in training squadrons VT-10 and VT-86 to train Naval Flight Officers (NFO). The T-47 replaced the T-39D Sabreliner in that role; in 1991, the T-47 was succeeded by the T-39N Sabreliner. The T-47 was contractor maintained and operated.

See 14th Edition/page 426 for characteristics.

T-45A GOSHAWK

The Goshawk is the Navy's basic undergraduate jet training aircraft, replacing the T-2C and TA-4J. The T-45 is a variant of British Aerospace's Hawk series 60 trainer. Despite using an off-the-shelf aircraft, the first flight of a U.S. Navy Goshawk took place almost five years behind the original schedule. Employing the T-45 reduces flight training by about 15 hours per student compared to the T-2C/TA-4J. The first student pilots flew in the T-45A on 11 February 1994.

The Navy initially planned to procure 253 carrier-compatible T-45A trainers and 54 land-based T-45B variants. However, Congress directed that they all be T-45A "wet"—carrier-capable—models. Accordingly, the current program provides for a total of 268 training aircraft and two prototypes (plus 32 flight simulation devices).

Developed by Hawker Siddeley Aviation before it was merged into British Aerospace, the Hawk entered RAF service in 1976 and is also flown by several other air forces. The U.S. Navy's program was originally designated VTX-TS: the VTX for a new training aircraft and TS for Training System, i.e., the simultaneous development of simulators and related training equipment.

Initial T-45 flight tests revealed several shortcomings. Consequently, among other changes, the original Adour Mk 861/F405-RR-400 engine was replaced in production aircraft with the Adour Mk 871/F405-RR-401.

Design: The U.S. Navy's Goshawks differ from the British Hawk design in that they have a small ventral fin, an arresting hook, and modified wings, landing gear, and speed brakes. Endurance is approximately four hours. Leading-edge slats are fitted to bring carrier approach speeds within acceptable limits. A pylon is fitted under each wing for small bombs, rockets, or drop tanks. Provision has also been made for a centerline store.

The wing and after fuselage sections of the T-45A are built in Britain by British Aerospace; Rolls-Royce produces the engines there. (The Hawk continues in production in Britain.)

The first production T-45B Goshawk in flight. The wing pylons are for carrying practice munitions. The nose and tail are red to help students sight other aircraft during training cycles. (McDonnell Douglas)

Rear aspect of a T-45A Goshawk aboard the KENNEDY. The "JFK" now serves as a reserve-training carrier. (McDonnell Douglas)

Name: The name Goshawk was previously assigned to the Navy's Curtiss-built F11C fighter of the 1930s.

Status: Operational; in production. First flight T-45A on 16 April 1988. IOC (VT-21) was in 1994. (First flight of British T 1 on 21 August 1974.) The British Hawk is flown by ten other countries.

Manufacturer:	British Aerospace and McDonnell Douglas	
Crew:	(1) pilot + student	
Engines:	1 Rolls-Royce Adour Mk 871/F405-RR-401 turbofan; 5,845 lbst (2,651 kgst)	
Weights:	empty	9,834 lbs (4,461 kg)
	maximum T/O	14,081 lbs (6,387 kg)
Dimensions:	length	35 ft 9 in (10.89 m) + probe
	wing span	30 ft 9¾ in (9.39 m)
	wing area	179.6 ft² (9.39 m²)
	height	13 ft 6⅛ in (4.12 m)
Speed:	maximum	609 mph (980 km) at 8,000 ft (2,439 m)
Ceiling:	42,500 ft (12,957 m)	
Range:	805 miles (1,296 km)	
	ferry 1,840 miles (2,963 km) with external tanks	
Armament:	25-lb (11-kg) Mk 76 target bombs and 2.75-inch (70-mm) rockets	
Radar:	none	

A T-45A Goshawk on the KENNEDY showing the aircraft's leading-edge flaps. (McDonnell Douglas)

A T-45A Goshawk lands on the JOHN F. KENNEDY. The tail hook has just caught on arresting cable; the nose wheels are not on the deck. The plane's dive brakes (just above the fuselage) are open. (McDonnell Douglas)

T-44A KING AIR

The T-44A was procured as a replacement for the TS-2/US-2 Tracker employed in the multi-engine training role.

Design: The aircraft is a modification of the commercial King Air 90, with a straight wing mounting twin turboprop engines relatively far forward and a conventional tail configuration. The aircraft can be configured as a transport carrying two pilots and three passengers. During development the military version was designated VTAM(X).

Status: Operational. From 1977 the Navy took delivery of 61 T-44A aircraft, all being assigned to squadrons VT-21 and VT-31; only the latter squadron now flies the T-44A. The U.S. Army procured unpressurized versions as the U-21A, while the Air Force obtained one as the UC-6A for special missions and a VC-6 as a VIP transport.

Manufacturer:	Beech	
Crew:	(3) pilot, copilot, instructor + 2 students	
Engines:	2 Pratt & Whitney of Canada PT6A-34B turboprops; 550 hp each	
Weights:	empty	6,326 lbs (2,869 kg)
	maximum T/O	9,650 lbs (4,377 kg)
Dimensions:	length	35 ft 6 in (10.82 m)
	wing span	50 ft 3 in (15.32 m)
	wing area	293.9 ft² (27.3 m²)
	height	14 ft 3 in (4.33 m)
Speed:	cruise	276 mph (444 km) at 15,000 ft (4,573 m)
Ceiling:	29,500 ft (8,994 m)	
Range:	1,455 miles (2,343 km)	
Radar:	navigation	

A T-44A King Air and T-34C Mentor from Training Wing 4 squadrons fly in formation over Corpus Christi, Texas. The Army and Air Force also fly variants of the T-44 and T-34. (U.S. Navy)

T-39N SABRELINER

The Navy operates several of the long-serving T-39s to train Naval Flight Officers (NFO) who will fly in F-14, EA-6B, S-3A/B, and two-seat F/A-18 aircraft. The T-39N is a basic T-39A that's been upgraded with advanced radar and the CT-39E/G engines.

Design: The T-39 has a low, swept-wing configuration, with two turbojet engine nacelles mounted on the after fuselage. The aircraft is not carrier capable.

The N variant is distinguished from the basic T-39A by being fitted with the Westinghouse APG-66NT radar, a modification of the APG-68 currently installed in several combat aircraft. The T-39N also has engine thrust reversers.

A few CT-39s serve as high-priority transport aircraft (see page 393 for basic characteristics).

Status: Operational, flown by training squadrons VT-10 and VT-86. The first of 17 T-39N aircraft were delivered in late 1991. The aircraft are flown by Tracor Flight Services, Inc., under contract to the Navy.

Manufacturer:	North American Rockwell	
Crew:	(3) pilot, 2 instructors + 3 students	
Engines:	2 Pratt & Whitney J60-P-3A turbojets; 3,000 lbst (1,361 kgst) each	
Weights:	maximum T/O	approx. 18,000 lbs (8,165 kg)
Dimensions:	length	44 ft (13.41 m)
	wing span	44 ft 6 in (13.57 m)
	wing area	342.1 ft^2 (31.77 m^2)
	height	16 ft (4.88 m)
Speed:	cruise	501 mph (806 km/h)
	maximum	554 mph (892 km/h)
Ceiling:	45,000 ft (13,720 m)	
Range:		
Radar:	APG-66NT	

A pair of CT-39E Sabreliner aircraft, ex-trainers used as short range transports by the Navy. These VRC-30 aircraft have the American flag on their tails, as do VR/VRC aircraft. (U.S. Navy)

T-38A TALON

The T-38 is the standard U.S. Air Force trainer, flown in small numbers by the Navy for test-pilot proficiency and air combat maneuver training.

The T-38 is closely related to the design of the Northrop F-5 Freedom Fighter and F-5E/F/G (now F-20) Tiger II aircraft.

Status: The YT-38 first flew in April 1959. More than 1,187 were produced, the majority for the U.S. Air Force, which still flies more than 500 in the training role; others remain in foreign service. The Air Force also flew an AT-38B attack version.

Manufacturer:	Northrop	
Crew:	(1) pilot + student	
Engines:	2 General Electric J85-GE-5A turbojets; 3,850 lbst (1,746 kgst), each with afterburner	
Weights:	empty	7,594 lbs (3,445 kg)
	maximum T/O	12,000 lbs (5,443 kg)
Dimensions:	length	46 ft 10 in (14.13 m)
	wing span	25 ft 3 in (7.7 m)
	wing area	170 ft² (15.80 m²)
	height	12 ft 11 in (3.92 m)
Speed:	maximum cruise 630 mph (1,014 km/h) at 40,000 ft (12,195 m)	
	economical cruise 594 mph (956 km/h) above 40,000 ft (12,195 m)	
Ceiling:	53,600 ft (26,341 m)	
Range:	1,310 miles (2,111 km)	
Radar:	none	

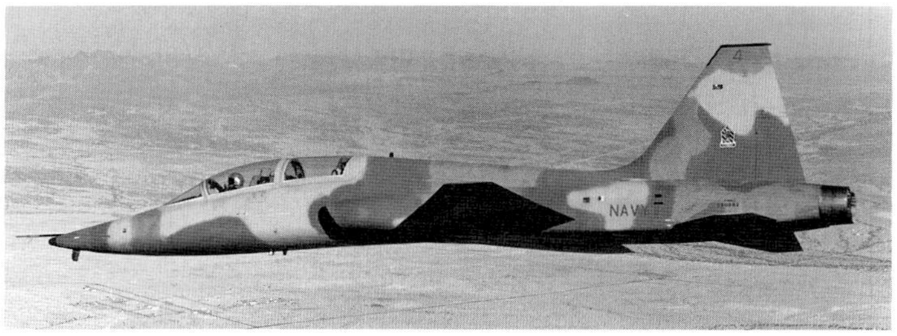

A T-38A Talon—camouflaged for adversary training—assigned to VF-43. (Robert L. Lawson)

T-34C MENTOR

The Mentor is the Navy's primary, basic flight training aircraft. A few T-34C aircraft are used for recruiting and utility activities, while the Light Attack Wing Atlantic employs a few others for spotting duties.

The low-wing, turboprop C model has replaced the earlier piston-engine aircraft in Navy service. The plane is not carrier capable. The Navy selected the Beechcraft Model 45 as a primary trainer in 1953, which led to procurement of the T-34A/B/C series. Two T-34B aircraft were converted to YT-34C prototypes (turboprop engine) in 1973.

Status: Operational. First flight YT-34C on 21 September 1973. IOC (T-34C) was in July 1976. A total of 352 T-34C aircraft were delivered from 1976 to 1988. (The earlier, piston-engine aircraft have been retired.)

Variants are flown by the U.S. Air Force and several foreign air services.

Manufacturer:	Beech	
Crew:	(1) pilot + student	
Engines:	1 Pratt & Whitney of Canada PT6A-25 turboprop; 400 shp	
Weights:	empty	2,940 lbs (1,334 kg)
	maximum T/O	4,300 lbs (1,950 kg)
Dimensions:	length	28 ft 8½ in (8.75 m)
	wing span	33 ft 3⅞ in (10.16 m)
	wing area	179.6 ft² (16.69 m²)
	height	9 ft 7 in (2.92 m)
Speed:	maximum	257 mph (413 km/h) at 5,335 ft (1,627 m)
	cruise	247 mph (397 km/h) at 5,335 ft
Ceiling:	30,000 ft (9,146 m)	
Range:	850 miles (1,370 km)	
Radar:	none	

A T-34C Mentor, the turboprop version of a long-serving Navy and Air Force basic training aircraft. (Beech)

T-2C BUCKEYE

The T-2C variant of the Buckeye is used by the Navy for undergraduate jet pilot training; a few aircraft are also flown by fleet readiness squadrons for spin-recovery training, the Navy's aggressor training squadron, and the Naval Test Pilot School at NAS Patuxent River, Maryland.

Design: The Buckeye has straight wings, generally with wing tip tanks fitted; the twin engines are buried in the bottom of the fuselage. Wing pylons can be fitted for carrying small bombs, rockets, or gun pods. The aircraft is carrier capable.

The T-2A was a single-engine aircraft; the T-2B/C were similar, with twin engines. All earlier aircraft have been phased out of U.S. Navy service. A T-2D variant was developed from the T-2C for the Venezuelan Navy, a T-2E attack variant for the Greek Air Force.

Designation: The Buckeye was originally designated T2J, which was changed to T-2 in 1962.

Status: Operational. The Navy took delivery of 217 T-2A and 97 T-2B aircraft before procuring 231 T-2C variants from 1969 to December 1975. The aircraft's service life has been extended, at considerable cost, from 7,500 to 12,000 hours, pending availability of the T-45 Goshawk for the training role.

The Buckeye is currently flown in six training squadrons (VT) of the undergraduate jet training program and in the aggressor training squadron (VF-43), as well as other units. The aircraft is no longer in production.

Manufacturer:	North American Rockwell	
Crew:	(1) pilot + student	
Engines:	2 General Electric J85-GE-4 turbojets; 2,950 lbst (1,338 kgst) each	
Weights:	empty	8,115 lbs (3,681 kg)
	maximum T/O	13,191 lbs (5,983 kg)
Dimensions:	length	38 ft 3½ in (11.67 m)
	wing span	38 ft 1½ in (11.62 m)[27]
	wing area	255 ft² (23.69 m²)
	height	14 ft 10 in (4.51 m)
Speed:	maximum	530 mph (853 km/h) at 25,000 ft (7,622 m)
Ceiling:	45,500 ft (13,970 m)	
Range:	1,045 miles (1,683 km)	
Armament:	up to 640 lbs (290 kg) of bombs or rockets on 2 wing stations + wingtip tanks	
Radar:	none	

27. Span over wingtip tanks.

A T-2C Buckeye from Training Wing 1. These aircraft will be replaced by the T-45 Goshawk. (U.S. Navy)

A T-2C Buckeye from VT-19 showing the arresting hook. These twin-engine trainers normally have wingtip tanks. (U.S. Navy)

A T-2C Buckeye from VT-10. That squadron has since changed aircraft (see chapter 28). (Peter B. Mersky)

TA-4J SKYHAWK

The Skyhawk was developed in the early 1950s as a lightweight, daylight-only, nuclear strike aircraft for strikes against the Soviet Union. The aircraft subsequently evolved into a highly versatile attack aircraft, widely used by the Navy and Marine Corps as well as several foreign air forces. It survives in Navy service only in the TA-4J configuration as a training aircraft; the last Marine A-4M aircraft were retired in 1992.

The Navy TA-4J variant will be replaced by the T-45 Goshawk.

Design: The basic Skyhawk was a single-seat, single-engine aircraft with a delta wing, which did not fold for carrier stowage. A pair of 20-mm cannon were fitted in the wing roots with external attachment points for ordnance or external fuel tanks.

The TA-4J was a simplified version of the TA-4F variant, which was fully combat capable. Some weapons capability and avionics have been deleted from the TA-4J. Early TA-4J aircraft were built with a single 20-mm gun; all retain pylons and an in-flight refueling probe. The TA-4J is carrier capable.

Designation: The Skyhawk was originally designated A4D; that was changed to A-4 in 1962.

Operational: The Israeli Air Force has made extensive use of A-4s in Middle East combat, as did the Argentine Navy and Air Force during the 1982 conflict in the Falklands. The A-4 was used extensively by the Navy and Marine Corps in the Vietnam War.

Status: Operational. First flight XA4D-1 on 22 June 1954. Navy IOC (VA-72) was in September 1956. TA-4J first flight in May 1969; the IOC was on 6 June 1969.

A total of 2,960 A-4s were built for U.S. and foreign use, 555 of which were two-seaters, including 293 TA-4J aircraft, used by the Naval Air Training Command. The last Skyhawk delivery, an A-4M for the Marine Corps, was made in 1979. This was one of the longest production runs of any combat aircraft in history. The last U.S. combat aircraft were Marine A-4M variants; the last plane was retired on 30 June 1992. Many A-4s survive in foreign air forces.

A TA-4J Skyhawk from VT-7—in camouflage markings—demonstrates the agility of this outstanding attack aircraft. (U.S. Navy)

Manufacturer:	McDonnell Douglas	
Crew:	(1) pilot + student	
Engines:	1 Pratt & Whitney J52-P-6A turbojet; 8,500 lbst (3,856 kgst)	
Weights:	empty	10,602 lbs (4,809 kg)
	loaded	15,783 lbs (7,159 kg)
	maximum	24,500 lbs (11,113 kg)
Dimensions:	length	42 ft 7 in (12.99 m)
	wing span	27 ft 6 in (8.38 m)
	wing area	260 ft² (24.155 m²)
	height	15 ft 3 in (4.65 m)
Speed:	maximum	660 mph (1,062 km/h) at sea level
Ceiling:	38,700 ft (11,795 m)	
Range:	normal	1,350 miles (2,175 km)
	maximum	2,200 miles (3,540 km)
Armament:	none	
Radar:	none	

TC-18F

The Navy flies two training versions of the Boeing 707 to prepare air crewmen for the E-6A Mercury TACAMO aircraft. Both TC-18F aircraft were flown in this role in 1987–1991 and again from 1993; the "break" in service, when they were grounded, resulted from a lack of funding.

The Air Force also flies an EC-18 electronics aircraft.

Status: Operational. TC-18Fs are assigned to Navy Strategic Communications Wing 1.

Manufacturer:	Boeing	
Crew:	(2) pilot, flight engineer + 2 students	
Engines:	4 Pratt & Whitney JT3D turbofan	
Weights:	empty	135,000 lbs (61,236 kg)
	normal T/O	225,000 lbs (102,060 kg)
	maximum T/O	326,000 lbs (147,873 kg)
Dimensions:	length	152 ft 11 in (46.62 m)
	wing span	145 ft 9 in (44.435 m)
	wing area	
	height	42 ft 5½ in (12.94 m)
Speed:		
Ceiling:	42,000 ft (12,800 m)	
Range:		
Armament:	none	
Radar:	APS-133 weather	

A quartet of TA-4J Skyhawks from VT-7 fly over their home base of Meridian, Mississippi. Although scheduled for replacement in the near future, the TA-4J will probably still be flying in the U.S. Navy at the start of the 21st century. (U.S. Navy)

One of the two TC-18F trainers flown by Navy Strategic Communications Wing 1 to train E-6A Mercury TACAMO pilots. The aircraft's JT3D turbofans are much smaller than the F108-CF-100 turbofans of the E-6A. (U.S. Navy)

The Navy and Marine Corps flew the C-4 series aircraft only in the TC-4C Academe configuration to train A-6 Intruder bombardier/navigators. The elongated nose has a TRAM sphere fitted in the bottom. The code letters AD are worn by Atlantic Fleet readiness-transition squadrons. (U.S. Navy)

TC-4C ACADEME

The Navy previously operated several TC-4C trainers for A-6E Intruder bombardier/navigators. These aircraft were discarded in 1995 in anticipation of the A-6E being phased out of Navy service in 1996. The Marines transferred their TC-4s to the Navy, and the Coast Guard will soon retire its single, long-serving VC-4A Gulfstream VIP transport. (All variants of the aircraft in military service are generally referred to as Gulfstreams; the Coast Guard aircraft officially retained the name Gulfstream I.)

Design: Originally developed as a business aircraft, the Gulfstream I is a low-wing, twin turboprop aircraft with the long nacelles common to Rolls-Royce engines. The TC-4C variants had a simulated A-6E cockpit, with pilot and bombardier/navigator positions in the after section of the cockpit, plus four identical bombardier/navigator training consoles. In addition to the A-6E radar (upgraded from the original APQ-92 and APQ-88 radars), these planes had the TRAM and FLIR fitted in the A-6Es.

The T-41A (later TC-4B) was a navigation training version of the Gulfstream I ordered by the Navy, but that program was canceled.

See 15th edition/pages 428–29 for characteristics.

ROTARY-WING AIRCRAFT

In addition to the rotary-wing aircraft described below, the Navy has earmarked funds in the fiscal 1998 budget to initiate procurement of a Vertical Replenishment (VERTREP) helicopter to replace the UH-46D Sea Knight. A variant of the Sikorsky H-60 series appeared to be the leading candidate for this role as this edition of *Ships and Aircraft* went to press. Also proposed were the Kaman K-Max helicopter, which uses twin, inter-meshing main rotors; the EH Industries EH 101 shipborne helicopter; the Aérospatiale AS 332 Super Puma; and an improved model of the Bell UH-1 Huey series.

Of these candidates, only the H-60 variant would have a high degree of commonality with existing Navy helicopters, an important factor for flight training, maintenance, and logistics support. That aircraft would be mainly an Army UH-60L outfitted with T700-GE-401(C) and certain HH-60H features.

MV-22 OSPREY

The MV-22 Osprey is a high-speed, rotary-wing aircraft being developed for the Marine Corps assault role, primarily to replace the CH-46 Sea Knight. In addition, the Air Force plans to procure the CV-22 as a special operations aircraft. The Navy had planned to procure V-22 variants, initially for the Search-and-Rescue (SAR) role, with the potential for both the AEW and ASW missions, but at this writing the Navy had no procurement plans.

The Navy–Marine Corps had the lead in developing the aircraft under the project designation JVX. The Marine Corps initially planned to procure 552 aircraft for vertical assault and the Navy an additional 50 for combat SAR.[28] The other Navy missions could have added some 200 to 300 aircraft to the Navy program. The Air Force at one point envisioned a buy of 80 aircraft for special operations and the Army about 230 for medical evacuation as well as for Special Electronic Mission Aircraft (SEMA). Thus, the V-22 program could have reached 900 to 1,200 aircraft.

The Army and Air Force withdrew from the program in the late 1980s, and on 25 April 1989 Secretary of Defense Cheney eliminated all funding for the Navy-Marine program. At the time, his staff proposed a replacement force of 602 MV-22s, with a combination of 376 CH-53E and 590 H-60 helicopters. Department of Defense opposition to the V-22 continued as late as September 1994.

The Marine Corps opposed all alternatives to the V-22, and Congress continued to support and fund the V-22 program. Production is now approved for a Marine buy of 425 MV-22s and Air Force procurement of 48 CV-22s—a total acquisition of 473 aircraft.

MV-22 procurement is scheduled to begin with the fiscal 1997 aircraft procurement program, with Marine buys reaching a peak production rate of nine aircraft per year beginning in 2001.

Design: The V-22, developed from the XV-15A technology-demonstration aircraft, has twin rotor-engine nacelles mounted on a connecting wing. The nacelles rotate to a horizontal position for conventional aircraft flight and are vertical for vertical takeoffs and landings or hovering.

The basic aircraft will have an internal cargo capacity of 10,000 pounds (4,536 kg) and an external (slung) capacity of 15,000 pounds (6,804 kg). Rolling takeoffs and landings are the normal operating mode, although VTOL operations are feasible. Thus, the design has the advantages of both a conventional aircraft and a helicopter. An in-flight refueling probe is provided.

The Marine Corps has proposed a gunship variant of the MV-22 that could carry a variety of guns, rockets, and missiles. The proposed Navy SV-22 would carry Mk 50 ASW torpedoes and operate a number of anti-submarine sensors, including APS-137 radar, dipping sonar, sonobuoys, and FLIR.

The Royal Navy has expressed interest in the AEW variant of the V-22 for operation from the INVINCIBLE-class VSTOL carriers. That AEW aircraft would loiter at about 15,000 feet (4,500 m), have a radius of some 230 miles (370 km), and have two and a half hours on station. In-flight refueling could extend the on-station time to five and a half hours. The aircraft would carry the APS-138 or APS-145 radar.

28. The original Marine requirement was based on:

16 HMM squadrons × 15 aircraft	240
2 reserve squadrons × 15 aircraft	30
2 HMT squadrons × 20 aircraft	40
1 VMX squadron × 15 aircraft	15
RDT&E, pipeline, 20-year attrition	227

A prototype V-22 Osprey in Marine markings. The aircraft is in the high-speed mode, with engine nacelles in the horizontal position. (Bell Boeing)

A V-22 Osprey prototype on a helicopter carrier's deck-edge elevator with rotor blades folded for shipboard stowage. Shipboard trials were fully successful. (Bell Boeing)

A V-22 prototype with its engine nacelles in the vertical or helicopter mode. The main landing gear retracts into faired housing along the side of the fuselage to provide maximum internal cargo space. (Bell Boeing)

(Potential U.S. Navy AEW configurations provided for conformal-array radars on the fuselage of the aircraft.)

The following data for aircraft range reflect a shortfall in the original MV-22 requirements.

Operational: The No. 4 development aircraft began shipboard flight trials on the USS Wasp (LHD 1) on 4 December 1990; they were highly successful.

The No. 5 development aircraft crashed on its initial flight on 11 June 1991; the cause was not considered a design flaw, but rather an assembly problem.

The No. 4 aircraft crashed into the Potomac River near MCAS Quantico, Virginia, on 20 July 1992, killing all seven on board. That crash, which began with an in-flight fire, was attributed to pilot error.

Status: In development. First flight on 19 March 1989; first full conversion flight on 14 September 1989. First flight of a production MV-22 is expected in December 1996.

Six development aircraft have been built, with procurement of 425 MV-22 and 48 CV-22 aircraft planned.

Manufacturer:	Bell-Boeing	
Crew:	(3) pilot, copilot, crew chief + 24 troops	
Engines:	2 Allison T406-AD-400 turboshafts; 6,150 shp each (continuous rating 5,890 shp)	
Weights:	maximum T/O	59,000 lbs (26,762 kg)
Dimensions:	fuselage length	56 ft 10 in (17.33 m)
	span (over engine nacelles)	46 ft 6 in (14.18 m)
	height	17 ft 4 in (5.28 m)
	rotor diameter	36 ft (10.98 m)
	aircraft width (including rotor blades)	84 ft 6 in (25.76 m)
Speed:	dash	approx. 345 mph (156 km/h)
	maximum cruise	approx. 300 mph (483 km/h) at 18,000 ft (5,488 m)
Ceiling:	30,000+ ft (9,146+ m)	
Range:	radius	230 miles (370 km) with 24 troops
	radius	57.5 miles with 8,300 pounds (3,765 kg) external cargo
	ferry 1,980 miles (3,185 km) without refueling	
Radar:	none	

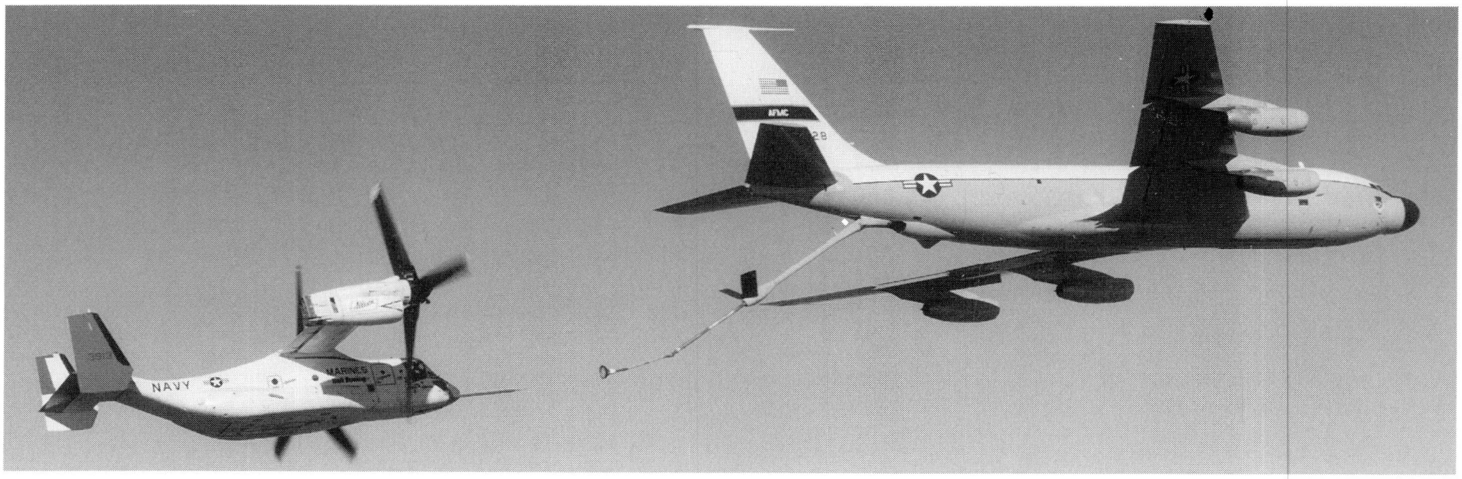

A prototype V-22 Osprey closes on an Air Force KC-135 Stratotanker during tests of the Osprey's in-flight refueling capability. The MV-22 variant is belatedly entering production for the Marine Corps, with Navy and Air Force variants to follow. (Bell Boeing)

S-92M MEDIUM-LIFT HELICOPTER

The Sikorsky S-92M had been proposed to meet the Marine Corps medium-lift helicopter requirement to replace the CH-46 Sea Knight. The S-92M design was revealed in April 1992 in response to a Department of Defense decision at that time not to proceed with development of the MV-22 Osprey.

The S-92M design incorporated technology and features from the H-60 Black Hawk/Seahawk series, with more cabin volume than the H-60 and a rear ramp for loading small vehicles and palletized cargo. As a troop carrier the S-92M could accommodate 18 to 20 troops for a 200-n.mile (370-km) lift. The four-blade main rotor would fold for shipboard stowage, as does the tail boom. The S-92M design had a fully retractable landing gear and could be fitted for in-flight refueling.

With the decision to proceed with procurement of the MV-22, Sikorsky has converted the S-92 design to a civilian configuration, given the company name "Helibus." It would carry 19 to 22 passengers and feature highly simplified maintenance. Assembly began in 1995 on the first of five flying prototypes; the first flight is scheduled for 1998.

See 15th Edition/pages 438–39 for characteristics.

HH-65A DOLPHIN

The French-designed Dolphin is flown by the Coast Guard in the short-range SAR role. It replaced the HH-52A. The HH-65A is flown in larger numbers than any other Coast Guard aircraft.

Developed by Aérospatiale as model SA 366G Dauphin, the helicopter was selected in a Coast Guard competition in 1979.

Those HH-65A helicopters that embark in icebreakers are fitted with skis in addition to their standard landing gear, giving them more stability for snow and ice operations.

Design: This is a streamlined helicopter with fully retractable landing gear, twin turboshaft engines, and a fan-in-fin *fenestron* tail rotor (i.e., an 11-blade tail rotor within a shroud). Engine problems led to replacement (beginning in 1991) of the original LTS101 with Allison-Garrett LHTEC T800-800 turboshaft engines.

In Coast Guard service they have a 3.5-million candlepower searchlight, an infrared system, and droppable rescue equipment. Maximum mission endurance is four hours.

Status: First flight SA 360 on 2 June 1972; SA 366G/HH-65A (prior to installation of avionics) on 23 July 1980. Coast Guard IOC was in November 1984.

The Coast Guard has procured 96 Dolphins, with deliveries delayed from an originally planned IOC of late 1981 because of engine problems.

Several nations fly the helicopter in the military role; some variants have been fitted with anti-ship missiles and ASW equipment. The Israeli Navy procured two H-65A helicopters for shipboard evaluation that were funded by the United States. Israel later procured 20 additional helicopters, all built by Aérospatiale to HH-65A standards.

29. IGE = In Ground Effect; OGE = Out of Ground Effect.

An HH-65A Dolphin during a rescue training flight off Annapolis, Maryland. (Joseph Handleman)

Manufacturer:	Aérospatiale	
Crew:	(3) pilot, copilot, crewman + 3 passengers	
Engines:	2 Allison-Garrett LHTEC T800-800 turboshafts; 1,200 shp each	
Weights:	empty	5,992 lbs (2,718 kg)
	maximum T/O	9,200 lbs (4,173 kg)
Dimensions:	fuselage length	37 ft 6 in (11.43 m)
	overall length	43 ft 9 in (13.33 m)
	height	12 ft 9 in (3.89 m)
	main rotor diameter	39 ft 2 in (11.9 m)
Speed:	maximum	201 mph (324 km/h)
	cruise	160 mph (257 km/h)
Ceiling:	7,510 ft (2,290 m) hover IGE[29]	
	5,340 ft (1,627 m) hover OGE	
Range:	radius	175 miles (280 km) with 30 minutes loiter
	maximum	470 miles (760 km)
Radar:	none	

HH-60J JAYHAWK

The HH-60J is the Coast Guard's medium-range SAR variant of the ubiquitous Black Hawk/Seahawk helicopter series. The HH-60J replaced the HH-3F Pelican and CH-3E Sea King in Coast Guard service. The Jayhawk is flown in larger numbers than any Coast Guard aircraft except the HH-65A helicopter.

Design: The HH-60J configuration is similar to the Navy's SH-60F variants, with generally the same characteristics, except that the

The HH-60J Jayhawk is a SAR-configured version of the Navy's H-60 Seahawk series. The standard access door is on the starboard side; the port-side opening permits litters to be loaded. The nose radome houses an RDR-1300 weather radar. Up to three external fuel tanks can be fitted. (Sikorsky)

A Coast Guard HH-60J Jayhawk flying fast and low. These helicopters are deployed in cutters of the Hamilton (WHEC 715) and Bear (WMEC 901) classes. (Sikorsky)

HH-60J can be fitted with three external fuel tanks for long-range operations (see maximum range, below). The helicopter has an external lift of 4,000 pounds (1,814 kg).

Like all H-60 series helicopters, the HH-60J has a fixed, tail-wheel landing gear. It can operate on board the 12 "Famous" (WMEC 270)-class Coast Guard cutters and larger ships. The helicopter has FLIR and a large searchlight.

Standard SH-60F data apply except as indicated below.

Designation: The Japanese Maritime Self-Defense Force flies the SH-60J and UH-60J helicopters. The former is a copy of the U.S. SH-60B Seahawk ASW aircraft and the latter a utility variant. The J indicates Japanese, in an improper use of the suffix letter.

Status: Operational; no longer in production. HH-60J IOC was in July 1991. The Coast Guard procured 42 Jayhawks through 1995.

Manufacturer:	Sikorsky	
Engines:	2 General Electric T700-GE-401C turboshafts; 1,900 shp each	
Crew:	(4) pilot, copilot, 2 crewmen + 6 rescuees	
Weights:	maximum T/O	21,884 lbs (9,927 kg)
Range:	radius	345 miles (556 km) with 45 minutes loiter
Radar:	Bendix RDR-1300C weather	

HH-60H SEAHAWK

The HH-60H is the Navy's combat SAR variant of the H-60 series. It has replaced the HH-3A Sea King as a specialized SAR helicopter. The HH-60H variants are flown by reserve squadrons HCS-4 and HCS-5; two HH-60H variants (in addition to four SH-60F helicopters) are assigned to all carrier HS squadrons.

These helicopters can carry eight SEALs and their equipment when operating in support of special operations.

Design: The HH-60H variants have the APR-39 radar warning receiver, the ALE-39 chaff/flare dispenser, and the ALQ-144 infrared jammer, as well as sophisticated communications gear. Although these helicopters were initially armed with machine guns, proposals are being considered to provide them additionally with 2¾-inch (70-mm) rockets and Hellfire missiles and a growth potential for air-to-air missiles.

Planned upgrades to the HH-60 include a FLIR/laser designator-range finder and Hellfire missiles.

Standard SH-60B/F data apply except as indicated below.

Status: Operational; no longer in production. First flight on 17 August 1988. HH-60H IOC (HCS-5) was in July 1989.

Manufacturer:	Sikorsky
Crew:	(3) pilot, copilot, crew chief + rescuees
Range:	radius 290 miles (465 km)
Armament:	2 7.62-mm machine guns M60D (8,000 rounds)
or	1 7.62-mm rotary machine gun GAU-2B/A
Radar:	none

An HH-60H Seahawk combat SAR aircraft with low-visibility markings. The tail-wheel landing gear (with double tail wheels) is nonretracting. (Sikorsky)

Details of an HH-60H from squadron HCS-4 with a 7.62-mm, six-barrel GAU-2B/A Minigun mounted in the door. Alternatively, conventional 7.62-mm machine guns can be fitted in both side doors. (Peter B. Mersky)

SH-60 SEAHAWK (LAMPS III)

In naval service the Seahawk is primarily an ASW helicopter. The SH-60B is the component of the Navy's ship-based LAMPS III ASW and over-the-horizon targeting system, and the SH-60F is a carrier-based ASW aircraft. The SH-60R is a planned "remanufacture" of the two helicopters, combining their capabilities into a single platform to serve in both HS and HSL squadrons.

The SH-60B is embarked in active cruisers, destroyers, and frigates in two-plane detachments from HSL squadrons; the SH-60F is combined with two HH-60H Seahawks in six-plane HS squadrons aboard aircraft carriers.

An SH-60B Seahawk LAMPS III helicopter, showing the port-side door (closed) and the 25-cell sonobuoy dispenser. The projection on the fuselage aft of the dispenser is an ALQ-142 ESM antenna; the small pods under the nose and the tail boom are data-link antennas. (Sikorsky)

The following ships were each configured to carry two SH-60B helicopters:

25	CG 47	TICONDEROGA class
31	DD 963	SPRUANCE class
26	FFG 7	OLIVER HAZARD PERRY class

In addition, the improved ARLEIGH BURKE (DDG 51)-class ships will carry the SH-60.

Design: The Seahawk is adopted from the UH-60A Black Hawk, the U.S. Army's basic transport helicopter. The SH-60B carries 2,000 pounds (907 kg) of avionics, including the ALQ-142 ESM sensor (similar to the SLQ-32 found on most U.S. surface warships). This system permits the helicopter to provide over-the-horizon detections and missile targeting for the launching ship. It also has a 25-sonobuoy dispenser, APS-124 radar, FLIR, ASQ-81 MAD, and a UYS-1(V)2 Proteus acoustic processor. No dipping sonar is fitted in the SH-60B. Beginning in 1990 the SH-60B variants have been fitted to carry the Penguin anti-ship missile. Some helicopters will be further modified to fire the Hellfire missile.

From 1995 on, these helicopters are also being fitted to mount a 7.62-mm M60D machine gun, AAR-47 missile detection system, ALE-39 chaff/flare dispenser, and ALQ-144 infrared jammer.

A YSH-60B was modified in 1984 to test the AQS-13F active dipping sonar and automated flight control system for the SH-60F. The carrier-based SH-60F has AQS-13F dipping sonar with a 1,500-foot (457-m) cable. The radar, MAD, sonobuoys, and some other equipment of the SH-60B have been deleted. The UYS-1(V)2 acoustic processor is fitted in the F variants.

Early plans called for a crew of four in the SH-60B, but in the event the aircraft has three (there is only one sensor operator). Although designed to carry nuclear depth bombs, the Seahawks have not been "wired" for this weapon. The IBM corporation was the prime contractor for the LAMPS III/SH-60B, this being the first time that the airframe manufacturer did not perform this role for a U.S. Navy helicopter. Sikorsky is the prime contractor for the SH-60F variant.

Designation: LAMPS = Light Airborne Multi-Purpose System, a term originally coined for the SH-2 LAMPS I helicopter (see below). The LAMPS II was a design study that did not reach fruition.

Status: Operational; no longer in production. First flight YUH-60 test bed on 17 October 1974; prototype SH-60B on 12 December 1979. Navy SH-60B IOC (HSL-41) was in September 1983; SH-60F IOC (HS-10) was in June 1989. The SH-60R is expected to become operational about 2001.

Australia, Greece, and Spain have purchased the SH-60B, while Japan is producing the SH-60J for shipboard use and the UH-60J for land basing. (A total of 16 nations other than the United States fly H-60 variants.)

Manufacturer:	IBM/Sikorsky	
Crew:	(3) pilot, copilot/airborne tactical officer, sensor operator	
Engines:	2 General Electric T700-GE-401 turboshafts; 1,690 shp each; helicopters procured after 1988 have 2 T700-GE-401C turboshafts; 1,900 shp each	
Weights:	empty	13,648 lbs (6,191 kg)
	loaded	19,500 lbs (8,845 kg) in ASW role
		18,000 lbs (8,165 kg) in Harpoon targeting role
		21,000+ lbs (9,526 kg) in utility role
Dimensions:	fuselage length	50 ft (15.26 m)
	overall length	64 ft 10 in (19.76 m)
	height	17 ft 2 in (5.23 m)
	main rotor diameter	53 ft 8 in (16.36 m)
Speed:	maximum cruise	145 mph (233 km/h)
Ceiling:	19,000 ft (5,790 m)	
	9,500 ft (2,896 m) hover IGE	
	10,400 ft (4,390 m) hover OGE	
Range:	radius 50 n.miles (92.5 km) with 3-hour loiter	
	radius 150 n.miles (278 km) with 1-hour loiter	
Armament:	2 Mk 46/50 ASW torpedoes	
or	2 Penguin anti-ship missiles	
Radar:	APS-124 in SH-60B (none in SH-60F)	

Carrying two dummy Mk 46 ASW torpedoes, an SH-60B Seahawk hovers for the camera. Outboard of the starboard torpedo is a towed MAD antenna in its stowed position. This is the only H-60 variant to have the APS-124 radar, mounted in a circular radome between the main landing gear. (Sikorsky)

An SH-60F Seahawk from HS-2 aboard the carrier NIMITZ lowers the AQS-15F active dipping sonar. The F model Seahawks do not have sonobuoys because active sonar is more effective when in the area of friendly ships, which reduce the effectiveness of passive detection. (Sikorsky)

An SH-60B carrying a Penguin anti-ship missile. Mounted in the chin position on the Seahawk are two ALQ-142 antennas, flanking the forward data-link pod. The after data-link pod is visible next to the tail wheels. (Norsk Forvarsteknologi A/S)

VH-60N "WHITE TOP"

The Marine Corps flies nine VH-60 variants of the H-60 series as executive transports. Assigned to squadron HMX-1 at Quantico, Virginia, these are "white top" helicopters that provide transportation for the president and other senior national officials. They replaced VH-1A Huey helicopters previously employed in this role. When the president is embarked in an HMX-1 helicopter, it is designated "Marine One."

Design: The VH-60N has a VIP interior configuration and is fitted with weather radar, cabin soundproofing, and Electromagnetic Pulse (EMP) hardening.

Name: These helicopters do not have an official name; they are generally referred to as "White Tops."

Status: IOC was on 30 November 1988.

Manufacturer:	Sikorsky	
Crew:	(4) pilot, copilot, flight engineer, radio operator + passengers	
Engines:	2 General Electric T700-GE-700 turboshafts; 1,560 shp each	
Weights:	empty	11,284 lbs (5,118 kg)
	loaded	16,994 lbs (7,708 kg)
Dimensions:	fuselage length	50 ft ¾ in (15.26 m)
	overall length	64 ft 10 in (19.76 m)
	height	16 ft 10 in (5.13 m)
	main rotor diameter	53 ft 8 in (16.36 m)
Speed:	maximum	184 mph (296 km/h)
	maximum cruise	167 mph (268 km/h)
Ceiling:	19,000 ft (5,790 m)	
	9,500 ft (2,896 m) hover IGE	
	10,400 ft (4,390 m) hover OGE	
Range:	370 miles (600 km) with 30 minutes loiter	
Radar:	weather	

A "white top" VH-60N configured as a VIP transport and flown by Marine squadron HMX-1. The weather radar is housed in the small radome under the nose. This relatively lightweight variant has only a single tail wheel, positioned farther aft than in SH-60 variants. (Sikorsky)

TH-57 SEARANGER

The SeaRanger is a training version of the commercial Bell 206 JetRanger series. The JetRanger was originally designed to compete in a U.S. Army 1961 light observation helicopter competition. Bell lost that competition, but the Model 206 was commercially successful and was later produced in large numbers for the Army as the OH-58 Kiowa.

Design: The TH-57 is fitted with dual controls; the TH-57C models have improved avionics and controls. The latter are upgraded TH-57A variants (their designation was changed to TH-57C in February 1983).

Status: TH-57A IOC was in 1968, TH-57C IOC in November 1982. The Navy purchased 40 off-the-shelf commercial aircraft as the TH-57A in 1968; 89 improved TH-57C models were procured in the 1980s. The latter replaced the TH-1L Hueys in the training role.

Manufacturer:	Bell	
Crew:	(1) pilot + 4 students	
Engines:	1 Allison T63-A-700 turboshaft; 317 shp	
Weights:	empty	1,464 lbs (664 kg)
	maximum T/O	3,000 lbs (1,361 kg)
Dimensions:	fuselage length	32 ft 7 in (9.94 m)
	overall length	41 ft (12.5 m)
	height	9 ft 7 in (2.91 m)
	main rotor diameter	35 ft 4 in (10.78 m)
Speed:	maximum	138 mph (222 km/h)
	cruise	117 mph (188 km/h)
Ceiling:	18,900 ft (5,762 km)	
	13,600 ft (4,146 m) hover IGE	
Range:	345 miles (483 km)	
Radar:	none	

A TH-57 SeaRanger, the Navy's principal training helicopter. (Bell)

A TH-57 SeaRanger about to land on the helicopter training craft IX 514. (U.S. Navy)

A Marine CH-53E Super Stallion showing the large sponsons that are fitted with auxiliary fuel tanks and the three turboshaft engine nacelles mounted above the fuselage. (Sikorsky)

CH-53E/MH-53E SUPER STALLION/SEA DRAGON

Developed specifically for the U.S. Navy and Marine Corps, this is the heaviest lift helicopter in service outside of Russia. It is flown by the Marines in the CH-53E assault/heavy cargo roles and by the Navy in the CH-53E cargo/VERTREP and MH-53E mine countermeasures roles.

Design: The CH-53E can lift 16 tons (16,330 kg) of external load. These helicopters have the same basic configuration as the D-model Sea Stallion, but with three engines, a seven-blade main rotor (vice six in the CH-53A/D), larger rotor blades, an in-flight refueling probe, and improved transmission. Two 650-gallon (2,470-liter) external tanks can be fitted to the sponsons. The CH-53E can lift 93 percent of the heavy equipment in a Marine division, compared to 38 percent for the CH-53D.

The MH-53E can handle the Mk 103 moored sweep gear, Mk 104 acoustic sweep, Mk 105 magnetic sweep, Mk 106 magnetic/acoustic

A Marine CH-53E Super Stallion with landing gear retracted. Note the fixed refueling probe fitted to the starboard side of the aircraft. The H-53E series have a greater lift capacity than any helicopters produced outside of Russia. (Sikorsky)

sweep, ALQ-166 Lightweight Magnetic Sweep (LMS), and AQS-14 towed minehunting sonar. The improved AQS-20 minehunting sonar will be provided for these helicopters in place of the AQS-14. It is capable of night operations, with a six-hour mission capability. (The RH-53D can operate strictly in daylight.)

Designation: The M prefix indicates its multi-mission capability.

Historical: The RH-3A Sea King was the first airborne MCM helicopter to be approved for U.S. Navy service. It was replaced by the CH-53A Sea Stallion in the early 1970s; those helicopters participated in Operation End Sweep, the 1972–1973 mine clearance of North Vietnamese ports.

The CH-53A was succeeded by the RH-53D in 1972; these helicopters were deployed to the Suez Canal in 1974–1975 (Operations Nimbus Star/Stream); to the Red Sea/Gulf of Suez in 1984 (Operation Intense Look); and to the Persian Gulf in 1987 (Operation Earnest Will).

In turn, the RH-53D has been succeeded in the MCM role by the MH-53E.

Operational: Six MH-53E Sea Dragons were airlifted by C-5A Galaxy transports to the Persian Gulf in early October 1990 to participate in Desert Shield/Desert Storm. They then operated from the helicopter carrier TRIPOLI (LPH 10). In doing so, of course, the MH-53Es displaced Marine helicopters and troops.

Status: Operational; no longer in production. First flight YCH-53E on 1 March 1974; first flight CH-53E on 13 December 1980; first flight MH-53E on 1 September 1983 (a CH-53E in the MCM configuration flew on 23 December 1981). IOC CH-53E (HMH-464) was in February 1981.

The last of 48 MH-53E helicopters was delivered in late 1994. The last of 160 CH-53E helicopters were being delivered in 1996. (The Marines hope to procure an additional 18 helicopters for active squadrons and 12 for reserve units.)

Manufacturer:	Sikorsky	
Crew:	(3) pilot, copilot, crew chief + 55 troops	
Engines:	3 General Electric T64-GE-416 turboshafts; 4,380 shp each	
Weights:	empty CH-53E	33,685 lbs (15,280 kg)
	MH-53E	36,336 lbs (16,482 kg)
	maximum T/O	73,500 lbs (33,340 kg)
Dimensions:	fuselage length	73 ft 4 in (22.33 m)
	overall length	99 ft ½ in (30.18 m)
	height	27 ft 9 in (8.46 m)
	main rotor diameter	79 ft (24.08 m)
Speed:	maximum	195 mph (315 km/h) at sea level
	cruise	172 mph (278 km/h) at sea level
Ceiling:	18,500 ft (5,640 m)	
	11,550 ft (3,520 m) hover IGE	
	9,500 ft (2,895 m) hover OGE	
Range:	radius	57.5 miles (92.5 km) with 16 tons of external cargo
	radius	575 miles (926 km) with 10 tons of external cargo
	ferry	1,150 miles (1,852 km)
Radar:	none	

A Navy MH-53E Sea Dragon from squadron HM-14. The sponson configuration differs from the CH-53E configuration; a refueling probe is fitted, as are mirrors extending from the nose to enable the pilots to monitor sweep gear. (Sikorsky)

An MH-53E Sea Dragon during a high-speed mine countermeasures operation tows a Mk 105 hydrofoil sled fitted with the ALQ-166 system for countering magnetic mines. These helicopters can be deployed to forward areas in C-5 Galaxy cargo aircraft, by ferrying (with in-flight refueling), or aboard ship. (U.S. Navy)

Mk 105 hydrofoil sleds for MH-53E Sea Dragons are stowed in the hangar deck of the helicopter carrier Tripoli (LPH 10) during Operation Desert Storm. The Tripoli was flagship for the Coalition's mine countermeasures efforts, and she was one of two U.S. warships to strike mines in the Persian Gulf during the conflict. (U.S. Navy)

CH-53D/RH-53D SEA STALLION

The H-53 series has served as the Marine Corps' heavy assault helicopter and the Navy's mine countermeasures helicopter. Both are now flown in limited numbers, having been replaced by the CH-53E Super Stallion and MH-53E Sea Dragon, respectively. The D models are now flown only by active and reserve Marine squadrons (the latter flying ex-Navy RH-53D helicopters).

All earlier Navy/Marine CH-53A helicopters have been retired.

Design: The basic dimensions of the D variant are similar to the E, except that the later helicopter has a third engine and other propulsion improvements. These helicopters have a large cargo compartment with a rear ramp. The RH-53D variants are similar to the CH-53D but have upgraded T64-GE-415 engines and automatic flight controls for sustained low-level flight. The MCM versions have provisions for two swivel .50-cal machine guns, and they can stream Mk 103 cutters for countering contact mines. A Mk 104 acoustic countermeasures, a Mk 105 hydrofoil sled for countering magnetic mines, a Mk 106 sled with acoustic sweep equipment, the SPU-1 Magnetic Orange Pipe (MOP) for countering shallow-water mines, and the AQS-14 dipping/towed sonar are also available for the RH-53D.

Operational: Eight RH-53D helicopters, flying from the carrier NIMITZ, were used in the aborted April 1980 attempt to rescue hostages from the American embassy in Tehran; seven of those helicopters were destroyed in the operation.

Refueling five times in flight from KC-130 tankers, an RH-53D has made an 18½-hour flight across the United States.

Status: Operational. First flight CH-53A on 14 October 1964. Marine Corps IOC (HMH-463) was in November 1966.

The Navy and Marine Corps took delivery of 384 H-53A/D series helicopters; others were flown by the U.S. Air Force and foreign services. In addition to the 30 RH-53D models delivered to the U.S. Navy, six more MCM versions went to Iran prior to the 1979 Islamic revolution.

A Marine CH-53D Sea Stallion from HMH-362 takes off from the carrier THEODORE ROOSEVELT. Although far less capable than the H-53E series, these helicopters still provide a major component of the Marines' helicopter lift. (U.S. Navy, PHAA Chris J. Purtee)

Manufacturer:	Sikorsky	
Crew:	(3) pilot, copilot, crewman + 38 troops or 24 litters + 4 attendants (7 crewmen in RH-53D)	
Engines:	2 General Electric T64-GE-413 turboshafts; 3,925 shp each	
Weights:	empty	23,628 lbs (10,718 kg)
	loaded	34,958 lbs (15,857 kg)
	maximum T/O	42,000 lbs (19,051 kg)
Dimensions:	fuselage length	67 ft 2 in (20.48 m)
	overall length	88 ft 3 in (26.92 m)
	height	24 ft 11 in (7.59 m)
	main rotor diameter	72 ft 3 in (22.04 m)
Speed:	maximum	196 mph (315 km/h)
	cruise	173 mph (278 km/h)
Ceiling:	21,000 ft (6,402 m)	
	13,400 ft (4,085 m) hover IGE	
Range:	620 miles (1,000 km)	
	ferry 1,020 miles (1,641 km)	
Radar:	none	

HH-52A SEA GUARD

The HH-52A was a commercial helicopter adopted by the Coast Guard for the SAR mission. The H-52 was not flown by any other U.S. military service. The Sikorsky-designed helicopter was in service from 1963 to 1989; the last unit flew for the last time on 12 September 1989. Ninety-nine helicopters were procured.

The HH-52A was replaced in Coast Guard service by the HH-65A Dolphin.

Designation: Originally designated HU2S-1G; that was changed to HH-52A in 1962. The suffix G indicated Coast Guard under the pre-1962 system.

See 14th Edition/pages 437–38 for characteristics.

CH-46E/UH-46D SEA KNIGHT

The CH-46E is the Marine Corps' principal assault helicopter, and the UH-46D is flown by the Navy in the VERTREP role. The Marine variant will be replaced by the long-delayed MV-22 Osprey tilt-rotor aircraft. The Navy is seeking a replacement for the UH-46D in the VERTREP role; these are flown by five HC squadrons. (The Navy also flies a small number of other CH-46 variants; see chapter 28.)

Design: The Sea Knight has a tricycle landing gear and small, wheel-housing sponsons aft, distinguishing it from the similar, widely flown CH-47 Chinook cargo helicopter. The Sea Knight is a tandem-rotor helicopter with a rear ramp for the rapid loading and unloading of cargo, including small vehicles; the rotor blades fold for shipboard stowage. The H-46 series has demonstrated the capability of remaining afloat for more than two hours in two-foot (0.6 m) waves, with the rotors stopped.

The Marines have upgraded 273 CH-46A/D troop helicopters to the CH-46E configuration. Provided in the upgrade are improved engines, crash attenuating seats for pilots, a more survivable fuel system, and an improved rescue winch. Subsequent upgrades have been undertaken to extend the service life of these aircraft.

Designation: Originally designated HRB; the naval variants were changed to H-46 in 1962.

Status: Operational. First flight YHC-1A prototype on 22 April 1958. Marine IOC (HMM-265) was in June 1964.

The Navy took delivery of 264 Sea Knights and the Marine Corps received 360 helicopters from 1961 to 1977.

CH-46E

Manufacturer:	Boeing Vertol	
Crew:	(3) pilot, copilot, crewman + 25 troops or 15 litters + 2 attendants	
Engines:	2 General Electric T58-GE-16 turboshafts; 1,870 shp each	
Weights:	empty	15,198 lbs (6,894 kg)
	maximum T/O	24,300 lbs (11,022 kg)
Dimensions:	fuselage length	46 ft 8 in (13.92 m)
	overall length	84 ft 4 in (25.72 m)
	main rotor diameter	25 ft 6 in (7.81 m)
	height	16 ft 8 in (5.08 m)
Speed:	maximum	161 mph (259 km/h)
	cruise	158 mph (254 km/h)
Ceiling:	9,400 ft (2,866 m)	
Range:	radius 86 miles (139 km) with payload	
	ferry 690 miles (1,111 km)	
Armament:	2 .50-cal machine guns can be fitted	

A CH-46E Sea Knight from squadron HMM-261 lifts off the helicopter carrier Saipan (LHA 2). The H-46 series is similar to the U.S. Army's CH-46 Chinook. The rear ramp is closed in this view. (U.S. Navy, JO1 Kip Burke)

A Navy UH-46D Sea Knight lands cargo on the helicopter carrier Essex (LHD 2). VERTREP operations are carried out on a regular basis, saving considerable time in replenishment operations. Note the fixed tricycle landing gear and the rescue hoist over the starboard-side door. (U.S. Navy, PHAN Jeffrey Viano)

A pair of Marine CH-46E Sea Knights show the ungainly appearance of these helicopters. After many delays, they are to be replaced by the MV-22 Osprey as the principal Marine rotary-wing assault aircraft. (U.S. Marine Corps)

A UH-46E Sea Knight from squadron HC-3 crosses the wake of a replenishment ship. The aircraft wears the older, darker colors of Navy VERTREP helicopters. The UH-46E has a rescue hoist over the door, on the starboard side, with the upper half open. These helicopters also have a stern ramp. (Leo Van Ginderen collection)

OH-6B CAYUSE

Four OH-6B Cayuse helicopters were acquired by the Naval Test Pilot School at NAS Patuxent River, Maryland, on loan from the Army for use in test pilot training. The Cayuse was developed for the Army's 1961 Light Observation Helicopter (LOH) competition. The helicopter proved a highly versatile aircraft, and the commercial Model 500 set 23 international records for helicopters in 1966.

The Navy aircraft have been discarded.

Designation: The OH-6 was designated HO-6 prior to 1962.

See 15th Edition/page 446 for characteristics.

HH-3F PELICAN

This version of the Sea King was built specifically for the U.S. Coast Guard SAR role. It was similar to the HH-3E Jolly Green Giant rescue version flown by the U.S. Air Force. The HH-3F carried droppable rescue supplies and had a modified boat-type hull and sponson-floats for water operations.

Forty of these helicopters were built for the Coast Guard. The HH-60J Jayhawk has replaced the HH-3F.

See 15th Edition/page 446 for characteristics.

SH-3 SEA KING

From the early 1960s into the early 1990s the Sea King was the U.S. Navy's standard carrier-based ASW helicopter. It has been replaced aboard aircraft carriers by the SH-60F Seahawk and in the SAR and utility roles by other variants of the H-60 series. The Sea King is now flown only in the utility and VIP roles, although several SH-3Hs remain in service. The later, VH-3D variants are flown by Marine squadron HMX-1 to transport the president.

Design: The Sea King has a "boat" hull but does not normally alight on the water (unlike the Coast Guard HH-3F, listed separately). The tail pylon and main rotor blades fold for carrier stowage. In the ASW role the ultimate ASW-configured SH-3H had AQS-13B dipping sonar, sonobuoys, APN-130 Doppler radar, ASQ-81 MAD, and ALE-37 chaff dispenser. A total of 145 Sea Kings were converted to the ultimate SH-3H configuration.

Two Sea Kings (designated YSH-3J) were used to test sensors for the SH-60B.

Earlier SH-3A/D ASW variants, the HH-3A rescue variant, and the RH-3A mine countermeasures version have all been discarded.

Designation: Formerly the HSS-2, the Sea King was redesignated SH-3 in 1962. The HSS-1 was the redesignation of the SH-34 Seabat, a very different helicopter.

Operational: During Operations Desert Shield/Desert Storm in 1990–1991, SH-3H helicopters aboard participating aircraft carriers were fitted with a flexible 7.62-mm M60D machine gun, mounted in the (starboard) door opening.

A VH-3D from HMX-1 was used to transport Pope John Paul II during his October 1995 visit to the United States.

Status: First flight XHSS-2 on 11 March 1959; first flight SH-3H in April 1972. Navy IOC (HS-1) was in June 1961.

The helicopter is flown by several foreign services.

SH-3H

Manufacturer:	Sikorsky	
Crew:	(4) pilot, copilot, 2 systems operators	
Engines:	2 General Electric T58-GE-10 turboshafts; 1,400 shp each	
Weights:	empty	13,465 lbs (6,108 kg)
	maximum T/O	21,000 lbs (9,526 kg)
Dimensions:	fuselage length	54 ft 9 in (16.69 m)
	overall length	72 ft 8 in (22.15 m)
	height	16 ft 10 in (5.13 m)
	main rotor diameter	62 ft (18.9 m)
Speed:	maximum	166 mph (267 km/h)
	cruise	136 mph (219 km/h)
Ceiling:	14,700 ft (4,482 m)	
	10,500 ft (3,201 m) hover IGE	
Range:	620 miles (1,000 km)	
	ferry 745 miles (1,198 km)	
Armament:	2 Mk 46 ASW torpedoes	
Radar:	LN-66HP search	

An SH-3G Sea King from squadron HC-2 lifts off of the helicopter carrier New Orleans (LPH 11). The SH-3G helicopters have been stripped of ASW equipment; there is a rescue hoist over the large, starboard-side door. The tail wheel does not retract. (U.S. Navy)

A VH-3D from Marine squadron HMX-1 passes the Lincoln Memorial in Washington, D.C. The president normally flies in a Sea King, which has more head room than the VIP-configured VH-60N "White Top" does. The presidential seal is on the nose of the helicopter. (U.S. Navy)

An SH-3H Sea King from squadron HS-9 and a Brazilian SH-3D both trail their AQS-13 dipping sonar during a joint naval exercise. At the time, HS-9 was with CVW-8 aboard the carrier NIMITZ. All deploying HS squadrons now fly the SH-60F and HH-60H Seahawks. (U.S. Navy, PHAA P. Silver)

CH-3E SEA KING

The Coast Guard acquired six CH-3E cargo helicopters from the Air Force in the 1980s because of the increase in rotary-wing aircraft required for drug interdiction operations.

A variant of the basic H-3 design, this helicopter was widely used by the Air Force in the cargo and transport roles. The helicopter was capable of water landing and takeoff and has a hydraulically operated rear loading ramp. Three of the Coast Guard helicopters were modified for the SAR role, being fitted with auxiliary fuel tanks, Loran-C navigation gear, and APN-215 radar. The three other CH-3Es were held in storage for possible use or to provide parts for the active helicopters. They have been discarded.

See 15th Edition/page 448 for characteristics.

SH-2G LAMPS I

The SH-2G LAMPS I is an ASW helicopter flown from OLIVER HAZARD PERRY-class (FFG 7) frigates operated by the Naval Reserve Force. The original SH-2D LAMPS I was developed for the ASW role, operating from surface warships. The subsequent SH-2F and SH-2G variants were carried in ships that could not accommodate the larger SH-60B LAMPS III helicopter. Only the SH-2G variant is now in U.S. Navy service.

Primarily employed in the ASW role, the helicopter can also carry out over-the-horizon targeting of anti-ship missiles and has a limited VERTREP capability.

The Navy's need for ship-based ASW helicopters in the early 1970s led to the conversion of 20 single-engine HU2K/UH-2 Seasprite utility helicopters to the SH-2D configuration and another 85 conversions to the SH-2F variant. Subsequently, 54 additional SH-2F helicopters were procured. The surviving D models were later upgraded to an F configuration, the last in 1983. A small number of SH-2s were further upgraded to the SH-2G configuration for exclusive service aboard NRF frigates. The six fiscal 1987 helicopters were built as SH-2G variants; these were the last H-2 series helicopters to be built.

(Two aircraft were modified to a YSH-2E configuration; they were later changed to SH-2F. One SH-2F without ASW avionics became an NHH-2D test aircraft. One SH-2F to YSH-2G conversion in 1985 tested the ultimate LAMPS I configuration.)

Previously, the SH-2 LAMPS I was embarked in or planned for the following ships (one helicopter per ship except for the FFG 7, which could carry two):

4	CGN 38	VIRGINIA class
1	CGN 35	TRUXTUN
2	CG 47	TICONDEROGA class
8	CG 26	BELKNAP class
4	DDG 993	KIDD class
25	FFG 7	OLIVER HAZARD PERRY class
6	FFG 1	BROOKE class
48	FF 1052	KNOX class
6	FF 1040	GARCIA class
1	FF 1098	GLOVER
12	WHEC 378	HAMILTON class (Coast Guard)

In addition, the 12 "Famous"-class Coast Guard cutters were to have a LAMPS I upgrade capability; the LAMPS I program was halted before those ships were modified.

Design: The SH-2 LAMPS are employed to localize and attack submarine contacts initially made by surface ASW ships. The helicopters have no sonobuoy analysis capability, the data being data linked to the supporting warship for analysis. The SH-2G is fitted with the LN-66 radar, a 15-sonobuoy dispenser, ASQ-81C(V)2 MAD, ALR-66 ESM, ALE-39 chaff/flare dispenser, AAQ-16 FLIR, APN-217 Doppler radar, and upgraded avionics, including the ASN-150 tactical management system. With the sonobuoy dispenser removed, the cabin can accommodate four passengers or two litters. In the VERTREP role the SH-2F can lift 2,000 pounds (907 kg) of cargo.

Designation: The original designation HU2K was changed to UH-2 in 1962 and to SH-2 upon conversion to ASW configuration.

Name: The name Seasprite was officially assigned to both the HU2K and H-2 series; it is rarely used.

Operational: The SH-2 has also served as the test and limited operational platform for the Magic Lantern laser mine-detection system. During Operation Desert Storm in 1991 SH-2F helicopters used the Magic Lantern device to detect sea mines in the Persian Gulf. The laser device is fitted in a large pod that is attached to the right side of the helicopter.

Status: Operational. First flight HU2K-1 on 2 July 1959. Navy IOC (HU-2) was in December 1962. First flight SH-2D on 16 March 1971; the IOC SH-2D (HC-4) was in October 1971. First flight SH-2G on 28 December 1989; the IOC SH-2G was in March 1991.

One hundred eighty-six UH-2 utility helicopters were built for the Navy through 1965. The 54 subsequent new SH-2F helicopters produced by Kaman were the first helicopters built by that firm in 15 years and the first of this series to be manufactured in an ASW configuration. They were followed by the production of six SH-2G helicopters. Kaman also converted 17 SH-2F aircraft to the G configuration.

Egypt, Pakistan, and Portugal have likewise procured the SH-2 for the ASW role.

Manufacturer:	Kaman	
Crew:	(3) pilot, copilot/tactical coordinator, systems operator	
Engines:	2 General Electric T700-GE-401 turboshafts; 1,790 shp each	
Weights:	maximum T/O	13,500 lbs (6,124 kg)
Dimensions:	fuselage length	40 ft 2 in (12.24 m)
	overall length	52 ft 6 in (16.0 m)
	height	15 ft 1 in (4.6 m)
	main rotor diameter	44 ft (3.66 m)
Speed:	maximum	172.5 mph (278 km/h) at sea level
Ceiling:	20,400 ft (6,220 m)	
	17,600 ft (5,365 m) hover IGE	
	14,600 ft (4,450 m) hover OGE	
Range:	radius 40 miles (65 km) with 1 Mk 46/50 torpedo with 2½-hour loiter	
	radius 40 miles (65 km) with 2 Mk 46/50 torpedoes with 1½-hour loiter	
	maximum 621 miles (1,000 km) with 3 external 100-gallon (378.5-liter) tanks; endurance 5.3 hours	
Armament:	2 Mk 46/50 ASW torpedoes	
Radar:	LN-66HP search	
	APN-217(V)3 Doppler navigation	

An SH-2G LAMPS I with an auxiliary fuel tank and towed MAD antenna in stowed position mounted on the starboard side. These helicopters are retained in service to provide a LAMPS capability to Naval Reserve frigates. The tail wheel does not retract. (Kaman)

A now-discarded SH-2F LAMPS I carries a Magic Lantern laser mine-detection system on its starboard side. The landing gear is extended in this view; there is a fuel tank mounted on the port side. Compare the engine nacelles of this SH-2F with the more powerful SH-2G. (Kaman)

AH-1W SEACOBRA

The SeaCobra is a specialized gunship helicopter that evolved from the widely used Huey series. It is flown by the Marine Corps' utility and attack helicopter squadrons (HMLA).

The AH-1G variant was the first specialized gunship of the Huey series, being produced for both the Army and Marine Corps. (UH-1 series helicopters have been heavily armed, including Navy variants flown in the Vietnam War.)

The AH-IW is generally referred to unofficially as the "Super Cobra."

Design: The SeaCobra has a narrow fuselage that provides a minimal cross section; it also features stub wings for carrying rocket packs or gun pods, a nose turret with a 20-mm three-barrel cannon, and tandem seating for a gunner (forward) and pilot. The 20-mm cannon has a helmet-sight system.

All AH-1W helicopters are being fitted with FLIR/laser designator-range finder and a video camera/recorder as part of a Night Targeting System (NTS).

The now-standard AH-1W has a weapons payload of 3,000 pounds (1,361 kg), including the Army-developed Hellfire missile, TOW anti-tank missile, Sidearm radar-homing missile, and Sidewinder AAM. Alternatively, drop tanks can be fitted to extended range. An ALE-39 chaff/flare dispenser is fitted. This helicopter can take off on a single engine and climb at more than 800 feet (244 m) per minute.

Surviving AH-1T helicopters were upgraded to the AH-1W configuration, with new procurement following.

Designation: The AH-1W was originally designated AH-1T+.

An AH-1W SeaCobra carries a full payload of missiles and rockets. There is a laser range finder above the three-barrel, 20-mm M197 gun mounted in a chin turret. (Bell)

An AH-1W SeaCobra from HMLA-167 fires a Sidewinder missile. These helicopters will be further upgraded to enable them to serve into the 21st century. A gunship variant of the MV-22 Osprey is a candidate for their eventual successor. (Bell)

Status: Operational; in production. First flight Army AH-1G on 7 September 1965; first flight AH-1T+ on 16 November 1983. IOC (AH-1G) with the Marine Corps was in 1969, AH-1T in October 1977, and AH-1W in March 1986.

Marine procurement of the AH-1W has ended with the fiscal 1995 budget. When the last AH-1W helicopters are delivered in 1999, the Marines will have 225 aircraft. Weapon upgrades are expected to provide for a service life through at least the year 2020.

More than 2,500 Cobra gunships have been built for U.S. and foreign military services, with the AH-1S model being coproduced by Fuji in Japan.

Manufacturer:	Bell	
Crew:	(2) pilot, gunner	
Engines:	2 General Electric T700-GE-401 turboshafts; 1,690 shp each	
Weights:	empty	10,200 lbs (4,627 kg)
	maximum T/O	14,750 lbs (6,690 kg)
Dimensions:	fuselage length	45 ft 6 in (13.87 m)
	overall length	58 feet (17.68 m)
	height	14 ft 2 in (4.32 m)
	main rotor diameter	48 ft (14.63 m)
Speed:	maximum	219 mph (352 km/h) at sea level
Ceiling:	17,500 ft (5,335 m)	
	14,750 ft (4,497 m) hover IGE	
	3,000 ft (915 m) hover OGE	
Range:	330 miles (528 km)	
Armament:	1 20-mm cannon M197 (750 rounds)	
	8 TOW or Hellfire missiles	
or	38 2.75-inch rockets	
or	32 5-inch Zuni rockets	
plus	2 Sidewinder AAMs	
Radar:	none	

Rear aspect of an AH-1 SeaCobra on the helicopter carrier GUADALCANAL (LPH 7). There is a Sidewinder AAM on the starboard pylon and Hellfire missiles on the port pylon. (Department of Defense)

HH/UH-1N HUEY (IROQUOIS)

The Huey series is the most widely used military helicopter in the Western world. The HH-1N and UH-1N are the only variants now flown by the Navy and Marine Corps, employed in the utility role from ships and ashore.

The Navy TH-1L training and HH-1K rescue variants have been discarded, as have the Marine VH-1N variants used for VIP transport with squadron HMX-1.

Designation: The Huey, originally designated HU-1 by the Army, was changed to UH-1 in 1962. In 1991 many of the UH-1Ns employed for SAR operations aboard amphibious ships and at air stations were redesignated HH-1N.

Name: Officially named Iroquois in accord with the Army scheme of naming helicopters for American Indian tribes. Invariably, the helicopter is called "Huey," derived from the designation HU-1E.

Status: Operational. First flight XH-40 on 22 October 1956. Marine IOC (VMO-1) was in March 1964.

More than 9,000 Hueys have been produced for U.S. and foreign service since the Bell design won the U.S. Army's competition for a turbine helicopter in 1955.

UH-1N

Manufacturer:	Bell	
Crew:	(3) pilot, copilot, crew chief + 12 to 15 troops	
Engines:	2 United Aircraft of Canada PT6T turboshafts; 900 shp each	
Weights:	empty	5,549 lbs (2,517 kg)
	maximum T/O	10,500 lbs (4,763 kg)
Dimensions:	fuselage length	42 ft 5 in (12.93 m)
	overall length	57 ft 3 in (17.47 m)
	height	14 ft 5 in (4.39 m)
	main rotor diameter	48 ft 2 in (14.7 m)
Speed:	126 mph (203 km/h)	
Ceiling:	15,000 ft (4,573 m)	
	12,900 ft (3,933 m) hover IGE	
Range:	290 miles (463 km)	
Armament:	various combinations of machine guns and rockets can be mounted	
Radar:	none	

EXPERIMENTAL AIRCRAFT

X-31A ENHANCED FIGHTER MANEUVERABILITY (EFM) DEMONSTRATOR

This is an advanced research aircraft intended to demonstrate whether it is possible to exploit the high-angle-of-attack flight regime to enable a fighter to achieve tighter, faster turns and earlier weapon-firing opportunities.

Flight testing of the two X-31A aircraft is carried out by an international test organization made up of representatives from NASA, the Advanced Research Projects Agency (ARPA), the U.S. Navy and Air Force, Germany, and the firms of Rockwell International and Messerschmitt-Bolkow-Blöhm (MBB).[30] ARPA has overall program management; the Navy serves as ARPA's agent and provides on-site direction.

Design: The basic aircraft design is relatively conservative, featuring a delta-wing configuration with canards (forward fuselage-mounted planes). The aircraft has a deep fuselage with a large variable-capture air intake beneath it. An F/A-18 Hornet-type HUD is provided. To the maximum extent possible, off-the-shelf components were employed to reduce costs. The initial costs of developing and producing the aircraft were shared: the United States contributed 75 percent and Germany 25 percent.

The aircraft is unarmed.

Designation: The designation X-31 was assigned on 23 February 1987.

Status: Flight test. First flight on 11 October 1990. The initial test phases were carried out in 1990–1991 at the Rockwell International facility in Palmdale, California; in late 1991 it was moved to the NASA Ames-Dryden research facility at Edwards AFB, California, to continue tests.

Two aircraft were built; one X-31 crashed at Edwards AFB, California, on 19 January 1995.

30. Now part of Deutsche Aerospace.

A Marine UH-1N Huey from squadron HMLA-267 during flight operations with a Royal Navy Lynx helicopter. Army and Navy Hueys were heavily armed during the Vietnam War; the Navy's armed UH-1B variants were called Sea-wolves. (U.S. Navy, PH1 Charles W. Alley)

Manufacturer:	Rockwell and Messerschmitt-Bolkow-Blöhm	
Crew:	(1) pilot	
Engines:	1 General Electric F404-GE-400 turbojet; 16,000 lbst (7,257 kgst)	
Weights:	empty	10,212 lbs (4,632 kg)
	mission T/O	11,830 lbs (5,366 kg)
	maximum T/O	13,968 lbs (6,335 kg)
Dimensions:	length	43 ft 4 in (13.21 m)
	wing span	23 ft 10 in (7.26 m)
	wing area	226.3 ft^2 (20.37 m^2)
	canard area	23.6 ft^2 (2.12 m^2)
	height	14 ft 7 in (4.44 m)
Speed:		
Ceiling:	35,000+ ft (10,670+ m)	
Range:		
Radar:	none	

One of two X-32 EFM demonstration aircraft in its original markings with its sponsors—DARPA, MBB (BMVg), and Navy—emblazoned on its fuselage. A Marine pilot from the Naval Air Test Center was piloting the aircraft when this photo was taken. (U.S. Navy)

XV-15A

The XV-15A is a tilt-rotor demonstration aircraft that serves as a technology prototype for the V-22 Osprey series. Developed by Bell Helicopter Textron, the XV-15A has successfully demonstrated the ability of a rotary-wing aircraft to fully convert in flight to a conventional aircraft configuration.

Design: The aircraft has twin rotor-engine nacelles mounted on a connecting wing; the nacelles rotate to the horizontal position for conventional aircraft flight and are vertical for takeoffs and landings or hovering. Rolling takeoffs and landings are possible. Thus, the design has the advantages of both a conventional aircraft and a helicopter.

Bell built two XV-15A aircraft under NASA and Army sponsorship. Subsequently, the Navy and Marine Corps supported the project.

Operational: The two XV-15A aircraft have achieved their flight-demonstration goals in extensive testing by NASA and the armed services. One was airlifted in 1982 in a C-5A Galaxy transport to the Paris air show, where it performed for international audiences. Aircraft No. 702 crashed on 20 August 1992; aircraft No. 703 continues in the flight test program.

In a key XV-15A evaluation, one aircraft flew 54 takeoffs and landings from the helicopter carrier Tripoli (LPH 10) in August 1982. Although the aircraft was not intended for shipboard operation, the tests succeeded with only minor difficulties.

Status: Operational. First flight 3 May 1977.

An XV-15A during shipboard compatibility trials on the helicopter carrier Tripoli. The engine nacelles are in the vertical position for takeoff. (U.S. Navy)

Manufacturer:	Bell	
Crew:	(2) pilot, copilot	
Engines:	2 Avco Lycoming LTC1K-4K turboshafts; 1,800 shp each	
Weights:	empty	9,670 lbs (4,386 kg)
	loaded	13,000 lbs (5,897 kg)
	maximum T/O	15,000 lbs (6,804 kg)
Dimensions:	length	42 ft 2 in (12.83 m)
	wing span (over engine nacelles)	35 ft 2 in (10.72 m)
	height	15 ft 4 in (4.67 m)
	rotor diameter	25 ft (7.62 m)
	aircraft width (including rotor blades)	57 ft 2 in (17.4 m)
Speed:	maximum	382 mph (615 km/h) at 17,000 ft (5,183 m)
	maximum cruise	345 mph (555 km/h)
Ceiling:	29,000 ft (8,841 m)	
Range:		
Radar:	none	

One of two XV-15 tilt-rotor technology demonstration aircraft in the horizontal flight mode with engine nacelles in the horizontal position. The XV-15A was the precursor to the V-22 Osprey. (Bell)

LIGHTER-THAN-AIR

The Navy and Coast Guard Lighter-Than-Air (LTA), or airship, programs have been halted. The Navy's development of a surveillance airship was canceled in early 1992, shortly before completion of the first flight of a full-size prototype (the YEZ-2A/Sentinel 5000). The Coast Guard's fully operational aerostat surveillance program was "grounded" on 31 December 1991 for transfer to the Army. On that date the five Coast Guard sea-based aerostat vessels were brought into the ports of Miami and Key West, Florida, pending completion of studies on the future of the program. Subsequently, the ships were briefly returned to service, operated by civilian contract crews and uniformed Army personnel on board for technical duties.

The lack of funds in the post–Cold War era makes it unlikely that airship programs will be pursued by either the Navy or Coast Guard in the foreseeable future. Nevertheless, several Navy studies have supported airship development, primarily in an AEW/missile targeting role.

See 15th Edition/pages 453–55 for characteristics.

UNMANNED AERIAL VEHICLES

The Department of Defense has a large, multifaceted program of Unmanned Aerial Vehicles (UAV), previously known as Remotely Piloted Vehicles (RPV). The UAV program enjoys relatively substantial funding, in part because of the highly successful U.S. Army, Navy, and Marine Corps use of the Pioneer UAV in the Gulf War in January–February 1991.

The Department of Defense has restructured the UAV effort to provide a four-tier program of vehicles that will encompass the broadest possible spectrum of roles and missions. Several aspects of the UAV program are being carried out in conjunction with Israeli firms and government agencies. The Joint Tactical Unmanned Aerial Vehicle (JT-UAV) program tiers are:

Tier	Type[31]	Altitude	Endurance	Payload
1		5,000–25,000 ft (1,524–7,620 m)	24–40 hours	141 lbs (64 kg)
2	MAE	25,000 ft (7,620 m)	24–40 hours	441 lbs (200 kg)
2+	HAE	25,000+ ft (7,620 + m)		
3−		45,000 ft (13,720 m)	8 hours	795 lbs (360 kg)

The Tier 1, a project directed by the Central Intelligence Agency, rapidly fielded the General Atomics Gnat 750 UAV with a relatively small payload for carrying out operations from Albania in early 1994; the CIA-sponsored UAV apparently resumed operations over Bosnia in the winter of 1994–1995, employing an RG-8 motorized glider as a manned aerial relay platform.

Several firms are still competing for the Tier 2 program.

The Tier 3 was a huge, expensive, and stealthy UAV that was canceled in the concept stage; some of the technology investment from the project was applied to the Tier 3− effort.

Another aspect of the U.S. UAV development program is the RAPTOR (Response Aircraft Program for Theater Operations). This is a High-Altitude, Long-Endurance (HALO) vehicle intended to destroy theater ballistic missiles by boost-phase interception. A demonstration has been planned for 1995–1996; the interceptor would be mounted on a Tier 2+ or a Tier 3− UAV.

31. HAE = High Altitude Endurance; MAE = Medium Altitude Endurance.

There are also short-range UAV programs: the battle-tested Pioneer and Hunter and the so-called Maneuver vehicle. The 1995 Department of Defense plan for the UAV order of battle in the year 2001 was:

20	Pioneers
216	Hunters
92	Maneuvers
10	MAE (Predators)
10	HAE

This changed in February 1996 with cancellation of the Hunter program (see below).

Additional force-level data are classified. These UAVs will be employed by the different services, as required. Details of the major vehicles are provided below (listed in alphabetical order).

The Navy's interest in UAVs includes support of special operations, surveillance, reconnaissance, mine detection, and ASW in shallow water. Most of these vehicles are low observable ("stealth") and have modular payloads, which allow the interchanging of sensors.

Historical: Previously, U.S. armed forces had made extensive use of target drones as well as reconnaissance drones, the latter usually of a highly classified (black) nature. These recce drones were used in large numbers by the Air Force in the Vietnam War.[32] Also in the 1960s, the Navy had a large drone program known as DASH (Drone Anti-Submarine Helicopter). Although those drones—designated DSN and, after 1962, QH-50—were successful aerial vehicles, problems with training and operating procedures resulted in a large number of losses. The DASH project was short-lived (and U.S. ASW ships were left without helicopters until the LAMPS program was initiated in the early 1970s.) However, the Japanese Maritime Self-Defense Force continued to employ DASH vehicles after they were discarded by the U.S. Navy, and several were employed for gunfire spotting for the battleship New Jersey (BB 62) during her brief service in the shore bombardment role off South Vietnam in 1968.[33]

During the 1970s and early 1980s the U.S. Navy resisted proposals for RPV/drones except for use as target vehicles. However, following the extensive use of RPVs by the Israelis in the 1982 invasion of Lebanon, especially against anti-air gun and missile systems in the Bekaa Valley, Secretary of the Navy John Lehman directed that the Navy look into the pilotless aircraft. As a result, in January 1984 the Navy ordered a Mastiff III drone system produced by Tadiran Israeli Electronics, Limited, for gunfire spotting. In June 1984 the Marine

32. From August 1964 through June 1975 the 100th Strategic Reconnaissance Wing flew 3,435 combat sorties with the Teledyne Ryan–produced AQM-34 "Buffalo Hunter" drone. Adapted from a target drone, the vehicle was employed in photographic and electronic reconnaissance.
33. Subsequently, the Navy tested a "Snoopy DASH" configuration, fitting the drone for reconnaissance with a TV camera and data link.

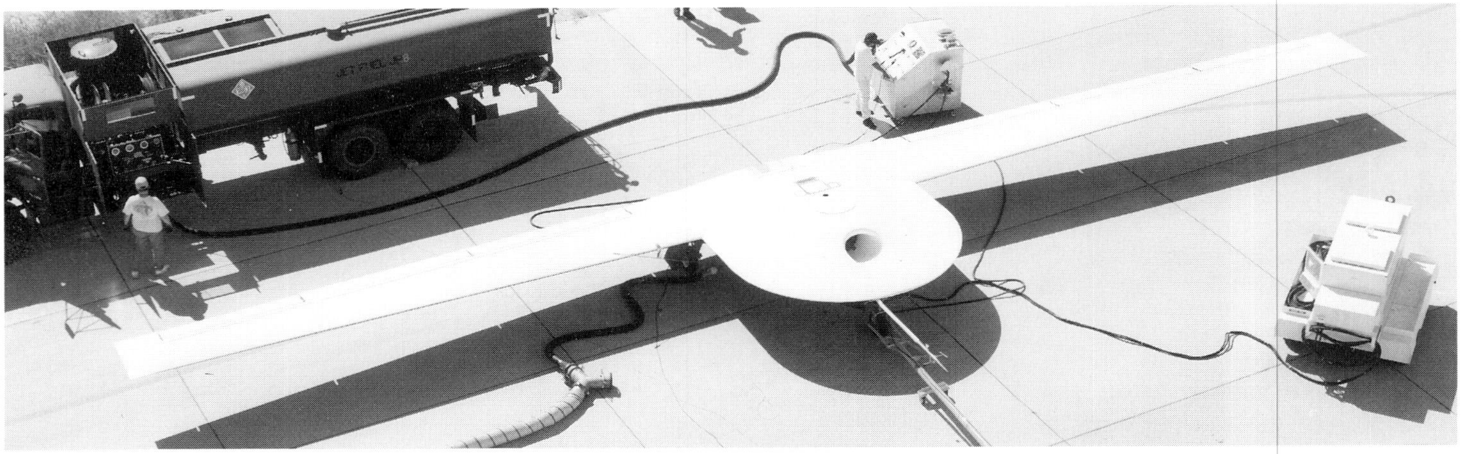

The prototype DarkStar UAV is prepared for flight. This is undoubtedly the most unusual configuration of the UAVs being developed for the U.S. military services. (Lockheed Martin, Denny Lombard)

Rollout of the high-flying, long-endurance DarkStar at the Lockheed Martin "Skunk Works" in June 1995. The wide-wing design is reminiscent of the Lockheed U-2 spyplane and the strategic reconnaissance variants of the English Electric-Martin B-57 Canberra. (Lockheed Martin, Eric Schulzinger)

Corps established the 1st RPV Platoon at Camp Lejeune, North Carolina, to evaluate and operate the Mastiff RPVs in support of Marine requirements. The first shipboard launching of an Israeli Mastiff (a development of the Scout) occurred in March 1984 from the helicopter carrier GUAM (LPH 9), with Israeli controllers. Marine Corps trials were carried out in February 1986 on the helicopter carrier TARAWA (LHA 1).

Subsequently, the Navy awarded a contract to provide the fleet with the Israeli-developed Pioneer RPV. This vehicle was extensively used from ashore and from the battleships MISSOURI (BB 63) and WISCONSIN (BB 64) in the Gulf War. The Marine Corps deployed all three of their RPV companies to Saudi Arabia for the Gulf War, with the Army deploying a UAV platoon to the theater. The Navy assigned detachments from squadron VC-6 to the two battleships to operate Pioneers from those ships during the conflict. About five vehicles and 40 personnel were assigned to each of these six units. According to the Department of Defense report to Congress on the Gulf conflict, "Pioneer proved to be valuable and appears to have validated the operational employment of UAVs in combat. . . ."[34]

Also during the gulf conflict, at the start of air operations, the U.S. Air Force launched 38 Northrop BQM-74C "Chukar" target drones into Iraq, and the Navy launched a number of TLAD target drones from aircraft. These were used to trick the Iraqis into turning on their radars so they could be attacked by U.S. radar suppression aircraft; Air Force F-4G Wild Weasels and Navy EA-6B Prowlers armed with HARM missiles. The BQM-74Cs were ground launched while A-6E Intruders air launched the TLADs.

On the ground, Marines flew a number of small, lightweight FQM-151 Pointer and Brandebury Exdrone vehicles during the Gulf War. (See 15th Edition/page 458 for characteristics.)

34. Department of Defense, *Conduct of the Persian Gulf Conflict* (July 1991), p. 6–8.

DARKSTAR UNMANNED AERIAL VEHICLE

The DarkStar is a Tier 3− vehicle developed under a highly classified program. It is one of two high-altitude UAVs being developed by the Department of Defense.

Estimated procurement cost in 1995 was $10 million per vehicle.

Design: Payload includes Synthetic Aperture Radar (SAR) or Electro-Optic (E-O) sensors; communications links are both line-of-sight and satellite relay. Mission duration is eight hours.

Status: Development; first flight on 29 March 1996. (During the 20-minute first flight, the UAV operated completely autonomously, with no updates to the on-board flight program.)

The prototype Dark Star crashed on take off on its second flight, 22 April 1996. The crash delayed the program by several months.

Manufacturer:	Lockheed Martin (Skunk Works) and Boeing	
Engines:	1 Williams International FJ44 turbofan; 1,900 lbst (862 kgst)	
Weights:	maximum	8,600 lbs (3,900 kg)
Dimensions:	length	15 ft (4.57 m)
	wing span	69 ft (21.04 m)
	height	5 ft (1.52 m)
Speed:	subsonic	
Ceiling:	45,000+ feet (13,720+ m)	
Range:	2,000+ n.miles (3,730+ km)	

ENCHANTMENT

U.S. Navy proposal for a non-stealthy, long-range, over-ocean UAV. It was to have a wingspan of approximately 200 feet (61m). The proposal was not pursued.

EAGLE EYE UNMANNED AERIAL VEHICLE

This is a tilt-rotor UAV—based in part on XV-15 technology—developed for shipboard use. It is particularly attractive to the Navy because of its VTOL capabilities.

Design: The Eagle Eye is a tilt-rotor vehicle with twin engines in nacelles that rotate to the vertical position for takeoff and landing and to the horizontal position for conventional flight. The UAV is based partially on the Bell-Boeing Pointer UAV, which flew for the first time in November 1988.

Up to 300 pounds (136 kg) of sensors can be carried.

Status: Development. First flight on 10 July 1993; first full conversion flight February 1994.

Manufacturer:	Bell Helicopter Textron	
Engines:	1 Allison 250-C20R recuperative turboshaft; approx. 450 shp	
Weights:	maximum T/O	2,260 lbs (1,025 kg)
Dimensions:	length	16 ft 5 in (4.99 m)
	wing span	13 ft 5 in (4.08 m)
	height with nacelles in vertical position	5 ft 2 in (1.58 m)
	rotor diameter	8 ft 2½ in (2.5 m)
Speed:	maximum	approx. 230 mph (370 km/h)
	cruise	approx. 115 mph (185 km/h)
Ceiling:	20,000+ ft (6,100+ m)	
Range:	8-hour endurance with 100 lbs (45.4 kg) of sensors	

The Eagle Eye—seen here in vertical flight with its twin rotors in the horizontal plane—reveals its V-22 Osprey/XV-15 design progenitors. The bicycle landing gear, with outriggers extending from the rear of the twin-engine nacelles, is fully retractable. (Bell Helicopter Textron)

The Eagle Eye in horizontal, high-speed flight. The twin rotors are rotating to the horizontal plane, which gives the UAV the appearance of a high-speed propeller aircraft. The landing gear is fully retracted. (Bell Helicopter Textron)

GLOBAL HAWK HIGH ALTITUDE ENDURANCE VEHICLE

The Teledyne Ryan Aeronautical entry for the Tier 2+/HAE vehicle was selected in 1995 for development following a Department of Defense competition.

The following are the tentative specifications developed by the Advanced Research Projects Agency (ARPA) and may not reflect the actual UAV characteristics.

Design: This is one of the largest and highest-flying UAVs yet conceived. It will have fully retractable landing gear.

Status: Development.

Manufacturer:	Teledyne Ryan	
Engines:	2 Williams FJ44-2E turbofans	
Weights:	empty	6,035 lbs (2,737 kg)
	gross	17,100 lbs (7,711 kg)
Dimensions:	length	44 ft 5 in (13.54 m)
	wing span	110 ft (33.54 m)
	wing area	526 ft² (48.92 m²)
	height	
Speed:	400 mph (643 km/h)	
Ceiling:	65,000 ft (19,817 m)	
Range:	radius	1,150 miles (1,850 km) with 36-hour loiter
		3,440 miles (5,535 km) with 24-hour loiter
		5,750 miles (9,255 km) with 10-hour loiter

HUNTER UNMANNED AERIAL VEHICLE

This was an enlarged version of the highly successful Pioneer. The Hunter experienced technical problems in development, however, and the project was canceled by the Department of Defense on 1 February 1996. Under Secretary of Defense for Acquisition and Technology Paul Kaminski has stated that the Hunter is too large, too expensive, and requires too much operational support. He told a Pentagon press conference, "This is a vehicle that doesn't have the flexibility [the Pentagon wants]."

The Hunter program, including development and production, was expected to have cost $4 *billion.* The Hunter's unit cost was approximately $2 million. (The Pentagon has spent nearly $667 million on the Hunter.)

Kaminski directed that the final two of seven Hunters the Pentagon must purchase under an existing contract be accepted; of the seven, five will be placed in storage and two will be used for training.

The Hunter will be replaced by the Predator UAV.

Design: The Hunter had an extremely simple design. The UAV was to carry a variety of sensors, including daylight television, FLIR, laser range finder-designator, ELINT, and optical systems.

Status: Canceled. Under development for the U.S. Army and Marine Corps. First flight took place in 1991.

A Hunter UAV makes a landing approach with its arresting hook extended; arresting cables are used ashore. The aircraft can land aboard a flight-deck ship without arresting wires. The drone has a fixed tricycle landing gear. (TRW)

Soldiers maneuver a Hunter UAV, a development of the Israeli-developed Pioneer that was used extensively in the 1991 war in the Persian Gulf. (TRW)

Manufacturer:	IAI and TRW	
Engines:	2 Teledyne Continental GR-18 rotary piston; 68 hp each	
Weights:	gross	1,250 lbs (567 kg)
	payload	250 lbs (113 kg)
Dimensions:	length	22 ft 10 in (6.95 m)
	wing span	29 ft (8.9 m)
	height	5 ft 5 in (1.65 m)
Speed:	maximum	126.5 mph (204 km/h)
	cruise	103.5 mph (167 km/h)
Ceiling:	19,000 ft (5,790 m)	
Range:	radius	93 miles (150 km)
	12-hour endurance	

PIONEER UNMANNED AERIAL VEHICLE

The Pioneer is a highly effective unmanned, tactical reconnaissance vehicle that was flown extensively in the Persian Gulf conflict. The Navy and Marine Corps expect to operate Pioneers until the year 2000.

Following a fly-off completion of aerial vehicles, the Navy awarded contracts in January 1986 to produce 21 Pioneer RPVs to the AAI Corporation of Cockeysville, Maryland, and Mazlat, Limited, the latter a joint venture of Israel Aircraft Industries (IAI) and Tadiran.

Originally flown from battleships and shore launchers, with the demise of the battleship the vehicles have been flown by Navy squadron VC-6 from a variety of amphibious ships. The Navy has also begun to investigate the feasibility of vertical launch of UAVs, and in 1995 the Navy experimented with a submarine controlling an airborne Predator UAV.

The Pioneer has been modified to target the SLAM missile; when this edition went to press the Navy was examining the possibility of targeting the Tomahawk TLAMs with the Pioneer.

Design: The Pioneer, modeled on the IAI Scout vehicle, carries its sensors and engines in a fuselage section fitted with twin tail booms. The vehicle is powered by a reciprocating engine with a small pusher propeller. The vehicle can be launched with rocket assistance and can be recovered on a runway or by a net. It has a fixed tricycle landing gear. The metal and fiberglass construction of the vehicle presents a low radar cross section. The Pioneer is transported in a disassembled condition and can be rapidly put together with minimum tools.

The Pioneer's payload is 100 pounds (45.4 kg). At the time of the Gulf War the Pioneer was fitted with a daylight television camera or, alternatively, a FLIR sensor. The existing control/data link is a C-band system that is resistant to jamming and has a range of 100 n.miles (185 km).

A Pioneer UAV is launched from a battleship during the Gulf War. Previously, the Israelis had made extensive use of small drone aircraft in Middle East combat. (U.S. Navy)

Operational: The first shipboard trials of the Pioneer were held on the battleship IOWA (BB 61) in the Chesapeake Bay in December 1986. During "proof-of-concept" tests in the Caribbean in January–February 1987, the IOWA's 16-inch (406-mm) guns fired on targets detected by the RPV. In that exercise four of the five embarked RPVs were lost in accidents.

During the Gulf conflict from 16 January to 27 February 1991 some 40 Pioneer UAVs flew 552 sorties for a total mission duration time of 1,641 hours. *At least one Pioneer UAV was airborne at all times during Operation Desert Storm.* The vehicles were employed for adjusting naval gunfire, battle damage assessment, reconnaissance, and force coordination. On 27 February, after a Pioneer detected two Israeli patrol boats off Faylaka Island and naval aircraft were called in to destroy the craft, a large number of Iraqi soldiers on the island surrendered to a UAV launched by the battleship MISSOURI (BB 63). Apparently, the soldiers knew that their detection by the drone would be followed by air or naval gunfire attack. It was history's first known surrender of enemy troops to an unmanned vehicle.

The following summary of Pioneer sorties was compiled by the Navy:

Unit	Sorties	Hours
VC-6 Det. 1 in USS WISCONSIN (BB 64)	100	342.9
VC-6 Det. 2 in USS MISSOURI	64	209.7
1st Marine RPV Company (commenced operations 26 Sep 1990)	94	330.3
2nd Marine RPV Company (operations 27 Nov 1990 through 1 Mar 1991)	69	226.6
3rd Marine RPV Company	147	380.6
U.S. Army UAV Platoon[35] (commenced operations 1 February 1991)	48	150.8

A total of 12 Pioneers were destroyed during the conflict:

airframe/engine failures	6
electromagnetic interference	3
operator error	2
enemy fire	1

Eight of the losses were from the ten Pioneers embarked in the two battleships.

In addition, 14 Pioneers were damaged during Desert Storm (all repairable):

operator error	6
engine/general failure	3
enemy gunfire	3
electromagnetic interference	2

The Department of Defense's final report on the Gulf War (April 1992) stated: "The Navy Pioneer UAV system's availability exceeded expectations. Established sortie rates indicated a deployed unit could sustain 60 flight hours a month."

In late 1992 the Navy operated Pioneers from the helicopter carrier NEW ORLEANS (LPH 11). During the launch and recovery operations, two arresting wires were set up on the flight deck (as well as the standard recovery net), and the drones snagged the arresting wires, as done ashore. All shipboard recoveries had previously been made into nets.

35. Assigned to the U.S. Army's 82nd Airborne Division.

During a six-month deployment to the Mediterranean–Adriatic Sea area in 1995–1996, Navy Fleet Composite Squadron (VC) 6, embarked in the amphibious ship SHREVEPORT (LPD 12), operated Pioneer UAVs in support of Marines ashore in Bosnia-Herzegovina.

Status: Operational. U.S. Navy IOC was in May 1986.

Manufacturer:	AAI and Mazlat	
Engines:	1 Sachs 2-stroke piston; 26 hp	
Weights:	maximum launch	430 lbs (195 kg)
	payload	100 lbs (45.4 kg)
Dimensions:	length	16 ft 3 in (4.96 m)
	wing span	16 ft 9½ in (5.12 m)
	height	3 ft 3 in (1.0 m)
Speed:	maximum	115 mph (185 km/h)
	cruise	55 to 81 mph (89 to 130 km/h)
Ceiling:	15,000 ft (4,573 m)	
Range:	8-hour endurance	

Marines in the Saudi Arabian desert prepare a Pioneer UAV for a reconnaissance flight. The Pioneer is a simple system to maintain and operate. (U.S. Marine Corps)

A Pioneer UAV is recovered into a shipboard net after a successful reconnaissance mission. (U.S. Navy)

PREDATOR MEDIUM ALTITUDE ENDURANCE VEHICLE

The Predator UAV is a versatile platform capable of performing a number of missions. It is the most sophisticated UAV currently flying for the United States.

Design: The vehicle carries a maximum payload of 400 pounds (181 kg); it is capable of day/night operations with a variety of sensors, including video and infrared (with ground link). The vehicle has retractable landing gear, being designed to take off and land on highways or other open areas.

Up to 450 pounds (204 kg) of sensors can be carried.

The use of the Predator over Bosnia has accelerated fitting the UAV with synthetic aperture radar because of flights being hampered by overcast and ground fog.

Operational: The Predator began intelligence collection missions in July 1995, flying from Albania to observe targets in Bosnia and Herzegovina. Four disassembled Predators were flown into Gjader Airfield near Tirana in C-130 Hercules. The UAVs were assembled and flown by civilian contract personnel.

One of the Predators was lost over Bosnia on 11 August 1995; a second was deliberately destroyed on 14 August after suffering an engine failure over Bosnia, which may have been caused by hostile ground fire.

A second Predator deployment to Bosnia began in March 1996. The three UAVs, operating from Sarmellek, Hungary, were fitted with Synthetic Aperture Radar (SAR), permitting more effective reconnaissance through clouds and fog.

In 1996 the Navy was to conduct tests with a submarine controlling an Predator UAV. The drone would be launched from land, fly out to an ocean operating area, and then be controlled by the submarine, running submerged with an antenna raised above the surface for the data link to the Predator. The data link could be direct or via satellite relay.

Status: Operational and in production. The Department of Defense awarded General Atomics Aeronautical a $31.7 million contract in January 1994 to build ten UAVs and three ground control stations; these were delivered by mid-1995.

Manufacturer:	General Atomics	
Engines:	Rotax 912 turbojet with fuel injection; 85 hp	
Weights:	empty	773 lbs (350.63 kg)
	normal T/O	1,873 lbs (849.6 kg)
Dimensions:	length	26 ft 8 in (8.14 m)
	wing span	48 ft 4 in (14.75 m)
	wing area	
	height	
Speed:	maximum	100 mph (161 km/h)
	cruise	65 mph (105 km/h)
Ceiling:	40,000 ft (12,195 m)	
Range:	575 miles (925 km) with 8-hour loiter maximum endurance 40+ hours	

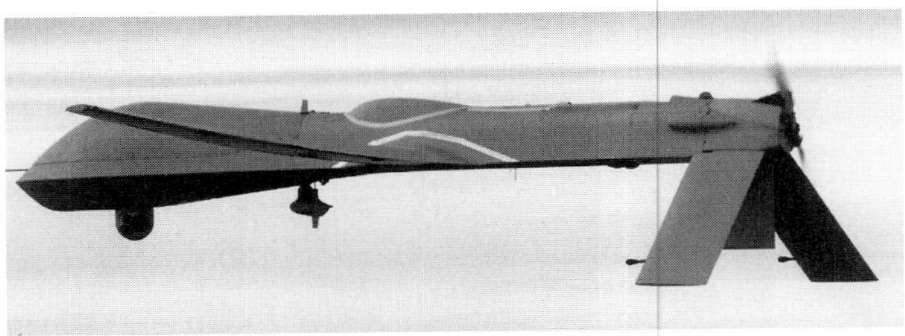

With its tricycle landing gear fully retracted, a Predator UAV takes part in a fleet evaluation in December 1995. Controllers were aboard ship as well as ashore. The pusher propeller is at the rear of the fuselage. (U.S. Navy, PH3 Jeffrey S. Viano)

A Predator UAV warms up on a runway at San Nicholas Island—off the coast of southern California—for a simulated aerial reconnaissance mission in conjunction with the CARL VINSON (CVN 70) carrier battle group. (U.S. Navy, PH3 Jeffrey S. Viano)

BQM-145 UNMANNED AERIAL VEHICLE

This will be a mid-range vehicle for carrying out electro-optical and infrared reconnaissance. The Teledyne Ryan Model 350 was selected for this role in May 1989.

The BQM-145 is fabricated of fiberglass and composites; however, in 1991 the UAV Executive Committee decided that the fuselage should be all metal. The wing has no movable control surfaces. The payload consists of FLIR, an IR line-scanning device, and meteorological sensors. In 1991 digital flight avionics were added, including a radar altimeter and Mk IV Identification Friend or Foe (IFF).

The vehicle can be air- or ground-launched; aircraft platforms include the F/A-18 Hornet and DC-130 Hercules. After a mission, the UAV returns to base and deploys a parachute. It can also be recovered in flight by a specially configured aircraft.

Status: Development. IOC is planned for the late 1990s. It is expected that the BQM-145 will be employed by the Army, Air Force, and Marine Corps, and possibly the Navy.

Manufacturer:	Teledyne Ryan	
Crew:	unmanned	
Engines:	1 Teledyne CAE382-10 turbofan; 970 lbst (440 kgst)	
Weights:	max launch 1,950 lbs (885 kg)	
Dimensions:	length	17 ft 11⅓ in (5.47 m)
	wing span	10 ft 6 in (3.20 m)
	wing area	25 ft^2 (2.32 m^2)
	height	2 ft 10 in (0.86 m)
Speed:	maximum	562 mph (904 km/h)
Ceiling:	13,720 ft (4,183 m)	
Range:	700 miles (1,125 km)	

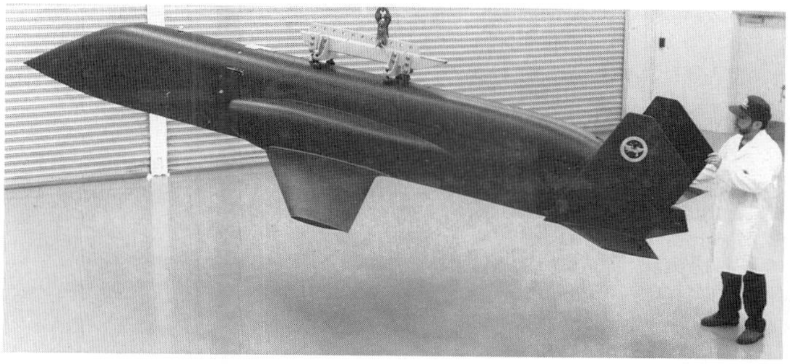

A YBQM-145A test vehicle is being prepared. The drone will be air-launched for high-altitude missions. (Teledyne Ryan)

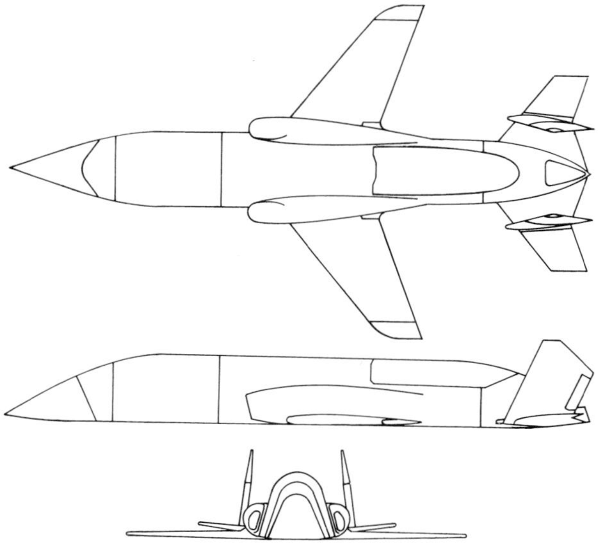

A BQM-145A reconnaissance drone. (William Clipson)

FQM-151 POINTER UNMANNED AERIAL VEHICLE

The Pointer is a small, very-low-cost, hand-launched UAV. Resembling a model aircraft, the Pointer is man-portable; the entire system can be carried in two backpacks—one for carrying the air vehicle (45 lbs/20.25 kg) and one containing the control unit (50 lbs/22.5 kg).

In 1988 the Marine Corps purchased one unit for tests. The Department of Defense joint program office procured 24 Pointers in December 1989. Several of these units were deployed to Saudi Arabia with the Marines in 1991. The Pointer's sensor payload is a black-and-white television camera that uses an 8-mm video cassette. The Pointer can be modified to carry a chemical agent detector.

The system can be fully prepared for flight in about five minutes. Flight endurance exceeds one hour. For recovery, the Pointer is directed into a deep stall. The crew on the ground consists of an operator and an observer.

Status: Operational.

Manufacturer:	AeroVironment (Simi Valley, Calif.)	
Crew:	unmanned	
Engines:	1 electric motor; 300 watts; 2-blade pusher propeller	
Weights:	9 lbs (4 kg)	
Dimensions:	length	6 ft (1.83 m)
	wing span	9 ft (2.74 m)
Speed:	maximum	approx. 45 mph (72 km/h)
	cruise	approx. 23 mph (37 km/h)
Ceiling:		
Range:		

A Marine hand-launches a Pointer, one of the smallest UAVs in existence. It is fitted with a black-and-white television camera. The mini-drone has a pusher propeller. (U.S. Marine Corps, courtesy *Marine Corps Gazette*)

An FQM-151 Pointer mini-drone is prepared for flight. (U.S. Marine Corps, courtesy *Marine Corps Gazette*)

CHAPTER 30

Weapon Systems

Ordnance waits on the deck of the aircraft carrier THEODORE ROOSEVELT (CVN 71), cruising in the Adriatic Sea, in anticipation of strikes during 1995 air operations over Bosnia. Three Navy fliers can be seen climbing to the flight deck. (John R. Anderson/Army Times Publishing)

BOMBS AND UNGUIDED MISSILES

U.S. Navy and Marine Corps aircraft carry Mk 80-series bombs and unguided Rockeye and APAM (Anti-Personnel/Anti-Material Munitions) rockets. Three Mk 80-series bombs are in use:

Mk 82	500 lbs (227 kg)
Mk 83	1,000 lbs (454 kg)
Mk 84	2,000 lbs (907 kg)

The Mk 80 weapons have both standard (fixed) tail assemblies and low-drag tails; the latter extend upon release to slow the bomb and enable a low-flying aircraft to escape the bombs' explosions. Laser-Guided Bomb (LGB) kits can be fitted to these bombs to enable the launching aircraft or other forces to guide a bomb to a target illuminated by a laser designator. Laser designation can be accomplished by the launching aircraft, an accompanying aircraft (including helicopter), surface ship, or troops on the ground. (The last can include SEAL-type special forces operating behind enemy lines, as was done in the 1991 war in the Persian Gulf.)

The Rockeye II Mk 20 is an unguided rocket that dispenses bomblets to attack "soft" targets such as anti-aircraft sites and lightly armored vehicles. Each rocket carries 247 bomblets with shaped-charge warheads; the bomblets each weigh 1.02 pounds (0.46 kg). The earlier Rockeye I was designated Mk 15.

The APAM is an improved rocket carrying a bomblet dispenser.

Navy and Marine aircraft employed the following weapons in the January–February 1991 air war in the Persian Gulf:

Mk 82 bombs	17,730
Mk 83 bombs	18,619
Mk 84 bombs	1,962
LGB	880
Rockeye/APAM	21,746

A large number of the Mk 82 and Mk 83 bombs were fitted with Destructor mine kits (Mk 36 and Mk 40, respectively) and dropped on Iraqi airfields. (This was in addition to mines planted in Iraqi rivers; see page 434.)

Nuclear bombs are no longer available to U.S. naval forces (see page 464).

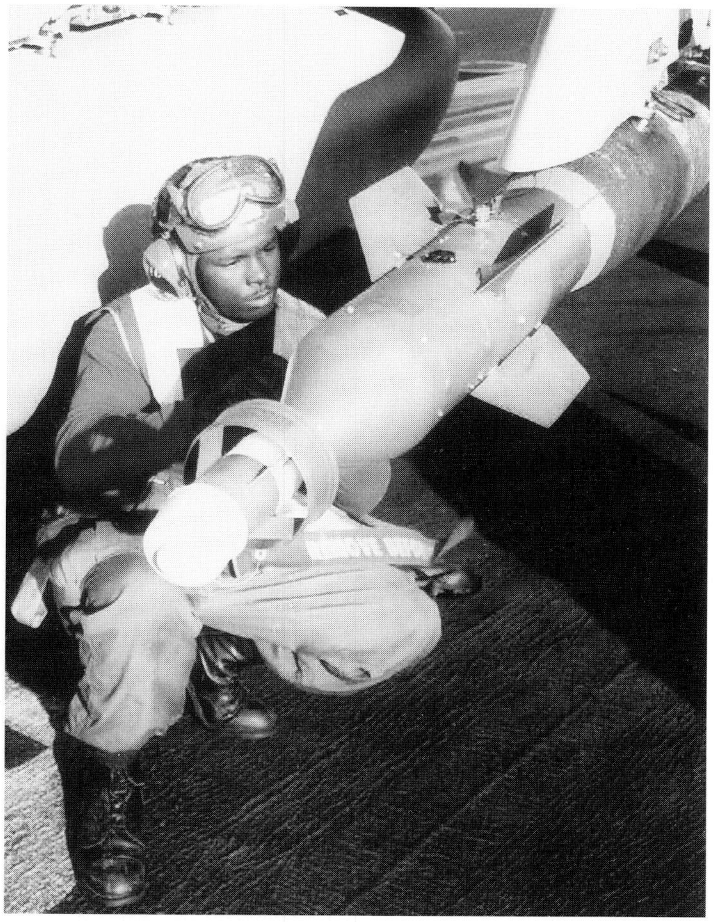

An aviation ordnanceman makes adjustments to a Mk 83 1,000-pound (454-kg) bomb fitted with laser guidance on the deck of the carrier America (CV 66). A short time after this photo was taken, the F/A-18 Hornet was launched for operations over Bosnia. Note the size of the guidance/fin package. (U.S. Navy, PH3 Brandon Teeples)

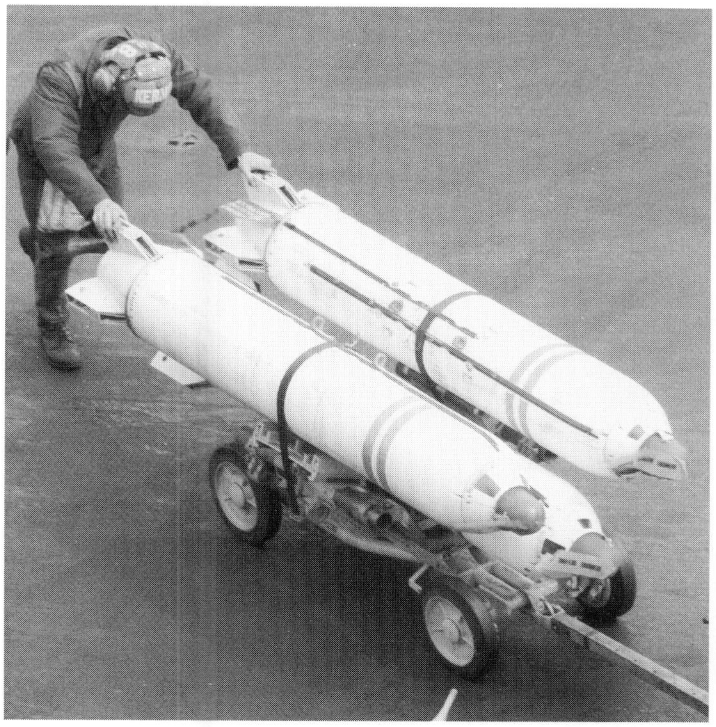

Three Mk 20 Rockeye II cluster bombs are moved across the flight deck of the carrier Saratoga (CV 60). Carrier air operations require a considerable amount of manual labor, often at night and in foul weather on a moving flight deck. (U.S. Navy, PH3 Mac M. Thurston)

An aviation ordnanceman pushes two Mk 82 low-drag bombs across the flight deck of the carrier Constellation (CV 64). The folding fins extend upon release to slow the bombs' descent, enabling the launch aircraft to escape the explosions. (U.S. Navy)

Sailors load Mk 82 500-pound (227-kg) bombs on an A-6E Intruder aboard the carrier INDEPENDENCE (CV 62) while steaming off the coast of Thailand in a 1995 exercise. The fuzing mechanism is being screwed into the upper bomb; note the nose cavity in the lower bomb. (U.S. Navy, PH1 David Tucker)

An F/A-18 Hornet from the naval air test complex at Patuxent River, Maryland, releases a salvo of Mk 83 1,000-pound (454-kg) bombs while in a 60° dive. The F/A-18 has proven to be a versatile attack as well as fighter aircraft. (Randy Hepp)

Laser-guided, low-drag bombs are prepared for loading on A-6E Intruders on the flight deck of the GEORGE WASHINGTON (CVN 73) during 1996 operations in the Adriatic Sea. This was one of the last deployments for the A-6E. (U.S. Navy, Airman Joe Hendricks)

NAVAL GUNS

The largest naval guns in U.S. warships are 5-inch (127-mm) weapons. The Navy's shipboard firepower had increased dramatically in the 1980s with the reactivation of the four battleships of the IOWA (BB 61) class. Those ships each carry nine 16-inch (406-mm)/50-cal guns and, as modernized in the 1980s, 12 5-inch/38-cal guns. With the mothballing of the MISSOURI (BB 63) in early 1992, however, all four of these behemoths were again laid up in reserve (and subsequently stricken). The largest guns remaining in active U.S. Navy service are thus 5-inch weapons.

The Marine Corps' requirement for naval gunfire support has led to a renewed interest in deployment of the 8-inch (203-mm) Major Caliber Lightweight Gun (MCLWG), which is suitable for installation in ships of cruiser and destroyer size, as well as several other naval gunfire support systems. Austere budgets and possible adaption of other gun and rocket systems (some already in Army or Marine use) make the deployment of the 8-inch MCLWG doubtful.

The principal rocket candidate during the 1980s was the ABRS (Assault Ballistic Rocket System), an unguided rocket and launcher adopted from the LTV Corporation's Multiple Launch Rocket System (MLRS) used by the U.S. Army, Marine Corps, and several NATO countries. The ABRS had been proposed for installation on the IOWA-class battleships and NEWPORT (LST 1179)-class landing ships, with one concept providing for full conversion of LSTs to "rocket monitors." See 14th Edition/page 466 for ABRS/MLRS characteristics.)

Currently proposed for the fire support role is the Army's ATACMS (Army Tactical Missile System). Previously proposed have been ten existing and candidate guns of 5-inch, 8-inch, and 155-mm, employing a variety of propellants (e.g., Rocket-Assisted Projectiles [RAP]).

A 1993 review by the Center for Naval Analyses identified eight gun systems that—combined with missiles—were capable of attacking at least 95 percent of targets in postulated major regional conflicts.[1] Five of these systems were 155-mm gun variants and three were 8-inch gun variants with differing propellants, projectiles, and calibers. The analysis concluded that a 155-mm/60-cal gun system with an advanced propellant and precision guided munitions, in combination with the Tomahawk TLAM missile, was the most cost effective option for naval gunfire support.

Beyond the retiring of the battleships there has been a steady decline of naval guns as older cruisers and destroyers have been decommissioned. Newer ships generally have fewer guns of smaller caliber. All cruisers armed with 8-inch and 6-inch (152-mm) guns have been retired, as have all pre-SPRUANCE (DD 963)-class destroyers, which carried up to six 5-inch guns. The last active U.S. ship with 8-inch/55-cal guns was the NEWPORT NEWS (CA 148), decommissioned in 1978, and the last active ship with 6-inch/47-cal guns was the cruiser-flagship OKLAHOMA CITY (CG 5), retired in 1979. All mothballed cruisers with these guns have been stricken.

(The only warships in service today in foreign navies with guns larger than 5-inch are in the Russian Navy: the later KIROV-class battle cruisers, SLAVA-class missile cruisers, and SOVREMENNYY-class destroyers mount 130-mm/70-cal dual-purpose guns. All cruisers of the SVERDLOV class mounting from 6 to 12 152-mm guns have been discarded.)

The largest guns now fitted in active U.S. Navy ships are the 5-inch Mk 45 lightweight guns in cruisers and destroyers. All frigates armed with 5-inch guns have been retired, and the Coast Guard cutters armed with 5-inch guns have either been retired or rearmed. The 5-inch guns are considered primarily shore-bombardment weapons and have only a limited anti-air capability. The 76-mm guns in Navy frigates and the larger Coast Guard cutters are primarily anti-aircraft weapons, but they do have an anti-surface capability. Most Navy surface warships and several auxiliary classes are armed with the Mk 15 20-mm Close-In Weapon System (CIWS) for close-in defense against anti-ship missiles. In addition, various types of 25-mm, 20-mm, .50-cal, and 7.62-mm machine guns are fitted in naval ships, primarily for defense against small craft in restricted waters.

Ammunition: In the following lists AP = Armor Piercing and HC = High Capacity (for shore bombardment).

Classifications: Guns are classified by their inside barrel diameter and gun-barrel length. Diameters traditionally have been listed in inches for weapons larger than one-inch diameter and in millimeters for smaller weapons. Thus, a 5-inch/38-cal gun has a barrel length of 190 inches (bore [5] × caliber [38] = barrel length [190]). The Italian-developed OTO Melara 76-mm gun retains its metric measurement in U.S. naval service.

Guns smaller than one-inch diameter are measured in millimeters or calibers, the latter being fractions of an inch (e.g., .50 cal = ½ inch).

Nomenclature: A mount is an assembled unit that includes the gun barrel(s), housing(s), slide(s), carriage, stand, sights, elevating and training drives, ammunition hoists, and associated equipment. Mounts include guns from 20-mm caliber up to, but not including, 6-inch guns. A mount differs from a turret in that a mount does not have a barrette structure within the hull.

The unmanned, unarmored mounting for the 8-inch Mk 71 MCLWG is considered a mount rather than a turret.

Saluting guns: U.S. aircraft carriers, cruisers, missile destroyers, amphibious ships, and auxiliaries have 40-mm Mk 11 saluting guns. This weapon is for saluting only and has no combat capability.

The following entries are arranged by gun size (i.e., bore diameter).

16-INCH/50-CAL (406-MM) GUN

These guns, which were the main gun battery of the IOWA-class battleships, were the largest guns ever mounted in warships except for the 18.1-inch (460-mm) guns of the Japanese YAMATO-class battleships of World War II and the single 18-inch (457-mm) gun of the British carrier FURIOUS of World War I.

The U.S. 16-inch/50s were also intended for the five never-built battleships of the MONTANA (BB 67) class.

See 15th Edition/pages 462–63 for characteristics.

8-INCH/55-CAL (203-MM) MAJOR CALIBER LIGHTWEIGHT GUN MK 71

Single mount. The Mk 71 Major Caliber Lightweight Gun (MCLWG) is a comparatively small and lightweight mount intended for installation in destroyer-size ships. The Navy's plan to install the 8-inch/55-cal Mk 71 MCLWG in the 31 SPRUANCE-class destroyers, as well as possibly some later ship classes, died when Secretary of Defense Harold Brown canceled the gun project in July 1978. A prototype gun had been successfully evaluated in the SHERMAN (DD 933)-class destroyer HULL (DD 945) from 1975 to 1979. It is listed here because of historical interest and recent proposals that it be considered for deployment to provide a gunfire support capability.

The Mk 71 could automatically fire 75 rounds from the ready service loader. The gun was specifically designed to fire laser-guided projectiles and rocket-assisted projectiles as well as conventional rounds.

Status: Development; no procurement or deployment plans.

Gun barrel:	Mk 39 Mod 2
Muzzle velocity:	2,800 ft/sec
Crew:	6
Weight:	172,895 lbs (78,425 kg)
Rate of fire:	12 rounds/minute (guided projectiles 6 rounds/minute)
Maximum range:	31,408 yds (28,727 m) at 45° elevation
Projectile weight:	260 lbs (118 kg)
Fire control:	Mk 86 GFCS
Ships:	(program canceled)

1. This was the Cost and Operational Effectiveness Analysis (COEA).

The 8-inch/55-cal MCLWG on the destroyer HULL (DD 945) during the gun's at-sea evaluation. The SPRUANCE (DD 963)-class destroyers—for which the guns were planned—are considerably larger than the HULL. (U.S. Navy)

The 8-inch/55-cal MCLWG on the HULL during firing trials. The gun is now at Dahlgren, Virginia. (Giorgio Arra)

5-INCH/54-CAL (127-MM) GUN MK 45

Single mount. The Mk 45 is capable of engaging air or surface targets. The gun mount is unmanned; the gun crew is stationed below deck. The mount stows up to 20 rounds of ready service ammunition that can be fired quickly by a single individual at the below-deck control console. The magazine can be reloaded while the gun is firing without interrupting the firing sequence. The maximum rate of fire is 16 to 20 rounds per minute with fixed ammunition. Firing Rocket Assisted Projectiles (RAP) and other separated, multi-part ammunition reduces the gun's firing rate.

The gun is now being installed in new-construction ARLEIGH BURKE (DDG 51) surface combatants. Note that while the TARAWA (LHD 1)-class large amphibious ships mount this weapon, the successor WASP (LHA 1) class mounts only the 20-mm CIWS and lighter weapons.

The Navy awarded a contract for $49,600,000 in 1996 to United Defense/Armament Systems to modify Mk 45 guns for extended range and enhanced performance. The modified guns will be capable of firing extended-range guided munitions out to 63 n.miles (117 km). United Defense will build one partially updated gun for delivery in mid-1997 and two full-up prototypes in 1998. The latter will be for both land firing (at Dahlgren, Virginia) and for installation aboard ships.

The Navy plans to introduce the updated Mk 45 to the Fleet aboard ARLEIGH BURKE and Improved ARLEIGH BURKE destroyers in the year 2000. A buy of 18 to 28 guns is envisioned, plus a possible upgrade to existing guns for the Naval Surface Fire Support (NSFS) mission.

Status: Operational; in production.

Gun barrel:	
Muzzle velocity:	2,500 ft/sec
Crew:	6
Weight:	47,820 lbs (21,691 kg)
Rate of fire:	16 to 20 rounds/minute
Maximum range:	25,909 yds (23,697 m) at 47° elevation 48,700 ft (14,848 m) at 85° elevation
Projectile weight:	70 lbs (31.75 kg)
Fire control:	Mk 86 GFCS
Ships:	CGN 38 CGN 36 CG 47 DDG 993 DD 963 LHA 1

The forward 5-inch/54-cal DP gun in the destroyer DAVID R. RAY (DD 971). All 5-inch guns in the U.S. Fleet are now Mk 45 weapons. (W. Donko)

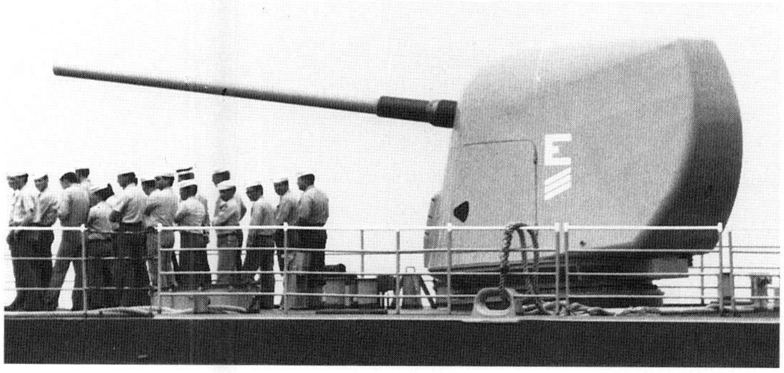

The forward 5-inch/54-cal DP gun in the destroyer CALLAGHAN (DDG 994). The mount—all of its crewmen serve below decks—has won "E" awards for battle efficiency. (W. Donko)

76-MM/62-CAL GUN MK 75

Single mount. The OLIVER HAZARD PERRY (FFG 7)-class frigates, as well as Coast Guard cutters, are fitted with the 76-mm/62-cal Mk 75 gun mount. The gun system was designed by OTO Melara SpA of Italy and is generally identified by the firm's name.

The 76-mm gun is specifically designed for use in ships as small as 200 tons and is capable of engaging air or surface targets. (They were previously fitted in the U.S. PEGASUS/PHM 1 hydrofoil missile combatants.) The gun is remotely controlled with a small, unmanned mount.

The Mk 75 gun is also used by several foreign navies.

Status: Operational; no longer in production for U.S. ships.

Gun barrel:	Mk 75
Muzzle velocity:	3,000 ft/sec
Crew:	4
Weight:	13,680 lbs (6,205 kg)
Rate of fire:	75 to 85 rounds/minute
Maximum range:	approx. 21,000 yds (19,207 m) at 45° elevation
	approx. 39,000 ft (11,890 m) at 85° elevation
Projectile weight:	14 lbs (6.35 kg)
Fire control:	Mk 92 GFCS
Ships:	FFG 7
	WHEC 715
	WMEC 901

The 76-mm/62-cal OTO Melara gun is now found only in the Navy's frigates of the OLIVER HAZARD PERRY (FFG 7) class; they are also carried in the two larger classes of Coast Guard cutters. This mount is in the now-discarded AQUILA (PHM 4). (Giorgio Arra)

3-INCH/50-CAL (76-MM) GUN MK 33

Twin mount. The large number of 3-inch/50-cal anti-aircraft guns fitted from the early 1950s onward in large numbers of surface combatants, amphibious ships, and fleet auxiliaries have been entirely removed, except for several amphibious ships that are in reserve.

The guns were generally ineffective and difficult to maintain. Amphibious ships and auxiliaries have been refitted with the Phalanx CIWS and/or Sea Sparrow point-defense missiles in place of some 3-inch mounts.

These are open or shielded (unarmored) mounts. They have two open, drum-type magazines for each barrel, which are hand loaded.

Status: Operational; no longer in production.

Gun barrel:	Mk 22
Muzzle velocity:	2,650 ft/sec
Crew:	12
Weight:	approx. 33,000 lbs (14,969 kg)
Rate of fire:	50 rounds/minute per barrel
Maximum range:	14,041 yds (12,842 m) at 45° elevation
	29,367 ft (8,953 m) at 85° elevation
Projectile weight:	7 lbs (3.2 kg)
Fire control:	local control only
Ships:	LKA 113
	LST 1179

The only U.S. Navy ships that retain 3-inch/50-cal guns are inactive amphibious ships. This 3-inch mount—aboard the command ship MOUNT WHITNEY (LCC 20)—has a blast shield. The guns are hand-loaded and have very limited effectiveness against air targets. (U.S. Navy)

81-MM MORTAR MK 2

This weapon is generally mounted in tandem with a .50-cal machine gun in some Navy patrol craft and Coast Guard cutters.

Status: Operational; no longer in production.

Gun barrel:	
Muzzle velocity:	
Crew:	2
Weight:	580 lbs (263 kg)
Rate of fire:	10 rounds/minute in trigger mode
	18 rounds/minute in drop-fire mode
Maximum range:	2,200 yds (2,012 m)
Projectile weight:	10.85 lbs (4.9 kg)
Ships:	PB
	WPB

A sailor drop-loads an 81-mm mortar of an over/under mounting of a .50-cal machine gun and a mortar. (U.S. Navy)

60-MM ELECTROTHERMAL TECHNOLOGY DEMONSTRATOR

This is a technology demonstration model of a 60-mm Electrothermal (ET) gun intended for shipboard use in the CIWS role. After initial ET testing, the gun was delivered to the Naval Surface Warfare Center at Dahlgren, Virginia, for additional test firings and tests with advanced projectile propellants and "smart munitions."

The ET gun and automatic loader are mounted on a Mk 15 CIWS trunnion assembly. The barrel length is 16 feet 11 inches (5.16 m). The propelling charge for the gun has an electrical energy output of 1.0 to 2.0 megajoules; the projectile acceleration rate is 30,000 to 45,000 g's.

In operational use the gun would fire in bursts of ten rounds, using command-guided projectiles or conventional ammunition.

The gun is produced by United Defense (formerly FMC).

Gun barrel:	
Muzzle velocity:	4,265 ft/sec
Crew:	
Weight:	
Rate of fire:	200 rounds/minute
Maximum range:	
Projectile weight:	6 lbs (2.7 kg)
Fire control:	

Preview of the next Navy gun system? A test firing of the technology demonstration model of a 60-mm Electrothermal (ET) gun at Elk River, Minnesota. Note the muzzle blast. (United Defense/FMC)

The breech of the 60-mm ET gun technology demonstrator. The rotary magazine is visible in this view. (United Defense/FMC)

40-mm grenade launcher Mk 19 on a tripod mount. (U.S. Marine Corps)

40-MM GRENADE LAUNCHER MK 19

Numerous Navy auxiliaries and small combatants and Coast Guard cutters have the 40-mm Mk 19 grenade launcher. It is usually fitted to the Mk 64 machine-gun mount. The Mk 19 barrel is 43 inches (1.1 m) long.

The launcher is manually fired and shoots high-velocity 40-mm grenades from linked belts. The rounds are configured in an armor-piercing shape, having been initially designed to counter lightly armored vehicles. (The Mk 19 can also be mounted on land vehicles and helicopters.)

Effective range is generally cited as 1,650 yards (1,509 m).

Status: Operational; in production.

Gun barrel:	
Muzzle velocity:	800 ft/sec
Crew:	1
Weight:	72.5 lbs (33 kg)
Rate of fire:	325 to 375 rounds/minute
Maximum range:	2,400 yds (2,195 m)
Projectile weight:	0.75 lb (0.34 kg)
Fire control:	open sight
Ships:	various

Cleaning the barrel of a Mk 19 Mod 3 40-mm grenade launcher aboard a PB Mk III patrol craft. The craft was in the Persian Gulf at the time, high and dry aboard a support barge. (U.S. Navy)

25-MM/87-CAL GUN MK 38

This is a rapid-fire cannon known as the "Bushmaster" or "Chain gun." It is provided for close-in defense in a number of Navy ships and small craft. In the larger Navy surface combatants (up to battleships) and amphibious ships, the guns are installed on a temporary basis as the ships deploy to areas where they are subject to enemy small craft attack (e.g., Persian Gulf).

The gun has an M242 single barrel fitted on the Mk 88 mount. It can be selected to fire at different rates. The Mk 88 mount is not stabilized and the gun is manually aimed. The weapon is also fitted in the Army's Bradley Armored Fighting Vehicle (AFV) and the Marine Corps' Light Armored Vehicle (LAV).

Status: Operational; in production by McDonnell Douglas Helicopter Company (formerly Hughes Helicopter Corporation).

Gun barrel:	M242
Muzzle velocity:	3,600 ft/sec
Crew:	2
Weight:	1,250 lbs (567 kg)
Rate of fire:	variable; single shot or 100 or 200 rounds/minute
Maximum range:	2,500 yds (2,287 m) effective range
Projectile weight:	1.1 lb (0.5 kg)
Fire control:	optical
Ships:	various

A 25-mm/87-cal Bushmaster on the landing ship MOUNT VERNON (LSD 39) in the Persian Gulf. The mount is stabilized but visually aimed, making its use on small craft in rough seas extremely difficult. Here an SH-3 Sea King flies over the smooth waters of the gulf. (U.S. Navy)

20-MM GUN MK 68

The similar, single-barrel 20-mm Mk 67 and Mk 68 cannon are fitted on auxiliary and amphibious ships and Coast Guard cutters and patrol boats for close-in defense against surface craft. These are refinements of the Oerlikon design.

Status: Operational; in production.

Gun barrel:	Mk 16 Mod 5
Muzzle velocity:	2,740 ft/sec
Crew:	2
Weight:	900 lbs (408 kg)
Rate of fire:	800 rounds/minute
Maximum range:	4,800 yds (4,390 m)
Projectile weight:	0.75 lbs (0.3 kg)
Fire control:	open sight
Ships:	various

20-MM GUN MK 67

The Mk 67 is similar to the Mk 68 but has a lightweight mounting. Earlier 20-mm guns fitted in U.S. Navy ships included the Mk 10 and Mk 24; all have been withdrawn from U.S. service.

Gun barrel:	Mk 16 Mod 5
Muzzle velocity:	2,740 ft/sec
Crew:	2
Weight:	475 lbs (215 kg)
Rate of fire:	800 rounds/minute
Maximum range:	4,800 yds (4,390 m)
Projectile weight:	0.75 lbs (0.3 kg)
Fire control:	open sight
Ships:	various

A sailor stands watch at a 20-mm gun on the fantail of a PB Mk III in the Persian Gulf. (U.S. Navy)

20-MM/76-CAL CLOSE-IN WEAPON SYSTEM MK 16

The Phalanx Close-In Weapon System (CIWS) is intended to defeat attacking anti-ship missiles. The installation of the Phalanx CIWS followed by several years the appearance of similar rapid-fire gun systems, of larger caliber, in Soviet surface warships.

The Phalanx underwent initial at-sea tests in the destroyer KING (DDG 41, then-DLG 10) from August 1973 to March 1974; operational suitability tests were conducted in the destroyer BIGELOW (DD 942) from November 1976 to 1978. Production was initiated in December 1977.

The Phalanx CIWS is a totally integrated weapon system that includes the VPS-2 search-and-track radar, gun, magazine, weapon control unit, and associated electronics, all fitted into a single unit 15 feet (4.6 m) high and weighing about six tons. Thus, it is suitable for small combat craft (and is fitted in Saudi Arabian and Israeli missile craft) as well as larger warships. It can also be rapidly installed—in 24 hours in an emergency situation. The U.S. Navy plans to fit the Phalanx in some 300 ships, from single guns in frigates to four mounts in IOWA-class battleships and certain aircraft carriers. (Some Phalanx-armed ships have been mothballed.)

The CIWS is designated both Mk 15 and Mk 16 by the U.S. Navy, with the 20-mm gun subsystem designated Mk 26. The gun is a six-barrel Gatling gun adopted from the Air Force M61 Vulcan gun series used in several types of aircraft and ground mounted for airfield defense.

The gun is hydraulically powered, having a theoretical firing rate of 3,000 rounds per minute, a very low dispersion rate, and initially a 980-round magazine; later guns have a 1,550-round magazine. The earlier weapons are being upgraded. The gun fires a depleted-uranium bullet or penetrator manufactured from the waste products of nuclear energy programs; the depleted-uranium penetrator is 2.5 times heavier than steel. This penetrator has been phased out in favor of a tungsten penetrator, which is slightly heavier. The penetrator, whose diameter is only 12.75 millimeters, is fired in a nylon sabot via an aluminum pusher that imparts spin to the projectile. The sabot and pusher break away after the round leaves the muzzle.

The built-in J-band, pulse-doppler radar combines several functions and follows the bullets in flight to make corrections for the next burst being fired. Early Navy analyses indicated that about 200 rounds would be fired per gun in each engagement against a missile.

All engagement functions are performed automatically with a high-speed digital computer. When active, the CIWS will engage any incoming, high-speed target unless the operator holds fire. Reaction time for the CIWS is less than two seconds from when the threat is first detected and identified.

Designation: The Phalanx CIWS is designated Mk 15 and consists of one to four CIWS Weapon Groups Mk 16. The latter is the designation of the above-deck portion of the system, consisting of the actual gun, magazine, radar, and weapons control unit. The below-deck components of the Mk 15 are control panels.

Status: Operational; in production. IOC was in 1980 on the CORAL SEA (CV 43).

In 1981 the Japanese destroyer KURAMA became the first foreign ship to mount the Phalanx; it is also used by Australia, Canada, Great Britain, Greece, Israel, Portugal, Saudi Arabia, and Taiwan.

Manufactured by General Dynamics/Pomona and General Electric Corporation.

Gun barrel:	Mk 26
Muzzle velocity:	3,650 ft/sec
Crew:	(unmanned)
Weight:	approx. 12,000 lbs (5,443 kg)
Rate of fire:	3,000 rounds/minute
Maximum range:	1,625 yds (1,486 m)
Projectile weight:	0.22 lbs (0.1 kg)
Fire control:	self-contained Ku-band search radar; digital Moving Target Indicator (MTI)
Ships:	various

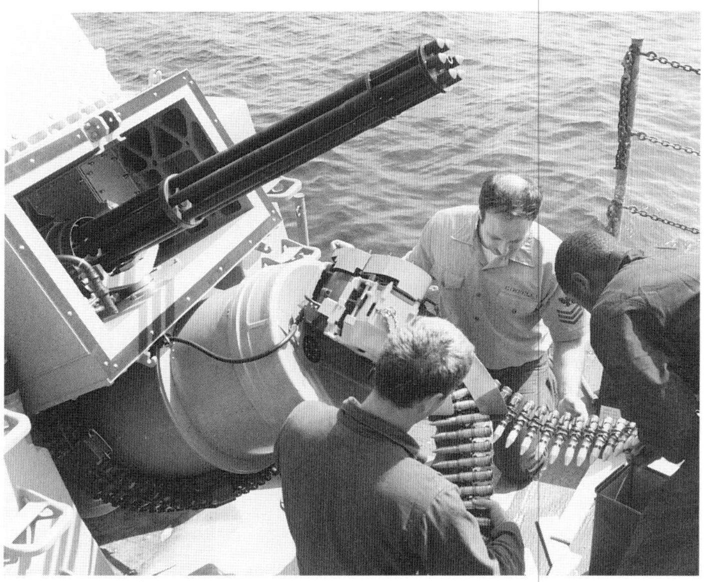

Sailors load a Phalanx CIWS on a U.S. warship. (General Dynamics/Pomona)

A Phalanx CIWS on an Australian destroyer spews forth bullets during a test firing in the Persian Gulf. There is an enlarged magazine under the gun barrels. (Royal Australian Navy)

At rest, a Phalanx CIWS is installed in a U.S. warship. Each above-deck weapon group is designated Mk 16; the entire Phalanx installation in a ship (one to four guns) is designated Mk 15. (General Dynamics/Pomona)

NAVAL MINES

The U.S. Navy has a significant inventory of mines.[2] Except for the CAPTOR (Encapsulated Torpedo) anti-submarine mine, however, these weapons are rapidly reaching obsolescence and have limited effectiveness against modern, quiet submarines.

Most of the Navy's mines are based largely on technology of the 1950s and 1960s. There are three types of mines in U.S. Navy use besides the CAPTOR: the Mk 67 Submarine-Launched Mobile Mine (SLMM), adapted from the Mk 37 torpedo; and the Quickstrike and Destructor series of aircraft bombs modified for use as medium- and shallow-water mines. (The CAPTOR is the Navy's only deep-water mine, i.e., suitable for use down to depths of some 3,000 feet/915 m).

The SLMM is launched from a submarine torpedo tube at "stand-off" ranges and travels underwater like a torpedo. After reaching the end of its run, the SLMM dives to the bottom, the engine shuts down, and the mine is armed. It is a shallow-water bottom mine, activated by magnetic, seismic, and/or pressure influences.

The Quickstrike and Destructor mines were revolutionary in that they permit the rapid adaptation of standard aircraft bombs to use as mines. Further, standard bomb-handling facilities on aircraft carriers can ready the mines, and standard carrier-based and maritime patrol aircraft can carry them.

No mines are currently being procured, the last procurement having been CAPTOR mines in fiscal 1986. Neither are any mines currently under development nor are any advanced mines planned for procurement. Of the funding appropriated for mine warfare in the early 1990s, for example, less than 10 percent went to offensive mine warfare and less than 2 percent was invested in mine research and development. The remainder went mainly to mine countermeasures activities.

The Quickstrike mine series, with the exception of the Mk 65, are Mk 80-series streamlined aircraft bombs with kit conversions that enable them to be used as shallow-water bottom mines. These mines can be activated by one or more influence firing mechanisms and are fitted with Target Detection Devices (TDDs) that are inserted prior to laying the mines. These weapons are effective against surface ships as well as submarines. Further, the Mk 57 TDD enables these mines to be dropped on land targets. (The Mk 58 and Mk 71 TDDs are also in use; see individual mine entries.)

The Mk 65 was the only weapon of the Quickstrike series designed specifically for use as a mine.

The Destructor (DST) mine series was developed during the Vietnam War in response to the need for large numbers of mines. These mines also employ the standard Mk 80-series aircraft bombs that, with the insertion of the Mk 42 firing mechanism and Mk 32 safing/arming device, could be employed as mines. The Destructor mines are obsolete and are being succeeded by the Quickstrike weapons.

Aircraft. The principal U.S. means of minelaying is by aircraft. The Navy's carrier-based A-6E Intruder (being phased out in 1996) and S-3B Viking aircraft, in addition to the land-based P-3 Orion patrol/ASW aircraft, are configured for minelaying. The F/A-18 Hornet can also carry mines, but the availability of that aircraft for an offensive mine mission is questionable, and its mine payload is less than half that of the A-6E.

The U.S. Air Force will operate just over 200 "strategic" bombers in the year 2000, in both active and reserve units.

21 B-2A Spirit (stealth) bombers
97 B-1B Lancer bombers
95 B-52H Stratofortress bombers

Of these, the B-1B can carry the Mk 62 and DST Mk 36 mines; the B-52H can carry all air-launched mines (i.e., all mines now in Navy service except the SLMM).

2. The author is in debt to Dr. Scott C. Truver, coauthor with Gregory Hartmann of *Weapons That Wait: Mine Warfare in the U.S. Navy* (Annapolis, Md.: Naval Institute Press, 1991), and to Stephen H. Keller for their assistance in writing this section. Dr. Truver and Mr. Keller are participants in the development of the Navy's official Mine Warfare Plan.

AIRCRAFT MINE CAPACITIES*

Aircraft		Mk 65	Mk 60	Mk 56	DST 41	Mk 63 DST 40	Mk 62 DST 36
A-6E	Intruder	5	5	5	5	5	5
B-1B	Lancer	—	26	—	—	—	84**
B-52H	Stratofortress	#	#	4/#	8/#	18/#	18/#
F/A-18	Hornet	4	—	4	—		
P-3C	Orion	3/6	3/6	3/6	—	3/8	6/8
S-3B	Viking	2/0	2/0	2/0	—	2/2	6/4

*6/8 indicates internal/external carriage.
**DST 36 AIR configuration.
#The number is classified.

See the accompanying table for a breakdown of the mine capabilities of combat aircraft. The F/A-18 Hornet and A-6E Intruder carry mines externally; the P-3C Orion and S-3B Viking carry mines in their weapons bay and on wing pylons. The B-1B and B-52H carry mines internally; the B-52H also has wing pylons for bombs/mines.

The Department of Defense has also examined the feasibility of employing C-130, C-141, and C-5 cargo aircraft in the minelaying role under a program called CAML (Cargo Aircraft Minelaying). A C-130 Hercules with the CAML rig fitted could carry 16 2,000-pound (907-kg) mines.

Submarines. U.S. submarines of the STURGEON (SSN 637) and improved LOS ANGELES (SSN 751) classes are configured to launch the SLMM and CAPTOR mines. However, mines can be carried by submarines only at the expense of torpedoes or Harpoon or Tomahawk weapons. Submarines at sea at the time a mining decision is made would have to return to port, unload some or all of their other weapons, load mines, and then undertake the mining mission. Depending upon how many mines were carried, they could be required to return to port and rearm before undertaking anti-submarine or anti-shipping operations. Alternatively, during a period of crisis some submarines could be pre-loaded with mines, again at the expense of other weapons.

Surface ships. No U.S. surface ships are employed to lay mines except in exercises for minesweepers or swimmers. Only the CAPTOR mine can be laid from surface ships.

In the following listings, shallow mines are laid to a maximum depth of approximately 600 feet (182 m), medium-depth mines down to about 1,000 feet (305 m), and deep-water mines down to about 3,000 feet (915 m).

Operational: The Destructor mine series was used in large numbers during the Vietnam War, being dropped in coastal waters, river deltas, and rivers as well as along roads and trails.

During the Persian Gulf War in 1991 naval aircraft reportedly employed bombs modified with Destructor kits for use in attacking Iraqi airfields.

An aerial mining operation was also undertaken in an attempt to isolate Iraqi naval craft in the northern Persian Gulf from the port facilities and naval bases at Al-Basrah, Az-Zubayr, and Umm Qasr, and to prevent Iraqi naval craft from leaving those bases. On 18 January 1991 the mining operation was flown against the mouth of the Khawr Az-Zubayr River. The mission consisted of 18 aircraft from the carrier RANGER (CV 61), including four A-6E Intruders carrying a total of 48 Destructor Mk 36 mines. Forty-two of the mines were successfully dropped at four separate locations in the river. (Six mines on one aircraft failed to release; the plane was diverted to an airfield in Bahrain, where the mines were off-loaded before the A-6E returned to the RANGER. One A-6E was lost to enemy fire during the mission.)

MOBILE MINE MODIFIED MK 48 TORPEDO

The Navy is developing a mobile mine version of the Mk 48 torpedo that will carry two warheads (i.e., mines). The torpedo will be: (1) submarine launched; (2) capable of traveling greater distances than the Mk 67 mobile mine; and (3) capable of releasing one warhead at a preset location, after which the weapon will proceed to a second location carrying the second warhead.

SLMM MK 67

The Submarine-Launched Mobile Mine (SLMM) is a torpedo-like mine that permits covert mining by submarines in waters that are inaccessible to other means of delivery. It is a shallow-water bottom mine for use against surface ships as well as submarines. This is the U.S. Navy's only self-propelled mine; it has an electric motor that provides a range of up to 17,500 yards (16,000 m).

The SLMM is based on the Mk 37 Mod 2 torpedo: the wire guidance has been removed, and sensor, arming device, exploder, and associated battery have been installed.

Procurement of the SLMM ended far short of the goal of 2,400 weapons announced in the early 1980s.

Status: Operational; IOC was in 1983.

Type:	self-propelled, shallow/bottom	
Targets:	surface ships	
Weight:	1,765 lbs (801 kg)	
Length:	$13\frac{5}{12}$ ft (4.1 m)	
Diameter:	21 in (533 mm)	
Warhead:	515 lbs (233.6 kg) PBXN-103 high explosive	
Depth:	maximum 328 ft (100 m)	
Sensor:	TDD Mk 70	magnetic/seismic
	TDD Mk 71	magnetic/seismic/pressure
Delivery platforms:	submarines	

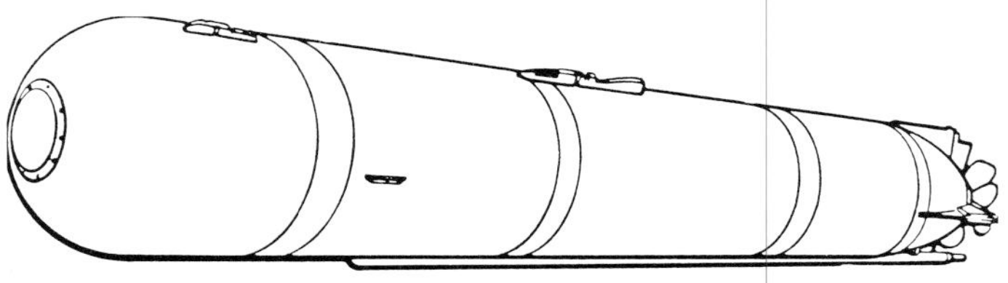

QUICKSTRIKE MK 65

The only weapon in the Quickstrike series designed specifically as a mine, the Mk 65 is the U.S. Navy's largest mine. With a thin-wall mine casing in lieu of the thick-wall casing of the Mk 80-series bombs, the Mk 65 is fully compatible with naval aircraft as well as the Air Force B-1B Lancer.

Status: Operational.

Type:	shallow/bottom		
Targets:	surface ships		
Weight:	2,390 lbs (1,084 kg)		
Length:	$9\frac{1}{6}$ ft (2.8 m)		
Diameter:	20.9 in (531 mm)		
Warhead:	HBX high explosive		
Depth:	maximum 300 ft (91.5 m)		
Sensor:	Mod 0	TDD Mk 57	magnetic/seismic
	Mod 1	TDD Mk 58	magnetic/seismic/pressure
		TDD Mk 70	magnetic/seismic
		TDD Mk 71	magnetic/seismic/pressure
Delivery platforms:	aircraft		

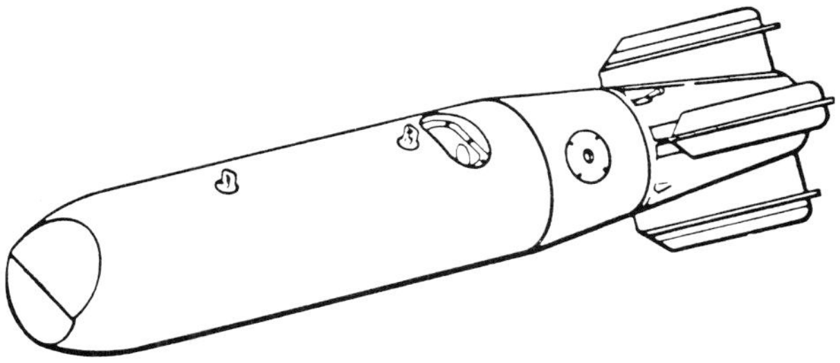

QUICKSTRIKE MK 64

This mine, a modified Mk 84 2,000-pound bomb with a thick-walled casing, is no longer available.

See 15th Edition/page 472 for characteristics.

QUICKSTRIKE MK 63

This is a modified Mk 83 1,000-pound bomb fitted with various target detection devices.

Status: Operational.

Type:	shallow/bottom	
Targets:	surface ships	
Weight:	985 lbs (447 kg) CF[3]	
	1,105 lbs (501 kg) LD	
Length:	$9\frac{5}{12}$ ft (2.9 m)	
Diameter:	14 in (355.5 mm)	
Warhead:	450 lbs (204 kg) H-6 high explosive	
Depth:	maximum 300 ft (91.5 m)	
Sensor:	TDD Mk 57	magnetic/seismic
	TDD Mk 58	magnetic/seismic/pressure
	TDD Mk 70	magnetic/seismic
	TDD Mk 71	magnetic/seismic/pressure
Delivery platforms:	aircraft	

3. CF = Conical Fixed tail assembly; LD = extending Low Drag tail assembly.

QUICKSTRIKE MK 62

The Mk 62 is a modified Mk 82 500-pound bomb fitted with various target detection devices.

Status: Operational.

Type:	shallow/bottom	
Targets:	surface ships	
Weight:	531 lbs (241 kg) CF	
	570 lbs (258.5 kg) LD	
Length:	$7\frac{5}{12}$ ft (2.3 m)	
Diameter:	10.8 in (274 mm)	
Warhead:	196 lbs (89 kg) H-6 high explosive	
Depth:	maximum 300 ft (91.5 m)	
Sensor:	TDD Mk 57	magnetic/seismic
	TDD Mk 58	magnetic/seismic/pressure
	TDD Mk 70	magnetic/seismic
	TDD Mk 71	magnetic/seismic/pressure
Delivery platforms:	aircraft	

CAPTOR MK 60

The CAPTOR (Encapsulated Torpedo) is one of the Navy's principal anti-submarine mines. It is a deep-water weapon normally laid by aircraft or submarine. Upon being laid, the CAPTOR is anchored to the ocean floor. (Aircraft-laid mines are lowered to the water by parachute.)

The Mk 60 acoustically detects passing submarines, ignoring surface ships (or submarines on or near the surface). Upon detecting a hostile submarine the CAPTOR launches a Mk 46 Mod 4 torpedo. A mine's life in water can be several months; detection range is credited as 1,093 yds (333 m).

The CAPTOR comes in two versions: Mod 0 and Mod 1. The latter has improved effectiveness against shallow-water targets. All Mod 0 mines are being upgraded to the Mod 1 configuration.

An F/A-18 Hornet releasing Mk 63 Quickstrike mines during an evaluation mission. The last major U.S. mining operation was flown in 1972 against Haiphong and other North Vietnamese ports; it was executed by carrier-based aircraft. Naval mines were used against *land* targets in the Gulf War of 1991. (Randy Hepp)

The mine suffered from significant development and operational problems. These led to several production delays. A related problem has been the relatively small warhead of the Mk 46 torpedo.

Status: Operational; IOC was in September 1979.

Type:	deep/moored
Targets:	submarines
Weight:	2,321 lbs (1,053 kg)
Length:	$12\frac{1}{12}$ ft (3.7 m) aircraft launch 11 ft (3.35 m) submarine launch
Diameter:	21 in (533 mm)
Warhead:	96 lbs (43.5 kg) PXBN-103 high explosive (in Mk 46 Mod 4 torpedo)
Depth:	maximum 3,000 ft (915 m)
Sensor:	acoustic
Delivery platforms:	aircraft submarines

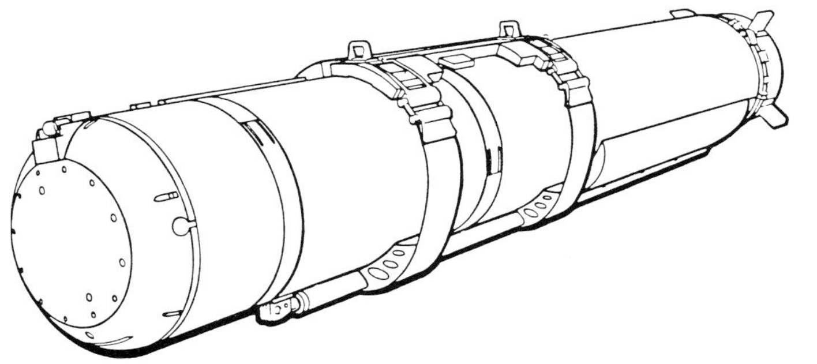

A CAPTOR mine with a parachute pack fitted at its back end (at right). (U.S. Navy)

CAPTOR mines mounted on wing pylons of a B-52 Stratofortress bomber. When rigged for conventional bombing/minelaying, a B-52 could carry eight CAPTORs under its wings and 18 in its weapons bays. (U.S. Air Force)

MINE MK 57

This was a medium-depth, moored mine similar to the Mk 56 but developed for launching from submarine torpedo tubes. It had a fiberglass casing. Operational from 1964, these mines have been discarded.

See 15th Edition/page 474 for characteristics.

MINE MK 56

This is an air-dropped mine capable of being used against surface ships and submarines. It was designed specifically for use against high-speed, deep-operating submarines of the 1960s.

This is the only U.S. mine now in service suitable for medium-depth water. When laid, the mine sinks to the bottom, where the case and anchor separation takes place. Should the mine become embedded in the bottom sediment before the case/anchor separation and mooring take place, a slow-burning propellant in the anchor is ignited that frees the mine from the bottom. As the case rises, a hydrostat senses the preset mooring depth and arrests the cable payout.

Status: Operational; IOC was in 1966.

Type:	medium/moored
Targets:	submarines, surface ships
Weight:	2,135 lbs (968 kg)
Length:	$9\frac{1}{2}$ ft (2.9 m)
Diameter:	23.4 in (594 mm)
Warhead:	357 lbs (162 kg) HBX-3 high explosive
Depth:	maximum 1,200 ft (366 m)
Sensor:	magnetic
Delivery platforms:	aircraft

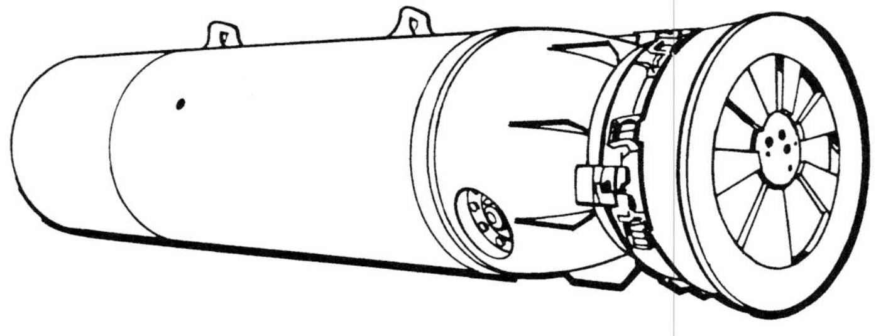

MINE MK 55

This was a modified 2,000-pound aircraft bomb, similar in concept to the Mk 52 mine except that the casing was larger and the flight equipment differed. It has now been discarded.

See 15th Edition/page 474 for characteristics.

MINE MK 52

The first of a series of post–World War II ASW mines, the Mk 52 was a modified 1,000-pound aircraft bomb. Operational from 1955, it has now been discarded.

See 15th Edition/page 475 for characteristics.

DESTRUCTOR MK 41

The Destructor (DST) weapons are bombs converted to mines through the installation of a modular arming kit that contains a Mk 32 safing/arming device fitted in the nose fuze well and a Mk 42 mine-firing mechanism inserted in the tail fuze well.

The Mk 41 is a modified Mk 84 2,000-pound bomb.

Status: Operational; IOC was in the 1960s.

Type:	shallow/bottom
Targets:	surface ships
Weight:	Mods 0–3 2,093 lbs (949 kg) CF Mods 4, 5 2,030 lbs (907 kg) CF
Length:	$12\frac{5}{12}$ ft (3.8 m)
Diameter:	25 in (635 mm)
Warhead:	990 lbs (449 kg) H-6 high explosive
Depth:	maximum 300 ft (91.5 m)
Sensor:	Mods 0–3 magnetic Mods 4–6 magnetic/seismic
Delivery platforms:	aircraft

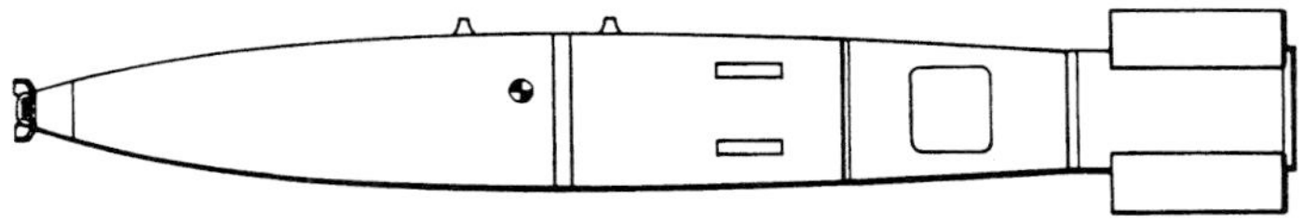

DESTRUCTOR MK 40

This is a Mk 83 1,000-pound bomb fuzed and modified for aerial minelaying.

Status: Operational; IOC was in the 1960s.

Type:	shallow/bottom	
Targets:	surface ships	
Weight:	985 lbs (447 kg) CF	
	1,105 lb (501 kg) LD	
Length:	$9\frac{3}{4}$ ft (3.0 m)	
Diameter:	22.5 in (571.5 mm)	
Warhead:	445 lbs (202 kg) H-6 high explosive	
Depth:	maximum 300 ft (91.5 m)	
Sensor:	Mods 0–3	magnetic
	Mods 4, 5	magnetic/seismic
Delivery platforms:	aircraft	

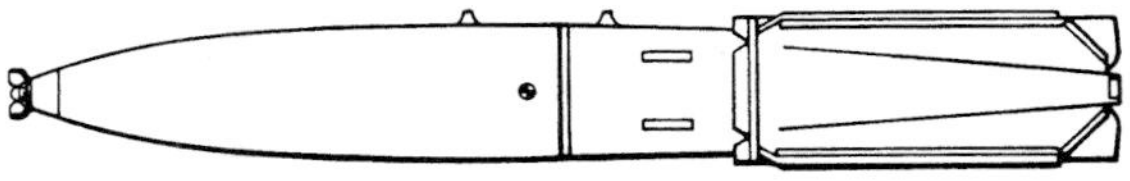

DESTRUCTOR MK 36

A modified Mk 82 500-pound bomb, this weapon was widely used in the Persian Gulf conflict of 1991. The Air Force version of this weapon—designated DST 36 AIR—is the only mine now planned for carriage by the Air Force B-1B bomber.

The principal difference in the various Mods lies in their tail assembly and firing mechanism. More than 4,000 Mk 36 conversion kits were procured.

Status: Operational; IOC was in the 1960s.

Type:	shallow/bottom	
Targets:	surface ships	
Weight:	531 lbs (241 kg) CF	
	570 lbs (258.5 kg) LD	
Length:	$7\frac{5}{12}$ ft (2.3 m)	
Diameter:	15 in (381 mm)	
Warhead:	192 lbs (87 kg) H-6 high explosive	
Depth:	maximum 300 ft (91.5 m)	
Sensor:	Mods 0–3	magnetic
	Mods 4–6	magnetic/seismic
Delivery platforms:	aircraft	

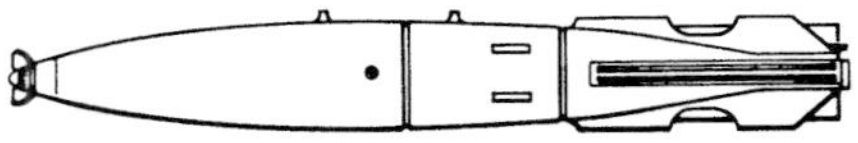

MISSILE LAUNCHING SYSTEMS

Several types of missile launchers are fitted in U.S. warships. They are of three generic types: (1) the traditional above-deck launchers, wherein missiles are pushed upward from below-deck magazines onto the launcher, which is then trained and elevated; (2) various "box"-like launchers, such as the Armored Box Launcher (ABL) and ASROC launcher; and (3) the below-decks Vertical Launching System (VLS). The Harpoon canisters fitted in a variety of Navy ships (as well as numerous foreign ships) can be considered a variation of the box launcher concept.

Only VLS and Harpoon canisters are currently installed in new U.S. surface combatants, i.e., the Arleigh Burke-class destroyers and the planned SC 21 surface combatant. The new Mk 49 RAM launcher is being fitted in a variety of surface combatants and amphibious ships.

The VLS provides a high degree of missile launch flexibility, more rapid launching, reduced maintenance requirements, and fewer crewmen in comparison with earlier above-deck surface-to-air missile launch systems. The Mk 41 VLS can accommodate Standard and Tomahawk missiles and the Vertical-Launch ASROC (VLA). In the future it may be configured to fire the Army's ATACMS missile as well as a four-pack container with the Evolved Sea Sparrow Missile (ESSM).

The VLS has numerous advantages: (1) total flexibility in missile selection; (2) rapid reselection if a weapon fails to launch (without having to unload or jettison the missile); (3) some protection for the missile from weather and shrapnel—in comparison with a missile on an above-deck launcher; and (4) more efficient use of space than below-deck rotary magazines.

The VLS consists of a series of eight-cell launch modules, plus launch control units and a missile loading/strikedown module. The strikedown module takes the space of three missile cells. Thus, the 61-missile launch system actually consists of 64 cells, three of which are devoted to the loading/strikedown module; in the 29-missile launcher there are 32 cells, with a three-cell loading/strikedown module.

The standard eight-cell VLS module weighs 29,300 pounds (13,290 kg); each module contains two rows of four missile cells separated by an exhaust uptake. The 61-missile VLS installation (i.e., eight standard modules) is $28\frac{7}{12}$ feet long, $12\frac{5}{12}$ feet wide, and $25\frac{1}{4}$ feet high ($8.7 \times 3.8 \times 7.7$ m). The maximum missile length that can be accommodated is 22 feet (6.7 m). The launchers are manufactured by the Northern Ordnance Division of the FMC Corporation, Minneapolis, Minnesota, and Martin Marietta (now Lockheed Martin) in Georgia.

Two new missile launcher designs have been developed for the RAM surface-to-air missile (see page 437).

In the following entries, the system weight does not include missiles or hydraulic fluids, except that missiles are included for the Mk 16, Mk 25, Mk 29, and Mk 141 launchers.

LAUNCHER MK 143

IOC:	1980
Type:	ABL
Missiles:	4 Tomahawk
System weight:	
Ships:	CGN 38
	DD 963 (7 ships)

LAUNCHER MK 141 MOD 1

This is a canister-type launcher, normally fitted in two groups of four canisters that are arranged in an X-configuration. This launcher, previously on the Hamilton (WHEC 715)-class cutters, was the first missile launching system to be installed in U.S. Coast Guard ships.

These canisters are fitted in numerous foreign warships. The Mk 141 Mod 0 was fitted in the Pegasus-class hydrofoil missile combatants.

IOC:	1977
Type:	canister
Missiles:	4 Harpoon
System weight:	13,000 lbs (5,897 kg)
Ships:	cruisers
	destroyers

A Tomahawk Land-Attack Missile (TLAM) is launched from an Armored Box Launcher (ABL) on the stern of the cruiser MISSISSIPPI (CGN 40). The battleships of the IOWA class each had eight ABLs, for a total of 32 Tomahawk missiles. (U.S. Navy)

Eight Harpoon canisters in two four-missile mounts are the standard armament of all U.S. cruisers and destroyers. The Harpoons are "wooden rounds" in sealed canisters, which are also used for shipping the missiles and storing them ashore. These Harpoons and the 5-inch/54-cal Mk 45 gun mount are in the cruiser MOBILE BAY (CG 53). (Giorgio Arra)

LAUNCH SYSTEM MK 49

A total of 30 launchers are planned for U.S. ships; they are also being fitted in German patrol boats. Early proposals called for firing the RAM from a modified Mk 29 NATO Sea Sparrow launcher as well (i.e., configured for both weapons).

IOC:	1992
Type:	box
Missiles:	21 RAM
System weight:	12,736 lbs (5,777 kg)
Ships:	LHD 1 (some units)
	LHA 1
	DD 963 (some units)
	LSD 41

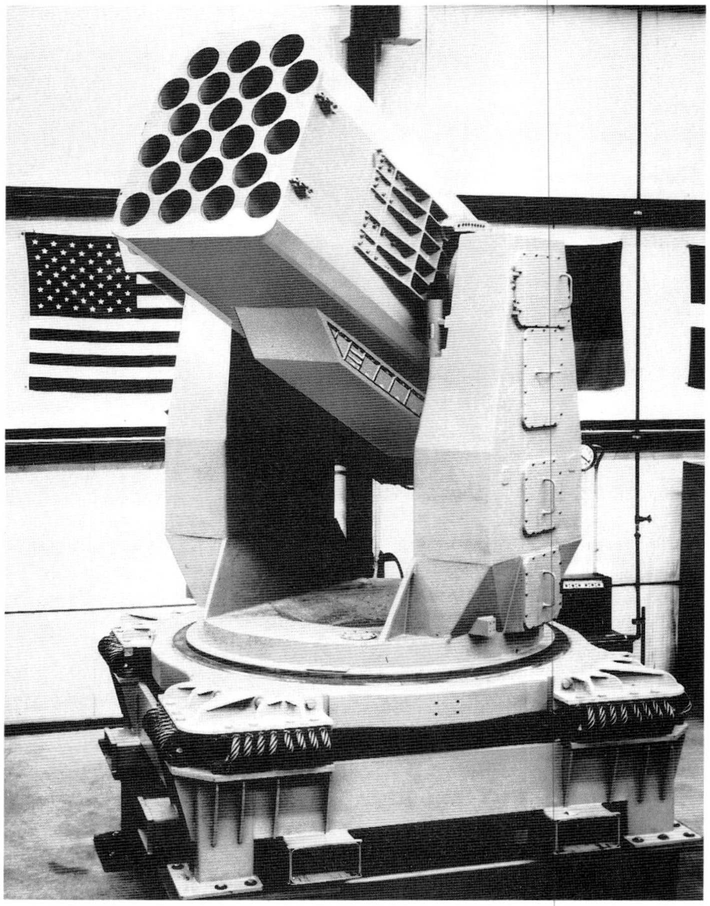

The 21-cell Mk 49 launcher for the RAM. The launcher uses components from the Phalanx CIWS mount. (General Dynamics/Pomona)

LAUNCH SYSTEM MK 41 (29 CELL)

IOC:	1991
Type:	VLS
Missiles:	29 Standard/Tomahawk/VLA
System weight:	approx. 94,000 lbs (42,638 kg)
Ships:	DDG 51

LAUNCH SYSTEM MK 41 (61 CELL)

IOC:	1986
Type:	VLS
Missiles:	61 Standard/Tomahawk/VLA
System weight:	approx. 188,000 lbs (85,277 kg)
Ships:	CG 52
	DDG 51
	DD 963 (29 ships)

A Tomahawk TLAM launches from the VLS of the destroyer FIFE (DD 991). The FIFE fired 60 Tomahawks during the Gulf War, more than any other ship and 21 percent of the TLAMs launched. (U.S. Navy, STG3 Mark D. Cooper)

The after 61-cell VLS on an Aegis guided missile cruiser. This launch concept provides more efficient use of space and a high degree of flexibility in missile selection and use. (United Defense/FMC)

Eight-cell units of the Mk 41 VLS are installed in a destroyer of the SPRUANCE (DD 963) class. Most SPRUANCES have been fitted with VLS for 61 missiles without reducing any of the ships' combat capabilities. Each of the eight cells is 25 × 25 inches (635 × 635 mm); the two box-like units on the module (at left) are launch sequencers, part of the launch control subsystem. (Litton/Ingalls Shipbuilding)

LAUNCH SYSTEM MK 29 MOD 0

All active U.S. aircraft carriers have two or three Mk 29 launchers; other ships have one. (Note that the mothballed carrier MIDWAY/CV 41 has two Mk 25 BPDMS launchers.)

The launcher box is designated Mk 132. It was derived from the Mk 16 ASROC launchers. Missiles are reloaded "by hand."

This weapon launcher is fitted in numerous foreign warships.

IOC:	1974
Type:	box
Missiles:	8 NATO Sea Sparrow
System weight:	24,000 to 28,000 lbs (10,886 to 12,700 kg)
Ships:	carriers
	DD 963
	LHD 1
	AOE 1
	AOE 6
	AOR 1 (some ships)

LAUNCH SYSTEM MK 26 MOD 1

IOC:	1976
Type:	twin-arm
Missiles:	44 Standard-MR/ASROC
System weight:	208,373 lbs (94,518 kg)
Ships:	CGN 38 (forward)
	CG 47–51
	DDG 963 (forward)

LAUNCH SYSTEM MK 26 MOD 0

The Mk 26 was first installed in the missile test ship NORTON SOUND (AVM 1).

IOC:	1976
Type:	twin-arm
Missiles:	24 Standard-MR/ASROC
System weight:	162,028 lbs (73,496 kg)
Ships:	CGN 38 (aft)
	CG 47–51 (forward and aft)
	DDG 963 (aft)

LAUNCH SYSTEM MK 25 MOD 0

The Basic Point Defense Missile System (BPDMS) launcher is derived from the ASROC launcher. Two launchers that are reloaded "by hand" are fitted in each of the ships listed below.

The launcher box is designated Mk 112.

IOC:	1967
Type:	box
Missiles:	8 Sea Sparrow
System weight:	32,081 lbs (14,552 kg)
Ships:	CV 41
	LHA 1
	LPH 2
	MCS 9

The eight-cell Mk 29 launch system for the Sea Sparrow point-defense missile on the destroyer COMTE DE GRASSE (DD 974). Point-defense guided missile systems do not qualify ships for the "G" designation. (Leo Van Ginderen collection)

A Mk 26 launcher on board the cruiser VALLEY FORGE (CG 50); these are Standard SM-1 missiles, derivatives of the Tartar SAM. The later Aegis cruisers have VLS. (Jürg Kürsener)

Loading a Sea Sparrow missile in a Mk 25 "box" launcher. Several foreign navies have vertical-launch Sea Sparrow systems, a launch mode that will be adopted by the U.S. Navy. (U.S. Navy)

LAUNCH SYSTEM MK 16 MODS 1–6

These were the standard ASROC "box launchers" introduced into the U.S. Fleet in 1961. During the 1960s, 1970s, and into the 1980s this weapon was fitted in all U.S. cruisers, destroyers, and frigates that were ASW capable. Some ASROC box launchers were modified to additionally fire Standard-ARM and Harpoon surface-to-surface missiles. There are no ASROC box launchers remaining in the U.S. Fleet. The last ships to carry them were the California (CGN 36) and Spruance (DD 963) classes; they were deleted in the early 1990s. The box launcher is still in use in several other navies.

ASROCs can be launched from the forward Mk 26 twin-arm launcher of cruisers and destroyers as well as from vertical-launch systems (VLA in the latter ships). See 15th Edition/page 476 for launcher characteristics.

LAUNCH SYSTEM MK 13 MOD 4

This was the last conventional missile launcher to be fitted in U.S. warships.

IOC:	1978
Type:	single-arm
Missiles:	40 Standard-MR/Harpoon
System weight:	134,704 lbs (61,102 kg)
Ships:	FFG 7

LAUNCH SYSTEM MK 13 MOD 3

IOC:	1974
Type:	single-arm
Missiles:	40 Standard-MR
System weight:	135,012 lbs (61,241 kg)
Ships:	CG 36

The Mk 13 launch system with a Harpoon anti-ship missile. The Mk 13 launcher loads missiles in a vertical position from a below-deck, cylindrical magazine. (John Bouvia)

MISSILES

The missiles currently available or under development for the Navy and Marine Corps for use from aircraft, surface ships, and submarines are listed below.[4] (Ground- and vehicle-launched missiles used by the Marine Corps are not listed.)

The missiles are arranged alphabetically by their names. All missiles in U.S. service or advanced development have letter-number designations explained in the accompanying table. There is a designation series for missiles and a separate series for rockets. Of the weapons described here, the ASROC RUR-5A is the only one from the latter designation series.

The term anti-radiation is officially used for missiles that home on enemy radar transmissions; because of the widespread confusion over the term radiation, which is normally associated with nuclear weapons, the term *anti-radar* is used throughout this volume.

The Israeli-developed Barak surface-to-air missile will be evaluated by the U.S. Navy in 1996 as a possible alternative to the Evolved Sea Sparrow Missile (ESSM) and RAM systems.

Six missiles are currently being procured for Navy-Marine use as shown in the accompanying table.

MISSILE ACQUISITION PROGRAM

	FY 1993 Actual	FY 1994 Actual	FY 1995 Actual	FY 1996 Authorized	FY 1997 Authorized
AMRAAM	140	44	106	115	220
Harpoon-SLAM	70	75	58	30	15
Hellfire	1,000	1,931	—	—	—
RAM	—	240	240	230	235
Standard	330	220	202	151	116
Tomahawk	200	216	217	164	164
Trident D-5	21	24	18	6	7

Explanation of Symbols

YAIM-120A

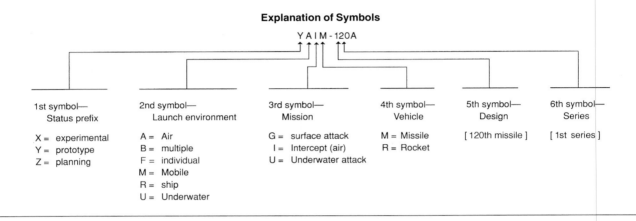

1st symbol—Status prefix	2nd symbol—Launch environment	3rd symbol—Mission	4th symbol—Vehicle	5th symbol—Design	6th symbol—Series
X = experimental	A = Air	G = surface attack	M = Missile	[120th missile]	[1st series]
Y = prototype	B = multiple	I = Intercept (air)	R = Rocket		
Z = planning	F = individual	U = Underwater attack			
	M = Mobile				
	R = ship				
	U = Underwater				

AAAM (ADVANCED AIR-TO-AIR MISSILE)

The AAAM was intended to replace the Phoenix long-range AAM; it has been canceled. Tentative planning provided for the F-14D variant of the Tomcat to carry up to eight AAAMs and the F/A-18 Hornet at least four; a total U.S. Navy procurement of 4,000 missiles was envisioned. Congress had proposed that AAAM also be adopted by the U.S. Air Force for the F-15C/D Eagle and F-22 Advanced Tactical Fighter (ATF), although the Air Force contended that there is no requirement for the weapon on its aircraft.

See 15th Edition/page 480 for characteristics.

ABRS (ASSAULT BALLISTIC ROCKET SYSTEM)

The ABRS—in use by the Army and Marine Corps—was proposed by the LTV Corporation for installation on the IOWA-class battleships and NEWPORT-class landing ships to provide fire support for amphibious assaults. One concept provided for full conversion of LSTs to "rocket monitors."

In the event, the project was not pursued for shipboard use.

See 14th Edition/page 466 for characteristics.

AIWS (ADVANCED INTERDICTION WEAPON SYSTEM)

The AIWS was intended as a stand-off weapon to replace the SLAM, Maverick, Walleye, Skipper II, and Paveway guided bombs. It has been canceled.

See 15th Edition/page 480 for characteristics.

AMRAAM AIM-120A

The Advanced Medium-Range Air-to-Air Missile is a joint Navy–Air Force weapon intended to succeed the Sparrow AAM. The missile has a high resistance against enemy ECM and a "snap-down" capability to engage low-flying aircraft and possibly anti-ship missiles.

Design: The AMRAAM is smaller than the Sparrow and, unlike the Sparrow's semi-active radar guidance, the new missile uses a mid-course inertial reference system with a sophisticated monopulse radar seeker for terminal guidance. Maximum speed is approximately Mach 4. The AIM-120B has added infrared guidance, and the AIM-120C adds improved aerodynamic performance.

Estimated cost for Air Force–Navy procurement of 15,450 missiles is $12.2 *billion.*

Status: Operational; in production. Also used by British air forces, and sales to Israel and the United Arab Emirates have been approved.

It is anticipated that production of the missile will total 15,450 weapons for Air Force and Navy-Marine requirements, with about a 75–25 percent split between the two services, plus allied requirements. The Hughes Aircraft Company also proposed the possible use of the missile from surface ships (called Sea AMRAAM), but that concept has not been pursued. European coproduction is planned.

Manufacturer:	Hughes and Raytheon
Weight:	approx. 300 lbs (156.5 kg)
Length:	12 ft (3.65 m)
Span:	1 ft 8¾ in (526 mm)
Diameter:	7 in (178 mm)
Propulsion:	solid-propellant rocket
Range:	approx. 40 n.miles (74 km)
Guidance:	inertial + active terminal radar homing
Warhead:	50 lbs (22.7 kg) high explosive
Platforms:	*aircraft* F-14
	F/A-18

4. The author is in debt to Mr. Edward L. Korb, editor of *The World's Missile Systems* (Pomona, Calif.: General Dynamics Corp.), for his assistance in this section.

An F/A-18 Hornet from Air Test and Evaluation Squadron (VX) 4 carrying ten AMRAAMs mounted on four wing pylons and two fuselage points. Two Sidewinder missiles are mounted on the plane's wingtips. (Hughes Aircraft)

AMRAAMs are moved from a weapons magazine of the carrier George Washington during 1996 operations in the Adriatic Sea in support of NATO peacekeeping operations in Bosnia. AMRAAM replaces the long-serving Sparrow missile. (U.S. Navy, PH/A Ryan Child)

ASROC RUR-5A

The ASROC—Anti-Submarine Rocket—was a ship-launched, ballistic ASW weapon that can be fitted with a conventional Mk 46 homing torpedo. From the early 1960s onward ASROC was fitted to all U.S. Navy cruisers, destroyers, and frigates until the advent of the PERRY-class frigates. The ASROC was a short-range weapon; almost continuous proposals for an extended-range ASROC have been deferred.

The weapon was phased out of U.S. Navy service in the early 1990s. The Mk 16 box launchers were removed from two CALIFORNIA-class cruisers and seven SPRUANCE-class destroyers, the last U.S. ships to have that launcher. Five TICONDEROGA-class cruisers and four KIDD-class destroyers could also fire ASROC from their Mk 26 launchers.

A Vertical-Launch ASROC (VLA) has been developed for use in warships with Vertical Launch Systems (VLS); see separate entry.

The standard ASROC was fired from an eight-tube box launcher (Mk 16) and from the Mk 26 surface-to-air missile launcher. It has been employed by 11 foreign navies with the Mk 44/46 torpedoes.

Design: As delivered to the U.S. Navy the ASROC could carry a W44 nuclear depth bomb as an alternate payload to a conventional homing torpedo. The surviving nuclear warheads were removed from the Fleet in the late 1980s.

Operational: The ASROC was tested on only one occasion with a nuclear warhead, being fired from the destroyer AGERHOLM (DD 826) on 11 May 1962 in a Pacific weapons test.

Status: Operational; IOC was in 1961. It is used with conventional torpedoes by several foreign navies. No longer in U.S. Navy service.

ASW STAND-OFF WEAPON

See Sea Lance entry.

ATACMS (MGM-140)

The Army Tactical Missile System (ATACM)S is a long-range tactical semi-ballistic missile. The Navy is considering the employment of ATACMS from surface ships (surface combatants with VLS and amphibious ships) and possibly submarines as a battlefield/naval fire support weapon for the Marine Corps. The missile would be launched from VLS.

Design: ATACMS is a semi-ballistic missile, with inertial guidance provided by a laser gyroscope system. Launch can be as much as 30° off-axis, and the missile is steered aerodynamically during the descent by electrically actuated control fins, thus modifying the flight path from a ballistic parabola. Offsetting the launch angle and descending in a semi-ballistic mode complicates enemy trajectory plotting to find the launch vehicle. The disadvantage of this system, however, is that accuracy is less precise than a straightforward flight path would achieve.

Proposed upgrades for a Navy ATACMS would incorporate Global Positioning System (GPS) updated navigation. The GPS guidance package for the land-based variant would increase its range to more than 173 statute miles (280 km). The Army also plans to fit ATACMS with the BAT (Brilliant Anti-Tank) submunition.

The missile has an M74 warhead that dispenses 950 M42 Anti-Personnel/Anti-Material (APAM) submunitions.

Operational: A standard Army tracked M270 two-missile ATACMS launcher was placed on the dock landing ship MOUNT VERNON (LSD 39) for missile test firings on 12 February 1995.

Status: Operational; in production for the U.S. Army. IOC for the Army was in 1990.

Manufacturer:	Loral Vought Systems
Weight:	3,687 lbs (1,672 kg)
Length:	13 ft (3.96 m)
Span:	(ballistic)
Diameter:	24 in (610 mm)
Propulsion:	solid-propellant rocket
Range:	150+ n.miles (280+ km) in ship-launched variant
Guidance:	inertial
Warhead:	950 M42 bomblets
Platforms:	

An Army ATACMS is launched from its tracked launch vehicle during a test firing. ATACMS—which was used in the Gulf War—is being proposed for naval use. It could be carried in large numbers by the proposed "arsenal ship." The tail fins fold to fit in the launch canister. (Loral Vought Systems)

GRAND SLAM

See SLAM entry.

HARM AGM-88

The HARM, or High-Speed Anti-Radiation Missile, was developed by the Naval Weapons Center at China Lake, California, for attacking hostile radars. The missile is a successor to the Shrike AGM-45A and Standard-ARM AGM-78D missiles, providing greater range, increased velocity, more frequency coverage, and additional flexibility—through an on-board computer—in reacting to threats. HARM uses the computer to automatically calculate threat priorities and engage the one that poses the greatest threat to friendly aircraft. It can also engage radiating targets detected at any angle from the aircraft.

Note that HARM is the only weapon carried by the EA-6B Prowler electronic jamming aircraft. (The U.S. Air Force's EF-111A electronics countermeasures aircraft cannot carry missiles.)

Design: The latest version, the AGM-88C, is an updated AGM-88B; 750 of the new guidance units have been procured.

The HARM has been criticized for high costs, and in early 1986 the Navy briefly stopped accepting the missile because of manufacturing flaws.

Operational: In the Gulf War of 1991 a total of 895 HARMs were launched by Navy and Marine aircraft, more than any other missile used by U.S. naval forces in the conflict. The Tactical Air Launched Decoy (TALD) was employed in conjunction with HARMs to entice Iraqi forces to use their radars against the decoys, marking them as

HARM targets. A total of 137 TALDs were used in this manner by naval aircraft during the conflict.[5]

Status: Operational; IOC was in 1984, AGM-88C in 1993. The last HARM is to be delivered in late 1997. Some 21,000 have been delivered, plus more than 1,000 guidance packages to upgrade earlier missiles.

HARMs are also used by several foreign air forces.

Manufacturer:	Texas Instruments
Weight:	796 lbs (361 kg)
Length:	13 ft 7 in (4.17 m)
Span:	3 ft 8 in (1.13 m)
Diameter:	10 in (253 mm)
Propulsion:	solid-propellant rocket
Range:	approx. 80 n.miles (148 km)
Guidance:	radar homing
Warhead:	145 lbs (65.8 kg) high explosive
Platforms:	*aircraft* F/A-18 A-6E EA-6B

A HARM on an A-7E Corsair aircraft. The anti-radar missile was highly effective in the Gulf War, the finale for the Corsair. The missile can be carried by the EA-6B Prowler, which will perform ECM missions for both the Navy and Air Force. (U.S. Navy, PH1 William Shaya)

HARPOON AGM/RGM/UGM-84A

The Harpoon is a versatile, widely used anti-ship missile. It is the first U.S. Navy missile designed for shipboard launch against surface targets since the Regulus I, which was deployed in the 1950s—albeit primarily for the strategic, land-attack role. The Harpoon was initially conceived for aircraft use against surfaced Soviet Echo-class cruise missile submarines. Subsequently, the missile was developed for air, surface, and submarine launch against surface targets.

The missile is carried in most U.S. surface combatant classes, being launched from surface-to-air missile launchers (Mk 13), vertical launchers (Mk 41), ASROC box launchers (Mk 29), and stand-alone canisters (Mk 141). In shipboard (and submarine) launch, the missile has a rocket booster fitted. Submarines can launch the Harpoon encapsulated from standard 21-inch (533-mm) torpedo tubes; in submarine launch the capsule rises to the surface and the missile ignites, leaving the canister. The F/A-18, A-6E, P-3C, and S-3B aircraft can carry the Harpoon.

Design: From 1982 onward the U.S. Navy took delivery of the Block 1B Harpoon with improved radar guidance and a lower flight altitude. The subsequent 1C version, delivered from 1984, had improved guidance and burned a higher-density fuel, resulting in an increase in range—to almost 80 n.miles (148.2 km).

The Block 1D improvements backfit of earlier missiles from 1992 allows the missile to re-attack a target by flying a clover-leaf pattern if the missile does not acquire the target on its first approach. The 1D variant also has a 23-inch (0.6-m) fuel tank extension that almost doubles the missile's range.

Shown here launched from an A-6E Intruder, the Harpoon is a highly versatile missile that has been adopted by numerous Western navies. It can be launched from most combat aircraft, surface ships, and submarines. (McDonnell Douglas)

The maximum Harpoon flight velocity is Mach 0.85. For surface ship and submarine launch the booster burn is approximately three seconds, after which it falls off and the sustaining engine starts. Flight reliability is in excess of 93 percent.

The Harpoon forms the basis for the Standoff Land Attack Missile (SLAM).

Operational: The first combat use of the Harpoon was by U.S. naval forces against Libyan missile craft in the Gulf of Sidra in 1986.

The only known use of the Harpoon during the 1991 campaign in the Persian Gulf occurred when the Saudi Arabian missile craft FAISAL launched a single missile, which sank an Iraqi minelayer. The engagement took place early on 23 January, with the detection and missile launch being made by radar in the pre-dawn darkness; the target ship was identified by Iraqi survivors.

Status: Operational; IOC was in 1977 for surface ships and submarines, 1979 in land-based aircraft (P-3C), and 1981 in carrier-based aircraft (A-6E).

Twenty other nations employ the Harpoon from surface ships and submarines (with the submarine-launched Harpoon called Sub-Harpoon in foreign navies); the Coast Guard briefly had Harpoon launchers on its larger cutters; and the U.S. Air Force has carried Harpoon missiles on B-52G and F-111C bombers in the anti-shipping role.

More than 6,000 Harpoon *and* SLAM missiles have been produced for the United States and 23 other countries.

A Harpoon fitted to the wing of a P-3C Orion maritime patrol aircraft. The letter "T" in the designation ATM-84A indicates that this is a training missile. (McDonnell Douglas)

5. In addition to attack aircraft launching TALDs, during the Gulf War they were launched by S-3B Vikings working in conjunction with HARM-armed aircraft to attack Iraqi radar sites.

Manufacturer:[6]	McDonnell Douglas
Weight:	1,390 lbs (631.8 kg) for air launch 1,757 lbs (798.6 kg) for surface/submarine launch
Length:	14 ft 7 in (4.4 m) for air launch 17 ft 2 in (5.2 m) for surface/submarine launch
Span:	3 ft (0.9 m)
Diameter:	13½ in (343 mm)
Propulsion:	turbojet (Teledyne CAE J402-CA-400); 600 lbst (272 kgst) + solid-propellant booster of 12,000 lbst (5,443 kgst) for surface/submarine launch
Range:	75+ n.miles (105.6 km)
Guidance:	active radar
Warhead:	510 lbs (231 kg) high explosive
Platforms:	*aircraft* F/A-18, A-6E, P-3C, S-3B *submarines* SSN 637 and later classes *cruisers* all CG/CGN *destroyers* all DD/DDG *frigates* FFG 7

6. Data for 1D variant, unless otherwise indicated.

A Harpoon blasts out of its canister after being launched by a submarine. The spring-loaded fins and stub wings are fully deployed in this photo. (McDonnell Douglas)

An aviation ordnanceman prepares a Harpoon under the wing of a P-3C Orion. The Harpoon was designed initially for attacking surfaced Soviet cruise missile submarines. (McDonnell Douglas)

HELLFIRE AGM-114

The Hellfire (derived from the term Helicopter-Launched Fire and forget) is an anti-tank missile launched from Marine attack helicopters. The missile is intended to replace the wire-guided TOW, with the Hellfire being a free-flight weapon with a longer-range that permits launch-and-leave tactics.

When the Army initiated development of the Hellfire in the mid-1970s, Rockwell International was the prime contractor for the sole-source program; Martin Marietta provided the laser seeker for the missile. From the mid-1980s, however, Martin became a second production source for the missile.

Design: The Hellfire is a modular missile that allows a variety of sensors to be fitted. The Marines will use the laser-guided variant. The target can be designated for helicopters by ground-based or airborne laser designators; it affords additional survival to the launching helicopter by a lock-on-after-launch feature. A land-launched version has been developed.

Operational: Hellfire missiles fired by Army AH-64 Apache helicopters against Iraqi radar sites were the first coalition weapons launched in Operation Desert Storm in January 1991.

Status: Operational; IOC for the Army was in 1985.

Manufacturer:	Rockwell International and Martin Marietta (now Lockheed Martin)
Weight:	99.6 lbs (45.2 kg)
Length:	5 ft 4 in (1.625 m)
Span:	1 ft 1 in (0.33 m)
Diameter:	7 in (178 mm)
Propulsion:	solid-propellant rocket
Range:	3+ n.miles (5.55 km)
Guidance:	laser tracking
Warhead:	20 lbs (9 kg) high explosive
Platforms:	*helicopters* AH-1W, SH-60B

A Marine AH-1J SeaCobra carrying eight Hellfire anti-tank missiles. (Bell Helicopter Textron)

JDAM (JOINT DIRECT ATTACK MUNITION)

The JDAM is a joint Navy–Air Force program to develop an air-launched attack munition based on employing Mk 83 1,000- and Mk 84 2,000-pound bombs with guidance kits. The guidance will be a combined inertial/GPS navigation package. Expected accuracy will be less than ten feet (three meters).

In 1995 the estimated cost was $40,000 per weapon.

Status: Development; IOC is planned for about 2000.

An AH-1W SeaCobra flown by VX-5 fires a Hellfire anti-tank missile. U.S. Army AH-56 Apache helicopter gunships fired Hellfires to destroy Iraqi border radar installations at the start of the air war over Iraq on the morning of 17 January 1991. (U.S. Navy)

JSOW (JOINT STAND-OFF WEAPON) AGM-154

The JSOW is a joint development effort by the Navy and Air Force to produce the next generation of stand-off missiles. The Navy is the lead service in developing the weapon. The baseline JSOW would replace the Rockeye and APAM; the planned improved JSOW would replace laser-guided bombs and the Maverick, Skipper, and Walleye missiles.

Design: The JSOW program is developing a baseline weapon for use against fixed area targets. It will have an inertial/GPS navigation capability and will carry a variety of warheads. (The BLU-97 is a general-purpose submunition, while the BLU-108 is an anti-armor submunition; 145 BLU-97s are carried.)

Several seekers are being considered, including Synthetic Aperture Radar (SAR), Imaging Infrared (IIR), laser radar, or millimeter-wave radar. Baseline accuracy is considered less than 33 feet (ten meters).

The wings fold atop the missile; the tail fins do not fold.

More than 20,000 weapons are planned for Navy–Air Force procurement, with the first acquisition being funded about fiscal 1998. Consideration is also being given to employing the missile in an electronic jamming role.

Status: Development; IOC is planned for 1998.

Manufacturer:	Texas Instruments
Weight:	
Length:	13 ft 4 in (4.06 m)
Span:	
Diameter:	
Propulsion:	
Range:	35 n.miles (65 km)
Guidance:	inertial/GPS + seeker
Warhead:	500–1,000 lbs (227–454 kg) unitary high explosive or BLU-97/BLU-108 bomblets or BAT (Brilliant Anti-Tank) submunition
Platforms:[7]	*aircraft* AV-8B F/A-18

LRDMM (LONG-RANGE DUAL-MODE MISSILE)

The proposed LRDMM was envisioned as a long-range (more than 100-mile/161-km) missile for launching from Aegis ships. The missile would have been used against incoming anti-ship missiles launched at long ranges, attack bomber aircraft, and electronic jamming aircraft. At one point it was also envisioned that the airframe could be used for the ASW Stand-Off Weapon (SOW).

The project was not pursued because of technical difficulties and uncertainty over how to conduct the outer air battle to defend battle groups against attacking Soviet cruise missile aircraft.

MAVERICK AGM-65

This is an air-to-surface missile derived from an Air Force anti-tank missile for use by Marine aircraft in the close air support role and by the Navy in the anti-ship role.

The Marines have the AGM-65E laser-guided version, compatible with air- and ground-based laser designators; the Navy's AGM-65F combines the Imaging Infrared (I^2R) of the Air Force AGM-65D missile with the warhead and propulsion sections of the AGM-65E.

Design: The Maverick is a modular missile produced in several variants that employ one of three guidance packages (television, laser, infrared), one of two warheads, and the same rocket motor. The Navy-Marine variants have a 300-pound (136-kg) penetrating blast warhead in place of the 125-pound (57-kg) shaped charge used for attacking tanks in the Air Force versions.

Status: Operational; IOC for the AGM-65E was in 1985. Eighteen other nations employ the Maverick.

Manufacturer:	Hughes	
Weight:	AGM-65E	
	AGM-65F	645 lbs (293 kg)
Length:	8 ft 2 in (2.49 m)	
Span:	2 ft 4½ in (0.72 m)	
Diameter:	12 in (300 mm)	
Propulsion:	solid-propellant rocket	
Range:	12 n.miles (22 km)	
Guidance:	infrared	
Warhead:	300 lbs (136 kg) high explosive	
Platforms:	*aircraft*	A-6E
		AV-8B
		F/A-18
	helicopters	AH-1W

7. Also to be carried by Air Force F-15E, F-16, and B-1B aircraft.

An infrared Maverick is launched from a P-3C Orion during a feasibility test. Although the Maverick is suitable for the anti-ship role, the value of launching the missile from a large, slow, relatively vulnerable Orion is questionable at best. (U.S. Navy)

An infrared variant of the Maverick missile is checked on the pylon of an A-7E Corsair aircraft. The missile has demonstrated its effectiveness in night attacks against large and small ships during live-round tests. (Hughes Aircraft)

MRASM (MEDIUM-RANGE AIR-TO-SURFACE MISSILE) AGM-109

The MRASM was a joint Navy–Air Force program to develop an air-launched missile with a 250-n.mile range for delivering submunitions against runways. Originally to be a (shortened) variant of the Tomahawk, during early development significant changes were made to most components, reducing the commonality with Tomahawk. The Navy's interest in MRASM was minimal, while the Air Force's position was divided: the Tactical Air Command (TAC) had limited interest, the Strategic Air Command (SAC) envisioned the MRASM as a useful weapon for the B-52G strategic bomber.

The MRASM program was terminated by Congress in 1983. Other weapons that could be adopted to the MRASM role at that time included the Air Force GBU-15, an air-launched glide bomb, and the Navy's Harpoon.[8] The Air Force Advanced Cruise Missile (ACM)—a "stealth" weapon—could be used by strategic aircraft. Also being planned is an Army–Air Force effort to develop a common Joint Tactical Missile System (JTACMS) that could be ground launched and carried by strategic and tactical aircraft for "deep attack."

The designation AGM-109H was intended for the Air Force airfield attack weapon and AGM-109L for a projected Navy anti-ship and land-attack version.

PHOENIX AIM-54

The Phoenix was developed for long-range fleet air defense against attacking Soviet bomber aircraft. It is the most sophisticated and longest-range AAM in service with any nation. The missile can be carried only by the F-14 Tomcat fighter using the AWG-9 radar/fire-control system. The AWG-9 is capable of simultaneously guiding all six Phoenix missiles that can be carried by an F-14 (although six-missile loadouts are rare).

Design: The AIM-54A, with analog electronics, has been replaced in U.S. service with the AIM-54C/C+ models. The C/C+ have a digital system to allow software programing for more rapid target discrimination, improved beam attack, better resistance to electronic countermeasures, longer range, increased altitude, and increased reliability. The previously used expanding, continuous-rod warheads of the early Phoenix missiles have been replaced by controlled fragmentation warheads (entering production in fiscal 1983). The AIM-54B was an interim model, similar to the AIM-54A but without the earlier missile's liquid cooling system; it did not go into production. The missile's designed range was 60 n.miles (111 km); intercepts have been made out to at least 110 n.miles (204 km). Maximum speed is approximately Mach 5.

The AIM-54C model was delayed in delivery to the fleet by quality control problems that resulted in several hundred missiles being delivered, but none was considered acceptable by the Navy until certain modifications were made. Production ended with the fiscal 1992 order.

Hughes Aircraft Company proposed a shipboard short-range defensive missile system in the 1970s based on the Phoenix/AWG-9; that option was not pursued.

Operational: The AIM-54A was compromised by having been provided to the Iranian Air Force prior to the fall of the Shah in 1979.

Status: Operational; IOC was in 1974. More than 2,500 AIM-54A missiles were produced, as were more than 1,000 AIM-54C/C+ models.

Manufacturer:	Hughes
Weight:	1,020 lbs (463 kg)
Length:	13 ft (4.0 m)
Span:	3 ft (0.915 m)
Diameter:	15 in (380 mm)
Propulsion:	solid-propellant rocket
Range:	110 n.miles (204 km)
Guidance:	semi-active radar in cruise phase; active terminal radar homing
Warhead:	133 lbs (60 kg) high explosive
Platforms:	*aircraft* F-14

8. GBU = Guided Bomb Unit.

A Phoenix is launched from an F-14A Tomcat. The missile, developed to provide long-range air defense of carrier battle groups, has limited value in tactical situations that are likely to be encountered by U.S. naval forces in the late 1990s. (Hughes Aircraft)

PENGUIN MK 3 AGM-119

The Penguin Mk 3, an anti-ship missile developed by the Norwegian Navy, is being procured for U.S. Navy use from the SH-60 Seahawk helicopter.[9] The missile has also undergone U.S. Navy evaluation for use on small craft, but that application is not being pursued. The missile was considered too heavy for use on small combatants.

9. The Mk 3 was originally designated as the Mk 2 Mod 7.

An AIM-54C+ Phoenix missile undergoes final inspection before delivery to the Navy. The various sections of the missile are clearly visible; the technician is working on the guidance section. (Hughes Aircraft)

Design: The missile is a "fire-and-forget" weapon with several unusual features, including an indirect flight path to target. On board ship the Penguin is fired from a storage/launcher container that weighs 1,100 pounds (499 kg). The Mk 3 has a greater weight but a smaller wing span than the Mk 2 that was evaluated for shipboard use (see 13th Edition/page 441).

The Penguin carries a Bullpup ASM warhead.

Maximum missile speed is approximately Mach 1.2.

Status: Operational; IOC for the Mk 3 in the Norwegian Air Force was in 1987. IOC in the U.S. Navy was in April 1994.

The original Penguin became operational on Norwegian fast attack boats in 1972; it is also used by the Greek, Swedish, and Turkish Navies. The improved Mk 2 became operational in 1979, and the Mk 3 has been developed for launch from F-16 strike fighters of the Norwegian Air Force.

Current U.S. Navy procurement is 101 missiles.

Manufacturer:	Kongsberg Vaapenfabrikk (Norway) and Grumman
Weight:	820 lbs (372 kg)
Length:	10 ft 6 in (3.2 m)
Span:	3 ft 3 in (1.0 m)
Diameter:	11 in (280 mm)
Propulsion:	solid-propellant rocket + solid-propellant booster
Range:	30+ n.miles (55+ km) air launch mode
Guidance:	inertial + infrared homing
Warhead:	265 lbs (120 kg) high explosive
Platforms:	*helicopters* SH-60B

A Penguin in flight, moments after being released by an SH-60B Seahawk. The Norwegian-developed Penguin provides SH-60B/F/R helicopters with a potent anti-ship capability. (U.S. Navy, PH2 Danny Lee)

This Penguin missile has just been released from a VX-1 SH-60B Seahawk. The missile's wings are still folded and the rocket engine has not yet ignited. (U.S. Navy, PH2 Danny Lee)

POLARIS UGM-27

The Polaris SLBM has been retired from U.S. Navy service. It was deployed as the U.S. sea-based strategic deterrent weapon from 15 November 1960—the start of the first deterrent patrol of the GEORGE WASHINGTON (SSBN 598) with 16 A-1 missiles—to 1 October 1981—when the submarine ROBERT E. LEE (SSBN 601) was taken off alert status (she had been carrying 16 A-3 missiles). (She did not return to port until several days later.)

The Polaris missile was produced for the U.S. Navy in three variants: A-1/2/3. The A-1 and A-2 were single-warhead missiles; the A-3 was the only Western Multiple Reentry Vehicle (MRV) ballistic missile to be deployed. Five U.S. submarines carried the A-1 (SSBN 598–602), 13 submarines carried the A-2 (SSBN 608–611, 616–620, 622–625), and 23 submarines were originally fitted with the A-3 (SSBN 626–636, 640–645, 654–659). The first 18 submarines were subsequently rearmed with A-3 missiles (with several later being rearmed with Poseidon C-3, and some of those with Trident C-4 missiles; see below).

The Royal Navy procured the A-3 variant which, fitted with a British warhead, entered service in June 1968 when the submarine RESOLUTION began the first British SSBN patrol. The Chevaline A3TK variant is being phased out of British service in favor of the Trident C-4 SLBM.

See 12th Edition/pages 336–37 for characteristics.

POSEIDON (C-3) UGM-73

The Poseidon SLBM, derived from the Polaris missile, had an increased strike capability through a Multiple Independently targeted Reentry Vehicle (MIRV) warhead, the first strategic missile of any nation to have that feature. The Poseidon MIRV could carry up to 14 RVs, with 8 to 10 being a common loadout. The RVs could be directed at specific targets within range of the warhead's "footprint." The missile range was reduced when the larger numbers of RVs were carried.

Going to sea in 1971, the Poseidon replaced the Polaris A-2 and A-3 missiles in the 31 LAFAYETTE (SSBN 616)-class submarines. Subsequently, 12 submarines of that class were upgraded to fire the Trident C-4 missile. The Poseidon patrols were terminated on 1 October 1991 when two submarines were taken off alert status; they returned to port on 15–16 October 1991. A total of 1,182 submarine patrols were carried out with Poseidon missiles from 1971 to 1991.

See 14th Edition/page 473 for characteristics.

RAM RIM-116A

The Rolling Airframe Missile (RAM) is a rapid-reaction, short-range missile for shipboard defense using off-the-shelf components. The RAM is the first U.S. Navy shipboard fire-and-forget missile and the only Navy missile that rolls (i.e., is not stabilized) in flight.

Design: The RAM has the infrared seeker from the Army's Stinger missile and the rocket motor, fuze, and warhead from the Sidewinder AAM. The RAM is also provided with multi-mode guidance. The missile is supersonic.

The complete RAM round consists of the RIM-116A missile and the Ex-8 sealed canister, together designated Ex-44. The RAM missile is fired from a 24-missile Mk 49 launcher. The launcher uses the mount and elevation/train assemblies from the Phalanx CIWS. The launcher is reloaded by hand.

It had been proposed to also fire the missile from two of the eight cells of the NATO Sea Sparrow launcher (five missiles per cell).

Status: Operational; in production. IOC was in 1992.

The Ex-31/Mk 49 launcher was evaluated in the destroyer DAVID R. RAY (DD 971) in the late 1980s. The first two production launchers were installed in the helicopter carrier PELELIU (LHA 5) in 1992 (the Sea Sparrow launchers were removed). The Navy plans to provide 50 ships with one or two RAM launchers.

The missile is also fitted in German small combatants.

A RAM is fired from the 24-missile launcher evaluated in the destroyer DAVID R. RAY. The missile encountered major development problems but is now being installed in U.S. ships. (General Dynamics/Pomona)

Manufacturer:	General Dynamics/Pomona
Weight:	162 lbs (73.5 kg)
Length:	9 ft 2 in (2.79 m)
Span:	1 ft 5 in (434 mm)
Diameter:	5 in (127 mm)
Propulsion:	solid-propellant rocket
Range:	approx. 5 n.miles (9 km)
Guidance:	passive RF acquisition + mid-course guidance with IR terminal or passive RF all the way
Warhead:	25 lbs (11.3 kg) high explosive
Platforms:	*destroyers* DD 963 (planned)
	amphibious ships LHD 1 (some units)
	LHA 1
	LSD 41

SEA LANCE UUM-125B

Formerly the ASW Stand-Off Weapon (SOW), the Sea Lance was to be a long-range ASW weapon. It has been canceled.

The weapon was conceived of as a common ship/submarine–launched weapon and, subsequently, a submarine-only weapon. It was to mate a rocket booster with a Mk 50 anti-submarine torpedo. Although often labeled a successor to SUBROC, the Sea Lance was to initially have only a conventional (torpedo) warhead, whereas the SUBROC carried only a nuclear depth bomb. A conventional (Mk 50) warhead would have inhibited its use at longer ranges because of the limited target localization capability of the Mk 50. Plans to provide a nuclear warhead for Sea Lance were considered but never funded.

The Sea Lance was designed for attacks out to the third sonar Convergence Zone (CZ), i.e., approximately 90 to 100 n.miles (167 to 185 km). When fitted with the conventional Mk 50 torpedo the effective range would probably have been only the first CZ (i.e., some 30 to 35 n.miles/55.6 to 65 km). The weapon was to be stowed and launched from a standard 21-inch torpedo tube in a canister, much like the Harpoon anti-ship missile and the CAPTOR encapsulated mine. When the capsule reached the surface, the missile booster was to ignite, launching the missile on a ballistic trajectory toward the target area. At a designated point the torpedo would separate from the booster, would be slowed to reenter the water, and would seek out the hostile submarine.

The technical and program difficulties proved too great for a dual surface/submarine–launched weapon, and the surface-launched weapon evolved into the Vertical-Launch ASROC (VLA). Subsequently, technical difficulties led to complete cancellation of the project.

The Navy's procurement goal for Sea Lance was some 2,400 missiles.

Name: Boeing had used the name Seahawk for the weapon before the Navy designated it Sea Lance.

See 15th Edition/page 474 for characteristics.

SEA SPARROW RIM-7

The Sea Sparrow is a modification of the Sparrow AAM employed as an anti-ship missile defense system. The concept was developed in the 1960s to counter the threat from Soviet anti-ship weapons and is fired from the eight-cell Mk 25 box launcher of the Basic Point Defense Missile System (BPDMS) or the Mk 29 launcher of the NATO Sea Sparrow Missile (NSSM). The RIM-7M and RIM-7P missiles are currently used in this role.

The RIM-7R Evolved Sea Sparrow Missile (ESSM) is now being developed for VLS in U.S. ships. A four-pack ESSM canister would be fitted in each standard missile tube.

The Sea Sparrow launchers are not fitted in ships that have Standard missile capabilities. The Mk 25/29 launchers are not automatically reloaded, and many ships do not have reloads on board. Several foreign navies use vertical-launch systems for the Sea Sparrow. A compact jet vane control unit is attached to the rear of the missile for VLS launching. This device has four independent jet vanes that interact with the rocket exhaust plume to provide initial pitch-over, roll, and slew of the missile. Once the missile has achieved the proper heading for intercept and speed for normal fin control, the vane unit is jettisoned through the activation of four explosive bolts.

Design: The Sea Sparrow launchers are derived from the ASROC box launcher.

The Mk 91 missile FCS is used with the NSSM, the Mk 115 with the BPDMS. Beginning in 1980 the Mk 23 Target Acquisition System (TAS) was added to the NSSM on U.S. ships to provide a self-contained system (with TAS providing a dual-mode radar and digital processor for automatic threat detection).

The RIM-7P has a combined semi-active radar homing and infrared seeker package.

Operational: The carrier SARATOGA (CV 60) accidently launched two Sea Sparrow missiles during an exercise in the Aegean Sea on 1 October 1992. One missile struck the Turkish destroyer MAUVENET, killing five men (including the commanding officer) and injuring at least 14 others. Initial reports cited personnel failures as the cause of the accidental launches. There were no U.S. casualties in the firing.

Status: Operational. IOC was in 1969; IOC for the RIM-7M was in 1983. The Sea Sparrow launchers have been removed from several U.S. amphibious and command ships.

Thirteen other navies employ the Sea Sparrow in the missile-defense role; some ships have been armed with vertical-launch Sea Sparrow launchers.

The following data apply to the RIM-7M. See listing for Sparrow missile for additional data.

Manufacturer:	Raytheon
Weight:	450 lbs (204 kg)
Length:	12 ft (3.7 m)
Span:	3 ft 4 in (1.0 m)
Diameter:	8 in (203 mm)
Propulsion:	solid-propellant rocket
Range:	approx. 10 n.miles (18.5 km)
Guidance:	radar homing
Warhead:	90 lbs (40.8 kg) high explosive
Platforms:	*aircraft carriers* CV/CVN
	destroyers DD 963
	amphibious ships LHD 1
	LHA 1
	LPH 2
	auxiliaries AOE 1
	AOR 1

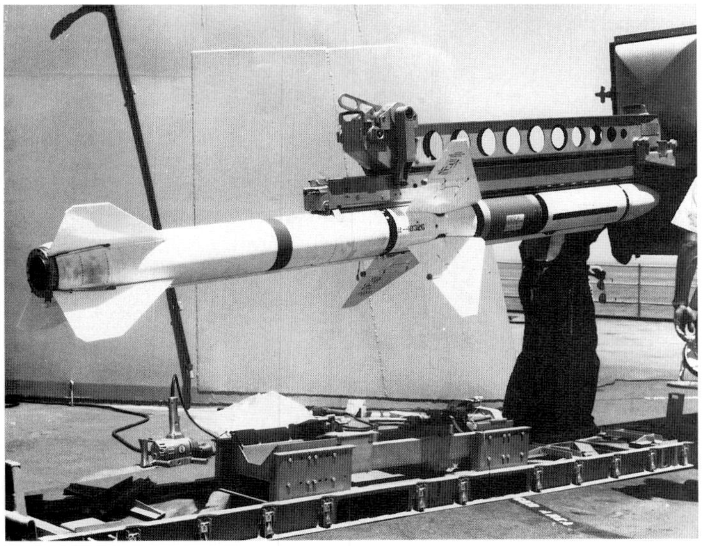

A Sea Sparrow missile is loaded into a launcher on board the replenishment ship KANSAS CITY (AOR 3). No ships have automatic reloading for their Sea Sparrow missiles. (U.S. Navy)

A NATO Sea Sparrow launcher on the carrier NIMITZ (CVN 68) launches a missile during an exercise in the fall of 1995. (U.S. Navy, PH2 Brian Aliffi)

SHRIKE AGM-45

The Shrike was an anti-radar missile designed to home on hostile radar emissions. The missile was derived from the AIM-7 Sparrow for the U.S. Navy and was used in the Vietnam War from 1964 onward. The Royal Air Force used Shrike missiles (ineffectively) in the 1982 Falklands conflict. More than a dozen variants reflect changes in the guidance seeker to counter different electronic threats. The Shrike suffered from a short range and in the mid-1980s was replaced by the HARM.

See 14th Edition/page 476 for characteristics.

SIAM (SELF-INITIATING ANTI-AIRCRAFT MISSILE)

The Advanced Research Projects Agency (ARPA) sponsored the development of technology for the SIAM for use from a submerged submarine against an ASW fixed-wing aircraft or helicopter. The weapon was to be launched from special tubes in the submarine and home on the attacking aircraft. The towed acoustic arrays now used by submarines could detect low-flying aircraft to initiate SIAM launch.

The concept was not new; one earlier U.S. Navy experiment using variants of the Sidewinder missile was dubbed "Subwinder." The Royal Navy and Vickers have developed the SLAM (Submarine-Launched Air Missile) in which the submarine surfaces or at least broaches her sail to extend a six-tube Blowpipe missile launcher. The SIAM concept calls for missile launch while the submarine remains completely submerged.

During demonstrations, test vehicles were successfully launched against QH-50 drone helicopters. No deployment occurred.

See 14th Edition/page 476 for characteristics.

SIDEARM AGM-122

The Sidearm is an anti-radar missile developed to counter ground-based air-defense weapons at short ranges. The missile is based on the outdated AIM-9 Sidewinder AAMs that had been placed in storage in the 1970s.

Design: The missiles have been fitted with a relatively broad band, passive-only, radar-homing plus active optical target-detection device from the AIM-9L missile. These, in turn, have been refitted with newer, in-production rocket motors, warhead, and fins.

Upon launch the Sidearm executes a pitch-up maneuver that permits launch from very-low altitudes, an important feature for helicopters flying in the nap-of-the-earth mode. It can be used by essentially all fixed-wing fighter and aircraft. Maximum speed is Mach 2.3.

The Sidearm was developed by the missile-prolific Naval Weapons Center at China Lake, California. Motorola converted several hundred AIM-9 missiles to the Sidearm configuration; future new production is envisioned. An improved AGM-122B version was canceled because of funding problems. The first production/remade Sidewinders were funded in fiscal 1986.

Status: Operational.

Manufacturer:	Motorola (Tempe, Ariz.)
Weight:	approx. 200 lbs (90.7 kg)
Length:	9 ft 6 in (2.9 m)
Span:	2 ft 1 in (635 mm)
Diameter:	5 in (127 mm)
Propulsion:	solid-propellant rocket motor
Range:	18,000 yds (16,463 m)
Guidance:	radar homing + electro-optical
Warhead:	10 lb (4.5 kg) high-explosive fragmentation
Platforms:	*helicopters* AH-1W

Sidearm anti-radar missile fitted on an AH-1 SeaCobra helicopter. (U.S. Navy)

SIDEWINDER AIM-9

The Sidewinder is the most widely used missile outside of Russia: several hundred thousand missiles have been produced for 37 nations in addition to the United States. The air-to-air weapon was used extensively by the U.S. Navy in the Vietnam War, as well as by Allied forces in other conflicts. In the 1991 Persian Gulf War it was responsible for 24 percent of the air-to-air kills (see below).

Design: Developed by the naval research center at China Lake, California, the Sidewinder is a simple, effective, infrared-homing missile. The AIM-9M version is currently in production in the United States, although the AIM-9L is being built by a European consortium and by Mitsubishi in Japan. The AIM-9M features improved resistance to electronic countermeasures and can engage targets against hot backgrounds. The guidance includes digital electronics, electronic reprograming for future software upgrades, imaging, and autotracking. In 1991 the Department of Defense approved full-scale development of the AIM-9R until additional upgrades become available in a variant known as AIM-9X. AIM-9 series missile speed is approximately Mach 2.5.

In late 1995 the Department of Defense schedule called for an IOC of the AIM-9X and its associated helmet-mounted sight of 2002. The AIM-9X budget has remained intact, while other missile programs have been cut back or canceled in the early post–Cold War era. The viability of the AIM-9X program has been due in large part to the appearance of the Russian AA-11 Archer missile with its helmet-mounted sight, which gave Russian fighters a significant advantag over the U.S. F-15 Eagle armed with the AIM-9M missile. (The AA-11 was first seen by Western observers—carried by the MiG-29 Fulcrum fighter—in 1985; its Russian designation is R-73 Vympel.)

The AIM-9X is an "off-boresight" missile with improved Infrared Counter-Countermeasures (IRCCM); its seeker is intended to acquire targets out to 90°.

An AIM-9C with a modified anti-radar seeker is called Sidearm (see page 452).

Operational: The Sidewinder scored most of the air-to-air kills by U.S. Navy and Air Force aircraft in the Vietnam War and by the Israeli Air Force in the 1967 and 1973 wars in the Middle East. During the 1982 fighting over Lebanon's Bekaa Valley, Israeli aircraft used Sidewinders to shoot down 51 of 55 Syrian-flown MiG aircraft destroyed in aerial combat. The Sidewinder was also highly successful when used by British Harrier VSTOL aircraft in the 1982 Falklands conflict.

In the 1991 Gulf War, Sidewinders were responsible for 12 air-to-air kills against Iraqi aircraft, two of which were by Navy fighters: on 17 January 1991 a MiG-21 was downed by a Navy F/A-18 Hornet,[10] and on 6 February 1991 an Mi-8 Hip helicopter was downed by a Navy F-14A Tomcat. (In addition, eight Iraqi high-performance aircraft were downed by U.S. Air Force F-15C Eagles and two by Saudi F-15Cs firing Sidewinder missiles.)

Status: Operational. IOC was in 1956; IOC for the AIM-9M was in 1983. More than 125,000 missiles have been produced for all users.

10. On the same mission this F/A-18 also shot down a second MiG-21 with a Sparrow missile.

AIM-9M Sidewinder missiles on the carrier George Washington await loading onto aircraft. Protective nose cones are fitted; they are bright yellow to avoid being inadvertently left on when a plane is cleared for takeoff. The basic Sidewinder design has been in service for 40 years! (U.S. Navy, Kris White)

The AIM-9X version is in joint development by the Navy and Air Force.

The data below are for the AIM-9L variant, except where noted.

Manufacturer:	Raytheon and Ford Aerospace	
Weight:	88 lbs (40 kg) for AIM-9H	
	86½ lbs (39 kg) for AIM-9L/M	
Length:	9 ft 6 in (2.87 m)	
Span:	2 ft ¾ in (0.63 m) for AIM-9H	
	2 ft 1 in (0.635 m) for AIM-9L/M	
Diameter:	5 in (127 mm)	
Propulsion:	solid-propellant rocket	
Range:	approx. 10 n.miles (18.5 km)	
Guidance:	infrared passive homing	
Warhead:	25 lbs (11.3 kg) high explosive for AIM-9H	
	20.8 lbs (9.4 kg) high explosive for AIM-9L/M	
Platforms:	*aircraft*	A-6E
		AV-8B
		F-14
		F/A-18
	helicopters	AH-1W

A Sidewinder is launched by a TA-4J Skyhawk from Fleet Composite Squadron (VC) 10. (U.S. Navy)

SKIPPER II AGM-123A

The Skipper was a laser-guided propelled bomb made up of off-the-shelf components. Created by the Naval Weapons Center, the Skipper II was an effort to produce a low-cost weapon with a short development time for the air-to-surface role. This weapon was carried by the A-7E Corsair and A-6E Intruder, both of which have been phased out of service. (See 15th Edition/page 494 for characteristics.)

Design: The missile used a 1,000-pound warhead from a Mk 83 general-purpose bomb and the propulsion motor of the Shrike ARM; the laser guidance and control sections are from the Air Force Paveway II (unpowered) laser-guided bomb.

Status: Operational. IOC was in 1985.

First launch tests of the Skipper were conducted between June and November 1984, and the first production models were delivered to the Navy in July 1985.

SLAM (STAND-OFF LAND-ATTACK MISSILE) AGM-84E

The SLAM is a derivative of the Harpoon anti-ship missile. It is intended for use by carrier-based aircraft in "surgical strikes" against high-value fixed targets or enemy ships at sea and is considered the most accurate air-to-surface weapon in the Navy's arsenal.

SLAM has the airframe, propulsion, and control systems of the Harpoon missile, with a combination of existing missile guidance systems: the Maverick IIR (Imaging Infrared) seeker, Walleye II data link, and Global Positioning System (GPS) receiver/processor. The missile's inertial guidance system is updated in flight by GPS fixes to ensure that the infrared seeker is pointed directly at the target. When the infrared seeker is activated, it sends a video image to the launching aircraft, which selects the specific aim point for the missile. After the target is locked in, the missile steers to the target. The missile can be controlled by an aircraft other than the launching plane.

The SLAM-ER (Expanded Response—*not* Extended Range) has a 50 percent increase in range that is accomplished by planar wings, an improved warhead for penetrating hardened targets, and an improved data link that increases stand-off range of the controlling aircraft by 100 percent and enhances resistance to jamming. It has a speed of Mach 0.8.

SLAM is intended for aerial launch as well as shipboard launch from canisters or VLS installations.

SLAM-ER kits are being used to upgrade the basic SLAM weapons. A further improvement of the Harpoon/SLAM weapon has been proposed by McDonnell Douglas, whose officials call it the "Grand Slam." The range of this variant is on the order of 185 n.miles (343 km) while carrying a 1,000-pound (454-kg) warhead.

The data provided below show the air-launched configuration for SLAM-ER; a solid-propellant rocket booster is added for shipboard launch.

Operational: The SLAM was first used in combat from A-6E Intruder and F/A-18 Hornet aircraft, controlled by A-7E Corsair attack aircraft using AAW-9 pods. The seven SLAMs used in the Gulf War all struck their targets, with the infrared video providing verification of their accuracy. This was achieved despite the unreliability of the AAW-9 data-link pods (since replaced by the improved AAW-13 pods).

In a March 1995 test, four SLAM missiles were launched simultaneously by four F/A-18C Hornets; all struck the single target.

Status: Operational; in production. IOC was in November 1988.

Manufacturer:	McDonnell Douglas
Weight:	SLAM 1,385 lbs (628 kg)
	SLAM-ER 1,600 lbs (727 kg)
Length:	14 ft 4 in (4.37 m)
Span:	SLAM 3 ft (0.9 m)
	SLAM-ER 7 ft 11½ in (2.4 m)
Diameter:	13½ in (343 mm)
Propulsion:	turbojet (Teledyne CAE J402-CA-400); 600 lbst (272 kgst)
Range:	SLAM approx. 50 n.miles (92.65 km)
	SLAM-ER approx. 75 n.miles (105.6 km)
Guidance:	inertial + infrared/video command homing
Warhead:	510 lbs (231 kg) high explosive
Platforms:	*aircraft* F/A-18

A SLAM is launched from a shipboard canister. A derivative of the Harpoon missile, it was—like the Harpoon—originally developed for air launch. An additional section with fins is added for shipboard launch. (McDonnell Douglas)

A mockup of the SLAM-ER advanced air-to-surface missile. The missile has large gull wings and cruciform tail fins. (McDonnell Douglas)

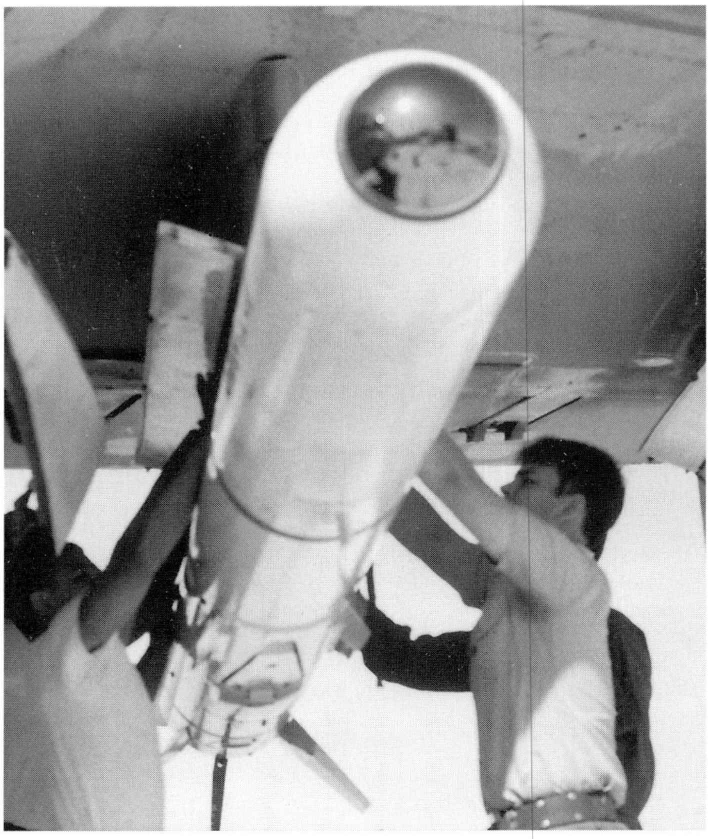

An air-launched SLAM is fitted to an aircraft pylon. Note the infrared seeker in the missile's nose. (McDonnell Douglas)

An artist's concept of the SLAM-ER missile in flight. Note the large guidance window and the wing and tail configuration. (McDonnell Douglas)

SPARROW III AIM-7

The Sparrow is an all-weather, medium-range AAM. It has been adopted for surface launch in the Sea Sparrow variants for use in the anti-ship missile defense role (see page 451).

Design: The AIM-7M combines the heavy warhead and large rocket motor introduced in the AIM-7F with an advanced monopulse seeker, better look-down/shoot-down capability, and improved resistance to ECM. The early, expanding continuous-rod warhead of these missiles has been replaced by a fragmentation warhead.

The AIM-7R is the latest variant, combining infrared terminal guidance with semi-active radar guidance (the latter was fitted in earlier versions).

Missile speed is reportedly in excess of Mach 4.

Operational: The weapon had minimal use in air-to-air engagements until the 1991 war in the Persian Gulf, when it was credited

A Sparrow III is launched from an F-4 Phantom. Sparrows scored 26 of the 38 air-to-air missile kills in the Gulf War. (U.S. Navy)

with 68 percent of the air-to-air kills—28 of the 41 air-to-air kills against Iraqi aircraft. Only two of those kills were credited to the Navy: on 17 January 1991, an Iraqi MiG-21 was shot down by a Sparrow from a Navy F/A-18 Hornet, which, in the same engagement, used a Sidewinder to kill a second MiG-21. (U.S. Air Force F-15C Eagles used Sidewinders to shoot down 22 high-performance Iraqi aircraft and 3 helicopters; in addition, one Saudi F-15C Eagle used Sparrows to kill two Iraqi fighters in the same engagement.[11]) The USAF hit rate for Sparrows fired was nearly triple the rate in the Vietnam War.

Status: Operational. IOC was in 1958; AIM-7F IOC was in 1976; AIM-7M IOC was in 1983.

The AIM-7E/F/M variants are in wide U.S. Marine Corps and Navy service, although production of those variants has ended.

The missile has been produced for U.S. and foreign air forces. In addition to the two U.S. producers, the Sparrow is manufactured in Japan by Mitsubishi. The data given below are for the AIM-7M model, except where indicated.

Manufacturer:	Raytheon and General Dynamics/Pomona
Weight:	508 lbs (230 kg)
Length:	12 ft (3.7 m)
Span:	3 ft 4 in (1.1 m)
Diameter:	8 in (203 mm)
Propulsion:	solid-propellant rocket
Range:	approx. 30 n.miles (55.5 km)
Guidance:	semi-active radar homing (plus infrared in AIM-7R)
Warhead:	85 lbs (39 kg) high explosive with continuous rod
Platforms:	*aircraft* F-14
	F/A-18

11. In addition to the 28 Sparrow and 10 Sidewinder air-to-air kills, one Iraqi MiG-29 crashed while maneuvering to escape a USAF F-15C, and two Iraqi helicopters were shot down by USAF A-10 Thunderbolt (Warthog) attack aircraft using 30-mm Gatling guns, for a total of 41 air-to-air kills in the Gulf War.

STANDARD SM-1 MR RIM-66B

The Standard series of missiles is the principal surface-to-air weapon of U.S. cruisers, destroyers, and frigates. The Standard series was developed to replace the 3-T missiles—the Talos, Terrier, and Tartar. Initially, the MR (Medium Range) missiles were to replace the Tartar and the ER (Extended Range) missiles the Terrier and Talos. However, various modifications and production blocks with varying characteristics of Standard missiles have blurred model distinctions.

Standard missiles are currently in use by the U.S. Navy and nine other navies.

The SM-1 MR is a single-stage missile, replacing the Tartar SAM. It is launched only from the Mk 13 launcher, which has a 40-round vertical magazine.

Design: The Block VI is the current production variant, using the SM-2 monopulse seeker for better resistance to enemy jamming and improved fuzing. It can engage low-altitude targets at ranges out to about ten n.miles (18.5 km).

Status: Operational; Block VI is in production. IOC was in 1970.

Manufacturer:	General Dynamics/Pomona and Hughes-Raytheon
Weight:	1,378 lbs (625 kg)
Length:	14 ft 9 in (4.47 m)
Span:	3 ft 6 in (1.1 m)
Diameter:	13½ in (342 mm)
Propulsion:	solid-propellant rocket
Range:	25 n.miles (46 km)
Guidance:	semi-active radar homing
Warhead:	high explosive
Platforms:	*cruisers* CGN 36
	frigates FFG 7

A Standard MR missile is launched from the VLS of a TICONDEROGA (CG 47)-class cruiser. (United Defense/FMC)

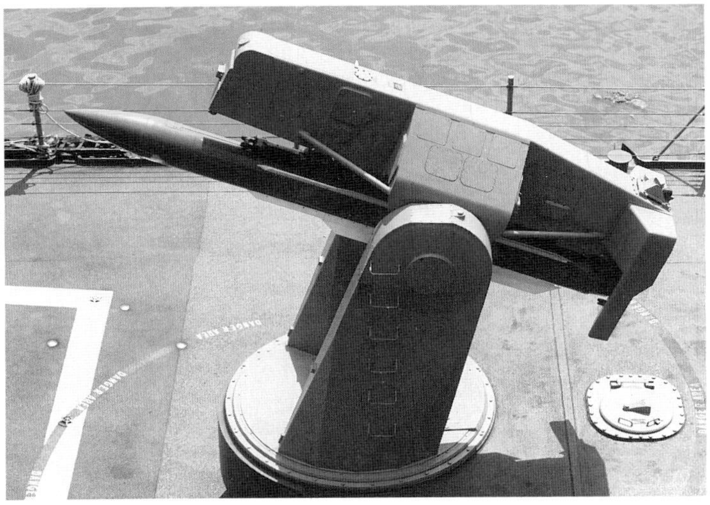

A Standard MR missile on the Mk 13 launcher of the frigate Stephen W. Groves (FFG 29). A missile loading hatch for the circular magazine is visible at right. (Giorgio Arra)

STANDARD SM-2 MR RIM-66C

This missile has an increased range over the SM-1 MR as well as the addition of mid-course guidance and enhanced resistance to electronic countermeasures. It is intended specifically for use on Aegis missile ships.

Design: The Block IV variant provides significantly increased performance over all previous versions of the Standard. It is launched with a solid-propellant booster rocket.

The traditional expanding, continuous-rod warheads of the Standard missiles have been succeeded by controlled fragmentation warheads.

The Block IVA missile is configured for use in the Theater Ballistic Missile Defense (TBMD) role.

Status: Operational; in production. IOC was in 1981. The first at-sea firing of the SM-2 Block IV occurred in July 1994 from the Lake Erie (CG 70). IOC was in 1995. Block III entered production in 1988; Block IV is currently in production.

Manufacturer:	General Dynamics/Pomona and Hughes-Raytheon	
Weight:	1,554 lbs (705 kg)	
Length:	15 ft 6 in (4.72 m) + booster	
Span:	3 ft 6 in (1.1 m)	
Diameter:	13½ in (342 mm)	
Propulsion:	solid-propellant rocket	
Range:	approx. 40 n.miles (74 km)	
Guidance:	semi-active radar homing	
Warhead:	high explosive	
Platforms:	*cruisers*	CG 47
		CGN 38
	destroyers	DDG 51
		DDG 993

STANDARD SM-2 ER RIM-67B

The SM-2 ER version of the Standard has extended range, mid-course guidance, an inertial reference system, and improved resistance to electronic countermeasures compared to earlier missiles. This missile is now carried in the U.S. Navy only by the four destroyers of the Kidd (DDG 993) class, being launched from their Mk 26 launcher systems.

Design: This is the largest missile of the Standard series. It is a two-stage missile that can reach an altitude of approximately 80,000 feet (24,390 m). Approval to develop a missile with the W81 nuclear warhead—designated SM-2(N)—was given in 1979 but canceled in 1985.

The Block III incorporated low-altitude intercept enhancements; the Block IV had a new booster rocket motor with guidance, control, and airframe changes.

Status: Operational. IOC was in 1981. Production of the less capable SM-1 ER missile ended in 1974. The SM-2 ER Block III entered production in 1988, Block IV in 1991. All of these missiles are no longer in production.

Manufacturer:	General Dynamics/Pomona and Hughes-Raytheon	
Weight:	3,705 lbs (1,680 kg)	
Length:	26 ft 2 in (7.98 m)	
Span:	5 ft 3 in (1.6 m)	
Diameter:	13½ in (342 mm)	
Propulsion:	solid-propellant rocket + solid-propellant booster	
Range:	75–90 n.miles (139–167 km)	
Guidance:	inertial, with semi-active radar homing	
Warhead:	high explosive	
Platforms:	*destroyers*	DDG 993

Standard ER missiles are loaded onto a Mk 10 launcher on the destroyer Farragut (DDG 37). The missiles were carried in horizontal circular magazines, similar to the later Mk 26 arrangement. The angled fittings on the deck are for jettisoning dud missiles. (Giorgio Arra)

STANDARD SM-3

A Standard SM-3 missile was considered to provide a very-long-range missile for intercepting Soviet stand-off jamming aircraft and possibly missile-carrying aircraft at ranges greater than those possible with the SM-2 ER. This was similar in concept to the LRDMM (see above); a concept called Thor was similar. They were not pursued.

STANDARD-ARM AGM-78

This was an Anti-Radiation Missile (ARM) adopted from the Standard RIM-66A Surface-to-Air Missile. It was also employed briefly by the U.S. Navy as an interim surface-to-surface missile pending availability of the Harpoon. In the mid-1980s the Standard-ARM was replaced by the HARM.

STINGER FIM-92

The Stinger is an advanced, shoulder-held surface-to-air missile that resembles the World War II–era bazooka rocket launcher. The missile was placed aboard several U.S. naval ships in the eastern Mediterranean beginning in the winter of 1983–1984 in reaction to threatened terrorist attacks against U.S. ships; it was subsequently carried in Navy ships operating in the Persian Gulf area. (The Russian Navy similarly uses the shoulder-held SA-7 Grail missile, formerly Strela, in various ships.)

Design: Originally designated Redeye II, the missile is tube-launched, with four pop-out vanes at the front and four folding fins at the rear.

Status: Operational. IOC was in 1981. The Stinger is used by the U.S. Marine Corps, Army, and Air Force, as well as by several foreign services. The missile is replacing the Redeye in U.S. service. An improved Stinger-Post (Passive Optical Seeker Technique), with increased resistance to countermeasures, entered production in fiscal 1984.

A Stinger missile in flight with its wings extended. (U.S. Army)

A Stinger shoulder-fired missile. (U.S. Army)

Manufacturer:	General Dynamics/Pomona
Weight:	34.5 lbs (13.6 kg)
Length:	5 ft (1.5 m)
Span:	8 in (203 mm)
Diameter:	2¾ in (70 mm)
Propulsion:	solid-propellant rocket
Range:	approx. 3 n.miles (5.5 km); effective range is probably less
Guidance:	infrared homing
Warhead:	6.6 lbs (3 kg)
Platforms:	various ships

SUBROC UUM-44A

The SUBROC (Submarine Rocket) was a rocket-propelled nuclear depth bomb that could be launched from standard 21-inch submarine torpedo tubes. The weapon was analog and hence not compatible with U.S. attack submarines having the Mk 117 digital fire-control system. Thus, only about 25 submarines of the PERMIT (SSN 594) and later classes fitted with the Mk 113 fire-control system carried the weapon. The missile, which became operational in 1984, was taken out of Navy service in 1989. (The Sea Lance ASW stand-off weapon was to have replaced the SUBROC, with alternative nuclear or conventional warheads, but in the event the nuclear variant is no longer planned for development.)

See 14th Edition/pages 481–82 for characteristics.

TOMAHAWK BGM-109

The Tomahawk is a long-range cruise missile developed for both surface and submarine launch against surface ship and land targets. It was initially known as the Sea-Launched Cruise Missile (SLCM), but in 1979 the Navy began using the terms Tomahawk Land-Attack Missile (TLAM) and Tomahawk Anti-Ship Missile (TASM) to distinguish the principal variants.

The TASM is scheduled to be phased out of the fleet when the Block IV Tomahawk Multi-Mission Missile (TMMM) comes into the Fleet after the year 2000. That weapon will have a common terminal sensor that is capable of attacking targets on land and at sea.

The missile has been deployed in Armored Box Launchers (ABL) on four battleships, five cruisers, and seven SPRUANCE-class destroyers; it is carried in the vertical launchers (Mk 41) of later TICONDEROGA-class cruisers, BURKE-class destroyers, and most of the SPRUANCES. It can also be fired from 21-inch submarine torpedo tubes and, in the later LOS ANGELES (SSN 688) class, from vertical launch tubes.

Design: The Block III version now in production features a smaller but more lethal warhead with an extended range permitted by additional fuel. These missiles also have a GPS receiver for improved accuracy and time-of-arrival control to permit coordinated missile or aircraft and missile strikes. That variant also has a Williams 402 turbofan engine with a 19 percent increase in thrust and a 2 percent decrease in fuel consumption.

The Navy variants are:

Mode	Launch mode	Type	Warhead
BGM-109A	ship/submarine	TLAM(N)	nuclear (W80 warhead)
BGM-109B	ship/submarine	TASM	conventional (1,000-lb Bullpup)
BGM-109C	ship/submarine	TLAM-C	conventional (1,000-lb Bullpup)
BGM-109D	ship/submarine	TLAM-D	conventional (bomblets) or fiber spools

The TLAM-D dispenses 166 bomblets, each weighing 3.4 pounds (1.5 kg), in packets of 24. These submunitions can be armor-piercing, fragmentation, or incendiary.

In April 1992 it was revealed that a warhead containing carbon-fiber spools had also been developed for the Tomahawk. Several of the 116 missiles fired on the first day of the Gulf War carried the

During the Gulf War two U.S. attack submarines fired a total of 12 Tomahawk missiles against land targets in Iraq. This series shows a TLAM launch from the PITTSBURGH (SSN 720), photographed through a periscope. Clockwise from upper left: A missile emerges from the water; the missile clears the water; the wings, fins, and air scoop begin to deploy; and the missile streaks toward its target. (U.S. Navy)

still-experimental warheads which, upon detonation, disrupted Iraqi electric power, helping to blind air-defense and command-and-control activities.

The warhead, developed under a highly classified "black" program, showered outdoor switching and transformer areas of electric generating plants with thousands of rolls of very fine carbon fibers. When released by the Tomahawks, the fiber spools unwound in the wind and the fibers then dropped onto power lines and transformers, causing massive short circuits but not permanent damage. Reportedly, each Tomahawk could spread thousands of the mini-spools over a single target when the warhead detonated to spread the spools. (They were not "dispensed" as are the BLU-97 bomblets; see below.) Accuracy of the TLAM missile is on the order of 33 feet (ten meters); GPS and other guidance modifications should improve this significantly in the Block IV missile.

General Dynamics has proposed an ASW variant of the Tomahawk as an alternative to the Sea Lance project (for both surface ship and submarine use).

An air-launched Tomahawk competed unsuccessfully with the Boeing Air-Launched Cruise Missile (ALCM) for use on B-52 strategic bombers. The Ground-Launched Cruise Missile (GLCM) version, however, was selected as a theater nuclear weapon for deployment in Western Europe under Air Force control, but those weapons were discarded under the Intermediate-range Nuclear Forces (INF) treaty.

The TLAM(N), fitted with the W80 nuclear warhead, has been removed from ships (see page 464).

In late 1983 McDonnell Douglas was selected as a second source to produce the missile.

Operational: The U.S. Navy fired 288 Tomahawks in the 1991 Gulf War—276 from surface combatants and 12 from submarines (see individual ship classes for launching ships and number fired). Of the 288 missiles, approximately 80 percent were daylight attacks and 20 percent night attacks. Of those missiles, 282 transitioned to a cruise profile for a successful launch rate of 98 percent. Reportedly, the Iraqis recovered one Tomahawk virtually intact.

Tomahawks were employed both to destroy or specifically damage targets (in addition to the microwave warhead being used for electronic disruption activities). The TLAM-D missiles carried BLU-97 bomblets and were able to attack multiple targets; for example, one submarine-launched TLAM-D struck three separate targets and then performed a terminal dive to strike a fourth target.

According to the official Department of Defense report on the Gulf War, the Tomahawk's "demonstrated accuracy was consistent with results from pre-combat testing. The observed accuracy of TLAM, for which unambiguous target imagery is available, met or exceeded the accuracy mission planners predicted."

During the conflict an estimated 477 TLAMs were available in theater.

On 17 January 1993 three destroyers launched another 45 missiles (plus one that failed to launch) at targets in Iraq. On 26 June 1993 an additional 23 missiles (plus one that failed to launch) were fired at Iraqi targets by a cruiser and a destroyer.

Tomahawk missiles were used in the Bosnian conflict on the night of 10 September 1995, when the cruiser NORMANDY (CG 60) fired 13 TLAMs against Serbian air defense positions around Banja Luka. One missile did not function properly. The NORMANDY launch came after another surface ship and the submarine OKLAHOMA CITY (SSN 723) were unable to fire Tomahawks because of equipment malfunctions.

Status: Operational; in production. IOC for TASM in surface ships was in 1982; for TASM in submarines 1983; for TLAM in surface ships 1984; for TLAM(N) 1987.

A Tomahawk cruise missile was successfully launched from the submarine BARB (SSN 696) on 1 February 1978; the GUITARRO (SSN 665) was the first submarine armed with Tomahawk. The MERRILL (DD 976) was fitted with the first Tomahawk installation in October 1982 for at-sea evaluation; the battleship NEW JERSEY (BB 62) was the second ship, receiving the Tomahawk in March 1983.

Manufacturer:	General Dynamics/Convair and McDonnell Douglas	
Weight:	2,650 lbs (1,200 kg) + 550-lb (250-kg) booster + 1,000-lb (454-kg) capsule for submarine launch	
Length:	18 ft 2 in (5.55 m) for TASM + 2 ft (0.6 m) booster	
Span:	8 ft 8 in (2.6 m)	
Diameter:	21 in (533 mm)	
Propulsion:	turbofan + solid-propellant booster	
Range:	TASM	250+ n.miles (463+ km)
	TLAM	750+ n.miles (1,390+ km)
	TLAM(N)	1,200+ n.miles (2,225+ km)
Guidance:	active radar homing in TASM (same as Harpoon SSM)	
	inertial and TERCOM (Terrain Contour Matching) in TLAM	
Warhead:	1,000 lbs (454 kg) high explosive in TASM and TLAM	
Platforms:	*attack submarines*	SSN 637
		SSN 688
		SSN 21
	cruisers	CGN 38
		CG 52–73
	destroyers	DDG 51
		DD 963

A Tomahawk in flight with stub wings, air scoop for turbofan engine, and tail fins fully extended. (U.S. Navy)

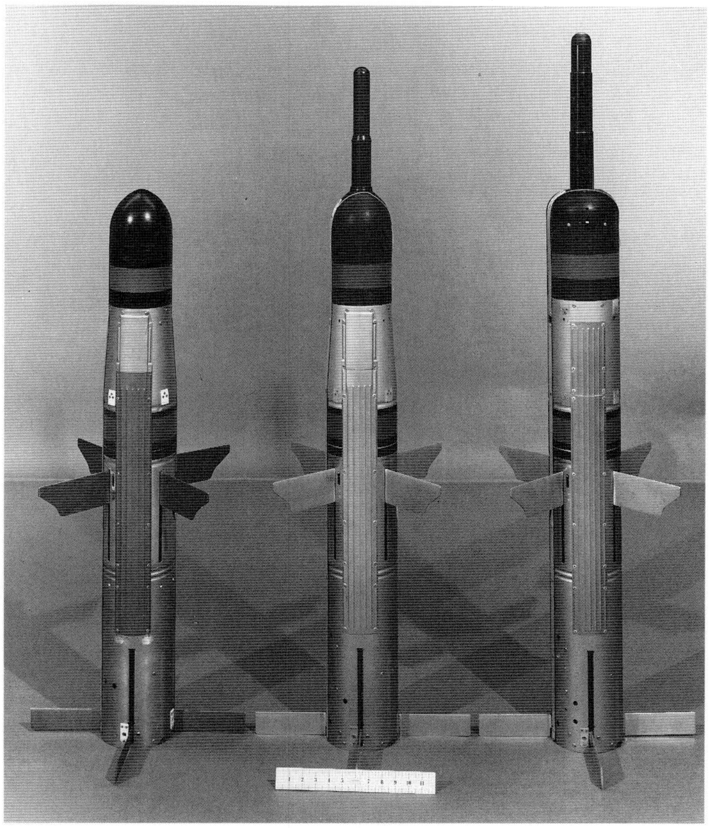

TOW missiles: from left, the basic TOW, Improved TOW, and TOW 2. The TOW and I-TOW have 5-inch (127-mm) diameter warheads; the TOW 2 has a 6-inch (152-mm) warhead. The spikes provide improved penetration of armor (see following page). (Hughes Aircraft)

TOW MGM-71

The TOW—for Tube-launched, Optically tracked, Wire-guided—is an anti-tank missile fired from Army and Marine Corps helicopters, as well as ground and vehicle mounts.

Design: Improved versions, designated Improved TOW (I-TOW) and TOW 2, have an upgraded warhead and an upgraded warhead plus higher impulse motor, respectively. The missile has a high subsonic speed.

Status: Operational. IOC was in 1970.

Manufacturer:	Hughes and Emerson Electric
Weight:	54 lbs (24.5 kg)
Length:	3 ft 8 in (1.1 m)
Span:	3 ft 9 in (1.1 m)
Diameter:	6 in (152 mm)
Propulsion:	solid-fuel rocket + solid-fuel booster
Range:	1.5 n.miles (2.8 km); 2 n.miles (3.7 km) for TOW 2
Guidance:	optical/wire
Warhead:	8 lbs (3.6 kg) high explosive (shaped charge)
Platforms:	*helicopters* AH-1W

This classic photo of a TOW anti-tank missile being launched from a light truck shows the weapon in great detail. The tail fins have not fully deployed; the control wires are clearly visible. (U.S. Marine Corps)

A TOW 2 anti-tank missile in flight. Successive variants of the TOW have increased accuracy and armor penetration. The latter has become increasingly difficult because of improved tank armoring techniques. (Hughes Aircraft)

TRIDENT (D-5) UGM-96

The Trident II, or D-5, is the principal U.S. sea-based strategic missile. It provides a greater range and more accuracy than the Trident C-4 SLBM. Also, the D-5 can deliver 75 percent more payload than the C-4, carrying eight of the Mark 5 reentry bodies, each fitted with a W88 nuclear warhead that has an explosive force of about 300–475 kilotons. (Only some 400 W88 warheads have been produced; the remaining missiles are to be fitted with the W76 warhead, which will result in a yield of about 100 kilotons.)

In the future, the D-5 missiles will be downloaded to only four warheads, reflecting the agreed-upon U.S.–Soviet arms control limit of 1,728 warheads in submarines.

The longer-range and more accurate D-5 version of the Trident missile was approved for development by the Secretary of Defense in October 1981 and fitted in the ninth and subsequent submarines of the Ohio (SSBN 726) class. The first eight submarines of that class were to be retrofitted to fire the D-5 missile, but those plans were canceled in 1991 because of fiscal considerations.

The D-5 missile will eventually be fitted to the 14 submarines of the Ohio (SSBN 726) class that will be retained after the year 2000.

Trident D-5 missiles with British-made warheads are being fitted to the four Royal Navy SSBNs of the Vanguard class, completed from 1993 to 1996. The C-4 missile was originally planned to succeed the Polaris A-3 in British service.

Operational: The Tennessee (SSBN 734) began the first Trident D-5 patrol on 29 March 1990.

Status: Operational; in production.

The first test flight of the Lockheed D-5 missile from Cape Canaveral, Florida, on 21 March 1989 was a failure, as was the third launch, on 15 August 1989. (The failures were due to a design flaw; the water pressure on the missiles' nozzles caused them to tumble after leaving the water.) The second, fourth, and later launches were successful. The first submarine launch occurred on 22 March 1989 from the TENNESSEE; that test launch also failed. Following a series of successful test launches, the missile became operational.

Manufacturer:	Lockheed (now Lockheed Martin)
Weight:	approx. 130,000 lbs (58,968 kg)
Length:	44 ft (13.4 m)
Span:	(ballistic)
Diameter:	83 in (2.1 m)
Propulsion:	3-stage solid-propellant rocket
Range:	4,000+ n.miles (7,400+ km); possibly up to 6,000 n.miles (11,120 km) with downloading of MIRVs.
Guidance:	inertial
Warhead:	nuclear Mk 5 with 8 W88 or W76 MIRVs (being reduced; see text)
Platforms:	*submarines* SSBN 734–743

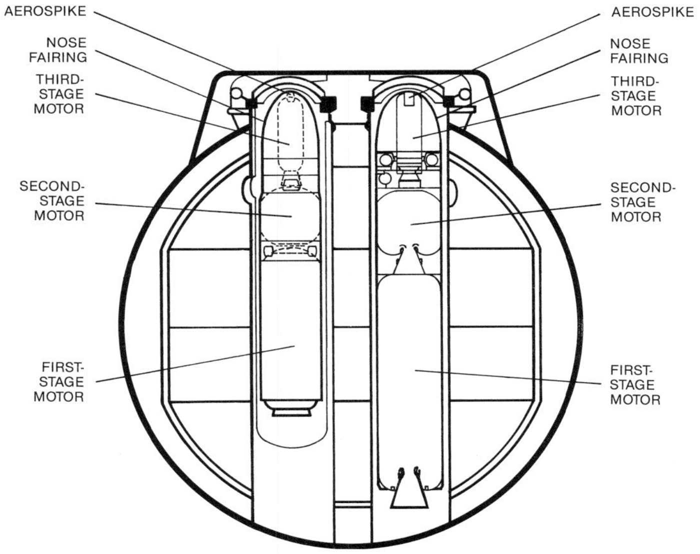

Comparison of the Trident C-4 (left) and Trident D-5 missiles shown in the cross section of an OHIO-class submarine.

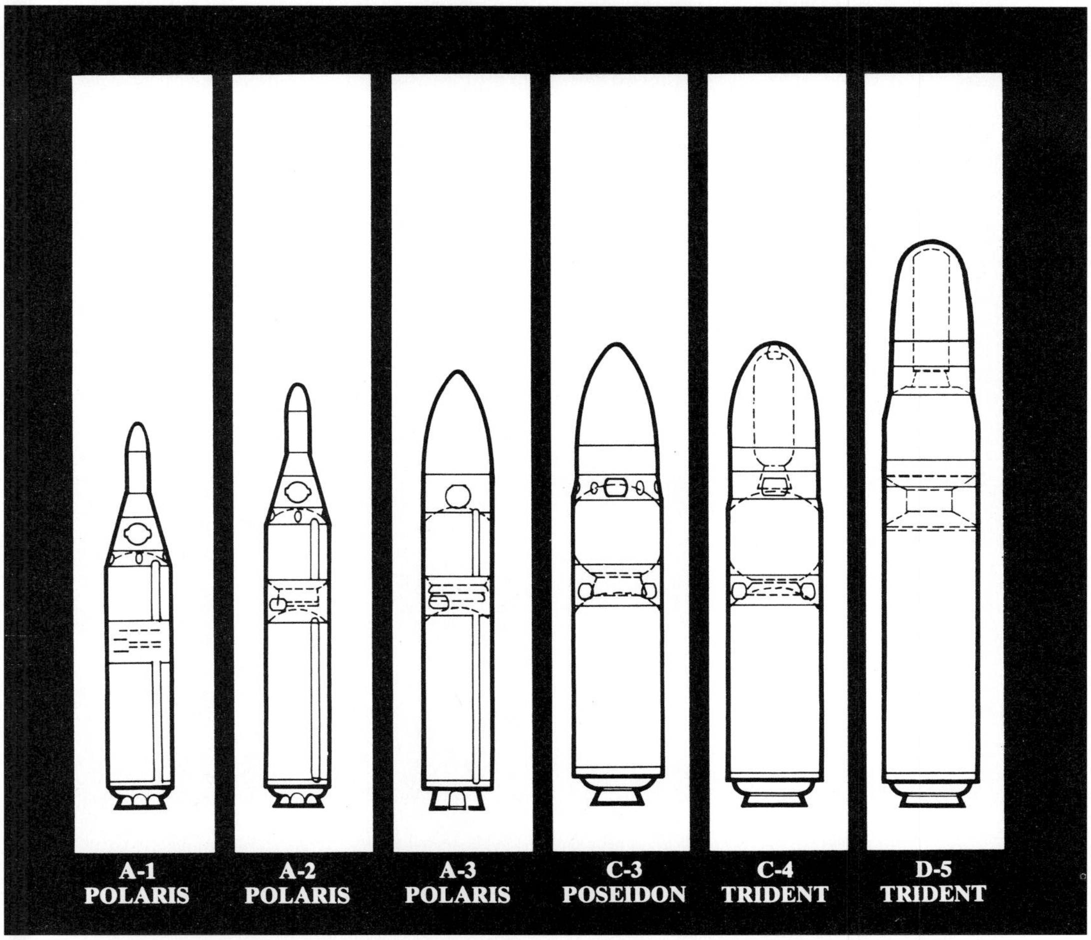

U.S. submarine-launched ballistic missiles.

TRIDENT C-4

The Trident I, or C-4, SLBM evolved from the Department of Defense STRAT-X study of the late 1960s that proposed an advanced SLBM, with a range of 6,000 n.miles (11,120 km), to be carried in a new class of submarine. Subsequently, the Navy proposed a two-phase program: the Trident C-4 (also called Trident I), based on an Extended-range Poseidon (EXPO) missile with a range of some 4,000 n.miles (7,410 km), and the more capable Trident D-5, to be developed at a later date with the longer range.

Design: The C-4 missile has a MIRV warhead with eight Mk 4 independently targeted reentry bodies. It has double the yield and twice the accuracy of the previous Poseidon C-3 missile. It was designed to alternatively carry the Mk 500 Evader *Maneuvering* Reentry Vehicle (MaRV) warhead; this warhead was intended to overcome ballistic missile defenses but was not developed.

The C-4 is a three-stage missile. After it reaches a certain altitude, an aerospike extends from the nose. This spike cuts the friction of the air flowing past the missile, extending its range by about 300 n.miles (556 km).

Status: Operational. IOC was on 31 March 1972 on board the JAMES MADISON (SSBN 627). Twelve LAFAYETTE (SSBN 616)-class submarines were refitted with the Trident missile, and the first eight OHIO-class submarines were armed with the missile. Four of the latter submarines will be rearmed with the Trident D-5 missile.

Manufacturer:	Lockheed (now Lockheed Martin)
Weight:	73,000 lbs (33,110 kg)
Length:	34 ft (10.4 m)
Span:	(ballistic)
Diameter:	74 in (1.9 m)
Propulsion:	3-stage solid-propellant rocket
Range:	approx. 4,000 n.miles (7,400 km)
Guidance:	inertial
Warhead:	nuclear Mk 4 with 8 W76 MIRVs
Platforms:	*submarines* SSBN 726–733

A Trident D-5 SLBM in a test launch from Cape Canaveral, Florida. In flight, an aerospike will extend from the missile's nose to reduce air resistance. All 14 Trident submarines will be armed with the D-5 missile. (Department of Defense)

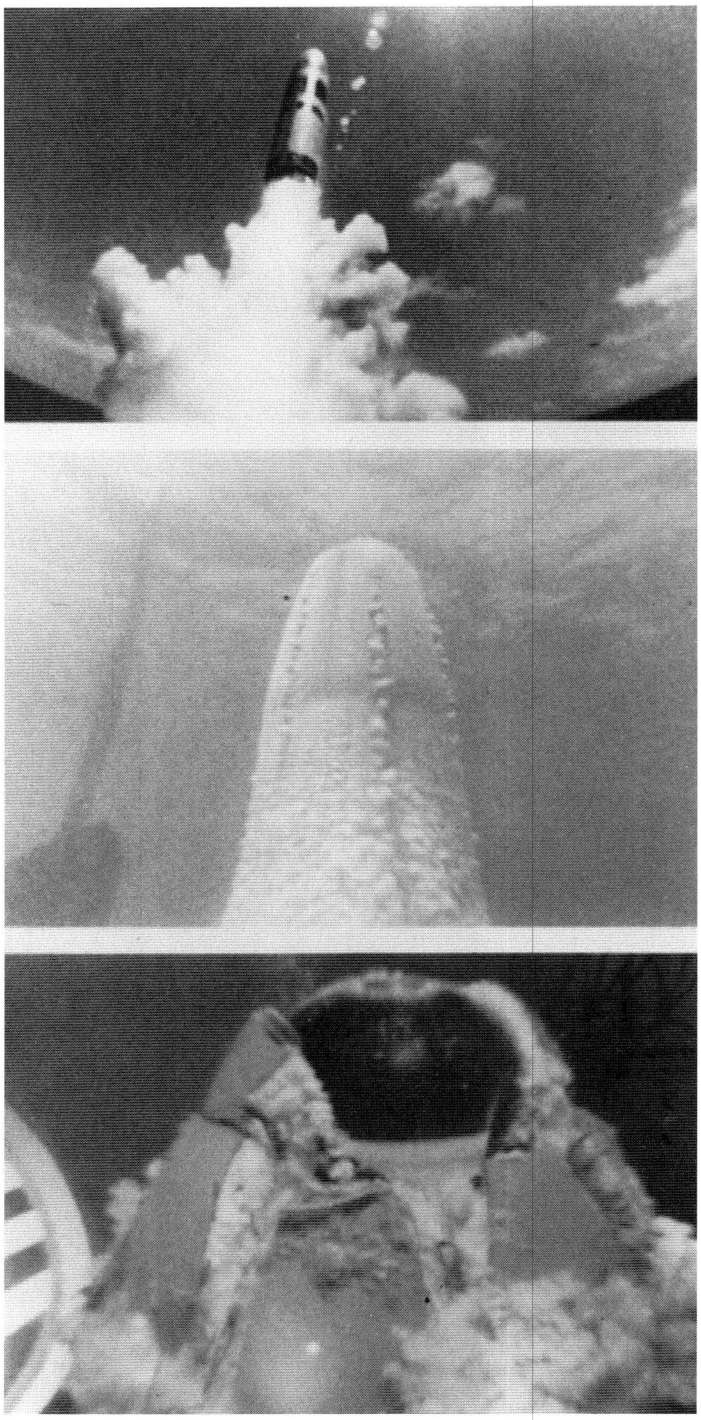

The underwater launch sequence of a Trident C-4 missile. (Courtesy Los Alamos National Laboratory)

A Trident C-4 engine ignites after the missile clears the water during a launch from the submarine MICHIGAN (SSBN 727). (U.S. Navy)

TRI-SERVICE STAND-OFF ATTACK MISSILE (TSSAM) AGM-137

Formerly a highly classified "black" program, the TSSAM was revealed by the Department of Defense in June 1991, in part to help justify procurement of the B-2 "stealth" bomber. TSSAM was to provide a precision stealth weapon for the suppression of enemy air defenses. However, the Northrop-developed weapon was canceled in January 1995 because of higher-than-expected costs.

In development since 1986, the low-observable (stealth) TSSAM was intended to provide precision guidance with a conventional warhead to ranges of more than 100 n.miles (185 km). Apparently, a variety of warheads were to be available, i.e., penetrating, multiple submunitions, and conventional high explosive.

The missile was to be compatible with the Army–Marine Corps Multiple Launch Rocket System (MLRS); the Air Force B-2, B-52 Stratofortress, and F-16 Fighting Falcon aircraft; and the Navy F/A-18 Hornet and A-6E Intruder aircraft.

The procurement of 9,050 missiles was planned—2,250 for the Navy, 1,800 for the Army, and 5,000 for the Air Force. In June 1991 the Department of Defense estimated a TSSAM procurement of 8,650 missiles for all services at a cost of $15.1 *billion,* or an average of $1.7 million per round, including research, tooling, support, etc. Subsequently, the unit cost increased to $2 million per missile.

In place of the TSSAM the Navy plans to procure additional Stand-off Land-Attack Missiles (SLAM/SLAM-ER).

VERTICAL-LAUNCH ASROC (VLA) RUM-139A

This is a short-range ASW weapon, the vertical-launch successor to the ASROC RUR-5A ASW rocket for use in later TICONDEROGA-class cruisers and ARLEIGH BURKE-class destroyers. Only small numbers of the weapon are being procured.

Design: The VLA has more than double the basic ASROC range. The VLA would also be suitable for launch from modified ASROC launchers. The VLA carries a Mk 50 ASW torpedo as its warhead, although tests are being conducted with the earlier Mk 46 Mod 5 torpedo.

The Navy had originally sought to combine the replacement for ASROC and SUBROC in a single weapon. This proved too difficult,

Test launch of a Vertical-Launch ASROC (VLA) from the destroyer ELLIOT (DD 967). This long-delayed weapon will not be deployed in large numbers; rather, manned helicopters—and possibly future drones—will provide U.S. warships with a stand-off ASW attack capability. (Loral)

however, and the VLA was to be surface launched and the Sea Lance ASW stand-off weapon submarine launched. In the late 1980s, however, the VLA was labeled as an interim weapon (only 300 were to be produced) while an attempt was again made to develop the Sea Lance as a common surface/submarine ASW weapon.

Status: Operational. Congress approved a one-time procurement of 300 missiles in fiscal years 1987 and 1989. The Japanese Aegis destroyers of the KONGO class are also VLA capable.

Manufacturer:	Loral	
Weight:	1,409 lbs (634 kg)	
Length:	16 ft (4.9 m)	
Span:	2 ft 3⅖ in (0.7 m)	
Diameter:	14 in (356 mm)	
Propulsion:	solid-propellant rocket	
Range:	approx. 15 n.miles (27.8 km)	
Guidance:	ballistic; terminal acoustic homing with Mk 50 torpedo	
Warhead:	Mk 50 torpedo	
Platforms:	*cruisers*	CG 52–73
	destroyers	DDG 51
		DD 963 (24 ships)

A VLA rising from the deck of the ELLIOT. The exhaust is being vented at left. Vertical-launch provides many advantages over conventional missile launchers. The ELLIOT retains a full ASW capability with installation of a 61-cell VLS. (Loral)

WALLEYE II AGM-62

The Walleye is an unpowered glide bomb formerly used by the Navy. It was listed in the missile designation series and was operationally considered as such against surface ships and hardened ground targets.

Operational: Although being phased out of service by 1991, it was employed in the Gulf War; 133 missiles were launched by Navy A-7E Corsair aircraft from the carrier JOHN F. KENNEDY (CV 67). With the demise of that aircraft immediately after the Gulf War, the missile is no longer in naval service.

The Navy and Marine Corps used the Walleye only with conventional warheads, while the Air Force also had a nuclear version. The Walleye was also used by the Israeli Air Force.

Status: IOC was in 1967; the Walleye was phased out of naval service in 1991.

See 14th Edition/pages 488–89 for characteristics.

NUCLEAR WEAPONS

All nuclear weapons—except for submarine-launched ballistic missiles—have been taken off U.S. Navy warships and removed from land-based naval air squadrons. This action and the similar large-scale cutback of Army and Air Force tactical and strategic nuclear weapons were announced in a dramatic television speech by President George Bush on 27 September 1991. (At the time, the president also proposed the elimination of all multiple warheads on land-based missiles by both the United States and the Soviet Union.)

The president's announcement of the massive, unilateral nuclear weapons and readiness reductions was hailed by then-Secretary of Defense Dick Cheney, who said that the president's initiative was, in his opinion, "the biggest single change in the deployment of U.S. nuclear weapons since they were first integrated into our forces. . . ."[12]

The U.S. action came one month after the abortive Soviet right-wing, political-military coup. The victory of democratic forces in the Soviet Union has, said Cheney, permitted a "sweeping package" of nuclear arms reductions by the United States.

At the time of President Bush's statement, the Navy had the following nuclear weapons in service:

Strategic missiles: 656 SLBMs in 35 strategic missile submarines:

176 Poseidon C-3 in 11 LAFAYETTE class
192 Trident C-4 in 12 LAFAYETTE class
192 Trident C-4 in 8 OHIO class
96 Trident D-5 in 4 OHIO class

Land-attack missiles: Approximately 100 Tomahawk TLAM(N) missiles were in attack submarines, cruisers, and destroyers; all were to be placed in storage ashore. The Navy's inventory goal for TLAM(N) missiles prior to the president's statement was reported as 637, with 399 already funded through fiscal 1991. No additional missiles were to be procured.

Bombs: Some 400 nuclear strike bombs (B57 and B61) and anti-submarine depth bombs (B57) were embarked in aircraft carriers. All were to be withdrawn; most of the B61s were to be placed in storage and the B57s eliminated.

Additional B57 weapons were at shore bases for use by P-3 Orion maritime patrol aircraft; these weapons were to be eliminated.

Development of the advanced B90 dual-purpose bomb was halted. With cancellation of the B90 bomb, no nuclear weapons were under development for naval use.

(There were similar, far-reaching cuts of U.S. Army and Air Force tactical nukes. The only tactical nuclear weapons left with U.S. operational forces were the B57 and B61 bombs of Air Force fighter-bomber squadrons. The only U.S. tactical nuclear modernization program that was under way at the time of the president's speech, the Air Force SRAM-T missile, was also terminated by the president's action.[13])

Department of Defense officials contend that in the future the Tomahawks and B61 bombs could be taken out of storage and

12. Secretary of Defense Dick Cheney, Pentagon press briefing, 28 September 1991.
13. SRAM = Short-Range Attack Missile. The follow-on SRAM II strategic weapon had also been terminated by President Bush's action.

returned to the Fleet within a very short time—perhaps days. However, with the weapons removal, the ongoing personnel reductions, and severe budget constraints, it was unlikely that the capability could be retained to rapidly bring nuclear weapons back aboard submarines and surface ships and use them effectively.

The only nuclear weapons that remain in the U.S. Fleet are Trident C-4 and D-5 SLBMs. This force will be reduced to 14 submarines by the beginning of the 21st century, carrying a total of 336 D-5 missiles.

The other U.S. strategic weapons in the year 2000 are expected to consist of: 500 Minuteman III missiles, each with three MIRVs; 50 MX Peacekeeper missiles, each with ten MIRVs; 97 B-1B bombers; and 21 of the controversial B-2 "stealth" bombers. However, the cancellation of the SRAM II missile, which is carried by strategic bombers, should raise further questions about pursuing production of the B-2 aircraft.

Longer-term plans call for "de-MIRVing" all land-based strategic missiles, i.e., downloading the 500 Minuteman IIIs and 50 MX Peacekeepers to one reentry vehicle per missile.

Historical: The U.S. Navy had a theoretical nuclear strike capability as early as 1948 with the Mk 4 atomic bomb and a dozen land-based P2V-3C Neptune bombers. These twin-engine piston aircraft could fly from airfields in Europe or North Africa or be loaded by cranes aboard carriers for shipboard launch. It was a primitive force with a questionable capability. At the time, atomic bombs had to be assembled by teams of up to 40 men, who required several hours to "glue" them together.

Beginning in 1951 with the Mk 6 atomic bomb and AJ-1 Savage piston-engine attack aircraft, the Navy has continuously had nuclear weapons on board surface ships, although the early carrier deployments were made without certain nuclear materials. In a crisis (or war) they would be flown by B-47 jet bomber from storage sites in the United States to airfields in the Mediterranean area, and then be flown aboard carriers by Carrier On-board Delivery (COD) aircraft for bomb assembly. Subsequently, surface combatants and submarines were fitted with nuclear-armed anti-ship and anti-air missiles; land-attack and anti-ship cruise missiles; antisubmarine torpedoes and rockets; and 16-inch projectiles for the four IOWA-class battleships.

The 1991 decision to remove the remaining tactical weapons from warships follows the 1989 decision to dismantle the surviving ASROC anti-submarine rockets and Terrier-BTN anti-aircraft missiles fitted with nuclear warheads. Those weapons, like some of the bombs later taken out of service, were overage, and their remaining "shelf life" was severely limited, while their effectiveness was questionable.

The accompanying table lists all nuclear weapons previously available to the U.S. Navy.

NAVAL NUCLEAR WEAPONS*

Warhead	Weapon	Type	In stockpile
Mk 4	bomb	strike	1948–1953
Mk 5	Regulus missile	strike/ASUW	1952–1963
Mk 6	bomb	strike	1951–1962
W7	Betty depth bomb	ASW	1955–1963
W7	BOAR bomb	strike	1956–1963
Mk 8	bomb	strike	1951–1956
W23	16-inch shell	strike	1956–1961
W27	Regulus missile	strike/ASUW	1958–1965
W30	Talos missile	AAW	1958–1979
W34	Lulu depth bomb	ASW	1958–1971
W34	ASTOR torpedo	ASW	1958–1977
B43	bomb	strike	1961–1991
W44	ASROC rocket	ASW	1961–1989
W45	Terrier missile	AAW	1962–1989
W47	Polaris missile	strike	1960–1975
W55	SUBROC rocket	ASW	1964–1989
B57	bomb	strike/ASW	1963–1992
W58	Polaris missile	strike	1964–1982
B61	bomb	strike	1966–1992
W68	Poseidon missile	strike	1970–1991
W76	Trident I missile	strike	1979–present
W80	Tomahawk missile	strike	1984–1992
W81	SM-2 Standard missile	AAW	not developed
W88	Trident II missile	strike	1990–present
B90	bomb	strike/ASW	(not developed)

*Artillery shells and Atomic Demolition Munitions (ADM) used by the Marine Corps are not included.

TORPEDOES

The U.S. Navy has two series of torpedoes in service: the lightweight Mk 46 and Mk 50, used by aircraft and surface ships and in the CAPTOR mine, and the heavyweight Mk 48 ADCAP, carried in all submarines. These torpedoes are intended primarily for the anti-submarine role, although the Mk 48 can be used against surface ships.

No torpedoes are currently being procured; Mk 48 torpedoes are being upgraded to the ADCAP configuration.

Both the heavy- and lightweight torpedo programs have encountered major problems, most related to the nature of the Soviet-Russian submarine threat. The problems with U.S. torpedoes have been identified publicly. By some criteria, U.S. torpedoes have lagged behind the potential threat since the appearance of the first Soviet nuclear-powered submarines in the late 1950s. In a 1981 congressional colloquy between a senator and the Deputy Chief of Naval Operations (Surface Warfare), Vice Admiral William H. Rowden, the senator noted that then-new Soviet submarines of the Alfa class could travel at "40-plus knots and could probably outdive most of our anti-submarine torpedoes." He then asked what measures were being taken to redress this particular imbalance.[14]

The admiral replied, "We have modified the Mark 48 torpedo . . . to accommodate to the increased speed and to the diving depth of those particular submarines." The admiral was less confident about the Mk 46 used by aircraft, helicopters, and surface ships, however. "We have recently modified that torpedo to handle what you might call the pre-Alfa. . . ."[15]

Russian undersea craft are difficult targets for several reasons. The large size, double hull, and multiple compartments of Soviet submarines reduce the effectiveness of the small Mk 46 and Mk 50 warheads. Both heavy and light torpedo effectiveness also suffer from the Soviet use of anechoic coatings on their submarine hulls that degrade torpedo acoustic guidance, and the extensive use of acoustic decoys. Finally, the Mk 48's capability is reduced in the under-ice environment of the Arctic ice pack.

Submarines carry the Mk 48 torpedo. Modern U.S. Navy SSNs have a capacity of some 25 tube-launched weapons (4 tubes + 22 reload spaces, with one rack left free to facilitate weapons handling). The later, improved LOS ANGELES (SSN 688)-class submarines additionally have 12 vertical-launching tubes for Tomahawk missiles, making more reload spaces available within the submarine. The SEAWOLF (SSN-21) class has space for 50 weapons (8 tubes + 42 reload spaces). The New Attack Submarine (NSSN) will have 4 torpedo tubes and 12 vertical-launch Tomahawk cells; about 25 torpedoes will be carried.

While weapon loadouts will vary with the submarine's mission and operating area, a nominal loadout for a standard SSN is torpedoes plus four Harpoons and four Tomahawks.

Surface ships have the Mk 46 or Mk 50 torpedo as an ASW weapon, launched by (1) over-the-side Mk 32 torpedo tubes, (2) LAMPS helicopters, or (3) ASROC/VLA. Until the late 1950s U.S. surface combatants had long torpedo tubes for anti-ship torpedoes. For a brief period in the 1960s the Mk 48 was intended for tube-launch from surface warships to provide a long-range, wire-guided ASW torpedo. Several surface warships were fitted with torpedo-handling gear and 21-inch tubes in their stern counter or after deckhouse. However, this aspect of the Mk 48 program was canceled, and only Mk 32 tubes for lightweight torpedoes have been retained in U.S. cruisers, destroyers, and frigates.

ASW Aircraft and Helicopters carry the Mk 46 or Mk 50 torpedo, externally on the SH-2G and SH-60B/F helicopters and in internal weapons bays in the S-3B and P-3C fixed-wing aircraft.

14. The Alfa SSN, with six units completed from 1979–1982, had a submerged speed of 43 knots and an operating depth of 2,000–2,500 feet (610–760 m). The prototype Alfa, completed in 1972, suffered major engineering problems and never became operational.

15. Vice Adm. William H. Rowden, USN, Deputy Chief of Naval Operations (Surface Warfare), hearings before the Appropriations Committee, Senate, 8 April 1981.

MK 50 LIGHTWEIGHT TORPEDO

The Mk 50—formerly known as the Advanced Lightweight Torpedo (ALWT)—is the successor to the Mk 46 for use by ASW/patrol aircraft and helicopters and surface warships. (It was also intended for the submarine-launched Sea Lance ASW missile.) The torpedo has enhanced kill capability over the Mk 46, but it still suffers from some of the shortcomings, such as size of warhead, of the older torpedo.

The ALWT program was initiated in August 1975 with a design competition subsequently being held between Honeywell (Ex-50 design) and McDonnell Douglas (Ex-51). The former firm was selected to develop the torpedo. During the competition the torpedo was also designated Mk XX. Concept development began in 1975 and advanced development was approved in 1979; limited production began in March 1989.

Design: Special features of the Mk 50 include the AKY-14 programable digital computer.

The torpedo can be used by all Mk 46 launchers/attachment points without platform modification.

Name: The Mk 50 is referred to as Barracuda by the producer.

Status: Operational. Manufactured by Alliant Techsystems (formerly Honeywell) and Westinghouse Electric Corporation.

Production of the Mk 50 for the U.S. Navy ended in mid-1996.

Weight:	approx. 800 lbs (363 kg)	
Diameter:	12¾ in (324 mm)	
Length:	9 ft 6 in (2.9 m)	
Propulsion:	Stored Chemical Energy Propulsion System (SCEPS)	
Speed:	50+ knots	
Range:		
Guidance:	active/passive acoustic homing	
Warhead:	approx. 100 lbs (45 kg) conventional shaped charge	
Platforms:	*aircraft*	P-3C
		S-3B
		SH-2G
		SH-60B/F
	ships	cruisers
		destroyers
		frigates

A Mk 50 lightweight torpedo fitted on a Seahawk-type helicopter. Two Mk 50s can be carried by an SH-60 Seahawk or SH-2G LAMPS I helicopter. (Alliant Techsystems)

A Mk 50 lightweight torpedo is launched from the fixed torpedo tubes of a Knox (FF 1052)-class frigate. Mk 32 tubes—launching Mk 46 or Mk 50 torpedoes—are a last-ditch weapon, especially against submarines armed with anti-ship cruise missiles. (Alliant Techsystems)

MK 48 ADCAP TORPEDO

This is the U.S. Navy's submarine-launched torpedo. The Mk 48 ADCAP (Advanced Capability) version of the Mk 48 heavy torpedo has been in production since fiscal 1985 as successor to the standard Mk 48 versions. The ADCAP version was developed from 1978 onward to counter the high-speed, deep-diving Alfa SSN and other advanced Soviet submarines. The ADCAP performance requirements were to: (1) improve target acquisition range; (2) reduce the effect of enemy countermeasures; (3) minimize shipboard constraints such as warmup and reactivation time; and (4) enhance effectiveness against surface ships.

In 1996 the Navy revealed that an advanced mobile mine is being developed based on the Mk 48 ADCAP. This weapon would have two warheads; after the mine released one warhead at a preset location, it would continue to another location to place the second warhead.

Design: The principal changes from the Mk 48 to the ADCAP configuration to meet these requirements were made to the torpedo's acoustic transducer (guidance) and control system. The higher-powered active sonar enables the torpedo to search a much greater volume of water to attain a target submarine. And, the sonar is electrically steered, reducing the need for the torpedo to maneuver while searching. The torpedo retains the Gould (swashplate) motor, with a larger fuel capacity. However, in November 1986 the Navy began seeking proposals for developing a quieter, closed-cycle propulsion system for the ADCAP, a requirement apparently caused by the recent Soviet submarine quieting efforts.

The ADCAP program has suffered both delays and severe cost increases. In 1982 the Chief of Naval Operations, Admiral Thomas B. Hayward, said that the problems included: (1) the original R&D program being significantly underestimated; (2) the scope of effort increasing because of the evolving Soviet submarine threat; (3) an attempt being made to accelerate the IOC; (4) too little emphasis being placed on cost control; and (5) the prime contractor (Hughes) being new to torpedo business and underestimating the effort required.

Reliability problems with the ADCAP surfaced in early 1991 but, according to Navy officials, they were solved the following year. An under-ice capability has been provided in the ADCAP upgrade.

In 1995 the Navy proposed an upgrade to the ADCAP propulsion program to enhance the torpedo's effectiveness against diesel-electric submarines operating in littoral or shallow water. The upgrade reduces the range at which an adversary is alerted by the torpedo's engine sounds to an attack and thus is able to undertake evasive action or to counterfire. An analysis by the General Accounting Office stated:

> [B]ecause of the short ranges at which diesel submarines are likely to be detected in littoral or shallow water, the technological improvement to be contributed by the propulsion upgrade—that is, torpedo quieting—will neither improve the performance of the ADCAP nor reduce the vulnerability of the launching submarine to enemy attack. Moreover, the Commander, Operational Test and Evaluation Force, already considers the current ADCAP operationally suitable and effective in shallow water, and the Navy did not establish a requirement to improve the ADCAP's propulsion system for use in open ocean, deep water in its operational requirements document for the upgrade.[16]

Status: Operational; in production. IOC was in 1989. Manufactured by Westinghouse Corporation and Hughes Aircraft. Production for the U.S. Navy was completed in December 1995.

Weight:	3,450 lbs (1,564 kg)
Length:	19 ft 2 in (5.8 m)
Diameter:	21 in (533 mm)
Propulsion:	piston engine (liquid monopropellant fuel); pump-jet
Speed:	maximum 55 knots
Range:	approx. 35,000 yds (32,012 m)
Guidance:	wire + active/passive acoustic homing
Warhead:	approx. 650 lbs (295 kg) PBXN-103 high explosive
Platforms:	*submarines* SSN/SSBN

16. General Accounting Office, *Navy Torpedo Programs: MK-48 ADCAP Upgrades Not Adequately Justified,* GAO/NSIAD-95-104, June 1995, p. 1.

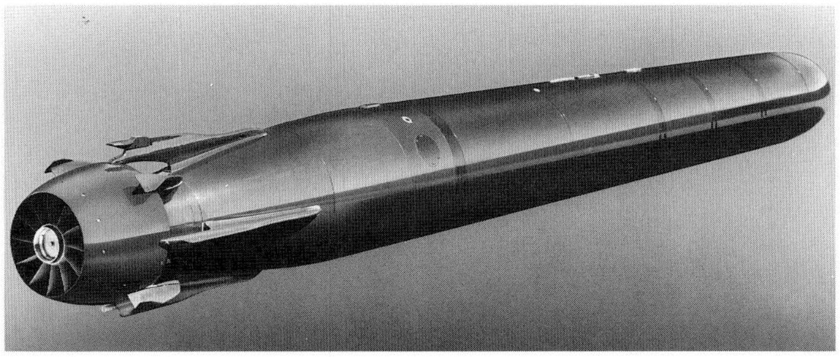

Mk 48 torpedo showing the shrouded propeller or "propulsor" configuration. (Gould)

Mk 48 torpedoes are prepared for loading aboard an SSN at Port Canaveral, Florida. (U.S. Air Force)

Rear aspect of a Mk 48 torpedo; the guide for the control wire is at top. (Gould)

MK 48 HEAVY TORPEDO

This was the latest weapon in a long series of heavy torpedoes. It is 21 inches (533 mm) in diameter and up to 21 feet (6.4 m) long. The immediate predecessor of the Mk 48 was the Mk 37, which remains in foreign naval service. The Mk 48 also replaced the Mk 45 ASTOR (Anti-Submarine Torpedo), the U.S. Navy's only nuclear torpedo, which was in service from 1958 to 1977 with a W34 warhead. The long range and improved guidance of the Mk 48, with a large conventional warhead, made it as effective as the Mk 45 in most situations. Also, the Mk 48's anti-surface ship capability was considered sufficient to cancel the purely anti-surface Mk 47 torpedo.

Development of the Mk 48 began in the early 1960s as the Navy-sponsored RETORC (Research Torpedo Configuration) research project of the Applied Research Laboratory of Pennsylvania State University and the Westinghouse Electric Corporation (Baltimore, Maryland). The project was initially designated Ex-10. This effort led to the Mk 48 Mod 0 torpedo with a turbine propulsion system. This was subsequently refined into the Mk 48 Mod 2.

In 1967 the Gould Corporation of Cleveland, Ohio, and the Naval Surface Warfare Center (White Oak, Maryland) began developing the Mod 1 with a redesigned acoustic homing guidance and a piston (swashplate) engine. This torpedo uses an Otto fuel that contains its own oxidizer for combustion. After evaluation of the two versions, the Mod 1 was selected for production by Gould for Fleet use.

Design: The Mk 48 had a guidance wire that spun out simultaneously from the submarine and the torpedo to permit the submarine to exercise control over the "fish," at least during the initial stages of its run. The Mod 3 introduced several improvements including TELECOM (Tele-Communications) to provide two-way data transmissions between submarine and torpedo. Thus, the torpedo could transmit acoustic data back to the submarine for processing. See above ADCAP listing for basic characteristics.

The Mod 4 version was an upgrade to provide more capability against the Alfa-class and other advanced Soviet SSNs.

The Mk 48 is also used in Australian and Dutch submarines.

Status: Succeeded in U.S. service by the Mk 48 ADCAP. Mk 48 IOC was in 1972.

MK 46 LIGHTWEIGHT TORPEDO

The Mk 46 is a lightweight torpedo intended for use against submarines by helicopters, aircraft, and surface ships; it is also fitted in the CAPTOR deep-water mine.

The lightweight torpedo concept dates to the late 1940s when it was envisioned that future convoys would be protected from submarine attack by helicopters with dipping sonar and airships (blimps) with towed sonar. For this application, weight (initially a maximum of 350 pounds/159 kg) became a primary consideration for ASW torpedoes. In addition, the concept would require large numbers of torpedoes, hence cost was also an important factor in torpedo design. Subsequently, surface combatants were fitted with "short" torpedo tubes for launching these torpedoes, and the ASROC was fitted with the lightweight torpedo. The first lightweight ASW torpedo to enter fleet service was the Mk 43 Mod 1 (260 lbs/118 kg), in 1951. The Mk 43 Mod 3 and the Mk 44 Mod 0 (425 lbs/193 kg), introduced in 1957, were followed by the Mk 44 Mod 1. The Mk 46 is thus the third generation of lightweight ASW torpedoes.

The Navy procured kits for the conversion of 172 Mk 46 torpedoes to function as anti-torpedo weapons as part of the Surface Ship Torpedo Defense (SSTD) project.

The Mk 46 was developed by the Naval Ordnance Test Station (Pasadena, California) and Aerojet General (Azusa, California). Subsequent production was undertaken at the Naval Ordnance Plant (Forest Park, Illinois) and Honeywell, as well as Aerojet. The Mk 46 has a higher speed, twice the range, deeper operating depth, and better acoustic performance than its predecessor, the Mk 44.

Design: The Mk 46 propulsion is provided by a thermal piston engine, with the Mod 0 using a solid propellant grain and the Mod 1 having a liquid monopropellant fuel, the latter providing improved performance. The Mod 2 introduced the PBXN-103 warhead (providing 27 percent more explosive power over the Mods 0/1). There was no Mod 3 torpedo.

The Mod 4 version of the Mk 46 is especially configured for the CAPTOR (Encapsulated Torpedo) naval mine. In 1981 Secretary of Defense Harold Brown stated that "because the existing Mk 46 torpedo will not meet the submarine acoustic and countermeasures threat through the early 1980s, we have budgeted for a new version called the Near-Term Torpedo Improvement Program (NEARTIP)."[17] This program included modification kits for earlier Mk 46s, as well as new torpedo procurement. The NEARTIP or Mod 5 has an improved

17. *Department of Defense Annual Report Fiscal Year 1982* (19 January 1981), p. 160.

A Mk 46 torpedo fitted on an SH-3D Sea King helicopter; the contra-rotating propellers are at left. Russian ASW helicopters carry their torpedoes in internal weapons bays. (U.S. Navy)

sonar transducer, new guidance and control group, and engine upgrades. Overall performance, in addition to shallow-water effectiveness, is enhanced with these changes.

Status: Operational. IOC for the Mod 0 was in October 1965, for Mods 1 and 2 in 1967. The last Mk 46 Mod 5 torpedoes were delivered to the U.S. Navy in 1992; they were produced by Alliant Techsystems, which was part of the defense-product spinoff from Honeywell in October 1990. In addition, the firm produced several hundred conversion kits for the Navy to upgrade earlier Mod 1 and Mod 2 torpedoes to the Mod 5 configuration.

The Mk 46 is used by numerous other countries.

Weight:		
Diameter:	12.75 in (324 mm)	
Length:	8 ft 6 in (2.6 m)	
Propulsion:	cam engine (liquid monopropellant) contra-rotating propellers	
Speed:	approx. 45 knots maximum	
Range:		
Guidance:	active/passive acoustic homing	
Warhead:	approx. 95 lbs (43 kg) PBXN-103 high explosive	
Platforms:	Mod 4	CAPTOR mine
	Mod 5	aircraft (P-3C, S-3B, SH-2G, SH-60B/F), cruisers, destroyers, frigates

Mk 46 torpedoes in the weapons bay of a P-3 Orion maritime patrol aircraft. Parachute packs are fitted to the rear of the torpedoes. (U.S. Navy)

Mk 46 torpedoes about to be inserted in Mk 32 torpedo tubes on a surface combatant. Additional torpedoes are stowed at left. (Alliant Techsystems)

ANTI-SURFACE WARFARE TORPEDO

The Navy promulgated a requirement for a low-cost, anti-surface ship torpedo on 2 December 1985 at the urging of then-Secretary of the Navy John Lehman. The torpedo was intended for use against surface ships that did not require the more complex (and higher-cost) Mk 48 ADCAP torpedo, which was developed specifically for attacking maneuvering submarines, a much more difficult type of target.

Known as the "no frills" torpedo, the ASUW weapon encountered delays primarily because of the contractual restrictions on potential contractors, such as each finalist having to provide seven test torpedoes at its own expense for a "swim-off" competition. The torpedo was also opposed by the submarine community, which questioned the utility of a weapon that would displace Mk 48 torpedoes and other weapons from the limited reload space in attack submarines. The program was eventually canceled.

The ASUW torpedo had a program goal of 2,000 weapons at a cost of $200,000 each (compared to a $2.43-million unit cost for the Mk 48 ADCAP torpedo in the fiscal 1988 budget, plus continuing research and development costs). The initial procurement was set for fiscal 1987, with 34 torpedoes. The program was canceled, however, after Mr. Lehman's departure from office in 1987.

The parachute deploys from a Mk 46 torpedo as it is released from an SH-3D Sea King helicopter. Lightweight torpedoes, originally developed for use from blimps, are now the only ASW weapons carried by U.S. Navy surface ships and aircraft. (U.S. Navy)

CHAPTER 31

Electronic Systems

The SPY-1 Aegis radar—shown here on the destroyer MITSCHER (DDG 57) with an F-14 Tomcat fighter overhead—is the world's most advanced shipboard radar. But will the SPY-1 and its derivatives be able to cope with the very-low-level Mach 3+ anti-ship missiles that could proliferate in the 21st century? Even less capable missiles will be a serious threat in the littoral areas, where land clutter and other factors will present major challenges to radars. (Greg Harper/Litton/Ingalls Shipbuilding)

The U.S. Navy depends heavily upon electronic systems for navigation, communications, and, most especially, combat operations (including both offensive and defensive operations). This chapter lists the Navy's principal electronic warfare systems, radars, sonars, torpedo countermeasures, and weapon control systems now fitted in U.S. surface ships and submarines. Sonobuoys are listed as a subset of the sonar entries.

ELECTRONIC DESIGNATIONS

Most U.S. Navy electronic systems are identified by the joint electronics type designation system shown in the accompanying chart. This system was previously called the joint Army-Navy nomenclature system, and the three-letter-plus-number designations are still prefixed by the AN/ of the World War II era. In this volume the AN/ is omitted from three-letter designations. The electronic systems designated in various mark (Mk) series do not have the AN/ prefix.

Variants of basic radars are indicated by suffix letters or (V)-series numbers.

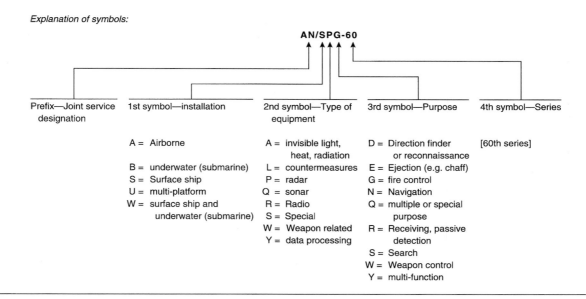

Explanation of symbols:

AN/SPG-60

Prefix—Joint service designation	1st symbol—installation	2nd symbol—Type of equipment	3rd symbol—Purpose	4th symbol—Series
	A = Airborne	A = invisible light, heat, radiation	D = Direction finder or reconnaissance	[60th series]
	B = underwater (submarine)	L = countermeasures	E = Ejection (e.g. chaff)	
	S = Surface ship	P = radar	G = fire control	
	U = multi-platform	Q = sonar	N = Navigation	
	W = surface ship and underwater (submarine)	R = Radio	Q = multiple or special purpose	
		S = Special	R = Receiving, passive detection	
		W = Weapon related	S = Search	
		Y = data processing	W = Weapon control	
			Y = multi-function	

ELECTRONIC WARFARE SYSTEMS

Electronic Warfare (EW) consists of efforts to detect, locate, exploit, reduce, or prevent an enemy's use of the electromagnetic spectrum, as well as actions that retain one's own use of the electromagnetic spectrum. There are several categories of electronic warfare:

Electronic Warfare Support Measures (ESM)
Signals Intelligence (SIGINT)
Electronic Countermeasures (ECM)
Electronic Counter-Countermeasures (ECCM)

Because EW deals with electromagnetic energy, and not just electronics, infrared, laser, and optical systems are also included. However, radiation produced by nuclear weapons is usually classified as nuclear effects, not EW.

Electronic Warfare Support Measures (ESM) activities are the portion of EW that seeks to detect, intercept, locate, record, and analyze enemy electromagnetic radiations. Thus, ESM provides the information required to conduct electronic countermeasures and counter-countermeasures or for immediate threat recognition. Generally passive, ESM seeks to detect the enemy through "listening" to an enemy's radio and radar emissions.

The U.S. Navy has a variety of ESM systems that are used in ships, submarines, aircraft, and ashore. Being passive, ESM offers a number of obvious tactical advantages: (1) it permits the ESM collection platform to remain electronically silent; and (2) it can detect a hostile radar transmission beyond the radar's detection range because the radar requires much of its power to return a signal to the transmitter after it detects a target.

Certain ESM systems are highly specialized—and highly classified—such as the ALR-series receivers in the Navy's ES-3A Viking[1] and EP-3E Orion aircraft that support fleet operations.

ESM capabilities are also incorporated into multifunction systems. For example, according to published Navy manuals, a Los Angeles (SSN 688)-class submarine has equipment for the collection of Electromagnetic Intelligence (ELINT), including Acoustic Intelligence (ACINT) and Communications Intelligence (COMINT):

- BQQ-5 sonar system, which has a passive classification processor that can continuously evaluate low-frequency acoustic data from sonars
- BLD-1 radio direction finder
- BRD-7 radio direction finder
- WLR-8 receiver that can detect enemy fire-control radars as well as radio communication frequencies (reportedly having a 50 MHz to 18 GHz frequency range)
- WLR-9 acoustic intercept receiver that can detect active search sonars and acoustic-homing torpedoes
- WLR-10 countermeasures

Several of these systems are multipurpose, especially the BQQ-5 system. It is the submarine's tactical sonar, having both active and passive modes. Additional ESM equipment can be installed for special collection missions.

Electronic surveillance and collection equipment have special design characteristics, among them:

Wide-spectrum or bandwidth capability: Because the frequency of a foreign radar may not be known before it operates, a wide bandwidth should be covered. With modern technology, this means a frequency spectrum from 30 MHz to 50 GHz. This range is too large for a single receiver; thus, several receivers with different tuning ranges must be used or a single receiver in which different tuning units can be inserted to cover the frequency range.

Wide dynamic range: The ESM receiver must be able to receive very weak signals and very strong signals. The receiver may be at different distances from different signals at the same time, and widely dissimilar signals could impair both collection and analysis unless the equipment is designed specifically for the role.

Unwanted signal rejection: This characteristic—also called narrow band-pass—is desirable because it enables the receiver to discriminate between the target frequency and signals at other, nearby frequencies.

Good angle-of-arrival measurement: The ability of a receiver to accurately take bearings on a distant transmitter permits different bearings (taken by the same or several surveillance platforms) to be plotted to give the precise location of the transmitter. Airborne,

1. The ES-3A Vikings are unofficially known as "Shadows."

shipboard, or ground-based digital computers can be programed to perform this function rapidly.

The receiver should be designed to immediately alert the operator to the presence of a signal of possible interest, to sort out the signal of interest, and to analyze the signal. The alerting and sorting are particularly important because an airborne ESM platform may be exposed to the signal for a short time compared to a ship or shore facility, or the signal may be on the air for only a very short time. The current trend in ESM is to automatically record the intercepted signal for later analysis and, if appropriate, for reproduction for use in EW libraries.

The submarine is an excellent ESM platform because it is difficult for an enemy to detect her by conventional radar and visual means, and even by acoustic sensors under some conditions. And, of course, a submarine is not impeded by surface weather. Submarines are particularly useful in gaining acoustic intelligence on enemy submarines. The periodic press reports of U.S. and Soviet submarines "scraping" one another in close encounters in northern waters suggest that U.S. submarines are used in such surveillance missions in areas such as the Arctic and the Norwegian Sea.

An ACINT capability is also found in the Navy's seafloor Sound Surveillance System (SOSUS). In addition to providing a peacetime warning system of submarine movements, the SOSUS networks in the Atlantic, Pacific, and regional seas can record data on surface ship and submarine noise characteristics.

Specialized electronic reconnaissance aircraft have long conducted ESM missions along the peripheries of the Soviet Union (and now Russia), China, and North Korea. The current U.S. naval aircraft in this category are the ES-3A Viking and EP-3E Orion from fleet air reconnaissance squadrons (VQ). These aircraft, with the Vikings able to operate from forward-deployed aircraft carriers, also provide electronic surveillance of surface ships and submarines for fleet commanders. The primary advantage of aircraft ESM platforms is their altitude, permitting them to detect distant electronic emissions, including those originating inside enemy territory.

Aircraft—and surface ships—also are used to stimulate enemy radars and communications as they near enemy territory. In turn, this stimulation permits the aircraft or ship to record the electromagnetic responses of an enemy, that is, which of their radars they turn on, which of their communications channels they use, etc.

Signals Intelligence (SIGINT) includes the collection of intelligence information for Navy and national requirements, including all Communications Intelligence (COMINT), Electronics Intelligence (ELINT), Acoustic Intelligence (ACINT), and Telemetry Intelligence (TELINT). The National Security Agency (NSA) is the national program manager for the collection, analysis, and dissemination of SIGINT. However, the platforms and personnel involved in SIGINT belong to the armed services, and some systems obviously have both ESM and SIGINT collection capabilities. Thus, the actual operation of SIGINT activities is conducted by the services and, in wartime, the operational control of some dedicated SIGINT platforms would be assigned to tactical commanders.

Surface warships are used extensively for SIGINT activity. Two U.S. destroyers engaged in SIGINT—the TURNER JOY (DD 951) and MADDOX (DD 731) on the so-called De Soto patrols off the North Vietnamese coast in August 1964—were involved in the Gulf of Tonkin incidents that led to a dramatic escalation of American involvement in the Vietnam conflict.[2] Because of the hostile nature of the North Vietnamese and the guerrilla war then going on, destroyers were deemed the appropriate ESM platforms.

In the supposedly more benign environment of international waters off North Korea, the U.S. Navy carried naval and National Security Agency teams on board the "passive" SIGINT surveillance ships BANNER (AGER 1) and PUEBLO (AGER 2), while the LIBERTY (AGTR 5) was used in 1967 to monitor Israeli communications during the Six-Day War. The United States and the Soviet Union had long believed that such ships operated by the two superpowers were immune to hostile actions by the Third World. However, attacks on the PUEBLO and LIBERTY demonstrated that a superpower's ships are not immune from so-called Third World powers. The U.S. Navy has ceased to operate such "passive" intelligence ships, although almost 50 of these intelligence collectors are reportedly still active in the Russian Navy (designated AGI by NATO).

Land-based aircraft, satellites, and ground intercept facilities also provide SIGINT collection of foreign naval activities.

Electronic Countermeasures (ECM) are intended primarily to detect threats to friendly forces and to inhibit or degrade the effectiveness of enemy weapons and sensors. Most surface warships, submarines, and combat aircraft have ECM systems to help protect them against hostile detection and attack. In addition, specialized ECM aircraft assist other aircraft in penetrating heavily defended areas.

Different ECM techniques are used to reduce the effectiveness of enemy radars. The three basic techniques are to: (1) interfere with the radar through jamming and deception; (2) change the electrical properties of the air between the radar and (friendly) target, mainly through chaff; and (3) change the reflective properties of the (friendly) target through radar-absorbing materials or paint, and through electronic and mechanical echo (blip) enhancers or decoys.

Although the above discussion concentrates on ECM techniques against radar, to some extent these concepts are usable against electromagnetic communications and sonar. For example, the properties of shipboard noise can be reduced. Modern U.S. surface warships use the Prairie and Masker systems of creating small air bubbles around a ship's hull and wake to reduce her acoustic signature. Advanced submarine hull designs reduce noise created by submarine movement, while special internal mountings reduce propulsion and auxiliary machinery noises. Russian submarines additionally use anechoic coatings—intended to reduce the effectiveness of hostile acoustic homing torpedoes—which can also reduce submarine-generated noises, as can polymers discharged from a submarine. Of course, surface ships and, especially, submarines can slow or stop to reduce their self-generated noises.

A large number of threat warning and countermeasures systems are installed in U.S. surface ships and submarines, most numbered in the SLQ and WLR series.

The U.S. Navy and Marine Corps fly the EA-6B Prowler in the ECM role. The EA-6B is easily distinguished from the A-6 Intruder, from which it was developed, by the housing atop its tail fin and up to five jammer pods carried on its wings and fuselage. The pods are ALQ-99 tactical jammers, each with an exciter/processor and a minicomputer to detect, identify, and jam a broad spectrum of hostile radars. The aircraft also has the ALQ-100 multiband track-breaking system and ALQ-92 communications jammer. The EA-6B is probably the most capable EW aircraft in the West (although Grumman has provided these systems in the Air Force EF-111A). The basic EA-6B aircraft has had its frequency coverage extended through a series of updates (see chapter 29).

The EA-6B aircraft are designed to provide ECM support for strike aircraft attacking defended targets. The strike aircraft can themselves carry chaff, ECM pods, and radar-homing missiles to further enhance their survivability. Each carrier air wing has a squadron of four EA-6B Prowlers, while the Marine Corps has five squadrons, each assigned five EA-6B aircraft; there is also one Naval Reserve EA-6B squadron. (Other naval aircraft have built-in or pod-mounted ECM systems for self-defense.)

In 1995 the Navy and Air Force reached an agreement whereby the Navy would assume the responsibility for all airborne ECM. This agreement leads to the retirement of the Air Force's EF-111A Raven aircraft; 40 EF-111s were in service in 1995.[3]

Electronic countermeasures are costly, not only in resources (especially for research and development as well as production) but also because of tactical uncertainties and limitations that they impose.

---

2. Apparently, on the night of 2 August 1964 the destroyers were, in fact, attacked by North Vietnamese motor torpedo boats, and on the night of 5 August 1964 U.S. naval commanders thought the destroyers again were under torpedo boat attack.

3. Grumman converted 42 EF-111A ECM aircraft from standard F-111A strike aircraft. The F-111A was developed and produced by General Dynamics under the controversial TFX program.

For example, it may be undesirable to employ ECM against an enemy's communications, for by doing so, one denies communications intercept to one's own side. Or, firing chaff and decoys to defend against a possible enemy missile attack can degrade one's own radar effectiveness.

Also, ECM produces "soft kills." It is not always possible for the ECM operator to detect or determine if his efforts are successful. Further, ESM/SIGINT/ECM/ECCM are undertaken with a continuous interaction. Those who allocate resources are not always eager, for example, to spend funds on an ECM system that may be a counter to a threat the intelligence community predicts may have a certain capability. Somehow, it seems easier to buy a new ship or missile or aircraft rather than a new "black box."

Electronic Counter-Countermeasures (ECCM) are those actions taken to retain the effectiveness of one's own use of the electromagnetic spectrum against hostile electronic warfare efforts.

The following are the principal U.S. Navy EW systems fitted in surface ships and submarines.

APR-39A(V)1 RADAR WARNING RECEIVER

The APR-39 is an omni-directional Radar Warning Receiver (RWR) fitted in helicopters and fixed-wing aircraft, including several Navy-Marine helicopters. It is also fitted in the coastal patrol ships of the CYCLONE (PC 1) class.

The system can determine the frequency, Pulse Repetition Frequency (PRF), pulse-width, persistence, and threshold power level of missiles and radars.

The APR-39(V)1 consists of a blade antenna, four spiral antennas in hemispheric radomes, two dual video receiver units, an indicator unit, an analog comparator, and a control unit.

Manufacturer: E-Systems
Ships: PC 1

BLD-1 RADIO DIRECTION FINDER

This is a mast-mounted radio direction finder. The BLD-1 and BRD-7 will be replaced by the Integrated ESM Mast (ISM) under development for backfitting on SSN 21 and SSN 688 submarines.

Manufacturer: Litton
Ships: submarines

BLQ-SERIES ACOUSTIC COUNTERMEASURES

These are submarine systems that perform a variety of countermeasures against hostile sonars.

The BLQ-3 is a low-frequency acoustic jammer, BLQ-4 a high-frequency acoustic jammer, BLQ-5 a low-frequency acoustic repeater, BLQ-6 a high-frequency acoustic repeater, and BLQ-8 acoustic countermeasures.

Manufacturer: General Electric, except BLQ-8 Bendix/Aerojet
Ships: submarines

BLR-SERIES RADAR WARNING RECEIVERS

Mast mounted, these systems provide warning of hostile radar emissions from aircraft, surface ships, or (surfaced) submarines.

The BLR-14 is known as the Submarine Acoustic Warfare System (SAWS). It provides an integrated receiver, processor, display, and countermeasures launch system.

Manufacturer: BLR-1–10 various
BLR-12 Kollmorgan
BLR-13 Kollmorgan
BLR-14 Sperry
BLR-15 Kollmorgan
Ships: submarines

BRD-SERIES RADIO DIRECTION FINDERS

These are mast-mounted RDF systems. The BRD-7 is currently in U.S. Navy use.

Manufacturer: Lockheed-Sanders
Ships: SSN 637
SSN 671
SSN 688

SLQ-32A(V) ELECTRONIC COUNTERMEASURES

The principal U.S. surface ship ECM system is the SLQ-32 "design-to-cost" EW suite. Variations of this system are fitted in most surface combatant and amphibious ships as well as several underway replenishment types. The SLQ-32 is considered a short-range, omnidirectional, self-defense system that evaluates electronic emissions and can, in some variants, initiate countermeasures.

Several variants of the SLQ-32 are based on modular "building blocks" for different types of ships. The (V)1 variant provides warning, identification, and bearing of radar-guided cruise missiles and their launch platforms. The (V)2 variant has the (V)1 capability and expanded ESM capabilities. An add-on ECM transmitter called "Sidekick" is fitted to SPRUANCE and OLIVER HAZARD PERRY (FFG 7)-class frigates to augment the SLQ-32(V)2, thus creating the (V)5 variant. The Sidekick is an active ECM system intended to confuse enemy threats. (Sidekick was designed, produced, and delivered by Raytheon within 11 weeks of the Navy's request for the system.)

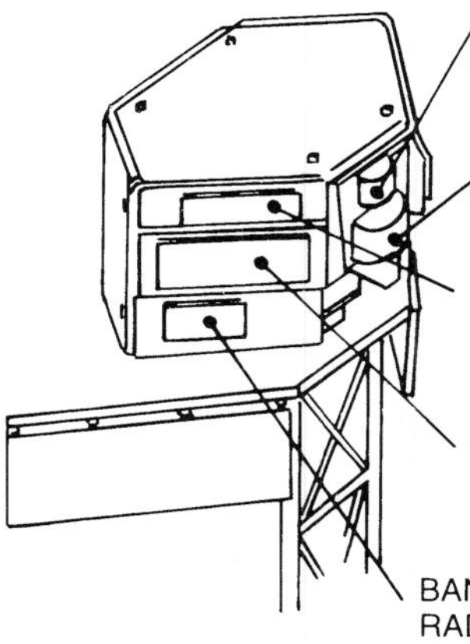

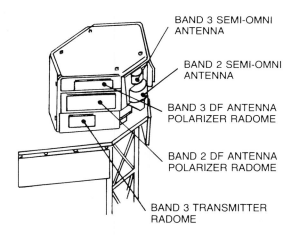

The (V)3 configuration has combined the (V)1 and (V)2 capabilities and the means to counter or deceive missile guidance radars. The (V)3 has a quick-reaction mode that permits the initiation of jamming against a target signal before its characteristics are fully analyzed. This feature could be particularly useful against "pop-up" submarine-launched missiles or those fired by missile craft hiding in coastal shore "clutter."

The (V)4 combined most features into a set intended for aircraft carriers, which had not previously been intended for SLQ-32 installation. These sets are provided only in the last few ships of the NIMITZ (CVN 68) class, plus the recently rebuilt ENTERPRISE (CVN 65).

The SLQ-32 antennas are fitted in two boxlike enclosures, port and starboard, high in the ship's superstructure. The (V)2 and (V)3 are fitted with twin Rotman lens direction-finding receiving antennas. The SLQ-32 systems employ UYK-19 computers.

The proposed follow-on system to the SLQ-32 series is the SLQ-54, previously known as the Advanced Integrated EW System

SLQ-32(V)3 ECM antenna on board the Aegis cruiser YORKTOWN (CG 48) with two Mk 36 multi-tube launchers for Super Rapid Blooming Offboard Chaff (SRBOC) in the foreground. (N. Polmar)

SLQ-32(V)5 ECM system in a PERRY-class frigate. The system consists of the SLQ-32(V)2 antenna mounted on a platform above the smaller "Sidekick" antenna. The latter is an add-on ECM transmitter that enhances the SLQ-32's capabilities. (Raytheon)

(AIEWS). The SLQ-54 is envisioned to counter hostile threats of the 21st century.

The SLQ-32 and other ECM systems are used in conjunction with Mk 36 Super Rapid Blooming Offboard Chaff (SRBOC) launchers that fire either semiautomatically or on manual direction from a ship's ECM operators. Large ships have four Mk 36 launchers and smaller ships have two, each consisting of six fixed barrels. (Infrared decoys and flares can also be fired in response to detections by threat warning devices.)

The ALQ-142 fitted in the SH-60B helicopter is similar to SLQ-32, with two Rotman-lens antennas. Data are transmitted via data link to SLQ-32 ships.

The bands covered by the SLQ-32 are:

(V)1	H/I/J
(V)2/5	B through J
(V)3	B through J; countermeasures in H/I/J

Manufacturer:	Raytheon		
	Hughes		
Ships:	(V)1	LPD 4	LKA 113
		LSD 41	AE 26
		LSD 36	AO 177
	(V)2	DDG 51–67	
		FFG 7 (some ships)	
		AGF 11	
		LSD 49	
	(V)3	CG 47	LHA 1
		CGN 38	LPH 2
		CGN 36	LPD 17
		DDG 79	MCS 12
		DDG 68–78	AOE 6
		LCC 19	AOE 1
		AGF 3	AOR 1
		LHD 1	
	(V)4	CVN 65, 70–76	
	(V)5	DD 963 (some ships)	
		FFG 7 (some ships)	

SLQ-32(V)3 ECM antenna in the cruiser MISSISSIPPI (CGN 40); the smaller antenna at left is a telemetry receiver. The modular SLQ-32 is found in most U.S. Navy surface combatants. (Stefan Terzibaschitsch)

SLQ-29 ELECTRONIC COUNTERMEASURES

Consisting of the SLQ-17A Deceptive ECM, WLR-1H, WLR-8, and WLR-11, this suite was developed for aircraft carriers to provide a broad spectrum of ECM capabilities. Later ships (CVN 70 and later) have the SLQ-32(V)4 in place of the SLQ-29.

Manufacturer:		
Ships:	CV 41	CV 67
	CV 62–CV 64	CVN 68
	CV 66	CVN 69

SLQ-25A NIXIE TORPEDO COUNTERMEASURES

See page 000.

SLQ-17 DECEPTIVE ELECTRONIC COUNTERMEASURES

See SLQ-29.

SLR-23 RADIO DIRECTION FINDER

Associated with the WLR-1 and SLQ-32 systems, the SLR-23 intercepts signals in the D/E/J bands.

Manufacturer:
Ships: surface ships

SLR-16 SIGINT RECEIVER

This is a high-frequency receiver for SIGINT activities, employing the SRD-19 antenna array. It is part of the SSQ-72 system.

Manufacturer:
Ships: surface ships

SLR-12 RADIO DIRECTION FINDER

Manufacturer:
Ships: surface ships

SRD-19 SIGINT RECEIVER

Part of the Classic Outboard system, this is a low/medium/very high–frequency SIGINT exploitation system. It has 24 small, deck-edge antennas and a masthead Adcock-type very-high-frequency direction-finding array. It is used in conjunction with the SLR-16 and is part of the SSQ-72 system.

Manufacturer: Sanders
Ships: surface ships

SRS-1 COMBAT DIRECTION-FINDING RECEIVER

A less capable version of the SSQ-72/108 Classic Outboard system, the SRS-1 is intended to detect anti-ship missiles. The basic system is designated Block 0, while the Block 1 (SRS-1A) incorporates the Automated Digital Acquisition Subsystem (ADAS) to enable the exploitation of unconventional and low-probability-of-intercept signals. Five shore sites will also be fitted with the Block 1 system.

Manufacturer:	Lockheed-Sanders	
Ships:	Block 0	LHD 1
	Block 1	DDG 51

SSQ-74 CLASSIC OUTBOARD SIGINT SYSTEM

Manufacturer: ITT Avionics
Ships: surface ships

SSQ-72 CLASSIC OUTBOARD SIGINT SYSTEM

This is a combat direction-finding system with SRD-19 and SLR-16 antennas. The SSQ-108 is a more advanced version.

Manufacturer: Lockheed-Sanders
Ships: surface ships

WLQ-4 SEA NYMPH ESM SYSTEM

Manufacturer:	GTE-Sylvania	
Ships:	WLQ-4E	SSN 637
	WLQ-4(V)	SSN 21

WLR-13 INFRARED/ELECTRO-OPTICAL WARNING

Intended to warn surface ships of attack by anti-ship missiles with infrared and electro-optical guidance systems.

Manufacturer:
Ships: surface ships

WLR-11 RADAR WARNING/SIGINT SYSTEM

Manufacturer: ARGO Systems
Ships: surface ships

WLR-10 RADAR WARNING RECEIVER

Submarine radar warning receiver fitted to a mast; it is collocated with the WLR-8.

Manufacturer: Astro Labs
Ships: SSBN 726
SSN 642
SSN 645
SSN 688

WLR-9 SONAR WARNING RECEIVER

Manufacturer: Norden (United Technologies)
Ships: submarines

WLR-8(V) RADAR WARNING RECEIVER

The WLR-8(V) provides coverage of 0.5–18 GHz frequencies. A surface ship version was canceled in 1983, although it was installed in the ENTERPRISE. Trident submarines have the (V)5, and LOS ANGELES-class submarines have the (V)2 variant.

Manufacturer: GTE-Sylvania
Ships: SSBN 726
SSN 642
SSN 645
SSN 688

WLR-6 WATERBOY RADAR WARNING, SIGNAL COLLECTION

Manufacturer: GTE-Sylvania
Ships: submarines
surface ships

WLR-1 RADAR WARNING RECEIVER

This radar warning receiver originally covered the 50 MHz to 10.75 GHz frequency range. Most sets are now WLR-1H variants, covering 0.55–20 GHz. It is employed with the WLR-11.

Manufacturer:		
Ships:	submarines	SSN 688
	surface ships	

MK 70 MOSS (MOBILE SUBMARINE SIMULATOR)

MOSS is a torpedo-shaped device that simulates the sounds of a nuclear-propelled submarine to mislead enemy sonars.

Manufacturer:	Gould Electronics
Ships:	SSBN 726
	SSNs

MK 23 TORPEDO DECOY

This device is launched from submarine signal ejection tubes to mislead enemy sonars and acoustic homing torpedoes.

Manufacturer:	
Ships:	SSNs

MINE COUNTERMEASURES SYSTEMS

Two surface-ship acoustic mine neutralization systems are listed with electronic system designations, the SLQ-37(V) and SLQ-53.

SLQ-48 MCM SYSTEM

The remote-controlled Mine Neutralization System (MNS) is given the designation SLQ-48(V). Carried by MCM and MHC ships, it is produced by Honeywell (see page 207).

SLQ-38(V) MCM SYSTEM

The U.S. Navy's standard mechanical minesweeping gear, in use since the early 1940s, this device has recently been given the designation SLQ-38.

SLQ-37(V) MCM SYSTEM

The SLQ-37(V) consists of the combined "magnetic tail" Mk 5A and the Mk 4(V) and/or Mk 6(V) acoustic sweep gear.

SHIPBOARD RADARS

U.S. Navy shipboard radars are used principally for surface and air search, height finding, weapons fire control, target illumination, and aircraft control. In a few radars, two functions can overlap, with the advanced SPY-1 series providing multiple radar functions in a single system.

Aircraft control radars are unique to aviation ships (CV/CVN/LHA/LHD/LPH) and are designated in the SPN-series, informally referred to as "spin" radars. They are used to guide aircraft into the proper approach pattern or glide path to the ship. The SPN-41 and SPN-42 in the K band, SPN-43 in the S band, and SPN-44 in the X band are currently in service.

Numerous shipboard radars have been deleted from the previous edition, reflecting, in part, the large number of ships and classes deleted in the past few years. Radars that will be found in the 15th Edition are:

SPG-35/Mk 35
SPG-53
SPG-55
SPS-53
SPS-66
Mk 13
Mk 25

Designations: Fire-control radars were assigned mark (Mk) numbers beginning in 1941. This series ran through Mk 47, with the next radar initiating the SPG series. Subsequent versions of some earlier radars were given the SPG prefix, thus Mk 35 and SPG-35 were the same radar.

RADAR BANDS

NATO Band Designations
Megahertz

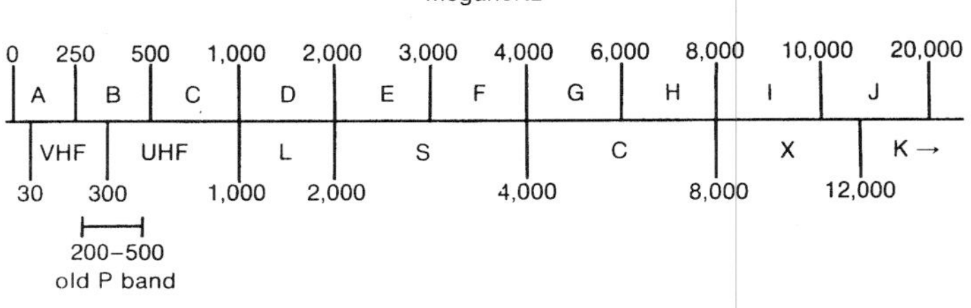

Conventional Band Designations

BPS-16 RADAR

This advanced submarine search and navigation radar was evaluated in the ATLANTA (SSN 712) in 1991–1992. The BPS-16 has an outer "sleeve" that mounts the radar and reduces problems with retraction equipment and leakage. The radar also has multiple frequencies that reduce the unique signature common to previous BPS-series radars that enabled a hostile ESM system to easily identify submarine radar emissions.

Manufacturer:	Sperry
Band:	X
Operational:	1991
Ships:	SSBN 726 (3 ships; to be backfitted in 11 early units beginning about 1997)
	SSN 21

An air traffic controller in the carrier GEORGE WASHINGTON (CVN 73) operates a "spin"-series air traffic control radar during operations in the Adriatic Sea in 1996. (U.S. Navy, AN Joe Hendricks)

BPS-15 RADAR

The BPS-15 submarine search and navigation radar has replaced all older radars in U.S. submarines except for later units of the OHIO (SSBN 726) class and the SEAWOLF (SSN 21) class. The principal differences among the various BPS-series radars are the pedestal mounting. Peak power is 35 kW.

Manufacturer:	Sperry	
Band:	X	
Operational:		
Ships:	BPS-15A/E	SSN 688
	BPS-15B	SSBN 726–740
	BPS-15E	SSN 637
		SSN 642
		SSN 645
		SSN 671

BPS-15 series radar in the raised position at the forward edge of the sail of the ANNAPOLIS (SSN 760). The speckled camouflage on the mast and periscope "sleeves" makes them more difficult to see when projecting above the water. The dark panel on the front of the sail is an antenna for the BQS-15 short-range sonar. (Giorgio Arra)

SPG-62 RADAR

This is the illumination radar for the Standard SM-2 missile in Aegis warships. The Aegis ships have three (DDG 51) or four (CG 47) Mk 99 missile-control directors that use the SPG-62 illumination channel to provide radar reflections for Standard missiles. They are "slaved" to the SPY-1 radar. The antenna is 7½ feet (2.3 m) wide. Peak power is 10 kW.

Manufacturer:	Raytheon
Band:	X
Operational:	1983
Ships:	CG 47
	DDG 51

The forward SPG-62 illumination radar in the ARLEIGH BURKE-class destroyers is fitted above the bridge, at the base of the tripod mast; two SPG-62s are mounted amidships. The forward SPY-1D antennas are visible (on either side of the Phalanx CIWS mount) and the bar-type antennas for the SPS-64 and SPS-67(V)3 radars are above the SPG-62. (Giorgio Arra)

SPG-60 RADAR

The SPG-60 radar both provides gun control data and permits Standard-MR missile tracking with the addition of an illuminator to the Mk 86 FCS. The SPG-60 is a monopulse, pulse-doppler radar that is combined with the SPQ-9A in the Mk 86 weapon control system and can illuminate targets for the Standard and Sea Sparrow missiles. Thus, a single fire-control system can serve several functions. The X-band SPG-60 is credited with a nominal range of some 50 n.miles (92.5 km) and is able to track Mach 3 targets out to 100 n.miles (185 km). (The Mk 86 system can simultaneously track up to 120 incoming targets in a track-while-scan mode.)

The Separate Target Illumination Radar (STIR), using the SPG-60 antenna mount, is found in the PERRY-class frigates to provide two missile control channels for the Mk 86.

The antenna is 13⅓ feet (4 m) across. Peak power is 5.5 kW.

Manufacturer:	Lockheed Electronics
Band:	X
Operational:	
Ships:	CGN 36
	CGN 38
	DDG 993
	DD 963

The STIR in the Perry-class frigates uses the SPG-60 antenna. The antenna is mounted just forward of the Mk 75 76-mm gun. (Giorgio Arra)

SPG-51D RADAR

The SPG-51 is a pulse-doppler tracking/illumination radar used with the Standard-MR in cruisers and destroyers armed with that missile. (Originally, this radar was developed for use with the Tartar missile). It is associated with the Mk 74 missile FCS. The two operating modes share a common antenna; the C-band is a pulse-doppler monopulse tracker. An SPG-51E was developed as a "universal" fire-control radar for use with the Tartar-Terrier-Talos missiles; it was not deployed in significant numbers because of the availability of more advanced radars.

The antenna is 7⅔ feet (2.3 m) in diameter. Peak power is 81 kW in tracking and 5 kW in illumination.

Manufacturer:	Raytheon
Band:	C for tracking
	X for illumination
Operational:	1960
Ships:	CGN 36
	CGN 38
	DDG 993

SPG-51D antennas on the amidships superstructure of the cruiser Mississippi (CGN 40). (Stefan Terzibaschitsch)

SPQ-9 RADAR

The SPQ-9A is the fire-control radar associated with the Mk 86 GFCS. It provides surface search functions as well as weapons control, operating in a high-resolution, pulse-doppler, track-while-scan mode. The SPQ-9A operates from a minimum of 150 yards (137 m) out to 20 n.miles (37 km) against aircraft-size targets. The high scan rate of 60 revolutions per minute can detect and track incoming missiles as well as aircraft and surface targets. The Mk 86 system, with the SPG-60/SPQ-9, is found in new missile cruisers, the Spruance-class destroyers, and the Tarawa (LHA 1)-class helicopter ships. The battleship Iowa mounted the SPQ-9A without the Mk 86 system.

The antenna is housed in a 120-inch (3-m) diameter plastic radome. Peak power is 1.2 kW. The Mean Time Between Failures (MTBF) is given as about 800 hours.

An SPQ-9B variant has been developed by the Navy and preproduction "kits" ordered from Westinghouse-Norden. The SPQ-9B can better detect low-altitude (sea-skimming) missiles in a clutter environment, which should be of particular value in littoral areas. The basic SPQ-9A reflector was replaced by a larger unit with multiple feeds and new processor and receiver/exciter; the transmitter was replaced by an APG-68 radar transmitter as used in the F-16 Fighting Falcon aircraft.

A shore-based SPQ-9B ADM (Advanced Development Model) was tested at Wallops Island, Virginia, and has since been installed for at-sea tests in the stricken destroyer Decatur (DD 936/DDG 31), which serves as a test hulk for the Ship Self-Defense System (SSDS) that operates out of the Puget Sound (Washington). See photo page 131.

Spherical SPQ-9A radome and the SPG-60 radar antenna on the destroyer Elliot (DD 967). Note the exhaust configuration of the ship's forward/port funnel. An OE-82 SATCOMM antenna is mounted atop the port bridge wing. (Giorgio Arra)

Manufacturer:	SPQ-9A	Lockheed Electronics
	SPQ-9B	Westinghouse-Norden
Band:	X	
Operational:	1970	
Ships:	CG 47	DDG 993
	CGN 36	DD 963
	CGN 38	LHA 1

SPS-69 RADAR

This solid-state radar is a modified commercial Raytheon R41X small craft navigation radar. Maximum power is 4 kW.

The Coast Guard has several hundred sets in service. It is no longer fitted in Navy ships.

Manufacturer:	
Band:	X
Operational:	1990
Ships:	Coast Guard cutters and craft

SPS-67(V) RADAR

This surface search/navigation radar was developed as a successor to the long-serving and widely used SPS-10 radar. The newer radar has a high degree of automation and can instantly distinguish between moving and stationary targets.

It has solid-state electronics with an MTBF in excess of 1,000 hours.

Manufacturer:	Norden (United Technologies)	
Band:	C	
Operational:	1982	
Ships:	CVN 68 (3 ships)	LSD 49
	CGN 36	LSD 41
	DDG 51	AH 19
	LCC 19	AOE 6
	LHD 1	

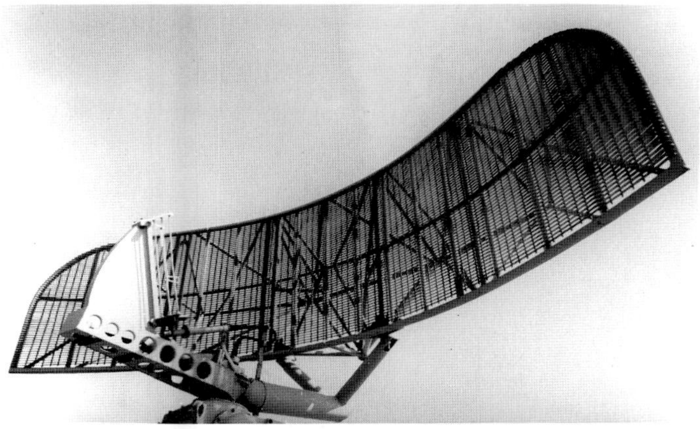

An SPS-67(V) antenna, a search/navigation radar widely used on surface combatants and a few aircraft carriers. (United Technologies/Norden)

SPS-64(V) RADAR

This surface search/navigation radar uses a bar-type antenna. The size of the four available antennas varies from four feet (1.2 m) to 12 feet (3.7 m), depending on the capability/size of the system. Variants have different frequency bands and operating characteristics.

The commercial variants have a four-digit number following the letters RM. The radar's commercial name is Raypath.

The SPS-64 can automatically track up to 20 targets. The variants are:

Variant	Band	Transmitter	User
(V)1	S-band	single 20 kW transmitter	Coast Guard
(V)2, 3	S-band	two 20 kW transmitters	Coast Guard
(V)4	S/X-bands	two 20 kW transmitters	Coast Guard
(V)5	X-band	single tunable 20 kW transmitter	Army
(V)6	X-band	single 50 kW transmitter	Coast Guard
(V)7, 8	S-band		Coast Guard
(V)9	X-band		Navy
(V)10, 11	S-band		Coast Guard
(V)12–14	X-band		Army
(V)15	X-band		Navy
(V)16, 17	X-band		Army
(V)18	X-band		Navy

Manufacturer:	Raytheon			
Band:	S and X			
Operational:				
Ships:	CVN 65	LPD 17	LCC 19	MCM 1
	CVN 68	LSD 36	AGF 3	AE 26
	CG 47	LSD 41	AGF 11	AOE 1
	CGN 36	LSD 49	LHD 1	AOE 6
	CGN 38	LST 1179	LHA 1	AOR 1
	DDG 51	MCS 12	LPH 2	ARS 50
	DDG 993	MHC 51	LPD 4	ATS 1

An SPS-64(V)9 antenna, widely used on Army, Navy, and Coast Guard small ships and craft. (Raytheon)

SPS-59 RADAR/LN-66

SPS-59 is the Navy designation for the LN-66 commercial navigation radar; both designations are used for the radar. This is a short-range navigation radar adopted from a commercial design. It has been installed in a variety of U.S. ships, from battleships to small riverine craft. The radar is also fitted in the SH-2G LAMPS I ASW helicopter.

The radar is being replaced by the SPS-69 and other, more modern radars.

Manufacturer:	Canadian Marconi	
Band:	X	
Operational:		
Ships:	DD 963	AFS 1
	LKA 113	AO 177
	LCAC	AS 32
	Mini-ATC	AS 33
	AD 37	

SPS-58/SPS-65(V) RADAR

The SPS-58/SPS-65 are low-level, high-speed radars for both detecting attacking anti-ship cruise missiles and acquiring targets for the Sea Sparrow point-defense missile system. A pulse-doppler radar, the SPS-65 can "share" the SPS-10 antenna, while the SPS-58 has its own 16-foot (4.9-m) antenna. These radars have no integral display; in aircraft carriers the SPS-65 uses those of the ship's Naval Tactical Data System (NTDS); frigates have the SPS-58, duplexing with the SPS-10.

The SPS-65(V)1 has a specified MTBF of 400 hours.

Manufacturer:	Westinghouse
Band:	D
Operational:	
Ships:	CV 41

An SPS-65(V) antenna. This radar is now found in the U.S. Fleet only in the mothballed aircraft carrier MIDWAY (CV 41). (Westinghouse)

SPS-55 RADAR

This is a surface search radar intended to replace the widely used SPS-10. The SPS-55 has a slotted-array antenna six feet (1.8 m) across.

Manufacturer:	Cordion	
Band:	X	
Operational:		
Ships:	CG 47	DD 963
	CGN 38	FFG 7
	DDG 51	MCM 1
	DDG 993	AO 177

SPS-52 RADAR

A 3-D air search radar with Frequency Scanning (FRESCAN) in elevation, the SPS-52 was developed from the SPS-39 radar. Since 1963 the SPS-52 has been installed in several aircraft carriers plus missile-armed cruisers, destroyers, frigates, and the five TARAWA (LHA 1)-class helicopter carriers. The carriers and LHAs use this radar for aircraft control. The SPS-52 has now been replaced mainly by the SPS-48 3-D radar; it is retained only in large helicopter carriers.

The SPS-52 is credited with a range of 60 n.miles (111 km) against small, high-speed aerial targets, and out to much greater distances—about 250 n.miles (463 km)—against larger, high-flying aircraft. It has a high data rate and clutter rejection features including Moving Target Indicator (MTI). Later versions with solid-state components have MTBF in excess of 200 hours.

The SPS-72 was to have been an improved version with a more advanced antenna.

Manufacturer:	Hughes	
Band:	S	
Operational:	1963	
Ships:	SPS-52B	LHA 1
	SPS-52C	LHD 1 (1 ship)

SPS-49(V) RADAR

The most effective rotating 2-D air search radar in the U.S. Navy is the SPS-49, a lower L-band radar. It is the principal air search radar in most large U.S. warships and is a complementary radar to the SPY-1 in the TICONDEROGA (CG 47) class. Note that the ARLEIGH BURKE (DDG 51) class does not have the SPS-49; it was deleted from the design primarily because of cost constraints.

The SPS-49 was evaluated in 1965 on board the experimental destroyer GYATT (DD 712), and an advanced version was installed in the guided missile cruiser DALE (CG 19) in 1975. This radar features high reliability, with an MTBF reported to exceed 300 hours.

It is a very long-range radar and has a narrow beam, which helps to counter hostile jamming efforts. The antenna, which is 24 × 14 feet (7.3 × 4.3 m), is easily identified, with its large, lower feed horn (the similar-looking SPS-40 antenna has an overhead feed horn). Frequency range is 851–942 MHz.

The SPS-50 was a modified SPS-49 intended to replace the earlier SPS-6 and SPS-12 radars; it failed its operational evaluation.

Manufacturer:	Raytheon	
Band:	L	
Operational:	1975	
Ships:	(V)1	LSD 41 (some ships)
	(V)2	DD 997
	(V)4	FFG 7 (some ships)
	(V)5	aircraft carriers
		CGN 38
		CGN 36
		DDG 993
		LHD 1
		LPD 17
		LSD 41 (some ships)
		FFG 7 (some ships)
	(V)6/7/8	CG 47

An SPS-52C antenna mounted forward on the island structure of the helicopter carrier WASP. The later ships of this class have the SPS-48E in place of this radar. An SPS-67(V)3 is seen on the mast, above the SPS-52C. (Giorgio Arra)

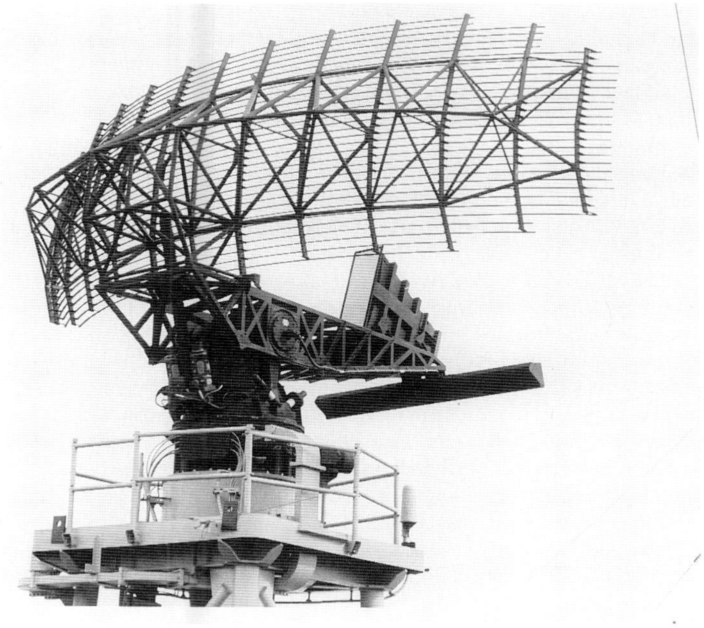

An SPS-49(V) antenna on the frigate JACK WILLIAMS (FFG 24). This is one of the most widely used—and effective—radars in the U.S. Fleet. (Giorgio Arra)

SPS-48 RADAR

The SPS-48 is a 3-D radar used for aircraft control in carriers and command ships; it also supports the air defense role of missile ships. A FRESCAN radar, the older SPS-48A sets were upgraded with Automatic Detection and Tracking (ADT) features and are designated SPS-48C. This radar is more capable than the SPS-52 and can support the longer-range Standard missiles.

The rectangular antenna is 17 × 17½ feet (5.2 × 5.3 m). Frequency band is 2900–3100.5 MHz. Maximum range is about 220 n.miles (407 km).

Manufacturer:	ITT Gilfillan	
Band:	S	
Operational:	1962	
Ships:	SPS-48C	CV 41
		CV 66
		LCC 19
	SPS-48E	CV 63 (3 ships)
		CVN 65
		CVN 68
		CGN 36
		CGN 38
		DDG 993
		LHD 1 (5 ships)

SPS-40 RADAR

The SPS-40 is a widely used 2-D air search radar capable of very long detection ranges. It was previously fitted in about 125 cruisers, destroyers, and frigates, plus amphibious and auxiliary ships. One SPRUANCE-class destroyer has had the SPS-40 replaced by an SPS-49 radar.

Frequency range is 400–450 MHz. Range against medium-size aircraft is 150–200 n.miles (280–370 km). The SPS-40B has been upgraded to an SPS-40C, with higher power and improved ECCM. The SPS-40E is an updated SPS-40B/C/D with a solid-state transmitter, very low failure rate, and reliability increased to some 200 hours MTBF.

The SPS-40 was developed from the SPS-31.

An SPS-48E antenna on the forward "mack" of the cruiser VIRGINIA. Beneath the square antenna is a spherical SPQ-9A antenna; an SPS-40B is just visible on the after "mack." Some ships were refitted with the SPS-49(V)5; the VIRGINIA, shown here in 1993, was not upgraded. (Giorgio Arra)

Manufacturer:	SPS-40	Lockheed Electronics
	SPS-40A	Sperry
	SPS-40B	Norden (United Technologies)
	SPS-40E	Westinghouse
Band:	B	
Operational:	1961	
Ships:	DD 963 (30 ships)	LPH 2
	LCC 19	LPD 4
	AGF 3	LSD 36
	AGF 11	MCS 8
	LHA 1	

An SPS-40 antenna mounted beneath an SPS-67. (Giorgio Arra)

SPS-10 RADAR

The most widely used post–World War II radar in the Navy was the SPS-10 surface search, found in most surface combatants, amphibious ships, and auxiliaries. Its 11-foot (3.35-m)-wide antenna has been a familiar sight on U.S. and allied ships since late 1953. It is generally considered a horizon-range radar, although significantly longer-range detections are routinely made.

Few of the SPS-10E/F variants remain in U.S. Navy service; all of them are in amphibious-type ships and fleet auxiliaries. The improved I-band SPS-55 (similar to the SPS-10 but with higher resolution) and the solid-state SPS-67 (using the same antenna) have replaced the SPS-10.

Manufacturer:	GTE-Gilfillan	
	Raytheon	
Band:	C	
Operational:	1953	
Ships:	AGF 3	AO 180
	AGF 11	AO 186
	LSD 36	AS 32
	LST 1179	AS 33
	LKA 113	AS 36
	AFS 1	AS 39

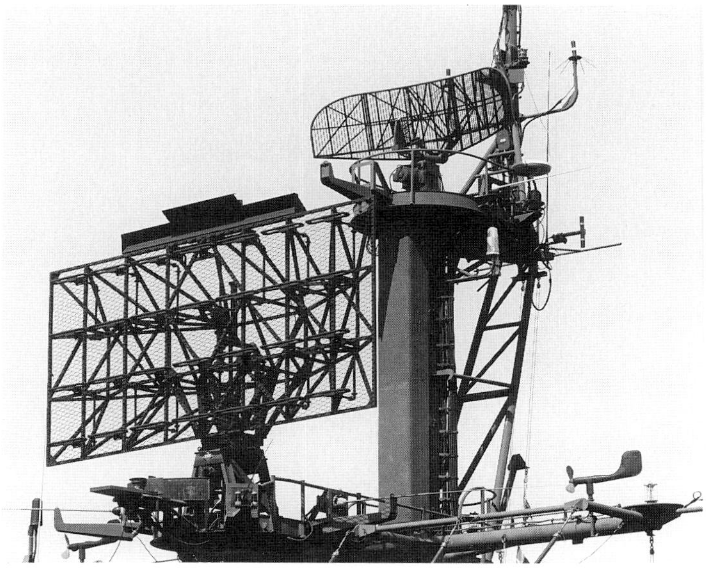

An SPS-10 antenna mounted above an SPS-37 antenna on the destroyer Edson (DD 946). The SPS-10 was mounted in more Navy ships than probably any radar. Only amphibious-type and auxiliary ships now mount the SPS-10. (Giorgio Arra)

SPY-1 RADAR

The SPY-1 is a multifunction, phased-array (fixed-antenna) radar that is the heart of the Aegis AAW system. The SPY-1 combines azimuth and height search, target acquisition, classification, and tracking functions and can provide command guidance to ship-launched missiles. The replacement of several different radars with the single SPY-1 reduces or eliminates several complex interfaces between specialized radars, speeds up all functions, and provides a very large target-handling capability.

The SPY-1 radar—consisting of the antenna, transmitter, signal processor, control groups, and auxiliary equipment—employs four fixed antennas ("faces") and operates in the F (formerly S) band. The antennas each contain 4,480 separate radiating elements in an octagonal face only 12½ feet (3.7 m) across. This small size facilitates ship design: the Ticonderoga has two antennas on a forward deckhouse (facing forward and to starboard) and two on an after deckhouse (facing aft and to port); the Arleigh Burke (DDG 51) has four antennas fitted on a single deckhouse. These four antennas each cover a 90° quadrant from horizon to zenith for total scanning around the ship.

The SPY-1 has a wide frequency bandwidth that randomly radiates different frequencies across it on a pulse-to-pulse basis. The radar has very low sidelobes in comparison with its main lobe, and it also has an extremely complex signal structure. All of these characteristics present great challenges to anti-radar missiles. The SPY-1 radar is also highly resistant to electronic countermeasures because of its frequency diversity, and it can "sense" jamming and automatically shift to different frequencies where less interference is present. Also, digital signal-processing techniques are employed to counter or suppress jamming as well as sea clutter. The latter feature is vital for an effective defense against sea-skimming missiles whose radar return is often lost to conventional radars because sea clutter can mask the target's signal.

Control of the SPY-1 is exercised by four UYK-7 digital computers that schedule and direct the beams; this is necessary because the SPY-1 can project hundreds of pencil-thin radar beams in rapid sequence, far too many for manual control or coordination. Beam steering is a mathematical problem that requires the calculations of a computer system. The computer capacity is a practical limitation on the number of targets that the SPY-1 can handle at one time. When a target is detected, the computers automatically schedule several more beams to "dwell" on the target within a second of the initial detection, thus initiating a track. Hundreds of targets can thus be identified and tracked simultaneously, out to ranges on the order of 200 n.miles (370 km).

In earlier missile ships the surface-to-air missiles had to be guided all the way from launch to the target. Missile ships could thus be characterized by the number of guidance channels, i.e., separate guidance radars available. The modern Standard missiles have an "autopilot" that is set at the moment of launch. The SPY-1 continuously tracks both the missiles in flight and the targets, and the missile guidance can be updated while in flight. Specific radar guidance is required only for the last few seconds before the missile detonates. With this concept the Ticonderoga's four guidance radars can handle perhaps 20 separate targets simultaneously. This provides a vast improvement over previous AAW ship capabilities.

The SPY-1 F-band covers 3100–3500 MHz with a beam measuring $1.7 \times 1.7°$. Its peak power is four to six megawatts, with an average power of 58 kilowatts. Control is exercised by the UYK-7 computer in the CG 47–64 and the UYK-43/UYK-44 series in the CG 65–74 and the DDG 51 class.

There are five production versions of the SPY-1:

SPY-1A	initial design (CG 47–58)
SPY-1B	possessing upgraded antenna, improved transmitter and signal processor for increased effectiveness against low-flying and small radar–cross section missiles, and low sidelobe levels for enhanced ECM resistance (CG 59–73)
SPY-1C	designation not used
SPY-1D	single deckhouse version in Arleigh Burke class
SPY-1D(V)	littoral operations upgrade
SPY-1E	single deckhouse version for DDG 87 and later ships; greater effectiveness against sea-skimming missiles and low-observable targets; IOC about 1999.

Inserting electronic elements in a SPY-1 radar. (RCA)

The reverse side of a SPY-1 radar during assembly. (RCA)

There have been proposals to install the SPY-1 radar in the NIMITZ-class carriers, primarily for aircraft control, and in some nuclear-propelled cruisers. However, no installations have been made in the carriers for fiscal reasons; the cruiser installations were opposed by the Navy's nuclear propulsion community, which sought the construction of nuclear-propelled Aegis ships.

The SPY-1 was developed from the SPG-59 phased-array radar intended for the aborted Typhon missile frigate (DLGN) program. Development of the Aegis SPY-1 began in the late 1960s. The SPY-1 (one radar face) began operation at the RCA-development facility in Cherry Hill, New Jersey, in 1973, followed a year later by a single face being installed in the missile test ship NORTON SOUND (AVM 1).

Manufacturer:	Lockheed Martin (formerly Martin Marietta, General Electric-RCA)
Band:	S
Operational:	1983
Ships:	CG 47
	DDG 51

VPS-2 RADAR

This radar is fitted in the Mk 16 Phalanx gun system, with a single transmitter supporting separate search and tracking radars mounted above the actual Gatling gun. The radar tracks both incoming targets and outgoing bullets, detects the angular error between them, and automatically corrects gun aim. It has a Moving Target Indicator (MTI) with the ability to track very high speed targets and has a very rapid reaction capability. (The radar is also used with the U.S. Army's Vulcan air-defense gun system.)

The radar's search range is approximately 5,500 yards (5,030 m). Its frequency range is 9200–9250 MHz with a peak power of 1.4 kW.

Manufacturer:	Lockheed Electronics
Band:	Ku and X
Operational:	1980
Ships:	various

STIR—SEPARATE TARGET ILLUMINATION RADAR

STIR is an SPG-60 radar modified for use with a Mk 92 gun/missile fire-control system in the PERRY-class frigates.

Manufacturer:	FMC
Band:	X
Operational:	1974
Ships:	FFG 7

SHIPBOARD SONARS

Sonar is the U.S. Navy's principal means for detecting and targeting submarines. All active U.S. surface warships and submarines are fitted with sonars. Anti-submarine aircraft employ expendable sonobuoys, with the SH-60F ASW helicopter using a "dipping" sonar as well as sonobuoys. The CAPTOR sea mines employ sonar for submarine detection. Mine countermeasures forces use sonars to detect mines. And ASW forces make extensive use of seafloor Sound Surveillance Systems (SOSUS). These sonars are either passive or active; some equipment, however, is capable of operating in both modes.

Several sonar entries have been deleted in this edition because of the large number of ships stricken since the previous, 15th Edition. Those sonars are:

BQR-7
BQR-15
SQS-35 IVDS
SQS-23

Submarine sonars. Contemporary U.S. submarine sonars are derived principally from the passive array sonars developed by the Germans just prior to and during World War II. These sonars have a series of fixed transducers that form beams in various directions by the electrical phasing of the transducer inputs.[4] U.S. submarines have traditionally operated in the passive mode in the era of nuclear-propelled submarines, generally being able to detect relatively noisy Soviet nuclear submarines before they themselves could be detected by their opponents. However, the appearance of quiet Soviet nuclear submarines from the early 1980s, of which the Akula class was the harbinger, has resulted in a new interest in active sonar techniques. The Soviet Navy's modern diesel-electric submarines—when operating submerged on electric propulsion—have a very low acoustic signature. (Of course, operating techniques, environmental conditions, and other factors can make even the relatively noisy submarines difficult to detect.)

Although the towed-array sonars were developed by the U.S. Navy primarily for use in surface ships, they were quickly adapted to submarine use and have now been fitted in most of the current SSN and SSBN types.

Surface ship sonars. Surface ship sonars vary considerably in type and installation. The principal hull-mounted sonars in the U.S. Navy today are the SQS-23, SQS-26/SQS-53 series, and SQS-56. The SQS-23/26/53 sonars had their origins in the early 1950s, when the first Soviet post–World War II submarines began going to sea in large numbers. These are relatively large sonars, with long-range passive and some active capabilities.

During the later 1950s the U.S. Navy developed two additional types of surface ship sonars: Variable Depth Sonar (VDS) and Towed Array Sonar (TAS). The VDS is lowered over the stern of the ship to place the sonar dome below the near-surface thermal layers that reflect sonar beams. Towed array development has led to the highly successful Tactical Towed Array Sonar (TACTAS), which consists of a passive (hydrophone) system in a cable towed behind the ship. By using convergence zone detection techniques, TACTAS has long-range capabilities against submarines, especially when employed by screening ships away from the noisy task force center. (If the ocean depth is sufficient, sound will travel down and back to the surface at an annular about 30 n.miles/55.5 km away, i.e., to the first convergence zone. An advanced passive sonar system can be effective out to three convergence zones, or some 90–100 n.miles/167–185 km.)

A further development of the towed-array concept is the Surveillance Towed Array Sonar System (SURTASS), which is a longer, more capable hydrophone array. While the TACTAS is carried by combatant ships (cruisers, destroyers, and frigates), the SURTASS is an area surveillance system towed by slow-speed, tug-type ships designated T-AGOS (see page 226). The SURTASS/T-AGOS concept is intended for use in areas where the seafloor SOSUS detection system has been destroyed or does not exist (see below). The SURTASS AN-series designation is UQQ-2.

Mine countermeasures sonars. Sonar is also used in mine countermeasures: high-resolution sonars are fitted in minesweepers and helicopters (see below).

BQG-5 WIDE APERTURE ARRAY

The Wide Aperture Array (WAA) will enhance submarine fire-control solutions against hostile submarines. The first BQG-5 was installed in the submarine Augusta (SSN 710) in 1992 for at-sea evaluation. WAA components were also evaluated in the research ship Glover (T-AGFF 1).

The Seawolf will be fitted with the BQG-5 and the follow-on New Attack Submarine (NSSN) design will have a lightweight WAA.

Manufacturer: Martin Marietta
Operational: 1992
Ships: SSN 688 (1 ship)
SSN 21

BQQ-6 SONAR

Adapted from the BQQ-5 for use in strategic missile submarines of the Ohio class, this sonar system is primarily passive, with a limited active capability (see BQS-13). The BQQ-6 includes a bow sphere with 944 hydrophones, plus flank arrays and a towed array.

Manufacturer: IBM
Operational: 1981
Ships: SSBN 726

BQQ-5 SONAR

This active/passive sonar system is currently fitted in all U.S. attack submarines except the two converted Polaris/Poseidon submarines employed as transports for special operations forces. The BQQ-5 was built in the Los Angeles class (through SSN 750) and was backfitted in the Permit (SSN 594) and Sturgeon (SSN 637) classes, which originally had the BQQ-2.

The BQQ-5 is a digital system that integrates the bow-mounted array, the conformal (hull-mounted) array, and the towed array. A computer-driven signal processor is used to select the hydrophones and to steer the beams. With this method the number of beams that can be formed is limited only by computer capacity. Also, the digital BQQ-5 suffers far less from internal noises than the BQQ-2 with manual switching, thus enhancing the detection of weaker acoustic signals. The BQQ-5 digital computer's processing allows a reduction in the number of normal watch standers.

Developed from the BQQ-2 system, there is a large spherical bow array fitted in a 15-foot (4.6-m) sphere mounting 1,241 transducers (the BQS-11, 12, or 13), a "chin" array with 104 hydrophones, and TB-series towed array (see below).

BQQ-5 variants have provided improved display consoles as well as integrated towed array processing. The latest variant is the BQQ-5E modification, having been fitted in all Los Angeles-class submarines; the improved SSN 688 class has the BQQ-5 integrated in the BSY-1 system. The BQQ-5E is referred to as the "QE-2" system.

Manufacturer: IBM
Loral
Operational: 1976
Ships: ISSN 688
SSN 688
SSN 671
SSN 637

BQR-21 SONAR

A passive detection sonar, the BQR-21 is a highly capable sonar with DIMUS (Digital Multi-beam Steering). It is now found only in two converted SSBNs. It is used with BQR-24 processor.

Manufacturer: Honeywell
Operational:
Ships: SSN 642
SSN 645

BQR-19 SONAR

This short-range passive navigation sonar is mounted on a submarine mast and has 24 hydrophones in a cylindrical housing.

Manufacturer: Raytheon
Operational:
Ships: SSBN 726

4. The first "modern" array sonar installations were fitted in German submarines and surface ships beginning in the late 1930s. After the war the first U.S. array sonar developed for operational use was the BQR-4, which was fitted in the hunter-killer submarine K-1 (SSK 1) in 1951.

BQS-24 SONAR

The BQS-24 is a high-frequency active array fitted in the sail structure of the SEAWOLF.

Manufacturer:	
Operational:	1996
Ships:	SSN 21

BQS-14/BQS-15 SONAR

A short-range sonar for under-ice and mine-avoidance operations, the BQS-14/15 has a cylindrical transducer housing and operates in both high- and low-frequency ranges. It is fitted in the forward section of the sail structure.

Manufacturer:	Hazeltine	
Operational:		
Ships:	BQS-14	SSN 637
		SSN 671
	BQS-15	SSBN 726
		SSN 688

BQS-13 SONAR

This is the bow-sphere sonar of the BQQ-5 system. It is a narrow-band, active search sonar.

Manufacturer:	Raytheon
Operational:	
Ships:	SSN 637
	SSN 671
	SSN 688

BQS-4

This active/passive sonar features seven large transducers that serve as receivers. Now fitted only in the two ex-Polaris/Poseidon submarines employed as transports for special operations forces.

Manufacturer:	EDO
Operational:	1955
Ships:	SSN 642
	SSN 645

BSY-2 COMBAT SYSTEM (formerly SUBACS/Fiscal 1989 System)

The BSY-2 system is an advanced sonar and fire-control system for attack submarines of the SEAWOLF class. This system was originally part of the SUBACS (Submarine Advanced Combat System); see BSY-1 entry for background information.

The functions of the BSY-2 are to detect, classify, track, and launch weapons against hostile submarine targets. It is intended to permit the SEAWOLF to detect and locate targets faster, to allow operators to perform multiple tasks and address multiple targets concurrently, and—ultimately—to reduce the time between detecting a threat and launching weapons. The principal antennas of the BSY-2 are a large spherical array, conformal hull array, separate active transmitter, high-frequency mine/under-ice sonar, towed arrays, and Wide Aperture Arrays (WAA). The WAAs consist of three large, flat arrays mounted along each side of the submarine; they employ low-frequency, passive sensing capabilities to rapidly determine the locations of targets in both azimuth and depth to provide more accurate target range and tracking data. (The BSY-1 is similar in concept, although the configuration is different; see below.)

The BSY-2 has been plagued by a number of problems, including increasing costs and technical problems associated with the UYS-2 Enhanced Modular Signal Processor (EMSP), database management system, and computer network. Of particular concern has been the unprecedented number of lines of computer (software) code required for the BSY-2 system: namely, some 3.2 million lines, over two million of which are in the new Ada language, for which there were inadequate numbers of experienced programmers available.[5] The BSY-2 computer code requirement is about twice the amount needed for the BSY-1. A recent investigation by the General Accounting Office into the BSY-2 concluded:

> The risks that the Navy has allowed in the development of its BSY-2 combat system are serious. . . .
>
> In its endeavor to meet BSY-2 delivery schedules, tied closely to the submarine's delivery, the Navy is not following some sound management principles and practices, and is pushing forward not only with development of the first three systems but also for approval of three additional systems. By doing so, the Navy could find itself with combat systems that fall short of their promised capability and could cost millions to enhance.[6]

The delays in completion of the first submarine of the class, however, could permit time to remedy some or all of these problems, many of which can be traced directly to its predecessor, the BSY-1.

The estimated cost of the BSY-2 program has *decreased* over the past few years, from about $16 *billion* to some $14 *billion.* The reduction was due mainly to the Navy eliminating one base at which SEAWOLFS would operate (with a reduction in BSY-2 spares, training equipment, personnel, etc.). Those costs, however, were based on the procurement of 29 sets; far fewer will be procured for the truncated SEAWOLF program.

BSY-2 component systems include the BQS-24 high-frequency active array in the sail, BQG-5 Wide Aperture Array (three per side), and the TB-12X and TB-16D towed-array sonars.

Manufacturer:	Martin Marietta (formerly General Electric)
Operational:	1996
Ships:	SSN 21

5. The only Department of Defense program known to exceed the SEAWOLF in lines of Ada code is the F-22 Advanced Tactical Fighter.
6. General Accounting Office, *Submarine Combat System: BSY-2 Development Risks Must Be Addressed and Production Schedule Reassessed* (Washington, D.C.: August 1991), p. 2.

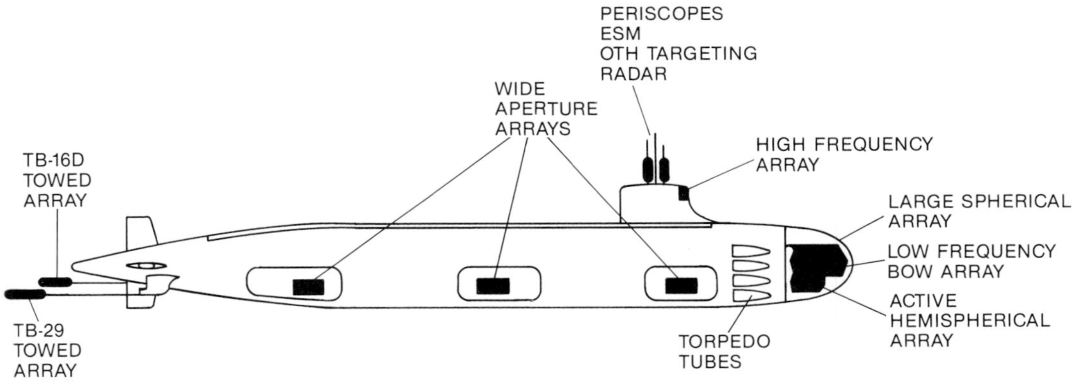

BSY-2 Combat System in the SEAWOLF. (William Clipson)

BSY-1 COMBAT SYSTEM (FORMERLY SUBACS)

The BSY-1 is an advanced sonar and fire-control system intended for installation in 20 Los Angeles submarines, beginning with the SSN 751. The system was known as SUBACS until 1986, when the name was changed to BSY-1. As the SUBACS/BSY-1 program, it was one of the most poorly run programs in recent Navy history.

Early in 1986 the Secretary of Defense told Congress that SUBACS "will maintain our [submarine] force's edge in undersea detection and targeting." Employing advanced computer hardware and software, the system is intended to exploit advanced acoustic sensors—such as Wide Aperture Arrays—to analyze acoustic detection data, identify targets, and make fire-control calculations.

When conceived in the early 1980s there were to be three versions of SUBACS: The *Basic* version for the SSN 751–759, the *B* version for the SSN 760 (fiscal 1986) and later Los Angeles-class submarines, and the *B-prime* variant for the SSN 21 class. The need to restructure the program because of major problems led to a two-part program: the BSY-1 for the improved Los Angeles class (SSN 751–773) and BSY-2 for the Seawolf.

The program has suffered severe technical, cost, and management problems. The planned optical data bus—using fiber-optic technology to transmit data—encountered difficulties, causing a redesign effort to employ more conventional electronic technology. Next, there were difficulties in producing the multilayer computer circuit boards. And,

The spherical, bow-mounted array that will hoist components of the BSY-2 sonar/combat system. This system will be fitted only in the Seawolf class. (Newport News Shipbuilding)

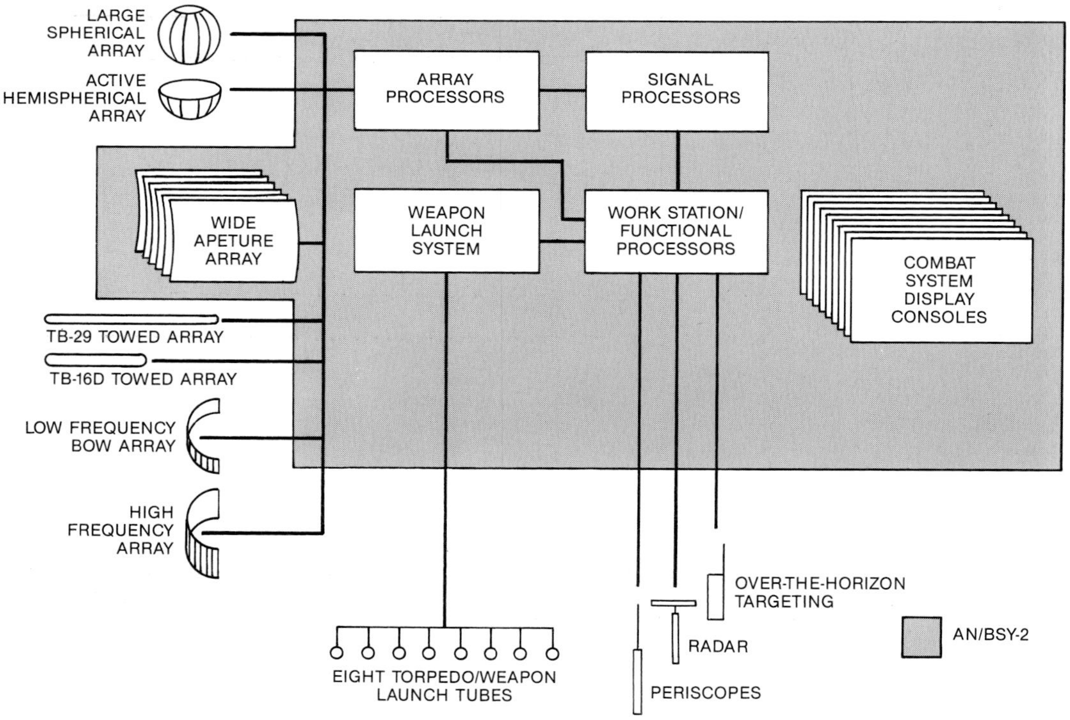

BSY-2 Combat System. (William Clipson)

there were management problems, both on the part of IBM, which had been contracted to develop and produce SUBACS, and the Navy. A late 1985 congressional report on the situation stated, "[S]evere technical and management problems have significantly increased costs, delayed schedules, and degraded planned system capability." Navy and other government agency reviews of SUBACS indicated that research and development for the system would cost $2.4 *billion,* and shipbuilding costs for the submarines already authorized were estimated to be 40 percent more than appropriated. The House and Senate Armed Services Committees at the time reported, "[T]he constrained capability of the SUBACS is no longer worth the investment."

The problems led the Secretary of the Navy and the Chief of Naval Operations to personally take over the management of the contract and renegotiate it. In late 1985 the Navy restructured the program. The BSY-1 is being developed by IBM for the SSN 751 and later (improved) LOS ANGELES-class submarines. In January 1986 the Navy renegotiated the IBM contract to complete seven sets at a fixed price of $1.3 *billion.* In his February 1986 testimony to Congress, Admiral James Watkins, then Chief of Naval Operations, spoke of the "restructured" and "relabeled" SUBACS program becoming the BSY program. Watkins described SUBACS as originally having three steps, but the program was reorganized. "The middle step was not deemed necessary; it was very expensive and there was no way we could have managed the transition from step 2 to 3, which is to the SSN 21 class suite."

When installation of the first BSY-1 set began on the SAN JUAN (SSN 751) late in 1986, it was found that the cabling would not fit into the spaces allocated for the equipment in the submarine. This situation has further increased costs and delayed completion of that submarine. Moreover, the first four installations (SSN 751–754) were not complete when fitted in submarines having only limited self-defense capabilities; they were upgraded to provide full BSY-1 capabilities after the submarines went to sea.

Manufacturer:	IBM General Electric Lockheed Missile and Space Loral
Operational:	1989
Ships:	SSN 751–773

SQQ-89(V) ASW COMBAT SYSTEM

The SQQ-89 surface ship ASW combat system is the first integrated ASW combat system for surface ships, combining sensors and weapons control systems with sophisticated data processing and display. Known as the "Squeak 89," the system correlates and manages acoustic sensor input from hull-mounted sonar and towed array, and it forwards track data to the ship's combat direction system.

There are four variants of the SQQ-89. The (V)1 is in the SPRUANCE (DD 963) and KIDD (DDG 993) destroyers; the (V)3 is in the TICONDEROGA-class cruisers and the BURKE-class destroyers; and the (V)4, intended for the PERRY-class frigates, was canceled in 1990 because of budgetary constraints. (That variant was also known as the SQQ-89I, the suffix indicating "improved"; it was subsequently designated SQY-1.) The (V)2 was to be installed in both active and Naval Reserve Force frigates of the PERRY class. In those ships the limited-capability SQS-56 sonar was to be integrated with the SQQ-89. In the event, only the FFG 7, 9, 20, and 48–52 were fitted with the (V)4.

The large, SQS-53B/C sonars of the cruisers and destroyers are integrated into the SQQ-89, as are the SQR-19 towed arrays, SQQ-28 shipboard acoustic processing component of the LAMPS III (helicopter) system, and the ships' ASW weapons control system.

The destroyer MOOSBRUGGER (DD 980) was the first ship to have the SQQ-89 installed.

Manufacturer:	General Electric Westinghouse
Operational:	1985
Ships:	CG 47 DDG 51 DD 963 FFG 7 (some ships)

SQQ-32 SONAR

The SQQ-32 is a high-resolution mine detection and classification sonar provided in new construction minesweepers and to be backfitted in early MCM ships. The sonar antenna is a "towed" body lowered through the hull of the carrying ship (the SQQ-14/SQQ-30 arrangement is similar). The sonar can be employed in a hull-mounted (retracted) mode for shallow-water operation. There are 48 acoustic arrays in a "stave" arrangement around the barrel-like towed body, with the bar-type classification antenna at the bottom of the body. The towed body weighs 7,845 pounds (3,530 kg).

The first operational use of the SQQ-32 was by the AVENGER (MCM 1) in the Persian Gulf in early 1991. The SQQ-32 provided successful mine detections in the gulf operations.

Manufacturer:	Raytheon/Thomson CSF
Operational:	1991
Ships:	MCM 1 (5 ships) MHC 51

An SQQ-32 towed body prior to installation in a mine countermeasures ship. (Raytheon)

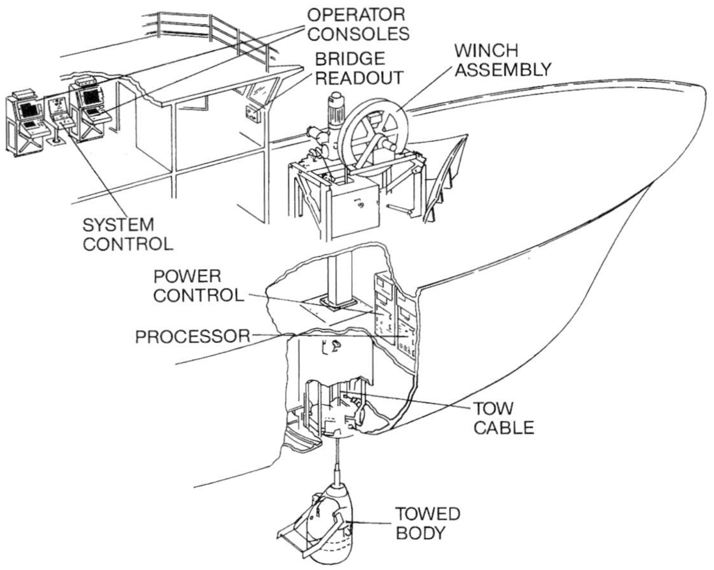

An SQQ-32 arrangement in MCM/MHC–type ships. (William Clipson)

An artist's concept of the SQQ-32 minehunting sonar examining a seafloor object. This "hunting" technique is necessary to detect and identify objects on the seafloor that could be mines. (Raytheon)

SQQ-30 SONAR

This mine detection and classification sonar was developed from the SQQ-14. The antenna is cable-lowered from under the minesweeper. The SQQ-30 has limited capabilities and is being succeeded in service by the SQQ-32.

Manufacturer:	General Electric
Operational:	1987
Ships:	MCM 1 (9 ships)

SQQ-28 SONAR PROCESSOR

The SQQ-28 is a shipboard acoustic processor and data link for the SH-60B LAMPS III anti-submarine helicopter.

Manufacturer:	
Operational:	
Ships:	CG 47
	DDG 51
	DD 963
	FFG 7

TB-SERIES TOWED ARRAY SONARS

Submarine towed array sonars are now designated in the TB-series (for Towed Body). These passive arrays are fully retractable into "sleeves" on submarine decks.

The original TB-16 array is 240 feet (73 m) long and is towed at the end of a 2,600-foot (793-m) cable and mounts 50 hydrophones. Later variants have longer arrays, with the TB-16D being a thin-line array.

The TB-23 is a thin-line array about 1,500 feet (457 m) long and towed by a 2,600-foot cable. It has 98 hydrophones, the smaller diameter of the array permitting the greater length to be accommodated by the submarine.

Manufacturer:		
Operational:		
Ships:	TB-16	SSBN 726 (being replaced by TB-29)
		SSN 671
	TB-16D	SSN 21
	TB-16 or TB-23	SSN 637
		SSN 688
	TB-29	SSN 21

SQR-19A/B TACTAS

This Tactical Towed Array Sonar (TACTAS) is a passive hydrophone array deployed from cruisers, destroyers, and frigates. The towed array, or "tail," locates the sonar away from ship-generated noises that could otherwise mask a target's acoustic signals. The modular construction of the array permits hydrophone components that fail or are damaged to be replaced aboard ship.

The SQR-19 is fitted in the Ticonderoga-class cruisers, Burke and Spruance destroyer classes, and the active Perry-class frigates. Installation in the Kidd-class destroyers was considered but will not occur.

The array can be effective at relatively high ship's speed and in sea states up to four. The SQR-19 array has a nominal diameter of 3¼ inches (82.5 mm) and is towed at the end of a 5,600-foot (1,700-m) cable. The array section weighs about 10,000 pounds (4,536 kg).

The "wet end" (cable systems) of the SQR-19 is also fitted in Canadian and Spanish frigates.

Manufacturer:	Gould Electronics
Operational:	
Ships:	CG 47
	DDG 51
	DD 963 (several ships)
	FFG 7 (33 ships)

SQR-18A(V) TACTAS

This version of the TACTAS is a passive hydrophone system employed by frigates. Similar to the SQR-19, the SQR-18A(V)2 is streamed from the PERRY-class ships assigned to the Naval Reserve Force. The array—which is 730 feet (223 m) long—is towed from a 5,000-foot (1,525-m) cable rather than the VDS towed body, as in the earlier frigates of the KNOX (FF 1052) class. The system can be effective in sea states up to four.

The SQR-18A is fitted in Japanese ASW ships.

The basic SQR-18 was an interim towed array that evolved into the SQR-18A TACTAS.

Manufacturer:	Gould Electronics
Operational:	
Ships:	FFG 7 (Naval Reserve)

SQR-17 ACOUSTIC PROCESSOR

An acoustic processor for sonobuoys and related display for use with SH-2G LAMPS I helicopters, the SQR-17A is being succeeded in newer ships by the SQQ-89. In 1986 Congress voted funds for the procurement of 20 SQR-17A sets for Naval Reserve frigates.

Manufacturer:	Diagnostic Retrieval Systems
Operational:	
Ships:	DDG 993 DD 963 FFG 7 (Naval Reserve units)

SQS-56 SONAR

Ships fitted with this active/passive sonar—with its severely limited capabilities—are expected to detect submarines primarily with their towed array sonar.

The severe cost and size constraints imposed by the Chief of Naval Operations when the PERRY-class frigates were designed led to the small, higher-frequency and thus shorter-range SQS-56 being employed in this class. Raytheon had developed the SQS-56 as a totally company-funded project to provide a modern, lightweight sonar for smaller warships. The use of the SQS-56 saved perhaps 600 tons of displacement in the FFG 7, while requiring far less electrical power than the 66 kilowatts needed for the SQS-53. The cost is effective range, with the SQS-56 being capable of direct path detections only on the order of five miles (8 km)—far too little for effective use with ship-based ASW helicopters. The SQS-56 operates at 5.6, 7.5, and 8.4 kHz.

During the 1980s the set was modified to provide a capability for short-range mine detection; the modification is known as the "Kingfisher."

(Other factors in the decision to reduce the PERRY-class sonar effectiveness were the availability of large numbers of SQS-26/SQS-53 sonars in other ASW ships and the potential of towed array sonars.)

SQS-56 sonars have been fitted in the warships of several other navies, some with the Raytheon commercial designations DE-1160B/C.

Manufacturer:	Raytheon
Operational:	1977
Ships:	FFG 7

SQS-53 SONAR

An improved SQS-26CX sonar, the SQS-53 is a large active/passive sonar that became the bow-mounted sonar of the SPRUANCE variants (DD 963/DDG 993/CG 47 classes) as well as the VIRGINIA (CGN 38)-class nuclear-propelled cruisers and the subsequent ARLEIGH BURKE-class destroyers.

The principal difference between the SQS-26CX and SQS-53 is the digital interface with the Mk 116 ASW weapon control system in the latter sonar. The SQS-53B has an improved, digital, solid-state display; the SQS-53C has an improved active performance, multiple target capability, automatic target tracking, and a higher systems availability (2,000 hours MTBF).

The SQS-53B is fitted in the TICONDEROGA class (beginning with CG 56) and backfitted in the SPRUANCE class (beginning with DD 980). The SQS-53C is being procured for the BURKE-class destroyer and will eventually be backfitted in ships with SQS-53/SQS-53B.

Manufacturer:	General Electric Hughes
Operational:	1975
Ships:	CG 47 CGN 38 DDG 51 DDG 993 DD 963

SQS-38 SONAR

A hull-mounted version of the SQS-35 developed for Coast Guard cutters, this set has now been deactivated because those ships have discarded their ASW capability. The solid-state sonar was developed specifically to replace the vacuum-tube SQS-36 sonar in the HAMILTON (WHEC 715)-class cutters. The sonar could operate in both active and passive modes.

This was the only sonar fitted in U.S. Coast Guard cutters.

The SQS-38 was manufactured by EDO Corporation, College Point, New York; 14 sets have been delivered for shipboard installation and training from 1967.

An SQS-53 transducer housing on a SPRUANCE-class destroyer. (Litton/Ingalls Shipbuilding)

SQS-26 SONAR

The SQS-26 is an active/passive sonar with a nominal direct-path range of 20,000 yards (18,292 m). Major delays in delivery and technical problems resulted in the SQS-26 finally being approved for service in November 1968—six years after its introduction. By that time more than a score of ships had been fitted with the sonar. The sonars were of limited effectiveness during this period, while the ships' long-range ASW delivery capability was nil because of the short range of ASROC and the short-lived Drone Anti-Submarine Helicopter (DASH) program.

The large SQS-26 then went into the subsequent 46 ships of the KNOX class and the two nuclear cruisers of the CALIFORNIA (DLGN/CGN 36) class. With these installations a number of improvements were made to the SQS-26. A major advance was made with a shift to solid-state electronics, resulting in the new designation SQS-53. The SQS-26 variants are AXR, BX, and CX.

An SQS-26 sonar dome on the frigate KNOX. This sonar will soon depart the U.S. Fleet, although the similar and improved SQS-53 remains in large numbers in cruisers and destroyers. (U.S. Navy)

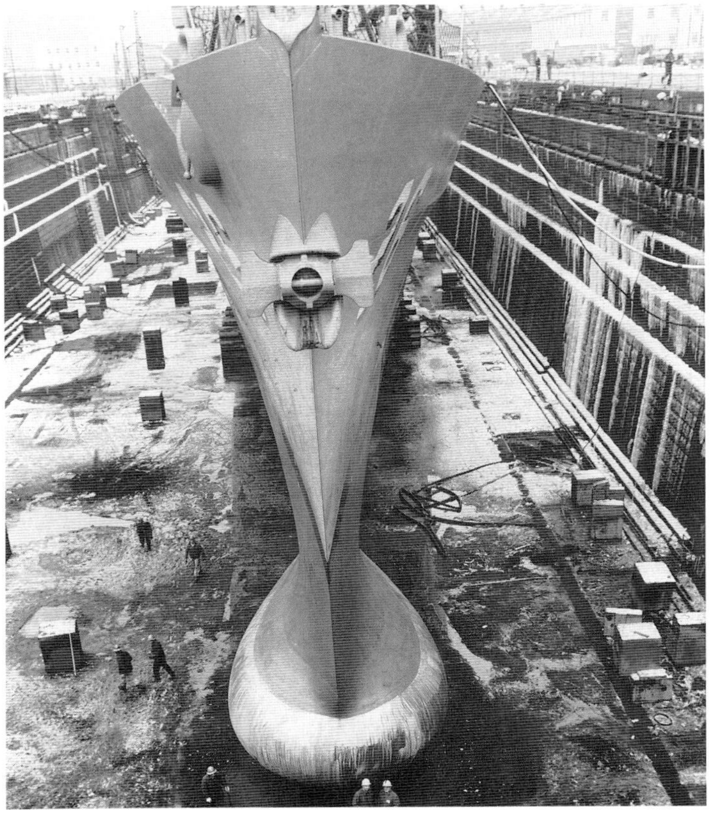

An SQS-26 sonar dome in the cruiser BELKNAP (CG 26). The stem anchor is placed specifically to reduce possible damage to the dome. (U.S. Navy)

Manufacturer:	General Electric
Operational:	1962
Ships:	CGN 36

SQY-1 ASW COMBAT SYSTEM

This was to be an integrated ASW combat system intended for major ASW ships as the successor to the SQQ-89. It was to integrate all ASW sensors and fire-control systems in surface combatants.

The SQY-1 was terminated by the Department of Defense in January 1992 as a cost-saving measure, permissible in view of the demise of the Soviet Union and the reduced threat from its submarine force. Accordingly, there will be some changes in the SQQ-89 modernization program to reflect the SQY-1 cancellation.

The initial operational capability was planned for the mid-1990s, but it was delayed because of funding issues until after the year 2000 and subsequently canceled. The system was originally intended for the 51 frigates of the PERRY class, as well as cruisers and destroyers. The subsequent decision not to provide the system to ASW frigates reduced the program to some 80 ships, with a related increase in unit costs.

Like the BSY-2, the SQY-1 was to incorporate the UYS-2 Enhanced Modular Signal Processor (EMSP) to handle the large amount of data processing required for the system. (When developed, the EMSP will also be used for an upgrade of the SURTASS and other ASW systems.)

The system was previously designated SQQ-89 Improved (SQQ-89I).

Operational:	canceled
Ships:	planned CG 47
	DDG 51
	DDG 993
	DD 963

UQQ-2 SURTASS

The Surveillance Towed Array Sensor System (SURTASS) is a submarine detection system towed by slow surface ships to supplement the SOSUS. These ships operate where SOSUS coverage is inadequate or where the seafloor arrays are damaged or destroyed. The SURTASS data are sent via satellite link to shore facilities for processing and further transmission to ASW forces; however, the ships can provide "raw" acoustic data to ASW ships in the area. The SURTASS concept differs from the tactical TASS/TACTAS systems in that the latter are tactical hydrophone arrays towed by warships to supplement hull-mounted sonars.

The oceanographic research ship MOANA WAVE (AGOR 22) conducted sea trials of the UQQ-2 in 1979–1984; the ex-missile submarine SAM HOUSTON (SSB 609) was employed in the mid-1980s as an underwater test platform for the UQQ-2.

So-called block upgrades are expanding the acceptability of SURTASS for the T-AGOS 23 ships.

See page 226 for additional characteristics.

Manufacturer:	Hughes
	Lockheed-Sanders
Operational:	1984
Ships:	T-AGOS 1
	T-AGOS 19
	T-AGOS 23

SEAFLOOR ACOUSTIC SYSTEMS

The U.S. Navy operates several seafloor Sound Surveillance Systems (SOSUS) in various parts of the Atlantic and Pacific, as well as across the Strait of Gibraltar and off North Cape (north of Norway).[7] In the late 1960s then-Secretary of Defense Robert S. McNamara first publicly acknowledged the existence of SOSUS, although installation began in the 1950s.

SOSUS is used to detect transiting submarines and, in wartime, would be used to direct air, surface, and submarine ASW forces to their targets. However, the SOSUS arrays are vulnerable to active and passive (i.e., jamming) attacks by hostile naval and possibly merchant forces.

During World War II the American and British (and Soviet) navies installed limited-capability acoustic arrays on the ocean floor in shallow waters, especially near harbors. Immediately after the war the U.S. Navy began development of deep-ocean arrays. By 1948 arrays were being tested at sea, and by 1951 the first SOSUS arrays were being implanted at sea. Also termed Project Caesar, the first set of operational hydrophones were installed at Sandy Hook, south of Manhattan, followed in 1952 by a deep-water (1,200-foot/365.85-m) installation off Eleuthra in the Bahamas. That year the Chief of Naval Operations directed the establishment of six arrays in the Western Atlantic, all to be ready by the end of 1956. The first arrays in the Pacific were operational in 1958. Installations in other areas followed.

Initially, a number of Naval Facilities (NAVFAC) were established as the shore terminals for SOSUS, with NAVFACs being located along both U.S. coasts, and in the Caribbean, Iceland, and Japan, as well as at other overseas locations. Subsequently, the seafloor hydrophones have been replaced, and the NAVFACs in the United States and Caribbean have been consolidated as more capable arrays and computers have been developed.

The SOSUS system and SURTASS (T-AGOS) ships are integrated into the so-called Integrated Undersea Surveillance System (IUSS). Acoustic data from the NAVFACs and Regional Evaluation Centers (REC) are provided through the Ocean Surveillance Information System (OSIS) to the Atlantic, Pacific, and European area Fleet Command Centers (FCC) and to the Naval Ocean Surveillance Information Center (NOSIC), in Suitland, Maryland, near Washington, D.C., as well as the National Command Authorities (NCA). Thus, SOSUS information is provided at several levels: to tactical as well as theater and national commanders, and for technical evaluation.

Published sources cite detection ranges of "hundreds" of miles by SOSUS, with arrays reported in the Atlantic and Pacific areas, as well as some regional seas. Several update programs have been announced; one, especially, is related to a computer capability to more rapidly provide data with an improved signal-to-noise ratio.

An improved SOSUS-type system known as the Fixed Distributed System (FDS) is under development. The system is intended to detect quiet, deep-running Soviet/Russian submarines. A shallow-water FDS variant is being developed, with a greater emphasis on fiber-optics than in the SOSUS-type systems, and possible integration of non-acoustic sensors.

These acoustic systems are to be linked into the IUSS. The FDS was in advanced development in the early 1990s at the time of massive defense funding reductions. Beginning in mid-1990, Congress began cutting the funding for the IUSS and FDS programs despite traditional congressional support for major ASW programs. At the same time, the Navy began examining the feasibility of employing FDS in coastal and shallow-water areas.

An Advanced Deployable System (ADS) is now under development. ADS is intended to provide an undersea surveillance system to detect diesel-electric submarines operating in shallow waters, to observe minelaying activity, and to track surface contacts. The system will interface directly with tactical forces (ships and aircraft). During a crisis or conflict ADS is to be deployed within ten days to the operational area.

The obvious vulnerabilities of SOSUS in wartime, as well as some coverage limitations, have led to the T-AGOS/SURTASS program, in addition to proposals for smaller arrays that could be planted by surface ships or aircraft. The latter idea has been an on-again, off-again program, identified by such acronyms as MSS (Moored Surveillance System) and RDSS (Rapidly Deployable Surveillance System). The RDSS was formally canceled by the Navy on 26 December 1984. This form of sonar would probably have been quite useful, in view of the increased Soviet naval operating areas predicted at that time and the growing Third World submarine forces.

Current upgrades to SOSUS include transitioning from single-beam paper displays to multi-beam CRT-based displays and improved communication links. These upgrades are being undertaken by AT&T.

7. The locations of U.S. SOSUS arrays have been identified in Soviet magazines.

HELICOPTER SONARS

AQS-22

In December 1991 the Navy selected the French-based Thomson-CSF firm to develop the advanced helicopter sonar, called Airborne Low Frequency Sonar (ALFS) by the U.S. Navy. Designated AQS-22 by the U.S. Navy, it will be used in the SH-60F/R ASW helicopters. The French system is known as FLASH for Folding Light Acoustic Sonar for Helicopters. The FLASH system was chosen over proposals by several U.S. firms and, when this edition went to press, the selection was being contested by some of the competitors.

The Thomson system will be developed under a subcontract from Hughes Aircraft Company. The lead systems will be delivered in the late 1990s.

The airborne low-frequency sonar program calls for 429 systems at a production cost of $1.2 *billion,* which includes the costs of spares, training, and fitting the system to SH-60B/F helicopters. The Navy plans to combine the capabilities of the SH-60B and SH-60F into a single aircraft through a remanufacture program.

(A towed version of this array has been proposed; such a system could have been employed from airships.)

AQS-20

This improved mine detection sonar is intended for use by MH-53E Sea Dragon helicopters, replacing the AQS-14. Produced by Westinghouse, it will enter service in the late 1990s.

AQS-14

The AQS-14, produced by Westinghouse, is a helicopter-towed sonar employed by the MH-53E Sea Dragon and RH-53D Sea Stallion mine countermeasures helicopters. The AQS-14 towed body weighs 555 pounds (251 kg). The system's control console and winch are mounted on pallets and can be rapidly installed or removed from a helicopter. The system can also be fitted to small surface craft.

The proposed use of LCAC landing craft for mine countermeasures would employ the AQS-14 as a towed array.

AQS-13

The Navy's SH-60F Seahawk ASW helicopter is fitted with the AQS-13 active "dipping" sonar. This sonar is generally used in areas where ship-generated noises are high and passive sonar or sonobuoy effectiveness is limited (e.g., near a carrier battle group). The latest variant to be fitted in these helicopters is the AQS-13F.

An airborne low-frequency sonar is under development to succeed the AQS-13 series of sonars. This system is intended for use with the SH-60B LAMPS III helicopter as well as the SH-60F carrier-based variant. However, the weight of the dipping sonar would require an increase of the operating weight of the SH-60B to an estimated 23,500 pounds (10,660 kg).

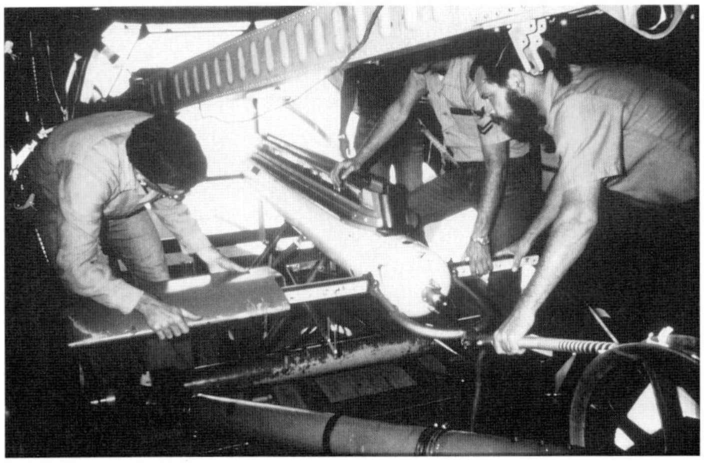

An AQS-14 minehunting sonar "fish" being prepared for deployment from an MH-53E Sea Dragon helicopter. (Westinghouse)

An AQS-13 dipping sonar being deployed from an SH-3 Sea King. (U.S. Navy)

SEA MINE SONAR

Another significant use of sonar in ASW is mine warfare, with the U.S. Navy's CAPTOR (encapsulated torpedo) being fitted with sonar to detect hostile submarines passing through the "attack envelope" of the mine's Mk 46 homing torpedo. The Mk 60 initially uses a passive sonar to detect targets and an active acoustic set to identify the hostile submarine before launching an acoustic-homing Mk 46 torpedo.

(In addition to the Mk 46 Mod 5 launched by the CAPTOR mine, other versions of the torpedo launched from surface ships [Mk-32 tubes or ASROC] and aircraft are fitted with active-passive acoustic guidance, as is the larger, submarine-launched Mk 48 torpedo.)

SONOBUOYS

Naval aircraft employ expendable, short-duration sonobuoys for the localization of submarines. Sonobuoys are generally employed after an initial submarine contact is gained by other means. However, there are sonobuoy barrier tactics in which a string of sonobuoys is periodically planted ahead of a task force. The Navy's S-3B Viking, P-3C Orion, SH-2G LAMPS I, and SH-60B/F Seahawk aircraft all can launch and monitor sonobuoys; the SH-2 helicopters, which cannot analyze sonobuoy data, relay that data to their supporting warship.

The principal types of sonobuoys now in U.S. Navy service are listed in the accompanying table. When released by aircraft, the buoys fall to the water and are slowed by parachute or a retardation device. Upon reaching the water the buoy's battery is activated, the transmission antenna extends, and the hydrophone is lowered by cable. Buoys either activate upon hitting the water or are command activated. The data are for the latest production models, unless a variant is indicated; the term "depth" indicates the level to which the buoy's hydrophone (or XBT sensor) is lowered by cable. After a specified number of minutes or hours the buoy canister floods and sinks. Most current sonobuoys are of a standard "A"-size—three feet (0.9 m) in length and 4⅞ inches (122 mm) in diameter—that fits launch chutes on board ASW aircraft. The SSQ-75, however, is larger—7½ feet (2.3 m) in length, with a diameter of 10 inches (254 mm). Efforts are being made to reduce sonobuoy size; dwarf "B" versions of the SSQ-53/77/79 are being developed that will permit three sonobuoys to be carried in a standard "A"-size aircraft launcher.

Ice-penetrating sonobuoys have also been developed for use in the Arctic ice pack to detect Russian submarines operating under ice. These air-launched buoys are known to have successfully penetrated ice up to 10 feet (3 m) thick. At least one concept for ice-penetrating buoys employs a two-pound (0.9-kg) lithium nose cone for penetrating the ice cover. Housed in an A-size sonobuoy, the ice-penetrator has an oversized parachute and shock absorber to reduce impact upon landing. After landing on the ice the lithium nose cone melts through the ice; the sensor deploys through the hole in the ice, the nose cone falls away, and the antenna, which remains above the ice, extends and the sonobuoy becomes operational.

Sonobuoys are used in a complementary manner; some are laid down to attain initial detection of a possible submarine target, while others provide shorter-range, more precise data on the target's exact depth and bearing. The SSQ-36 Expendable Bathythermograph (XBT) is used to determine the acoustic conditions of the water column, a vital datum in ASW operations. The principal buoys currently used in air ASW operations are the SSQ-53 Directional Finding and Ranging (DIFAR) and SSQ-62 Directional Command Active Sonobuoy System (DICASS) types. The SSQ-77 is a deep-searching sonobuoy with a long-line array, as is the SSQ-79 Steered Vertical Line Array (SVLA). The SSQ-75 Expendable Reliable Acoustic Path Sonobuoy (ERAPS) is a command-activated buoy that actively seeks very quiet submarines. During its three-hour service life it produces about 100 active acoustic "pings." The SSQ-57 is a small, passive-detection sonobuoy intended for relatively shallow waters. The current U.S. Navy interest in regional naval operations could lead to renewed attention to this type of buoy.

The earlier SSQ-50 CASS buoy has been succeeded by the SSQ-62 DICASS. The SSQ-73 was an experimental deep-DIFAR buoy based on the SSQ-53; the SSQ-73 passive Vertical Line Array DIFAR (VLAD) was procured in its place.

A large, 103-pound (46 kg) active pinging buoy designated SSQ-90 is in limited production for the Navy.

The SSQ-101 is a Horizontal-Line Array (HLA) sonobuoy that holds promise of long-range submarine detections. If development is successful, the buoy would be used for long-range detections ahead of surface naval forces. Development began in the mid-1980s (as did development of the TSS and LCS buoys in response to the emergence of several Soviet quiet submarine classes).

Sonobuoys are loaded into the dispensing chutes on the port side of an SH-60B Seahawk helicopter. (U.S. Navy)

An advanced submarine detection program known as the SSQ-102 Tactical Surveillance Sonobuoy (TSS) was canceled in late 1991 because of the reduced Soviet/Russian submarine threat. The TSS was to have an onboard mini-computer to analyze and record probable submarine noises and transmit them to ASW aircraft when so directed. This transmit-on-command was necessary because of the expected service life of TSS, on the order of five to seven days. (In effect, the TSS would have been a scaled-down version of the MSS and RDSS concepts.)

Although TSS has been canceled, some of the technologies being developed under the program will be applicable to other ASW projects.

Also under development is the SSQ-103 Low-Cost Sonobuoy (LCS), a multiple-buoy device in which an "A"-size buoy would consist of a field of six mini-buoys, each of which would suspend a hydrophone 300 feet (91 m) below the surface. The individual buoys would be 5½ inches (140 mm) in length and 4½ inches (114 mm) in diameter.

The LCS system would seek out submarine flow noises, i.e., the water flow over a submarine's hull, a gross, broad-band noise. This requires less sophisticated sensors and analyses than those needed for narrow-band noises (produced by a submarine's machinery and propellers), and they are very short range against slow-moving submarines.

The SSQ-58A is a moored surveillance buoy used by the Navy's Mobile Inshore Undersea Warfare units to form surveillance barriers to detect swimmers or small craft. The buoy itself is a fiberglass float 24 inches (0.6 m) in length and 36 inches (0.9 m) in diameter, carrying a standard, omni-directional hydrophone, up-link transmitter, antenna, etc. It can be recovered and its battery recharged; it does not sink at a predetermined time as do other buoys discussed here. (The designation SSQ-58 was previously applied to a Low-Frequency Acquisition and Ranging [LOFAR] buoy.)

The U.S. Navy also employs several communication buoys for submarine use. The BRC-6 Expendable Submarine Tactical Transceiver (XSTAT) is a two-way expendable buoy for ultra-high-frequency (UHF) communications between a submarine and aircraft. The BRT-1 Submarine-Launched One-way Transmitter (SLOT) is ejected by a submarine to broadcast, with a preset delay, a four-minute taped message. The BRT-3/4/5 buoys transmit a signal to identify a submarine in night/bad weather. The BRT-6 is a one-way transmission buoy to uplink prerecorded UHF transmissions to a communications satellite. The SSQ-71 and SSQ-86 are "A"-size two-way aircraft-submarine communications buoys that are carried in aircraft sonobuoy dispensers.

A technician loads an *internal* sonobuoy dispenser in a P-3C Orion. This is the only U.S. naval aircraft that has a sonobuoy dispenser that can be re-loaded in flight (in addition to non-reloadable chutes external to the cabin). (U.S. Navy)

A sonobuoy falls from an SH-2F helicopter. The retardation fins are open to slow its descent. Note the 15 sonobuoy chutes fitted into the port side of the helicopter. There is a Mk 46 torpedo mounted below the sonobuoy chutes. (U.S. Navy)

Designation	Type	Manufacturer	Weight	Depth	Frequency Range	Endurance
SSQ-36	bathythermograph; XBT (water temperature profile)	Sparton	18 lbs (8.2 kg)	1,000 ft (305 m)	—	few minutes
SSQ-41A	omni-directional passive detection; LOFAR (Jezebel)	Hermes, Magnavox, Sparton	21 lbs (9.5 kg)	60 or 300 ft (18 or 91 m)	10 Hz to 20 kHz	1, 3, or 8 hours
SSQ-41B	same		29 lbs (13 kg)	60 or 1,000 ft (18 or 305 m)	10 Hz to 10 kHz	
SSQ-47B	active range-only		29 lbs (13 kg)	60 or 800 ft (18 or 244 m)		30 minutes
SSQ-53B	passive directional (DIFAR)	Canadian Commercial, Magnavox, Sparton	22 lbs (10 kg)	100, 400 or 1,000 ft (30.5, 122 or 305 m)	10 Hz to 2.4 kHz	1, 3, or 8 hours
SSQ-57	passive for restricted waters	Hermes, Sparton	14 lbs (6.35 kg)	60 or 400 ft (18 or 122 m)		1, 3, or 8 hours
SSQ-58	surveillance buoy	Sparton		20 ft (6.1 m)	50 Hz to 10 kHz	100 hours
SSQ-62B	Directional Command Activated Sonobuoy System (DICASS)	Raytheon	34 lbs (15.4 kg)	90, 400 or 1,500 ft (27, 122 or 457 m)		30 hours
SSQ-75	Expendable Reliable Acoustic Path Sonobuoy (ERAPS)	ERAPSCo*	325 lbs (147 kg)	60 to 16,500 ft (18 to 5,030 m)		3 hours
SSQ-77B	passive Vertical Line Array DIFAR (VLAD)	Sparton, Magnavox	29 lbs (13 kg)	1,000 ft (305 m)	10 Hz to 2.4 kHz	1 or 8 hours
SSQ-79	Steered Vertical Line Array (SVLA)	Hazeltine		1,000 ft (305 m)		4 or 8 hours
SSQ-102	Air-Deployed Active Receiver Tactical Surveillance Sonar**					

*ERAPSCo is a joint venture by Magnavox and Sparton formed in 1987 to produce the ERAPS buoy.
**Can operate in bistatic or multistatic mode, with a shipboard sonar providing active signal.

TORPEDO COUNTERMEASURES

Torpedo countermeasures include electronic systems and decoys to reduce the effectiveness of enemy torpedoes or to "replace" the ship or submarine target in the torpedo's target-acquisition process. U.S. surface warships, amphibious ships, and certain auxiliary ships have the SLQ-25 Nixie.

U.S. attack submarines are reported to carry the Mk 23 acoustic countermeasures device to decoy homing torpedoes, while ballistic missile submarines can also launch the Mk 70 MOSS (Mobile Submarine Simulator) from torpedo tubes to simulate a full-size submarine to hostile sonar.

SURFACE SHIP TORPEDO DEFENSE

After several false starts, the Surface Ship Torpedo Defense (SSTD) project is providing U.S. ships with a limited hard-kill torpedo defense system using modified Mk 46 torpedoes launched from Mk 32 torpedo tubes (see chapter 30). In the fall of 1988 the U.S. and British governments signed a Memorandum of Understanding (MOU) to establish a four-phase, joint research SSTD project. When signed on 26 October 1988, the MOU was hailed by a U.S. Navy spokesman as providing "an excellent opportunity to improve mutual defense capabilities, reduce development and acquisition costs and to provide for increased compatibility and interoperability between the U.S. and Royal navies."[8]

The joint program immediately ran into shoal water, however. While the U.S. Navy has pushed for a hard-kill approach, the British believe that soft-kill is more viable for SSTD. The British fear that a convoy escort firing weapons to intercept an incoming torpedo would put other ships in the convoy at risk. More threatening to the joint effort is the U.S. House Appropriations Committee's decision to kill funding for several Anglo-American projects, among them SSTD. The House report stated that the "committee does not consider such a joint project to be feasible given the security consideration regarding the sharing of acoustic signal data and countermeasure development, which the program would ultimately require."[9] Such language was highly inflammatory and counterproductive because of the close technical and operational relationship of the U.S. and British submarine communities and the large amount of acoustic data on Soviet/Russian undersea craft provided to the United States by the Royal Navy!

The U.S. Navy has converted 172 Mk 46 ASW torpedoes for an active anti-torpedo system for carrier defense against Russian wake-homing torpedoes.

Three American-led consortia were formed to develop SSTD systems: General Electric teamed with Alliant Techsystems (formerly defense products of Honeywell) and Marconi Underwater Systems; Westinghouse joined with AT&T, Dowty Maritime, and Ferranti; and Martin Marietta worked with Hughes Ground Systems, British Aerospace Dynamics, and Frequency Engineering Laboratories (USA). After a series of initial contracts in the torpedo defense area, in early 1992 the first two teams were awarded contract extensions for the program.

SLQ-25 NIXIE

A towed torpedo countermeasures systems, the Nixie is found on most U.S. Navy surface combatants and other ships, including replenishment ships that would normally operate with surface warships.

The effectiveness of Nixie was demonstrated in the 1982 war in the Falklands. A Nixie being towed by the British carrier HERMES attracted and was blown up by a British ASW torpedo that had been launched against a suspected Argentine submarine contact.

Manufacturer: Aerojet
Operational: 1974
Ships: aircraft carriers
cruisers
destroyers
frigates
command ships
LCC 19
amphibious ships

LHD 1	LSD 36
LHA 1	LSD 41
LPH 2	LSD 49
LPD 4	LKA 113 (1 ship)
LPD 17	

auxiliary ships

AE 26	AOE 6
AO 177	AOR 1
AOE 1	

WEAPON CONTROL SYSTEMS

Weapon control systems are designated in several series, and several mark series are also used. The major systems are identified in this section.

CCS-SERIES COMBAT CONTROL SYSTEMS

These are multiple-function control systems for weapons in LOS ANGELES-class submarines. The original Mk 1 CCS developed for the LOS ANGELES class has been replaced in some units by the upgraded Mk 2 CCS (see chapter 12). The CCS integrates the submarine's torpedo fire-control system (Mk 117) with the central computer complex.

The original CCS Mk 1 was the Mod 0; the Mod 1 (using UYK-7 computers) integrated the Tomahawk missile; the Mod 2 (using

8. Caleb Baker, "U.S., Royal Navy to explore torpedo defense systems," *Navy Times* (19 December 1988), p. 26.
9. "House cites 'security concerns' in cutting U.K. from SSTD," *Navy News* (21 August 1989), p. 8.

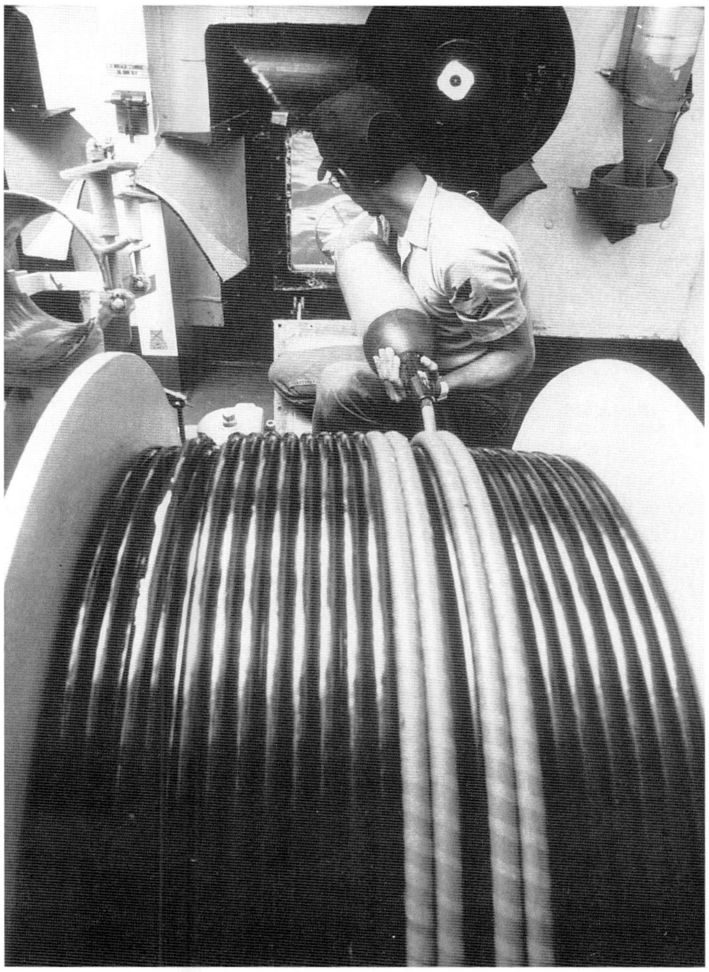

A sailor holds the towed "fish" of the SLQ-25 Nixie torpedo countermeasures system; the towing cable is in the foreground. The Nixie was used in a combat environment by the Royal Navy in the Falklands in 1982. (Aerojet General)

A pair of Mk 70 MOSS acoustic decoys is loaded aboard an attack submarine. These decoys were originally developed for use by strategic missile submarines. (U.S. Navy)

UYK-44 computers) added the vertical-launching capability; the Mod 3 adds Mk 48 ADCAP capability; and the Mods 4 and 5 add the Sea Lance missile capability.

The CCS Mk 2 has improved displays and workstations over the Mk 1. The Mod 0 was rapidly succeeded by the Mod 1, with its provisions for over-the-horizon targeting (Tomahawk and Harpoon missiles); the Mod 2 intended for Trident submarines has modified consoles/controls.

The software is modular, facilitating adaption for various submarine/weapon configurations.

Manufacturer:	Raytheon
Operational:	
Ships:	SSBN 726 SSN 688

SYS-SERIES INTEGRATED DETECTION AND TRACKING SYSTEMS

The SYS-1(V)2 and SYS-2(V) Integrated Automatic Detection and Tracking (IADT) systems integrate various radars in non-Aegis guided missile ships and large amphibious ships to facilitate command and control in high-threat environments. Each shipboard radar is fitted with a video converter in which the images pass through a processor and are integrated for display in the ship's combat information center.

The SYS-1 was developed specifically for the ADAMS-class destroyers and the SYS-2 for guided missile cruisers. The latter was subsequently selected for the PERRY-class frigate upgrade and is also installed in the WASP-class amphibious ships. (The SYS-3 system is being procured for the Israeli SA'AR V-class missile corvettes being built in the United States.)

The follow-on Integrated Radar Detection and Identification System (IRDIS) will integrate non-radar data (e.g., ESM) into the system.

Manufacturer:	Norden (United Technologies)
Operational:	SYS-1 in 1977
Ships:	DDG 993 FFG 7 (some ships) LHD 1

MK 160 GFCS

The Mk 160 is an advanced gunfire control system.

Manufacturer:	
Operational:	1991
Ships:	DDG 51

MK 118 TORPEDO FCS

An all-digital torpedo fire-control system developed for Trident SSBNs, the Mk 118 controls both torpedo launches and the release of 3-inch (76-mm) and 6-inch (152-mm) torpedo countermeasures and the Mk 70 MOSS target simulators.

Manufacturer:	
Operational:	1981
Ships:	SSBN 726

MK 117 TORPEDO FCS

The U.S. Navy's first all-digital torpedo fire-control system, the Mk 117 was first installed in submarines of the THRESHER/PERMIT class. Installation of the digital Mk 117 prevented use of the analog SUBROC missile, although an attempt was made to correct this interface, but it had only limited use.

The Mk 117 Mods 6 and 7 are compatible with the Tomahawk missile; the Mod 8 is compatible with the Tomahawk and SUBROC, and could have handled the Sea Lance, had that missile been procured.

This system was originally known as the All-Digital Attack Center (ADAC).

Manufacturer:
Operational:
Ships: Mod 0 SSN 700–715
Mod 6 SSN 637–639
SSN 646–653
SSN 660–670
SSN 672–677
Mod 7 SSN 671
SSN 678–687
Mod 8 SSN 716–720

MK 116 ASW FCS

This is an advanced ASW weapons control system for surface ships. The all-digital system is linked to the SQS-53 sonar and controls ship-launched weapons (ASROC and Mk 32 torpedo tubes) and interfaces with the LAMPS helicopters (SH-2G and SH-60B).

Mods 1 through 4 are for various ship types; Mod 5 integrates the SQQ-89 sonar system; Mod 6 integrates the Vertical-Launch ASROC (VLA) potential for the later TICONDEROGA-class cruisers; and Mods 7, 8, 9, and 10 introduced the UYK-43B computer and are for use in the BURKE-class destroyers as well as non-VLS ships.

Manufacturer: Librascope
Operational:
Ships: CG 47, DDG 51, CGN 38, DDG 993, CGN 36, DD 963

This photo shows the Mk 92 weapon direction system as mounted in the frigate STARK (FFG 31). (Giorgio Arra)

MK 115 FCS

The Mk 115, associated with the Sea Sparrow BPDMS, is a director/illuminator adapted from the older Mk 51 gun director mount. It also has side-by-side antennas. Tracking is manual.

Manufacturer:
Band: X
Operational:
Ships: CV 41
LHA 1
LPH 2
MCS 8

MK 113 TORPEDO/MISSILE FCS

This was a torpedo fire-control system widely used in SSNs and SSBNs; in attack submarines it was replaced by the Mk 117 system. The only active U.S. submarines with the Mk 113 are the two remaining LAFAYETTE (SSBN 616)-class submarines, which are employed as transports for special operations forces. They were not upgraded to the Mk 117 system because of their limited sonar capabilities and limited remaining service life.

Manufacturer: Librascope
Operational:
Ships: SSN 642
SSN 645

MK 99 MISSILE FCS

Fire-control directors associated with the Aegis weapon system (Mk 7), the Mk 99 is operated in conjunction with SPG-62 radar.

The Mods 0 and 3 were fitted in the missile test ship NORTON SOUND (AVM 1); Mod 1 was the prototype for the TICONDEROGA class; Mod 2 was the production model for that class; and Mod 4 was a production model.

Manufacturer:
Band: X
Operational: 1983
Ships: CG 47
DDG 51

MK 98 MISSILE FCS

The Mk 98 is a missile control system for Trident missile submarines.

Manufacturer:
Operational: 1981
Ships: SSBN 726

MK 92/MK 94 WEAPON DIRECTION SYSTEMS

The Mk 92 and Mk 94 are both combined tracking and illuminating systems that incorporate two antennas, one for air and one for surface target tracking. The Mod 2 version, in the PERRY-class frigates, is combined with the STIR radar to provide a second missile guidance channel in those ships; Mods 0 and 2 can control guns or missiles. Mods 1 and 3–5 are for gun control only, with the Mod 1 in the PEGASUS (PHM 1) class (except for the lead ship, which had the Mk 94 prototype), the Coast Guard's BEAR (WMEC 901) class, and the modernized Coast Guard HAMILTON (WHEC 715) class. The Mk 94 prototype is fitted in the missile ship PEGASUS and the PERRY-class frigates. In the latter ships, those refitted with the Mk 92 Mod 6 system—featuring a Coherent Radar Transmitter (CORT) in conjunction with the SYS-2(V)2 automatic target tracking system—have increased weapons control capabilities.

Manufacturer:	Sperry
Band:	X
Operational:	
Ships:	FFG 7
	Coast Guard cutters

MK 91 WEAPON DIRECTION SYSTEM

The Mk 91 is a weapon direction system for the NATO Sea Sparrow missile system. The antenna system has side-by-side receiving and transmitting antennas; it typically has targets designated automatically by the SPS-58/SPS-65 radars or the Mk 23 TAS.

Manufacturer:	
Band:	X
Operational:	
Ships:	all aircraft carriers except CV 41
	DD 963
	LHD 1
	AOE 6
	AOE 1

Paired antennas for the Mk 91 weapon direction system with convex and concave domes—on the carrier KITTY HAWK (CV 63). (Giorgio Arra)

MK 86 GUN/MISSILE FCS

This weapons control system is fitted with SPQ-9A radar. The complete Mk 86 system includes an electro-optical sensor (closed-circuit low-light-level television) and SPG-60 tracker-illuminator radar. Reportedly, up to 120 target tracks can be monitored simultaneously.

The Mk 86 was evaluated in 1965 in the destroyer BARRY (DD 933). The Mods 0 through 10 were developed with various target/tracking capabilities for various ship/radar/computer configurations.

Manufacturer:	Lockheed	
Band:	X	
Operational:	1970	
Ships:	CG 47	DDG 993
	CGN 38	DD 963
	CGN 36	LHA 1

MK 74 MISSILE FCS

The weapons control system associated with Tartar/Standard-MR missiles, the Mk 74 is fitted with SPG-51D radar.

Mods 0 through 15 were developed for various ship/radar/computer configurations. Some mods were fitted with low-light-level television.

Manufacturer:	
Band:	G
Operational:	1960
Ships:	CGN 38
	CGN 36
	DDG 993

MK 25 TARGET ACQUISITION SYSTEM

This is an improved version of the Mk 23 Target Acquisition System (TAS).

Manufacturer:	Hughes
Operational:	1994
Ships:	AOE 6
	AOR 6

MK 23 TARGET ACQUISITION SYSTEM

The Mk 23 Target Acquisition System (TAS) supports the NATO Sea Sparrow launcher Mk 29; the Mk 92/Mk 94 weapon FCS adopted from the Dutch M28 system; and the Mk 115 director/illuminator for the basic Sea Sparrow launcher Mk 25.

The Mk 23, intended for automatic reaction/target designation of incoming sea-skimming missiles, has a maximum range of almost 100 n.miles (185 km) and a minimum designation range of 20 n.miles (37 km). It incorporates pulse-doppler radar. Designed to operate in a high-clutter environment, it can simultaneously track up to 54 targets with a two-second scan rate. The Mk 23 first went to sea in the frigate DOWNES (FF 1070) in 1975.

Manufacturer:	Hughes	
Band:	L	
Operational:	1975	
Ships:	CV 63	LHD 1
	CVN 65	LHA 5
	CVN 68	LPD 17
	DD 963	AOE 3

CHAPTER 32

Coast Guard

A half dozen "black hull" oceangoing buoy tenders of the BALSAM class gather for a portrait. It is unusual for these hard-working "cutters" to be seen in this manner. They are highly versatile ships that have even served in a combatant role. Naval planners tend to consider only "white hull" cutters when planning maritime-naval operations. (U.S. Coast Guard)

The U.S. Coast Guard is a military service under the Department of Transportation. Federal statute states that in the national security role, the Coast Guard "shall maintain a state of readiness to function as a specialized service in the Navy in time of war, including the fulfillment of Maritime Defense Zone command responsibilities."

The Coast Guard is responsible for the enforcement of U.S. laws in coastal waters and on the high seas subject to the jurisdiction of the United States. At the direction of the President, the Coast Guard becomes a part of the Navy (as in 1798–1801, for the Quasi War with France, and in both World Wars). Alternatively, Coast Guard forces can operate in a war zone while remaining an independent service (as during the Korean and Vietnam Wars and the 1991 conflict in the Persian Gulf).

The principal peacetime missions of the Coast Guard are: (1) enforcing recreational boating safety; (2) conducting search and rescue operations; (3) maintaining aids to navigation (3 manned and 454 unmanned lighthouses, some 13,000 minor navigational lights, plus other navigation aids); (4) implementing merchant marine safety; (5) carrying out environmental protection; (6) being responsible for port safety; and (7) enforcement of laws and treaties.

Admiral Robert E. Kramek, Commandant of the Coast Guard since 1 June 1994. (U.S. Coast Guard)

That last mission comprises the enforcement of the nation's customs and immigration laws, including the prevention of smuggling drugs and narcotics, and also the enforcement of fisheries laws, including international treaties related to the 200-n.mile (370-km) offshore Exclusive Economic Zone (EEZ).

In addition, as a military service the Coast Guard carries out those military missions assigned by the Joint Chiefs of Staff, with the Commandant of the Coast Guard attending those JCS meetings that address issues of interest to the Coast Guard. Since 1985 the Coast Guard has had coastal defense responsibilities for the U.S. Atlantic coast and, since 1986, for the U.S. Pacific coast under the concept of Maritime Defense Zones (see below).

Historical: The Coast Guard was established on 4 August 1790 as the Revenue Marine of the Department of the Treasury. In 1885 it was renamed the Revenue Cutter Service and, since 1915, the Coast Guard. The service incorporated the Lighthouse Service in 1939.

The Coast Guard was a component of the Treasury Department from its formation until being transferred to the newly established Department of Transportation in 1967.

ORGANIZATION

The major U.S. Coast Guard operating commands are the Atlantic Area (headquarters on Governor's Island in New York harbor) and the Pacific Area (headquarters in San Francisco), with ten subordinate district commands (see below). Each area command—in addition to its component districts—has a Maintenance and Logistics Command assigned to it.

District	*Headquarters*	*Area*	*Personnel*[1]
1st District	Boston, Mass.	northeast	3,000
2nd District	St. Louis, Mo.	central	800
5th District	Portsmouth, Va.	middle Atlantic	2,400
7th District	Miami, Fla.	southeast	4,000
8th District	New Orleans, La.	gulf coast	2,950
9th District	Cleveland, Ohio	northern–Great Lakes	2,200
11th District	Long Beach, Calif.	southwest	1,350
13th District	Seattle, Wash.	northwest	3,300
14th District	Honolulu, Hawaii	Hawaii	1,200
17th District	Juneau, Alaska	Alaska	2,000

The district commanders control all shore, air, and sea activities in their area of responsibility. In addition, in 1985–1986 the commanders of the Coast Guard Atlantic and Pacific Areas were designated as commanders of the newly established Maritime Defense Zone (MDZ) Atlantic and Pacific, respectively. The MDZ commanders report to their respective Navy fleet commanders.[2]

The MDZ commanders are responsible for: (1) planning, conducting, and coordinating wartime operations in and around U.S. harbors and coasts; (2) ensuring an integrated defense plan for the MDZs' areas of responsibility; and (3) protecting coastal and nearby sea lines of communication. Within each MDZ are operating sectors that are commanded by Coast Guard district or base commanders.

The MDZ organization sought to rectify a long-standing shortfall in U.S. defense policy, namely, that of defending U.S. harbor and coastal waters from hostile activity, particularly submarine operations. However, the threat from submarine mining and the use of Coast Guard forces in forward crisis and combat areas does raise the question of whether the Coast Guard should additionally have control of the surface mine countermeasures forces, which are now, of course, a Navy activity.[3]

Coast Guard Headquarters, located in Washington, D.C., provides overall supervision and support for the operating districts. The headquarters, as shown in the accompanying figure, was reorganized in 1995–1996, reflecting a staff reduction of some 300 Coast Guard officers and civilians, with an estimated savings of $15 to $20 million per year in personnel costs. There are now five major directorates for Coast Guard activities.

(Previously Coast Guard Headquarters had ten major directorates, or "offices," an awkward command structure for efficient management of the Coast Guard in the rapidly changing maritime-defense environment. See 15th Edition/page 550 for previous headquarters organization.)

1. Active-duty Coast Guard men and women.
2. A detailed description of the Maritime Defense Zones is found in Comdr. Lawson W. Brigham, USCG, "U.S. Coast Guard in 1985," U.S. Naval Institute *Proceedings* [Naval Review issue] (May 1986), pp. 42–49.
3. This issue was examined in N. Polmar, "The U.S. Navy: Mine Warfare Problems . . . And a Solution," U.S. Naval Institute *Proceedings* (December 1991), pp. 105–6.

COAST GUARD ORGANIZATION

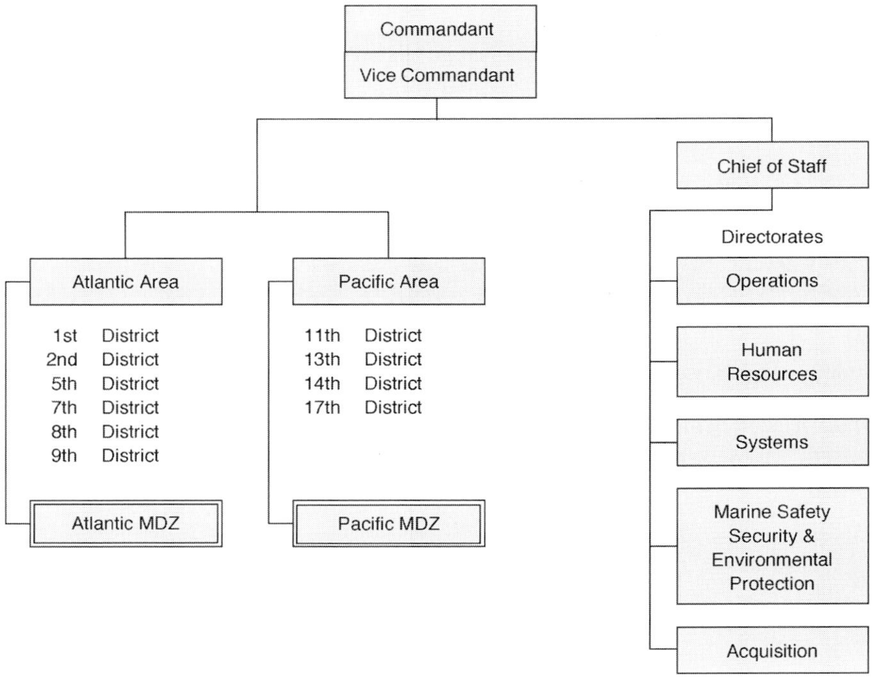

Notes: ═══ signifies under Navy operational control.

OPERATIONS

The Coast Guard has had a major role in coping with the Haitian and Cuban refugee waves that attempted to reach U.S. territory in the early 1990s. Tens of thousands of refugees were taken in custody by Coast Guard cutters, often plucked from makeshift rafts and sinking boats.

The Coast Guard also made major contributions to U.S. military operations during Desert Shield and Desert Storm in the Persian Gulf area. Its contributions were:

- Ten four-man Law Enforcement Detachments (LEDet) were placed on board Navy ships to go aboard ships suspected of carrying contraband cargoes to Iraq.
- Three reserve Port Security Units (PSU), each with some 100 men and women, with patrol craft, were deployed in the gulf.[4]
- Two HU-25C Falcon surveillance aircraft were deployed to Bahrain to monitor the oil pollution caused by Iraqi forces.

No Coast Guard cutters were deployed to the gulf area. (In 1987 the deployment of 110-foot/33.5-m patrol craft to the gulf was proposed, but the proposal was quickly abandoned in the face of Navy opposition.)

In the Western hemisphere, Coast Guard activities include the service's traditional law-enforcement, safety, and merchant marine inspection activities. The Coast Guard is a major participant in drug interdiction operations with Joint Task Forces 4 and 5, the multi-agency anti-drug forces. Both task forces are commanded by Coast Guard rear admirals.

CUTTERS AND BOATS

The Coast Guard operates a large number of oceangoing, coastal, and inland ships, as well as small craft, for a variety of purposes.

Two major ship procurement programs were completed in the early 1990s: 13 medium endurance cutters of the Bear, or Famous, class, and 49 large patrol boats of the Island class. The former ships equate to corvettes in many navies; those ships have limited military capabilities. Coast Guard plans to construct a larger "patrol boat" known as the Heritage class have come to a full stop. That program was not adequately thought out and had suffered severe criticism from other government agencies.

The Coast Guard is now considering designs for a smaller patrol boat to replace the popular and useful 82-foot (25-m) patrol boats of the Point class. The new design is referred to as a coastal patrol boat. All of the older 95-foot (29-m) patrol boats of the Cape class have been discarded.

Other procurement programs include a long-delayed third large icebreaker, a series of seagoing buoy tenders, and another series of coastal buoy tenders.

The large Hamilton high endurance cutters and Reliance medium endurance cutters have been extensively modernized, thus extending their service life. There are no plans at this time to develop a replacement for the excellent Hamilton-class cutters, and if they are not replaced, the Coast Guard will in fact as well as name evolve into a coastal patrol force.

Most cutters are painted white; the larger icebreakers are painted red; and buoy tenders and harbor tugs are painted black, with white superstructures.

The Coast Guard insignia—a narrow blue stripe and a wide orange stripe, with the Coast Guard shield superimposed on the latter—is carried on the bows of all vessels except lightships. The words "Coast Guard" are painted on the sides of all ships.

Designations: The Coast Guard uses the term *vessels* for all watercraft operated by the service. Within that classification, the term *cutter* is used for ships that have "an assigned personnel allowance and that [have] installed habitability features for the extended support of a permanently assigned crew." In practice, this includes 65-foot (19.8-m) tugs and larger vessels, except ferries. The term "cutter" comes from the early British revenue service ships that were cutter-rigged sailing vessels, although the original U.S. revenue cutters were sailing schooners.

Craft less than 65 feet (19.8 m) in length are considered "boats" and have hull numbers whose first two digits indicate the vessel's length overall. However, the designation "patrol boat" (WPB) is used for craft up to 120 feet (36.6 m) long.

4. These units, which were flown to the Persian Gulf with their boats, served as port security forces in Bahrain and Saudi Arabia. It was the first time in the 50-year history of the Coast Guard Reserve that its personnel had served outside of the United States. The units were No. 301 from Buffalo, N.Y., No. 302 from Cleveland, Ohio, and No. 303 from Milwaukee, Wisc.

The Coast Guard classifies all of its ships and small craft by length (shown in this volume in parentheses after the class name). The Coast Guard vessel classification scheme is derived from that of the U.S. Navy (see chapter 3). All Coast Guard cutters and boat classifications are prefixed by the letter W (unofficially for White-painted ships). The larger cutters are numbered in a single, sequential series that was initiated in 1941–1942, with new classes initiating new number blocks.

Cutter names are prefixed by USCGC for U.S. Coast Guard Cutter.

COAST GUARD CUTTERS, PATROL BOATS, AND AUXILIARIES

Number	Class/Ship	Class	Commissioned	Active	Notes
WHEC 715	Hamilton	378	1967–1972	12	
WMEC 901	Bear	270	1983–1990	13	
WMEC 615	Reliance	210	1964–1969	16	
WMEC 38	Storis	230	1942	1	ex-WAGB type
WMEC 6	Escape	213	1943–1944	2	ex-Navy ARS
WMEC 62	Balsam	180	1942–1944	1	ex-WLB type
WPB 1400	Heritage	120	canceled	—	canceled
WPB 1301	Island	110	1986–1990	49	
WPB 82301	Point	82	1960–1970	41	
WAGB 20	Healy	460	1998	—	1 building
WAGB 10	Polar	399	1976–1978	2	
WAGB 83	Mackinaw	290	1944	1	Great Lakes
WIX 327	Eagle	295	1936	1	sailing bark
WLB 601	Juniper	225	1996–	1	more units building
WLB 62	Balsam	180	1942–1944	26	plus 1 WMEC
WLM	coastal buoy tenders			12	more units building
WLI	inland buoy tenders			5	
WLIC	inland construction tenders			16	
WLR	river buoy tenders			18	more units building
WTGB	icebreaking tugs			9	
WYTL	small harbor tugs			14	

AVIATION

The Coast Guard air arm operates about 170 aircraft based at 27 air stations in the continental United States, Hawaii, Alaska, and Puerto Rico. Characteristics of Coast Guard aircraft are provided in chapter 29 of this volume.

Although the Coast Guard has traditionally flown aircraft of the same type operated by the Navy, in the 1980s the Coast Guard procured two French-designed aircraft: 41 HU-25 Guardian fixed-wing aircraft, acquired to replace the HU-16 Albatross amphibian and HC-131 Samaritan; and 96 HH-65A Dolphin Short-Range Recovery (SRR) helicopters, acquired to replace the HH-52A Sea Guard helicopters. They are not flown by any other U.S. military service.

The Coast Guard's latest series-produced aircraft, the HH-60J Jayhawk, is a search-and-rescue variant of the widely flown H-60 helicopter series. This is the only aircraft currently flown by all five U.S. military services—Army, Navy, Marine Corps, Air Force, and Coast Guard.

The cutters of the Hamilton and Bear classes, as well as the two Polar-class icebreakers, regularly embark helicopters, while some of the other cutter classes have landing decks but cannot support helicopters. In wartime the Hamilton and Bear classes were intended to carry Navy SH-2F LAMPS I anti-submarine helicopters. However, they have lost their effectiveness in that role because of the lack of towed-array sonars for the Coast Guard cutters and the deletion of ASW data links from the Hamilton class. HH-60J search-and-rescue helicopters are now carried aboard the Hamilton and Bear classes.

The Coast Guard has a single CASA 212-300 turboprop transport, acquired in the summer of 1990 to evaluate the aircraft for possible use in the logistics support role. That aircraft is leased from CASA (Construcciones Aeronauticas) of Spain. The long-serving VC-11A Gulfstream VIP transport was replaced in 1995 by a much improved C-20B Gulfstream III, transferred from the Air Force.

The Coast Guard also operates three RU-38A motorized gliders for anti-drug surveillance. These replaced two highly successful RG-8A Condor motorized gliders. The motorized gliders can operate from any runway 3,000 feet (915 m) or longer, with only minimal support requirements.

The Coast Guard has pioneered in the development of unmanned airships, or aerostats, for ocean surveillance. A 1985 agreement between the Navy and Coast Guard assigned the responsibility for development of manned airships to the Navy and for unmanned craft to the Coast Guard. The Coast Guard's mobile aerostat program was

An HH-60J comes aboard the cutter Escanaba, steaming on a smooth sea. The Coast Guard has a sizeable air arm, but it has paid too high a price to acquire and maintain a French-designed helicopter and land-based, fixed-wing search aircraft. (Sikorsky)

An HH-60J Jayhawk helicopter refuels in flight from the 378-foot cutter MORGENTHAU. These are large, versatile cutters with the ability to operate large helicopters, which greatly enhances their effectiveness. But the issue of follow-on large cutters has yet to be decided. (Courtesy *Naval Aviation News*)

transferred to the Army in 1992 and promptly disbanded. See 15th Edition/pages 603–5 for characteristics of the aerostat tenders.

Coast Guard aviators are trained by the Navy, with specialized aircraft-type training being given at the Coast Guard Aviation Training Center in Mobile, Alabama.

The following table lists the aircraft in active Coast Guard service. Several additional HU-25 and HH-65A aircraft are in storage. The single EC-130V "Herk"—evaluated by the Coast Guard for anti-drug surveillance operations—was transferred to the Air Force in late 1993. The E-2C Hawkeye airborne early warning aircraft operated by the Coast Guard were returned to the Navy in 1991. (One aircraft crashed at Roosevelt Roads, Puerto Rico, on 24 August 1990, killing the four-man crew.)

All Coast Guard–flown CH-3E Sea King and HH-3F Pelican helicopters have been retired.

No aircraft are flown by the Coast Guard Reserve.

COAST GUARD AIRCRAFT

Active	Type	Mission
26	HC-130H Hercules	Long-Range Search (LRS)
20	HU-25 Guardian	Medium-Range Search (MRS)
1	C-20B Gulfstream III	executive transport
1	VC-4 Gulfstream	executive transport
1	CASA 212-300	cargo aircraft
80	HH-65A Dolphin	Medium-Range Recovery (MRR)
35	HH-60J Jayhawk	Medium-Range Recovery (MRR)
3	RU-38A	motorized glider

PERSONNEL

Uniformed Coast Guard personnel operate all cutters and boats as well as aircraft. Medical personnel are provided by the U.S. Public Health Service on assignment to the Coast Guard.

Active-duty Coast Guard strength at the beginning of 1996 totaled almost 35,700: 5,757 officers, 1,538 warrant officers, and 28,401 enlisted men and women. Also counted as active-duty personnel were 841 cadets at the Coast Guard Academy in New London, Connecticut, and 160 medical officers of the Public Health Service.

About 7 percent of the Coast Guard's active-duty personnel are women. The Coast Guard was the first U.S. military service to accept women at its service academy and the first to assign women as commanding officers of armed vessels (WPB patrol boats).

The Coast Guard has 8,000 selected reservists who attend periodic drills in addition to summer active-duty training. There is also a civilian auxiliary of 35,650 men and women. The Coast Guard Auxiliary consists of expert boaters, amateur radio operators, and licensed aircraft pilots who use their own equipment to support Coast Guard activities. Their efforts include conducting free courtesy marine inspections of recreational boats, teaching a variety of boating courses, and assisting the Coast Guard in search and rescue.

Coast Guard personnel have Navy-style ranks: the Commandant has the rank of full admiral, and the Deputy Commandant is a vice admiral. There are 3 other vice admirals (the chief of staff and the commanders Atlantic and Pacific Areas, with additional duty as commanders of the Atlantic and Pacific MDZs, respectively), 9 rear admirals (upper half) and 12 rear admirals (lower half), plus 4 rear admiral selectees.

HIGH ENDURANCE CUTTERS

These cutters are the largest ships operated by the Coast Guard except for icebreakers. All high endurance cutters prior to the HAMILTON class have been stricken; no new construction of this type is planned. The HAMILTONS will reach the end of their nominal service life from about 2005 on.

With the cutback in active Navy frigates, the proposal had been made for some Navy FF/FFG-type ships to be transferred to the Coast Guard, with at least one to serve as a training cutter. Such transfers are unlikely, however.

12 HIGH ENDURANCE CUTTERS: "HAMILTON" CLASS (378)

Number	Name	Builder	Laid down	Launched	Commissioned	Modernized	Status
WHEC 715	HAMILTON	Avondale Shipyards, New Orleans, La.	4 Jan 1965	18 Dec 1965	20 Feb 1967	Oct 1985–Nov 1988	**PA**
WHEC 716	DALLAS	Avondale Shipyards, New Orleans, La.	7 Feb 1966	1 Oct 1966	1 Oct 1967	Nov 1986–Dec 1989	**AA**
WHEC 717	MELLON	Avondale Shipyards, New Orleans, La.	25 July 1966	11 Feb 1967	22 Dec 1967	Oct 1985–June 1989	**PA**
WHEC 718	CHASE	Avondale Shipyards, New Orleans, La.	15 Oct 1966	20 May 1967	1 Mar 1968	July 1989–Mar 1991	**PA**
WHEC 719	BOUTWELL	Avondale Shipyards, New Orleans, La.	12 Dec 1966	17 June 1967	14 June 1968	Mar 1989–Apr 1991	**PA**
WHEC 720	SHERMAN	Avondale Shipyards, New Orleans, La.	13 Feb 1967	23 Sep 1967	23 Aug 1968	May 1986–Feb 1990	**PA**
WHEC 721	GALLATIN	Avondale Shipyards, New Orleans, La.	17 Apr 1967	18 Nov 1967	20 Dec 1968	Mar 1990–Jan 1992	**AA**
WHEC 722	MORGENTHAU	Avondale Shipyards, New Orleans, La.	17 July 1967	10 Feb 1968	14 Feb 1969	Nov 1989–Dec 1991	**PA**
WHEC 723	RUSH	Avondale Shipyards, New Orleans, La.	23 Oct 1967	16 Nov 1968	3 July 1969	July 1989–Sep 1991	**PA**
WHEC 724	MUNRO	Avondale Shipyards, New Orleans, La.	18 Feb 1970	5 Dec 1970	10 Sep 1971	Dec 1986–Nov 1989	**PA**
WHEC 725	JARVIS	Avondale Shipyards, New Orleans, La.	9 Sep 1970	24 Apr 1971	30 Dec 1971	Mar 1991–Dec 1992	**PA**
WHEC 726	MIDGETT	Avondale Shipyards, New Orleans, La.	5 Apr 1971	4 Sep 1971	17 Mar 1972	Sep 1990–Mar 1992	**PA**

Displacement:	2,716 tons standard 3,050 tons full load
Length:	350 feet (106.7 m) waterline 378⅚ feet (115.4 m) overall
Beam:	42¾ feet (13.0 m)
Draft:	20⅓ feet (6.2 m) over sonar dome
Propulsion:	CODOG: 2 gas turbines (Pratt & Whitney FT4-A6); 28,000 shp + 2 diesel engines (Fairbanks Morse 38TD8 1/8); 7,200 bhp; 2 shafts
Speed:	28.4 knots
Range:	2,400 n.miles (4,445 km) at 29 knots 9,600 n.miles (17,790 km) at 19 knots (gas turbines) 14,000 n.miles (25,930 km) at 11 knots (diesel)
Manning:	178 (20 officers + 158 enlisted)
Helicopters:	1 HH-60J Jayhawk
Guns:	1 76-mm/62-cal DP Mk 75 2 40-mm grenade launchers Mk 19 (2 single) 2 25-mm Bushmaster cannon Mk 38 (2 single) 1 20-mm Phalanx close-in Mk 16 (multi-barrel) 4 .50-cal machine guns M2 (4 single)
ASW weapons:	removed
Missiles:	removed
Radars:	1 SPS-40B air search 2 SPS-64(V)6 navigation
Sonars:	inactivated
Fire control:	Mk 92 Mod 1 GFCS
EW systems:	WLR-1C WLR-3

The DALLAS entering Portsmouth, England. These are attractive ships, highly suitable for the patrol/search-and-rescue roles, but they have been stripped of most of their military capabilities. An antenna dome for the Mk 92 Mod 1 gunfire control system sits atop the bridge. (1994, Leo Van Ginderen collection)

These cutters are capable of long-range patrol and rescue operations. They were intended to serve during wartime in the frigate role as ocean escorts. However, on 31 July 1992 the Commandant of the Coast Guard announced that all ASW weapons would be removed from these cutters.

> The requirement to maintain the WHEC ASW mission/capability, was reviewed by the Navy–Coast Guard Board (NAVGARD) on 23 July 1992. The Board determined that ASW should be retained as a mission for WHECs, but in [the] absence of a global ASW threat, the requirement to maintain an ASW capability can be eliminated. The Navy has sufficient assets to respond to regional contingencies requiring ASW and there will be enough warning time to regenerate the WHEC capability if needed for future global scale conflicts.[5]

The Commandant concluded: "The decision to eliminate the ASW capability requirement . . . was a hard one. The Coast Guard has been effectively prosecuting the ASW mission in the defense of our country since before World War II. However, the world has changed and we must change with it."[6]

In accord with this decision, the ships' ASW weapons were removed and the sonar was inactivated. The Harpoon missile capability was also deleted from these ships.

All 12 cutters have been upgraded under a Fleet Rehabilitation and Modernization (FRAM) program.

Armament: As built, these ships had a single 5-inch/38-cal Mk 30 gun mount, Mk 56 Gunfire Control System (GFCS), and two ahead-firing hedgehog ASW projectile launchers; an SQS-36 sonar was provided. Major armament/sensor/electronics upgrades to the class were:

1967–1987 ASW upgrade:
Installation of six 12.75-inch (324-mm) torpedo tubes Mk 32 (triple) and Mk 309 torpedo control panel (hedgehogs deleted)
Installation of SQS-38 sonar (a hull-mounted version of the SQS-35 variable-depth sonar).

5. Message from Commandant, Coast Guard, to All Coast Guard, 31 July 1992, COMDTNOTE 1430.

6. Ibid.

The GALLATIN shows the long, graceful lines of the 378-foot design. Early designs provided for a twin mast aft with an upper cross section; instead, a tripod mast was fitted, now supporting the large SPS-40B radar antenna. A small TACAN pod tops the main portion of the forward mast. (1994, Leo Van Ginderen collection)

The GALLATIN, showing the Mk 75 76-mm gun forward and the Phalanx CIWS aft. The latter is of little value for the ships in their current patrol/search-and-rescue roles and will probably be removed in the near future. Note the helicopter deck and expanding hangar to support helicopter operations. (1994, Leo Van Ginderen collection)

1985–1992 FRAM modernization:
5-inch/38-cal DP gun replaced by the 76-mm OTO Melara Mk 76
Mk 56 GFCS replaced by Mk 92 GFCS
SPS-29D air search radar replaced by SPS-40 air search radar
Flight deck upgraded to accommodate SH-2F LAMPS I helicopter
Installation of telescoping helicopter hangar and TACAN
Installation of SQR-17A(V)1 acoustic processor for LAMPS
Communications equipment upgraded
Installation of Harpoon SSM canister mountings
Installation of SQR-4 and SQR-17 sonobuoy data link and analysis equipment
Installation of Mk 36 SRBOC chaff/flare launchers
(The planned SLQ-32(V)2 EW and SLQ-25 Nixie systems were canceled.)

Class: Originally, 36 cutters of this class were planned. Additional ships were deferred as the ocean station program was drawn down, i.e., Atlantic and Pacific open-ocean weather and rescue patrol stations were ended. Subsequently, construction of the smaller and less capable BEAR-class cutters was undertaken.

Design: The superstructures of these ships are fabricated largely of aluminum. They are fitted with oceanographic and meteorological facilities. The helicopter hangars were used as balloon shelters prior to their FRAM modernization.

Engineering: These were the largest U.S. combat ships to have gas-turbine propulsion prior to completion of the SPRUANCE (DD 963) in 1975. The gas turbines are FT-4A marine versions of the J75 aircraft engine. The propulsion machinery is CODOG (Combination Diesel or Gas turbine). Maximum speed was 29 knots prior to modernization.

A 350-hp bow propeller pod is fitted.

Guns: These were the last active ships in U.S. service to mount 5-inch (127-mm)/38-cal DP guns. (The last active U.S. Navy ships with this weapon were the frigates of the BROOKE/DEG 1 and GARCIA/FF 1040 classes.)

Missiles: On 16 January 1990 the MELLON became the first Coast Guard cutter to fire a guided missile, launching a Harpoon SSM. Five cutters were fitted with Harpoon through 1992; all of the ships were scheduled for the installation of fittings for eight Harpoon canisters forward, between the bridge and 76-mm gun. In the event, the Harpoon installation was canceled and the missiles were removed from the five ships that had them.

Modernization: These cutters have been updated under a FRAM program and the related Harpoon/CIWS weapons upgrade. With the FRAM update the manning standards for these cutters was increased from 152 (15 officers + 137 enlisted) to 171.

The FRAM work was undertaken at the Bath Iron Works, Maine, shipyard for four East Coast ships (see *Operational* notes) and at the Todd Pacific yard in Seattle, Washington, for eight West Coast ships. A large deck structure was fitted to the forecastle to mount the 76-mm gun and the Harpoon canisters; the Phalanx CIWS mount was fitted aft of the flight deck.

Details of the HAMILTON showing the Harpoon and 76-mm gun arrangement; there is an OE-82 SATCOMM antenna between the Harpoon canisters and bridge structure. Only five ships were fitted with Harpoons before the concept was dropped. (1991, Giorgio Arra)

The FRAM upgrades experienced major delays and cost increases over the original estimates. The entire program has run about two years behind schedule, and the original cost of $30 million per ship has increased to between $50 and $70 million per ship.

Names: The first nine ships were named for Secretaries of the Treasury; the last three ships honor heroes of the Coast Guard. Accordingly, the cutters have been referred to as the Hero class.

Signalman 1st Class Douglas A. Munro was the only Coast Guardsman to receive the Medal of Honor in World War II. He was honored posthumously for having helped evacuate Marines under heavy Japanese fire at Guadalcanal.

Operational: The HAMILTON and CHASE were transferred from the East Coast (homeported in Boston, Massachusetts) to the West Coast (San Pedro, California) in late 1991, bringing 10 of the 12 ships of this class to the Pacific. The DALLAS and GALLATIN remain on the East Coast, based at Governor's Island in New York harbor until 1995, when both shifted to Charleston, South Carolina.

The DALLAS deployed to the Mediterranean in July 1995 for a three-month assignment as a fully integrated unit of the U.S. Sixth Fleet. This is believed to be the first time such an assignment has occurred in peacetime.

HIGH ENDURANCE CUTTERS: "CASCO" CLASS (311)

The UNIMAK (WHEC 379, ex-AVP 31), the last of 18 seaplane tenders of the World War II–built BARNEGAT (AVP 10) class transferred to the Coast Guard in 1946–1948, was stricken on 29 April 1988. She was returned to the Navy for disposal. The UNIMAK was completed as the Navy AVP 31 in 1943; she was transferred to the Coast Guard in 1946 as WAVP 31, then changed to WHEC 379 in 1966. She operated as a training cutter (WTR 379) from 1969 until her decommissioning in May 1974.

She was recommissioned as a WHEC in August 1977 to support the 200-n.mile (370-km) U.S. offshore resource zone. She was in service until 1988.

Historical: During World War II, ships of this class served as seaplane tenders and motor torpedo boat tenders; only one was an amphibious command ship. One ship of this class continues to serve in the Vietnamese Navy (ex-ABSECON/WHEC 374, ex-AVP 23).

See 14th Edition/page 535 for characteristics.

HIGH ENDURANCE CUTTERS: SECRETARY CLASS (327)

All of the large, venerable cutters of the so-called Secretary class have been stricken.[7] Seven of these cutters were completed in 1936–1937; all saw service in World War II as ocean escorts (WPG) and, except for the ALEXANDER HAMILTON (WPG 34), as amphibious command ships (WAGC). The HAMILTON was sunk by a German U-boat in 1942. The six survivors were changed to high endurance cutters (WHEC) on 1 May 1968.

The cutters were stricken from 1981 to 1988. The last were the DUANE (WHEC 33) on 1 August 1985; BIBB (WHEC 31) on 1 September 1985; TANEY (WHEC 37) on 7 December 1986; and INGHAM (WHEC 35) on 27 May 1988 (after 52 years of active service!).

See 14th Edition/pages 535–36 for characteristics.

MEDIUM ENDURANCE CUTTERS

MEDIUM ENDURANCE CUTTERS: EX-NAVY "STALWART" CLASS

A plan to provide six former Navy ocean surveillance ships of the STALWART (T-AGOS 1) class to the Coast Guard for employment as medium endurance cutters has been canceled. The former T-AGOS ships were rejected for the WMEC role because of their slow speed (11 knots) and lack of a helicopter capability. These ships were to replace former Navy ARS-type ships in Coast Guard service.

The VINDICATOR (T-AGOS 3) and PERSISTENCE (T-AGOS 6) were

7. They were named for Secretaries of the Treasury. Details of the World War II configurations of these cutters and other Coast Guard units will be found in Robert L. Scheina, *U.S. Coast Guard Cutters & Craft of World War II* (Annapolis, Md.: Naval Institute Press, 1982), and *U.S. Coast Guard Cutters & Craft, 1946–1990* (Annapolis, Md.: Naval Institute Press, 1990).

the first to have been modified; they were transferred to the Coast Guard on 30 March 1993 and 11 October 1994, respectively. The VINDICATOR was temporarily commissioned in Coast Guard service on 20 May 1994 for the U.S. blockade of Haiti. She was decommissioned on 19 August 1994 to await conversion.

Subsequently, the entire program was canceled. The six ships were to be modified, especially their berthing and galley areas, and new electronic equipment, as well as minimal armament, was to have been added. Their crew in Coast Guard service was to be 45. The cost of converting the first two ships was estimated at $3.7 million.

Class: Originally a class of 18 ships, all are being taken out of service as surveillance ships, with several ships being transferred to NOAA and to academic institutions.

See page 229 for characteristics.

13 MEDIUM ENDURANCE CUTTERS: "BEAR" CLASS (270)

Number	Name	Builder	Laid down	Launched	Commissioned	Status
WMEC 901	BEAR	Tacoma Boatbuilding, Tacoma, Wash.	23 Aug 1979	25 Sep 1980	4 Feb 1983	AA
WMEC 902	TAMPA	Tacoma Boatbuilding, Tacoma, Wash.	2 Apr 1980	19 Mar 1981	16 Mar 1984	AA
WMEC 903	HARRIET LANE	Tacoma Boatbuilding, Tacoma, Wash.	15 Oct 1980	6 Feb 1982	20 Sep 1984	AA
WMEC 904	NORTHLAND	Tacoma Boatbuilding, Tacoma, Wash.	9 Apr 1981	7 May 1982	17 Dec 1984	AA
WMEC 905	SPENCER (ex-SENECA)	Robert E. Derecktor, Middletown, R.I.	26 June 1982	17 Apr 1984	28 June 1986	AA
WMEC 906	SENECA (ex-ESCANABA)	Robert E. Derecktor, Middletown, R.I.	16 Sep 1982	17 Apr 1984	4 May 1987	AA
WMEC 907	ESCANABA (ex-TAHOMA)	Robert E. Derecktor, Middletown, R.I.	1 Apr 1983	2 June 1985	27 Aug 1987	AA
WMEC 908	TAHOMA (ex-SPENCER)	Robert E. Derecktor, Middletown, R.I.	28 June 1983	2 June 1985	6 Apr 1988	AA
WMEC 909	CAMBELL (ex-ARGUS)	Robert E. Derecktor, Middletown, R.I.	10 Aug 1984	29 Apr 1986	19 Aug 1988	AA
WMEC 910	THETIS (ex-TAHOMA)	Robert E. Derecktor, Middletown, R.I.	24 Aug 1984	29 Apr 1986	30 June 1989	AA
WMEC 911	FORWARD (ex-ERIE)	Robert E. Derecktor, Middletown, R.I.	11 July 1986	19 Aug 1987	4 Aug 1990	AA
WMEC 912	LEGARE (ex-MCCULLOCH)	Robert E. Derecktor, Middletown, R.I.	11 July 1986	19 Aug 1987	4 Aug 1990	AA
WMEC 913	MOHAWK (ex-EWING)	Robert E. Derecktor, Middletown, R.I.	18 June 1987	18 May 1988	20 Mar 1990	AA

Displacement:	1,200 tons light 1,820 tons full load
Length:	255 feet (77.8 m) waterline 270 feet (82.3 m) overall
Beam:	38 feet (11.6 m)
Draft:	14 feet (4.3 m)
Propulsion:	2 geared diesel engines (Alco 18V-251E); 7,200 bhp; 2 shafts
Speed:	19.5 knots
Range:	3,850 n.miles (7,130 km) at 19.5 knots 9,900 n.miles (18,335 km) at 12 knots
Manning:	100 (11 officers + 89 enlisted) + 16 air crew
Helicopters:	1 HH-60J Jayhawk
Guns:	1 76-mm/62-cal AA Mk 75 2 .50-cal machine guns M2 (2 single)
ASW weapons:	none
Radars:	2 SPS-64(V)1/6 navigation
Sonars:	none
Fire control:	Mk 92 Mod 1 GFCS
EW systems:	SLQ-32(V)1

These are multipurpose cutters, but their lack of ASW weapons and sensors makes them unsuitable for employment in the ASW role. They have also been criticized for their slow speed, and they ride poorly in heavy seas.

The first four ships were ordered from Tacoma Boatbuilding, with the remainder planned for procurement from the Tacoma yard. The Coast Guard was forced into competitive bidding, however, and the subsequent ships were then awarded to the Derecktor yard.

The BEAR was not delivered to the Coast Guard for service until late in 1983. The entire class is based along the Atlantic coast.

Aircraft: A landing deck and expanding hangar permit these cutters to handle any of the Coast Guard's helicopters.

The LEGARE shows the large helicopter deck of these ships (the hangar is fully retracted). The railing/safety nets are in the raised position around the helicopter deck. The LEGARE has OE-82 SATCOMM antennas forward of the mast and aft of the funnels. (1994, Giorgio Arra)

It was originally intended that in wartime an SH-2F LAMPS I ASW helicopter would be assigned to each ship for convoy escort. The ESCANABA conducted trials with a Navy SH-60B LAMPS III helicopter in 1988. (Plans to install associated sonar and ASW data links were not carried out to support the LAMPS III evaluation.)

The Recovery Assistance and Traversing System (RAST) is fitted to facilitate helicopter operations in rough seas.

Class: The lead ship was authorized in fiscal 1976, WMEC 902–904 in fiscal 1977, and WMEC 905–913 in fiscal 1980. The class, officially known as the Famous class, is generally referred to as the BEAR class.

Design: Design criteria for this class included 14-day law enforcement patrols in areas out to 400 n.miles (740 km) from base. Maximum normal at-sea endurance is 21 days.

These cutters have a very short forecastle with a large, two-level superstructure that gives them a humpback shape. Active fin stabilizers are fitted.

The BEAR-class ships were the first Coast Guard cutters since World War II to be completed with a contemporary EW suite. They were designed to be fitted in wartime with the following military systems: SH-2F LAMPS I anti-submarine helicopter, eight Harpoon anti-ship missiles, 20-mm Phalanx CIWS, Tactical Towed Array Sonar (TACTAS), and chaff launchers. It is unlikely that the ship could accommodate all of these systems simultaneously, in part because of the number of additional personnel required as well as the probable lack of available systems during a conflict.

Accommodations are provided for 109 personnel.

Guns: Six positions are provided for installing machine guns or 40-mm Mk 19 grenade launchers.

Names: The Coast Guard initially named all 13 ships of the class. Subsequently, these prematurely awarded names for WMEC 905 and later ships were withdrawn and those cutters were renamed, as indicated above.

The BEAR honors a long-serving Navy and Coast Guard screw steamer. Built in Scotland in 1874 as a sealing vessel, she was purchased by the U.S. Navy in 1884 and operated successively in the Navy, Revenue Cutter Service, Coast Guard, and, again, the Navy (designated AG 29). The BEAR was used extensively in Arctic operations and by Rear Admiral Richard E. Byrd during his Antarctic expedition of 1933–1935. She was decommissioned in 1944 and transferred to the Maritime Commission in 1948.

Operational: Note that the entire class is based on the Atlantic coast.

The stern of the THETIS clearly showing the helicopter hangar and railing/safety nets. There is a Rigid Inflatable Boat (RIB) and its handing crane on the fantail along with miscellaneous gear. RIBs are found on Coast Guard cutters for use in ship boardings and inspections. (1994, U.S. Navy, PH2 John Sokolowski)

The THETIS under way off the coast of Haiti in support of U.S. military operations in the Caribbean nation. The Mk 92 Mod 1 radar sphere is atop the bridge, and the SLQ-32(V)1 ECM antenna is immediately aft of the bridge. The hangar is extended in this view. (1994, U.S. Navy, PH2 John Sokolowski)

16 MEDIUM ENDURANCE CUTTERS: "RELIANCE" CLASS (210)

Number	Name	Launched	Commissioned	Status
A series (5)				
WMEC 615	Reliance	25 May 1963	20 June 1964	**AA**
WMEC 616	Diligence	20 July 1963	31 Aug 1964	**AA**
WMEC 617	Vigilant	24 Dec 1963	1 Oct 1964	**AA**
WMEC 618	Active	21 July 1965	17 Sep 1966	**PA**
WMEC 619	Confidence	8 May 1965	19 Feb 1966	**AA**
B series (11)				
WMEC 620	Resolute	30 Apr 1966	8 Dec 1966	**PA**
WMEC 621	Valiant	14 Jan 1967	28 Oct 1967	**AA**
WMEC 622	Courageous	18 Mar 1967	19 Apr 1968	**AA**
WMEC 623	Steadfast	24 June 1967	7 Oct 1968	**PA**
WMEC 624	Dauntless	21 Oct 1967	10 June 1968	**AA**
WMEC 625	Venturous	11 Nov 1967	16 Aug 1968	**AA**
WMEC 626	Dependable	16 Mar 1968	22 Nov 1968	**AA**
WMEC 627	Vigorous	4 May 1968	23 Apr 1969	**AA**
WMEC 628	Durable	29 Apr 1967	8 Dec 1967	**AA**
WMEC 629	Decisive	14 Dec 1967	23 Aug 1968	**AA**
WMEC 630	Alert	19 Oct 1968	28 July 1969	**PA**

Builders:	WMEC 615–617	Todd Shipyards, Houston, Texas
	WMEC 618	Christy Corp., Sturgeon Bay, Wisc.
	WMEC 619, 625, 628, 629	Coast Guard Yard, Curtis Bay, Md.
	WMEC 620–624, 626, 627, 630	American Shipbuilding, Lorain, Ohio
Displacement:	950 tons standard 1,007 tons full load except WMEC 616–619 970 tons	
Length:	210½ feet (64.2 m) overall	
Beam:	34 feet (10.4 m)	
Draft:	10½ feet (3.2 m)	
Propulsion:	2 turbo-charged diesel engines (Alco 251B); 5,000 bhp; 2 shafts	
Speed:	18 knots	
Range:	A series	2,100 n.miles (3,890 km) at 18 knots 6,100 n.miles (11,300 km) at 13 knots
	B series	2,700 n.miles (5,000 km) at 18 knots 6,100 n.miles (11,300 km) at 13 knots
Manning:	74 (8 officers + 66 enlisted)	
Helicopters:	landing area	
Guns:	1 25-mm Bushmaster cannon Mk 38 2 .50-cal machine guns M2 (2 single)	
ASW weapons:	none	
Radars:	2 SPS-64(V)1 navigation	
Sonars:	none	

These are search-and-rescue cutters. They can land helicopters but have no hangar.

Armament: No ASW armament is provided in these cutters. Their design included space and weight provisions for hedgehogs and, subsequently, Mk 32 ASW torpedo tubes.

As built, they carried a 3-inch/50-cal Mk 22 gun forward; this was replaced by a 25-mm Bushmaster chain gun.

Classification: These ships were originally classified as patrol craft (WPC); the designation changed to WMEC—with the same hull numbers—on 1 May 1966. The Reliance was changed to WTR on June 1975 (the TR indicating *T*raining of *R*eserves); she reverted to WMEC on 16 August 1982.

Design: The Reliance design has a small island superstructure with 360° visibility from the bridge to facilitate helicopter operations and towing.

The Alert was fitted with the Canadian-developed "Beartrap" helicopter haul-down system.

Engineering: The WMEC 615–619 were built with CODAG (Combination Diesel and Gas) turbine plants to provide experience in operating mixed propulsion plants. Those cutters had a high acceleration rate from all stop or, with their engines shut down, could be at full speed in a few minutes; they could make 15.25 knots on gas turbines alone. The cost factor influenced the decision to make the remaining ships all diesel.

The five ships were reengined during their mid-life modernization (see below).

Modernization: These cutters have been upgraded under a Mid-life Maintenance Availability (MMA) program. The upgrade included an enlarged superstructure; installation of a larger, improved engine exhaust (funnel); improved living spaces; redesigned engine room; upgraded firefighting system; new refrigeration and air-conditioning units; and a new electronics suite.

The MMA required approximately 18 months and cost about $20 million per cutter. The work was done at the Coast Guard Yard, Curtis Bay, Maryland. Modernization of the lead ship, the Active, began in October 1984 and was completed in February 1987. The last cutter, the Resolute, was completed in 1996.

The Vigorous after her extensive MMA upgrade. She now has a 25-mm Bushmaster cannon Mk 38 forward, a large funnel aft of the mast, and the radio-direction-finding loop moved from aft of the "island" structure to a position forward of the bridge. Internal changes are much more extensive. (1994, Giorgio Arra)

Stern aspect of the VIGOROUS showing her new funnel structure and clear stern counter, which previously had twin diesel engine exhausts. These cutters are well into their third decade of service. (1994, Giorgio Arra)

1 MEDIUM ENDURANCE CUTTER: "STORIS" (230)

Number	Name	Launched	Commissioned	Status
WMEC 38	STORIS	4 Apr 1942	30 Sep 1942	**PA**

Builders:	Toledo Shipbuilding, Ohio
Displacement:	1,715 tons standard 1,925 tons full load
Length:	230 feet (70.1 m) overall
Beam:	43 feet (13.1 m)
Draft:	15 feet (4.6 m)
Propulsion:	diesel-electric (3 Fairbanks Morse 38D 8¼ diesel engines); 1,800 shp; 1 shaft
Speed:	14 knots
Range:	12,000 n.miles (22,225 km) at 14 knots 22,000 n.miles (40,745 km) at 8 knots
Manning:	
Helicopters:	no facilities
Guns:	1 25-mm Bushmaster cannon Mk 38 4 .50-cal machine guns M2 (4 single)
Radars:	2 SPS-64 navigation

The STORIS was built specifically for offshore icebreaking and patrol in the Greenland area. She has been employed since 1949 in the Alaskan area for search, rescue, and law enforcement. She is currently the oldest Coast Guard cutter in active service.

Classification: The STORIS originally was classified as WAGL 38 and then WAG 38; she was changed to WAGB 38 on 1 May 1966. She was reclassified as a medium endurance cutter (WMEC) on 1 July 1972 to emphasize her role in law enforcement off the Alaskan fishing grounds.

Design: The ship was designed specifically for operation in northern waters and for icebreaking, although she is generally similar in design to the Coast Guard's 180-foot (54.9-m) buoy tenders. During World War II the STORIS carried a single J2F Duck scouting biplane.

Guns: As built, the STORIS was armed with two 3-inch guns and four 20-mm guns, plus ASW weapons. A single 3-inch gun was retained into the 1980s.

Names: The ship was initially named the ESKIMO, but the name was changed to STORIS during construction at the request of the State

The very-long-serving STORIS in Alaskan waters. She is the oldest cutter in Coast Guard service, except for the sailing bark EAGLE. Note her icebreaking prow, cargo crane forward of the bridge, and 3-inch/50 gun mount aft of the funnel (since removed). In World War II she carried a second 3-inch gun forward, 20-mm AA guns, depth charges, and Mousetrap ASW rocket projectors, plus a floatplane. (U.S. Coast Guard)

Department, which feared that the name might offend the natives of Greenland.

Operational: During World War II the STORIS served in the North Atlantic as an ocean escort ship.

The STORIS and the seagoing buoy tenders BRAMBLE and SPAR carried out the first circumnavigation of the North American continent and transited the Northwest Passage in 1957, departing from Unimak Pass, Alaska, on 1 July and reaching Argentia, Newfoundland, on 19 September.

2 MEDIUM ENDURANCE CUTTERS: EX-NAVY SALVAGE SHIPS (213)

Number	Name	Launched	Navy Comm.	Status
WMEC 167 (ex-ARS 9)	ACUSHNET	1 Apr 1943	5 Feb 1944	**PA**
WMEC 168 (ex-ARS 26)	YOCONA	8 Apr 1944	3 Nov 1944	**PA**

Builders:	Basalt Rock, Napa, Calif.
Displacement:	1,557 tons standard
	1,745 tons full load
Length:	213½ feet (65.1 m) overall
Beam:	39 feet (12.8 m)
Draft:	15 feet (4.9 m)
Propulsion:	4 diesel engines (Cooper Bessemer GSB-8); 3,000 bhp; 2 shafts
Speed:	15.5 knots
Range:	9,000 n.miles (16,670 km) at 15.5 knots
	20,000 n.miles (37,040 km) at 7 knots
Manning:	
Helicopters:	no facilities
Guns:	2 40-mm grenade launchers Mk 19 (2 single)
Radars:	2 SPS-64 navigation

These are former Navy salvage ships that were permanently transferred to the Coast Guard after World War II: the WMEC 167 on 29 June 1946 and WMEC 168 on 28 June 1946.

Class: A third ship of this type, the ESCAPE (ARS 6), was transferred on loan to the Coast Guard on 4 December 1980 (redesignated WMEC 6). She was decommissioned for disposal on 29 June 1995.

Classification: Upon transfer to the Coast Guard, these two ships were classified as tugs (WAT). They were changed to WMEC on 1 May 1966, with the ACUSHNET modified to handle environmental data buoys and changed to an oceanographic cutter (WAGO 167) in 1969. She was redesignated WMEC in 1978.

Names: The two ships permanently transferred were renamed in Coast Guard service; their Navy names were SHACKLE (ARS 9) and SEIZE (ARS 26). The ex-ARS 6 retained her Navy name.

MEDIUM ENDURANCE CUTTERS: EX-NAVY FLEET TUGS (205)

Number	Name	Navy Comm.	USCG Comm.	Notes
WMEC 153 (ex-ATF 153)	CHILULA	1945	1956	stricken 27 June 1991
WMEC 165 (ex-ATF 66)	CHEROKEE	1940	1946	stricken 28 Feb 1991
WMEC 166 (ex-ATF 95)	TAMAROA	1943	1946	stricken 1 Feb 1994

These are former Navy fleet tugs that were transferred to the Coast Guard and employed as medium endurance cutters. (The TAMAROA was named ZUNI in Navy service; the others retained their Navy names.)

They were returned to Navy custody for disposal; the TAMAROA was transferred to the INTREPID Sea-Air-Space Museum in New York City.

Class: Two additional Navy ATFs transferred to the Coast Guard on loan on 30 September 1980 also served as cutters: the UTE (WMEC 76, ex-ATF 76) and LIPAN (WMEC 85, ex-ATF 85). Both were returned to the Navy, on 26 May 1988 and 9 June 1988, respectively, and have subsequently been stricken.

Classification: These ships were classified ATF by the Navy; upon transfer to the Coast Guard they became WAT, with two having new hull numbers assigned. All three were changed to WMEC on 1 May 1966.

See 15th Edition/page 562 for characteristics.

1 MEDIUM ENDURANCE CUTTER: "BALSAM" CLASS (180)

The CITRUS (WMEC 300), a buoy tender of the BALSAM (WLB 62) class, is employed as a medium endurance cutter (see page 520).

SURFACE EFFECT SHIPS

SES CUTTERS: "SEA HAWK" CLASS

Number	Name	Commissioned	Notes
WSES 2	SEA HAWK	1982	decomm. 28 Jan 1994
WSES 3	SHEARWATER	1982	decomm. 28 Jan 1994
WSES 4	PETREL	1983	decomm. 28 Jan 1994

The three Surface Effect Ships (SES) acquired by the Coast Guard and used primarily in the drug enforcement role have been decommissioned and discarded. They were acquired after evaluation of a prototype ship, the DORADO (designated WSES 1), which was commissioned in the Coast Guard in 1981 and, after extensive trials, retransferred to the Navy.

The three SEA HAWK-class cutters were overweight and did not achieve their specified speed of 33 to 35 knots. They were based at Key West, Florida.

See 15th Edition/page 563 for characteristics.

The ACUSHNET is one of two ex-Navy tug/salvage ships remaining in Coast Guard service. Long ago she beached all of her salvage gear and has been extensively remodeled for her role as a patrol cutter. (1990, Giorgio Arra)

PATROL BOATS

PATROL BOATS: HERITAGE CLASS (120)

Number	Name	Launched	Completed	Status
WPB 1400	Leopold	—	(1993)	canceled
WPB	95 units			canceled

Builders:	Coast Guard Yard, Curtis Bay, Md.
Displacement:	157 tons full load
Length:	118 feet (36.0 m) overall
Beam:	23 feet (7.0 m)
Draft:	8 feet (2.5 m)
Propulsion:	2 diesel engines; 2 shafts
Speed:	30 knots
Range:	720 n.miles (1,333 km) at 30 knots
Manning:	17 (2 officers + 15 enlisted)
Guns:	1 20-mm cannon 2 .50-cal machine guns M2 (2 single)
Radars:	1 SPS-64(V)1 navigation

This class of Coast Guard patrol boats was intended to replace the older and smaller Cape-class and Point-class patrol boats. The Heritage-class design was expected to be faster, to serve longer, and to be less expensive to build and maintain than the Island class.

The Leopold was ordered in March 1989 and was laid down on 27 August 1990. Series production of 35 follow-on units was expected to begin in 1992 if the prototype proved successful; long-range plans called for a total of up to 96 units. However, the Coast Guard halted work on the Leopold on 25 November 1991 because of the rapidly changing world situation. A Coast Guard spokesman stated, "The reason that we're suspending it at this point—and most likely it will be canceled—is basically times have changed."

The Coast Guard decision came four months after a report of the General Accounting Office (GAO) questioned the need for the craft. That report stated: "There were weaknesses in identifying mission needs and the capabilities the replacement vessels [Heritage class] would require to meet these needs. The Coast Guard also could not support its decision for the number of patrol boats needed because agency officials could not provide support for the calculations of the computer model used to determine the need for 96 vessels."[8] The GAO report also noted that the Coast Guard underestimated the time and cost required to acquire the Heritage class.

Classification: The class was rated at 120 feet (36.58 m), although the actual length is 118 feet (36 m).

Cost: In October 1991 a government report revealed an expected cost of $13 million for the lead unit, or almost double the initial estimate of $7.7 million. In comparison, the Island-class boats are about $6.5 million each. In series production the Heritage class was expected to cost some $6 million per unit.

Design: The design's "deep-V" hull has a raked bow, low bow bulwark, and a full hull form farther aft. The forward half of the deckhouse is protected by a full-beam shield with a ladder in its face that leads to bridge wings. A tripod mast is stepped abaft the bridge, which has 360° visibility. The design provided for a steel hull with an aluminum deckhouse.

The new class was to have the towing capability that the Island-class patrol craft lack.

The new boats were expected to have an estimated life of 30 years vice the 15 to 20 years of the Island class because the heavier hull plating takes longer to wear from corrosion.

Names: These ships were to be named for former Coast Guard cutters that were part of the service's heritage.

8. General Accounting Office, *Coast Guard: Adequacy of the Justification for Heritage Patrol Boats* (Washington, D.C.: 12 July 1991), pp. 1–2.

Artist's concept of the Leopold, lead ship for an abortive class of 118-foot patrol boats. The craft were to have had a streamlined superstructure compared to the boxy appearance of the Island class. (U.S. Coast Guard, T. Freeman)

The largest class of cutters in the Coast Guard is the Island class of 110-foot patrol *boats.* Despite the age of their design and some structural problems, these cutters are well liked in the Coast Guard. Here, the crews of the Adak (nearer camera) and Staten Island man the rails. (1994, Leo Van Ginderen collection)

49 PATROL BOATS: ISLAND CLASS (110)

Number	Name	Launched	Commissioned	Status
A series (16)				
WPB 1301	Farallon	27 Aug 1985	21 Feb 1986	AA
WPB 1302	Manitou	9 Oct 1985	28 Feb 1986	AA
WPB 1303	Matagorda	15 Dec 1985	25 Apr 1986	AA
WPB 1304	Maui	13 Jan 1986	9 May 1986	AA
WPB 1305	Monhegan	15 Feb 1986	16 June 1986	AA
WPB 1306	Nunivak	15 Mar 1986	4 July 1986	AA
WPB 1307	Ocracoke	12 Apr 1986	4 Aug 1986	AA
WPB 1308	Vashon	10 May 1986	15 Aug 1986	AA
WPB 1309	Aquidneck	14 June 1986	26 Sep 1986	AA
WPB 1310	Mustang	11 July 1986	29 Aug 1986	PA
WPB 1311	Naushon	22 Aug 1986	3 Oct 1986	PA
WPB 1312	Sanibel	3 Oct 1986	14 Nov 1986	AA
WPB 1313	Edisto	21 Nov 1986	7 Jan 1987	PA
WPB 1314	Sapelo	9 Jan 1987	24 Feb 1987	PA
WPB 1315	Matinicus	26 Feb 1987	16 Apr 1987	AA
WPB 1316	Nantucket	17 Apr 1987	4 June 1987	AA
B series (21)				
WPB 1317	Attu	4 Dec 1987	9 May 1988	AA
WPB 1318	Baranof	15 Jan 1988	20 May 1988	AA
WPB 1319	Chandeleur	19 Feb 1988	8 June 1988	AA
WPB 1320	Chincoteague	25 Mar 1988	8 Aug 1988	AA
WPB 1321	Cushing	29 Apr 1988	8 Aug 1988	AA
WPB 1322	Cuttyhunk	3 June 1988	15 Oct 1988	PA
WPB 1323	Drummond	8 July 1988	19 Oct 1988	AA
WPB 1324	Key Largo	12 Aug 1988	24 Dec 1988	AA
WPB 1325	Metomkin	16 Sep 1988	12 Jan 1989	AA
WPB 1326	Monomoy	21 Oct 1988	16 Dec 1988	AA
WPB 1327	Orcas	25 Nov 1988	14 Apr 1989	PA
WPB 1328	Padre	6 Jan 1989	24 Feb 1989	AA
WPB 1329	Sitkinak	10 Feb 1989	31 Mar 1989	AA
WPB 1330	Tybee	17 Mar 1989	9 May 1989	PA
WPB 1331	Washington	21 Apr 1989	1989	PA
WPB 1332	Wrangell	26 May 1989	24 June 1989	AA
WPB 1333	Adak	30 June 1989	17 Nov 1989	AA
WPB 1334	Liberty	4 Aug 1989	22 Sep 1989	PA
WPB 1335	Anacapa	8 Sep 1989	13 Jan 1990	AA
WPB 1336	Kiska	13 Oct 1989	1 Dec 1989*	PA
WPB 1337	Assateague	17 Nov 1989	1 Jan 1990*	PA
C series (12)				
WPB 1338	Grand Isle	1989	14 Dec 1990*	AA
WPB 1339	Key Biscayne		27 Apr 1991	AA
WPB 1340	Jefferson Island		17 Apr 1991	AA
WPB 1341	Kodiak Island	8 Feb 1991	21 June 1991	AA
WPB 1342	Long Island	19 Mar 1991	27 Aug 1991	PA
WPB 1343	Bainbridge Island	19 Apr 1991	14 June 1991*	AA
WPB 1344	Block Island		19 July 1991*	AA
WPB 1345	Staten Island		23 Aug 1991*	AA
WPB 1346	Roanoke Island		27 Sep 1991*	AA
WPB 1347	Pea Island		1 Nov 1992*	AA
WPB 1348	Knight Island	6 Sep 1991	6 Dec 1991*	AA
WPB 1349	Galveston Island	15 Nov 1991	17 Jan 1992*	PA

*These are delivery vice commissioning dates.

Builders:	Bollinger Shipyard, Lockport, La.
Displacement:	A series 117 tons light
	B series 107 tons light
	C series 107 tons light
	A series 165 tons full load
	B series 155 tons full load
	C series 153 tons full load
Length:	110 feet (33.5 m) overall
Beam:	21 feet (6.4 m)
Draft:	7⅓ feet (2.2 m)
Propulsion:	2 diesel engines (Paxman Valenta 16CM RP200V); 5,820 bhp except C series 2 diesel engines (Caterpillar 3516); 5,324 bhp; 2 shafts
Speed:	30 knots
	except C series 26.5 knots
Range:	900 n.miles (1,670 km) at 30 knots
	2,700 n.miles (5,000 km) at 12 knots
	except C series 840 n.miles (1,555 km) at 26.5 knots
	2,400 n.miles (4,445 km) at 12 knots
Manning:	16–18 (2 officers + 14–16 enlisted)
Guns:	1 25-mm Bushmaster cannon Mk 38
	2 7.62-mm machine guns M60 (2 single)
Radar:	1 SPS-64(V)1 navigation

Bow aspect of the Chandeleur. Beyond their boxy superstructure, these craft are distinguished by their open bridge atop the enclosed bridge and quadrapod lattice mast. The bar-type antenna for the SPS-64(V)1 navigation radar tops the mast. (1994, Giorgio Arra)

A RIB and its handling crane stowed aft of the island structure of the Chandeleur. (1994, Giorgio Arra)

The Coast Guard acquired this class for offshore surveillance, law enforcement, and search-and-rescue operations, replacing the 95-foot (29-m) and 82-foot (25-m) WPBs. However, some ports available for the smaller craft cannot accommodate the Island-class WPBs.

The contract for these boats was originally awarded in May 1984 to the Marine Power and Equipment Company, Seattle, Washington, for 16 boats. A U.S. District Court set aside the award because of irregularities in the procurement process. Bollinger was awarded a contract for the first 16 units in August 1984.

The basic design was 20 years old when the contract was awarded, and critics have claimed that more capable designs were available. Also, early operational experience with the Island-class WPBs revealed hull problems, i.e., cracks developing in heavy seas.

Design: The design is based on an existing patrol boat developed by Vosper-Thornycroft in Britain to minimize cost and to reduce technical risks. The craft have a steel hull with aluminum deck and superstructure; they have a flush-deck, round-bilge hull, with some bow sheer, and a low bow combing. The WPB 1317 and later units have heavier bow plating to correct a hull-cracking problem. A quadripod mast is fitted.

Manning: The Vashon undertook a historic manning experiment in 1994–1995, employing Naval Reserve personnel to help provide shore support and maintenance for the patrol boat, as well as undertaking their at-sea drills on board for 12 to 17 days.[9] The Vashon is based at Roosevelt Roads, Puerto Rico.

Operational: The Island-class units in the Caribbean area normally conduct 10- to 12-day patrols followed by an in-port period.

9. See Lt. Joe DiRenzo III, USCG, "The Ultimate Odd Couple," U.S. Naval Institute *Proceedings* (June 1995), pp. 65–67.

The CHANDELEUR off the coast of Florida displays the boxy lines of these 110-foot patrol boats. The 25-mm Bushmaster cannon is under canvas. (1994, Giorgio Arra)

(50) PATROL BOATS: NEW CONSTRUCTION (87)

Builders:	Bollinger Shipyard, Lockport, La.
Displacement:	approx. 89.5 tons full load
Length:	86 11/12 feet (26.5 m) overall
Beam:	17 1/3 feet (5.29 m)
Draft:	5 5/6 feet (1.78 m)
Propulsion:	2 diesel engines; 2 shafts
Speed:	25 knots
Range:	approx. 1,225 n.miles (2,270 km)
Manning:	10 (1 or 0 officers + 9 or 10 enlisted)
Guns:	2 7.62-mm machine guns M60 (2 single)
Radars:	surface search X-band navigational

These will replace the 82-foot WPBs, complementing the 110-foot cutters of the Island class as the Coast Guard's principal patrol craft after the year 2000.

The Coast Guard revealed details of the new 87-foot craft in early 1996. Bollinger was awarded a contract on 22 March 1996 to design and construct the lead unit.

Design: The 87-foot WPBs will have improved habitability, intended for mixed-gender crews. Accommodations will consist of four two-person and one three-person berths (with one spare berth).

Engineering: Range is calculated at 15 hours at 25 knots and 85 hours at 10 knots.

The CAPE HATTERAS was the last Cape-class WPB in U.S. Coast Guard service. The Cape class had a distinctive funnel aft of the bridge and a stub mast and boat boom aft of the superstructure. The HATTERAS has since been transferred to Mexico. (1990, Georgio Arra)

PATROL BOATS: CAPE CLASS (95)

Number	Name	Status
WPB 95300	CAPE SMALL	decomm. 13 Apr 1987; to Marshall Is. 1987
WPB 95302	CAPE HIGGON	decomm. Jan 1990; to Uruguay 1990
WPB 95303	CAPE UPRIGHT	decomm. 6 Jan 1989; to Bahamas 1989
WPB 95304	CAPE GULL	decomm. 15 May 1988
WPB 95305	CAPE HATTERAS	decomm. 14 Mar 1991; to Mexico 1991
WPB 95306	CAPE GEORGE	decomm. 3 Sep 1989; to Micronesia 1990
WPB 95307	CAPE CURRENT	decomm. 1 May 1989; to Bahamas 1989
WPB 95308	CAPE STRAIT	decomm. 21 Jan 1983
WPB 95309	CAPE CARTER	decomm. 19 Jan 1990; to Mexico 1990
WPB 95310	CAPE WASH	decomm. 1 June 1987; to U.S. Navy
WPB 95311	CAPE HEDGE	decomm. 7 Jan 1987; to Mexico 1990
WPB 95312	CAPE KNOX	decomm. 10 Feb 1989
WPB 95313	CAPE MORGAN	decomm. 20 Oct 1989; to Bahamas 1989
WPB 95316	CAPE FOX	decomm. 30 June 1989; to Bahamas 1989
WPB 95317	CAPE JELLISON	decomm. 12 Dec 1986; to U.S. Sea Scouts
WPB 95319	CAPE ROMAIN	decomm. 11 Aug 1989; to U.S. Navy 1989
WPB 95320	CAPE STARR	decomm. 16 Jan 1987
WPB 95321	CAPE CROSS	decomm. 20 Mar 1990; to Micronesia 1990
WPB 95322	CAPE HORN	decomm. 25 Jan 1990; to Uruguay 1990
WPB 95324	CAPE SHOALWATER	decomm. 9 Dec 1988; to Bahamas 1989
WPB 95326	CAPE CORWIN	decomm. 6 Apr 1990; to Micronesia 1990
WPB 95328	CAPE HENLOPEN	decomm. 28 Sep 1989; to Costa Rica 1989
WPB 95332	CAPE YORK	decomm. 26 May 1989; to Bahamas 1989

All 95-foot (29-m), steel-hull patrol boats of the Cape class have been discarded, with many having been transferred to other navies and coastal patrol agencies. The above units were those in service when the last edition of *Ships and Aircraft* was published (see appendix D for details on foreign transfers). Previous transfers of this class went to Ethiopia, Haiti, South Korea, Saudi Arabia, and Thailand.

The CAPE HEDGE (WPB 95311) was transferred to the U.S. Navy on 7 January 1987 and served as a pilot boat in 1987–1989 (renamed VANGUARD); she was transferred to Mexico in 1990. The CAPE ROMAIN (WPB 95319) went to the U.S. Navy as a pilot boat on 11 August 1989. The CAPE WASH (WPB 95310) went to the U.S. Navy in 1987 (see page 318 for details).

Class: A total of 36 of these craft, originally intended primarily for harbor patrol and coastal ASW, were constructed between 1953 and 1959. Plans to discard this class in the 1970s in favor of new construction were dropped and all surviving units were modernized. They have been replaced from the mid-1980s on by the Island-class WPBs.

See 14th Edition/page 544 for characteristics.

41 PATROL BOATS: POINT CLASS (82)

Number	Name	Commissioned	Status
A series (1)			
WPB 82302	Point Hope	5 Oct 1960	to Costa Rica 1991
WPB 82311	Point Verde	15 Mar 1961	to Mexico 1991
WPB 82312	Point Swift	22 Mar 1961	**AA**
WPB 82314	Point Thatcher	13 Sep 1961	stricken 13 Mar 1992
C series (31)			
WPB 82318	Point Herron	14 June 1961	to Mexico 1991
WPB 82332	Point Roberts	6 June 1962	stricken Feb 1992
WPB 82333	Point Highland	27 June 1962	**AA**
WPB 82334	Point Ledge	18 July 1962	**PA**
WPB 82335	Point Countess	8 Aug 1962	**AA**
WPB 82336	Point Glass	29 Aug 1962	**AA**
WPB 82337	Point Divide	19 Sep 1962	**PA**
WPB 82338	Point Bridge	10 Oct 1962	**PA**
WPB 82339	Point Chico	29 Oct 1962	**PA**
WPB 82340	Point Batan	21 Nov 1962	**AA**
WPB 82341	Point Lookout	12 Dec 1962	stricken 24 Mar 1994
WPB 82342	Point Baker	30 Oct 1963	**AA**
WPB 82343	Point Wells	20 Nov 1963	**AA**
WPB 82344	Point Estero	11 Dec 1966	**AA**
WPB 82345	Point Judith	26 July 1966	to Venezuela 1992
WPB 82346	Point Arena	26 Aug 1966	**AA**
WPB 82347	Point Bonita	12 Sep 1966	**AA**
WPB 82348	Point Barrow	4 Oct 1966	to Panama 1991
WPB 82349	Point Spencer	25 Oct 1966	**AA**
WPB 82350	Point Franklin	14 Nov 1966	**AA**
WPB 82351	Point Bennett	19 Dec 1966	**PA**
WPB 82352	Point Sal	5 Dec 1966	**AA**
WPB 82353	Point Monroe	27 Dec 1966	**AA**
WPB 82354	Point Evans	10 Jan 1967	**PA**
WPB 82355	Point Hannon	23 Jan 1967	**AA**
WPB 82356	Point Francis	3 Feb 1967	**AA**
WPB 82357	Point Huron	17 Feb 1967	**AA**
WPB 82358	Point Stuart	17 Mar 1967	**PA**
WPB 82359	Point Steele	26 Apr 1967	**AA**
WPB 82360	Point Winslow	3 Mar 1967	**AA**
WPB 82361	Point Charles	15 May 1967	stricken 13 Dec 1991
WPB 82362	Point Brown	30 Mar 1967	stricken 30 Sep 1991
WPB 82363	Point Nowell	1 June 1967	**AA**
WPB 82364	Point Whitehorn	13 July 1967	**AA**
WPB 82365	Point Turner	14 Apr 1967	**AA**
WPB 82366	Point Lobos	29 May 1967	**AA**
WPB 82367	Point Knoll	27 June 1967	to Venezuela 1991
WPB 82368	Point Warde	14 Aug 1967	**AA**
WPB 82369	Point Heyer	3 Aug 1967	**PA**
WPB 82370	Point Richmond	25 Aug 1967	**PA**
D series (7)			
WPB 82371	Point Barnes	21 Apr 1970	**AA**
WPB 82372	Point Brower	21 Apr 1970	**PA**
WPB 82373	Point Camden	4 May 1970	**PA**
WPB 82374	Point Carrew	18 May 1970	**PA**
WPB 82375	Point Doran	1 June 1970	**PA**
WPB 82376	Point Harris	22 June 1970	stricken 12 Apr 1992
WPB 82377	Point Hobart	13 July 1970	**PA**
WPB 82378	Point Jackson	3 Aug 1970	**AA**
WPB 82379	Point Martin	20 Aug 1970	**AA**

Builders:	Coast Guard Yard, Curtis Bay, Md., except WPB 82345–82349 J. Martinac Shipbuilding, Tacoma, Wash.
Displacement:	A series 67 tons full load C series 66 tons full load D series 69 tons full load
Length:	83 feet (25.3 m) overall
Beam:	17⅙ feet (5.2 m)
Draft:	5¾ feet (1.8 m)
Propulsion:	2 diesel engines (Cummins VT-12-M); 1,600 bhp or (Caterpillar 3412); 1,480 bhp; 2 shafts
Speed:	A series 23.5 knots C series 23.7 knots D series 22.6 knots
Range:	A and C series 490 n.miles (910 km) at 20 knots 1,500 n.miles (2,780 km) at 8 knots D series 320 n.miles (590 km) at 20 knots 1,200 n.miles (2,220 km) at 6 knots
Manning:	10 (see notes)
Guns:	2 .50-cal machine guns M2 (2 single)
Radars:	SPS-64(V)1 navigation

The Point Barnes under way off the Florida coast. These 30-year-plus patrol boats will serve into the 21st century. The Point Barnes has a machine gun forward, two life-raft canisters forward of the bridge, and a RIB and crane amidships. (1994, Giorgio Arra)

The Point Whitehorn, without a .50-cal machine gun mounted forward. Two guns can be mounted forward in these craft. (1992, Leo Van Ginderen collection)

The Point Franklin shows the simple arrangement of these long-serving patrol boats. (1990, Leo Van Ginderen collection)

These are 82-foot cutters used for port security and search and rescue. Several additional units planned for disposal have been retained on a temporary basis because of asbestos problems.

Class: Originally, this class contained 78 units. Beginning in 1965, 26 units were deployed to South Vietnamese waters; these units were transferred to South Vietnam in 1969–1970.

Recent disposals are listed above (see also appendix E). Some survivors will be in Coast Guard service beyond the year 2000.

The Point Charles was transferred to Texas A&M University and the Point Brown to Kingsborough Community College, Brooklyn, New York, for training. The Point Harris was heavily damaged by Hurricane Iniki at Kauai, Hawaii, on 11 September 1992 and was subsequently stricken.

Design: These patrol boats have steel hulls and aluminum superstructures. There are no noticeable differences among the various series of the Point class. A tripod mast is fitted atop the bridge roof.

Engineering: The POINT THATCHER originally had two gas turbines generating 1,000 shp and capable of making 27 knots; they are fitted with controllable-pitch propellers. She was refitted with diesels.

The Coast Guard had planned to reengine 43 of these craft, beginning in the late 1980s, to extend their service lives. All were completed with two Cummins VT-12-M diesel engines. Starting in 1989, the 43 units were to be refitted with two 750-bhp Caterpillar 3412 V-12 diesel engines, but that effort is behind schedule, and only 26 units will be upgraded. The POINT HIGHLAND was the first unit to be reengined.

Guns: Earlier, these WPBs had a single 20-mm gun forward of the deckhouse. During the 1960s and 1970s, however, many units carried two .50-cal machine guns or an 81-mm mortar mounted "piggyback" with a .50-cal machine gun. Subsequently, they carried only the single machine guns. Only small arms are now carried.

Manning: About half of the Point-class WPBs are commanded by commissioned officers and the remainder by an officer-in-charge, who is normally a chief petty officer.

Names: The WPB 82301–82344 were assigned geographical point names in January 1964; later cutters were named as built.

ICEBREAKERS

Coast Guard icebreakers operate in the Arctic and Antarctic regions in support of U.S. national requirements for military and scientific activities. The Coast Guard had long planned to construct two Polar-class icebreakers to replace the GLACIER and two additional Wind-class icebreakers, thus providing a force of four modern icebreakers to meet national requirements. But the GLACIER and two surviving Wind-class ships were decommissioned without replacements.

In late 1986 the Coast Guard expressed interest in leasing two large polar icebreakers as an alternative to building and operating government-owned ships. Such a build-and-charter concept was similar to that used by the Navy for tankers and maritime prepositioning ships. The concept, however, was rejected in favor of a single new construction ship. Named HEALY, the new ship will be larger and more powerful than the Polar-class icebreakers.

(1) ICEBREAKER: "HEALY"

Number	Name	FY	Launch	Commission	Status
WAGB 20	HEALY	90	1997	1998	Building

Builders:	Avondale Industries, New Orleans, La.
Displacement:	17,710 tons full load
Length:	400 feet (121.95 m) waterline 460 feet (140.2 m) overall
Beam:	94½ feet (28.8 m)
Draft:	32 feet (9.75 m)
Propulsion:	diesel-electric: 4 diesel engines; 40,000 bhp + electric motors; 60,000 shp; 2 shafts
Speed:	12.5 knots
Range:	34,500 n.miles (63,900 km) at 12.5 knots 37,000 n.miles (68,525 km) at 9.25 knots
Manning:	133 (19 officers + 114 enlisted) + 30 scientists
Helicopters:	2 HH-65A Dolphin
Guns:	2 .50-cal machine guns M2 (2 single)
Radars:	2 navigation

The HEALY is intended primarily as an Arctic research and support ship. This is the first specialized icebreaker to be built for the U.S. Navy or Coast Guard in more than two decades.

Congress voted $275 million in the fiscal 1990 budget for construction of this ship; the remainder of the necessary funding, $60 million, was authorized by Congress in fiscal 1992. The Navy lists the ship as being in the fiscal 1993 shipbuilding program.[10]

Cancellation of the planned shipyard selection and award of a contract for construction of the HEALY was announced on 20 March 1992. The Naval Sea Systems Command, procurement agent for the Coast Guard for icebreakers, canceled the procurement because the responses received from shipyards were in excess of appropriated funds. The Coast Guard and Navy stated that they would "continue to examine alternatives for procuring the icebreaker. . . ." A contract to construct the ship was awarded to Avondale Industries on 15 July 1993.

Although a second ship was planned, no authorization has been forthcoming.

Design: Intended to break ice 4½ feet (1.4 m) thick at a continuous speed of three knots. The ship has extensive laboratory spaces.

Engineering: The ship will have an endurance of 180 days.

10. Various editions of the *Naval Sea Systems Command Quarterly Progress Report for Shipbuilding and Conversion,* NAVSEA 250-574 (Washington, D.C.).

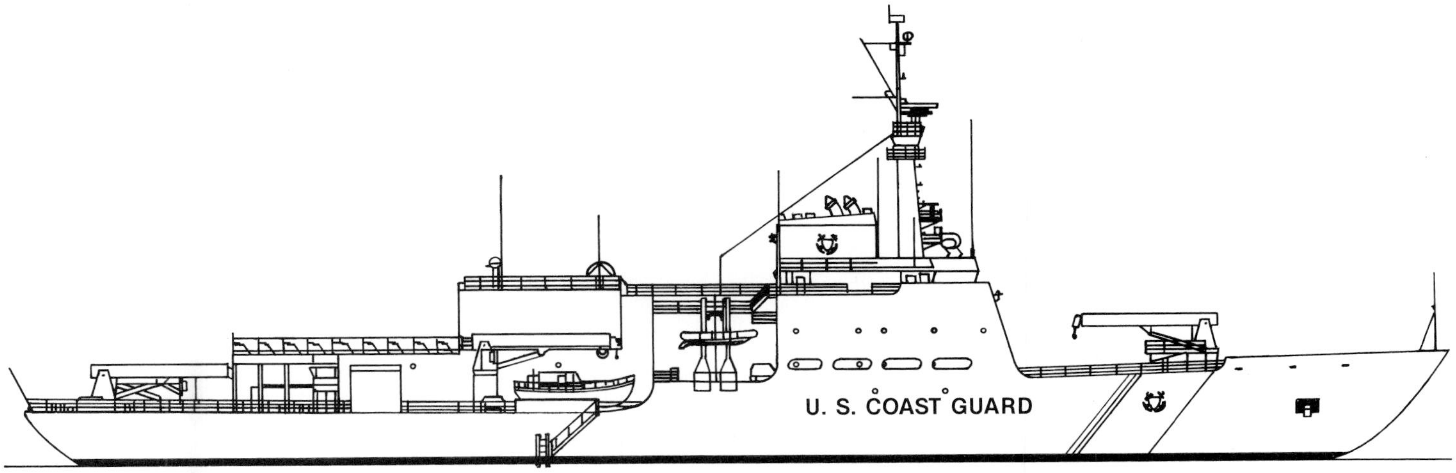

Line drawing of the icebreaker HEALY. After a prolonged gestation period, the Navy canceled the ship in March 1992 because of higher-than-expected cost estimates from U.S. shipyards. Nevertheless, a contract was awarded on 15 July 1993. (William Clipson)

2 ICEBREAKERS: POLAR CLASS (399)

Number	Name	Launched	Commissioned	Status
WAGB 10	Polar Star	17 Nov 1973	19 Jan 1976	**PA**
WAGB 11	Polar Sea	24 June 1975	23 Feb 1978	**PA**

Builders:	Lockheed Shipbuilding, Seattle, Wash.
Displacement:	10,430 tons standard 13,190 tons full load
Length:	399 feet (126 m) overall
Beam:	83½ feet (25.5 m)
Draft:	33½ feet (10.2 m)
Propulsion:	CODOG: 6 diesel engines (Alco); 18,000 bhp + 3 gas turbines (Pratt & Whitney); 60,000 shp; 3 shafts
Speed:	18 knots
Range:	16,000 n.miles (2,963 km) at 18 knots 28,000 n.miles (51,855 km) at 14.5 knots
Manning:	138 (13 officers + 125 enlisted)
Helicopters:	2 HH-65A Dolphin
Guns:	2 40-mm grenade launchers Mk 19 (2 single)
Radars:	2 SPS-64 navigation

These are the largest icebreakers now in service outside of Russia. Additional ships were originally planned in this class as replacements for the Wind-class icebreakers. No more ships of this class were built, in part because of the higher-than-anticipated construction costs.

Design: These ships have conventional icebreaker hull forms. A hangar and flight deck are fitted aft, and two 15-ton-capacity cranes are abaft the hangar. Arctic and oceanographic laboratories are provided.

Both icebreakers underwent an upgrading of their scientific capabilities in 1987–1992. Improvements were made to their laboratory spaces, oceanographic instrumentation, and communications equipment, and new oceanographic and trawling winches were fitted.

Engineering: CODOG (Combination Diesel or Gas turbine) propulsion is provided, with diesel engines for cruising and rapid-reaction gas turbines available for surge-power requirements. The controllable-pitch propellers allow propeller thrust to be reversed by reversing the direction of shaft rotation. Both ships have experienced problems with their controllable-pitch propellers and control systems.

The original design provided for a speed of 21 knots; it has not been achieved in service.

Operational: Both icebreakers are based at Seattle, Washington.

The Polar Sea circumnavigated the North American continent in 1985. The icebreaker departed Seattle on 6 June, sailed through the Panama Canal, up the East Coast to Greenland, and through the Northwest Passage to pass into the Bering Sea and the Pacific, returning to Seattle on 2 October. The ship required just under seven days, including a brief stop at the village of Resolute, to transit the 850-n.mile (1,575-km) Northwest Passage.

The Polar Sea and the Canadian Coast Guard icebreaker Louis St. Laurent reached the North Pole in August 1994 as part of a joint U.S.–Canadian scientific research mission. This was the first U.S. surface ship to ever reach the North Pole.[11] (The Coast Guard icebreaker Westwind/WAGB 281 came within 375 n.miles/690 km of the North Pole in 1979.)

11. The Soviet nuclear-propelled icebreaker Arktika was the first surface ship in history to reach the geographic North Pole, doing so on 17 August 1977. The Arktika spent 15 hours at the North Pole. Her sister ship Sibir' reached the North Pole in May 1987; sister ship Yamal in August 1994.

The Polar Sea is one of the two largest icebreakers ever to fly the U.S. flag. The Polar design has a large, enclosed crow's nest, uneven funnels, and a large helicopter deck aft. Two helicopters are normally embarked in these cutters for ice operations; they often lead the ship through ice fields. (1993, Leo Van Ginderen collection)

The POLAR STAR. These ships have red hulls and orange funnels to facilitate locating them in ice. Both ships have suffered numerous mechanical problems. (1991, Leo Van Ginderen collection)

ICEBREAKER: "GLACIER" (310)

The one-of-a-kind icebreaker GLACIER (WAGB 4, ex-AGB 4) was decommissioned on 17 June 1987 and, when this edition went to press, was laid up at the Mare Island Naval Shipyard awaiting disposal.

The GLACIER was the only icebreaker built for U.S. naval service after World War II, being commissioned as the AGB 4 on 27 May 1955. She was transferred to the Coast Guard on 30 June 1966 (and stricken from the Navy Register on 1 July 1966, the day after her transfer to the Coast Guard). The ship may become a memorial.

See 14th Edition/page 547 for characteristics.

1 ICEBREAKER: "MACKINAW" (290)

Number	Name	Launched	Commissioned	Status
WAGB 83	MACKINAW	4 Mar 1944	20 Dec 1944	GL

Builders:	Toledo Shipbuilding, Ohio
Displacement:	5,320 tons full load
Length:	290 feet (88.4 m) overall
Beam:	75 feet (22.9 m)
Draft:	19 feet (5.8 m)
Propulsion:	diesel-electric (Fairbanks Morse diesel engines, Westinghouse electric motors); 10,000 shp aft + 3,000 shp forward; 2 shafts aft + 1 shaft forward
Speed:	18.7 knots
Range:	10,000 n.miles (18,520 km) at 18.7 knots 41,000 n.miles (75,930 km) at 9 knots
Manning:	75 (8 officers + 67 enlisted)
Helicopters:	landing area
Guns:	none

The MACKINAW was designed and constructed specifically for Coast Guard use on the Great Lakes. The ship is homeported in Cheboygan, Michigan. She will be decommissioned in 1996.

Classification: The ship originally was classified WAG 83; she was changed to WAGB on 1 May 1966.

Design: The MACKINAW has many features of the Wind class; being designed for the Great Lakes, however, the ship is longer and wider than the oceangoing ships and has significantly less draft. Two 12-ton-capacity cranes are fitted. The ship has a clear deck aft for a helicopter, but no hangar is provided.

Name: Originally named MANITOWOC.

The MACKINAW and a Bay-class icebreaking tug in Great Lakes ice. The MACKINAW was designed specifically for Great Lakes operation; no armament was planned because of the U.S.–Canadian agreement on demilitarization of their common border. (U.S. Coast Guard)

ICEBREAKERS: WIND CLASS (269)

The Wind-class icebreakers WESTWIND (WAGB 281, ex-Navy AGB 6) and NORTHWIND (WAGB 282) were stricken in 1989. These were the last of seven sister ships, two built for the Navy and the remaining five to Coast Guard specifications; three of the latter ships served with the Soviet Navy after World War II. A table showing their service assignments and designations is found in the previous edition of *Ships and Aircraft.*

These were effective icebreakers. They were also built with a relatively heavy gun armament and could carry a floatplane (the ships were later provided with a helicopter capability).

See 14th Edition/pages 547–49 for characteristics.

The Wind-class ships were the principal U.S. icebreakers for more than three decades. Originally seven ships were in this class: two were built for the Navy, and the remaining five were built to Coast Guard specifications. Three of the latter ships served with the Soviet Navy after World War II. This is the NORTHWIND in her final configuration, shortly before being stricken. Note the massive, extended helicopter hangar. (1988, Leo Van Ginderen collection)

TRAINING CUTTERS

1 TRAINING BARK: "EAGLE"

Number	Name	Launched	USCG Comm.	Status
WIX 327	EAGLE	13 June 1936	15 May 1946	**TRA-A**

Builders:	Blohm and Voss, Hamburg (Germany)
Displacement:	1,784 tons full load
Length:	231 feet (67.8 m) waterline 295 feet (89.9 m) over bowsprit
Beam:	39½ feet (11.9 m)
Draft:	17 feet (5.2 m)
Masts:	fore and main 150½ feet (45.7 m) mizzen 132 feet (40.2 m)
Propulsion:	1 auxiliary diesel engine (Caterpillar D-399 V-16); 1,000 bhp; 1 shaft
Speed:	up to 18 knots under sail; 10 knots on auxiliary diesel engine
Range:	5,450 n.miles (10,100 km) on diesel
Manning:	50 (12 officers + 38 enlisted) + 150 cadets
Guns:	none

The EAGLE is the former German naval training bark HORST WESSEL. Taken by the United States as reparation after World War II, she was acquired in January 1946 at Bremerhaven and assigned to the Coast Guard. Based at the Coast Guard Academy in New London, Connecticut, she is employed to train Coast Guard cadets on summer practice cruises.

This is the oldest ship in U.S. government service except for the relic CONSTITUTION.

Class: Three other ships were built to this design. The ALBERT LEO SCHLAGETER (launched 1937) was also taken over by the United States in 1945 but was sold to Brazil in 1948 and resold to Portugal in 1962 (now in service as the SAGRES).

The GORCH FOCK (1933) was taken over by the Soviet Union in 1946 and renamed the TOVARISCH; she remains in Russian service.[12]

The generally similar MIRECA (1938) was built for Romania and also remains in service.

A later ship of the same general design, also named the GORCH FOCK, was built at the same German yard for the West German Navy (launched in 1958).

Design: The EAGLE is steel hulled. She carries up to 21,350 square feet (1,921.5 m²) of sail.

12. The TOVARISCH is employed as a sail training ship for the Russian merchant marine; see *Guide to the Soviet Navy,* 5th Edition (Annapolis, Md.: Naval Institute Press, 1991), pp. 332–33.

The training bark EAGLE. (1994, Giorgio Arra)

The training bark EAGLE. Her fore- and mainmasts are square-rigged; the mizzenmast has a fore-and-aft rig. Note the small radome near the base of the mizzenmast. (1994, Giorgio Arra)

BUOY TENDERS

Many of the buoy tenders listed as Atlantic or Pacific are based on rivers. All coastal and inland buoy tenders listed below are in active service. The entries are arranged by type and by length, i.e., Coast Guard class designation.

No coastal or inland buoy tenders are armed.

1 + 15(?) SEAGOING BUOY TENDERS: "JUNIPER" CLASS (225)

Number	Name	FY	Launched	Commissioned	Status
WLB 201	JUNIPER	93	24 June 1995	12 Jan 1996	**AA**
WLB 202	WILLOW	94	15 June 1996	1997	Building
WLB 203	KUKUI	95		1997	Building
WLB 204	ELM	96		1998	Building
WLB 205	WALNUT			1999	Planned
WLB 206	DOGWOOD			1999	Planned
WLB 207	HICKORY			1999	Planned
WLB 208	FIR			2000	Planned
WLB 209	SYCAMORE			2000	Planned
WLB 210	ASPEN			2000	Planned
WLB 211	CYPRESS			2000	Planned
WLB 212	OAK			2001	Planned
WLB 213	MAPLE			2001	Planned
WLB 214	ALDER			2001	Planned
WLB 215	HOLLYHOCK			2001	Planned
WLB 216	SEQUOIA			2002	Planned

Builders:	Marinette Marine, Wisc.
Displacement:	2,000 tons full load
Length:	225 feet (68.58 m) overall
Beam:	46 feet (14.0 m)
Draft:	13 feet (4.0 m)
Propulsion:	2 diesel engines (Caterpillar 3608); 6,200 bhp; 1 shaft
Speed:	15 knots
Range:	6,000 n.miles (11,110 km) at 12 knots
Manning:	40 (6 officers + 34 enlisted)
Guns:	see notes
Radars:	1 SPS-64(V)1 navigation

These are the first seagoing buoy tenders built for the U.S. Coast Guard since the BALSAM class of World War II. In 1991 the Coast Guard awarded contracts to build the new tenders to several shipyards. In August 1992 the Marinette yard was chosen to build the lead tender; construction began in November 1993.

The JUNIPER plows through light ice on Green Bay in Wisconsin during trials. The JUNIPER and her sister buoy tenders will replace BALSAM-class tenders more than 50 years old. (1996, U.S. Coast Guard, CWO2 Craig Heilman)

Class: The final number of tenders to be built to this design has not been determined. About 16 units are currently planned.

Design: A 440-shp bow thruster and 550-shp stern thruster are fitted. These tenders have a 30,000-pound (13,605-kg) lift capacity, a large deck area for handling buoys, and the ability to work buoys in eight-foot (2.4-m) seas.

These tenders have a built-in oil-spill recovery system.

Endurance is 45 days.

Guns: There are provisions for installing a single 25-mm Bushmaster cannon Mk 38.

The JUNIPER at high speed on Green Bay, Wisconsin. Buoy tenders are distinguished by a heavy-lift crane or derrick and open working space forward for handling buoys and other navigation aids. Two smaller derricks are fitted aft for handling the tender's two small boats and other gear. (1996, U.S. Coast Guard, CWO2 Craig Heilman)

1 MEDIUM ENDURANCE CUTTER
26 SEAGOING BUOY TENDERS } **"BALSAM" CLASS (180)**

Number	Name	Builder	Launched	Commissioned	Status
A series (10)					
WLB 277	COWSLIP	MI	11 Apr 1942	17 Oct 1942	**AA**
WLB 290	GENTIAN	ZD	23 May 1942	3 Nov 1942	**AA**
WLB 291	LAUREL	ZD	4 Aug 1942	24 Nov 1942	**AA**
WLB 296	SORREL	ZD	28 Sep 1942	15 Apr 1943	**AA**
WMEC 300	CITRUS	MI	15 Aug 1942	30 May 1943	**PA**
WLB 301	CONIFER	MI	3 Nov 1942	1 July 1943	**PA**
WLB 302	MADRONA	ZD	11 Nov 1942	30 May 1943	**AA**
WLB 306	BUTTONWOOD	MI	30 Nov 1942	24 Sep 1943	**AA**
WLB 308	PAPAW	MI	19 Feb 1943	12 Oct 1943	**AA**
WLB 309	SWEETGUM	MI	15 Apr 1943	20 Nov 1943	**AA**
B series (2)					
WLB 297	IRONWOOD	CG	16 Mar 1943	4 Aug 1943	**PA**
WLB 307	PLANETREE	MI	20 Mar 1943	4 Nov 1943	**PA**
C series (15)					
WLB 388	BASSWOOD	MI	20 May 1943	12 Jan 1944	**PA**
WLB 389	BITTERSWEET	ZD	11 Nov 1943	11 May 1944	**AA**
WLB 392	BRAMBLE	ZD	23 Oct 1943	22 Apr 1944	**GL**
WLB 393	FIREBUSH	ZD	3 Feb 1944	20 July 1944	**PA**
WLB 394	HORNBEAM	MI	14 Aug 1943	14 Apr 1944	**AA**
WLB 395	IRIS	ZD	18 May 1944	11 Aug 1944	**PA**
WLB 396	MALLOW	ZD	9 Dec 1943	6 June 1944	**PA**
WLB 397	MARIPOSA	ZD	14 Jan 1944	1 July 1944	**PA**
WLB 401	SASSAFRAS	MI	5 Oct 1943	23 May 1944	**PA**
WLB 402	SEDGE	MI	27 Nov 1943	5 July 1944	**PA**
WLB 403	SPAR	MI	2 Nov 1943	12 June 1944	**AA**
WLB 404	SUNDEW	MI	8 Feb 1944	24 Aug 1944	**GL**
WLB 405	SWEETBRIER	MI	30 Dec 1943	26 July 1944	**PA**
WLB 406	ACACIA	ZD	7 Apr 1944	1 Sep 1944	**GL**
WLB 407	WOODRUSH	ZD	28 Apr 1944	22 Sep 1944	**PA**

Builders: CG = Coast Guard Yard, Curtis Bay, Md.
MI = Marine Iron and Shipbuilding Co., Duluth, Minn.
ZD = Zenith Dredge, Duluth, Minn.
Displacement: 697 tons light
1,038 tons full load
Length: 180 feet (54.9 m) overall
Beam: 37 feet (11.3 m)
Draft: 13 feet (4.0 m)
Propulsion: diesel-electric (2 General Motors 8-645E6A diesel engines); 1,200 shp; 1 shaft; see *Modernization* notes
Speed: 13 knots
Range: 4,500 n.miles (8,335 km) at 13 knots
13,500 n.miles (25,000 km) at 7.5 knots
Manning: 52 (7 officers + 45 enlisted)
Guns: 2 .50-cal machine guns M2 (2 single)

The PAPAW at Fort Lauderdale, Florida. The space booster recovery craft RSB-1 is in the background. These tenders have working space forward for handling buoys and other aids to navigation. (1992, Giorgio Arra)

The SORREL showing the arrangement for her 20-ton-capacity boom, used to lift buoys onto her forward deck. The boom structure is removed in the medium endurance cutter CITRUS and the research cutter EVERGREEN. (1991, Giorgio Arra)

These are tenders that service navigation buoys and other aids to navigation in coastal waters. They have proven to be highly versatile ships, having served as convoy escorts, in the SAR role, and as salvage ships, as well as having assisted in constructing and servicing LORAN navigation stations. Some have a light icebreaking capability.

Nine A-series tenders (WLB) have been modernized under a Service Life Extension Program (SLEP); see below.

Class: Thirty-nine ships of this design were completed in 1942–1944.

The COWSLIP (WLB 277) was stricken on 23 March 1973 (she was sold). She was repurchased by the Coast Guard in January 1981 and recommissioned in November 1981. She replaced the BLACKTHORN (WLB 391), which was rammed and sunk on 28 January 1980.

CLOVER (WLB/WMEC 292), decommissioned in June 1990.

EVERGREEN (WLB/WAGO/WMEC 295), decommissioned on 13 June 1990.

MESQUITE (WLB 305) ran aground in Lake Superior on 5 December 1989 and was a total loss.

BLACKHAW (WLB 390), stricken on 26 February 1993.

SAGEBRUSH (WLB 399), stricken on 26 April 1988.

SALVIA (WLB 400), stricken on 12 April 1991.

Classification: Several ships were temporarily reclassified as medium endurance cutters (WMEC) and engaged in patrol work during the 1970s and 1980s. The EVERGREEN was refitted as an oceanographic cutter in 1973 and reclassified WAGO; she was changed to WMEC on 1 May 1982. The only BALSAM-class cutter rated as a WMEC at this time is the CITRUS, which was changed to WMEC in June 1979.

Design: The WLB 296, 300, 390, 392, and 402–404 have strengthened hulls for icebreaking. They are fitted with a 20-ton-capacity boom. (In SLEP ships, a hydraulically powered system replaces the electrically powered boom.) These ships are highly effective for breaking through light ice.

Engineering: The WLB 277, 389, 394, and 395 are fitted with controllable-pitch, bow-thrust propellers.

Guns: As completed, these tenders had one 3-inch/50-cal AA gun and four 20-mm AA guns (two in A-series ships); the 3-inch gun was fitted in a raised "tub" aft of the funnel. They additionally carried depth charges, and some ships had ahead-throwing Mousetrap ASW projectors.

Modernization: Nine tenders of the A series have been upgraded under a SLEP effort. They have been fitted with new main engines, electronics, and other systems, plus improved habitability. These tenders have General Electric EMD 8-645E6A diesel engines. Endurance is increased to 5,500 n.miles (10,200 km) at 10 knots.

The modernizations, accomplished at the Coast Guard Yard, were:

Cutter	*Start*	*Complete*
COWSLIP	Jan 1983	July 1984
GENTIAN	Nov 1979	Aug 1983
LAUREL	July 1986	Feb 1990
SORREL	Oct 1979	Jan 1983
CONIFER	Aug 1983	Jan 1986
MADRONA	Apr 1984	Sep 1989
BUTTONWOOD	Mar 1991	Jan 1993
PAPAW	Sep 1989	Nov 1990
SWEETGUM	Feb 1990	Dec 1991

The SORREL was the first ship to be modernized, with her 16-month SLEP being completed in January 1983. Five other SLEP upgrades were canceled.

Names: The ACACIA originally was named THISTLE; her name was changed in 1944 because that former name was also carried at the time by an Army hospital ship.

The CITRUS was one of several oceangoing buoy tenders employed as medium endurance cutters. With the removal of the bridge boom, the superstructure has an unusual appearance. (The EVERGREEN was also painted white when employed as an oceanographic ship.) (1986, Giorgio Arra)

1 + 13 COASTAL BUOY TENDERS: "IDA LEWIS" CLASS (175)

Number	Name	Launched	Commissioned	Status
WLM 551	IDA LEWIS	13 Oct 1995	9 Dec 1995	**Active**
WLM 552	HANNA	1996	1997	Building
WLM 553	KATHERINE WALKER	17 Aug 1996	1997	Building
WLM 554	ANTHONY PETTIT	1997	1997	Building
WLM	10 units			Planned

Builders:	Marinette Marine, Wisc.
Displacement:	916 tons full load
Length:	155 feet (47.24 m) waterline 175 feet (53.34 m) overall
Beam:	36 feet (11.0 m)
Draft:	8 feet (2.4 m)
Propulsion:	2 diesel engines (Caterpillar 3508 TA); 1,920 bhp; 2 azimuth propellers (Z-drive)
Speed:	12 knots
Range:	2,000 n.miles (3,700 km) at 10 knots
Manning:	18 (1 warrant officer + 17 enlisted)

This is a new class of coastal buoy tenders being built to replace the outdated craft of the Red and White classes. Fourteen of these tenders are planned.

The IDA LEWIS was ordered on 22 June 1993.

Design: These are a smaller version of the JUNIPER class. They are capable of fresh-water icebreaking. A 500-shp through-bow thruster is fitted. The hydraulic crane forward provides a 10-ton lift capacity.

Names: Idawalley Zorada Lewis was a lighthouse keeper in the Lighthouse Service. In 1858, at age 16, she had performed a single-handed rescue of four young boys.

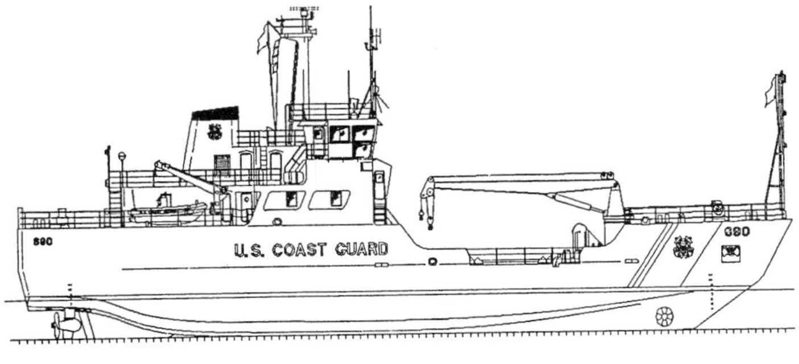

The IDA LEWIS. (Marinette Marine)

5 COASTAL BUOY TENDERS: RED CLASS (157)

Number	Name	Launched	Commissioned	Status
WLM 685	Red Wood	4 Apr 1964	6 Aug 1964	**AA**
WLM 686	Red Beech	6 June 1964	20 Nov 1964	**AA**
WLM 687	Red Birch	19 Feb 1965	7 June 1965	**AA**
WLM 688	Red Cedar	1 Aug 1970	18 Dec 1970	**AA**
WLM 689	Red Oak	19 June 1971	10 Dec 1971	**AA**

Builders: Coast Guard Yard, Curtis Bay, Md.
Displacement: 371 tons light
525 tons full load
Length: 157 feet (47.8 m) overall
Beam: 33 feet (10.1 m)
Draft: 6 feet (1.8 m)
Propulsion: 2 diesel engines (Caterpillar); 1,800 bhp; 2 shafts
Speed: 12.8 knots
Range: 2,250 n.miles (4,170 km) at 12.8 knots
3,055 n.miles (5,660 km) at 11.6 knots
Manning: 31 (4 officers + 27 enlisted)

These buoy and navigation aid tenders have strengthened steel hulls for light icebreaking and are fitted with bow thrusters. Each is fitted with a 10-ton-capacity derrick.

The Red Beech in New York harbor. Like most buoy tenders, the Red-class ships have a light icebreaking capability. (1990, Giorgio Arra)

6 COASTAL BUOY TENDERS: WHITE CLASS (133)

Number	Name	Launched	Commissioned	Status
WLM 540 (ex-YF 416)	White Sumac	14 June 1943	6 Nov 1943	**AA**
WLM 543 (ex-YF 341)	White Holly	8 Apr 1944	6 June 1944	**AA**
WLM 544 (ex-YF 444)	White Sage	9 June 1943	29 May 1944	**AA**
WLM 545 (ex-YF 445)	White Heath	21 July 1943	9 Aug 1944	**AA**
WLM 546 (ex-YF 446)	White Lupine	28 July 1943	31 May 1944	**AA**
WLM 547 (ex-YF 448)	White Pine	28 Aug 1943	11 July 1944	**AA**

Builders: Erie Concrete and Steel Supply, Penna., except White Sumac by Niagara Shipbuilding, Buffalo, N.Y.; White Holly by Basalt Rock, Napa, Calif.
Displacement: 435 tons standard
600 tons full load
Length: 133 feet (40.5 m) overall
Beam: 31 feet (9.4 m)
Draft: 9 feet (2.7 m)
Propulsion: 2 diesel engines (Union); 600 bhp; 2 shafts
Speed: 9.8 knots
Range: 2,100 n.miles (3,890 km) at 9.8 knots
4,500 n.miles (8,340 km) at 5.1 knots
Manning: 23 (1 officer + 22 enlisted)

These buoy and navigation aid tenders are converted Navy self-propelled lighters (YF). They were transferred to the Coast Guard in August–September 1947.

Class: White Bush (WLM 542) was stricken on 16 September 1985.

The White Sumac shows the typical buoy tender configuration working space forward, with a heavy lift boom. There is a RIB aft of the deckhouse and a life-raft canister aft. (1992, Giorgio Arra)

COASTAL BUOY TENDERS: "HOLLYHOCK" CLASS (175)

The last of three tenders of this class, the Fir (WLM 212) was decommissioned on 1 October 1991. Her sister ships Hollyhock (WLM 220) and Walnut (WLM 252) were decommissioned on 31 March 1982 and 15 June 1982, respectively.

See 14th Edition/page 551 for characteristics.

4 INLAND CONSTRUCTION TENDERS: "PAMLICO" CLASS (160)

Number	Name	Number	Name
WLIC 800	Pamlico	WLIC 802	Kennebec
WLIC 801	Hudson	WLIC 803	Saginaw

Builders: Coast Guard Yard, Curtis Bay, Md.
Displacement: 416 tons
Length: 160 feet (48.8 m) overall
Beam: 30 feet (9.1 m)
Draft: 4 feet (1.2 m)
Propulsion: 2 diesel engines (Cummins); 1,000 bhp; 2 shafts
Speed: 10 knots
Manning: 14 (1 officer + 13 enlisted)

These large inland construction tenders were completed in 1976–1977.

The Hudson under way on the Inland Waterway. She has a large crane forward, a pilothouse with all-around vision, and twin funnels. (1992, Giorgio Arra)

1 INLAND BUOY TENDER: "BUCKTHORN" (100)

Number	Name	Launched	Commissioned
WLI 642	Buckthorn		17 July 1964

Builders:	Mobile Ship Repair, Ala.
Displacement:	200 tons full load
Length:	100 feet (30.5 m) overall
Beam:	24 feet (7.3 m)
Draft:	4 feet (1.2 m)
Propulsion:	2 diesel engines (Caterpillar); 600 bhp; 2 shafts
Speed:	11.9 knots
Manning:	15 (1 officer + 14 enlisted)

The Buckthorn is a single-ship design that operates on the Great Lakes. She is fitted with a five-ton-capacity boom.

Names: Inland tenders were named in 1963.

The one-of-a-kind Buckthorn. (1989, Leo Van Ginderen collection)

1 INLAND BUOY TENDER / 3 INLAND CONSTRUCTION TENDERS } "COSMOS" CLASS (100)

Number	Name	Launched	Commissioned
WLIC 298	Rambler	6 May 1943	26 May 1943
WLI 313	Bluebell	28 Sep 1944	24 Mar 1945
WLIC 315	Smilax	18 Aug 1944	1 Nov 1944
WLIC 316	Primrose	18 Aug 1944	23 Oct 1944

Builders:	Dubuque Boat & Boiler, Iowa, except Bluebell by Birchfield Boiler, Tacoma, Wash.
Displacement:	178 tons full load
Length:	100 feet (30.5 m) overall
Beam:	24 feet (7.3 m)
Draft:	5 feet (1.5 m)
Propulsion:	2 diesel engines; 600 bhp; 2 shafts
Speed:	10.5 knots
Range:	1,400 n.miles (2,600 km) at 10.5 knots 2,700 n.miles (5,000 km) a 7 knots
Manning:	14 (1 officer + 13 enlisted)

All were formerly designated WLI; three of these tenders were changed to inland construction tenders (WLIC) on 1 October 1979. All are fitted with a five-ton-capacity crane. The Primrose is fitted with a pile driver on her bow.

Class: This was originally a class of eight tenders. The Cosmos (WLI 293) was decommissioned on 16 August 1985.

9 INLAND CONSTRUCTION TENDERS: "ANVIL" CLASS (75)

Number	Name	Number	Name
A series (2)		*C series* (4)	
WLIC 75301	Anvil	WLIC 75306	Clamp
WLIC 75302	Hammer	WLIC 75307	Wedge
B series (3)		WLIC 75309	Hatchet
WLIC 75303	Sledge	WLIC 75310	Axe
WLIC 75304	Mallet		
WLIC 75305	Vise		

Builders:	WLIC 75301, 75302	Gibbs Shipyard, Jacksonville, Fla.
	WLIC 75303–75305	McDermott, Morgan City, Mich.
	WLIC 75306, 75307	Sturgeon Bay Shipbuilding, Wisc.
	WLIC 75309, 75310	Dorchester Shipbuilding, N.J.
Displacement:	145 tons	
Length:	75 feet (22.9 m) overall, except C series 76 feet (23.2 m) overall	
Beam:	22 feet (6.7 m)	
Draft:	4 feet (1.2 m)	
Propulsion:	2 diesel engines; 600 bhp; 2 shafts	
Speed:	A series 8.6 knots B series 9.1 knots C series 9.4 knots	
Range:	A series 1,300 n.miles (2,400 km) at 9 knots 2,400 n.miles (4,450 km) at 5 knots B series 1,000 n.miles (1,850 km) at 9 knots 2,200 n.miles (4,075 km) at 5 knots C series 1,050 n.miles (1,950 km) at 9 knots 2,500 n.miles (4,630 km) at 5 knots	
Manning:	13 (enlisted)	

The Hatchet pushing a work barge. (U.S. Coast Guard)

The Bluebell. (1993, George R. Schneider)

2 INLAND BUOY TENDERS: IMPROVED BERRY CLASS (65)

Number	Name	Launched	Commissioned
WLI 65400	Bayberry	2 June 1954	28 June 1954
WLI 65401	Elderberry	2 June 1954	28 June 1954

Builders:	Reliable Welding Works, Olympia, Wash.
Displacement:	68 tons light
	71 tons full load
Length:	65 feet (19.8 m) overall
Beam:	17 feet (5.2 m)
Draft:	4 feet (1.2 m)
Propulsion:	2 diesel engines (General Motors 6-71); 400 bhp; 2 shafts
Speed:	11.3 knots
Range:	800 n.miles (1,480 km) at 11.3 knots
	1,700 n.miles (3,150 km) at 6 knots
Manning:	8 (enlisted)

Similar to the basic Berry-class design, these tenders have a more powerful propulsion plant. Originally designed for fresh-water operation, these craft have been modified for saltwater operation.

The Elderberry. (U.S. Coast Guard)

2 INLAND BUOY TENDERS: BERRY CLASS (65)

Number	Name	Launched	Commissioned
WLI 65303	Blackberry		24 Aug 1946
WLI 65304	Chokeberry	23 May 1946	30 Aug 1946

Builders:	Dubuque Boat & Boiler, Iowa
Displacement:	68 tons full load
Length:	65 feet (19.8 m) overall
Beam:	17 feet (5.2 m)
Draft:	4 feet (1.2 m)
Propulsion:	1 diesel engine (General Motors); 220 bhp; 1 shaft
Speed:	9 knots
Range:	1,500 n.miles (2,780 km) at 5 knots
Manning:	8 (enlisted)

The third tender of this craft, the Loganberry (WLI 65305), was decommissioned in 1977.

The Chokeberry. (U.S. Coast Guard)

RIVER BUOY TENDER: "LANTANA" (80)

The Lantana (WLR 80310), the single tender of this design (completed in 1943), was decommissioned on 27 October 1991.

See 14th Edition/page 555 for characteristics.

1 RIVER BUOY TENDER: "SUMAC" (115)

Number	Name	Launched	Commissioned
WLR 311	Sumac	14 Oct 1944	11 Nov 1944

Builders:	Peterson and Haecker, Blair, Neb.
Displacement:	478 tons full load
Length:	115 feet (35.0 m) overall
Beam:	30 feet (9.1 m)
Draft:	6 feet (1.8 m)
Propulsion:	3 diesel engines (General Motors); 2,250 bhp; 3 shafts
Speed:	10.6 knots
Range:	11,600 n.miles (21,500 km) at 5 knots
Manning:	22 (enlisted)

A single tender of this type was built. The largest tender rated as a river craft (WLR), the Sumac is based at St. Louis, Missouri.

The Sumac is the only tender of this design; the Coast Guard also has a buoy tender named White Sumac. (U.S. Coast Guard)

RIVER BUOY TENDERS: "DOGWOOD" CLASS (114)

The three tenders of this class, completed 1941–1943, have been discarded: Forsythia (WLR 263) was decommissioned on 12 August 1977; Dogwood (WLR 259) was decommissioned on 11 August 1989; and Sycamore (WLIC 268) was decommissioned 30 June 1977.

See 14th Edition/page 555 for characteristics.

2 + 3 RIVER BUOY TENDERS: "KANKAKEE" CLASS (75)

Number	Name	Launched	Commissioned
WLR 75500	Kankakee	8 July 1989	Jan 1990
WLR 75501	Greenbrier		12 Apr 1990
WLR	3 units		Planned

Builders:	Avondale Industries (Small Boat Division), New Orleans, La.
Displacement:	172 tons full load
Length:	75 feet (22.9 m) overall
Beam:	24 feet (7.3 m)
Draft:	5 feet (1.5 m)
Propulsion:	2 diesel engines (Caterpillar 3412-DIT); 1,080 bhp; 2 shafts
Speed:	12 knots
Range:	600 n.miles (1,110 km) at 11 knots
Manning:	19 (enlisted)

Improved Gasconade-class river tenders, these craft push 130-foot (39.6-m) work barges. They are fitted with six rudders to provide a high degree of maneuverability.

Three additional units of this design are planned.

The Greenbrier, resembling a houseboat. There are twin engine exhausts on the upper deck, abaft the bridge. The mast is offset to port. (1990, Avondale Shipyards)

INLAND BUOY TENDER: "TERN" (80)

The single tender of this design, the Tern (WLI 8080), was decommissioned in July 1977. Completed in 1969, the Tern has a unique stern-crane configuration for buoy handling; after evaluation and service use, the concept was discarded.

See 14th Edition/page 586 for characteristics.

9 RIVER BUOY TENDERS: "GASCONADE" CLASS (75)

Number	Name	Number	Name
WLR 75401	Gasconade	WLR 75406	Kickapoo
WLR 75402	Muskingum	WLR 75407	Kanawha
WLR 75403	Wyaconda	WLR 75408	Patoka
WLR 75404	Chippewa	WLR 75409	Chena
WLR 75405	Cheyenne		

Builders:	WLR 75401 St. Louis Shipbuilding & Dry Dock, Mo. WLR 75402–75405 Maxon Construction, Tell City, Ind. WLR 75406–75409 Halter Marine, New Orleans, La.
Displacement:	141 tons full load
Length:	75 feet (22.9 m) overall
Beam:	22 feet (6.7 m)
Draft:	4 feet (1.2 m)
Propulsion:	2 diesel engines (Caterpillar); 600 bhp; 2 shafts
Speed:	7.6 or 8.7 knots
Range:	3,100 n.miles (7,740 km) at 6.5 knots
Manning:	19 (enlisted)

These tenders were completed from 1964 to 1970. They work in tandem with a 90-foot (27.4-m) barge.

The Cheyenne with a buoy barge. (U.S. Coast Guard)

6 RIVER BUOY TENDERS: "OUACHITA" CLASS (65)

Number	Name	Number	Name
WLR 65501	Ouachita	WLR 65504	Scioto
WLR 65502	Cimarron	WLR 65505	Osage
WLR 65503	Obion	WLR 65506	Sangamon

Builders:	Gibbs Corp., Jacksonville, Fla., except WLR 65501, 65502 by Platzer Shipyard, Houston, Texas
Displacement:	143 tons
Length:	65½ feet (20.0 m) overall
Beam:	21 feet (6.4 m)
Draft:	5 feet (1.5 m)
Propulsion:	2 diesel engines; 600 bhp; 2 shafts
Speed:	10.5 knots
Range:	3,500 n.miles (6,485 km) at 6 knots
Manning:	12 (enlisted)

These tenders were completed in 1960–1962. They were designed specifically to operate with work barges.

The Osage with a buoy barge. (U.S. Coast Guard)

TUGS

9 ICEBREAKING TUGS: BAY CLASS (140)

Number	Name	Launched	Commissioned	Status
WTGB 101	Katami Bay	8 Apr 1978	8 Jan 1979	**GL**
WTGB 102	Bristol Bay	22 July 1978	5 Apr 1979	**GL**
WTGB 103	Mobile Bay	11 Nov 1978	6 May 1979	**GL**
WTGB 104	Biscayne Bay	3 Feb 1979	8 Dec 1979	**GL**
WTGB 105	Neah Bay	2 Feb 1980	18 Aug 1980	**GL**
WTGB 106	Morro Bay	11 July 1980	25 Jan 1980	**AA**
WTGB 107	Penobscot Bay	27 July 1984	2 Jan 1985	**AA**
WTGB 108	Thunder Bay	15 Aug 1985	4 Nov 1985	**AA**
WTGB 109	Sturgeon Bay	12 Sep 1987	20 Aug 1988	**AA**
WTGB 110	Curtis Bay	canceled		

Builders: Tacoma Boatbuilding, Wash., except WTGB 107, 109 by Bay City Marine, Tacoma, Wash.
Displacement: 662 tons full load
Length: 140 feet (42.7 m) overall
Beam: 37 feet (11.3 m)
Draft: 12 feet (3.7 m)
Propulsion: diesel-electric (2 Fairbanks Morse 38D8 1/8 diesel engines); electric drive (Westinghouse); 2,500 shp; 1 shaft
Speed: 14.7 knots
Range: 1,800 n.miles (3,333 km) at 14.7 knots
4,000 n.miles (7,410 km) at 12 knots
Manning: 17 (3 officers + 14 enlisted)
Radars: SPS-64(V)1 navigation

These were the largest tugs to be constructed specifically for Coast Guard service. They are designed to provide general towing and support services and can break through ice up to 20 inches (0.5 m) thick.

The planned tenth unit was not built.

Classification: These tugs were originally designated WYTM. The Katami Bay was changed to WTGB on 5 February 1979; the others were changed to WTGB upon completion.

Design: These tugs are fitted with a hull air-lubrication system to enhance their icebreaking capability.

The Sturgeon Bay. (1991, Giorgio Arra)

MEDIUM HARBOR TUGS: "MANITOU" CLASS (110)

All of these 110-foot (33.5-m) tugs have been stricken, having been replaced by the WTGB type. They were designated WYTM. One series was completed from 1939 to 1943, and a second, four-ship series in 1986.

See 14th Edition/page 557 for names and characteristics.

14 SMALL HARBOR TUGS: 65-FT TYPE

Number	Name	Commissioned	Status
WYTL 65601	Capstan	19 July 1961	**AA**
WYTL 65602	Chock	12 Sep 1962	**AA**
WYTL 65603	Swivel	27 Oct 1961	**AA**
WYTL 65604	Tackle	1962	**AA**
WYTL 65605	Towline	27 Mar 1962	**AA**
WYTL 65606	Catenary	Apr 1962	**AA**
WYTL 65607	Bridle	3 Apr 1963	**AA**
WYTL 65608	Pendant	Aug 1963	**AA**
WYTL 65609	Shackle	7 May 1963	**AA**
WYTL 65610	Hawser	17 Jan 1963	**AA**
WYTL 65611	Line	21 Feb 1963	**AA**
WYTL 65612	Wire	19 Mar 1963	**AA**
WYTL 65614	Bollard	10 Apr 1967	**AA**
WYTL 65615	Cleat	10 May 1967	**AA**

Builders: WYTL 65601–65606 Gibbs Corp., Jacksonville, Fla.
WYTL 65607–65612 Barbour Boat Works, New Bern, N.C.
WYTL 65614, 65615 Western Boatbuilding, Tacoma, Wash.
Displacement: 62 tons light
72 tons full load
Length: 65 feet (19.8 m) overall
Beam: 19 feet (5.8 m)
Draft: 7 feet (2.1 m)
Propulsion: 1 diesel engine; 400 bhp; 1 shaft
Speed: 10.5 knots, except WYTL 65607–65609 9.8 knots
Range: 3,600 n.miles (6,670 km) at 6 knots, except WYTL 65607–65609 2,700 n.miles (5,000 km) at 5.8 knots
Manning: 8 (enlisted)

These are steel-hull tugs. Originally a class of 15 tugs, the Bitt (WYTL 65613) was decommissioned on 4 October 1982.

The Line, fitted with an SPS-66A or SPS-69 bar-type navigation radar on the mast and a commercial "pot" type navigation radar atop the bridge. Note the "short stack" fitted amidships, forward of the life-raft canister. (1994, Leo Van Ginderen collection)

1 SMALL HARBOR TUG: EX-ARMY TYPE

Number	Name	USA in service
WYTM 85009	Messenger (ex-ST 710)	5 Sep 1945

Builders: Equitable Equipment, New Orleans, La.
Displacement:
Length: 85 feet (26.2 m) overall
Beam: 23 feet (7.0 m)
Draft: 10 feet (3.05 m)
Propulsion: 1 diesel engine; 650 bhp; 1 shaft
Speed: 9 knots
Manning:

This former Army tug is assigned to the Coast Guard Yard.

Her sister ship Research (WYTM 85010) was stricken on 23 May 1973.

FERRIES

These ferries are used to transport personnel and vehicles between lower Manhattan and Governor's Island, New York. Located off the southern tip of Manhattan, the island has been the site of a major Coast Guard station since 1966 and serves as headquarters for the Commander, Atlantic Area. Previously, it was also headquarters for the 3rd Coast Guard District.

These ferries are civilian manned. They do not have Coast Guard hull numbers assigned and are not in commission.

1 FERRY: "GOVERNOR"

Number	Name	USCG in service
(none)	GOVERNOR	1985

Builders:	Moore Drydock, Oakland, Calif.
Displacement:	1,600 tons standard
Length:	$242\frac{2}{3}$ feet (74.0 m) overall
Beam:	$65\frac{1}{2}$ feet (20.0 m)
Draft:	14 feet (4.3 m)
Propulsion:	diesel-electric (2 diesel engines); 2 shafts
Speed:	
Manning:	

The ship was built in 1954 and was used by the Navy in San Diego as the CROWN CITY. She was subsequently sold to the State of Washington, renamed KULSHAN, and employed in the Puget Sound area. She was acquired by the Coast Guard in 1982 and rehabilitated by the Coast Guard yard at Curtis Bay from late 1982 until early 1985.

The GOVERNOR can carry 55 automobiles and 150 passengers.

The GOVERNOR transiting between lower Manhattan and Governor's Island; Brooklyn is in the background. The GOVERNOR did not have the Coast Guard shield on her blue-and-red stripes when this photo was taken; ferries do not have "Coast Guard" on their sides. (1991, Giorgio Arra)

2 FERRIES: EX-U.S. ARMY

Number	Name
(ex-FB 812)	LT SAMUEL S. COURSEN
(ex-FB 813)	PVT NICHOLAS MINUE

Builders:	John H. Mathis, Camden, N.J.
Displacement:	869 tons full load
Length:	172 feet (52.4 m) overall
Beam:	48 feet (14.6 m)
Draft:	14 feet (4.3 m)
Propulsion:	diesel-electric (2 diesel engines); 1,000 bhp; 2 shafts
Speed:	12 knots
Manning:	

Both are former U.S. Army ferries that were completed in 1956.

The LT SAMUEL S. COURSEN. (1990, Giorgio Arra)

1 FERRY: "THE TIDES"

Number	Name
(none)	THE TIDES

Builders:	
Displacement:	774 tons full load
Length:	185 feet (56.3 m) overall
Beam:	55 feet (16.8 m)
Draft:	9 feet (2.7 m)
Propulsion:	diesel-electric (2 diesel engines); 1,350 bhp; 2 shafts
Speed:	12 knots
Manning:	

THE TIDES is a former commercial ferry that was launched in 1946.

THE TIDES. (1991, Giorgio Arra)

SMALL CRAFT

The Coast Guard operates several hundred small craft in the patrol, search, rescue, oil cleanup, and navigation support roles. Only craft 21 feet (6.4 m) and larger are listed, although there are smaller boats in service.

The buoy tenders and aids-to-navigation craft—as well as the single-cable craft—have black hulls and white superstructures; the other craft are all white.

The Interceptor and Raider types are the only units normally armed and are listed first in this section.

5 FAST COASTAL INTERCEPTORS

Number	Number	Number
WFCI 43501	WFCI 43503	WFCI 43505
WFCI 43502	WFCI 43504	

Builders:	Tempest Marine, North Miami Beach, Fla.
Displacement:	7 tons standard
Length:	43½ feet (13.3 m) overall
Beam:	9½ feet (2.9 m)
Draft:	3⅙ feet (1.0 m)
Propulsion:	2 diesel engines (Caterpillar 3208 TA); 750 bhp; 2 shafts
Speed:	50+ knots
Range:	
Manning:	4 to 6
Guns:	small arms
Radars:	1 Raytheon 1900 navigation

These are small, high-speed boats built specifically for Coast Guard use in intercepting drug smugglers off the Florida coasts. Four units were placed in service in 1987 and the WFCI 43505 in 1988.

Twenty additional units were planned but not built.

Design: The design is based on the Riviera-class "cigarette boats," but these craft have diesel engines in lieu of the gasoline engines normally found in the Riviera class.

The craft have a 25° V-bottom monohull fabricated of fiberglass. These are extremely stable craft at high speeds and in heavy sea conditions. They are fitted with fixed-pitch, super-cavitating propellers.

Operations: All are based in Florida.

The fast coastal interceptor WFCI 43505. Note the commercial navigation radar "pot" mounted atop her "roll bar." (1990, Giorgio Arra)

A Coast Guard 22-foot raider craft makes a sharp turn during an exercise. (U.S. Coast Guard)

24 PATROL CRAFT: 22-FT RAIDER TYPE

Builders:	NAPCO International, Hopkins, Minn.
Displacement:	1.5 tons light 2 tons full load
Length:	22⅓ feet (6.8 m) overall
Beam:	7$\frac{5}{12}$ feet (2.25 m)
Draft:	
Propulsion:	2 outboard gasoline engines; 360 hp
Speed:	40 knots
Range:	165 n.miles (305 km) at 40 knots
Manning:	3+
Guns:	1 .50-cal machine gun M2 1 7.62-mm machine gun M60 small arms
Radars:	1 navigation

These are modified Boston Whalers built of Glass-reinforced Plastic (GRP). They were delivered to the Coast Guard between 1987 and 1989.

They are craft operated by reserve Port Security Units (PSU); several were airlifted to the Persian Gulf during Operation Desert Shield in 1990.

A Coast Guard–manned 22-foot raider craft passes the flagship La Salle (AGF 3) in the Persian Gulf. These high-speed craft have radar and a high degree of maneuverability, and they can carry several machine guns. (1991, U.S. Navy, CWO2 Ed Bailey)

20 AIDS-TO-NAVIGATION BOATS: 58-FT TYPE

Builders:	
Displacement:	28.8 tons full load
Length:	58 feet (17.68 m) overall
Beam:	17 feet (5.2 m)
Draft:	5 feet (1.5 m)
Propulsion:	2 diesel engines (General Motors 12V71 TI); 1,080 bhp; 2 shafts
Speed:	22 knots
Manning:	
Radars:	1 Raytheon 1900 navigation

These are aluminum-hull craft that support navigation aids on inland waterways.

A 58-foot aids-to-navigation boat passes the frigate Stark (FFG 31) as the "black hull" goes about putting down channel markers, which cram her deck. Note the hydraulic crane amidships. (1994, Giorgio Arra)

1 CABLE REPAIR CRAFT: CONVERTED NAVY LCM(6)

Builders:	
Displacement:	50 tons full load
Length:	56 feet (17.07 m) overall
Beam:	$14\frac{1}{3}$ feet (4.37 m)
Draft:	$3\frac{5}{6}$ feet (1.17 m)
Propulsion:	2 diesel engines (General Motors 6-71); 330 bhp; 2 shafts
Speed:	10 knots
Range:	130 n.miles (240 km) at 10 knots
Manning:	5 (enlisted)

Designated 560500, this is a former Navy landing craft that was converted in 1986 at the Coast Guard Yard for service at South Portland, Maine. A pilothouse has been added aft and the bow has been modified. The 560500 is painted black.

The cable repair craft 560500 is a converted landing craft that has a small deckhouse amidships and handling gear installed aft. (1994, Leo Van Ginderen collection)

25 AIDS-TO-NAVIGATION BOATS: 55-FT TYPE

Builders:	Robert E. Derecktor, Mamaroneck, N.Y.
Displacement:	28.8 tons light
	31.25 tons full load
Length:	58 feet (17.68 m) overall
Beam:	17 feet (5.18 m)
Draft:	5 feet (1.5 m)
Propulsion:	2 diesel engines (General Motors 12V71 TI); 1,080 bhp; 2 shafts
Speed:	22 knots
Range:	350 n.miles (650 km) at 18 knots
Manning:	4 (enlisted)

Numbered 55101 through 55125, these craft were placed in service in 1976–1977. They have a cargo capacity of 4,000 pounds (1,814 kg) and a 1,000-pound (453-kg) capacity crane fitted aft.

The aids-to-navigation craft 55103, one of the smaller "white hull" craft often seen on inland waterways and in harbors to maintain navigation markers. (U.S. Coast Guard)

4 MOTOR LIFEBOATS: 52-FT TYPE

Number	Name	Number	Name
52312	Victory	52314	Triumph II
52313	Invincible	52315	Intrepid

Builders:	Coast Guard Yard, Curtis Bay, Md.
Displacement:	31.7 tons light
	35 tons full load
Length:	52 feet (15.85 m) overall
Beam:	$14\frac{1}{2}$ feet (4.4 m)
Draft:	$6\frac{1}{4}$ feet (1.9 m)
Propulsion:	2 diesel engines (General Motors 6-71); 340 bhp; 2 shafts
Speed:	11 knots
Range:	495 n.miles (920 km) at 11 knots
Manning:	5 (enlisted) + 35 survivors
Radars:	1 navigation

These are "self-righting" lifeboats with steel hulls and aluminum superstructures. The Victory was built in 1956, the others in 1960–1961.

Highly capable craft, they can operate in heavy sea conditions and are fitted with fire-fighting pumps.

These are the only small craft assigned names.

One of the few small Coast Guard craft to be named, this is the motor lifeboat Intrepid. (U.S. Coast Guard)

1 SEARCH AND RESCUE BOAT: 50-FT TYPE

Builders:	Munson Manufacturing, Edmonds, Wash.
Displacement:	26 tons full load
Length:	$50\frac{5}{12}$ feet (15.37 m) overall
Beam:	$16\frac{1}{3}$ feet (4.97 m)
Draft:	4 feet (1.2 m)
Propulsion:	2 diesel engines (General Motors 8V92 TI); 1,300 bhp; 2 shafts
Speed:	26 knots
Range:	300 n.miles (555 km) at 18 knots 200 n.miles (370 km) at 26 knots
Manning:	4 or 5 (enlisted)

The 502001 is a small SAR craft, procured in record time by the Coast Guard to evaluate the potential for a live-aboard boat to replace small shore stations. The craft was placed in service on 1 May 1992 at Station Taylors Island in Chesapeake Bay, Maryland. With the availability of the 502001, the station's number of assigned personnel was reduced from 19 to 8.

The craft was adopted from a commercial design; its cost was $550,000.

The one-of-a-kind search-and-rescue boat 502001 at high speed in Chesapeake Bay, Maryland. (1992, U.S. Coast Guard, PA3 Richard Matthews)

The 502001 at rest. There is a stern gate to assist in rescue operations; a life-raft canister and navigation radar are fitted atop the cabin. (1994, U.S. Coast Guard, PA3 Richard Matthews)

17 BUOY SERVICING BOATS: 49-FT TYPE

Builders:	Maritime Contractors, Bellingham, Wash.
Displacement:	31.65 tons light
Length:	$49\frac{1}{4}$ feet (15 m) overall
Beam:	$16\frac{5}{6}$ feet (5.13 m)
Draft:	$6\frac{5}{6}$ feet (2.08 m)
Propulsion:	1 diesel engine; 305 bhp; 1 shaft
Speed:	10.5 knots
Range:	300 n.miles (556 km) at 10 knots
Manning:	4 (enlisted)

The first of these craft, designated 49401–49417, were completed in August 1994. They have a stern crane for handling buoys.

1 + 105(?) MOTOR LIFEBOATS: 47-FT TYPE

Builders:	Textron Marine Systems, New Orleans, La.
Displacement:	18.1 tons full load
Length:	47 feet (14.33 m) overall
Beam:	14 feet (4.3 m)
Draft:	4 feet (1.2 m)
Propulsion:	2 diesel engines (General Motors 6V92); 900 bhp; 2 shafts
Speed:	25 knots (20 knots sustained)
Range:	200 n.miles (370 km) at 25 knots
Manning:	4 (enlisted) + 5 survivors
Radars:	1 SPS-69 navigation

These craft are numbered in the 47200 series. Constructed of aluminum, they are "self-righting" lifeboats capable of flipping end-over-end or rolling up to 360° and self-righting in 30 seconds or less. They can withstand 20-foot (6.1-m) breaking waves. There are inside and outside helm control stations.

The lead boat was delivered in August 1990; five additional prototypes are being built, and production of about 100 more units is planned.

The 47-foot motor lifeboat 47201 at high speed. On her trials off the coast of Oregon, the prototype rescued four fishermen when their ship sank in 20-foot seas. (1993, Textron Marine Systems)

The prototype 47-foot motor lifeboat successfully self-righted in 5.3 seconds during rollover tests. This is the Coast Guard's first all-aluminum rescue craft. (1990, Textron Marine Systems)

9 BUOY SERVICING BOATS: 46-FT TYPE

Builders:	46301–46306 Hunt Shipyard 46307–46309 Coast Guard Yard, Curtis Bay, Md.
Displacement:	20 tons light 27 tons
Length:	$46\frac{1}{3}$ feet (14.1 m) overall
Beam:	$16\frac{1}{6}$ feet (4.9 m)
Draft:	$5\frac{2}{3}$ feet (1.7 m)
Propulsion:	1 diesel engine (General Motors 6-71); 180 bhp; Schottel rudder-propeller unit
Speed:	9 knots
Range:	440 n.miles (815 km) at 9 knots
Manning:	4 (enlisted)

These craft have steel hulls and superstructures. They are numbered 46301–46309. The above data are for later units; the initial 46301–46306 have reduced fuel capacities, for a range of only 320 n.miles (590 km).

Cargo capacity is $7\frac{1}{4}$ tons of buoys and navigation aids; a 4,000-pound (1,814-kg) lifting frame is aft.

The 46-foot buoy boat 46314 based in New York City. (1991, Giorgio Arra)

32 AIDS-TO-NAVIGATION BOATS: 45-FT TYPE

Builders:	Coast Guard Yard, Curtis Bay, Md.
Displacement:	21.5 tons light
	31.27 tons full load
Length:	$45\frac{1}{4}$ feet (13.8 m) overall
Beam:	15 feet (4.6 m)
Draft:	3 feet (0.9 m)
Propulsion:	1 diesel engine (General Motors 6-71); 150 bhp; 1 shaft
Speed:	8.5 knots
Range:	550 n.miles (1,020 km) at 8.5 knots
Manning:	4 (enlisted)

These are steel-hull craft with steel superstructures. The above characteristics relate to the units 45302–45312; the similar 45313–45316 carry less fuel, and their GM 6-71 engine is rated at 180 bhp, with a range reduction to 520 n.miles (960 km).

These boats can carry about $9\frac{1}{2}$ tons of buoys and navigation aids.

The 45-foot buoy boat 45306. (1988, Leo Van Ginderen collection)

105 MOTOR LIFEBOATS: 44-FT TYPE

Builders:	Coast Guard Yard, Curtis Bay, Md.
Displacement:	14.9 tons light
	17.7 tons full load
Length:	44 feet (13.4 m) overall
Beam:	$12\frac{2}{3}$ feet (3.9 m)
Draft:	$3\frac{11}{12}$ feet (1.2 m)
Propulsion:	2 diesel engines (General Motors 6-71); 372 bhp; 2 shafts
Speed:	15 knots (11.8 knots sustained)
Range:	185 n.miles (340 km) at 11.8 knots
Manning:	4 (enlisted) + survivors
Radars:	1 navigation

These are "unsinkable" lifeboats, assigned hull numbers 44300 to 44409. They were delivered from 1961 to 1973.

These craft will be replaced by the 47-foot (14.3-m) design.

The 44-foot motor lifeboat 44306 in calm waters. These craft are constructed of alloy steel. (U.S. Coast Guard)

A 44-foot motor lifeboat going to sea. A bar-type radar antenna is visible atop the open control position. (U.S. Coast Guard)

207 UTILITY BOATS: 41-FT TYPE

Builders:	Coast Guard Yard, Curtis Bay, Md.
Displacement:	13–14 tons full load
Length:	$40\frac{2}{3}$ feet (12.4 m) overall
Beam:	$13\frac{1}{2}$ feet (4.1 m)
Draft:	4 feet (1.2 m)
Propulsion:	2 diesel engines (Cummins V903M or VT903M); 560 or 636 bhp; 2 shafts
Speed:	22–26 knots (see notes)
Range:	300 n.miles (555 km) at 18 knots
Manning:	3 (enlisted)
Radars:	1 Raytheon 1900 navigation

These are aluminum utility craft completed from 1973 on. Hull numbers begin with 41300. The later units have vanes on their propeller shafts, adding 2.5 knots.

Their rescue equipment includes a fire pump.

The 41-foot utility boat 41352 off Fort Lauderdale, Florida. (1990, Giorgio Arra)

The 41-foot utility boat 41411 at high speed. She has a bar-type antenna, compared to the "pot" configuration in the 41352. (1995, Leo Van Ginderen collection)

2 UTILITY BOATS: 38-FT TYPE

Builders:	Munson Manufacturing, Edmonds, Wash.
Displacement:	11 tons full load
Length:	38 feet (11.58 m) overall
Beam:	$12\frac{1}{2}$ feet (3.8 m)
Draft:	$2\frac{5}{12}$ feet (0.7 m)
Propulsion:	2 diesel engines (Caterpillar 3208 TA); 750 bhp; 2 shafts
Speed:	30 knots
Manning:	4

The 380501 and 380502 were placed in service in April 1991. They are based in New York City and patrol against illegal dumping of hazardous material.

Eight passengers/inspectors can be carried.

The 38-foot utility boat 380502, one of two similar craft that patrol against the dumping of toxic materials in the New York City area. (1991, Giorgio Arra)

365 PORT AND WATERWAYS BOATS: 32-FT TYPE

Builders:	
Displacement:	7.5 tons light
	8.6 tons full load
Length:	$33\frac{1}{3}$ feet (10.2 m) overall
Beam:	$11\frac{3}{4}$ feet (3.6 m)
Draft:	$2\frac{5}{6}$ feet (0.9 m)
Propulsion:	2 diesel engines (Caterpillar 3208); 406 bhp; 2 shafts
Speed:	25 knots
Manning:	3
Radars:	1 Raytheon 1900 navigation

These boats were built in the late 1970s and are equipped for firefighting. They are of GRP construction.

The 32-foot port and waterways boat 32328 based in New York City. (1990, Giorgio Arra)

The port and waterways boat 32328. (1990, Giorgio Arra)

28 PORT SECURITY BOATS: 31-FT TYPE

Builders:	31001–31004 Bertram Boat, Miami, Fla. 31005–31028 Coast Guard Yard, Curtis Bay, Md.
Displacement:	7.4 tons full load
Length:	$30\frac{5}{12}$ feet (9.27 m) overall
Beam:	$11\frac{1}{2}$ feet (3.5 m)
Draft:	$3\frac{11}{12}$ feet (1.2 m)
Propulsion:	1 diesel engine (General Motors); 197 bhp; 2 shafts
Speed:	14 knots
Range:	165 n.miles (305 km) at 12.5 knots
Manning:	3 (enlisted)
Radars:	1 navigation

These GRP craft were completed in the 1960s and are used primarily for training. They are numbered from 31001 to 31028.

19 SURF RESCUE BOATS: 30-FT TYPE

Builders:	Coast Guard Yard, Curtis Bay, Md.
Displacement:	4.6 tons full load
Length:	$30\frac{1}{3}$ feet (9.25 m) overall
Beam:	$9\frac{1}{3}$ feet (2.8 m)
Draft:	$3\frac{2}{3}$ feet (1.1 m)
Propulsion:	2 diesel engines (General Motors 6VT92T); 375 bhp; 1 shaft
Speed:	31 knots
Range:	150 n.miles (280 km) at 25 knots
Manning:	2 (enlisted) + survivors

Employed in short-distance operations, these rescue boats were placed in service 1986–1990. Their hull numbers are 30201–30220.

A 30-foot surf rescue boat—in the surf. (U.S. Coast Guard)

1 LAKE CHAMPLAIN PATROL BOAT: 28-FT TYPE

Builders:	SeaArk Boat, Monticello, Ark.
Displacement:	
Length:	$28\frac{1}{2}$ feet (8.69 m) overall
Beam:	$11\frac{2}{3}$ feet (3.56 m)
Draft:	$1\frac{5}{6}$ feet (0.56 m)
Propulsion:	2 diesel engines (Volvo AQAD 41/290); 400 bhp; 2 outboard drives
Speed:	38 knots
Range:	
Manning:	3

Based at Burlington, Vermont, this boat is used for search and rescue on Lake Champlain.

A 28-foot Lake Champlain patrol boat. (1987, SeaArk)

1 HONOLULU PERSONNEL LAUNCH: 26-FT TYPE

Builders:	Munson Manufacturing, Edmonds, Wash.
Displacement:	3.2 tons full load
Length:	26 ft (7.9 m) overall
Beam:	10 feet (3.05 m)
Draft:	2 feet (0.6 m)
Propulsion:	1 diesel engine (Volvo AQAD 41/200); 1,200 bhp; 1 outboard drive
Speed:	25 knots
Range:	
Manning:	1 + 12 passengers

This personnel launch is used in the Honolulu, Hawaii, area to transport Coast Guardsmen. She has been assigned hull number 266200.

The Coast Guard's unique Honolulu harbor launch. (Munson)

206 SURF BOATS / 41 CARGO BOATS } 25-FT TYPE

Builders:	Coast Guard Yard, Curtis Bay, Md.
Displacement:	2.3 tons light 3.4 tons full load
Length:	$25\frac{2}{3}$ feet (7.8 m) overall
Beam:	7 feet (2.16 m)
Draft:	2 feet (0.64 m)
Propulsion:	1 diesel engine (General Motors 3-53); 80 bhp; 1 shaft
Speed:	11 knots
Range:	60 n.miles (110 km) at 11 knots
Manning:	surf boats 2 (enlisted) + survivors cargo boats 3 (enlisted)

More than 200 surf boats of this design, plus 41 similar cargo craft, entered Coast Guard service from 1969 to 1983. They have hull numbers 253301–253517. They are of GRP construction.

2 HAMMERHEAD PATROL CRAFT: 24-FT TYPE

Builders:	Munson Manufacturing, Edmonds, Wash.
Displacement:	2.8 tons full load
Length:	24 feet (7.3 m) overall
Beam:	8½ feet (2.6 m)
Draft:	2 feet (0.6 m)
Propulsion:	2 gasoline outboard motors (Evinrude V-6)
Speed:	45 knots
Range:	
Manning:	

One of the two Hammerhead 24-foot patrol craft based on Lake Tahoe, California. (Munson)

These craft are employed for search and rescue on Lake Tahoe, on the California-Nevada state line.

14 SEARCH AND RESCUE BOATS: 21-FT TYPE

Builders:	SeaArk Boat, Monticello, Ark.
Displacement:	1.9 tons full load
Length:	21 feet (6.4 m) overall
Beam:	8 feet (2.44 m)
Draft:	
Propulsion:	2 gasoline outboard motors (Evinrude)
Speed:	32 knots
Range:	
Manning:	

These trailer-transportable patrol craft are used on inland waterways.

58 AIDS-TO-NAVIGATION BOATS: 21-FT TYPE

Builders:	SeaArk Boat, Monticello, Ark.
Displacement:	1.6 tons light 3.17 tons full load
Length:	21½ feet (6.56 m) overall
Beam:	7⅓ feet (2.24 m)
Draft:	1⅙ feet (0.36 m)
Propulsion:	1 gasoline outboard motor; 228 bhp
Speed:	28 knots
Range:	100 n.miles (328 km) at 20 knots
Manning:	

Designed to be transported on trailers, these craft are used in inland waterways.

The Coast Guard regularly provides law enforcement detachments to U.S. Navy ships when police-type operations are being carried out, as in the Persian Gulf, Adriatic Sea, and Caribbean. Here, Coast Guard personnel are seen handling the captain's gig of the destroyer GOLDSBOROUGH (DDG 20) when that ship was on patrol in the Persian Gulf. (1990, John Bouvia)

CHAPTER 33

Miscellaneous U.S. Ships

The Army's vehicle landing ship MAJ GEN CHARLES P. GROSS is typical of the large number of ships and craft operated by various government agencies beyond the Navy and Coast Guard. Many of these are research ships; the Army has a large fleet of amphibious-type ships for inter-theater/coastal operations. (1994, Leo Van Ginderen collection)

In addition to the Navy and Coast Guard, several U.S. government agencies operate a variety of ships and craft. The more significant ships as well as landing craft are listed in this chapter.

NATIONAL OCEANIC AND ATMOSPHERIC ADMINISTRATION

The National Oceanic and Atmospheric Administration (NOAA), an agency within the Department of Commerce, conducts ocean surveys and other research and surveying activities for the U.S. government. NOAA conducts nonmilitary research operations in U.S. coastal waters as well as overseas. NOAA maps and charts are used by the armed forces, however, and during time of war or national emergency the President may transfer NOAA ships, shore stations, and personnel to the Navy or to other military services.

NOAA's National Ocean Survey currently has 16 ships in operating status. One specialized research ship, appropriately named RESEARCHER, is under construction; another ship is in the yard for modernization. Additional new construction for NOAA, long delayed for budgetary reasons, is now unlikely because of the availability of ex-Navy T-AGOS surveillance ships for NOAA service.

Historical. The Survey of the Coast was established as a U.S. government agency by an act of Congress on 10 February 1807; its name was changed to the Coast Survey in 1834 and to the Coast and Geodetic Survey in 1878.

Rear Admiral William L. Stubblefield, Director, Office of NOAA Corps Operations, since May 1995.

The commissioned officer corps was established in 1917. The Coast and Geodetic Survey was made a component of the Environmental Science Services Administration (ESSA) on 13 July 1965, when that agency was established within the Department of Commerce. ESSA became the National Oceanic and Atmospheric Administration in October 1970, with the Coast and Geodetic Survey being renamed the National Ocean Survey, which is today the ship-operating branch of NOAA.

SHIPS

The status of NOAA ships varies from year-to-year, with research and survey operations dependent upon specific budget allocations. These ships are supported by the NOAA Atlantic Marine Center at Norfolk, Virginia, and the Pacific Marine Center at Puget Sound, Washington.

Designations: All NOAA ships are designated by a three-digit number preceded by the letter R for Research or S for Survey, with the first digit indicating the Horsepower Tonnage (HPT) class. The HPT is the numerical sum of the vessel's shaft horsepower plus her gross tonnage.

Class I ships are 5501–9000 HPT; Class II are 3501–5500 HPT; Class III are 2001–3500 HPT; Class IV are 1001–2000 HPT; Class V are 501–1000 HPT; and Class VI are up to 500 HPT.

The accompanying table lists the NOAA research and survey ships, their HPT class, current hull numbers, and previous designations.

Guns: NOAA ships are unarmed.

Helicopters: Only the DAVID STARR JORDAN has a helicopter platform. The ship periodically deploys with a helicopter.

NOAA SHIP DESIGNATIONS

The following are NOAA ships that are either in active service, undergoing modernization, or under construction. They are arranged in the following table in numerical order.

Class	Number	Name	Former Number
I	R102	DISCOVERER	OSS 02
I	R103	MALCOLM BALDRIGE	OSS 03
I	R104	RONALD H. BROWN	
II	S221	RAINIER	MSS 21
II	R223	MILLER FREEMAN	
III	S329	WHITING	CSS 29
III	S330	MCARTHUR	CSS 30
III	S331	DAVIDSON	CSS 31
III	R332	OREGON II	
III	R333	KA'IMIMOANA	T-AGOS 15
III	R342	ALBATROSS IV	
IV	R443	TOWNSEND CROMWELL	
IV	R444	DAVID STARR JORDAN	
IV	R445	DELAWARE II	
IV	R446	CHAPMAN	
IV	S492	FERREL	ASV 92
V	R552	JOHN N. COBB	
V	S590	RUDE	ASV 90

AIRCRAFT

NOAA operates several light fixed-wing aircraft and helicopters, plus two extensively modified WP-3D Orion weather reconnaissance aircraft. These aircraft operate under the direction of the NOAA Aircraft Operations Center at MacDill Air Force Base in Florida.

The aircraft operate throughout the United States and in overseas areas, supporting scientific and cartographic activities. Three of the helicopters are employed to transport scientific and technical personnel to remote areas. The single MD-500D helicopter is deployed for about four months each year aboard the DAVID STARR JORDAN, flying dolphin surveys in the eastern Pacific area.

Whereas the two WP-3D Orions can accommodate up to 17 personnel, they normally fly with crews of 8: 2 pilots, 1 flight engineer, 1 navigator, 1 chief scientist, 1 camera operator, 1 flight director, and 1 mission scientist. WP-3D Orions generally resemble Navy P-3 Orions, but with an enlarged "tail stinger" that houses an X-band Doppler radar (the aircraft also have a C-band radar fitted in the nose). The aircraft also carry expendable bathythermographs and have satellite data transmission links, Loran-C and Global Positioning System (GPS) navigation, and various in-flight sensors.

The current NOAA aircraft are:

Active	*Type*	*Base*
(fixed wing)		
2	Lockheed WP-3D Orion	MacDill AFB, Fla.
1	Cessna Citation I	MacDill AFB, Fla.
1	Cessna Citation II	Dulles Airport, Va.
1	Gulfstream IV	MacDill AFB, Fla.
1	Turbo Commander	Dulles Airport, Va.
2	Twin Otter	MacDill AFB, Fla.
1	Aero Commander Shrike	Frederick, Md.
1	Aero Commander Shrike	Eden Prairie, Minn.
(helicopters)		
2	Bell 212	MacDill AFB, Fla.
1	Hughes MD-500D	MacDill AFB, Fla.
2	Lake Seawolf	MacDill AFB, Fla.

PERSONNEL

NOAA has 400 commissioned officers, approximately 120 of whom are assigned to shipboard duty. Ninety licensed civil service personnel and about 625 unlicensed personnel are also assigned to ships. Medical officers from the U.S. Public Health Service are provided to ships when necessary.

NOAA is commanded by a rear admiral of the NOAA commissioned officer corps.

NOAA's two WP-3D Orion weather reconnaissance aircraft fly formation. Note the aircraft's large C-band search radar (under forward fuselage), elongated probe (fitted to starboard side of nose), and X-band tail Doppler radar. The Orions can release expendable bathythermographs through their sonobuoy chutes. (NOAA)

The ADVENTUROUS at the NOAA pier in Norfolk, Virginia, with NOAA markings. NOAA and the Coast Guard had initially planned to take over a large number of the Navy's discarded T-AGOS sonar surveillance ships; however, few will be employed by U.S. agencies. (1994, U.S. Navy, Don S. Montgomery)

(1) RESEARCH SHIP: "THOMAS G. THOMPSON" CLASS

Number	Name	FY	Launch	Commission	Status
R104	RONALD H. BROWN	94	30 May 1996	1997	Building

Builders:	Trinity/Halter Marine, Moss Point, Miss.
Displacement:	2,100 tons light 3,250 tons full load
Length:	274 feet (83.5 m) overall
Beam:	52 feet (15.85 m)
Draft:	17 feet (5.2 m)
Propulsion:	diesel-electric (3 diesel generators/Caterpillar 3516TA; 2 electric motors/General Motors CD6999); 6,000 shp; 2 azimuth propellers
Speed:	15 knots
Range:	11,300 n.miles (20,940 km) at 12 knots
Manning:	
Helicopters:	no facilities
Radars:	. . . . navigation
Sonar:	Krupp-Atlas seafloor mapping

The BROWN is one of several ships of this class, the others being built by the Navy for operation by academic institutions on behalf of naval research projects (see page 000). This is the first ship built specifically for NOAA in nearly 15 years.

The ship was laid down on 21 February 1995.

Design: The ship is being built to commercial standards and is designed for extended at-sea operations. Four laboratory/accommodation vans can be carried on deck in addition to more than 4,000 square feet (372 m^2) of laboratory space.

Endurance is 60 to 70 days.

Designation: Assigned Navy hull number AGOR 26 for accounting purposes.

Engineering: In addition to three diesel generators for propulsion, the ship has three ships' service power generators (3508TA) plus one emergency generator (3406TA).

She is fitted with azimuth, or Z, drives, with 360° rotating propellers; there is also a rotating 360°, 1,180-shp bow thruster to provide precise station keeping.

Names: The ship was originally named RESEARCHER, that name having previously been assigned to the NOAA research ship MALCOLM BALDRIGE (see below). The ship was renamed HAROLD H. BROWN when christened to honor the Secretary of Commerce, who died in a plane crash in Bosnia on 3 April 1996.

3 SURVEY SHIPS: EX-NAVY "STALWART" CLASS

Number	Name	FY	Launched	USN in service	Status
R . . . (T-AGOS 13)	ADVENTUROUS	85	23 Sep 1987	19 Aug 1988	PR
R333 (T-AGOS 15)	KA'IMIMOANA	86	18 June 1988	8 Mar 1989	**PA**
R . . . (T-AGOS 18)	RELENTLESS	87	12 May 1989	12 Jan 1990	AR

Builders:	Trinity/Halter Marine, New Orleans, La.
Displacement:	1,600 tons light 2,285 tons full load
Tonnage:	1,584 GRT 786 DWT
Length:	203⅔ feet (62.1 m) waterline 224 feet (68.3 m) overall
Beam:	43 feet (13.1 m)
Draft:	15 feet (4.6 m)
Propulsion:	diesel-electric (4 Caterpillar D-398B diesel generators with General Electric motors); 3,200 shp; 2 shafts
Speed:	11 knots
Range:	3,000 n.miles (5,556 km) at 11 knots + 90 days on station at 3 knots
Manning:	KA'IMIMOANA 21 (5 officers + 16 civilians)
Helicopters:	no facilities
Radars:	2 . . . navigation
Sonars:	removed

These ships were built for the Navy's Surveillance Towed Array Sensor System (SURTASS) program (see page 229). With the massive cutbacks in that program, three ships have been transferred to NOAA. Up to eight transfers were planned, but it is unlikely that NOAA will acquire additional ships for the foreseeable future.

When this edition of *Ships and Aircraft* went to press, one ship was in active service with NOAA and two others were laid up as "cold iron," their futures uncertain. The KA'IMIMOANA is employed as an oceanic and atmospheric research vessel.

The ships and their dates taken out of Navy-MSC service/strike/to NOAA are indicated below (note that some ships were stricken from the Naval Vessel Register *after* their transfer).

	Out of service	*Stricken*	*To NOAA*
T-AGOS 13	1 June 1992	3 June 1992	5 June 1992
T-AGOS 15	31 Aug 1993	3 Sep 1993	31 Aug 1993
T-AGOS 18	20 May 1993	20 May 1993	17 Mar 1993

Class: Originally a class of 18 ships, all are being taken out of service as surveillance ships.

Design: The T-AGOS hull is similar to that of the T-ATF 166 class. A high degree of crew habitability is provided: as built, there were 19 single staterooms for the ships' civilian (MSC) crew, with 3 single and 4 double staterooms for the ten Navy technicians. (There were several additional berths available.)

Upon transfer to NOAA, the T-AGOS 15 was extensively outfitted with hydrographic survey gear, and some structural modifications are being made to the after section of the ship.

Endurance is rated at 98 days.

Engineering: The four diesel generators drive two main propulsion motors. A bow-thruster powered by a 550-hp electric motor is fitted for station keeping. There are special features to reduce machinery noise.

Names: Only one ship has been renamed by NOAA; KA'IMIMOANA is Hawaiian for "ocean seeker." In naval service the T-AGOS 15 was the USNS TITAN.

Operational: The ADVENTUROUS was employed in 1993–1994 for training NOAA officers.

The ADVENTUROUS, also at the NOAA piers in Norfolk, "fully dressed" for Independence Day celebrations, a tradition for U.S. government ships. (1993, Don Montgomery)

The former Navy ocean surveillance ship RELENTLESS at the NOAA piers in Norfolk, Virginia. Another former T-AGOS is moored adjacent to her. Although the ship carries NOAA markings, she is laid up awaiting funds and decisions on how she and the ADVENTUROUS will be employed. (1994, Jürg Kürsener)

1 RESEARCH SHIP: "OCEANOGRAPHER" CLASS (S2-MET-MA62A)

Number	Name	Launched	Commissioned	Status
R102	DISCOVERER	29 Oct 1984	29 Apr 1967	**PA**

Builders:	Aerojet-General Corp., Jacksonville, Fla.
Displacement:	4,033 tons full load
Length:	303½ feet (92.4 m) overall
Beam:	52 feet (15.8 m)
Draft:	18½ feet (5.6 m)
Propulsion:	diesel-electric (2 Westinghouse diesel engines; 2 Westinghouse electric motors); 5,000 shp; 2 shafts
Speed:	18 knots
Range:	12,250 n.miles (22,690 km) at 15 knots
Manning:	79 (13 officers + 66 civilians) + 24 scientists

This is NOAA's largest ship. The R-series, Class I ships conduct worldwide oceanographic research, primarily in physical and chemical oceanography, air-sea interactions, and marine geology.

The DISCOVERER has graceful, yacht-like lines.

Class: Her sister ship OCEANOGRAPHER (R101), commissioned in 1966, was taken out of service in 1995 and is being discarded.

Design: The DISCOVERER has an underwater observation chamber.

Engineering: The ship is fitted with a 400-hp through-bow thruster.

The DISCOVERER, showing the yacht-like lines of the OCEANOGRAPHER class. These were the largest ships to be operated by NOAA or its several predecessor agencies. (NOAA)

1 RESEARCH SHIP: "MALCOLM BALDRIGE" (S2-MT-MA7A)

Number	Name	Launched	Commissioned	Status
R103	MALCOLM BALDRIGE	5 Oct 1968	8 Oct 1970	**AA**

Builders:	American Shipbuilding, Lorain, Ohio
Displacement:	2,875 tons full load
Length:	278¼ feet (84.8 m) overall
Beam:	51 feet (15.5 m)
Draft:	16¼ feet (5.0 m)
Propulsion:	2 diesel engines; 3,200 bhp; 2 shafts
Speed:	16 knots
Range:	10,800 n.miles (20,000 km) at 12.5 knots
Manning:	68 (13 officers + 55 civilians) + 14 scientists

The BALDRIGE will be taken out of service in 1996 and subsequently discarded.

Design: The ship is fitted with a bow sonar dome.

Engineering: The BALDRIGE is fitted with a 450-hp 360° retractable bow thruster for precise maneuvering and "creeping" speeds up to seven knots.

Names: Originally named RESEARCHER, the ship was renamed on 5 March 1988.

The MALCOLM BALDRIGE in Wellington, New Zealand. Note the handling gear amidships and at her stern for research equipment. (1990, Leo Van Ginderen collection)

The MALCOLM BALDRIGE alongside a pier with the destroyer tender SHENANDOAH (AD 44). (1994, Leo Van Ginderen collection)

SURVEY SHIP: "SURVEYOR" (S2-S-RM28A)

The SURVEYOR (S132), commissioned in 1960, was taken out of service in late 1995 for disposal. See 15th Edition/page 589 for characteristics.

3 SURVEY SHIPS: "FAIRWEATHER" CLASS (S1-MT-MA72A)

Number	Name	Launched	Commissioned	Status
S220	FAIRWEATHER	15 Mar 1967	2 Oct 1968	PR
S221	RAINIER	15 Mar 1967	2 Oct 1968	**PA**
S222	MT. MITCHELL	29 Nov 1966	23 Mar 1968	AR

Builders:	Aerojet-General Corp., Jacksonville, Fla.
Displacement:	1,798 tons full load
Length:	231 feet (70.4 m) overall
Beam:	42 feet (12.8 m)
Draft:	13⅝ feet (4.2 m)
Propulsion:	2 diesel engines; 2,400 bhp; 2 shafts
Speed:	14.5 knots
Range:	7,000 n.miles (12,965 km) at 13 knots
Manning:	69 (12 officers + 57 civilians) + 4 scientists

The Class II ships are outfitted primarily for hydrographic surveys involving charting operations. Two ships have been taken out of service and will be disposed of in 1996.

Engineering: These ships have a 200-shp through-bow thruster.

The MT. MITCHELL, showing her small radome mounted above the forward edge of her short, squat funnel. (1992, Stefan Terzibaschitsch)

1 RESEARCH SHIP: "MILLER FREEMAN"

Number	Name	Launched	Completed	Status
R223	Miller Freeman	1967	1974	**PA**

Builders: American Shipbuilding, Lorain, Ohio
Displacement: 1,920 tons full load
Length: 216½ feet (66.0 m) overall
Beam: 41 feet (12.5 m)
Draft: 20 feet (6.1 m)
Propulsion: 1 diesel engine (General Motors); 3,200 bhp; 1 shaft
Speed: 14 knots
Range: 13,800 n.miles (25,560 km) at 14 knots
Manning: 41 (7 officers + 34 civilians) + 11 scientists

A fisheries research ship, the Freeman is scheduled to be replaced during the late 1990s.

Design: The ship is fitted with a stern trawl ramp.

Engineering: A 400-hp Schottel bow thruster can be lowered for precise station keeping.

The Miller Freeman. (1985, NOAA)

1 SURVEY SHIP: "PEIRCE" CLASS (S1-MT-59A)

Number	Name	Launched	Commissioned	Status
S329	Whiting	20 Nov 1962	8 July 1963	**AA**

Builders: Marietta Manufacturing, Point Pleasant, W.Va.
Displacement: 760 tons full load
Length: 164 feet (50.0 m) overall
Beam: 33 feet (10.1 m)
Draft: 10 feet (3.0 m)
Propulsion: 2 diesel engines; 1,600 bhp; 2 shafts
Speed: 12.5 knots
Range: 5,700 n.miles (10,555 km) at 12 knots
Manning: 41 (8 officers + 33 civilians) + 2 scientists

This ship primarily conducts hydrographic surveys of the 200-n.mile (237-km) exclusive economic zone for bathymetric maps and nautical charts.

Class: The Peirce (S328), completed in 1963, was laid up in 1993, transferred to New York City for use as a school ship, and renamed Elizabeth A. Fisher.

The Whiting under way. The ship has a crane forward, davits for two boats amidships, and a smaller boat on the fantail. There is a small radome forward of the funnel. (1992, Stefan Terzibaschitsch)

2 SURVEY SHIPS: "McARTHUR" CLASS (S1-MT-MA70a)

Number	Name	Launched	Commissioned	Status
S330	McArthur	15 Nov 1965	15 Dec 1966	**PA**
S331	Davidson	7 May 1966	10 Mar 1967	PR

Builders: Norfolk Shipbuilding and Dry Dock, Va.
Displacement: 995 tons full load
Length: 175 feet (53.3 m) overall
Beam: 38 feet (11.5 m)
Draft: 11½ feet (3.5 m)
Propulsion: 2 diesel engines; 1,600 bhp; 2 shafts
Speed: 13 knots
Range: 6,000 n.miles (11,110 km) at 12 knots
Manning: 38 (8 officers + 30 civilians) + 2 scientists

The Davidson has been laid up and will be disposed of in the near future.

The McArthur. (NOAA)

1 RESEARCH SHIP: "OREGON II"

Number	Name	Launched	Completed	Status
R332	Oregon II	1967	1967	**AA**

Builders: Ingalls Shipbuilding, Pascagoula, Miss.
Displacement: 952 tons full load
Length: 169¹¹⁄₁₂ feet (51.8 m) overall
Beam: 34¹⁄₁₂ feet (10.4 m)
Draft: 14¹⁄₁₂ feet (4.3 m)
Propulsion: 2 diesel engines (Fairbanks Morse); 1,600 bhp; 1 shaft
Speed: 12 knots
Range: 9,500 n.miles (17,600 km) at 12 knots
Manning: 16 civilian + 6 scientists

The Oregon II is a far-ranging fisheries research ship.

The Oregon II. (NOAA)

1 RESEARCH SHIP: "ALBATROSS IV"

Number	Name	Launched	Completed	Status
R342	ALBATROSS IV	Apr 1962	May 1963	**AA**

Builders:	Southern Shipbuilding, Slidell, La.
Displacement:	1,089 tons full load
Length:	187 feet (57.0 m) overall
Beam:	32⅚ feet (10.0 m)
Draft:	16 feet (4.9 m)
Propulsion:	2 diesel engines (Caterpillar); 1,130 bhp; 1 Kort nozzle propeller
Speed:	12 knots
Range:	4,300 n.miles (7,965 km) at 12 knots
Manning:	22 (7 officers + 15 civilians) + 15 scientists

This is a fisheries research ship.

Engineering: The ship has a 125-hp bow thruster.

The ALBATROSS IV. (NOAA)

1 RESEARCH SHIP: "TOWNSEND CROMWELL"

Number	Name	Launched	Completed	Status
R443	TOWNSEND CROMWELL	1963	1963	**PA**

Builders:	J. Ray McDermott, Morgan City, La.
Displacement:	652 tons full load
Length:	163 feet (49.7 m) overall
Beam:	32⅚ feet (10.0 m)
Draft:	12⅚ feet (3.9 m)
Propulsion:	2 diesel engines (White Superior); 800 bhp; 2 shafts
Speed:	11.5 knots
Range:	8,300 n.miles (15,370 km) at 11.5 knots
Manning:	17 (4 officers + 13 civilians) + 9 scientists

Taken over by NOAA in June 1975, the CROMWELL, a fisheries research ship, is scheduled to be replaced in the 1990s.

The TOWNSEND CROMWELL. (NOAA)

1 RESEARCH SHIP: "DAVID STARR JORDAN"

Number	Name	Launched	Completed	Status
R444	DAVID STARR JORDAN	Dec 1964	Jan 1966	**PA**

Builders:	Christy Corp., Sturgeon Bay, Wisc.
Displacement:	993 tons full load
Length:	170 11/12 feet (52.1 m) overall
Beam:	36¾ feet (11.2 m)
Draft:	15¾ feet (4.8 m)
Propulsion:	2 diesel engines (White Superior); 1,086 bhp; 2 shafts
Speed:	11.5 knots
Range:	8,560 n.miles (15,850 km) at 11.5 knots
Manning:	16 civilian + 13 scientists

This is another of NOAA's fisheries research ships.

Design: The ship can operate a helicopter and periodically deploys with an MD-500D for dolphin surveys.

Engineering: A retractable 200-hp Schottel bow thruster is fitted.

The DAVID STARR JORDAN. (NOAA)

1 RESEARCH SHIP: "DELAWARE II"

Number	Name	Launched	Completed	Status
R445	DELAWARE II	Dec 1967	Oct 1968	Yard

Builders:	South Portland Engineering, Maine
Displacement:	758 tons full load
Length:	154⅚ feet (47.2 m)
Beam:	30⅙ feet (9.2 m)
Draft:	14¾ feet (4.5 m)
Propulsion:	1 diesel engine (General Motors); 1,230 bhp; 1 shaft
Speed:	11.5 knots
Range:	6,600 n.miles (12,220 km) at 11.5 knots
Manning:	15 civilian + 9 scientists

A fisheries research ship, the DELAWARE II is laid up, pending modernization to add an estimated ten years to her service life. The availability of ex-Navy T-AGOS ships, however, makes the future NOAA modernization program questionable.

The DELAWARE II. (NOAA)

1 RESEARCH SHIP: "CHAPMAN"

Number	Name	Launched	Completed	Status
R446	Chapman	Dec 1979	July 1980	**AA**

Builders:	Bender Shipbuilding, Wash.
Displacement:	520 tons full load
Length:	$126\frac{11}{12}$ feet (38.7 m) overall
Beam:	$29\frac{5}{6}$ feet (9.1 m)
Draft:	$14\frac{1}{12}$ feet (4.3 m)
Propulsion:	1 diesel engine (Caterpillar); 1,250 bhp; 1 shaft
Speed:	11 knots
Range:	6,000 n.miles (11,110 km) at 11 knots
Manning:	11 (3 officers + 8 civilians) + 6 scientists

The Chapman is a fisheries research ship.

Engineering: A 150-hp Omnithruster bow-mounted waterjet thruster is installed.

The Chapman. (NOAA)

1 RESEARCH SHIP: "JOHN N. COBB"

Number	Name	Launched	Completed	Status
R552	John N. Cobb	Jan 1950	Feb 1950	**AA**

Builders:	Western Boatbuilding, Tacoma, Wash.
Displacement:	250 tons full load
Length:	$92\frac{5}{6}$ feet (28.3 m) overall
Beam:	$25\frac{11}{12}$ feet (7.9 m)
Draft:	$10\frac{5}{6}$ feet (3.3 m)
Propulsion:	1 diesel engine (Fairbanks Morse); 325 bhp; 1 shaft
Speed:	9.3 knots
Range:	2,900 n.miles (5,370 km) at 9.3 knots
Manning:	8 civilian + 4 scientists

The Cobb, a fisheries research ship, is scheduled to be replaced during the 1990s.

The John N. Cobb. (NOAA)

1 SURVEY SHIP: "FERREL" (S1-MT-MA83A)

Number	Name	Launched	Commissioned	Status
S492	Ferrel	4 Apr 1968	4 June 1968	**AA**

Builders:	Zigler Shipyard, Jennings, La.
Displacement:	363 tons full load
Length:	$133\frac{1}{4}$ feet (40.5 m) overall
Beam:	32 feet (9.7 m)
Draft:	7 feet (2.1 m)
Propulsion:	2 diesel engines (Caterpillar); 750 bhp; 2 shafts
Speed:	10.6 knots
Range:	2,200 n.miles (4,075 km) at 10 knots
Manning:	19 (5 officers + 14 civilians)

The Ferrel conducts near-shore and estuarine-current surveys. She employs data collection buoys in her work, and there is a large open buoy stowage area aft, as well as a comprehensive workshop.

Engineering: The ship is fitted with a 100-hp through-bow thruster.

The Ferrel. (NOAA)

1 SURVEY SHIP: "RUDE" CLASS (S1-MT-MA71A)

Number	Name	Launched	Commissioned	Status
S590	Rude	17 Aug 1966	29 Mar 1967	**AA**

Builders:	Jakobson Shipyard, Oyster Bay, N.Y.
Displacement:	214 tons full load
Length:	90 feet (27.4 m) overall
Beam:	22 feet (6.7 m)
Draft:	7 feet (2.1 m)
Propulsion:	2 diesel engines (Cummins); 800 bhp; 2 Kort nozzle propellers
Speed:	11.5 knots
Range:	800 n.miles (1,480 km) at 10 knots
Manning:	11 (3 officers + 8 civilians)

The surveying ships Rude and Heck (S591) formerly worked as a pair, using wire drags to locate underwater navigational hazards. In that role one commanding officer was assigned to the two vessels; he normally rode one ship, and the executive officer the other.

Class: The Heck, completed in 1967, was taken out of service in 1995; she will be discarded.

Engineering: The propellers on these ships are protected by shrouds, similar to Kort nozzles. Auxiliary propulsion provides 70 hp to each propeller for slow-speed dragging operations.

The RUDE. (NOAA)

The HECK. (1988, Leo Van Ginderen collection)

RESEARCH SHIP: "MURRE II"

The fisheries research and logistic support ship MURRE II (R663) was sold in 1991 for private use. A converted Army craft, she had operated in Alaskan waters.

RESEARCH SHIP: EX-ARMY TUG

The research tug SHENAHON (R693), the former U.S. Army tug T-465, was taken out of service in early 1996. She was replaced on the Great Lakes by the HALCYON, a former Army "swamp."

TRAINING CRAFT: EX-ARMY SUPPLY SHIP

The VIRGINIA KEY (ex-U.S. Army T-433), employed as a training ship by the NOAA Training Center at Fort Eustis, Virginia, has been discarded.

RESEARCH CRAFT

NOAA laboratories operate several small research craft that are 65 feet (19.8 m) or less in length.

ENVIRONMENTAL PROTECTION AGENCY

The Environmental Protection Agency (EPA) operates two major research ships.

1 RESEARCH SHIP: EX-NAVY GUNBOAT

Number	Name	FY	Launched	USN Comm.	To EPA
(ex-PG 86)	PETER W. ANDERSON	63	18 June 1966	4 Nov 1967	17 Jan 1978

Builders:	Tacoma Boatbuilding, Wash.
Displacement:	approx. 250 tons full load
Length:	164½ feet (50.2 m) overall
Beam:	23¾ feet (7.28 m)
Draft:	9½ feet (2.9 m)
Propulsion:	2 diesel engines (Cummins VT12-875M); 1,400 bhp; 2 shafts
Speed:	16 knots
Range:	2,400 n.miles (4,445 km) at 14 knots on diesel engines
Manning:	30 (civilian contractor)

The ANDERSON is a former ASHEVILLE-class patrol combatant/gunboat now employed in the pollution research role. Three sister ships serve as Navy research ships with the David Taylor Research Center (see chapter 25).

This ship was decommissioned as a Navy gunboat on 1 October 1977 and transferred to the EPA in 1978.

All weapons have been removed.

Class: Originally, this was a class of 17 units (see page 195). The CROCKETT (PG 88), previously operated by the EPA, is now a museum at Muskegon, Michigan.

Design: The ANDERSON has an aluminum hull with a fiberglass superstructure. For the research role the ship has been fitted with three laboratories and a computer center.

Names: The ANDERSON was named ANTELOPE (PG 86) in naval service.

Operational: Under the EPA the ship originally operated on the Great Lakes; she is now based at Annapolis, Maryland.

Propulsion: Originally a CODOG-propelled ship; the ANDERSON no longer has a gas turbine.

The PETER W. ANDERSON, showing the handling gear for sampling equipment mounted on the stern. (1990, Giorgio Arra)

The PETER W. ANDERSON at sea, showing the modified Coast Guard–type ship markings used by ESSA. (1992, Giorgio Arra)

1 RESEARCH SHIP: EX-COAST GUARD BUOY TENDER

Number	Name	Launched	USCG Comm.	To EPA
ex-WAGL 234	ROGER R. SIMONS	29 Apr 1939	June 1939	1974

Builders:	Marine Iron and Shipbuilding, Duluth, Minn.
Displacement:	342 tons full load
Length:	122¼ feet (37.26 m) overall
Beam:	27 feet (8.23 m)
Draft:	7½ feet (2.29 m)
Propulsion:	2 diesel engines (Superior); 430 bhp; 2 shafts
Speed:	10 knots
Range:	3,500 n.miles (6,480 km) at 6 knots
Manning:	

A former Coast Guard buoy tender, the SIMONS is employed by the EPA in pollution survey and water studies. The ship was decommissioned and stricken by the Coast Guard on 1 June 1973, transferred to the U.S. Navy on 8 August 1973, and transferred to the EPA in 1974.

Names: Coast Guard name was MAPLE (WAGL 234).

Operational: The ship is based at Cleveland, Ohio, on Lake Erie.

GEOLOGICAL SURVEY

The Geological Survey of the Department of Interior previously operated one major research ship, the former Navy survey ship S. P. LEE.

SURVEY SHIP: "KELLAR" CLASS

The survey ship S. P. LEE (ex-U.S. Navy AG 192, T-AGS 31) was returned to the Navy from the Geological Survey on 1 August 1992; the ship was stricken from the Naval Vessel Register on 1 October 1992 and transferred to Mexico on 7 December 1992.

The LEE was built as a naval surveying ship and placed in service with the Military Sealift Command (USNS) upon completion in 1968. The ship was reclassified as a miscellaneous research ship (AG 192) on 25 September 1970. She was taken out of naval service on 29 January 1973 and was transferred on loan to the National Geological Survey on 27 February 1974.

Under the Geological Survey, the LEE conducted deep-sea seismic surveys, seafloor coring, and seafloor bottom sampling.

NATIONAL SCIENCE FOUNDATION

1 ARCTIC RESEARCH SHIP: "NATHANIEL B. PALMER"

Number	Name	Launched	Completed
(none)	NATHANIEL B. PALMER	1991	May 1992

Builders:	North American Shipbuilding, Larose, La.
Displacement:	6,800 tons full load
Length:	308 feet (93.9 m) overall
Beam:	60 feet (18.29 m)
Draft:	22½ feet (6.86 m)
Propulsion:	4 diesel engines (Caterpillar); 13,200 bhp; 2 shafts
Speed:	15 knots
Range:	
Manning:	approx. 25 + 37 scientists

This ship was built specifically for NSF operation.

Design: Icebreaking hull. A helicopter deck and hangar are provided.

The NATHANIEL B. PALMER.

1 ARCTIC RESEARCH SHIP: "POLAR DUKE"

Number	Name	Launched	Completed
(none)	POLAR DUKE	1983	1983

Builders:	Vaagen Verft (Norway)
Displacement:	1,645 tons full load
Length:	219 feet (66.77 m) overall
Beam:	43 feet (13.1 m)
Draft:	19 feet (5.79 m)
Propulsion:	2 diesel engines; 4,500 bhp; 2 Kort nozzle propellers
Speed:	12 knots
Range:	29,950 n.miles (55,470 km) at 12 knots
Manning:	14 civilian + 23 scientists

The POLAR DUKE was constructed specifically for the NSF. The ship supports multidiscipline research in the Antarctic area.

Design: Icebreaking hull. The ship has a helicopter deck, but no hangar. Endurance is 90 days.

The POLAR DUKE. (National Science Foundation)

ARMY TRANSPORTATION CORPS

The Army operates logistic support ships, landing craft, and small tugs under the Transportation Corps, and a number of dredges under the Corps of Engineers. Numerous motorboats are also used by engineer units to assist in the assembly of pontoon bridges. Only self-propelled ships and craft of the Transportation Corps are listed in this chapter.

The Army Transportation Corps had, until 1950, operated a large number of oceangoing troop transports, cargo and supply ships, minelayers, and large tugs. The troop transports and some cargo ships and tugs were transferred to the newly established Military Sea Transportation Service (now Military Sealift Command). Other ships were transferred to the Navy. A few ex-Army transports, barges, and one tug remain on the Naval Register as service craft (see chapter 25).

Designations: The Army uses a ship and craft designation series derived in part from the Navy's designation scheme. The designations are:

BC	barge, dry cargo (non–self-propelled)
BCDX	barge, deck enclosure
BD	floating crane
BDL	beach discharge lighter
BG	barge, liquid cargo (non–self-propelled)
BK	barge, dry cargo (non–self-propelled)
BPL	barge, pier, self-elevating
BR	barge, refrigerated (non–self-propelled)
FMS	floating marine repair shop (non–self-propelled)
FS	freight and supply vessel (over 100 ft/30.48 m)
FSR	freight and supply vessel, refrigerated
J	workboat (under 50 ft/15.24 m)
LARC	lighter, amphibious, resupply, cargo
LCM	landing craft, mechanized
LCU	landing craft, utility
LCV	landing craft, vehicle
LSV	landing ship, vehicle
LT	large tug (over 100 ft/30.48 m)
Q	workboat (over 50 ft/15.24 m)
ST	small tug (under 100 ft/30.48 m)
T	small freight and supply vessel (under 100 ft/30.48 m)
Y	liquid cargo vessel

Guns: No Army ships are armed.

Names: Army ships and craft are generally named for campaigns and battles in which the Army participated, except the LT 130-series large tugs, named for signers of the American Constitution who had a military affiliation. Several battle names are carried by both Navy ships and Army craft.

Operational: Four LCUs, three LT-series tugs, ten LCMs, and one floating crane[1] are normally carried on board the Military Sealift Command–operated repositioning ship AMERICAN CORMORANT (T-AK 2062), prepositioned at Diego Garcia in the Indian Ocean (see page 263).

A large number of Army ships and craft are based at the Army Transportation Center at Fort Eustis, Virginia.

1. The crane is the non–self-propelled ALGIERS (BD 6072).

1 HEAVY LIFT SHIP: C1-MT-123A TYPE

Number	Name	Launched	In service
(none)	JAMES MCHENRY		1978

Builders:	Peterson Builders, Sturgeon Bay, Wisc.
Displacement:	5,453 tons full load
Tonnage:	2,640 DWT
Length:	278 11/12 feet (85.01 m) waterline 300 1/6 feet (91.49 m) overall
Beam:	55 1/6 feet (16.82 m)
Draft:	16 11/12 feet (5.16 m)
Propulsion:	2 diesel engines (General Motors 16-645-E2); 5,750 bhp; 2 shafts
Speed:	14 knots
Range:	10,100 n.miles (18,700 km) at 11 knots
Manning:	approx. 30

This is a unique heavy lift ship employed by the Army primarily as a training ship for cargo handlers at Fort Story, Virginia. The ship has a vehicle ramp aft, with a drive-through tunnel in the superstructure to provide access to the forward cargo deck.

The JAMES MCHENRY has a vehicle ramp aft, with a drive-through tunnel in the superstructure to provide access to the forward cargo deck. (1990, Giorgio Arra)

The stern aspect of the JAMES MCHENRY. (1990, Giorgio Arra)

6 VEHICLE LANDING SHIPS: "BESSON" CLASS

Number	Name	Launched	In service
LSV 01	Gen Frank S. Besson, Jr.	30 June 1987	20 Jan 1988
LSV 02	CWO3 Harold C. Clinger	16 Sep 1987	20 Apr 1988
LSV 03	Gen Brehon B. Somervell	18 Nov 1987	26 July 1988
LSV 04	Lt Gen William B. Bunker	11 Jan 1988	1 Sep 1988
LSV 05	Maj Gen Charles P. Gross	11 July 1990	12 Dec 1990
LSV 06	SP4 James A. Loux	7 Apr 1994	1994

Builders:	Halter-Moss Point Marine, Escatawpa, Miss.
Displacement:	1,612 tons light 4,199 tons full load
Tonnage:	1,800 DWT
Length:	256 feet (78.03 m) waterline 272⅔ feet (83.14 m) overall
Beam:	60 feet (18.28 m)
Draft:	12 feet (3.66 m)
Propulsion:	2 diesel engines (General Motors EMD 16-645-E2); 3,900 bhp; 2 shafts
Speed:	12 knots
Range:	5,500 n.miles (10,185 km) at 11 knots
Manning:	29 (6 officers + 23 enlisted)
Radars:	2 SPS-64(V) navigation

The Gen Frank S. Besson, Jr. (1988, Giorgio Arra)

These are small LST-type ships based on the Australian roll-on/roll-off ship Frances Bay. They transport vehicles and containers (48 TEU) or 1,815 tons of vehicles or other cargo.

Class: The large beach discharge lighter Lt Col John D. Page was discarded in 1989.

Design: These ships have an LST-like design, with a superstructure aft. A tunnel runs through the superstructure to permit vehicles to drive from the stern ramp into the open cargo well. A bow ramp is fitted. The ships are built to commercial shipbuilding standards.

This Besson-class landing ship shows the twin funnels, island structure aft, and long bow ramp of these ships. Two LARC wheeled amphibious vehicles are parked on the ship's "tank deck." (U.S. Army)

35 "LCU 2000" CLASS

Number	Name	Number	Name
LCU 2001	Runnymede	LCU 2019	Fort Denelson
LCU 2002	Kennesaw Mountain	LCU 2020	Fort McHenry
LCU 2003	Macon	LCU 2021	Great Bridge
LCU 2004	Aldie	LCU 2022	Harpers Ferry
LCU 2005	Brandy Station	LCU 2023	Hobkirk
LCU 2006	Bristoe Station	LCU 2024	Hormigueros
LCU 2007	Broad Run	LCU 2025	Malvern Hill
LCU 2008	Buena Vista	LCU 2026	Matamoros
LCU 2009	Springfield	LCU 2027	Mechanicsville
LCU 2010	Cedar Run	LCU 2028	Missionary Ridge
LCU 2011	Chickahominy	LCU 2029	Molino Del Rey
LCU 2012	Chickasaw Bayou	LCU 2030	Monterey
LCU 2013	Churubusco	LCU 2031	New Orleans
LCU 2014	Coamo	LCU 2032	Palo Alto
LCU 2015	Contreres	LCU 2033	Paulus Hook
LCU 2016	Cornith	LCU 2034	Perryville
LCU 2017	El Caney	LCU 2035	Port Hudson
LCU 2018	Five Forks		

Builders:	LCU 2001–2003 Lockheed Shipbuilding, Savannah, Ga. LCU 2004–2035 Trinity-Moss Point Marine, Escatawpa, Miss.
Displacement:	672 tons light 1,102 tons full load
Length:	156 feet (47.55 m) waterline 174 feet (53.03 m) overall
Beam:	42 feet (12.8 m)
Draft:	8½ feet (2.6 m)
Propulsion:	2 diesel engines (Cummins KTA-50M); 2,500 bhp; 2 Kort nozzle propellers
Speed:	11.5 knots
Range:	4,500 n.miles (8,333 km) at 11.5 knots empty
Manning:	12 (2 officers + 10 enlisted)

These large landing craft, with a deckhouse aft, are too large to be carried by Navy amphibious ships with docking wells (as can the smaller LCU designs). Completed in 1990–1992, the craft are intended to replace the LCU 1466-class landing craft.

Each craft has a bow ramp for unloading onto the beach; beaching draft forward is four feet (1.2 m).

The first three units were completed at Trinity Marine after the demise of the Lockheed shipbuilding yard.

Class: LCU 2001–2007 were ordered in 1986; LCU 2008–2017 in 1987; LCU 2018–2023 in 1988; and LCU 2024–2035 in 1989. Two additional craft, which were authorized but not ordered, were to have been named Sackett's Harbor and Sayler's Creek.

Design: Built to commercial shipbuilding standards specifically for the U.S. Army. All other U.S. LCU/LSU types were built to Navy designs.

Engineering: These craft have a 300-shp bow thruster.

Names: The LCU 2009 was originally named Calaboza.

The Bristoe Station showing the low gunwales and large superstructure of this class. (1990, Giorgio Arra)

The Bristoe Station. (1990, Giorgio Arra)

UTILITY LANDING CRAFT: "LCU 1466" CLASS

The 38 landing craft of this class have been disposed of by the Army. These were the survivors of a large series of Navy-designed LCUs. Two still serve in the Navy (see page 175).

Class: This class covered hull numbers LCU 1466–1609, with 14 units constructed in Japan. Numerous units were transferred to other nations; others became Navy service craft (YFU).

See 15th Edition/page 600 for characteristics.

13 UTILITY LANDING CRAFT: "LCU 1610" CLASS

Number	Name	Number	Name
LCU 1667	Manassas	LCU 1674	St. Mihiel
LCU 1668	Belleau-Wood	LCU 1675	Commando
LCU 1669	Marseilles	LCU 1676	Birmingham
LCU 1670	San Isidro	LCU 1677	Brandywine
LCU 1671	Catawba Ford	LCU 1678	Naha
LCU 1672	Bushmaster	LCU 1679	Chateau Thierry
LCU 1673	Double Eagle		

Builders:	General Ship & Engine Works, East Boston, Mass.
Displacement:	190 tons light 390 tons full load
Length:	134¾ feet (41.1 m) overall
Beam:	29¾ feet (9.1 m)
Draft:	6 11/12 feet (2.1 m)
Propulsion:	4 diesel engines (General Motors Detroit 6-71); 1,200 bhp; 2 Kort nozzle propellers
Speed:	11 knots
Range:	1,200 n.miles (2,222 km) at 11 knots empty 1,200 n.miles (2,222 km) at 8 knots loaded
Manning:	6 (enlisted)
Troops:	8
Radars:	LN-66 or SPS-53 navigation

These are Navy-designed LCUs completed in 1976–1978.

The Commando has been modified to serve as a diver support ship. She is assigned to the Army's 558th Transportation Company at Fort Eustis.

Class: This class originally consisted of hull numbers LCU 1610–1624 and 1627–1681; many still serve in the Navy (see chapter 20).

Design: These craft have unloading ramps forward and aft.

Names: Note that the Army spells Belleau-Wood with a hyphen; the Navy's LHA 3 with the same name does not have a hyphen.

The San Isidro showing the starboard-side bridge structure of this class, used by the Army as well as the U.S. Navy and several other nations. (1989, Leo Van Ginderen collection)

The Naha carrying Army cranes and trucks; note the stern ramp and starboard-side island structure. (1983, Giorgio Arra)

126 MECHANIZED LANDING CRAFT: LCM(8) TYPE

Builders:	
Weight:	varies 34–36.5 tons light 111–121 tons full load
Length:	$73\frac{7}{12}$ feet (22.4 m) overall
Beam:	21 feet (6.4 m)
Draft:	$4\frac{7}{12}$ feet (1.4 m) aft
Propulsion:	2 diesel engines (General Motors Detroit 6-71); 600 bhp; 2 shafts (see notes)
Speed:	12 knots empty 9.2 knots loaded
Range:	150 n.miles (278 km) at 12 knots empty 150 n.miles (278 km) at 9.2 knots loaded
Manning:	2–4 (enlisted)

These are standard landing craft intended to carry vehicles and cargo. Capacity is one M60-series tank or about 60 tons of cargo. No accommodations are provided in these craft.

Completed between 1954 and 1972, eighteen of these craft are in reserve.

An LCM(8)-type landing craft. (1986, Leo Van Ginderen collection)

LANDING AIR CUSHION VEHICLE (LACV) CRAFT

The Army's LAMP-H enlarged, advanced prototype vehicle capable of carrying 89 tons of cargo was canceled on 18 October 1991, prior to completion. The craft had been ordered in 1990. The Army's 26 LACVs were offered for sale during August 1994.

The Army's air cushion landing craft were based at Fort Story, Virginia, and were intended for the ship-to-shore movement of troops and equipment. The Army uses the term Logistics-Over-The-Shore (LOTS) for this evolution.

See 15th Edition/page 601 for characteristics.

30 LARC XV TYPE AMPHIBIOUS VEHICLES

Builders:	
Weight:	20.8 tons empty 35.7 tons loaded
Length:	45 feet (13.72 m) overall
Beam:	$14\frac{1}{2}$ feet (4.42 m)
Propulsion:	2 diesel engines; 600 bhp; 1 propeller
Speed:	8.25 knots water 29.5 mph land
Range:	45 n.miles (83 km) water at 8.25 knots 300 miles (483 km) land at 29.5 mph
Manning:	2 (enlisted)
Troops:	50+

These wheeled/propeller driven vehicles are the successors to the DUKW ("duck") amphibious trucks of World War II fame. They were introduced into amphibious landings by the U.S. Army in Operation Huskey, the 1943 Allied landings on Sicily.

The LARC XV type are large, four-wheel cargo vehicles with an aluminum hull. They can carry 15 tons of cargo, which is unloaded over a stern ramp.

These craft are based at Fort Story and Palatka, Florida; a few are in storage.

19 LARC LX TYPE AMPHIBIOUS VEHICLES

Builders:	
Weight:	88 tons empty 190 tons loaded
Length:	$62\frac{1}{2}$ feet (19.07 m) overall
Beam:	$26\frac{7}{12}$ feet (8.1 m)
Propulsion:	4 diesel engines; 660 bhp; 2 propellers
Speed:	6.5 knots water 15 mph land
Range:	75 n.miles (139 km) water at 6 knots 150 miles (241 km) land at 15 mph
Manning:	8 (enlisted)
Troops:	125

The LX type are very large, four-wheel cargo vehicles. They can normally carry 60 tons of cargo or an overload of up to 90 tons. The craft are fitted with a bow ramp and have limited maneuverability.

All are based in California.

The LARC LX 16 carrying a fuel truck while traversing shallow water. (U.S. Army)

3 LARC V TYPE AMPHIBIOUS VEHICLES

Builders:	
Weight:	8.9 tons empty 13.4 tons loaded
Length:	35 feet (10.67 m) overall
Beam:	10 feet (3.05 m)
Propulsion:	1 diesel engine; 300 bhp; 1 propeller
Speed:	9 knots water 29.5 mph land
Range:	60 n.miles (111 km) water at 9 knots 200 miles (322 km) land at 29 mph
Manning:	2 (enlisted)
Troops:	20

This type of four-wheel cargo vehicle can carry up to five tons of cargo. The craft are fitted with a bow ramp and are built of aluminum. Troops are not normally carried in these vehicles.

3+5 LARGE HARBOR TUGS: LT 130 DESIGN

Number	Name	Launched	Completed	Status
LT 801	Maj Gen Nathanael Greene	4 July 1989	Sep 1993	Active
LT 802	Maj Gen Henry Knox	Oct 1989	1994	Active
LT 803	Maj Gen Anthony Wayne	2 Aug 1990	1994	Active
LT 804	Brig Gen Zebulon Pike			Planned
LT 805	Maj Gen Winfield Scott			Planned
LT 806	Col Seth Warner			Planned
LT 807	Sgt Maj John Champe			Planned
LT 808	Maj Gen Jacob Brown			Planned

Builders:	Trinity/Halter Marine, Moss Point, Miss.
Displacement:	924 tons full load
Length:	128 feet (39.0 m) overall
Beam:	36 feet (10.97 m)
Draft:	15½ feet (4.73 m)
Propulsion:	2 diesel engines (General Motors EMD 12-645FMB); 2,550 bhp; 2 shafts
Speed:	12 knots
Range:	5,000 n.miles (9,260 km) at 12 knots
Manning:	

This series of large tugs has been delayed; the five planned additional units will probably not be built.

Builders: Beginning in 1988, contracts for these tugs were awarded by the Navy to the Robert E. Derecktor yard at Middletown, Rhode Island. The lead unit was "conditionally" delivered to the Army on 30 August 1991, with the yard responsible for correcting certain deficiencies. On 3 January 1992 the Derecktor yard filed for bankruptcy protection under Chapter 11. The contract was then transferred to the Trinity/Marine yard.

The Maj Gen Nathanael Greene, lead ship of a series of large tugs built for the Army and the largest tugs yet acquired by that service. Army tugs are intended to assist merchant and landing ships, and to move barges in overseas ports. (1993, U.S. Army)

18 LARGE HARBOR TUGS

Number	Name	Number	Name
LT 1937	Sgt William W. Seay	LT 1977	Attleboro
LT 1953	Salerno	LT 2076	New Guinea
LT 1956	Fredericksburg	LT 2081	San Sapor
LT 1959	Murfreesboro	LT 2085	Anzio
LT 1960	Lundy's Lane	LT 2086	Bataan
LT 1970	Okinawa	LT 2088	Petersburg
LT 1971	Normandy	LT 2090	SP4 Larry G. Dahl
LT 1972	Gettysburg	LT 2092	North Africa
LT 1973	Shiloh	LT 2096	Valley Forge
LT 1974	Champagne-Marne		

Builders:	
Displacement:	295 tons light 390 tons full load
Length:	107 feet (32.61 m) overall
Beam:	26½ feet (8.08 m)
Draft:	12⅙ feet (3.71 m)
Propulsion:	1 diesel engine (Fairbanks Morse); 1,200 bhp; 1 shaft
Speed:	12.75 knots
Range:	3,325 n.miles (6,160 km) at 12 knots
Manning:	16 (enlisted)

Sixty-five tugs of this design were built in the 1950s (LT 1936–1977, 2202, and 2075–2096). Several units are in storage at Hythe (Kent), England.

The North Africa. (1989, Leo Van Ginderen collection)

11 SMALL HARBOR TUGS

Number	Name	Number	Name
ST 1988	Bemis Heights	ST 2116	King's Mountain
ST 1989	Eutaw Springs	ST 2118	Guilford Court House
ST 1990	Mohawk Valley	ST 2119	Bennington
ST 1991	Oriskany	ST 2126	Stony Point
ST 1993	Cowpens	ST 2130	Fort Mifflin
ST 2014	Monmouth		

Builders:	
Displacement:	100 tons light 122 tons full load
Length:	69 11/12 feet (21.31 m) overall
Beam:	19½ feet (5.94 m)
Draft:	8⅙ feet (2.5 m)
Propulsion:	1 diesel engine; 600 bhp; 1 shaft
Speed:	12 knots
Range:	3,500 n.miles (6,480 km) at 12 knots
Manning:	6 (enlisted)

These are the survivors of a large class of Army tugs built in the 1950s. Some units stricken in the early 1990s were in storage at Hythe (Kent), England.

The MOHAWK VALLEY high and dry for maintenance. Army landing craft and tugs often have the last two digits of their hull number on their bow or funnel. (1995, Leo Van Ginderen collection)

The VALCOUR ISLAND; now stricken. (1986, Leo Van Ginderen collection)

2 SMALL TUGS

Number	Number
ST 2154	ST 3000

Builders:	
Displacement:	25.2 tons light
	29 tons full load
Length:	$45\frac{1}{6}$ feet (13.77 m) overall
Beam:	$12\frac{5}{6}$ feet (3.91 m)
Draft:	6 feet (1.83 m)
Propulsion:	1 diesel engine; 170 bhp; 1 shaft
Speed:	10 knots
Range:	700 n.miles (1,300 km) at 10 knots
Manning:	4 (enlisted)

These small, unnamed tugs were built in the 1950s.

The SANTIAGO (ST 2028) of this type was stricken in 1990.

SERVICE CRAFT

The Army's Transportation Corps and Corps of Engineers operate a large number of small, self-propelled craft for local transportation and supply, as well as dredges and barges of various types.

AIR FORCE

The Air Force operates a large number of small craft, all managed by the San Antonio Air Logistics Center at Kelly Air Force Base (AFB) in Texas. In addition to the craft listed here, the Air Force operates several small personnel craft, utility boats, and miscellaneous barges, plus one Army LARC V-type amphibious craft (designated L-35-2212).

Designations: Air Force craft are designated according to their length (rounded up).

5 MISSILE RETRIEVERS: 120-FT TYPE

Number	Number
MR-120-8801	MR-120-8803
MR-120-8802	MR-120-8805

Builders:	Swiftships, Morgan City, La.
Displacement:	91 tons light
	133 tons full load
Length:	$117\frac{1}{3}$ feet (35.78 m) overall
Beam:	$24\frac{2}{3}$ feet (7.51 m)
Draft:	$6\frac{3}{4}$ feet (2.06 m)
Propulsion:	4 diesel engines (Detroit Diesel 16V92 MTA); 5,600 bhp; 4 shafts
Speed:	30 knots
Range:	600 n.miles (1,111 km) at 27 knots
Manning:	10 (enlisted)

These retrieval craft are employed to recover practice missiles. They can carry 20 tons of cargo and are constructed of aluminum.

The craft were completed in 1988–1989.

The MR-120-8801 at speed. These craft have white hulls, red superstructures, and yellow decks. (1988, Swiftships)

A pair of 120-foot missile retrievers at Tyndall Air Force Base near Panama City, Florida. (1991, Staff Sgt. Rick Fligort, USAF)

1 MISSILE RETRIEVER: 85-FT TYPE

Number
MR-85-1603

Builders:	
Displacement:	90 tons full load
Length:	85 feet (25.91 m) overall
Beam:	18 feet (5.49 m)
Draft:	$5\frac{1}{6}$ feet (1.57 m)
Propulsion:	2 diesel engines (Detroit 16V92); 2 shafts
Speed:	17 knots
Range:	400 n.miles (740 km) at 17 knots
Manning:	10 civilian

This is the survivor of a small class of missile recovery craft. She was completed in 1967.

The 85-foot missile retriever MR-85-1603 at Tyndall AFB. (1991, Staff Sgt. Rick Fligort, USAF)

MISSILE RETRIEVERS: 65-FT TYPE

The 65-foot (19.8-m) missile retrievers have been discarded.

See 15th Edition/page 606 for characteristics.

1 SMALL HARBOR TUG

Number
TG-45-1919

Builders:	
Displacement:	25.2 tons light
	29 tons full load
Length:	$45\frac{1}{6}$ feet (13.77 m) overall
Beam:	$12\frac{5}{6}$ feet (3.91 m)
Draft:	6 feet (1.83 m)
Propulsion:	1 diesel engine; 170 bhp; 1 shaft
Speed:	10 knots
Range:	700 n.miles (1,300 km) at 10 knots
Manning:	4 (enlisted)

Similar to the Army ST-series tugs, this is the last tug in Air Force service. She is based at Thule, Greenland. The tug was completed in 1953.

4 MECHANIZED LANDING CRAFT: LCM(8) TYPE

Number	Number
C-74-2205	C-74-8601
C-74-2206	C-74A-2113

Weight:	116 tons full load
Length:	$73\frac{7}{12}$ feet (22.4 m) overall
Beam:	21 feet (6.4 m)
Draft:	$4\frac{7}{12}$ feet (1.4 m) aft
Propulsion:	2 diesel engines (General Motors Detroit 6-71); 600 bhp; 2 shafts
Speed:	12 knots empty
	9.2 knots loaded
Range:	150 n.miles (278 km) at 12 knots empty
	150 n.miles (278 km) at 9.2 knots loaded
Manning:	2 to 4 (enlisted)

The cargo capacity of each craft is 57 tons. They were completed between 1954 and 1987.

Three units are at Wake Island; the C-74A-2113 is at Homestead AFB in Florida.

APPENDIX A

Navy Force Levels, 1945–1995

The following are ships in active commission as of the end of the fiscal year indicated. Beginning in 1965, operational Naval Reserve/Naval Reserve Force (NRF) ships manned by composite active-reserve crews are indicated by the plus (+) symbol.

Large frigate-type warships (DL-DLG-DLGN) are listed separately prior to 1975; from that year onward they are included with missile cruisers and destroyers based on their reclassification in that year (see page 000).

Ship Type	1945	1950	1953[1]	1955	1960	1965	1970	1975	1980	1985	1990	1995
Submarines—*conventional*												
SS-SSK-SSR	237	73	122	121	131	83	59	11	6	4	—	—
SSG	—	—	1	2	4	—	—	—	—	—	—	—
auxiliary	—	—	7	18	20	15	26	2	1	1	1	1
Submarines—*nuclear*												
SSN-SSRN	—	—	—	1	7	22	48	64	73	94[2]	87	77
SSGN	—	—	—	—	1	—	—	—	—	—	—	—
SSBN	—	—	—	—	2	29	41	41	40	37	34	16
auxiliary[3]	—	—	—	—	—	—	—	—	—	2	2	2
(total submarines)	(237)	(73)	(130)	(142)	(147)	(149)	(174)	(118)	(120)	(138)	(124)	(96)
Aircraft Carriers												
CVB-CVA-CVAN-CV-CVN	20	7	17	16	14	16	15	15	13	13	12	11 + 1[4]
CVS	—	—	—	5	9	9	4	—	—	—	—	—
CVL	8	4	5	1	—	—	—	—	—	—	—	—
CVE	70	4	17	3	—	—	—	—	—	—	—	—
Battleships												
BB	25[5]	1	4	3	—	—	—	—	—	2	3	—
Cruisers												
CAG-CG-CLG-CGN	—	—	—	—	6	12	10	27	27	30	43	32
CA (8-inch guns)	24	9	15	10	6	2	2	—	—	—	—	—
CL (6-inch guns)	42	3	3	3	—	—	—	—	—	—	—	—
CLAA (5-inch guns)	6	1	1	—	—	—	—	—	—	—	—	—
Frigates[6]												
DL	—	—	—	5	5	5	—	—	—	—	—	—
DLG-DLGN	—	—	—	—	4	20	20	—	—	—	—	—
Destroyers[7]												
DD-DDE-DDK-DDR	372	142	246	244	211	189 + 17	122	32	43	31 + 1	31	31
DDG	—	—	—	—	1	33	37	38	37	37	22	17
Escort Ships/Frigates												
DE-DER/FF-FFR[8]	365	11	89	64	41	39 + 21	41	58	59	53 + 6	36 + 12	—
DEG/FFG	—	—	—	—	—	—	6	6	13	47 + 4	35 + 16	15 + 14
Flagships/Command Ships												
AGC-CC-CLC-LCC-AGF	18[9]	6	226[10]	175[10]	113[10]	7	3	3	3	4	4	4
Amphibious Ships	~3,300	83				132	95	62	58 + 5	58 + 2	59 + 3	37 + 2

1. End of Korean War (June 1953).
2. Beginning in 1983, SSNs were armed with Tomahawk anti-ship and land-attack cruise missiles (TASM and TLAM, respectively).
3. Includes transport submarines.
4. The NRF carrier is the John F. Kennedy (CV 67), manned primarily by active-duty personnel.
5. The 1945 force included two large cruisers (designated CB); they were often referred to as battle cruisers (armed with 12-inch guns).
6. Frigates (DL-DLG-DLGN) were reclassified as CG-CGN-DDG in 1975.
7. Additional destroyer-type ships were employed as mine warfare ships (DM-DMS-MMD) until 1958; they retained most of their guns and some ASW weapons.
8. Includes one AGDE-AGFF from 1966 until classified as an FF in 1975.
9. In addition, six large Coast Guard cutters were configured as amphibious force flagships.
10. Includes amphibious force flagships (AGC).

APPENDIX B

Navy Shipbuilding Programs Fiscal 1947–1996

This appendix lists U.S. Navy shipbuilding programs since World War II. Only those ships actually constructed are listed, except where noted; ships transferred to other navies upon completion are not included.

The SCB (Ships Characteristics Board) numbers are sequential for Navy ship designs reaching the advanced planning stage; numbered in a single series from 1947 (SCB No. 1 was the NORFOLK/CLK 1, later DL 1) through 1964 (SCB No. 252 was the FLAGSTAFF/PGH 1). From 1964 on, the SCB used numbered blocks: 001–099, cruisers; 100, carriers; 200, destroyers/frigates (DL); 300, submarines; 400, amphibious; 500, mine warfare; 600, patrol; 700, auxiliary; 800, service craft; 900, special purpose. The latter numbers have a suffix representing the fiscal year of the first ship; for example, 303.70 for the LOS ANGELES (SSN 688)—the first submarine under the new system, ordered in fiscal year 1970.

Number	Class name	SCB No.	Notes
Fiscal Year 1947			
2 SS 563, 564	TANG	2	
Fiscal Year 1948			
2 SS 565, 566	TANG	2	
1 SSK 1	K-1	35	
(1) CVA 58	UNITED STATES	6A	*construction canceled*
1 CLK 1	NORFOLK	1	completed as DL 1
(1) CLK 2	NORFOLK	1	*construction canceled*
4 DD 927–930	MITSCHER	5	completed as DL 2–5
Fiscal Year 1949			
2 SS 567, 568	TANG	2	
2 SSK 2, 3	K-1	35	
Fiscal Year 1950			
1 AGSS 569	ALBACORE	56	
1 MSO 421	AGILE	45A	
Fiscal Year 1951			
1 SST 1	MACKEREL	68	
28 MSO 422–449	AGILE	45A	
Fiscal Year 1952			
1 SSN 571	NAUTILUS	64	
2 SSR 572, 573	SALMON	84	changed to SS
1 SST 2	MACKEREL	68	
1 CVA 59	FORRESTAL	80	changed to CV/AVT 59
1 DE 1006	DEALEY	72	
1 IFS 1	CARRONADE	37	changed to LFS 1
4 LSD 28–31	THOMASTON	75	
15 LST 1156–1170	TERREBONNE PARISH	9	
20 MSO 455–474	AGILE	45A	
2 MSC 121, 122	BLUEBIRD	69	
1 AGB 4	GLACIER	11A	changed to WAGB 4
6 AO 143–148	NEOSHO	82	
Fiscal Year 1953			
1 SSG 574	GRAYBACK	161	changed to LPSS 574
1 SSN 575	SEAWOLF	64A	
1 CVA 60	FORRESTAL	80	changed to CV 60
3 DD 931–933	FORREST SHERMAN	85	
2 DE 1014, 1015	DEALEY	72	
9 MSO 488–496	AGILE	45A	
20 MSC 190–199, 201, 203–209, 289, 290	BLUEBIRD	69	

Number	Class name	SCB No.	Notes
Fiscal Year 1953 (cont.)			
2 AF 58, 59	RIGEL	97	
Fiscal Year 1954			
1 SS 576	DARTER	116	
1 CVA 61	FORRESTAL	80	changed to CV 61
3 DD 936–938	FORREST SHERMAN	85	
2 DE 1021, 1022	DEALEY	72	
2 LSD 32, 33	THOMASTON	75	
1 LST 1171	DE SOTO COUNTY	119	
1 MHC 43	BITTERN	109	
4 MSO 508–511	ACME	45A	
2 AE 21, 22	SURIBACHI	114	
Fiscal Year 1955			
1 SSG 577	GRAYBACK	161	
2 SSN 578, 579	SKATE	121	
1 CVA 62	FORRESTAL	80	changed to CV 62
5 DD 940–944	FORREST SHERMAN	85	
8 DE 1023–1030	DEALEY	72	
2 LSD 34, 35	THOMASTON	75	
6 LST 1173–1178	DE SOTO COUNTY	119	
2 T-AOG 81, 82	ALATNA	—	
Fiscal Year 1956			
3 SS 580–582	BARBEL	150	
2 SSN 583, 584	SKATE	121	
1 SSN 585	SKIPJACK	154	
1 SSRN 586	TRITON	132	changed to SS 586
1 SSGN 587	HALIBUT	137A	changed to SS 587
1 CVA 63	KITTY HAWK	127	changed to CV 63
6 DLG 6–11	COONTZ	142	changed to DDG 37–42
7 DD 945–951	FORREST SHERMAN	85	
2 DE 1033, 1034	CLAUD JONES	131	
2 AE 23, 24	SURIBACHI	114A	
Fiscal Year 1957			
5 SSN 588–592	SKIPJACK	154	
1 SSN 593	THRESHER	188	
1 CVA 64	KITTY HAWK	127A	changed to CV 64
1 CLGN 160	LONG BEACH	169	completed as CGN 9
4 DLG 12–15	COONTZ	142	changed to DDG 43–46
8 DD 952–959	CHARLES F. ADAMS	155	completed as DDG 2–9
2 DE 1035, 1036	CLAUD JONES	131	
1 AE 25	SURIBACHI	114A	
Fiscal Year 1958			
3 SSN 594–596	THRESHER[1]	188	originally ordered as SSGN 594–596 (SCB-166A)
1 SSN 597	TULLIBEE	178	
3 SSBN 598–600	GEORGE WASHINGTON	180A	
1 CVAN 65	ENTERPRISE	160	changed to CVN 65
3 DLG 16–18	LEAHY	172	changed to CG 16–18
5 DDG 10–14	ADAMS	155	
1 LPH 2	IWO JIMA	157	
Fiscal Year 1959			
2 SSBN 601, 602	GEORGE WASHINGTON	180A	
5 SSN 603–607	THRESHER	188	1 unit originally planned as SSGN (SCB-166A)
4 SSBN 608–611	ETHAN ALLEN	180	

Number	Class name	SCB No.	Notes
Fiscal Year 1959 (cont.)			
6 DLG 19–24	Leahy	172	changed to CG 19–24
1 DLGN 25	Bainbridge	189	changed to CGN 25
5 DDG 15–19	Adams	155	
1 LPD 1	Raleigh	187	
1 LPH 3	Iwo Jima	157	
Fiscal Year 1960			
4 SSN 612–615	Thresher	188	
3 DDG 20–22	Adams	155	
2 DE 1037, 1038	Bronstein	199	changed to FF 1037, 1038
1 PCH 1	High Point	202	
1 LPD 2	Raleigh	187	
1 LPH 7	Iwo Jima	157	
2 AGOR 3, 4	Conrad	185	academic ships
1 AS 31	Hunley	194	
Fiscal Year 1961			
1 SSBN 618	Ethan Allen	180	
4 SSBN 616, 617, 619, 620	Lafayette	216	
1 SSN 621	Thresher	188	
5 SSBN 622–626	Lafayette	216	FY 1961 supplemental
1 AGSS 555	Dolphin	207	
1 CVA 66	Kitty Hawk	127B	changed to CV 66
3 DLG 26–28	Belknap	212	changed to CG 26–28
2 DDG 23, 24	Adams	155	
2 DE 1040, 1041	Garcia	199A	changed to FF 1040, 1041
1 LPD 3	Raleigh	187	changed to AGF 3
1 AG 163	Glover	198	completed as AGDE 1; changed to FF 1098/ AGFF 1
1 AFS 1	Mars	208	
2 T-AGOR 5, 6	Conrad	185	academic ships
1 AOE 1	Sacramento	196	
Fiscal Year 1962			
3 SSN 637–639	Sturgeon	188A	
10 SSBN 627–636	Lafayette	216	
6 DLG 29–34	Belknap	212	changed to CG 29–34
1 DLGN 35	Truxtun	222	changed to CGN 35
3 DE 1043–1045	Garcia	199A	changed to FF 1043–1045
3 DEG 1–3	Brooke	199B	changed to FFG 1–3
3 LPD 4–6	Austin	187B	
1 LPH 9	Iwo Jima	157	
1 AFS 2	Mars	208	
1 AGEH 1	Plainview	219	
1 T-AGOR 7	Conrad	185	
1 T-AGS 25	Kellar	214	
1 AS 32	Hunley	194	
Fiscal Year 1963			
8 SSN 646–653	Sturgeon	188A	
6 SSBN 640–645	Lafayette	216	
1 CVA 67	John F. Kennedy	127C	
5 DE 1047–1051	Garcia	199A	changed to FF 1047–1051
3 DEG 4–6	Brooke	199B	changed to FFG 4–6
4 LPD 7–10	Austin	187B	
1 LPH 10	Iwo Jima	157	
1 T-AK-278	Meteor	236	changed to T-LSV/T-AKR 9
2 PGM 84, 85	Asheville	229	changed to PG 84, 85
2 AGOR 9, 10	Conrad	185	academic ships
1 T-AGS 26	Silas Bent	226	
1 AOE 2	Sacramento	196	
1 AS 33	Simon Lake	238	
Fiscal Year 1964			
5 SSN 660–664	Sturgeon	188A	
1 SSN 671	Narwhal	245	
6 SSBN 654–659	Lafayette	216	
10 DE 1052–1061	Knox	199C	changed to FF 1052–1061
3 LPD 11–13	Austin	187C	LPD 11 changed to AGF 11
2 PGM 86, 87	Asheville	229	changed to PG 86, 87
1 AD 37	Samuel Gompers	244	
1 AFS 3	Mars	208	
1 T-AGS 27	Silas Bent	226	
1 AS 34	Simon Lake	238	
Fiscal Year 1965			
6 SSN 665–670	Sturgeon	188M	
16 DE 1062–1077	Knox	200	new SCB series; changed to FF 1062–1077

Number	Class name	SCB No.	Notes
Fiscal Year 1965 (cont.)			
1 AGC 19	Blue Ridge	400	changed to LCC 19
4 AKA 113–116	Charleston	403	changed to LKA 113–116
2 LPD 14, 15	Austin	402	new SCB series
1 LPH 11	Iwo Jima	157	
1 LSD 36	Anchorage	404	new SCB series
1 LST 1179	Newport	405	new SCB series
3 PGM 88–90	Asheville	600	new SCB series; changed to PG 88–90
1 AD 38	Samuel Gompers	700	new SCB series
2 AE 26, 27	Kilauea	703	new SCB series
2 AFS 4, 5	Mars	705	new SCB series
2 T-AGOR 12, 13	Conrad	710	new SCB series
1 AGS 29	Chauvenet	723	built in Scotland
1 T-AGS 31	Kellar	709	
1 AOE 3	Sacramento	196	
2 AOR 1, 2	Wichita	707	
(1)AS 35	Simon Lake	738	*canceled*
1 AS 36	L.Y. Spear	702	
Fiscal Year 1966			
6 SSN 672–677	Sturgeon	188M	
10 DE 1078–1087	Knox	200	changed to FF 1078–1087
1 AGC 20	Mount Whitney	400	changed to LCC 20
1 LKA 117	Charleston	403	changed to LKA 117
1 LPH 12	Iwo Jima	157	
3 LSD 37–39	Anchorage	404	
8 LST 1180–1187	Newport	405	
2 PGH 1, 2	Flagstaff/Tucumcari	601	competitive prototypes
10 PGM 92–101	Asheville	600	changed to PG 92–101
2 AE 28, 29	Kilauea	703	
1 AFS 6	Mars	705	
2 AGOR 14, 15	Melville	710	academic ships
1 T-AGS 32	Chauvenet	723	built in Scotland
1 AOE 4	Sacramento	196	
2 AOR 3, 4	Wichita	707	
1 AS 37	L.Y. Spear	702	
1 ATS 1	Edenton	719	built in England
Fiscal Year 1967			
5 SSN 678–682	Sturgeon	188M	
1 CVAN 68	Nimitz	102	changed to CVN 68
1 DLGN 36	California	241	changed to CGN 36
10 DE 1088–1097	Knox	200	changed to FF 1088–1097
1 LSD 40	Anchorage	404	
11 LST 1188–1198	Newport	405	
2 AE 32, 33	Kilauea	703	
1 AFS 7	Mars	705	
1 T-AGOR 16	Hayes	726	changed to T-AG 195
2 T-AGS 33, 34	Silas Bent	725/728	
2 AOR 5, 6	Wichita	707	
1 ASR 21	Pigeon	721	
2 ATS 2, 3	Edenton	719	built in England
Fiscal Year 1968			
2 SSN 683, 684	Sturgeon	188M	
1 SSN 685	Glenard P. Lipscomb	302	new SCB series
1 DLGN 37	California	241	changed to CGN 37
(10)DE 1098–1107	Knox	200	*canceled;* No. 1098 assigned to the Glover
2 AE 34, 35	Kilauea	703	
(2)AGOR 19, 20	Melville	710	*canceled*
1 ASR 22	Pigeon	721	
Fiscal Year 1969			
2 SSN 686, 687	Sturgeon	188M	
1 LHA 1	Tarawa	410	
Fiscal Year 1970			
3 SSN 688–690	Los Angeles	303	
1 CVAN 69	Nimitz	102	changed to CVN 69
1 DLGN 38	Virginia	—	changed to CGN 38
3 DD 963–965	Spruance	224	
2 LHA 2, 3	Tarawa	410	
Fiscal Year 1971			
4 SSN 691–694	Los Angeles	303	
1 DLGN 39	Virginia	—	changed to CGN 39
6 DD 966–971	Spruance	224	
2 LHA 4, 5	Tarawa	410	
2 AGOR 21, 22	Gyre	734	academic ships

Number	Class name	SCB No.	Notes
Fiscal Year 1972			
5 SSN 695–699	Los Angeles	303	
1 DLGN 40	Virginia	—	changed to CGN 40
7 DD 972–978	Spruance	224	
1 AOR 7	Wichita	707	
1 AS 39	Emory S. Land	737	
Fiscal Year 1973			
6 SSN 700–705	Los Angeles	303	
1 PF 109	Oliver Hazard Perry	261	changed to FFG 7
1 PHM 1	Pegasus	602	
(1)PHM 2	Pegasus	602	*canceled;* reauthorized in FY 1976
1 AS 40	Emory S. Land	737	
Fiscal Year 1974			
5 SSN 706–710	Los Angeles	303	
1 SSBN 726	Ohio	304	
1 CVN 70	Nimitz	102	
7 DD 979–985	Spruance	224	
Fiscal Year 1975			
3 SSN 711–713	Los Angeles	303	
2 SSBN 727, 728	Ohio	304	
1 CGN 41	Virginia	—	
7 DD 986–992	Spruance	224	
3 FFG 8–10	Perry	261	
4 PHM 3–6	Pegasus	602	
1 AD 41	Samuel Gompers	700	
Fiscal Year 1976			
2 SSN 714, 715	Los Angeles	303	
1 SSBN 729	Ohio	304	
6 FFG 11–16	Perry	226	
1 PHM 2	Pegasus	602	
1 AD 42	Samuel Gompers	700	
2 AO 177, 178	Cimarron	739	
4 T-ATF 166–169	Powhatan	744	
Fiscal Year 1977			
3 SSN 716–718	Los Angeles	303	
1 SSBN 730	Ohio	304	
8 FFG 19–26	Perry	261	
1 AD 43	Samuel Gompers	700	
1 AO 179	Cimarron	739	
1 AS 41	McKee	737	
Fiscal Year 1978			
1 SSN 719	Los Angeles	303	
2 SSBN 731, 732	Ohio	304	
1 DDG 47	Ticonderoga	226	changed to CG 47
1 DD 997	Spruance[2]	224	
8 FFG 27–34	Perry	261	
2 AO 180, 186	Cimarron	739	
3 T-ATF 170–172	Powhatan	744	
Fiscal Year 1979			
1 SSN 720	Los Angeles	303	
4 DDG 993–996	Kidd[3]	—	
8 FFG 36–43	Perry	261	
1 AD 44	Samuel Gompers	700	
2 T-AGOS 1, 2	Stalwart	—	
1 T-ARC 7	Zeus	—	
Fiscal Year 1980			
2 SSN 721, 722	Los Angeles	303	
1 SSBN 733	Ohio	304	
1 CVN 71	Nimitz	102	
1 CG 48	Ticonderoga	226	
5 FFG 45–49	Perry	261	
1 T-AGOS 3	Stalwart	—	
Fiscal Year 1981			
2 SSN 723, 724	Los Angeles	303	
1 SSBN 734	Ohio	304	
2 CG 49, 50	Ticonderoga	226	
6 FFG 50–55	Perry	261	
1 LSD 41	Whidbey Island	—	
1 ARS 50	Safeguard	—	
5 T-AGOS 4–8	Stalwart	—	
Fiscal Year 1982			
2 SSN 725, 750	Los Angeles	303	
3 CG 51–53	Ticonderoga	226	
3 FFG 56–58	Perry	261	
1 LSD 42	Whidbey Island	—	

Number	Class name	SCB No.	Notes
Fiscal Year 1982 (cont.)			
1 MCM 1	Avenger	—	
4 T-AGOS 9–12	Stalwart	—	
1 T-AO 187	Henry J. Kaiser	—	
2 ARS 51, 52	Safeguard	—	
Fiscal Year 1983			
1 SSBN 735	Ohio	304	
2 SSN 751, 752	Los Angeles	303	improved design
2 CVN 72, 73	Nimitz	102	
3 CG 54–56	Ticonderoga	226	
2 FFG 59, 60	Perry	261	
1 LSD 43	Whidbey Island	—	
1 MCM 2	Avenger	—	
1 T-AO 188	Henry J. Kaiser	—	
1 ARS 53	Safeguard	—	
Fiscal Year 1984			
1 SSBN 736	Ohio	304	
3 SSN 753–755	Los Angeles	303	improved design
3 CG 57–59	Ticonderoga	226	
1 FFG 61	Perry	261	
1 LHD 1	Wasp	—	
1 LSD 44	Whidbey Island	—	
(1)SWCM 1	(Sea Viking class)	—	*canceled*
3 MCM 3–5	Avenger	—	
(1)MSH 1	Cardinal	—	*canceled*
2 T-AO 189, 190	Henry J. Kaiser	—	
Fiscal Year 1985			
1 SSBN 737	Ohio	304	
4 SSN 756–759	Los Angeles	303	improved design
3 CG 60–62	Ticonderoga	226	
1 DDG 51	Arleigh Burke	—	
2 LSD 45, 46	Whidbey Island	—	
4 MCM 6–9	Avenger	—	
2 T-AGOS 13, 14	Stalwart	—	
2 T-AGS 39, 40	Maury	—	
3 T-AO 191–193	Henry J. Kaiser	—	
Fiscal Year 1986			
1 SSBN 738	Ohio	304	
4 SSN 760–763	Los Angeles	303	improved design
3 CG 63–65	Ticonderoga	226	
1 LHD 2	Wasp	—	
2 LSD 47, 48	Whidbey Island	—	
2 MCM 10, 11	Avenger	—	
1 MHC 51	Osprey	—	
2 T-AGOS 15, 16	Stalwart	—	
2 T-AO 194, 195	Henry J. Kaiser	—	
Fiscal Year 1987			
1 SSBN 739	Ohio	304	
4 SSN 764–767	Los Angeles	303	improved design
3 CG 66–68	Ticonderoga	226	
2 DDG 52, 53	Arleigh Burke	—	
(1)SWCM 1	(Sea Viking class)	—	*canceled*[4]
1 AOE 6	Supply	—	
1 AGOR 23	Thomas G. Washington	—	academic ship
2 T-AGOS 17, 18	Stalwart	—	
1 T-AGOS 19	Victorious	—	
2 T-AO 196, 197	Henry J. Kaiser	—	
Fiscal Year 1988			
1 SSBN 740	Ohio	304	
3 SSN 768–770	Los Angeles	303	improved design
2 CVN 74, 75	Nimitz	102	
5 CG 69–73	Ticonderoga	226	
1 LHD 3	Wasp	—	
1 LSD 49	Harpers Ferry	—	
3 MCM 12–14	Avenger	—	
2 T-AO 198, 199	Henry J. Kaiser	—	
Fiscal Year 1989			
1 SSBN 741	Ohio	304	
1 SSN 21	Seawolf	—	
2 SSN 771, 772	Los Angeles	303	improved design
5 DDG 54–58	Arleigh Burke	—	
1 LHD 4	Wasp	—	
2 MHC 52, 53	Osprey	—	
3 T-AGOS 20–22	Victorious	—	
5 T-AO 200–204	Henry J. Kaiser	—	
1 AOE 7	Supply	—	

Number	Class name	SCB No.	Notes
Fiscal Year 1990			
1 SSBN 742	OHIO	304	
1 SSN 773	LOS ANGELES	303	improved design
5 DDG 59–63	ARLEIGH BURKE	—	
1 LSD 50	HARPERS FERRY	—	
8 PC 1–8	CYCLONE	—	
2 MHC 54, 55	OSPREY	—	
3 AGOR 24–26	THOMAS G. WASHINGTON	—	2 academic ships
1 T-AGOS 23	IMPECCABLE	—	
3 T-AGS 60–62	PATHFINDER	—	
1 AOE 8	SUPPLY	—	
Fiscal Year 1991			
1 SSBN 743	OHIO	304	last ship authorized in basic SCN series
1 SSN 22	SEAWOLF	—	
4 DDG 64–67	ARLEIGH BURKE	—	
1 LHD 5	WASP	—	
1 LSD 51	HARPERS FERRY	—	
5 PC 9–13	CYCLONE	—	
2 MHC 56, 57	OSPREY	—	
Fiscal Year 1992			
(1)SSN 23	SEAWOLF	—	*canceled* in January 1992; reauthorized as a FY 1996 ship
5 DDG 68–72	ARLEIGH BURKE	—	
3 MHC 58–60	OSPREY	—	
(1)AOE 9	SUPPLY	—	*canceled;* reauthorized as a FY 1993 ship
Fiscal Year 1993			
4 DDG 73–76	ARLEIGH BURKE	—	
1 LHD 6	WASP	—	
Fiscal Year 1993 (cont.)			
1 LSD 52	HARPERS FERRY	—	
2 MHC 61, 62	OSPREY	—	
1 AGOR 24	THOMAS G. WASHINGTON	—	
1 AOE 10	SUPPLY	—	
1 WAGB 12	HENLEY	—	for Coast Guard operation
Fiscal Year 1994			
1 DDG 79	Improved ARLEIGH BURKE	—	
2 DDG 77, 78	ARLEIGH BURKE	—	
1 AGOR 25	THOMAS G. WASHINGTON	—	
1 T-AGS 63	PATHFINDER	—	
Fiscal Year 1995			
1 CVN 76	NIMITZ	—	
3 DDG 80–82	Improved ARLEIGH BURKE	—	
Fiscal Year 1996			
1 SSN 23	SEAWOLF	—	
2 DDG 83, 84	Improved ARLEIGH BURKE	—	
1 LHD 7	WASP	—	
LPD 17		—	

1. Class renamed for PERMIT (SSN 594) after loss of the USS THRESHER in April 1963.
2. Congress authorized two improved SPRUANCE-class destroyers with enhanced aviation capabilities; in the event, the Navy built only one ship, to a standard SPRUANCE configuration.
3. Taken over while under construction for Iran.
4. The SWCM/Sea Viking program was restructured in 1987 and the lead ship reordered that same year. No ships of this design were completed.

The supercarrier CARL VINSON (CVN 70) refuels from the oiler PECOS (T-AO 197) during an underway replenishment in the Persian Gulf. Another warship steams astern, waiting to hook up to the PECOS's fuel hoses. (U.S. Navy, PH3 David C. Lloyd)

APPENDIX C

Foreign Ship Transfers, 1990–1996

With the end of the Cold War and the availability of large numbers of destroyers and frigates for transfer, some before the end of their nominal 30-year service life, the U.S. Navy is transferring a large number of these ships to foreign navies. Among the new customers for these types of ships from the U.S. Navy are Thailand, Egypt, and several Persian Gulf states; more traditional buyers of U.S. warships, who are restocking their fleets, are Greece, Taiwan, and Turkey. Also, the extremely useful landing ships of the NEWPORT (LST 1179) class are available for transfer and, as indicated below, are highly coveted by other navies.

In addition to ships transferred for service are several ships being transferred for spare parts (i.e., "hangar queens"). The large numbers of ships being scrapped by the U.S. Navy make replacement parts and spares readily available for ships being transferred for service.

The transfer of three guided missile frigates of the OLIVER HAZARD PERRY (FFG 7) class to Turkey was placed on "hold" in the summer of 1996.

Number	Name	Recipient	Transfer date
Destroyers			
DDG 15	BERKELEY	Greece	30 Sep 1992
DDG 16	JOSEPH STRAUSS	Greece	1 Oct 1991
DDG 18	SEMMES	Greece	12 Sep 1991
DDG 20	GOLDSBOROUGH	Australia[1]	17 Sep 1993
DDG 23	RICHARD BYRD	Greece[1]	1 Oct 1991
DDG 24	WADDELL	Greece	1 Oct 1992
Frigates			
FFG 10	DUNCAN	Egypt	1996–1997
FFG 16	CLIFTON SPRAGUE	Turkey	1996 (?)
FFG 20	ANTRIM	Turkey	1996 (?)
FFG 21	FLATLEY	Turkey	1996 (?)
FFG 24	JACK WILLIAMS	Bahrain	1996
FFG 25	COPELAND	Egypt	1996
FFG 27	MAHLON S. TISDALE	Oman	1996
FF 1037	BRONSTEIN	Mexico	1 Oct 1993
FF 1038	MCCLOY	Mexico	1 Oct 1993
FF 1056	CONNOLE	Greece	30 Aug 1992
FF 1063	REASONER	Turkey	28 Aug 1993
FF 1068	VREELAND	Greece	25 July 1992
FF 1073	ROBERT E. PEARY	Taiwan	7 Aug 1992
FF 1075	TRIPPE	Greece	30 July 1992
FF 1076	FANNING	Turkey	31 July 1992
FF 1077	OUELLET	Thailand	19 Aug 1994
FFT 1078	JOSEPH HEWES	Taiwan	30 June 1994
FFT 1079	BOWEN	Turkey	3 June 1994
FF 1082	ELMER MONTGOMERY	Turkey[1]	13 Dec 1993
FF 1083	COOK	Taiwan	31 May 1994
FFT 1084	MCCANDLESS	Turkey	6 May 1994
FFT 1085	DONALD B. BEARY	Turkey	20 May 1994
FF 1086	BREWTON	Taiwan	23 July 1992
FF 1087	KIRK	Taiwan	6 Aug 1993
FF 1088	BARBEY	Taiwan	21 June 1994
FF 1089	JESSE L. BROWN	Egypt	27 July 1994
FFT 1090	AINSWORTH	Turkey	27 May 1994
FF 1092	THOMAS C. HART	Turkey	30 Aug 1993
FF 1093	CAPODANNO	Turkey	30 July 1993
FFT 1095	TRUETT	Thailand	30 July 1994
FFT 1097	MOINESTER	Egypt	28 July 1994
Amphibious Ships			
LSD 33	ALAMO	Brazil	20 Nov 1990[2]
LST 1180	MANITOWOC	Taiwan	14 July 1995
LST 1181	SUMTER	Taiwan	14 July 1995
LST 1183	PEORIA	Venezuela	Jan 1996
LST 1186	CAYUGA	Brazil	26 Aug 1994
LST 1188	SAGINAW	Australia	24 Aug 1994
LST 1189	SAN BERNARDINO	Chile	30 Sep 1995
LST 1192	SPARTANBURG COUNTY	Malaysia	16 Dec 1994
LST 1193	FAIRFAX COUNTY	Australia	27 Sep 1994
LST 1196	HARLAN COUNTY	Spain	14 Apr 1995
LST 1197	BARNSTABLE COUNTY	Spain	26 Aug 1994
LST 1198	BRISTOL COUNTY	Morocco	16 Aug 1994
Mine Countermeasures Ships and Craft			
MSO 455	IMPLICIT	Taiwan	30 Sep 1994
MSO 488	CONQUEST	Taiwan	3 Aug 1994
MSO 489	GALLANT	Taiwan	3 Aug 1994
MSO 492	PLEDGE	Taiwan	3 Aug 1994
CT-3	(unnamed; also 103WB831)	Panama	22 July 1992
MSB 25, 28, 29, 41		Panama	3 Mar 1993
Auxiliary Ships			
AG 192	S.P. LEE (ex-AGS 31)	Mexico	7 Dec 1992
AGOR 10	THOMAS WASHINGTON	Chile	28 Sep 1992
T-AGOR 12	DE STEIGUER	Tunisia	2 Nov 1992
T-AGOR 13	BARTLETT	Morocco	26 July 1993
ATF 88	NARRAGANSETT	Taiwan[1]	30 Oct 1990[3]
ATF 113	TAKELMA	Argentina	30 Sep 1993
ATF 118	WENATCHEE	Taiwan	30 Oct 1990[3]
ATF 148	ACHOMAWI	Taiwan	30 Oct 1990[3]
Service Craft			
YTM 776	HIAMONEE	Philippines	30 June 1990
YFU 97	(unnamed)	Bahamas	19 June 1991
105UB821	ERLINE	Panama	July 1992
Floating Dry Docks			
AFDL 40	(unnamed)	Philippines	30 June 1990
Coast Guard Cutters			
WMEC 300	CITRUS	Dominican Republic	16 Sep 1995
WPB 82302	POINT HOPE	Costa Rica	3 May 1991
WPB 82311	POINT VERDE	Mexico	19 July 1991
WPB 82318	POINT HERRON	Mexico	26 July 1991
WPB 82345	POINT JUDITH	Venezuela	15 Jan 1992
WPB 82348	POINT BARROW	Panama	7 June 1991
WPB 82367	POINT KNOLL	Venezuela	18 Oct 1991[2]
WPB 95302	CAPE HIGGON	Uruguay[2]	25 Jan 1990
WPB 95305	CAPE HATTERAS	Mexico	Mar 1991
WPB 95306	CAPE GEORGE	Micronesia	30 Mar 1990
WPB 95309	CAPE CARTER	Mexico	Feb 1990[2]
WPB 95311	CAPE HEDGE	Mexico	Jan 1990
WPB 95318	CAPE HERRON	Mexico	June 1991
WPB 95321	CAPE CROSS	Micronesia	30 Mar 1990
WPB 95322	CAPE HORN	Uruguay	25 Jan 1990
WPB 95326	CAPE CORWIN	Micronesia	30 Mar 1990

1. Transferred for spare parts.
2. Correction to previous edition.
3. All three ATFs were delivered to Taiwan on 30 June 1991.

APPENDIX D

Navy and Coast Guard Ships Preserved as Memorials and Museums

These ships are arranged alphabetically by name.

The NS SAVANNAH, the world's first nuclear-propelled merchant ship, was located at Patriot's Point, Charleston, South Carolina, until being towed away in 1995, having failed to attract a significant number of visitors.

(The world's first civilian nuclear ship, the SAVANNAH was launched in 1959 and went to sea in 1962 to demonstrate peaceful uses for nuclear power. She was retired from active service in 1971.)

Efforts were under way when this edition of *Ships and Aircraft* went to press to preserve some or all of the four battleships of the IOWA (BB 61) class. The MISSOURI (BB 63) is the most likely to be preserved, probably at San Francisco or Pearl Harbor.

When this edition went to press, the Soviet-built, former German missile corvette HIDDENSEE was to be transferred to the Sea-Air-Space Museum (see chapter 21). After the German U-505, she is believed to be the first foreign navy ship to go on permanent display in the United States. (Several ex-German, Italian, and Japanese mini-subs and manned torpedoes are on exhibition in the United States.)

Number	Name	Completed	Location
BB 60	Alabama	1942	Battleship Memorial Park, Mobile, Ala.
AGSS 569	Albacore	1953	Portsmouth Naval Shipyard, Maine
BB 39	Arizona	1916	Sunken remains and memorial off Ford Island, Pearl Harbor, Hawaii
DD 933	Barry	1956	Navy Yard, Washington, D.C.
SS 310	Batfish	1943	Muskogee War Memorial, Okla.
SS 319	Becuna	1944	Cruiser Olympia Association, Philadelphia, Penna.
SS 581	Blueback	1959	Oregon Museum of Science and Industry, Portland, Ore.
SS 287	Bowfin	1943	Submarine Memorial Park, Honolulu, Hawaii
CVL 28	Cabot	1943	Cabot/Dedalo Museum, New Orleans, La.
	Cairo[1]	1862	Vicksburg National Park, Miss.
DD 793	Cassin Young	1943	Boston Historical National Park, Mass.
SS 244	Cavalla	1944	U.S. Submarine Veterans, Galveston, Texas
	Chattahoochee[2]	1862	Confederate Naval Museum, Columbus, Ga.
SS 343	Clamagore	1945	Patriots Point, Charleston, S.C.
WAL 538	Chesapeake[3]	1930	Baltimore Maritime Museum, Md.
SS 245	Cobia	1944	Manitowoc Maritime Museum, Wisc.
SS 224	Cod	1943	Cleveland, Ohio
WATA 202	Comanche	1934	Patriots Point, Charleston, S.C.
IX 20	Constellation[4]	1855	Constellation Dock, Baltimore, Md.
IX 21	Constitution[5]	1798	Boston National Historical Park, Mass.
SS 246	Croaker	1944	Buffalo Naval and Servicemen's Park, N.Y.
PG 88	Crockett	1967	Great Lakes Naval and Maritime Museum, Muskegon, Mich.
SS 228	Drum	1941	Battleship Memorial Park, Mobile, Ala.
DD 946	Edson	1958	Sea-Air-Space Museum, New York, N.Y.
WLM 212	Fir	1940	Seattle, Wash.
SSG 577	Growler	1958	Sea-Air-Space Museum, New York, N.Y.
LPH 7	Guadalcanal	1961	Sea-Air-Space Museum, New York, N.Y.
AM 240	Hazard	1944	Freedom Park, Omaha, Neb.
AM 242	Inaugural	1944	Gateway Arch, St. Louis, Mo.
WPG 35	Ingham	1936	Patriots Point, Charleston, S.C.
CVS 11	Intrepid	1943	Sea-Air-Space Museum, New York, N.Y.
	Intelligent Whale[6]	1863	Navy Museum, Navy Yard, Washington, D.C.
	Jackson[7]	1864	Confederate Naval Museum, Columbus, Ga.
DD 850	Joseph P. Kennedy, Jr.	1945	Battleship Cove, Fall River, Mass.
DD 661	Kidd	1943	Louisiana War Memorial, Baton Rouge, La.
DD 724	Laffey	1944	Patriots Point, Charleston, S.C.
AVT 16	Lexington (ex-CV 16)	1943	Corpus Christi, Texas
SS 297	Ling	1945	Submarine Memorial, Hackensack, N.J.
SS 298	Lionfish	1944	Battleship Cove, Fall River, Mass.
CLG 4	Little Rock (ex-CL 92)	1945	Buffalo Naval and Servicemen's Park, N.Y.
WMEC 416	McLane	1927	Great Lakes Naval and Maritime Museum, Muskegon, Mich.
SST 2	Marlin	1953	Freedom Park, Omaha, Neb.
BB 59	Massachusetts	1942	Battleship Cove, Fall River, Mass.
WPG 78	Mohawk	1934	City piers, Wilmington, Del.
	MSB 5	—	Pate Museum of Transportation, Fort Worth, Texas
WAL 534	Nantucket	1936	Sea-Air-Space Museum, New York, N.Y.
SSN 571	Nautilus	1954	Naval Submarine Base, Groton, Conn.
	Neuse[7]	1864	Caswell-Neuse State Historic Site, Kingston, N.C.
	Niagara[8]	1813	Erie, Penna.
BB 55	North Carolina	1941	North Carolina Battleship Memorial, Wilmington, N.C.
CA 15	Olympia	1895	Cruiser Olympia Association, Philadelphia, Penna.
SS 383	Pamanito	1943	Fisherman's Wharf, San Francisco, Calif.
	PCF 1	1965	Navy Museum, Navy Yard, Washington, D.C.
	Philadelphia[9]	1776	Smithsonian Institution, Washington, D.C.
	Pioneer[10]	1862	Cabot/Dedalo Museum, New Orleans, La.
	PT 309	1944	LaPorte, Texas
	PT 617	1945	Battleship Cove, Fall River, Mass.
	PT 796	1945	Battleship Cove, Fall River, Mass.

Number	Name	Completed	Location
SS 383	PTF 17	1968	Buffalo Naval and Servicemen's Park, N.Y.
WAL 605	RELIEF[3]	1950	Oakland, Calif.
SSR 481	REQUIN	1945	Carnegie Science Center, Pittsburgh, Penna.
CA 139	SALEM	1949	Naval Shipbuilding Museum, Quincy, Mass.
SS 573	SALMON	1956	Naval Shipbuilding Museum, Quincy, Mass.
SS 236	SILVERSIDES	1941	Great Lakes Naval and Maritime Museum, Muskegon, Mich.
DE 766	SLATER	1944	Sea-Air-Space Museum, New York, N.Y.
ARL 24	SPHINX (ex-LST 963)	1944	Rio Grande Military Museum, Mission, Texas
DE 238	STEWART	1943	SEAWOLF Park, Galveston, Texas
WMEC 166	TAMAROA (ex-ATF 95)	1943	Sea-Air-Space Museum, New York, N.Y.
WPG 37	TANEY	1936	Baltimore Maritime Museum, Md.
BB 35	TEXAS	1914	Battleship TEXAS State Historical Park, Laporte, Texas
DD 537	THE SULLIVANS	1943	Buffalo Naval and Servicemen's Park, N.Y.
SS 423	TORSK	1944	Baltimore Maritime Museum, Md.
	TRIESTE I[11]	1953	Navy Museum, Navy Yard, Washington, D.C.
DSV 1	TRIESTE II[11]	1971	Naval Undersea Museum, Keyport, Wash.
DD 951	TURNER JOY	1959	Puget Sound Naval Shipyard, Bremerton, Wash.
	U-505[12]	1941	Museum of Science and Industry, Chicago, Ill.
AG 16	UTAH (ex-BB 31)	1911	Sunken remains off Ford Island, Pearl Harbor, Hawaii
	X-1[13]	1955	Naval Academy, Annapolis, Md.
CV 10	YORKTOWN	1943	Patriots Point, Charleston, S.C.

1. Union Navy ironclad, paddewheel gunboat.
2. Confederate Navy gunboat.
3. Lightship.
4. Not the original ship built in 1797, but a ship constructed at the Gosport (Norfolk) Navy Yard (Va.) in 1853 (see chapter 25).
5. Remains in full commission as a Navy ship.
6. Submersible.
7. Confederate Navy ironclad ram.
8. American brig from Battle of Lake Erie.
9. Gondola gunboat built on Lake Champlain during the American Revolution.
10. Confederate Navy submersible.
11. Bathyscaph.
12. Former German submarine captured at sea during World War II.
13. Midget submarine.

The aircraft carrier YORKTOWN of the ESSEX (CV 9) class, the destroyer LAFFEY of the ALLEN M. SUMNER (DD 692) class, and the nuclear merchant ship SAVANNAH at Patriots Point. The SAVANNAH has since been removed, having attracted too few visitors. The submarine CLAMAGORE, a GUPPY III conversion of the BALAO (SS 285) class, is moored inboard of the LAFFEY. (Patriots Point Development Authority)

General Index

Note: An asterisk indicates additional comments are provided in the addenda to this edition. A percent sign indicates additional illustrations are provided in the addenda.

Ship Name and Class Index

Notes: In the following entries the T- prefix indicating a ship's assignment to the Military Sea Transportation Service/Military Sealift Command has been deleted, in part because many ships have served as both active Navy and MSTS/MSC units.

An asterisk indicates additional comments are provided in the addenda to this edition. A percent sign indicates additional illustrations are provided in the addenda.

Addenda

Two views of the USS Seawolf (SSN 21) on sea trials in July 1996. (General Dynamics/Electric Boat)

STATE OF THE FLEET

In response to Iraqi incursions into the Kurdish area of northern Iraq, on 3 September 1996 two U.S. warships in the Persian Gulf joined a flight of two B-52H strategic bombers flying from Guam to strike targets in the Baghdad area. The missile cruiser Shiloh (CG 67) and missile destroyer Laboon (DDG 58) fired six and eight Tomahawk TLAM missiles, respectively; the B-52s launched 13 CALCM cruise missiles, all fitted with conventional warheads.[1]

Rear Admiral Edward Moore, Jr., Commander, Cruiser-Destroyer Group 3, said: "The strikes were ordered as a warning to Iraq to adhere to requirements outlined in United Nations resolutions." The Shiloh and Laboon were part of the Carl Vinson (CVN 70) battle group. The two B-52s were escorted by F-14 Tomcat fighters from the Vinson, with three relays—each with four fighters—covering the bombers' arrival and departure from their launch points.

Another Tomahawk strike followed on 4 September, with 17 additional missiles being fired from four U.S. warships:

Jefferson City (SSN 759)	2 missiles
Hewitt (DD 966)	2 missiles
Laboon	5 missiles
Russell (DDG 59)	8 missiles

Again, all of the ships were operating in the Persian Gulf. A Pentagon spokesman said that President Clinton authorized the strikes to suppress air defenses over southern Iraq and to provide greater safety for U.S. and allied pilots who police the expanded no-fly zone over Iraq.

No Air Force aircraft participated in the second missile strike.

"Mating" the island structure of the Harry S. Truman (CVN 75) with the carrier's hull on 11 July 1996. (Newport News Shipbuilding, Mike Dillard)

SUBMARINES

SSN 21	Seawolf	commission	11 Nov 1996
SSN 773	Cheyenne	launch	13 Sep 1996

Submarines in stand-down status during deactivation, in preparation for decommissioning and strike (ICIR = In Commission, In Reserve):

SSN 639	Tautog	ICIR	1 Nov 1996
SSN 649	Sunfish	ICIR	1 Oct 1996
SSN 668	Spadefish	ICIR	30 Sep 1996
SSN 670	Finback	ICIR	1 Oct 1996
SSN 694	Groton	ICIR	19 Sep 1996

(Note: "Decommissioning" ceremonies are usually held before the official ICIR date.)

AIRCRAFT CARRIERS

The John F. Kennedy (CV 67)—in a training/Naval Reserve Force status—is expected to continue to forward deploy. The ship is tentatively scheduled to deploy from April to October 1997. At that time the ship will have some 300 TAR (Training and Administration of Reserves) personnel on board; after the deployment, approximately 300 selected reservists will also be assigned to the ship, providing a reserve complement of about 20 percent of the ship's total personnel.

ARSENAL SHIPS

The Advanced Research Projects Agency (ARPA) has selected five industry teams to begin Phase I of the joint Navy/ARPA arsenal ship program. Each team is being awarded $1 million as part of the $520 million development effort.

During the six-month Phase I program, which began in July 1996, the five industry teams will perform tradeoff studies and will undertake the initial arsenal ship design concept. After the designs are evaluated, two of the teams will be selected for Phase II of the effort to further develop their designs. Phase II will last one year.

One team will be selected for Phase III, to complete detail design of the ship and undertake construction of an arsenal ship "demonstrator," with an option to construct five additional ships (Phase V). Phase IV is performance testing and fleet evaluation. The demonstrator ship is expected to be subsequently upgraded to a full combat capability.

The five teams are (team leaders are in italic type):

- *General Dynamics/Marine, Bath Iron Works,* GD/Electric Boat Raytheon Electronic Systems, and Science Applications International Corporation.
- *Hughes Aircraft Corporation,* Avondale Shipyards, Advanced Marine Enterprises, Booze-Allen & Hamilton, and McDonnell Douglas.
- *Lockheed Martin Government Electronic Systems,* Litton Industries/Ingalls Shipbuilding, and Newport News Shipbuilding.
- *Metro Machine Corporation,* Rockwell International/Collins International, Trinity Marine Group, Composite Ships, and Marinex International.
- *Northrop Grumman Corporation,* National Steel and Shipbuilding, Vitro Corporation, Solipsys, and Band Lavis & Associates.

BATTLESHIPS

The issue of retaining and possibly reactivating the two surviving battleships of the Iowa class–the New Jersey (BB 62) and Wisconsin (BB 64)—continues in the press and, to a lesser degree, in Congress. The advocates of reactivating the battleships appear to be supporters of the U.S. Air Force, who see the dreadnoughts as a means of halting or delaying development of the arsenal ship (which they feel is a threat to manned "strategic" bombers), and "battleship whiners," those who feel the grandeur of the battleship somehow equates to military effectiveness for the 21st century.

Congress has provided $400 million in the fiscal 1997 budget to retain the New Jersey and Wisconsin in mothballs, that is, mobilization category B. Available data indicate that beyond the cost of reactivating the battleships are expenses involving the manufacture of certain components, as all spares were used up in their reactivation during the Reagan-Lehman naval buildup of the 1980s. Navy leaders are also reluctant to use the existing powder supplies in light of the explosion on the battleship Iowa in 1989 that killed 47 men. Restarting powder production will cost tens of millions of dollars.

1. CALCM = Conventional Air-Launched Cruise Missile.

But the most significant factors remain (1) the limited capabilities of the battleships and (2) the large manning requirements—nearly 1,600 officers and enlisted personnel per ship (compared to 390 for a TICONDEROGA-class cruiser and 360 for an ARLEIGH BURKE-class destroyer).

In August 1996 Secretary of the Navy Dalton announced that the MISSOURI would be moored as a permanent memorial-museum at Pearl Harbor. The alternative sites, either San Francisco or San Diego, would have provided a more suitable location for visits by the American population. (The remains of the battleships ARIZONA [BB 39] and UTAH [AG 16, ex-BB 31] are already at Pearl Harbor.)

CRUISERS

CGN 35	BAINBRIDGE	decomm./stricken 30 Sep 1996
CGN 40	MISSISSIPPI	decomm./stricken 6 Sep 1996

DESTROYERS

DDG 66	GONZALEZ	commission 12 Oct 1996
DDG 69	MILIUS	commission 26 Oct 1996
DDG 73	DECATUR	commission Nov 1996

FRIGATES

FFG 25	COPELAND	decommissioned 18 Sep 1996
FFG 26	GALLERY	decommissioned 30 Sep 1996
FFG 27	TISDALE	decommissioned 30 Sep 1996

AMPHIBIOUS SHIPS

LPD 17		named SAN ANTONIO
T-LKA 115	MOBILE	to MSC-ROS 1 Oct 1996

A sad ending: The hulk of the nuclear-propelled, guided missile cruiser LONG BEACH (CGN 9) is towed to the breakers—backwards. Her masts, superstructure, missile systems, guns, and reactor have already been stripped away. (Newport News Shipbuilding, Jim Hemeon)

The INCHON (MCS 12) during work up off Norfolk, Virginia, following her conversion to a mine countermeasures support ship—and her incorrect reclassification as MCS 12 instead of MCS 8. (Litton/Ingalls Shipbuilding)

MINE COUNTERMEASURES SHIPS

MHC 56	Kingfisher	commission 26 Oct 1996
MHC 61	Raven	launch 28 Sep 1996

AUXILIARY SHIPS

AD 44	Shenandoah	decommissioned 13 Sep 1996
AE 34	Mount Baker	to MSC Dec 1996
AOE 10	Bridge	launch 24 Aug 1996
AOR 6	Kalamazoo	decommissioned 16 Aug 1996
AS 32	Holland	decommissioned 30 Sep 1996
AS 36	L.Y. Spear	decommissioned 6 Sep 1996

The Navy's three British-built salvage and rescue ships have been decommissioned: the Edenton (ATS 1) on 29 March 1996, and the Beaufort (ATS 2) and Brunswick (ATS 3) on 8 March 1996. Plans to operate them with civilian crews under the aegis of the Military Sealift Command were dropped; the ships will be discarded.

SEALIFT SHIPS

T-AKR 297	Yano	MSC in service 30 Nov 1996
T-AKR 298	Soderman	MSC in service 20 Dec 1996

NAVAL AVIATION

ATTACK SQUADRONS

VA-115	Eagles	changed to VFA-115 on 30 Sep 1996

As VFA-115, the squadron entered cadre status; it is scheduled to be reactivated on 1 October 1998, flying the F/A-18E Hornet and shifting its base to NAS Lemoore, California.

VA-165	Boomers	disestablished 30 Sep 1996

FIGHTER SQUADRONS

VF-24	Fighting Renegades	disestablished 31 Aug 1996

PATROL SQUADRONS

The decommissioning of Patrol Squadron (VP) 11 at NAS Brunswick, Maine, has been delayed by congressional legislation as part of the fiscal 1997 defense authorization bill. (VP-11's squadron name is Pegasus.)

Reserve, VP-68, based at NAF Washington, D.C., had also been scheduled for decommissioning in 1996–1997; it, too has been named for retention in congressional legislation.

TRAINING SQUADRONS

Training Squadrons (VT) 4 and 10 took delivery of their first Air Force T-1A Jayhawk trainer at NAS Pensacola on 1 May 1996. The aircraft are part of the consolidation plan to create a joint Navy Air Force navigator/naval flight officer training program.

The ten T-1A aircraft will be "owned" and maintained by the Air Force. They will make T-39N Sabreliner aircraft available to VT-86 for advanced navigator/NFO training.

Air Force personnel are being assigned to the squadrons. The joint program has a goal of providing navigation/NFO training to 360 Air Force, 365 Navy and Marine Corps, and 105 German, Italian, and Saudi Arabian personnel every year.

(The T-1A Jayhawk is a militarized version of the Beechjet 400A corporate aircraft, powered by twin turbofan engines. The Air Force designation T-1A and the name Jayhawk violate Department of Defense guidance because T-1A was previously used by the Navy Sea Star [formerly T2V-1] and Jayhawk is currently used for the HH-60J helicopter.)

NAVAL AIRCRAFT

In preparing the fiscal year 1997 budget, the House of Representatives funded the Joint Strike Fighter (JSF) program—successor to the

An Air Force T-1A Jayhawk, of the type now being flown—with their Air Force livery—by Navy training squadrons VT-4 and VT-10. (Robert F. Dorr)

JAST. It is questionable, however, that there will be an Advanced STOVL variant of the JSF aircraft. This failure to develop a successor to the AV-8B Harrier STOVL would be a severe blow to Marine tactical aviation. It was expected that the British—the Royal Navy and possibly the Royal Air Force—would be partners in developing the ASTOVL, with several other countries possibly procuring the aircraft for operation from their VSTOL carriers.

Meanwhile, the Navy has formally rejected the proposed A/F-117X variant of the Air Force stealth attack aircraft for carrier operation. The Navy contends that the F/A-18E Hornet would have the capability of first-day-of-war strikes against defended targets.

The Navy–Marine Corps requirement for F/A-18E and F variants has been put at approximately 1,000 aircraft, replacing the F-14, F/A-18C/D, and A-6E in carrier and Marine air wings.

F-14 TOMCAT

Fighter Squadron (VF) 103 became the first F-14 unit to be equipped with the LANTIRN (Low-Altitude Navigation and Targeting Infrared for Night) targeting system, enabling the aircraft to deliver laser-guided weapons. LANTIRN was developed by the Air Force.

WEAPON SYSTEMS

JASSM (JOINT AIR-TO-SURFACE STAND-OFF MISSILE)

Plans are for tactical Navy and Air Force aircraft to use this missile. It is to have a range of 156–173 n.miles (290–320 km), flying autonomously after launch with a low-level flight profile.

McDonnell Douglas and Lockheed Martin will jointly develop the missile and compete for the final development and production contract. Initial JASSM production contracts are expected to be awarded in the year 2000 for 2,400 missiles; IOC will be in 2002.

JSOW (JOINT STAND-OFF WEAPON)

Weight:	1,065–1,500 lbs (483–651 kg); varies with warhead
Length:	13 ft 4 in (4.065 m)
Span:	8 ft 10 in (2.69 m)
Diameter:	
Propulsion:	1 William International WJ-24-8 turbojet
Range:	15–40 n.miles (28–74 km) glide flight; varies with altitude and speed of launch aircraft
	120 n.miles (200 km) powered flight
Guidance:	Global Positioning System (GPS)/inertial
Warhead:	AGN-154A 145 BLU-97A/B submunitions
	AGM-154B 6 "sticks" BLU-108/B sensor-fuzed submunitions
	AGM-154C BLU-111/B 500-lb (226.8-kg) unitary warhead
Platforms:	aircraft F/A-18
	AV-8B

A Joint Stand-Off Weapon (JSOW) in flight after being launched on a 1996 test flight. As with the Tomahawk cruise missile, wings and air scoop extend after launch. (Texas Instruments Defense Systems & Electronics)

An F/A-18C Hornet on the deck of the carrier CONSTELLATION (CV 64) with a Joint Stand-Off Weapon (JSOW) mounted under its left wing. The Air Force will also use this missile. (Texas Instruments Defense Systems & Electronics)

FAST HAWK

The Navy plans to demonstrate the feasibility of a land-attack missile that will provide a precision, hard-target strike weapon at a relatively low cost. Dubbed Fast Hawk, the missile will have a terminal speed in excess of Mach 4 and be capable of attacking targets almost 40 feet (12 m) underground. It would thus have a considerably greater speed than the subsonic Tomahawk and be capable of more effective attacks against hard targets.

An Advanced Technology Demonstration (ATD) is planned under the fiscal 1997 budget. The Fast Hawk would have a warhead of about 750 pounds (340 kg) and a range of 700 n.miles (1,265 km); smaller warheads would permit greater ranges. The missile would be fabricated of steel tubing and would use thrust vectoring from its advanced turbojet/combuster engine; the missile would not have conventional wings or fins. It would use Global Positioning System (GPS) and inertial guidance to achieve a high degree of accuracy. The Naval Air Warfare Center at China Lake, California, is the lead agency for development of the Fast Hawk.

The missile would be compatible with vertical-launch cells in cruisers, destroyers, and submarines, as well as the proposed arsenal ship.

COAST GUARD

WMEC	168	YOCONA	decommissioned for disposal 30 May 1996
WLB	296	SORREL	decommissioned for disposal 20 June 1996
WLM	544	WHITE SAGE	decommissioned for disposal 28 June 1996

ABOUT THE AUTHOR

Norman Polmar is an analyst, historian, and author specializing in naval and strategic issues.

Since 1980 Mr. Polmar has been a consultant to several senior officials in the Navy Department and the Department of Defense. He has also directed studies for U.S. and foreign shipbuilding and aerospace firms. From 1982 to 1986 he was a member of the Secretary of the Navy's Research Advisory Committee and additionally served on the steering group for the Secretary's analysis of the Falklands War. Mr. Polmar was also a consultant to the Director of the Los Alamos National Laboratory and a panel member of the Naval Studies Board of the National Academy of Sciences.

Mr. Polmar has served as a consultant to three U.S. senators and one member of the House of Representatives and as a consultant, or adviser, to three Secretaries of the Navy and one Chief of Naval Operations. He was also a consultant to the deputy counselor to President Ronald Reagan.

Prior to 1980, Mr. Polmar was an executive and before that an analyst with research firms that specialize in strategic, naval, and intelligence issues, topics that he has covered in numerous books and magazine articles.

For the U.S. Naval Institute he has produced several editions of *Ships and Aircraft* and its companion reference, *Guide to the Soviet Navy,* as well as other books. A frequent lecturer and television commentator on military affairs, Mr. Polmar also writes a column for the Naval Institute *Proceedings.*

The **Naval Institute Press** is the book-publishing arm of the U.S. Naval Institute, a private, nonprofit, membership society for sea service professionals and others who share an interest in naval and maritime affairs. Established in 1873 at the U.S. Naval Academy in Annapolis, Maryland, where its offices remain today, the Naval Institute has members worldwide.

Members of the Naval Institute support the education programs of the society and receive the influential monthly magazine *Proceedings* and discounts on fine nautical prints and on ship and aircraft photos. They also have access to the transcripts of the Institute's Oral History Program and get discounted admission to any of the Institute-sponsored seminars offered around the country. Discounts are also available to the colorful bimonthly magazine *Naval History*.

The Naval Institute's book-publishing program, begun in 1898 with basic guides to naval practices, has broadened its scope in recent years to include books of more general interest. Now the Naval Institute Press publishes about 100 titles each year, ranging from how-to books on boating and navigation to battle histories, biographies, ship and aircraft guides, and novels. Institute members receive discounts of 20 to 50 percent on the Press's nearly 600 books in print.

Full-time students are eligible for special half-price membership rates. Life memberships are also available.

For a free catalog describing Naval Institute Press books currently available, and for further information about joining the U.S. Naval Institute, please write to: